EMBEDDED SYSTEMS

The teacher, who is indeed wise, does not bid you to enter the house of his wisdom but rather leads you to the threshold of your mind.

—Khalil Gibran

EMBEDDED SYSTEMS

An Integrated Approach

LYLA B DAS

DEPARTMENT OF ELECTRONICS AND COMMUNICATION ENGINEERING
NATIONAL INSTITUTE OF TECHNOLOGY CALICUT
KOZHIKODE, KERALA

Pearson

Assistant Editor—Acquisitions: R. Vijay Pritha
Associate Editor—Production: M.R. Ramesh

ISBN 978-81-317-8766-3

First Impression, 2012
Twelfth Impression, 2020
Thirteenth Impression, 2025

Published by Pearson India Education Services Pvt. Ltd, CIN: U72200TN2005PTC057128

Head Office: 1st Floor, Berger Tower, Plot No. C-001A/2, Sector 16B, Noida – 201 301,Uttar Pradesh, India.

Registered Office: Featherlite, 'The Address' 5th Floor, Survey No 203/10B, 200 Ft MMRD Road, Zamin Pallavaram, Chennai - 600044

Website: in.pearson.com; Email:companysecretary.india@pearson.com

Digitally printed in India by Trinity Academy for Corporate Training Ltd, New Delhi in the year of 2025.

This book is dedicated
to my children
and
to all my students

CONTENTS

PREFACE

Preamble

Writing a book on Embedded Systems is not easy—let me list a few reasons to substantiate this statement. The first reason is that the field of embedded systems is very vast. The second is that there is no clear understanding on what exactly a student of engineering should learn about embedded systems. A great number of products which are classed as embedded systems are available, and the field is very sophisticated, well developed and rapidly expanding. Anything from a printer to an iPhone is an embedded system. To write a book on all this is quite difficult on account of not having a clear idea of where to start and where to end.

To complicate matters further, there are different families of embedded processors. A student cannot be expected to learn all of them, or even some of them. To make a decision on what to include and what not to, has been difficult, Besides that, 'embedded processors' is not the only topic to learn. There is a large set of various kinds of sensors, actuators, buses, operating systems, design methodologies, view points, development models and what not.

But after a lot of contemplation, finally, I converged on a few popular and upcoming processors, latest buses, new approaches, traditional as well as modern peripherals, real time operating systems and the like. A lot of literature for all these is available in the form of technical documents, data sheets and user manuals—right from the USB technical spec to PSoC's data sheets

Rummaging through all these highly sophisticated technical information, trying to make sense of it all, and finally presenting it in a way that a student, albeit an eager and enthusiastic one, will be able to enjoy reading and studying it—this is the challenge involved in writing this book. I have tried my best to address this challenge of making it a student-friendly presentation.

There are a number of books available under the title of 'Embedded Systems'. Except for a few, most of them have simply concentrated on the architecture and application details of one particular processor. Others have concentrated on the software aspects alone. There are certain others that deal with both, but since the field of embedded systems is one in which fast evolution is the rule rather than the exception, some topics become outdated quite fast.

Approach

I have started from the hardware basics, proceeded to discuss some important processors and systems, and then moved on to the software aspects. The book ends with a presentation on embedded design from a system point of view. Along with the basics, I have also tried to focus on the latest and most relevant topics in the field, from the latest processors and buses to the latest trends in embedded computing.

Pre-requisite

A student of CS, EC or EE branch who has done a first course in digital logic and a second course in 'microprocessors and microcontrollers', is best placed to take up a course on Embedded Systems.

But it is possible also to study Embedded Systems as a second course—that is why some very basic ideas of microprocessors and microcontrollers are included in the initial chapters.

Organization of the Book

This book is organized as twenty chapters numbered from 0 to 19. It is divided into five logical parts from Part I to Part V.

Part I

This part, which includes chapters 0 to 6, deals with the basics, the hardware aspects including sensors, actuators, buses etc. and the tools commonly used in system development.

Chapter 0 is a revision of computer arithmetic and computer architecture. One needs to be very thorough in these two basic topics—then the path ahead becomes very comfortable.

Chapter 1 introduces readers to what an embedded system is, and what its mandatory parts are. Examples of practical and popularly used embedded systems are listed to make the introduction clear. The classifications, history and current trends in the embedded industry are also touched upon.

Chapter 2 is a very important chapter—any student who needs to use/learn embedded hardware should become conversant and confident about all the topics covered in this chapter. Not only are the important aspects of typical embedded processors covered here, related topics such as semiconductor memory (RAM and Flash), low power design, concepts of pullup and pulldown resistors are also touched upon.

Chapter 3 is very important for practical design of systems. Most students are likely to do hardware based projects as part of academic requirements—this chapter, which gives an in-depth discussion on sensors and actuators will definitely find use then.

Chapter 4 is meant for a light reading on some of the applications of embedded systems. Mobile phones, robotics, RFIDs, automotive electronics, medical electronics etc. are discussed as popular applications. A new idea called 'brain machine interface' is also introduced in this chapter.

Chapter 5 is meant to be studied as a very important topic. It contains explanations of some of the popular buses used in embedded systems. A student is not expected to study all buses in detail, but a general idea of buses, and a study of some of the important ones is advised. On-board and off-board buses, wired and wireless buses, bus standards, bus arbitration etc are the important topics covered here.

Chapter 6 is a brief introduction to the development tools that are needed to take a project to completion. The discussion is meant to guide students in the right direction when they are confused about the techniques for writing programs, testing them and burning them into hardware.

Part II

This is the second part of the book, and there are three chapters here. This part deals with software design aspects. Chapter 7 is quite lengthy, but it should mandatorily be learned because it gives answers to many aspects of computers and embedded systems that are seen and experienced in everyday life. This chapter covers operating system concepts in detail and then offers codes/pseudo codes where OS concepts are tried out.

Chapter 8 is about 'real time operating systems'. This should be considered as a continuation of the previous chapter, But here the special requirements and scheduling policies for a special class of embedded systems i.e., real time systems, are taken up. Numerical problems are worked in both these chapters to understand the scheduling mechanism used in operating systems.

Chapter 9 is a short chapter, being at best a basic introduction to Embedded C. It assumes that the reader has a basic knowledge of the constructs of 'C'. How this high-level language is used for processor programming is the focus of the discussion, which is based on the 8051 architecture. Some codes for PIC are also included. Later chapters of PSoC and ARM contain more coding using Embedded C, but basic ideas are introduced here, in Chapter 9.

Part III

This part consists of Chapter 10 to Chapter 15. The architecture, programming and applications of some of the most widely used and popular processors are covered in reasonable depth.

Chapters 10 and 11 are devoted to the ARM processor, which is the most popular processor used in 32-bit and high-end applications. Chapter 10 explains the core of ARM and follows it up with assembly language programming. Chapter 11 expands ARM architecture to make it a microcontroller. A specific ARM-based MCU is chosen and its peripherals are studied. Programming of some peripherals using C is done. These two chapters are likely to be sufficient to get a good grip on ARM architecture.

Chapter 12 is about a new processor. It is not new in the embedded design world, but the academic world is just getting familiarized with it – the chapter discusses PSoC, an MCU series, which makes life easier for a product designer. This is because of the graphical IDE it has, and other special features that are covered (with programming examples in Embedded C) in the chapter.

Chapters 13 and 14 are about one of the most widely used 8-bit microcontroller i.e., the 8051. This MCU is simple and the first that a student should study. These two chapters discusses this MCU with assembly language programming. All the peripherals are covered, and programming is explained with worked-out examples.

Chapter 15 contains a general coverage of DSP processors. Such processors are increasing in relevance and the time is just right to learn the special features of such chips. The special features of such processors are first explained, and then some popular DSP processors (BlackFin, SHARC, OMAP etc) have been identified, and their features elaborated.

Part IV

This part includes Chapters 16, 17 and 18.

Chapter 16 deals with ASIC design. It starts with the classification of digital ICs, continues with programmable devices and then gives a step-by-step explanation of how a digital IC is designed, tested and fabricated. The reader can get a good idea of what terms such as front-end design, back-end design etc. mean, without going very deep into the process of ASIC design.

Chapter 17 introduces two new terminology. One is 'Hardware Software Co-design' and the other is 'Embedded Product Development Lifecycle'. Both these terms are explained and elaborated upon, with relevant examples.

Chapter 18 is very special. After all the previous chapters, it looks upon an embedded product as a system, and suggests the steps needed to apply embedded systems to make useful products as demanded by users. The user/users might have their viewpoint expressed before the design starts. New concepts like user research, ergonomics, anthropometry etc are introduced. Starting from the desires of users, the design steps reach the final stage of product manufacture and resting.

Part V

This part has just one chapter. Chapter 19 has a concise discussion of three projects done by students. The projects pertain to embedded hardware and software and use advanced processors—ARM, OMAP and PIC. This chapter is meant to encourage students to take up challenging and innovative ideas and build products based on these ideas.

Appendices

The book has appendices from A to K. Only Appendix A to D are in the text book, The rest are available in the website of the book www.pearsoned.co.in/lylabdas/embeddedsystems.

The contents of the appendices are as listed:

A - The instruction set of 8051
B - A step-by-step guide to using the Keil RVDK for 8051 and ARM
C - A step-by-step guide to using the PSoC Designer
D - Pin configuration and PINSEL register configuration of LPC 2148
E - A manual with experiments for PSoC1
F - A step by step guide to using PSoC Creator
G - A tutorial on Keil RVDK for 8051 and ARM
H - A program for interfacing a Graphical LCD to PSoC3
I - A program for interfacing an SD card to ARM7 (LPC 2148)
J - A program for using the I2HC interface of PSoC1
K - User manual of ARM LPC 2148

In addition, PowerPoint presentations and solution manual of the chapters are available for instructors.

Contact

Your suggestions and feedback are welcome. In spite of my best efforts, it is possible that some errors may have crept in. Please point them out to me.

My contact id is lbd@nitc.ac.in

ACKNOWLEDGEMENTS

This is my second major book, and as I complete it, I would like to acknowledge all those who have helped and encouraged me in this Herculean task. Truly, it has been a great effort to write it, and there are a lot of people who have directly or indirectly helped me. Let me start from the beginning.

The team at Pearson Education provided a lot of inputs, suggestions and support and brought the project to fruition. I feel that Sojan Jose, my editor, and Ramesh M. R and Vijay Pritha, the production editors have done a tremendous job.

The first batch of students I taught Embedded Systems was the B070EC batch and the next year, the B080EC batch came in. Both batches expressed enthusiasm and interest in the topics I taught, and this is the primary factor that gave me the courage to embark on the venture of writing a book on the subject. I would like to thank each and every one of them for this.

During the process of writing, a few students helped me directly in bringing the book to this form. They gave suggestions, performed reviews, and three of them have contributed by writing a few sections of the book. All of them are working in reputed companies and I would like to list their names, along with expressing my heartfelt thanks to them.

Nithin Gopinath (Texas Instruments, Bangalore), Sabu Paul (Texas Instruments, Bangalore) and Sai Krishna K. (Broadcom, Bangalore) are the three who have contributed directly by writing a few sections in the book.

The list of those who have done reviews of the chapters are: Nithin Gopinath (Texas Instruments, Bangalore), Jayalal Vijayan (Synopsis, Bangalore), Sai Krishna K. (Broadcom, Bangalore), Harikrishnan M. (McAfee, Bangalore), Srijit R. (Deloitte, Hyderabad) and Sushmitha Dandeliya (Assistant Professor, Engineering College, Gwalior).

A few of my colleagues also have helped me in this endeavor, and I extend my gratitude to them. Raghu C. V., my colleague in the department, has done the writing of Chapter 18, and has also given me suggestions at various stages of this work. The names of others with whom I have had discussions on some topics are Sameer S. M., Deepthi P. P., Sudheesh George, Bhuvan B. and Rajiv T. R., my department colleagues, and Jayaraj B. and Anu Mary Chacko of the Computer Science Department. I am grateful to Anand, senior mechanic at the Embedded Systems Lab, who assisted me in all the hardware work associated with the book. I thank Beljit, Anju and Aswathi who have drawn the diagrams in the book. I would also like to make a note of acknowledgement to my son Sagar, for his suggestions on the theme of the front cover of the book.

Two engineers at Cypress Semiconductors, Narayana Swamy, and Geethesh N. S., made a detailed review of the chapter on PSoC. Their inputs have enhanced the quality of the chapter. I am obliged to them and also to Benoy Jose, and Karthikeyan Mahalingam of Cypress Semiconductors for co-ordinating this activity.

It is only because my department gave me free time without the hassles of regular work that I have been able to complete the book on schedule. All my colleagues have been helpful in this and I feel that words are not sufficient to express my feelings of gratitude to all of them. I am deeply indebted to my institute for giving me the freedom to grow and follow the path I chose.

Chapter 19 of the book contains the project work of a few teams of students. They have worked systematically and enthusiastically to do projects of good standard, which require a lot of background study. I congratulate them for the work they have done and would like to mention their names here. They are: Nithin Gopinath, Jayalal Vijayan, Ashwin Harikumar, Kurian Abraham, Ebin George, Sushmita Dandeliya, Fahim Bin Basheer, Jinu J. Alias, Mohammed Favas C., Navas V. and Naveed Farhan K.

I am happy that my family has always been a source of solace for me.

Last, but not the least, I thank all my students once again for the inspiration they have always been, and continue to be.

Lyla B. Das

ABOUT THE AUTHOR

Lyla B. Das is Associate Professor, Department of Electronics Engineering, National Institute of Technology Calicut (NITC), Kerala. She has a diverse mix of industrial, teaching and research experience spanning about 30 years. As a young graduate specializing in Electronics and Communications from the College of Engineering, Trivandrum, Lyla B. Das joined Keltron Controls as Deputy Engineer in 1981. She joined NITC (then Regional Engineering College, Calicut), as lecturer in 1985 and proceeded to complete her master's degree in digital communications from the same college. Over the years, she was successively elevated as Assistant Professor and then Associate Professor, a position which she currently holds.

Keen to actively seek and impart knowledge, Lyla B. Das currently teaches courses on microprocessors, microcontrollers, digital system design using VHDL, and system design using embedded processors at the undergraduate as well as postgraduate level. She has presented research papers in conferences of national and international stature and has worked on numerous projects based on microprocessors and microcontrollers, such as microprocessor-based voting machines and microcontroller-based rail track switching system. An avid reader of contemporary research material, she keeps herself abreast of the current trends in her chosen field and guides students in their M.Tech. research theses. This book on *Embedded Systems* is her second book with Pearson Education, the first one being *The X86 Microprocessors*, which was published in 2010 and received with wide acclaim.

Lyla B. Das has worked on various projects funded by the ministry of human resource development (MHRD) in thrust areas of growth including the setting up of an embedded systems laboratory in 2005–2008. She has delivered expert lectures on image compression using wavelets, advanced microprocessors and microcontrollers, FPGA based systems and embedded systems at several engineering colleges across Kerala. She has also participated in numerous tutorials and workshops conducted by the Indian Institute of Technology (IIT) and the Indian Institute of Science (IISc). She was a Fellow in the national conference on 'VLSI Design and Embedded Systems' held at IISc Bangalore (2003) and IIT Mumbai (2004). She is a life member of the System Society of India and a member of the Indian Society for Technical Education and the Computer Society of India.

PART-I

DESIGN ASPECTS OF EMBEDDED SYSTEMS

0 BASICS OF COMPUTER ARCHITECTURE AND THE BINARY NUMBER SYSTEM

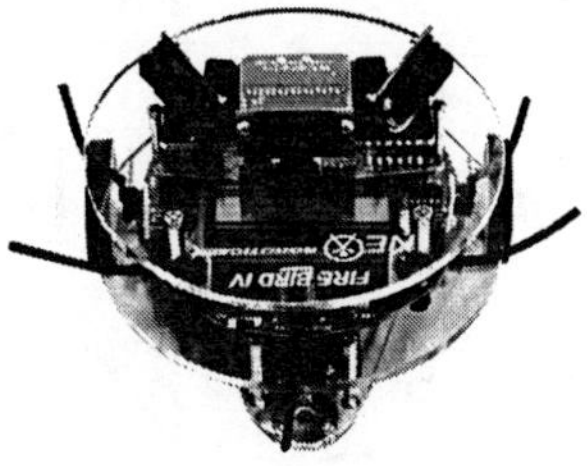

In this chapter, you will learn

- The general principles of computer architecture
- The operation of the data, address and control buses of a computer
- The distinction between RISC and CISC computing
- The comparison between assembly and high level language programming
- The binary, hexadecimal and BCD number systems
- Number format conversions

0.1 | Basics of Computer Architecture

0.1.1 | The Block Diagram of a Computer

A computer, as its name indicates is a machine used for computing. Computing, which many years ago meant arithmetic calculations, has now given way to large amounts of 'data processing'. As such, it is more reasonable to designate the computer now as a 'data processing machine'. For performing its designated tasks, this machine requires many components, which can broadly be divided as hardware and software. Hardware is obviously, the physical constituents of a computer. Software is the collection of programs which directs the hardware to perform its tasks.

Let us first look at a computer in terms of its hardware. Figure 0.1 shows the architectural description of a computer system. It shows the major parts of the computer and also indicates how these parts are connected together, to form the computing machine. The major parts are the CPU, memory and input/output devices.

The heart of a computer is the 'central processing unit'. It is this unit which gives 'life' to a computer. The CPU usually is a 'microprocessor', which means that it is usually a separate and self contained chip. The CPU processes the data given to it, according to the programs meant to operate on these data. The program consists of 'instructions'. These instructions are decoded by the CPU, which generates control signals necessary

Chapter-opening image: Firebird robotic platform (Courtesy: Nex Robotics, Mumbai).

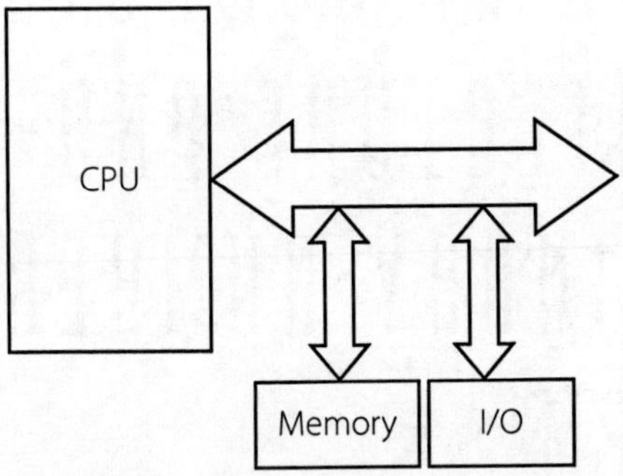

Figure 0.1 | The block diagram of a computer

to activate the arithmetic and logic units of the CPU. As such, the CPU contains the arithmetic logic unit and the control unit. All these activities are timed and synchronized by a pulse train of fixed frequency. This is the clock signal, and it also has the job of synchronizing the activity of the CPU with the activity on the bus.

0.1.2 | The System Bus

A bus is collection of signal wires which connect between the components of the computer systems—Figure 0.2 shows that the CPU is connected to the memory as well as I/O through the system bus, but only one at a time—if the memory and I/O wants to use the bus at the same time, there is a conflict, as there is only one system bus. The system bus comprises of the address bus, data bus and the control bus.

The Data Bus The set of lines used to transfer data is called the data bus. It is a bidirectional bus, as data has to be sent from the CPU to memory and I/O, and has to be received as well by the CPU. The width of the data bus determines the data transfer rate, size of the internal registers of the CPU and the processing capability of the CPU. In short, it is a reflection of the complexity of the processor. As we see, the 8086 has a data bus width of 16 bits, while the 80486 has a 32-bit bus width. Thus the 80486 can process data of 32 bits at a time while the 8086 can only handle 16 bits.

The Address Bus The address bus width determines the maximum size of the physical memory that the CPU can access. With an address bus width of 20 bits, the 8086 can address 2^{20} different locations. It can use a memory size of 2^{20} bytes or 1 MB. For Pentium with an address bus width of 32 bits, the corresponding numbers are 2^{32} bytes i.e., 4 GB. When a particular memory location is to be accessed, the corresponding address is placed on the address bus by the CPU. I/O devices also have addresses. In both cases, it is the CPU which supplies the address, and as such, the address bus is unidirectional.

The Control Bus The control bus is a set of control signals which needs to be activated for activities like writing/reading to/from memory/I/O, or special activities of the CPU like interrupts and DMA. Thus, we see signals like Memory Read, I/O Read, Memory Write and Interrupt Acknowledge as part of the control bus. These control signals dictate

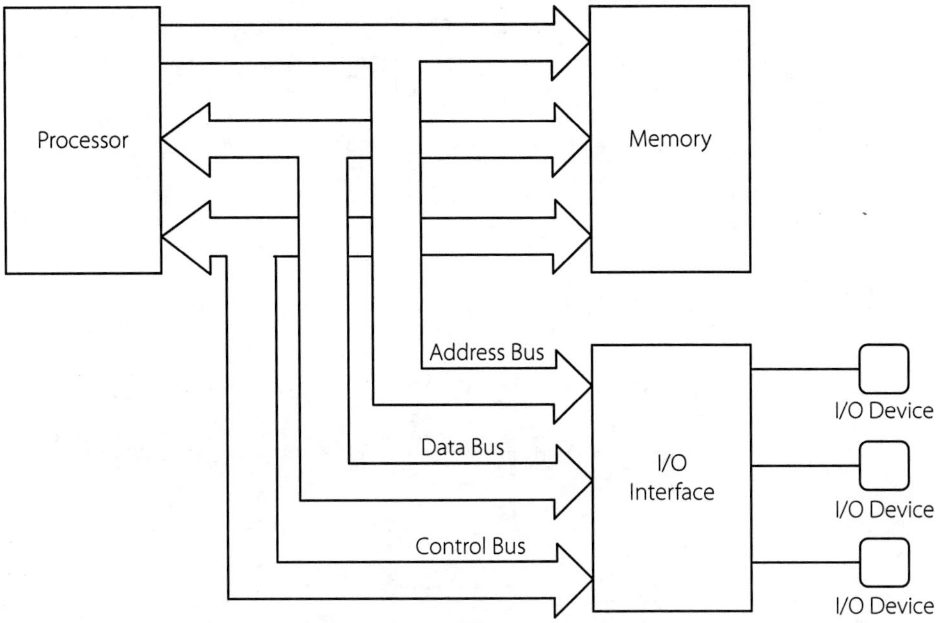

Figure 0.2 | The system bus and its components

the actions taking place on the system bus that involve communications with devices like memory or I/O. For example, the Memory Read signal will be asserted for reading from memory. It is sent to memory from the processor. A signal such as 'Interrupt' is received by the processor from an I/O device. Hence in the control bus, we have signals traveling in either direction. Some control lines may be bidirectional too.

Now that we have discussed a computer system in general, let us go a bit deeper into its individual constituents.

0.1.3 | The Processor

The processor or the microprocessor as we might call it, is the component responsible for controlling all the activity in the system. It performs the following three actions continuously. See Figure 0.3.

i) Fetch an instruction from memory.
ii) Decode the instruction.
iii) Execute the instruction.

When we write a program, it is stored in memory. Our code has to be brought to the processor for the required action to be performed. The first step obviously, is to 'fetch' it from memory. The next step i.e., decoding, involves the interpretation of the code as to what action is to be performed. After decoding, the action required is performed. This is termed 'instruction execution'. The sequence of these three actions is called the 'execution cycle'. To do all this, the processor has 'control circuitry' to fetch and decode instructions. The ALU part of the processor performs the required arithmetic/logic

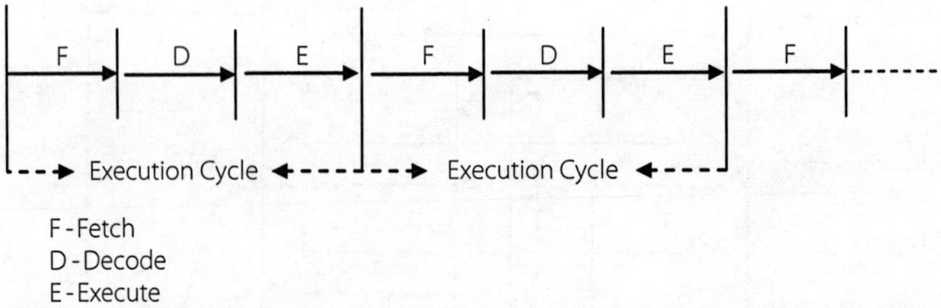

Figure 0.3 | The execution cycle

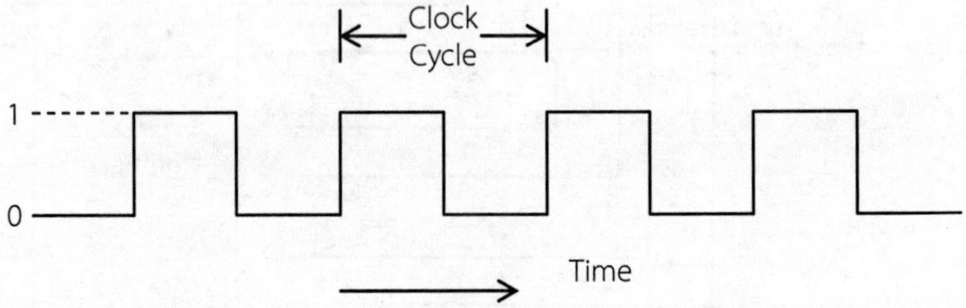

Figure 0.4 | System clock

operations. The sequence of fetch-decode-execute is done continuously and infinitely by the processor. An important implication of this cycle is that instruction execution is 'sequential' in nature—it is only after the first instruction is dealt with, will the second one be taken up. However, there will be situations when the sequential nature of program execution is disturbed. This is when a 'branch' instruction appears in the sequence, and a new sequence of instructions will be taken up starting from a new location.

0.1.4 | System Clock

All the activities of the processor and buses are synchronized by a clock, which is as shown in Figure 0.4 a square wave with a particular frequency. The reciprocal of the clock frequency is the cycle time T, also called the clock period. $T = 1/f$ where f is the clock frequency. An execution cycle may require many clock periods. This depends on the architectural features of the processor, as well as the complexity of the instruction to be executed. Since an execution cycle also involves fetching instructions and data from memory, it also depends on how many clock cycles are needed to access memory. Obviously, the time for execution depends on the clock speed as well. i.e., a clock speed of 3 GHz implies faster processing than a clock of 1 GHz. However, the technology used for the processor must be able to support the clock frequency used.

0.1.5 | Memory

The memory associated with a computer system includes the primary memory as well as secondary memory. However, for the time being, we will think of memory as constituting the primary or main memory only, which is usually RAM (Random Access

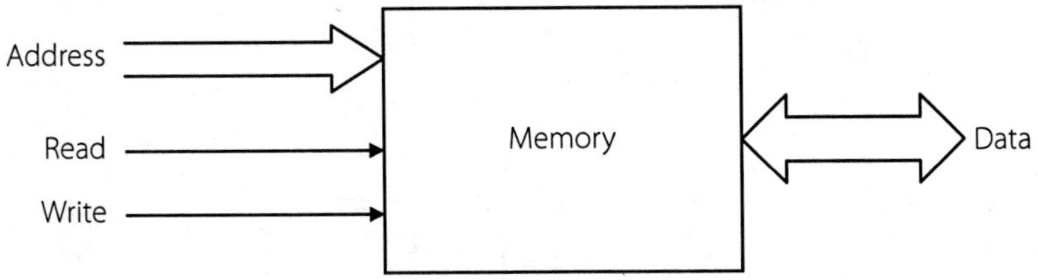

Figure 0.5 | Memory and associated control signals

Memory). Memory is organized as bytes, and the capacity of a memory chip is stated in terms of the number of bytes it can store. Thus, we can have chips of size 256 bytes, 1KB, 1MB and so on. If a computer has a total memory space of 20 MB it can use RAM chips of the available capacity to get that much of memory.

There are two basic operations associated with memory—read and write. Reading causes a data stored in a memory location to be transferred to the CPU, without erasing the content in memory. Writing causes a new data to be placed in a memory location (it overwrites the previous value). There is a certain amount of time required for these operations and this is termed as 'access time'.

Memory Read Cycle The steps involved in a typical read cycle are:

i) Place on the address bus, the address of the memory location whose content is to be read. This action is performed by the processor.
ii) Assert the memory read signal which is part of the control bus.
iii) Wait until the content of the addressed location appears on the data bus.
iv) Transfer the data on the data bus to the processor.
v) De-activate the memory read signal. The memory read operation is over and the address on the address bus is not relevant anymore.

Memory Write Cycle As a continuation, let us also examine the steps in a typical write cycle.

i) Place on the address bus, the address of the location to which data is to be written.
ii) On the data bus, place the data to be written.
iii) Assert the memory write signal which is part of the control bus.
iv) Wait until the data is stored in the addressed location.
v) De-activate the memory write signal. This ends the memory write operation.

At this stage, we should remember that these operations are synchronized with the system clock. An 8086 processor takes at least four clock cycles for reading/writing. These four cycles constitute the 'memory read' and 'memory write' cycles for the processor. Other processors may require more/less clock cycles for the same operations.

0.1.6 | The I/O System

For a computer to communicate with the outside world there is the need for what are called peripherals. Some of these peripherals are purely input devices like the keyboard and mouse; some are purely output devices like the printer and video monitor and some

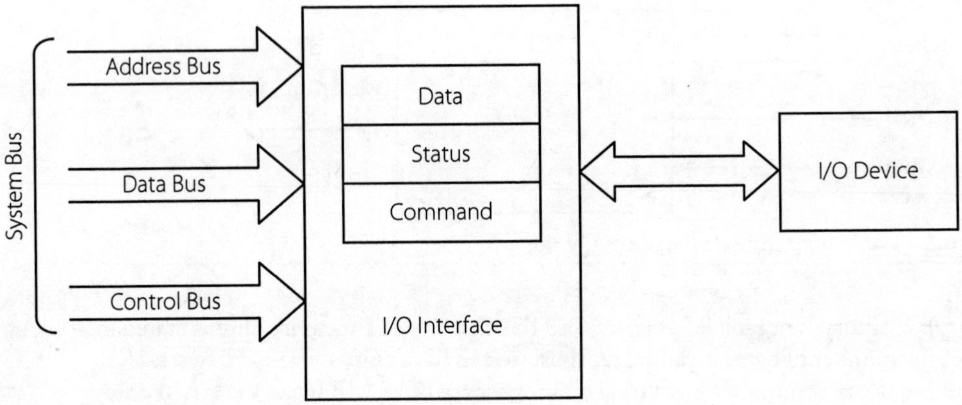

Figure 0.6 | The I/O system

like the modem transfer data in both directions. All this just means that such I/O devices are needed for us to use a computer. However, it is difficult for a processor to deal directly with I/O devices, because of their incompatibility with the processor—each peripheral is different and the operating conditions, voltages, speeds and standards are not understandable to the processor. The processor does not have the necessary control signals to deal with different peripherals. Hence, the normal practice is for each peripheral to have a controller which acts as an interface between the peripheral and the processor. This controller, which may be a special purpose chip, understands the characteristics of the particular device and provides the necessary control signals to the processor to communicate with the peripheral. Thus, we have specialized controllers for most peripherals—like the keyboard display interfacing chip, parallel port interfacing chip and serial communication chip. All these chips are programmable—they have registers for commands, data and status. By suitably programming these chips, we can get the processor to communicate correctly with any peripheral. Figure 0.6 shows the use of an I/O interface between an I/O device and a processor. The processor is not shown in the figure, but the system bus which comes from the processor is shown.

In the final analysis, we can think of a computer that we usually use, as a conglomeration of components which include memory and I/O devices of various types, applications and specifications.

0.2 | Computer Languages

0.2.1 | Machine Language, Assembly Language and High Level Language

The computer is just a dumb piece of equipment unless we are able to make it work for us. For that, we must be able to 'program' it, so that it will perform the tasks we assign it. Programming a computer entails the use of a language that the computer understands. The language native to computers is 'machine language' which consists of binary ones and zeros. The computer knows this language, and the series of ones and zeros fed to it are 'operation codes' for it, which tells it what action is to be performed. Thus there is one binary code for addition and another one for subtraction. These operation codes are called 'opcodes' and this language is called 'machine language'. Programming in machine language means writing the opcodes of the tasks we want to get done by the computer.

However, the problem with machine language, as is obvious, is that it is cumbersome and error-prone. Human beings are not good at remembering or using binary codes. Programming using machine language is not something that any one of us is likely to enjoy. To make it easier for us to communicate with computers, there is a language at a slightly higher level and that is called 'assembly language'. This is more intelligible to users than machine code. This language uses 'mnemonics' for specifying the operation the computer is to perform. These mnemonics are a direct translation of the machine code to a symbol. For example, the binary code for addition is replaced by the symbol 'ADD'—the binary code for multiplication is given the symbolic name 'MUL'. The exact mnemonic used depends on the processor type, but it will be related to the operation to be done.

How does this help? A user does not have to remember binary codes or enter binary code for programming. He only needs to remember the symbolic codes and the associated syntax. We say that assembly coding is at a higher level than machine coding. However, does the computer understand the mnemonics? No, which means that should be an interface between assembly language and machine language. This interface converts the symbolic codes fed in by the user into machine codes. The software which does this is called an 'assembler'.

Since machine language is native to a processor, each processor will have its own machine language and thus it has its own assembly language also. Translating from assembly language to machine language and vice versa is a one to one process—one opcode translates to a unique machine code for a particular processor.

However, we human beings always look for easier ways to get things done. So there are 'higher level languages' which has the vocabulary and grammar similar to the language spoken by us. Such languages are very easy to use because the communication process is similar to English. We have heard of languages like C, FORTRAN, COBOL and many, many such 'high level languages'. The features of such languages are that they are

i) easy to understand and write,
ii) are not processor specific.

Thus if we write a program in C, we can use it to run on any processor—as long as the 'compiler' for the language is available. The compiler is the software which 'translates the high level language statements' to statements in a lower level language. The lower level may be assembly or machine language. However, finally the processor needs the machine code.

The program that we write in assembly or high level language is called the source program or source code. A compiler or assembler converts this into an object code which is 'executable' in the sense that the processor understands the code and performs the tasks indicated.

0.2.2 | Comparison

Programming in machine language is too cumbersome and hence ruled out in the present world. However, assembly language programming is frequently done, so let us now make a comparison between assembly language programming and high level language programming.

Assembly code is specific to a processor—which means that the assembly code of 8086 does not make any sense to 8085 (though both are Intel made). Assembly programs need the programmer to know the architecture of the processor intimately. He should know the registers and flags and the way each instruction handles data. So doing assembly coding involves the study of the concerned processor. However, once this part is done, coding is very efficient, compact and executes very fast. Speed advantage of a hundred times or more, is fairly common. Assembly language programming also gives direct access to key machine features essential for implementing certain kinds of low level routines, such as an operating system kernel or microkernel, device drivers, and machine control.

High level language programming, on the other hand, is not processor-specific. It is easy to learn and master. However, high level languages are abstract. Typically a single high level instruction is translated into several (sometimes dozens or in rare cases even hundreds) executable machine language instructions. The object code generated by a compiler is usually not compact. However, the advantage of high level languages is that since it is easy to learn, semi-skilled designers can be employed for development activities, and so development and maintenance times are much less.

This book focuses on the x86 architecture and on assembly language programming. The aim is to impart good assembly language skills and a thorough knowledge of the x86 architecture.

0.3 | RISC and CISC Architectures

Two terms that are likely to be encountered frequently while reading about computer architecture are RISC and CISC. RISC stands for Reduced Instruction Set Computer and CISC means Complex Instruction Set Computer. Since a lot of controversy surrounds these two terms, let us try to find out what it is all about.

In the early days of microprocessor development, the trend was to have complex instructions implemented fully using hardware. For example, the multiply instruction is a complex instruction which needs a dedicated hardware multiplier. Because hardware is fast, execution is fast, but with lots of such complex instructions, the hardware budget is naturally high. This is the philosophy and the main feature of CISC.

RISC on the other hand, views this matter in a different way. On an average, the number of complex instructions a computer uses is relatively less. So, why not realize a complex instruction using a set of simple instructions? This is possible, and the advantage is that the hardware budget is much less. The instruction set is also small. However, software is to be written to realize complex instructions with simple instructions. This amounts to trading software for hardware.

There exists a long history of controversy regarding which is better. The x86 architecture was based on the CISC philosophy, right from the beginning. By the time RISC principles became popular and software development for RISC became established, the x86 CISC processors had already carved a niche for themselves in the processor market. So, even though the supporters of RISC were able to establish their point, most developers did not want to take the risk of switching over to an untested domain. However, most of the newer processors used the RISC philosophy for their architectures—examples are ARM, Power PC, Sun's Sparc processors and the like. Many of them found their applications in the embedded processing field.

The main features of RISC are that they have only simple instructions implemented in a single clock. However, there is an irony in that, many RISC processors have as many complex instructions as CISC processors. Probably this can be justified by explaining that such complex instructions have been implemented using microprogramming rather than a direct hardware realization. Microprogramming is a method of implementing the control unit of a computer by breaking down instructions into a sequence of small programming steps.

While the RISC versus CISC controversy is still raging, the distinction between what exactly is RISC and what is CISC is reducing to the extent of being almost indistinguishable except at the basic philosophical level. Intel which held on to CISC for many years, bowed down to the RISC architecture by designing its Pentium Pro with complex instructions which internally were broken down to simple RISC like instructions. So the comment on it is that Pentium Pro is a RISC processor than runs CISC instructions.

0.4 | Number Systems

Motivation In the study of microprocessors, we will have to use many different number systems, and conversions from one system to the other. Clarity of these ideas is very important for correct computation and the right interpretation of results. This is the motivation for a review on it, though most of you have had an introduction to it already.

We have become quite used to the number system which we call the decimal number system, which is a system with a base (radix) 10. We are so used to this system of numbers that our visualization of quantity is always based on this. Our mental faculties are tuned to perform all calculations in this number system. In contrast, computers are not comfortable with this system—we know that they use the binary system of numbers and all computations are done in the binary format. Thus we have a problem when we use computers to perform computations for us. So let us start this discussion by first understanding the intricacies of each of the commonly used number systems. We will discuss the ones that we most often might have to use in the context of computers.

0.4.1 | The Decimal System

The base of this system is 10 (ten)—and it naturally follows that there are ten defined symbols in this system—the combinations of these ten symbols give us various values. The ten symbols here are 0, 1, 2, 3, 4, 5, 6, 7, 8 and 9, and they are called 'digits'. The position of a digit in a number is what gives its value.

For example, how does the number 346 get its value?

$$\begin{aligned} 346 &= 3 \times 10^2 + 4 \times 10^1 + 6 \times 10^0 \\ &= 300 + 40 + 6 \end{aligned}$$

This means that, associated with each position, there is a weight. Here the weight is a power of 10. Thus

$$\begin{aligned} 56785 &= 5 \times 10^4 + 6 \times 10^3 + 7 \times 10^2 + 8 \times 10^1 + 5 \times 10^0 \\ &= 50000 + 6000 + 700 + 80 + 5 \end{aligned}$$

What about fractional numbers? The positions on the right side of the decimal number also have weights, but the powers (of 10) are negative.

$$\begin{aligned} 6.785 &= 6 \times 10^0 + 7 \times 10^{-1} + 8 \times 10^{-2} + 5 \times 10^{-3} \\ &= 6 \times 1 + 7 \times 0.1 + 8 \times 0.01 + 5 \times 0.001 \\ &= 6 + 0.7 + 0.08 + 0.005 \end{aligned}$$

These are things that we know very well. They have been reviewed here to show that the same concept applies to other number systems as well.

0.4.2 | The Binary Number System

The base of this system is 2, and so it has two symbols, 0 and 1, each of them being called a bit. So each position has a weight which is a power of 2. Take the number 110110. Let us find its value. Since there are 6 bits, there are six positions with weights as shown for the bits:

Power of 2:	2^5	$+2^4$	$+2^3$	$+2^2$	$+2^1$	$+2^0$
Weight:	32	+16	+8	+4	+2	+1
Number:	1	1	0	1	1	0
Value:	1×32	$+1 \times 16$	$+0 \times 8$	$+1 \times 4$	$+1 \times 2$	$+0 \times 1$

Adding the values in all the bit positions gives $32 + 16 + 0 + 4 + 2 + 0 = 54$. This is the equivalent value in the decimal system. We cannot help putting back everything into the decimal system, because this is the number system with which we are most familiar and comfortable.

Note Sometimes binary numbers are suffixed with B to indicate that they are binary numbers e.g., 110110B, 1010110B. Sometimes the notation 110110_2 is also used.

Note Keep the calculator in the PC (Accessories of Windows) open in the scientific mode. This will help to verify all the calculations we are going to do from now on.

Next, let us try to understand the concept of fractional binary numbers.

Example 0.1

Find the decimal values of the binary number 1001.011 B

Solution

Power of 2:	2^3		2^2		2^1		2^0		2^{-1}		2^{-2}		2^{-3}
Weight	8		4		2		1		0.5		0.25		0.125
Number	1		0		0		1	.	0		1		1
Value	8	+	0	+	0	+	1	.	0	+	0.25	+	0.125
	= 9.375												

Example 0.1 shows 1001.011 in binary (often written as 1001.011_2).

It also shows the power and weight or value of each digit position. Thus 1001.001 is equivalent in decimal to 9.375 (8 + 1 + 0.25 + 0.125).

Notice that this is the sum of $2^3 + 2^0 + 2^{-2} + 2^{-3}$, but 2^2 and 2^1 are not added, as the bit under these positions is 0. The fractional part is composed of 2^{-2} and 2^{-3}, but there is no digit under 2^{-1}, so 0.5 is not added.

0.4.3 | The Hexadecimal Number System

Next is the hexadecimal system of numbering which has 16 symbols namely 0, 1, 2, 3, 4, 5, 6, 7, 8, 9, A, B, C, D, E, F. The base of the system is 16 and each symbol is called a 'hex digit'. Each position in the hexadecimal number system has a weight which is a power of 16. Let us find the value of 240FCH. The letter 'H' is suffixed to the number if it is needed to make clear that it is a hexadecimal number. A to F have the decimal values of 10 to 15.

Power of 16:	16^4	$+16^3$	$+16^2$	$+16^1$	$+16^0$
Weight:	63536	+4096	+256	+16	+1
Number:	2	4	0	F	C
Value:	2×65536	$+4 \times 4096$	$+0 \times 256$	$+15 \times 16$	$+12 \times 1$
i.e.,	131072	+16384	+0	+240	+12
	= 147708				

So we have calculated the equivalent decimal value of the given hex number by using the concept of positional weights.

Example 0.2

Find the decimal value of the hex number 25.1H

Solution

Power of 16:	16^1	$+16^0$		$+16^{-1}$
Weight:	16	+1		+0.0625
Number:	2	5	.	1
Value	2×16	$+5 \times 1$	.	$+1 \times 0.0625$
i.e.,	32	+5	.	+0.0625
	= 37.0625			

There is also an octal system whose base is 8. The equivalent calculations involved in this are left as an exercise for the interested student. In all the above, we have done the conversion to decimal form from other number systems. Now we will see how we will convert a decimal number to other systems of numbering.

Note i) In most computers, the default number system for writing numbers is decimal. When we mean decimal numbers, we simply write it as it is—like 35, 687 and 234 and so on. A number in hex form is suffixed with the letter H, for example, 56H, 8FH, 0AH and so on.

ii) The numbers from 0 to 9 are the same in the decimal and the hexadecimal system. So, in the forthcoming chapters, you will see that no 'H' is added when writing numbers from 0 to 9, though there is nothing wrong in writing 7H, 8H, 01H and so on.

0.5 | Number Format Conversions

0.5.1 | Conversion from Decimal to Binary

The method is to divide the decimal number by 2, until the quotient is 0. See the technique illustrated below.

Example 0.3

Find the binary value of 13.

Solution

Divide 13 by 2 repeatedly and save the remainders

2)13	remainder = 1
2)6	remainder = 0
2)3	remainder = 1
2)1	remainder = 1
0	

Now write the remainders from bottom to top, as one line from left to right. We get 1101 as the converted binary number.

Thus, we have been able to convert from decimal to binary by repeated division by 2, the base of the binary number system. To verify, try converting this binary number back to decimal. It should be 13. Or simply use the scientific calculator to verify the conversion. (Make sure it is kept open on your PC's desktop.)

Example 0.4

Convert the number 213 to binary form.

Solution

2)213	remainder = 1
2)106	remainder = 0
2)53	remainder = 1
2)26	remainder = 0
2)13	remainder = 1
2)6	remainder = 0
2)3	remainder = 1
2)1	remainder = 1
0	

Now write the remainders from bottom to top in one line, from left to right. The number is 11010101.

0.5.2 | Conversion from Decimal to Hexadecimal

Conversion from decimal to hexadecimal is accomplished by dividing by 16 and finding the remainders. Remainders ranging from 10 to 15 will be written using the hexadecimal symbols A to F. See how 225 is converted to a hexadecimal form.

16)225	remainder = 1
16)14	remainder = E
0	
	Result = E1

The method for this is obvious i.e., divide repeatedly the decimal number by 16, keep the remainders. Do this until the quotient is 0.

Example 0.5

Convert the decimal number 4152 to hexadecimal.

Solution

16)4152	remainder = 8
16)259	remainder = 3
16)16	remainder = 0
16)1	remainder = 1
0	

Take the remainders from bottom to top and write it in a single line from left to right. The number is 1038H.

0.5.3 | Converting from Binary to Hexadecimal

If we take any hex digit, note that its decimal value ranges from 0 to 15. For example F is 15, A is 10 and so on. If a hex digit has to be converted to a binary number, the maximum number of bits required is 4.

See Table 0.1. Any hex digit can be written as a group of four bits. Taking an example, 4C57FH can be written in binary, by writing the equivalent binary of each of the digits

Hex	4.	C	5	7	F
Binary	0100	1100	0101	0111	1111

The binary value of 4C57FH is 01001100010101111111. Looking at both the representations tells us the biggest problem with binary numbers—they are long and cumbersome to handle. Putting them into a hex form makes the representation short and concise—we conclude that the binary representation is an expanded form of the hexadecimal representation where each hex digit is expanded to its 4-bit binary form.

If we have a long binary number, what we can do to convert it into hex form is to divide it into groups of 4 bits (starting from the right i.e., the LSB). Then write the hex representation of each 4-bit binary group. Try this technique with the following binary number: 11100101010100011101.

1110	0101	0101	0001	1101	B	i.e., binary
E	5	5	1	D	H	i.e., hex

Table 0.1 | Hex, Binary and Decimal Representations

Decimal	Hex	Binary	Decimal	Hex	Binary
0	0	0000	8	8	1000
1	1	0001	9	9	1001
2	2	0010	10	A	1010
3	3	0011	11	B	1011
4	4	0100	12	C	1100
5	5	0101	13	D	1101
6	6	0110	14	E	1110
7	7	0111	15	F	1111

Example 0.6

Convert the following binary number to hex form.
10111110000111110001.

Solution

It is the practice to write binary as groups of four with a space between the groups. This increases the readability of the binary number.

1011	1110	0001	1111	0001
A	E	1	F	1

The equivalent hex number is AE1F1H.

Example 0.7

Convert the following hexadecimal number to binary form.
3AF24H

Solution

Take each hexadecimal digit and write its equivalent four-bit binary value.

3	A	F	2	4
0011	1010	1111	0010	0100

From all this, we should realize that the hexadecimal notation is a contracted form of rebinary number representation. Computers do all their processing using binary numbers, but it is easier for us to represent that binary number in hex form. So when we ask the computer to add 34H and 5DH, it actually expands these into binary form and does the addition.

0.5.4 | BCD Numbers

BCD stands for 'Binary Coded Decimal' but there is more to it than being just a binary representation of a decimal number. Let us look into the details.

Decimal numbers are represented by 10 symbols from 0 to 9, each of them being called a digit. We know the binary code for each of these decimal numbers. Suppose we represent one decimal digit as a byte, it is called 'unpacked BCD'. Consider the representation of 9—it is written as 00001001. Now if we want to write 98 in unpacked BCD, it is written as two bytes:

9	8
00001001	00001000.

Thus the binary code of each decimal digit is in one byte.

Packed BCD What, then, is 'packed BCD'? When each digit is packed into 4 binary bits, it is packed BCD. Thus 98 is

9	8
1001	1000.

Each digit needs a nibble (four bits) to represent it. The packed BCD form of 675 is 0110 0111 0101. The important point to remember is that since there is no digit greater than 9, no BCD nibble can have a code greater than '1001'. Computers do process BCD numbers, but the user must be aware of the number representation that is being used.

Can we write BCD numbers in hex? Yes, because the hex representation is just a concise representation of binary numbers. The decimal number 675 when written as 675H represents the packed BCD, in hex form. There is no need to be confused about this, because the steps involved are:

i) write the binary equivalent of each decimal number, as a nibble,
ii) write the hex equivalent of each nibble.

675 is

0110	0111	0101	
6	7	5	H

Spend a few moments thinking, to make it clear. One important point to keep in mind is that when we represent BCD in hex form, no digit will ever take the value of A to F, since decimal digits are limited to 9. So there will never be a BCD number such as 8F5H or 56DH or A34H.

Example 0.8

Find the binary, hex and packed BCD representation of the decimal numbers 126 and 245. Also write the packed BCD in the hex format.

Solution

Number form	Binary	Hex	BCD	BCD in hex
126	0111 1110	7EH	0001 0010 0110	126H
245	1111 0101	F5H	0010 0100 0101	245H

Example 0.9

Find the packed BCD value of the decimal number 2347654, and represent the BCD in hex format.

Solution

To find the BCD, each digit is to be coded in 4-bit binary.
Hence 2347659 is
0010 0011 0100 0111 0110 0101 1001 i.e., 2347659H is the hex representation of the BCD number.

It is very important to keep this in mind, when we do programs using BCD arithmetic. Whenever you have doubts then, just refer back to this chapter.

0.5.5 | ASCII Code

This word pronounced as 'ask-ee' is the abbreviation of the words 'American Standard Code for Information Interchange'. This is the code used when entering data through the keyboard and displaying text on the video display. It is very important to know what it is and how this code is used.

ASCII is a seven bit code, which is written as a byte. It has representations for numbers, lower case and upper case English alphabets, special characters (like # , ^ . &) and control characters. For example, there are ASCII codes for 'new line', carriage return and the space bar. A number of characters are related to printing. When we type a character on the keyboard, it is the ASCII value of the key that is read in. The computer must convert it from this form to binary form, for processing. The list of ASCII codes is shown in Table 0.2. Note that the ASCII value of numbers from 0 to 9 is 30H to 39H. The ASCII of upper case alphabets starts from 41H and that for lower case starts from 61H. This table will be needed as quick reference for various calculations we will do in the programming chapters.

0.5.6 | Representation of Negative Numbers

There are various ways of representing negative numbers—like signed magnitude, one's complement, two's complement and so on, but we will straightway discuss the representation used by computers for this. Computers use the 'two's complement' representation for negative numbers. The method is to complement each bit of the number and add a '1' to this. Let us see how it is done.

We will start with 4-bit numbers. Say we want to represent –6.

i) Write the 4-bit binary value of 6: 0110.
ii) Complement each bit: 1001.
iii) Add '1' to this: 1010.

So –6 is '1010', for computers.

Let us try this for all the numbers from 0 to 7. See Table 0.3 which shows the positive and negative number representation of numbers possible to be represented in four bits. A number of observations can be made from Table 0.3.

i) The range of numbers that can be represented by 4 bits is –8 to +7. For an n-bit number, this range works out to be (-2^{n-1}) to $(+2^{n-1}-1)$.
ii) In this notation, the most significant bit (MSB) is considered to be the sign bit. The MSB for positive numbers is '0' and for negative numbers is 1.
iii) There is a unique representation for 0.

Since we will deal mostly with bytes and words (16-bit) let's have a feel of 8-bit negative number representation.

Example 0.10

Find the two's complement number corresponding to –6 when 6 is represented in 8 bits as 0000 0110.

Solution

The steps: 0000 0110

```
1111 1001        ;complement each bit
1111 1010        ;add '1' to it
F    A           ;in hex
```

Thus –6 is FAH in 8-bit form, while it is AH in 4-bit form (from Table 0.3)

Note H is the notation for 'hexadecimal'.

Table 0.2 | The ASCII Code—Symbols versus Hex Value

Symbol	ASCII (Hex)	Symbol	ASCII (Hex)	Symbol	ASCII (Hex)	Symbol	ASCII (Hex)
NUL	0	DLE	10	(Space)	20	0	30
SOH	1	DC1	11	!	21	1	31
STX	2	DC2	12	"	22	2	32
ETX	3	DC3	13	#	23	3	33
EOT	4	DC4	14	$	24	4	34
ENQ	5	NAK	15	%	25	5	35
ACK	6	SYN	16	&	26	6	36
BEL	7	ETB	17	.	27	7	37
BS	8	CAN	18	(	28	8	38
Tab	9	EM	19	)	29	9	39
LF	A	SUB	1A	*	2A	:	3A
VT	B	ESC	1B	+	2B	;	3B
FF	C	FS	1C	,	2C	<	3C
CR	D	GS	1D	-	2D	=	3D
SO	E	RS	1E	.	2E	>	3E
SI	F	US	1F	/	2F	?	3F
@	40	P	50	`	60	P	70
A	41	Q	51	a	61	q	71
B	42	R	52	b	62	r	72
C	43	S	53	c	63	s	73
D	44	T	54	d	64	t	74
E	45	U	55	e	65	u	75
F	46	V	56	f	66	v	76
G	47	W	57	g	67	w	77
H	48	X	58	h	68	x	78
I	49	Y	59	i	69	y	79
J	4A	Z	5A	j	6A	z	7A
K	4B	[	5B	k	6B	{	7B
L	4C	/	5C	l	6C		7C
M	4D	]	5D	m	6D	}	7D
N	4E	^	5E	n	6E	~	7E
O	4F	–	5F	o	6F		7F

Table 0.3 | Negative and Positive Number Representation in 4-bit Binary

Negative Numbers	Binary	Hex	Positive Numbers	Binary	Hex
−8	1000	8			
−7	1001	9	+7	0111	7
−6	1010	A	+6	0110	6
−5	1011	B	+5	0101	5
−4	1100	C	+4	0100	4
−3	1101	D	+3	0011	3
−2	1110	E	+2	0010	2
−1	1111	F	+1	0001	1
−0	0000	0	+0	0000	0

One very important point we need to observe and keep in mind is that, when a 4-bit number is expanded into an 8-bit form, its sign bit has to be extended into the 8 bits. The sign bit in the 4-bit representation of −6 is '1'. When expanding the number to fill into 8 bits, the 1 is replicated 4 more times to fill the whole byte. Thus −6 which is AH in 4-bit form, becomes FAH in byte form, and will be FFFAH in 16-bit format, and FFFF FFFAH in 32-bit format. We need to understand this for negative numbers. For positive numbers, we do it without much thinking. So +6 is 0110, which expands to be 0000 0110 (byte) or 06H, and 0006H in 16-bit format and 0000 0006 H in the 32-bit format. Note that for positive numbers, the sign bit is 0; effectively we are doing sign extension here too. This concept of 'sign extension' is important and we will deal with it in greater detail later.

Conversion from Two's Complement Form Given the two's complement representation of a decimal number, how do we find the decimal number which it represents? The answer is—two's complement it again.

Take FA

1111 1010		...the number
0000 0101	+	...invert each bit
1		...add 1
0000 0110		...its 2's complement

This is 6. Thus FA is the two's complement representation of −6.

Example 0.11

Find the decimal number whose two's complement representation is given.

i) FFF2H
ii) F9H

Solution

i) FFF2H
   Taking two's complement gives 000E
   which is 1110. i.e., 14—which means that −14 is the number represented by FFF2H.

ii) F9H
Taking two's complement gives
0111 i.e., 7, which means that –7 is the number represented by F9H.

Question Looking at the result of various arithmetic operations on binary numbers, how do we know whether it is a positive or a negative number? What is your observation regarding signed numbers?

Answer We should know how many bits are used for the representation of a signed number in the system. Then, if the MSB is a '1', it is a negative number, if the MSB is a '0', it is a positive number.

0.6 | Computer Arithmetic

0.6.1 | Addition of Unsigned Numbers

When we say that a number is unsigned, it implies that the sign of the number is irrelevant, which actually means that we consider the numbers as having no sign bit—all the bits allotted for the data are used for the magnitude alone, in effect, it turns out that these refer to positive numbers. With 8 bits, numbers from 0 to 255 can be used.

Binary addition is something that you have already learnt. Here we are reviewing it to bring into focus some important points which we may have to be taken care of, in the study of microprocessor programming.

Binary addition is done by adding bits column wise. We will consider byte sized data.

Case 1

Binary	Decimal	Hexadecimal
0101 1001 +	89 +	59H +
0110 1001	105	69H
1100 0010	194	C2H

Addition of the same numbers in the binary, decimal and hexadecimal formats is shown. Since the sum lies within a value of 255, there is no special problem in this case.

Case 2

0111 1000	120 +	78H +
1001 1001	153	99H
10001 0001	273	111H

In this case, the sum is greater than the number of bits allotted for the operand, and the extra bit, beyond the 8 bits of the sum, is called a 'carry'. Whenever a carry appears, it indicates the insufficiency of the space allocated for the result. In microprocessors, there is a flag that indicates this condition.

0.6.2 | Addition of Packed BCD Numbers

Now let us add packed BCD numbers

Case 1

Consider the case of two packed BCD bytes that are to be added, say 45 and 22.

Packed BCD	Packed BCD in hex form	Decimal
0100 0101 +	45H +	45 +
0010 0010	22H	22
0110 0111	**67H**	**67**

In this case, the upper nibble and lower nibble are within 0 to 9. So the addition proceeds just like normal decimal addition.

Case 2

Consider the case of two packed BCD bytes that are to be added, say 45 and 27. In BCD form, the correct answer should be 72. However, this is not obtained directly.

Packed BCD	Packed BCD in hex form	Decimal
0100 0101 +	45H +	45 +
0010 0111	27H	27
0110 1100	**6CH**	**72**

When adding in binary form, the lower nibble of the sum is greater than 9. Since no BCD digit can have a value greater than 9, a correction needs to be applied here. The correction to get the sum back to BCD form is to add 6 (0110) to the lower nibble alone.

Correction

0110 1100	+
0000 0110	
0111 0010	

This gives the correct sum of 72.

Case 3

This is when the upper nibble of the sum is greater than 9. The correction is to add 6 to the upper nibble alone.

Add BCD 76 and 62. In binary form, the additions are

0111 0110 +	76H +	
0110 0010	62H	
1101 1000 +	D8H +	Now adding 6 to the upper nibble,
0110 0000	60H	
1 0011 1000	138H	

However, note that the data size exceeds 99, which is the maximum s number that 8 bits can accommodate for a packed BCD number. Thus there is a 'carry' generated from the addition operation. However, if the carry is also included in the answer, the sum of 138 is correct. However, more than 8 bits are needed for the sum.

Case 4

When both the upper and lower nibbles of the sum are greater than 9, add 6 to both nibbles. Add BCD 89 and 72.

1000 1001 +	89H +	
0111 0010	72H	
1111 1011	FBH	add 06 to both nibbles
0110 0110	66H	
1 0110 0001	1 61H	

The right answer of 161 is obtained. However, the sum needs more than one byte space.

Example 0.12

Perform the addition of the following numbers, after converting to decimal and hexadecimal forms.

i) 39 and 99
ii) 117 and 156

Solution

	Decimal	Binary	Hexadecimal
i)	39 +	0010 0111 +	27H +
	99	0110 0011	63H
	138	1000 1010	8AH
ii)	117 +	0111 0101 +	75H +
	156	1001 1100	9CH
	273	1 0001 0001	1 1 1H

In the second addition, the data has exceeded the size which can be accommodated in 8 bits. Hence a carry will be generated. In microprocessors, there is a flag which indicates this condition.

0.6.3 | Addition of Negative Numbers

We know now that negative numbers are represented in two's complement notation. Let's consider adding two negative numbers.

Example 0.13

Add –43 and –56

Solution

Convert the two numbers into their two's complement form, as both are negative numbers.

–43 +	1101 0101 +
–56	1100 1000
–99	1 1001 1101

We are adding two 8-bit numbers. If the sum exceeds 8 bits, an extra bit is generated from the addition. Ignore this carry and look at the eight bits of the sum. (This is the rule for two's complement addition.)

It is 1001 1101. The MSB is found to be '1'. So we know that it is a negative number. To find the decimal number whose two's complement representation this is, take the two's complement of the sum. This comes to be 0110 0011 i.e., 99. Thus, we verify the correctness of our addition procedure.

Example 0.14

Add +90 and –26.

Solution

One number is positive and the other is negative.

+90	0101 1010	+
–26	1110 0110	
64	1 0100 0000	

Ignore the end around carry. The sum is 0100 0000. Since the MSB of the number is '0', we understand that the sum is positive. So convert it to decimal. The result is 64.

Example 0.15

Add –120 and +45

Solution

–120	1000 1000	+
+45	0010 1101	
–75	1011 0101	

Look at the sum—the MSB of the sum is '1'. Hence, it is a negative number. The two's complement of this is 0100 1011 i.e., 75. Thus, the result of the calculation is –75.

Note In all the above calculations, we have used data of 8 bits. The result of the calculations was in the range of –128 to +127. Thus, the answers are correct. If the sum goes outside this (for eight-bit data), the answers will be wrong, and havoc will be created if one is not aware of that. Computers have 'flags' to let us know of this. This will be discussed in later sections.

0.6.4 | Subtraction

Unsigned Numbers

i) Binary numbers
ii) Hexadecimal numbers
iii) BCD numbers

The procedure here is similar to addition i.e., bit by bit, column by column subtraction. Sometimes, borrows from the columns on the left are needed.

Example 0.16

Subtract 56 from 230. Do this subtraction after converting numbers to binary and hex.

Solution

230 –	1110 0110 –	E6H –
56	0011 1000	38H
174	**1010 1110**	**AEH**

In the above subtraction, we are subtracting a smaller number from a bigger number. However, when subtracting column-wise, sometimes there is the issue of having to subtract a bigger number from a smaller number. We know the idea of 'borrow' from the left-hand column. However, for the borrowing with which we append the number, depends on the base of the number system. For the decimal system, we borrow 10, for binary 2 and for hex we borrow 16.
Check this hexadecimal subtraction:

E6H –
38H
AEH

Starting from the rightmost column, we see that we cannot subtract 8 from 6. So, borrowing from E is needed. Borrowing from E leaves E to become D and 6 becomes 6 + 16 = 22 (in decimal). Subtracting 8 from 22 gives 14 which is E in hex. That is how we get E in rightmost column of the result. Then, going over to the left, subtract 3 from D (13 in decimal). This is 10 (in decimal) and A in hex. That is how the result of the subtraction is A.

This idea has been explained here in detail, so that we can use a similar idea in BCD subtraction.

0.6.5 | Packed BCD Subtraction

Let us use the same numbers for BCD subtraction as we did in Example 0.16. i.e., subtract 56 from 230. The BCD representation is shown below. Each decimal digit is packed in to 4-bit binary bits.

Decimal	Packed BCD
230 –	0010 0011 0000 –
56	0000 0101 0110
174	**0001 0111 0100**

The point to remember here is that each group of 4 bits represents a 'decimal number', the base of which is ten. Thus, when we try to subtract a bigger number from a smaller number, we have to consider the 'four bits together' as a decimal number. Let us review the steps in the above subtraction.

First step

Thus, when we have to subtract 6 from 0 in the rightmost group of four bits, we need to borrow. Borrow from the group on the left a decimal 10, and add it to the '0000' on the right. That makes it '1010' (because of borrowing, the 0011 on the left is now '0010'). Then subtract 0110 from this. The result is 0100 as seen (within the group, binary subtraction is done).

```
0010 0010 1010  –
          0110
          0100
```

Second step

This is the second group. For subtracting 0101 from 0010, borrowing of decimal 10 is taken from the leftmost group. Thus 0010 is '1100', 12 in decimal. Subtracting '0101' (5) from it, gives '0111' (7) as shown.

```
0001 1100 1010  –
     0101 0110
     0111 0100
```

Third step

The leftmost group is now 0001. Subtract 0000 from it. Thus, the final answer is 174 in packed BCD form.

```
0001 1101 1010  –
0000 0101 0110
0001 0111 0100
```

All this shows that BCD subtraction also needs extra care as BCD addition. In computers, special instructions take care of this.

Example 0.17

Express the numbers 53 and 18 in packed BCD and subtract the latter from the former.

Solution

Decimal	Packed BCD
53 –	0101 0011 –
18	0001 1000

First step

Borrowing from the left side nibble to the nibble on the right side gives

```
0100 1101  –
0001 1000
     0101
```

Second step

```
0100 1101  –
0001 1000
0011 0101
```

The result is 35, as it should be.

0.6.6 | Subtraction of Signed Numbers

Subtraction is the process of changing the sign of the second number and adding to the first. 65–34 is 65 + (–34).

So when we do subtraction, we actually add the two's complement form (i.e., the negative) of the second number to the first number. This is what computers actually do when they perform subtraction. In the discussion of subtraction in Section 0.6.4, this was not explicitly mentioned, because the idea then was to present certain other intricacies related to subtraction. Now let us discuss subtraction for 8-bit signed numbers. Keep in mind that the range of signed numbers usable with 8 bits is –128 to + 127.

Example 0.18

Perform subtraction of the following signed numbers:

i) +26 from +68
ii) +26 from –68

Solution

i) +26 from +68

This comes to be a computation in the form of 68 + (–26). For this, the two's complement form of 26 should be added to 68.

Decimal		Binary	
68	is	0100 0100	+
–26	is	1110 0110	
		1 0010 1010	

Ignore the extra bit generated. Since the MSB is '0', the result is positive. The result is 0010 1010 i.e., 42.

ii) +26 from –68 i.e., –68 – (26) –68 + (–26)

–68 is (in two's complement form)	1011 1100	+
–26	1110 0110	
–94	**1 1010 0010**	

Ignore the extra bit generated. Since the MSB of the 8-bit result 1010 0010 is '1', the difference of the two numbers is negative. Take the two's complement of this. 0101 1110 i.e., 94. So the result of the computation is –94.

Example 0.19

Find the result of the following subtraction:

i) –56 from + 23
ii) –56 from –23

Solution

i) –56 from + 23

The computation to be done is +23 – (–56) i.e., 23 + 56. This turns out to be the addition of the two positive numbers 23 and 56.

23	+	0001 0111	+	
56		0011 1000		
79		**0100 1111**		i.e., 79

ii) –56 from –23

The computation to be done is –23 – (–56) i.e., –23 + 56.

–23	+	1110 1001	+
56		0011 1000	
33		**1 0010 0001**	

Ignore the extra bit generated. The MSB of the 8-bit result 0010 0001 is '0'. So the number is positive and is 33 in decimal, as it should be.

Overflow into the Signed Bit

Whenever we use 8-bit signed numbers in addition or subtraction, the result is found to be correct in sign and magnitude if it is within the range of –128 to +127. However, suppose this is violated? What happens then? A typical case is when two negative numbers are added. Try adding –100 and –55. Both the operands are within the allowed range. See the addition.

–100	+	1001 1100	+
–55		1100 1001	
–155		**1 0110 0101**	

Ignore the extra carry bit and look at the 8-bit result. The MSB of the result is '0' indicating that it is a positive number. However, we know that the answer is negative. What caused the error? Because the sum was too large (larger than –128) to fit into the 8 bits allotted to it, there was an 'overflow into the sign bit' causing the sign bit to be changed. (A similar issue occurs when we add two positive numbers and the sum is greater than + 127). In computers there is a flag which tells us when there is an overflow into the sign bit causing it to be inverted. These matters will be discussed in detail when we do programming.

0.6.7 | Addition of Numbers of Different Lengths

We have discussed computer arithmetic in detail, because it is very important to be clear about it, so as to be able to understand how the microprocessor responds to different data types and arithmetic operations. Now let's try to understand how data of different data widths are dealt with.

Data can have different sizes depending on the processor. The 8086 can have data of 8 bits and 16 bits, while Pentium can handle 8, 16 and 32 bits internally. Sometimes it may be required to add/subtract data of different widths. In these cases, the important thing to do is to equalize the size of the data involved. Processors do not allow addition/

subtraction of data of different widths. So a byte will have to be converted to a 16-bit word, if it has to be added to a 16-bit number. The way it is done depends on whether the data is signed or unsigned. For unsigned data, the byte is appended with zeros in the upper byte, and converted to a 16-bit word. For signed data, the byte should be 'sign extended' to make it a 16-bit word. Refer Section 0.5.6 once again to convince yourself of the necessity for this.

Example 0.20

Add the unsigned numbers 35H and 7890H.

Solution

In this, 35H is appended with zeros to make it 0035H.

```
 0035H   +
 7890H
      78C5H
```

Example 0.21

Add the following signed numbers:

i) 45H and A87CH
ii) A8H and 1045H
iii) F5H and B45CH

Solution

i) In this 45H should be made into a 16-bit number. Check the MSB of this byte. It is '0', meaning that it is a positive number. The sign bit when extended to 16 bits makes the number 0045H. Then the addition is

```
 0045H   +
 A87CH
 A8C1H
```

ii) In this the byte is A8H, which has an MSB of '1'. Thus, sign extension makes it FFA8H. Now the addition is

```
  FFA8H   +
   1045H
 1 0FEDH
```

The extra bit generated is ignored, like we have done in Section 0.7.3 on signed number computation.
To be sure that this is correct, verification can be done as below.

A8H is −88
1045H is +4165

Adding the two, gives us 4077 whose hex representation is 0FEDH.

iii) Add F5H and B45CH
In this, F5H is sign extended to be FFF5H
Adding

FFF5H +
B45CH ... note that this is a negative number
1 B451H

Ignoring the extra carry bit, the sum is B451H, a negative number. To verify, find the decimal equivalents of the numbers which are –11 and –19364, which when added, give –19375.

Note You may also verify that, without extending the negative sign, a wrong result is obtained.
All the calculations we have done can be verified easily using the scientific calculator available on the PC. So, try to be adept in the use of that calculator.

0.7 | Units of Memory Capacity

A memory device is one in which data is stored. How much data a memory device can store depends on its capacity. The capacity of memory is specified as multiples of bytes since memory is byte organized, which means that one byte is stored in one location in memory. So, if there are 100 locations in a memory device, 100 bytes are stored. We all have heard of memory capacity being mentioned in terms such as bytes, kilobytes and megabytes. Now let us quantify these terms. You will be hearing these terms throughout the use of this book.

A byte is 8 bits. A word is not really defined. It depends on the processor used. For the 8086, a word size is 16 bits. A 32-bit processor may claim to have a word size of 32 bits. Memory capacity is always specified in bytes.

$2^8 = 256$ bytes
$2^{10} = 1024$ bytes = 1KiloByte or 1KB
$2^6 \times 2^{10} = 2^{16} = 64$ KB $= 65,536$ bytes
$2^{10} \times 2^{10} = 2^{20}$ = one Mega Byte (1MB) $= 1024 \times 1024 = 1,048,576$ bytes
$2^{10} \times 2^{20} = 2^{30}$ = one Giga Byte (1 GB) $= 1024 \times 1024 \times 1024 = 1,073,741,824$ bytes
$2^{10} \times 2^{30} = 2^{40}$ = one Terra Byte (TB) $= 1024 \times 1024 \times 1024 \times 1024$
$= 1,099,511,627,776$ bytes

There are also higher units, which are not so common in usage as yet, but things will change soon, no doubt about it. Some of these units are:

Peta Byte (PB) = 2^{50} bytes
Exa Byte (EB) = 2^{60} bytes
Zetta Byte (ZB) = 2^{70} bytes

KEY POINTS OF THIS CHAPTER

- A computer system consists of a CPU, memory and I/O which communicate with one another through the system bus.
- The system bus comprises the data bus, address bus and the control bus.
- A processor's activities are restricted to fetching, decoding and executing instructions.
- For reading and writing from/to memory, a number of clock cycles of time are required. The time expended for this is called the memory access time.
- When comparing assembly language programming with high-level language programming, we conclude that the former is faster in execution and more efficient and compact, but is more difficult to learn and master.
- RISC and CISC are two different philosophies in computer design, and even though a lot of controversy still rages around which is better, the two seem to have merged, more or less.
- Computers do all the computations in binary, but for entering data through the keyboard and for displaying it on the monitor, ASCII codes are used.
- Negative numbers are represented in two's complement form by all computers.

QUESTIONS

1. Name the three most important components of a computer system.
2. Have you heard of the term 'bus contention'? What does it mean in the context of a computer system?
3. If the data bus width of a processor is 64 bits, what would you say about its complexity and capability?
4. If the address bus of a processor is 64 bits, what is its address space?
5. What could be a 'multi processing' system?
6. What is the first step in the execution cycle of a processor?
7. How does the system clock frequency influence the speed of processing?
8. If a system uses a 1.5-GHz clock, what is its clock period?
9. What is meant by the word 'system bus'?
10. Why should a computer have an I/O controller?
11. What are the difficulties involved in learning and using assembly language programming?
12. Name one distinguishing feature each of RISC and CISC computers.
13. How are the hexadecimal and binary number systems related?
14. When two signed positive numbers are added and the sum exceeds 127, what is the problem that arises?
15. What is the range of signed numbers that can be represented in 12 bits?

EXERCISES

1. Write the decimal equivalent of the following numbers:
   a) 31.3H
   b) 1100.101B
   c) A32.3H
   d) 100101B
2. Convert the following numbers to binary form:
   a) 34
   b) 200
   c) 90
3. Convert to hexadecimal format.
   a) 3454
   b) 4523
   c) 789
4. Write the binary values for:
   a) 34ADH
   b) 78FH
   c) 407BH
5. Write the hexadecimal values of:
   a) 1100010101011100 01B
   b) 1001111110000101 0B
6. Find the packed BCD representation of the following decimal numbers:
   a) 45
   b) 4678
   c) 802345
7. Represent the packed BCD of the following numbers in hex:
   a) 235
   b) 9123
8. What is the ASCII of each of the following?
   a) 7
   b) 8
   c) 0
   d) A
   e) Z
   f) y
   g) d
   h) *
   i) &
9. Find the two's complement representation of the following numbers in 8 bits:
   a) −45
   b) −90
   c) −12
   d) −34

10. Represent the following negative numbers using 16 bits:
    a) −267
    b) −4
    c) −5676
    d) −675
11. Perform binary addition for the following numbers:
    a) 34 and 56
    b) −52 and −70
    c) −47 and +120
12. Convert to packed BCD and add,
    a) 46 and 23
    b) 55 and 67
    c) 34 and 49
    d) 99 and 44
13. Subtract after converting to binary form,
    a) −20 from −75
    b) +49 from +97
    c) E5H from A4H
14. Add the following signed numbers:
    a) F3H and 3245H
    b) AH and F45H
    c) B2H and 123EH
15. How many bytes constitute
    a) 5 MB
    b) 4 KB
    c) 32 MB
    d) 32 KB
    e) 8 GB

1 INTRODUCTION TO EMBEDDED SYSTEMS

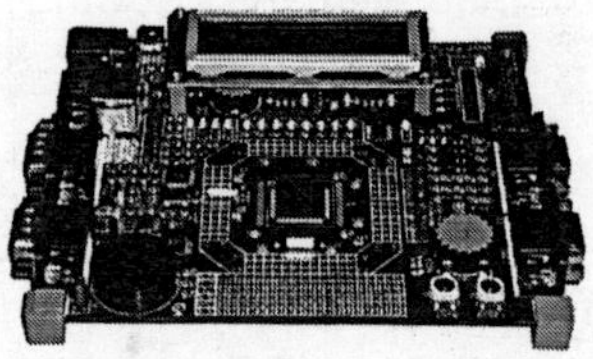

In this chapter, you will learn

- What is meant by the term 'embedded systems'
- The application domain of embedded systems
- The model of an embedded system
- The difference between an MCU and an MPU
- The working of a simple embedded system
- The figures of merit for an embedded system
- Classification of MCUs on the basis of data bus widths
- The history and current trends of the embedded systems industry

Introduction

The term 'embedded systems' has become very common, but is quite difficult to 'define', because of the large variety of devices included in this class. So, let us make an attempt to understand it, rather than make an attempt to 'define' it.

An embedded system is an electronic system which is designed to perform one or a limited set of functions, using hardware and software. Thus, let's examine the vast domain of embedded systems.

Having hardware and software makes an embedded system a computer, but this computer performs only a limited set of functions. Thus, we exclude the PC from the embedded system world, and name it as a general purpose computer. Therefore, an embedded system is a 'special purpose' computing unit—meaning that it will have a processor and associated software. The software associated with the application is 'burned' into the ROM of the processor; therefore, it is better to designate it as a 'firmware'.

Take the case of an automobile, for example, a car. It has a number of 'electronic control units (ECUs)' as part of what is called 'automobile electronics'—each of these units has a processor, which controls one or other of the various parts of the car such as engine, brakes, lights, doors and so on. Thus, embedded systems are ubiquitous, that is, omnipresent within an automobile, and adds intelligence to the operation of the vehicle.

Chapter-opening image: Development board of TI's low power MSP 430 microcontroller.

1.1 | Application Domain of Embedded Systems

The application domain of embedded systems percolates every element of modern life—it will be easier to understand its features once we take a tour of the world of embedded systems. The following is a list:

i) **Consumer electronics**: Cameras, music players, TVs, DVD players, microwave ovens, washing machines, refrigerators and remote controls.
ii) **Household appliances/home security systems**: Airconditioners, intruders and fire alarm systems.
ii) **Automobile controls**: Anti-lock braking system, engine and transmission control, door and wiper control, etc.
iv) **Handheld devices**: Mobile phones, PDAs, MP3 players, digicams, etc.
v) **Medical equipments**: Scanners, ECG and EEG units, testing and monitoring equipments.
vi) **Banking:** ATMs, currency counters, etc.
vii) **Computer peripherals**: Printers, scanners, webcams, etc.
viii) **Networking:** Routers, switches, hubs, etc.
ix) **Factories**: Control, automation, instrumentation and alarm systems.
xi) **Aviation**: Airplane controls, guidance and instrumentation systems.
xii) **Military:** Control and monitoring of military equipments.
xiii) **Robotics:** Used in factories, household and hobby-related activities.
xiii) **Toys**.

Figure 1.1 depicts some embedded products. It is only a sample of the products in the galaxy of embedded systems.

This list is incomplete, and on perusing it, you are likely to feel that anything and everything that involves modern day electronic control is an 'embedded system'. This is not far from the truth. In fact, the only electronic equipment that we simply and easily exclude from the list is the home PC.

Why do we exclude the PC from this list?

We will first list out the general features of an embedded system before attempting to answer this question.

1.2 | Desirable Features and General Characteristics of Embedded Systems

i) It should have one or a small set of functions which it is expected to perform efficiently.
ii) It should be designed for low-power dissipation, because many systems are battery powered.
iii) It has limited memory and limited number of peripherals.
iv) Applications are not meant to be alterable by the user.
v) Many of them are not accessible directly, that is, they may be part of the control unit of a larger system, so no interference in operation is possible.
vi) They need to be highly reliable.
vii) Many of them need to operate with time constraints.

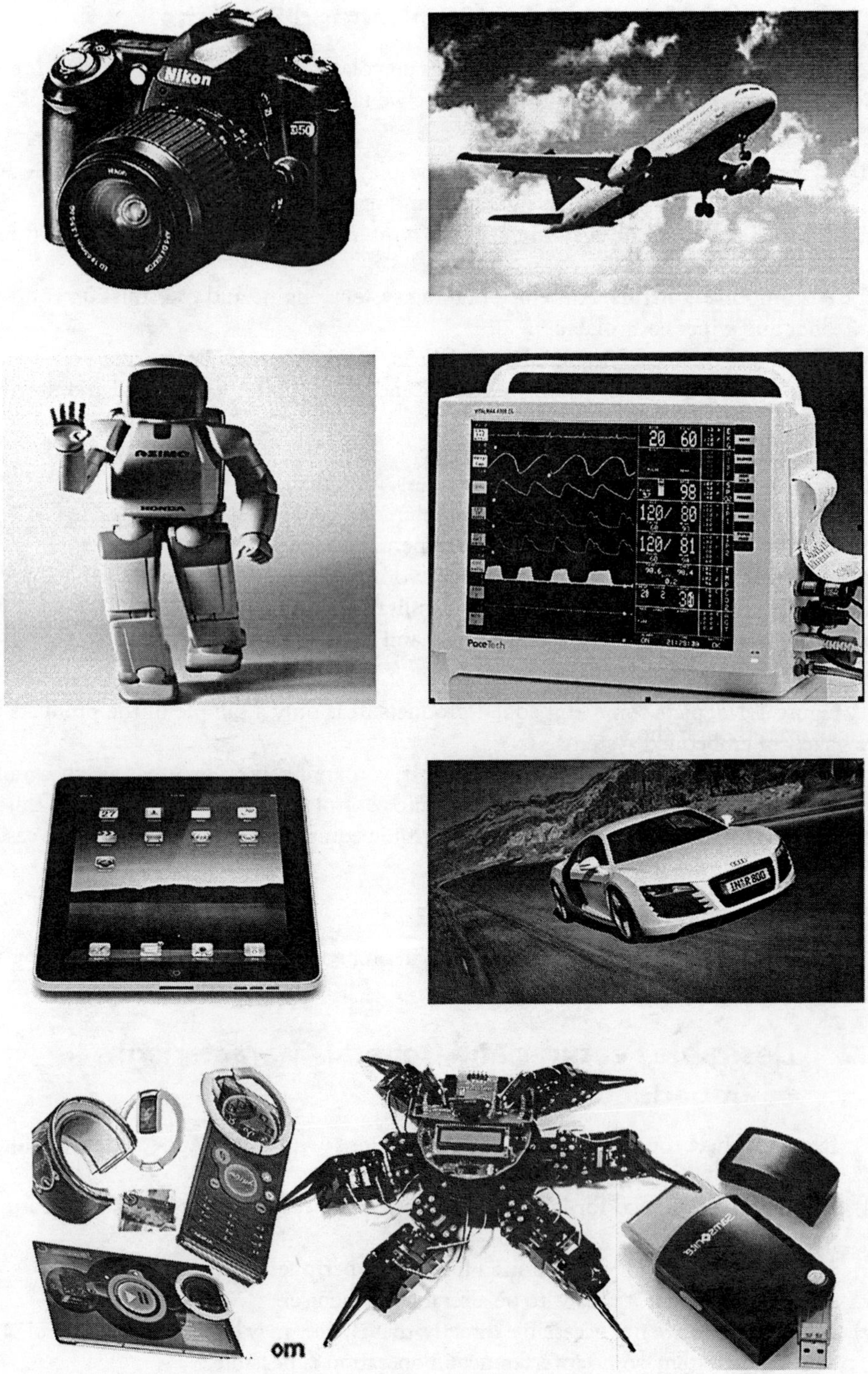

Figure 1.1 | Some application fields of embedded systems

Now let's try to understand why a PC is not considered to be an embedded system.

i) The PC has a large application set, from word processing and computation to communications, printing, scanning and many more.
ii) Low power consideration is a good idea, but that is not the guiding principle in its design.
iii) Memory is available in various forms: RAM, ROM and secondary memory devices like the hard disk, CDROMs and the like. More memory can be added if the user desires.
iv) Since the PC is used for various applications, more applications can be added as and when needed.
v) The PC can be accessed by input devices like the keyboard, mouse, modem, etc.
vi) Like any other system, the PC also needs to be reliable, but since it is unlikely to be the part of a very critical system, it can afford to fail once in a while (not a very good idea, though because PCs are used in critical monitoring applications sometimes).
vii) The applications on the PC need to be fast for better performance, but usually there is no time criticality involved.

Now that we have eliminated the general purpose PC from the list of embedded systems, the next question is whether the new handheld devices such as advanced mobile phones, PDAs, etc. can be included in the list of 'embedded systems'. The answer is that gradually these devices are also being used for 'general purposes', just like a PC. But the other side of the argument is that the design of such handheld devices is similar to that of embedded systems, where processor power, memory, size, are limited, and timing is critical, even though the applications may resemble that of a PC. As such, such devices can also be thought of as embedded systems.

1.3 | Model of an Embedded System

In its simplest and most general form, an embedded system consists of a processor, sensors, actuators and memory. The idea is that any application should be able to provide solution to a real-world problem, for which some data is definitely to be read in. For this, sensors are needed. This data is processed by the processor and the result of it is given to actuators which perform appropriate actions. See Figure 1.2, which is a very simple model of an embedded system.

1.4 | Microprocessor vs Microcontroller

We have already talked about a processor as being the brain of an embedded system. This simply means that there should be a computational engine as the core of the system, to make it 'intelligent'. There are two types of 'processor units' commonly mentioned in the literature.

1.4.1 | Microprocessor Unit (MPU)

A processor like the 8086, or its advanced version, that is, Pentium, has very high computational capability, but it does not have pins or the internal architecture to interface with the external world. For such 'microprocessors', external chips act as peripheral

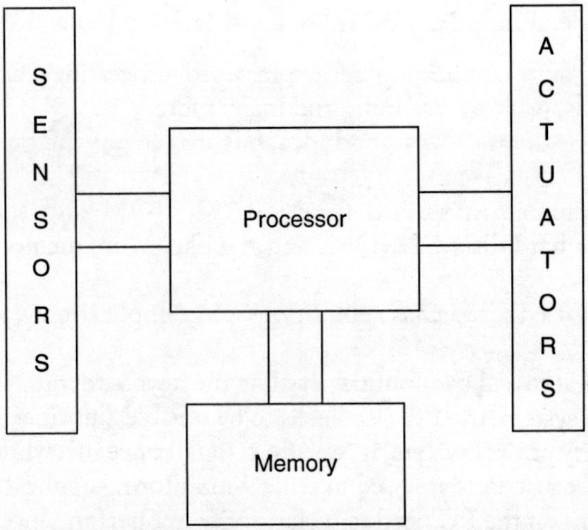

Figure 1.2 | General model of an embedded system

controllers. For example, to connect an LCD display to an MPU, a parallel port IC is to be connected externally—to have a serial transmission facility, an external serial controller is necessary—for timing and counting, external timers are needed. Memory can also be connected externally. Figure 1.3 shows an MPU chip connected to peripherals and memory which are physically external to the chip. Such MPUs are used as the core of general purpose computation systems, where the emphasis is on 'computational power' rather than interfacing capability. A PC uses an MPU, and a number of external chips together as a 'chipset' which acts as controllers to various peripherals.

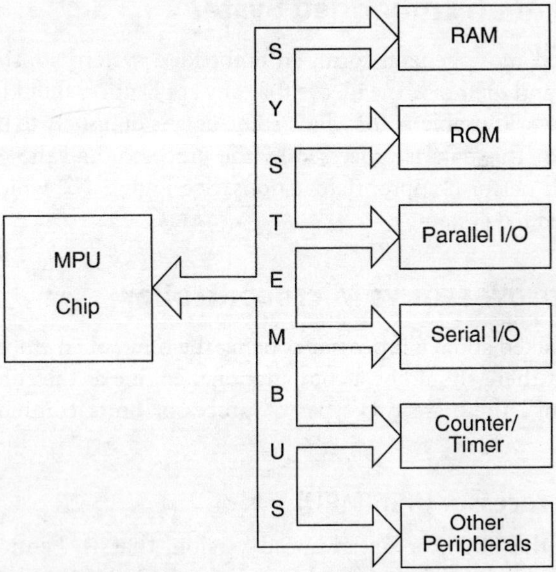

Figure 1.3 | An MPU with peripherals and memory external to the chip

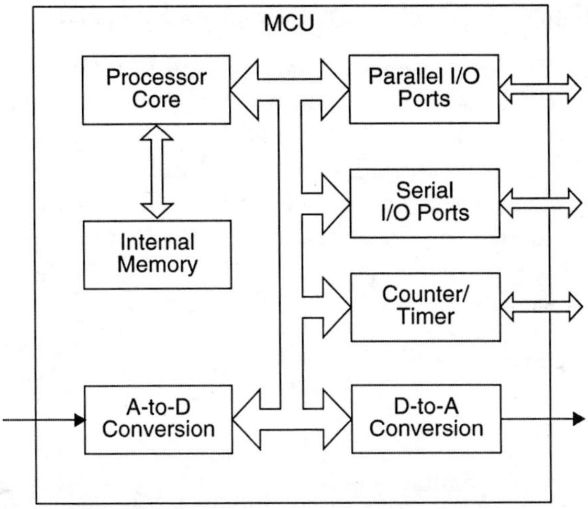

Figure 1.4 | An MCU with peripherals and memory inside the chip

1.4.2 | Microcontroller Unit (MCU)

See Figure 1.4. Here the processing unit has along with it (in the same chip), timers, parallel ports, serial ports, RAM, ROM, etc. So, no external controller chips are needed. Memory is also available inside the chip—the program code is burned into the internal ROM, and application code is run with the help of internal RAM. Thus, this is more or less a self-contained single chip computer. Popular microcontrollers include 8051, PIC, AVR, ARM, etc. When such an MCU has a lot of peripherals inside, such that the design of a large system is possible with these peripheral controllers itself, the chip is called a System on Chip (SoC). We usually hear terms like ARM SoC, Cypress's PSoC (Programmable System on Chip), etc. which are very popular in the embedded system market. Figure 1.5 is a photograph of a few MCU chips.

Figure 1.5 | Some popular MCUs

1.5 | Example of a Simple Embedded System

Let's examine the embedded system in detail. We will think of a very simple system, as in Figure 1.6. An MCU is considered the brain of this system, which functions as a temperature monitor/controller. A sensor reads the temperature, and an ADC inside the MCU converts it to digital form. This data is compared to a reference temperature, and if it is above the allowed value, an alarm is activated. Also an output from the MCU is used to start a cooling fan to reduce the temperature. There is a digital display of the temperature as well.

Thus, the output actuation consists of the following:

i) Display of the temperature value
ii) Alarm
iii) Motor which controls a cooling fan

The input is just a temperature sensor.

This is a very simple system. The program continuously measures the temperature at the sensor with a delay of T, between the readings. This 'delay' is obtained from the timer inside the MCU. There is an ADC inside the MCU to convert the analog value of the temperature into a digital number. The output display also is refreshed at the same rate as the rate of reading the input temperature. The program is written, tested and burned into the ROM (usually flash ROM) of the MCU. The program runs continuously. The circuitry is put on a PCB, packed inside an enclosure, and it becomes a product. The user simply places it in the area that he wants to measure the temperature. Now, if the program is to be changed, the designer has to interfere. The user cannot do anything to the finished product.

This product can have a user interface, by adding a keyboard at the input side. For example, if the 'reference temperature' is allowed to be changed by the user, this keyboard input, with a password (optional) can be used. The keyboard is interfaced with an interrupt, that is, when a key is pressed, an ISR (interrupt service routine) (Section 2.2.9) is activated, which checks the password and allows the user to change the 'reference' temperature settings.

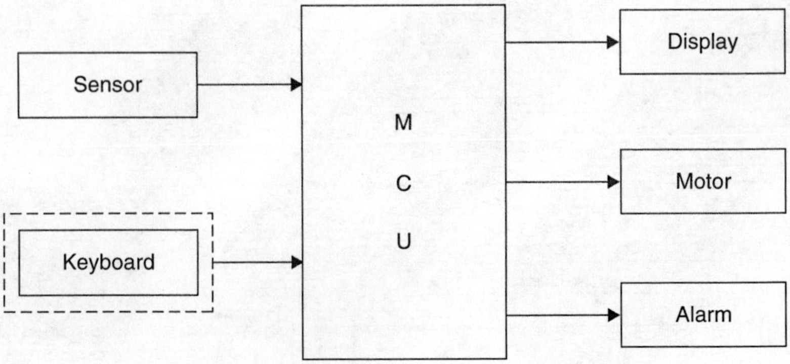

Figure 1.6 | A simple temperature monitor

This kind of approach in 'programming', where a program continually and repeatedly runs in memory, is termed 'the superloop approach'. This is how a simple embedded system is designed to meet its requirements. Any aperiodic input is accepted by the mechanism of interrupts.

Next let's take the case of a more complex system, for example, a mobile phone, which has a number of functions to perform: handling voice calls, messaging, the Internet, video and music players, reminders and a lot more. Some of the applications may be time critical, others may not be. Such a complex system needs a 'manager' and usually has an operating system. Most of us are aware that mobile phones have some version of an operating system. Symbian, Android, etc. are some popular mobile phone operating systems.

Other complex systems like PDAs, telecom networks, wireless sensor networks, etc., also have operating systems. Operating systems are needed only when system complexity due to multiple tasks of different types and criticality of response times dictate the need for it.

1.6 | Figures of Merit for an Embedded System

Embedded system design is usually aimed to achieve the following objectives:

i) Low-power dissipation
ii) Small physical size
iii) Small code size
iv) High speed of response

Low-power Dissipation Many embedded devices are battery powered, and hence low-power dissipation is an important figure of merit. Even in cases where the embedded system is part of a larger system (like in a washing machine), it is important to keep power dissipation low to avoid excessive heating. Thus, embedded designs should be low-power designs and the first step in this is achieved by choosing an MCU with low-power features. What has made the ARM MCU (used in many mobile phones, IPads, etc.) very popular is its 'low power' feature. Taking care of the power requirement of the MCU is not the only thing. Peripherals like displays, motors, relays, etc. should also be chosen with the same consideration.

Small Physical Size Many embedded systems are handheld devices, and others are allotted only small spaces within large systems such as the electronic unit which controls a printer, scanner, etc. It is obvious that the smaller the size of the unit, the better it will be. As such, the trend is to choose an MCU with most of the peripheral controllers inside the chip itself—thus the PCB is very small, with very few extra chips—there is also the trend in chip design to focus on 'small dies'.

Small Code Size The system code, after testing and debugging, is to be embedded as firmware, and it is best if it fits inside the (flash) ROM of the MCU. Thus, the code size is to be minimized, as on-chip ROM is expensive and a scarce resource. If the code size is large, external memory will have to be added, which will defeat the very purpose of using an MCU. If an operating system is being used for the system, its 'footprint' should be small.

High Speed As a general case, we would like systems to respond fast. For an embedded MCU, fast response implies high clock frequency—but the higher the clock frequency, higher will be the power dissipation—so the trick is not to choose an unnecessarily high clock frequency unless the application needs it. For simple applications, if PIC and 8051 MCUs are used, we find that frequencies in the range of 12–20 MHz are common. This is not a high frequency compared to clock frequencies of general purpose processors (2 to 3 GHz). But higher end systems are likely to use MCUs (like ARM) with much higher clock frequencies for faster response.

Real Time Response There is another aspect to response time and that is defined by a 'deadline'—if an operation is stipulated to have to be completed within a deadline, the system must be able to produce the result within this time frame—if not, it becomes either a useless system or a system with low performance quotient.

1.7 | Classification of MCUs: 4/8/16/32 Bits

We can classify embedded systems on the basis of their complexity. Complex operations imply large amounts of data, usually. For example, image and video operations need large word lengths and higher clock rates. This needs MCUs also with wide data buses. MCUs of different data and address bus widths are available. Here we classify MCUs on the basis of their data word lengths.

i) **4-bit MCUs:** Some applications deal with very little computation, and in that case 4 bits of data could be sufficient. Simple toys and applications which use just switch inputs and directly perform actuation don't need to handle large volumes of data.
ii) **8-bit MCUs:** The highest volumes of MCUs used are the ones with 8-bit data buses. For moderately complex operations, this is sufficient. The most popular of this is the 8051 family, which was developed by Intel, but which is now manufactured by various other companies as well. Microchip's PIC is another popular family with many different series with varying capabilities. Newer versions of PIC with more and newer peripherals are being developed which makes the PIC series very attractive. Incidentally, the PIC series includes 8-bit, 16-bit and 32-bit MCUs.
iii) **16-bit MCUs:** There are a few 16-bit MCUs like Intel's 8096, 80196, some versions of PIC, etc. MSP 430 (manufactured by Texas Instruments) is a new 16-bit series, which has very low-power dissipation, and can compete effectively in the new embedded market, which is very particular about power dissipation.
iv) **32-bit MCUs:** 'ARM' is the most popular 32-bit MCU in use today; it is used in complex applications requiring low power, high speed and good computing capability. The 32-bit MCUs are the ones used in image and video applications and thus find use in the latest mobile phones, IPods, PDAs, etc.

In the following section, we will discuss some other devices which are also included in the category of embedded systems.

1.7.1 | ASIC: Application Specific Integrated Circuit

This is an IC in which complex functional blocks are integrated to make it a complete application. The IC is designed from basics, after defining its application. It can even be that it is tailor-made for a particular customer by the designer company.

A video codec (coder decoder) is an example of an ASIC. What we get here is a hardware implementation of a complex algorithm, and this hardware implementation will be very efficient and fast (in the case of a sturdy design). ASICs are generally expensive to make, especially because of 'strict' specifications and limited application market.

What is an ASIP?

ASIP stands for 'Application Specific Instruction Set Processor'. It is a processor whose instructions set is tailor-made for a specific application, like graphics, for example. Thus, it will be a sort of tradeoff design between the programmability features of a CPU and the performance of an ASIC.

1.7.2 | FPGA (Field Programmable Gate Array)

These devices also are included in the domain of embedded systems. As the name indicates, it is a programmable hardware— a type of hardware which is programmable, that is, reconfigurable even while it is part of a circuit. It is an advanced form of complex programmable logic devices. Here the device density is very high.

In this, a number of logic cells are interconnected—the logic cells as well as interconnects are programamable using hardware description languages and synthesis tools. This makes hardware design cheap and flexible, but the end result is not as efficient or as fast as ASICs. There are a number of well-advanced companies supplying FPGAs—Xilinx, Altera, Altec, etc.

1.7.3 | DSP Processors

The above-said processors belong to the set of 'general purpose processors'. They have instruction sets which cater to general arithmetic and logical computations. But for many applications like signal processing where floating point operations and complex arithmetic operations are involved, their performance is unlikely to be sufficiently fast and efficient. Here comes the necessity for processors with instruction sets which are designed for signal processing and complex math operations. They are called DSP processors.

Where real-time processing of speech, image, video, etc. are involved, they perform superbly. There are many companies manufacturing such DSP processors: Texas Instruments is the leader in the design of DSP processors, and Analog Devices, Nvidia, Lucent, Freescale, etc. also some of them. For many applications, the current trend is to have a general purpose core and a DSP core on the same chip, so that tasks can be partitioned. See Figure 1.7 which is a very popular setup for advanced operations—an ARM core and a DSP core handling different types of computations, along with a number of peripheral controllers—all on the same chip.

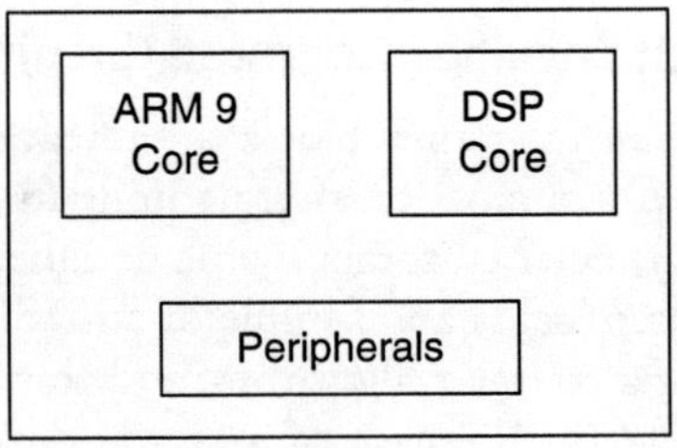

Figure 1.7 | Typical embedded dual core setup

1.8 | History of Embedded Systems

To trace the history of embedded systems, one does not need to look very far back. When Intel and other companies started their design and manufacture of microprocessors, it was realized that programmability features could ease computations and also that interfacing with input and output devices was possible. All this led to the development of computers or what we now call the personal computer. The immense possibility of using computers for control and actuation soon grew into realization and many possibilities were tried out.

With this realization, the personal computing sector grew and along with that, the idea of embedding intelligence into computer chips took new wings. It was realized that along with a computational engine, other functions can be incorporated into a single chip. Memory and other functional blocks, when added to a microprocessor gave it the name microcontroller or embedded processor. It was actually the development of the concept of such types of processing units with peripherals and memory on a single chip that gave the necessary impetus for the growth of embedded systems.

Two engineers in TI (Texas Instruments), Gary Boone and Michael Cochran, are credited with creating the first microcontroller TMS 1000, which became a commercial product in 1974. It had ROM, RAM and clock circuitry on the chip along with the processing unit.

In 1977, Intel emerged in this field with the 8048, a microcontroller which had RAM and ROM and which became widely used used in PC keyboards. In 1980, Intel introduced the 8051 MCU and called it MCS-51 architecture. Over the years, it became very popular especially because Intel allowed others also to manufacture and sell it. In 1982, Intel introduced the 80186 and called it an embedded processor. It had the same computing engine as the 8086, but had a number of peripherals inside it, like timers, DMA controllers, clock generators and so on. This chip was never used in PCs—all its applications were in embedded products. Other popular microcontroller series are PIC by Microchip and ATMega by AVR. Besides this there are a number of smaller players also in the market.

This outlook that microcontrollers alone paved the way for the development of the embedded industry development may not very true, however. If we look at any embedded system today, we know that it is not 'electronics' alone that has made miraculous strides. Along with electronics, sensors, actuators, displays, mechanical parts and software developments have also made giant strides to fuel the growth of the embedded industry.

What are the challenges in this field now?

New and innovative products are continually appearing in the market. The three Ps of innovation frequently highlighted are 'Price, Performance and Power'. This obviously means that performance needs to be increased, but keeping power dissipation and price as low as possible. This translates to using low-power dissipating processors, sensors and actuators, all of which must be able to boast of high performance. Performance implies high computational capability at the highest possible speed. The factors performance and power dissipation directly conflict each other, and keeping prices low is an additional issue. But in spite of all these challenges, the embedded industry is moving ahead in leaps and bounds.

1.9 | Current Trends

To address the challenges just mentioned, various trends are being adopted.

i) **Multi-core processors:** It has become very clear that trying to improve processor performance by increasing clock frequencies is fraught with difficulties, because the direct result of higher clock frequency is high power dissipation. Thus, the option of using more than one processor core (at lower clock frequencies) is being tried out. Thus, the current smart phones and gaming consoles use multi-core processors. It may be understood that if there are two cores, one may be a DSP core while the other is a general purpose core. The design of multi core systems requires new design environments which are being developed at a rapid rate.

ii) **Embedded and real-time operating systems:** With the emergence of complex applications, many new embedded and real-time operating systems have become popular. Linux has emerged as a popular embedded OS, and others like Android and newer versions of Symbian have came up for mobile applications and hand-held devices.

iii) **Newer areas of deployment of embedded devices:** Embedded devices have applications in the entertainment, healthcare and automotive segments. Besides that, there are applications in the communication and military fields as well. Research and development in these fields is going ahead.

Conclusion

In the forthcoming chapters, we will try to get some insight into this exciting field of embedded systems and learn how we can make its study fruitful and interesting.

KEY POINTS OF THIS CHAPTER

- Embedded systems have made their presence felt in every area of modern life.
- There are some desirable features for an electronic system to be included in the list of embedded systems.
- A general purpose PC is not an embedded system.

- Any embedded system has a sensor and an actuator.
- MCUs are MPUs with peripherals and memory designed to be inside the chip.
- The embedded systems industry is relatively new, but marching forward at a rapid rate.
- Making use of multi-core processors has become a trend in the embedded industry.

QUESTIONS

1. Explain what an embedded system is, with few examples.
2. How is software embedded into an ES?
3. Name four fields of applications for an embedded system.
4. List three characteristics that an embedded system should possess.
5. Can an electronic tablet be listed as an embedded system? Substantiate your answer.
6. What is the difference between an MCU and an MPU?
7. Why is power dissipation a very important factor in embedded design?
8. Why are DSP processors used in embedded design?
9. Name two new areas of deployment for embedded systems.
10. Name two commercial products based on the ARM processor.

EXERCISES

1. Draw a block diagram of an embedded system which can be used for measuring short distances.
2. Name a few embedded products in the field of bio-medical engineering.

2 EMBEDDED SYSTEMS—THE HARDWARE POINT OF VIEW

In this chapter, you will learn

- The hardware aspects of an embedded system
- The ideas of power-on-reset and brown-out-reset
- The importance of the clock and general purpose I/O
- The working principle of timers and counters
- The necessity of watchdog timers, real-time clock and DMA
- The concept of interrupts
- Semiconductor memories like SRAM, DRAM, Flash and EEPROM
- The necessity and techniques of low power design
- Important concepts like pullups, pulldowns and Hi-Z

Introduction

In Chapter 1, the model of an embedded system was defined and discussed. In this chapter, we will probe a bit deeper. By now, it must be clear that embedded systems include both hardware and software. This chapter plans to delve into the hardware aspects and discuss the hardware building blocks of typical systems.

Anyone who wants to design a system starts with a suitable MCU which must meet his requirements. The MCU should address all the needs of the application for which the design is to be done. There is no point in choosing an MCU which is much more advanced than what the application needs. We should not use a 32-bit MCU for an application for which the data involved is very little. It is also important to ensure that, as far as possible, all the controllers for the peripherals are available within the chip. It should also be confirmed that there are sufficient numbers of I/O pins for connecting all the peripherals. The clock frequency should be high enough, but not excessively high because power dissipation tends to increase as clock frequency increases. In short, a number of factors are to be kept in mind when hardware design is envisaged.

This chapter discusses the MCU as a hardware unit and examines the important components in an MCU. Though the discussion is very general, the 8051 is used (in certain sections) as an example to highlight some general features of MCU hardware. This microcontroller has been chosen because it is one of the simplest and most popular

---

Chapter-opening image: PIC and 8051 MCUs.

of the available ones—there is also a chance that some of you have already done a course on the 8051 MCU. Some features of PIC are also referred to in some parts of this chapter.

Those who already have had some exposure to microcontrollers will be able to connect well with these discussions if some example MCUs are referred to. For others, this chapter is meant to be the first step towards understanding embedded systems hardware. It is important to keep in mind that when designing a system, the data sheet of the chosen MCU should be referred and a thorough understanding of the pin diagram, register structure, modes of operation, etc. should be gained.

In this chapter, a detailed discussion of semiconductor memory has also been attempted. Different types of memory, and the relevance of each type, has been probed into—this is necessary, because various types of memory are used in any system, and even inside an MCU. Finally, low power design has also been elaborated upon.

2.1 | Microcontroller Unit (MCU)

In Chapter 1, it was made clear that a processing unit is needed for an embedded system. An 'embedded processor' which is another name for a 'microcontroller unit', is used at the heart of the system design.

There is a processor part inside the MCU block—this is the CPU or the computing engine of the MCU. Figure 2.1 shows this. The other blocks inside it are memory and peripheral controllers (the term peripheral is the term usually used, though we really mean 'peripheral controllers'). The number and kind of peripheral controllers is not standard—various MCUs have different sets of peripherals, but there are some peripherals which are more or less a standard feature-like timers and the serial communication interface.

2.1.1 | The Processor

The processor is the unit which acts as the 'brain'—it is the central processing unit which performs the required computations and controls the peripherals. Since memory and peripheral controllers are also inside the chip, the data bus as well as the address bus are internal.

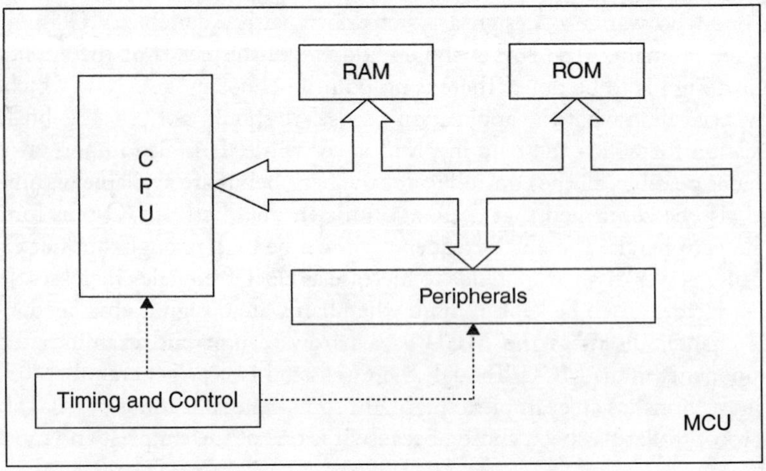

Figure 2.1 | The internal structure of an MCU

The 'performance' of the processing unit of an MCU is dependant on many factors, like instruction set architecture (ISA), data bus width and addressing space. Its capacity to perform complex computations at a fast rate is decided by the ISA. The ISA can be defined as that aspect of computer architecture which is related to programming, including the native data types, instruction registers, addressing modes, memory architecture and interrupt handling. In short, it specifies the way in which an assembly language programmer or a compiler designer views the processor.

2.1.2 | The Harvard Architecture

There are architectural variations in processors; the two classical divisions are the Von Neumann and the Harvard architectures. In the former, both code and data share the same address space and hence they are accessed using the same bus. Many MPUs use this architecture, for example, the x86 series.

In the Harvard architecture, code and data are considered distinct and hence are accessed by separate buses, and also have separate storage spaces. Figure 2.2 illustrates this aspect. Microcontrollers achieve this physical separation by having instructions stored in flash ROM and data in RAM.

Microcontrollers are single chip computers, and memories (RAM and ROM) are inside the chip. As such, the buses for accessing data and instructions are inside the chip.

If the processor is an 8-bit one (like the 8051), it means that the data bus is 8 bits wide and all computations are possible only for an 8-bit data, which means that for arithmetic operations like addition, subtraction, multiplication, etc., the operands can be only 8 bits in size. This also means that the data bus (internal) is 8 bits wide. If two 16-bit numbers are to be added, a program should be written to add the lower two bytes, save the carry, and then add the upper two bytes and the carry. Obviously, a processor with 16-bit data capability can do this with a single instruction. Thus, the second processor is naturally superior to the first. A 32-bit processor will do still better, when large numbers are involved.

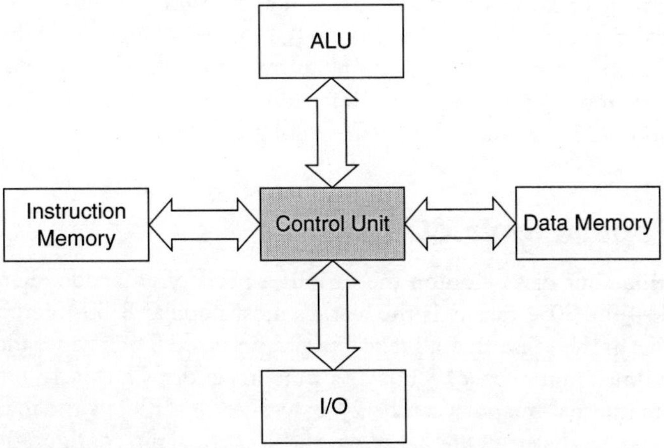

Figure 2.2 | The Harvard architecture

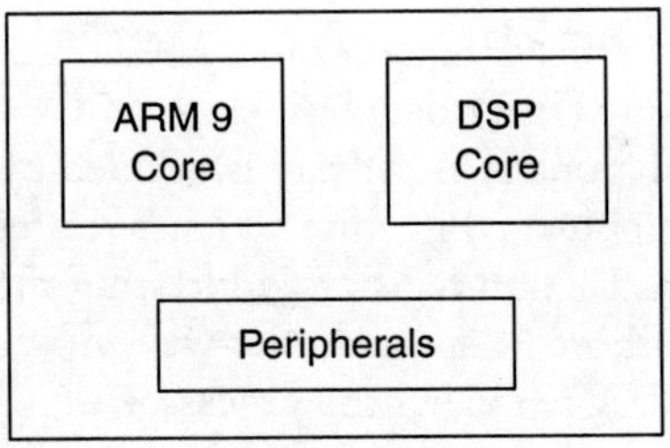

Figure 2.3 | An MCU with two CPU cores

Now about the address bus: If the address bus (internal) is 16 bits as is the case of 8051, a maximum of 2^{16} bytes, that is, 64K of internal memory, can be addressed by the CPU. The memory, in this context, is ROM, where the code will finally reside. Besides this, there is RAM available inside the chip. This is relatively small and is divided as general purpose registers, R/W memory area and special function registers (SFRs). The latter refers to the registers associated with the peripherals.

Corresponding to every peripheral, a number of registers are needed. As an example, think of a timer. A timer unit allows the generation of a square wave which can be taken out from one of the pins. Inside the MCU, the timer unit has registers for fixing up the period, mode, etc. The registers associated with the timer operation are called the 'special function registers' (SFRs) of the timers—similarly, there are SFRs for all other peripherals.

The choice of MCU is dictated by the application requirement. Many applications don't require a lot of computation; so using a 32-bit MCU where the amount of data and the complexity of processing is trivial, is a waste. The reason why 8-bit MCUs have the biggest share in the embedded market is because many low end embedded systems have to deal more with interfacing than with complex computations.

It is when large amounts of data have to be processed at high rates and the computations are complex do we go for 32-bit processors with powerful ISAs. ARM (refer to Chapters 10 and 11) is one such processor. ARM is a computationally intensive processor, but it performs integer computations. If floating point arithmetic operations and complex signal processing is involved, the MCU may be augmented by a DSP core. Many of the newer embedded applications warrant the use of such a system in which there is more than one processing unit. Refer to Figure 2.3 which shows an MCU with two cores—an ARM core and a DSP core—along with the peripherals.

2.2 | A Popular 8-bit MCU

We will continue our discussion on the various aspects of embedded hardware using a sample MCU—the 8051 family is the world's most popular 8-bit microcontroller. It is an 8-bit MCU, in the sense that all registers and ports are 8 bits wide, and data transfer can occur at a maximum rate of 8 bits at a time. Its address bus is 16 bits wide, which means that its internal memory can be 2^{16} bytes, i.e. 64K. This is the maximum size of internal ROM it can have. Figure 2.4 shows the functional pin configuration of the 8051 chip. It has four ports named P0, P1, P2 and P3. All these pins can be used as input or

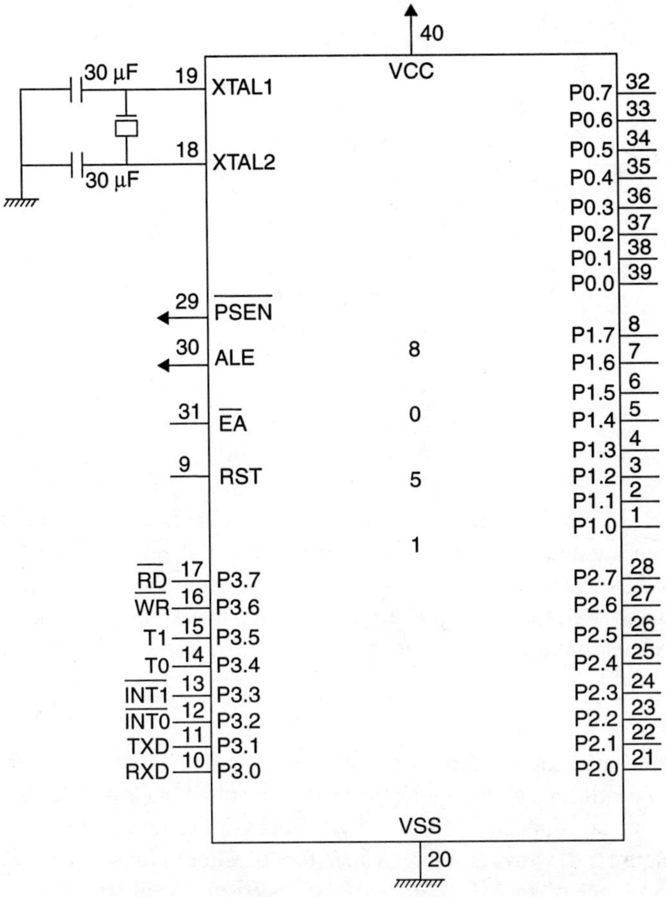

Figure 2.4 | The functional pin diagram of the 8051

output, and many of the pin lines have dual functions. In Figure 2.4, Port3 pins have been shown to have two functions each: they act either as I/O or act as signal lines for the functions shown in the diagram. The 'dual' functions of the other ports have not been shown here.

2.2.1 | General Purpose I/O (GPIO)

All MCUs have a set of pins on which external peripherals can be connected. This is a set of ports which can be used as a group or as a single pin, all of which are programmable as inputs or outputs. Each port pin may have more than one function, and the user can decide the functionality. Refer the pin configuration of 8051 in Figure 2.4. It has four 8-bit ports P0 to P3. If used as a group, all eight bits of a port can be addressed to work in unison. In that case, we use the nomenclature P0, P1, etc., in programs. If used individually, P1.0 and P1.1 indicate the 0th and 1st bits of Port 1. Similar notations are used for the pins of the other ports. Each port and each pin can be used to connect peripherals.

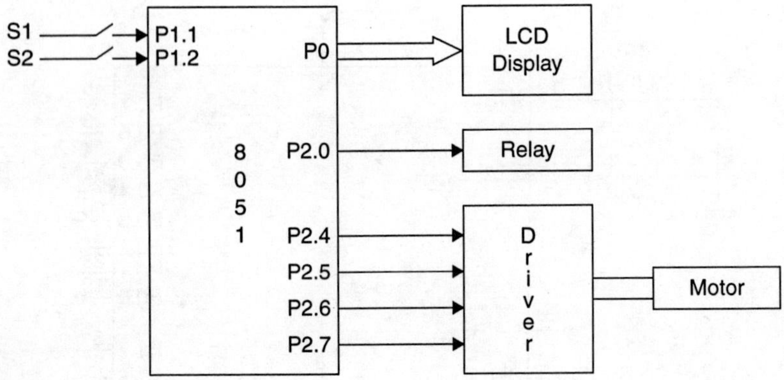

Figure 2.5 | I/O devices connected to the GPIO pins of 8051

Figure 2.5 shows various peripheral devices connected to some of the ports of an 8051 chip. Port 0 is used as the 8-bit data port for an LCD display, P1.2 and P1.1 are used for connecting switches. Port 2.0 is connected to a relay, and P2.4 to P2.7 to a stepper motor driving circuit. This figure and the discussion are meant only to show that GPIO pins can be used for any application as decided by the user. In this case, only P1.0 and P1.1 have been programmed to be inputs, all the others are output pins.

2.2.2 | Clock

All processor activities are synchronized by a clock. Usually, there is an oscillator inside the chip, which produces a clock signal, the frequency of which is decided by the resonant frequency of a crystal connected outside. Note the crystal connected between pins 18 and 19 of 8051 (Figure 2.4) with stabilizing capacitors of values ranging from 20pF to 40pF.

The performance of an MCU, in terms of 'speed of computation' is directly related to the clock frequency. Each MCU has a specification as to what is the maximum frequency of the crystal it can use. All timing calculations of timers, counters, serial port baud rate, etc., are based upon the frequency of this clock.

2.2.3 | Power on Reset

Every processor has a power on reset circuit. 'Power on reset' means that when the power is switched on, the processor should be reset. Otherwise, the system may operate initially in an unpredictable fashion because flip-flops (inside the MCU) are not designed to power-on in any particular state. The meaning of reset generally implies that internal registers (constituted by flip flops) are cleared, and that the processor gets ready to execute. Because the program counter is cleared by reset, for almost all MCUs the particular location from which the processor takes its first instruction from, is the first address itself.

Each MCU needs a specific pulse for reset to occur—it is specific in the sense that the reset pulse is either high or low and also needs to have a minimum period. This reset pulse should appear just once, when the power is switched on, and then it should disappear. But there should be a provision for manual reset also, if necessary. There is a reset pin for the MCU chip, but the 'power on reset' circuit is to be provided externally.

Figure 2.6 is a typical POR circuit. Let us analyse the circuit. Figure 2.7 a, b and c show the voltage waveforms at the capacitor and at RES and $\overline{RES}$. When power is first switched on, C starts charging as shown in Figure 2.7a. The presence of the Schmitt trigger makes the exponential charging pulse to be a rectangular pulse, V_H is the voltage at which the Schmitt switches (changes state). The value of R and C decide the value

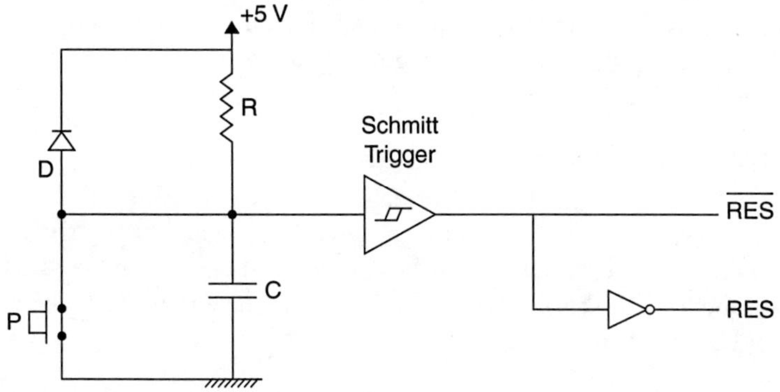

Figure 2.6 | A typical power on reset circuit

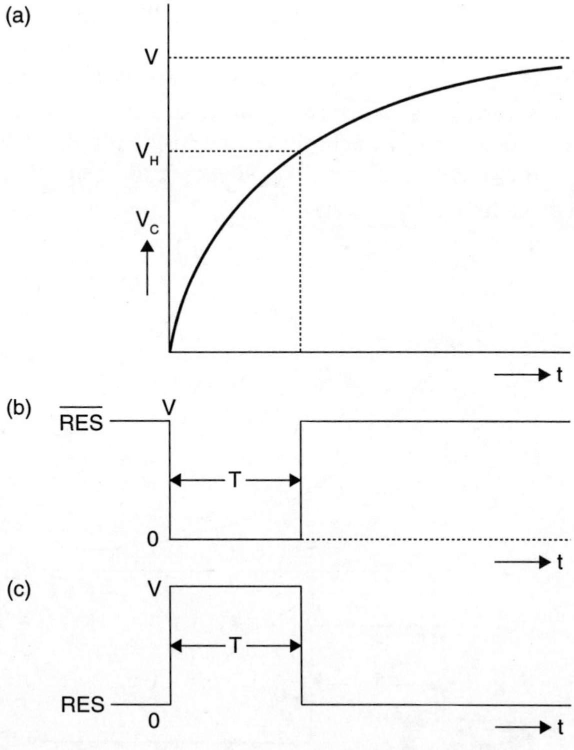

Figure 2.7 | **(a)** The voltage waveform across the capacitor, **(b)** The pulse at $\overline{RES}$ and **(c)** The pulse at RES

of T of the pulse. This pulse obtained at the point $\overline{RES}$ of Figure 2.6 can be used by any MCU which needs an active low reset. By using an inverter, a high pulse can be obtained at RES, which can be used for an MCU which needs an active high reset.

Note that once the capacitor is fully charged, the voltage at the RES point is zero and that at the $\overline{RES}$ point is V. Thus, after the reset pulse is over, the circuit behaves normally as is needed in its operational mode.

Now see the other components in Figure 2.6. P is a push button connected across the capacitor. This is for manual reset, if needed. Pressing the push button discharges the capacitor, and on push button release, once again the capacitor gets recharged and generates the reset pulse.

What is the need for the Diode D in Figure 2.6?

This diode is called a flywheel diode. Normally the diode is reverse biased by the +5V at its cathode. Now, if the capacitor is made to discharge suddenly by the push button switch, the sudden change in polarity of the capacitor voltage can make the point A to have a voltage above +5V. This makes the diode conducting and protects the MCU from being damaged by the voltage surge.

2.2.3.1 | *Power on Reset for 8051*

Figure 2.6 is a general circuit which shows the principle behind power on reset circuits. We can use any circuit which achieves the same result. The usually suggested POR circuit for the 8051 is very simple and consists just of a resistor and a capacitor. As the capacitor gets charged from the power supply, the voltage at the reset pin, that is, across the resistor falls exponentially as shown in Figure 2.8a. This functions as the high reset pulse. It is quite likely that there is a Schmitt trigger inside the IC to convert this exponential pulse to be a pulse with steep sides (see Figure 2.8b). You can add a push button for reset and a flywheel diode, if necessary.

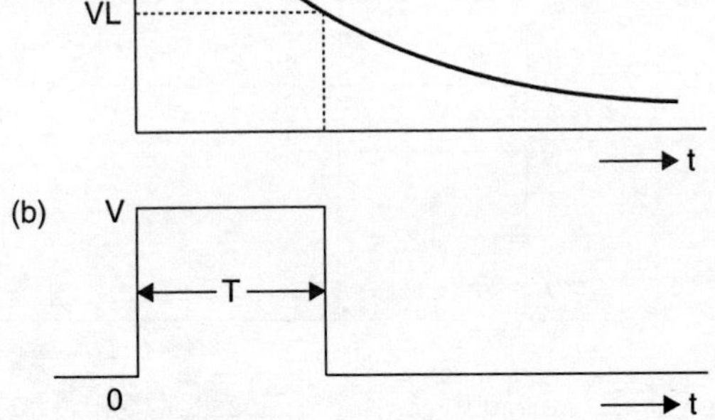

Figure 2.8 | **(a)** Waveform at pin 9 of 8051 and **(b)** Reset pulse obtained internally

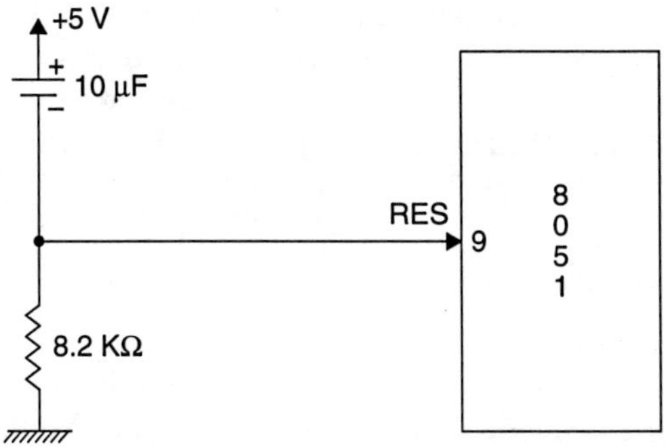

Figure 2.9 | A commonly used POR circuit for 8051

The typical values used for an 8051 with a crystal frequency of 12 MHz are shown in Figure 2.9. This MCU needs an active high pulse for reset, which is to be long enough for its oscillator to start, plus two machine cycles (this is as per the specifications given by the manufacturer). One machine cycle is 12 clock cycles. You can verify if the RC value as used in the circuit of Figure 2.8 satisfies this condition.

2.2.4 | Brown Out Reset

Many embedded systems work on battery power. It may happen that the battery gets drained and then the MCU does not work correctly. This may give wrong results leading to wrong decisions and actions. To protect the system from occurrences of such a situation, it is to be ensured that if the power supply voltage goes below a specified level, the MCU should be reset. This is called 'brown out reset'. The PIC family of MCUs has an inbuilt facility for 'brown out reset'. The 8051 family does not have this. In such cases, an external circuit is needed to ensure brown out reset. In certain other cases, it may also be that the brown out voltage level needs to be different from that ensured by the inbuilt circuitry of an MCU. Figure 2.10 shows a typical brown out reset circuit.

The circuit uses an analog comparator. The reference voltage is 2.25V, which is defined by the breakdown voltage of the zener diode D. The voltage at A (the inverting terminal of the op-amp) is half the power supply voltage V. If V = 5V, A has a voltage $V_A = 2.5V$. The circuit is designed in such a way that if the voltage V goes below 4.5 V, V_A

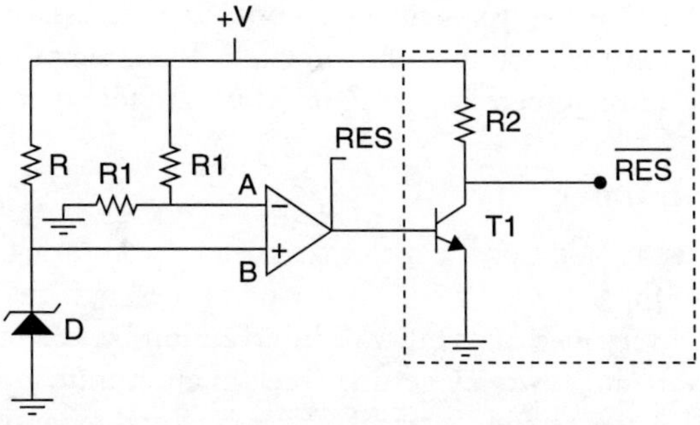

Figure 2.10 | A simple circuit for brown out reset

will become less than 2.25V. Then the comparator changes state from low to high. This can be used as the reset signal (RES) for an MCU which requires an active high reset.

For an MCU which requires the opposite polarity for reset ($\overline{RES}$), transistor T1 acting as an inverter, can be added which goes low when the voltage at the output of the comparator is high.

2.2.5 | Timers and Counters

All MCUs have timers as one of its peripherals. A timer is a dedicated hardware for 'timing' events, to generate waveforms and so on. Once a timer is started, the CPU does not have to interfere, as the timer hardware will take care of it. A number of registers may be associated with timers, but basically there is a timer count register and a mode register to decide between different options.

In its most basic form, the method of working of a timer is this: The processor clock acts as the reference clock, and in many cases this clock frequency is divided by a constant to get a lower frequency clock. In the timer count register, a number is loaded, and the timer is then 'started'. The count keeps increasing (or decreasing) until it reaches the maximum (or minimum) value. At this point, the count register resets to 0, and this is indicated by a flag bit or an interrupt. The time elapsed between the starting of counting and the resetting of the count register can be used as a 'measure' of a delay.

In many MCUs, there is a prescaler that reduces the clock frequency used as the reference, so that a longer delay is obtained—how much of prescaling is required can be indicated in a prescale register.

What Is a counter?

In 'timing' applications, the reference clock is taken from the processor clock. But there is another duty for timer units—to get it to act as a **counter**. A counter counts external events; as such it does not use the processor clock. For example, if the frequency of an external square wave is to be measured, the square wave is given as an input to a specific MCU pin, and then the timer is started. The number in the count registers gets incremented for every edge (leading or trailing) of the incoming square wave, and doing this for say, one second, gives us the number of edges counted during that time. This is the frequency of the incoming square wave. When the timing unit is used in this manner, it is called an event counter.

For more sophisticated MCUs, there are advanced 'compare and capture' units which perform counting in a very systematic manner. It is necessary to know the details of individual MCUs for understanding it completely. The attempt here is only to give a 'feel' of the functions of the timer/counter units which are found in every MCU.

2.2.6 | Watchdog Timer

A watchdog timer is an additional timer that does a 'monitoring' job and resets the system, if necessary. The scenario is this. Most embedded systems are expected to be 'self-reliant'. There is very little possibility of intervention by a human operator in case the associated software goes awry by getting stuck in an infinite loop. Some embedded systems are placed in inaccessible sites like factory environments, space probes, etc. When the software is detected to be malfunctioning, the best way is to reset and start

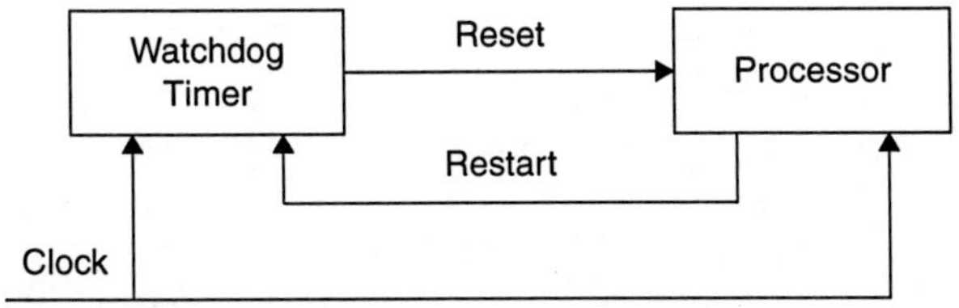

Figure 2.11 | A watchdog timer setup

again. Such anomalies can occur due to various reasons like deadlocks (in a multitasking environment), a noise voltage on some pin which may cause wrong triggering and so on. The point is that, if such a situation arises, there should be a mechanism by which this is automatically detected and gets the system to reset.

The watchdog timer is like any other timer. It can be loaded with a 'count' which decrements down to zero. When it reaches zero, it resets the processor. For a system which is doing its job correctly, the watchdog timer will never count down to zero. Before that, the 'correctly operating' software will re-start it periodically and re-load its original count, so as to prevent it from counting down to zero. What is the number loaded as the 'count' in a WDT? This is decided by considering how much time is to be allowed for the system to recover (on its own) before it is to be forcibly reset.

Figure 2.11 shows the way a watchdog timer operates. This is the case when the WDT is external to the processor. The 8051 family of MCUs don't have an internal WDT, but most other MCU families like PIC, AVR, ARM, etc., have it as an internal timer. When the processor gets reset by the WDT, it is called a 'soft reset' or a warm boot.

2.2.7 | Real-time Clock (RTC)

Many systems need to have a clock which refers to the 'real' time. For example, our PCs give us a display of the system clock which refers to real world time. This clock gives a reading in terms of seconds, minutes and hours. In the PC, there is a dedicated IC which keeps count of 'real' time in such a way that even if the PC is off, the IC keeps working and the time reference is not lost. This implies that this IC has an inbuilt battery which keeps the clock ticking always.

Many embedded systems also need a reference to real time. Operating systems loaded into memory need a timing tick at regular intervals. There are a lot of time referenced operations for which embedded systems are used. There are specialized ICs for keeping time (like the Dallas DS series) which can be programmed to count time in terms of seconds, minutes and hours. Of course, it is possible to count time by using just a counter IC with a clock. But a dedicated RTC IC will make the task simpler and the code compact. For an embedded system which needs such an RTC, such dedicated chips may be used.

Besides that, there are some MCUs which have RTC peripherals on the chip itself. Timing then occurs with respect to an oscillator which is derived from the system clock frequency. For example, many ARM MCUs have on the chip, a real-time clock (RTC) which is a set of counters for measuring time when system power is on, and optionally when it is off (by supplying a battery back up). To use this RTC, the only action needed is to write appropriate words into the associated registers.

2.2.8 | Stack

Associated with any system, there should be a stack. A stack is an area in RAM which is used to store some important data temporarily, and from a software point of view it is just a data structure. The operation of a stack is different from ordinary memory operations. Only two operations are normally defined for stacks: they are PUSH and POP (the exact instructions used may vary from processor to processor). They can be either LIFO (Last In First Out) or FIFO (First In First Out) stacks. In the case of the former, the data that was last pushed in, is the one that can be taken out first. The data structure of the latter is just the reverse. Most stacks are LIFO stacks.

It is obvious from the above that, in a stack, data cannot be written to or read from random locations. The 'top of the stack' is the reference location, with respect to which all accesses are done.

2.2.8.1 | *Ascending/Descending Stacks*

There is also another classification: the stack is either a descending or ascending type. An **ascending** stack grows upwards. It starts from a low memory address and, as items are pushed onto it, progresses to higher memory addresses. A **descending** stack grows downwards. It starts from a high memory address, and as items are pushed onto it, progresses to lower memory addresses.

Descending Stack

For any system, a stack must be defined before it can be used. Defining it amounts to just giving an address to the stack top—this address must be in the 'stack pointer', i.e. SP which is a processor register.

Let us have a look at the operation of a descending stack (see Figure 2.12). The stack is in the RAM of the MCU. Let us consider a case of a RAM with 8-bit addresses. We first load the number 0 × 42 (the notation 0 × 42 is for hex and is the same as 42H) in SP. Thus, the beginning of the stack is finalized. Now let us push two bit numbers xx and yy into the stack (which may now be in some registers). This entails the decrementing of SP, writing xx into 0 × 41 and repeating the same for the next data byte. such that the new value of SP is 0 × 40. This is how the PUSH instruction functions (see Figure 2.12a).

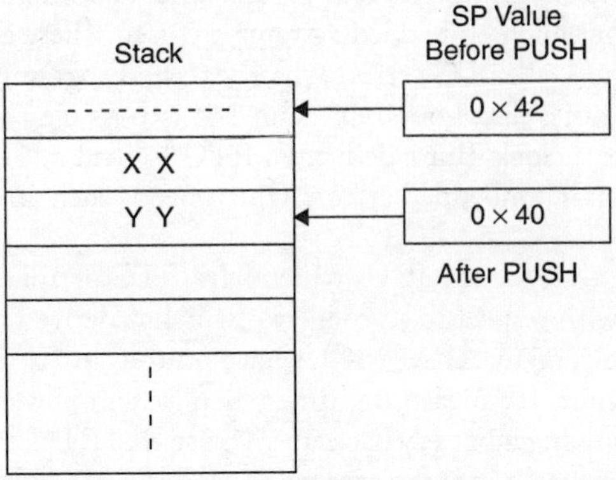

Figure 2.12a | PUSH operation in a descending stack

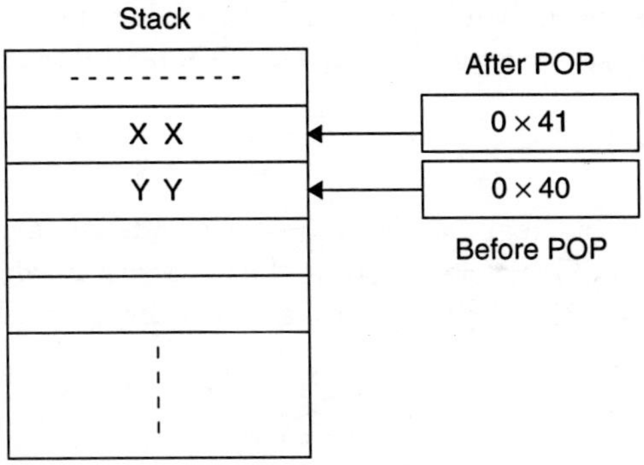

Figure 2.12b | POP operation in a descending stack

What about taking data out from the stack? SP is first incremented, then the data at the top is read. Referring to Figure 2.12b. If one byte alone is to be popped out, yy is read and loaded into a register. The content of SP is 0 × 41 now

Ascending Stack

For an ascending stack, the operation is just the reverse. This is the kind of stack available in the 8051 MCU. If the stack top is defined as 0 × 42 (SP = 0 × 42), pushing two bytes changes its content to 0 × 44; popping out one byte decrements it to 0 × 43. Figure 2.13 shows the operations for such a stack.

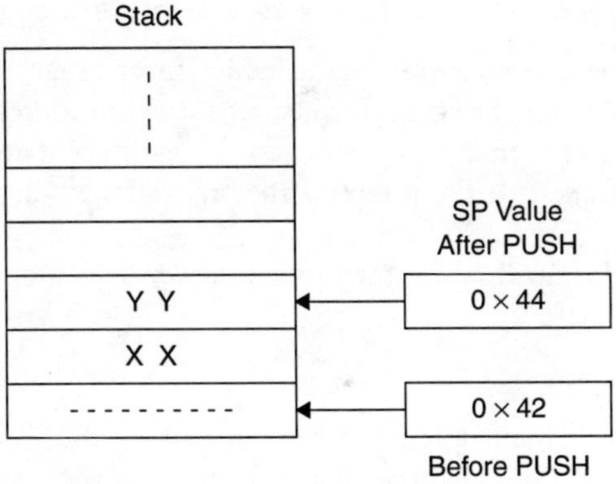

Figure 2.13a | PUSH operation in an ascending stack

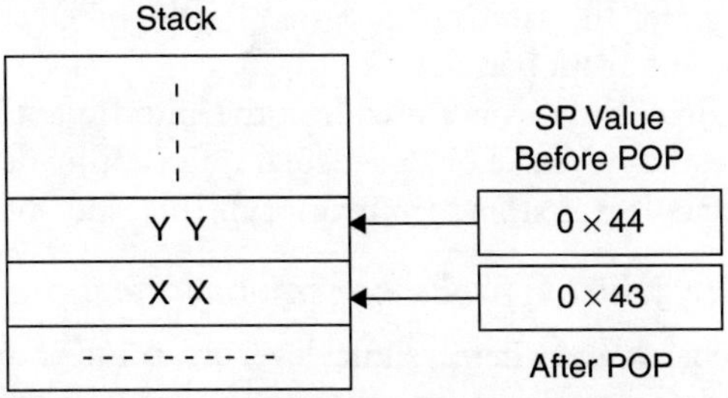

Figure 2.13b | POP operation in an ascending stack

The above discussion is only to give you a feel about stacks in general. More details of stack operation, the exact instructions used etc., should be learned with respect to a specific processor.

Where are stacks used?

A stack is used to store data 'temporarily'—so that it finds use in storing addresses and processor status (content of registers including the flag register) when function calls and interrupts occur. A programmer can find various other uses of stacks when he wants to write intelligent and interesting programs.

2.2.9 | Interrupts

This is a very commonly used term in embedded processing, and thus it is very important to understand it thoroughly. Let us start with the whole philosophy of this term with respect to processor activity.

A processor in its operating state is normally performing some activity, that is, executing a program. Now, if another more important activity is to be done, it is imperative that the current activity be stopped and that the new one be taken up. For this, the mechanism of 'interrupts' is needed.

When the processor is interrupted, it completes the instruction it is currently executing and takes up the new task which it has been asked to do. This is actually a temporary matter, because once the interrupting task is done, the processor must return and continue from where it had been interrupted.

So there are a number of matters to be settled before 'interrupting' gets through.

i) The processor must save its current status which means that the content of registers it is currently using must be saved. It must also save the address of the next instruction in the sequence, so that it can return to the right point at which it had left off.
ii) It should then 'branch' to the program that the interrupting device wants to get executed.
iii) After executing this, it should 'return' to the earlier program and resume execution from where it had left off.

Let us see how all this is done.

i) When a processor is interrupted, it saves the value of the working registers on the stack (Section 2.2.8), and also the current content of the program counter (which will point to the next instruction in the sequence).
ii) The program counter will then be loaded with the address of the first instruction of the interrupt program. The interrupt program is designated as an 'Interrupt Service Routine' (ISR) or 'Interrupt handler'.
iii) The first instruction of the ISR is available at the 'interrupt vector'. The word 'vector' in this context means 'address'. For a particular interrupting device, there is a specific location at which its ISR is stored (in memory). This is its interrupt vector.

What are the ways by which a processor can be interrupted?

i) It can be done by hardware, where a signal level on an 'interrupt pin' can be activated. For example, if a keyboard wants to cause an interrupt, it can activate an interrupt pin of the processor. See Figure 2.4 for the 8051 in which Pin No. 12 is an interrupt pin. For most MCUs, interrupts are vectored, which means that there is a definite and pre-defined address at which the ISR is expected to be. For the interrupt in $\overline{INT0}$ the 'vector' is 0 × 03 (see Table 2.1), and so control branches to that location, and the ISR therein will be executed to completion. The last instruction in any ISR is a return instruction and that will take control back to the 'interrupted program'.

ii) In MCUs, there are a number of inbuilt peripherals, and most of these peripherals have interrupts associated with them. For example, consider the case of the timer which is a standard peripheral in almost all MCUs. The timer has a register which keeps counting by increasing/decreasing the number in the register. When it reaches its limit called the 'terminal count', a flag is set in another register. Along with this, an interrupt can also be generated. This mans that control branches to its 'vector' and an ISR is taken from there. For 8051, the interrupt vector of its timer 0 is 0 × 0B (Table 2.1).

iii) There is also the facility to write instructions which are called software interrupts. This is more applicable to general purpose CPUs. The x86 series can be interrupted by instructions INT0, INT1 ...INT255.

Why are interrupts very important in embedded processing?

Interrupts are extremely important in embedded systems. In fact, interrupting is 'the' way by which the processor interacts with the real world.

Think of a system in which a number of input peripherals are present. Each of these peripherals can be made to act only on the basis of interrupts. In this case, the processor can be simply kept in a waiting loop, or doing some activity. Any peripheral that needs service can interrupt and get its ISR executed after which once again the processor goes back to its waiting loop until the next peripheral wants service and interrupts it, and so on and so forth.

Note that many issues can come up here, like two (or more) peripherals interrupting at the same time. How do you think this will be handled? Obviously one of them should be defined as a more important peripheral and given priority. A well-designed system will take care of all such possibilities and eventualities. Most systems have an 'interrupt controller' called a PIC (Programmable Interrupt Controller) which is a dedicated hardware taking care of multiple interrupts by assigning and resolving priorities, fixing up interrupt vectors and the like. Many embedded processors have such interrupt controllers inside them, while general purpose systems have external chips.

Can reset be considered as an interrupt?

All processors have a reset pin. On being reset, control branches to a particular address (usually 0 for most MCUs) and this address is called the 'reset vector'. So, considering reset as a hardware interrupt seems quite reasonable.

2.2.9.1 | *The Interrupt Structure of 8051*

Now, let us take a look at the interrupt structure of the 8051. This will help to bring in an additional level of clarity to our discussion on interrupts.

The 8051 has 5 interrupts excluding reset. Two are external hardware pins $\overline{INT0}$ and $\overline{INT1}$ which use pin no. s 12 and 13, respectively. Note that they are active low interrupts. An external device can be connected to these pins and cause the processor to be

Table 2.1 | Interrupt Vectors of 8051

Sl. No.	Interrupt	Vector
1	Reset	0 × 000
2	$\overline{INT0}$	0 × 0003
3	Timer 0	0 × 000B
4	$\overline{INT1}$	0 × 0013
5	Timer1	0 × 001B
6	Serial R/T	0 × 0023

interrupted by making the pin low for a minimum time as specified in the manual of the chip. The interrupt vectors of these hardware interrupts are listed in Table 2.1.

There are three other interrupts for this MCU. Two are timer interrupts. For each of the timers, when its terminal count is reached, the timer flags are set and a corresponding interrupt is also activated. Whatever is the action that needs to be done when the timer count is reached, can be included in the corresponding ISR.

The other interrupt is the serial communication interrupt. As a matter of fact, this interrupt pertains to both serial transmission as well as reception. Whenever a byte is received or transmitted, this interrupt is activated and control branches to its interrupt vector (Table 2.1).

For all the five interrupts, it is up to the user to decide whether the interrupt mechanism is to be used or not—this means that there are ways and means to disable them if they are not to act. This and many other options can be exercised by using the bits of interrupt related registers.

The above discussion is about the interrupt structure of 8051, but most MCUs have a similar structure. Of course, where are there more peripherals, you can expect to find more number of interrupts, obviously.

Now look at Table 2.1 once again. Note the interrupt vectors. You will find there is only an 8 byte space for the ISR of $\overline{INT0}$. Will that space be sufficient to store a program which needs to take care of an external peripheral? Quite unlikely. So usually, in the vectored location, a jump instruction is written and then control gets re-directed to some other address in memory. This is so, for all the interrupt vectors.

2.2.10 | DMA

DMA stands for 'direct memory access'. So far, we have seen the processor communicating with either memory or I/O, that is, any communication always involves the processor. Is it possible for data in memory to be sent directly to I/O or vice versa without involving the processor? For example, we might need to print a large chunk of data which is in memory. This data can be sent to the output device (printer) directly from memory. In this case, there is no necessity to involve the processor in the data transfer and the data transfer is faster. This is called 'direct memory access'.

However, since the processor is in the system, it must be isolated from this process. This means that, when DMA is to take place, the connection of the processor to memory and I/O is blocked, that is, the buses of the processor are to be tri-stated (in the high

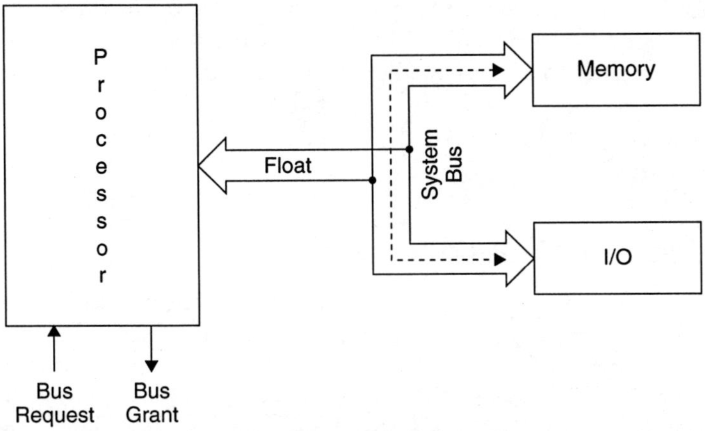

Figure 2.14 | Processor buses in float state during DMA operation

impedance state), leaving the path open for data to be transferred directly between I/O and memory. Figure 2.14 shows the typical scenario. Data transfer occurs between the memory and I/O, in either direction. The processor cannot do any bus-related operation, as its buses are in the float state.

A system which uses DMA should have a DMA controller which co-ordinates this activity. When DMA operation is to be done, the DMA controller places a DMA request on the 'Bus Request' line of the processor. This is essentially a request for permission to take control of the system bus. Since DMA is a high priority service, the processor stops whatever it is doing and acknowledges the request by activating the 'Bus Grant' signal, and then DMA is initiated.

Except for low end applications, most embedded systems require DMA. The whole process is managed and controlled by a DMA controller, usually available inside the embedded processor. A number of registers also are needed to set up and get the DMA operation done. The code for it will set up destination and source pointers denoting the starting address of where the data is coming from and where it is be moved to. A counter must be programmed to track the number of bytes in the transfer and give an indication when the transfer is complete.

DMA is a standard feature in embedded and general purpose computing systems, and the respective peripheral buses have pins for initiating and controlling the operation of direct memory access. The transfer of data can be between I/O and memory, and also from memory to memory. Having this kind of data transfer facility gives a significant speed advantage, compared to what would have been obtained by writing code to get the CPU to do it.

2.2.11 | Communication Ports

In this context, communication means 'serial communication'. All MCUs have the UART (Section 5.3.3) as a standard peripheral. There are registers, pins and interrupts associated with this peripheral. See Figure 2.4 in which the 8051 has pins 10 and 11 for serial reception and transmission. The pins are T × D for transmission and R × D for reception. Serial communication with a baud rate as decided by the register settings and processor clock frequency, is possible with this communication setup.

More sophisticated MCUs have other communication ports as well. You may see ports and peripheral controllers for protocols like SPI, I2C, bluetooth, USB, etc., for some of the advanced MCUs like ARM, PIC, etc. The principles of these protocols are dealt with, in Chapter 5.

2.3 | Memory for Embedded Systems

In general purpose computing systems, memory is outside the processor chip. Consider a PC with a Pentium processor. It has primary memory in the form of RAM and ROM, which are on the motherboard of the PC, but outside the processor. But for an embedded processor (MCU), we know that RAM and ROM are inside the processor chip. The amount of such memory available varies from chip to chip, and a designer is expected to choose a processor which has sufficient amount of memory available on-chip, as required for his application. But in case the memory requirements are much larger than that can be provided on-chip, adding external memory is possible. Now, before we go into such issues, a brief review of different kinds of semiconductor memory devices will be in place.

2.3.1 | Semiconductor Memory

First let us discuss some general aspects of semiconductor memories. Data is stored in memory, and it is usually defined to be 'byte oriented' (in most cases). This means that one address corresponds to one byte of memory. Thus, when one address is accessed, one byte is either read or written into it. This suggests that for getting a word of four bytes from/to memory, four consecutive locations with four addresses have to be accessed.

There are also memory devices in which memory is organized as 16 bits. In such a case, each 16-bit data has one address.

Reading and writing takes a certain amount of time which is termed 'memory access time'. For reading, this is the time interval from the instant the address is placed at the address pins to the time the data is available at the data pins. A similar definition applies to write access time as well. The access time of any memory device depends on the technology involved. Another term frequently encountered is 'memory cycle time'. This is the time interval between two consecutive memory accesses. These terms will be used frequently throughout this chapter.

2.3.2 | Random Access Memory (RAM)

The word RAM stands for 'Random Access Memory' in which any location can be accessed randomly (in contrast to serial access like in the case of magnetic tapes) with the same latency (delay). It is a volatile memory which means that when power is removed, the stored data is lost. There are different types of RAM depending on the technology used. The fastest and hence the most expensive RAM is SRAM which stands for 'Static RAM'.

2.3.2.1 | *Static RAM (SRAM)*

Each cell holds either a '0' or a '1', and this content is static, because the content is stored as a voltage, which does not change with time. Memory is realized using MOSFETS and

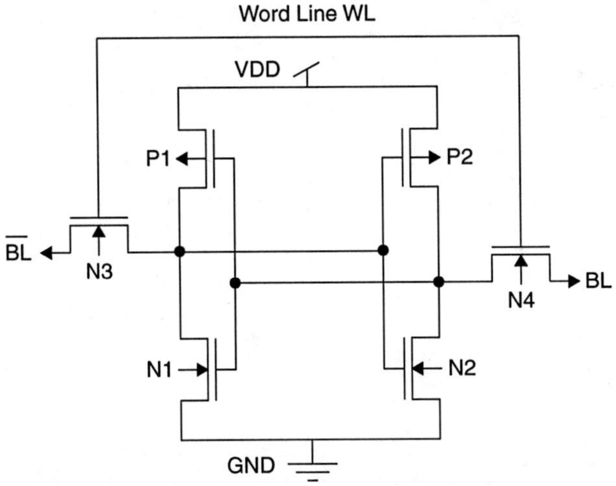

Figure 2.15 | An SRAM cell storing one bit

the most commonly used type of memory cell (for storing one bit) needs six transistors and is called the 6T cell. Figure 2.15 shows this cell—it has two cross coupled NMOS transistors (N1 and N2) acting as a bistable multivibrator and two PMOS transistors (P1 and P2) acting as their loads. The output of N1 or N2 can be considered as the cell output. (In many cases, a differential output is taken, which is better for noise immunity.)

The access transistors N3 and N4, and the word line WL and bit lines BL and $\overline{BL}$, are used to read and write from or to the cell. Normally (when no reading or writing is required), the word line is low, turning the access transistors (N3 and N4) off. To write into the cell, the logic data is placed on the bit line BL and the complementary data on the inverse bit line, $\overline{BL}$. Then the access transistors are turned on by setting the word line to high. As the driver of the bit lines is strong, it will assert this information on the cross coupled transistors. As soon as the information is thus stored in the bistable multivibrator, the access transistors can be turned off and the information in the cell is preserved.

For reading, the word line is turned on to activate the access transistors while the information is sensed at the bit lines.

This (Figure 2.15) is the cell for storing a single bit; for a byte, we need 8 such cells, which needs $8 \times 6 = 48$ transistors for just a single byte. This is one of the reasons why SRAM is very expensive.

2.3.2.2 | *An SRAM Chip*

Figure 2.16 shows a typical SRAM chip which has N address lines, 8 data lines and control signals for reading and writing. Only when the $\overline{CE}$ ((Chip Enable) line is activated will the chip become usable (selected or enabled). $\overline{WR}$ is the write control signal and $\overline{OE}$ is the read control signal (OE stands for 'output enable'). It enables the data lines for reading, i.e. it is the read control signal)

Now, observe the read and write timings for SRAM (Figures 2.17 and 2.18) for which the steps are listed. Note that the timing is 'asynchronous' because there is no reference clock.

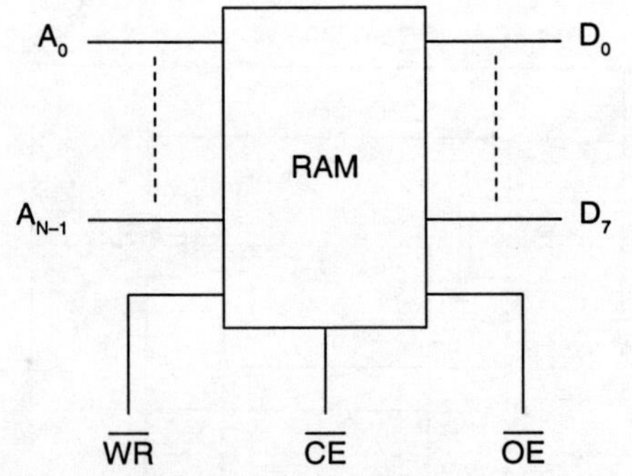

Figure 2.16 | An SRAM chip with control signals

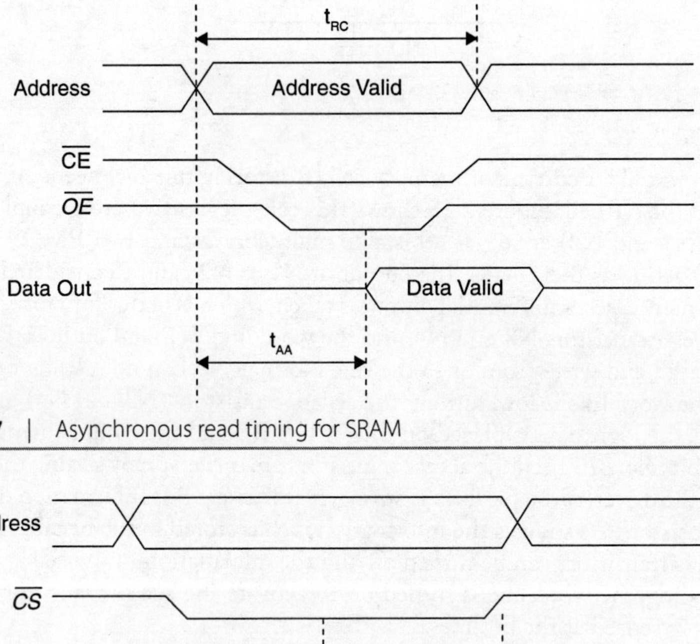

Figure 2.17 | Asynchronous read timing for SRAM

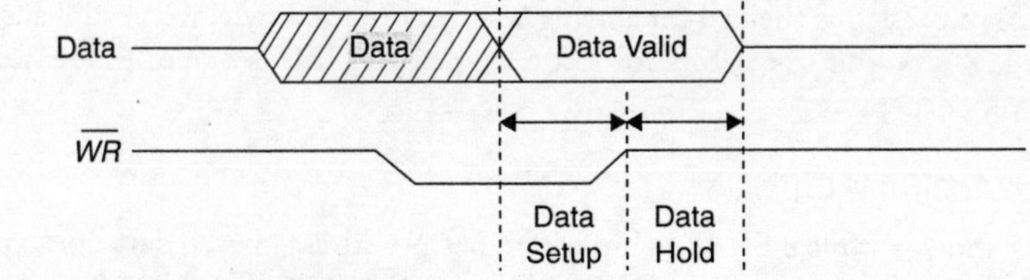

Figure 2.18 | Asynchronous write timing for SRAM

2.3.2.3 | *Memory Read Cycle*

The steps in a read cycle of SRAM are as follows:

i) Place the address of the byte to be read, on the address bus.
ii) Ensure that the chip is activated by making $\overline{CE}$ low.

iii) Activate the $\overline{OE}$ pin which is the $\overline{RD}$ pin itself. This ensures that data is read.
iv) The required data then appears on the data bus.

In the timing diagram, two timing figures are shown: one is t_{AA}, the **read access time**. This is the time measured from the instant the address is placed on the address bus to the point in time when the required data is available on the data pins.

The other timing figure is t_{RC}, the **read cycle time**, which is the minimum time between two read cycles. These two timing figures can be equal for SRAM because, as soon as data is available at the data pins, it can be read by the processor, and a new read cycle may be initiated. (This is pointed out here to contrast it with DRAM timing, where we will see another element of delay.)

2.3.2.4 | *Memory Write Cycle*

A write cycle has also a similar timing. The steps in writing are as follows:

i) Place the address of the byte to be read, on the address bus.
ii) Ensure that the chip is activated by making $\overline{CE}$ low.
iii) Place the data to be written on the data bus.
iv) Activate the $\overline{WR}$ line. Only then the data is considered to be valid.
v) The data then gets written into the addressed location.

What are the merits and de-merits of SRAM?

To achieve low levels of power consumptions, CMOS is typically used for SRAM technology. It uses less power than DRAM (which we will discuss in the following sections), but at high frequencies, it can also consume significant amounts of power. Because each cell needs at least six transistors, SRAMs are quite expensive. They are as fast as typical CPUs because of using the same technology as the CPU. Any MCU will have a certain amount of SRAM inside it by the name 'on chip RAM'. For many MCUs this SRAM includes the internal registers which are arranged as 'banks'.

2.3.2.5 | *Synchronous SRAM (SSRAM)*

Ordinary SRAMs are asynchronous in the sense that there is no clock signal for timing the read and write operations. But recently, synchronous SRAM (called SSRAM) has been produced for high speed applications. In such SRAMs, processor clocks create the timing for read and write. SSRAMs are used in high speed applications. They are used as the 'cache' for Power PC and Pentium-based workstations.

2.3.3 | Dynamic RAM (DRAM)

Another very popular and widely used RAM is 'dynamic RAM'. It is designated as dynamic because its content does not remain unchanged or static as in SRAM, and hence frequent 'refreshing' is necessary.

To understand this point, let us see what is contained in a typical DRAM cell (Figure 2.19). A DRAM memory cell consists of a single field effect transistor (FET) and a capacitor. It is the amount of charge stored in the capacitor that decides whether the cell stores a '1' or a '0'. One of the problems with this arrangement is that the capacitor does not hold charge indefinitely as the charge in a capacitor 'leaks off' and needs to be replenished. This action of replenishing the charge that gets lost is done by 'refreshing'

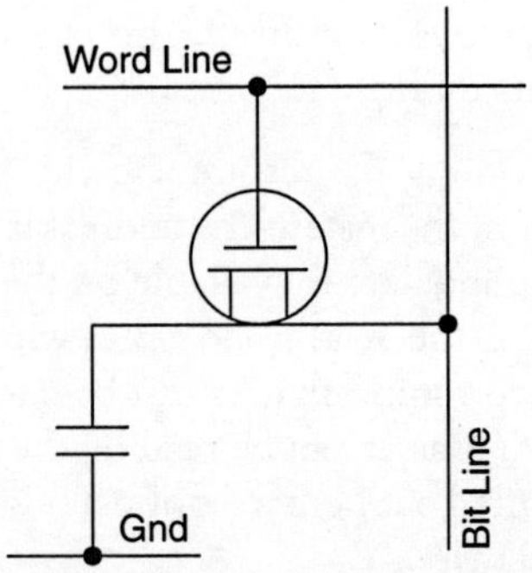

Figure 2.19 | A DRAM cell

the cell at regular intervals. The data is sensed and written and this then ensures that any leakage is overcome, and the data is re-instated. The two lines, the Word Line and the Bit Line are connected as shown, so that the required bit within the memory can be selected to be read or written to.

In a DRAM chip, there are multitudes of such cells which form words consisting of bits. Refreshing for the cells is done at one go, in a particular sequence. Memory addresses are decoded and converted as rows and columns of the matrix that memory elements are arranged in.

2.3.3.1 | *Read Cycle of DRAM*

Let us see the steps involved in a typical memory read of a DRAM chip. Recollect that a processor when addressing memory sends the complete address on its address pins. Between the processor and a DRAM chip, there is a memory controller whose function is to split the address into two, as columns and rows. **A DRAM has only half the number of address pins as the address supplied by the processor, because the address lines of the DRAM chip are multiplexed in time for the row and column addresses.** The memory controller should also generate the signals necessary for reading and writing to the DRAM.

Figure 2.20 displays the memory controller of a DRAM. Because the row and address information is placed on the same address lines (multiplexed in time) the pin count of the

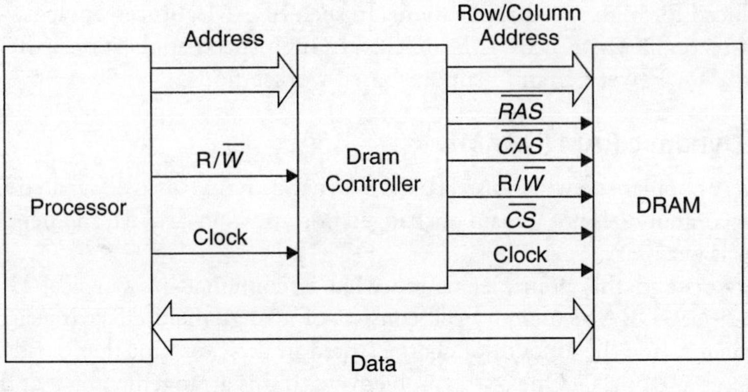

Figure 2.20 | Memory control for DRAM

DRAM chip is reduced. DRAM chips are large rectangular arrays of memory cells with support logic that is used for reading and writing data in the arrays, and refresh circuitry to maintain the integrity of stored data. Memory arrays are arranged in rows and columns of memory cells called word lines and bit lines, respectively. Each memory cell has a unique location or address defined by the intersection of a row and a column.

Let us see the steps in a typical read cycle of DRAM. Refer to the internal diagram of a DRAM chip (Figure 2.21) and the timing diagram in Figure 2.22.

i) The row address is placed on the rows and given sufficient time to stabilize and be latched.
ii) The row address strobe $\overline{RAS}$ signal is then activated.
iii) The row address decoder selects the proper row.
iv) Next, the column address is placed on the same address lines and allowed to stabilize and be latched.
v) The column address strobe $\overline{CAS}$ signal is then activated.
vi) The $\overline{CAS}$ pin also serves as the output enable, so once the $\overline{CAS}$ signal has been stabilized, the sense amps place the data from the selected row and column, on the data bus.
vii) With this, the data in the selected address is available at the output buffers of the chip, and it is transferred to the data bus.

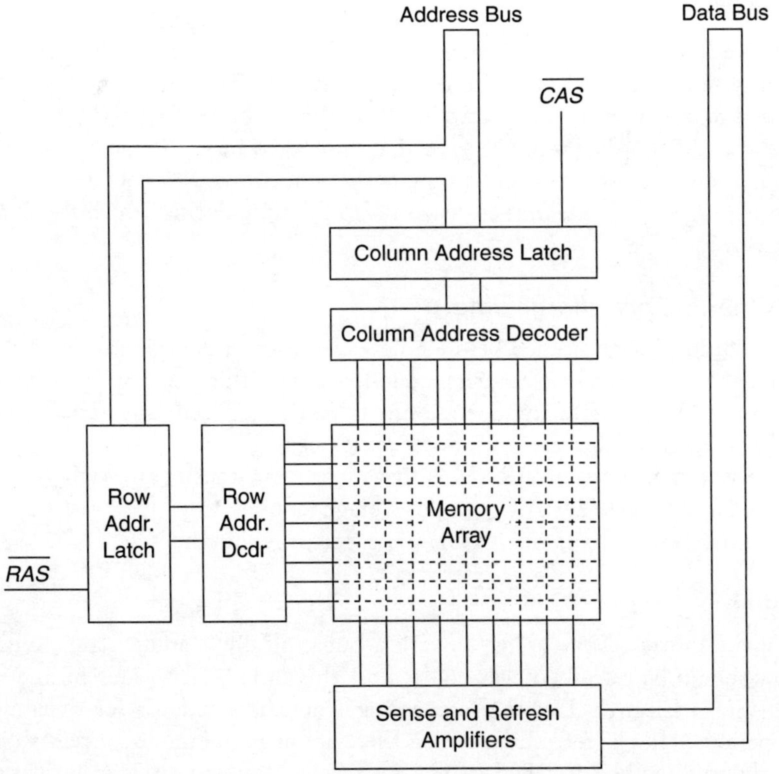

Figure 2.21 | Internal diagram of a DRAM chip

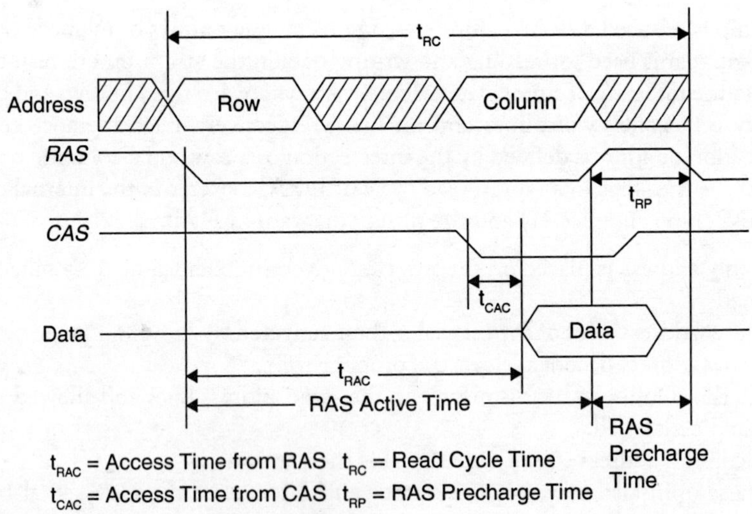

Figure 2.22 | Read timing diagram for DRAM

viii) Before the read cycle can be considered complete, CAS and RAS must return to their previous state.

This is a conventional **asynchronous read,** because the timing signals are not tied to the main system clock. The access time (t_{RAC}) is the time from the time the *RAS* signal is activated to the time the data is available on the data bus. The read cycle time (t_{RC}) is also shown in the diagram. Observe that another time t_{RP} is included within this read cycle time. The total read cycle time is the sum of the 'RAS active time', and the 'RAS pre-charge time'. The first corresponds to the time during which the *RAS* signal is active (low).

What Is the 'RAS pre-charge time', (t_{RP})?

It is the additional time needed before a new read (or write) cycle can be started. This is because there is a parasitic capacitance for each cell. This parasitic capacitance must be pre-charged high before any operation is to be commenced. **The access time is also referred to as latency.** This applies to write cycles also.

One important merit of DRAM is that its packing density is very high compared to SRAM. Note that for DRAM, one-bit storage requires only one transistor, while for SRAM a minimum of six (at least four) transistors is required.

Refreshing

What about the refreshing rate? It varies, but typically manufacturers specify that each row should be refreshed every 64 msecs. This time interval falls in line with the JEDEC (Joint Electron Device Engineering Council) standards for dynamic RAM refresh periods. How is refreshing done? There are many methods for refresh, and one commonly used method is called ROR (RAS Only Refresh). Practically, it is done by activating each row using *RAS.*

The DRAM controller takes care of scheduling the refreshes and making sure that they do not interfere with regular reads and writes. So to keep the data in DRAM chip from leaking away, the DRAM controller periodically sweeps through all of the rows by cycling repeatedly and placing a series of row addresses on the address bus. This method is designated as ROR or RAS Only Refresh. To reduce the number of refresh cycles, one method of design is to split the address such that there are fewer rows and more columns. So, the DRAM array is then a rectangular array, rather than a square one.

2.3.3.2 | *Synchronous DRAM (SDRAM)*

You might have noted the word 'asynchronous' when we talked about the read timing cycle of DRAM. This meant that the access timing is not related to the system clock at all. In around 1996, a new type of DRAM started making headway in the memory arena and that technological innovation in DRAMs is called Synchronous DRAM. For this type of DRAM, accesses are synchronized with the system clock and SDRAM is currently 'the' RAM that is used as the primary (main) memory in general purpose computer systems.

Embedded processors do not have SDRAM inside them. But many embedded boards do have SDRAM as external memory.

Now, let us see what SDRAM has to offer in terms of improvements over asynchronous DRAM. Technologically, they are similar, but SDRAM has incorporated certain new features and modes of operations.

Synchronous Operation All operations are synchronized to the leading edge of the system clock and thus controls are made easier.

Mode Register There is a command register for this RAM into which command words are written to specify various operating modes and also generate various control signals. This is an entirely new concept for memory chips and thus allows a level of control based on the level of performance needed from the RAM. In effect, it makes the RAM performance 'programmable'.

2.3.3.3 | *Synchronous vs Asynchronous DRAMs*

Let us conclude by saying that in terms of the basic technology and principle of operation of a basic DRAM memory cell, both types are the same, but SDRAM scores higher only because of the way it is used. Since asynchronous DRAM does not share any sort of common clock signal with the CPU, the controller chips have to manipulate the DRAM's control pins based on all sorts of timing considerations. SDRAM, however, shares the bus clock with the CPU. Commands can be placed (or, certain predefined combinations of signals) on its control pins on clock edges.

A significant difference between conventional DRAM and SDRAM is the way in which memory access is executed. In a standard DRAM, the toggling of the external control inputs has a direct effect on the internal memory array. In an SDRAM, the input signals are latched into a control logic block which functions as the input to a state machine. Therefore, the state machine actually controls the memory access. Basic operations of the SDRAM, such as read, write and refresh, are initiated by loading control commands into the device.

2.3.3.4 | *DDR*

This stands for 'Double Data Rate' SDRAM and the difference it has from regular SDRAM is that it can be made to transfer data at both the rising and falling edges of the clock, instead of just at the rising edge. This should double the data rate and hence the designation DDR. It achieves higher throughput by using differential pairs of signal wires to allow faster signalling without noise and interference problems. DDR SDRAM first came to market in 2000, but it did not really catch on until 2001 with the advent of mainstream motherboards and chipsets supporting it. DDR found initial support in the graphics card market and since then has become the mainstream PC memory standard. As such, DDR SDRAM is supported by all the major processors and memory manufacturers.

DDR–2 and DDR–3 These are just faster versions of DDR SDRAMs and use special techniques for speed up, considering that the basic latencies of a DRAM cell can never be done away with completely. DDR2 is still double data rate just as with DDR, but the modified signalling method enables higher speeds to be achieved with more immunity to noise and crosstalk between the signals. The additional signals required for differential pairs add to the pin count of DDR2 and DDR3.

2.3.4 | ROM (Read Only Memory)

This is a very commonly used term and we know it stands for 'Read Only Memory'. The user has the option to 'burn in' the contents of this, which is not lost when power is switched off. Current terminology is 'firmware' for the ROM and its contents together.

ROM is a type of 'programmable' memory. It has internal fuses which when blown, create a bit pattern which is permanent and hence can be read whenever needed. However, if it is an OTP (one time programmable) ROM, its contents can never be changed again. This statement implies that there are other kinds of ROM into which data can be re-written. This is EPROM. EPROMs are 'Erasable and Programmable'– their contents can be erased by exposing them to ultraviolet radiation. Such ROMs have a window through which UV light penetrates the chip.

2.3.4.1 | *EEPROM*

This is 'Electrically Erasable' PROM, and erasure can be done while the chip is on the circuit board. The predominant feature of EEPROM is that the programmer can change the data embedded on the memory one byte at a time, giving him more control on how he enters the data. However, this method takes a very long time especially when erasing all the data in it.

The advantage of EEPROM is that it is non-volatile, but also erasable and reprogrammable. Because of this, EEPROMs are used for data storage in small quantities in embedded systems, where this data may have to be referenced (read) frequently by the application software, but may not have to be changed normally. There are dedicated EEPROM chips available which may be connected to MCUs, on an embedded board.

EEPROMs are of two types: parallel and serial. The data lines of parallel EEPROMs can be directly connected to the processor's data lines for data transfer. In the case of serial EEPROMs, there are only one/two data lines. For transferring data between a processor and the serial chip, serial protocols like SPI, I2C (refer Section 5.2) can be used.

There are PIC MCUs with EEPROMs inside the chip. The size of this is not very large, but this has a special place in the system, in that it is used to store data like certain constants, tables, identification numbers, etc. Frequent reading of this data may take place in the course of program execution.

2.3.4.2 | *Flash Memory*

Flash memory is the most popular of the non-volatile types of memory available currently. In technology, it is similar to EEPROM, but there is the difference between the two, in that EEPROM can be erased and written only one byte at a time, while for flash, these operations are 'block oriented'.

The Flash Memory Cell

Flash memory stores data in an array of memory cells. The memory cells are made from floating-gate MOSFETS (known as FGMOS). These FG MOSFETs can store electrical charge (as '1' or '0') for years, without the need for a power supply. This is the secret of the robustness of flash storage.

Principle of Data Storage in Flash Memory A flash cell stores the data by removing or putting electrons on its floating gate (Figure 2.23). The charge on the floating gate affects the threshold of the memory element. When electrons are present on the floating gate, no current flows through the transistor. This denotes a '0'. When electrons are removed from the floating gate, the transistor starts conducting, indicating a '1'. This is achieved by applying voltages between the control gate and source or drain. There are some tunnelling phenomena associated with all this, but a more detailed explanation is beyond the scope of this chapter (and book).

There are two types of flash memory: the NOR flash developed by Intel and NAND flash, which originated from Toshiba technology. The names, NOR-flash and NAND-flash, came from the structure used for the interconnections between memory cells as shown in Figure 2.24.

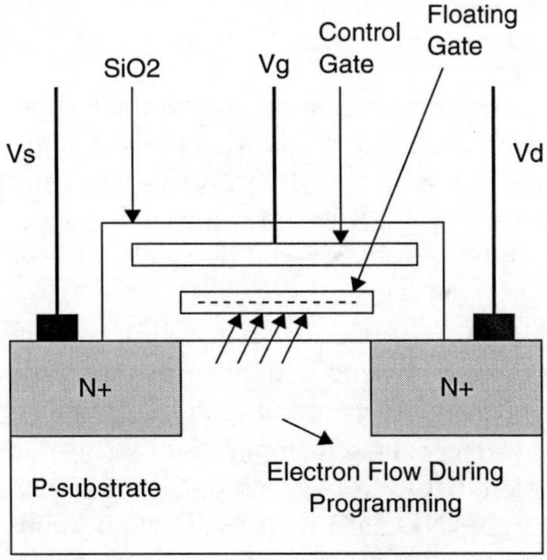

Figure 2.23 | A flash memory cell

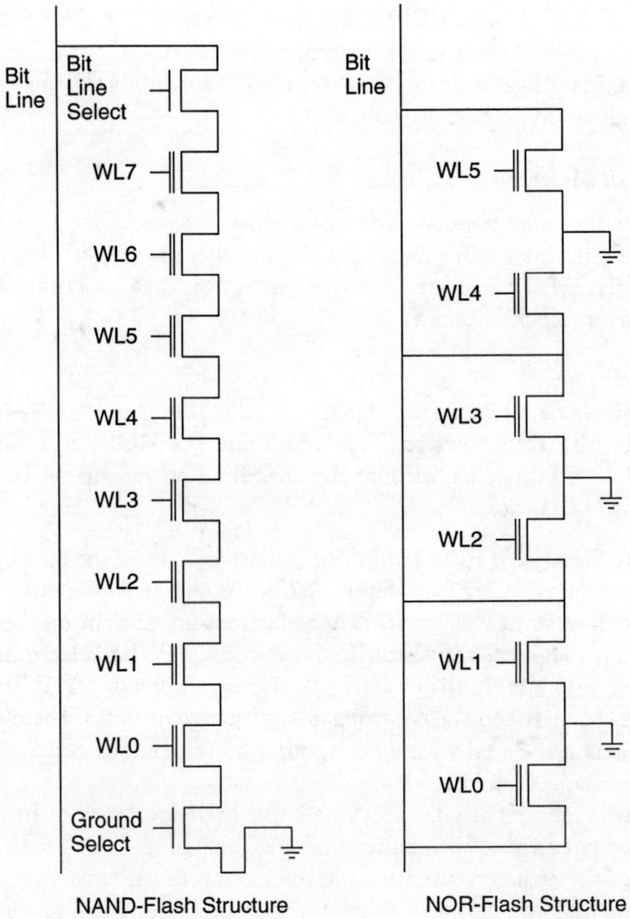

Figure 2.24 | NAND and NOR Flash

In NOR-flash, cells are connected in parallel to the bit lines facilitating the reading/writing/erasing of each cell individually. This parallel connection is similar to the parallel connection of transistors in a CMOS NOR array, and hence the name 'NOR flash'. In contrast, cells in a NAND flash are connected in series. This difference is the reason for differences in the way of usage and the application domain of the two types of cells.

NOR flash is relatively higher speed (than NAND), and here random access is possible such that data can be read or written in quantities as small as a byte. NAND flash, on the other hand, does sequential access and can read or write only as blocks.

Because of this, the former is used in applications where data needs to be randomly accessed—it is used to store BIOS in PCs and operating systems in PDAs and mobile phones. The latter, that is, NAND flash finds use in applications where data is sequentially stored and retrieved, that is, for data storage in digital cameras, mobile phones, MP3 players, USB memory sticks and so on.

Have you heard about SD cards?

SD stands for 'Secure Digital' and such cards are flash memory cards with security features incorporated. The SD format includes several important technological features. These include the addition of cryptographic security protection for copyrighted data/music. There is an SD Card Association, which sets the specifications for SD cards. Such cards are available in various capacities and also sizes—that's why we have cards designated as mini SD, micro SD. MMC (multi media card), mobile MMC, etc.

Appendix I elaborates the interfacing of an SD card to an ARM MCU.

Comparing Volatile and Non-volatile Memory

Now that we have taken a brief tour of both volatile and non-volatile memory, it should be quite evident that each of these memory types have different application domains. Table 2.2 summarizes the differences between these types.

Which of these memory types are available in MCU chips?

All MCUs have a small amount of SRAM, and a relatively large amount of flash. SRAM is used for a small amount of storage of intermediate data during computations. The flash is the area where code is burned. A part of it may be used for data storage, as well.

Besides this, some MCUs have a small amount of EEPROM used to hold data which is unlikely to change once the system is designed and launched.

As an example, have a look at the on chip memory structure of the PIC 18 F series of MCUs. This series has a maximum SRAM size of 4KB, EEPROM of 1024 bytes and flash ROM of 128KB. Individual members of this series have different amount of these types of memory. The 8051 family, on the other hand, has a maximum size of SRAM of 256 bytes, flash ROM of 64KB and no EEPROM.

Memory Shadowing—What does it mean?

In PCs, the BIOS is in flash, which is a relatively slow memory device. Usually, device drivers which are part of BIOS are frequently used, so having to access ROM each time

Table 2.2 | Comparison of Different Memory Types

Memory Type	Features	Usage
SRAM	Volatile, high speed	Cache On chip RAM in MCUs
DRAM	Volatile, speed lower than SRAM	Primary memory in PCs External memory in embedded boards
EEPROM	Non-volatile, very low speed	Storage of small amounts of data which remains more or less constant
FLASH ROM	Non-volatile, lower speed than RAMs	i) Storage of large amounts of data which may have to be changed frequently ii) Storage of the program code of embedded systems

creates quite a delay. To circumvent this, the BIOS is copied to RAM and ROM accesses are disabled. Thus access becomes very fast. The RAM used for this is called shadow RAM and the technique is called memory shadowing.

There can be a similar problem for embedded systems which are expected to perform high speed applications. All code and most data are in the flash, the response time of which is slow. To hasten up the system, memory shadowing will be necessary here too.

2.3.5 | Caches

Cache is a word you might have heard in various contexts. Most of you might already have studied the operation of caches with respect to 'computer architecture'. The purpose of this section is not to discuss it in detail, but to stress the importance of cache in embedded systems architecture.

We know that general purpose computing systems have a cache in the system. The memory hierarchy in such a system is as shown in Figure 2.25.

Whenever the processor needs an instruction or data, the ideal condition is to find it in the cache (this is called a hit). It is also possible that at certain times, the required information is not found in the cache. This is called a miss and then, it will have to be taken from main memory, and this is a relatively slow access. The cache mapping policy is designed to maximize hits, and one important point to keep in mind is that a cache is entirely managed by hardware—as the cache size increases or the mapping policy becomes more stringent, the amount of hardware for managing this, increases. Thus, the amount of cache required for a system and the amount it can afford (in terms of the increased hardware budget) have to be carefully balanced.

Cache is the memory closest to the processor and also the fastest. But remember that the content of cache is only a 'copy of a portion' of the main memory. In a general purpose computing system, cache memory uses SRAM, while main memory is DRAM technology—there are also different levels of caches—L1, L2 and L3, with L1 being closest and L3 being farthest from the CPU.

2.3.5.1 | *Embedded Systems and Cache*

Do embedded systems have caches? The answer is that only the mid and high range systems possess it or need it. Thus, many high end processors, specifically DSP processors have it in their cores.

Consider a system as shown in Figure 2.26. This system could be an embedded processor board or a node in a networked system. Other blocks present in the system are not

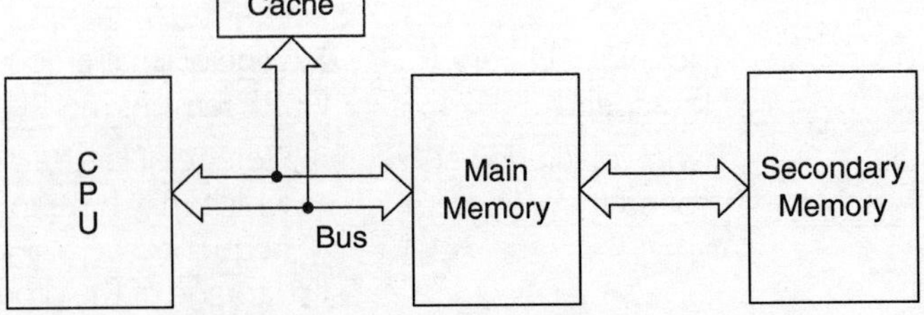

Figure 2.25 | Memory hierarchy in a system with cache

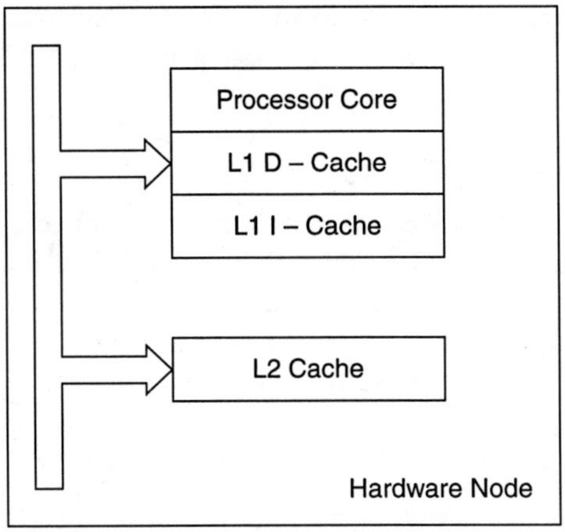

Figure 2.26 | A hardware node of an embedded system

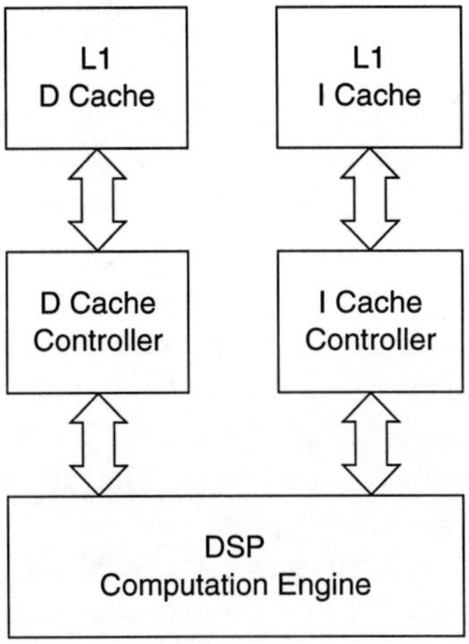

Figure 2.27 | A DSP processor with cache

shown in the figure. There is a processor in the system, and the processor has an on chip L1 cache which is divided into an instruction cache and a data cache. L2 cache is outside the processor. DSP processors are one class of processors which mandatorily use cache internally.

Figure 2.27 shows the internals of a DSP processor with L1 caches and their respective controllers.

2.3.5.2 | *Caches and Real-time Systems*

Caches, however, are not a preferred item for real-time systems (Section 8.2). The reason can be explained to be because of the probabilistic nature of operations of caches. Everything is fine for a hit—but in case of a miss, access becomes very slow. Since the data in the cache is continually changed, there is no way of guaranteeing that a particular item will be there when needed. Real-time systems are 'time critical' and are to be designed to be deterministic. Processors used for 'real-time' applications usually have a 'tightly coupled memory' which gives deterministic performance in contrast to the probabilistic performance of caches.

2.3.5.3 | *Tightly Coupled Memory*

This is just a fast memory directly connected to the processor core (inside the chip). It is meant to provide low-latency memory that the processor can use without the unpredictability associated with caches. Actually, it is an area of memory in which important and critical items like interrupt handlers, real-time task codes, etc., are stored. It can also hold important data which is needed frequently. Many ARM processors which are designated to be specific for real-time applications have TCM and associated registers. Such systems might have caches as well, but the caches may be disabled if they are not to be used.

2.4 | Low Power Design

This is the age of handheld devices and the consequent requirement for miniaturization. More and more applications are being built into devices which are small and can be carried around—this requires more powerful processors, and also needs peripherals which are very small. We need tiny keys, touch screens with good resolution and small packaging. But beyond all this, there is one important factor which is a key issue in any design, and that is 'power'. All these appliances are battery operated and hence the need to preserve the battery power is a matter of high priority.

So the current focus of research is on low power design. Every device used in the system must be able to work with the lowest possible power supply voltage and the lowest current. This applies to the processor and to the peripherals. Besides this, techniques must be looked at so that when a device is not doing anything, it is in the sleep or dormant state and wakes up only when alerted by an interrupt. Here, let us have a quick look at what low power design entails.

The first point to take into account while designing a system aimed to dissipate minimum power is to choose an MCU with a low power processor core. The 32-bit ARM core is claimed to be one such processor. TI's MSP 430 is a 16-bit low power processor. There are many other processors in the market with 'low power' claims tagged to them.

What are the steps to be taken into consideration when there is the need to design systems which are power limited?

To get a grip on this, let us think of the factors which tend to increase power dissipation and then attempt to reduce the effect of these factors.

i) **High frequency:** The higher the clock frequency, higher is the power. In fact, doubling the clock frequency translates to doubling the power. But when high performance is needed, high frequencies cannot be avoided. The point then, is to use only the minimum clock rate that is actually needed.

   In the same design, some applications don't need the same high clock rates as certain others. The trick is to use a processor whose clock frequency can be dynamically changed. Many of the modern day processors have internal PLLs (phase locked loops) that can change the clock frequency on the fly.

ii) **High power supply voltage:** High power supply causes high currents and so more power. The trend now is to have low supply voltages in the range of 3V. This reduces noise margins, but 'differential signalling' (Section 5.3.1.5) has helped to improve noise resilience.

ii) **Complex hardware:** Having simpler hardware directly translates to low power; there are less number of transistors and so less is the power dissipated. RISC cores are comparatively low power cores, and choosing such a core (if it can satisfy the performance criteria also) is the first major step in this direction.

iii) **Higher bus widths:** Since more bus lines means more capacitances getting charged and discharged for change of logic states (which does not translate to useful power), it is best to reduce bus widths of the external (off chip) buses.

iv) **I/O devices:** Certain I/O device like optical isolators, electromechanical relays, back lit displays, etc., are not ones that favour low power; it is best to avoid such devices. In I/O selection, leakage and quiescent current ratings should be verified and those which offer the lowest, should be chosen.

v) **Circuit design:** In the design of the processor, it is likely that the designers have used ideas to switch off parts of the circuitry which are not being actively used. The same ideas should be used in the circuits in the system design. Using gated clocks help when the clock is removed from that part of the circuit—it doesn't function and thus needs no power.

vi) **Using low power modes of the processor:** Most embedded systems don't need to operate continuously. Many of them wake up when a stimulus (in the form of an interrupt) is obtained. Thus, it is important to use the sleep and power down modes of the processor effectively.

vii) **Battery type:** Choosing the right type of battery is important and it depends on the application as well. In some applications, recharging is possible, in others (like a monitoring device placed in an inaccessible location), it is not possible. The above two cases need different types of batteries.

2.5 | Pullup and Pulldown Resistors

These are words which are commonly heard and popularly used, but not many people have a clear idea of what they really mean. Here is an attempt to bring in a bit of clarity to these terms.

2.5.1 | Floating State of an Input

Consider a gate, say an AND gate connected as in Figure 2.28. One of the inputs is connected to the supply, and the other is left unconnected. Many people have the notion that leaving the pin open is equal to a '0' level. So their expectation is of getting a '0' at the output, for this logic connection. On finding that the output is a '1', the natural tendency is to doubt the gate as being faulty. But the fault is not of the gate, but is because one input is left 'floating'. A floating input truly floats, and cannot take on any fixed voltage level permanently, and usually it is found to have a voltage corresponding to a high level. It may even be susceptible to accepting noise voltage pulses and may keep changing.

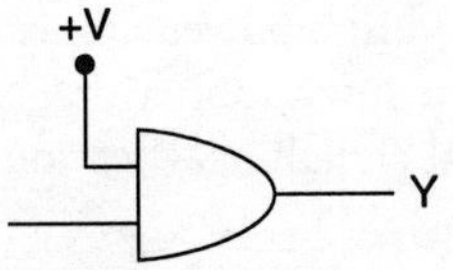

Figure 2.28 | Floating state of an input

The solution to this predicament is to ground the other input if it is to be considered a '0'. All '1' levels inputs are to be connected to V and '0' levels to ground. In this case, no input is 'floating', and the correct logic is obtained at the output. But sometimes, we need to connect these terminals through a resistance if we want to limit current through the circuit. This is where pulldown and pullup resistances come to the picture.

2.5.2 | Pulldown and Pullup Resistances

See the inverter in Figure 2.29. It can be connected either to a '1' or '0' depending on which switch is closed. This is what we usually do when using digital gates, but in some cases, there may be reasons to limit the current that flows to the input. Figure 2.30a shows a circuit in which the input is connected to V through a resistor R1, which is called a pullup resistor. This resistor's function is to limit the amount of current that flows through the circuit.

The term 'pullup resistor' implies that the input has been pulled 'up' to high through the resistor. It is clear that when the input is to be high, the switch S2 is to be kept open. The value of the pullup resistance can be calculated by considering the maximum current allowed, If 5 mA is the maximum current allowed, 5V/5 mA =10K for the pullup.

See Figure 2.30b; here R2 is called a 'pulldown' resistor as it is connected to the ground. It is obvious that when S1 is open, the input is truly grounded, and when S1 is

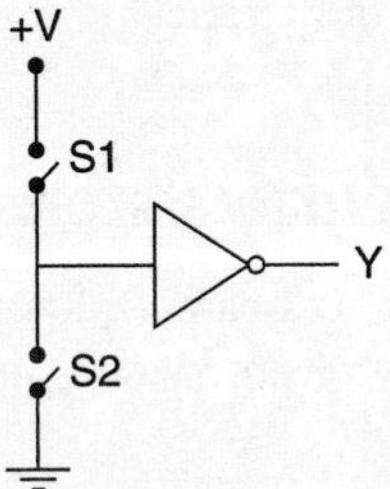

Figure 2.29 | Inverter with two switches

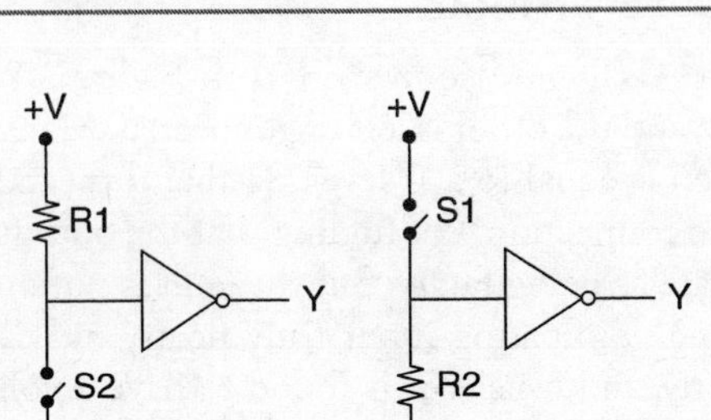

Figure 2.30 | **(a)** Inverter with a pullup resistor and **(b)** Inverter with a pulldown resistor

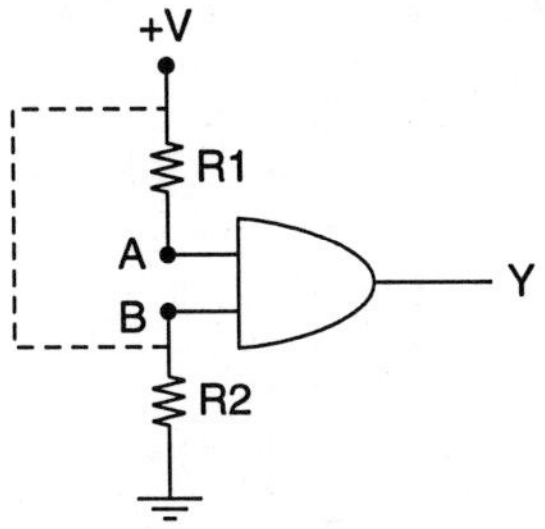

Figure 2.31 | AND gate with pullup and pulldown resistors

closed, voltage V is fully dropped across R2 corresponding to a '1' input, but the current is limited by R2.

Figure 2.31 shows an AND gate with a pullup resistor R1 and a pulldown resistor R2. In this set up (ignore the dotted line), the logic levels at A and B are 1 and 0, respectively. If B is also to be made '1', it is just enough to connect B to the supply voltage (note the dotted line). Then the full V is available at B, but the current is limited by the resistance R2.

Normally, in digital circuits, most of you might not have connected pullup and pulldown resistors at the input because the available TTL gates have inbuilt protection at the inputs, but there can be cases when power dissipation is a consideration. Also GPIOs of some MCUs insist on such resistors—use it only then.

2.5.3 | Open Collector/Open Drain Gates

In MCUs, GPIO pins are used to connect input and output devices. These pins have internal pullups ('active' pullups rather than resistive), so external resistors are not needed in most cases but there is a necessity for pullup resistors for gates with a 'open' output, and that is what we will discuss next.

Logic gates are based on TTL or MOS technology. For most logic gates, there is an output stage (remember the totem pole output for TTL?), but there are certain gates with outputs left open. They are called 'open collector' or 'open drain' depending on whether the technology is TTL or MOS. See Figure 2.32a, where the collector of the output transistor (of the gate) is left open, that is, unconnected to any power source. To use such a gate to get a '1' when the transistor is OFF, it must be connected to +V through a resistor, and that resistor is called a pullup resistor (see Figure 2.32b). The same discussion applies to open drain outputs, also.

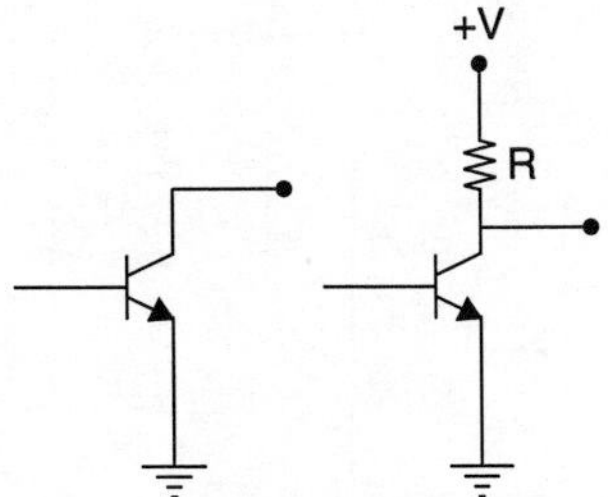

Figure 2.32 | **(a)** An open collector gate output and **(b)** An open collector gate with a pullup resistor

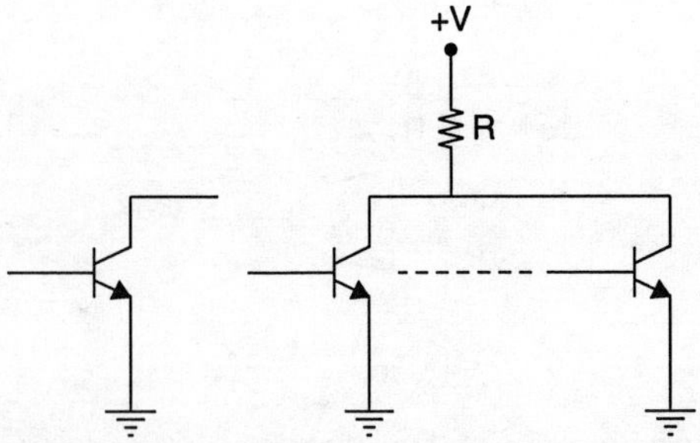

Figure 2.33 | Wired AND logic

What is the need for such open collector/drain circuits?

A wired AND or dot AND logic can be very easily obtained by having a number of 'open collector' gates connected to the power supply using just one pullup resistor. See Figure 2.33, which shows a number of transistors using a common pullup resistance. If any of the switches is ON, that is, any transistor is conducting, the output is '0' and thus we get an AND logic, with this simple wiring. Many protocols use this sort of logic. Section 5.2 provides a note on how the I2C protocol uses wired AND logic. Pullup resistors are widely used in such output configurations.

Port 0 of the 8051 is an open drain configuration. This port needs pullup resistances as the drains of the output transistors are left open. See Figure 2.34, which shows pullup resistors connected externally to P0.0 to P0.7. Separate pullup resistors are used, as the port pins may have to be used as single bit port lines.

The other ports P1 to P3 are not open drain configuration. Each of these port pins have an output stage which consists of active devices and have an effective internal pullup. (The data sheet can be looked at to find the amount of current such an output pin sources or sinks.)

2.5.4 | Weak and Strong Pullup

When the current drawn through the pullup is small, it is called a weak pullup, that is, a high resistance, otherwise it is a strong pullup. A weak pullup has a high R and since there is a capacitance associated with any signal lead, it constitutes a high RC. Thus

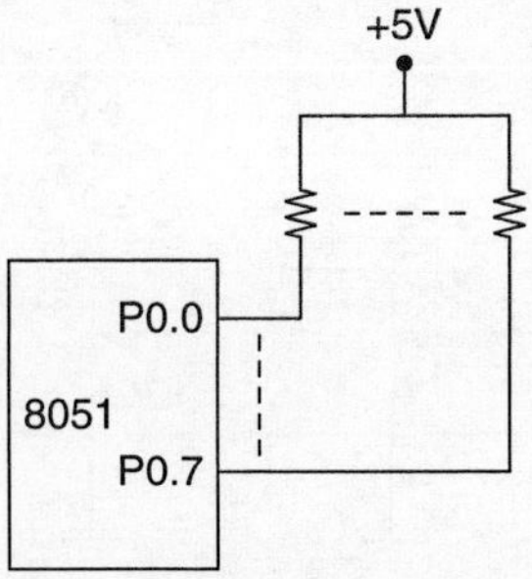

Figure 2.34 | Pins of port 0 of 8051 with pullup resistors

where switching speed is important, like in the case of buses like the I2C bus, a weak pullup is not advisable as it will cause slow switching between levels.

Thus, values of pullup resistances should be calculated on the basis of speed requirements, current specification of the gates and also on the number of outputs to be connected together.

2.5.5 | High Impedance State, Hi-Z

In digital systems, the two logical states are 1 (high) and 0 (low). Depending on the type of logic family used, there are voltage levels defined for these states. Besides this, one more logic state is usually used in most bus-oriented designs. The third logic is the 'high impedance' state also called the Hi-Z or floating state. If a particular device is connected to a line which is in the high impedance state, that device is as good as 'not connected'. Thus, a Hi-Z state is an open circuited state.

See Figure 2.35a for a tri state buffer. The signal E is the enable signal. If it is put in the enabling state (can be defined to be high or low, as per the circuit design), the signal at A is transferred to Y. Otherwise, the buffer acts like an open circuit (Figure 2.35b).

There are many chips which have multiple tri state buffers in them. The chip 74LS244 is one of them. A control pin is used to activate/disable the buses. See Figure 2.36, which shows a functional view of this chip. It has two sets of four bit inputs and corresponding outputs. For each set, there is an enable pin $\overline{OE}$. When the pin $\overline{OE}$ is low, the output pins are active and will take on the logical levels of the input pins. When the $\overline{OE}$ pin is high, the output pins are at high impedance or blocked or floating state. Any device that

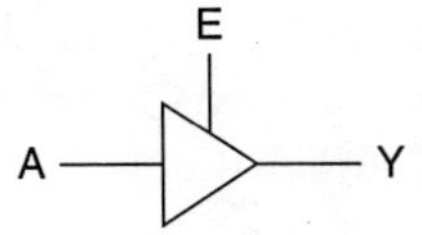

Figure 2.35a | A tri-state buffer

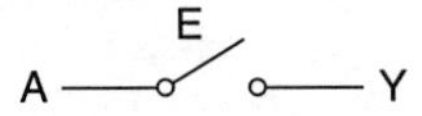

Figure 2.35b | An open circuit

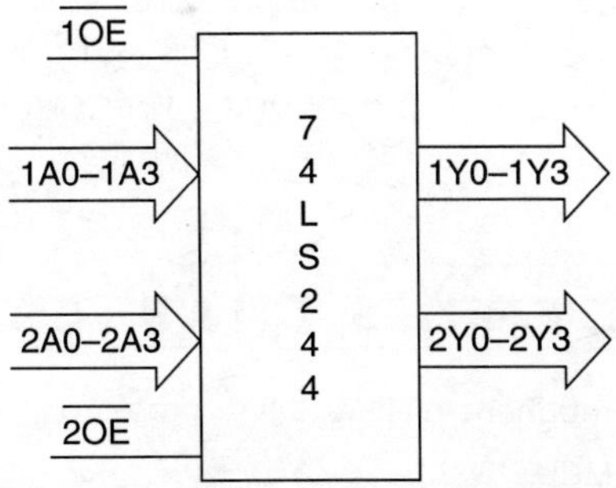

Figure 2.36 Functional pin diagram of the 74LS244 tri-state buffer IC

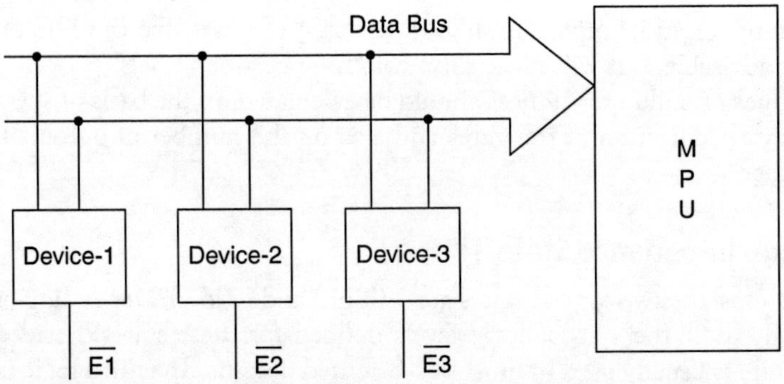

Figure 2.37 | Example of a bus-oriented system using the Hi-Z logic

is connected to these output pins is 'disconnected', in the sense that the interconnection lines are actually 'open circuit'.

The Hi-Z state is very important in bus-oriented systems, where a number of devices are connected to the same set of lines. See Figure 2.37, in which three input devices are attached to the data bus of an MPU. Only one of the devices should be really 'connected' to the bus. All the devices have an enable pin each. Only if the enable pin of the respective device is activated will that device's output lines be activated. Then only will the particular device be connected to the data bus.

It is to be understood that at a time, only one of the devices should be 'connected' to the data bus, and this is achieved by selectively enabling each device. When the enable pin of a device is inactive, the output lines of the device are in the high impedance (Hi-Z) state, and hence no connection exists between the device output and the data bus of the MPU. This setup is to ensure that only one device can send data to the MPU at a time.

Conclusion

With this, we come to the end of our discussion on the general hardware aspects of embedded systems. For each of the topics discussed here, more (intense) study will be required, if and when a project is to be done and a hardware is to be completely developed. For that, the data sheets of the processor, memory and I/O devices will have to be studied. It is very important to understand the concepts in this chapter well, because it will go a long way in developing your confidence to understand any MCU with ease.

KEY POINTS OF THIS CHAPTER

- The most important component in an MCU is its processor.
- 8051 is a popular 8-bit MCU.
- The stack of an MCU is defined in RAM and is a very useful data structure.

- Interrupts are a way by which peripherals can get the attention of the processor.
- Timers and counters are found in most MCUs as a standard peripheral.
- DMA is a type of operation that is done in mid- and high-range processors.
- There are serial communication ports in all MCUs.
- MCUs have semiconductor memory on the chip in the form of flash, RAM and EEPROM.
- Many embedded systems prefer tightly coupled memory to caches.
- Designing embedded systems for very low power is the trend now.
- Gates with open collector outputs need pullup resistors.
- Bus-oriented systems have a high impedance state besides '0' and '1' logic.

QUESTIONS

1. What are the types of registers available in an MCU?
2. What is meant by the word GPIO? What is it used for?
3. What is the use of a real-time clock for an OS?
4. Give two uses of the processor stack.
5. Distinguish between software and hardware interrupts.
6. Explain how a typical timer operates.
7. Why is serial communication needed? Give some contexts in which it is used.
8. Distinguish between SRAM and DRAM.
9. Why is SRAM the preferred memory technology for caches?
10. How is tightly coupled memory different from cache?
11. List a few applications for NAND flash.
12. Specify a context in which a pullup resistor is used.
13. Explain why bus-oriented systems need the Hi_Z logic level.
14. Explain the concept of wired AND logic.

EXERCISES

1. Draw an MCU with the following peripherals connected to its GPIO pins:
   a) A single digit LED
   b) Four toggle switches
   c) A relay
2. List the numbers and manufacturers of:
   a) Two SRAMs
   b) Two SDRAMs
   c) One SSRAM
3. Choose a specific PIC IC and list out how much of RAM, flash and EEPROM it contains.
4. What are the trends in embedded design for low power dissipation?

3 SENSORS, ADCs AND ACTUATORS

In this chapter, you will learn

- The working principle of a number of sensors
- The use of temperature and light sensors in practical circuits
- How an LED is used in sensing circuits
- Circuits which use photodiodes and photo transistors
- The working principle of proximity and range sensors
- How an optical encoder works
- The data and control interface of an ADC
- The use of parallel and serial ADCs
- The use of seven segment LEDs and OLEDs
- The ways of using Character and Graphical LCDs
- Usage of stepper motors, DC motors, current drivers and optocouplers
- The working principle of a relay and some practical circuits

Introduction

In our discussion on general purpose I/O (GPIO) in Chapter 2, it was mentioned that depending on the application, the GPIO pins can be used as output or input pins, and various peripheral devices can be connected to these pins. In this chapter, we discuss a few standard and widely used I/O devices, that is, sensors which are input devices and actuators which are output devices. Sensors are required for getting data from the real world and actuators are needed to get the embedded system to 'act' based on this data.

We also devote a small amount of space to 'Analog to Digital Converters' or ADCs as they are commonly referred to. All sensors have analog outputs. But for using them with MCUs, their analog voltages are to be converted to digital numbers. ADCs perform this function, which is a very critical part of the whole system. Without an ADC of good resolution and sensitivity, the whole point in having good sensors is lost. Taking this aspect into consideration, the important aspects of A to D conversion have been looked into.

Chapter-opening image: Two ADC chips.

3.1 | Sensors

Remember the block diagram (Figure 1.2) that we started with. Any embedded system needs sensors—depending on the application, it may be just one sensor or as in most cases, many sensors. A sensor converts a physical quantity into a corresponding voltage. Take an application like a home security system—there should be sensors for sensing temperature, light, motion, humidity, etc. The data obtained from these sensors decide the course of action for the actuators of the system. In this section, we take a quick look at some of the commonly used sensors.

3.1.1 | Temperature Sensors

3.1.1.1 | *Thermistor*

A thermistor is a thermally sensitive resistor, which means that its resistance is 'affected' by the temperature variations around it. Thermistors are made with semi-conductor materials and there are two kinds of thermistors—those with NTC (negative temperature coefficient) and PTC (positive thermal coefficient). For the former, the resistance of the thermistor decreases with increase in temperature, and for the latter, it is just the reverse.

Figure 3.1 is a very simple circuit which uses a NTC thermistor. At normal temperatures, the transistor is OFF, because the high resistance of the thermistor prevents it from getting sufficient base current. When the temperature increases, the resistance of the thermistor decreases and at a certain value of thermistor resistance, the base current needed to turn on the transistor is obtained. This switches the transistor ON. The collector voltage goes low, and the LED lights up. Since the collector is connected to the input pin of an MCU, the port P1.1 switches from high to low at a particular 'triggering temperature'. The exact value of this temperature can be varied by varying the value of R. That is why, it is shown as a variable resistor. Figure 3.2 is the photograph of a thermistor.

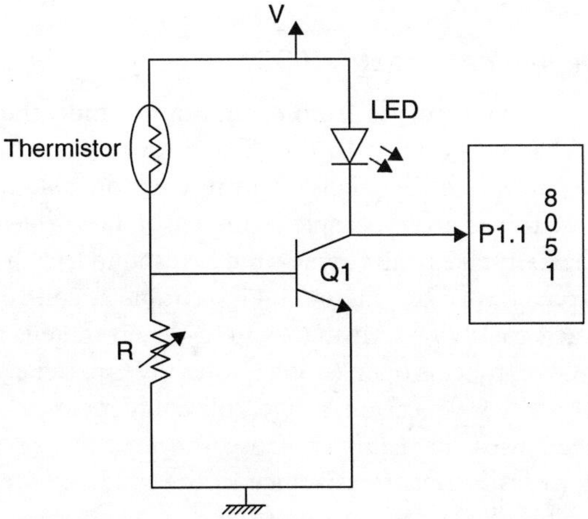

Figure 3.1 | A simple circuit using a thermistor

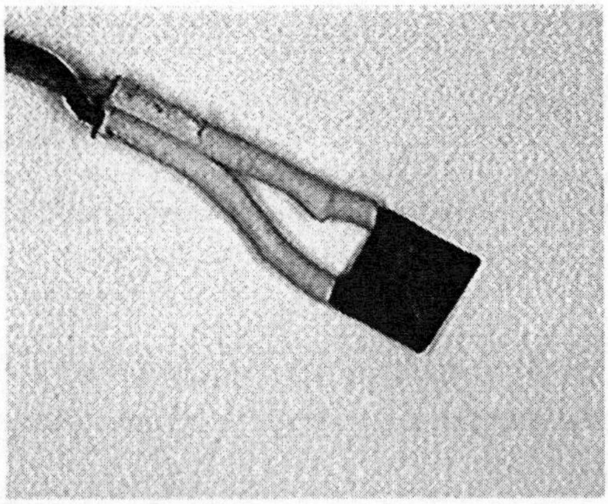

Figure 3.2 | Photograph of a thermistor

3.1.1.2 | *Thermocouple*

A thermocouple is also a sensor for measuring temperature. In this, there are two dissimilar metals, joined together at one end and they produce a voltage proportional to the temperature difference between the two ends of the pair of conductors. One junction is kept at a constant temperature and is called the reference (cold) junction, while the other is the measuring (Hot) junction. When the two junctions are at different temperatures, a voltage is developed across the junction.

Thermocouples are used in many high temperature applications like furnaces, turbines and engine temperature measurements in industries and automobiles.

3.1.2 | Light Sensors

Sensing of light, or rather the blocking of the light that is being sensed continuously is an important feature in many systems. Let's make a review of some of the popular light sensors.

3.1.2.1 | *Light Dependent Resistor (LDR)*

LDRs are very popular devices, made from cadmium sulphide, the resistance of which changes from several thousand ohms in the dark to only a few hundred ohms in the presence of bright light. When light falls upon it, electron hole pairs are created and conductivity increases. This is a very simple light sensor, but it has the disadvantage of 'sluggish' response, that is, it takes quite some time to respond to a change in illumination. Fig 3.3 is a photograph of an LDR. Figure 3.4 is a simple circuit which uses an LDR as a sensor. The circuit acts as a light activated switch. When there is no ambient lighting, the relay (Section 3.3.4) contact is open (it is a 'Normally Open', i.e., NO contact) When the light level increases beyond a certain range, this contact closes.

This simple circuit uses the LDR to sense the presence or absence of light. In the absence of light, the LDR has a resistance in the range of Mega ohms and so the transistor does not get sufficient bias to be ON. But when there is ambient lighting, the resistance of the LDR falls and the transistor gets the bias current to conduct. The

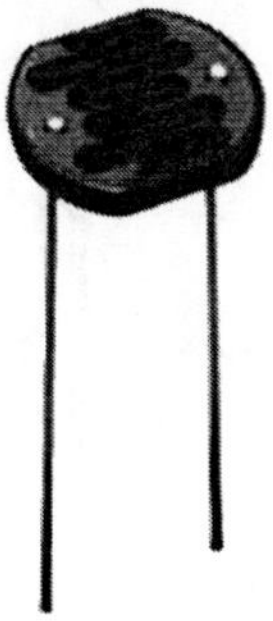

Figure 3.3 | Photograph of an LDR

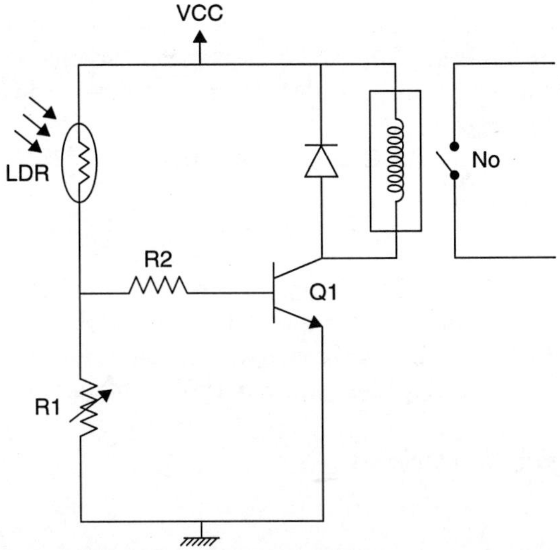

Figure 3.4 | A circuit which uses an LDR for sensing light

transistor switches ON and the relay gets energized—its contact closes. This 'closing' can be used to activate some action, as needed. The amount of illumination required to cause the 'switching' may be adjusted by using the variable resistance R1.

3.1.2.2 | *Light Emitting Diodes (LED)*

LEDs are light generating devices, and as such do not act directly as sensors. Fig 3.5 shows the photograph of an LED. But they can be made to emit light, which is detected by a photo detecting device. This 'detection' can be used as a sensor value. Let's think of some typical applications which use this technique for sensing.

In what is called a line following robot, a robot is made to move continuously on a white line (drawn on a black surface). An LED is fixed under the robotic vehicle. The light from this LED strikes the white line on the ground and reflects it back. There is a photo detecting circuitry to receive this, and the corresponding activation circuitry ensures that the vehicle moves continuously on the white line.

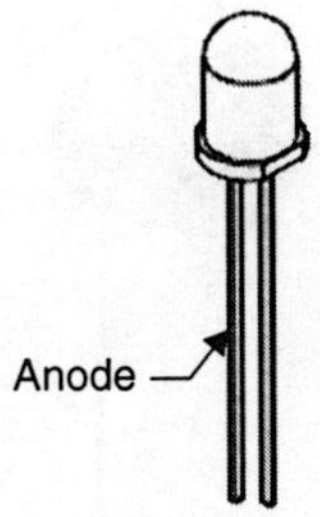

Figure 3.5 | A photograph of an LED

But when the path becomes a curve, the moving vehicle which is moving in a 'straight path' will deviate from the path defined by the white line. This will be sensed by the photodetecting circuitry which no longer receives the reflected light, because the black background absorbs it all. This can be used to create the necessary logic to bring the vehicle back on the white line, and due to this feedback mechanism, it is made to navigate along the curve.

This example was just to make clear the idea of how an LED can be part of a 'sensor' mechanism.

Infra Red LED

For many sensor circuits, infra red LEDs are preferred as the light source. This is because it can be used in the same manner at night and day, as visible light does not affect its operation. Common IR LEDs have a wavelength of 850nm, 940~980nm. The light generated by this is sensed by an IR receiver, which is usually a photodiode or phototransistor.

3.1.2.3 | *Photojunction Devices*

Photodiodes

This is a diode similar to regular semiconductor diodes except that its outer casing is either transparent or has a clear lens to focus the light onto the PN junction for exposure to light, i.e. it is packaged with a window to allow light to reach the sensitive part of the device. It is designed to operate in reverse bias, so that reverse current flows. When light energy strikes the junction, it is this current that increases.

Photodiodes are very smart light sensors that can switch from 'ON' and 'OFF' in nanoseconds. They are commonly used in very many applications from robotics to cameras, TV remote controls, scanners, fax machines, copiers, etc.

Phototransistors

A phototransistor is basically a photodiode with gain. The phototransistor light sensor has its collector-base PN-junction reverse biased and is also exposed to radiant light source. Any normal transistor can be easily converted into a phototransistor light sensor by connecting a photodiode between the collector and base. Now, let's think of an application where light sensing is used.

Intrusion Detection In this circuit (Figure 3.6), an infra red LED output which is activated by an astable oscillator (using the IC NE555, for example) is used to generate a

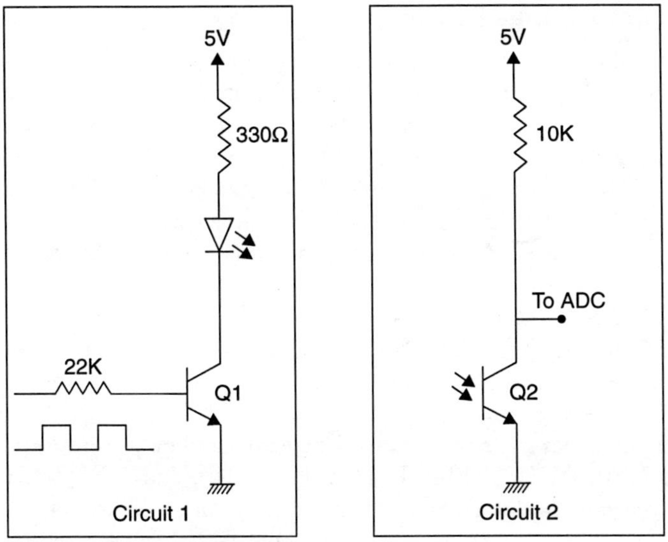

Figure 3.6 | An intrusion detection setup

pulse of some particular frequency. This LED is in Circuit 1 which is the light transmitter circuit.

This pulse train is continuously detected by an infra red detector in Circuit 2. When an intruder blocks the path of light (between circuits 1 and 2), the momentarily absence of light is sensed by the IR sensor in Circuit 2 and this information can be used as an indication that an intruder has blocked the path of light. Any action can be initiated by this, for example, a relay can be activated to trigger an alarm on sensing the intruder.

There is a standard IC acting as an infra red receiver, and it is the TSOP series. For using this, the signal transmitted by the IR LED should have a standard format (refer to its data sheet). The TSOP IC package contains a PIN photodiode, a bandpass filter and a demodulator which converts the signal to a format that a microcontroller can use, i.e. a high or low pulse. Because of the preamplifier and bandpass filter inside, the received signal is robust and free of noise. Such receivers are very popular in simple intruder detector systems, and also in remote control systems, proximity detectors, etc. Fig 3.7 is a photograph of the TSOP (SM0038) IC.

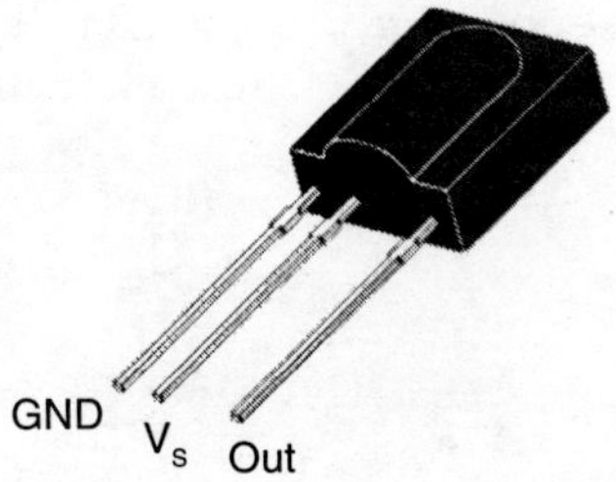

Figure 3.7 | Photograph of a TSOP IC

3.1.3 | Proximity/Range Sensors

Detection of an object and determination of its range are very important, especially in the field of robotics. Visible or infra red light can be used successfully for this. To detect whether there is some object in the proximity, the simple method used is to send a beam of light (usually IR) which the object will reflect back to the receiver. The reflected light is detected by a photo detector, and the information can be used to confirm that there is an object within the path of the emitted light (within a certain range). This is what we call a proximity sensor. To make it a range sensor, there should be a method to find its range, as well.

Recently SHARP (the company) has produced a series (GP2DXX) of IR range finder ICs which are very powerful and easy to use. Its merits are that it is quite accurate, easy to use, affordable, small, has good range measurement capability from inches to metres, and also low-power consumption.

The GP2DXX series has both proximity detectors and range sensors. The GP2D12, GP2D120, GP2Y0A02 ('0A02'), GP2Y0A21 ('0A21'), and GP2Y0A700 ('0A700') sensors offer true ranging information in the form of an analog output. The GP2D15 and GP2DY0D02 ('0D'), by contrast, offer a single digital value based on whether an object is present or not. None of the detectors require an external clock or signal.

3.1.3.1 | *Range Sensing Technique*

The Sharp IR Range Finder (the photograph of which is shown in Fig 3.8) works by the process of triangulation, which is a technique in which a region is divided into a series of triangular elements based on a line of known length, so that accurate measurements of distances and directions may be made by the application of trigonometry.

A pulse of IR light is emitted and then is reflected back if it strikes an object in its path. The reflected beam returns at an angle that is dependent on the distance of the reflecting object. Triangulation works by detecting this reflected beam angle—by knowing the angle, the distance can be determined (Fig 3.9). This type of IR range finder receiver has a special precision lens that transmits the reflected light onto an enclosed linear CCD array based on the triangulation angle. The CCD array then determines the angle and causes the rangefinder to give an analog value, which corresponds to the distance of the object. Additional to this, the 'Sharp IR Range Finder' circuitry applies a modulated frequency to the emitted IR beam. This ranging method is almost (not 100% true!!) immune to interference from ambient light, and is indifferent to the colour of the detected object.

Note These sensors can measure range between 20 to 150 cms (approximate), which means that there is not only a 'maximum' but also a minimum for the range measurement.

Figure 3.8 | Photograph of a SHARP sensor

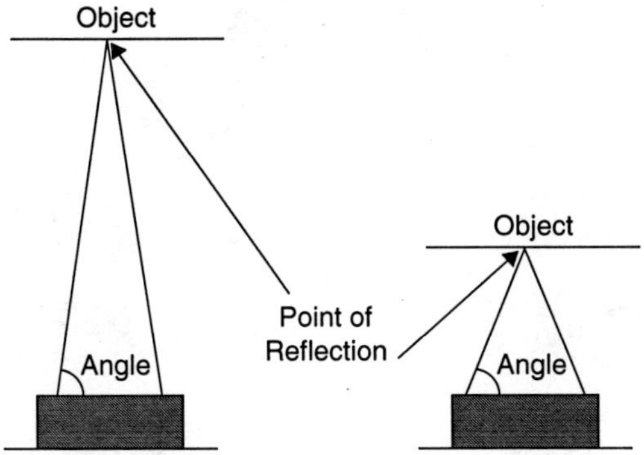

Figure 3.9 | The technique for sensing range

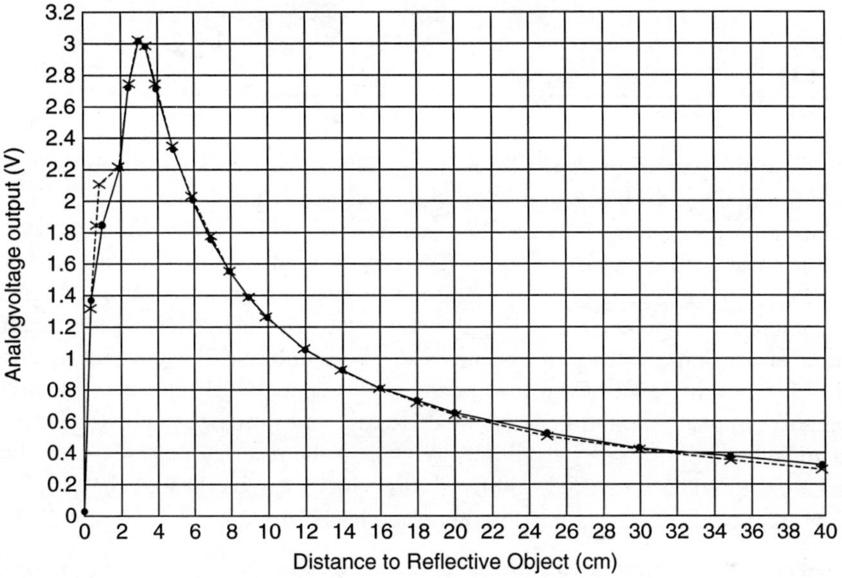

Figure 3.10 | Graph of voltage vs range for a range sensor

For example, observe the voltage output (Figure 3.10) from the GP2D120 sensor which has the range specified to be between 4 and 13 cms.

The characteristic shows that below 4 cm, the output falls and may be wrongly interpreted as a large range. In robotics, the best method would be to use more than one range finder and then to cross fire them.

3.1.4 | Encoders

There is a sensor for finding the speed and direction (and thus the position and distance travelled) of a moving vehicle. This is an 'encoder' which can be fitted to the shaft of the wheel of the vehicle. It uses optical principals and is called an 'optical encoder'. Such encoders work on the principle of counting the number of transitions across a black and white pattern.

Figure 3.11 | Pattern used in an optical encoder

Look at the pattern in Figure 3.11. If we calibrate the black and white patterns in terms of 1 and 0 –(0 for block, and 1 for white), we get a square pulse.

The pattern in Figure 3.11 has 12 black and 12 white blocks. Assume that this pattern is embedded on a disk which is fitted to the shaft of the wheel and that there is a sensor from which pulses can be obtained corresponding to the pattern. When the wheel rotates once, a pulse train of 12 pulses are obtained. Thus, if the pulses are counted, the number of rotations that have occurred can be found out. If the wheel diameter is known, the circumference of the wheel can be calculated, which measures the distance covered with one wheel rotation. In effect, this simply means that by knowing how much is the angle turned for one received pulse, counting the received pulses is equivalent to measuring the distance travelled, and from this velocity can be calculated.

For an optical encoder, two components are necessary

i) A disk with a pattern as shown in Figure 3.11. Now see Figure 3.12 which shows such a disk.
ii) An LED which generates light which passes through the holes in the disk, or is blocked by the disc.
iii) An optical sensor which receives these light pulses and converts it to electrical signals.

Figure 3.12 shows a pattern disk with a few holes, which can be attached to the shaft of a moving wheel. As the wheel rotates, the light passes through the holes and this is sensed by the receiver on the PCB shown. The pulse train obtained can be used to calculate the distance travelled (from which velocity can be obtained).

IC s are available, with an IR LED and a photodetector in one package, which act as the receiver. See the optical interruptor switch in Figure 3.13 (also called the break beam switch) with a U-shaped slot using which it can be fixed to the rotating wheels.

Such an IC is the H21A1/H21A2/H21A3 series which consist of a gallium arsenide infrared emitting diode coupled with a silicon phototransistor in a plastic housing.

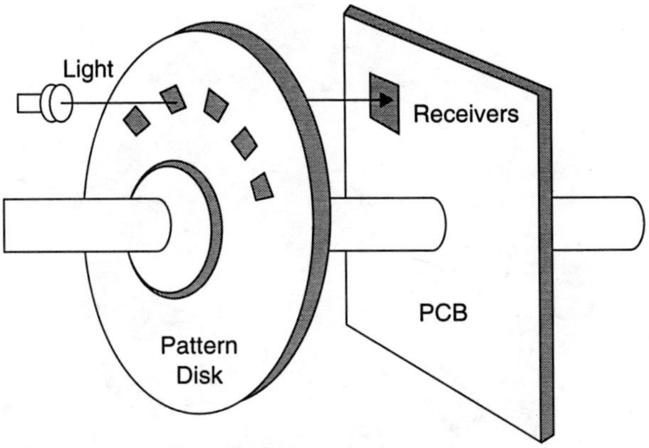

Figure 3.12 | Optical encoder transmitter and receiver

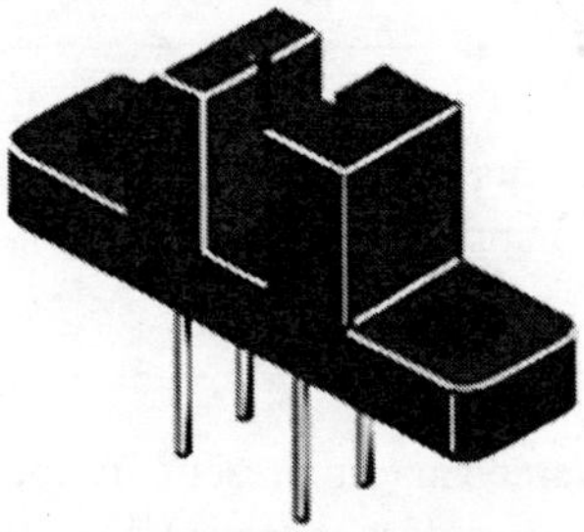

Figure 3.13 | Photograph of an optical interruptor switch

The gap in the housing provides a means of interrupting the signal with an opaque material, switching the output from an 'ON' to an 'OFF' state.

Figure 3.14 shows the arrangement of the pattern disk and the switch connected to a wheel of a robot.

The type of pattern disk that we have just discussed is non-directional because it cannot decipher the direction of movement. For directionality, a quadrature phase

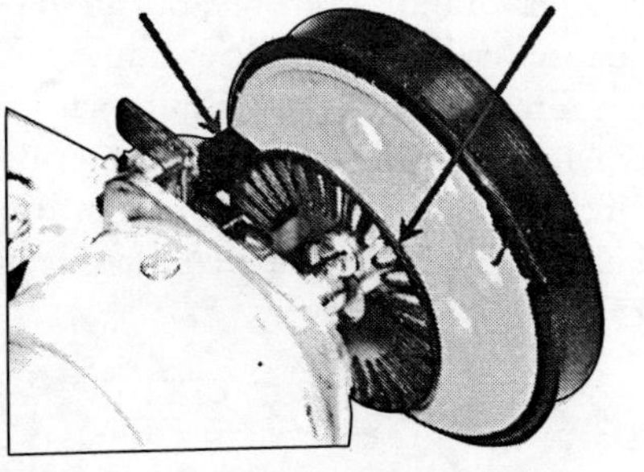

Figure 3.14 | Optical Encoder fixed to the wheel of a robot
(Reproduced with permission from Nex Robotics, Mumbai)

Figure 3.15 | A directional pattern

pattern with two staggered patterns is necessary, so that the system can tell which way the wheel is turning. Figure 3.15 shows such a pattern.

3.1.5 | Humidity Sensors

Humidity is the quantity of water vapour present in air. It can be expressed as being 'absolute' or 'relative'. Absolute humidity expresses the water vapour content of the air using the mass of water vapour contained in a given volume of air. Relative humidity is a ratio that compares the amount of water vapour in the air with the amount of water vapour that would be present in the air at saturation. Thus, humidity sensors measure the amount of water vapour present in air, but what are the applications for it?

In home automation systems, humidity is monitored so as to bring it to a level which makes it a comfortable environment—other applications are in the semiconductor industry where moisture levels need to be continuously monitored during wafer processing—in the household, it is used for intelligent control of living environment, microwave cooking, laundry, etc. In automobiles, this sensor information forms the basis for window de-fogging control.

There are different types of humidity sensors, but in general, sensing of humidity involves a change of impedance (capacitance, for example). For this principle, the sensor element is built out of a film capacitor on different substrates (glass, ceramic, etc.). The dielectric is a polymer which absorbs or releases water proportional to the relative environmental humidity, and thus changes the capacitance of the capacitor, which is measured by an on-board electronic circuit. One commonly available relative humidity sensor is the HS12P, HS15P series.

3.1.6 | Other Sensors

In this section, only a few types of sensors have been covered. Besides these, there are sensors for many other physical quantities—there are gas sensors, smoke sensors, piezo-electric sensors (for sensing stress, strain etc), touch sensors and so on. As per the requirements of the applications, standard sensors for these can be easily sought out.

3.2 | Analog to Digital Converters

All sensors give an analog voltage proportional to the physical quantity sensed—to convert it to a digital number which an MCU can use, an Analog to Digital Converter (ADC) is used. Many MCUs have ADCs inside the chip (PIC, ARM, AVR, etc.), while there are MCUs like 8051 where an external ADC might be needed. In this section, we review some important aspects of ADCs.

3.2.1 | ADC Interfacing *

ADCs [Analog-to-Digital Convertors] convert analog voltages into digital codes which can be processed by embedded systems. ADCs are required for all systems that need to interface with real-world (analog) signals.

ADCs usually have two separate interfaces that are accessible to an embedded system.

i) Control interface
ii) Data interface

3.2.1.1 | *Control Interface*

ADCs vary widely in complexity, performance and speed. They have various modes and states which need to be managed to make them operate in the manner we need them to. For example, an ordinary SAR (Successive Approximation Register) ADC might continuously convert the input signal, generate codes and put them out on the data bus. However, the ADC might have different modes like 10-bit/12-bit/14-bit (resolution), various offset correction modes, power modes, latency modes (which determines how many clock cycles it takes for a given input to appear at the output), input clock modes (single ended/differential), etc. There might be a huge number of modes depending on the complexity of the ADC. Some might have elaborate schemes for tweaking various aspects of their operation to improve or tailor performance to our needs.

Register Control

All these modes and states are managed with the help of registers and register controlled fuses inside the ADC.

Hence, we need some way of writing into and reading from these registers. For this, we depend on the control interface which is essentially a register interface.

Various industry standards exist for such interfaces. A few among them are (Section 5.1.3)

i) SPI
ii) I2C
iii) UART

---

*The section 3.2.1 is written by Sabu Paul, Analog Design Engineer, Texas Instruments, Bangalore.

Pin Control

For very simple ADCs, there might not be enough number of states or modes to justify the usage of a register interface. They might simply have a few pins which control the state of the ADC. Typically, the number of such pins will be less than or equal to 4, which allows us to select between 16 different states. Some such devices might have a simple state machine inside which allows the ADC to respond to the sequence of inputs applied at the input pins. This is frequently used in ADCs used for compact biomedical applications. The ADC might be combined with an AFE (Analog Front End) and/or transceiver. The entire module can be controlled through the pin interface mentioned earlier.

3.2.1.2 | *Data Interface*

ADCs vary widely in their speed of conversion, from a few samples per second to several GSPS (Giga Samples per Second). In the case of very slow ADCs, separate data and control interfaces are not usually used. In such devices, the register interface is used to read out both the data and to write and read state information. For example, most microcontrollers contain a built-in ADC which has a register interface through which both control signals like start conversion/stop conversion as well as data can be sent and read out, respectively.

In the case of high speed ADCs, the transmission speeds of conventional register interfaces and their signalling overheads together make them unsuitable for data. Also, in most of the cases where high speed ADCs are used, control signals will have to be sent without interrupting the flow of data.

In such cases, a separate dedicated data interface is used.

Two types of interfaces used are:

i) Parallel
ii) Serial

Parallel Interface

In a parallel data interface, each data word is transmitted over several physical lines with each line carrying one data bit. There is also a clock line which is used to latch the data when it is ready. These systems are losing popularity and are used mainly in applications where the resolution and/or speed is low. In such cases, parallel interfaces make sense since they can be directly transmitted without a lot of digital manipulation by the ADC and directly read by the controller. This is unlike serial systems which require a SERDES (Serializer-Deserializer) for data transfer. A clearer picture of its pros and cons vis-à-vis the serial system will emerge during the discussion of serial systems.

Parallel interfaces can be classified based on the clock edge used for latching data.

i) **Positive edge:** The data is latched on the positive edge of the clock.
ii) **Negative edge:** The data is latched on the negative edge.
iii) **Dual edge:** The data is latched on the positive and negative edges of the clock. This is also known as a DDR [Dual Data Rate] scheme. This can reduce the number of data lines by half (at the cost of some extra hardware) or increase the speed by two.

Based on the number of lines used to transmit a single bit, we have

i) **Single ended:** A single line is used to transmit one bit and the voltage is referred to the common ground.

ii) **Differential:** A matched pair is used to transmit 1-bit. One line carries bit+V and the other bit -V. This improves noise immunity and can allow for reduced signal swing. A differential system requires twice the number of lines as a singled ended system.

Based on the voltage levels, these interfaces are classified into

i) **CMOS (1.8 -3.3V):** Modern ADCs have digital modules made using MOS technology. So, this voltage level is commonly used by a lot of ADCs for signalling.
ii) **TTL (5V).**
iii) **LVDS (700mV peak-to-peak):** Low Voltage Differential Signalling is used in differential systems. Both bit+ and bit- lines have a swing of 350mV peak-to-peak each. The noise immunity afforded by the matched pair of lines is what allows the usage of this reduced swing without compromising on BER (Bit Error Rate).

The LVDS scheme requires 2X (twice) the number of lines. To work around this problem, it normally is used in conjunction with the DDR scheme mentioned earlier. It is then called a DDR LVDS scheme. This allows us to have the exact same pin count while at the same time getting the reduced power consumption and EMI (Electro Magnetic Interference) levels of an LVDS scheme. The advantages of the LVDS scheme will become more apparent after the discussion of its use in serial systems. ICs are available which are capable of translating between voltage levels and signal modes (Differential/Single-ended).

Serial Interface

A lot of the modern day high performance devices use the serial mode of data transfer.

Here, instead of each data line carrying 1-bit of the data word, all the bits are sent serially over one single line. There are many advantages to this approach when compared to a parallel system.

Advantages

i) Fewer number of physical connections.
ii) Smaller die size made possible by reduced pin count.
iii) The size is a big advantage for some of the higher resolution (<14 bits)/multi-channel ADCs.
iv) Serial interfaces can operate differentially as the increase in the number of wires is minimal. This drastically cuts down noise pick-up and allows for lower signalling voltages.
v) The EMI generated by a balanced differential pair is much lesser than that by a large number of single ended parallel data lines. This is because the opposing currents in the pair cancel out the magnetic fields caused due to each other.
vi) The lower signal swing made possible by the common mode noise rejection in a differential system reduces power consumption.
vii) Serial interfaces allow for features like clock recovery. This makes it unnecessary to have a separate clock line. The clock is recovered from the data. This is possible because serial interfaces switch at a much higher speed than parallel buses.
viii) Quite a few high-quality serial interface standards are there which allow for easy interoperability.

Disadvantages

i) Requires a deserializer to convert the serial data to data words.
ii) Features like clock recovery require the data to be modified to make sure that there are sufficient number of transitions for the PLL (Phase Locked Loop) to lock on to and to ensure that there are an equal number of 1s and 0s in a specified number of bits to ensure that the input common mode of the receiver does not change.
iii) Parallel data has to be converted to serial data and a high speed clock generated inside the device.
iv) The speed of transmission is higher by a factor equal to the resolution of the ADC when compared to a parallel scheme. So, reliability of data transfer becomes very sensitive to clock jitter and board parasitics.

Serial interfaces are also classified into the following:

- **Single-ended:** There is only one data line and signal voltage is referred to the common ground. The zero crossings are susceptible to noise. But, the number of lines is less. Single ended interfaces come with different signalling levels. A couple of them are
  - CMOS (1.8-3.3V)
  - TTL (5V)
- **Differential:** Data is transmitted over a matched differential pair. This reduces noise and EMI generation. Signal swing can be lower because of improvement in noise. This can save power. These systems require special interfacing ICs to convert the differential signal into a single ended one for use in the embedded system. Differential systems are further classified based on voltage swing.
  - Rail-Rail Swing (e.g. USB)
  - LVDS (Low Voltage Differential Signalling 700mVpp)

Nowadays, high speed multi-channel ADCs are available which convert several input signals simultaneously into corresponding digital codes. They give out output codes serially over several output data channels. Sometimes, hybrid systems are used to get around speed limitations. These systems are mainly of the following two types:

- **Multiplexed output:** Data from several input channels is multiplexed onto one output channel to save on pin count.
- **Interleaved output:** Data from one channel can be split up into 2 or more streams which are then sent serially over multiple output data channels. This is done to support higher sampling speeds.

Conventional serial standards like USB and Firewire (Section 5.3) are not used in data converters. This is because ADCs are a special category of devices sending out one single type of data. Hence, the complications, overheads and limitations of these serial standards make them unsuitable for use in ADC interfacing. The JEDEC (*Joint Electron Devices Engineering Council)* JESD204 is the upcoming standard for serial data interfaces in high speed data convertors. This is an LVDS scheme supporting very high data transfer speeds over multiple synchronized lanes and from multiple ADCs.

The complexity of the interfacing, depends on the speed and resolution of the ADCs used. It varies from simple singled ended CMOS/TTL parallel interfaces to JEDEC SERDES interfaces. The cost also increases correspondingly.

3.2.1.3 | *Interfacing an ADC to 8051*

ADCs may be 'parallel' or 'serial', as we have just discussed. First we consider a parallel ADC.

3.2.1.4 | *An ADC with a Parallel Data Interface*

Our interest is to interface an ADC to an 8051 MCU using Port2 as the data lines, and some pins of Port 1 for the control signals needed by the ADC. When an analog voltage is given as an input to an ADC, it gets converted to a digital number which is transferred to the 8051. The digital value can be stored in the RAM of the system and may be displayed or used in further computations. See the block diagram of such a setup in Figure 3.16.

ADC 0808/0809

We choose here, the ADC0808/ADC0809 which is an 8-bit parallel ADC and is microprocessor compatible. Its functional pin diagram is shown in Figure 3.17. It is designated as an '8-Bit μP Compatible A/D Converter with 8-Channel Multiplexer'. It uses the successive approximation technique for analog to digital conversion.

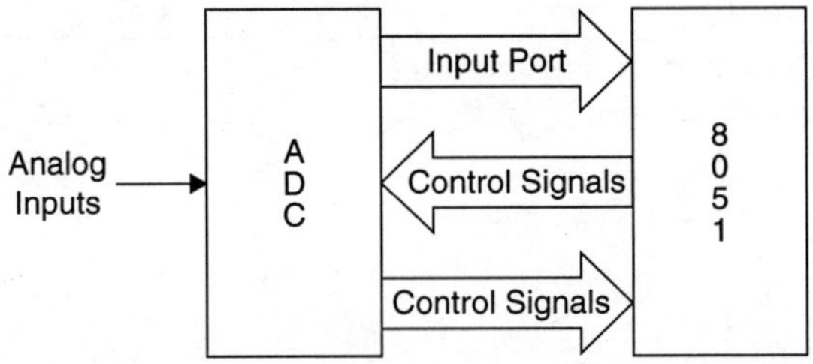

Figure 3.16 | General block diagram of the connection between an ADC and a MCU (8051)

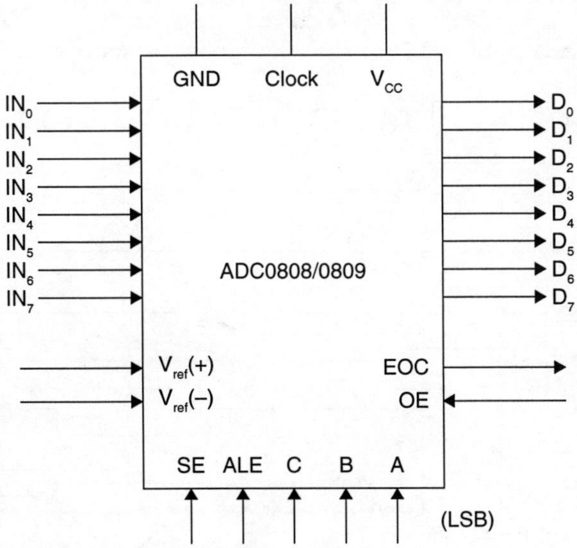

Figure 3.17 | Functional pin diagram of ADC 0808/0809

Its key specifications are given as:

1. Resolution 8 Bits
2. Total Unadjusted Error +/_ ½ LSB and +/_ 1 LSB
3. Single Supply 5 VDC
4. Low Power 15 mW
5. Conversion Time 100 μsecs

It is an 8-input multiplexed ADC, which means that it has 8 input analog signal lines, though only one of them can be operational at a time. This is selected by three address inputs A, B, C. Table 3. 1 shows the address bit configuration for selecting specific input channels. For example, if IN0 is to act as the input, the address lines C, B and A all have to be low; for IN1, the values of CBA is to be 001 and so on.

The first requirement in using the ADC is to select an input channel by giving the appropriate logic on the address pins. To latch this on to the chip, a signal called ALE (Address Latch Enable) is to be supplied on the ALE pin. ALE is to be a low to high transition (refer to Figure 3.18). After the address is latched and the analog input is

Table 3.1 | Channel Selection Logic

Selected analog channel	C	B	A
IN0	0	0	0
IN1	0	0	1
IN2	0	1	0
IN3	0	1	1
IN4	1	0	0
IN5	1	0	1
IN6	1	1	0
IN7	1	1	1

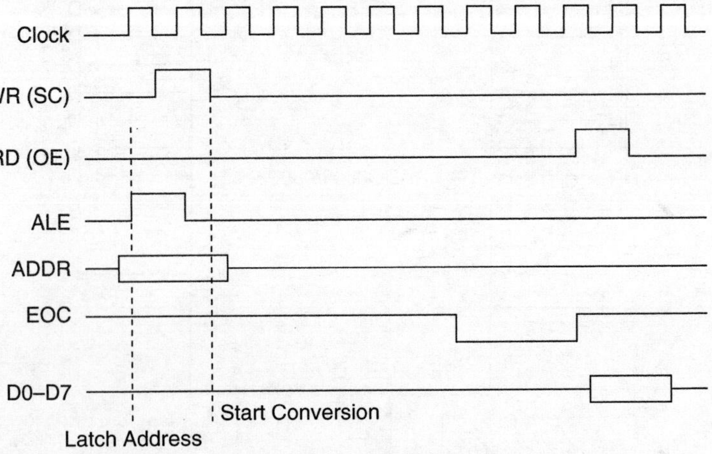

Figure 3.18 | Timing diagram for the ADC 0808/0809

available at the selected input line, the ADC must be signalled to start conversion. This (SC) is a low to high pulse of minimum specified duration (as mentioned in the data sheet). The ADC requires a clock and the speed of conversion depends on the clock rate. The maximum clock frequency is specified in the data sheet. The clock of the MCU can be divided to get the right frequency for the ADC.

The ADC takes a finite time to complete the conversion and then it notifies this fact by lowering the pin called EOC (End of Conversion). This should be brought to the notice of the MCU. The EOC signal can be used to interrupt the MCU, and allow the converted data to be transferred to the 8086 or this signal can be polled continuously.

To receive the digital data, the output lines of the ADC are to be activated. This is done by making high the line OE (Output Enable). Once, the output lines are activated, the converted digital data can be transferred to the 8051. The above is the sequence of actions necessary to use the ADC chip 0809 to perform analog to digital conversion and then to transfer the digital data to the microprocessor.

Let us now use the pins of 8051 for the purposes specified above. Make the connections between the 8051 and the ADC as shown in Figure 3.19. The salient points regarding the connection are as follows:

i) Port 2 is used in the input mode to get the converted digital data from the ADC to 8051.
ii) The port pins P1.7.P1.6 and P1.5 are used in the output mode as the address selection pins A, B, C of the ADC.
iii) The port pin P1.0 is used as ALE. It is to be an output pin.
iv) The port pin P1.1 is used to give the start conversion (SC) pulse to the ADC. Hence it is to be an output pin.
v) The port pin P1.2 is used in the input mode, to receive the End of Conversion (EOC) signal from the ADC.
vi) Port pin P1.3 is used as OE for the ADC. It is defined as an output pin.

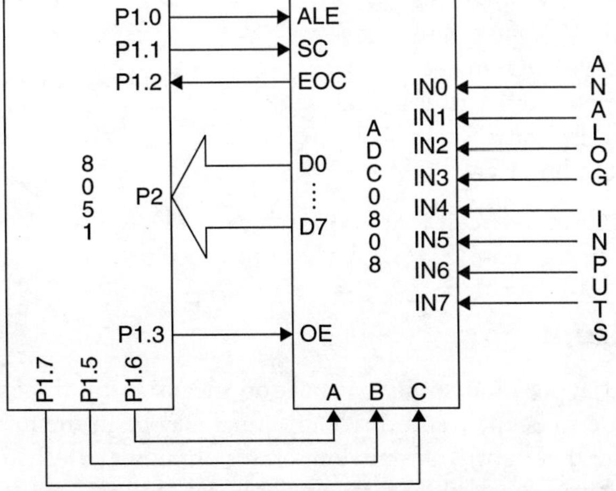

Figure 3.19 | Connections between the ADC and the 8051 MCU

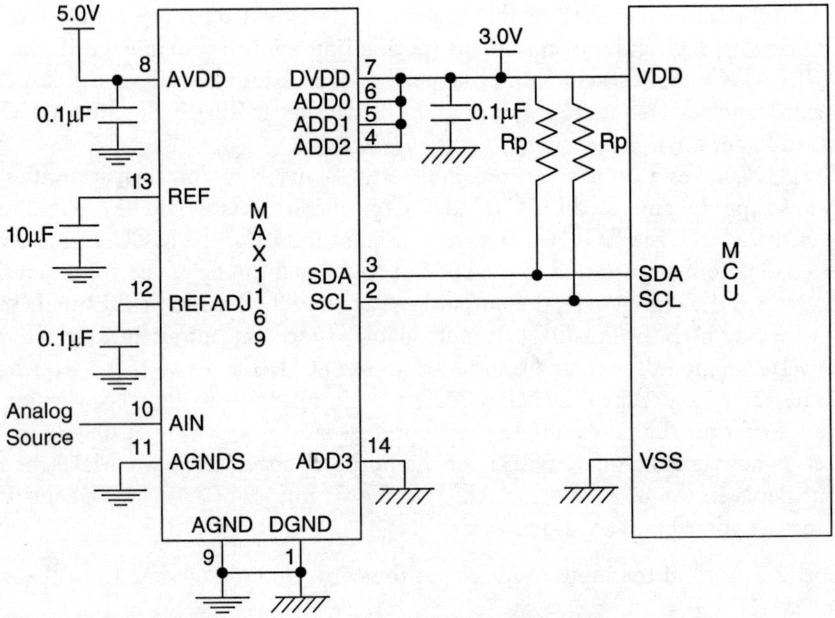

Figure 3.20 | Application circuit for the serial ADC MAX 1169 (Courtesy: Maxim Semiconductors)

3.2.1.5 | *Serial ADC*

An example for a serial ADC is the MAX 1169 which uses the I2C protocol (Section 5.2.1) for transfer. The specifications of this chip is given as

i) High-Speed I2C-Compatible Serial Interface
ii) 400kHz Fast Mode
iii) 1.7MHz High-Speed Mode
iv) +4.75V to +5.25V Single Supply
v) +2.7V to +5.5V Adjustable Logic Level
vi) Internal +4.096V Reference
vii) External Reference: 1V to VAVDD
viii) Internal 4MHz Conversion Clock
ix) 58.6ksps Sampling Rate

A typical application circuit for the IC is shown in Figure 3.20 Note that the MCU to be used needs an I2C port (SDA and SDC are I2C pins).

3.3 | Actuators

In the embedded application scenario, actuation means many things—it implies that something is made to happen, and this 'happening' may be in the form of a motion or display, alarm (sound or light), transmission to a distant unit etc. When the actuation is a 'motion', motors have to be used for rotational or linear motion. Let's start the discussion with display devices, related techniques and simple circuits where necessary.

3.3.1 | Displays

For most systems, some sort of display is necessary. Displays like LEDs, LCDs, etc. are very common. There is a lot of range and variety in the displays used in embedded systems.

Let's examine the features of some of the most popular displays.

3.3.1.1 | *Light Emitting Diodes (LED)*

A light emitting diode or LED as it is designated, works just as an ordinary semiconductor diode. It is usually made of Gallium Arsenide and is available in different colours. When it is forward biased, it conducts and also emits light which is used as a 'display unit'.

A single LED is used as an indication, of the state of a switch, the activation of any signal, reception of some data/signal, etc. It can also be made to act as an alarm by switching it on and off continuously at a certain rate. LEDs are easy to use and give a very bright and pleasing display which can be viewed equally well from any viewing angle, (unlike LCDs). The only drawback with LED displays is the high amount of current they need, unlike LCDs which need very low power. Figure 3.21 shows that a single LED can be connected to a positive power supply as shown. The value of the current limiting resistor depends on the current rating of the LED.

In case we need a number of LEDs for displays, we still use only one power source for all of them. In that case, they are connected together in either the 'common anode' or 'common cathode' LED configuration. In Figure 3.22a, the anodes of the three LEDs are connected together, and it is a 'common anode' connection. If we want to light up only the first and third LEDs, i.e., apply a '0' (i.e. ground), only at K1 and K3.

Figure 3.21 | A single LED circuit

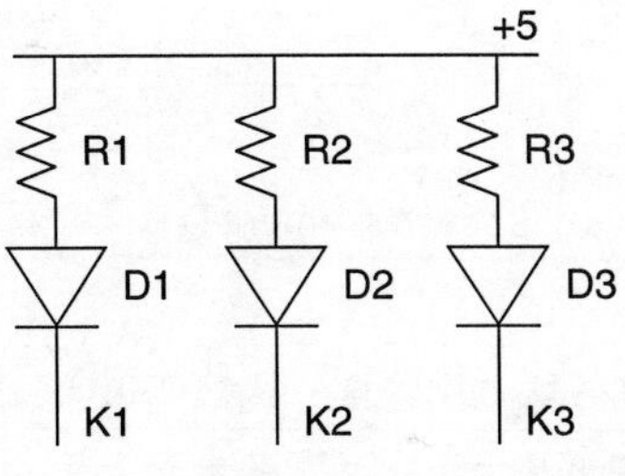

Figure 3.22a | Common anode connection

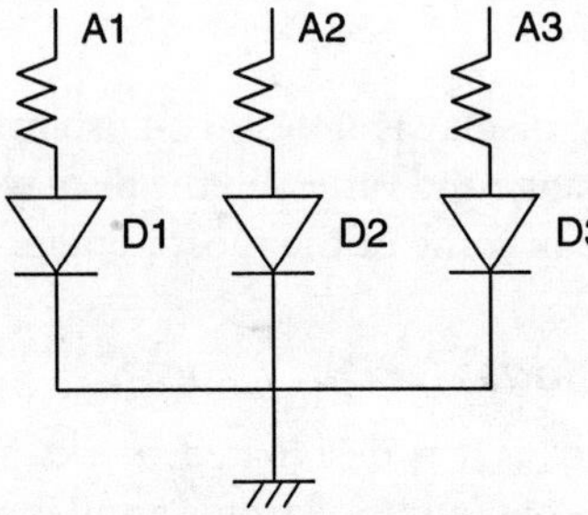

Figure 3.22b | Common cathode connection

In Figure 3.22b, which is 'common cathode', A1 and A3 alone should be given a '1' for the same result.

3.3.1.2 | *Seven Segment LED*

However, more important applications of LEDs are as alphanumeric displays. For that, seven segment LEDs are used, in which seven LEDs are arranged as the segments of a display arranged in a particular shape (see Figure 3.23a). When segments are selectively lighted up, the display of all alphanumeric characters is possible. By lighting up all the segments, we get '8' displayed. We can have one more segment in this display and it is for the decimal point. In Figure 3.23a, you can see that there are eight segments, including the segment for the decimal point. In spite of this, such displays are still designated as 'seven' segment displays. Such LED modules also can be used in either the common anode or common cathode configuration.

To light up a seven segment display LED of the common cathode type, ensure that the cathode is grounded, and give a '1' to the segments which are to be lit up. It is obvious that the opposite logic is to be used for common anode type.

Figure 3.23b shows the segments of a seven segment LED, arranged as a data byte D0 to D7.

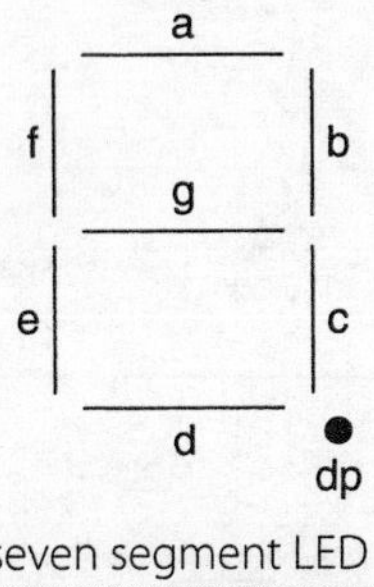

Figure 3.23a | The segments of a seven segment LED

D_7	D_6	D_5	D_4	D_3	D_2	D_1	D_0
dp	g	f	e	d	c	b	a

Figure 3.23b | The data byte for the seven segment LED

Example 3.1

a) Assuming a common cathode type of display, find the seven segment codes to be used for displaying
   i) 8, ii) A and iii) b.
b) How will the code change of it is a common cathode display?

Solution

(a) Since it is a common cathode type, the common cathode of the LEDs of a digit is to be grounded. Then, supply the segment information to the anodes. For displaying 8, the segments to be lighted up are a, b, c, d, e, f, g. Since, we are using a common cathode type of display, the data to light up a segment is '1'. Hence, the bits from D0 to D6 is '1'.
Thus, the seven segment code for the display of 8 is 0111 1111, i.e., 7 FH.

   i) Similarly for 'A' it is 0111 0111, i.e., 77 H.
   ii) For 'b' it is 0111 1100, i.e., 7 CH.

b) For common anode displays, the code for '8' is 1000 1000, for 'A' is 1000 1000 and for 'b' is 1000 0011.

3.3.1.3 | *Static Seven Segment Displays*

Now, suppose we want to use such a module to display a single character. Let us think of a scenario wherein, the number to be displayed is sent from an 8051 port to the display module. We just send the code (called seven segment code) corresponding to the segments of the LED. This code gives the information as to which of the segments are to be lighted up for the display of a specific character. In Example 3.1, if 77H is outputted through a port, the character 'A' is displayed on the segment LED connected to the port lines.

Assume we use only a one digit display module. If it is a common cathode type, we ground the common cathode and then we send the seven segment code directly to activate the required segments. This causes some of the segments to be ON and some to be OFF. Either way, as long as the display is ON, the module draws its required current from the power source. This may be in the range of 5 to 30 mA for a single segment to be lighted up. The display is ON all the time, and hence it is called a 'static' display.

Assume now that we need an eight digit display. If we use the same kind of static display, the current drawn is multiplied by 8, and this becomes quite a large amount. Multiply $7 \times 25 \times 8$ mA. This gives a value of 1.4 A, which is much too large for an electronic circuit. For this reason, static displays are not preferred for multiple digit displays.

3.3.1.4 | *Dynamic Displays*

When there is an array of digit display units, say 4 seven segment LEDs arranged in digit form in a row, a continuous display can be obtained by lighting up just one digit at a time. The next instant this digit is switched off and the next one is lighted up. This is done continuously and cyclically from digits 1 to 4 and repeated at a rapid rate. Because of the property of persistence of vision of the eyes, an illusion of continuous display is obtained. This is also called a multiplexed display.

The important points to note here are:

i) The common anode/cathode of a digit is to be activated for a digit to be active.
ii) At a time, only the segments of one digit are 'ON'.
iii) After a specified delay, this digit is switched off and the segments of the next digit are ON. The information displayed here is different from that of the previous case.
iv) Thus, for display multiplexing, consecutive digits should be switched on in a cyclic fashion, and for each digit, the segment information should be supplied.

Now, let us use this concept in a system in which an 8051 handles a dynamic display (Figure 3.24). This is an 4-digit display, of the common cathode type. The ports of 8051 are used in such a way that Port 1 supplies the digit information and Port 2 supplies the segment information. Digit information through Port 1.0 to P1.3 is to select which digit is being activated at a particular time. For segment information, the seven segment code of each digit should be sent as a byte through Port 2.

Figure 3.25 shows the complete set up. Four pins of port 1 are used for 'digit driving'. These pins are connected to the bases of the four transistors Q1 to Q4. At

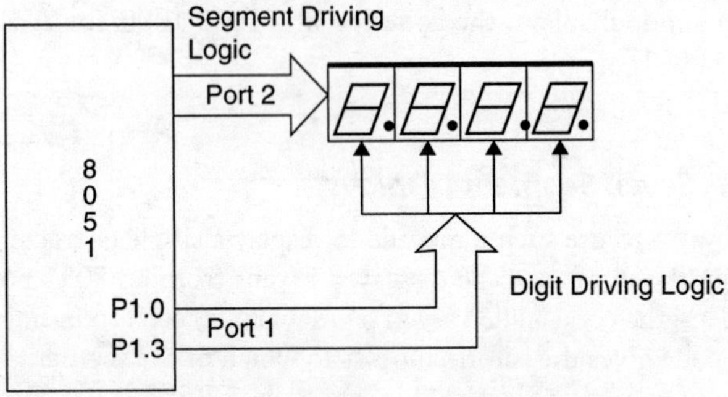

Figure 3.24 | A dynamic display for an 8051-based system

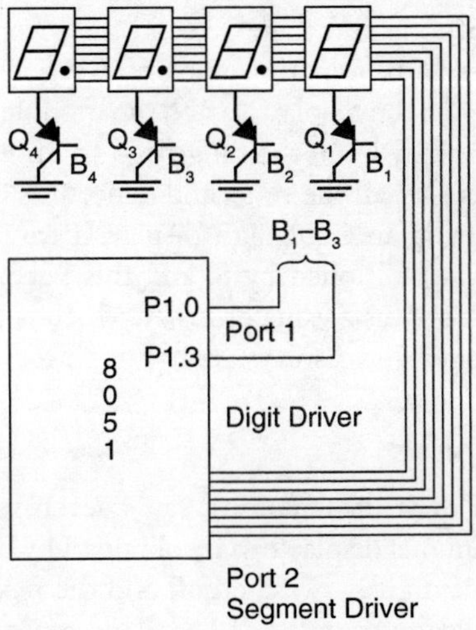

Figure 3.25 | A four digit dynamic display using the 8051.

a time, only one particular transistor is to be ON. These are PNP transistors and are turned ON if a '0' is applied to the bases. This '0' goes to the emitters of the transistor which is connected to the common cathode of the segment LEDs, of a particular digit. At a time, Port 1 gives a '0' only on one of its port lines. To understand this clearly, observe Figure 3.25. The most significant digit (or the left most digit of the display) is activated by a '0'on pin P1.0. When this pin is cleared, P1.1 to Pi1.3 should be set. At the same time, the segment information for displaying the left most digit should be placed on Port 1. If Port 2 gives the data 77 H, the first digit displays 'A'.

This technique is to be repeated for all digits continuously. The steps are:

1. Select the first digit to be displayed and send a suitable logic through P1.0 to P1.3 to activate a digit.
2. Send the segment code through Port 2.
3. Call a delay of say, 3msecs.
4. Repeat this sequence for all four digits.
5. Then start again from the first step.

With 4 digits and 3 msecs delay, we can get back to the first digit every 12 msecs.

This corresponds to a refresh rate of around 83 times per second, which is sufficient to fool the eye into believing that all the digits are ON at the same time [The persistence of human vision is $(1/16)^{th}$ of a second–(62.5 msec)].

3.3.1.5 | *Organic LED (OLED)*

This is a relatively new type of display which has gained acceptance in mobile phones, PDAs, digital media players, cameras and similar portable applications. OLED-based TVs are also making their foray into the consumer market.

The physical structure of an OLED consists of a layer of organic material (which is emissive electroluminescent) is sandwiched between two conductors (an anode and a cathode), which in turn are sandwiched between a glass top plate (seal) and a glass bottom plate (substrate). See Figure 3.26. When electric current is applied to the two conductors, a bright, electro-luminescent light is produced directly from the organic material. There are two types of OLEDs- small molecule OLED, and polymer OLED. The small molecule type is considered to have a longer lifespan. The OLED primary colour matrix is arranged in red, green and blue pixels, which are mounted directly to a printed circuit board. It expresses pure colours when an electric current stimulates the relevant pixels.

Thin organic layers serve these displays as a source of light, which offers significant advantages in relation to conventional technologies. The nature of its technology lends itself to extremely thin and lightweight designs, which makes its application domain very wide. To list out a few plus points of OLEDs:

i) Unlimited viewing angle
ii) Low power consumption
iii) Fast 'response time'
iv) Brighter and more brilliant picture

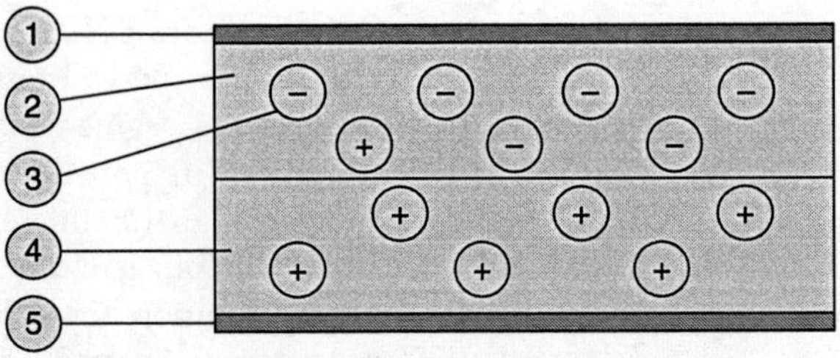

Figure 3.26 | Schematic of a bilayer OLED: 1. Cathode 2. Emissive Layer 3. Emission of radiation 4. Conductive Layer 5. Anode

When comparing it with standard display technologies, the notable points are that:

i) They require no backlighting as for LCDs because they are emissive devices.
ii) The fabrication process is easy, and devices are thinner and lighter than those fabricated by cathode ray tube (CRT) display technology.

3.3.1.6 | *Liquid Crystal Displays (LCDs)*

Liquid crystal displays called LCDs are very popular, with their qualities of low power dissipation and ease of use. The only problem normally encountered is the problem of the viewing angle. The display is not equally clear at all viewing angles. They are available as character LCDs for displaying ASCII characters, and as graphical LCDs which contain display elements as dots or pixels which can be selectively illuminated, so as to display any pattern.

Character LCD

Character LCD modules of many different specifications (mostly differing in the number of lines, number of characters per line and so on) are available. An LCD module has registers, writing into which the display can be easily programmed and controlled. Here, we will discuss a 16 × 2 character LCD which looks as shown in Figure 3.27.

Pins of the LCD The LCD that we have selected, has 16 pins as shown in Table 3.2. We see that DB0 to DB7 correspond to the data pins. The others are the pins for control signals and the power supply. VEE is a pin used to adjust the contrast of the display. It is usually connected to a potentiometer, so that contrast can be adjusted. Besides that, there

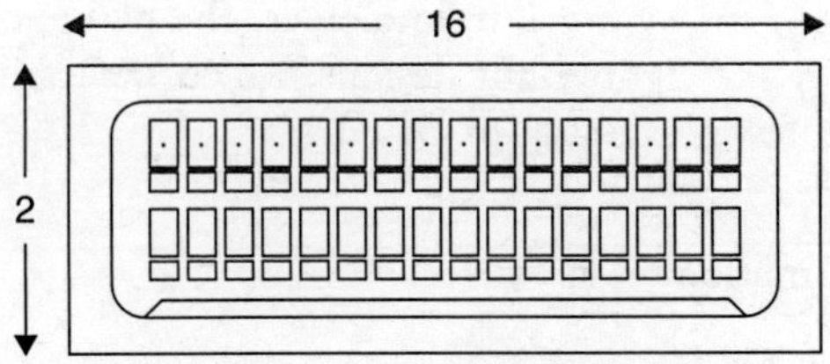

Figure 3.27 | A 16 x2 character LCD module

Table 3.2 | Pins of the 16 × 2 LCD Module

No	Symbol	Function
1	Vss	Power supply ground (0V)
2	Vcc	Power supply (5V)
3	VEE	Power supply for adjusting contrast
4	RS	Register select signal
5	R/W	Read write select signal
6	E	Enable signal
7	DB0	Data bus line
8	DB1	Data bus line
9	DB2	Data bus line
10	DB3	Data bus line
11	DB4	Data bus line
12	DB5	Data bus line
13	DB6	Data bus line
14	DB7	Data bus line
15	AV_{EE}	Positive voltage for back light
16	K	0V for back light

are the VCC and ground pins. There are two pins for backlight adjustment, if necessary. Backlighting means extra lighting behind the LCD panel (usually LEDs) so that the display is visible in the dark also.

- **RS–Register Select:** This pin selects between a command register and a data register. RS = 0 corresponds to the command register and RS = 1 to the data register. The data to be displayed is to be sent to the data register.
- **R/W–Read/Write:** This pin allows the user to write to or read from the display. When there is no necessity for reading the display, this pin is grounded. If both reading and writing is required, this pin is made programmable.
- **E–Enable:** The enable pin has to be given a high to low pulse, which is maintained high for at least 450 ns (may be different for other LCD modules).
- **DB0 to DB7:** These are the data pins of the LCD. Data to be written is to be sent through these pins, and data to be read will be received from the LCD through these pins. The data to be written for display are sent as ASCII characters. For writing into the command registers, there are predefined codes for the LCD. The codes for the specific LCD considered here, are given in Table 3.3.
- **Busy Flag:** It is seen that there is a minimum time required to latch one data on the LCD and get it displayed. Suppose we want to give a new data for display, the simplest way would be to introduce a small delay between sending the two display data (which can be given only one character at a time). However, another method for sending consecutive characters is to check what is called the 'Busy' flag of the LCD. For testing the busy flag, make RS = 0 first. The 'Busy' flag is DB7 and can be read

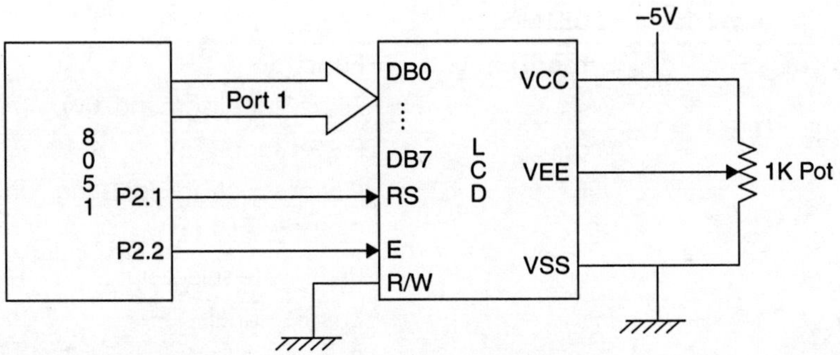

Figure 3.28 | Connecting the LCD module to the pins of 8051

when R/W = 1 and RS = 0. If DB7 is found high, it means that the LCD is busy doing its operations, and will not accept any new information. Keep checking this flag until it is low. Then, the next data can be written to it.

Note If the busy flag is to be read, the R/W pin has to be made programmable.

Now, let us do some display activities using a 16 × 2 LCD. Data and commands are sent from the ports of 8051. See Figure 3.28. Port1 is used as the data lines, and pins P2.1 and P2.2 are used for RS and E.

The connections are done as follows. Refer to Figure 3.28.

i) VSS and R/W is connected to ground.
ii) VCC is connected to 5 V supply.
iii) VEE is connected through a 10 K pot to the supply for contrast adjustment.
iv) RS is connected to P2.0 and E is connected to P2.1.
v) Pin 7-14 (DB0 to DB7) of the LCD module are connected to Port 1 of 8051.
vi) Pins 15 and 16 of the LCD are used for backlight adjustment (not shown in Figure 3.28).

Backlight There is a lamp here instead of reflected light. If backlighting is provided by LEDs as in the case of many 16 × 2 LCDs, connect pin 16 to ground, and pin 15 to Vcc through a 100 Ω resistor.

Getting a Character Displayed on the LCD To display characters on the LCD, the ASCII value of the character should be sent to the data register. But before sending the data, appropriate control signals should be activated by giving the required logic levels on the port pins. Also, first the LCD is initialized, then cleared, and then the cursor is positioned. This is done by sending command words to the LCD command register. (Refer Table 3.3).

Algorithm

i) Send command word to Port 1. The command word are 38 H (initializing LCD), 0EH (making the LCD and cursor ON), 01 (clearing the screen), 06 (shifting the cursor right) and 81 H (moving the cursor to line 1, position 1).

Table 3.3 | Command Codes of the LCD

Code (Hex)	Command
01	Clear display screen
02	Return home
04	Shift cursor left (decrement cursor)
05	Shift display right
06	Shift cursor right (increment cursor)
07	Shift display left
08	Display off, cursor off
0A	Display on, cursor on
0C	Display on, cursor off
0E	Display on, cursor blinking
0F	Display off, cursor blinking
10	Shift cursor position to left
14	Shift cursor position to right
18	Shift the entire display to the left
1C	Shift the entire display to the right
80*	Force cursor to the beginning of the fi rst line
C0*	Force cursor to the beginning of the second line
38	2 lines and 5 × 7 matrix

* For a 16 × 2 line display, the addresses of the cursor positions are 80 to 8F for the fi rst line, and C0 to CF for the second line

ii) Make RS = 0 (by clearing P2. 1) for selecting the command register.
iii) Make R/W = 0 to write to LCD (if this line is grounded as in Figure 3.28, this step can be skipped).
iv) Send a H to L pulse at the E pin to complete the writing. For this, make P2.2 high for a short while and then clear it.
v) With this, the writing of commands is over. Now the required data must be written.
vi) Make RS = 1 for selecting the data register.
vii) Repeat steps 3 and 4.

In this setup (Figure 3.28), one whole 8-bit port was used up for LCD data. To save on pins, it is possible to use LCDs with just 4 data pins of a port. The data and command words are sent as in the previous case, but the method here is to send the 8 bits as two nibbles—thus only four lines of an MCU port need to be used. See Figure 3.29, which shows that only 7 port pins are needed in total, to connect an LCD module to an MCU.

Graphical LCD (GLCD)

Character LCDs have their limitations in that they can display characters only. Graphical LCDs are currently used to display customized characters and images. Graphical LCDs

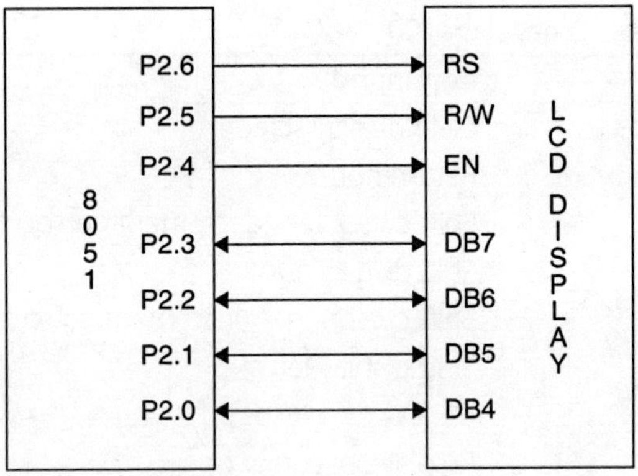

Figure 3.29 | A 4-bit LCD interface

find use in many applications; they are used in video games, mobile phones, etc. as display units. The customization is possible because the LCD has dots or pixels which may be selectively lighted up to generate the display we need. Thus, their size is specified as MxN dots or pixels.

Such LCD displays come in a variety of sizes, ranging from 32 × 80 to 240 × 320. dots/pixels. Larger displays offer more display area, cost more and take longer to refresh the entire screen with new data.

Graphical LCD modules come with inbuilt controllers which will allow us to interface the display with an MCU, for selectively lighting up the required pixels. Figure 3.30 shows the picture of a 128 × 64 dots graphical LCD manufactured by 'Vishay', with built-in controllers which are two ICs of KS0108 or equivalent. Table 3.4 gives the pin functions of this LCD display module.

Two controllers are needed because the display is split logically as half-left half and right half. It then needs two controllers with IC1 (Chipselect1) controlling the left half of the display and IC2 (Chipselect2) controlling the right half. Each controller must be addressed independently. Each half consists of 8 horizontal pages each of which is 8 bits (1 byte) high. The page addresses, 0-7, specify one of the 8 pages. That is illustrated in Figure 3.31.

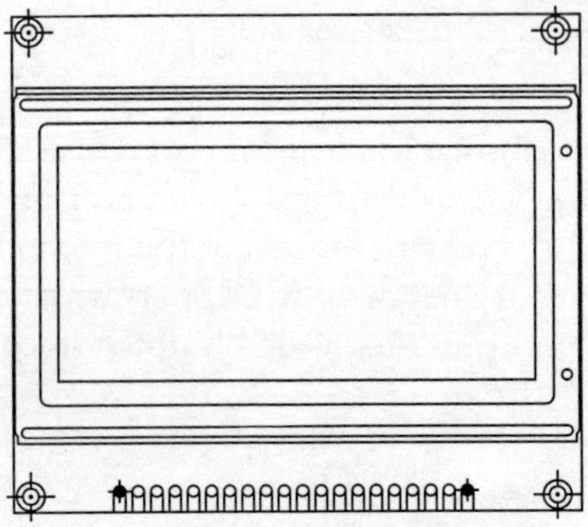

Figure 3.30 | A 128 × 64 dots (pixels) graphical LCD

Table 3.4 | Pin functions of the LCD module of Figure 3.30

Pin Number	Symbol	Function
1	Vss	GND
2	Vdd	Power Supply (+5V)
3	Vo	Contrast Adjustment
4	D/L	Data/Instruction
5	R/W	Data Read/Write
6	E	H L Enable/Signal
7	DB0	Data Bus Line
8	DB1	Data Bus Line
9	DB2	Data Bus Line
10	DB3	Data Bus Line
11	DB4	Data Bus Line
12	DB5	Data Bus Line
13	DB6	Data Bus Line
14	DB7	Data Bus Line
15	CS1	Chip Selector for IC1
16	CS2	Chip Selector for IC2
17	RST	Reset
18	Vee	Negative Voltage Output
19	A	Power Supply for LED (4.2V)
20	K	Power Supply for LED (0V)

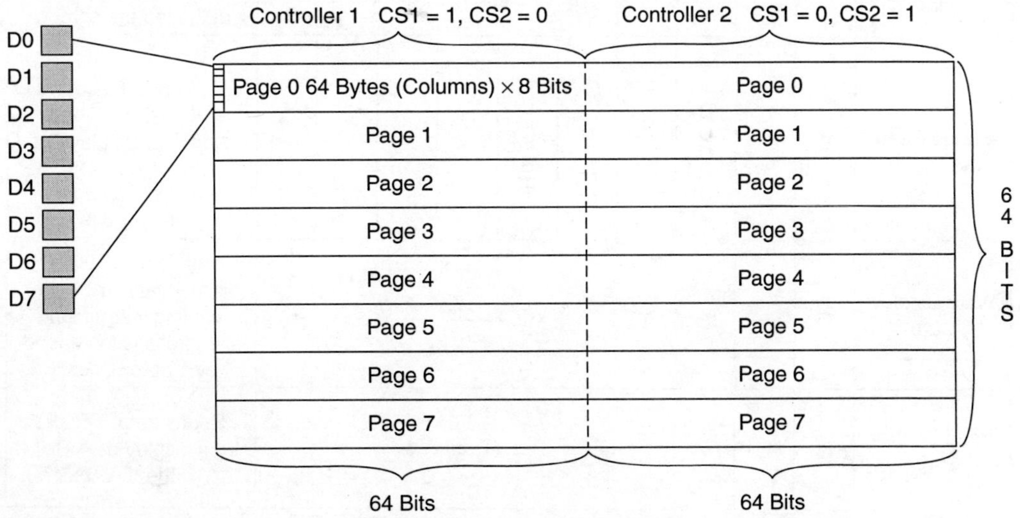

Figure 3.31 | Division into two halves, and the vertical pages of the GLCD

The Controller IC The KS0108B is a LCD driver with 64 channel output for dot matrix liquid crystal graphic display system. This device consists of the display RAM, 64-bit data latch, 64-bit drivers and decoder logic. It has the internal display RAM for storing the display data transferred from an 8-bit MCU and generates the dot matrix LCD driving signals corresponding to stored data.

Commands of the Controller The following are the KS0108 commands. See Figure 3.32.

- **Y address (0 to 63):** The Y address counter designates address of the internal RAM. An address is set by instructions and is increased by 1 automatically by read or write operations of display data. Y address 0 is the leftmost byte, and Y address 63 is the rightmost byte of a page.
- **X address (0 to 7):** This is the page address and has no count function.
- **Display line (0 to 63):** The display start line register specifies the line in RAM which corresponds to the top line of LCD panel, when displaying contents in display data RAM on the LCD panel. It is used for scrolling of the screen.

Instruction	RS	R/W	DB7	DB6	DB5	DB4	DB3	DB2	DB1	DB0	Function
Display On/Off	L	L	L	L	H	H	H	H	H	H	Controls the display on or off internal status and display RAM data is not affected
Set Address	L	L	L	H	Y Address(0-63)						Sets the Y address in the Y addresss counter
Set Page (X Address)	L	L	H	L	H	H	H	Page (0–7)			Sets the X address at the X address register
Display Start Line	L	L	H	H	Display Start Line (0–63)						Indicates the display data RAM displayed at the lop the screen
Status Read	L	H	BUSY	L	ON/OFF	RESET	L	L	L	L	Read status Busy L: Ready H: In Operation On/Off L: Display On H: Display Off Reset L: Normal H: Reset
Write Display Data	H	L	Write Data								Writes data (DB0:7) into dispaly data RAM after writing instruction Y address is increased by 1 automatically
Read Display Data	H	H	Read Data								Reads data (DB0:7) from display data RAM To the data bus

Figure 3.32 | Commands of the controller

With this information, and an in-depth reading of the data sheets of the controller, it should now be possible for you to interface graphical LCD to an MCU like 8051, PIC, etc.

The algorithm for use is similar to that of the character LCD, i.e., send the initialization signals as commands, and then send the data.

How to light up pixels selectively?

Figure 3.33a shows the left half of the display (for one column only). There are 8 pixels in one column and there are eight such columns, one for each page. The total number of pixels in a column is numbered as P0 to P63.

Figure 3.33 b shows the eight pixels (named P0 to P7) corresponding to Page 0 of Figure 3.33a Assume we want to light up P0, P1 and P7 of this column. The data for this is to be sent as a byte. It is 1100 0001, i.e., 0xC1. Now for the next page (for pixels P8 to P15) if all the pixels except P8 and P15 are to be lighted up, the data is 0111 1110, i.e., 0x7E. This is continued for all the eight pages (one column of the display).

Thus, we write data (in bytes) for all the pixels of one column, and then go on to the next column. This is done first for the left part of the display, and then for the right half. The display will then appear to start from the left, and move to the right. We see that for any pattern, we have to generate a bit map and load it into the display RAM of the LCD controller.

Connecting a Graphical LCD to an 8051 MCU

Figure 3.34 shows the connections between a graphical LCD and 8051. Note that the connections are similar to Figure 3.28 but here two extra connections are for CS1 and CS2.

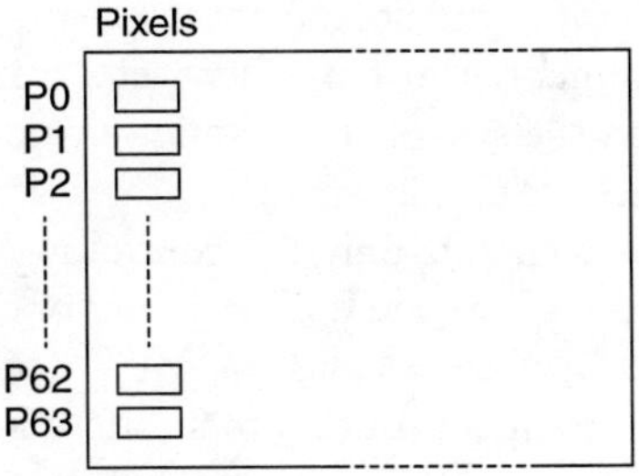

Figure 3.33a | Pixels in one column of the GLCD

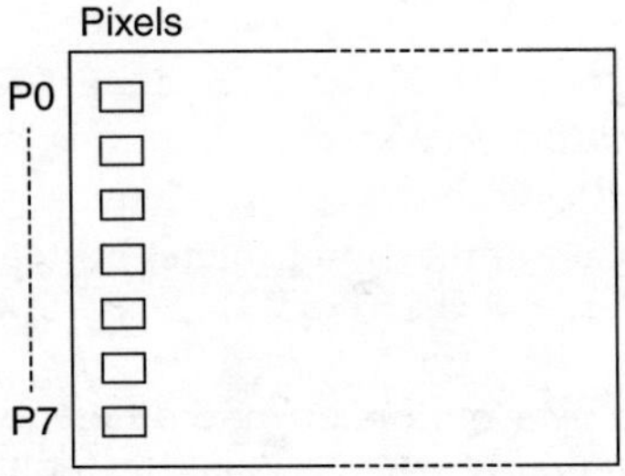

Figure 3.33b | Pixels of Page 0

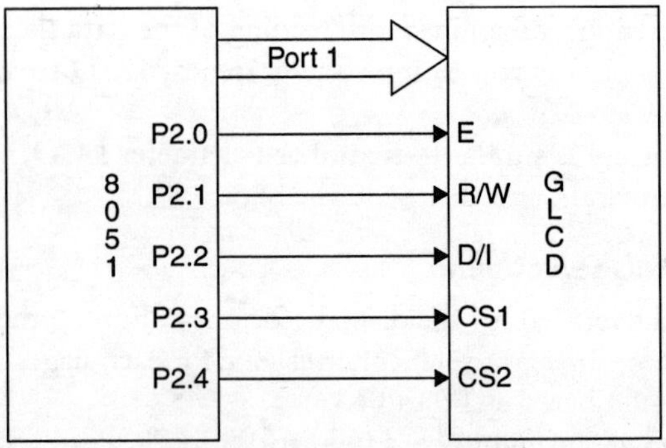

Figure 3.34 | Connections of a GLCD to 8051

D/I is the pin which selects between data and commands (similar to pin RS in Figure 3.28). Pins 19 and 20 of the LCD module are for backlighting, and are not shown in Figure 3.34.

Note Appendix H contains the program for interfacing this graphic LCD to PSoC3. The program is also given.

3.3.2 | Motors

Motors are used for rotational motion, which can be converted to linear motion when the application calls for it. In embedded systems, the rating (voltage, current, torque, etc.) of the motor to be used, depends on the application. For example, we might use a motor in a home security system to get a door opened or closed. This might require a heavy duty motor depending on the weight of the door. Another very common application is hobby robotics where vehicle movement, arm movement, etc. are required. The rating of the motor to be used depends on the size of the robotic vehicle and its activity. The motors used by hobbyists for robotics are usually small and rated at 6 to 12 V supply.

MCUs are used in motor circuits only for 'controlling' the motor. Motors may be made to rotate clockwise/anti-clockwise at different rpms or it may be that a movement by a small angle alone is needed. In all these cases, the MCU can be programmed to generate the driving logic for motor movement. But motors cannot be driven directly by a MCU because the current output from an MCU is relatively small. So there should be arrangements to get higher driving currents, and additional circuitry is usually necessary. We will examine all such aspects for two types of motors—stepper motors and DC motors.

3.3.2.1 | *Stepper Motors*

Introduction to Stepper Motors A stepper motor is an electromechanical device which converts electrical pulses into discrete mechanical movements. When electrical pulses are applied to it, the shaft of the motor rotates in steps and this type of movement gives the motor its name.

Principle of Operation Stepper motors operate differently from normal DC motors. A DC motor rotates continuously when voltage is applied to its terminals. Stepper motors, have multiple toothed electromagnets arranged around a central gear-shaped piece of iron (see Figure 3.35). The electromagnets are energized by an external control circuit which sends pulses to the motor.

To turn the motor shaft, one of the electromagnets is given power first, which makes the gear's teeth magnetically attracted to the electromagnet's teeth. When one tooth of the gear is thus aligned to the energized electromagnet (Electromagnet 'B' and tooth '6' are aligned in Figure 3.35), others are slightly offset from the corresponding electromagnets. When the next electromagnet is turned on and the first is turned off, the gear rotates slightly to align with the next one, and from there the process is repeated. Each of those slight rotations is called a step, with an integral number of steps making a full rotation. In this way, the motor can be turned by a precise angle.

The rotation of the motor is related to the sequence of the input pulses:

i) The order in which a particular sequence is applied, decides the direction of rotation (clockwise or anti-clockwise).
ii) The speed of stepping depends on the frequency of the pulses applied, i.e., higher the frequency, faster the stepping motion.

We can use stepper motors for movement which needs to be finely controlled. The fine control is obtained because these motors move in steps, and the steps can be quite small in size. For example, one step can be 2 degrees and, for one complete (360 degree) rotation, 180 steps are obviously needed. For one such step, the motor needs to get a 'pulse' from a control circuit. In order to obtain a 90 degree rotation for such a motor, we must write a program to supply only 45 pulses to it.

This type of stepping motion can be used to advantage when it is needed to control aspects such as rotation angle, speed, position and synchronism. As such, they are used in applications such as printers, plotters, high end office equipment, hard disk drives, medical equipment, fax machines, and automotive and industrial applications where precise and controlled rotation is required. Robotics is another area where it is used for precise and controlled motion.

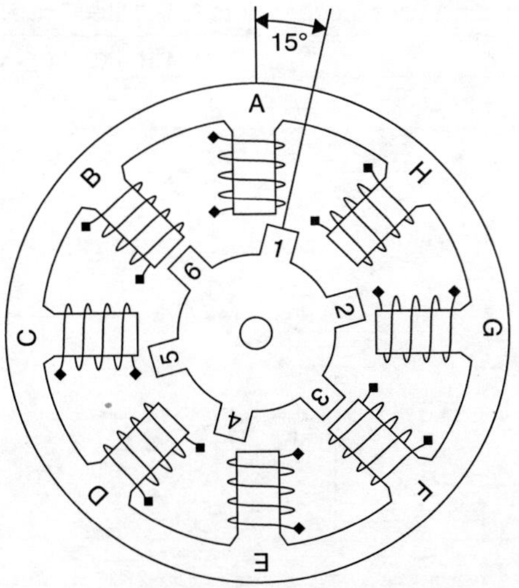

Figure 3.35 | Figure showing the operating principle of a stepper motor

Driving a Stepper Motor

Full Step Drive (two phases on) This is the usual method for full step driving of the motor. Both phases are always ON. The motor will thus have the full rated torque. This is achieved by the sequence of ones and zeros as shown in Table 3.5 which is to be repeatedly applied. (Note the presence of two '1's in each row of the table corresponding to 'two phases' being ON at any time.) Reversing the order in which the sequence is applied gives anti-clockwise rotation.

In short, for clock wise rotation, the sequence to be applied repeatedly is 09, 0CH, 06, 03. For anti-clock wise rotation, it is 03, 06, 0CH, 09. If you read about stepper motors from any other source, there is a possibility that you might see another 'sequence' being suggested. Neither that nor this is wrong. The 'sequence numbers' just depend on the way we have named the phase windings. There are four wires available at the output of any stepper motor winding and they are named A, $\overline{A}$, B and $\overline{B}$ corresponding to Figure 3.36.

Wave Drive In this drive method, only a single phase is activated at a time. It has the same number of steps as the full step drive, but the motor will have significantly less than rated torque. This sequence is 8, 4, 2, 1 for clockwise and 1, 2, 4, 8 for anti-clockwise rotation. Table 3.6 is the driving sequence for this.

Half Stepping When half stepping, the drive alternates between two phases ON and a single phase ON. This increases the angular resolution, but the motor also has less torque at the half step position (where only a single phase is on). The advantage of half stepping is that the drive electronics need not change to support it. The step-angle is half that of the previous two cases—thus the stepping resolution is increased. For anti-clockwise rotation, the order of the above sequence should be reversed. Table 3.7 is the driving sequence for this.

Table 3.5 | Driving Sequence for a Stepper Motor—Full Step Drive

	Clockwise			
Step No.	**A**	**B**	**$\overline{A}$**	**$\overline{B}$**
1	1	0	0	1
2	1	1	0	0
3	0	1	1	0
4	0	0	1	1

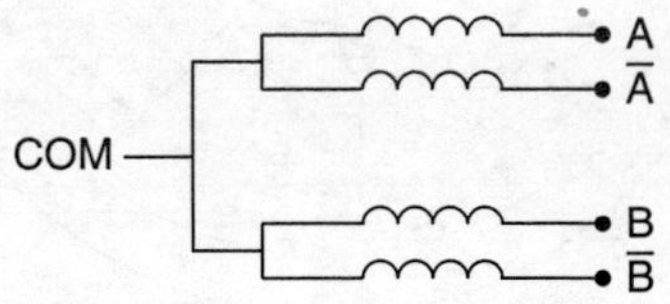

Figure 3.36 | Stepper motor windings

Table 3.6 | Driving Sequence for a Stepper Motor—Wave Drive

	Clockwise			
Step No.	**A**	**B**	$\bar{A}$	$\bar{B}$
1	1	0	0	0
2	0	1	0	0
3	0	0	1	0
4	0	0	0	1

Table 3.7 | Driving Sequence for a Stepper Motor—Half Stepping

	Clockwise			
Step No.	**A**	**B**	$\bar{A}$	$\bar{B}$
1	1	0	0	1
2	1	0	0	0
3	1	1	0	0
4	0	1	0	0
5	0	1	1	0
6	0	0	1	0
7	0	0	1	1
8	0	0	0	1

Using an 8051 to Interface a Stepper Motor

We can run a motor using a sequence generated by an MCU, say 8051. The motor, however, cannot be driven directly from its port pins, because the motor requires a current much more than can be supplied by the MCU. (The exact current requirement depends on the specifications of the particular motor being used.) As such, current drivers are needed between the 8051 port lines and the leads of the motor. Transistors with high current capability (e.g. Darlington pair or power transistors) can be used. Besides this, there are special motor driving ICs available. One such IC is the ULN 2003 driving IC whose pin diagram is shown in Figure 3.37. This IC contains an array of seven Darlington pair transistors. Figure 3.38 shows the 8051 MCU generating a sequence for energizing a stepper motor, with the IC ULN 2003 being used to raise the current level. Four pins of Port1 have been used for sending the driving sequence to the motor.

Other Issues Regarding Stepper Motors

An important issue to take care of when using stepper motors is that there is a chance of back emf being produced during the de-energization of the coils. This can damage the circuits producing the sequence and hence diodes are connected which block these spikes. Such diodes are called by various names as flywheel, fly back, free wheeling or snubber diodes (Section 3.3.4.2) When discrete Darlington pair transistors are used for

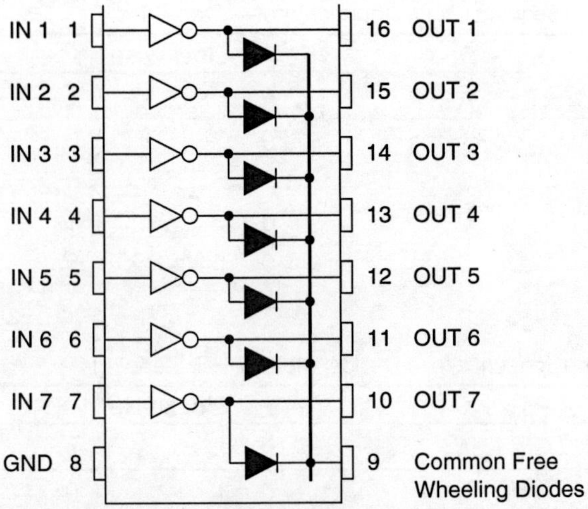

Figure 3.37 | Functional pin diagram of the driver, IC ULN2003

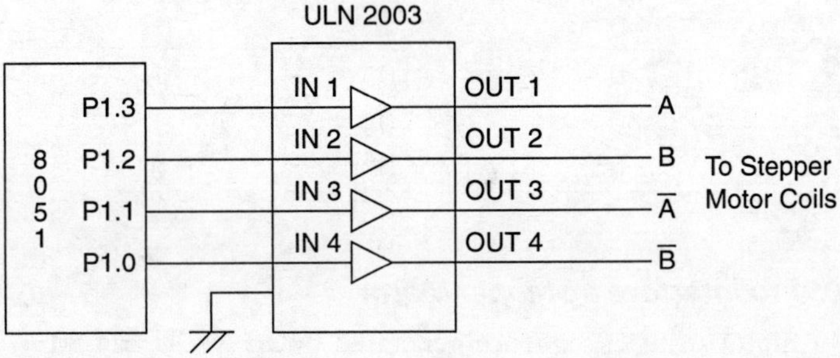

Figure 3.38 | Connections between 8051 and the stepper motor through a current driver

producing the high current required to drive the motors, diodes are connected to block this back emf. Such a diode is also in-built within the motor driving IC ULN 2003. Note the diode connected at pin 9, which is the freewheeling diode, corresponding to all the seven Darlington transistors inside the chip.

3.3.2.2 | *DC Motors*

This is a type of motor which operates on direct current and is very commonly used in embedded systems, when continuous movement is needed. The movement may be made 'controlled', in the sense that the speed and direction can be changed as per the requirements of the application. Robotics is an area where DC motors are widely used, but this is not the only application. Any type of movement is possible to be achieved with dc motors.

The DC motor has two basic parts: the rotating part that is called the armature and the stationary part called the stator that includes coils of wire called the field coils.

Figure 3.39 | Photograph of a small DC motor

The armature is made of coils of wire wrapped around the core, and the core has an extended shaft that rotates on bearings. The ends of each coil of wire on the armature are terminated at one end of the armature. The termination points are called the commutator, and this is where the brushes make electrical contact to bring electrical current from the stationary part to the rotating part of the machine. Figure 3.39 is a photograph of a light weight DC motor.

Characteristics of DC Motors

DC motors are non-polarized; this means that its power supply voltage can be reversed. The characteristics of a DC motor that we use in applications are as follows:

Speed Varies with Applied Voltage This feature is important for running a motor at different speeds. This can be done by increasing or decreasing the power supply voltage. But when we use electronic control, PWM (pulse width modulation) is the method for varying motor speed.

The method is to apply a pulse train to the power terminals of the motor. The average voltage obtained at the terminals is then proportional to the duty cycle of the pulse train, which is proportional to the speed of rotation (rpm) of the motor. Thus, as the duty cycle is increased, the motor rpm increases and vice versa. When the power supply is constant, it runs at 100% of its power rating (at no load). As the duty cycle reduces, the speed and the power reduce. Figure 3.40 shows pulse trains of various duty cycles.

When it is necessary to do speed control of DC motors for embedded applications, an MCU can be made to generate the PWM waveform based on some criterion, or depending on sensor output values. Many MCUs have a PWM unit as an integrated peripheral—the user just needs to use a few registers to specify the pulse repetition time (T) and the duty cycle. The 8051 does not have PWM unit—but such a waveform can be generated easily by a simple program.

Torque Varies with Current The torque of a motor is the rotary force produced on its output shaft. Torque increases with increased current, which means that it increases with increase in power supply voltage.

Reversal of Polarity of the Supply Voltage Causes Reversal of Direction of Rotation This aspect is very important in many applications, especially in robotics, when the motor

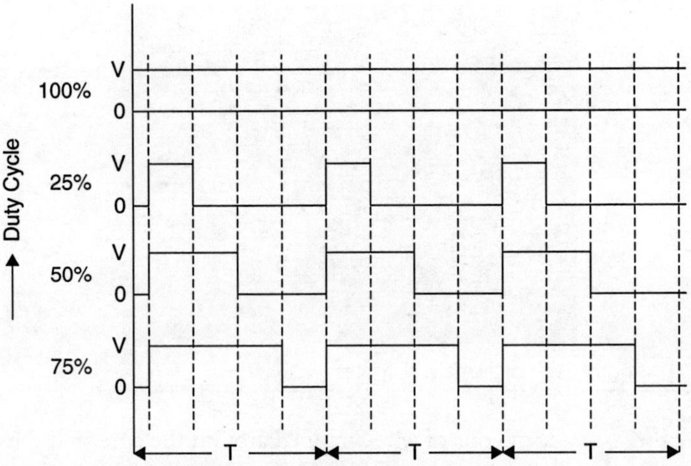

Figure 3.40 | PWM waveforms at various duty cycles

needs to reverse its direction of rotation. For example, a robotic vehicle will have to change from forward motion to reverse motion when an obstacle comes in its path. To do this dynamically, some sort of controlling switch is necessary, and this is available in the form of the H bridge.

3.3.2.3 | *H Bridge*

The H bridge is so named because it has four switching elements at the limbs of the H and the motor forms the cross bar. Figure 3.41 shows the 'idea' of the H bridge. There are two switches at the top (left and right) and two more switches at the bottom. They are named S1, S2, S3 and S4.

When the motor is not expected to rotate, all the switches are to be kept open. When switches S1 and S4 alone are closed, the motor rotates in the clockwise direction, with switches S2 and S3 closed, the rotation is anti-clockwise. In the positions when the top two switches and/or the bottom two switches are closed, the motor gets short circuited and such a situation should not be allowed.

The valid states of the switch are shown in Table 3.8, assuming that activation by a '1' corresponds to a switch closure.

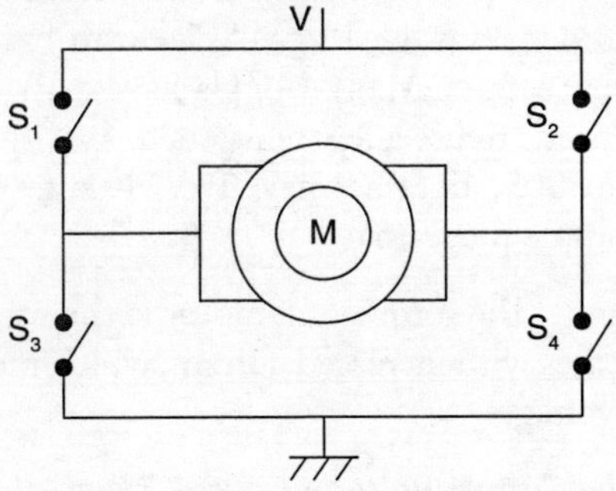

Figure 3.41 | The principle of operation of an H bridge

Table 3.8 | Switch status for direction of motor rotation

S1	S2	S3	S4	Motor Rotation
1	0	0	1	Clockwise
0	1	1	0	Anti-clockwise

What is the mechanism to realize an H bridge?

It can be done using any device that has switching properties like relays, transistors, MOSFET, etc. But if you are trying to run a DC motor from an MCU output, the best bet would be a motor driving IC with H bridge. The IC L293D is a dual H bridge IC which also provides sufficient current to drive a small motor.

The L293D IC whose pin configuration (shown in Figure 3.42) is a dual H Bridge motor driver. With one such IC, two DC motors can be driven which can be controlled in both clockwise and counter clockwise directions.

For applications that don't need reversal of direction, the four output pins can be used for driving four separate motors. This IC is rated for an output current of 600 mA and peak output current of 1.2A per channel. Moreover for protection of the circuit against back EMF, snubber/flywheel diodes (Section 3.3.4.2) are included within the IC. A simple schematic for interfacing a DC motor using L293D is shown in Figure 3.43. Refer Table 3.9 for the status of A and B.

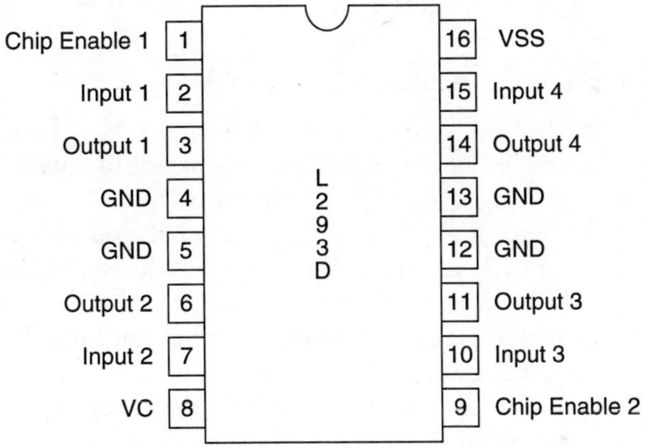

Figure 3.42 | Pins of the L293D motor driver

Table 3.9 | Action Performed for the Four Combinations of A and B

A	B	Action Performed
0	0	Motor is in the stop/brake condition
0	1	Motor rotates anti-clockwise
1	0	Motor rotates clockwise
1	1	Motor is in the stop/brake condition

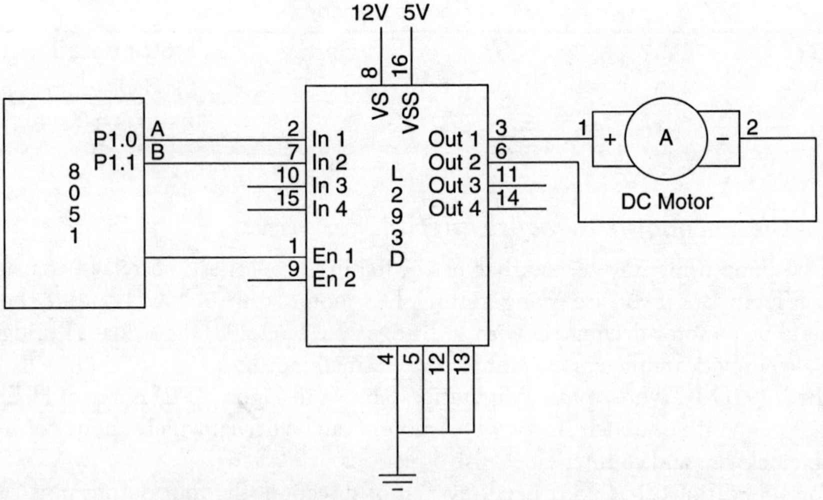

Figure 3.43 | Connections between an 8051, an H bridge and a DC motor

Three pins of the chip are needed as inputs from the MCU. The enable pin has to be set, and the pins A and B are to be controlled by the port lines P1.0 and P1.1, which generates the necessary logic to get the motor to rotate as required.

Embedded applications may use either stepper or DC motors. But when it comes to speed, weight, size and cost, DC motors are always preferred over stepper motors.

3.3.3 | Optocouplers/Opto Isolators

An optocoupler is another device helpful in damping the back EMF produced in a motor circuit. An optocoupler or optical isolator is a device that uses an optical transmission path to transfer a signal between elements of a circuit, while keeping them electrically isolated. An optocoupler is essentially a combination of two distinct devices: an optical transmitter, typically a gallium arsenide LED (light-emitting diode) and an optical receiver such as a phototransistor or light-triggered diac. The two are separated by a transparent [insulator] barrier which blocks any electrical current flow between the two, but does allow the passage of light.

The basic idea is shown in Figure 3.44. Usually the electrical connections to the LED section are brought out to the pins on one side of the package and those for the

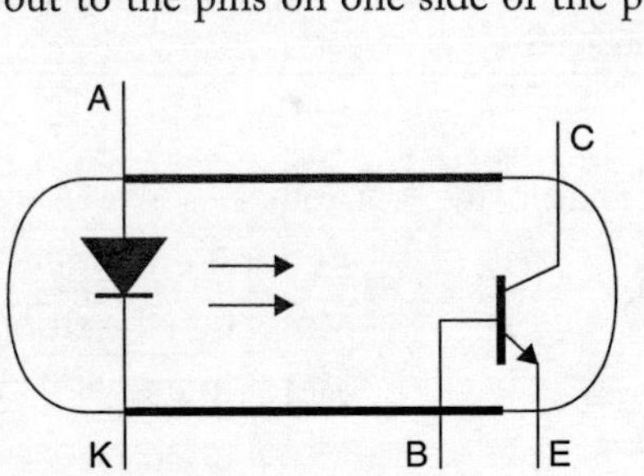

Figure 3.44 | Operating principle of an optocoupler

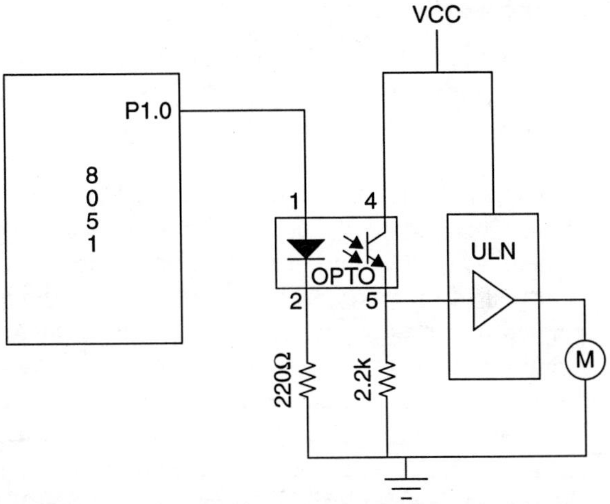

Figure 3.45 | A DC motor connected to 8051 through a current driver and an optocoupler

phototransistor or diac to the other side, to physically separate them as much as possible. Figure 3.45 shows the K817. optocoupler used in a stepper DC motor interfacing circuit, along with a driving IC ULN 2003.

3.3.4 | Relays

Switches which can be turned ON and OFF without manual control constitute a 'relay'. Relays can be used to connect and disconnect between points in a circuit, by using electrical control logic. Relays allow one circuit to switch a second circuit which can be completely separate from the first. For example, a low voltage circuit can use a relay to switch a high voltage (say, 230V AC mains) circuit. There is no electrical connection inside the relay between the two circuits, the link is magnetic and mechanical. Such relays are 'electromechanical'. Figure 3.46 is a photograph of such a relay. Newer relays are of the semiconductor type.

Figure 3.46 | Photograph of a relay

3.3.4.1 | *Electromechanical Relays*

This is the earliest type of relay, and is still is use today. We will discuss the types with specifications that enable it to be used in embedded systems, where voltages and currents are low. By using these low voltages and currents, relays can make and break connections in higher voltage circuits.

Electromechanical relays convert a magnetic flux created by an electrical signal into a mechanical force. This mechanical force causes switches to 'close' or 'open'

See Figure 3.47. There is a coil wound around a permeable iron core. One end of the iron core is fixed (and called the yoke), while the other end is end is free and spring loaded (or gravity operated in certain cases), and is called the armature. The armature is hinged to the yoke and mechanically linked to one or more sets of moving contacts. When the coil is de-energized there is an air gap in the magnetic circuit. In this condition, one of the two sets of contacts in the relay is closed, and the other set is open.

In Figure 3.47, two sets of electrical contacts are shown. The contacts which are open, when the coil is de-energized are called 'Normally open (NO)' contacts–similar to this, there are 'Normally closed (NC)' contacts as well. This is shown in Figure 3.48.

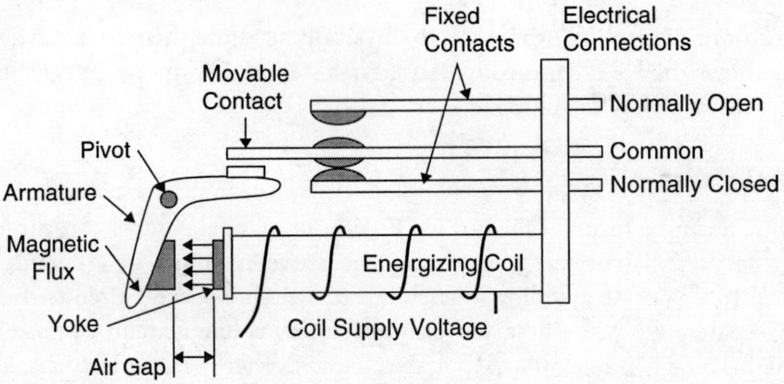

Figure 3.47 | The principle of operation of a relay

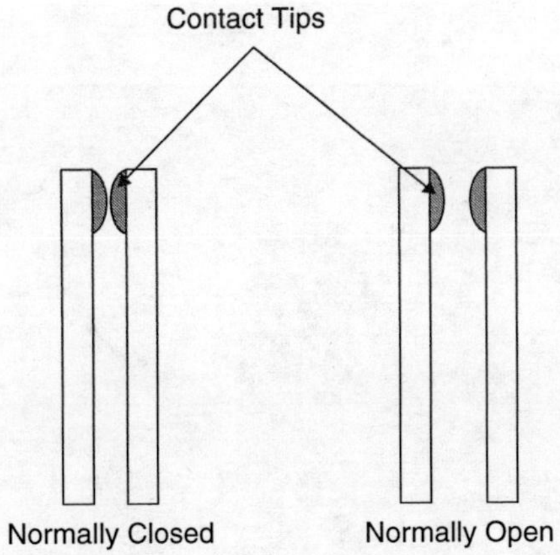

Figure 3.48 | NC and NO contacts

In a relay, there can be many NC and many NO contacts. When a contact closes, the contact is like a short circuit (zero resistance) and when open, it is an open circuit (infinite resistance). This is the ideal condition, but which may not hold true in practice.

3.3.4.2 | *Contact Types*

The energization and de-energization of a relay can open or close one or more switch contacts. Each 'contact' may be referred to as a 'pole'. Many of these contacts or poles can be connected or **'thrown'** together and this gives rise to the description of the contact types as being SPST (single pole single throw), DPST (double pole single throw) and DPDT (double pole double throw). See Figure 3.49.

For many applications, we connect a relay to the output side of a BJT or FET circuit, as in Figure 3.50. Here a diode is seen to be connected across the relay. This is the 'flywheel diode' which saves the transistor or FET from getting damaged, when there is a back emf from the coil. This is produced when the current in the coil is turned off. The magnetic flux collapses within the coil and results in a back emf which may be very high in comparison with the switching voltages used for the active device in the circuit, The diode is connected with such a polarity that the back emf makes it conduct and dissipates the story energy in it, thus preventing damage to the BJT/FET. The diode now is called the flywheel/freewheeling/snubber diode. Motors are another type of inductive load which require such a flywheel diode.

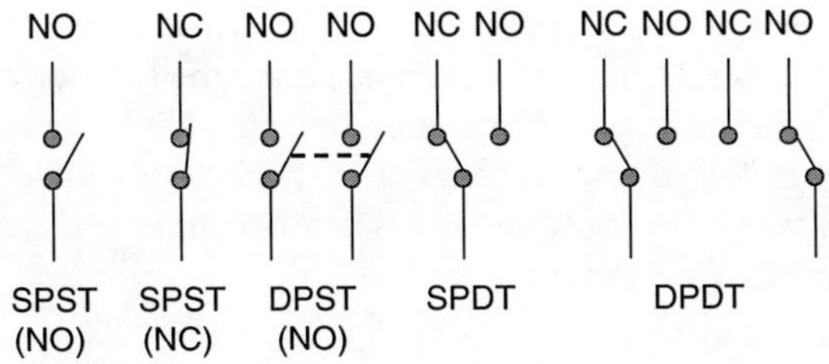

Figure 3.49 | Contact types

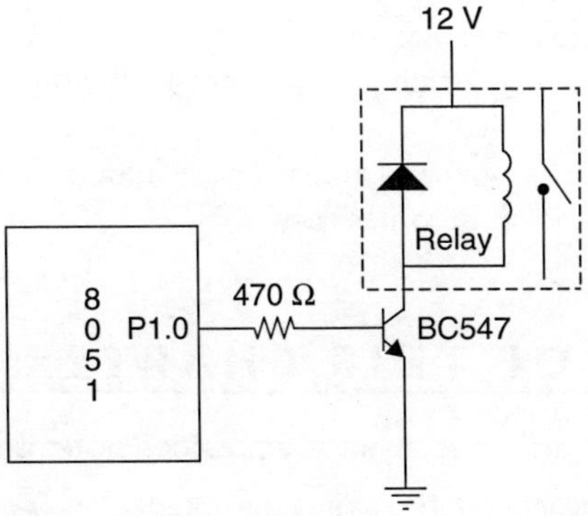

Figure 3.50 | A simple relay circuit

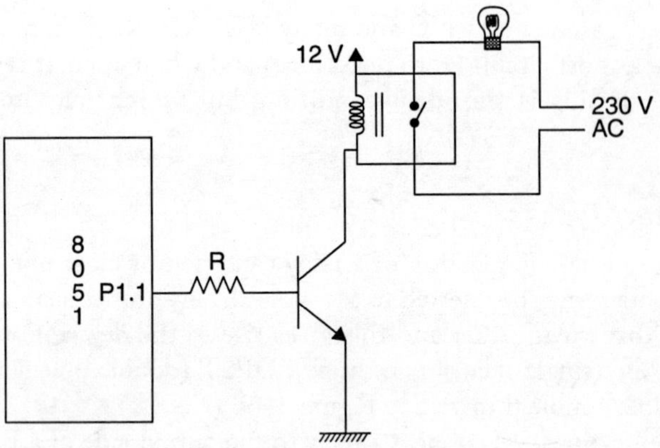

Figure 3.51 | A relay circuit switching a high voltage circuit

Relays in embedded systems are connected to output pins of microcontrollers. In many cases, it is used to control high power circuits, that is, high voltage/current, by using the lower voltage levels in the MCU. See Figure 3.51 which shows a relay used to control the switching of a bulb rated for 230V. In this case, the contacts of the relay should be able to withstand the high current passing through it.

3.3.4.3 | *Solid State Relays*

Electromechanical relays have problems such as large physical size and mechanical parts which tend to wear out with time. Solid state relays are the solution to these problems.

They have the same principle of operation, but they differ by having semiconductor switching elements like thyristors, triacs, diodes and transistors. Most of them have optoisolators incorporated internally, so as to isolate the input and output. Thus, they are smaller, noiseless, bounce free and more reliable.

Conclusion

With this, we come to the end of this chapter. This chapter has covered many commonly used sensors and actuators. The explanation for each of them is aimed at a level of knowledge with which a student can attain a confidence level sufficient to let him endeavour to do practical projects.

Once a few particular sensors and actuators are understood well, choosing the right one for a particular application becomes easy.

KEY POINTS OF THIS CHAPTER

- Sensors and actuators are necessary in all embedded systems.
- Sensors convert physical quantities to analog voltages.
- Some popular temperature sensors are thermistors and thermo couples.

- Commonly used light sensors are LDRs and photo junction devices.
- Sharp (the Company) has developed a good set of proximity and range sensors.
- Optical encoders are fixed to the wheels of moving vehicles to measure velocity.
- Humidity sensors are used in homes, factories and automobiles.
- A to D converters have data and control interfaces
- The data interface of ADCs may be parallel or serial.
- Displays are a necessity in many embedded systems.
- LEDs may be used singly or as seven segment ones.
- Seven segment LEDs may operate in the static or dynamic modes.
- OLEDs are a new kind of display devices
- LCDs are very popular and are available as Character LCD or Graphical LCD modules.
- Motors which are used in embedded systems are stepper motors or DC motors.
- Relays are either electromagnetic or solid state types.

QUESTIONS

1. What is the role of sensors in an embedded system? Name the sensors used in two popular embedded systems.
2. How does an LDR work?
3. Why are infra red LEDs preferred to ordinary LEDs in sensing circuits?
4. How can an ordinary transistor be converted to a photo transistor?
5. How does a proximity sensor work?
6. Explain the principle by which range is calculated by the Sharp range sensor?
7. What is the operating mechanism of an optical encoder? Where is such an encoder used?
8. List two applications of humidity sensors.
9. Distinguish between the terms 'control interface' and 'data interface' for an ADC.
10. Why are serial ADCs becoming more popular than the parallel ones?
11. How can a static seven segment LED system be made 'dynamic'?
12. In what ways is a Graphical LCD superior to a Character LCD?
13. What is the role of drivers in the Graphical LCD module?
14. What role does an optocoupler have in a motor driving circuit?
15. Why are current drivers needed in motor circuits driven by MCUs?
16. What is the need for an H bridge in a DC motor circuit?
17. How does an H bridge work?
18. What do you understand by the terms NO and NC contacts of a relay?
19. Discuss two simple applications of relays.
20. What are the merits of a semiconductor relay over an electromagnetic relay?

EXERCISES

1. Refer to the data sheet of the TSOP (SM0038) light sensor, and find out how it is used. Draw typical circuits in which it is used.
2. Make a review of the use of Sharp range sensors and their use in hobby robotics.
3. List the names of five serial ADCs and discuss the data interface of each of them.
4. Are OLEDs used in consumer electronic products? Find out the details.
5. Design a robotic platform with wheels driven by
   i) stepper motors and
   ii) DC motors.

   Compare the merits and de-merits and the differences in the use of these two kinds of motors, for this application.

4 EXAMPLES OF EMBEDDED SYSTEMS

In this chapter, you will learn

- The working of a few embedded products
- The working principle and components of a mobile phone
- The role of embedded systems in automobiles
- How an RFID system works
- Bio-medical applications of embedded systems
- What a wireless sensor network is
- The principle and working of the brain machine interface

Introduction

Embedded systems form an integral part of our modern day life. As mentioned in Chapter 1, the applications are very vast, ranging from small toys to huge machines. This chapter focuses on a few important applications of embedded systems.

4.1 | Mobile Phone

It is an undeniable fact that the most depended upon and the most sought after gadget of modern times is the **mobile phone**. Initially arriving as a wireless mode of data (mainly voice) communication, and then eventually transforming into a handheld device which now encompasses the uses of a camera, music player, note book, GPS, map, etc. (the list grows longer each day), the mobile phone (or cell phone), has come a long way. There was a time when mobile phones only had monochromatic LCD displays and provided only basic functions like making calls and texting (SMSes). Today, mobile phones are much more advanced with bright and colourful displays, touch screens, and are capable of many video and audio processing applications. This metamorphosis has been mainly due to the evolution of modern day embedded processors which have powerful processing capabilities and at very high clock speeds. The advent of fine sensors, very good displays and A to D converters with high resolutions also have their role in gearing up the mobile revolution. Needless to say, the modern day cell phone has changed lives and lifestyles. Figure 4.1 shows a number of cell phones of different grades and brands.

Chapter-opening image: An ARM9 development board.

Nithin Gopinath, Analog Design Engineer, Texas Instruments, Bangalore.

Figure 4.1 | A photograph of different cell phones (Courtesy: www.geek.com)

4.1.1 | Block Diagram

Let's look at the basic block diagram of a mobile phone. Figure 4.2 shows the functional block diagram of a mobile phone receiver,

The fundamental blocks of a mobile phone are the following:

i) **Central processing block** consisting of the Microcontroller Unit (MCU), Digital Signal Processing Unit (DSP) and memory. This forms the 'embedded processor' of a mobile phone.
ii) **RF transceiver** consisting of RF modem, transmitter, synthesizer and receiver. It uses a low noise amplifier for boosting signals and an RF antenna for transmitting/receiving.
iii) **Power management block** takes care of all power-related issues (analog and digital power) of the device.
iv) **Analog baseband block** is responsible for dealing with the analog signals coming from the microphone and going to the speaker.

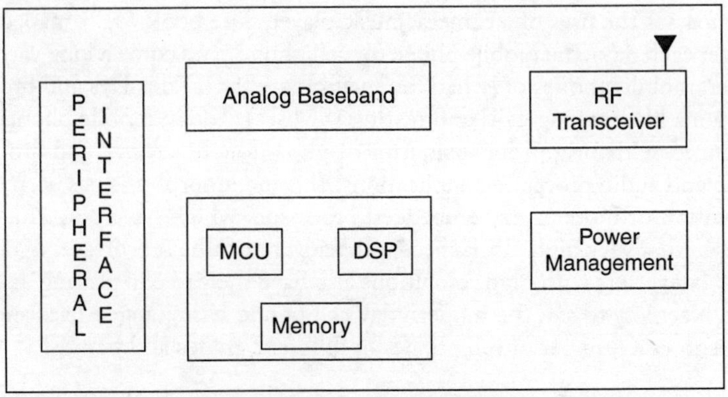

Figure 4.2 | The functional block diagram of a mobile phone

v) **Display** consists of LCDs, LEDs and other such hardware.
vi) **Peripheral interface** consists of USB port, audio jack, etc. which facilitate the connection of peripherals to the phone.

We are mainly concerned with the 'embedded processing' part of the phone. Hence, let us focus on the first block.

The central processing block consists of ARM core based general purpose processors (single or dual core) and some co-processors which take charge of signal processing. The same SoC handles the MCU and DSP applications. The processors used in today's smart phones are powerful enough to run operating systems like Linux, Android, etc. The modern day phone does almost as many as, if not more, than the number of applications done by the PC.

Some of the popular processors used in mobile phones are Texas Instruments' OMAP (Refer Section 15.6), Samsung's Exynos, Qualcomm's Snapdragon, Apple Inc.'s Ax series and Nvidia's Tegra platform. Intel is also keen to enter the mobile/tablet market with its Medfield platform. Figure 4.3 shows photographs of some of these processors.

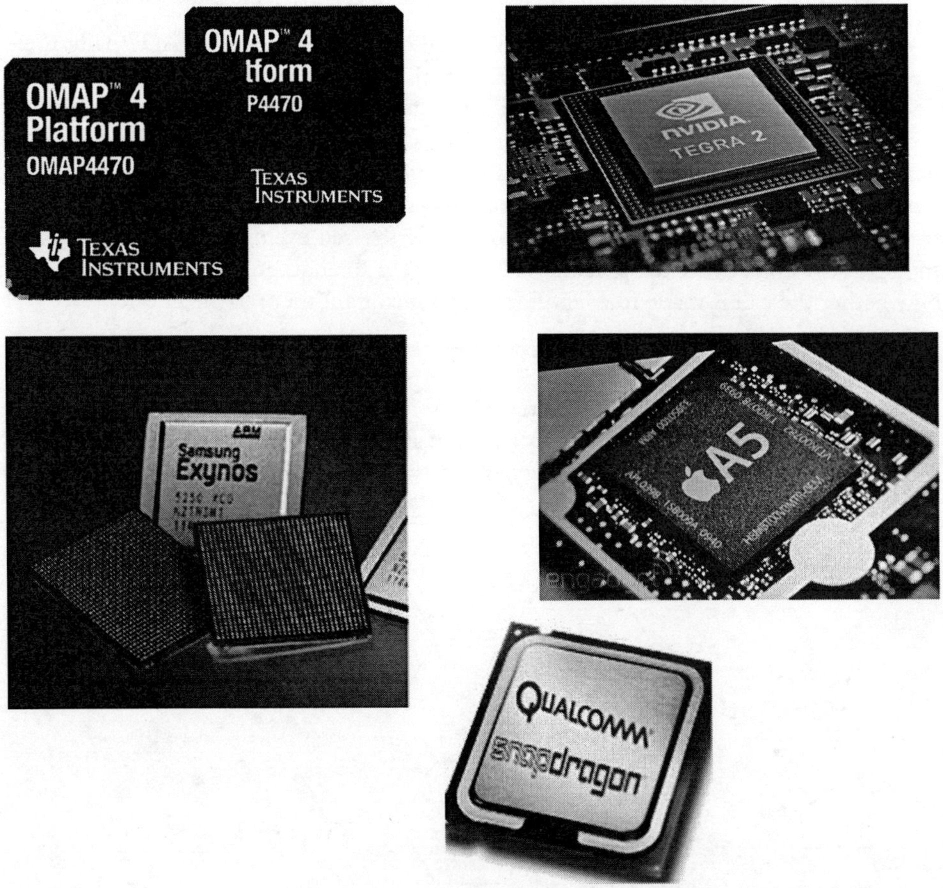

Figure 4.3 | Photographs of some of the popular SoCs used in mobile phones

4.1.2 | The Cellular Concept

In a cellular network, the area over which the network has coverage is divided into sub-units called 'cells'. These sub-units are of a particular shape—hexagon, square, circle, etc. Usually, hexagonal cells are used (see Figure 4.4). Each cell has a centrally located base station controller (BSC) which is responsible for handling calls. A group of base stations are controlled by a mobile switching centre (MSC).

4.1.3 | Multiple Access

In any form of communication (wireless or wired), the same channel is shared by many transmitters for transmitting their messages. In such cases, access to the channel has to be given to the different transmitters in an organized manner. Some of the types of shared medium accesses are as listed below.

i) **FDMA (Frequency Division Multiple Access):** Here, each user is allocated a single distinct central frequency with a certain bandwidth around it (for all the time).
ii) **TDMA (Time Division Multiple Access):** In this case, each user is allocated a single time slot during which the user can use all the available bandwidth.

Today's cellular networks use a combination of FDMA and TDMA. Usually, there are multiple antennae in a base station. Each of the antennae will have transceiver units. Each of the transceiver units is assigned a frequency. Each of the frequency channels is divided into time slots. When a person makes a call using his cell phone, the call is handled by the nearest base station. The call is assigned a time slot on one of the frequencies on one of the antennae (if all are directional antennae, then the call will be assigned to that antenna which covers the user's location). The call eventually gets connected to the PSTN (Public Switched Telephone Network) or to another base station depending on whether the call is made to a landline telephone or another mobile phone.

4.1.4 | Frequency Re-use

As power of the signal transmitted varies inversely with square of the distance from the signal source, the signal transmitted by the base station dies out after a certain distance. This allows us to use the same frequency for two other base stations which are at a

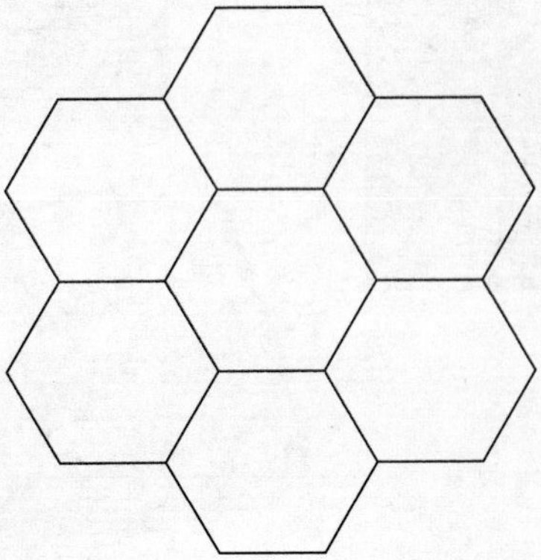

Figure 4.4 | A hexagonal cell cluster

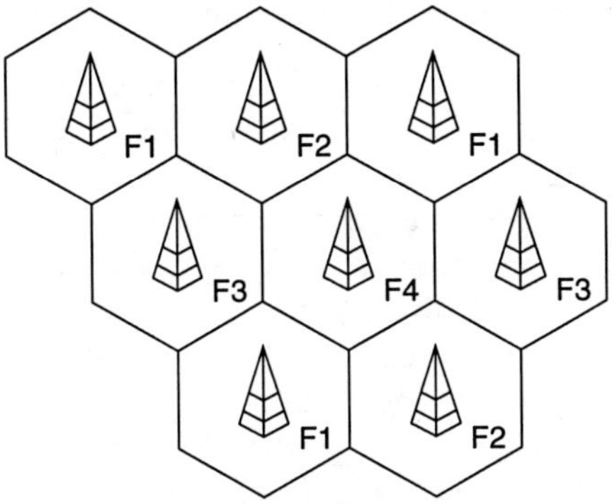

Figure 4.5 | Illustration of the concept of frequency re-use

minimum distance from each other. This is called frequency re-use. This may not be possible for two adjacent base stations as there might be locations where signals from both base stations arrive with power greater than the minimum power required. This type of interference is called **co-channel interference.** This is prevented by utilizing frequency re-use only after a certain minimum distance. Hence, with a couple of frequencies, a service provider can provide coverage to a large area using frequency re-use. Figure 4.5 illustrates this concept.

4.1.5 | Handoff (Handover)

Consider the case of a person talking on the phone, and is travelling. If he moves out of the cell (area of coverage of the base station handling the call), one would expect the call to be dropped by the base station. The cellular network architecture uses a technique called handover (handoff) to take care of this situation and to ensure that the call is not dropped. The base station near the previous position of the person will communicate with the base station near the new position of the person, and will effectively hand over the call to the new base station.

4.1.6 | Spread Spectrum Techniques

In spread spectrum techniques, signals which are limited to a certain bandwidth are spread across a wider bandwidth. This is advantageous for two main reasons:

i) **Narrowband interference:** Consider the case when there is some interference around a certain frequency. If the frequency allotted to all base stations are fixed, then the base station allotted this particular frequency will always have the same high value of interference. However, if the frequencies are switched from time to time, this narrowband interference gets averaged over all base stations and hence, each of base station receives only a small amount of interference. This is known as spread spectrum technique. This also helps to take care of jamming noise.
ii) **Eavesdropping:** The frequency switching takes place according to a pseudo-random sequence known only to the sender and the receiver. Hence, 'third person eavesdropping' on the communication is impossible without knowing the pseudo-random sequence. This helps in making the communication secure.

Some of the different types of spread spectrum are as follows:

i) **Frequency hopping spread spectrum:** Frequency hopping is a technique in which the frequency assigned to a base station is changed frequently among a set of frequencies. The switching of frequencies is done according to a pseudo-random sequence known only to the sender and the receiver.
ii) **Direct sequence spread spectrum:** In this technique, the signal is multiplied with a pseudo-random sequence (chirp signal) which is known only to the sender and receiver. At the receiver side, the correlation of the received signal with the pseudo-random sequence is determined to demodulate the signal. This process is known as de-spreading and it relies heavily on the orthogonality of the pseudo-random sequences. This is the basis for CDMA (Code Division Multiple Access).

4.1.7 | Set Up and Maintanence

The setup and maintenance of mobile networks is an extensive and complicated process.

Usually, mobile service providers outsource the engineering aspects of their mobile networks to telecommunication companies like Ericsson, Nokia-Siemens, Huawei, etc. The latter companies are responsible for setting up BSCs, MSCs, user databases, etc.

Figure 4.6 shows the photograph of a mobile tower.

4.1.8 | Conclusion

The modern mobile phone is no longer 'just a phone'. Many of the smartphones have functionalities of what may be thought of to be 'handheld computers' with multimedia, computing and data processing capabilities. Multitudes of applications run on it

Figure 4.6 | Photograph of a mobile tower

and many important aspects of life like banking, for instance, find mobile phone and mobile communications to be safe and secure. The future will definitely bring many more 'solutions' to be handled by mobile phones.

4.2 | Automotive Electronics

Electronic systems in automobiles have been available for quite some time. The earliest electronic equipments to be used in automobiles were AM radios and 2-way radios. With the invention of the integrated circuit (IC), there have been major developments in the field of automotive electronics. Electronic systems today are involved in almost every aspect of the car. They are used for safety purposes, better driving comforts, fuel usage efficiency, infotainment purposes, and so on. The industry is constantly driven by consumer demand and hence, a great deal of advancement is still happening in this field.

The electronic systems inside an automobile are controlled by electronic control units (ECU). There are about 50 to 100 ECUs in a modern car. These ECUs form the 'brain centres' of the electronic system of the automobile. The ECU mainly consists of a microprocessor and necessary software stored on memory (EEPROM or flash). As any faulty reading or delayed reading can potentially harm the passengers of the automobile, the sensor inputs are processed in real time. As a result of this, the OS assigns hard deadlines to the applications. Communication between devices is done using the controller area network (CAN) bus (Section 5.4.1). Let us discuss some of the important electronically controlled units in a modern automobile.

4.2.1 | Electronic Fuel Injection (EFI)

Electronic fuel injection was one of the major developments that took place in the latter part of the twentieth century. EFI is a mechanism for regulating the amount of fuel supplied to the engine for combustion. Prior to the development of electronic mechanisms, this was done by a carburetor and a floating mechanism. The floating mechanism would regulate the amount of fuel supplied to the engine. The carburetor would evaporate the fuel so that it mixes with the air for combustion. The EFI mechanism, on the other hand, measures the fuel amount so that the exact amount is given to the engine. It then forcibly pumps the fuel through a tiny nozzle under high pressure to atomize it. Hence, it gives only the proper amount of fuel needed for the engine.

EFI has great advantages over the carburetor mechanism:

- EFI prevents the flooding of the engine by not allowing too much fuel into the engine.
- EFI is more efficient and emission-friendly.
- With EFI, similar hardware can be used for diesel and petrol engines, which is not the case for carburetors.

4.2.2 | Anti-lock Braking System (ABS)

Anti-lock braking system [ABS] is one of the most popular systems in automotive electronics. ABS is a mechanism to prevent skidding due to locking up of the wheels. Consider a situation in which a vehicle is moving at a high speed and is suddenly confronted by an obstacle in its path. In a moment of panic, the driver applies full brakes and turns the steering wheel with the intention of turning the vehicle away from the obstacle. As the driver has applied full brakes, the wheels are locked (i.e. they are not turning) and hence, they start skidding on the road. As a result of this, the vehicle does not change direction (even though the driver has turned the steering wheel) but skids in the direction of the obstacle. If the wheels hadn't got locked up, the vehicle would have changed direction and this collision could have been prevented. This is the basic concept behind ABS.

An ABS consists of an ECU, wheel sensors and hydraulic brakes. Figure 4.7 shows the important parts of ABS. The wheel sensors inform the ECU about the speed of the wheels. The speed of the wheels relative to each other is important and hence their differentials are analyzed. Whenever a wheel is moving significantly slower or faster than the other wheels, (this is an indicator of wheel lock up) the ABS applies hydraulic brakes appropriately. If one wheel is moving faster than the other wheels, the ABS increases the brakes applied on this wheel and if one wheel is moving slower than the other wheels, the ABS decreases the brakes applied on this wheel. After a few accelerations and decelerations, all the wheels will be having similar speeds. The latest ABS mechanisms make use of brake pulsing in which the wheels are subject to a sequence of quick alternate accelerations and decelerations.

The main advantage of ABS is that it prevents wheel lock-up and hence, gives the driver steering control, even after application of the full brake. This reduces the risk of accidents. ABS also has the added advantage of lesser braking distance as compared to vehicles without ABS. Braking distance is the distance a vehicle travels after application of brakes before coming to a stop. This also depends on road conditions. On snow-covered roads, vehicles without ABS have lesser braking distance than the ones with ABS. However, ABS still gives the driver better control over the car on such roads.

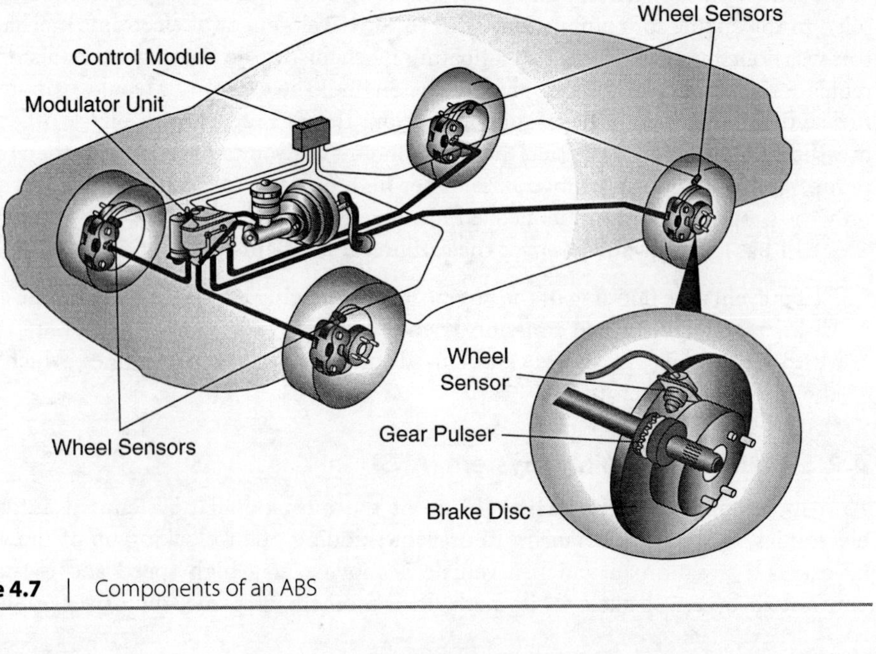

Figure 4.7 | Components of an ABS

4.2.3 | Electronic Stability Control

Electronic stability control (ESC) is very similar to ABS. It also provides the driver better control of the vehicle. It has wheel sensors and braking mechanisms similar to ABS. It also has a steering wheel orientation sensor and a gyroscopic sensor. The gyroscopic sensor detects the directional changes of the vehicle. The ECU of the ESC checks if the vehicle is moving in the direction the driver intends to move, that is, whether the gyroscopic sensor senses the vehicle in the direction of the steering wheel orientation or not. If they agree with each other, the ESC does not intervene. If they do not match, it indicates that the driver does not have control over the vehicle at the moment. Then the ESC applies brakes appropriately on the wheels so that the vehicle moves in the direction intended by the driver. ESC can work on any surface and is mostly seen in high-end vehicles, trucks, etc.

4.2.4 | Adaptive Cruise Control

Cruise control is a mechanism in which the vehicle speed is maintained at a constant value without the driver having to constantly keep his foot on the accelerator pedal. Whenever brakes are manually applied, the cruise control mechanism gives control of the throttle to the driver. This mechanism can be very useful for drivers while driving through highways with low traffic levels. Ordinary cruise control is not very useful when there is a significant amount of traffic. Modern cruise control mechanisms take into account other vehicles in front of them. These mechanisms are called adaptive cruise control mechanisms.

Adaptive cruise control units consist of an ECU and RADAR headway sensor (usually placed somewhere in the front of the car, behind the grill). When there is no vehicle in front, adaptive cruise control behaves like normal cruise control. When there is a vehicle in front, adaptive cruise control comes into play. With the help of the RADAR sensor, the ECU measures the speed and distance of the vehicle ahead and accordingly accelerates or decelerates. This will ensure that the vehicle is at a safe distance from the vehicle in front.

Another type of cruise control called 'hill descent control' helps the driver in descending down hilly roads in difficult terrain. The control mechanism applies brakes appropriately to drive downhill without the driver having to apply brakes.

4.2.5 | Airbag Deployment

Airbags are one of the earliest safety mechanisms used in vehicles. Airbags are to be deployed whenever there is an automobile collision. They prevent the passengers in the vehicle from hitting the inside of the car—window, dashboard, etc. The airbag mechanism makes uses of the speed sensors (accelerometers, gyroscopic sensors, wheel speed sensors, etc.) and impact sensors. Whenever there is a sudden decrease in the speed of the vehicle in a very small amount of time, that is, large amount of deceleration, it indicates a collision. The impact sensor may also report a collision. In either case, the ECU actuates the ignition of a gas generator propellant. The gas is usually nitrogen which then inflates a nylon fabric bag. The airbags are thus deployed preventing injury. Figure 4.8 illustrates this.

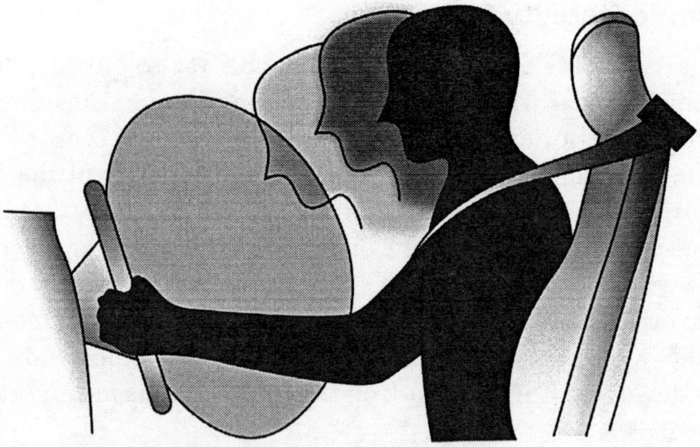

Figure 4.8 | Airbag deployment

4.2.6 | Automotive Navigation Systems

Automotive navigation systems are electronic systems which provide a whole lot of useful information to the driver. It can provide real-time information about routes, traffic congestion, etc. These systems consist of an ECU, gyroscopic sensor and GPS. A touch-screen user interface is also provided. GPS (Global Positioning System) makes use of satellites in space to triangulate the position (in terms of latitude and longitude) of the vehicle. The gyroscopic sensor is used to detect the direction in which the vehicle has turned. These systems also provide details about driving restrictions (one-ways, etc.), signboards, warning boards, nearby fuel stations, car wash shops, workshops, restaurants, etc. Figure 4.9 is a photograph of the details seen on the screen of a navigation system developed by Sony Corporation.

Figure 4.9 | The screen of a navigation system developed by Sony

The current position of the vehicle is known to the ECU using the GPS. The software has knowledge of all routes. When the user enters the destination details into the system using the user interface, the ECU finds the shortest route from the current point to the destination. The driver can choose any route and not necessarily the shortest one. Once the driver has selected the route, it shows the driver the path to be taken and also informs the driver when and where a turn is to be taken. If the driver takes a wrong turn, the system recalculates and finds the shortest route from that point to the destination.

The modern versions of the navigation systems also show traffic details. These details are usually communicated in real-time to the navigation system using Bluetooth or such wireless communication protocols.

4.2.7 | Conclusion

With this, we end our discussion of automotive electronics. Note that we have included only a few items of control in this. But keep in mind that, automotive electronics has come to occupy a major share of the embedded systems market. Consider the case of cars alone. All cars manufactured these days come with automatic fuel injection and related electronic control in the engine. Besides safety and navigation features, there is the 'infotainment' system also in a car. High end cars have electronic controls for almost everything, right from door locking to engine starting key. The number of processors used in an S class Mercedes Benz is likely to be, more than 100. These processor circuits are interconnected by buses like CAN, LIN, MOST and Flex-Ray. In short, the automobile industry is one of the biggest users of embedded systems.

4.3 | Radio Frequency Identification (RFID)

Radio frequency identification is a method of identifying, tracking or verifying objects/persons with the help of electronic tags/labels attached to them. These electronic tags are capable of receiving and transmitting radio frequencies and are called RFID tags or RFID labels. The ID information from these tags is obtained using RFID readers.

Refer to Figure 4.10 to see how an RFID system works. The system consists of a reader, tag and antennae. Each RFID tag has a transmitter and receiver, called a transponder because it 'transmits and responds'. The RFID reader transmits a signal to interrogate

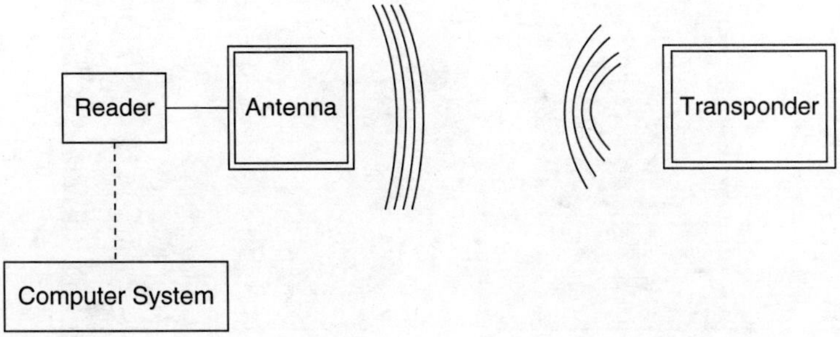

Figure 4.10 | Working of an RFID system

the tag (or tags). The tag receives the signal and responds by transmitting its identity information. The system than takes some action based on this information. The action may be simply to display a number/name on a handheld device, or it may be that the information is passed on to a system for authentication/counting of a person, items etc.

Most systems utilize three general bands:

i) Low frequency from 125 KHz to 134 KHz
ii) High frequency at 13. 56 MHz
iii) Ultra high frequency at 860 to 930MHz

There may be some difference in frequency use due to some regulations in any particular country. The frequency band used also influences the practical size of the antenna and the power transmissions that can be used.

4.3.1 | RFID Architecture

4.3.1.1 | *Tag/Label*

RFID tags units belong a class of radio devices known as 'transponders'. A transponder is a combination of a transmitter and a receiver, which is designed to receive a specific radio signal and automatically transmit a reply. In its simplest implementation, the transponder listens for a radio signal, and sends a signal of its own as a reply. More complicated system may send a letter or a digit back to the source, or even send multiple strings of letters and digits. Finally, advanced systems may do a calculation or verification process and include encryption to prevent eavesdroppers from obtaining the information being transmitted. Transponders used in RFID are commonly known as tag, chip or label. As a general rule, an RFID tag consists of following items:

i) Encoding/Decoding circuitry
ii) Memory
iii) Antenna
iv) Power supply
v) Communication control

A tag can take almost any physical form, like cards, keys, rods, etc., as desired, to perform the required function. The design may be influenced by the type of antenna, which in turn may be dependent on the frequency used for the system. Some typical tag types are card type, key fobs, etc. See Figure 4.11 which shows tags of various shapes.

Figure 4.11 | RFID tags of different physical shapes and sizes

RFID tags have risen as a major complement to the conventionally used barcode system. RFID provides many advantages over the barcode system such as:

- RFID can be used to read multiple tags at a time where as barcodes can read only one item at a time.
- RFID tags can be read even if the tagged object is inside a box or a cover, or other situations when there is no line of sight. Barcode requires the code to be scanned in the line of sight.

As electronic tags need to be working only when they are read, many RFID tags do not depend on a battery for power. Thus, there are two types of tags: active and passive. The active tags need a battery for power, while the passive tags don't. They make use of the power of the signal transmitted by the RFID reader. This prevents unnecessary power wastage during idle hours.

4.3.1.2 | *Reader*

The next component needed in the system is the RFID reader, that is, the interrogator. The reader is also a transceiver, that is, transmitter plus receiver. It is named as 'reader' by virtue of its function of querying the tag and reading data from it. Handheld systems have the reader and its antenna together as one unit, while larger systems usually separate antennas from the reader.

A reader may usually contains a system interface such as an RS-232 serial port or Ethernet jack, cryptographic encoding or decoding circuitry, a power supply or a battery and a communications control circuit. This depends on the requirement of the RFID system.

The reader retrieves the information from the RFID tag. The reader may be self-contained and may store information internally, But it may also be a part of localized system such as an authentication system or a large local area network (LAN) or a wide area network (WAN). Readers that send data to a LAN, do so by using a data interface such as Ethernet or serial RS-232.

4.3.1.3 | *Applications*

RFID tags have a huge variety of applications. Some of them are as follows:

i) Supply-chain product tracking
ii) Season parking tickets
iii) Toll booths
iv) Transportation services
v) Public transit (metro, railway, etc.)
vi) Hospitals and museums
vii) Person authentication

4.4 | Wireless Sensor Networks (WISENET)

As the name suggests, a wireless sensor network (WISENET) is a wireless network consisting of sensors meant for monitoring environmental conditions like temperature, pressure, humidity, level of gases, etc. They can also be used for auditory or visual

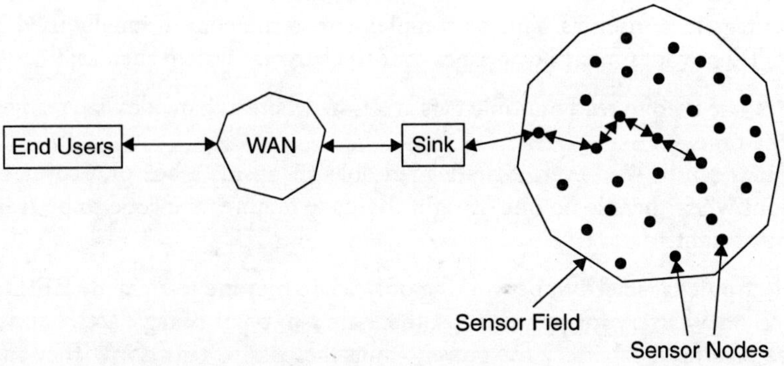

Figure 4.12 | A wireless sensor network

monitoring. This information is then transmitted to the main database. These networks are of great use in monitoring environmental conditions in places which are not easily accessible and in regions of difficult terrain.

A WISENET node consists of a wireless transceiver, antenna, microcontroller and battery. It is connected to a sensor or a collection of sensors. Refer to Figure 4.12 which shows a number of sensor nodes within a sensor field. The nodes communicate with each other and the information finally reaches the sink node (final node). The sink node is connected to the wide area network (WAN) and hence, reaches the end user. WISENET uses wireless communication protocols like ZigBee and IEEE 802.15.4. (Section 5.5.2). The algorithms used in WISENET software is such that it minimizes power consumption.

The first operating system software specifically designed for wireless sensor networks is the TinyOS. As the software is mainly responsible only for processing the sensor readings and transmitting the data packets, it need not be functioning all the time. Hence, TinyOS makes use of 'event-driven' programming. There are event handlers associated with each task. Whenever an event comes up, the OS assigns the event handler to handle the task.

4.4.1 | Applications

i) Vehicle tracking
ii) Energy monitoring

4.5 | Robotics

Robotics is the field of design and development of devices which can perform tasks on their own or with guidance. The devices which perform these actions are called **robots.** Robots are a subset of embedded systems. A robot is a mechanical system which has a sense of purpose. A typical robot

i) can sense its environment
ii) can manipulate things in its environment
iii) has intelligence embedded in it
iv) has motion or translation in one or more axes

The working of a robot has three main phases:

i) **Perception:** Obtaining information about the environment/stimulus. This action is done by the sensor, for example, vision, sound, touch, etc.
ii) **Processing:** The processor processes the input data from the sensor and generates the necessary control signals to be sent to the actuators which executes the necessary action.
iii) **Action:** Implementation of commands given by the processor. For example, motor, video, sound, etc.

4.5.1 | Sensors

Some of the sensors used by robots are as follows:

i) **Vision:** Robotic vision is mainly computer vision captured using a CMOS or CCD [Charge-coupled Device] array. The pixel information of the image is then processed by the processor.
ii) **Sound:** Robots which respond to audio signals have a microphone to gather input data which is then processed by the processor. Highly efficient algorithms have been developed for speech recognition applications.
iii) **Tactile sensors:** Robots which respond to touch, make use of tactile sensors for input data. These sensors have certain impedance measuring devices which help in detecting tactile information.

4.5.2 | Actuators

Some of the actuators used by robots are as follows:

i) **Motors:** Motors can be used to do mechanical functions like turning wheels, pumping water, move in any direction, etc.
ii) **Video and audio:** Robots can also provide visual and auditory data using LCD displays and speakers, respectively.

4.5.3 | Embedded Intelligence

All robots have some degree of intelligence attached to it. The intelligence to be embedded in a robot depends on its intended application as well as on the degree of sophistication and precision to which it is to perform.

To put it all together, let us say that for a robot, for example a mobile robot, to perform its intended applications, it needs

i) sensors to sense its environment and to move accordingly
ii) actuators for performing the movement, and the assigned task
iii) a control algorithm for moving and performing the intended task
iv) communication systems (optional, depending on the application)

4.5.4 | Types of Robots

i) **Stationary robots**: They are stationary as a whole, but have moving parts like a robotic arm, for example. Such arms may be used for picking up objects and/or perform similar activities.

ii) **Mobile robots** have the capability to move around in their environment and are not fixed to one physical location.
iii) **Humanoid robots** are those which have an appearance similar to a human body and can perform actions similar to human beings (e. g. dance and sing).

See Figure 4.13 for the image of two dancing robots developed by Sony Corporation. Figure 4.14 shows the pictures of two robotic research platforms developed by Nex Robotics, Mumbai (http://www. nex-robotics. com/).

4.5.5 | Open Loop and Closed Loop Systems

In open loop systems, the 'action' phase is executed based on the 'perception' phase but the 'perception' phase is not influenced by the 'action' phase. For example, consider a robot which translates from English to French. It has a microphone as the sensor and

Figure 4.13 | Dancing robots developed by Sony Corporation

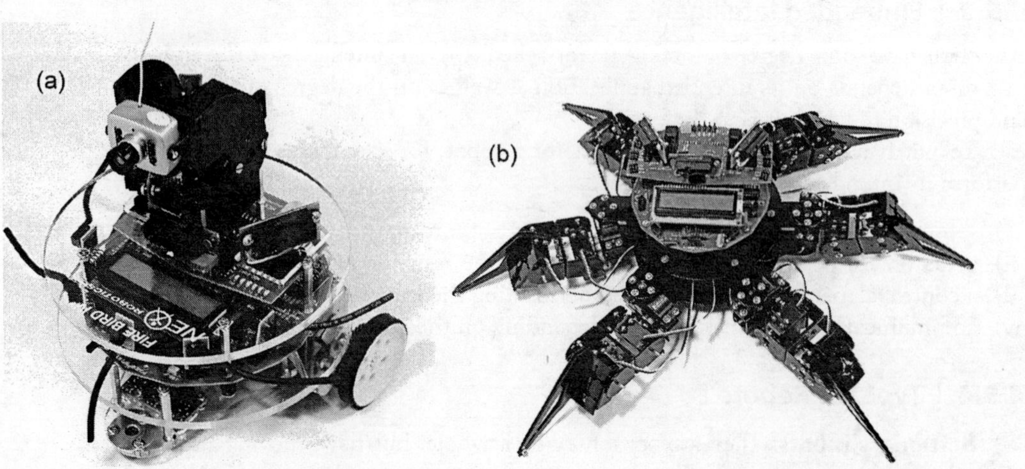

Figure 4.14 | Two robotic research platforms developed by Nex Robotics, Mumbai (a) Robotic platform with camera and (b) Craboide Robot (Reproduced with permission from M/s Nex Robotics)

speaker as the actuator. The robot takes in data in English via the microphone, translates it using its processor and gives the output in French via the speaker.

When the 'perception' phase is also made dependent on the previous 'action' phase(s), the loop becomes closed and hence there is a feedback mechanism in the system. For example, consider a mobile robot which follows a slow moving red-coloured ball. It has a video camera as sensor and motor as actuator to drive its wheels. The robot takes in visual data via the camera, finds the location of the red-ball using the algorithm burned in the processor and turns the wheel in such a way that the robot is still following the ball.

The simplest algorithm would be to ensure that the ball is always at the centre of the image captured by the camera. So, whenever the ball moves away from the centre, the robot adjusts its position such that the ball is at the centre of the image. Hence, the current image seen by the robot (current 'perception' phase) is dependent on the direction in which the robot moved in the previous instant (previous 'action' phase). This is an example of a closed loop system with negative feedback.

4.5.6 | Designing an Autonomous Robotic System

An autonomous robot is a robot which can perform desired tasks in unstructured environments without continuous human guidance. Different robots can be autonomous in different ways. An autonomous robot is an assembly of mechanical and electronic elements with artificial intelligence embedded in it. The mechanical structure of a robot must be controlled to perform tasks. The control of a robot involves various aspects such as path planning, pattern recognition, obstacle avoidance, etc.

The strategy for design consists of the following steps:

i) Identify various cost-effective applications
ii) Study various algorithms which can perform this job efficiently
iii) Test the chosen algorithms using modelling techniques
iv) Design the hardware and software
v) Choose the right sensors and actuators
vi) Integrate the whole system and test it

Figure 4.15 shows the picture of an autonomous robot capable of moving in a rough and hostile terrain. Section 19.1 contains a full description of the design of a vision controlled autonomous robot.

Figure 4.15 | Photograph of an autonomous robot (Reproduced with permission from M/s Nex Robotics)

4.6 | Biomedical Applications

Embedded systems are being used in a variety of medical applications. Their scope is being expanded by the improvements in sensor technology and by the miniaturization of Analog Front Ends (AFEs) and Analog to Digital Convertors (ADCs). A few of the biomedical applications are listed below:

i) **X-Ray:** X-ray machines used to be analog devices. The X-rays generated from a source are projected onto a film sensitive to the radiation, after passing it through the body part to be examined. Earlier, the film had to be developed to obtain the image. This has now given way to digital x-ray machines in which Flat Panel Detector (FPD) sensors replace the film. The analog output of the sensors are amplified and fed to ADCs which convert them into digital codes and pass it onto the digital modules which process the information and generate an image from it.

ii) **MRI (Magnetic Resonance Imaging):** Here magnetic waves generated by nuclei immersed in a strong magnetic field and disturbed by an RF pulse at their resonant frequency. This is sensed by coils and this information is processed to obtain the image.

iii) **CT (Computed Tomography):** This uses x-rays to generate 3D images of the body by rotating the sensor-detector pair around the body and taking multiple images at various angles.

iv) **Pulse oximetry:** Red and Infra Red (IR) light is passed through the user's finger or earlobe and the transmitted light is sensed and processed to obtain information about oxygen content in the blood and pulse rate.

v) **Blood glucose measurement:** A drop of blood is placed on a special strip and the strip is loaded into a device. The device applies various electrical inputs to the strip and then measures some quantity like total charge passed through the strip or its resistance to measure the glucose level in the blood.

vi) **Pedometer:** Miniature devices that can be embedded in special purpose shoes or carried/worn by the user can count the number of footsteps. This can be used by athletes to monitor their performance, on the go. Such devices might use accelerometers or pressure sensors to obtain the input signal, which is then filtered and processed to give the required information.

vii) **Wearable medical devices:** Compact light weight systems that can monitor important health parameters and transmit them for observation are being developed.

viii) **Emergency alert systems:** Systems are available that can monitor the vital statistics of a person and alert others in case of a problem. Such systems can also be manually triggered by the user. This is particularly useful for the elderly and the infirm, who are prone to dangers like falling or sudden and debilitating conditions like cardiac arrest.

ix) **Wheel chairs:** Wheel chairs with lots of flexibility of movement and control, and a lot of features, are now being manufactured. The complete control of the chair is done by high end processors with signal processing capabilities, and running very sophisticated algorithms for locomotion. See Figure 4.16 which is a photograph showing a modern wheel chair.

Figure 4.16 | A modern wheel chair

4.7 | Brain Machine Interface

Imagine a technology which would enable you to control objects without physically interacting with them, but could control them by just a thought. This popular concept in science fiction is soon to become a reality. In fact, many such devices have already translated human thought into prosthetic arm movements, computer cursor movements, etc. This is realized using what is called a Brain-Machine Interface (also called Brain-Computer Interface).

4.7.1 | Block Diagram

A brain-machine Interface (BMI) is a communication channel between the human brain and an external device. It serves as an interpreter or a translator which translates human thought into corresponding action. Figure 4.17 shows the block diagram of such a system.

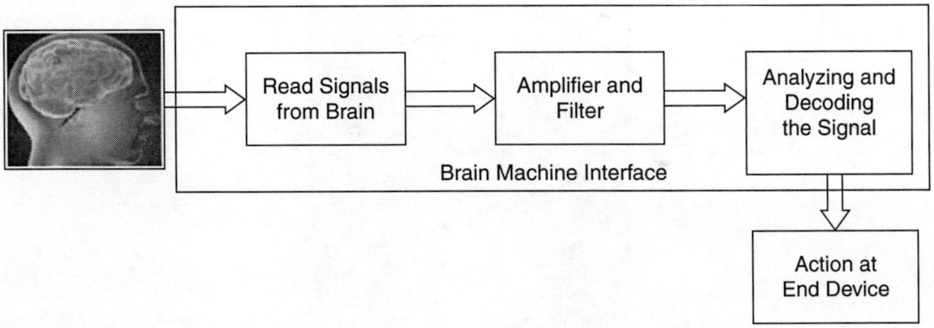

Figure 4.17 | Block diagram of a brain-machine interface

4.7.2 | Stages of a BMI

A BMI has the following stages:

4.7.2.1 | *Signal Reading Stage*

This is in the form of electrodes placed at different places on the scalp of the human head.

There are mainly two methods adopted for reading signals from the brain: non-invasive and invasive.

Non-invasive

Electroencephalography (EEG) EEG offers a **non-invasive technique** for reading brain activity, that is, reading signals without placing electrodes or any such devices inside the human body. Hence, there is no surgery required to connect a BMI to a person using EEG. However, only the signals which are obtained at the scalp can be read using EEG. These signals (originated from inside the brain) are heavily attenuated by the skull when they reach the scalp. These reasons make the signal obtained at the scalp weak and highly distorted. Hence, we need very high gain amplifiers to boost the signal and also very accurate filters to remove noise. The difficulty with such a method is that no non-invasive technique currently exists that approaches the spatial resolution needed to extract the finest neural details. Figure 4.18 shows a number of electrodes placed on a scalp.

Invasive

Electrocorticography (ECoG) The other alternative of ECoG provides a better option in terms of **spatial resolution**. Spatial resolution is a measure of the ability of the reading stage to differentiate between signals from two very close parts of the brain. This is of vital importance, considering the fact that different signals (sense, movement, etc.) come from different points on the brain surface which are often close to each other. As signals are read from the cortex directly, the attenuation caused by the skull is avoided. However, ECoG is an **invasive approach**, that is, the electrodes have to be surgically implanted inside the person's head. See Figure 4.19 which shows the signals inside the brain which are to be extracted, and the precise method is to place electrodes inside the brain.

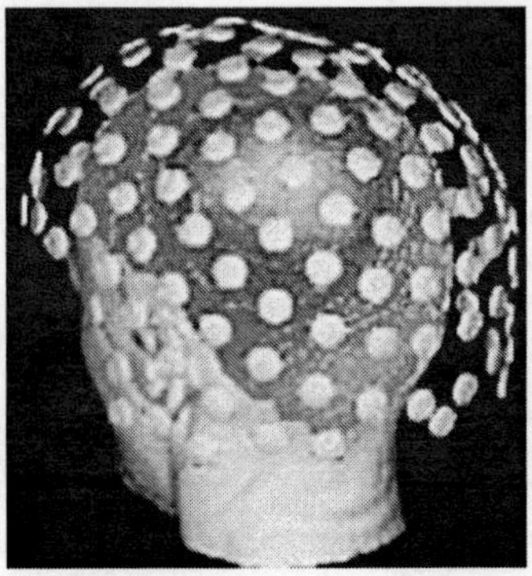

Figure 4.18 | Non-invasive reading of signal (EEG)

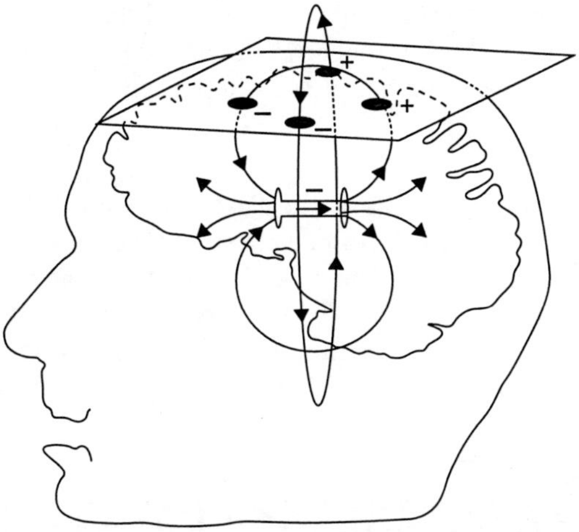

Figure 4.19 | Signals inside the brain which are to be 'invasively' read

4.7.2.2 | *Amplifier and Filter Stage*

The signals obtained from the scalp or cortex are weak, and need to be amplified. In EEG, usually differential amplifiers are used. These amplifiers have gain in the range of 60 dB to 100 dB, that is, a voltage gain of 1,000V/V to 100,000 V/V. This would facilitate the strengthening of a signal of μV range to a signal of mV range.

The EEG/ECoG signal obtained is not only a weak one, but is also corrupted with lots of noise. In order to decode the brain wave, it is very important that the signal be passed through a filter first and then only analysed. Analysing an EEG signal directly (even after amplification) is like listening to a bad telephone—there is a lot of static. Hence after amplification, the brain waves are passed through a filter with cut-off frequency, usually near the 30–70 Hz range. It depends on the type of waves expected. It is very important that the filters used here are very accurate as there are all sorts of noise in the signal. Sometimes, a notch filter is also used with the notch at the supply frequency, that is, the frequency at which the supply voltage operates (50 Hz in India and many other countries). This is done to avoid any noise creeping into the system via the power supply.

4.7.2.3 | *Analysing and Decoding the Signals*

Once the brain waves have been obtained, it is provided to the most important part of the brain-machine interface, that is, the decoding centre. It has the important job of analysing the signals, finding out what they are meant for and generating the necessary control signals to realize the corresponding movement/action in the end device.

There are a variety of parameters with the help of which the brain waves are analysed. Some of them are as follows.

Location of Electrode

One of the major parameters which help in decoding brain waves is the location on the brain from where the waves are read. Different parts of the brain have different functions. Signals received from the visual cortex of the brain are associated with vision, whereas signals received from the motor cortex of the brain are associated with voluntary limb movements. Spatial resolution becomes an important concept in this context.

Frequency of the Signal

The frequency of the brain waves tells us the class to which it belongs to (theta, alpha, beta, gamma, etc.). This in turn gives us some information about the kind of activity taking place in the brain. For example, alpha waves (frequency range 8–12 Hz) are obtained while closing or opening of the eye. When a person is in an alert state, beta waves (12–30 Hz) are obtained. Similarly, gamma waves (30–100+ Hz) are obtained during memory match.

Strength of the Signal

The strength of the signal obtained is also an important parameter in analysis of brain waves. The signal power is different for different types of brain activity. For example, while opening the eye, low signal power alpha waves are obtained, whereas while closing it, high power signals are obtained. This is one of the easiest methods which can be used for decoding brain waves.

Consider a robot which goes only forward and backward. Closing and opening of the eyes can serve as 'indicator thoughts' in order to tell the BMI to generate necessary control signals to make the robot move backward or forward.

This example is a very simple decoding algorithm. Actual algorithms, however, are very complex. This complexity is increased manifold by the fact that brain waves are usually subjective, that is, varies from person to person. To develop a BMI which can be readily used on any person would be impossible. The BMI has to fully 'understand' the person before actually being effective in aiding that person. For this to happen, the person and the BMI have to adapt to each other.

On one hand, the BMI has to understand the individual brain patterns characterizing the mental tasks executed by the subjects. On the other hand, the subject has to modulate his brain waves voluntarily through feedback to generate distinct brain wave patterns. This requires an adaptation time wherein the subject is made to visualize (think) about the necessary action being executed and his/her brain waves are recorded. This is done a number of times to get distinct brain wave patterns which are then fed into the BMI as indicators for the necessary action.

4.7.3 | End Device

The end device may be a robot, a prosthetic limb, a computer cursor, etc. In case of a computer cursor, the patient mentally visualizes the cursor moving to the target. The BMI understands this signal and then generates the necessary signals to make the computer cursor move to the target. For the brain-machine interface to understand the signal, a house of practice is required. The BMI has to be trained to decode the singles correctly.

The end device may also be a prosthetic limb. In this case, the patient visualizes the movement of the limbs which is interpreted by the software and the corresponding movement is generated in the prosthetic limb. See Figure 4.20 which shows both these cases.

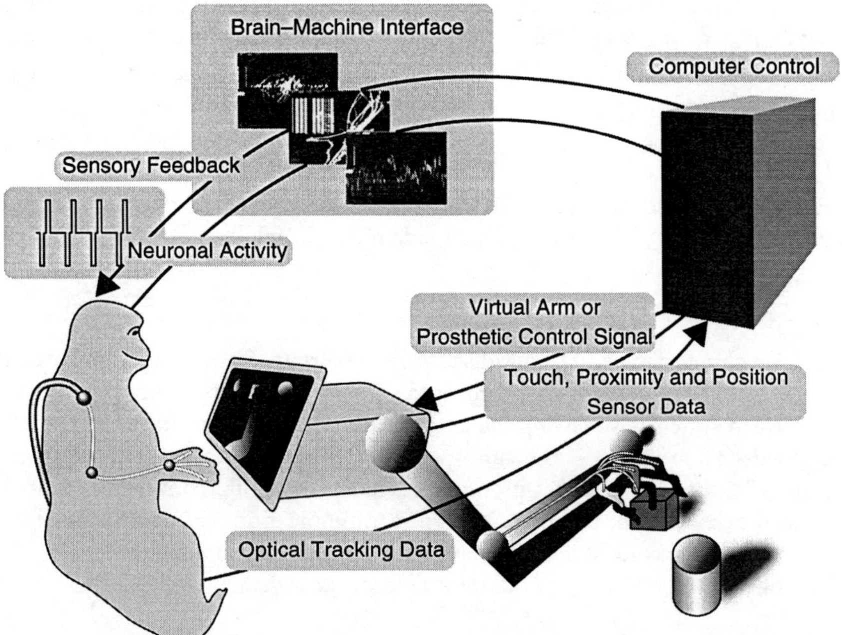

Figure 4.20 | Working of a BMI with computer cursor and prosthetic limb as end device

Sometimes BMIs are used to provide alternate neural pathways for persons whose natural neural pathways have been damaged or are dysfunctional. For instance, consider a case when the muscles near the elbow part of the arm are damaged. The signals from the brain cannot reach the hand part of the arm due to the blockage caused by the damaged muscles. A BMI can easily solve the problem by providing an alternate pathway between the brain and the human hand. Here the end device is not a prosthetic object or a robot, but a human organ.

4.7.4 | Important Milestones

In 2002, a man named Jens Neumann had his vision restored (imperfectly) using a BMI. Jens Neumann had lost his eyesight during adulthood. The device was in the form of camera attached to one of the glasses of his spectacles. The images captured by the camera were processed and sent to the visual cortex. Scientists targeted the 177 brain cells in the cortex which interpret the image falling on the retina (screen) of the eye.

The implant, however, offered only black-and-white vision and at a low frame rate. In spite of this, he was able to drive slowly in the parking lot of the research centre where he was given the BMI.

BMI technology for motor neuro-prosthetics created a whole new benchmark with the *BrainGate* BMI implanted into Matt Nagle's brain in 2005. Matt was paralysed neck down after his spinal cord had been severed, as a result of stabbing. It was done as part of the first nine-month human trial of *Cyber-kinetics Neuro-technology's* BrainGate chip-implant.

A 96 electrode BMI was implanted into his cortex. It required him some months to initially adapt to the BMI. His signals were read and were then used for moving a computer cursor. He could utilize the full functionality of the computer cursor including left-click, right-click, etc. He could then check e-mail, turn ON/OFF TV, lights, etc. He also became the first person to move a prosthetic hand (opening and closing of hand) with his thoughts.

These examples indicate that BMI seems to be quite promising, though many hurdles are left to be crossed before it can be made really useful.

Conclusion

With this, we come to the end of our discussion on certain specific and popular embedded systems. This chapter gives an insight into the various aspects involved in the design of an embedded system. By viewing the example of a mobile phone itself, we realize that an embedded system design is the culmination of the most complex technologies and knowledge of the fields of signal processing, analog to digital conversion technology, sensor and display design, processor design, communications principles, etc. Thus an embedded system does not stand alone as just a piece of electronics circuitry; it encompasses the finest and best in many different fields of knowledge.

KEY POINTS OF THIS CHAPTER

- This chapter introduces a few embedded systems in common use.
- One of the most popular devices we use today is the mobile phone.
- A mobile phone of modern times uses ARM processors with DSP co-processors.
- It uses the cellular concept and spread spectrum modulation technique.
- Modern automobiles have a lot of ECUs pertaining to different controls.
- ABS, EFI, ESC, ACC, etc. are systems used very commonly in many vehicles.
- RFID systems have a lot of advantages over the conventional barcode system.
- Wireless sensor networks are used for applications like environment monitoring.
- The field of robotics is one in which embedded systems are widely used.
- Robots are mechanical structures controlled by electronics.
- There are different types of robots like stationary, mobile, autonomous, etc.
- For autonomous robots, complex path following algorithms are needed.
- The biomedical field is one where embedded systems are widely used.
- Brain-machine interface is a new application which shows promise.

QUESTIONS

1. List out the fundamental blocks of a mobile phone and explain the function of each block.
2. Explain why the central processing block of a mobile phone needs processors of very high signal processing capability.

3. Why are mobile cells found to be hexagonal? Find out the reason.
4. What is the necessity for 'hand off'?
5. List at least five ECUs usually found in automobiles.
6. How does the ABS help in improving the safety of a vehicle?
7. Justify the name 'RFID' in terms of the functionality of the system.
8. List the most commonly used RFID frequencies.
9. What are the components likely to be present in a wireless sensor node?
10. Distinguish between open and closed loop robotic systems.
11. Name a few biomedical devices which used embedded systems.
12. Why is the wheel chair an apt example of the use of embedded systems?
13. Why do you think that BMI holds great promise for the future?
14. Why is the non-invasive method of reading brain signals not very effective?
15. What is the difficulty in the invasive method of brain signal reading?

EXERCISES

1. Name five service providers for cell phones in India.
2. Name five manufacturers of mobile phone receivers in the world.
3. What are the equipment likely to be present in a mobile phone tower?
4. In a car, find out which 'buses' are used for the following units.
   i) Infotainment
   ii) Engine Control
   iii) Body Electronics
5. How does the system of 'automatic gear' work in a typical 'gearless' car?
6. Explain how the GPS system in a vehicle (if present) works.
7. Find a few examples of the applications of wireless sensor networks.
8. Find the names of five manufacturers of biomedical appliances.
9. Find more examples of the practical results of using BMI.
10. Write an essay with information about the following topics.
    i) Robotic soccer
    ii) Humanoid robots and their future
    iii) Industrial robots
    iv) Robots for military applications

5 BUSES AND PROTOCOLS

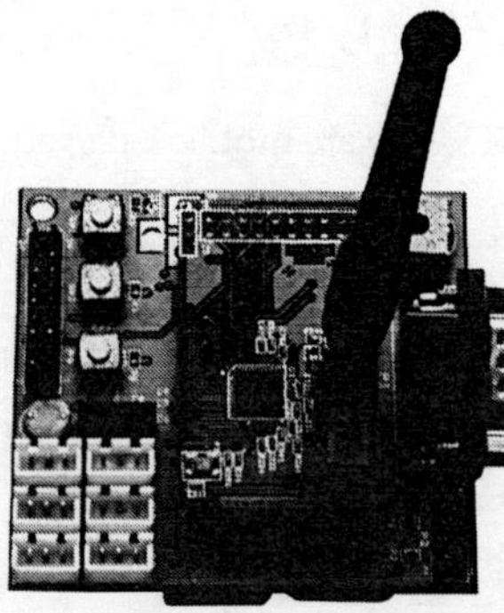

In this chapter, you will learn

- The definitions for buses and protocols
- The different types of buses in a computer system
- The reasons why serial buses are preferred currently
- The different methods of bus arbitration
- The protocols of two on-board buses, the I2C and SPI bus
- The working of the external serial buses USB and firewire
- The serial buses like RS 232, RS 422 and RS 485
- The concepts surrounding the Ethernet protocol
- The most important automotive bus, i.e., the CAN bus
- The wireless protocols for WLAN, Zigbee and Bluetooth

Introduction

In this chapter, we will discuss buses and protocols, two 'related' aspects that are very important for any system, whether it is a general purpose computer system or a special purpose embedded system. Let us start with some simple definitions.

5.1 | Defining Buses and Protocols

Bus In the simplest form, a bus is a collection of wires which carry electrical signals. The electrical signals may be defined in terms of voltage levels or current values. We are dealing with digital systems, and the signals involved in this carry information quantified as bits: either 0 or 1. In short, we say that a signal wire carries a '1' or a '0', and that a bus is a collection of such wires (we shall exclude the wires which carry power supply voltages).

Protocol A protocol is set of rules/specifications which govern the transmission and reception of information over a bus. These specifications are defined electrically, mechanically and also in terms of 'speed', that is, the rate at which data is transferred.

We will, in this section carry out an in depth review of these related terms and study different types of buses and associated protocols.

Chapter-opening image: A Zigbee module.

Since buses carry information, let us first have an idea of what kind of information can be carried by a bus. As a basic subdivision, the information carried can be classified as address, data and control. Remember that any computer system consists of a processor, memory and I/O. The system bus present in such a setup is subdivided into the following:

i) The address bus which carries the memory or IO addresses which the processor wants to access in order to read or write data. It is a unidirectional bus.
ii) The data bus carries data coming from or going to the processor. It is a bidirectional bus.
iii) The control bus also called command bus which transports control and synchronization signals. It is a bidirectional bus, that is, signals which travel in either or both directions are present in this group.

Figure 5.1 is a typical system showing the CPU connected to memory and I/O. In this figure, the system bus is shown connected to both I/O and memory.

5.1.1 | Processor-memory Bus

Over the years, the requirements of memory and I/O have become more and more distinct and separate, and you may hear terms like 'processor-memory bus' and 'peripheral bus', with respect to PCs or standard embedded systems. In any system the fastest unit is the CPU, that is, the processor. The next fast unit is main memory or cache (if present). The bus connecting the processor and memory (including cache, if present) is now called the processor-memory bus. It is also designated by terms such as internal bus, main bus, system bus, etc.

There is a continuous transport of information between a processor and its memory. For reading from memory, a processor (say, 8085) with an 8 bits data bus and a 16-bit address bus sends 16 bits of address on 16 separate address lines, and receives 8 bits of data on 8 physical wires. Control signals like memory read, chip enable, output enable, etc. are also activated. Thus, a number of physical wires are active at the same time, and contribute to the transfer of information. This is parallel communication between the processor and memory. Internal buses are almost always parallel buses.

5.1.2 | Peripheral Buses

Processors also need to communicate with peripherals, that is, external input and output devices, and this data pathway is called the I/O bus or peripheral bus. Since peripherals

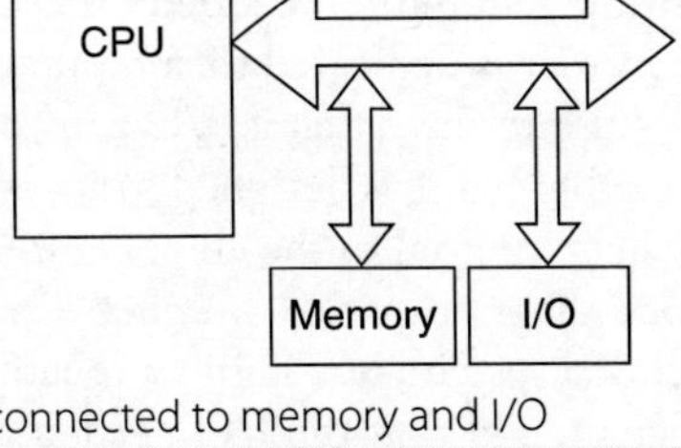

Figure 5.1 | A processor connected to memory and I/O

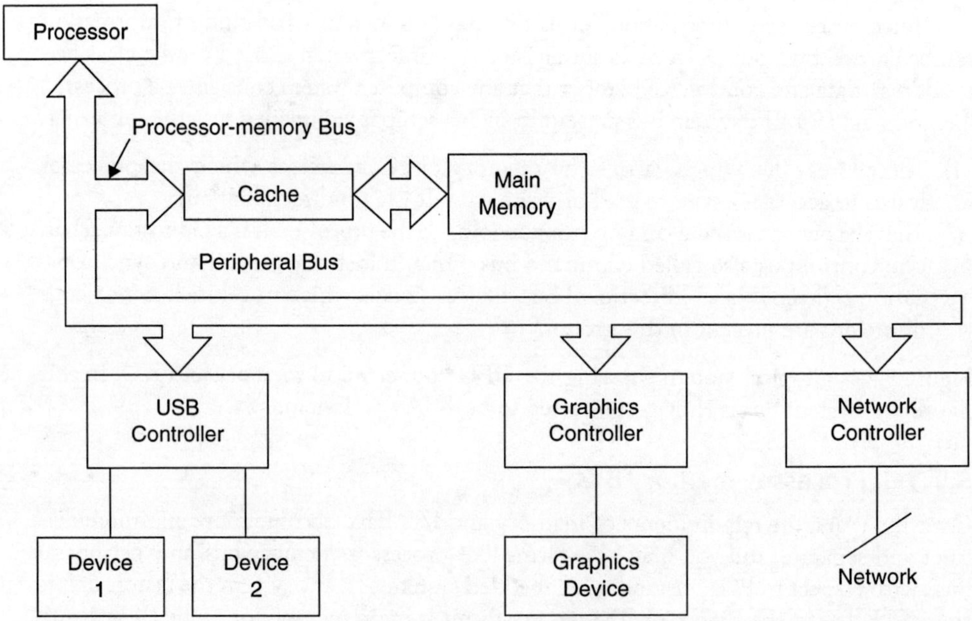

Figure 5.2 | The processor: memory bus and the peripheral bus

tend to be slower in response (compared to semiconductor memory), peripheral buses are slower compared to internal buses. Peripherals are of different varieties with differing electrical and mechanical characteristics, applications and are made from different materials, technologies, etc. This is the reason for having various kinds of peripheral buses, with different sets of control signals associated with them. For example, the requirements of a printer are quite different from the needs of a video monitor. All these also necessitate an extra 'controller' or an interfacing chip between the processor and the peripheral. This also dictates the need for different kinds of peripheral buses of different data rates, electrical specifications and mechanical dimensions. In Figure 5.2, we see that usually an I/O controller is needed to interface between the processor and I/O devices. The figure shows a USB controller, graphics controller, network controller, etc. connected to their respective devices.

5.1.3 | Embedded Processors/Microcontrollers

At this point of our discussion, we need to make a clear distinction between a general purpose processor (like Pentium) and an embedded processor or microcontroller (like 8051, PIC, ARM, etc). The former is dedicated to computation and for communicating with the external world, its 'I/O interface', that is, I/O controllers are external to the processor chip. The latter, on the other hand, is designed to act as a single chip computer, and has memory and I/O controllers internal to the chip. Figure 5.3 shows a typical embedded processor's internal block diagram with a number of peripheral controllers inside the chip. For a simple embedded system, it is highly probable that the RAM and ROM available internally are sufficient, and that the I/O needed can be directly connected to

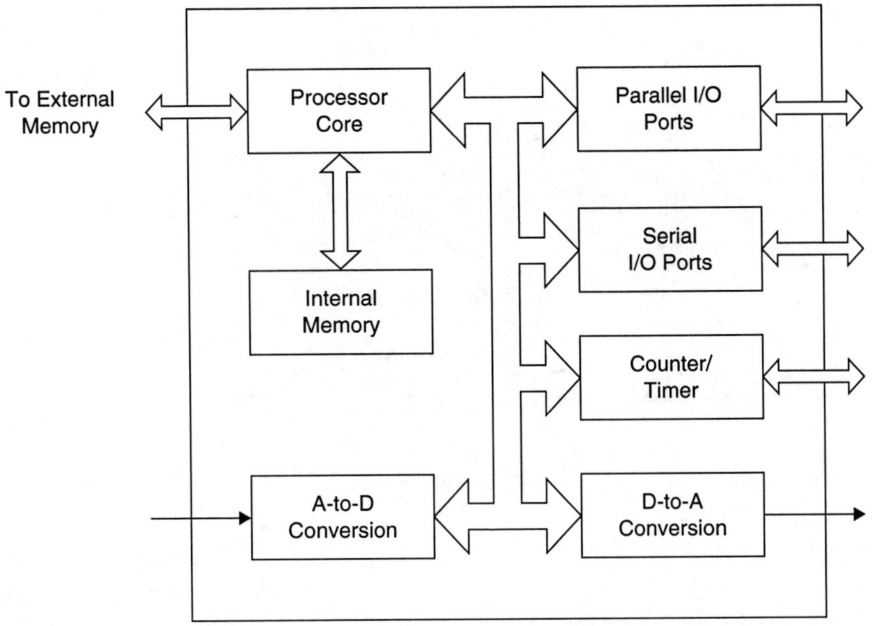

Figure 5.3 | Internal block diagram of an embedded processor

the port pins. In this case, the processor-memory bus is internal to the chip, and there is no need for an external peripheral bus.

Now, as embedded systems themselves have become big and complex, the resources available inside the processor chip may not be sufficient. Extra memory and more peripheral controllers become necessary. Then we need an **embedded board,** which needs at least one peripheral bus to connect to the extra peripherals and the memory needed. The major components that make up the embedded board, that is, the embedded processor, I/O components and memory are interconnected via buses on the embedded board. Such a bus is called an **on-board** bus. On an embedded board, an on-board bus will be the bus which connects between the MCU (microcontroller unit) and units like EEPROM, SD card, LCD display, etc. Typical examples of on-board buses are the SPI and I2C buses. Keep in mind that in this case, all the peripherals are on this board itself.

On more complex boards, multiple buses may be found on the same board. When different buses connect components that need to inter-communicate, **bridges** on the board act as the interface between the various buses and carry information from one bus to the other.

There are also **off-board** or expansion or external buses which connect the board with another board or with standard external peripherals. For example, the USB is an off-board bus. For such buses, there are connectors on the board. See Figure 5.4 which shows connectors for Ethernet, USB, RS-232, etc.

With this brief introduction, let us attempt to understand different types of 'peripheral' buses used in embedded systems. There are 'n' number of buses available in the industry. We will attempt a study of some of the standard and popular buses.

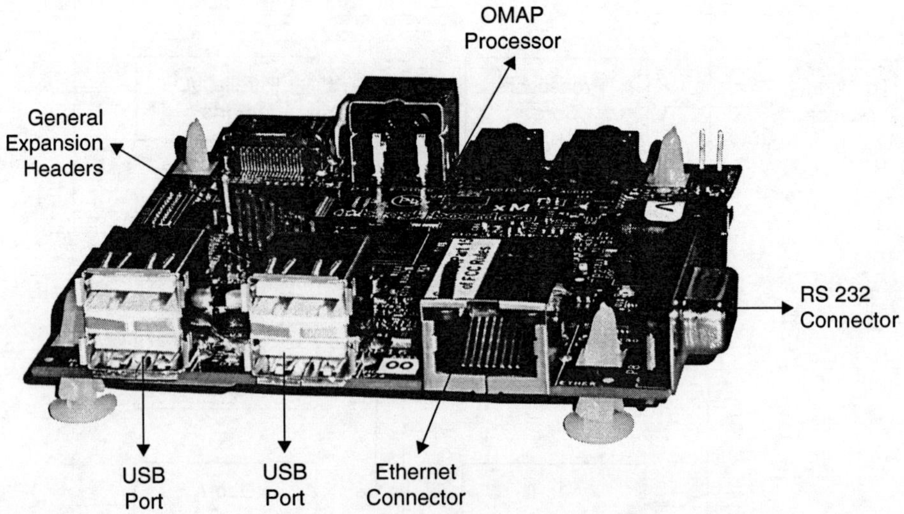

Figure 5.4 | An embedded board with connectors to many external buses

5.1.4 | Parallel vs Serial Buses

When data, address and control signals are transported in parallel, we have parallel buses. All the early buses were entirely parallel. To make this point clear, let's look at the buses of a general purpose computer (something that most of us are very familiar with). Some time back, many of the buses of the PC were parallel, for example, the printer port; all PCs had a parallel port to which a printer could be connected. Besides this, inside the PC also, the earlier buses for connecting expansions boards were all parallel, that is, the ISA, EISA (Industry Standard architecture and Extended Industry Standard architecture, which is now obsolete), PCI (Peripheral Component Interconnect bus for expansion boards), ATA (AT Attachment, for the hard disk) and so on. Other important buses like the multibus, VL bus, MCA buses, etc. were also parallel.

However, of late, things have changed, with all the above buses being replaced by serial buses. Thus, PCI has been replaced by the serial PCIe (Express), ATA by serial ATA (SATA, as it is called), the printer and many peripherals have accepted the USB as its standard bus. This is so for the PC.

Now for the embedded world—the on-board buses associated with embedded systems is all serial, for example, the I2C, SPI., so also the off-board buses like PCIe, USB and so on. Keep in mind that associated with each of these buses, there is a standard protocol. All the buses that we will discuss are serial buses.

What is the reason for the shift from parallel to serial buses?

i) The first reason is that parallel buses require more number of physical wires. So they take up more space on the PCBs and the ICs involved need a lot of pins.
ii) Over the years, the widths of the data and address buses have increased. The issue of 'skew' has become more prominent. Skew occurs when data travelling along

different physical wires reach the destination at different time instants, and tends to distort the received data. This problem becomes more acute with the increase in bus widths.

iii) When there are many physical wires, the possibility of crosstalk between them is also high.

All these problems are avoidable by serial communications, which, in its wake, has brought about a new and different set of issues to resolve.

5.1.5 | Serial Communications

Simplex, Half-Duplex and Full-Duplex Communication

A Simplex Connection is a connection in which the data flows in only one direction, from the transmitter to the receiver. This type of connection is useful if data does not need to flow in both directions (for example, from the computer to the printer or from the mouse to the computer.)

A Half-duplex Connection (sometimes called an alternating or semi-duplex connection) is a connection in which data flows in one direction or the other, but not both at the same time. At a time, transmission is done only in one direction and thus the full bandwidth of the line can be used for the transmission (like when talking on a radio).

A Full-duplex Connection is a connection in which data flows in both directions simultaneously.

Each end of the line can thus transmit and receive at the same time, which means that the bandwidth is divided by two for each direction of data transmission if the same transmission medium is used for both directions. Talking over a telephone line is a typical case of full-duplex transmission. The serial port on the PC is a full-duplex device meaning that it can send and receive data at the same time. In order to be able to do this, it uses separate lines for transmitting and receiving data.

Transmission Rate For parallel data transfer, the data rate is specified in bytes/second, but for serial communications, it always **bits per second (bps)** that is specified, because the data is sent one bit at a time. When you see the words Mbps and Kbps, translate it to Mega and Kilo 'bits per second'.

5.1.5.1 | *Some Features of Buses*

Synchronous and Asynchronous Buses A synchronous bus is timed by a clock signal. The bus can run very fast and the interface logic will be small. Every device on the bus must run at the same clock rate and the bus must necessarily be short to avoid clock-skew problems.

An asynchronous bus is not clocked. It follows a handshake protocol. It can accommodate a wide variety of devices, and the bus can be lengthened without worrying about clock-skew or synchronization problems.

5.1.6 | Bus Arbitration

When dealing with buses, a term that will frequently be encountered is 'bus arbitration'. Before discussing each of the buses, it will be apt to understand what this term means.

The activities that occur on a bus are called bus transactions. It amounts to putting up an address and sending/receiving data. The device that initiates a transaction is called a 'master' and the device that follows the orders of the master is called the slave. In a system, the main processor is the master; but for peripheral buses, the processor need not be called upon to initiate transactions, instead, the 'controllers' for the specific buses take charge of this activity. For example, the USB controller handles the USB transactions; similarly, we have controllers for I2C, SPI, etc.

The simplest system is one in which there is one master and one slave. A more complicated system will be one with one master and many slaves. Usually only one slave can respond to the master's initiation, and that will be decided by the address of the slave, only the 'addressed' slave need respond.

A complex system is one with many masters and many slaves. It can happen that more than one master will want to 'drive' the bus—this condition is called 'bus contention'—it is apparent that only one of the masters can be allowed 'grant' of the bus. The solution to this problem is 'bus arbitration'. When there are multiple masters, each master will have its own hardware arbiter to 'stake its claim' for the bus. There will also be a scheme for deciding which device ultimately gets the bus.

5.1.6.1 | *Bus Arbitration Schemes*

For any system, the arbitration scheme designed to be used must balance two factors.

i) **Priority:** The highest priority module must be serviced first.
ii) **Fairness:** Even the lowest priority module should be able to get service.

In all schemes, there is a central arbiter which will act to control and restrict bus access. This will be part of the I/O controller hardware and software. We will discuss three simple schemes for bus arbitration.

5.1.6.2 | *Daisy Chaining*

This scheme uses three lines: Bus request, bus grant and bus busy as shown in Figure 5.5. Each of these lines is shared by all the potential bus masters which are 'daisy chained', that is, connected in a cascaded fashion. The priority of the modules is fixed by their physical connection, left to right, meaning that the modules closer to the central bus arbiter have the higher priorities.

One or more modules may place a bus request on the common line and this is received by the central arbiter. It sends out a bus grant signal, provided the 'bus busy' line is inactive. This bus grant signal propagates from left to right and is accepted by the first module which had asked for the bus. It activates the bus busy signal and uses the bus. Thus, the bus grant signal does not propagate beyond this.

This scheme is very simple, but is obviously not a fair scheme. The priority of the modules is fixed up by the physical connection which cannot be changed once wired up, and a low priority module may be locked up permanently. The delay is propagating the

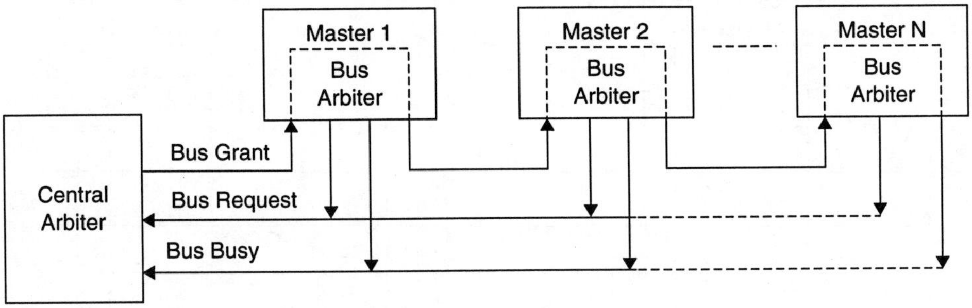

Figure 5.5 | Daisy chaining scheme of bus arbitration

bus grant signal from the left to right also limits the number of modules that can be accommodated in the system.

5.1.6.3 | *Parallel Arbitration Scheme*

This is also called the independent requests scheme. Here, a master module may output the request (REQ) only if the system bus is not busy. The centralized arbiter issues a bus grant signal to the module originating the highest priority request. Thus, this module can acquire the control of the system bus and it then activates the common 'bus busy' line. This is depicted in Figure 5.6. The priority may be preset (in this case, it can happen that low priority master modules cannot access the system bus at all, or after a long delay only), or it may use a round-robin scheme (the highest priority at a particular time

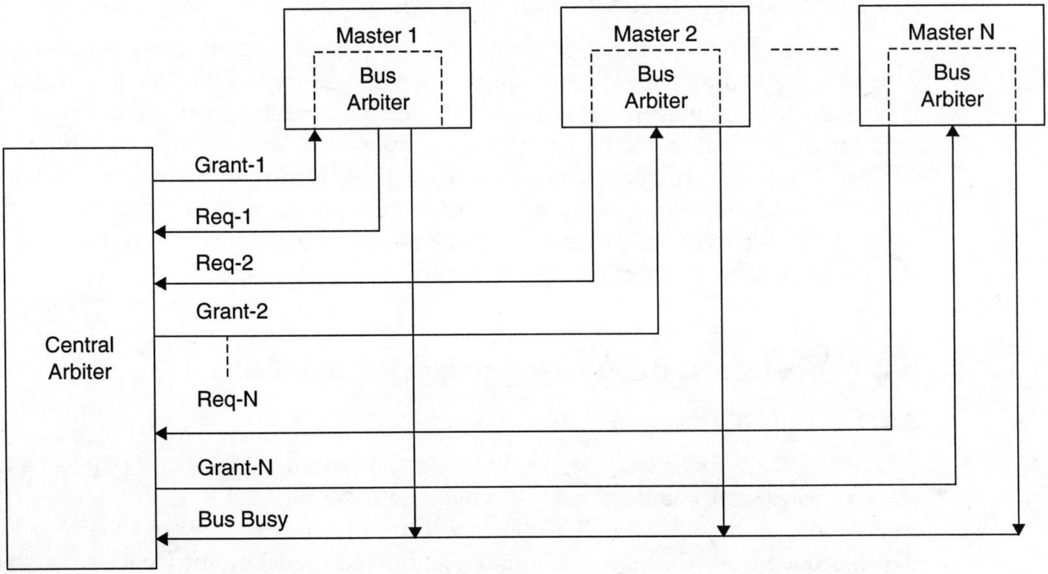

Figure 5.6 | Parallel arbitration scheme

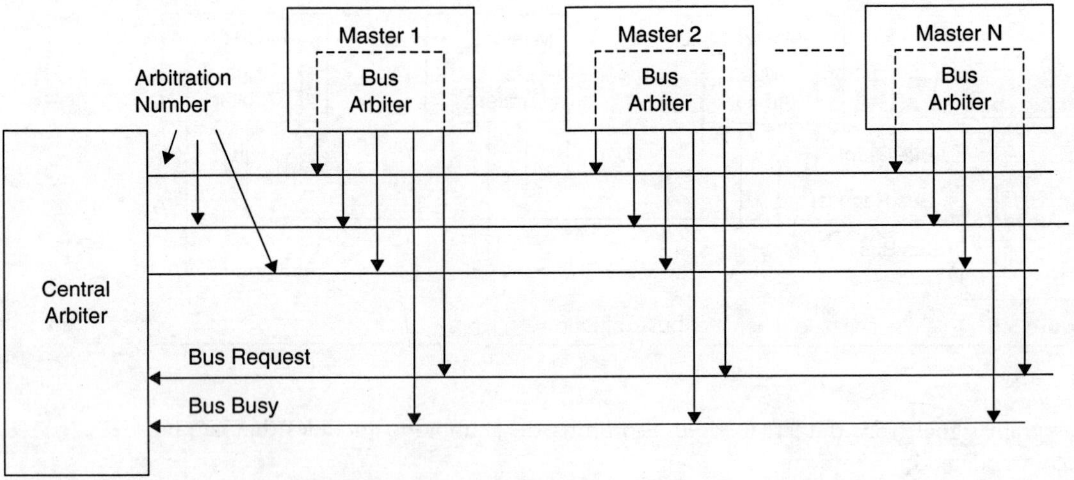

Figure 5.7 | Distributed arbitration by self-selection

instant is assigned to the right side neighbour of the master module currently using the system bus). In the latter case, all master modules have equal chance in accessing the system bus over a long time period. In the case of very large systems, a distributed version of the arbiter is used usually (the centralized version shown is failure critical).The demerit of this scheme is that each module needs one signal line for bus request and one for bus grant—two dedicated lines just for bus access.

5.1.6.4 | *Distributed Arbitration by Self-Selection*

This is a type of polling scheme. See Figure 5.7. Each module has an arbitration number with an associated priority. When multiple modules ask for the bus, the one with the highest arbitration number (not necessarily higher numerically) gets the bus. When bus conflicts arise, it will be resolved in favour of the module with the highest arbitration number. Along with a request, a module will also make known its arbitration number to the others. Each requesting device will compare this number to its own number and the one with the highest number wins. This scheme should allow dynamic reallocation of arbitration numbers to make it a truly fair scheme.

5.2 | On-board Buses for Embedded Systems

5.2.1 | The I2C Protocol

I2C or I^{2}C stands for 'Inter-Integrated Circuit' and is a simple 'two wire' protocol with just two wires, and was developed by Philips in 1980 for its TV applications which required the connection of a CPU to many ICs. Today, this bus is very widely used in the embedded field. This is a synchronous, half duplex, serial protocol and is also byte oriented, which means that one byte is sent, but one bit at a time in a serial fashion. After each byte, an acknowledgement is to be sent by the receiver IC to the sender IC.

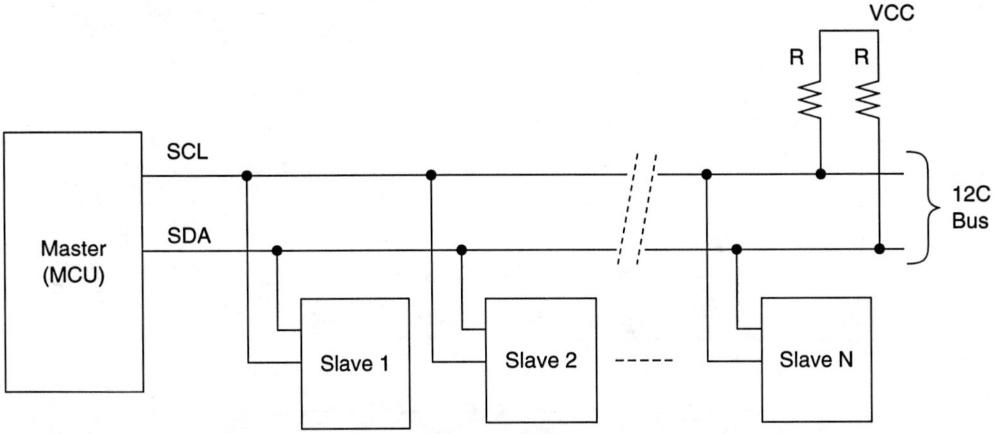

Figure 5.8 | I2C devices with one master and N slaves

In its simplest form, this can have one master and many slaves (Figure 5.8). The master, usually a microcontroller unit (MCU), can transmit as well as receive, so also the slaves depending on whether they are input or output devices. For example, a slave which is a ROM can only be read from, an LCD controller can only be written to, while an external RAM chip can be read and written into.

The two signal wires are bidirectional and carry the signals SCL, the serial clock and SDA the serial data. Each device has its own unique address, usually fixed by hardware. Figure 5.8. shows the two active wires connected to pullup resistors (wired AND connection), indicating that they are open collector or open drain connections, depending on whether the technology is BJT or MOS.

5.2.1.1 | *The I2C Protocol*

Now let's have a look at the talk session between a master and its slaves. Refer to Figure 5.9.

i) First, the master issues a START signal. This signal causes all the slaves to come to attention and listen. The start condition corresponds to the action of the master pulling the SDA line low, when the clock (SCL) is high.
ii) The first byte sent by the master is the address. This address (7-bit) is sent serially on the SDA line (MSB first). Note that the bits on the SDA line are synchronized by the clock signal on the SCL line which means that the data on the SDA line is read during the time that the clock on the SCL line is high (data is valid at the L to H transition of the clock).
iii) Just after this, the master also sends the R/W signal indicating the direction of data transfer (see Figure 5.9 a). Note that all activities are synchronized by the clock.
iv) Only one of the slaves will have the broadcasted address, and on realizing that its address matches with this address, the particular slave responds by sending an 'acknowledge' signal back to the master.
v) Now a byte can be received from the slave if the R/W bit is set to READ, or be written to the slave, if otherwise (see Figure 5.9b).

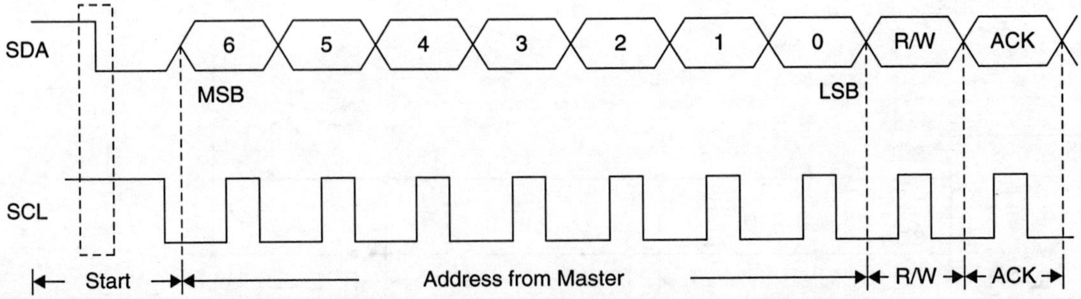

Figure 5 9a | The START condition and broadcast of the address by the master

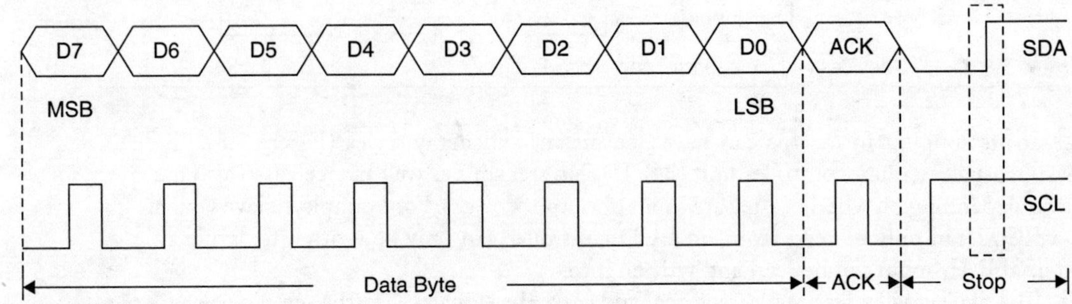

Figure 5.9b | Data transfer between the master and slave

vi) Once this data transfer is over, the device (master or slave) that has received the byte sends an acknowledge signal. Acknowledgement is when the receiver drives SDA low.

vii) If more bytes are to be transferred, steps v and vi are repeated.

viii) After this, the master pulls the SCL high, and then the SDA line also. This amounts to a STOP condition when the bus is idle, also indicating that it is available for use by other slaves.

The I2C bus was originally developed as a multi-master bus. This means that more than one device initiating transfers can be active in the system. In such a case, each master will have to arbitrate for the bus. I2C controllers have the additional hardware and protocol for this.

There are three standards for I2C bus and have the following three speeds:

i) Slow (under 100 Kbps)
ii) Fast (400 Kbps)
iii) High-speed (3.4 Mbps)

5.2.1.2 | *Extended Addressing*

Due to the popularity of the I2C bus, the 7-bit address space soon got exhausted. For those who are designing new I2C compatible ICs, this became a problem and so the I2C standard has been updated to implement a 10-bit addressing mode. A chip that conforms to the new standard, receives two address bytes. The first consists of the extended addressing reserved address including the 2 upper bits of the device address and the Read/Write bit. The second byte contains the 8 lower bits of the address. Any new design should implement this new addressing scheme.

The I2C protocol is very simple, but it is not as fast as the competing SPI scheme (Section 5.2.2.). I2C devices include EEPROMs, thermal sensors, real-time clocks and similar peripherals which can have one data line and a clock line, and can be programmed by an MCU. Many standard MCUs (PIC,AVR, PSoC, ARM, etc.) have I2C 'hardware' within and SDA and SCL lines as pins, so that the protocol can be implemented with ease. Since the hardware engine for this is already available, the user need only be concerned about writing the software for implementing it.

5.2.2 | The SPI Bus

This is a bus developed by Motorola.

SPI stands for 'Serial Peripheral Interface' and as the name suggests it is a serial data transfer protocol, which is synchronous and full duplex (data can be sent in both directions simultaneously), between a microcontroller unit (MCU) and a peripheral. As a system, it is a single master, multi-slave system, in which only one of the slaves is to be enabled at a time. It is a master slave protocol, in the sense that the master is the unit that generates the clock signal and initiates data transfer. When the master does this, data transfer occurs in both directions (simultaneously).

Figure 5.10a shows the signals of the SPI bus in a single slave configuration. There are four wires for the bus: SCLK, the clock generated by the master; MOSI, which carries data from the master to the slave; MISO which carries data from the slave to the master; and SS, the slave select signal. The last pin SS (Slave Select) of the master is to be connected to the chip enable pin of the slave to be selected, and is usually an active low signal.

MOSI stands for Master Out, Slave In
MISO stands for Master In, Slave Out

Now see Figure 5.10b which shows a multi-slave SPI configuration. The master is usually a microcontroller which has an SPI controller with the specified pins. The MCU's SPI controller unit has three SS pins, but only one slave is selected at a time. Slaves that are currently not selected should have their MOSI and MISO tristated and thus be isolated from the system.

5.2.2.1 | *The SPI Protocol*

The transfer of data using an SPI interface can be thought of as a large shift register shared between the master and slave devices. Data is clocked IN at the same time as it is clocked OUT of the devices (the clock is shared by the two devices). In addition, there should be a transmit buffer register at the transmitter side, and a receive buffer register at the receiver side.

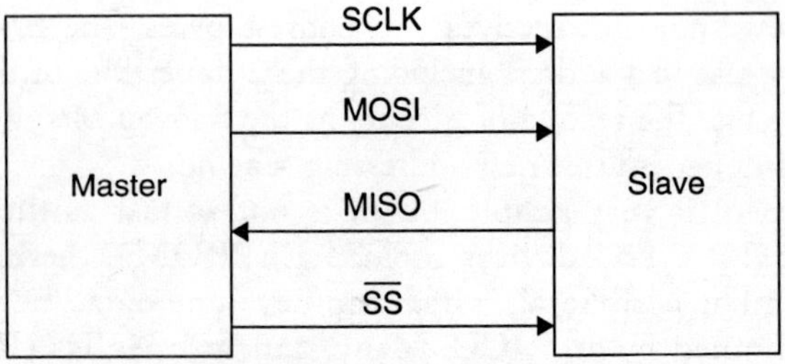

Figure 5.10a | SPI signals with the master and one slave

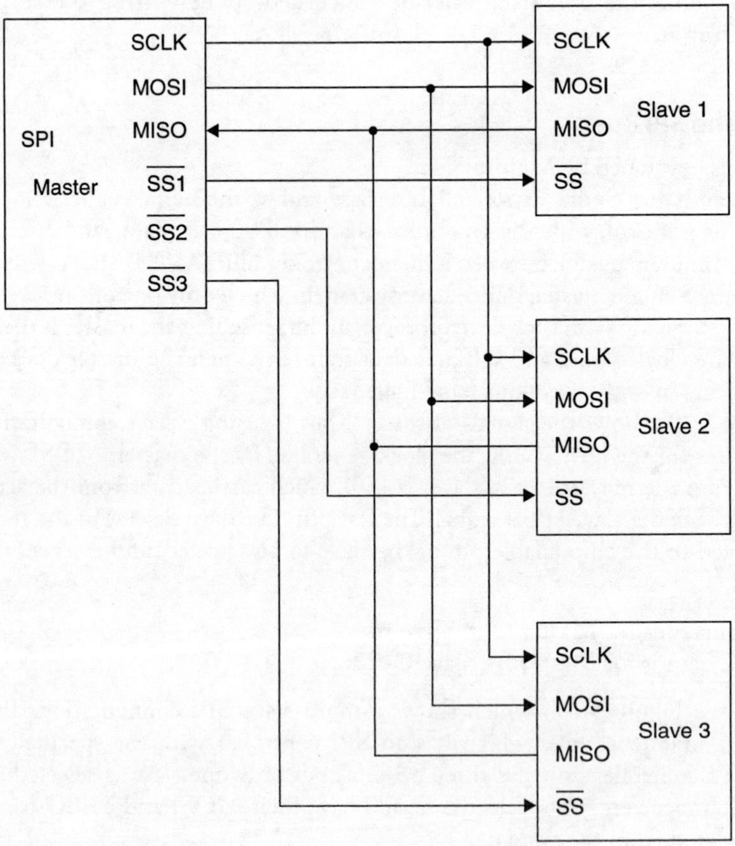

Figure 5.10b | SPI connections for one master and three slaves

The SPI protocol behaves like a ring buffer, so that whenever the master sends a byte to the slave, the slave sends a byte back to the master. Essentially, two actions take place in an SPI clock cycle which are as follows:

i) The master sends a bit on the MOSI line which the slave reads from the same line
ii) The slave sends a bit on the MISO line and the master reads it from that same line

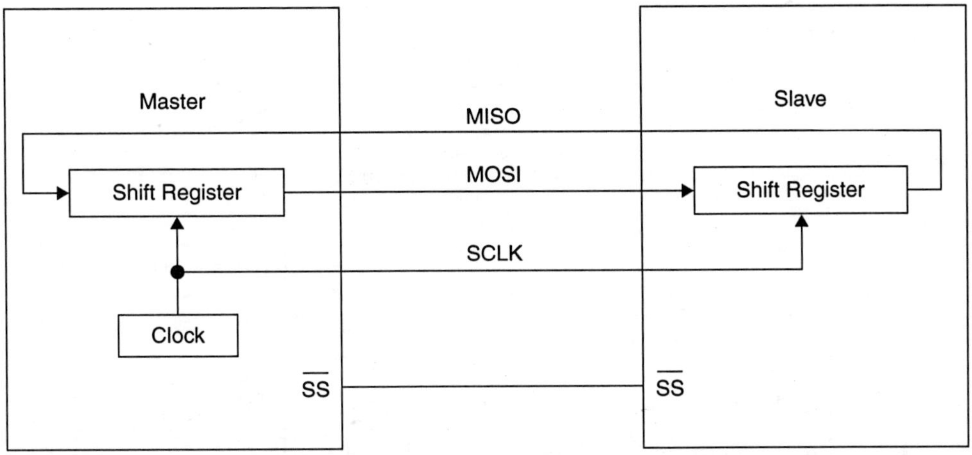

Figure 5.11 | SPI transactions using shift registers

Figure 5.11 shows the data transfer between a master and a slave. There are shift registers in the master and slave which are serially connected using the MOSI and MISO pins. In this interconnection, a bit is shifted from master to slave and slave to master simultaneously (full duplex). Not all transmissions require all these operations to be meaningful but this is the way the protocol works. If, say, the individual shift registers are 8 bits long, it is apparent that after 8 clock cycles, the data in the master and slave gets exchanged. The length of the shift registers is decided by the manufacturer of the SPI controller.

Once a set of data has been transmitted, the buffer at the transmitter side should get fresh data to be sent. Similarly, the received data should be copied and saved at the receiver side. This process can continue until the required block of data is transferred.

5.2.2.2 | *Points to Note*

i) SPI can operate at a higher speed compared to the I2C protocol, but it has a serious problem in that it has no acknowledge signal. So the master has no way of confirming the receipt of the data sent.
ii) The protocol works best for a single slave system.
iii) Clock frequencies up to 70 MHz are possible.
iv) Slave devices such as serial EEPROM, flash memory, LCD drivers, memory cards, serial ADCs, etc. are devices that frequently use the SPI protocol.
v) Popular MCUs like ARM, PIC, AVR, etc. have SPI controllers as a standard feature.

Figure 5.12 shows the connection between a PIC MCU and an SD card. Appendix I gives the details of SPI used with the ARM processor.

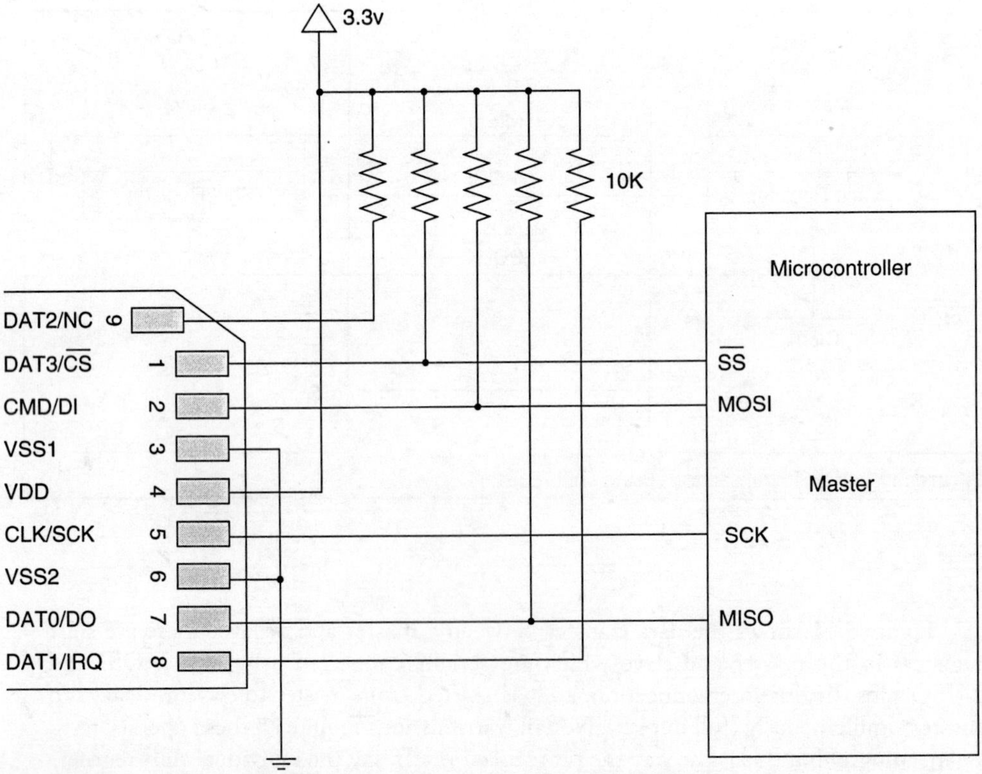

Figure 5.12 | SPI connections between a PIC MCU and an SD card

5.3 | External Buses

5.3.1 | The USB

The acronym USB stands for 'Universal Serial Bus', and it has become a very important interface for users. We have experienced the ease of plugging in different types of devices to the PC through the USB port. Many USB ports are available on the cabinet of the PC, and also on laptops, which are 'hot pluggable and hot swappable. These features make it very useful for the users. Now the trend is to shift a lot of the peripherals to the USB port. Thus we have printers, mice, keyboards, scanners, cameras, external hard disk and so on, all of which are interfaced to the PC through the USB port.

Let us start with its history. The USB 1.0 specification was introduced in 1996. The original USB 1.0 specification had a data transfer rate of 12 Mbps. USB, was created by a core group of companies that consisted of Compaq, Digital, IBM, Intel, Northern Telecom and Microsoft. One of the co-inventors of USB was Ajay Bhatt, who was later given credit by Intel. The USB 2.0 specification was released in April 2000 and was standardized at the end of 2001, with a data rate of 480 Mbps.

The USB 3.0 specification was released on 12 November 2008 by the USB 3.0 Promoter Group, and as of now in 2012, a number of USB 3.0 certified products have been released. They include host controllers, adapter cards, motherboards and hard drives. Its maximum transfer rate is up to 10 times faster than the USB 2.0. It has been dubbed the 'Super Speed USB'. The USB 3.0 port will be backward compatible with the current USB ones.

The USB 2.0 in current use, defines three data speeds:

i) **Low speed:** 1.5Mbps
ii) **Full speed:** 12Mbps
iii) **High speed:** 480Mbps

The low speed specification is meant for low speed devices like computer mouse. The full speed is for most other devices, and the high speed is meant to compete with the Firewire specifications. Firewire is a high speed port developed by Apple and is used in equipment like professional digital cameras.

5.3.1.1 | *Host and Devices*

USB is an 'asynchronous' bus which defines two components: a 'host', which is the master and many 'devices' which are slaves. The bus is host controlled and there can be only one host per bus.

Consider the case of a PC. It has a host controller in it, and thus is the host. Any peripheral plugged into the USB connector of a PC is a 'device'. Thus, memory sticks, cameras, external hard disks, etc., that we connect to the PC are devices. Only the host can act as the master—the host initiates transfers and communication takes place between a host and a device—but no communication is possible between 'devices' normally. (There is, however, a new mode named 'On the Go' mode, when a device can act as a host in a limited way).

A USB system consists of a **host controller** and **multiple devices** connected in a tree-like fashion using special hub devices. A hub is a device that contains one or more connectors or internal connections to USB devices along with the hardware to enable communicating with each device. See Figure 5.13 which shows a six-tier USB system of devices, connected through hubs at different levels.

Hubs may be cascaded, up to six levels. Up to 127 devices (including hubs) may be connected to a single host controller. To the user, this means that up to 127 devices can be connected to any one USB bus at any one given time. The limitation of 127 is because the address field in a packet is 7 bits long. The length of any cable used is limited to 5 metres.

5.3.1.2 | *USB Cables*

USB requires a shielded cable containing four wires, see Figure 5.14. The wires D+ and D-, which carry the differential signals, form a twisted pair. Besides this, there is the ground wire and also VBUS which carries a 5V supply used by a device for power.

5.3.1.3 | *USB Connectors*

The host and device have different types of connectors. Figure 5.15 shows the corresponding receptacles: the A receptacle on a host, and the B receptacle on a device or hub.

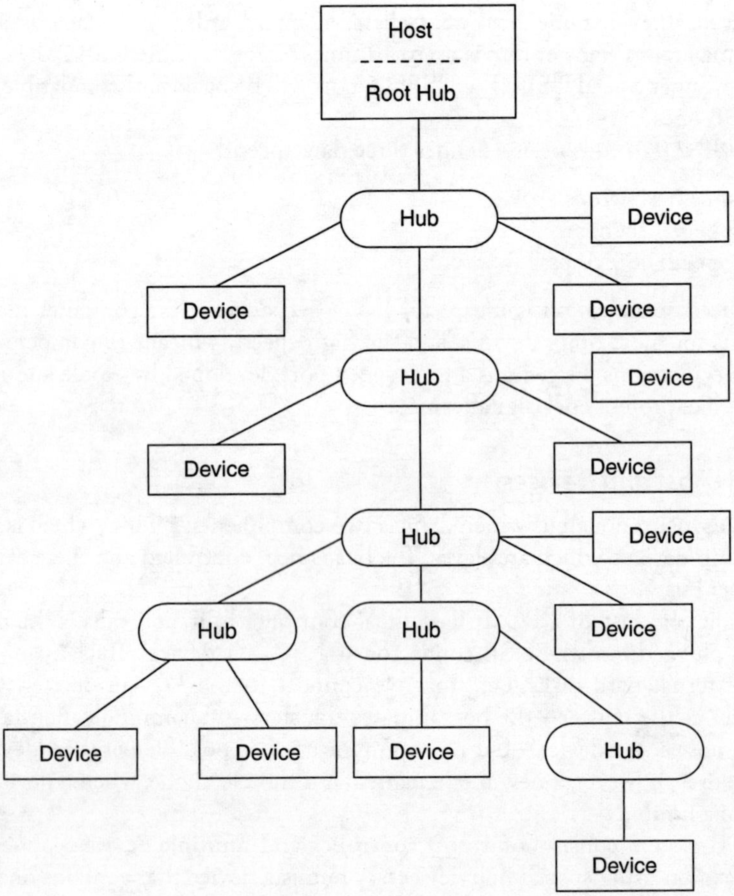

Figure 5.13 | A six-tier USB connection

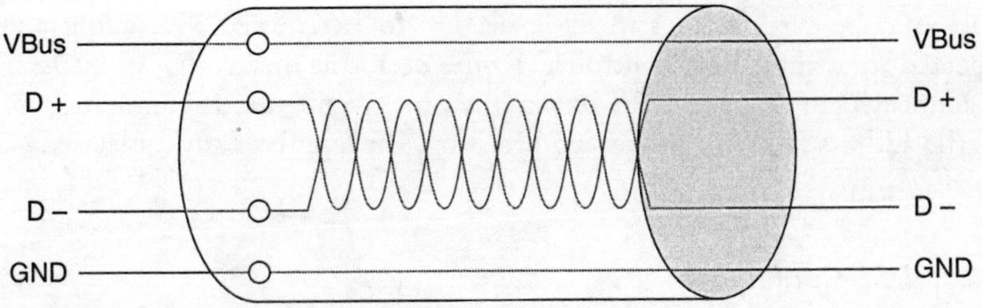

Figure 5.14 | Internal details of a USB cable

The mini-B plug and receptacle has also been defined as an alternative to the standard B connector on handheld and portable devices.

The A receptacle is what we see on a PC or laptop—the A plug on a flash memory, mouse, etc. plugs directly in to the A receptacle. The B/mini B receptacle is seen on a device like a digital camera, printer, etc. Figure 5.16 shows the connectors corresponding

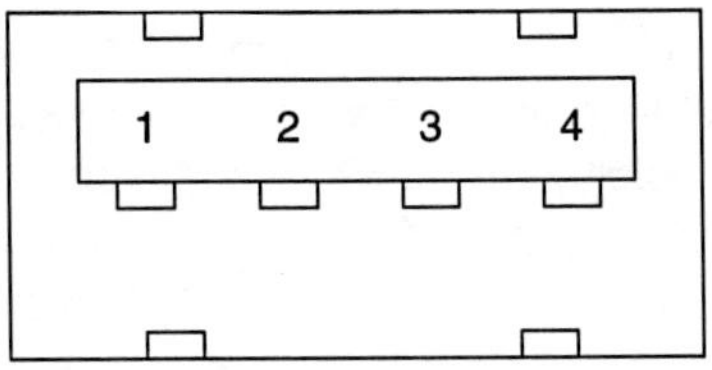

Figure 5.15a | The 'A' receptacle

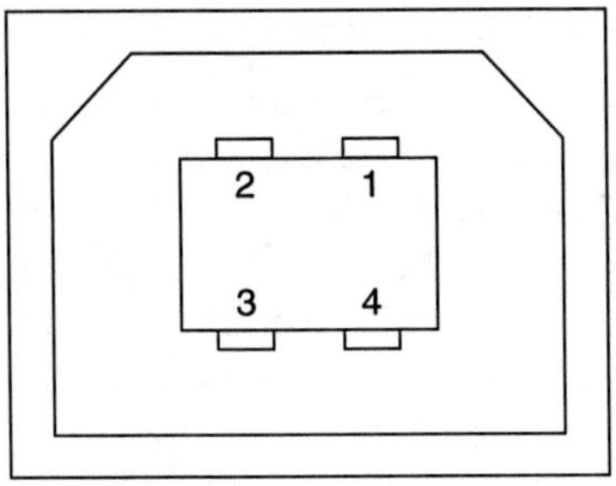

Figure 5.15b | The 'B' receptacle

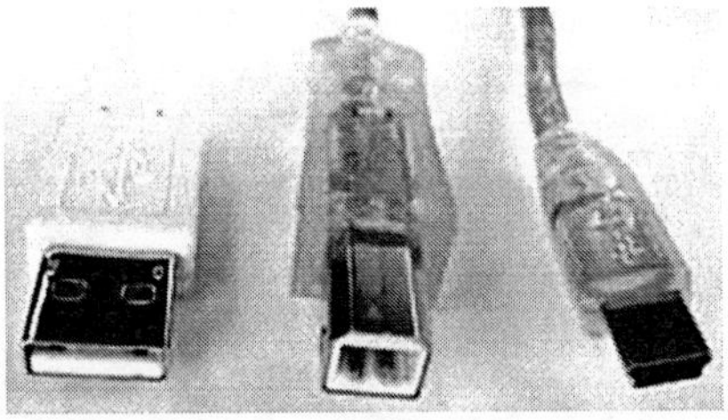

Figure 5.16 | The three types of USB connectors corresponding to A, B and mini B receptacles

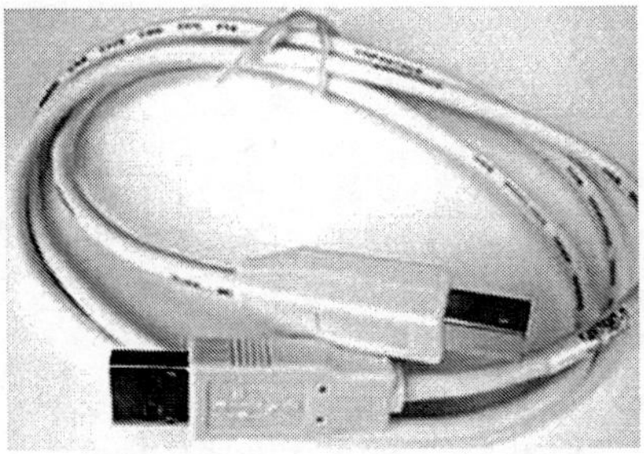

Figure 5.17 | USB cable with A and B plugs

Table 5.1 | USB Connector Pin Assignments

Pin No.	Name	Color
1	+5.0V	Red
2	Data–	White
3	Data+	Green
4	Ground	Black

to A, B and mini B receptacles. A cable with an A plug, at one end, and a B plug, at the other end, is used to connect between a host and devices like printers, digicams, etc., see Figure 5.17. Table 5.1 shows the pin numbers, the pin names and the corresponding colour codes.

5.3.1.4 | *USB–Power Issues*

The USB connector provides a single 5 volt wire from which connected USB devices may be powered. The bus is specified to deliver 100 mA current and even up to 500 mA, if the host permits it to be configured as a high powered device. This is often enough to power several devices, although this budget must be shared among all devices downstream of an unpowered hub. When USB devices (including hubs) are first connected, they are interrogated by the host controller, which enquires of each, their maximum power requirement. Devices that need more than 500 mA current must use an external power source. Thus, we see printers and certain external hard disks with external power supply, while USB-based mice and keyboards do not need any extra power.

When there is no communication between the host and a device for at least 3 msecs, the device goes to the 'suspend' state when it draws less than 0.5 mA current, until it is brought back to operation by a 'resume' signal or by a reset condition.

5.3.1.5 | *USB Signals*

The USB protocol uses differential signals for improving noise resilience. Differential signalling is when the effective signal is the difference of the signal in the two signal wires. In this case, common mode signals (usually noise) get cancelled out. USB signals are bi-phase, and signals use the NRZI (non-return to zero inverted) data encoding technique. In this technique, the signal level is inverted for each change to logic 0. The signal level for logic 1 is not changed. A '0' bit is 'stuffed' after every six consecutive ones in the data stream. This is for synchronization, when long strings of '1' appear. See Figure 5.18.

5.3.1.6 | *The USB Protocol*

USB is a protocol which is entirely host initiated—also there is only a single logical path at any one time—that path is between the host and 'one' device. All USB peripherals (devices) are slaves that obey a defined protocol.

At a time, either one 'device' or the 'host,' transmits. When a host transmits, and there are many devices in the system, only the device 'addressed' by the host can respond. This means that each device monitors the device address sent by the host. If the address broadcasted doesn't match the device's address, the device simply ignores the communication.

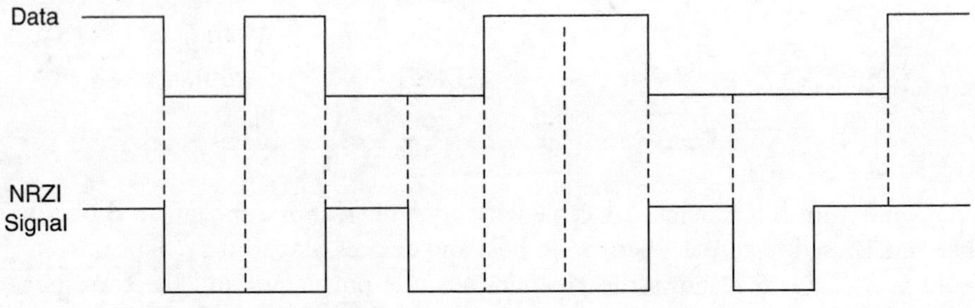

Figure 5.18 | Raw data and NRZI encoded data

When a USB device is first connected to a USB host, the device 'enumeration' process is started. This is a sort of 'interrogation' process in which the host asks the device to give complete information about itself. The enumeration starts by the host sending a reset signal to the USB device. If the device is supported by the host, the device drivers needed for communicating with the device are loaded from the operating system of the host computer and the device is set to a configured state. If, say, the host determines that the device is a 'standard' printer, the drivers for this should be available in the host computer—this is loaded into the USB system and then communication between the host and peripheral can continue, and data transfer can take place.

5.3.1.7 | *Data Transfer*

Transfer of data is designated as 'transactions' and is done using packets which are formats built up in a pre-determined way. A packet starts with a sync pattern, the data bytes of the packet follow, ending with an 'end of packet' signal. Remember that this is a serial protocol in which data is sent one bit at a time. Here, the LSB is sent first.

There are four ways in which data transfer can be done, and the chosen way depends on the type of data. Let's find out what this is all about.

i) **Control transfer:** A control transfer is a bidirectional data transfer, and is generally used for initial configuration of a device by the host. Control transfers enable the host to read information about a device, set a device's address, and select configurations and other settings. All other transfer types are unidirectional.

ii) **Bulk transfer:** Bulk transfers are intended for situations where the rate of transfer isn't critical, such as sending a file to a printer or receiving data from a scanner. Bulk transfers are designed to transfer large amounts of data with error-free delivery and no guarantee of bandwidth, which means that such applications can afford to wait, if the bus is busy handling other more important requests. Typical applications include scanners and printers.

iii) **Interrupt transfer:** Interrupt transfers are meant for devices that must receive the host's attention periodically. Low speed devices like the mouse and keyboard use this type of transfer where the device needs the attention of the host periodically. No 'interrupt' is involved here; only the type of transfer is like that in an interrupt-based system. Here, it is apparent that data should be transferred without any delay.

iv) **Isochronous transfer:** Isochronous in simple terms mean 'at regular intervals'. This is a sort of asynchronous data transmission, done at regular intervals, that is, a transmission service allowing the sending and receiving of data in equal time increments. Isochronous transfers have guaranteed delivery time but no error correcting facility. This is the only type of transfer that doesn't support automatic retransmitting of data received with errors, so occasional errors must be acceptable. Only full- and high-speed devices can do isochronous transfers. Audio and video streaming is done using this method, that is, real-time applications.

5.3.1.8 | *Plug and Play*

USB supports plug and play with dynamically loadable and unloadable drivers. This means that the user simply needs to plug the device on the bus. The host will detect this addition, interrogate the newly inserted device and load the appropriate driver, provided a driver is installed for the plugged-in device. The end user need not worry about terms such as IRQs and port addresses or rebooting the computer. Once the use is over, the user can simply plug the cable out, the host will detect its absence and automatically unload the driver.

The word 'hot pluggable and hot swappable' means that devices can be plugged in and/or swapped without switching off the power supply. For many of the buses available earlier (inside PCs and other systems), like ISA, EISA, etc., power had to be switched off before anything could be plugged in.

But then, why do we use the 'Safely Remove Hardware' utility before removing a USB device from a PC?

This is a USB device manager. When a device is plugged in a USB drive on a PC, the PC takes charge of writing and reading to/from the device. When writing, some of the data is cached, or say buffered. What this means is that the data to be written might be kept temporarily in the RAM of the PC. If the device is pulled out of the drive just as soon as you think that 'writing' is over and done with, there is a possibility that the data that is there in the disc is not actually the final and correct data. You are likely to get a corrupted file, then. But Windows automatically disables caching on USB devices, unless it has been specifically enabled. So this device manager is there simply as an extra level of security for USB 'storage devices'. The device manager causes the files to close properly preserving pointers and gives time for writing to complete fully.

5.3.1.9 | *USB And Embedded Systems*

All the time that we were discussing the USB port, we used the concept of a 'host' computer, which most of us would have visualized as the PC. But what about embedded boards? Most embedded boards have USB ports—as host ports and/or slave ports. See Figure 5.19 which shows many parts of a typical embedded board—a USB port (slave) is also seen.

Figure 5.19 | An embedded board showing a USB slave connector

In system design, usually a PC is used which has the required IDE (Integrated Development Environment). After cross compilation, the hex file is downloaded into the flash of the embedded board through the USB slave port. In early applications, the serial port was used for this. Now, that the serial port is more or less obsolete, the USB interface has become ubiquitous. Embedded boards can have host controllers also, using which embedded applications can use the board as the host (like a PC).

5.3.1.10 | *Developing USB-based Applications*

If you need to develop a USB-based application, a USB controller will be a necessity. The complexities and speed of the USB protocol are such that it is not practical to expect a general purpose micro-controller to be able to implement it using its instruction set. Dedicated hardware is required to deal with the time-critical portions of the specification, and in recent times, many MCU manufacturers have started integrating a USB controller in their products. There are some PIC and ARM chips which have this hardware built into them. Check the product range of the manufacturers of MCUs and choose the MCU which you think will solve your problem in the best way.

5.3.2 | The Firewire Port

Firewire, also known as IEEE 1394, is a high-performance serial bus originally developed by Apple in 1989. The baseline specification handles throughput rates of 100 Mbits/s, 200 Mbits/s and 400 Mbits/s. The IEEE 1394b specification increases this transfer rate to 3.2 Gb/s.

Firewire is hot-pluggable which means that devices can be connected and disconnected while the system is powered up. In addition, devices operating at different communication rates can exist on the same communications chain. It is a serial protocol which is much more complex than USB, though the connectors of both 'look' similar (see Figure 5.20).

But the difference between the USB and firewire protocols is in the speed. When large data blocks are to be transferred—such as video—from one device to another, firewire is the optimum solution. There are a number of upcoming applications which are the driving forces for the firewire standard. Following is a list of prospective applications.

5.3.2.1 | *Prospective Applications*

i) Digital television (DTV)
ii) Multimedia CDROM (MMCD)

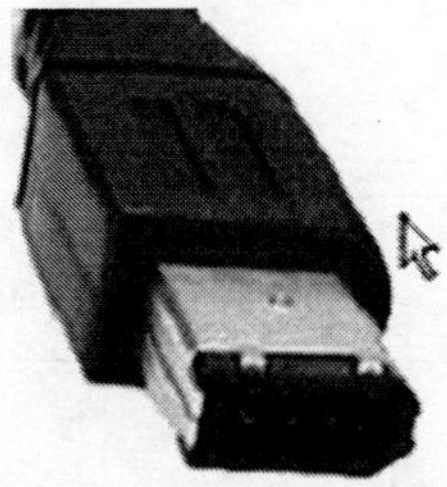

Figure 5.20 | A firewire plug-in connector

iii) Entertainment and video appliances
iv) Digital home networking
v) Printers for video and computer data
vi) Digital cameras and video conferencing cameras
vii) Industrial measurements

The range of possible applications is large. Most of the current PCs don't have a firewire port, but there are boards with firewire connectors which can be plugged inside in, if there is the need for high speed data transfer. One of the applications in which a firewire port is likely to be seen now is the professional digital camera.

5.3.2.2 | *Implementation*

Special integrated ICs are needed to implement the firewire protocol. Like ethernet, firewire is a layered transport system. The IEEE-1394 standard defines three layers: physical, data link and transaction. The physical layer provides the signals required by the firewire bus. The data link layer takes raw data from the physical layer and formats it into packets. The transaction layer takes the packets from the data link layer and presents them to the application. The remainder of the transaction functions is performed in software.

5.3.2.3 | *Topology*

The 1394 protocol is a peer-to-peer network with a point-to-point signalling environment.

A specific host is not required which means that data from a camera could be directly sent to a scanner or a printer. Similarly, a digital camera could easily stream data to a digital VCR and a DVD-RAM.

As seen in the Figure 5.21, each equipment on the bus is a node with several ports on them. Each of the nodes can act as a repeater, receiving and re-transmitting the packets received there.

Configuration of the bus occurs automatically whenever a new device is plugged in. During system initialization, each node in a 1394 bus carries out a process of bus initialization and self-identification.

Comparing USB and Firewire USB and 1394 are complementary buses, in the sense that they differ in their application focus

i) USB is the preferred connection for most PC peripherals and is used for relatively low-speed data transfer.
ii) Firewire caters to audio/visual consumer electronic devices such as digital camcorders, digital VCRs, DVD players and digital televisions which are high bandwidth applications.

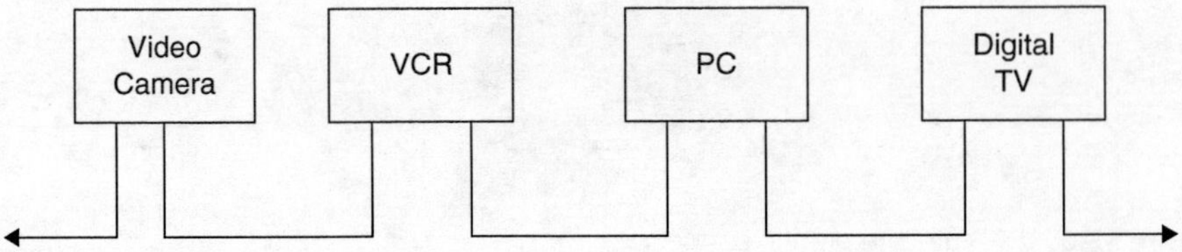

Figure 5.21 | Nodes connected through firewire

5.3.3 | The Standard Serial Port

For a long time, the standard serial port was available at the back of PCs and also in all embedded boards. This port is on its way to obsolescence, but it will be a good idea to have a look at this RS-232 compliant port. It is often called a 'legacy' port, but it is still used by hardware designed to connect to the serial port, especially for computers used as servers by companies. Laptops and Macs stopped being sold with serial ports several years before desktops did. However, if one needs a serial port, it is possible to buy one and install it.

But that is about the serial port of a general purpose computer. What about the relevance of this embedded systems? Usually embedded software is developed on a host computer and then downloaded to the MCU flash through the serial port of the computer. The connection between the PC and the target board has been replaced by the USB cable in recent cases, and for more advanced systems, there is the JTAG cable. But many embedded boards still have 'serial ports'. In some cases, it is probable that the PC does not have a serial port. In that case, a conversion cable (serial to USB and vice versa) can be used for communication between the two.

It is possible to have a two-way communication done between a PC and an embedded board using the serial cable and 'hyperterminal' software (or similar s/w) available in the PC. Refer Section 9.1.2.

Because of all these factors, let's have a 'light' discussion on RS-232, serial connectors and connections.

5.3.3.1 | *RS-232 Standards*

This is one of the early standards for serial communications. We have talked earlier, about sending data as bits as either '1' or '0'. As per TTL standards, these levels correspond to 5 V and 0 volts. However, during transmission over short distances (without a modem), say from one room to another, the TTL level signals will get corrupted easily by noise.

However, this problem does not occur normally, because we don't send or receive at TTL levels, instead we use a standard called **RS-232C**, which defines a different set of voltages/currents. RS-232 stands for **Recommend Standard Number 232** and C is the latest revision of the standard. By this standard, before being transmitted, the TTL voltage levels are changed to a level between −3 to −25 V for a '1', and +3 to +25 V for a '0' (the voltages between −3 V and +3 V is undefined). This means that before sending, the bits should be changed to this level and reconverted to TTL levels on receiving. There are some standard chips available for doing this.

5.3.3.2 | *RS-232 Level Converters*

Almost all digital devices that we use, require either TTL or CMOS logic levels. An IC for converting to and from these levels to RS-232 levels is the MAX232 (there are other ICs also for the same purpose) Figures 5.22a and b show the pinout and the connections for this chip.

5.3.3.3 | *RS-232 Connectors*

The pinout of the MAX 232 IC shows that we can get an RS-232 transmit signal and an RS-232 receive signal from it. These pins of the IC are terminated on the standard serial port. RS-232 defines a standard of 25 pins, leading to a 25 pin connector. But most serial ports need only a subset of the RS-232 standard. Most of these pins are not needed

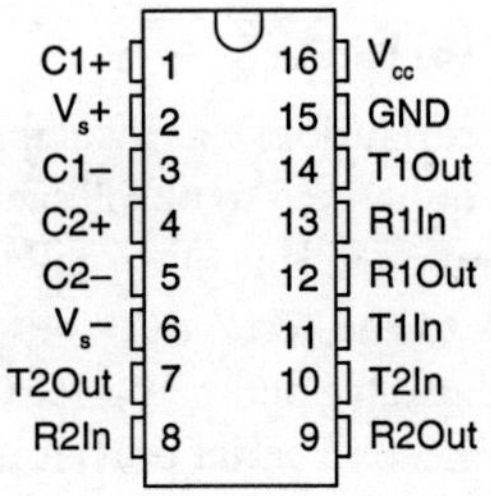

Figure 5.22a | The pin out of MAX232

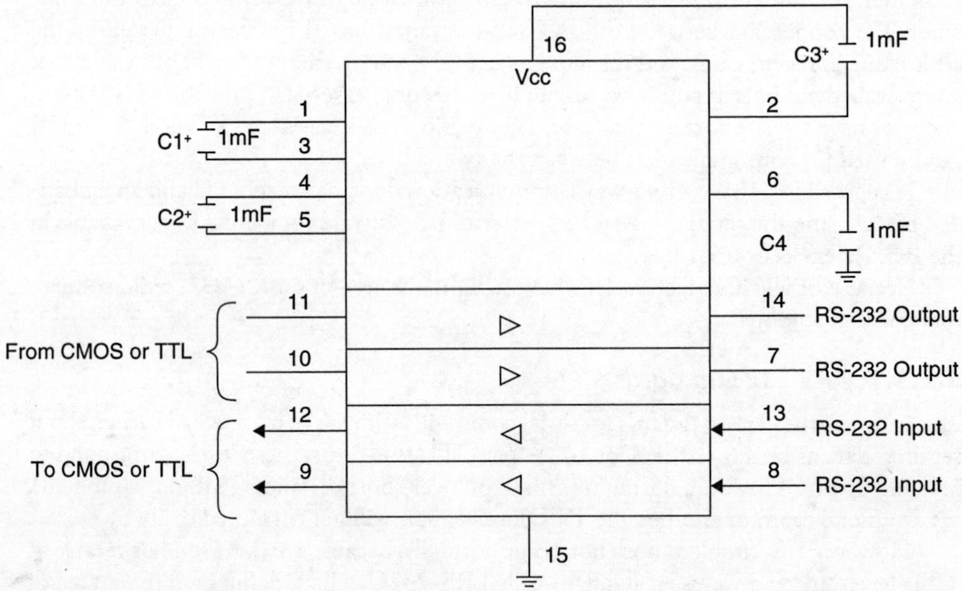

Figure 5.22b | Connections for using the chip

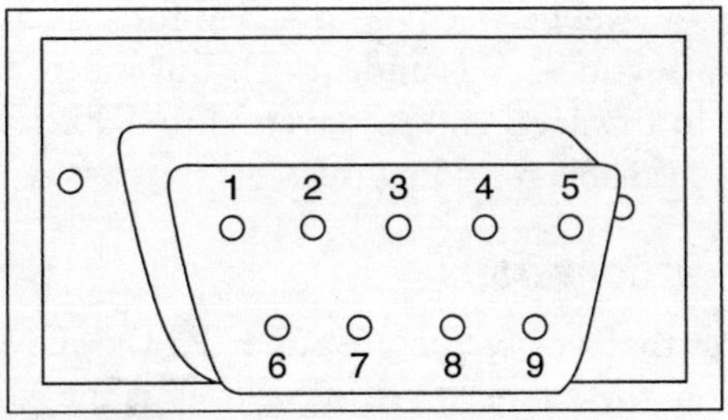

Figure 5.23 | The DB-9 connector

for normal PC communications, and indeed, most PCs are equipped with male D type connectors having only 9 pins. Figure 5.23 shows the DB-9 connector and Table 5.2 describes the pin functions of the DB9 connector. But again, even though the standard connectors have 9 pins, serial communication is possible with just 3 pins: T × D, R × D and ground. See Figure 5.24 which shows two serial ports (on two devices, say a PC and an embedded board) connected through a three wire cable.

Table 5.2 | Pin Functions of the DB-9 Connector

Pin No.	Description
1	Data carrier detect ($\overline{DCD}$)
2	Received data (R × D)
3	Transmitted data (T × D)
4	Data terminal ready ($\overline{DTR}$)
5	Signal ground (GND)
6	Data set ready ($\overline{DSR}$)
7	Request to send ($\overline{RTS}$)
8	Clear to send ($\overline{CTS}$)
9	Ring indicator (RI)

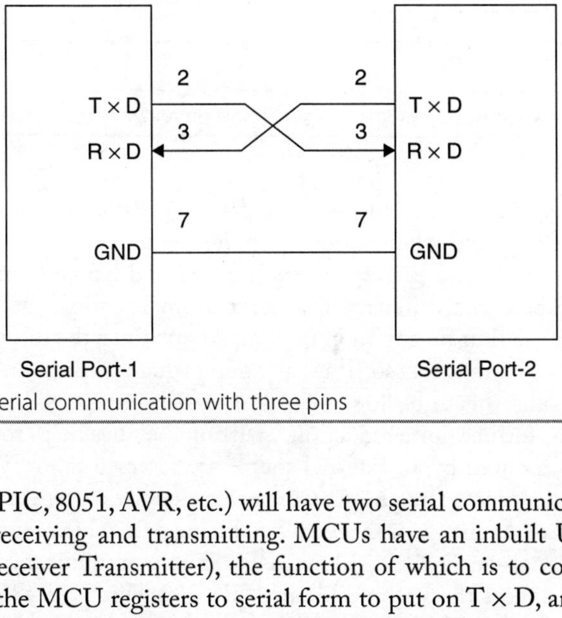

Figure 5.24 | Serial communication with three pins

Any MCU (PIC, 8051, AVR, etc.) will have two serial communication pins, R × D and T × D, for receiving and transmitting. MCUs have an inbuilt UART (Universal Asynchronous Receiver Transmitter), the function of which is to convert the parallel data available in the MCU registers to serial form to put on T × D, and also to convert the serial data received on R × D, back into parallel form. The rate at which serial data transfer occurs is determined by the 'baud rate' setting in the UART registers. To take the serial data out of the board, through the serial port, they have to be converted to RS-232 level signals, and this is done by the level converter MAX 232 IC or other ICs with similar functions.

Figure 5.25 shows the part of an embedded board which contains a MAX232 IC, an MCU, the connections of the MAX232 IC to the serial data pins of the MCU, and to the DB-9 male connector of the serial port.

5.3.4 | RS 422/RS 485

We have discussed the RS 232 serial interface in great detail, as this is a very popular interface, and long distance communication is achieved by having modems at the

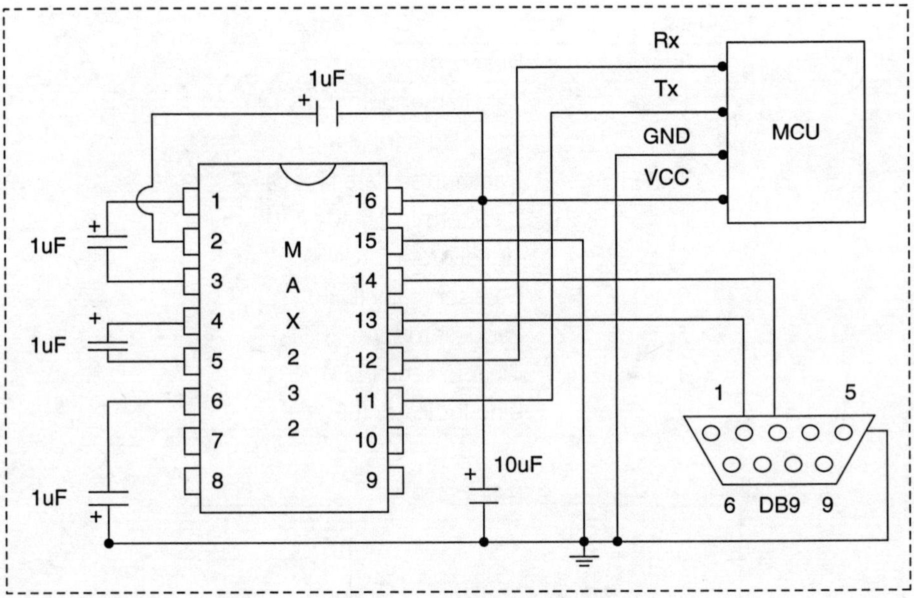

Figure 5.25 | The MAX232, an MCU and a serial port on an embedded board

transmission and reception ends. Now we talk of other serial protocols which are used in instrumentation systems and where modems are not used.

The prominent difference between these (RS 422 and RS 485) and RS 232 is that the signals here are 'balanced, differential' rather than single ended. There are two floating signal wires, V+ and V-, but no common ground. At any time, the difference in the voltages between the two wires is sensed. Thus, any noise which is common to both the wires is cancelled, and makes this to be 'low noise differential signalling'. In addition, the two wires are twisted for further noise reduction. Twisting the lines helps to reduce the noise. The noise currents induced by an external source are reversed in every twist. Instead of amplifying each other as in a straight wire, the reversed noise currents reduce each others' influence, that is, the currents get cancelled. See Figure 5.26 which illustrates this point.

Differential signals and twisting allows RS 485 to communicate over much longer communication distances than achievable with RS 232. With RS 485, communication distances of 1200m are possible.

5.3.4.1 | *RS 485 and RS 422—The Difference*

While many features of RS 485 and RS 422 are the same, there is one prominent difference. The former is a **multipoint** protocol, while the latter is **multidrop**. What do these terms mean?

Both of them allow the direct connection of intelligent devices, without the need of modems. But they are half duplex protocols. The RS 422 line driver can serve up to ten receivers in parallel. Thus, one central control unit can send commands in parallel to 10 slave devices. But these slave devices cannot send information back over a shared interface line. Thus, the network topology possible is only 'multi-drop'.

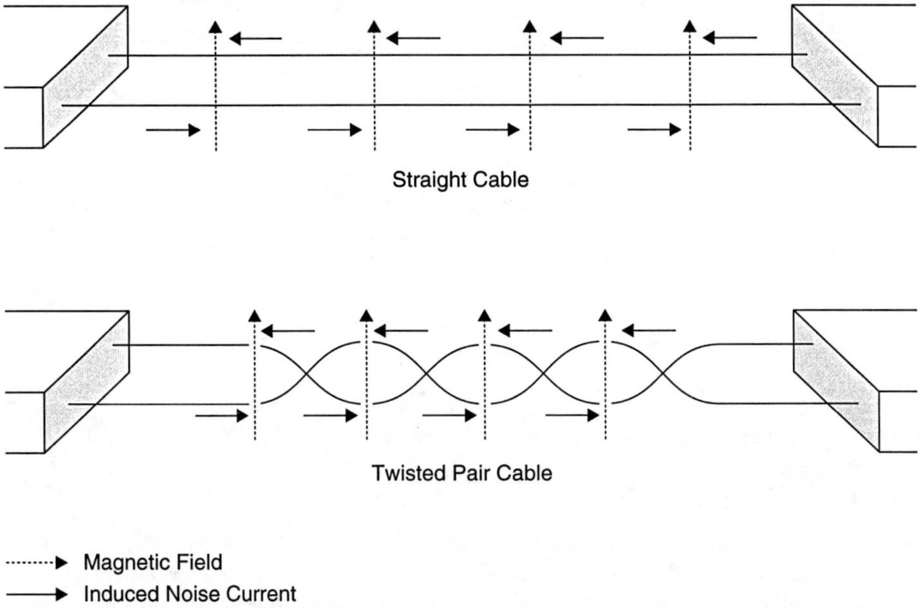

Figure 5.26 | Illustrating the effect of twisting wire pairs

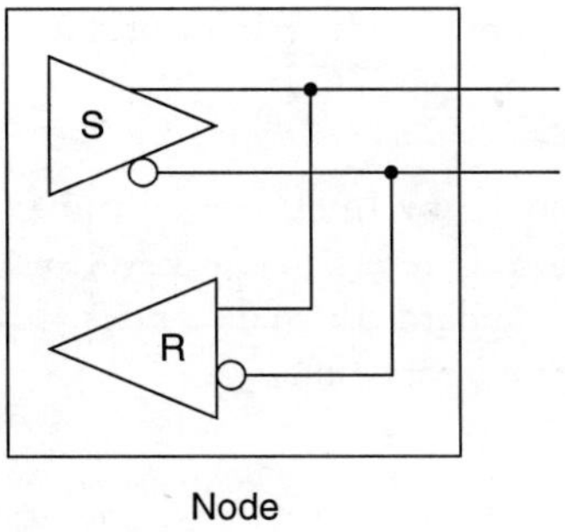

Figure 5.27 | Send and receive drivers in an RS485 node

For a multi-point network where all nodes are considered equal and every node has send and receive capabilities over the same line, an RS 485 interface can be used. Up to 32 parallel send and receive units can exist on one communication channel. Figure 5.27 shows the line driver and receiver in one node of RS 485.

Table 5.3 compares the important features of the three protocols.

5.3.5 | Ethernet

In the current world, networking between computers is very important in view of the fact that a very high percentage of personal and business communication is done electronically.

Table 5.3 | Comparison of RS 232, RS 422 and RS 485

	RS 232	RS 422	RS 485
Signal	Single ended	Differential	Differential
No of drivers (max)	1	1	32
No of receivers	1	10	32
Operation	Full duplex	Half duplex	Half duplex
Network topology	Point to point	Multidrop	Multipoint
Max distance	15m	1200m	1200m

As such, it is important to have some knowledge of the principles involved in the networking of computers and associated technology.

5.3.5.1 | *LAN, WAN and Internet*

Local area networks (LAN) are computer networks located within a small geographic area, for instance, a single building, a college campus or a business organization. The network can be as small as just three computers or as large as one that links hundreds of them. When such LANs located in different geographical areas are linked, it constitutes a Wide Area Network (WAN). The linking of LANs in WAN is accomplished by leased lines, dial up phones, satellite links, etc. The Internet, as we know, is a system of linked networks which has made the 'world wide web' a world in itself.

5.3.5.2 | *What is Ethernet?*

Ethernet was originally developed by Intel, Digital (now Compaq) and Xerox, and is now an open network standard. It refers to the LAN products covered by the IEEE 802.3 standard. It is a 'wired' standard. Three data rates are currently defined for operation over optical fibre and twisted-pair cables:

i) 10 Mbps-10Base-T Ethernet
ii) 100 Mbps-Fast Ethernet
iii) 1000 Mbps-Gigabit Ethernet

A new version named 10-Gigabit Ethernet was published in 2002. IEEE as 802.3ae supplement to the IEEE 802.3 base standard. This has slight differences from the older standard. We will discuss the type covered by the base standard.

Ethernet has been around for quite some time now, and there have been attempts to replace it by newer technologies. But the market for Ethernet is so strong that more than 85 per cent of wired LAN connected PCs use it still, because of its positive features which are listed as

i) It is easy to understand, implement, manage and maintain
ii) It allows low-cost network implementations
iii) It is a widely accepted industry standard, ensuring compatibility
iv) It is structured to allow compatibility with network operating systems (NOS)
v) It is very reliable
vi) Provides extensive topological flexibility for network installation

5.3.5.3 | *The OSI Model*

As Figure 5.28 shows, the Ethernet protocol is associated with only the data link and physical layers of the OSI model. The physical payer transforms data into bits that are sent across the physical media. The data link layer determines access to the network media in terms of frames. Its sub-layer Media Access Control (MAC) is responsible for physical addressing. The TCP/IP (Transmission Control Protocol/Internet Protocol) on Ethernet takes care of all the seven layers.

5.3.5.4 | *Network Topology*

The computers in a LAN network may be connected in the bus or star topology.

Bus In a bus topology, all devices on the network connect to one trunk cable. This makes it easy to install and configure, and is inexpensive. Ethernet in a bus topology requires no special equipment to amplify or regenerate the signal. The problem with this is that, if the trunk cable fails, all devices are affected. Figure 5.29 shows such a network.

Star In a star topology, a separate cable connects each device with a central device called a hub. Unlike the bus topology, if a cable fails, it affects only the one device connected

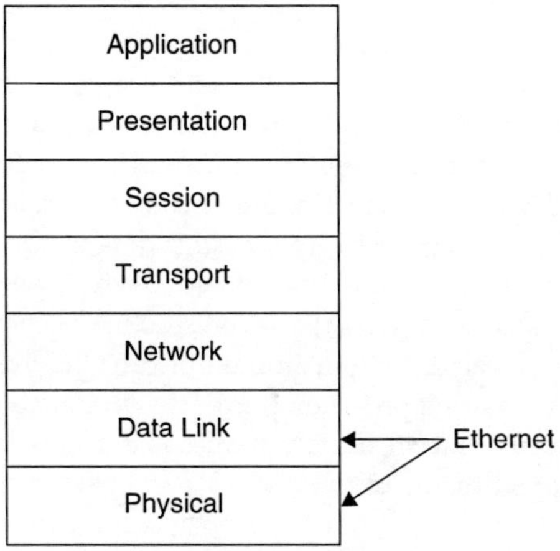

Figure 5.28 | Ethernet's association to the OSI model

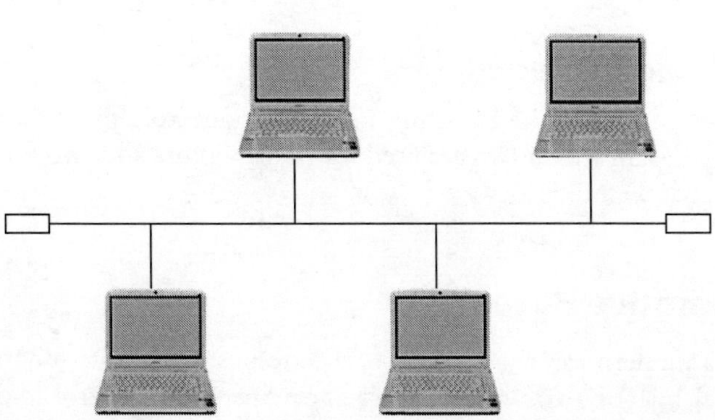

Figure 5.29 | Computers connected in a bus topology

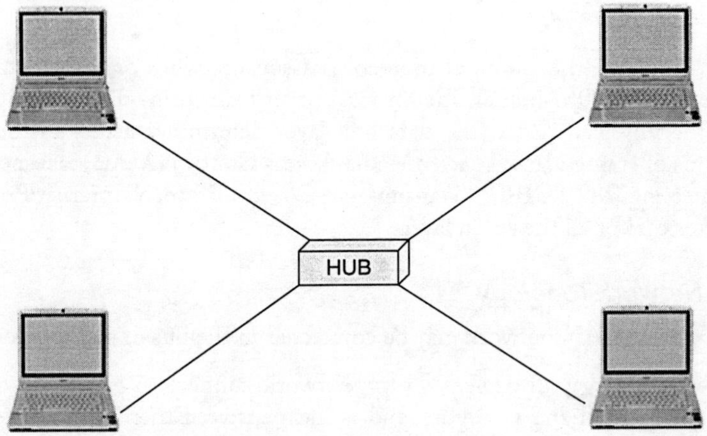

Figure 5.30 | Computers in a star connected LAN

to the failed cable. Star networks are easily expanded and are easier to troubleshoot. See Figure 5.30.

5.3.5.5 | *CSMA/CD*

CSMA/CD stands for Carrier Sense Multiple Access with Collision Detection (Refer Section 5.4.1.1). When more than two devices attempt to use the data channel simultaneously (i.e. a collision occurs), this protocol comes into action. Collision detection means that a sending device can 'detect' simultaneous transmission attempts of other senders. When two or more devices try to transmit data at the same time, a collision occurs and both transmissions become unreadable. Each device then transmits a jam signal, called a carrier, to alert all devices that a collision has occurred. All devices then go into a 'back off' mode and wait a random amount of time before attempting to retransmit. This 'random' time of waiting provision prevents simultaneous retransmissions.

Multiple access means that all devices have equal access to the network, that is, there is no priority assigned to any of the devices. Data packets can be sent at any time by any device. All devices receive the transmission and compare the packet's destination address. If the destination address matches the device's address, the device accepts the data. If the address does not match, the device simply ignores the transmission.

5.3.5.6 | *Ethernet Connector*

The network is connected to the PC using an RJ-45 connector. Inside the Ethernet cable there are eight wires, in which two are used for transmission, and two for reception. The rest are unused. See Figure 5.31.

5.4 | Automotive Buses

If you look at a modern car, the amount of electronics used in its functioning is huge. Right from fuel injection to window glass and wipers, the control is done electronically. 'Automotive electronics' has become a special field in which embedded processors,

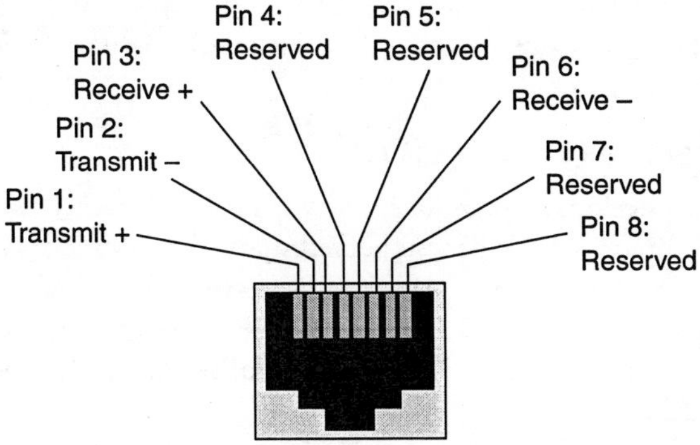

Figure 5.31 | An Ethernet connector

standard buses and the controllers for the innumerable peripherals in an automobile, have to work in unison. On-board electronics has contributed significantly to improved performance, travelling in comfort, ease of manufacture and testing, and also to 'cost effectiveness'.

Looking at a car, for instance, we can divide the requirements of electronic controls on the basis of priority (safety critical) and speed of response. Any electronic control involving the engine, brakes, etc. should have fast response and should be given priority, while door, wiper control, etc. can act much slower. Besides these, there is infotainment electronics, that is, the audio and video systems, radio, satellite navigation, etc. Some of the typical electronic modules in modern vehicles are the engine control unit (ECU), the transmission control unit TCU), the anti-lock braking system (ABS) and body control modules (BCM), and the infotainment unit.

The following are the ideas that should be apparent by now:

i) There are a number of embedded processors in any automobile, depending on the sophistication of the car—the higher the price of the car, the higher will be this number.
ii) All these processors have to communicate, and this means there are buses on which requests, grants and signals travel, and this interconnection will tend to become a 'network'.
iii) Depending on the requirements of a particular vehicle, it should be possible to plug in additional modules into the systems. This means that if 'air bag control' is not available, but is needed later, it should be possible to add the electronic module for this into the 'network'.
iv) Depending on the speed requirements of the data transfer, different kinds of buses are used in automobiles, catering to the different applications.

There are a number of vehicle buses available and popular now, some of which are as follows:

i) Controller area network (CAN), an inexpensive serial bus for interconnecting automotive components.
ii) Local interconnect network (LIN), a very low cost, low speed in-vehicle sub-network for body electronics.

iii) Media-oriented systems transport (MOST), a high-speed multimedia interface.
iv) FlexRay, a general purpose high-speed protocol with safety-critical features.

5.4.1 | Controller Area Network (CAN)

CAN is a protocol developed to reduce the wiring inside vehicles, around the year 1984 by Bosch, a company which has pioneered many developments in the automotive embedded market. For some years, it was in the testing and development stage, until finally it was installed on a Mercedes in the early 1990s. After that, the bus became very popular and is now the de facto standard for automotive buses. There are different standard versions for CAN, as shown as follows:

i) Low Speed CAN - 125 kbps - 11-bit identifier
ii) Standard CAN 2.0 A - 1 Mbps - 11-bit identifier
iii) Extended CAN 2.0 B - 1 Mbps - 29-bit identifier

In this section, we will take a look into the features of the CAN protocol, which is used in many units in a vehicle. Its interesting feature is that it is an 'interconnection network'. In vehicles, it may be used to interconnect between the engine control unit and the transmission control unit. A lower speed CAN is sufficient to connect the modules of door locks, seat control, climate control, etc. (this part is called the 'body electronics' of the vehicle). In one vehicle itself, there can be different CAN buses of different data rates. There can be other kinds of buses also in a vehicle. To connect between buses of different speeds and of different standards, 'bridges' are used. Figure 5.32 shows three different buses with different bit rates, catering to different sets of modules.

We start with saying that the CAN bus connects different nodes. What is a node? Figure 5.33 shows a CAN node, in which there is an MCU, a CAN controller and transceiver, connected to a CAN bus through line drivers. To the MCU I/O pins, sensors and actuators are connected. Because of its popularity, many microcontroller manufacturers have now added CAN controller units in their products, that is, inside the MCUs, making it a reliable, efficient and low cost option. Many PIC, AVR and ARM MCUs have CAN controllers as an integrated unit in them. CAN is now used in machine and factory automation products as well. Figure 5.34 shows a CAN bus and a number of CAN nodes connected to it.

5.4.1.1 | *The CAN Protocol*

How does CAN work?

Case 1: One Node Sends a Message CAN is a message based protocol. This means many things, let's look at it this way. One node 'broadcasts' a message, this means that every other node can use it. But unlike I2C, none of the nodes have addresses. So then, which node receives the broadcast message? That depends on the content of the message. The message has a field with an 'identifier', which also indicates a priority. The receiving nodes do an acceptance test for the identifier of the message to verify if the message is relevant for it, and accepts it if it is relevant. Otherwise the message is ignored. The selection processing is called 'acceptance filtering' at each station (node).

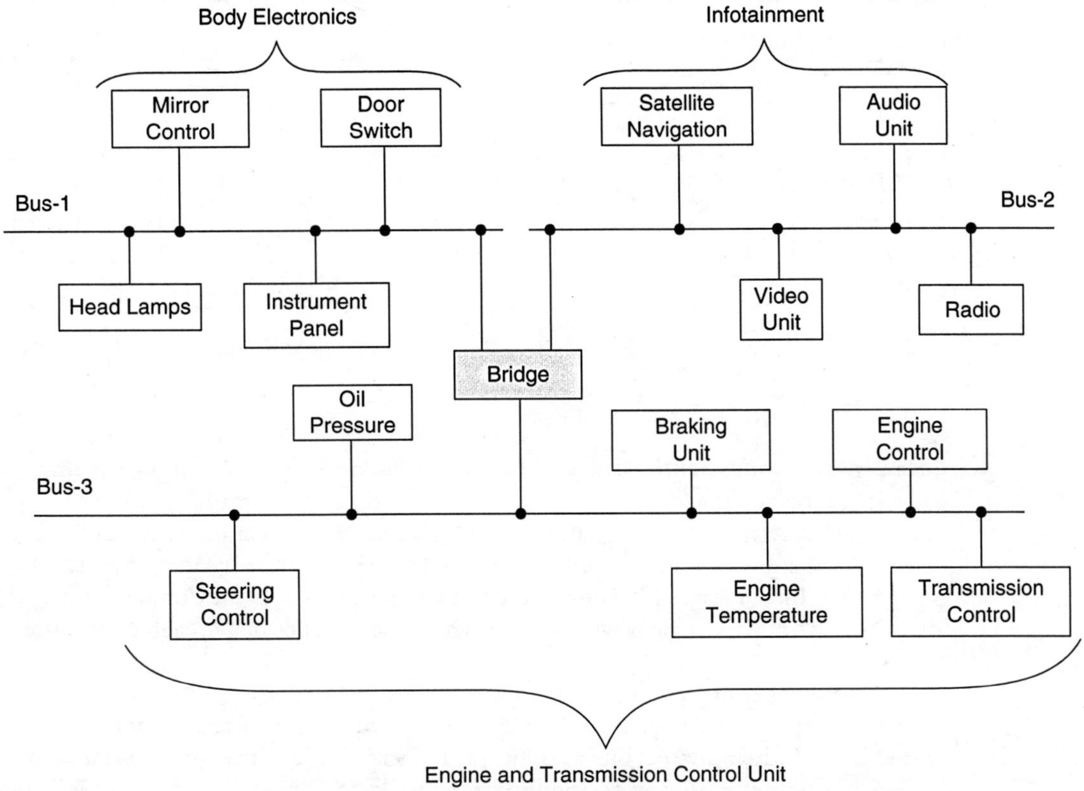

Figure 5.32 | Automotive electronic modules networked using different buses

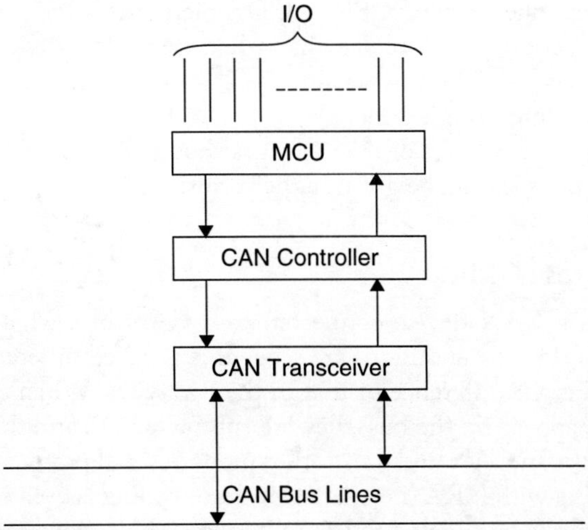

Figure 5.33 | A CAN node

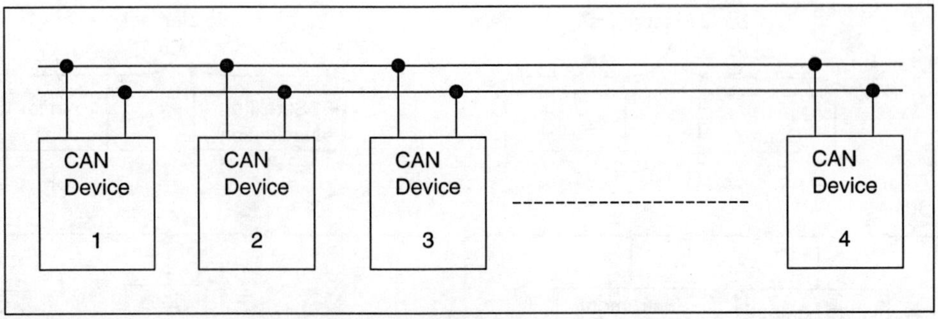

Figure 5.34 | Nodes connected through a CAN bus

Case 2: Many Nodes Send Messages When many nodes send messages simultaneously, it is necessary that only one node is allowed to do a valid 'broadcast'. Other transmitters should retreat, and try again later. Arbitration is the mechanism that handles bus access conflicts. The technique of arbitration used here is like this: The identifiers (11-bit or 29-bit) of the messages have dominant and recessive bits –0 is the dominant bit, and 1 the recessive bit. The logic is wired AND, where the presence of a 0, causes the output to be 0.

Let's use an example to understand this. Consider three nodes transmitting at the same time. Let's consider that the 11-bit identifiers of the 3 messages (from the three nodes) have all their lower 8 bits as 0. In the arbitration phase, the comparisons of the lower 8 bits do not cause any decision to be made. The 9th-bit of the identifier is 1 for node 2 alone. So, when contending for the bus, node 2 loses arbitration at this point of time. Then comes the 10th-bit, which is 1 for the message of node 3. Thus, node 3 also loses out, and node 1 is left with its message on the bus.

See Figure 5.35 for understanding this method in the case of the example message identifiers. The technique is called CSMA/CD which stands for carrier sense multiple access/collision detection. Here we see that when multiple access (to the CAN bus) occurs, collision detection is done by sensing the carrier (i.e. the encoded identifiers) and on the basis of this, arbitration is done.

The coding of the identifiers of the messages should obviously be in such a way that more important actions should be given higher priorities.

5.4.1.2 | *Features of CAN*

Figure 5.36 shows a CAN device connected to a CAN bus, where two signal wires CAN_L and CAN_H (low and high) are seen. This is called differential signalling and the effective signal is the difference of that in the two wires. When common mode signals, usually noise, appear on the bus, they are subtracted off, and this makes the CAN bus resistant to noise. In CAN and most other modern serial protocols (USB, PCIe, etc) differential signalling with NRZ (non return to zero) coding is used to reduce the effects of noise. A CAN bus is terminated to minimize signal reflections on the bus. The ISO-11898 requires that the bus has a characteristic impedance of 120 ohms.

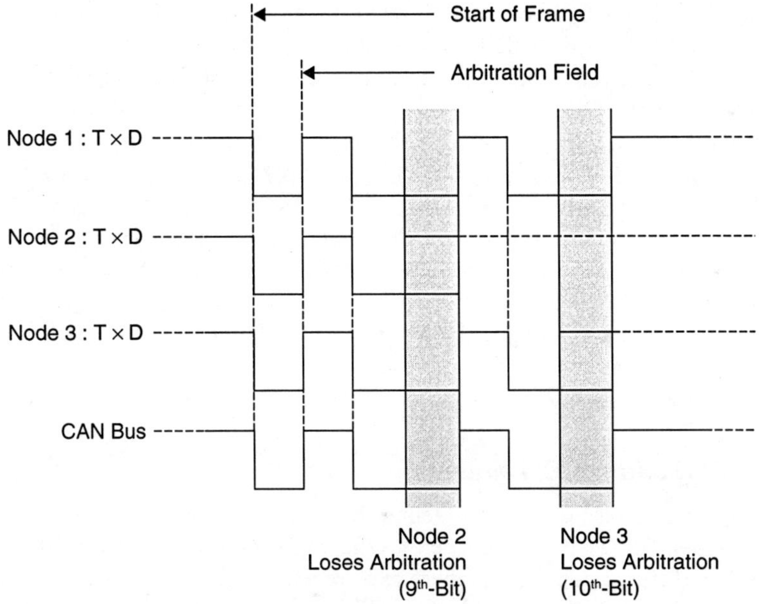

Figure 5.35 | The 'collision detection' and arbitration technique

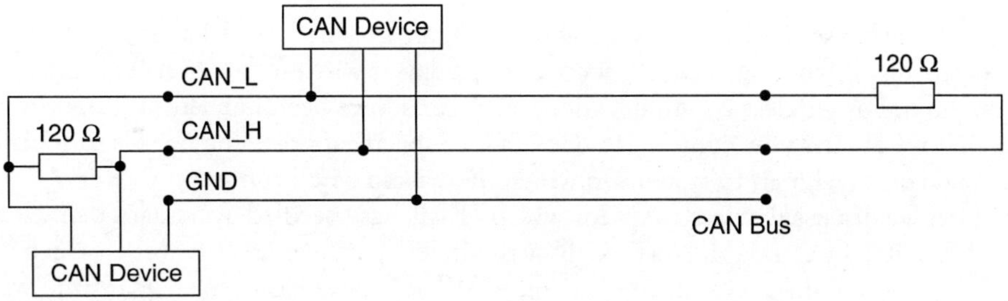

Figure 5.36 | CAN signals

SOF	Identifier	RTR	Control	Data	CRC	ACK	EOF

Figure 5.37 | A CAN 'data' frame

5.4.1.2 | *Message Frames*

CAN distinguishes four message formats: data, remote, error and overload frames. Figure 5.37 shows the data frame. A data frame begins with the start-of-frame (SOF) bit. It is followed by an eleven-bit identifier and the remote transmission request (RTR) bit. This bit can be used to tell any other node to 'transmit' instead of just listening. The identifier and the RTR bit form the arbitration field. The control field consists of six bits and indicates how many bytes of data follow in the data field. The data field can be zero to eight bytes. The data field is followed by the cyclic redundancy checksum (CRC) field, which enables the receiver to check if the received bit sequence was corrupted. The two-bit acknowledgment (ACK) field is used by the transmitter to receive an acknowledgment of a valid frame from any receiver. The message frame is terminated by a seven-bit end-of-frame (EOF). For CAN 2.0 B, the identifier is 29 bits long, instead of the eleven bits of CAN1.0.

You will need to know more about the different types of frames, if you are implementing a CAN-based application. But in that case also, you will be using a CAN controller IC (or a CAN controller in an MCU) which will take care of many implementation issues. CAN has become a very popular and widely used protocol because of its simplicity, low cost, sophisticated error detection and handling system. Its maximum range is typically 40 metres at 1Mbit/sec but the data rate decreases with increase in range.

5.4.1.4 | *CAN and The OSI Model*

Many network protocols are described using the seven-layer open systems interconnection (OSI) model. The CAN protocol defines the lowest two layers of the OSI model,i.e., the data link and the physical layer. There exist several CAN-based higher-layer protocols (application level) that are standardized. The user choice depends on the application.

5.5 | Wireless Communications Protocols

So far we have discussed serial protocols all of which are wired. Now let's see some wireless protocols which have become very relevant today, as wireless data transfer is the need of the hour. For wireless communications, standards have been defined, and the protocols that we discuss now conform to one of these specifications—the need is to transfer data and control signals to systems to which there is no wired connection.

First we discuss wireless LAN for which IEEE has specified a standard defined by the IEEE 802.11 standard. Next we discuss wireless personal area networks which are confined to small distances (in comparison to WLAN) and has been standardized with the number IEEE 802.15.

5.5.1 | WLAN (IEEE 802.11)

This is a standard defined for Wireless LANs (WLAN). The IEEE (Institute of Electrical and Electronic Engineers) released the 802.11 specification in June 1997. The initial specification, known as 802.11, used the 2.4 GHz frequency and supported a maximum data rate of 1 to 2 Mbps. Later, many changes and additions came, and are listed as follows:

i) **802.11b:** The first widely used wireless networking technology, known as 802.11b (more commonly called Wi-Fi), first released in 1999, but is still in use, though on the road to obsolescence.
ii) **802.11g:** In 2003, a follow-on version called 802.11g appeared offering greater performance (i.e. speed and range) and remains today's most common wireless networking technology.

iii) **802.11n:** Another improved standard called 802.11n is currently under development and is scheduled to be complete soon. The 802.11n standard has yet to be finalized, but products based on the draft 802.11n standard are available.

The 802.11 protocol covers the MAC (Media Access Control) layer and physical layer. The standard defines a single MAC which interacts with three types of physical layers.

i) Frequency Hopping Spread Spectrum in the 2.4 GHz Band
ii) Direct Sequence Spread Spectrum in the 2.4 GHz Band
iii) InfraRed

An 802.11 LAN is based on a cellular architecture where the system is subdivided into cells. The specification defines two types of operational modes: ad hoc (peer-to-peer) mode and infrastructure mode.

5.5.1.1 | *Infrastructure Mode*

Let us discuss the toplogy of a large wireless LAN network, while referring to Figure 5.38.

In the figure, a basic service set (BSS) is shown as a basic cell which has two components, which are the station and the access point.

Station This is the unit which communicates with the wireless medium. The most likely candidate to be a station is a PC with a network interface card (NIC). It is the presence of the NIC that qualifies a PC to be a station. Iphones, PDAs, tablets, etc. are new media devices which act as stations.

Access Point/Base Station Each cell is controlled by a base station, also called an access point (AP). Figure 5.38 shows three BSSs each with two to three stations in it. Note that,

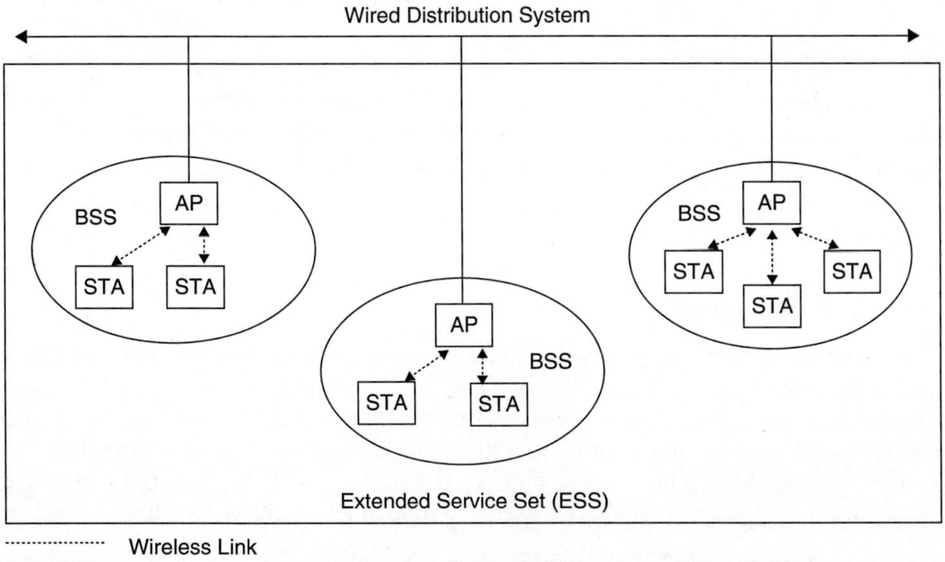

Figure 5.38 | A WLAN in the infrastructure mode

a BSS is not defined by a geographic area, but rather by connectivity. The AP is shown to form part of a wired system (through Ethernet). For stations in one BSS to connect to stations in another BSS, the communication is forwarded through their respectives base stations (APs). This forms an ESS.

5.5.1.2 | *Extended Service Set (ESS)*

It is a set of BSSs, where the APs communicate among themselves to forward traffic from one BSS to another and to facilitate the movement of mobile stations.

Distribution System A number of BSSs interconnected through some kind of backbone is called the distribution system (DS). In the figure, the DS is shown to be a wired (Ethernet) network but it can be a wireless system as well.

Roaming The 802.11 specification includes roaming capabilities that allow a computer to roam among multiple access points on different channels. Thus, roaming stations with weak signals can associate themselves with other access points with stronger signals. A wireless station's NIC may decide to associate itself with another access point within range, because the load on its current access point is too high for optimal performance.

5.5.1.3 | *CSMA/CA*

In a cell, multiple stations may try to transmit and this is prevented by the CSMS/CA protocol. This is slightly different from the CSMA/CD mechanism used in Ethernet where a collision is 'detected' and then, 'back off' is done. In WLAN, collision is 'avoided', however. A CSMA protocol works as follows: A station desiring to transmit, senses the medium. If the medium is busy (i.e. some other station is transmitting), then the station defers its transmission to a later time.

5.5.1.4 | *Ad hoc Mode*

In the ad hoc mode, also known as independent basic service set (IBSS) or peer-to-peer mode, all the computers equipped with an NIC can communicate with each other via the wireless link without an access point. The ad hoc mode is convenient for quickly setting up a wireless network in a meeting room, hotel conference centre, or anywhere else, when sufficient wired infrastructure does not exist.

5.5.1.5 | *Performance*

Wirelessly networked computers function best when located relatively close together and in the 'line of sight' of each other. The level of performance of WLAN is dependent on a number of important environmental and product-specific factors. 802.11b and g officially work over a distance of up to 320 feet indoors or 1300 feet outdoors, but it is practically difficult to achieve these figures. Access points will automatically negotiate the appropriate signalling rate based upon environmental conditions, such as:

i) Distance between WLAN devices (AP and NICs)
ii) Transmission power levels

iii) Building and home materials
iv) Radio frequency interference
v) Signal propagation
vi) Antenna type and location

5.5.2 | IEEE 802.15 for WPAN

These protocols belong to a class of applications called 'Wireless Personal Area Networks' (WPAN). WPAN is defined as a network meant to span a small area such as a private home or office building or an individual workspace. It is used to communicate over a relatively short distance. Ad hoc networking is one of the key concepts in WPANs. This allows devices to be part of the network temporarily; they can join and leave at will. WPAN standard ensures data security through data encryption, and so is resistant to unauthorized intrusions. Two important and popular protocols are Zigbee and bluetooth, which have similarities in their approach, but vary in their application domain.

The features of WPAN networks can be listed as follows:

i) Short-range
ii) Low Power
iii) Low Cost
iv) Small networks

Here we will take a look at two types of WPANs

5.5.2.1 | *Zigbee*

This is a wireless network of active modules, founded on a packet-based protocol known as the IEEE 802.15.4. ZigBee-compliant products operate in unlicensed bands worldwide, including 2.4GHz (global), 902 to 928 MHz (America) and 868 MHz (Europe). The transmission range is from 10 to 100 m, depending on the power output and environmental characteristics.

Communication Technology ZigBee uses direct sequence spread spectrum in the 2.4 GHz band, with offset-quadrature phase-shift keying modulation. The 868 and 900 MHz bands also use direct-sequence spread spectrum but with binary phase- shift keying modulation.

Application Arena The name Zigbee was suggested by the alliance which standardized and developed this protocol; the name was coined to compare the data movement in the network, to the zigzag movement that honey bees use to share information, such as the location, distance and direction of a newly discovered food source to fellow colony members.

The application arena of Zigbee is such that the focus is on low data rate and low power dissipation, to be useful for 'monitoring and control'. The applications lined up for using Zigbee are industrial control, embedded sensing, medical data collection, remote metering, smoke and intruder warning, building automation and domotics (The word domotics means home robotics, as 'domus' is the latin word for home).

The field of domotics covers the whole range of smart home technology, including the highly sophisticated sensors and controls that automate temperature, lighting, security systems, toys and so on. A special area of interest for Zigbee is 'wireless sensor networks' (Section 4.4).

To formalize and standardize the protocol, an alliance of interested groups was formed naming itself the 'Zigbee Alliance'. The initial eight promoter companies were Chipcon, Ember, Freescale, Honeywell, Mitsubishi, Motorola, Philips and Samsung. Now, things are looking up for Zigbee with a growing number of companies (over 175) expressing their commitment to providing Zigbee compliant products and solutions.

Understanding Zigbee Zigbee involves the interconnection of nodes. Each node has a processing unit and peripherals—some of the peripherals may be sensors, others may be actuators—besides this, nodes need to transmit and receive; as such, there is a transceiver and an antenna as well in each node.

Zigbee Nodes Zigbee is based on a master–slave configuration. Zigbee defines two different kinds of devices which act as the nodes in the network.

i) **Zigbee Full Function Device (FFD):** This device can act as a coordinator or router. The coordinators and routers have to listen to the network continuously.
ii) **Zigee Reduced Function Device (RFD):** Such devices can only act as slaves. They can find a network and transfer data from its application, if necessary. They are designed for energy saving and are typically battery powered.

A network consists of FFDs and RFDs connected in a mesh, star, cluster mesh or peer-to-peer topology. See Figures 5.39 and Figure 5.40 which show these topologies. The components of the network are defined as follows:

Zigbee Co-Ordinator Only one coordinator is required for a network—this is the node which initiates the formation of the network—new nodes can be added only at the behest of the coordinator. But once the network is formed, the coordinator becomes just a 'router'. It is a full function device. In a peer-to-peer network, there is no specific co-ordinator as all nodes are peers and have equal functionality, and all nodes use full function devices.

Zigbee Router As the name indicates, it participates in multi-hop routing of messages from one node to another. It should be a full function device. The number of routers depends on the application requirements. The idea is that messages from any point of the network must get routed to any other point of the network, through any path; so a series of routers are needed.

Zigbee End Device It is a reduced function device, in that it cannot do routing of messages. It can talk with a ZC or ZR but nothing more.

Figure 5.41 shows a typical Zigbee node. There is an RF transceiver module with an antenna and also a processor module connected to sensors/actuators. There are also components which take care of the Zigbee protocol.

The module which contains the MCU and the Zigbee network hardware is given the name 'MCU module'.

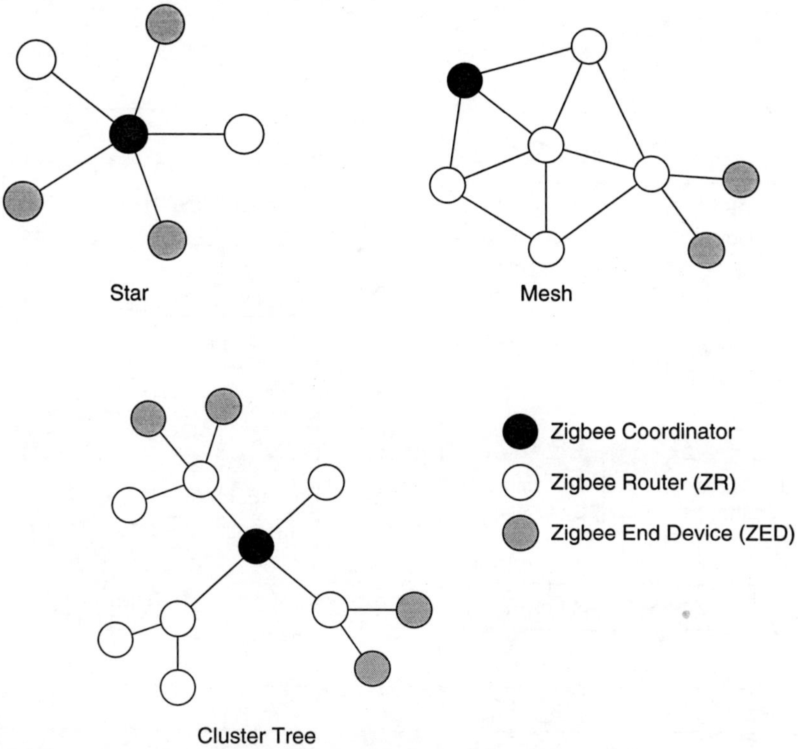

Figure 5.39 | Typical zigbee networks using star, mesh and cluster mesh

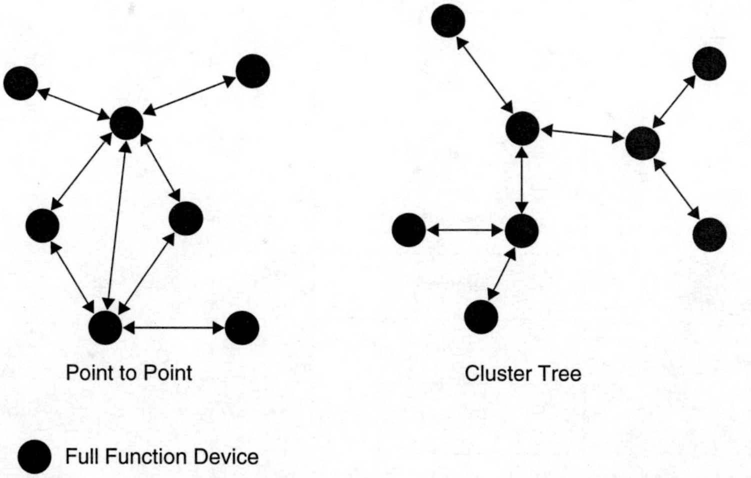

Figure 5.40 | Zigbee network in the peer-to-peer configuration

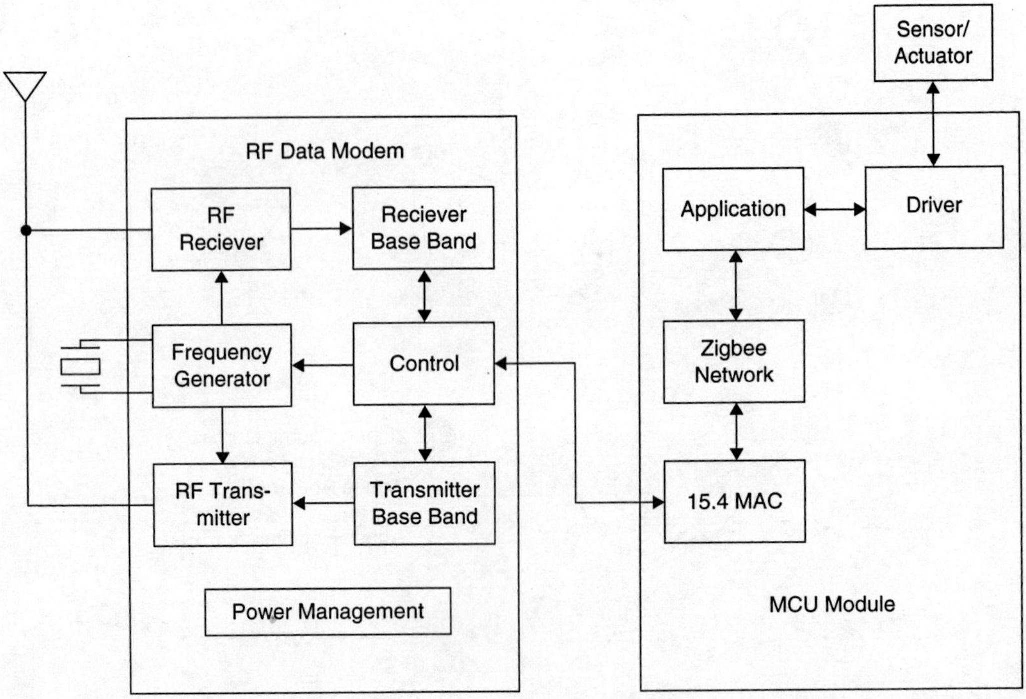

Figure 5.41 | Block diagram of a zigbee node

5.5.2.2 | *The OSI Model and Zigbee*

The Zigbee standard is loosely based on the OSI 7-layer model. The IEEE 802.15.4 wireless standard defines the lower two layers, the application is determined by the customer needs and the standards of the Zigbee Alliance, define the remaining three intermediate layers.

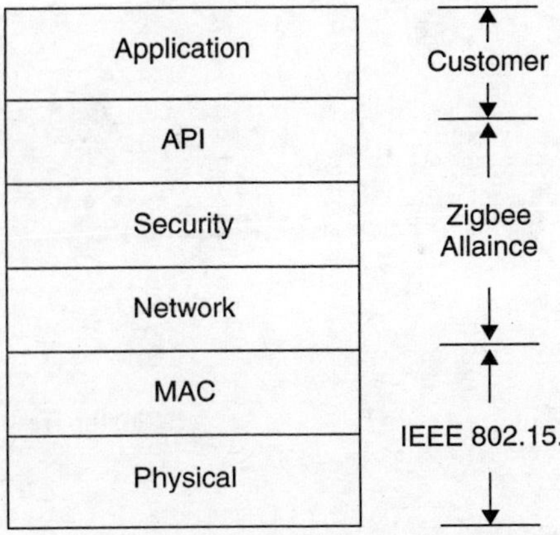

Figure 5.42 | The OSI layer, Zigbee and IEEE 802.15.14

Projects Using Zigbee From an academic point of view, projects can be done in which remote transmission is necessary. For this, the nodes with a microcontroller and peripherals can be developed. Since Zigbee is a high level protocol, it is not possible to implement it easily by using the instructions available in the processor. Dedicated hardware and firmware plus the RF section are needed. The solution is to buy a Zigbee module from any of the standard sources. Zigbee modules to fit your application are available at relatively low cost, from many sources.

5.5.2.3 | *Bluetooth*

All of us are very familiar with bluetooth, because most of us use it very frequently, as it is available in our laptops and mobile phones. Here we will attempt to have a glimpse of bluetooth as a 'technology' which has been standardized as the wireless standard IEEE 802.15.1 Bluetooth is a wireless PAN network similar to Zigbee but different in the area of application. This technology also offers wireless access to LANs, PSTN (*Public Switched Telephone Network,* which refers to the wired land line telephone network) the mobile phone network and the Internet, for a variety of home appliances and portable handheld interfaces. It supports a range of 10 m, which can be increased up to 100 m with the use of an amplifier.

The motivation for this technology was the necessity to avoid wires to connect peripherals. There was (and still is) a technology named IrDA (based on infra red signals) for wireless access, but this needs the transmitter and receiver to be within 'line of sight' of each other. Bluetooth does not have this limitation.

Bluetooth is a standard developed in 1998 by the members of the Bluetooth Special Interest Group (SIG) which consisted of the companies Ericsson, Intel, Toshiba, Nokia and IBM that allows electronic equipments to be interconnected without wires and cables. Today, more than 1000 companies have joined SIG to work for an open standard for the Bluetooth concept.

Communication Technology It operates in the unlicensed spectrum of 2.4 GHz. This spectrum is shared by other types of equipment (e.g. microwave ovens). In order to avoid interference, the Bluetooth specification employs frequency hopping spread spectrum (FHSS) techniques. Data is transmitted at a maximum rate of up to 1 Mb/s.

The Bluetooth Protocol Any Bluetooth device can be a master or a slave, depending on its application.

A master is the only one that may initiate the creation of a link. However, once a link is established, the slave has the permission to become the master if it needs to take charge of the network. Slaves are not allowed to talk to each other directly. All communication occurs between a slave and the master.

Any two Bluetooth devices that come within a range of each other can set up an ad hoc connection, which is called a piconet. Every piconet can consist of a maximum of eight units (because a three-bit MAC address is used). There is always a master unit in a piconet and the rest of the units act as slaves. The unit that establishes the piconet becomes the master unit. The master unit can change later but there can never be more than one master. Several piconets can exist in the same area. This is called a scatternet.

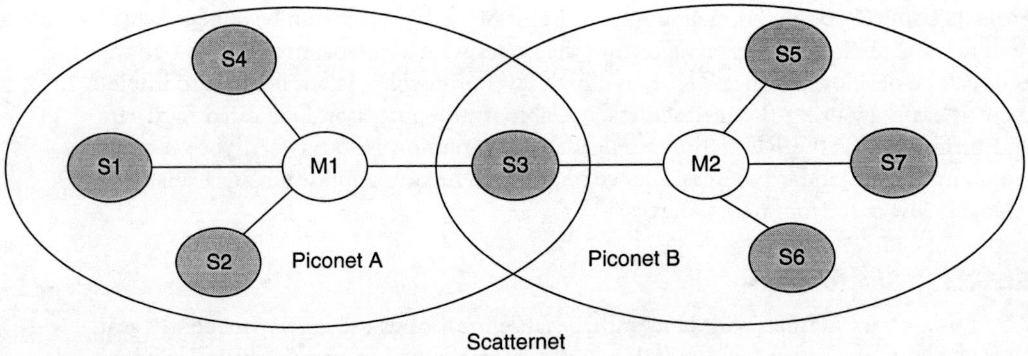

Figure 5.43 | A bluetooth network

Within one scatternet, all units share the same frequency range, but each piconet uses different hop sequences and transmits on different hop channels. See Figure 5.43.

Conclusion

With this, we come to the end of our discussion of buses and protocols. Only a few important buses and protocols have been covered here: as a sample of the large set of them available for various and varied purposes.

KEY POINTS OF THIS CHAPTER

- Buses carry signals inside a system, according to a set of well-defined rules called 'protocols'.
- Serial buses are gradually replacing parallel buses.
- When multiple masters need the same bus at the same time, techniques for bus arbitration must be sought.
- Two important on-board buses are the I2C and the SPI bus.
- The USB is a serial bus which has become very popular.
- Firewire is another serial bus similar to USB, but faster and more complex.
- The standard serial port has been around for a long time, but is rapidly being replaced by the USB port.
- RS 232, RS 422 and RS 485 are different serial communication standards with minor differences between them.
- The Ethernet is a wired LAN protocol which has stood the test of time and fierce competition.
- The CAN bus is the most popular automotive bus in use.
- WLAN is defined by the IEEE 802.11 standard.
- Two popular WPAN networks are Zigbee and Bluetooth.

QUESTIONS

1. Is the SPI a synchronous or asynchronous bus?
2. Why is UART considered an asynchronous protocol?
3. Why is cache needed for a computer system?
4. What is the purpose of having a bridge on an embedded board?
5. Make a clear distinction between on-board and off-board buses, with examples.
6. Name a few standard parallel buses you have heard of, and list their maximum transfer speeds.
7. What is the main difference between the PCI bus and PCIe bus?
8. What is meant by 'differential signalling' that is used for serial transmission and what are the advantages and disadvantages of such a signalling?
9. Compare the I2C and SPI buses in terms of their performance.
10. What is done in the enumeration phase of the USB protocol?
11. For what kind of data is isochronous data transfer used?
12. What is the arbitration technique used in CAN?
13. Why is the LIN protocol not very popular?
14. What is the use of the RTR bit in the CAN message format?
15. Why is the firewire considered to be a superior protocol?
16. In what way is RS 485 superior to RS 422 ?
17. What is the most significant advantage that RS 422/485 has over RS 232?
18. In what aspects are the Zigbee and bluetooth protocols different?

EXERCISE

1. Find the names of the PIC MCUs which have in them, I2C and SPI controllers. Draw a circuit diagram connecting an LCD display and an SPI controller in a PIC.
2. Find the names of ARM and PIC MCUs which have CAN controllers inside them.
3. Find applications of CAN which are not related to automotive embedded systems.
4. Draw the setup of a Zigbee network for a home security system. Explain the sensors that should be used, and the algorithm you will suggest for sensing and sending messages.
5. What do you know of the GSM network? Can you use a GSM module for home security applications? How?
6. What are the applications in which you have used bluetooth? Find out at least three more applications possible with bluetooth, but which you have not used.
7. Name at least 10 devices in which you have seen USB ports. Which of these ports are hosts and which of them are devices?
8. Where is the Ethernet protocol used? Does it have any similarity to CAN?
9. What do you know of Firewire? Where are Firewire ports seen?
10. Have you seen SATA ports? Where?
11. What types of communication techniques are used in WLAN? Explain.
12. To what applications does IEEE 802.11n cater to?

6 SOFTWARE DEVELOPMENT TOOLS

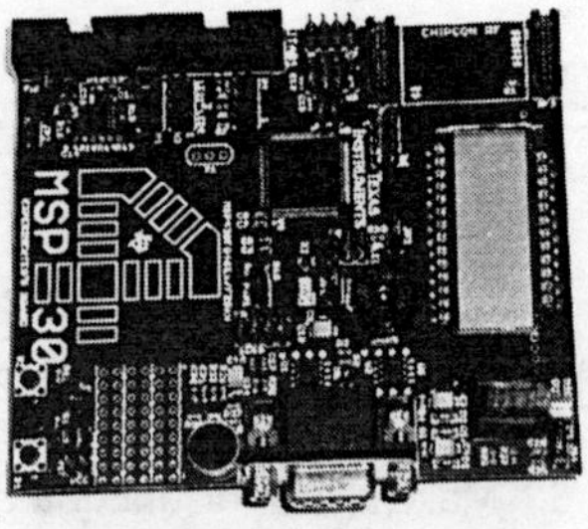

In this chapter, you will learn

- The steps in developing embedded systems software
- Cross compilation and cross assembly
- The set of actions involved in 'building' a program
- The methods of downloading the executable file into a non-volatile memory.
- Why a software simulator is very useful to a software developer
- Functions of an emulator
- The usefulness of a hardware simulator

Introduction

An embedded system, as we see, includes both hardware and software. To develop the hardware and software in unison, a number of tools become necessary. Another related term is 'firmware'. When software is embedded in hardware, it becomes a 'firmware'. The hardware involved here is a non-volatile memory which is part of an MCU or system board. Currently flash ROM is the device of choice for firmware.

In this chapter, we make a tour of the important tools used by an embedded system developer, which takes him step by step into writing and testing software, and finally embedding it as 'firmware'. We discuss software development alone in this chapter because hardware aspects have been covered in Chapter 2.

6.1 | Embedded Program Development

Let us first try to understand the program development steps. The assumption is that the hardware design is being done parallel, and we are out to develop, test and port the software onto the embedded systems board. It is only after the software is thoroughly tested can it be burned into the flash (ROM) of the target processor.

See Figure 6.1 which is a typical target board . The processor is on the board which contains a few more chips, and some connectors. There is the RJ-47 socket, USB socket,

---

Chapter-opening image: Development board of TI's low power MSP 430 microcontroller.

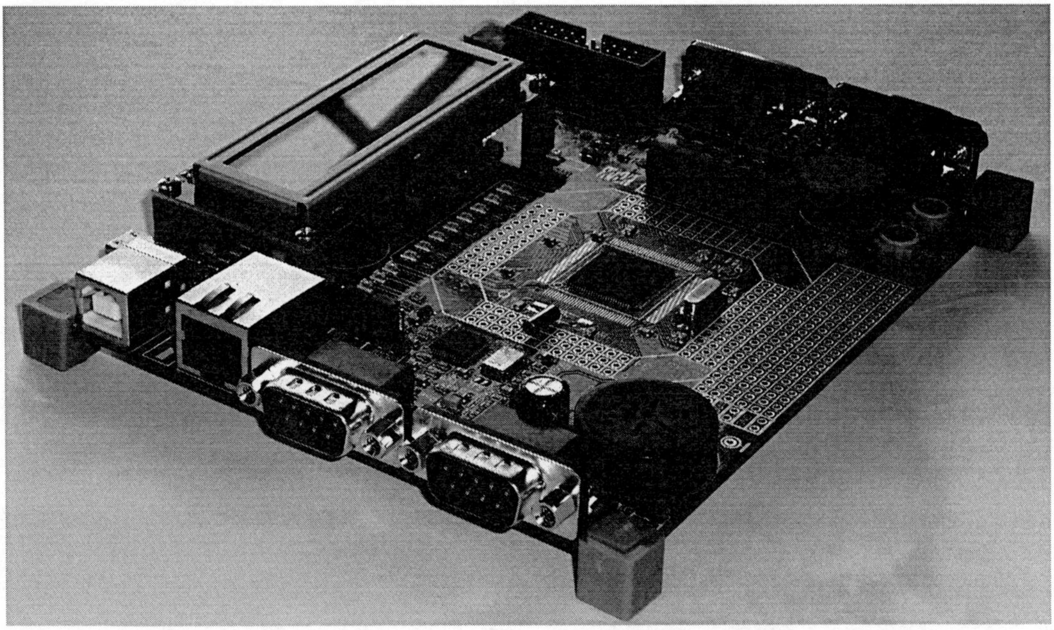

Figure 6.1 | An embedded board

serial port, other connectors, etc. seen on this board, besides the MCU and a few other chips and peripheral devices like an LCD, speakers, etc.

6.1.1 | The Initial Steps

Remember that the program to be run on the selected MCU cannot be simply burned on its flash without testing and making sure that it is working as per the required specifications. This part of developing a working and tested program called 'software development'. Let us assume that a high level language like say C is used for the programming.

The first part of development is carried out on a general purpose PC which is called the 'host' system which usually runs on an x86 processor. On this host system, we need an IDE (Integrated Development Environment) to 'build' the program for our embedded processor. An IDE is a tool chain which does cross compilation, linking and simulation for the program. Finally it generates an executable hex file. This executable file is downloaded on to the non-volatile memory, i.e., flash, of the MCU on the board, using a serial link as shown in Figure 6.2. (We call this file as a 'hex' file which is a transport file format for executable files or any binary information).Once this is done, the program is permanently available on the target board (as firmware), and the board then becomes a 'stand alone' system dedicated for the application.

These steps seem easy as long as we have all the 'development tools' for the MCU we use, that is, the IDE. With this brief introduction, let us attempt to understand the complete program development sequence and the role played by each 'part' of the tool chain. This chapter is meant to throw light on these aspects.

Figure 6.2 | A HOST computer and an embedded board

6.1.2 | The Integrated Development Environment

An integrated development environment (IDE) is a programming environment that has been packaged as an application program, consisting of a code editor, a cross compiler, a debugger, and a graphical user interface (GUI) builder. (An IDE is specific for a particular family of MCUs. One family of MCUs can have many different IDEs offered by many vendors.)

Table 6.1 lists some of the popular IDEs available. Some of them are open source ones, while others are proprietary. Some IDEs are very elementary, while others are very advanced and cater to professional requirements.

The Keil IDE has been suggested (in this book) for use by students because of its free availability (the student version), and ease of use. It caters to assembly and Embedded C for a wide range of MCUs including different versions of the 8051 and ARM. Appendix B gives the step by step method of using this IDE. It will be a good idea to gain familiarity with a typical IDE, before going further. That will go a long way in understanding the components of an IDE and the role of each component.

An IDE has at least the following:

i) Code Editor
ii) Builder
iii) Simulator
iv) GUI (Graphical User Interface)

Table 6.1 | A List of Popular IDEs

IDE	MCUs for Which They are Used	Supplier
Keil RVDK	ARM,8051	Keil Inc,
Eclipse	ARM	OPEN SOURCE
PSoC Creator	PSoC 3 and 5	CYPRESS SEMICONDUCTORS
PSoc Designer	PSoC 1	CYPRESS SEMICONDUCTORS
IAR	MSP 430, ARM, 8051	IAR SYSTEMS
Code Composer Studio	DSP Processors, MSP 430	TEXAS INSTRUMENTS
MPLAB	PIC	MICROCHIP TECHNOLOGY
AVR STUDIO	AVR MCU	ATMEL CORPORATION
CODEWARRIOR	ARM	FREESCALE SEMICONDUCTORS
VISUAL DSP++	Blackfin DSP processor	Analog Devices

6.1.3 | Code Editor

This editor allows code to be written, changed and saved as files in folders called 'projects'. During the course of the use of the IDE, the project folder will be found to contain all the different types of files associated with that project.

6.1.4 | GUI

Most windows based IDEs have a graphical user interface which makes it easy to use. This gives the facility to view all activities using the IDE. This is especially attractive in the debug mode, when the contents of registers, memory and peripherals have to be viewed.

6.1.5 | Compiler

A compiler is a program that translates one computer language program (called source code) into another (object code). Usually the name 'compiler' is used for programs that translate source code from a high-level programming language to a lower level language (assembly language or machine code.) **For a machine to 'run' the object code, the final conversion should be into the machine's machine code.** In that case, the conversion from a high level language to assembly code can be considered to be an intermediate step.

A C program running on an x86 processor (i.e on a PC) will be converted to the assembly language of the processor being used here, i.e. the x86. For embedded systems, it is 'cross compilation' that is done, however.

What is a cross compiler?

Assume that we have chosen 'ARM' as the processor of our target board. We write programs in Embedded C for the ARM processor. Then the compilation is done to convert the C program to the assembly/machine language of ARM rather than that of the x86 processor used by the host system. That is, the processor of the PC 'compiles' the program into the assembly code of 'another' processor. That is why it is called 'cross' compilation.

For any processor, different compilers are available. Compilation is not a one-to-one process. Each type of compiler may convert a single HLL line to many different assembly lines, (and thus to different sets of the machine code, finally). Essentially, this means that some compilers are more efficient than others because they might 'compile' to a lesser volume of the assembly/machine code. After compilation, the syntax errors are indicated.

6.1.6 | Assembler

This is the software which converts an assembly program into a machine code on a **one-to-one** basis. The term 'one to one' means that for a specific mnemonic, there is one and only one machine code.

6.1.6.1 | Cross Assembler

If the program for ARM, in the editor of the IDE is an assembly program, the 'cross assembler' in the IDE converts it to the machine language of ARM. Thus, the assembler software which runs on one processor (x86 of the PC) produces machine code for another processor, i.e., ARM. This is cross-assembly.

An assembler generates an 'object file' which contains the following information:

i) Machine code
ii) Re-locatable addresses of the code bytes

Typically, an assembler makes two 'passes' or readings over the assembly code. In the first pass, it reads each line and records labels (symbols corresponding to addresses) in a symbol table. In the second pass, it gets the actual addresses (displacements with respect to a reference) of each code line and fills in the missing portions of the symbol table. It is in this pass that the mnemonics are converted to machine code. Addresses are said to be relative because the actual physical addresses of locations in memory, to which these lines will be copied, will be a displacement with respect to a base address.

6.1.7 | Builder

Once the code has been written and saved as a file in a project, the next step is 'building the project'. A builder includes the compiler, and assembler that we have just talked about. There is also a linker. The project may contain a number of source files, which many be in C or assembly, and all of them are 'built' together, as we will soon see.

Now let us have a look at the general steps in converting a C program file, that is, the source file to an executable file. Figure 6.3 outlines the steps involved. The steps show the C source file being 'compiled' to an assembly file, which is then converted to machine code using an assembler.

The process of assembly also generates other files named as cross-reference, map and so on. Describing each one of them will tend to clutter this discussion with unnecessary details, and so is avoided. But any inquisitive reader can take a look at all these files in a typical IDE and easily understand the need for these extra files.

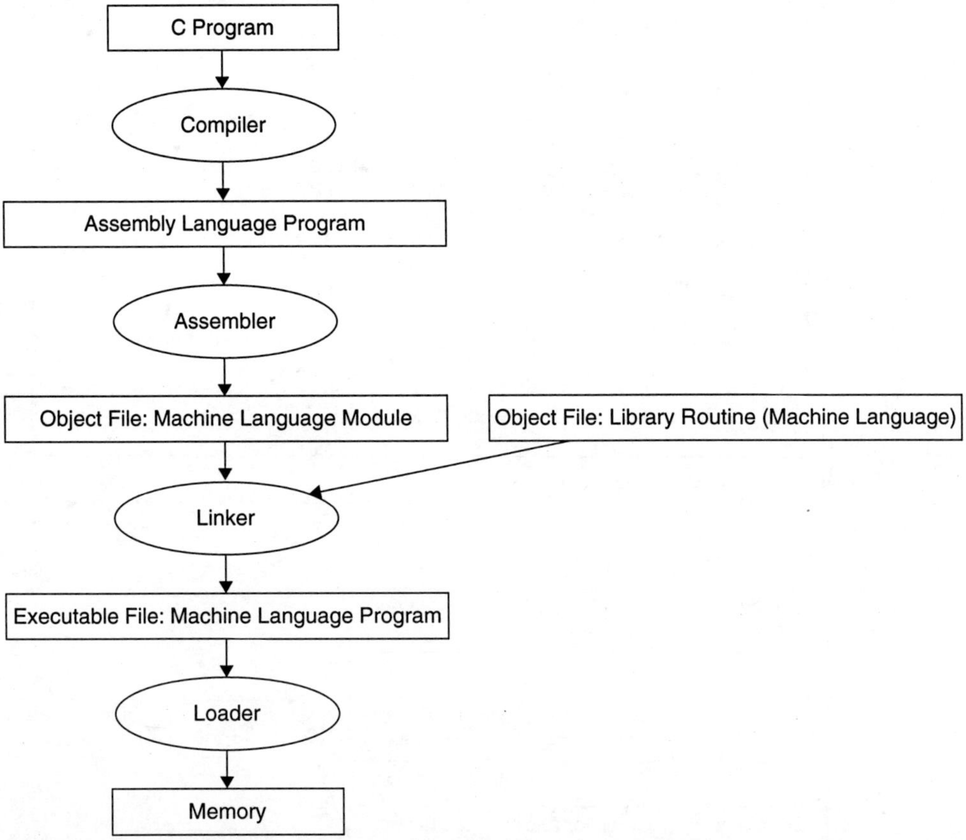

Figure 6.3 | Conversion steps from source file to an executable file

After the step of assembly, we have the machine language file. At this point, 'linking' is done with library routines (if needed), using a program called the 'linker'. At the end of all this, we get a single executable file which is to be 'loaded' into memory for execution by the processor.

6.1.8 | Disassembly

Disassembling is the reverse process of assembling. In the 'disassembly window', the addresses of the code lines, the machine code and the mnemonics can be seen. See such a typical window for the Keil µVision IDE (in the debug mode) in Figure 6.4.

Note the highlighted line, to understand each part of the line.

C:0x0000 is the address of this code line in the code memory

MOV R3, #0x14 is the code mnemonic and 7B 14 is the corresponding machine code in hex.

6.1.9 | Linker

This piece of software does the linking of many modules. There may be a number of source modules. Note Figure 6.5 where three source files are compiled and assembled.

```
Disassembly
     2:                      MOV R3,#20
C:0x0000      7B14     MOV       R3,#0x14
     3:                      CLR A
C:0x0002      E4       CLR       A
     4:                      MOV R2,#1
C:0x0003      7A01     MOV       R2,#0x01
     5: THERE:   ADD A,R2
C:0x0005      2A       ADD       A,R2
     6:                      INC R2
C:0x0006      0A       INC       R2
     7:                      DJNZ R3,THERE
C:0x0007      DBFC     DJNZ      R3,THERE(C:0005)
     8:                      MOV 40H,A
C:0x0009      F540     MOV       0x40,A
     9: HERE:     SJMP HERE
```

Figure 6.4 | A typical disassembly window

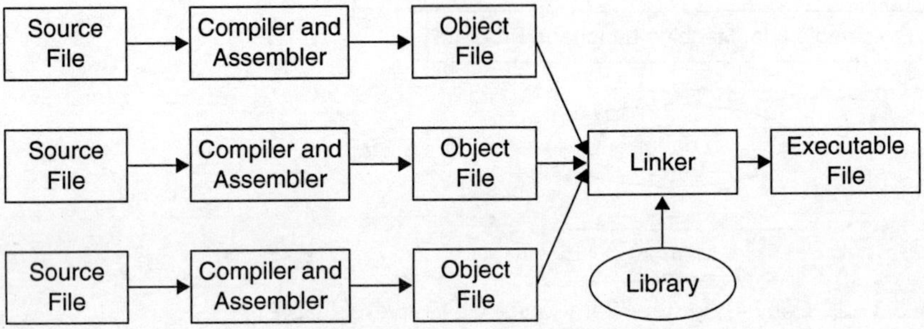

Figure 6.5 | Steps in building and converting to an executable file

There may also be a number of library functions being used. For example, if we started with a C program, we might be using the standard I/O or math library, which needs to be 'connected' to the object files. By linking, that is, combining all these, we get the executable file, which is usually designated as the 'exe file'. It is this file which will be 'loaded' to the processor memory to get executed.

For embedded processors, there is a reset vector and it is from that address in flash that the code gets executed (for 8051 it is the first address, i.e., 0x0). At the end of the linking process, the arrangement for loading the code into this specific address is also done. Now the hex file is ready to be downloaded into the non-volatile memory in the target board.

In an IDE (take a look at the Keil IDE, for example), the processes of 'compile, assemble and link' are together called 'build'. The output from the build process is the hex file which can be loaded into the flash of the processor or be simulated using the simulator of the IDE. Figure 6.3 shows the executable file being loaded into memory, using a 'loader'.

6.1.10 | Simulator

This is also called a software debugger. This is a software which allows debugging of code by identifying and correcting logical errors. Here setting break points and single step execution is possible. The most important aspect of a software debugger in an embedded system IDE is that the architecture of the selected processor is 'simulated'. What this means is that, if it is the 8051 MCU that has been selected, there is the facility to view the registers, RAM and ROM locations of this MCU after each step of execution. The available peripherals such as timers, GPIO, serial ports, etc. are also viewable. There is the facility for simulating the external input ports and logic values. This means that if to an input GPIO pin, applying a '1' as input is to be given, it can be done and the result of this (in memory or a register) can be observed.

With the help of a simulator, the developer can make himself very sure about the 'working', 'logical' of his code. But the simulator does not give a measure of time, though observation of generated waveforms is possible using the logic analyser in the simulator.

You can get a feel of all this, using the Keil Simulator by going to the 'debug' mode.

6.2 | Downloading the Hex File to the Non-volatile Memory

In Figure 6.3, a loader is shown to be loading the executable file to memory. In a general purpose system, the 'loader' is a software which find space in RAM to load the exe file. In the case of embedded systems, the final step in program development is burning the hex file into the non-volatile memory of the target board. Usually this is the flash memory of the MCU, but it is also possible that the target board contains flash memory external to the MCU.

Once the executable hex file is ready it can be downloaded into the flash of the MCU. This can be done in various ways:

i) OTP in factory environments
ii) Out of circuit programming
iii) In system programming

In the case of a factory environment where many chips have to be burned with the same code (for a standard product, for example), there is no need for re-programmability. All the chips are of type which is referred to as 'OTP or One Time Programmable'.

6.2.1 | Out of Circuit Programming

The MCU can be taken and plugged into a universal programmer. Refer to Figure 6.6. for the photograph of a **universal programmer** (SuperPro) with a chip plugged into it. Such a programmer is one which caters to different families of MCUs. The programmer is connected to the host PC and the hex code is burned onto the MCU. There are a number of such programmers available in the market having connectors for ICs of different numbers of pins and packaging.

The software associated with this is loaded into the host PC and the executable hex file is downloaded into the MCU's flash using a serial connection.

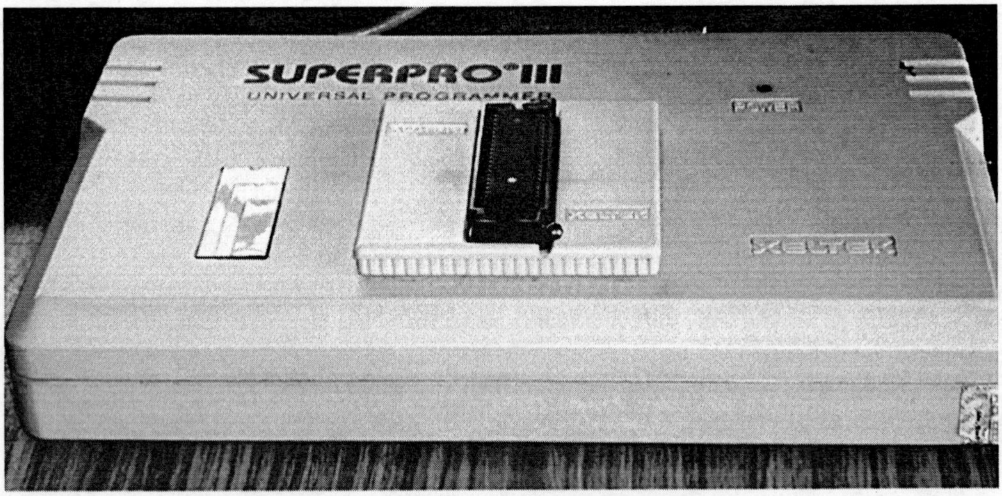

Figure 6.6 | An MCU plugged into the socket of a universal programmer

6.2.2 | In System Programming (ISP)

This is also called in-circuit programming. The idea here is that the MCU to be programmed remains on the target board itself, that is, it is in the system itself. This is very convenient and is in contrast to the out of circuit programming that we have just discussed. Many boards are supplied with the necessary ISP hardware and software (loaded in the host computer). For example, all MCU kits for educational purposes have it. Thus, students write, test and finalize their program on the host computer, and get the hex file ready. They then download it into the flash of the MCU on the kit. Erasing and re-loading can be done many times (limited only by the capability of the flash, which may be as high as 50,000 times).

What are the items included in ISP?

i) There is a software utility running on the host computer for controlling this programming interface.
ii) There is an adapter for connecting between the target board and any of the standard PC ports like the standard serial port, USB, etc. Sometime back, the standard serial port was the port of choice for downloading the exe file to the flash, but USB is more popular now. For more advanced processors like ARM, the JTAG interface is the one more common.
iii) There is a serial protocol in operation for the transfer from the host to the target. This may the SPI protocol (Section 5.2.2) or the JTAG protocol. This is indicated in Figure 6.7 as the 'programming interface'.

There is a large set of variants of ISP available, supplied by different board and chip manufacturers.

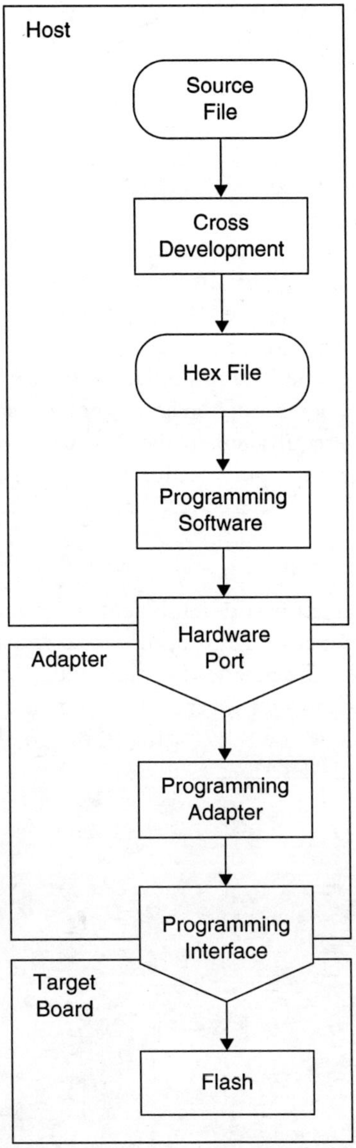

Figure 6.7 | The ISP interface

6.2.3 | Porting an OS to an Embedded Board

When the embedded board needs an embedded OS to be burned onto it, the complexity is more than just downloading an application program. A number of open source embedded operating systems are available on the web. We must do a thorough search and study to select the right OS for the board that we have, because some settings in the OS are hardware specific. These web sites offer a step-by-step procedure for porting the OS to the board. Section 19.1.13 gives the procedure for porting a Linux kernel to a beagle board (a board with a dual core processor, i.e., an ARM core and a DSP core).

6.2.4 | Emulator

The term 'emulate' means to 'imitate with effort'. Thus, what an emulator does in this context is to 'imitate hardware'. The hardware of interest is usually (but not necessarily) the MCU which is to be used in the embedded board under development. Thus, we use emulators for hardware debugging. In the emulator box, there is hardware which works exactly like the processor we use. Thus, our code is run on this emulator hardware and debugged in this, rather than in the actual hardware. An emulator can emulate the replaced uC in real time. The idea is similar to what we do with a simulator. The difference is that we read the contents of registers, memory, etc. from the emulator, which is a hardware which for us is equivalent to the target processor being used. Once the debugging is done (with single stepping, setting breakpoints, etc.), and the developer is confident about the performance of his code, it can be burned onto the target processor.

6.2.5 | ICE (In-Circuit Emulator)

An ICE is an emulator included in a development setup for a target board. A generic ICE box contains the emulator as well as the ISP for downloading the code to the target board. Many emulators have more advanced features like performance analysis, coverage analysis, a trace buffer and advanced trigger and breakpoint possibilities.

See Figure 6.8 which shows the ICE for the PSoC board. The ICE included in the PSoC development scenario is described as follows.

Figure 6.8 | A PSoC 3 board with an ICE

'The In-Circuit Emulator (ICE) consists of a base unit, USB 2.0 cable, and power supply. The base unit is connected to the host PC via the USB port. The ICE is driven by the Debugger subsystem of PSoC Designer IDE. This software interface allows the user to run, halt and single step the processor. It also allows the user to set complex event points. Event points can start and stop the trace memory on the ICE, as well as break the program execution'.

6.3 | Hardware Simulator

In the academic environment, where students want to develop hardware for their projects and innovative products, a hardware simulator is likely to be extremely useful. But what exactly is this? Before hard wiring and soldering a circuit, if it is possible to test the circuit and confirm that it works as per expectations, a lot of effort can be saved. There are some such simulators in common use, where the hardware of important MCUs are available into which the required program can be written and tested for the 'correctness' of the hardware connections and the associated software.

One such tool commonly used in the academic environment is the Proteus VSM which is a design suite which offers the idea of 'virtual modeling' of MCU-based circuitry with important external peripherals like LEDs, LCDs, etc. With such a tool, testing of the circuit can be started as soon as the schematic is ready, and once the software is also ready, the complete setup can be tested and verified. Once this is confirmed to be working correctly, PCB design can be started.

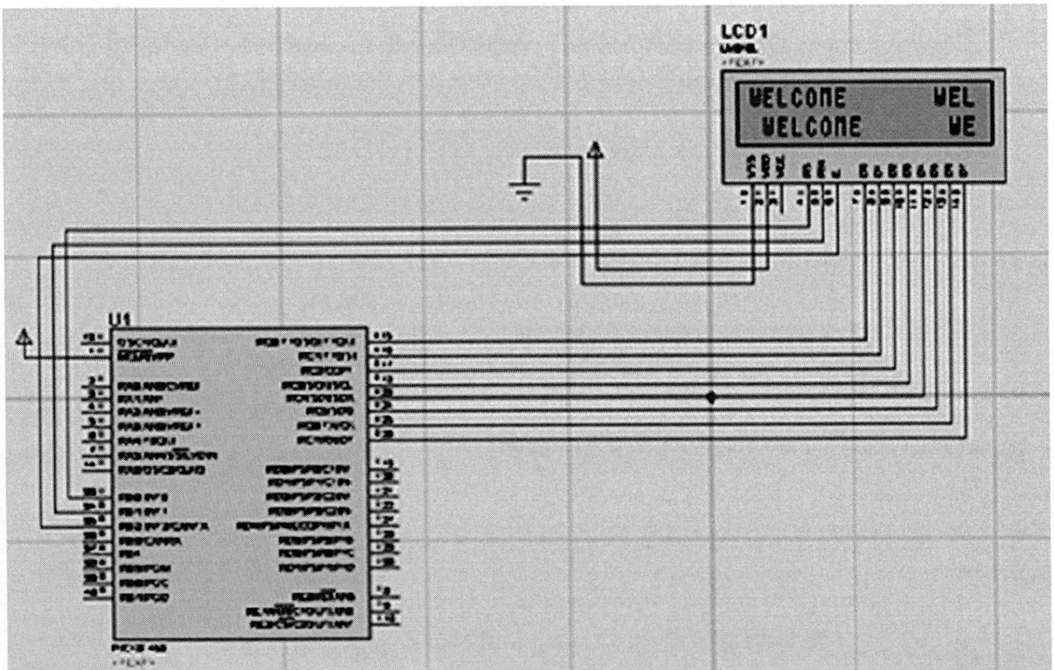

Figure 6.9 | A screenshot of a hardware connection simulated using Proteus VSM

Proteus VSM 'combines mixed mode SPICE circuit simulation, animated components and microprocessor models to facilitate co-simulation of complete microcontroller based designs'. MCUs of families like the 8051, PIC, ARM, HC11, etc. can be simulated and tested in terms of hardware and the programs burned into them. Figure 6.9 is a screenshot of the schematic of PIC 18F458 with an LCD display interfaced to it. The external connections between the MCU and the LCD unit have been simulated, and the display program has been loaded into it. Two character strings in two lines are shown on the display in the figure.

Conclusion

This chapter has dealt with some tools which are generally used in the development of embedded systems. Only a few simple tools have been covered because the target audience is expected to be university students. Do keep in mind that the embedded system industry is a multibillion dollar industry and many multinational companies develop very advanced products. For the development of very advanced systems, many sophisticated and elite tools are available which lets the developer have a very clear insight of the hardware and software he is in the process of developing. Such advanced tools are beyond the scope of this chapter as those tools are tuned to the requirements of professional developers working in the industry.

KEY POINTS OF THIS CHAPTER

- Embedded systems development needs a set of software tools.
- An IDE is a software tool chain used for software development, and is specific for a particular MCU.
- An IDE consists of an editor and a builder.
- The 'building' process includes the steps of compiling and linking.
- It is 'cross compiling' that is normally done in the case of embedded systems.
- A software simulator helps in checking the 'correctness' of the developed code.
- Downloading the executable file into the non-volatile memory can be done outside the circuit using a universal programmer.
- In circuit programming is the best solution for firmware embedding.
- An 'emulator' is a kind of hardware debugger.
- The Proteus VSM is a very popular hardware simulator.

QUESTIONS

1. Distinguish between hardware, software and firmware.
2. What is the role of a 'host system' in embedded system development?
3. What is an IDE?
4. Why should an IDE be 'specific' for a particular MCU family?

5. Define the process of 'assembly'.
6. What is the end product of the process of compilation?
7. Distinguish between compilation and cross compilation.
8. What is meant by the term 'disassembly'?
9. Where does 'linking' come in the steps of software development?
10. What are the components of ISP?
11. Where is OTP used and why?
12. What is the use of an ICE?

EXERCISES

1. Find the names of three popular IDEs not listed in Table 6.1.
2. Assuming you have done a project involving the development of an embedded board. Write down the names of the software tools you have used and your experiences while doing the development.

PART-II

SOFTWARE DESIGN ASPECTS

7 OPERATING SYSTEM CONCEPTS

In this chapter, you will learn

- Why a computer system needs an operating system
- The functions performed by an operating system
- What is meant by a kernel
- The concepts related to tasks and multitasking
- Calculations related to different scheduling algorithms
- The necessity and mechanisms of 'Inter Process Communications'
- The issues related to task synchronization
- The difficulties arising from racing, readers–writers problem and deadlock
- What is meant by 'bounded buffer' problem
- The concept and use of semaphores and mutexes
- Priority inversion and its solutions
- Methods of designing device drivers
- Codes and pseudo codes for OS functions

In this chapter, we will study the concepts of operating systems in general, and Chapter 8 will follow it up, by attending to the special requirements of what are called 'real-time' operating systems. The approach here will be to discuss concepts with numerical examples (wherever necessary), but codes/pseudo codes are presented separately, at the end of the chapter, and not within the conceptual discussions. Concepts regarding operating systems are very interesting, in that each one of them is related to some kind of real-world scenario and finding analogies from real life to understand underlying principles is easy.

Introduction

We have all heard of operating systems—we talk about their features and sometimes compare them—for example, we know that Windows 7 is available in the laptops and PCs we buy now; sometime back it was Vista, and recollect that the earlier Windows XP was a stable and reasonably good OS. Many of us still don't want to change to anything new.

Chapter-opening image: An 8051 based board.

Section 7.17 is written by Sai Krishna K., Design Engineer, Broadcom, Bangalore.

We recently have been hearing about the Android OS in the context of mobile phones and e-tablets. But there were other OSes in mobile phones earlier. For instance, there was Symbion in Nokia phones from quite a long time back, but it is only now that the public has become more aware of the word 'OS', and the features offered by different types of OSes. Apple has its own Mac OS for PCs and iOS for its IPhones and IPads. We will make a brief tour of the history of operating systems soon, to put the matter in the right perspective.

What exactly is an operating system and what does it do? In the simplest terms, we can consider it to be the **manager** of a system. For a PC, the OS manages the computer system which consists of the processor, memory and I/O devices like mouse, modem, keyboard, etc., and also the unlimited set of peripherals which are frequently plugged in, and unplugged from it. Another very important function that the OS has, is to hide the details of the hardware of the system from the user and his application program. Application programs can be written without much concern about the underlying hardware. This also means that the user does not have to know anything about the computer, except the application program that he is interested in.

This important aspect is what makes the computer, that is, the modern PC, a very convenient device—a child may be interested only in playing games on it, a salesman at the billing counter of a mall needs to bother only about entering prices of articles and printing bills, the design engineer at an engineering design centre is concerned about only the Computer Aided Design (CAD) program he currently uses. To each of these users, the OS hides the details of the intricate and complicated matters of the machine on which they works on. In short, the user needs to know only about how to run his application and nothing more.

This feature is called 'abstraction'—it means that at 'this' level, unnecessary details are hidden. The level can be different for different users. For example, the supervisory personnel at the computer centre of an institution will have to know more about setting and cancelling passwords of users, allotting each user a certain amount of memory and so on. Computer technicians have to go to a lower level and know greater details of the computer hardware, the software technician will have to know about the memory map of the system and so on. It is this feature of abstraction that makes computer usage a pleasure for all kinds of users.

An operating system is a special software (many processors provide a level of hardware support also, for its design) and is called the system software. In a computer system, the application software runs on top of system software using its support. That is why we frequently have to check whether an application software is compatible with a specific OS or not. There are many programs which run on Microsoft Windows but are not compatible with the Mac-OS (of Apple PCs) and vice versa. Linux OS users have a set of applications which run on Linux only. Such is the state of compatibility between system software and application software.

Currently there is also a transition occurring in terms of bit length. The earliest PCs had a data bus width of just 8 bits. Over the years that increased to 16, 32 and now 64 bits is standard and common. The OS code also has changed to using 64-bit word length. Thus, for instance, if we are offered a choice of 32-bit or 64-bit Windows 7, what do we choose? To 'move on' faster, it is best to use the 64-bit version, but there are a number of application programs which don't run on the 64-bit OS. Many cross compilers are not supported by 64-bit OSes. We may choose a 32-bit OS if we need to do embedded system development using low end IDEs, or may also consider having two OSes in the same machine, or have one OS and another one emulated for specific applications alone. These are choices that we can make for our own PC.

7.1 | Embedded Operating Systems

Till now, the concept of OS was talked about with reference to a PC. What about hand-held devices like mobile phones, PDAs, tablets, etc.? Why do they need an operating system? The answer is that each of them is almost as complex as a PC. A mobile phone has multiple tasks running concurrently, it has a number of I/O devices and a network, (the wireless mobile n/w) also to respond too. Besides that, we now run a number of applications on our phones right from bank software to entertainment software and games. There are mobile phones with an embedded version of the Windows 7 OS. Currently, Android is getting to be one of the most sought after OS for phones and tablets.

The Android and similar kinds of OS belong to a class named 'embedded OS' in contrast to the general purpose OS that computers use. The characteristics and special features needed for embedded and real-time OSes are covered in Chapter 8. In this chapter, we will be cover the important aspects of operating systems in general, and in the course of doing that, may point out some specific properties that embedded OSes should place more emphasis on.

7.2 | Network Operating Systems (NOS)

Each of us might have a PC (laptop or desktop), but we usually connect it to the Internet which is a 'network' of computers. Besides that, we find that institutions and organizations have computers connected as a 'local area network' and users have access to the resources locally available. Many OSes (UNIX, Mac OS, etc.) have networking features in it, but the ones that are designated as NOSes are those which are designed for networked systems alone. Examples are Novell Netware, Windows NT, Microsoft Server, etc.

7.3 | Layers of an Operating System

Figure 7.1 shows the functional layers of a computer system highlighting the 'level' at which the OS resides. The application is written by users, while 'software system programmers' have the responsibility of the design of the OS and software utilities. Examples of application programs are games, web browsers, word processors, etc. The user 'runs' these software for his needs—he doesn't design the 'software' package, however.

The systems programmer is the person who designs utilities like compilers, linkers, software packages, etc. for specific applications. He is a software developer who, with more expertise can design the kernel of the OS, as well.

The hardware design is done by a computer architect and the OS is meant to shield the user from having to know anything about the hardware and its complexities.

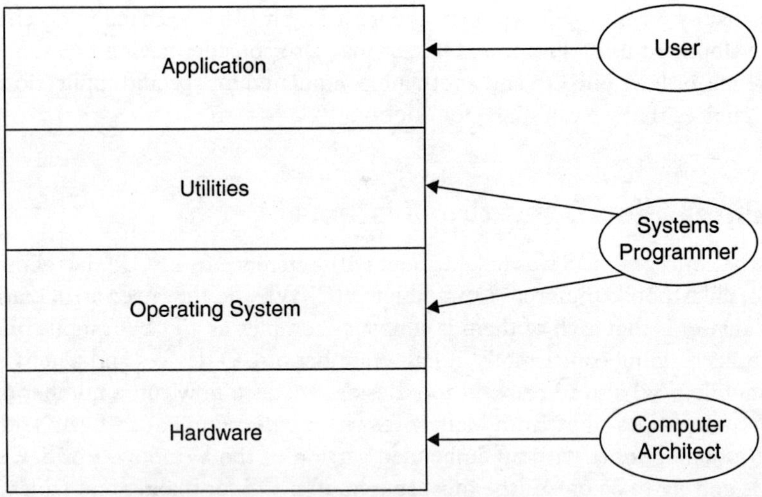

Figure 7.1 | Functional layers in a computer system

7.4 | History of Operating Systems

The earliest computers were quite small and simple and did not need an operating system, as the user directly talked (or rather, interacted) with hardware. But as computers became more complex and the range of users increased, having an interface for dealing with users on one side, and the hardware, on the other side, became necessary. If we look into the history of computers, we are likely to find numerous variants of OSes developed by various individuals and companies. Here we will talk only about the important ones which really made their presence felt. Let us make a list of such OSes catering to general purpose computer systems.

i) **MS-DOS:** In 1980–81, work began on the DOS (Disk Operating System) which later came to be associated with Microsoft and came to be named as MS-DOS. It is a command line based OS, and over the years has kept up by adding new features, and thus newer and newer versions of DOS keep on coming. It has been part of all Windows based OSes, except in the latest 64-bit Windows.

ii) **UNIX:** It was in 1970 that UNIX was developed using the C programming language, by Ken Thomson and Dennis Ritchie. It became very popular and was used in multiprogramming environments.

iii) **WINDOWS:** In the 1990s, Windows 3.0 was launched by Microsoft which is a GUI-based OS. GUI stands for 'Graphical User Interface'. Though Apple's PCs has already had such a GUI-based OS, it was the IBM PCs which made Windows popular. Over the years, newer versions of Windows keep coming up, each one claiming to have more and improved features with respect to the previous version. All in all, Windows is the most widely used OS in the world.

iv) **LINUX:** This is a very popular OS now, being used for small as well as very large applications. It started its development in 1991, the propounder being Linus Torvalds. Linux has similarities to Unix, but is not a version of Unix. Torvalds began work on the project while he was an undergraduate student on a part-time basis. He now works full-time for the Open Source Development Lab (OSDL) in Portland, Oregon (IBM is a member of OSDL, and thus helps support his work).

From that modest beginning 15 years ago, Linux has grown to be a complete modern operating system with a world-wide following. It is widely used on servers and PCs and embedded systems. Linux has also become the standard platform for developing and deploying open source software. There are embedded versions of linux as well as real-time versions.

7.5 | Functions Performed by an OS (Components of an OS)

Now let's make a survey of the functions that a general purpose operating system takes charge of. Figure 7.2 is a diagram which shows the important functional blocks of an operating system. The central function of an OS is 'resource management'.

What are the resources associated with a computer system?

There is the CPU, memory and I/O which are 'physical resources'. Logical resources are files, and defined variables like semaphores, mutexes, etc. (they are discussed in forthcoming sections).

7.5.1 | Processor Management

The most important resource in a computer is of course the processor. **We will assume a single processor system in our discussions here.** It is the processor which does computation and data processing, that is, it is the work horse in the system, and all the jobs (tasks) to be done are allocated to the processor.

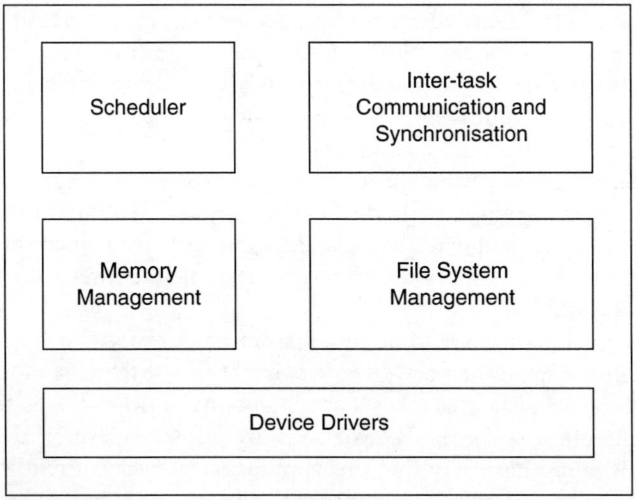

Figure 7.2 | Functional block diagram of an operating system

What then, is the need to 'manage' the processor?

The answer is that, almost always, a number of tasks are present in the system and all of them need the processor. But only one of then can get the service of the processor at a time. Thus, managing the processor translates to managing the tasks in the system efficiently, such that the processor is kept busy as long as there are tasks left to be done.

In addition to this, the different tasks in the system may need to communicate with each other and this needs synchronization between them.

7.5.2 | Memory Management

The processor is the most important resource, no doubt, but it cannot work in isolation. Memory is the next most important resource and there is constant interaction, that is, communication between memory and the processor. There are different types of memory in a system. Semiconductor memory is the primary or main memory. There is also the secondary memory which is the hard disk (for a PC).

The functions of an OS with respect to memory management can be listed as follows:

i) All programs are 'run' with code and data in the RAM. Thus for a program, RAM space has to be allocated when the program runs and de-allocated when the program terminates. The OS has to keep track of the RAM space when this is being done.
ii) Secondary memory is by and large, a storage space. The OS is expected to keep track of this storage space and allocate it aptly as required.
iii) The most important aspect of memory management is the virtual memory concept.
iv) The primary memory and secondary memories together constitute a system of 'virtual memory' which is a game played by the OS to get the user (i.e. the application) into believing that he has unlimited memory space. This needs a little more explanation.

What is virtual memory?

Some of you might have already learned this concept in 'computer architecture'.

Virtual memory is a concept by which the application (in effect, the user) is made to believe that it has much more memory than is physically available. In effect, there is this idea of an 'enlarged address space' which is called a 'virtual address space'. This space maps into a physical address space, ultimately.

Semiconductor memory, which is reasonably fast (RAM/ROM), is what we usually designate as 'primary memory', 'main memory' or 'physical memory'. The hard disk and other memory types are designated as 'secondary memory'. The processor directly communicates with the main memory only, but data movement between the secondary and main memory is possible.

Whenever an application is to be run, the processor expects to find the associated data and code in the main memory. In case it is not found there, it should be brought thereto from the hard disk. This takes a small amount of time. This is the reason why we find our computer 'slow' if the RAM size is low. However, even if the RAM is of a large capacity, it is not necessary that our application files are currently present there. Managing the system, such that important data and code are found in the main memory most of the time, is part of the 'cleverness' of the operating system. Figure 7.3 shows the

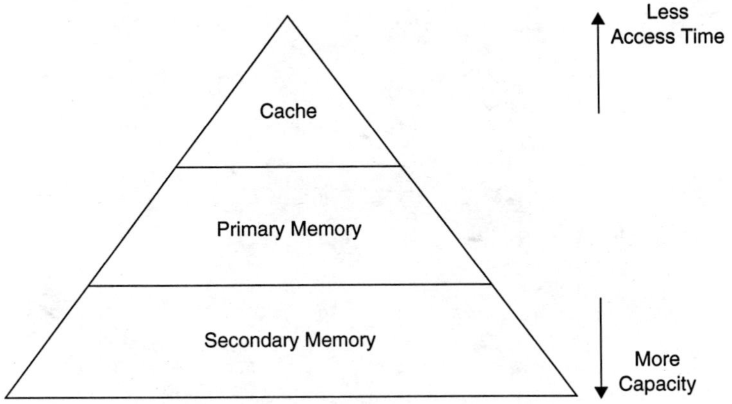

Figure 7.3 | Memory hierarchies

memory hierarchy in a computer system. In most computers today, there is an additional level in the memory hierarchy and that is the 'cache', which is a fast SRAM memory and which contains a copy of some parts of the RAM content.

7.5.2.1 | *Memory Management in An Embedded System*

In an embedded system, the kinds of memory available are RAM and ROM. Technologically there are different kinds of RAM and ROM—like RAM may be SRAM or SDRAM; ROM may be flash memory and/or EEPROM. The memory management involved in embedded systems is less complex than in general purposes PCs but there are some aspects to be managed when the system becomes complex, and dynamic memory allocation techniques may become necessary. But application programs for simple embedded systems (like those for 8-bit microcontrollers) almost always use static memory allocation. In such cases, there is no need for special techniques of memory management.

7.5.3 | IO Management

IO is the next important resource and is the one which allows the user to communicate with the computer. The number of I/O devices in common usage is increasing day by day as newer types and brands become available. Managing all this is quite cumbersome and requires skill. Figure 7.4 shows some I/O devices that are commonly used. It is obviously that there is no similarity between any of them, that is, the keyboard, mouse and video monitor. All work on different principles and protocols, and the voltage and current levels are different.

How does the OS get to manage all of them? The method is to have a device driver for each device. This is a set of routines written for the specific device. This routine takes care of the hardware setup and protocols associated with that device. The OS includes device drivers for most of the commonly used devices like printers, keyboard, mouse, video card, sound card, etc. The device drivers may be different for different brands of these I/O devices. If a new device is added to the system, the device driver also is loaded and when (if) the device is removed, the driver is unloaded. We will see more about this in Section 7.16.

Figure 7.4 | A keyboard, video monitor and mouse

7.5.4 | File Management

All of us are used to storing data in what are called files. Files are continuously created, deleted, modified, saved, opened, closed and stored in directories or folders. When a file in a particular folder has to be opened, it has to located and to get this done efficiently, file storage should be well structured. The file management system has to control access to data in files; certain files are to be password protected, some are 'read only' and certain files are to be restricted to be accessed only by specific programs. The file manager must attach a set of attributes to each file to control the access to it.

See Figure 7.5 which shows a file structure for a typical system. There is a root directory and directories within them, called subdirectories, for different applications like games, CAD, documents etc. The word 'directory' originated from MS-DOS. Windows calls them 'folders' and subfolders.

7.5.5 | Multiprogramming

This term refers to the fact that multiple users use the same CPU. There is the case that there is only one CPU, but multiple terminals on which multiple users work at the same time. In this case, each user is made to believe that it is his program that is running all the time, though actually all programs are running on a time shared basis.

Another case is when a user of the PC opens multiple windows and executes many different programs simultaneously. Here again, time sharing occurs but the user is not aware of this. The actions taken by the OS to create a time sharing environment should be transparent to the user. There is a task scheduler and dispatcher to take care of such matters.

7.5.6 | Protection and Security

The terms 'protection' and 'security' refer to two different aspects that the OS has to take care of.

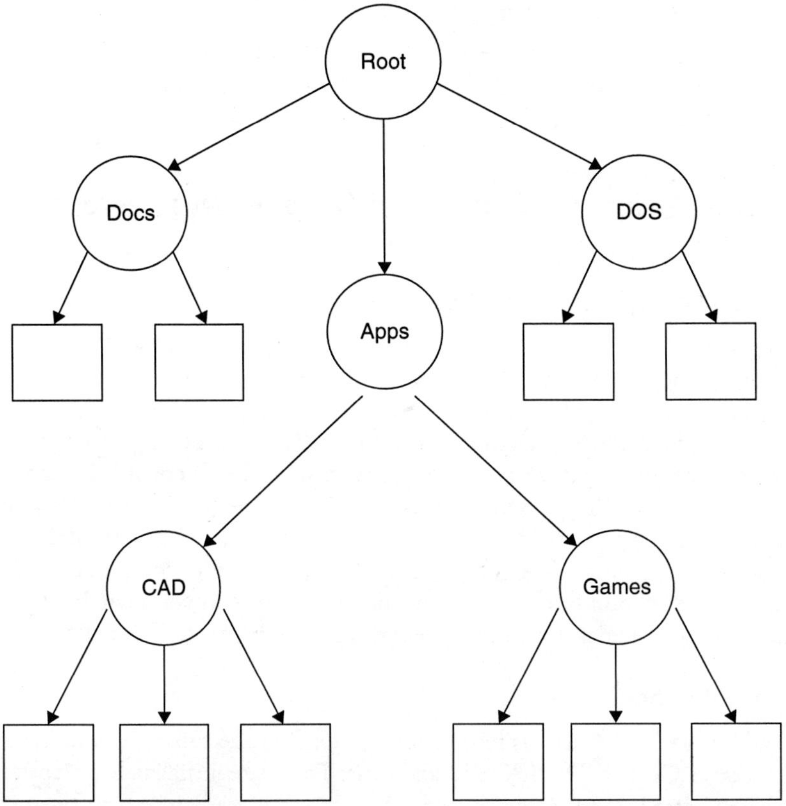

Figure 7.5 | A typical file system

Computers may be standalone or networked. In any case, multiple users and multiple programs use them, and there is the additional aspect that data and code from the same pool is shared across users. When this is being done, it is important to define and also maintain the rights of each of these users with respect to the shared information, and thus prevent unauthorized access. This aspect is called 'protection' and the OS has to implement this feature. This relates to protection between users. Another aspect of protection is when application level programs are not allowed to access system software and device drivers, etc. This aspect is for protecting the OS software from being tromped upon by users.

'Security' is something else. It is the capability of the system to keep itself safe from external attacks from viruses, malicious software and from intrusion by external agencies (who are not in the user set). A lot of security features may be incorporated in OSes itself, but for extra security, additional software like anti-viruses, spyware, etc. may be needed. It is obvious that computers dealing with defence information need more security incorporated into their operating systems that those used at home.

7.5.7 | Network Management

All computers are not connected to a LAN or WAN. But in the current world, every computer should be able to access the Internet and thus be part of the World Wide Web. Thus, 'network management' is part of the functionality of any operating system.

7.6 | Some Terms Associated with Operating Systems and Computer Usage

7.6.1 | Low Level Software Utility

This is a term very frequently used. What is its meaning and relevance?

A technical dictionary refers to 'software utility' as 'a program that performs a specific task related to the management of computer functions, resources, or files, such as password protection, memory management, virus protection, and file compression'. We have all used such software—they don't come as part of the OS, but these utilities can enhance computer usage by providing important services which are usable by users. Programs like disk cleanup, screen savers, disk partitioners, etc. are considered to be utilities which a user can use, provided he has a reasonably good knowledge about computers. Utilities are different from application programs like document, spreadsheet and database programs. Such programs are also developed by system developers. Refer to Figure 7.1.

7.6.2 | Boot Loader

A bootloader is a software that is responsible for loading the OS code onto main memory. Once Power On Self Test (POST) and other hardware initialization steps are done by the BIOS (Basic Input Output System), the system is ready to run software. For the OS itself to be run, it must be copied from secondary memory to primary memory. The bootloader is responsible for this. Once the OS kernel is loaded, the processor can start executing it. The kernel code will then continue to load and initialize other parts of the OS. A simple bootloader may consist of only a few assembly instructions that copy OS code from disk to RAM. More complex bootloaders can allow the user to select a particular OS (on a system with multiple OSes) or set options to the kernel.

For example, GRUB (Grand Unified Boot Loader), LILO (Linux loader).

Bootloaders are highly dependant on the hardware platform.

For embedded processors, a bootloader does the same thing, but here it loads application code (perhaps statically linked to an RTOS) onto the processor's execution space (usually flash). Bootloaders usually allow the code to be transferred via one of several interfaces like the serial port or JTAG port.

7.6.3 | User Interface

Users of a computer like to have an easy and a 'user friendly' interface to it, implying that, using a computer should be a pleasurable experience.

What is meant by the term 'user interface'?

It is the way the computer 'appears' to a user. It is through this interface that requests are sent to the operating system by the user for access to input devices and output devices.

Thus, the results of mouse clicks and key presses which are input devices are seen on the video monitor which is an output device. This is the case when the user interface is a GUI, that is, a Graphical User Interface, as we have in Windows type OSes. There is another user interface, that is, the command line interface (CLI) which is the interface for MS-DOS and sometimes used for Linux and Unix. In a CLI, we type commands for operations we need to perform. This may seem to be cumbersome, but has its plus points once the commands are mastered.

7.6.4 | Application Programming Interface (API)

An API is a set of functions, routines or protocols to simplify the process of building software applications. When a developer needs to write code, he doesn't have to start from first principles or the very basics to build an application. He can put together a set of routines from the API and get his application working. The API is the functional interface over which a programmer writing an application program in a high level language can get the service (data or functions) of the operating system or another application.

For example, in Chapter 12 on PSoC, for each user module, APIs are provided to help the programmer. For using the PWM module, for example (Section 12.7.3), the function PWM8_1_Start() is used. The internal details of this function need not be known to the programmer. Thus, an API provides a level of abstraction for the programmer and acts as an interface.

7.6.5 | POSIX

The words POSIX stands for 'Portable Operating System Interface'. This is a standard specified by IEEE to define the API and shell and utilities interfaces, to maintain portability between application programs and operating systems. It was started with the aim of developing an interface for UNIX compatibility, but now the standard has developed beyond this simple aim. By designing their programs to conform to POSIX, developers have some assurance that their software can be easily ported to POSIX-compliant operating systems. Complying to this standard is very important for embedded applications, because of the large variety of applications and many variants of operating systems available in the field.

7.7 | The Kernel

Figure 7.6 shows the 'onion skin' diagram of the operating system. The centre portion is the kernel. The kernel is the innermost part or core of an operating system, and it is that provides the basic services for all for all other parts of the system. The kernel is sometimes referred to as the supervisor, core or internals of the operating system. Outside the kernel is the less important part of the system software (Level-1), and the software utilities (Level-2). Outside all this are the application programs (Level-3).

The kernel of an OS performs the following services (most of which we discuss in the following section), though the last two items need not mandatorily be a part of the kernel.

- Interrupt handling
- Task creation and scheduling

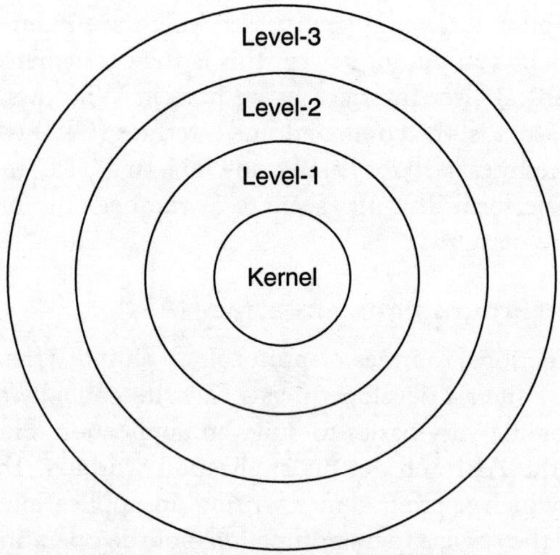

Figure 7.6 | 'Onion skin' diagram of the operating system.

- Inter process communication
- Support of I/O devices
- Memory allocation and deallocation
- File system management
- Network management

The kernel is the first part of the operating system to load into memory (RAM) during system startup. It remains there for the entire duration of the session because its services are required continuously. Less important system programs and utilities lie outside the kernel.

Because of its critical nature, the kernel has a privileged status as compared to normal user applications. It has a protected memory space and full access to hardware. This status and its memory space are collectively referred to as kernel-space. User applications, on the other hand, execute in user-space. These user applications do not have the privileges of kernel code, but can use kernel services using system calls. This relationship between an application program and the kernel through the system call interface is what prompts us to say that applications run on the OS. Figure 7.7 shows the user and kernel spaces. The system call interface is to enable applications to use kernel services. I/O is managed by device drivers on the other side.

Figure 7.7 shows that the kernel interacts with the hardware, on the one side, and the applications on the other.

With such a definition for the kernel, a number of questions need to be answered.

How does the kernel interact with the hardware?

Kernels usually implement some level of hardware abstraction for the underlying hardware. Thus for I/O, device drivers access the hardware, and for memory and the processor there are another set of kernel functions.

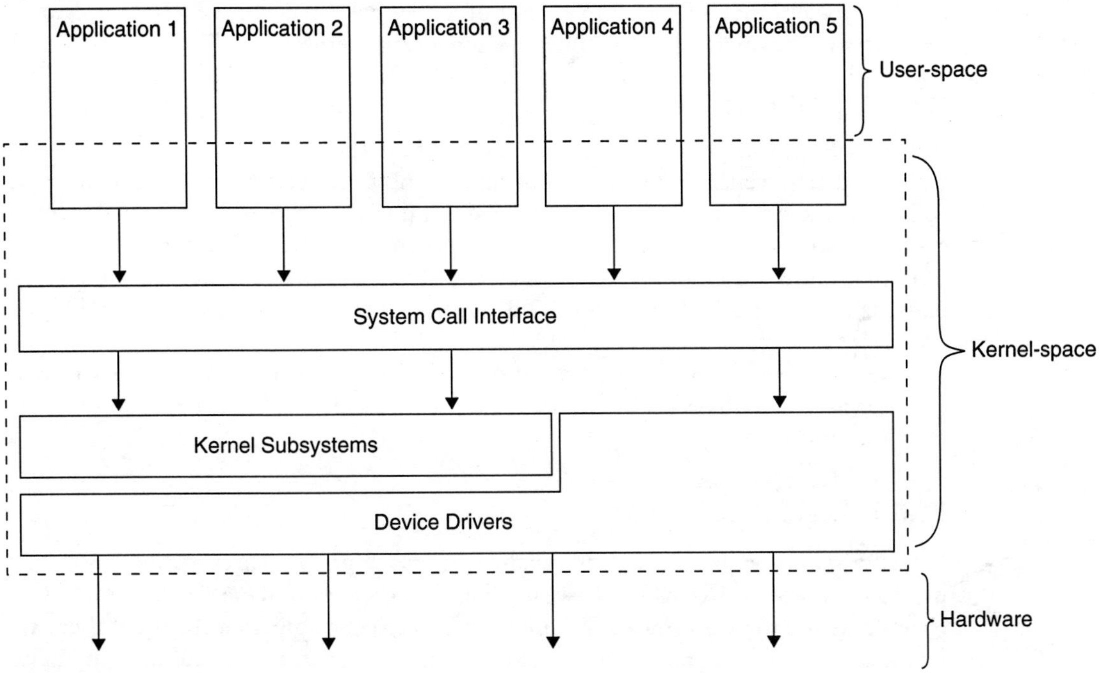

Figure 7.7 | Kernel and user spaces and I/O management for an OS

How specific is a kernel?

The kernel of an OS is very specific, that is, the kernel of Windows 98 and Windows XP are different and no migration is possible from one to the other.

Are kernels specific to the hardware they are loaded into?

Kernels are designed with a level of abstraction that that hide the details of the hardware below it and so permits them to be loaded into different kinds of hardware. But there are specific different kernel options that have to be configured when the OS is installed. This 'configuration' is related to the hardware onto which it is being installed. Changing major hardware components, such as the motherboard, processor or memory, often requires a kernel update. Such an aspect of the operating system may not be noticeable for a user who uses PCs with standard OSes, but when trying to load OSes into embedded boards, it is important to know the type of board being booted with the OS, and the configuration settings for it.

7.7.1 | Types of Kernels

There are two schools of thoughts with respect to kernel design.

7.7.1.1 | *Monolihthic kernel*

The word 'monolithic' means 'consisting of one piece'. A monolithic kernel implies that the kernel is one single entity and is loaded as a whole in the kernel space. Such a system has the problem that a failure in any part of the kernel can cause the whole system to crash. Kernels of solaris, unix and linux are monolithic kernels.

7.7.1.2 | *Microkernels*

In this, some processes of the kernel (i.e. the less important parts) are separated out and designated as 'servers'. The relatively more important of these servers run in kernel space, while the others run in user space. Because of this division, there is the need of interprocessor communication (IPC-Section 7.12) between these servers (i.e. processes) which can bring down the efficiency of the kernel. But the advantage is that the modularity prevents a 'total crash', if problems occur in some of the servers. Minix and BeOS are examples of microkernels.

Now that we have had a general introduction to the idea of operating systems as a whole. it is time to dissect it and learn the exact mechanism by which each of its functionalities is realized.

7.8 | Tasks/Processes

The activity of a computer is to 'run/execute' programs. A **program in execution** is **formally defined as a process.** Terms like 'task' and 'job' are also used to **denote a process. In this chapter, we use the words tasks and processes interchangeably.** In a system, if there are multiple programs that need execution at the same time, we call it a multiprogramming environment and the system is a multitasking system.

A task is defined in terms of the program counter which points to its code memory, the working registers (general purpose and status), stack and stack pointer. Another task will use a different area of code memory, a different stack but the same working registers (which are limited in number for any processor). We assume the single processor system, i.e., a system in which there is only one CPU to perform all the computations needed.

A process/task can be in any one of the following five states and there will be continual transition between the states, because a process is a dynamic item. The five states are named as new, ready, running, blocked and exit. Let's see what each state means.

i) **New:** A process has been created but it hasn't yet got admission into the 'ready' queue of executable processes.
ii) **Ready:** Here, the process has all the resources (like I/O) needed to execute, except the availability of the CPU for which it has to wait.
iii) **Running:** This is the state of the process that is currently being executed using the CPU.
iv) **Blocked:** In this state, the process cannot execute until a specified event such as an I/O completion occurs.
v) **Exit:** The process has terminated because its execution is complete, or because an error has occurred.

Figure 7.8 shows the state transition diagram, which may also be called the process life cycle, as it shows the possible states a process may traverse during its life time. A process when created is in the 'new' state. If then it gets all the necessary resources to run, it enters the 'ready' state. There may be many other processes in the ready state, which makes a 'ready queue'. Processes in this queue wait for their chance to get the CPU. But only one of them gets the CPU at a particular time. Which one of them (among the

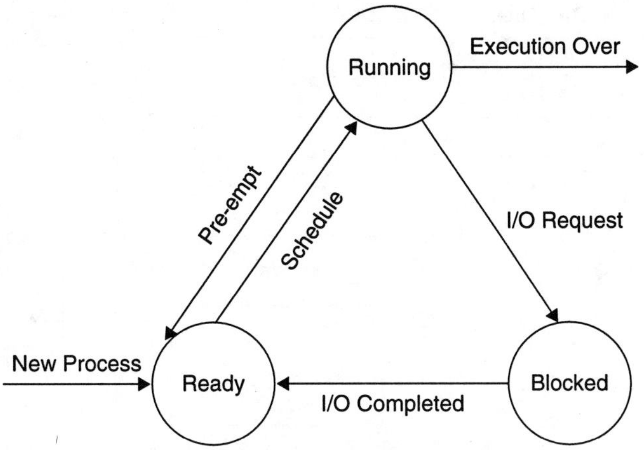

Figure 7.8 | The state transition diagram of a process

waiting tasks) gets the chance to execute, depends on the scheduling algorithm. The arrow marked 'schedule' shows a specific task getting its chance to use the CPU.

Figure 7.8 shows the transitions occurring between the ready, running and blocked states. Let's see the possibilities for the transitions to occur.

i) A process can exit from the running state when it finishes its stipulated use of the CPU.
ii) A process can be pushed back into the Ready queue. This is called 'pre-emption' and the reasons for this to happen will be that some other process is to be given the use of the CPU (depending on the scheduling algorithm).
iii) A process can be pushed into the 'blocked' state because of needing some additional resources, or an event from I/O, like a keyboard input or so. The arrow from the running to the blocked state shows this case.
iv) While in the blocked state, if the awaited I/O event occurs, it cannot go back to the 'running' state directly, rather, it waits in the ready queue until it gets its next chance to use the CPU.
v) Finally (many transitions can occur again), it goes to the exit state of successful completion or abnormal termination (due to some unforeseen error).

The OS is responsible for providing the support needed for creating a process and taking it to its termination. If for instance, a user task is taken up, say, a user opens a program window and wants to execute it, the OS prepares the task structure (called a task/process control block) for it, verifies the availability of resources and puts it in the ready queue.

7.8.1 | Task (Process) Control Block

This is a table that contains all the information about the task, and is prepared by the OS and placed in memory. It contains the following

i) The unique ID of the task
ii) The state of the task

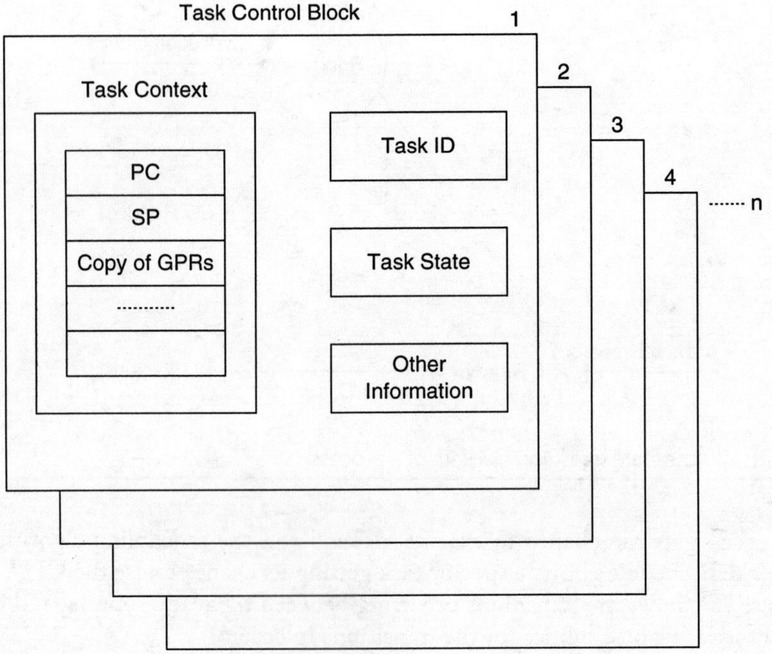

Figure 7.9 | Task control blocks for n tasks

iii) Scheduling information with respect to it
iv) The registers it uses and their contents
v) The I/O resources it has been allocated
vi) Pointers to the memory it uses
vii) Priority of the task
viii) Other information pertaining to the task

Thus for each task, there is a Task/Process control block (TCB/PCB). If there are n tasks, there are n TCBs in memory. Figure 7.9 shows the figure of TCBs for n tasks.

7.8.2 | Multitasking

We have assumed the case of 'a single CPU and multiple tasks' awaiting service from this CPU. Thus, it is clear that one task should not monopolize the use of the CPU, that is, the CPU must be shared between tasks. This is 'time multiplexing'. This is meant to create a feel of parallelism, with each task getting executed, but not at the same time. This is a sort of pseudo parallelism and is achieved by multitasking. It is imperative then that 'task switching' be done. Each task is allowed to use the CPU for some time, after which it relinquishes its claim and allows the next task to execute. In effect, chunks of each task get executed each time.

Recollect that there is a TCB associated with each task, which contains all the information of that task. This information is called the 'context' of the task. For a particular task, there are register contents, memory pointers, resource pointers, etc. This is what is meant by the context of the task at the time that it 'switches'. Task switching entails context switching which tells us that the context of the new task will be different from that of the abandoned task. So, it is obvious that all the information of the old task is to be saved, and the term used for this is 'context saving'. Because context saving is done, there is no difficulty in resuming this task from the point at which it had to stop, when it gets the service of the CPU once again, later.

When the CPU takes up a new task, the context changes to that of the new task. When an old task that was abandoned, is taken up again, context retrieval occurs. Thus in a multitasking system, context switching, context saving and context retrieval are activities that occur continuously. Note that these activities are time-consuming activities. All of them cause memory writes (for context saving) and memory reads (for context retrieval) as the TCBs are in memory.

The obvious side effect of multitasking is the additional time overhead in switching from one task to another. The operating system is a software but if the processor for which it is designed, provides hardware support for multitasking, the time overhead can be reduced. Most advanced processors provide this sort of support. The x86 processors from 80286 onwards have special registers and other support structures for multitasking. Embedded processors like ARM have modes for fast switching on interrupts. It is by using the mechanism of interrupts that task switching occurs—recollect that what an interrupt does is the abandoning of the current task and taking up a new task (Section 2.2.9).

How does multitasking affect the user?

There are single user operating systems like DOS, and multi user systems like Windows. In the latter, a number of tasks can run concurrently. The word 'concurrently' in this context means that all these tasks are placed for execution, but only one task is actually being executed by the CPU. The CPU is being 'time multiplexed' and with a high rate of this multiplexing, it appears that all the tasks are being run at the same time—this is the concurrent processing we talk about. The user is unaware that the CPU is being switched from one task to another. The user gets the feeling that all the tasks are executing in parallel. But as the number of tasks increase, one obvious effect is that of a 'system slowdown'.

7.8.3 | Task (Process) Scheduling

Now that we have discussed multitasking in principle, the next step is to get an idea of how it is accomplished in operating systems. What is the criterion on which task switching is done? A number of questions arise. Does each task gets a stipulated amount of time for executing before it is forced to relinquish its use of the CPU? Or are there some tasks which are more favoured such that they are allowed to use more CPU time? What is the order in which tasks are assigned to use the CPU? Are there tasks which are forced to wait because other more important tasks need to be executed earlier?

The answers to all these questions give us a clue as to what the scheduling policy of the operating system is. Note Figure 7.2 that shows that a scheduler is a specific and very important unit in an operating system. What a scheduler does (in general) is to share a 'resource' between the requestors. The scheduler does not want to give the resource to just one of the requesting parties alone, because all tasks are equally important to it.

Consider the common kitchen of a multiroomed apartment in which many families reside. Only one family can use the kitchen at a time, and if they all agree to use it on a time shared basis, the apartment manager can schedule it in a particular sequence based on the needs and time patterns of the different families.

In a computer system, when a number of tasks arise, the scheduler has the duty of allocating the services of the CPU to each one of them, based on a set of scheduling conditions. The conditions depend on the types of applications for which the operating system is used. The task scheduling conditions for a 'real time' embedded OS are much more stringent (Refer to Chapter 8) than for a non real-time OS.

Now we will go right into the heart of the matter by discussing the important task scheduling algorithms applicable for general purpose and non real-time embedded operating systems. The special and stringent task scheduling methods for real-time embedded systems are relegated to the next chapter.

7.8.4 | CPU and IO Bound Tasks

In a computer system, there are multiple tasks, one CPU and many I/O devices. A task usually needs to use the CPU as well as I/O devices. Some tasks are computationally intensive in which case they use the CPU for longer periods—they are termed CPU bound tasks—other tasks which need more I/O time are called I/O bound tasks. For example, a task which needs to do a lot of printing is an I/O bound task, because it uses the printer far more than it uses the CPU. But on the average, a typical task consists of a CPU burst followed by an I/O burst as in Figure 7.10, where a burst means the period of activity during which time a task uses the CPU or I/O as the case may be.

7.8.5 | Selection of a Scheduling Algorithm

Scheduling of tasks means that a decision is made regarding the order/sequence in which tasks are to be allocated the use of the CPU. We assume a system in which there are multiple tasks each of which is vying to get the service of the CPU. What are the objectives aimed to be achieved when a scheduling algorithm is chosen? Let's define some terms which will help us understand the qualities of a good scheduling policy, in a quantitative manner.

i) **CPU utilization:** There is only one processor and it should be utilized to the maximum; as far as possible, the CPU should never be allowed to idle. CPU utilization factor is defined as the percentage of time the CPU is working. When the CPU works all the time, the utilization is 100%.

ii) **Response time:** Consider a task which is waiting for the CPU from which it needs the response corresponding to the execution of the task. If this task gets its response

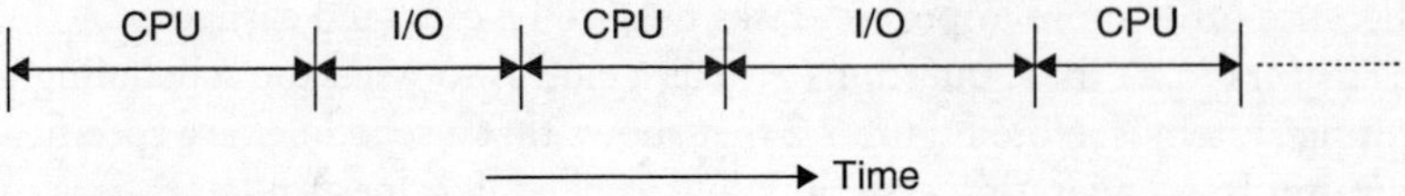

Figure 7.10 | Alternate CPU and I/O bursts

soon, the scheduling policy adopted for the system is assumed to be good—in principle, the response time should be minimum.

iii) **Turnaround time (TAT):** The time interval from the instant the task is presented to the system, to the instant that it exits after completion is defined as the 'turn around time'. This interval is likely to be quite eventful. Initially the task may have to wait to get the CPU. Even after getting the service of the CPU, it may go to the blocked state or back to the ready queue. Obviously then, the task may will not get executed in 'one go'. Parts of it may get executed until it reaches completion. Thus the TAT is the sum total of the 'execution' periods and the 'wait' periods. For a system, the average turnaround time indicates how well it can accommodate and execute multiple tasks efficiently.

iv) **Throughput rate:** This corresponds to the number of tasks processed in unit time. This will be the inverse of the average turnaround time.

In short, the ideal scheduling strategy should give a high throughput rate, minimum response and turn around times and should maximize CPU utilization. It should be a 'fair' policy, in that no task should be unnecessarily denied/delayed the use of resources, while keeping in mind that more important tasks should get priority. We will examine various strategies and compare them.

7.8.6 | CPU Scheduler and Resource Manager

We are talking about a system with just one CPU and multiple tasks. Because each task wants the CPU, there is a CPU scheduler which allocates the use of CPU to one of the tasks. After the task finishes with the CPU, it might need the service of an I/O device—like a printer. At that time, there are other tasks also needing the same resource. Thus to manage the use of resources (typically,/O), there is a resource manager too. Thus, you may now visualize multiple tasks with the following status:

i) Waiting in the 'ready' queue for the service of the CPU
ii) Waiting in the device queue for the service of a specific I/O device

These queues are dynamic, because as tasks are ready to execute, they enter the ready queue of the CPU scheduler and from there to the running state. This happens continuously. Similar is the case for the device queue—tasks enter and leave the queue continuously.

All information about a task including the pointer to its starting point is noted and kept in the TCB. Thus, when we say that tasks are in the queue, it means that the TCBs of tasks are placed in a queue in memory.

7.9 | Scheduling Algorithms

Now we will have a look at some popular scheduling algorithms. Note Figure 7.11. As far as scheduling is concerned, only three states are to be thought of and they are the ready, running and blocked states. Any task will be in one of these states, during the time when scheduling is 'meaningful' for the task.

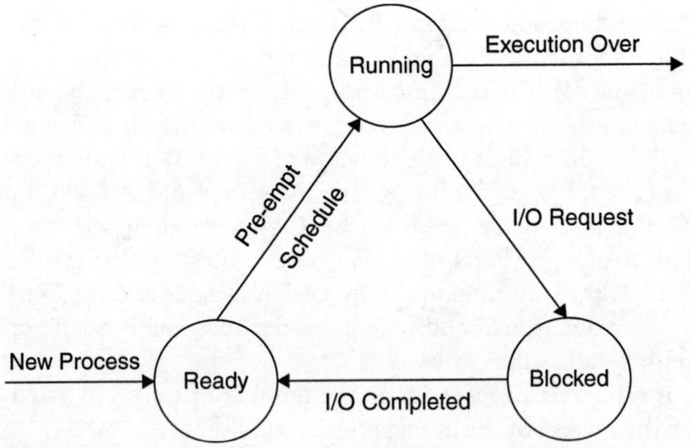

Figure 7.11 | The three important states of a task during scheduling

7.9.1 | Pre-emption

There is a word 'pre-emption' used frequently with respect to scheduling. The meaning of the word 'pre-empt' in this context is 'take the place after removing'. Thus, any task can 'pre-empt' the currently running task. Obviously in this context, the currently running task is forced to relinquish the use of the CPU and hand it over to some other task. The pre-empted task then waits in the ready queue (Refer Fig 7.11). With this possibility, scheduling policies may be non-preemptive or preemptive. We first consider non-preemptive scheduling methods.

7.9.2 | Assumptions

The assumptions that we make while calculating the results regarding a particular scheduling method are not realistic, in a true sense. Besides this, the calculation of 'times' ignores the 'scheduling latency'. Note the following:

i) The execution times of each task are to be known ahead of scheduling. This is neither realistic nor possible. Only some estimates of execution times may be made by the scheduler.
ii) Each time a new task comes into the ready queue, scheduling must be re-done.
iii) The scheduler needs some time to converge to a decision, and this adds a time overhead.

7.9.3 | Non-preemptive Methods of Scheduling

7.9.3.1 | *Co-operative Scheduling*

This is the simplest method of scheduling. Each task is allowed to execute to its finish, then only the next one is taken up. While one task executes, the others are willing to wait and this gives the name 'co-operative' to the scheduling algorithm. This is also a case of first come first serve scheduling (FCFS) or a first in first out scheme (FIFO). This is a very simple scheme, but the obvious disadvantage is that one task can monopolize the CPU if its service period is high.

Example 7.1

Consider a multitasking system which uses the FCFS scheduling algorithm. There are five tasks in the ready queue at a particular time, ordered from T_1 to T_5. Table 7.1 gives the tasks and the corresponding service times T_S for each. Find the average turn around time (TAT) and wait time. Comment on the CPU utilization.

Table 7.1

Task No	T_S (Time Units)
T_1	300
T_2	125
T_3	400
T_4	150
T_5	100

Solution

The tasks are serviced in the order in which they are placed in the ready queue. The Gantt chart (service time for each task) is shown in Figure 7.12.

Let us calculate the time for which each task waits. TAT for a task is its waiting time plus service time.

$$TAT = T_W + T_S$$

The first task T_1 has a waiting time of 0. All other tasks have to wait until the ones ahead in the ready queue are serviced.

T_1: $T_W = 0$, $T_S = 300$, $TAT = 300$
T_2: $T_W = 300$, $T_S = 125$, $TAT = T_W + T_S = 300 + 125 = 425$
T_3: $T_W = 425$, $T_S = 400$, $TAT = 825$
T_4: $T_W = 825$, $T_S = 150$, $TAT = 975$
T_3 $T_W = 975$, $T_S = 100$, $TAT = 1075$
Total TAT $= 3600$
Average TAT $= 3600/5 = 720$ time units

What is the total wait time?

$T_{TOTAL\text{-}W} = 0 + 300 + 425 + 825 + 975 = 2525$ time units
Average wait time $= 2525/5 = 505$ time units

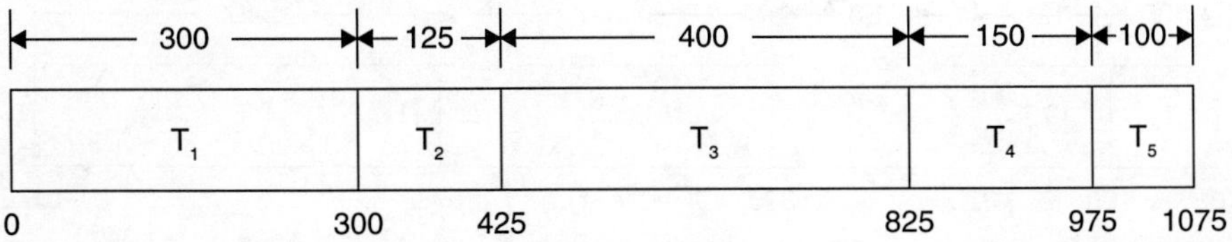

Figure 7.12 | Gantt chart of scheduling for Example 7.1

This example clarifies that this is a very simple algorithm. The problem that may occur is that if one process has a long execution time, it can monopolize the CPU.

7.9.4 | Shortest Job Next (SJN)

This is also called the shortest job first (SJF) algorithm. Here the method is to queue the tasks such that the one with the shortest service time gets to execute first. But the problem is that, usually the execution times of tasks are not known in advance. The method then is to estimate the service times by using the recent history of each of the tasks. The tasks are queued in the order of increasing service times.

Example 7.2 a

Let's use the data in the previous example itself. There are five tasks in the ready queue as we see in Table 7.2.

Table 7.2

Task No	T_S (Time Units)
T_1	300
T_2	125
T_3	400
T_4	150
T_5	100

Now to find the sequence in which the jobs are to be executed, just order them in the sequence of increasing service times. See the Gantt chart of Figure 7.13 which shows this. T_5, which is the shortest job, executes first; and T_3, with the longest execution time, comes last.

T_5: $T_W = 0$, $T_S = 100$, TAT = 100

T_2: $T_W = 100$, $T_S = 125$, TAT = $T_W + T_S = 100 + 125 = 225$

T_4: $T_W = 225$, $T_S = 150$, TAT = 375

T_1: $T_W = 375$, $T_S = 300$, TAT = 675

T_3: $T_W = 675$, $T_S = 400$, TAT = 1075

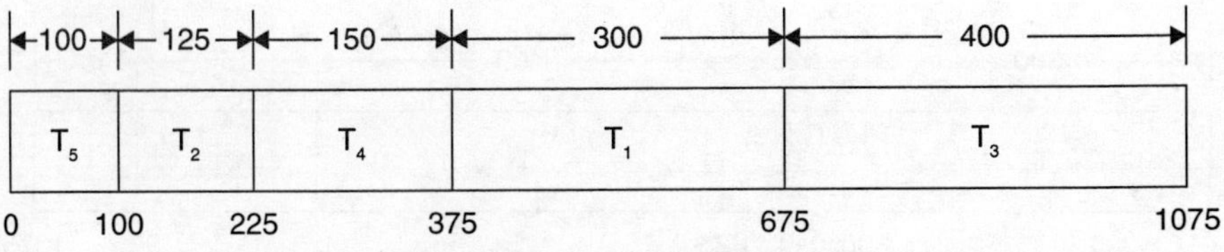

Figure 7.13 | Gantt chart of scheduling for Example 7.2a

Total TAT = 3600 time units

Average TAT = 3600/5 = 490 time units

What is the total wait time?

$T_{TOTAL\text{-}W} = 0 + 100 + 225 + 375 + 675 = 1375$ time units

Average wait time = 1375/5 = 275 time units

In this, the wait times are less than that in Example 7.1, and therefore the average TAT reduces.

Keep in mind that the service time is the same for any task, irrespective of the type of scheduling.

Example 7.2b

In Example 7.2a, we assumed that all the tasks are in the ready queue at time t = 0 and that no other tasks come in during the service periods of these tasks.

Now, let's change that assumption a bit. Assume that two new tasks enter the ready queue at time t = 350. At this time, T_4 is executing. Meanwhile, the ready queue is modified by adding T_7 and T_6 and ordered to have them execute before T_1 and T_3.

The new tasks are T_6 with a T_S of 250 and T_7 with a T_S of 200.

The scheduling is now re-ordered to be as shown in the Gantt chart of Figure 7.14

The waiting time of T_1 increases from 375 to 825

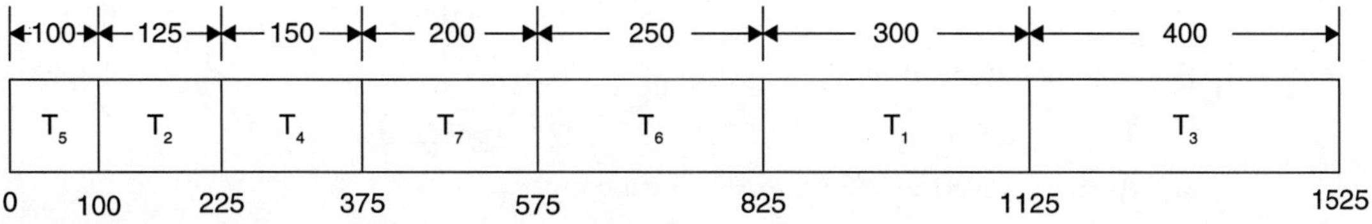

Figure 7.14 | Gantt chart of scheduling for Example 7.2b

The waiting time of T_3 increases from 675 to 1125

Thus, the effect of the new tasks is that the waiting times of T_1 and T_3 increase. If again tasks of shorter service periods come in to the ready queue, the execution of tasks of long periods gets delayed. **In the extreme case, there is the possibility of 'starvation' occurring for such tasks, by being deprived of the service of the CPU altogether.**

7.9.4.1 | *Priority-based Scheduling*

In such a system, tasks have priorities which are represented in terms of numbers. The convention is to have 0 to 255 as the numbers representing priorities, with 0 representing the highest priority, and higher numbers indicating lower priorities. Many systems use this scheme, and real-time operating systems (Chapter 8) use priority-based methods only.

Example 7.3a

See the task list in the ready queue in Table 7.3 with priorities as indicated.

Table 7.3

Task No	T_s (Time Units)	Priority
T_1	300	5
T_2	125	3
T_3	400	2
T_4	150	12
T_5	100	15

The scheduling will be in the order as shown in Figure 7.15

T_3: $T_W = 0$, $T_S = 400$
T_2: $T_W = 400$, $T_S = 125$, $TAT = T_W + T_S = 400 + 125 = 525$
T_1: $T_W = 525$, $T_S = 300$, $TAT = 825$
T_4: $T_W = 825$, $T_S = 150$, $TAT = 975$
T_5: $T_W = 975$, $T_S = 100$, $TAT = 1075$
Total TAT $= 3800$
Average TAT $= 3800/5 = 760$ time units

What is the total wait time?

$T_{TOTAL\text{-}W} = 0 + 400 + 525 + 825 + 975 = 2725$ time units
Average wait time $= 2725/5 = 545$ time units

The problem with such a scheme is that tasks of low priority tend to suffer. This condition is called 'starvation'. Note that the ready queue is dynamic, and as new tasks keep on coming, it may happen that some low priority tasks are kept in waiting. Every time that new tasks enter the ready queue, scheduling is re-done. If some higher priority tasks appear, the low priority tasks which have been waiting are forced to wait still more.

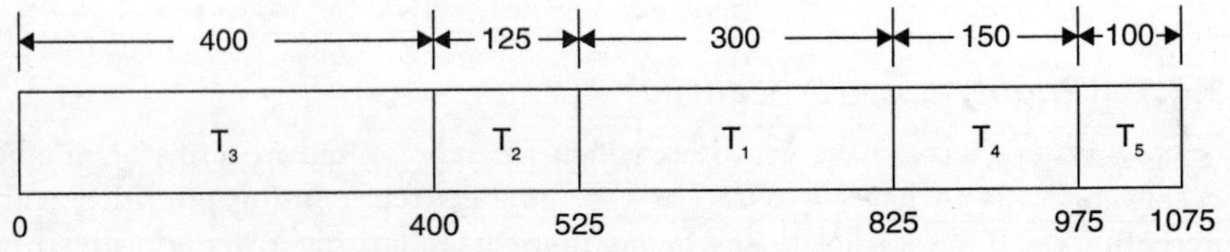

Figure 7.15 | Gantt chart of scheduling for Example 7.3a

Example 7.3b

Consider a situation when at t = 700, the ready queue of Table 7.3 gets appended with three new tasks T_6, T_7 and T_8, whose priorities are 0, 4 and 6, respectively. See Table 7.4. What is the change in the scheduling pattern?

Table 7.4

Task No	T_E (Time Units)	Priority
T_6	120	0
T_7	80	4
T_8	350	6

Solution

At t = 700, task T_1 is being serviced. It will continue to completion. Meanwhile, the scheduling order will be as shown in the Gantt chart of Figure 7.16.

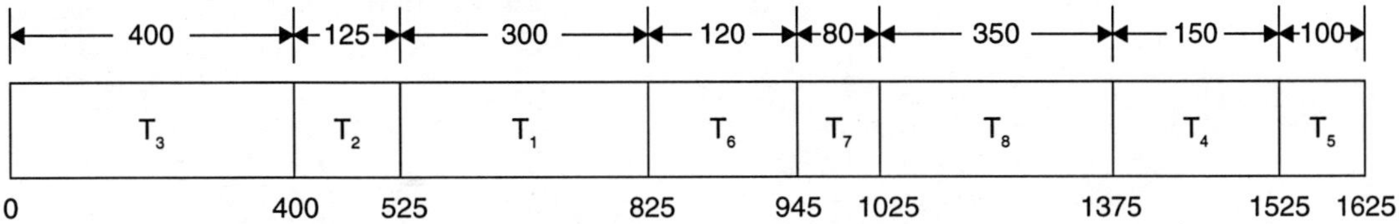

Figure 7.16 | Gantt chart of scheduling for Example 7.3b

After T_1, T_6, T_7 and T_8 are to be serviced. Only after these three are serviced, will T_4 and T_5 get the chance to use the CPU.

Now the waiting times of T_4 is changed from 825 to 825 + service times of T_6, T_7 and T_8.

That is, $825 + 120 + 80 + 350 = 1375$

The waiting time of T_5 is also changed from 975 to 975 + service times of T_6, T_7 and T_8.

That is, $975 + + 120 + 80 + 350 = 1525$

These waiting times can become bigger if more higher priority processes keep on coming in.

Comment: The solution to the problem of starvation occurring for low priority tasks is to change the priorities dynamically, and one technique is called 'aging'. In this method, the priority of a task increases as its waiting time increases, so at some time it finally gets the use of the CPU.

7.9.5 | Pre-emeptive Scheduling Strategies

In this set, when a task is running (i.e. using the CPU), it is pushed out from the 'running' state to the 'ready' state and another task from the ready queue is taken up. We say that the task has been pre-empted (removed and replaced). Let's examine some scheduling methods based on this pre-emptive approach.

7.9.5.1 | *Round Robin Scheduling*

Here, time slices are defined. Suppose there are n tasks in a system, each of them is allowed to execute for a period equal to the time slice. After this, the next task gets its turn, but can use the CPU only for a time equal to the defined time slice. This seems to be fair in the sense that all tasks get their chance at least once, in one round. This is also called a time sharing or time slice system.

Example 7.4

Draw the scheduling diagram corresponding to RR scheduling for the task set in Table 7.5. The time slice is defined to be 50 time units.

Table 7.5

Task No	T_S (Time Units)
T_1	150
T_2	100
T_3	200
T_4	50

Solution

Time quantum = 50

Note that this then acts like FCFS, in effect (Refer Figure 7.17).

T_1: $T_W = 0 + 150 + 100 = 250$, $T_S = 150$, TAT = 400

T_2: $T_W = 50 + 150 = 200$, $T_S = 100$, TAT = $T_W + T_S = 200 + 100 = 300$

T_3: $T_W = 100 + 150 + 50 = 300$, $T_S = 300$, TAT = 600

T_4: $T_W = 150 + T_S = 50$, TAT = 200

Total TAT = 1500

Average TAT = 1500/4 = 375 time units

What is the total wait time?

$T_{TOTAL\text{-}W} = 250 + 200 + 300 + 150 = 900$

Average wait time = 900/4 = 225 time units

In this, task T_4 needs only one time slice, while T_3 uses four time slices. Figure 7.17 shows the time periods taken by each task.

Are there problems in such a fair scheme?

The obvious problem is the amount of time to be spent in task switching, which is once every time slice. A lot of time is spent in context saving, switching and retrieval. If the time slices are small, the 'time overhead' is serious enough to be considered a system inefficiency. But if the time slice chosen is too large, the algorithm tends to being similar to FCFS.

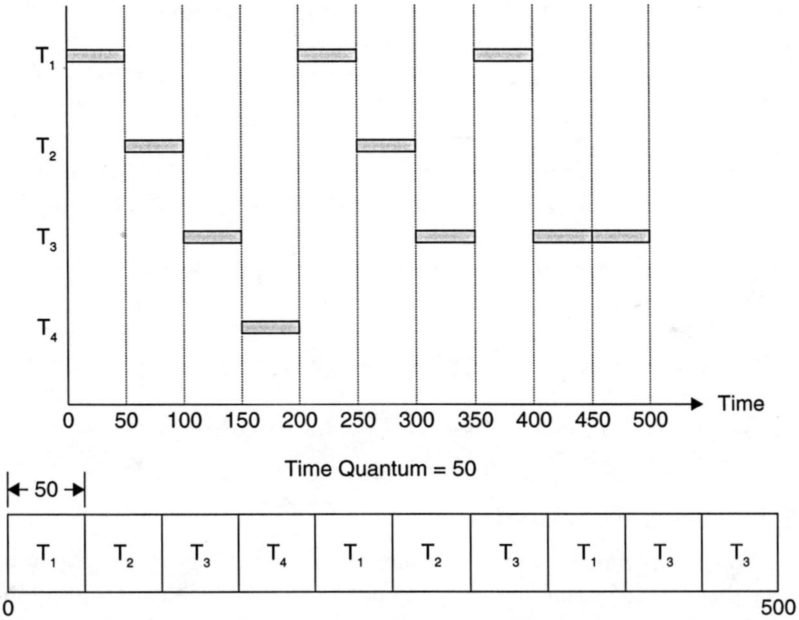

Figure 7.17 | Scheduling using the round robin technique

Example 7.5

Let's use the data of Example 7.1 for RR scheduling with a time slice of 100.

Table 7.6

Task No	T_s (Time Units)
T_1	300
T_2	125
T_3	400
T_4	150
T_5	100

Perform round robin scheduling with a time quantum of 100.

Solution

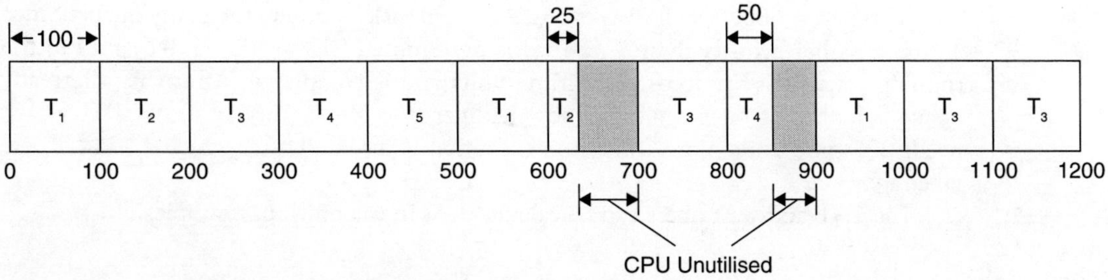

In round robin scheduling for this example, the OS gets a time tick every 100 time units—to mark the task switching times. If the service time of a task is less than the time quantum, for the rest of the time, the CPU remains free and unutilized. In this, one time slice is 100 time units.

T_1 gets its chance to execute at time points of 0, 500, and 900 time units.

T_2 has a total T_S of 125 time units. It executes at time points of 100 and 600. In the second time slice allotted to T2, only 25 time units are used by T2. For the remaining 75 time units, the CPU is unutilized.

T_3 has a T_S of 400 time units. It executes at time points of 200, 700, 1000 and 1100.

T_4 has a T_S of 150 time units. It executes at time points of 300, and 800. In the second time quantum, it uses only 50 time units. For the remaining 50 time units, the CPU is unutilized.

T_5 has a T_S of 100 time units. It uses the CPU for only one time quantum, at t = 400 time units.

7.9.5.2 | *Pre-emptive Priority*

In this method, at any time it should be ensured that it is the highest priority task in the ready queue that should be running. If, at any time, a task with a higher priority than the one that is currently running enters the ready queue, the current task is pre-empted and the new one is taken up. Example 7.6 shows how this is handled.

Example 7.6

Table 7.7 shows the tasks in the ready queue at time t = 0.

Table 7.7

Task No	T_E (Time Units)	Priority
T_1	300	5
T_2	125	3
T_3	400	2
T_4	150	12
T_5	100	15

At time t = 600, a new task T_6 of priority 1 and execution period 75 comes into the ready queue. What happens?

The task that was executing at that time is pre-empted. The final Gantt chart is as shown in Figure 7.18.

At time t = 600, task T_1 was executing when task T_6 enters the ready queue. Since T_6 has a higher priority than T_1, it (T_1) is pre-empted (at t = 600) and T_6 goes to the running state. It is serviced for 75 time units and is completed. After this, the ready queue is looked at once again by the scheduler. The highest priority task is T_1 which needs 225 time units more. Thus, T_1's execution is resumed after which T_4 and T_5 are taken up.

The TAT and wait times can be calculated as in the previous examples.

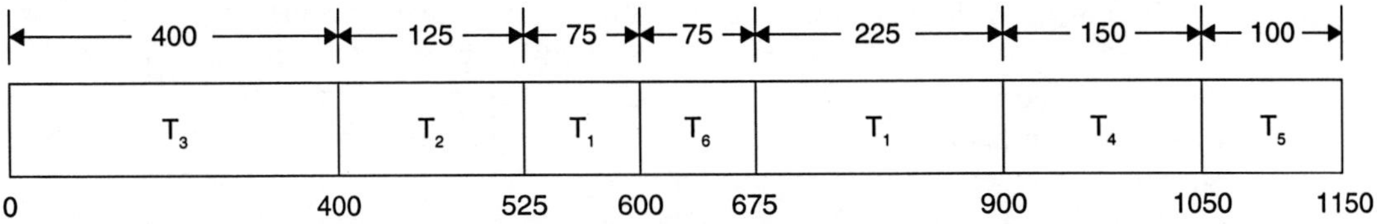

Figure 7.18 | Scheduling using pre-emptive priority technique

7.9.5.3 | *Pre-emptive SJN/Shortest Remaining Time (SRT)*

This is just like the previous example. Normally the scheduling is in the order of increasing service times. Thus, tasks with the shortest service times are executed earlier. In the midst of a schedule, if a new task enters the ready queue, its service time is compared with the remaining service time of the currently executing task. If the new task has a shorter service time than the remaining time of the current task, it (the current task) is pre-empted and the new one serviced until it completes.

Example 7.7

Let's use the data in Example 7.2 (Table 7.2 which is redrawn here)

Task No	T_S (Time Units)
T_1	300
T_2	125
T_3	400
T_4	150
T_5	100

At time t = 150, a new task T_6 with service time of 50 enters the ready queue. At this time instant, it was T_2 that was executing. It needs 75 time units more for completion. This is more than the service time of the new task T_6. So T_2 is pre-empted and T_6 is serviced. After this, T_2 is resumed once again. The resultant Gantt chart is as shown in Figure 7.19.

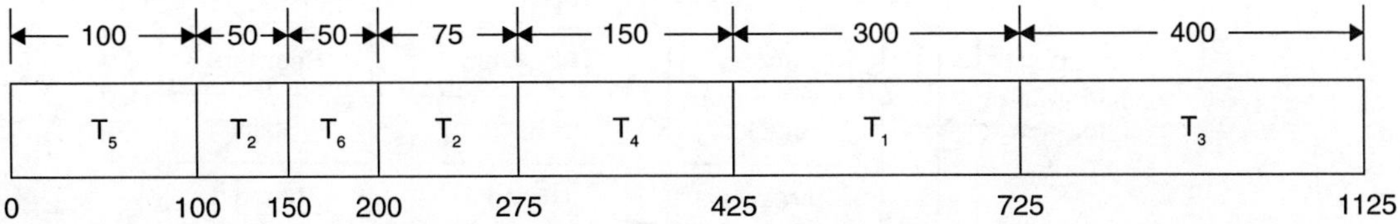

Figure 7.19 | Gantt chart for the SRT/SJN algorithm

The TAT and wait times can be calculated as in the previous examples.

It is obvious that scheduling is not a trivial job. It is a dynamic system with new entrants coming into the ready queue continuously. The scheduler also needs to make decisions based on a set of criteria and calculations. Anything extra that a scheduler has to do eats up valuable time. The delay involved in scheduling is referred to as scheduling latency. It includes interrupt latency (for task switching), deciding the task to be chosen and then the time involved in dispatching the chosen task to the CPU.

All the scheduling policies that we have discussed pertain more to general purpose operating systems. The specific policies that are used for real-time systems are discussed in Chapter 8.

7.10 | Threads

The word 'thread' is very commonly used in the discussion of different OS concepts. Now that tasks/processes have been discussed at great length, it will be easy to understand the idea of 'threads'.

What exactly is a thread? Where does it come into the picture? How is it useful?

A thread is sometimes called a 'lightweight process'. We now know what a process (i.e. task) is, what it entails, what it contains, what it comprises of, etc. We started by calling a process/task as a program in execution. In a program which goes into execution (and becomes a process/task), a number of subsidiary activities may be needed. For a process which deals with disk access, there can be one thread for reading and another thread for writing. We know that the CPU can do only one activity at a time. So then, it may read the disk for some time, and later may write. Thus, thread switching has to occur. The obvious question is 'Isn't this similar to task switching?' The answer is yes, but not entirely so. That is why we call a thread a lightweight process.

Each thread has its own program counter, general purpose registers and stack (see Figure 7.20). Each thread needs a separate stack because different threads do different activities and therefore handle a different set of procedures. But each thread belongs to a process. A process can have multiple threads and all these threads share the same 'address

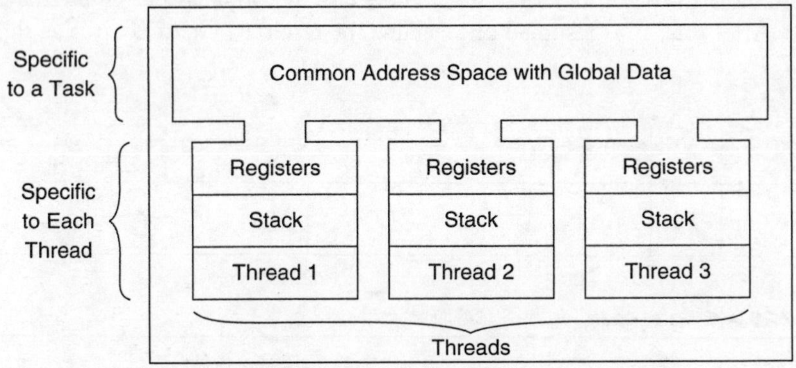

Figure 7.20 | Global and local resources for three threads

space', this aspect is what makes a thread 'lightweight'. *When thread switching takes place, there is no need to change the memory space, but the PC and stack do change.*

Having multiple threads is like having many specialists at work on the same object—only one of the specialists can work at one time, and each specialist does only one kind of work on the object. Thus, a thread is one line of activity. Multiple threads act serially, one after the other, doing separate activities. We can visualize a thread for reading a file, and another one for writing. Each of these threads executes the low level instructions needed for doing its assigned job.

The simplest process (task) is one which has just one thread. In general, most processes have multiple threads. Within a process, different threads might need to be scheduled and then most things that we discussed with respect to task scheduling apply for thread scheduling also. But the overhead involved in thread switching is less than in process (task) switching because all threads share the same memory space. Only registers (PC, SP and general purpose registers) needed to be saved and restored during thread switching.

Why threads?

The activities meant to be done by a process are subdivided into separate streams of activity done quite efficiently by a specific thread. This makes the process a subtotal of a number of threads.

Threads share the same data space and thus it is easy for threads to communicate with each other. Thus, we can see that threads assist each other, rather than compete with each other. But these advantages do not come free—the biggest drawback is that there is no protection between threads. But this may not be a big issue when we to refer to the previous statement that 'threads are meant to assist each other and pertain to the same process'.

There are kernel threads which form part of OS tasks, and user threads of application programs. Many times, user threads are supported by the threads of the kernels. We then say that the user thread runs over kernel threads.

7.11 | Interrrupt Handling

The mechanism of interrupt handling has been clearly described in Section 2.2.9. In that, the processor level activities for interrupt processing is described. But in a system with an OS, when the OS gets to know about a interrupt, it must co-ordinate all the actions to be done to save the context of the current program, get the interrupt handler, resume the previous activity once the Interrupt Service Routine (ISR) is over and done with, and also handle issues like multiple interrupts occurring simultaneously and so on. In short, even though processors have an inherent interrupt handling mechanism, the OS need to keep an eye over the whole scene because there are multiple sources for interrupts.

Most I/O devices use an interrupt mechanism to get access to the processor. For example, only if you type a key does the keyboard controller need to act. When it acts, it generates an interrupt to let the system know it. The corresponding interrupt handler is initiated to act, and after its duty it exits.

In the OS, interrupts are used either with hardware support (provided by the processor) or by pure software. Either way, an interrupt handler or ISR does the processing of the task initiated by the interrupt. In multitasking systems, task switching is usually accomplished by interrupts. For example, in the round robin method, every t seconds, an interrupt is generated and then the current task is pre-empted and the next task is taken up.

Interrupts are associated with a delay which is called 'interrupt latency'. Recollect the sequence of actions that follow an interrupt, which are as follows:

i) Saving the current context
ii) Determining the identity of the interrupt
iii) Switching to the new context
iv) Starting the execution of the Interrupt Handler

Interrupt latency is the sum total of the delays caused by each of these actions. The amount of 'interrupt latency' incurred depends on the speed of the hardware, as well as the efficiency of the software.

7.11.1 | Interrupts and Task Switching

Task switching is accomplished by the mechanism of interrupts. The first component of the latency involved is the interrupt processing time. Next, depending on the task scheduling method used, a certain amount of delay is incurred in deciding which task is to be switched to. This delay is called the dispatch latency. Thus, the total switching latency = interrupt latency + dispatch latency.

7.12 | Inter Process (Task) Communications (IPC)

We have been talking about tasks/processes and also about threads. Two important points to keep in mind with regard to them are as follows:

i) Processes are independent of each other. This means that one process does not share anything with another. They reside in separate memory spaces and are protected from being accessed by other processes.
ii) Threads of the same process share a common address space, and so there is the element of 'sharing' between threads. They are not protected with respect to one another, and so do not need any additional mechanism for communicating with one another.

Where then is communication needed?

Processes in the same machine, and processes in different machines might need to communicate —it might be to share data, or to send queries and receive responses. Let us first consider inter process communication as a general case and then discuss the additional aspects for 'remote communication'.

When sharing and communication occurs, there is bound to be some conflict between the activities of the processes that are involved. For example, reading and writing are conflicting actions when done in the same shared space. There are many other cases too, where inconsistencies and blockages occur. The resolving of such problems is grouped under 'process/task synchronization'. In practice, synchronization techniques should be included along with 'inter process/task communication techniques'. However, for the purpose of clarity in our discussion, we will deal with these two aspects separately. First we talk about task communication and then add task synchronization techniques to it.

7.12.1 | Task/Process Communication Methods

Two of the task communication methods are

i) Shared memory
ii) Message passing

7.12.1.1 | *Shared Memory*

This is a very simple concept. It simply means that an area of memory is allowed to be accessed by more than one task. See Figure 7.21, where N processes have access to a common area of memory. Let's assume that the processes involved are all on the same machine. Normally the address space of processes is separate and protected. When memory is shared, it assumes that this 'protection' is overridden and many co-operating tasks are allowed to read and write this area of memory. Shared memory communication is very efficient and fast, as the only actions needed are the setting up of this space (by the OS kernel) and allowing reading and writing to it, which are relatively fast operations. In practice, this sharing is a very dangerous condition which can lead to data inconsistencies and cause a race condition. These issues must be taken care of by synchronization techniques.

7.12.1.2 | *Message Passing*

This is just like our real-world courier service. The sender sends a message to a receiver through a courier. The courier in this case, is the IPC mechanism of the OS. The message is sent from the address space of the sender process to the address space of the receiver process. This is a case of a point-to-point message passing (see Figure 7.22). Messages may also be broadcast, that is, sent from one point to many receiving points (see Figure 7.23).

For message passing, the send and receive formats are as follows:

Send (destination, message)
Receive (source, message)

This means that the sender needs to know where the message is to be sent to. Similarly, the receiver should know the source of the message it receives. There are various mechanisms for message passing, with only minor differences between them. Two of them are message pipes and mailboxes.

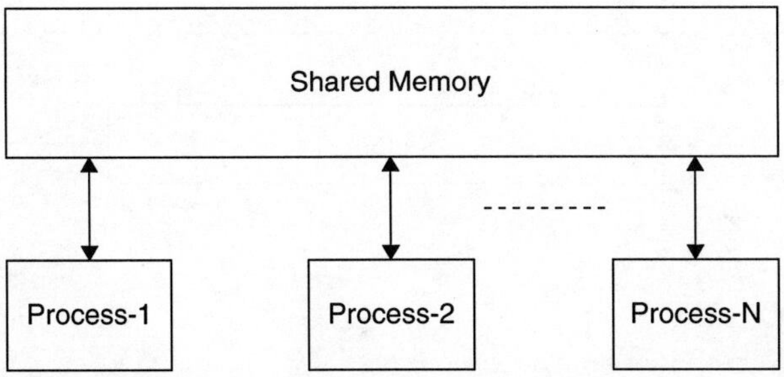

Figure 7.21 | N processes sharing a common area of memory

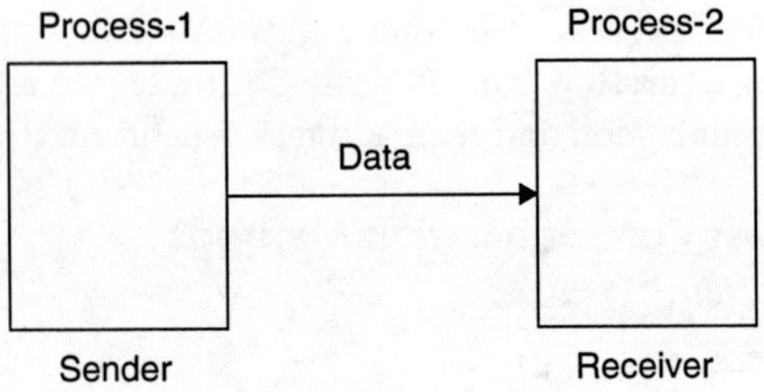

Figure 7.22 | Passing messages from a sender to a receiver process

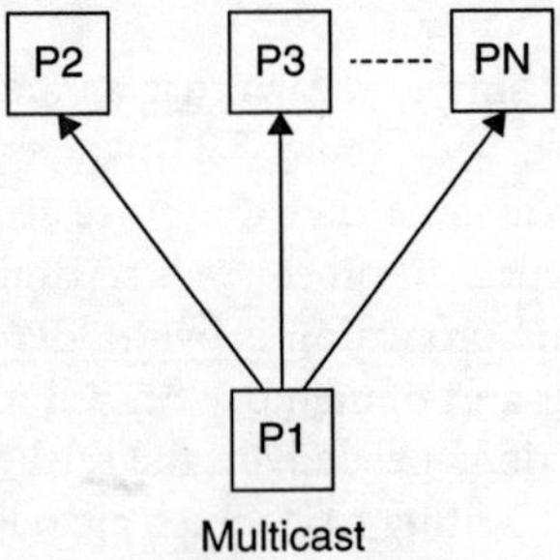

Figure 7.23 | Broadcasting of messages from one process

Message Pipes

This is a very simple concept which was first implemented in Unix, and is available in Windows and is part of POSIX compliance.

A pipe is a kernel data structure acting as a FIFO (First In First Out) buffer into which writing from one end and reading from the other end is possible (see Figure 7.24). As such it is a unidirectional transfer mechanism. If, between two tasks, bidirectional data transfer is needed, two pipes are needed, obviously. Creating a pipe is just a matter of defining the write point and the read point. The exact mechanism is implementation specific, meaning that Unix may do it in one way and Windows in another way.

Pipes may be anonymous or named. The former belongs to a process or its child process, and does not exist outside the process. Because of its association with a specific process, it does not need a name and that is why the terminology 'anonymous'.

A named pipe is a system concept. When a process creates a pipe, it is available as a name (similar to a filename) in the system space. A number of pipes, with names (similar to filenames) are available and any process is free to use any of them.

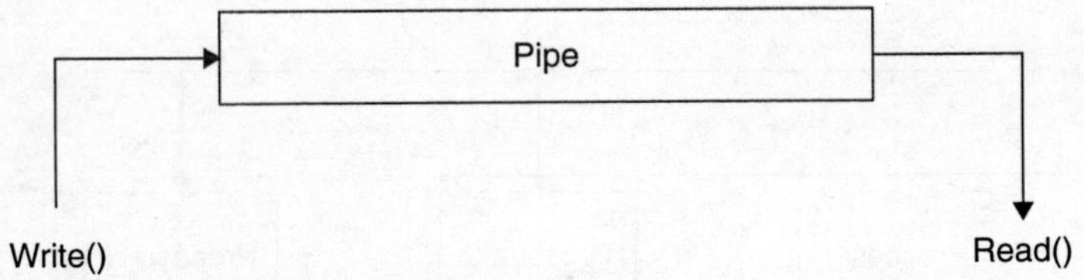

Figure 7.24 | Two ends of a message pipe

Mailboxes

This is an indirect way of sending messages. It is just like a mailbox available in post offices. The sender deposits the message in the box. The receiver should have the mechanism to receive it. If this is a common mail box, many receivers in the same locality can receive, but a receiver process can taken out only messages addressed to it. In the OS scenario, it is like having a mailbox maintained by the kernel. Thus the mailbox is common to the whole system, and the operating system manages the mailbox which is in the kernel space.

Another option is for each process to have its own mailbox in the address space of the process. This method is less popular. In a real-world analogy, it is like individuals having their own mailboxes placed in their own premises. We know that this is not done unless the receiver is a business establishment with the possibility of lots of mail being sent there.

Transfer Protocol

Since senders and receivers are involved in a communication setup, they have to agree on a protocol which can be synchronous (blocking) or asynchronous (non-blocking). Let us see what these terms mean to us here.

i) **Blocking sender, blocking receiver:** In this, when a sender sends a message, it expects the receiver to receive it (and maybe acknowledge it). Only then will it send the next message. Thus, the sender is blocked for further sending and the receiver is also blocked. The receiver has to 'receive' this message. Only then will it be sent any more messages. Thus, both the sender and receiver are blocked. This is a tightly synchronous system. See Figure 7.25 which shows process 1, the sender, and process 2, the receiver. In a synchronous system, the sender sends a message and the receiver receives (i.e. the execution of the receive process occurs). But only after the getting a response, that is, an acknowledge signal from the receiver, will the sender send again. At other times, both of them are blocked.

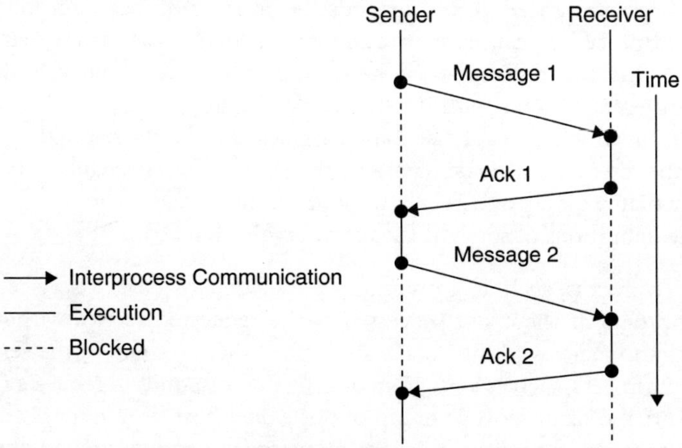

Figure 7.25 | Transfer protocol for synchronous communication

ii) **Non-blocking sender, blocking receiver:** Here the receiver process waits for a specific message, only then will it accept other messages. But the sender is allowed to send as long as the buffer is not full.

Producer Consumer Paradigm

The sender-receiver communication is a producer-consumer paradigm in which the consumer can consume only if the producer produces, and the producer need produce only as long as the consumer consumes it. When this condition does not hold, communication cannot take place.

Let's look at it from the side of the producer, that is, the sender. When a sender sends a message, it can be placed into a buffer for the receiver to pick it up when he wants it. The sender can continue to send, until the buffer is full, after which the sender will have to wait until the receiver receives some messages and the buffer is cleared for more messages to be sent.

Looking at it from the side of the receiver, the receiver can receive only if the sender has sent something into the buffer. As the sender keeps on sending data, the receiver can keep on receiving it (the received data is removed from the buffer). If all the messages are received and the sender does not send any more messages, the buffer is empty and no more reception can be done.

This whole scenario is highlighted as the 'bounded buffer problem'. There should be a mechanism for synchronizing the activities of the producer and consumer, and this is a classical OS problem with many kinds of solutions suggested, none of which are perfect or ideal.

Remote Procedure Call

In the cases of IPC discussed so far, the implied assumption is that of processes in the same computer that communicate. Now consider two physically separate computer systems that need to communicate. They will need a physical as well as a logical medium to communicate: the physical communication is either a wired or wireless network, and the protocols that govern the communication are what is meant by a logical medium.

The title 'remote procedure call' extends the concept of local procedure calling, so that the called procedure can exist in a different address space from that of the calling procedure. The two processes may be on the same system, but it is more sensible to consider different systems with a network connecting them. RPC is a standardized protocol by using which, users of distributed applications can be relieved of the necessity of knowing the finer and intricate details of the networking mechanism. In effect, RPC serves as a mediator for client/server communications.

Note the definitions of some of the terms involved in RPC.

i) **Client:** A process, such as a program or task that requests a service provided by another program. The client process uses the requested service without having to deal with too many working details about the other program or the service.
ii) **Server:** A process, such as a program or task, that responds to requests from a client.
iii) **Endpoint:** The name, port or group of ports on a host system that is monitored by a server program for incoming client requests. The endpoint is a network-specific address of a server process for remote procedure calls.

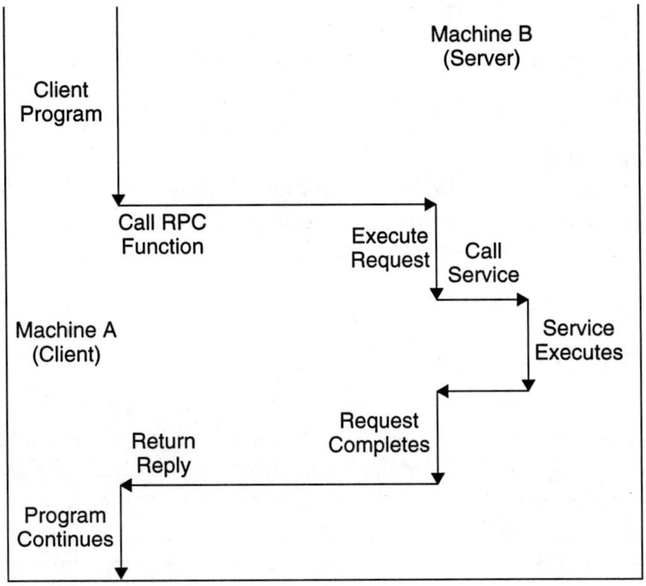

Figure 7.26 | Sequence of actions in RPC

RPC and Its Working

An RPC is similar to a procedure (function) call. When an RPC is made, the calling arguments are passed to the procedure in the remote machine and the caller waits for a response to be returned. Figure 7.26 shows the flow of activity between two networked systems.

The client makes a procedure call that sends a request to the server and waits. The thread is blocked from processing until either a reply is received or is timed out. When the request arrives, the server calls a dispatch routine that performs the requested service, and sends the reply to the client. After the RPC call is completed, the client program continues. RPC specifically supports network applications. It presumes the existence of a low-level transport protocol such as TCP or UDP (Transmission control protocol and user datagram protocol—both are commonly used in Internet protocols) for carrying the message data between communicating programs. RPC spans the transport layer and the application layer in the open systems interconnection (OSI) model of network communication.

RPC is usually adopted for calls between procedures in different machines. But the mechanism involved may be used in the same machine as well. Microsoft claims that much of its Windows architecture is composed of services that communicate with each other to accomplish a task and that these services use RPC to communicate with each other.

7.13 | Task Synchronization

We next consider a very important aspect of operating systems. There are three aspects to it.

First, how different tasks with conflicting actions can cause havoc. Second, how to avoid such situations and third, if such a situation occurs, how to get out of it.

7.13.1 | Parallelism aka concurrency

From our previous discussion on scheduling, it must be clear that what we try to achieve on a machine with just one CPU and multiple tasks is pseudo parallelism or concurrency, the latter being a better word for it. As far as users are concerned, a number of concurrent tasks are running, using the single available CPU. When such an illusion of parallelism is presented to the user, it must also be kept in mind that there is ample scope for clashes and confusion because of the conflicting interests of the concerned tasks. We will now look into such things which happen as a natural result of the concurrency we are out to achieve.

7.13.2 | The Race Condition

If we think of two or more tasks, we naturally assume them to be independent and residing in separate address spaces. Thus, they are independent of one another. But there will be cases when they use global or shared resources—global variables or code or data which is defined to be global, and thus allowed to be used by all tasks which need it.

Let's consider two tasks associated with railway ticket reservation. Task T_1 looks after 'reservation' while the other, T_2, deals with cancellation. After doing their parts, the respective tasks update a shared variable named A, which indicates the availability of seats. It is obvious that T_1 decrements A, and T_2 increments it. Now, what would happen in a scheduling system when T_2 is interrupted just after it does the ticket cancellation, and is midway in the computation to increment A?

T_1 starts the reservation process. When it tries to do it, the availability that it sees is not the right number. This is because T_1 interrupted T_2 before it (T_2) could complete the update of (write into) the shared variable A. Thus, the data read by T_1 is wrong. When it does the reservation, it does it using a wrong value of the shared variable A (the availability of seats). In a peak season, it is very difficult to get tickets, as we all have experienced. In an extreme case, the reservation program cannot do a reservation, because of finding the availability to be 0. Because of the cancellation, actually tickets are now available, but the reservation task T_1 does not know it.

Now the question is, when the interrupt came, why was T_2 not able to complete its updating of A? The updation is just a simple addition, isn't it? The answer is that, in a high level language it might be just one instruction, but we know that one HLL line corresponds to many low level assembly instructions. So incrementing A can get interrupted midway. Later, after the interrupting task T_1 completes the reservation part, it decrements the same variable A.

This situation creates an ambiguity and the value of A at any time depends on how the sequence of incrementing and decrementing by the two different tasks occurs. This is an example of what is called a called a race condition. Additional problems arise when more than two tasks are in the scene. The most common symptom of a race condition is unpredictable values of variables that are shared between multiple tasks/threads. This is because of the unpredictability of the order in which the tasks execute. At one time Task1 wins, at other times Task2 wins. At certain other times, execution works correctly. Also, if each task is executed separately without any interference, the variable value is always correct.

The ticket reservation issue is an example of how one task reads a wrong value of the shared variable and makes a wrong decision based on the value of the shared variable.

Figure 7.27 | Printer and two tasks

If it were a banking problem, and the shared variable is the 'balance' in the account of a customer, it will cause much more serious problems (in the practical world) than in the case of railway ticket reservation.

7.13.2.1 | *A Printer as a Shared Resource*

Let's try to understand the race problem with another example. Try to visualize this scene. A print command is given by one task, and printing starts. In between, another task interrupts and gives another print command. The first printing is stopped midway, and the printer prints the data given by the second task. You can see what will be the printed output—it will contain the printed output corresponding to both tasks, Figure 7.27 illustrates this. The two pages indicate the two tasks which needs separate printed outputs, but because of 'racing', it may turn out that the printed page contains the printed matter of both the tasks.

How could this have been prevented? For that, let's first try to understand some terms related to this problem.

7.13.3 | Critical Section

That part of the program where the shared memory/variable/device is accessed, is called the 'critical section'. Understand that it is the 'code' that uses the shared memory/variable that is the critical section (and not the area of memory). The critical section can be used by various tasks, as we have just seen. To avoid race conditions and flawed results, one must identify codes in critical sections in each task /thread. And then, when one task enters the critical section, it must be ensured that no other task interrupts it and enters it.

7.13.3.1 | *A Railway Track with a Critical Section*

See Figure 7.28, in which a common part of a railway track is the critical section. The part of the track which is common to the two railway lines is the 'critical section' with respect to railway traffic. It is obvious that only one train can use the common track at a time. The train in the other track has to wait. The same is the case with programming tasks which arrive at the critical section of code. Only one task is allowed to enter the critical section. Others have to wait.

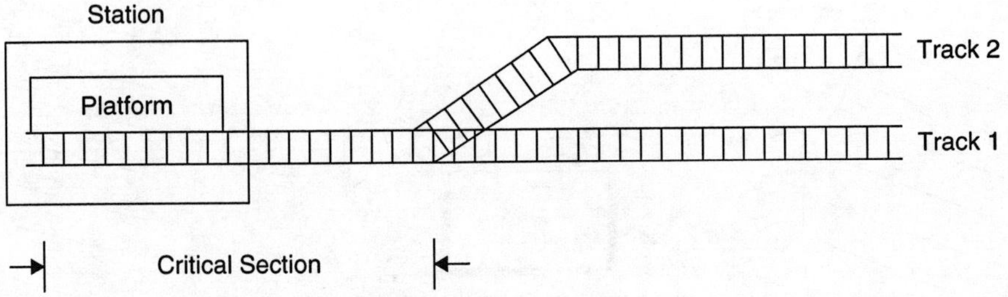

Figure 7.28 | A critical section of a railway track

7.13.3.2 | *Solutions to the Problem*

There can be hardware solutions to the racing condition

Atomicity

The code for the program in the critical section may be written in a high level language, but after compilation is converted to assembly instructions. If the increment and decrement operations are 'atomic', that is, uninterruptible or unbroken, then the racing condition does not occur. Assembly instructions are uninterruptible and therefore 'atomic', but one high level language line corresponds to a number of assembly instructions.

Let us look at an increment operation for a global variable A stored in memory. The code is

A++ ; increment A

When compiled, it is converted to assembly operations (processor dependant), such as the following:

i) Moving it to a register
ii) Incrementing the content of the register
iii) Copying it back to memory

If, by any chance, this task gets interrupted just after the move operation, another task uses the 'wrong' (unincremented) value of this global variable. This whole sequence is not atomic, and that is the real problem.

But if the three assembly operations 'together' are atomic, the second task will be able to interrupt the first one only after the global variable has been incremented. This is a solution possible if the processor hardware provided 'atomic' instructions for certain operations (not necessarily the increment and decrement instructions alone). Such a solution is possible, but having processors catering to such requirements in not always probable.

Disabling Interrupts

The second hardware method is to disable interrupts if a task/thread enters a critical section. That disallows a task/thread switching until the critical section part is done with. It is okay to do this, but interrupt disabling may affect other resources like I/O devices, and also affect the scheduling algorithms. Hence, this is not a feasible solution.

7.13.3.3 | *A Practical Solution-locks*

In practice, the actual solution is to lock out the critical section from contenders, once an operation therein is taken up by a certain task/thread. The important point is that when one task is executing programs involving shared modifiable data in its critical section, no other task is to be allowed to enter its critical section. This means that **execution of critical sections by tasks should be mutually exclusive.**

A locking mechanism called 'mutex' (mutual exclusion lock) is used to synchronize access to a resource, in this case the 'critical section'. Only one task (can be a thread also) can acquire the mutex. This means that there is the idea of ownership associated with mutex, and only the owner task can release the lock (mutex).

What does the above statement mean?

When a task needs to access a shared resource, it (the task) acquires the lock, and thus 'owns' the resource at the current time. When the task completes its use of the critical section, it releases the lock. Any other task can then take the lock, acquire access to the resource (keeping others away) and use it.

A simple pseudocode for a task to access a critical section is as shown

```
acquireLock();
Process Critical Section
releaseLock();
```

This shows that a task/thread acquires the lock prior to executing the critical section. This lock can be acquired by only one task.

7.13.4 | The Readers 'Writers' Problem

This is a classical problem in OS first identified by Djikstra in 1970.

Now that we know what is meant by a 'critical section', we should be able to understand this problem. If a number of readers and writers need access to a shared data area, how is it to be dealt with? We have already made an assumption that when a critical section is being used by one task, it is locked for other tasks. There are different types of tasks and they may be affected by being locked out. One classification of tasks is into readers and writers and the possible solutions too encompass the differences in the 'effects' on these two types of tasks.

7.13.4.1 | *Readers*

Consider that a reader is reading from the shared area, and before it exits the section, another task is scheduled which will also need to 'read' from the same area. Reading is a tame process. It does not change the content, and so more readers may be allowed, while the first reader's reading is not complete yet. So the reading of a shared section can be interrupted by another reader. This is one aspect.

7.13.4.2 | *Writers*

What if a writer now comes in? One way of sorting it out, is to let all readers finish reading—then only should a writer be allowed in. Once a writer enters its critical section, (wherein it writes into the shared area), further readers and writers should be blocked until this writer has completed. The point is that there is no danger in having several processes read data concurrently. But, writing or modifying data must be done under mutual exclusion to ensure consistency of data.

The above sequence seems quite logical, but both these solutions are prone to starvation. The first allows readers to indefinitely lock out writers and the second allows writers to indefinitely lock out readers. Because of this, many solutions have been proposed and used according to the approach decided in the specific OS design. Semaphores (Section 7.14) are used to do signalling between tasks, and also the sequence and priority of readers and writers can be decided according to a pre-decided OS policy.

7.13.5 | Deadlocks

This is another term commonly used in OS-related terminology.

What is a deadlock? What are the conditions necessary to consider it as a deadlock? What are the methods available to handle it?

We have all experienced deadlocks. It is a state in which we feel that nothing gets going. Everything is blocked. A typical case is a traffic junction (intersection) (see Figure 7.29). Assume that there are four roads meeting at the junction. Vehicles from all the four roads are waiting to go across the junction, as a result of which no movement is possible and it is a state of deadlock.

How does a deadlock occur in an operating system? Say, a task (A) needs to execute. It gets the CPU, but it also needs a resource (like a printer, display, etc.). But this resource is now in the possession of another task (B). What then? Task A cannot execute because of not getting the resource. And Task B cannot execute because of not having the CPU. Thus, neither Task A nor B gets to execute. This is obviously a deadlock, with neither A nor B being able to proceed at all.

We can generalize this case by saying that the first task needs a resource that the second task holds, and the second task needs the resource that the first one currently keeps. Thus, neither tasks get executed. The resources may be either physical (printers, memory, CPU, etc.) or logical (files, semaphores, etc.)

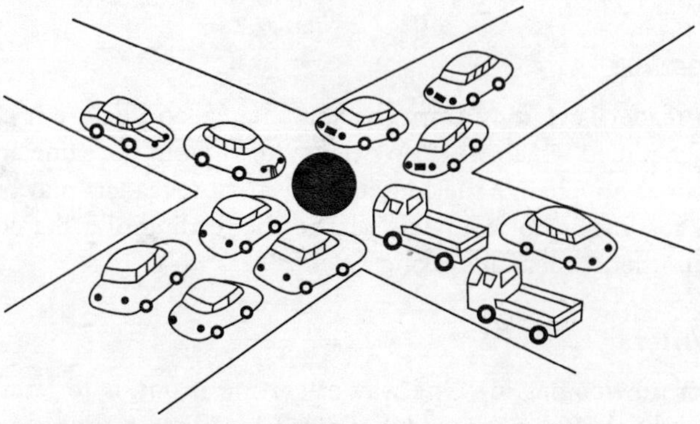

Figure 7.29 | A deadlocked traffic intersection

Both tasks need both the resources, then only can any one of them execute. But neither task is willing to let go of the resource that it currently holds. Each one waits for the other task to relinquish the resource that it holds. This does not happen and that is the issue with deadlocks.

Definition A set of tasks is deadlocked if each task in the set is waiting for an event that only another task in the set can cause. There are four conditions attributed to the occurrence of deadlocks, designated as 'necessary conditions'.

i) **Mutual exclusion:** The resource that is being contended for, is assigned to a specific task and no other task can expect to be allowed to share it. Thus, the resource has been kept locked by the task in question, and will not let it go.
ii) **Hold and wait:** This refers to the state that certain tasks are holding certain resources, but they need more resources to accomplish their execution. Such a task is in a 'hold and wait' state.
iii) **Non pre-emption:** The resources already allocated to some tasks cannot be forcibly taken away from them (cannot be pre-empted) by the OS—only when the task execution is complete, will the task release it.
iv) **Circular wait:** Try visualizing a set of tasks, each of them waiting for a resource held by the next task in the set. This forms a circular queue of waiting tasks.

The conditions listed above are called 'Coiffman conditions' and deadlock occurs on the combined occurrence of these conditions.

What can be done about deadlocks?

There are various ways of dealing with them. They are as follows:

i) **Ignore deadlocks:** This is a popular strategy employed by many operating systems and is called the 'Ostrich Approach' (guess why). But it may not be a good solution for systems which are safety critical.
ii) **Avoidance:** This is done by taking extra care in resource scheduling. It is just like having a traffic signal at traffic intersections, to avoid traffic jam.
iii) **Prevention:** Prevention, they say, is better than cure. Prevention is slightly different from 'avoidance'. This is done by negating one of the conditions that cause deadlock.
iv) **Detect and recover:** Yet another strategy allows deadlocks to occur and then gets the system to recover from it. At a traffic junction, when a deadlock happens, a policeman may force the vehicles on one side of the junction to back up, and allow vehicles from another direction to cross the junction. This implies interference by the OS for the recovery procedure.

Let's see how the latter two strategies can be applied to a computer system.

7.13.5.1 | *Detect and Recover*

In this, the idea is to frequently verify whether a deadlock has occurred. Once it is detected, deallocation of resources or pre-emption can be resorted to. Take the example of a bridge and traffic across it, as shown in Figure 7.30. Because the bridge is very narrow, traffic is allowed only in one direction. A deadlock occurs when two cars from opposite directions find themselves face to face with each other on the bridge.

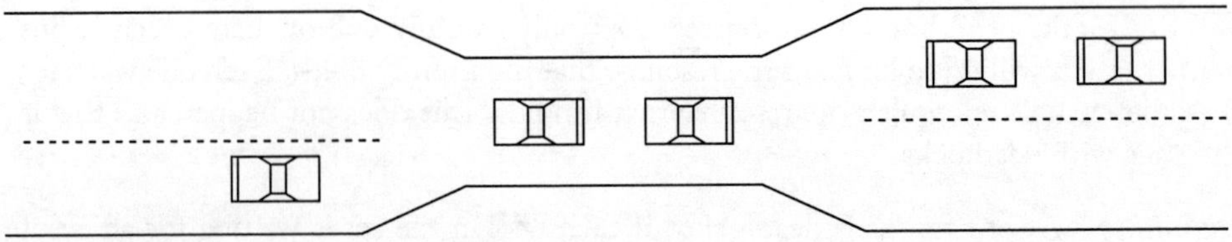

Figure 7.30

In this state, only one solution is possible: one of the vehicles should back up and clear the bridge. If there is a long line of traffic behind this car, a number of vehicles may have to back up. In the OS context, this is analogous to the case of detecting a deadlock and then, certain tasks which have been holding resources are forced to give them up, or it may be that some task which is using the CPU is pre-empted forcibly.

7.13.5.2 | *Deadlock Prevention*

This strategy looks potentially very simple, but the problem is that a certain amount of 'effort' is needed to implement it. This 'effort' tends to introduce inefficiency into the system. Why so? There are four conditions stipulated for deadlock occurrence. If one of these conditions is negated, deadlock cannot occur. But this will lead to inefficient utilization of resources because it prevents resources from being allocated in a normal sequence. It can force pre-emption of a resource held by a task. To prevent deadlock due to 'circular wait', some sequential order must be devised, which may not be optimal

In operating systems, there is a 'resource manager' which has all the information regarding resources and their allocation. The resource manager, with the help of resource graphs and other tools devise some solution.

The Dining Philosopher's Problem

This is a classical problem formulated by Djikstra. The dining philosophers problem is intended to illustrate the complexities of managing shared resources in a multitasking environment.

Here there are five brainy Chinese philosophers involved in discussions, but also are at a dining table wanting to eat. There are five bowls of rice placed before each of them, but each philosopher needs two chopsticks to eat. Chopsticks are a scarce resource and there is just one chopstick placed between two philosophers. The problem that arises is when all the five philosophers want to eat at the same time. Each one picks up the chopstick at his left, and then looks to the right for the second chopstick. It is not available, naturally. Thus, comes the deadlock with none of five philosophers being able to eat, and the ensuing starvation too.

In the OS context, each philosopher represents a task/thread and each chopstick is a shared resource.

Can this solution have a complete and perfect solution? The answer is 'No'. There are various suggestions for it, some which are as follows:

i) Have only four such philosophers
ii) Some philosophers are courteous enough to wait
iii) No philosophers eats indefinitely

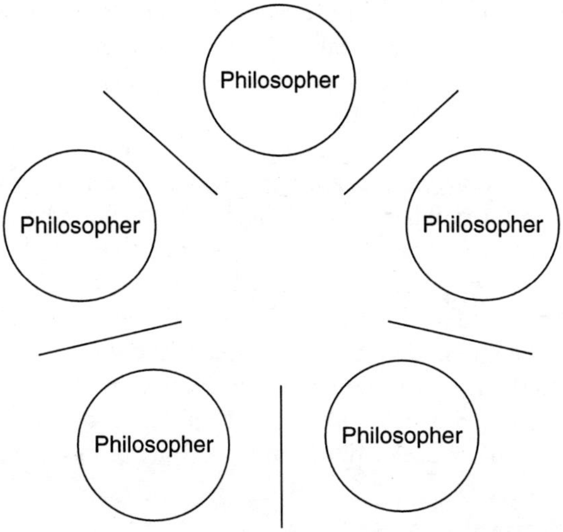

Figure 7.31 | Five philosophers at a dining table

This is just an example of a problem, and solutions may be chosen as per the discretion of the OS designer.

7.14 | Semaphores

The word 'semaphore' means 'signal'. In operating systems, a variable can be used as a semaphore which does signalling. But what kind of signalling do we mean? First let us try to understand a binary semaphore.

7.14.1 | Binary Semaphores

Assume two trains approaching a common area of a track. One train gets to use this track, and as it does so, it signals to the other train to wait. In this way, the first train acquires the associated binary semaphore and gives it a value of '0', that is, the semaphore is in the signalled state. The second train sees this signal (semaphore) and does not attempt to use the track. It simply waits. Meanwhile, the first train uses the critical section of the track, and after that, it releases the semaphore which now has the value '1'. The second train finds that the track is free and uses it, after making the semaphore to be '0' once again. This prevents other trains from using the same track, until the semaphore is released again.

So we see how the signalling occurs. In the case of an OS, if some task wants to run in a critical section, that task can acquire the corresponding semaphore, and signal to other tasks this matter. When this task exits the critical section, the semaphore is released and other waiting tasks can try to use the critical section.

7.14.2 | Counting Semaphores

The idea of using semaphores was formulated by Djikstra. The binary semaphore is only a special case of a counting semaphore.

To illustrate the idea of a counting semaphore, consider a car park with space for 50 cars. Thus, the semaphore is initialized to 50, meaning that 50 cars can come into the car park. The semaphore value is incremented or decremented as cars enter and leave the parking lot. Every time a car enters the car park, the value of the semaphore is decremented by one. When a car leaves the parking area, the semaphore is incremented by 1.

When, say, the semaphore value is 20, it implies that there is space for 20 more cars.

When the parking lot is full, the semaphore value is 0, and a new car entering it cannot park inside, as the semaphore value becomes negative.

Similar is the case of an operating system. This can be used in the bounded buffer problem. If the bounded buffer (memory with limited size) is divided into a number of blocks, each block can be accessed by a task (or thread) and the number of tasks accessing the buffer is limited to the number of blocks. This number can be used as the count N of the counting semaphore used by tasks to access the different blocks of the buffer. When N = 0, it implies that no more buffer blocks are available for tasks to access.

7.14.3 | Binary Semaphore vs Mutex

Are they the same? Both of them take only the values of 1 and 0. Some operating systems use them in the same way, but conceptually they are different. A mutex is a lock of a resource. A task (or thread) takes this lock (mutex is then set to '1'), and uses it for itself, to lock out other possible users from accessing the resource. At a particular time, the task owns the lock.

After using the resource, the task relinquishes ownership of the task by setting the mutex to '0'.

A binary semaphore, on the other hand, is used for signalling. When a task takes the semaphore of a resource (of I/O devices, critical section of code, etc.), it signals to other tasks that they should not try to access the resource. Once the task completes its action, it signals to the waiting tasks that the shared resource is free for use.

The binary semaphore acts like a gatekeeper to a room which has only one bed for sleeping. Once the occupant leaves the room, the gatekeeper indicates (signals) to others, that the room is free. In the OS context, tasks waiting to get access to the resource don't have to keep checking for its free status, the semaphore 'signals' to them the status. Thus, the waiting tasks can go to sleep and get awakened by the semaphore. This is a 'sleep and wake up' scenario.

In the case of a mutex, a prospective occupant gets the key of the room from the 'reception desk', uses the room and then returns the key to the reception when leaving. The issue here is there, when others want to use the same room, they have to continually check at the reception counter as to whether the key has been returned or not. In the OS context, this puts other waiting tasks in a test and wait loop, leading to inefficiency.

7.15 | Priority Inversion

This is something that is likely to occur in an OS, because of the many conflicting aspects that arise frequently. Let's try to visualize a situation that causes this.

A system has multiple tasks which are scheduled according to their priorities. Some tasks also need access to resources that are shared. Consider three tasks of low, medium

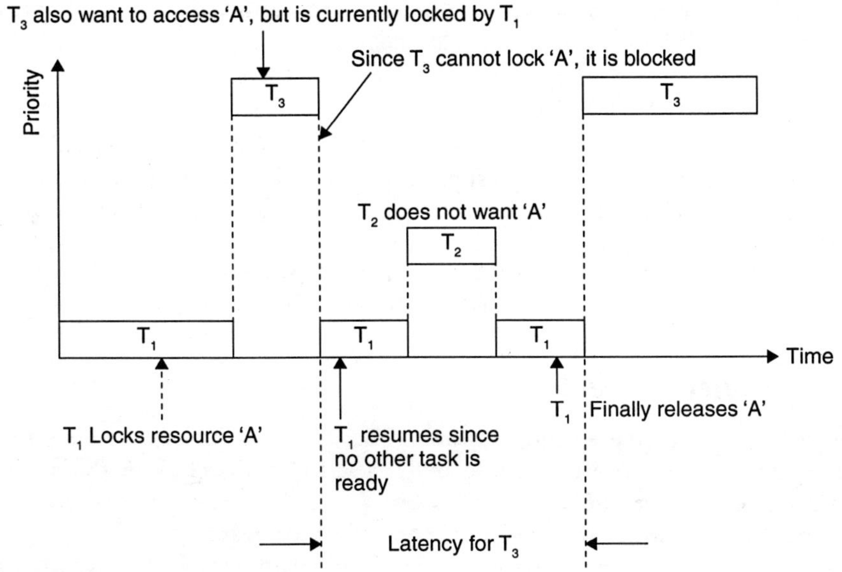

Figure 7.32 | An illustration of priority inversion

and high priorities with names T_1, T_2 and T_3, respectively. Let's say that the low priority task T_1 is running and is using a shared resource A by acquiring it semaphore. Task T_3 come in, and because it is a high priority one, can pre-empt T_1. But incidentally, T_3 also needs the shared resource held by T_1. There is no way to get T_1 to release the semaphore, and T_3 can run only after acquiring the semaphore. So T_3 waits and we say it is 'pending on the resource'.

One direct effect that will occur in a real-time system (Section 8.2) is that T_3 might miss its deadline due to this waiting. But that is not 'priority inversion'. The inversion occurs when a medium priority task T_2 comes in. T_2 does not need the resource, and so it can easily pre-empt task T_1 (because its priority is higher than that of T_1). This is priority inversion, because the medium priority task T_2 gets its chance to execute while the higher priority task is kept waiting. This is a very serious problem which totally upsets the balance of the system. Let us see what solutions are available.

7.15.1 | Solutions

7.15.1.1 | *Priority Inheritance*

Here, a lower-priority task inherits the priority of any higher-priority task which is 'pending on a resource' they share. As soon as the high priority task goes into its 'pending' state, the OS should get the low priority task to have the same priority as the pending task.

How does this help?

If a task of medium priority comes in during the pending period, it will not be able to pre-empt the currently executing low priority task. Then, once the semaphore is released, the pending high priority task takes it, and starts executing. At the same time, the low priority task is put back into its original priority. In this setup, no task of intermediate priority can come and upset the priority balance.

7.15.1.2 | *Priority Ceiling*

This is another solution. In this, each shared resource is given a priority called 'priority ceiling' which is higher than the highest priority of all tasks that can access the resource When a task uses this resource, the priority of the task is boosted (if it is a low priority task) to the ceiling value, thereby ensuring that a task owning a shared resource won't be preempted by any other task attempting to access the same resource. When the task releases the resource, the task is returned to its original priority level.

7.16 | Device Drivers

The above word has been used before (Section 7.5.3). Besides this, you are likely to have heard the term if you have attempted to attach new I/O devices to your PC. The point is that device drivers are associated with external devices that you want to add to your processing hardware, which may be a PC or an embedded board.

Think of a USB flash disk that we frequently use with our PC. This device is normally unknown to the PC's processor hardware and software. The processor does not know anything about its signals or its internal configuration. This implies that 'someone' should act as an intermediary so that the processor can interact with the flash disk and allow communication and data transmission between the two seemingly incompatible entities. Well, a device driver performs the role of this intermediary. It gets the processor and the flash disk to understand each other and then initiates communication between the two.

How is this done? Let's examine this in a philosophical sense. The USB is a well-defined protocol with well-defined modes of data transfer. The flash disk has four pins through which signals (including power) flow. The processor must be made aware of the intricate details of the flash disk's signal flow and the USB protocol. It is too much for an ordinary user to have to bother about such things, so the driver program does this.

The same principle applies to any I/O device that is used, right from a printer and scanner to a digital camera. In present times, when many device drivers are inbuilt in the OS, these devices have become 'plug and play' devices, that is, the user has only the job of plugging the device in – the OS detects the plugged in device and loads into RAM the appropriate device driver from the stored programs in the hard disk. When the device is unplugged, the driver can be unloaded (removed from main memory) until it is needed again. Thus, we see that device drivers for all possible (and probable) devices are available in a modern general purpose OS. For an embedded OS, such a large collection of device drivers is not available nor needed, because embedded systems are application specific.

Now let us go a bit deeper and try to answer various questions.

What is a device driver?

It is a software interface to a hardware device that handles requests from the kernel regarding the use of the particular I/O device. There is a well-defined interface for the kernel to make these requests. Because of this, adding new devices is easy. In short, there is a device driver for each and every hardware device that is to be used by the system.

Device drivers can be classified as follows.

i) **Block device drivers:** This is a driver that is well suited for 'block devices' which transfer data in blocks, like for example, disk drives. Such I/O devices have block-sized buffers as part of the buffer cache in memory.

ii) **Character device drivers:** As the name signifies, this is used for devices which move data as 'characters', and therefore does not need a buffer cache. A line printer is one such device, where data is sent as characters. But such drivers are not limited to applications that handle data as characters, some devices that handle data as large chunks of data are also within this class-the characteristic is that data is to transferred directly, without buffering. Most drivers belong to this class.

iii) **Network device drivers:** This type has to setup and prepare a network for data transmission and reception, and handle all the intricacies and protocols involved.

But what is this 'buffer cache'?

It is frequently needed to read data from the disk, and this reading is an extremely slow process. Sometime the same data will be read again and again within a short time frame, and the need to access the disk each time makes the system very slow. To circumvent this problem, the method of speed up is of reading the information from disk only once and then keeping it in memory until no longer needed. This is called disk buffering, and the memory used for the purpose is called the 'buffer cache'. A buffer cache is used in the case of 'writing' as well.

How does a hardware device communicate with a processor?

There is the 'polling' method by which a processor keeps waiting for a hardware to signal its need, but since this is very inefficient, mostly it is the interrupt based data transfer that is done. Whenever a I/O device 'acts', an interrupt is generated and an ISR or interrupt handler is awakened (Section 2.2.9 and Section 7.11). This ISR does the rest of the job.

7.16.1 | Reading a Key Pressed Using a Keyboard Driver

Consider a keyboard and its associated device driver. Let us examine how it is that when a key is pressed, it is identified and made known to the user program (like a document, for instance).

Let this be the scenario. The user (of a PC) opens a document file and wants to type in data into it. When a key is pressed, the ASCII value should reach the user program. For this, the identity of the key should be found out.

We know that there is a powerful processor in a PC.

But to get it involved in the key detection logic is a big waste on its time. Usually all keyboards have a dedicated keyboard controller (with a μC in it—this controller is usually a part of the motherboard chipset). Thus, when a specific key, say M, as in Figure 7.33 is pressed, its ASCII value is obtained in the data register of the keyboard controller. The fact that a key has been pressed and that the key code is available is to be

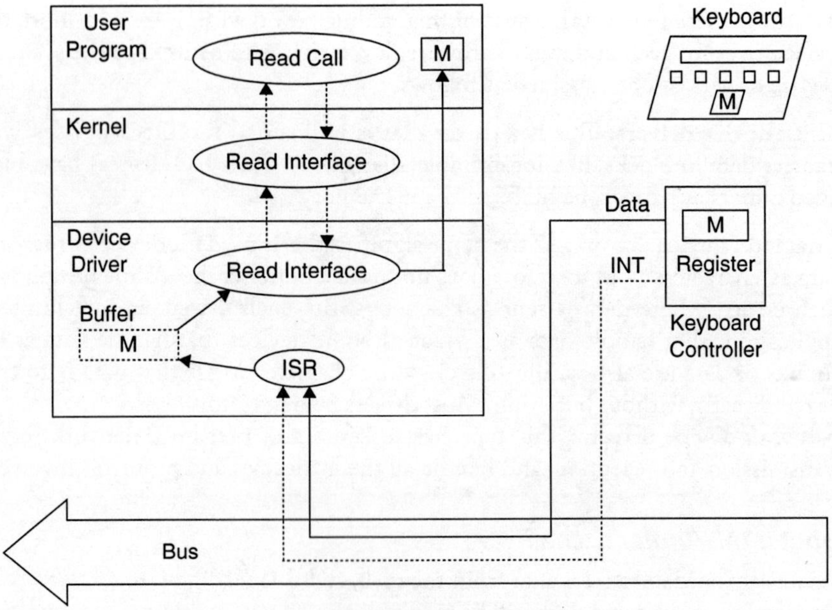

Figure 7.33 | The sequence of actions in reading a key pressed

made known to the user program. This 'knowledge' is passed through the levels as shown in Figure 7.33. The keyboard controller generates an interrupt which activates an ISR which is a part of the device driver code. This ISR gets the keycode in the buffer in the device driver level.

But how does the user program view it? The figure summarizes the flow of control between a user program, the kernel, the device driver and the hardware. The dotted lines show the flow of control signals, while the solid lines indicate the flow of data. The user program sends a read request, using a read function (maybe a printf). This passes through the kernel and is translated as a 'system call' to the device driver. Since the character (ASCII value of the key pressed) is available in the buffer of the device driver, it is sent to the user program, which is displayed on the video monitor (there is a device driver associated with the display device, as well).

What role has the device driver played here? Only the device driver software has any knowledge about the keyboard controller, its hardware signals, the format of the signals (control and data) it sends and so on. No other part of the OS need be bothered about trying to know or understand the keyboard controller.

7.16.2 | Purpose of a Device Driver

Figure 7.34 shows the different layers through which a user process has to go, to use a particular hardware. The steps involved are as follows:

i) The user process makes a request for I/O access
ii) The request is channelled through the OS, and is sent to the device driver as a system call.

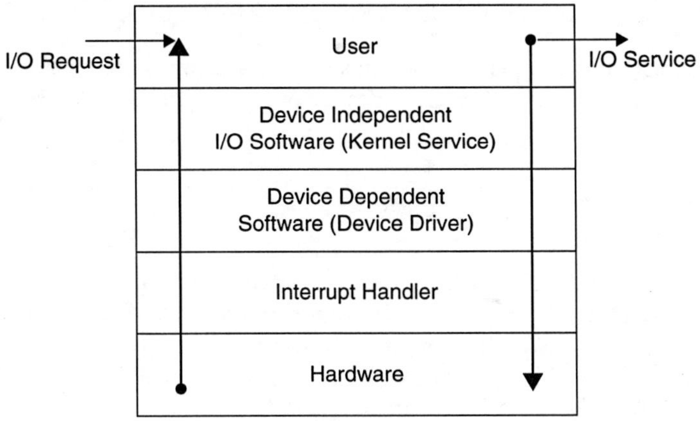

Figure 7.34 | Layers associated with a device driver

iii) The device driver understands what is needed and generates an appropriate interrupt to the hardware.
iv) The interrupt handler handles the interrupt request, gets the required service from I/O and wakes up the device driver which then communicates the matter to the user process.

Let us conclude by saying that the purpose of a device driver is to handle kernel requests with regard to a specific I/O device, through a well-defined kernel interface. On one side of this interface, is the device specific device driver code, and the other side, is a set of well-defined system calls. Because of this, adding new devices to a system is an easy task.

7.16.3 | Device Driver Design

The point is that, only the device driver needs to anything about the hardware, or rather the device driver should know everything about the device it is made for. Every other layer in Figure 7.34 is device independent.

Think of designing a parallel port driver. Such a parallel port will have a 'port controller'. This controller has control registers, status registers, mode controls, etc. The device driver should write appropriate bits in all these registers, for the chosen mode of operation. To arrange for data transfer, for a simple parallel port of 8086 with 8255 as the controller IC, this is reasonably simple.

As devices become more complex, it is likely that there are numerous registers to configure and many modes to choose from. This makes device driver design complex.

When a new embedded board is designed, drivers for its peripheral hardware and buses have to written from scratch, knowing the full details of the processor and other chips on the board.

Nowadays Linux has become the OS of choice for embedded systems, and writing device drivers based on Linux is very commonly done. A lot of standard functions are available for assisting the process of driver development.

7.17 | Codes/Pseudo Codes for OS Functions

A deeper understanding of operating systems concepts requires a 'hands on' experience of coding. A few sample codes /pseudo codes are presented here.

Note: All codes and pseudo codes discussed here, for 'RTOS' is applicable to GPOS as well.

7.17.1 | Multitasking

A task is a piece of code, from whose standpoint, appears to have full control of the CPU. A task can be thought of as the basic functional unit of an OS user application; the application is broken into modules whose functionality is described by tasks. A *multitasking* system will have several such tasks that are run according to the scheduling rule used by the system.

Almost all RTOSes and their application programs are written in C. A RTOS task is thus essentially a C function that returns nothing and usually takes no arguments. However, tasks may not be *called* in the same sense as a C function, and they never return. The common prototype of a RTOS task is as follows:

void some_task (**void**)

Note that some RTOS allow parameters to be passed to the task just like how parameters are passed to normal C functions, but here, for simplicity, we will assume that a task does not take any parameters.

A task describes a real-time activity, hence it must run as long as the system is active. Thus, task bodies are almost always infinite loops, within which the functionality of the task is coded. Thus, a task will look as follows:

```
void some_task (void)
{
    /* this part runs only once - usually something is
       initialized here */
    for(;;)
    {
            /*
            * code for the task's functionality comes here
            */
    }
}
```

The kernel is made aware that *some_task* is a RTOS task using an API such as *task_*create or *task_register*. The kernel passes control to the task when appropriate.

As stated earlier, a multitasking system will have several such tasks. One might wonder how they can execute, since each task is essentially an infinite loop. Once started, a task never stops executing! This is where the kernel does it's magic—the kernel is able to *pause* execution of a task, and can *resume* it at a later time.

A task need not run always—usually it will need to wait for an event, or may simply need to wait for a certain amount of time before it has to run again. Almost all RTOSes provide an API called *sleep* or *delay*, which causes the task to wait for a certain amount of time (specified as an argument to these API). Thus, when a task calls such an API, the kernel is notified that the task wants to sleep, and thus control of the CPU can be transferred to another task. If all tasks in the system are asleep, control is given to a special task called the *System Idle Task* or simply *Idle Task*. The Idle Task does nothing; the CPU can even be put in a low power mode till a scheduling interrupt arrives. The Idle Task can also be used to collect information about the RTOS performance (such as the CPU load). Usually, the Idle Task is not accessible to the application developer.

How is multitasking implemented?

To implement preemptive multitasking, the kernel must be able to *pause* the execution of a task, and *resume* the execution of another task. While this might seem difficult, it really isn't so.

Essentially, a task is just a piece of code; it will just be a sequence of CPU instructions that are to be fetched from memory. Consider the assembly equivalent of two tasks:

```
task1:
instruction-1
instruction-2
instruction-3
jmp task1

task2:
instruction-4
instruction-5
instruction-6
jmp task2
```

As stated earlier, both tasks are infinite loops. Assume that the CPU has started executing task1, and is currently processing instruction-2, and a need to run task2 arises. What needs to be done so that the CPU can *remember* it was about to execute instruction-3 before jumping into task2, and hence must return back to instruction-3 when task2 is done?

The answer is that the *Program Counter* needs to be saved.

If the PC is saved while the CPU is executing instructions of task1, control can be transferred to task2. When task1 needs to run again, this PC can be re-loaded and hence, the CPU continues from where it left off. The same is done for task2 as well. Thus for a system with N tasks, N different storage spaces are needed for the PC—one for each task. This is similar to a normal subroutine call (say using the CALL instruction), except that the PC is saved on both sides, and not just in the caller side of the code. The kernel code will be responsible for saving and restoring the PC.

If this switching is done fast enough, the system will appear to do multiple things simultaneously, and we say the system is multitasking.

Is it enough to save only the PC? The answer is usually no. If the instructions in each task do not share anything in common, then saving the PC alone is sufficient. However, almost all programs will require at least the CPU registers to be shared. If these registers are not saved, their values can get overwritten every time a different task gets control of the CPU. Thus, when the original task gets a chance to execute, the values in the CPU registers will not be the same as when it was previously executing, leading to inexplicable behavior. Thus, along with the PC, the shared registers must be saved as well. This is again similar to a sub-routine call, where registers that will be modified by the sub-routine are saved by the caller. Again, in this case, this saving is two-way.

If the code is written in a high-level language, it is difficult to predict what registers will be used where. Hence, generally, all the CPU registers are saved when a task is to be paused, and restored when the task resumes. In addition to CPU registers, the Stack Pointer is also commonly saved (this is a requirement for almost all C based systems), and in some rare cases, some extra information must be saved as well (such as some internal compiler symbols). Thus for N tasks, N such copies need to be maintained.

All this information (PC, Registers, Stack Pointer) is called a task's *Context*, and the activity of saving and restoring the context data is called *Context Switching*.

Where is the context stored? An obvious way is to use a region of memory that is reserved for this purpose. A more common approach is to use the stack itself.

For a multitasking system, the stack is split into smaller pieces, and each piece is given to a task. Thus, each task has it's *own* stack area. This means that the context information can be stored on the stack itself, without it needing to be copied elsewhere. The advantage is that the save is accomplished by simply pushing the data onto the stack. The stack pointer alone is saved elsewhere, in a known memory location. To restore the context, the stack pointer is retrieved, and then, the data can simply be popped off the stack. This method is employed for most processors (AVR, ARM, etc.).

For 8051 based systems, things are different. The *stack* exists in the IRAM portion of memory (which can be up to 256 bytes). This segment is too small to be partitioned to give multiple stacks, hence the context data needs to be stored in external RAM (XRAM). Since the 8051 has no instructions to move register contents to XRAM, the entire context needs to be pushed onto stack and then copied to XRAM. To restore the context, the context first needs to be copied onto stack from XRAM, and then popped.

7.17.1.1 | *The Kernel*

The kernel is the core of an RTOS. Again, the kernel is just a piece of code, but it does something very important. It is responsible for context switching, and hence, enabling multitasking. The basic work done by the kernel is shown in the following pseudo-code:

```
procedure Kernel is
begin
  Save_Context;
  Schedule;
  Restore_Context;
end procedure;
```

The first thing the kernel code does is to save the context. This involves pushing the context data onto stack. Once this is done, the kernel code is free to use the CPU registers to execute it's own instructions. The kernel then decides which task has to run next—an activity called *Scheduling*. Once a new task is scheduled, the kernel must start to relinquish control. It starts by restoring the context (popping context data from stack), and finally returning. This is somewhat similar to a function call, except that the kernel *may not* return to the caller.

Since the kernel code needs to access the CPU registers for context save/restore, that part has to be unavoidably written in assembly, since most high-level languages do not provide any direct means to access CPU registers or even the stack. The rest of the kernel code (scheduling) can be written in a high-level language.

The kernel code runs at special points in time called *scheduling points*. A scheduling point is simply something that causes the kernel to run—it can be a due to a API call (such as sleep), or a periodic interrupt.

Most systems employ a special timer that generates a periodic interrupt. This timer is called the *heart-beat* timer or the *tick* timer. Every time this timer generates an interrupt, the kernel code runs. This ensures that no task can take control of the CPU for longer than permitted.

The kernel can also run when a RTOS API is called. For example, if a task calls *sleep*, the kernel code can run so that the context of this task can be saved (the task is paused), and another task can be given control.

7.17.1.2 | *Task Control Blocks*

We have seen how basic multitasking is implemented. What else is required to complete the implementation? Looking at tasks as high-level entities, we can come up with some attributes they can have, such as the entry point of the task, state (running, sleeping, waiting), priority (for priority based systems), sleeping period (to implement *sleep*) and, of course, the copy of stack pointer (or context data).

To make writing kernel code easier, a structure or record is defined with the above fields as members. This structure is called a task control block (TCB). A TCB is the personification of a task—it is a way to look at a task in an abstract way (and not just as a piece of code). After all, the kernel needs to process only these attributes; it need not be concerned with the actual code of the task itself. A typical TCB looks like this:

```
struct tcb_t
{
  uint8_t *stack_pointer;
  uint8_t task_state;
  uint8_t task_priority;
  uint16_t sleep_ticks;
};
```

(uint8_t represents an 8-bit unsigned integer, uint16_t represents an unsigned 16-bit integer; data types used for the structure members depends on the architecture of the processor. The above example is for a typical 8-bit processor)

One TCB object is created for each task; it represents that task. These objects are usually part of an array, called the *TCB List*. The scheduler works with this TCB list to decide which task should run next. For a round-robin system, the next task is simply the next entry in the TCB List. If the current entry is the last one, the first entry is taken as next. For priority-based systems, scheduling involves finding out which entry in the TCB list has the highest priority among non-sleeping tasks.

A Complete Example

Consider a simple RTOS that supports only round-robin scheduling. The RTOS has the following API:

- *os_init*: initializes the RTOS
- *task_register*: registers a task with the kernel
- *task_sleep*: causes the task to sleep for a specified number of milliseconds
- *os_run*: starts up multitasking

Since the RTOS supports only round-robin scheduling, all tasks have equal priority. If two or more tasks are ready at the same time, they are run one after the other.

task_register takes three parameters:

- entry point of the task (address of the task function)
- start of the task's stack
- size of the task's stack

Each task's stack space is allocated statically; the stack is simply an array declared in the program.

The code for a simple application program: blinking two LEDs connected to two I/O ports is shown below:

(uint8_t is an unsigned 8-bit integer type)

```
/* declare the two tasks */

void task1 (void);
void task2 (void);

/*
*declare the stacks for each task
*
*each task has 40 bytes of stack space
*starting address of the stack is the address of the
 first element of the array
*/
uint8_t task1_stack[40];
uint8_t task2_stack[40];

int main (void)
{
    /* initializes the RTOS */
    os_init();

    /* register the two tasks with the kernel */
    task_register(task1, task1_stack, 40);
    task_register(task2, task2_stack, 40);

    /* start multitasking */
    os_run();

    return 0; /* will never reach here! */
}

/*
*define task1
*/
```

```
void task1 (void)
{
   for(;;)
   {
          IOPORT1 ^ = 1; / *toggle IOPORT1 */

          task_sleep(500);
   }
}

/*
*define task2
*/

void task2 (void)
{
   for(;;)
   {
          IOPORT2 ^ = 1; /* toggle IOPORT2 */

          task_sleep(1000);
   }
}
```

The application contains two tasks: task1 and task2. Each task toggle an I/O port and then sleep for an amount of time (task1 sleeps for 500 ms, task2 for 1000 ms).

Applications written for general purpose operating systems are distinct from the OS; they are not part of the OS itself. In this case, the operating system binary and application binary are different.

In contrast, there is no distinction between the RTOS application and the RTOS itself. Both are linked together to give a *single* binary image, which is then loaded onto the memory of the embedded processor. Hence, the RTOS exists as a library of code that is linked with the application code (similar to how a math library is linked when say the sin function is used). If a new task has to be added, the entire application code has to be re-compiled and re-linked.

Why use an RTOS?

The real advantage of using RTOS can be understood from a simple example:

Consider a system that has to do two tasks:

- **task1:** needs to execute only when an interrupt arrives
- **task2:** executes irrespective of whether the interrupt arrived or not

Without a RTOS, the code might be written as follows:

```
volatile uint8_t flag = 0; /* flag to indicate arrival of
                              interrupt */
void interrupt_handler (void)
{
   flag = 1;
}
```

```
int main (void)
{
    for(;;)
    {
            /* if interrupt has arrived, execute task1 */
            if (flag)
            {
                    task1();
                    flag = 0; /* reset the flag */
            }
            /* task2 runs irrespective of whether the
               interrupt arrived or not */
            task2();
    }
}
```

Looking at the code, we expect that task1 runs as soon as the interrupt arrives. However, this is true only if the interrupt arrived before *flag* is checked in the main loop. In such a case, the condition passes, and task1 runs as expected.

But what happens when the interrupt comes just after the condition was checked? Since at the time of checking, *flag* was zero, task1 was not executed. Instead, now task 2 has already started to execute when the interrupt arrived. Although *flag* is now set (by the interrupt handler), task1 has to wait until task2 finishes, so that the main loop sees that *flag* was set and that task1 can run.

An adhoc solution could be put in place, like checking for *flag* inside task2, but it does not really solve the problem. If the interrupts are completely asynchronous to the system (meaning it is hard to predict when they will arrive), no amount of checking will help. Things can get worse if another task needs to be added; where should the function call to that task be put?

If task1 has to run in *real-time*, that is, run as soon as the interrupt arrives (regardless of when it arrives), this code is of no use. Assume that the interrupt signals that a button was pressed, and task1 has to display a menu on a screen. Which the above code, a user will find that the menu appears on the screen after varying amounts of delay—sometimes it appears immediately, and at other times, it appears after a delay. Such a behaviour can be unacceptable in many cases.

In short, this type of code has is timing sensitive; adding or removing pieces of code will affect the time at which task1 actually executes.

Now let's see how the same code is written using a multitasking RTOS. Some new RTOS API are introduced here:

- **signal:** signals that a condition is fulfilled
- **wait:** causes a task to wait until a condition is fulfilled
- **os_interrupt_exit:** causes the kernel to run

signal and *wait* are what are called as *Semaphore* primitives. They are used for what their name suggests—signalling between tasks, or an interrupt handler and a task.

A task waiting on a semaphore will be blocked (paused) until another task signals it. This can be used for synchronization between two tasks. Note that an interrupt handler cannot be made to wait, it is always asynchronous to the rest of the code. However, an interrupt handler can signal a task. A *semaphore object* is used as parameters to *signal* and *wait*. This object contains some information about the signal state, what tasks are waiting on it, etc.

os_interrupt_exit contains some code to properly call the kernel, which reschedules the tasks. This can cause a signalled task to resume execution.

How are these primitives used to solve the above problem?

Since task1 has to run when the interrupt arrives, the interrupt handler has to *signal*, and task1 has to wait for that signal. When the signal does arrive, the kernel sees that task1 should run, and passes control to task1. If task2 is currently executing, it is paused until task1 completes. When task1 finishes executing, it goes back to waiting for the next signal, and task2 is resumed.

In this case, task1 always runs as soon as the interrupt arrives; task2 can no longer affect the time at which task1 executes. Hence, we can say task1 executes in *real-time*. The best part is that more tasks can be added or removed easily; the kernel takes care of scheduling, so that task1 always executes in real-time.

For simplicity, only the relevant task code is shown below; the main function, initialization of tasks, etc. are omitted.

```
void interrupt_handler(void)
{
   /* send the signal, s is a semaphore object */
   signal(&s);

   /* run the kernel code */
   os_interrupt_exit();

}

void task1 (void)
{
   for(;;)
   {
         /* wait for signal */
         wait(&s);

         /*
         * code for processing comes here
         */

   }
}

void task2 (void)
{
   for(;;)
```

```
        {
            /* some lengthy computation is done here */
        }
    }
```

Note that simply by using a RTOS does not magically make a non real-time system into a real-time system. The facilities provided by the RTOS must be used properly to ensure real-time behaviour.

7.17.2 | Mutex, Semaphore and Mailbox

Almost all RTOSes provide mutexes, semaphores and mailboxes. Typically, each has an associated data-type, and a set of API to operate on an object of that data-type. For example, the mutex implementation may have a data-type called *mutex_t* and a set of API such as *mutex_lock* and *mutex_unlock*. The exact names of the data-types and API are dependent on the RTOS, and hence, some general names are used here.

Assume that a particular RTOS provides the following:

i) **Semaphore**

- data-type: semaphore_t
- API: semaphore_create, semaphore_wait, semaphore_signal

ii) **Mutex**

- data-type: mutex_t
- API: mutex_create, mutex_lock, mutex_unlock

iii) **Mailbox**

- data-type: mailbox_t
- API: mailbox_create, mailbox_post, mailbox_wait

Each of these APIs operate on an object (variable) of the associated data-type. For example, *semaphore_signal* will require an object of type *semaphore_t* to be passed to it.

The following pseudo-code examples assume a C like language, where arguments are passed by value. Since all these APIs will need to modify the internal state of the object passed to them, the address of the object is passed to the API, instead of the object itself.

Semaphore Example

```
/* synchronizing producer-consumer tasks using
   semaphores */

/* number of items in buffer */
#define N 42

/* semaphore objects to indicate state of queue */
semaphore_t sem_fill, sem_empty;

void producer_task (void)
```

```
{
   for(;;)
   {
         /* wait till queue has atleast one empty space */
         semaphore_wait(&sem_empty);

         /* insert an item into the queue */
         insert_to_queue(item);

         /* signal that the queue has been filled with
            one item */
         semaphore_signal(&sem_fill);
   }
}

void consumer_task (void)
{
   for(;;)
   {
         /* wait for queue to be filled with atleast one
            item */
         semphore_wait(&sem_fill);

         /* remove item from queue and process it */
         item = remove_from_queue();

         /* signal that an item has been removed */
         semaphore_signal(&sem_empty);
   }
}

int main (void)
{
   /* create the semaphore with initial values */
   semaphore_create(&sem_fill, 0);
   semaphore_create(&sem_empty, N);

   /* code to register the tasks with the kernel and
      startup comes here */

   /* should never reach here! */
   return 0;
}
```

Here, two semaphore are used: *sem_fill* and *sem_empty*.

- *sem_fill* is initialized with value 0, and indicates the number of items currently in the queue.
- *sem_empty* is initialized with value N, and indicates the number of free slots left in the queue.

The producer task produces items (data) that are put in a common queue. Before items can be placed in the queue, the task must first ensure that the queue has *atleast* one empty slot. This is done by *wait*ing on the *sem_empty* semaphore: if this semaphore's count it zero, it means the queue is full (i.e. no free slots), and hence the producer task will be put to sleep by the RTOS. Once a slot if available, the producer task is automatically awakened by the RTOS. If free slots do exist, the execution continues normally. In either case, the item is placed in the queue *only* if it has a free slot. The task must then indicate that an item has been placed in the queue. This is done by *signall*ing the *sem_fill* semaphore. This operation simply increments the count of this semaphore. The operation of the consumer task is similar to the producer task, except that the consumer removes items from queue, and hence the condition is for the queue to be non-empty. This is done by *wait*ing on the *sem_fill* semaphore, and *signalling* the *sem_empty* semaphore indicates that one item has been removed (one more slot has been made free in the queue).

Mutex Example

```
/* guarding a shared serial communication line using
   mutexes */

/* mutex object representing the serial line */
mutex_t mx_serial;

void task1 (void)
{
    for(;;)
    {
            /* lock the serial port, or wait for lock */
            mutex_lock(&mx_serial);

            /* send the message */
            uart_puts("inside task1");

            /* unlock the serial port */
            mutex_unlock(&mx_serial);
    }
}

void task2 (void)
{
    for(;;)
    {
            /* lock the serial port, or wait for lock */
            mutex_lock(&mx_serial);

            /* send the message */
            uart_puts("inside task2");

            /* unlock the serial port */
            mutex_unlock(&mx_serial);
    }
```

```
}

int main (void)
{
   /* create the mutex object */
   mutex_create(&mx_serial);

   /* code to register the tasks with the kernel and
      startup comes here */

   /* should never reach here! */
   return 0;
}
```

Notice that the mutex API calls are symmetric: both tasks should try to lock and release the mutex object representing the serial port. The serial port itself is not aware of any mutex guarding it; the entire work is done by the mutex object *mx_serial* and the APIs *mutex_lock* and *mutex_unlock*. Using mutexes this way ensures that the serial port is accessed only by one task at a time, thus enforcing *mutual exclusion* of the serial port among the tasks.

Here, *task1* performs some lengthy calculations, and produces a result. This result is further used by *task2* to perform some other processing. *task1* can send this result using a mailbox, and *task2* simply needs to wait on this mailbox. Note that this is similar to using a semaphore, where one task signals and the other simply waits.

The mailbox object has a member called *contents*, which is usually a generic pointer (void pointer). Hence, to retrieve the data, this pointer has to be cast to the appropriate data-type pointer, and then dereferenced.

Mailbox Example

```
/* message passing using mailboxes */
/* declare the mailbox object */
mailbox_t mb;

void task1 (void)
{
   for(;;)
   {
         /* perform a lengthy calculation here */

         /* send the result using a mailbox */
         mailbox_send(&mb, &result);
   }
}

void task2 (void)
{
   for(;;)
   {
```

```
            /* wait for the result from task1 */
            mailbox_wait(&mb);

            /* read and process the results */
            data = *(int *)mb.contents;

            /* continue processing */
        }
    }

    int main (void)
    {
        /* create the mailbox object */
        mailbox_create(&mb);

        /* code to register the tasks with the kernel and
           startup comes here */

        /* should never reach here! */
        return 0;
    }
```

A Complete Example

Consider a music player that is driven by an RTOS. Two tasks that might exist are *play_task* and *glcd_gui_task*. *play_task* simply plays a song in the background, interacting only with the storage medium (say SD card) and the audio codec. *glcd_gui_task* runs in the foreground, always alert in responding to user actions.

Assume that the user selects a new song from the on-screen menu. *glcd_gui_task* will know of this, and has to send this information (i.e. the new file name) to *play_task*. This information is passed using a mailbox.

Both tasks send debugging messages through a serial line, and this serial line is protected using a mutex.

If some I/O error occurs during playback, *play_task* signals an error handling task to report the error to the user.

```
    /* declare objects */

    semaphore_t sem_error;

    mutex_t mx_serial;

    mailbox_t mb;
    char file_name[13];

    void glcd_gui_task (void)
    {
        for(;;)
        {
            Display_GUI();
```

```
        if(Menu_Button_Pressed)
        {
              Display_Menu();
              Get_Selection(file_name);

              /* send some debug information over
                 serial port */
              mutex_lock(&mx_serial);
              uart_printf("new file: %s", file_name);
              mutex_unlock(&mx_serial);

              /* send the new file name as a mail to
                 play_task */
              mailbox_post(&mb, file_name);
        }
  }
}

void play_task (void)
{
  for(;;)
  {
        /* wait for mail from glcd_gui_task */
        mailbox_wait(&mb);

        /* mail contents is the file name */
        Open_File(mb.contents);

        /* send some debug information over serial
           port */
        mutex_lock(&mx_serial)
        uart_printf("got file: %s", file_name);
        mutex_unlock(&mx_serial);

        for(;;)
        {
              /* read block from SD card */
              res = Read_File_Block(buffer, 512);

              /* in case of I/O error, signal the
                 error task */
              if(res! = RES_OK)
              {
                    semaphore_signal(&sem_error);
                    break;
              }

              /* forward the block to the audio codec */
              Forward_Block(&buffer);
        }
```

```
    }
}
void error_task (void)
{
    for(;;)
    {
            /* wait for I/O error signal */
            semaphore_wait(&sem_error)
            /* send a beep to the speakers to indicate
               error */
            Beep_Speaker();
    }
}
```

Some points to remember when using an RTOS

We have seen that an RTOS is very helpful when dealing with timing related code. However, an RTOS does have some disadvantages:

i) **Requires more memory:** since each task requires its own stack, stack space can get eaten up quickly as the number of tasks increase. Since the binary image also has the RTOS code, more ROM will be needed.

ii) **Overhead:** the Kernel is also a code that needs to execute: this adds some overhead to application code execution. Typically, (2–5%) of execution time is used up by the kernel itself.

For a preemptive RTOS, the stack space for each task is a major factor that affects the memory required. The stack is used to:

i) Store the context information
ii) Hold C automatic variables
iii)Hold copies of registers when an interrupt handler should run

The size of context information mainly depends on the number of processor registers: it can be quite high for RISC processors (in the order of 25 registers or so). Interrupt handlers are also required to push registers that they will use in their own code, so the stack must accommodate that as well. Things can get complicated with nested interrupts.

Conclusion

With this, we come to the end of the chapter on operating systems. Please note that most of the important concepts have been covered here.

In this chapter, the concepts presented apply to a general purpose operating system. Most of these concepts are used in embedded operating systems also. But additional constraints on time are to be added when an embedded OS is a real-time OS. These aspects are discussed in the next chapter. A **list of popular operating systems** is given by Table 7.8.

Table 7.8 | List of Some Popular Operating Systems

GPOS	EMBEDDED OS	RTOS
UNIX	SYMBION	uC/OS
LINUX VARIANTS	EMBEDDED LINUX	VxWorks
WINDOWS	ANDROID	FREE RTOS
MAC OC X	BADA (SAMSUNG)	RT LINUX
BSD VARIANTS	i OS	
	PALM OS	
	WINDOWS CE	
	TINY OS	

KEY POINTS OF THIS CHAPTER

- An operating system is the super manager of a computer system.
- The kernel is the core of the operating system.
- A task/process is defined as a program in execution.
- A notion of concurrency is achieved by using scheduling algorithms and multitasking.
- Scheduling may be pre-emptive or non-preemptive.
- Threads are light weight processes.
- Interrupts have an important role in operating system activities.
- It is necessary for processes to communicate with each other.
- IPC is performed using pipes, mailboxes and shared memory.
- Synchronizing various OS activities is a matter of priority.
- Racing, readers' writers' problem, producer consumer issue and deadlocks are matters to be resolved when designing operating systems.
- Semaphores are variables used for signalling.
- A binary semaphore and a mutex are not the same.
- Priority inversion can occur in systems where mutexes are used and pre-emption is allowed.
- Device drivers are an important part of any operating system and are used for interacting with I/O devices.

QUESTIONS

1. List three reasons why an operating system is desirable for a computer system.
2. List three functions that an operating system performs.
3. With the help of a suitable example, differentiate between protection and security.
4. Name three low level software utilities that you have used.
5. Why do I/O devices need the support of an OS?

6. How is concurrency achieved in a system which has multiple tasks to perform?
7. List two criteria for selecting a scheduling algorithm.
8. Why is pre-emption of tasks sometimes done by an OS?
9. How are threads different from tasks?
10. Name and explain two IPC mechanisms.
11. Distinguish between blocking and non-blocking send and receive in IPC.
12. Think of a practical situation which relates to the producer consumer paradigm.
13. Think of a situation in a computer system, in which 'racing' can affect the correctness of results.
14. How do deadlocks occur? How can they be avoided?
15. Is priority inversion a serious problem? Why?

EXERCISES

1. Three tasks T_1, T_2 and T_3, with service times as shown in Table 7.9 enter the ready queue in the order T_1, T_2 and T_3, respectively. Task T_4 with a service time of 50 time units, enter the queue after 50 time units.

Table 7.9

Task No	T_S (Time Units)
T_1	50
T_2	10
T_3	70

Calculate the average TAT and waiting time, for the following algorithms

i) Co-operative
ii) Shortest Job Next

2. Three tasks T_1, T_2 and T_3, with service times as shown in Table 7.10 enter the ready queue in the order T_1, T_2 and T_3. Task T_4 with a service time of 15 time units, enter the queue after 40 time units.

Table 7.10

Task No	T_S (Time Units)
T_1	60
T_2	50
T_3	10

Calculate the average TAT and waiting time, for the following algorithms

i) Co-operative
ii) Shortest Job Next
iii) Pre-emptive SJN (SRT)

3. Three tasks T_1, T_2 and T_3, with service times and priorities as shown in Table 7.11 enter the ready queue in the order T_1, T_2 and T_3, respectively. Task T_4 with a service time of 15 time units and priority 1 enter the queue after 40 time units.

Table 7.11

Task No	T_S (Time Units)	Priority
T_1	60	2
T_2	50	3
T_3	10	5

Calculate the average TAT and waiting time for the following algorithms

i) Non-preemptive priority-based scheduling
ii) Pre-emptive priority-based scheduling

4. Three processes with service times as shown in Table 7.12 enter the ready queue in the order T_3, T_1, T_2. Calculate their TATs for the FIFO (co-operative scheduling algorithm.)

Table 7.12

Task No	T_S (Time Units)
T_1	40
T_2	55
T_3	25

i) If they choose to use the round-robin scheme with a slice time of 10 time units, how will the scheduling change?

8 REAL-TIME OPERATING SYSTEMS

In this chapter, you will learn

- How to define a real-time task
- How to differentiate between soft, hard and firm real-time tasks
- The definitions of periodic, aperiodic and sporadic tasks
- The concept of real-time operating systems and their necessity
- The concepts of real-time scheduling algorithms
- The rate monotonic algorithm
- The earliest deadline first algorithm
- The qualities of a good real-time operating system (RTOS)

Introduction

The previous chapter focused on general purpose operating systems which are used in PCs. In this chapter, we will discuss real-time operating systems, or RTOS, as they are called, which have a rather restrictive domain. But most of the aspects of general purpose OSes are applicable in this as well. In this chapter, only the 'differences' will be highlighted and discussed.

Before we go into the intricacies of real-time operating systems, let us have a clear definition of what exactly we are talking about. First of all, what do we mean by the term 'real-time'? The answer is that it is 'time' measured by a physical clock. Things have to happen with relation to the actual time by which the universe is timed.

8.1 | Real-time Tasks

What is a real-time task?

It is a task in which the performance is judged on the basis of time; this means that the result of a computation is 'correct' only if has produced its correct output within the specified time constraint, that is, failure to meet the specified time constraints is designated either as 'system failure' or a reduced value for the 'quality of service'. This 'temporal' factor is the distinguishing feature of a real-time task.

Chapter-opening image: An EPROM IC.

Listed as follows are some examples of systems with real-time tasks:

- Process control in industrial plants
- Robotics
- Air traffic control
- Telecommunications
- Weapon guidance system
- Medical diagnostic and life-support systems
- Automobile engine control systems
- Anti-lock braking systems
- Real-time data bases

In all these applications, time is an important parameter. Think of air traffic control, where aircrafts are guided accurately for landing and navigation, and any delay in getting the right response will result in a disaster in terms of human life. This applies to all the other applications in the above-said sample list. A real-time data base is one which gets updated continually, for example, the flight data of an aircraft is to be continuously changed with new values of speed, direction, location, altitude and such data. Decisions on the navigation of the craft are made based on this data, and so this data is safety critical. Take another case—a queue of people needing service in a billing counter is not a real-time system, but if a time constraint is added that billing is to be completed within a certain amount of time, then the service for each customer becomes 'real time'.

What is real-time speech/video processing?

A speech or moving picture sample of 1 second, if processed in 1 second or less makes it real-time processing. If the processing takes more than 1 second, it is no longer real-time processing.

Are real-time systems and embedded systems the same?

No, embedded systems are systems designed for a specific set of applications (Ref Section 1.2). When such a system requires 'time constrained' operation, it becomes a real-time embedded system. All embedded systems are not real-time systems; a printer is not a real-time system, though it belongs to the class of embedded systems, but a robot which counts objects passing through a conveyor belt is a real-time system.

8.1.1 | Terms and Defintions

Now, let's define some terms which we will be using henceforth.

i) **Release time (or ready time):** This is the time instant at which a task is ready or eligible for execution.
ii) **Scheduling time:** This is the instant of time at which a task gets its chance to execute.
iii) **Completion time:** This is the time instant at which a task completes execution.
iv) **Deadline:** This is the instant of time by which execution of the task should be completed.
v) **Run time:** The time taken without interruption to complete the task, after the task is released.

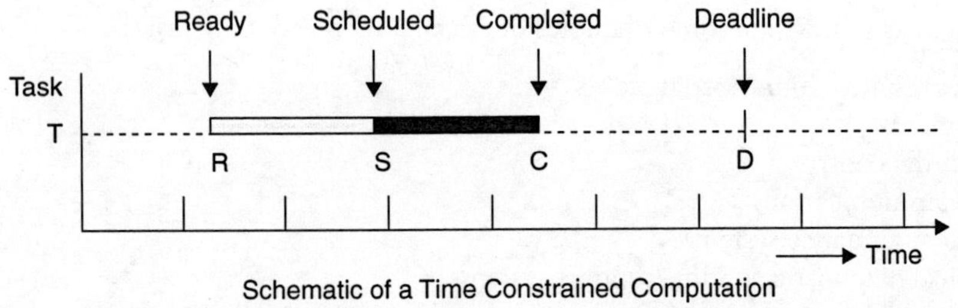

Figure 8.1 | Time components of a real-time task

vi) **Tardiness** specifies the amount of time by which a task misses it deadline. It is equal to the difference between the completion time instant and the deadline.

vii) **Laxity** is defined as the deadline minus the remaining computation time. The laxity of a task is the maximum amount of time it can wait, and still meet its deadline.

8.1.2 | Scheme of a Time Constrained Task Execution

Figure 8.1 shows the various time components of a real-time task. Each computation has a release/ready time *R*, at which the task becomes available for scheduling. At some point after the ready time, the task gets scheduled at the scheduling time *S*, and then the execution starts. Execution completes at time *C*, designated as the completion time. A deadline *D*, is typically associated with the task completion, and the aim is to complete the task before the deadline. Note that the task need not be scheduled just as soon as it is ready. It needs to wait in the ready queue, until it gets its chance to execute.

8.1.3 | Types of Real-time Tasks

We can classify real-time tasks as hard, soft and firm. Suppose there are n tasks in a system notated as T_1, T_2 .... T_n. Let the completion time instant and deadline for task T_i be C_i and D_i, respectively. We can differentiate between the three types, based on the following criteria.

8.1.3.1 | *Hard Real-time Task*

Task T_i is a hard real-time task if it is mandatory that $C_i < = D_i$. This implies that the failure to meet the deadline makes it a fatal fault. If the task misses the stipulated deadline, it is a failure, which means that the value of completing the task after the deadline, is zero, that is, the task is useless now, and may even be catastrophic. For a hard real-time task, the value of the task instantly reduces to zero as shown in Figure 8.2.

The value if the task is plotted on the Y axis, and completion time is plotted on the X axis, where release time *R*, and deadline *D*, are also marked. The task has the constant value *V*, if it is completed any time within the deadline *D*. After that, its value is zero.

An automobile braking system needs to have a 'hard' deadline—the calculation and decision for braking must be made before the expiry of the stipulated deadline—otherwise a collision occurs. Such an application is designated as 'safety critical', and all such tasks are hard real-time tasks.

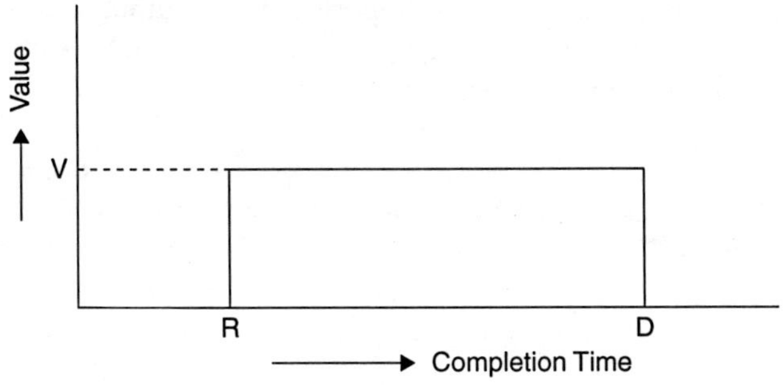

Hard Deadline Value Function

Figure 8.2 | A hard real-time task

8.1.3.2 | *Soft Real-time Task*

Task T_i is a soft real-time task if there is a penalty $P(T_i)$ associated with it if the condition $C_i <= D_i$ is not satisfied. The penalty increases as $(C_i–D_i)$ increases. The penalty is the inverse of the value of the task. If the completion time extends beyond the deadline, the value of the task starts falling until it is zero. Figure 8.3 illustrates this. It is seen that until the deadline is reached, the completion of the task has a value, which goes on reducing with time, till a point (in time) is reached when the result of execution of the task becomes useless, because it has come too late. The penalty and effects associated with missing the deadline are poorly defined and varies, depending on the application.

Imagine a game in which scores of the players have to be displayed continuously. If the scores are a bit late, no catastrophe occurs, but decisions have to be based on the scores; if scores are outputted beyond the deadline, we say that the performance of the scoring system is bad. Beyond a limit, the system becomes useless for gaming. Stock market updates are of the similar category with 'soft' deadlines.

8.1.3.3 | *Firm Real-time Task*

Task T_i is a firm real-time task, if its value reduces to zero if the stipulated deadline is not met. In practice, this means that the output of the task is discarded if the deadline is not met. This is slightly different from a 'hard' real-time task, in the sense that here,

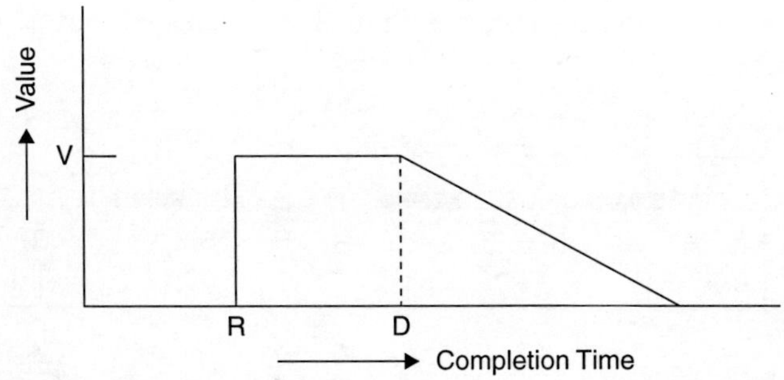

Figure 8.3 | The value of a soft real-time task

missing the deadline is not catastrophic, it simply is that the output of delayed execution is dropped. For such a system to be useful, the point is that deadlines are allowed to be missed once in a while, but not too frequently.

What could be considered as an example of a 'firm real-time task'? Think of a handheld device which receives/delivers video frames. The process of decoding a video frame may occasionally get delayed by reasons like unexpected interrupts and the like. When such video frames are delivered late, the playback does not look good. Skipping such frames and making sure that not too many such frames are delayed will be better, because the effect might be less noticeable to the user than playing back the delayed frames.

8.2 | Real-time Systems

In a system, there will be a number of tasks which will be taken up one by one for processing; do all these jobs need to be 'time constrained' to make it a real-time system? The answer is no. A real-time system is composed of many tasks, but there should be at least one task which can be categorized as one of the above three types (hard, soft or firm). Such a system can be designated as a real-time system.

Now let's see other types of classifications for real-time tasks.

8.3 | Types of Real-time Tasks

8.3.1 | Periodic Tasks

Periodic tasks are real-time tasks which are activated (released) regularly at fixed rates (periods). Periodic tasks must execute once per period. A very large set of real-time tasks are periodic. Consider a number of sensors in a chemical plant. These sensor inputs are sampled at regular intervals which are fixed 'a priori'. However, the periods of tasks can be dynamic as well. Figure 8.4 shows a task with period P.

8.3.2 | Aperiodic Tasks

An aperiodic task is a stream of jobs arriving at irregular intervals. The definition of aperiodic tasks indicates that the inter-arrival period between two such tasks can be zero, which means that two aperiodic tasks can arrive at the same time. Aperiodic tasks are also implied to have 'soft' deadlines, and the aim of scheduling them would be to provide

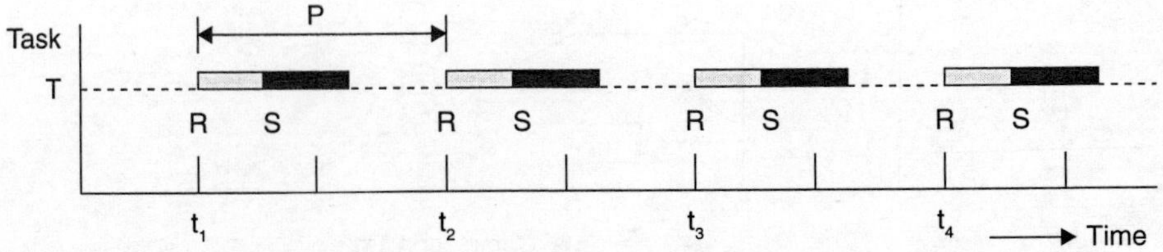

Figure 8.4 | A periodic task

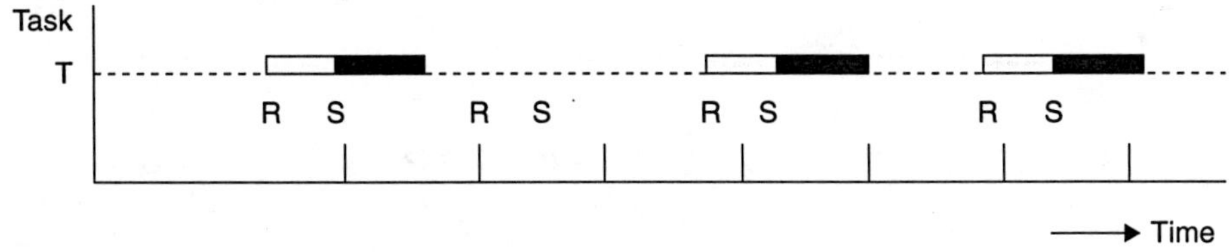

Figure 8.5 | An aperiodic task

fast 'average' response times. Signals generated by events from various devices in a system can constitute aperiodic tasks. An operator's command from a surveillance system (like radar) is an example. Along with processing the surveillance signals, this will also have to be taken care of. That's how two signals may arrive at the same time, and it is obvious that hard deadlines are not possible. See Figure 8.5 which shows a task whose instances arrive without any particular timing.

8.3.3 | Sporadic Tasks

A sporadic task is an aperiodic task with a hard deadline and a minimum inter-arrival time (between two such tasks). Without a minimum inter-arrival time restriction, it is impossible to guarantee that a deadline of a sporadic task would always be met. Examples of such tasks are emergency conditions like fire, over speed of critical machinery in a plant, etc.

8.3.4 | Preemptible/Non-preemptible Tasks

In some real-time scheduling algorithms, a task can be preempted if another task of higher priority becomes ready. In contrast, the execution of a non-preemptive task should be without interruption, once started.

In Figure 8.6, task T_1 was executing, and when the higher priority task T_2 comes in, the first one is preempted, that is, it is stopped in between, and the higher priority task T_2 is allowed to execute.

Now see Figure 8.7, in which T_1 is a task which cannot be preempted (because of the nature of the application). So, although the higher priority task T_2 comes in, T_1 continues till completion.

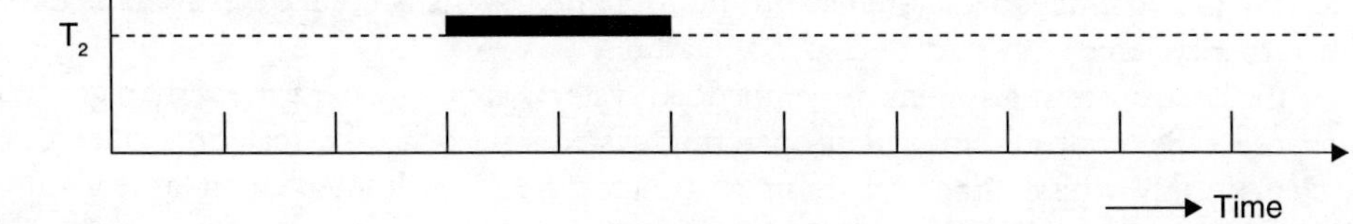

Figure 8.6 | A preemptible task

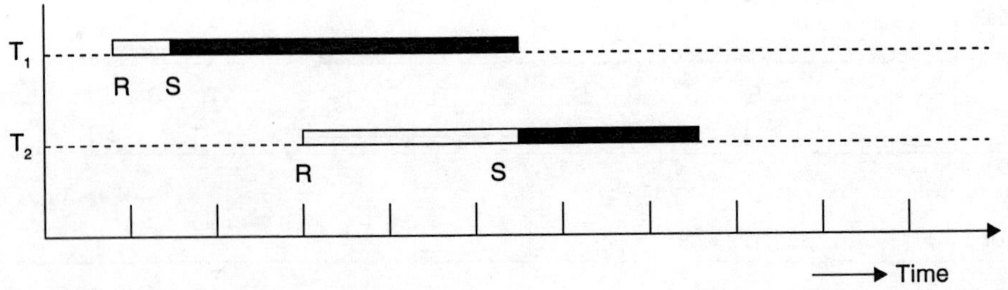

Figure 8.7 | A non-preemptible task

8.4 | Real-time Operating Systems

Now that you have got an idea of the different types of real-time tasks, it is time to be introduced to what is meant by a 'real-time operating system (RTOS)'.

All general purpose computers have operating systems, and the features of such systems have been dealt with, in Chapter 7. We note that any system which has a powerful processor, a number of peripherals, different types of memory and multiple users (amounting to multiple tasks) need a manager. The OS functions as the manager in a PC.

Do embedded systems need an operating system?

Simple embedded applications like printers, scanners, sensor-based home security systems, MP3 players and myriad such applications need only dedicated hardware and firmware.

Such embedded systems wait for sensor inputs and use interrupts to tell the CPU that it needs attention. This is called the **superloop-based approach**. In this, the whole code for the system is written as one loop which executes continuously. When external events (like key press, alarms, etc.) come, interrupts are generated to alert the processor and then the system responds appropriately. There can be a number of inputs and corresponding actuators, too. The code for the working of all these peripherals is there in the flash memory of the system.

But there are some classes of embedded systems which are complex and need a manager. If you visualize a mobile phone as an embedded system, you know that it is a 'computer' with less computing capabilities (than a PC), but more communicating capabilities—thus, it is a special function computer. It has a number of peripherals like key pad, display, camera, speakers, mic and so on; it also has memory in the form of RAM and flash. It needs to support different types of communication protocols. All this points to the necessity of having a manager for such a system, and that's why there are 'embedded operating systems'. An OS is a necessity in complex embedded systems.

Embedded systems are not limited to handheld devices (though that will be the first to come to our mind). In manufacturing/chemical plants, in communication networks, etc, distributed embedded systems with multiple processors is used. Such systems need operating systems with extra and special features.

In short, operating systems for embedded systems are of greater variety than general purpose OSes. But all embedded operating systems need not be real-time operating systems. Only where time constraint is a factor, need we bother about a 'real-time' OS. Thus, we may port a linux kernel into an embedded processor, but for a real-time application, it will be a real-time linux kernel that we port.

Most of the aspects of operating systems that we saw in Chapter 7 are relevant and applicable here, but this chapter gives an insight into real-time systems by introducing the aspect of 'time constraint'. The key difference between a GPOS and an RTOS is in the task scheduling scenario, and that is what is focused on, in this chapter. Many scheduling strategies are touched upon and a few are given an in-depth analysis with numerical examples.

What does an RTOS do?

Just as any OS functions, an RTOS also provides an abstraction layer between the embedded hardware and the application software. See Figure 8.8. This simply means that the users do not have to concern them self with the hardware—the RTOS manages the interaction between the applications and the hardware. The RTOS ensures that the multiple tasks that comes in, are managed and done 'on time'. RTOSes are a necessity in complex embedded real-time systems.

An RTOS has a kernel, which forms the core of the OS, besides that, there are other components in it. Figure 8.9 shows the basic services that must be provided by any RTOS kernel. As we see, managing multiple tasks, that is, task management is the core

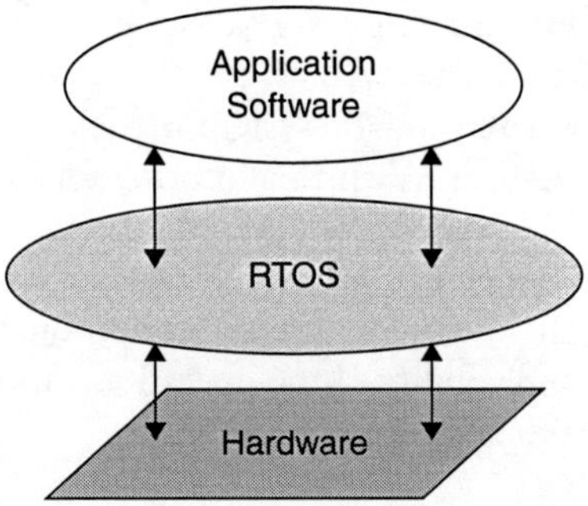

Figure 8.8 | Hardware–software hierarchy in a complex embedded system

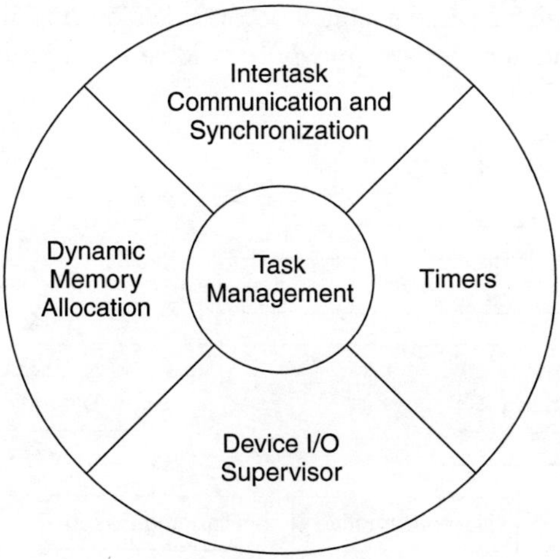

Figure 8.9 | Kernel services of an RTOS

issue. This unit takes charge of task scheduling with the timing information given by the timer. In this chapter, we will focus mainly on task scheduling. The other units of the kernel have the same functionality as discussed for general purpose operating systems in Chapter 7.

8.5 | Real-time Scheduling Algorithms

In the previous chapter, a number of scheduling algorithms for general purpose operating system have been discussed. Some of them are relevant for real-time systems as well, but here we will concentrate on algorithms which are specific for real-time systems. Let us classify the real-time scheduling methods which are in use. The flow chart in Figure 8.10 gives a classification.

Many real-time systems are multiprocessor systems—networked embedded sytems have processors at different locations. But here we dicuss only uniprocessor algorithms.

8.5.1 | Off Time Scheduling (Pre-run-time Scheduling)

They generate scheduling information prior to system execution. The scheduling is based on the knowledge of the release times, deadlines and execution times of all the tasks in the system. This is a deterministic system model. The exact timing characteristics of the tasks are known *a priori*. With this information, a scheduling algorithm can produce a precise schedule which optimizes one of several different measures and optimal algorithms can be used, which can guarantee very good system performance. Fixed factory jobs, where nothing changes under normal conditions, can use this approach. The obvious disadvantage is the inflexibility. If the operational mode or any other parameter changes, the policy will have to be re-done.

8.5.2 | On Line Scheduling

If the parameters of the tasks and the number and types of tasks that will come are not known a priori, the scheduling policy becomes an 'on line' policy. This is the only method that can be adopted by a system whose task list is not known in advance. Such a

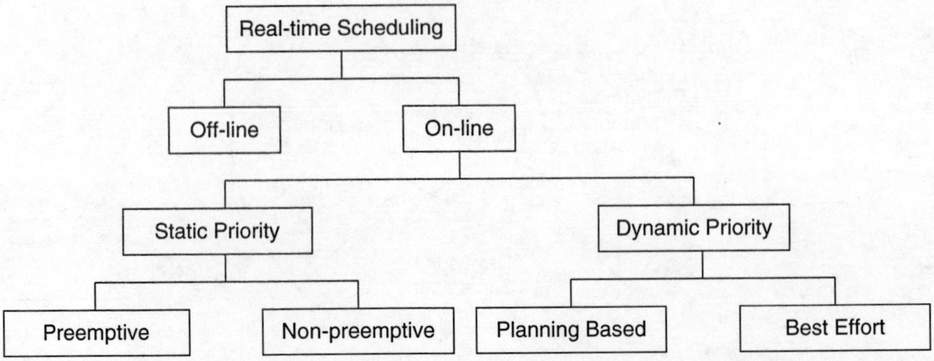

Figure 8.10 | Classification of real-time scheduling methods

scheduler must accommodate dynamic changes in the user demands and availability of resources. But it may not be able to make the best use of all the resources, because of the unpredictable nature of the incoming tasks.

8.5.2.1 | *Static Priority*

Using static priority and scheduling tasks such that those with higher priority gets the chance to execute first, is one of the most popular of the scheduling methods. The method can be preemptive or non-preemptive.

Non-preemptive Scheduling Here the task with the highest priority is run, until it is completed.

Preemptive Priority-based Execution The ready task with the highest priority is chosen for execution as in the previous case. But the difference is that execution of any task can be preempted if a task of higher priority becomes ready. **Thus, at all times the processor is either idle or executing the ready task with the highest priority.**

8.5.2.2 | *Dynamic Priority*

This allows priority to be changed at run time, and so scheduling requires more computation. Here also pre-emption may or may not be used. Flexibility is quite high in systems which adopt this method. There are two subsets for this method:

Planning-based techniques guarantee deadlines for all the accepted tasks. The best effort algorithm, as the name indicates does its best to maximize performance. It will guarantee the deadline of all the hard real-time tasks, while optimizing the performance of soft tasks. There are many algorithms which are used by different RTOSes, but we will concentrate on the most popular of them.

Now that we have had a broad discussion on task scheduling for real-time systems, let have a look at some numerical examples. In all our numerical examples, we imply hard real-time systems, in which meeting their respective deadline is what is meant by making a set of tasks to be schedulable.

First we consider a simple case of static priority.

Example 8.1

Consider three periodic tasks with priorities, periods and execution time as given in Table 8.1. Draw Gantt charts corresponding to how these tasks will be scheduled, assuming that all the jobs have the same release time (i.e. they arrive in the ready queue at the same time).

Table 8.1

Tasks	Priority	Period	CPU Burst
T_1	1	7	2
T_2	2	17	4
T_3	3	24	8

Schedule the tasks to meet their deadlines

i) Without pre-emption
ii) With pre-emption

Solution

The term 'CPU burst' means the time the particular task needs the service of the CPU. Each of the tasks has priorities, with Task1 having the highest and Task3, the lowest priority. Since each task is periodic, one burst of the task must be completed before its next period starts.

Figure 8.11 shows the chart with the three tasks shown on separate time axes, representing the scheduling without pre-emption. **The ready times of each burst of the tasks are marked with arrows at the respective time instants.**

The three tasks are ready at time t = 0. Task T_1, then T_2 and finally T_3 executes, one after the other, because T_1 has the highest priority and T_3, the lowest. Each task's burst is completely executed, and then only the next task is taken up. By the end of the time that T_3 has been completed, all the tasks have completed one round of execution. But a few 'bad' things have happened within this time.

i) At t = 7, the second burst of T_1 arrived, but it was not processed because at that time, the CPU was busy with Task T_3. So T_1 has to wait until time t = 14, for its second burst to be processed.
ii) At t = 14, the second and third bursts of T_1 are ready, but at this time, the CPU must execute the second burst of T_1. So the third burst of T_1 which will have to wait. In effect, T_1's deadline is missed at t = 7 and t = 14.
iii) Because the period of T_1 is relatively short, it is the task that suffers the most, even though it is the task with the highest priority.

This problem can be solved by using pre-emptive tactics. See Table 8.1. The second arrival of T_3 is only at t = 24, and therefore its first burst need not be completed in a hurry. Whenever T_1's burst arrives, T_3 can be preempted and T_1 can be processed. This is quite logical as T_1 is a higher priority task.

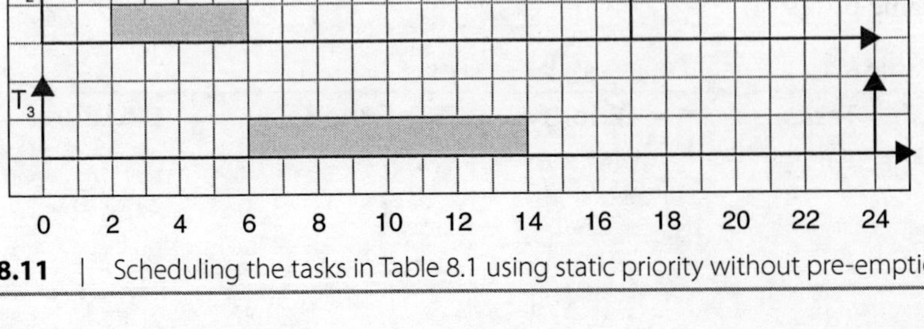

Figure 8.11 | Scheduling the tasks in Table 8.1 using static priority without pre-emption

See Figures 8.12 a and b.

i) T_1 is taken up at t = 0. It completes at t = 2.
ii) T_2 is taken up at t = 2. It completes at t = 6.
iii) T_3 is taken up at t = 6. It is preempted at t = 7, because the higher priority T_1 arrives again at t = 7.
iv) At t = 9, when the second burst of T_1 completes, T_3 is again take up for execution, and is able to perform execution up to t = 14.
v) At t = 14, the third burst of T_1 is ready. So T_3 is preempted once again.
vi) T_3 gets its next chance to execute at t = 16, after T_1 completes its third burst.
vii) At t = 17, the second burst of T_2 is ready and once again, T_3 is preempted.
viii) T_3 gets its chance again only at t = 23, after T_2 completes its second burst and T_1, its fourth burst.
ix) T_3 completes, with its last instance from t = 23 to 24, and is able to meet its deadline.

Note that neither T_1 nor T_2 had to be pre-empted, but T_3 had to be, three times. T_3 is taken up when neither T_1 nor T_2 needs to be processed. This is fine as T_3 is the lowest priority task. T_3 is completed, but in parts. The deadline of T_3 (i.e. 24) is not violated as the last instance of task T_3 completes just before this.

Figure 8.12a shows the time axes for the three tasks separately. The same information can be marked on the same time axis, as in Figure 8.12b. The first figure is easier for visualization of scheduling, while the second one will be easier, when you have to

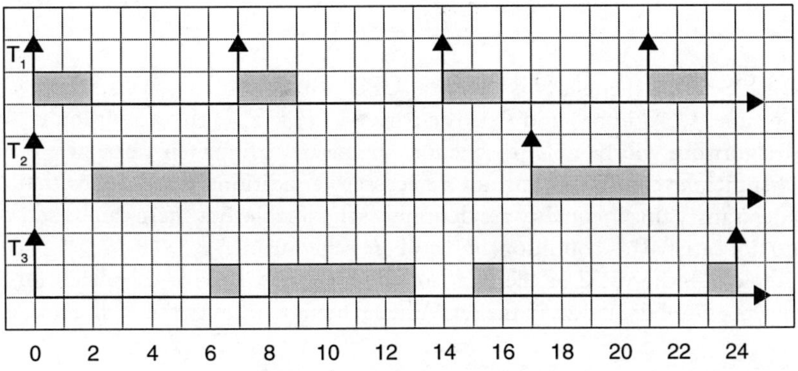

Figure 8.12a | Scheduling the tasks in Table 8.1 using static priority with pre-emption (Figure drawn with tasks on separate time axes)

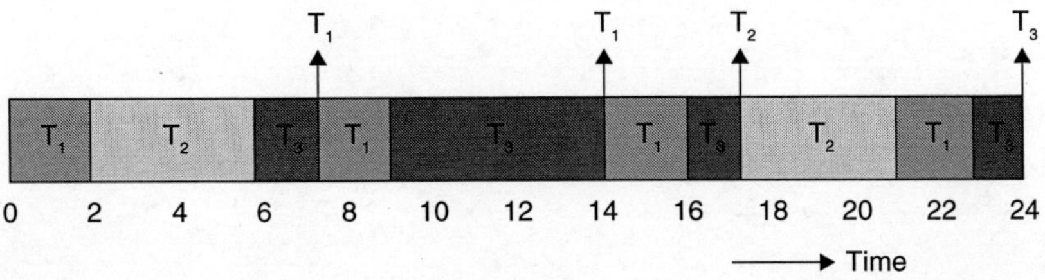

Figure 8.12b | Scheduling the tasks in Table 8.1 using static priority with pre-emption (Figure drawn with tasks on the same time axis)

draw scheduling diagrams. One point you will note is that the CPU is not idle for any time up to t = 24.

What is implicitly assumed in this example is that the deadline of a periodic task is the time when its next 'burst' arrives. Thus, effectively it means that the period of the task is its deadline also. This is the approach used in one of the most important real-time task scheduling algorithms, that is, the 'Rate Monotonic Scheduling', which we will discuss next.

8.6 | Rate Monotonic Algorithm

Rate Monotonic Theory

The notion of rate monotonic scheduling was first introduced by Liu and Layland in 1973. The term 'rate monotonic (RM)' is derived from a method of assigning priorities to a set of processes, that is, **assigning priorities as a monotonic function of the rate of a (periodic) process.** The term 'monotonic' means 'either increasing or decreasing' of a set of values.

In this, priorities are assigned according to the increasing period of a process; as the period increases, the priority decreases. This amounts to the fact that the process of lowest period will get the highest priority.

With this rule for assigning priorities, rate monotonic scheduling theory provides the following simple inequality (8.1), being the sufficient condition for 'scheduling' using the RM algorithm.

$$\sum_{i=1}^{n} C_i / P_i \leq n(2^{1/n} - 1) \tag{8.1}$$

The LHS of the inequality is the total CPU utilization for n tasks, where C_i is the execution time (CPU burst) and P_i is the period of task T_i. If this condition is satisfied, the RM algorithm will be able to schedule the tasks within their respective deadlines. This is a **sufficient condition, but not a necessary condition.** This implies that, sets of tasks which satisfy this inequality are definitely schedulable, but there can be sets of tasks which do not satisfy this condition, and still are schedulable.

In Table 8.2, the value of the RHS of the inequality (8.1) is calculated for various values of n, the number of tasks in the set. When n tends to infinity, the RHS reduces to ln2.

Table 8.2 | Rate Monotonic Schedulable Bound (RHS of Inequality 8.1)

Task Set Size (n)	Schedulable Bound
1	1
2	0.828
3	0.780
4	0.757
5	0.743
6	0.735
------	-----
infinity	ln2

Let's find the CPU utilization for the set of tasks in Example 8.1.

The LHS is $C_1/P_1 + C_2/P_2 + C_3/P_3 = 3/7 + 4/17 + 7/24 = 0.854$

The RHS is $= 3(2^{1/3} - 1) = 3 \times 0.26 = 0.78$ (see Table 8.2 for n = 3)

We see that the sufficient condition for the RM algorithm does not get satisfied. But still, this task set might be schedulable by the RM technique. Let us find out.

Looking closely, we find that the second part of Example 8.1 is the implementation of the RM algorithm itself, because the priorities are ordered in the decreasing order of their periods. T_1 has the least period and therefore, the highest priority. T_3 has the highest period and the least priority. We see that for this set of tasks, the RM algorithm was able to schedule the tasks using pre-emption—the condition being that, at any time, the task of the highest priority should be given the CPU (when it needs it). Thus, Figure 8.12 corresponding to the RM algorithm for the task set in Table 8.1. **The RM algorithm is a scheme catering to static priority with pre-emption.**

Example 8.2

For the task set in Table 8.3, find the CPU utilization, and verify whether it is schedulable using the RM algorithm.

Table 8.3

Tasks	Period	CPU Burst
T_1	12	5
T_2	7	3

Solution

CPU utilization = 5/12 + 2/7 = 0.844
For two tasks, the RHS of the inequality (8.1) is 0.828 (Table 8.2)

Since LHS > RHS, the sufficient condition for schedulability is not satisfied. But this task set is still schedulable using the RM algorithm, as shown in Figures 8.13a and b. Task T_2 has the higher priority (lower period) and so its burst is completed first. Next T_1 is taken up at t = 3. But at t = 7, the second burst of T_2 arrives. So T_1 is pre-empted, and T_2 is taken up. Once T_2 completes, T_1 is again taken up for execution, and it completes at t = 11, well before its deadline of t = 12.

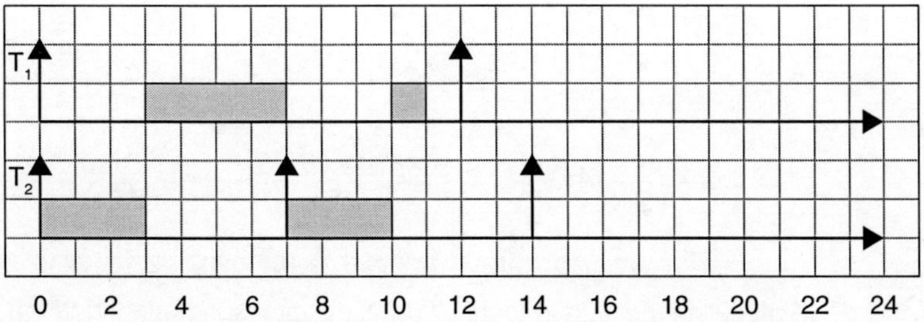

Figure 8.13a | Scheduling the tasks in Table 8.3 using the rate monotonic algorithm (Figure drawn with tasks on separate time axes)

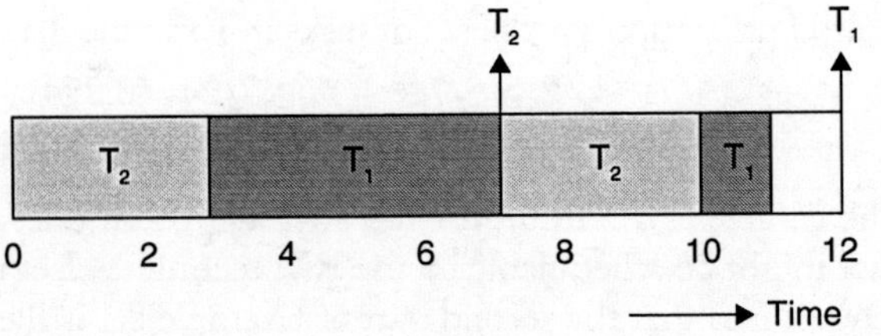

Figure 8.13b | Scheduling the tasks in Table 8.3 using the rate monotonic algorithm (Figure drawn with tasks on the same time axis)

Thus, we find that both tasks are able to finish before their deadline, But the processor is idle for certain periods (in the figure, the idle period is from t = 11 to t = 12).

Example 8.3

For the task set given in Table 8.4, find the CPU utilization, and find out whether it is schedulable using the RM algorithm

Table 8.4

Tasks	Period	CPU Burst
T_1	15	4
T_2	12	2
T_3	20	5

Solution

CPU utilization = 4/15 + 2/12 + 5/20 = 0.684.
The bound for scheduling for three tasks is 0.782.

Since LHS < RHS (of inequality 8.1), that is, the 'sufficient' condition is satisfied, this task set is definitely schedulable using the RM algorithm. See Figures 8.14a and b. Note that T_2 is the higher priority process and so it is executed first. The figures show

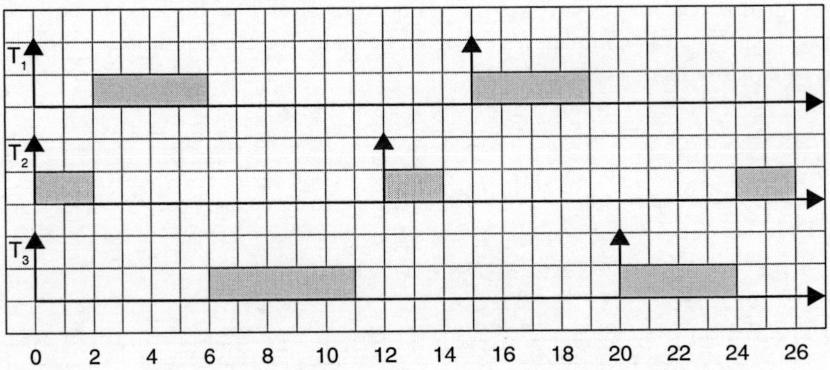

Figure 8.14a | Scheduling the tasks in Table 8.4 using the rate monotonic algorithm (Figure drawn with tasks on separate time axes)

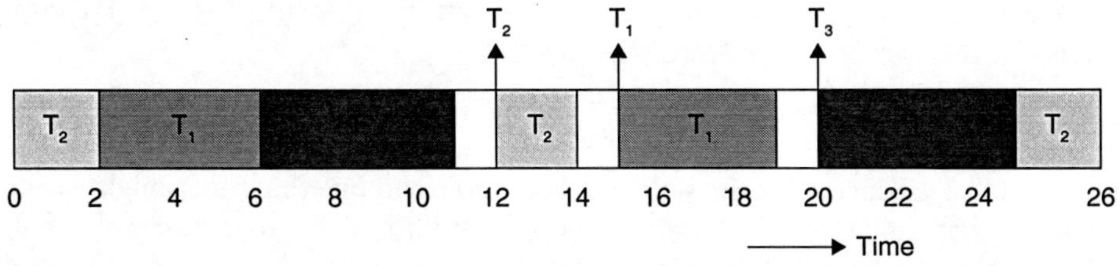

Figure 8.14b | Scheduling the tasks in Table 8.4 using the rate monotonic algorithm (Figure drawn with tasks on the same time axis)

that the CPU is idle for quite long periods; an ideal situation for the RM algorithm. During the second period of T_3, it is pre-empted at t = 24, because the higher priority task T_2 (which has a lower period) needs to be executed. T_3 is taken up again at t = 26.

Example 8.4

See Table 8.5 which shows three tasks, with different release times. This means that all the tasks are not ready at time t = 0. The next burst of each of the tasks is to be calculated with respect to its first release time. Try scheduling this with the RM algorithm.

Table 8.5

Tasks	Period	CPU Burst	Release Time
T_1	3	1	0
T_2	10	3	1
T_3	15	4	3

Solution

Figure 8.15 shows that scheduling is such that tasks T_2 and T_3 have to be preempted when the burst of the high priority task T_1 arrives, every three time units.

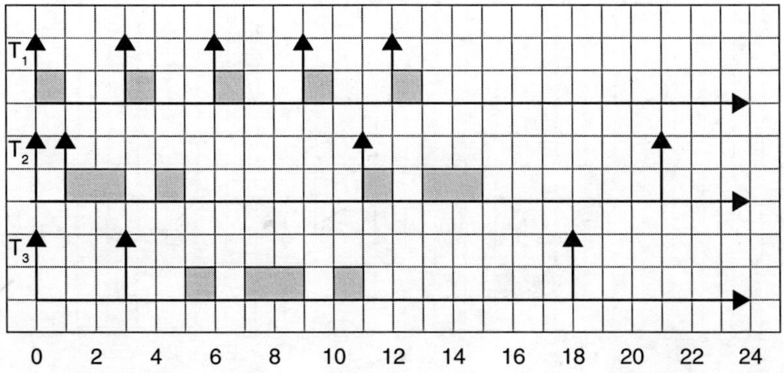

Figure 8.15 | Scheduling the tasks in Table 8.5 using the rate monotonic algorithm

Note that the release times of the tasks T_2 and T_3 are marked at t = 1 and 3, respectively. This task set is, therefore, schedulable.

Note: There is also a 'necessary' condition for verifying if a task set is schedulable by the RM algorithm. Since it involves a lot of calculation, it hasn't been included here. For now, we will be satisfied with the sufficient condition, and one thing that might strike us is that as the number of tasks increases, the CPU utilization has to reduce (Table 8.2) to ensure that it is 'schedulable' using the RM algorithm. This is inefficient, because maximizing CPU utilization is one of the aims for any scheduling scheme, and the RM algorithm takes advantage of low CPU utilization to ensure schedulability.

8.7 | The Earliest Deadline First Algorithm

This belongs to a class of dynamic priority allocation methods. Here the 'priority' of tasks changes at run time. At any instant, the highest priority task is one that has the closest deadline. Tasks that cannot be scheduled by the RM algorithm (because of high CPU utilization) can be scheduled by this method. Look at the task set in Table 8.6.

Example 8.5

Table 8.6

Tasks	Period	CPU Burst
T_1	4	1
T_2	6	2
T_3	9	4

Solution

The CPU utilization is $1/4 + 2/6 + 4/9 = 1.027$

We find that this set cannot be scheduled by the RM scheme. See Figure 8.16 which shows that task T_3 is unable to complete within its deadline of t = 9.

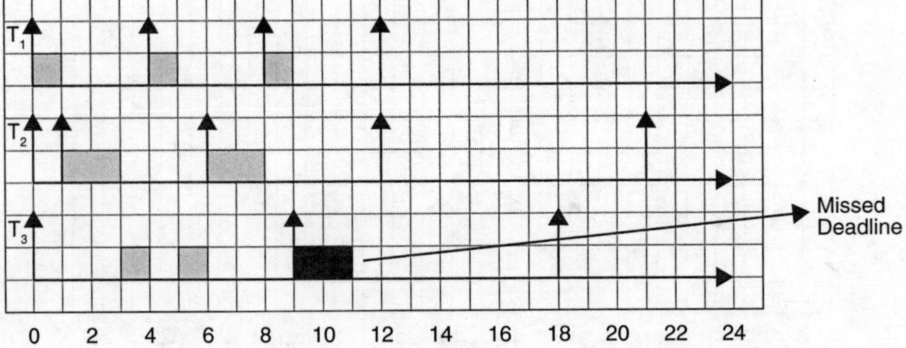

Figure 8.16 | Scheduling the tasks in Table 8.6 using the rate monotonic algorithm

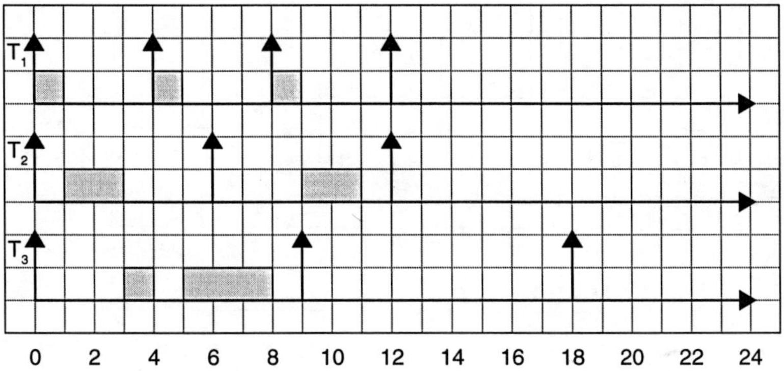

Figure 8.17 | Scheduling the tasks in Table 8.6 using the EDF technique

But we will see that it can easily be scheduled using the EDF technique (Figure 8.17). The idea is that at any time, the task which has the nearest deadline is to be scheduled, rather than the task whose new burst has been released. See the steps of scheduling with respect to Figure 8.17.

i) At $t = 0$, task T_1 is taken up for execution and then T_2 is taken up at $t = 1$.
ii) T_2 completes at $t = 3$, and then T_3 starts.
iii) At $t = 4$, the second burst of T_1 appears. Since T_1 has the earlier deadline (at $t = 8$), it is taken up first and then T_3 continues till it completes at $t = 8$.
iv) Meanwhile, the second burst of T_2 arrives at $t = 6$, but it will not be serviced now because the deadline of T_3 is nearer (at $t = 9$), that is, the second burst of T_2 need be completed only at $t = 12$. So T_3 continues till completion at $t = 8$.
v) At $t = 8$, there is a tie because the third burst of T_1 is ready, as well as the second burst of T_2, and both have the same deadline at $t = 12$. You can see that either of them can be taken up, and both of them are able to meet their deadlines.
vi) At the end, we see that none of the tasks have missed their deadlines.

Thus, the EDF algorithm can schedule the task set which was not schedulable with the static priority RM technique. **The necessary condition for schedulability with the EDF algorithm is that the CPU utilization must be less than 1.** There is no need to assume that tasks are periodic—aperiodic and sporadic tasks can also be scheduled with this.

EDF is an optimal algorithm, in the sense that if a task set can be scheduled, EDF will be able to do the scheduling.

8.7.1 | Disadvantages of EDF

It is a dynamic priority algorithm, and therefore requires dynamic determination of priorities. Thus, it is not as controllable as static priority algorithms. In effect, more overheads are required to implement this. Dynamic priority schemes are not usually used in systems which require absolute predictability. Such schemes have slightly greater scheduling overheads than fixed priority schemes. This is because the range of dynamic priorities is usually greater than the range of static priorities, and dynamic priorities must

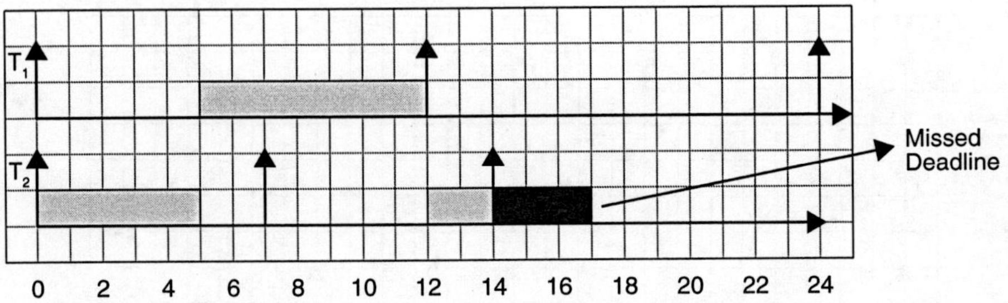

Figure 8.18 | Failure of EDF scheduling

also be recalculated at each decision point, whereas static priorities never change and never have to be recalculated.

Example 8.6

Verify if the task set in Table 8.7 is schedulable using the EDF algorithm.

Table 8.7

Tasks	Period	CPU Burst
T_1	12	7
T_2	7	5

CPU utilization of this is 7/12 +5/7 =1.297, that is, greater than 1. So the necessary condition for EDF is violated. This is thus not schedulable as Figure 8.18 shows. T_2 cannot meet its deadline for its second burst.

8.8 | Qualities of a Good RTOS

Since real-time applications are varied, RTOSes are also of different kinds and varieties. A set of qualities can be listed for an OS to 'qualify' as a good RTOS.

i) **Performance:** This factor implies that it must be capable of meeting the requirements of the application (for which is used)—it must be fast and cater to a high throughput. In short, it should aim to improve and support the performance of the real-time system.
ii) **Reliability:** This means that it should not fail or that the 'mean time between failures' should be very high.
iii) **Compactness:** Since the software and the OS will finally be ported to the memory (usually flash) of the real-time system, it is important that the size of the OS is as small as possible.
iv) **Scalability:** Many operating systems are large and cater to many types of applications. It is necessary that for a particular application, the unnecessary services are removed, that is, the OS must be scaled down. For example, if the application in

hand does not require network services, it must be possible to remove the network part of the OS. Thus, there should be a kind of modularity in the design of the OS, to allow it to be scaled down or up, as necessary.

Conclusion

This chapter reflects only a very small segment of the body of knowledge regarding real-time operating systems. The idea has been to present the vast ocean of knowledge in a small framework, and thus get you to understand the issues to be resolved when 'time' becomes a critical factor. Although only two algorithms have been discussed with a little depth, they are the important ones used in designing real-time kernels. Many other policies and techniques that are used have a reliance on these basic algorithms. This chapter is intended only to give an introduction, so as to motivate the reader to learn more about real-time systems.

QUESTIONS

1. Give two examples of systems which need 'real-time' capabilities.
2. Distinguish between laxity and tardiness.
3. Distinguish between 'release time' and 'scheduling time' of a task.
4. Distinguish (with examples) between hard and firm real-time tasks.
5. Distinguish (with examples) between aperiodic and sporadic tasks.
6. What is the importance of a 'timer' in a real-time kernel?
7. How do you define 'schedulability' of a set of tasks?
8. Under what condition would you say that static priority-based preemptive scheduling is the same as 'rate monotonic' scheduling?
9. What is meant by 'scalability' for an RTOS?
10. Name a few RTOSes.

EXERCISES

1. For the task set given in Table 8.8 what is the CPU utilization? Is it schedulable using (i) the RM algorithm (ii) the EDF method? Show the Gantt charts if it is schedulable.

Table 8.8

Tasks	Period	CPU Burst
T_1	20	6
T_2	60	20

2. For the task set given in Table 8.9, what is the CPU utilization? Is it schedulable using (i) the RM algorithm (ii) the EDF method? Show the Gantt charts if it is schedulable.

Table 8.9

Tasks	Period	CPU Burst
T_1	8	1
T_2	10	2
T_3	15	3
T_4	24	4
T_5	12	3

3. What is the CPU utilization for the following task set (Table 8.10)? Can it be scheduled using the EDF algorithm?

Table 8.10

Tasks	Period	CPU Burst
T_1	10	5
T_2	12	2
T_3	15	3
T_4	24	6

4. Try scheduling the task set in Table 8.9 using non-preemptive priority-based scheduling.
5. Find the names of four popular RTOSes.
6. Name the popular RTOSes used in mobile phones.
7. What is Tiny OS? Where is it used?

9 PROGRAMMING IN EMBEDDED C

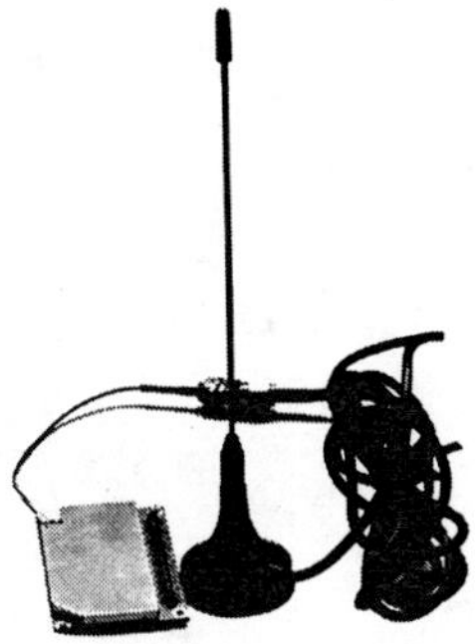

In this chapter, you will learn

- What is meant by the term 'Embedded C'
- Why it is specific for a particular processor
- How to understand the header file of a particular processor
- How to write delay programs for 8051
- The method of using the timers of 8051 in the status check and interrupt modes
- How to use logical and shift operators in C
- A few programs of PIC18F458

Introduction

This chapter is meant to provide an exposure to a high level language programming for embedded processors. In Chapters 13 and 14, programs written in assembly language for 8051 and ARM have been presented. We know that assembly programs are efficient but is also time-consuming because one needs to know the instruction set of the specific processor very intimately. Programming in a high level language is much easier. Here we use C as the high level language, because it is the most popular language in the embedded systems industry. This chapter is based on the assumption that you have a least a minimum level of knowledge of C constructs, looping structures and functions. It is from that point that we begin. All the 8051 programs in this chapter have been tested in the Keil RVDK.

9.1 | Embedded C

We use the kind of C called Embedded C. The name itself implies that an embedded processor is involved. Though the constructs that we use are that of the C language, the program lines need a certain amount of knowledge about the processor being used. The point is that we need to know at least the registers and settings needed for them, to get a particular application to be run. There are different compilers for the same processor. In this book, we use Keil C, which is freely downloadable and thus accessible for all students. Appendix B gives the step by step method of using the Keil Real View Development Kit (RVDK) for 8051 as well as for ARM.

Chapter-opening image: A GPS module setup.

In this chapter, we start with Embedded C for 8051 and end it with a few examples using a PIC 18F458 MCU. The architecture and interfacing details of 8051 are covered in Chapters 13 and 14. It is necessary to learn those chapters before you attempt to understand Embedded C for 8051.

9.1.1 | The Header File

To write a program, a specific processor is to be chosen. The processor chosen has a number of registers already defined in a header file, and we need to make this visible to our program. Let us, for instance, choose an 89C51 of Atmel. The 89C51 is a chip which has flash ROM, and hence is more likely to be used in projects and actual hardware design.

The header file is available in the directory C:\Keil\C51\INC\Atmel and is a notepad file of name 89X51. The 'X' in the processor names implies that any processor in the 89C51 series may be used

Open this file. The addresses (with names) of 8-bit registers and the single bits of bit-addressable registers are given in this file, and you will see the following set as in Table 9.1

Table 9.1 | Contents of the Header File for 89x51

```
/*--------------------------------------------------------------------------
--------------------------------------------------------------------------
AT89X51.H

Header file for the low voltage Flash Atmel AT89C51 and
AT89LV51.
Copyright (c) 1988-2002 Keil Elektronik GmbH and Keil
Software, Inc.
All rights reserved.
--------------------------------------------------------------------------
-----------------------------------------------------------------------*/

#ifndef__AT89X51_H__
#define__AT89X51_H__

/*---------------------------------------------
Byte Registers
--------------------------------------------*/
sfr P0   = 0x80;
sfr SP   = 0x81;
sfr DPL  = 0x82;
sfr DPH  = 0x83;
sfr PCON = 0x87;
sfr TCON = 0x88;
sfr TMOD = 0x89;
sfr TL0  = 0x8A;
```

```
sfr TL1  = 0x8B;
sfr TH0  = 0x8C;
sfr TH1  = 0x8D;
sfr P1   = 0x90;
sfr SCON = 0x98;
sfr SBUF = 0x99;
sfr P2   = 0xA0;
sfr IE   = 0xA8;
sfr P3   = 0xB0;
sfr IP   = 0xB8;
sfr PSW  = 0xD0;
sfr ACC  = 0xE0;
sfr B    = 0xF0;

/*------------------------------------------------
P0 Bit Registers
------------------------------------------------*/
sbit P0_0 = 0x80;
sbit P0_1 = 0x81;
sbit P0_2 = 0x82;
sbit P0_3 = 0x83;
sbit P0_4 = 0x84;
sbit P0_5 = 0x85;
sbit P0_6 = 0x86;
sbit P0_7 = 0x87;

/*------------------------------------------------
PCON Bit Values
------------------------------------------------*/
#define IDL_   0x01
#define STOP_  0x02
#define PD_    0x02    /* Alternate definition */
#define GF0_   0x04
#define GF1_   0x08
#define SMOD_  0x80

/*------------------------------------------------
TCON Bit Registers
------------------------------------------------*/
sbit IT0 = 0x88;
sbit IE0 = 0x89;
sbit IT1 = 0x8A;
sbit IE1 = 0x8B;
sbit TR0 = 0x8C;
sbit TF0 = 0x8D;
sbit TR1 = 0x8E;
sbit TF1 = 0x8F;
```

```
/*-----------------------------------------
TMOD Bit Values
-----------------------------------------*/
#define T0_M0_   0x01
#define T0_M1_   0x02
#define T0_CT_   0x04
#define T0_GATE_ 0x08
#define T1_M0_   0x10
#define T1_M1_   0x20
#define T1_CT_   0x40
#define T1_GATE_ 0x80
#define T1_MASK_ 0xF0
#define T0_MASK_ 0x0F
/*-----------------------------------------
P1 Bit Registers
-----------------------------------------*/
sbit P1_0 = 0x90;
sbit P1_1 = 0x91;
sbit P1_2 = 0x92;
sbit P1_3 = 0x93;
sbit P1_4 = 0x94;
sbit P1_5 = 0x95;
sbit P1_6 = 0x96;
sbit P1_7 = 0x97;

/*-----------------------------------------
SCON Bit Registers
-----------------------------------------*/
sbit RI  = 0x98;
sbit TI  = 0x99;
sbit RB8 = 0x9A;
sbit TB8 = 0x9B;
sbit REN = 0x9C;
sbit SM2 = 0x9D;
sbit SM1 = 0x9E;
sbit SM0 = 0x9F;
/*-----------------------------------------
P2 Bit Registers
-----------------------------------------*/
sbit P2_0 = 0xA0;
sbit P2_1 = 0xA1;
sbit P2_2 = 0xA2;
sbit P2_3 = 0xA3;
sbit P2_4 = 0xA4;
```

```
sbit P2_5 = 0xA5;
sbit P2_6 = 0xA6;
sbit P2_7 = 0xA7;

/*------------------------------------------------
IE Bit Registers
------------------------------------------------*/
sbit EX0 = 0xA8;    /* 1 = Enable External interrupt 0 */
sbit ET0 = 0xA9;    /* 1 = Enable Timer 0 interrupt */
sbit EX1 = 0xAA;    /* 1 = Enable External interrupt 1 */
sbit ET1 = 0xAB;    /* 1 = Enable Timer 1 interrupt */
sbit ES  = 0xAC;    /* 1 = Enable Serial port interrupt */
sbit ET2 = 0xAD;    /* 1 = Enable Timer 2 interrupt */
sbit EA  = 0xAF;    /* 0 = Disable all interrupts */

/*------------------------------------------------
P3 Bit Registers (Mnemonics & Ports)
------------------------------------------------*/
sbit P3_0 = 0xB0;
sbit P3_1 = 0xB1;
sbit P3_2 = 0xB2;
sbit P3_3 = 0xB3;
sbit P3_4 = 0xB4;
sbit P3_5 = 0xB5;
sbit P3_6 = 0xB6;
sbit P3_7 = 0xB7;

sbit RXD  = 0xB0;   /* Serial data input */
sbit TXD  = 0xB1;   /* Serial data output */
sbit INT0 = 0xB2;   /* External interrupt 0 */
sbit INT1 = 0xB3;   /* External interrupt 1 */
sbit T0   = 0xB4;   /* Timer 0 external input */
sbit T1   = 0xB5;   /* Timer 1 external input */
sbit WR   = 0xB6;   /* External data memory write strobe */
sbit RD   = 0xB7;   /* External data memory read strobe */

/*------------------------------------------------
IP Bit Registers
------------------------------------------------*/
sbit PX0 = 0xB8;
sbit PT0 = 0xB9;
sbit PX1 = 0xBA;
sbit PT1 = 0xBB;
sbit PS  = 0xBC;
sbit PT2 = 0xBD;
```

```
/*---------------------------------------------------
PSW Bit Registers
---------------------------------------------------*/
sbit P   = 0xD0;
sbit F1  = 0xD1;
sbit OV  = 0xD2;
sbit RS0 = 0xD3;
sbit RS1 = 0xD4;
sbit F0  = 0xD5;
sbit AC  = 0xD6;
sbit CY  = 0xD7;

/*---------------------------------------------------
Interrupt Vectors:
Interrupt Address = (Number * 8) + 3
---------------------------------------------------*/
#define IE0_VECTOR      0  /* 0x03 External Interrupt 0 */
#define TF0_VECTOR      1  /* 0x0B Timer 0 */
#define IE1_VECTOR      2  /* 0x13 External Interrupt 1 */
#define TF1_VECTOR      3  /* 0x1B Timer 1 */
#define SIO_VECTOR      4  /* 0x23 Serial port */
#endif
```

What we see is that the names of registers and ports and interrupt vectors have been defined here, and therefore 'including' the header file in our program makes the registers and other things visible to the compiler. With this structure, we can start writing simple programs for 8051 in C.

So let's write our first program in which we want to output specific values on port pins. Comments for important lines are given in the program itself.

Example 9.1

```
#include <AT89X51.H>
void main(void)
{
      for(;;)
      {
            P1 = 'H';        //copy 'H' to port P1
            P2 = 0x55;       //copy the value 0x55 to P2
            P3 = 0xF0;       //copy the value 0xF0 to P3
      }
}
```

The simple program in Example 9.1 gives values to the port pins, and this can be verified in the Keil simulator. Port 1 gets the binary value corresponding to the ASCII of H, and the other ports have values as required by the program. **The program is put in an infinite loop so that, when it is burned into the flash of the MCU, control does not go beyond the last line of the program** (otherwise unwanted data in addresses beyond this may be mistakenly taken as instructions).

Example 9.2

This program toggles P0 continuously between the values of 0 and 0xFF. This toggling can be observed in the simulator but if the program in burned on the 8051, it will be difficult to see the toggling because there is no time delay between the loading of the two different values in Port 0. Our next program creates a delay loop,

```
#include <AT89X51.H>
void main(void)
{
        for(;;)                 //Repeat forever
        {
                P0 = 0x00;      //Copy 0 to P0
                P0 = 0xFF;      //Copy 0xFF to P0
        }
}
```

Example 9.3

Write a program in which P2 is given two different values. The values should be passed to P2 with a delay.

Solution

```
#include <AT89X51.H>
void main(void)
{
        unsigned int x;
        for(;;)
        {
                P2 = 0xF0;          //Set the upper four bits alone
                for(x = 0;x<4000;x++);
                P2 = 0x0F;          //Set the lower four bits alone
                for(x = 0;x<4000;x++);
        }
}
```

Example 9.3 needs some explanation.

i) Here, a delay has been defined using an integer x, whose value changes from 0 to 4000. The time quantum of delay obtained with this will not be not clear now. To know that, the program has to be burned on an actual hardware and the calculations need to be done based on the clock frequency of the processor used.

Table 9.2 | Data Formats

Data Type	Size	Range
Unsigned char	8 bits	0 to 255
Signed char	8 bits	–128 to + 127
Unsigned int	16 bits	0 to 0xFFFF, i.e., 0 to 65,536
Signed int	16 bits	–32,768 to + 32,767
bit	1 bit	Used for bits of RAM
sbit	1 bit	Used for SFR bits

ii) The delay loop has been created using a C 'for' loop. In actual execution, these lines get converted to assembly instructions, and from this the delay can be calculated (Section 13.12).
   Different C compilers convert C program lines to different sets of assembly instructions. In the debug mode of the Keil simulator, it is possible to get the assembly code of this C program and from that, the delay can be calculated after knowing the clock frequency. We don't attempt to do such calculations here, as they are covered in Section 13.12.1.

iii) The variable x has been defined as unsigned int. In this context, let us list out the commonly used data types for 8051 C (Table 9.2).

Example 9.4

Write a program to toggle P2.2 with a delay between the states.

Solution

```
#include <AT89X51.H>
sbit LED = P2^2;
void wait(unsigned int);
void main(void)
{
        while(1)
        {
                LED = 0;            //Pin P2^2 = 0
                wait(5000);
                LED = 1;            //Pin P2^2 = 0
                wait(5000);
        }
}
void wait(unsigned int time)  //The function 'wait' is defined
{
        unsigned int i, j;
        for(i = 0;i<time;i++)
                for(j = 0;j<time;j++);
}
```

Example 9.4 shows a few new aspects.

i) The delay had been defined in a function named 'wait'. Whenever a delay is required the function with the parameter is called. Here wait (5000) is the function call. The function name is wait and the parameter is 5000.
ii) A port pin P2.2, a single bit has been name as 'LED'. The 'sbit' directive stands for single bit. Note that P2.2 is written as P2^2.
iii) This program generates a square wave at P2.2. If an LED is connected to the port hardware, it will go ON and OFF at the rate specified by the parameter.

9.1.1.1 | *Using a Character Array*

The next program uses the unsigned char data type. In this, the contents of the character array ARRAY are sent to Port 0 one after the other repeatedly. Note that the array is defined as an ASCII string.

Example 9.5

```
#include <AT89X51.H>
void main(void)
{
     unsigned char ARRAY[] = {"HELLO"}; //String to be displayed
     unsigned char x;
     for(;;)
     {
          for(x = 0;x<=5;x++)
              P0 = ARRAY[x];              //Displaying each
                                            character at P0
     }
}
```

When defined as a character, the corresponding hex number will be found to be in the RAM of the processor. This can be verified by viewing the 'RAM memory' in the simulator.

In this program, at a time, only one ASCII character will be in Port 0. Since no delay is available between different character movements to P0, it will be difficult to observe it (on an actual processor). But in the simulator, in the 'single step mode', it is possible to observe the characters on P0 one after the other.

Example 9.6

```
#include <AT89X51.H>
sbit SW = P2^3;
void main(void)
```

```
{
      bit B;                         //B is defined as a bit in
                                       bit-addressable RAM
      unsigned char Y;               //Y is defined as a character
                                       stored in RAM
      P1 = 0xFF;                     //make P1  an input port
      SW = 1;                        //make SW  an input pin

      {
            Y = P1;                   //copy the contents of P1
                                        to Y
            if(Y == 0x00 )           //verify if Y = 0
                  P3 = 0x0F;         //if yes, move a value to P3
            else                     //if Y is not = 0
                  P3 = 0xF0;         //move another value to P3
      }
      {
            B = SW;                  //the value on SW i.e P2.3
                                       is copied to B
            if(B == 1)               //verify if B = 1
                  P2 = 0x09;         //if yes, move a specific
                                       value to P2
            else                     //if B is not = 1,
                  P2 = 0x01;         //move another value to P2
      }
      while(1);
}
```

In this program, one 8-bit port and one single bit input have been defined as inputs. The contents in these ports and pin are read in and moved to RAM.

According to their values, specific numbers are moved to P3 and P2. The program makes it very clear.

Note The char Y and bit B are found in RAM locations.

Example 9.7

Now we will see a program which writes a message to an output port. This program outputs the ASCII value of the message MESG, written as an ASCII string, one character at a time at port P0. Note that we use #define to state that the port P0 has been named as LED. A delay is realized with a delay function named wait.

```
#include <AT89X51.H>
#define LED P0                        //name port P0 as LED
void wait(unsigned int);
void main(void)
```

```
{
      unsigned char MESG[] = "MY NAME IS LULLU";
      unsigned char x;
      while(1)                          //for all time
      {
            for(x = 0;x<=16;x++)
            {
                  LED = MESG[x]; //display all characters
                  wait(9000);
            }
      }
}
void wait(unsigned int time)      //delay routine named wait
{
      unsigned int i, j;
      for(i = 0;i<time;i++)
              for(j = 0;j<time;j++);
}
```

Note The MESG is in RAM and from there it is moved to Port 0.

You can check in the simulator, in the RAM, the values

4D 59 20
4E 41 4D 45 20
49 53 20
4C 55 4C 4C 55

So far, we considered programs in which delays are generated using software routines. Now let's use some of the peripherals of 8051. The timer is an important peripheral which can be programmed to operate in the status check mode as well as in the interrupt mode. The details of how the timers operate are given clearly in Chapter 14. This is the C version of Example 14.3 (done using assembly language).

Example 9.8

```
#include <AT89X51.H>
void timerdelay(void);
sbit OUTP = P2^4;
void main(void)
{
      while(1)
      {
            OUTP = ~OUTP;        //complement pin P2.4
            timerdelay();        //call the delay function
      }
}
```

```
void timerdelay(void)
{
     TMOD = 0x10;               //mode 1 timer 1
     TL1  = 0x42;               //load low byte of count
     TH1  = 0x80;               //load high byte of count
     TR1  = 1;                  //start timer
     while(TF1 == 0);           //wait as long as TF1 = 0
     TR1  = 0;                  //when TF1 = 1, stop timer
     TF1  = 0;                  //clear timer flag
}
```

The main program complements a pin (P2.4) and calls a delay function named 'timerdelay'. In this function, the SFRs of timer 1 are used. The mode word and the count values are loaded. The timer flag is continuously tested and when it becomes '1', the timer is stopped by clearing the timer start timer bit. Then the timer flag (TF) is cleared to make it ready for the next timing operation. Control then returns to the main program which complements the pin P2.4 and calls the delay function repeatedly.

This timer generates a symmetric square wave. For details of the frequency of the waveform, refer to Example 14.3.

Example 9.9

This program creates an unsymmetrical square wave at P1.4. These timing values are taken from Example 14.6. Since a timer in mode 1 is being used, timer count values are to be repeatedly re-loaded for each portion of the square wave. The two different counts are loaded in the two functions—timerdelay_ON and timedelay_OFF.

```
#include <AT89X51.H>
void timerdelay_ON(void);
void timerdelay_OFF(void);
sbit OUTP = P1^4;
void main(void)
{
     TMOD = 0x10;             //mode 1 timer 1
     while(1)
     {
          OUTP = 1;
          timerdelay_ON();
          OUTP = 0;
          timerdelay_OFF();
     }
}
void timerdelay_ON(void)      //function for ON time
{
     TL1 = 0x60;              //load low byte of count
     TH1 = 0xF0;              //load high byte of count
```

```
      TR1 = 1;                //start the timer
      while(TF1 == 0);        //wait as long as TF1 = 0
      TR1 = 0;                //when TF1 = 1, stop the timer
      TF1 = 0;                //clear the timer flag
}
void timerdelay_OFF(void)     //function for OFF time
{
      TL1 = 0x38;             //load low byte of count
      TH1 = 0xCD;             //load high byte of count
      TR1 = 1;                //start the timer
      while(TF1 == 0);        //wait as long as TF1 = 0
      TR1 = 0;                //when TF1 = 1,stop the timer
      TF1 = 0;                //clear the timer flag
}
```

Figure 9. 1 shows the unsymmetric waveform displayed on the logic analyser of the Keil simulator.

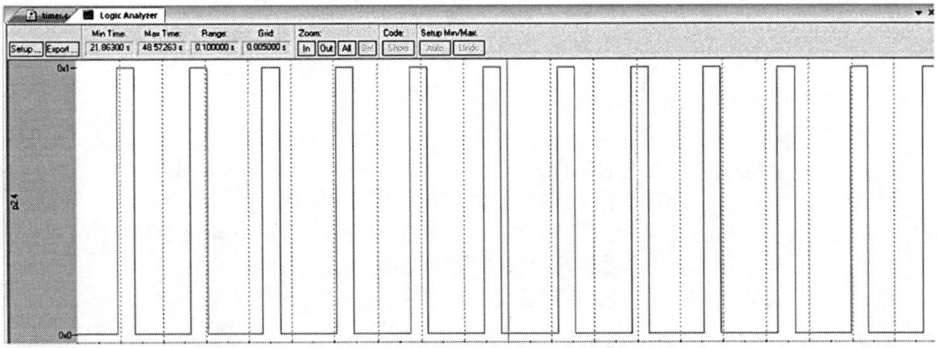

Figure 9.1 | The waveform of Example 9. 9 displayed in the logic analyser

The next example uses timer 0 in mode 2.

For mode 2, it is not necessary to re-load the count after each timer flag setting. The only action needed is to check if the flag is set, and then clear it when it is set. The count is automatically re-loaded and timing resumes.

Example 9.10

```
#include <AT89X51.H>
void timerdelay(void);
sbit OUTP = P1^3;
void main(void)
```

```
{
      TMOD = 0x02;                  //mode 2 timer 0
      THO  = 0;                     //load count = 0 ,for the
                                      largest delay
      TRO  = 1;                     //start timer
      while(1)
      {
            OUTP = ~OUTP;           //complement pin P1.3
            timerdelay();           //call time delay function
      }
}
void timerdelay(void)
{
      while(TF0 == 0);              //wait as long as TF0 = 0
      TF0 = 0;                      //clear TF0
}
```

9.1.1.2 | *Using Timers with Interrupts*

For using interrupts, look in the header file in Table 9.1. The part referring to interrupts is copied here.

Interrupt Vectors

```
Interrupt Address = (Number * 8) + 3
------------------------------------------------*/
#define IE0_VECTOR 0    /* 0x03 External Interrupt 0 */
#define TF0_VECTOR 1    /* 0x0B Timer 0 */
#define IE1_VECTOR 2    /* 0x13 External Interrupt 1 */
#define TF1_VECTOR 3    /* 0x1B Timer 1 */
#define SIO_VECTOR 4    /* 0x23 Serial port */
```

The interrupt numbers to be used in the interrupt functions are seen here. For example, for using timer 0, the vector is listed as 1. See how it is used in Example 9.11 here.

The event to occur when the interrupt of Timer 0 is activated is written in the interrupt function names as timer 0 (void) interrupt 1 (Any name can be given to the function, but the word interrupt 1 must be included in it. Here we have given the name timer 0, but that may be replaced by any label of our choice).

In Example 9.11, the only event that occurs is the complementing of pin P2.4. In the main program, the IE register is written so as to enable all the interrupts and specifically Timer 0 interrupt. Refer to Chapter 14 for the exact details of using timers in the interrupt mode.

Example 9.11

```
#include <AT89X51.H>
sbit OUTP = P2^4;
void timer 0(void)interrupt 1
```

```
{
      OUTP = ~OUTP;
}
void main(void)
{
      TMOD = 0x02;  //mode 2 timer 0
      TH0  = 0;     //load of count = 0 ,foe biggest delay
      IE   = 0x82;
      TR0  = 1;
      while(1);
}
```

Example 9.12

This is the C program corresponding to Example 14.19 in assembly. Both timers 0 and 1 are used and two square waves are simultaneously obtained at two output pins P2.0 and P2.1.

```
#include <AT89X51.H>
sbit OUTP = P2^1;
sbit OUTPP = P2^0;
void timer 0(void)interrupt 1
{
      OUTP = ~OUTP;
}
void timer 1(void)interrupt 3
{
      OUTPP = ~OUTPP;
}
void main(void)
{
      TMOD = 0x22;   //mode 2 timer 0 and 1
      TH0  = 0x0A;   //load count for timer 0
      TH1  = 0xCD;   //load count for timer 0
      IE   = 0x8A;   //activate interrupts for both timers
      TR0  = 1;      //start timer 0
      TR1  = 1;      //start timer 1
      while(1);      //for all time
}
```

9.1.1.3 | *Logical and Shift Operations in C*

When C is used for MCUs, it may be necessary to use logic operators and shift operators.

The notations for these are listed in Table 9.3a, and Example 9.12 shows a program which includes these operations.

Logical

Table 9.3a | Logical Operators

Data	OR	AND	EX-OR	INVERT
X,Y	X|Y	X&Y	X^Y	~X, ~Y

Shift

Table 9.3b | Shift Operators

A data may be left or right shifted, a fixed number of times.
The notation for left shift is << and for right shift, it is >>
The way to use is as shown

i) 0x34>>3 shifts the data right three times.

ii) 0x7E<<4 shifts the data 4 times to the left.

Example 9.13

```
#include <AT89X51.H>
unsigned char W, X, Y, Z;
void main(void)
{
      X  = 0x45;
      Y  = 0x78;
      Z  = 0x67;
      W  = 0xAB;

      P1 = X&Y;          //AND operation
      P2 = X|Y;          //OR operation
      P3 = Z<<3;         //Left shift
      P0 = W>>2;         //Right shift
}
```

9.1.2 | Serial Communication

Frequently, it is required to communicate serially between the PC and an embedded 8051 board. The 'hyperterminal' in the accessories of Windows allows the viewing of the data transmitted. Example 9.13 is a program to receive a character in RX and transmit the same character in TX, that is, to echo the input on the monitor via 'Hyperterminal'. To ensure baud rate compatibility between the two, the crystal frequency of 8051 should be 11.0952MHz.

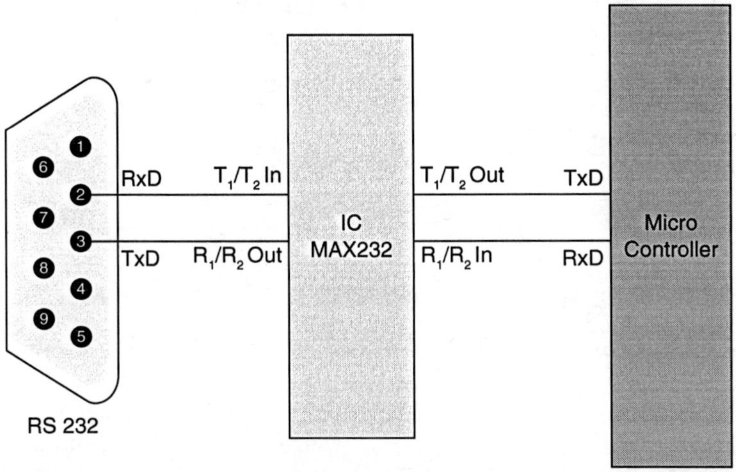

Figure 9.2 | Connections of a PC's serial port to the UART in a μC through a MAX 232 IC

The physical connection between the PC's RS-232 serial port and the 8051, through a MAX232 IC, is shown in Figure 9.2. A more detailed diagram is available in Figure 5.25.

Example 9.14

```
//With 11.0952MHz clock
#include <AT89X51.H>
unsigned char Send;
void Receive_Transmitt_Interrupt_Handler(void)interrupt 4
{
      if(RI == 1)
      {
            RI   = 0;
            Send = SBUF;
            SBUF = Send;
      }
      else
            TI = 0;
}
Initialise_UART()
{
      TMOD = 0x20;      //Timer 1 in Mode 2
      TH1  = 0xFD;      //Setting Baud rate 9600kbps, with
                          11.0952MHz
      SCON = 0x50;      //Serial mode 1 with 8-bit data,stop
                          bit and start bit.
                        //Baud rate is controlled by Timer 1
      IE   = 0x90;      //Enables serial communication flag
```

```
        TR1  = 1;        //Starting the Timer 1
}
int main(void)
{
        Initialise_UART();
        while(1);
}
```

9.2 | PIC Programming Using MPLAB

Next , three programs written for PIC 18F458 are included. Due to space limitations, it is not possible to include the details of the architecture of PIC in this book. However,these programs are presented here to show the structure of embedded C programs for another processor, besides 8051. For PIC, the most popular IDE is MPLAB, and this program has been tested in the C compiler of MPLAB.

Example 9.15

In this, the 8-bit Timer 2 is programmed to operate in the interrupt mode to generate a square wave on all pins of port B.

```
#include <p18f458.h>
void main(void)
{
        unsigned int chkint;
        WDTCON = 0x00;              //reset watchdog timer
        TRISB  = 0x00;              //configure PORTB as output
        TMR2   = 0x00;              //Timer 2 module register
                                      is cleared
        INTCON = 0x80;              //Global Interrupt Enable
                                      bit set
        PORTB  = 0x00;              //initialize PORTB as 00
        T2CON  = 0x04;              //Enable Timer 2 by setting
                                      the TMR2ON bit
        PIE1   = 0X02;              //set Peripheral Interrupt
                                      Enable register
        chkint = 0;
        while(1)
        {
              chkint = 0;
              PIR1   = 0x00;        //interrupt flag bits
                                      cleared in PIR register
              while(chkint == 0) //check for timer interrupt
              {
                    chkint = PIR1&0x02;
              }
```

```
        PORTB = 0xFF;       //when interrupt occurs
                              PORTB pins go high
        chkint = 0;
        PIR1 = 0x00;        //interrupt flag bits are
                              cleared
        while(chkint == 0)
        {
              chkint = PIR1&0x02;
        }
        PORTB = 0x00;       //when interrupt occurs
                              PORTB pins go low
    }
}
```

Example 9.16

This is a program for getting Timer 1 to act as a ring counter at Port B.

```
#include <p18f458.h>
void main(void)
{
      unsigned int chkint, n, p;
      WDTCON = 0x00;        //reset watchdog timer
      TRISB  = 0x00;        //make port B ,an output port
      TMR1L  = 0x8A;        //configured for some delay
      TMR1H  = 0XD0;
      INTCON = 0X80;        //Global Interrupt Enable bit
                              is set
      PORTB  = 0X00;        //initialize PORTB as 00
      T1CON  = 0X01;        //Enable Timer 1 by setting the
                              TMR1ON bit
      PIE1   = 0X01;        //set Peripheral Interrupt
                              Enable register
      chkint = 0;
      while(1)
      {
            WDTCON = 0x00;
            TMR1L  = 0x8A; //configured value for timer
            TMR1H  = 0XD0;
            chkint = 0;
            PIR1   = 0x00; //interrupt flag bits are cleared
            for(n = 0;n<8;n++)
            {
                  TMR1L  = 0x8A;
                  TMR1H  = 0XD0;
                  chkint = 0;
                  PIR1   = 0x00;
```

```
                    if(n == 0)
                          p = 1;
                    else
                          p = p*2;       //multiply by 2 for
                                           configuring as
                                         //ring counter
                    while(chkint == 0)
                    {
                          chkint = PIR1&0x01; //check for
                                                timer
                                                interrupt
                    }
                    PORTB = p;
              }
        }
}
```

Example 9.17

This program is for the 10-bit ADC, but using it as an 8-bit one, by using only the lower 8 bits. The 'end of conversion' is tested, and if conversion is found complete, the digital data is obtained at Port B.

```
#include <p18f458.h>
void main(void)
{
      unsigned int chkadc = 1;
      WDTCON = 0x00;
      TRISA  = 0x01;   //PORTA as input
      ADCON0 = 0x01;   //A/D converter module is powered up
      ADCON1 = 0x8E;   //Six (6) MSBs of ADRESH are read as
                       //'0' and A/D Port
                       //Control bits are configured
      TRISB = 0x00;    //PORTB taken as output
      while(1)
      {
            ADCON0|= 0x04;   //start ADC
            while(chkadc == 1)
            {
                  chkadc = (ADCON0&0x04);//check whether
                                           conversion is over
            }
            PORTB = ADRESL;                //digital output
                                             at PORTB
      }
}
```

Conclusion

This chapter has only dealt with simple C programs for 8051 and PIC. With more knowledge in C, many more constructs of the C programming language (including pointers) can be used in Embedded C. Programs using embedded C for PSoC are included in Chapter 12, and for ARM in Chapter 11.

KEY POINTS OF THIS CHAPTER

- Programming an MCU in a high level language like C is much easier than using assembly language, though the latter is more efficient.
- One needs to know about the architecture of the MCU to write a program for it.
- The header file which defines the names and addresses of the registers is to be 'included' in the C program.
- It is possible to address 8-bit ports, single bit ports and also memory.
- Since the final program will be burned on ROM, it is necessary to write programs with an infinite loop so that unused locations are not accessed.
- To write programs for 8051, the details of its ports and peripherals are to be known.
- The 'for, while and if' loops of C can be used to create delays.
- Timers are programmable using flag checking as well as using interrupts.
- Serial communication between a PC and an 8051 is possible and the data transferred can be observed using the hyperterminal facility of Windows.
- MPLAB is the most popular IDE for PIC MCUs.

QUESTIONS

1. Write a program to toggle all the bits of port B of 8051 alternately with a small delay.
2. Write a program to generate a square wave at pin P0.5. Observe the waveform in the logic anlayser of the Keil simulator. Use software delay loops.
3. Study the timers of 8051 as is given in Chapter 12, and write C programs to get the following.
   a) A symmetric square wave of 10 KHz at pin P2.3 using timer 1 in mode 1.
   b) A symmetric square wave of 15 KHz at pin P2.3 using timer 0 in mode 1.
   c) An unsymmetric square wave of period 10 msecs and duty cycle of 20 percent at pin P0.6, using timer 1 in mode 2.
4. Generate all the waveforms of question 3 using timers in the interrupt mode.
5. What do the following directives do?
   a) sbit
   b) bit

6. Write a program to do the following.
   a) Shift left thrice an 8-bit data, and move the result to port 0.
   b) Logically AND the 8-bit contents of two memory locations and move the result to port 1.
   c) Logically Ex-OR the 8-bit contents of two memory locations and move the result to port 0.

EXERCISES

1. Study the operation of the timers of any PIC MCU of the 18F series and write a program to generate square waves of different frequencies using the flag check mode as well as the interrupt mode.
2. Repeat the above for any PIC chip of the 16F and 21F series.

PART-III

POPULAR MICROCONTROLLERS USED IN EMBEDDED SYSTEMS

10 ARM—THE WORLD'S MOST POPULAR 32-BIT EMBEDDED PROCESSOR

PART I - ARCHITECTURE AND ASSEMBLY LANGUAGE PROGRAMMING

In this chapter, you will learn

- The history of the ARM processor
- The features and architecture of ARM
- The instruction set of ARM
- Assembly language programming for ARM
- The addressing modes of ARM
- How to use subroutines without a stack
- How to generate 32-bit constants using the rotation scheme
- The concept of literal pools
- How to access R/W and Read Only memory
- The use of different types of stacks

Introduction

This chapter gives an introduction to ARM, the very popular 32-bit processor, with a short account of its history, followed by details of where it stands in the embedded processor market now. ARM stands for 'Advanced RISC Machine'. The name explicitly states its characteristic of being a RISC processor. The first ARM processor actually was meant to be the 'Acorn RISC Machine' as it was manufactured by Acorn Computers Ltd., Cambridge, England, in 1985.

10.1 | History of the ARM Processor

In 1985, Acorn Computers Ltd. was in search of a new processor to put up in the desktop market. While the technocrats were contemplating various design options, they came across a few papers published by a set of students in the University of Berkley (USA) outlining a very simple processor design based on RISC principles. The computer architects of Acorn Computers found the design very attractive and decided to build

Chapter-opening image: An ARM7 LPC2140 board.

a new processor using some of these principles. This led to the development of ARM1, which had less than 25,000 transistors, and operated at 6 MHz.

This was followed by ARM2 (in 1987) with 30,000 transistors. Comparing this to an Intel/Motorola's processor of that time having 70,000 transistors, this was a beauty in terms of a smaller die size and lower power dissipation. This was thus, the first ARM processor which was produced in bulk. It had a 32-bit data bus, a 26-bit address space and sixteen 32-bit registers and was clocked at 8 to 12 MHz. It dissipated much less power, and performed much better than Intel's 80286 which came up around the same time (but focused on the desktop market).

ARM3, ARM4 and ARM5 were also designed, but never produced, because around this time, in 1990, Acorn Computers teamed up with Apple Computers and VLSI Technology group to form a company named Advanced RISC Machines Ltd. This company continued with ARM6, ARM7, etc. The latter was the processor which became very popular and led to ARM being used in exotic products such as mobile phones, PDAs, IPods, computer hard disks, etc. After this, ARM made rapid strides in the 32-bit embedded market, accounting for a very high percentage of applications in the high-end embedded systems market.

As of 2011, ARM processors account for approximately 90 per cent of all embedded 32-bit RISC processors. ARM processors are used extensively in consumer electronics, including PDAs, mobile phones, digital media and music players, handheld game consoles, calculators and computer peripherals such as hard drives and routers, etc.

The subsequent and more advanced processors of the ARM family (ARM9, ARM10, ARM11, Cortex) have been built on the success of the ARM7 processor, which is still the most popular and widely used member of the ARM family.

Over the years, many advanced features have been added to the ARM processor, but the core has remained more or less the same.

10.1.1 | The ARM Core

What is meant by the 'core'? The core is the 'processing unit' or the 'computing engine' which has all the computing power, and this aspect is decided by the architecture, which represents the basic design of the processor.

One special and unique feature of ARM as a company is that it designs the core and licenses this IP (Intellectual Property) to others. This simply means that the company does not 'fabricate' the chip, but sells only the design. This design is taken by the licensee, who may or may not add more features (usually peripherals) to the design. Sometimes the buyer can also modify the basic design to a minor extent. The buyer company fabricates the design and sells it/uses it for its products.

There are various ways in which ARM sells its IP. It could be in the form of a soft IP. In this case, the design is sold as RTL (VHDL/Verilog code), and this allows the buyer to modify the design to a certain extent. If the design is sold as a hard IP, it means the buyer gets only the layout or the net list (connection of nets or electronic wires). Thus, the buyer can add only peripherals to the 'black box' design he has purchased.

We can thus understand that ARM the company does not 'fabricate' ARM chips. (In contrast, Intel fabricates its processors and sells them as chips.) It is because of this, that we have ARM chips and boards of various companies—Samsung, Philips, Atmel, Texas Instruments, ST Microelectronics and so on—the list is very long.

10.1.2 | The ARM Microcontroller

ARM has been designated as a 'microprocessor' and indeed it is a processor which has very high computing capabilities. It has a rich set of features for handling complex computations.

However, for using it as an embedded processor, it needs many more capabilities and these come in the form of on-chip peripherals. To the ARM core, peripherals are added and thus it becomes a 'microcontroller' or an MCU (microcontroller unit), rather than an MPU (micro processor unit). Figure 10.1 shows the ARM MCU. The number and kind of peripherals added, depends on the requirements of the buyer of the IP. It is because of this that we have varying number of peripherals for ARM processors supplied by different companies. It could be obvious that to support more peripherals, the core has to be more powerful. That is why we generally find more peripherals around an ARM 9 core rather than around an ARM7 core. But as a rule, users have to spell out their requirements for the peripherals of an MCU.

When a chip has the core and the necessary peripherals to perform as a system, it is called a System on Chip (SoC)—and the term 'ARM SoC' is a very commonly used—understandably it has some version of the ARM core and a large set of peripherals.

10.1.3 | RISC vs CISC

The differences between these two schools of thought in computer architecture have been discussed in Section 0.3.

But to put the idea in a proper perspective in the context of ARM, some specific features of RISC are listed herein. These apply to most of the instructions of ARM, but not necessarily to all.

i) Instructions are of the same size, that is, 32 bits
ii) Instructions are executed in one cycle
iii) Only the load and store instructions access memory

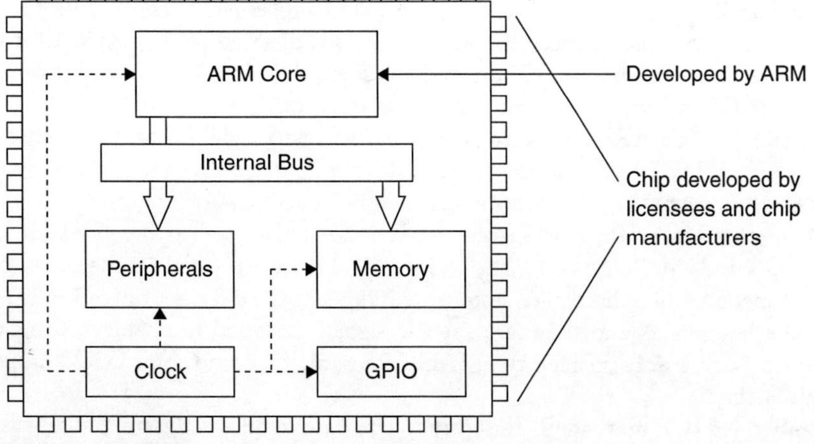

Figure 10.1 | ARM SoC—core with peripherals

Due to these simple guidelines in the design of the ISA (Instruction Set Architecture), the outstanding features of this RISC processor are as follows:

i) The number of transistors needed is much less than that of a CISC processor of comparable computational power.
ii) The die size is less because of the reduced hardware involved.
iii) Due to these aspects (and a few others, which will soon be elaborated), power dissipation is very low.

10.1.4 | Advanced Features

Once the basic ARM core was designed, later members of the family kept on having more and more features added. Over the years, some of these became 'standard' and some are still optional. To specify what features are available with a particular ARM core, naming conventions were adopted, but which have had to be changed over the years. Let us take a look into some of these features. *But if reading this section seems cumbersome, you can skip it now, but make sure you read it later.*

i) **Thumb:** A new 16-bit instruction set called 'Thumb' was made available. The logic of having this less powerful instruction set is that all applications do not need the full power of 32-bit ARM instructions. For such cases, the 16-bit Thumb set (which is a compressed form of the ARM instruction set) will be enough and the advantage obtained is that of high 'code density'.

But what is code density?

The higher the amount of code that can be contained in unit area of memory, the higher is the code density. Thus, when available memory is limited, it may be sufficient to use Thumb instructions, if the application is light. There is also present, the facility for mixing ARM and THUMB instructions, this is called 'ARM THUMB interworking'.

ii) **MMU and MPU:** These are two aspects related to memory. One is the 'memory management unit' and the other is the 'memory protection unit'. Such units are mandatorily available in all advanced desktop processors (like Pentium), but for embedded systems, the necessity of such units is dictated by the product for which the processor is to be used. Thus, we have some ARM processors with both MPU and MMU, and others with one or neither of them.
iii) **Cache:** The first ARM processor with a cache was ARM3. It had an on-chip cache of 4 KB. ARM 7 had a cache of 8 KB which was improved in ways other than just the size. Current ARM processors have cache as a standard component.
iv) **Debug interface:** There is an on chip unit for testing called the JTAG interface. JTAG stands for 'Joint Test Action Group' and defines a set of standards for testing the functionality of hardware. For any chip/system there is a set of scan cells located at the boundaries and there are specific signals designed to enable 'testing' of the device. Such a unit is called the JTAG debug interface, and some ARM chips have this facility.
v) **Embedded ICE macrocell:** The current hardware trend is to design a system as 'macrocells', which is a hardware unit. The ARM core could be considered as a macrocell,

while other units (peripheral units as well) may also be added as 'macrocells'. Some processors have an embedded ICE (In Circuit Emulator) macrocell to enable testing. This unit is powered by breakpoint and watch point registers and control and status registers. All this together can work to halt the ARM core to read status and thus do active debugging.

vi) **Fast muliplier:** Even though ARM is a RISC processor, there are many features in it which do not conform exactly to the RISC philosophy. Having dedicated hardware for complex operations is one such deviation. Multiplication is a complex operation, and for fast multiplication, there may be a fast multiplier unit.

vii) **Enhanced instructions:** Most advanced embedded systems require DSP operations, and for that a DSP unit with complex arithmetic operations, may be made available on the chip.

vii) **Jazelle DBX (Direct Bytecode eXecution):** allows some ARM processors to execute Java bytecode in hardware as a third execution state along with the existing ARM and Thumb mode. This is useful to increase the execution speed of Java ME games and applications. ARM claims that such Java applications get run in hardware (rather than software) so that 'more speed' is achieved.

viii) **Vector floating point unit:** This implies hardware support for floating point computation.

ix) **Synthesizable:** If an ARM processor is synthesizable, it means that its RTL code is available with the licensee, using which extensions and modifications are possible to the basic core.

See Table10.1 which summarizes the early naming conventions of ARM processors. (The { } notation means 'optional').

From Table 10.1, let's try to decipher what ARM7TDMI indicates. It is based on the ARM7 core, and has the Thumb instruction set (T), JTAG debugger (D), fast multiplier (M) and the embedded ICE macrocell(I). If the designation is ARM7TDMI-S, it means it is synthesizable. (Design available as VHDL/Verilog code.) Figure 10.2 shows two ARM cores which uses this naming convention.

Table 10.1 | Early Naming Conventions for ARM

ARM {x}{y}{z}{T}{D}{M}{I}{E}{J}{F}{H}{S}	
x	Family (7, 8, 9, 10, 11, ...)
y	Memory management/protection unit
z	Cache
T	Thumb 16-bit decoder
D	JTAG debug
M	Fast Multiplier
I	EmbeddedICE macrocell
E	DSP Enhanced instructions (assumes TDMI)
J	Jazelle
F	Vector Floating-point Unit
S	Synthesizable Version

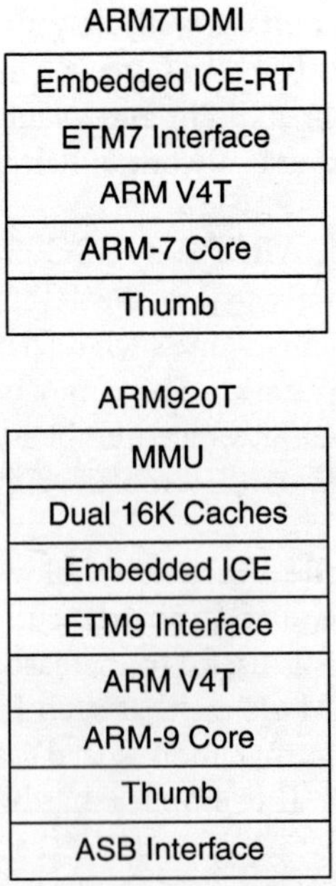

Figure 10.2 | Two ARM cores

Subsequently, it was decided to do away with these complex naming schemes, as the features corresponding to TDMI were expected to be mandatorily available in all ARM processors. But some numbers were added to imply the presence of memory interfaces, cache, tightly coupled memory and so on. For example, ARM with cache and MMU are now given the suffix 26 or 36, whereas processors with MPUs are suffixed with 46. Over the years, this type of naming convention has also changed. Refer to Table 10.2 for some more variants of ARM.

10.1.5 | Architecture Versions

Over the years, the architectural features have also been enhanced. Thus, later versions of the architecture are more powerful Versions v4 and v4T are the early versions, later versions are v5, v5E, v6 and v7. Table 10.3 lists various architecture variants of ARM.

10.1.6 | ARM CORTEX

ARM has come a long way from ARM2, which was the first one to be commercially produced. ARM7 was a resounding success which made ARM the dominant player in the 32-bit embedded processor market. ARM7 was followed by ARM9, ARM10 and ARM11, all of which boasted of more and more computing powers. The latest in the sequence is the CORTEX series which has the architecture v7 version. To make this series cater to well-defined application sets, the following three profiles have been defined:

i) **The A profile:** This profile which has the ARMv7-A architecture is meant for high end applications. It is meant to handle complex applications with high-end embedded operating systems, and typical applications requiring such a profile are mobile phones and video systems.

Table 10.2 | Variants of the ARM Processor

Processor Name	Architecture Version	Memory Management Features	Other Features
ARM7TDMI	ARMv4T		
ARM7TDMI-S	ARMv4T		
ARM7EJ-S	ARMv5E		DSP, Jazelle
ARM920T	ARMV4T	MMU	
ARM922T	ARMv4T	MMU	
ARM926EJ-S	ARMv5E	MMU	DSP, Jazelle
ARM946E-S	ARMv5E	MPU	DSP
ARM966E-S	ARMv5E	DSP	
ARM968E-S	ARMv5E		DMA, DSP
ARM966HS	ARMv5E	MPU (optional)	DSP
ARM1020E	ARMv5E	MMU	DSP
ARM1022E	ARMv5E	MMU	DSP
ARM1026EJ-S	ARMv5E	MMU or MPU	DSP, Jazelle
ARM1136J(F)-S	ARMv6	MMU	DSP, Jazelle
ARM1176JZ(F)-S	ARMv6	MMU+TrustZone	DSP, Jazelle
ARM11MPCore	ARMv6	MMU+Multiprocessor Cache Support	DSP, Jazelle
ARM1156T2(F)-S	ARMv6	MPU	DSP
Cortex-M0	ARMv6-M		NVIC
Cortex-M1	ARMv6-M	FPGA TCM interface	NVIC
Cortex-M3	ARMv7-M	MPU (optional)	NVIC

(Courtesy: The Definitive Guide to ARM Cortex-M3 by Joseph Liu, Newnes Publications)

Table 10.3 | Features of the Architecture Variants of ARM

Architecture Versions	Features
v4	ARM instructions only
v4T	THUMB instructions also added
v5	More advanced ARM and THUMB instructions
v5E	Advanced ARM instructions and enhanced DSP instructions
v6	Advanced ARM and THUMB. SIMD and memory support instructions added
v7	THUMB-2 technology, in which both 16-bit and 32-bit instructions are supported, and there is no need to switching between ARM and THUMB instruction sets

ii) **The R profile:** This profile which has the ARMv7-R architecture has been designed for high-end applications which require real-time capabilities. Typical applications are automatic braking systems and other safety critical applications.

iii) **The M profile:** This profile which has the ARMv7-M architecture has been designed for deeply embedded microcontroller type systems. This is to be used in industrial control applications where a large number of peripherals may have to be handled and controlled.

10.1.7 | The Features of ARM Which Make It 'Special'

Now that we have done a survey of the range of ARM processors, let's discuss the features which have made ARM a very popular processor in the high-end embedded market.

i) **Data bus width:** The processor has a 32-bit data bus width, which means that it can read and write 32 bits in one cycle. For high end applications, having a wide data bus corresponds to a high data bandwidth and is very important. When ARM first made its entry into the field, there were very few embedded processors which had such a wide bus width.

ii) **Computational capability:** The instruction set of ARM has been cleverly designed to facilitate very good computational capability. Many unique and new methods of fast computation without the necessity of extensive hardware is used. The design of the processor used the RISC approach, but over the years, this philosophy has been diluted to enable the addition of specialized hardware for computationally intensive tasks. In essence, ARM is a RISC processor which has a few CISC features as well.

iii) **Low power:** In the embedded field, power saving is very important, because a large number of devices operate on battery power. Designing lower power processor cores is thus a matter of high priority. How is it that a processor is designed to have low power capability? Embedded processors operate at low clock frequencies compared to desk top processors. While 3.3GHz is commonly used in the desktop processor field, ARM operates at relatively low frequencies from 60 MHz to at the most 1 GHz.

The other techniques in low-power design are explained in Section 2.4.

iv) **Pipelining:** Pipelining is a fundamental idea in computer architecture, for increasing the speed of operation. The idea is to get many activities to be done in tandem, by dividing the whole instruction processing stage into sub stages. The basic task that any processor does is 'fetch, decode and execute'. In the simplest form of pipelining (3 stage), all the three stages are active all the time. While the first stage is fetching an instruction, the next stage, that is,. the decode stage, is busy with the decoding of the previously fetched instruction, and the execute stage is executing the instruction which had been previously decoded. Thus at any time, there are three instructions simultaneously present in the pipeline, at different levels of processing.

If the processor clock frequency is f, the clock period (T) of the processor is divided by 3 to give a time of T/3 for each of the stages. In this sub-cycle (of period T/3), one instruction each is obtained as a throughput, which is essentially 3 instructions in the period T. It means that the processing speed is multiplied by 3.

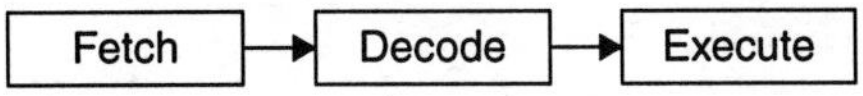

Figure 10.3a | A three stage pipeline

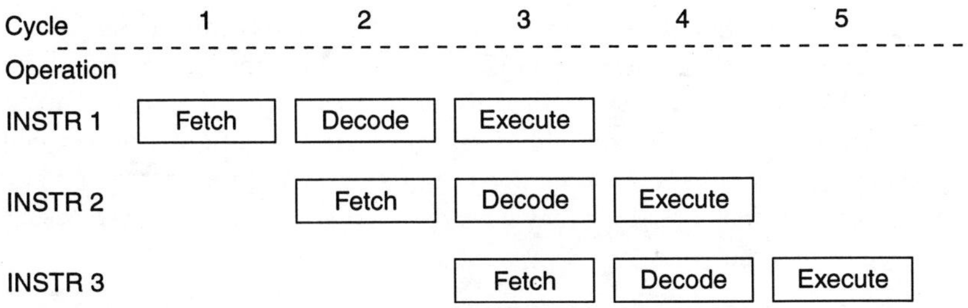

Figure 10.3b | The three stage pipeline with 3 instructions in operation

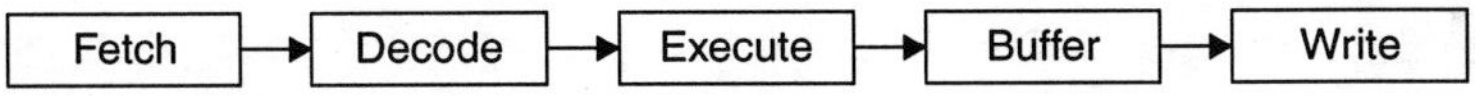

Figure 10.4 | A five-stage pipeline

Figure 10.3a shows a three stage pipeline, while Figure 10.3b shows three instructions in the pipeline. Any instruction needs three sub cycles to come out of the pipeline, which translates to a throughput of three instructions per clock period (T).

ARM7 has a 3-stage pipeline, while ARM9 has a 5-stage pipeline with more finely quantized stages (Figure 10.4), which are 'fetch, decode, execute, buffer data and write back'. As a general rule, more advanced processors have more pipeline stages. For example, ARM10 has 6 stages.

Pipelining is a great idea, but it has the drawback that when a branch instruction appears, the instructions following it are no longer needed to be executed in the normal sequence. So the instructions in the previous stage/stages have to be discarded, or we say that the pipeline is to be flushed. This creates a loss of speed, and the penalty is higher for pipelines with more number of stages.

v) **Multiple register instructions:** Since ARM is a RISC processor, it has instructions which process data which are in registers only – this simply means that data processing instructions do not use addressing modes in which one operand is in memory. But there are instructions which access memory and load data into multiple registers – also, contents of multiple registers can be stored in memory, with a single instruction.

vi) **DSP enhancements:** Our processor has RISC as its basic policy, but the more advanced members of the family have DSP (Digital Signal Processing) instructions as an enhanced feature. This is where ARM departs from its RISC philosophy, but is necessary for surviving in the embedded market. These DSP enhancements are signified by an 'E' in the name as of the ARMv5TE and ARMv5TEJ architectures.

10.2 | ARM Architecture

With this background, let us get started on the more intricate details of the processor.

10.2.1 | Instruction Set Architecture

It is likely that you have heard the term 'Instruction Set Architecture' (ISA) mentioned in some context or the other. The term implies the user's i.e. the programmer's view of the processor, which constitute the instruction set, addressing modes, registers, etc. ISA is the assembly programmer's or compiler designer's view of the processor. We will base most of our discussions on ARM7 which was the first and still the most popular of the ARM processors. Advanced versions may have more enhancements, but the basic architecture is more or less the same.

10.2.2 | Operating Modes

ARM has seven operating modes which are listed here. It is not important to understand the exact functions of each mode right now. But keep in mind that the user mode corresponds to the simplest mode, with least privileges, but is the mode under which most application programs run. The system mode is a highly privileged mode. This mode is used by operating systems to manipulate and control the activities of the processor. The other modes are entered on the occurrence of exceptions or rather, they are interrupt modes. See the list of the operating modes of ARM.

i) **User**: Unprivileged mode under which most tasks run
ii) **FIQ (Fast Interrupt Request):** Entered on a high priority (fast) interrupt request
iii) **IRQ (Interrupt Request):** Entered on a low priority interrupt request
iv) **Supervisor**: Entered on reset and when a software interrupt instruction (SWI) is executed
v) **Abort**: Used to handle memory access violations
vi) **Undef**: Used to handle undefined instructions
vii) **System**: Privileged mode using the same registers as user mode

10.2.3 | Register Set

ARM has 37 registers each of which is 32 bits long. They are listed as follows:

i) 1 dedicated program counter (PC)
ii) 1 dedicated current program status register (CPSR)
iii) 5 dedicated saved program status registers (SPSR)
iv) 30 general purpose registers

Now, let's go into the details of the listed registers

10.2.3.1 | *General Purpose Registers*

There are 30 of them, but they are distributed among different modes.

To understand this feature, see the case of one particular mode, say the user mode. In this mode, the registers act as shown in Table 10.4.

Table 10.4 | Registers in the User Mode

Register Numbers	Designations
R0–R12	General purpose registers
R13	Stack pointer (SP)
R14	Link register (LR)
R15	Program counter (PC)

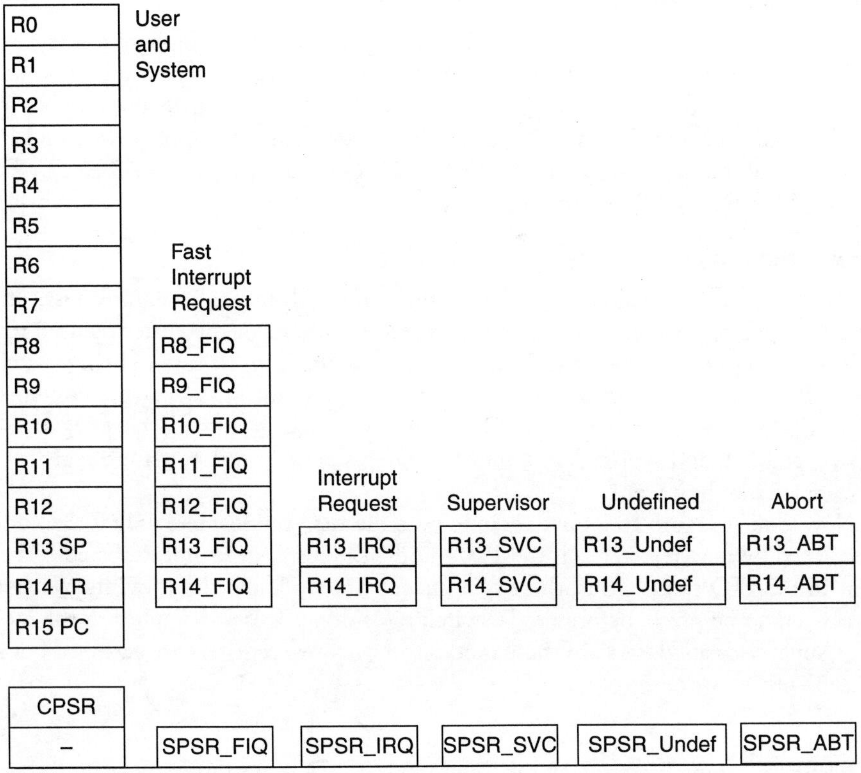

Figure 10.5 | Register set of ARM

Figure 10.5 shows the whole set of registers available for the processor. Look at the set of registers titled as 'user and system'. Let's discuss the specific functions of each of them.

R0–R12 are general purpose registers, or what may be designated as scratch pad' registers. These are the registers into which data and address are loaded. They are also 'the' registers used in computations.

R13 is the pointer to the stack, and is the stack pointer (SP).

R15 acts as the program counter (PC), which, like in any other processor, is the register which sequences instructions as they are fetched from memory.

R14 is the link register (LR), a special register. It is used whether there is a procedure call or an interrupt, that is, branching to a location. When branching becomes necessary, the value of PC is saved in the link register, and PC takes on the new branch address. When returning to the original sequence, the PC value can be retrieved from the link register. This is a very convenient option, because the necessity to push the PC value to the stack is avoided. The stack is a memory area, and saving and retrieving from stack is time consuming. Having such a register, that is, the LR, to store return addresses helps to reduce the delay associated with procedure calls and interrupts.

10.2.4 | Mode Switching

We know that there are seven modes for the processor, which implies that it can be switched to different modes, as decided by the requirement. When the processor switches, say, from the user to another mode, some of the user mode registers are replaced by another set of registers. See the FIQ_mode, for example, in this mode, R8 to R14 are replaced by another set of registers, and the names of these registers are suffixed by FIQ, like R14_FIQ, R12_FIQ and so on.

Why Is it that FIQ uses another set of registers?

Note that this mode is entered on a 'fast interrupt' which means it requires fast action. One action during interrupts would be to save the contents of the currently used registers. This 'saving' takes some time. To ensure fast operation, in the case of being switched to the FIQ_mode, new registers are used. No time is spent on saving the contents of register R8 to R14 of the user mode. Once the FIQ_mode is entered, those registers are just swapped out, and replaced by a set of new registers. Note also, that all registers are not swapped out, however.

Now look at Figure 10.5 once again to note the IRQ_mode. Here only R13 and R14 are replaced by new registers. In the IRQ_mode, the response is not expected to be, as fast as in the FIQ_mode. Thus, there is sufficient time to allow the contents of most of the registers to be saved, before mode switching is done. This also applies to the modes 'undef, supervisor and abort'. In these modes too, only two registers are swapped out and replaced with new ones.

CPSR

The CPSR (Current Program Status Register) is a very important register, and there is only one such register for the processor. Figure 10.6 and Table 10.5 gives its details.

The CPSR contains the information about the current state of the processor. It has bits which specify the mode, control bits to enable/disable interrupts, and also specifies whether the Thumb or ARM mode is currently in use.

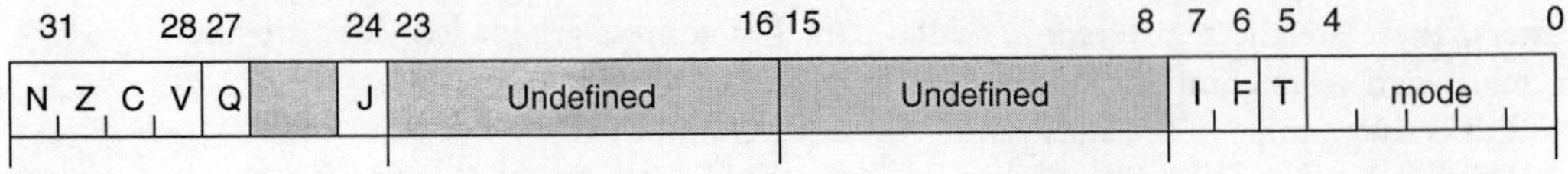

Figure 10.6 | Current Program Status Register (CPSR) bit configuration

Table 10.5 | CPSR Bits

Bit Nos.	Notation	Interpretation
0 to 4	Mode	Specifies the current mode of operation
5	T	Specifies whether in ARM(T = 1) or Thumb(T = 0) state
6	F	Disables (F = 1)FIQ
7	I	Disables (I = 1)IRQ
8 to 23, 25 to 26	Undefined	
24	J	In Jazelle state (J = 1)
27	Q	Sticky overflow flag
28 to 31	V, C, Z, N	Conditional flags

Bits 0 to 4 specify the current mode of operation. Since there are only 7 modes of operation, only seven mode numbers are valid.

The J bit is for indicating whether the Jazelle state is valid or not. The T bit specifies whether the current operation is in the ARM or Thumb mode.

The contents of this register can be modified only in the highly privileged system mode. It also contains the condition flag bits. Most of you are likely to know the relevance of the conditional flag bits. But for those who might be new to the concept of flags, here is a concise description.

10.2.5 | Conditional Flags

N: Negative Flag This flag indicates the status of the MSB of the result of an operation. If we are dealing with signed number N = 1 means that the sign bit = 1, which is a negative result.

C: Carry Flag This bit is set if there is an overflow from the MSB of the data being manipulated; this can happen in additions, shifts, rotates etc. It is also set when the result of subtraction is positive. If R1–R2 gives a positive result, C = 1, indicates that R1 is greater than R2. To be precise, let's say that 'A carry occurs if the result of an add, subtract or compare is greater than or equal to 2^{32}, or as the result of an inline barrel shifter operation in a move or logical instruction'.

Z: Zero Flag If the result of an arithmetic or logical operation is zero, then Z = 1.

V: Overflow Flag This is the overflow flag, which is relevant only for signed operations. It indicates that the sign bit has possibly been corrupted because the result has gone out of the range.

When signed numbers are used, only 31 bits are available for the magnitude of the numbers. With 32 bits, overflow occurs if the result of an add, subtract or compare is greater than or equal to $(2^{31}-1)$ or less than -2^{31}, which is the maximum range available for signed numbers.

To cite an example, say two positive numbers are added, and the magnitude of the sum becomes greater than 31 bits. There will be an overflow into the sign bit, which will change the MSB to '1' and get wrongly interpreted as a negative number. This overflow into the sign bit (MSB) with no overflow out of the MSB causes the overflow (V) bit to be set.

Q: Sticky Overflow Flag This flag indicates overflow itself, but it is 'sticky' in the sense that it remains set until explicitly cleared.

Saved Program Status Registers (SPSR) There are five 'Saved Program Status Registers', that is, one for each of the 'exception' modes of operation. When an exception, that is, an interrupt occurs, the corresponding SPSR saves the current CPSR value into it (so as to be able to retrieve it on returning to the previous mode). The system mode and user modes do not have SPSRs because they are not entered through the mechanism of interrupts.

10.3 | Interrupt Vector Table

We have seen that ARM has a number of exception modes. Exceptions are a class of interrupts which are internally generated due to the occurrence of some specific conditions. For example, when an undefined instruction is detected, the processor can't process it. The solution for such an undesired situation is to make the processor switch to another mode and generate an interrupt. This interrupt takes control to an interrupt service routine (ISR i.e. interrupt handler) residing in a specific location in memory. This specific location is termed the 'Interrupt Vector' corresponding to this exception.

Besides 'exceptions', the processor can be interrupted by instructions and this is called a software interrupt (SWI). There are hardware interrupts as well, which are activated by FIQ or IRQ.

The aforesaid discussion is just to clarify the fact that associated with all exceptions, hardware and software interrupts, there is a fixed interrupt vector which leads to the ISR or the interrupt handler.

See Table 10.6 which shows the pre-defined interrupt vectors.

Table 10.6 | List of Interrupt Vectors

Exception	Shorthand	Vector Address
Reset	RESET	0x00000000
Undefined instruction	UNDEF	0x00000004
Software interrupt	SWI	0x00000008
Prefetch abort	PABT	0x0000000c
Data abort	DABT	0x00000010
Reserved	–	0x00000014
Interrupt request	IRQ	0x00000018
Fast interrupt request	FIQ	0x0000001c

Note that the first entry in the table is 'Reset'. All processors have a address, termed 'reset vector' which is the location to which control branches to, when it is first powered on, or when reset in the midst of processor activity. For ARM, this is 0x0000 0000. Since this location is always fixed, RESET is usually included in the class of vectored interrupts.

10.4 | Programming the ARM Processor

Now that we have had a look at the concepts regarding the instruction set architecture (ISA) of ARM, we are in a position to understand it better by programming. Writing, running and testing programs is the key to understanding any processor. By doing programming, we become capable of understanding almost everything about how registers, memory and flags act on data. In short, we get a total feel about the processing activity done inside the processor.

To get to this, we need a programming environment, that is, an Integrated Development Environment (IDE). There are many IDEs available for ARM, some of which are free of cost (and freely downloadable) and some of which are proprietary and thus have to be paid for. However for students, an evaluation version is available which is freely downloadable and available from the website www.keil.com. Here, we will use the Keil IDE also called the RVDK (Real View Development Kit), which is very popular and easy to use. This version can be used for testing programs and for simulation also. We will do all our learning using this IDE. The step-by-step procedure for using this, is detailed in Appendix A. In this part of the chapter, we will assume that you have this IDE and also that you have already browsed through Appendix A.

10.4.1 | Programming—Assembly vs C

Programming can be done in assembly as well as in high level languages. In the embedded design world, high level languages are used in product design, and C is a very popular language. As such we will also do C programming (in the next chapter). But before that, let's have a stint in assembly programming. Our approach will be such that to understand the ARM core, that is, to use its registers, do memory access and so on, we will do assembly programming. This ensures that we get a good grip on the ARM core architecture. In this context, it will turn out that we focus on the computational capabilities of the core.

And when we start using ARM as a microcontroller, i.e. the core with a number of peripherals, we use C programming. This will allow us to use the processor in various practical applications involving peripherals and interaction with the external world. This part will be discussed in Chapter 11.

10.5 | ARM Assembly Language

As mentioned earlier, the ARM instruction set has been cleverly designed to get more than one operation to be done in a single instruction. Let's list out some features of the ARM instruction set.

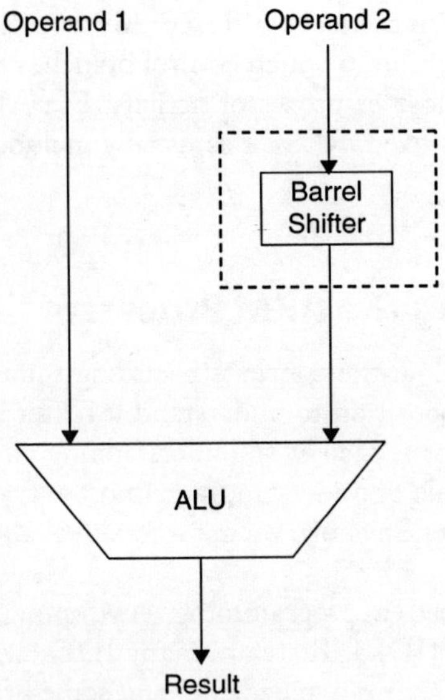

Figure 10.7 | Data processing unit

i) ARM is a RISC processor, in which every instruction has a maximum size of 32 bits. Instructions are expected to be executed in one cycle. This is true for most instructions, but not for all. Therefore it is better to say that ARM is a RISC processor with a few CISC type instructions as well.
ii) Another feature of RISC and therefore of ARM, is that it is a load–store architecture. This means that all computations are register based, that is, the operands are to be brought to registers from memory, using a load instruction. After computation, the result is to be stored in memory. For the user, this means that there is no data processing instructions in which one of the operands is in memory. All operands are to be available in registers before computation can be done.
iii) A third feature of ARM is that its ALU has a barrel shifter (Figure 10.7) associated with one of its operands. A barrel shifter is a unit that can perform more than one bit of shift/rotation, to the right or to the left on an operand. As we will soon see, the barrel shifter adds some clever processing techniques to data processing and allows shifting and an arithmetic operation to be combined in the same instruction.
iv) 'Conditions' can be appended to instructions: this implies that we can choose to 'do or not do' a particular operation based on the status of a condition flag, For most other processors, only branching operations depend on flag status. Here we will see that data movement as well as data processing instructions can be made 'conditional'.

10.5.1 | Data Types

ARM can operate on 32-bit data, which is termed a word, 16-bit data called a half word and also on byte operands. The processing tools offer the option of storing data as 'little endian', or 'big endian'. To clarify this concept, follow the forthcoming discussion, and observe Figure 10.8

Address	Data
0x00001200	A3
0x00001201	90
0x00001202	47
0x00001203	0E

Figure 10.8a | The little endian format

Address	Data
0x00001200	0E
0x00001201	47
0x00001202	90
0x00001203	A3

Figure 10.8b | The big endian format

A 32-bit data stored in memory needs 4 bytes of space which means 4 consecutive addresses are required, as one address can store only one byte. When the lowest byte of the 32-bit word is stored in the lowest of these four addresses, it is called the 'little endian' format. Otherwise, it is the 'big endian' format. See Figure 10.8. The 32-bit data word is 0x0E4790A3. The storage addresses are from 0x00001200 onwards.

In the processor industry, both formats are used. Intel prefers the little endian format, while Motorola uses the big endian format. ARM allows both formats (can be fixed up by software, in the initialization stage). In this book, we assume the little endian format.

10.5.2 | Data Alignment

Storing (and loading also) of 4 bytes in memory can be done in one cycle, because the processor has a 32-bit data bus. When 32-bit data is stored in memory, four addresses are needed. We need to specify only one address in our instruction; but there is an aspect called 'alignment'. For 32-bit data, 'alignment' implies that the last two bits of this address are zero. For example, the address 0x00001200 is an aligned address. When this address is used to store 32-bit data, this address and the next three addresses are automatically accessed. This is because of the way memory is organized, as four banks (see Figure 10.9).

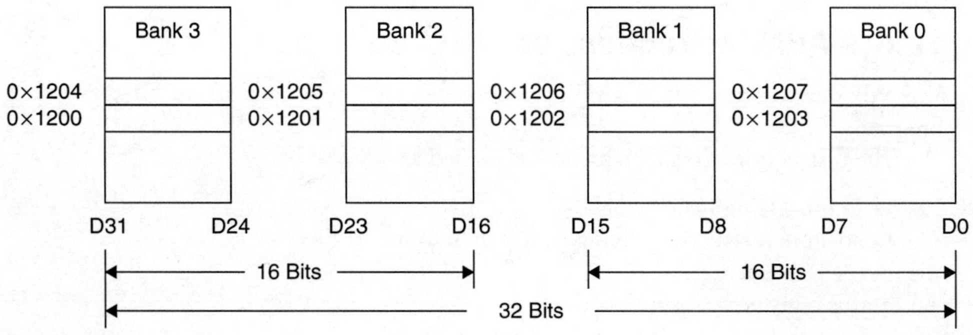

Figure 10.9 | Memory banks

If the address of a 32-bit number is given as 0x1200, the accessed addresses are 0x1200, 0x1201, 0x1202 and 0x1203. The 4 bytes in these addresses are considered to be in the same row, that is, aligned. In this case, one byte each from each bank is accessed and only one memory cycle is needed to access an aligned word.

For unaligned data, one more cycle is necessary. Think of the address 0x1201. The locations to be accessed will be 0x1201, 0x1202, 0x1203 and 0x1204. Note that the first three bytes will be in the same row, while the last will be in a different row (bank), and so one more cycle of access will be required.

We summarize the conditions for 'aligned data' as follows:

- For word (32-bit) data, the specified address should have its least significant two bits as 0.
- For half word (16-bit) accesses, the specified address should have the LSB equal to 0.

Most of the tools for ARM ensure that data is stored in aligned locations, so as to avoid unnecessary extra cycles of operation.

10.5.3 | Assembly Language Rules

An assembly language line has four fields, namely, label, opcode, operand and comment. A label is positioned at the left of a line and is the symbol for the memory address which stores that line of information. There are certain rules regarding labels that are allowed under the type of assembler being used. The manual of the specific assembler should be referred, to get this clear. The second field is the opcode or instruction field. The third is the operand field, and the last is the comment field which starts with a semicolon. The use of comments is advised for making programs more readable.

A typical assembly language statement is

```
BOSE    ADD    R1, R2, R3    ; add R2 and R3 and copy the sum to R1.
```

The label is BOSE, the opcode is ADD, the operands are R1, R2 and R3 and the line after the semicolon is the comment. While writing programs, make sure you don't write instructions at the extreme left of the page—that part is the 'label' field in this book. We will use the assembler which is part of the RVDK supplied by Keil. The steps in using it have been clearly described in Appendix A. More details are available in the 'Real view assembly guide'.

10.6 | ARM Instruction Set

We will now discuss the ARM instruction set, and gradually move on to writing programs.

The instruction set can be broadly classified as follows:

i) Data processing instructions
ii) Load store instructions—single register, multiple register
iii) Branch instructions
iv) Status register access instructions

The last set moves the contents of the CPSR or an SPSR to or from a general purpose register and are used only in privileged modes. We will discuss the first three sets in detail.

10.6.1 | Data Processing Instructions

ARM is a RISC processor, one of the features of which is that it processes, i.e., performs computations, on data which are in registers only. There are instructions which move data from one register to another. Such instructions have only two operands, that is, the source and the destination. Instructions which perform arithmetic/logical computations have three operands—two source operands and one destination operand.

10.6.1.1 | *MOV and MVN*

The 'MOV' instruction is a 'register to register' data movement instruction with the format MOV destination, source where both the source and destination have to be registers.

The mnemonic 'MVN' stands for 'move negated' which implies moving the complemented value of the source to the destination.

Registers R1 to R12 can be used for data movement as they are general purpose registers. The registers R13, R14 and R15, which are the stack pointer, link register and the program counter respectively, can also use the MOV instructions, but this must be done carefully and only for specific purposes.

Examples

```
MOV R11, R2     ;copy the contents of R2 to R11
MOV R12, R10    ;copy the contents of R10 to R12
MVN R0, R9      ;move the complemented value of R9 to R0
                ;if R9 = 0xFFF00000, R0 = 0x000FFFFF
```

Note Here we have discussed only the case of the MOV instruction used for moving data between registers. The MOV instruction is also used for copying immediate data into registers. That will be discussed in Section 10.17.

10.6.1.2 | *The Barrel Shifter*

Now, refer to Figure 10.7. We see that there is a barrel shifter associated with data processing. The figure shows two register operands, one of which can optionally be acted upon by a barrel shifter, before being admitted to the ALU. The barrel shifter can do shifting and rotation. Let us first have a general discussion on shifts and rotations.

10.6.2 | Shift and Rotate

Two types of shifts are possible: logical and arithmetic.

10.6.2.1 | *Logical Shift Left (LSL)*

Logical Shift Left of a (say) 32-bit number causes it to shift left, (a specified number of times) and the vacant bits on the right are filled with zeros. See Figure 10.10. The last bit

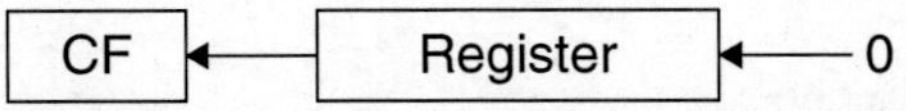

Figure 10.10 | Logical shift left

shifted out from the left is copied to the carry flag. Keep in mind that a left shift by one bit position corresponds to multiplication by 2. An LSL of 5 implies multiplication by 32.

10.6.2.2 | *Logical Shift Right (LSR)*

Logical Shift Right does a similar thing. The vacant bit positions on the left are filled with zeros, and the last bit shifted out is retained in the carry flag. This is shown in Figure 10.11. Shifting right by one, divides the number by 2. Two right shifts cause a division by 4.

10.6.2.3 | *Arithmetic Shift Right (ASR)*

Arithmetic Shift Right is different in the sense that the vacant bit positions on the left are filled with the MSB of the original number. See Figure 10.12. This type of shift has the function of doing 'sign extension' of data, because for positive numbers the MSB is 0, and for negative numbers, the MSB is 1. There is no instruction for arithmetic shift left, because of not having an application for it.

10.6.2.4 | *Rotate Right (ROR)*

In this, the data is moved right, and the bits shifted out from the right are inserted back through the left. See Figure 10.13. The last bit rotated out is available in the carry flag. There is no 'rotate left' instruction, because left rotation by n times can be achieved by rotating to the right (32 – n) times. For example, rotating 4 times to the left is achieved by rotating 32 – 4 = 28 times to the right.

10.6.2.5 | *Rotate Right Extended (RRX)*

This corresponds to rotating right through the carry bit, meaning that the bit that drops off from the right side is moved to C and the carry bit enters through the left of the data. This should be obvious from Figure 10.14.

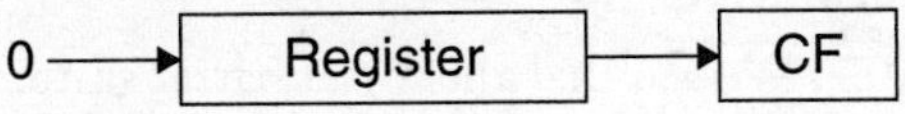

Figure 10.11 | Logical shift right

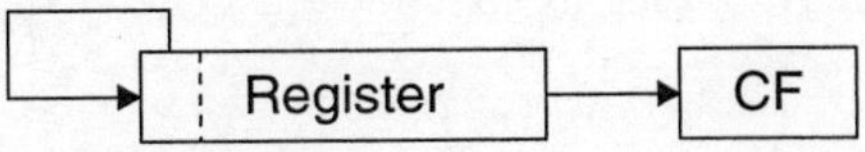

Figure 10.12 | Arithmetic shift right

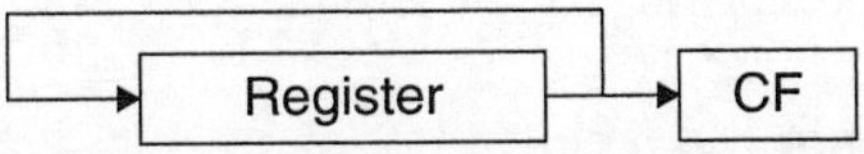

Figure 10.13 | Rotate right

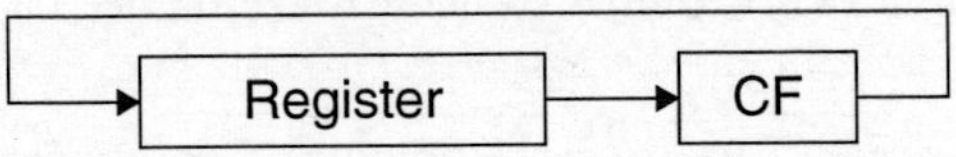

Figure 10.14 | Rotate right extended

10.6.3 | Format of Shift and Rotate Instructions

The number of bit positions by which shifts and rotations are to be done may be specified by a constant or may be indicated in another register.

Examples

```
LSL R2, #4     ;shift left logically, the content of R2 by 4 bit positions
ASR R5, #8     ;shift right arithmetically, the content of R2 by 4 bit positions
ROR R1, R2     ;rotate the content of R1, by the number specified in R2
```

Example 10.1

The content of some of the registers are given as:

R1 = 0xEF00DE12, R2 = 0x0456123F, R5 = 4, R6 = 28.

Find the result (in the destination register), when the following instructions are executed.

i) LSL R1, #8
ii) ASR R1, R5
iii) ROR R2, R6
iv) LSR R2, #5

Solution

i) Shifting R1 left 8 times causes 8 zeros in the 8 positions on the right. R1 now contains 0x00DE1200
ii) R5 contains 4. Arithmetically right shifting R1 4 times, causes the MSB (1, for the given number) to be replicated 4 times on the left, thus causing a sign extension of the shifted number. R1 now contains 0xFEF00DE1.
iii) R6 contains 28. Rotating R2 28 times to the right is equivalent to rotating it 32–28 = 4 times, to the left. After rotation, R6 contains 0x456123F0.
iv) Here, R2 is logically shifted right 5 times, and so 5 zeros enter through the left. R2 now has the value 0x0022B091.

10.6.4 | Combining the Operations of Move and Shift

Recollect the barrel shifter which is an integral part of the data processing unit of the processor. This allows shifting and data processing to be done in the same instruction cycle. We will first see how moving and shifting can be combined in one instruction itself.

```
MOV R1, R2, LSL #2
MOV R1, R2, LSR R3
```

In both the above instructions, R1 is the destination register. In the first instruction, the source operand, that is, the content of R2 is logically shifted twice and then moved to the destination register R1. In the second, the amount of 'shifting' is specified in register R3. After the shifting is done, the result is moved to R1.

Example 10.2

Find the content of the destination registers after the execution of each of the given instructions, given that the content of R5 = 0x72340200 and R2 = 4.

i) MOV R3, R5, LSL #3
ii) MOV R6, R5, ASR R2

Solution

The results here are similar to Example 10.1, except that the source and destination registers are not the same after execution of the instructions.

i) MOV R3, R5, LSL #3.
   The content of R5 is shifted left 3 times, and moved to R3.
   R3 now contains 0x91A01000
ii) MOV R6, R5, ASR R2
   R2 = 4, and so R5 is arithmetically shifted right 4 times. Since the MSB of the number in R5 is 0, when right shifting, this bit is replicated 4 times at the left of the number. After execution, R6 contains 0x07234020

10.7 | Conditional Execution

ARM has another interesting feature which can be designated as 'conditional execution'. This means that instructions are executed only if a specified condition is true, and here the important thing is that it is not branch instructions alone that are meant—any data processing instruction can be used in this way.

In general, all arithmetic and logic instructions are expected to affect conditional flags. But for ARM, we must suffix the instruction by S for this to happen. Otherwise the flags are unaffected. It is the S suffix on a data processing instruction that causes the flags in the CPSR to be updated.

In Example 10.2, in the instruction MOV R3, R5, LSL #3, there is a logical operation involved, that is, the left shift operation. This should cause the carry flag and N flag to be set. But since the MOV instruction is not appended with the suffix, 'S', the flags remain unaffected, that is, reset. The MOV instruction can be made conditional by writing it as MOVS R3, R5, LSL #3. After this is executed, we find the N and C flags to be set. This flag setting can be used to make an instruction following it, to be 'conditional'. We will soon see more aspects of this.

Figure 10.15 shows the format of a typical ARM instruction. In the instruction code, four bits are allotted for the condition under which the instruction is to be executed. If no condition is indicated, these bits assume the 'always' condition.

Table 10.7 lists the conditions, condition codes and the flag statuses for these conditions. We will discuss the use of condition codes for instructions.

Note that the conditions used for signed numbers and unsigned numbers are different. For unsigned numbers, we use the mnemonic 'higher' or 'lower', while for signed numbers, the conditions are specified as 'greater than' or 'lower than'. The flag settings are also different. The logic of this is very simple, that is, we know that 6 is higher than 3,

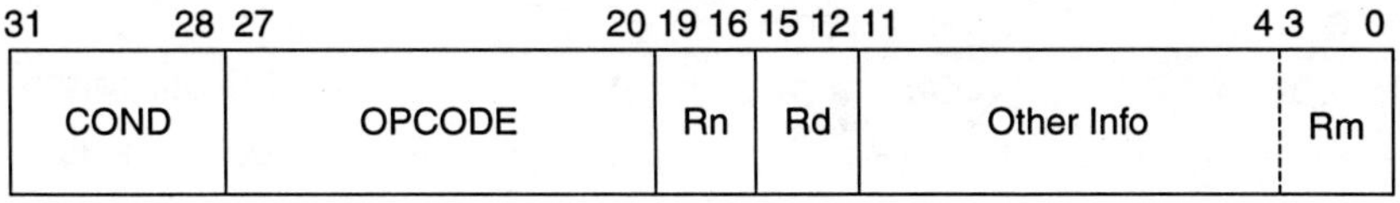

Figure 10.15 | Format of a typical instruction

Table 10.7 | List of Conditions, Codes and Corresponding Flag Status

Cond	Mnemonic	Meaning	Condition Flag State
0000	EQ	Equal	Z = 1
0001	NE	Not Equal	Z = 0
0010	CS/HS	Carry set/unsigned > =	C = 1
0011	CC/LO	Carry clear/unsigned <	C = 0
0100	MI	Minus/Negative	N = 1
0101	PL	Plus/Positive or Zero	N = 0
0110	VS	Overflow	O = 1
0111	VC	No overflow	O = 0
1000	HI	Unsigned higher	C = 1 & Z = 0
1001	LS	Unsigned lower or same	C = 0 | Z = 1
1010	GE	Signed > =	N = = V
1011	LT	Signed <	N! = V
1100	GT	Signed >	Z = = 0, N = = V
1101	LE	Signed < =	Z = = 1 or N! = V
1110	AL	Always	
1111	(NV)	Unpredictable	

but -3 is greater than -6. Thus, it is clear that unsigned and signed numbers have to be dealt with differently.

10.8 | Arithmetic Instructions

Now let's get a feel of the arithmetic instructions of ARM and the special ways in which they can be used.

10.8.1 | Addition and Subtraction

Addition and subtraction are three operand instructions. The destination is always a register. The source operands may both be registers or one of them may be an immediate data. There are some issues in using immediate data greater than 8 bits (Ref Section 10.17).

See Table 10.8 which gives examples of how the different addition and subtraction instructions work. Any of the general purpose registers may be used as operands, though in the table, only R3, R4 and R5 have been mentioned.

Table 10.8 | List of Arithmetic Instructions

Instruction	Operation	Calculation
ADD R3, R4, R5	Add	R3 = R4 + R5
ADC R3, R4, R5	Add with carry	R3 = R4 + R5 + C
SUB R3, R4, R5	Subtract	R3 = R4 – R5
SBC R3, R4, R5	Subtract with carry	R3 = R4 – R5 – C
RSB R3, R4, R5	Reverse subtract	R3 = R5 – R4
RSC R3, R4, R5	Reverse subtract with carry	R3 = R5 – R4 – C

Remember the concept of suffixing data processing instructions. This can be used ingenuously for making operations conditional. For example, the add instructions (just as any other data processing instruction) does not affect the conditional flags unless it is suffixed by S. Following such an ADD instructions, we can have instructions with conditions appended to it. The set of possible conditions are listed in Table. 10.7. For any instruction, the upper 4 bits are used to specify the condition (Figure 10.15).

Consider these program lines

```
SUBS R1, R2, R3      ;the suffix 'S' has been used
MOVEQ R2, R1         ;the EQ notation tests the Z = 1 condition
```

Here the move instruction is executed only if the result of the subtraction produces a zero and sets the zero flag. The condition EQ implies the setting of the zero flag (Refer Table 10.7)). Let's use this concept in a simple example.

Example 10.3

It is required to compare two numbers which are in registers R1 and R2. The bigger number is to be placed in R10. If the two numbers are equal, then the number is to be moved to R9.

Solution

Here we use the subtraction operation to do the comparison.

```
SUBS R3, R1, R2      ;R3 = R1 – R2
MOVEQ R9, R1         ;If R1 and R2 are equal (Z = 1) move R1 to R9
MOVHI R10, R1        ;if R1>R2, C = 1, R1 is moved to R10
MOV R8, R2           ;otherwise i.e., if R1 is less than R2, move R2 to R8
```

The salient points of this program are as follows:

i) First the operation, R1-R2 is performed and the result is placed in R3.
ii) Since the SUB instruction has been appended with S, the flags will be set accordingly.
iii) If the two numbers are equal, the zero flag gets set and the instruction MOVEQ will get executed. Otherwise it becomes a NOP (no operation) instruction. Here one of the numbers (R1) is to moved to R9 (as both numbers are equal).
iv) The next line checks whether the carry flag has been set. If R1>R2, the carry flag is set (C = 1) and the MOVHI (move if high) instruction gets executed.

Otherwise this also becomes a NOP. The move instruction gets the bigger number into R10.

v) If the carry flag is not set, and the Z flag is also not set, it means that R2 is bigger.

Note The last line does not need a condition. It can simply be MOV. If the other two conditions are not satisfied it is obvious that the last one will be.

Example 10.3 might seem much too simple to need such a lot of explanation, but the intention is to make this idea (of conditional execution) very clear, so as to enable you to tackle more difficult problems with ease.

One question that may come to your mind is 'why' such conditional execution?

The answer is that, with this the use of branch instructions can be avoided in many instances. This is a very great saving, as branching causes stalling of the pipeline (Section 10.2). It allows very dense code, without many branches. Not executing some of the conditional instructions does affect the speed, but the penalty is less than the overhead due to a branch.

Example 10.4

Find the result of the following instructions. What do these instructions accomplish?

i) ADD R1, R2, R2, LSL #3
ii) RSB R3, R3, R3, LSL #3
iii) RSB R3, R2, R2, LSL #4
iv) SUB R0, R0, R0, LSL #2
v) RSB R2, R1, #0

Solution

i) ADD R1, R2, R2, LSL #3
One source operand is R2, LSL #3. Left shifting 3 times accomplishes multiplication by $2^3 = 8$
The result of the whole operation is R1 = R2 + 8R2 = 9R2

ii) RSB R3, R3, R3, LSL #3
R3 = 8R3 – R3 = 7 R3

iii) RSB R3, R2, R2, LSL #4
R3 = 16R2 – R2 = 15R2

iv) SUB R0, R0, R0 LSL #2
R0 = R0 – 4R0 = -3R0

v) RSB R2, R1, #0
We get R2 = 0 – R1 = -R1. i.e., we get the negative value of R1

10.9 | Logical Instructions

Now, we will see the logical instructions of the processor. They also need to be suffixed with 'S' to have the flags updated. See Table 10.9.

Table 10.9 | List of Logical Instructions

Instruction	Operation	Logical Result
AND R3, R4, R5	Logical AND of 32 bit values	R3 = R4 AND R5
ORR R3, R4, R5	Logical OR of 32 bit values	R3 = R4 OR R5
EOR R3, R4, R5	Logical XOR of 32 bit values	R3 = R4 XOR R5
BIC R3, R4, R5	Logical bit clear	R3 = R4 (AND NOT) R5

Example 10.5

Given the contents of R3 and R4 as, R3 = 0x0FF00FF0, R4 = 0x0FF00FF0. and R0 = 0. Find the values in R1, R2 and R5 at the end of the sequence of instructions shown.

i) EORS R1, R3, R4
ii) ANDS R5, R3,

Solution

The content of the destination register and the affected flag is shown alongside the executed instruction

i) EORS R1, R3, R4 ;R1 = 0x00000000, Z = 1
ii) ANDS R5, R3, R0 ;R5 = 0x00000000 Z = 1

Note One of the source operands may be 8-bit immediate data as well. Refer to Section 10.17 for details of how to handle data bigger than 8 bits.

10.10 | Compare Instructions

This instruction compares two operands and causes the conditional flags to be affected, but neither the destination nor the source changes. Comparison is done by a subtraction operation, and the flags are set/reset according to the result of this. (ARM has four types of compare instructions as shown in Table 10.10). However, only two flags really matter and they are the zero flag and the carry flag. Refer to Table 10.11 to get an idea of the flag settings after a compare instruction.

Note Since the compare instructions explicitly affect the flags, the suffix S is not required for them.

Comparison is a very important operation, and we will use it very frequently. A number of programs using this instruction will be discussed subsequently.

Table 10.10 | List of 'Compare' Instructions

CMP R3, R4	Compare	R3 – R4, but only flags affected
CMN R3, R4	Compare negated	R3 + R4, but only flags affected
TST R3, R4	Test	R3 AND R4 but only flags affected
TEQ R3, R4	Test Equivalence	R3 OR R4 but only flags affected

Table 10.11 | Flag Settings After a Compare Instruction

If	C	Z
R3 > R4	1	0
R3 < R4	0	0
R3 = R4	1	1

What Is the use of the TST instruction?

TST is an instruction similar to compare, but it does ANDing and then sets conditional flags. If the result of ANDing is a zero, the Z flag is set. It can be used to verify if at least one of the bits of a data word is set or not. For that, 'test' the number with another one in which the required bit position has a '1'. For example, let's say we need to know if the LSB of the content of R1 is set or not. Use the instruction TST R1, #01 and verify the status of the Z flag. If Z = 1, it implies that the LSB of R1 is not set, because the AND operation for that bit, has produced a 0, not a 1.

What is the use of the TEQ instruction?

TEQ does exclusive ORing which tests for equality. If both the operands are equal, the Z flag is set. It verifies if the value in a register is equal to a specified number. The instruction TEQ R1, #45 verifies whether the content of R1 is 45.

10.11 | Multiplication

Multiplication is a complex operation which needs specialized hardware and takes more than one cycle to execute. ARM has a number of multiplication instructions, which uses this hardware. Let's examine how these instructions are used.

10.11.1 | Multiply

The format of the multiply instruction is

MUL Rd, Rm, Rs

where Rd is the destination register. Rm and Rs are source registers. A number of points are to be kept in mind when these instructions are used. Table 10.12 lists different types of multiplication instructions.

Table 10.12 | List of Multiply Instructions

Instruction	Operation	Calculation
SMLAL R0, R1, R2, R3	Signed multiply and accumulate	[R0, R1] = [R0, R1] + R2 * R3
SMULL R0, R1, R2, R3	Signed multiply	[R0, R1] = R2 * R3
UMLAL R0, R1, R2, R3	Unsigned multiply and accumulate	[R0, R1] = [R0, R1] + R2 * R3
UMULL R0, R1, R2, R3	Unsigned multiply	[R0, R1] = R2 * R3

i) The source and destination registers are 32 bits in length. If the product is longer than 32 bits, only the lower bits are preserved in the destination register.
ii) Immediate data cannot be used as a source operand.
iii) If the multiplicand and multiplier are signed numbers, it is up to the programmer to identify a logic to interpret the sign of the product.
iv) The instruction can be made conditional.

Example

```
MUL      R1, R2, R3    ;R1 = R2 × R3
MULS     R1, R2, R3    ;R1 = R2 × R3 and flags are also set
MULSEQ   R3, R2, R1    ;R3 = R1 × R2 is done only if the Z = 1
                       ;(because of the EQ suffix)
                       ;because of the S suffix, flags are updated
MULEQ    R4, R3, R5    ;if Z = 1, R4 = R3 × R5
```

10.11.2 | Multiply and Accumulate

The format of this instruction is

```
MLA Rd, Rm, Rs, Rn     ;Rd = (Rm * Rs) + Rn
```

This instruction does multiplication and accumulation (addition) as seen above. All the conditions specified for the MUL instruction are applicable here, as well.

Example

```
MLA R0, R1, R2, R3     ;R0 = R1 × R2 + R3
```

10.11.3 | Long Multiply/Long Multiply and Accumulate

In this, when 32-bit data are multiplied to get 64 bit results, the upper 32 bits are saved in a specified register. For signed data, the sign bit is also preserved in the upper register.

The format is

Instruction <RdLo>, <RdHi>, <Rm>, <Rs> Examples

Note That in all the above cases, two registers function as the destination

Since multiplication is a complex instruction, it takes many cycles for execution. So, it is best to realize multiplication using shifting and adding, rather than using any of the multiply instructions. Table 10.12 lists the available 'multiply and accumulate' instructions.

10.12 | Division

Division is another complex instruction requiring specialized hardware and extra clock cycles. As a policy, basic ARM architecture does not have a 'divide' instruction. Division can be realized using repeated subtraction. Compilers are given the responsibility of accomplishing division using the simple instructions of the processor.

10.13 | Starting Assembly Language Programming

If you have any previous experience of assembly language programming, you will know that there are two items used therein—instructions and directives—the former are executable statements which are 'executed' by the processor. The latter, that is, directives are non-executable statements relating to the assembler. They are used to give the assembler necessary information to perform the assembly process smoothly. For some processors, directives are also called pseudo instructions. For ARM, pseudo instructions are special directives issued to the processor which causes certain instructions to be executed. Thus, they are also executable statements. **Thus for ARM, an assembly language line will contain an instruction, directive or pseudo instruction.**

Writing and testing a program for ARM is done in a computer, usually a PC, which is called the host computer. The host computer should have the program development tools for ARM. Since the program written in ARM assembly language is assembled in a PC which has a different processor (usually some version of Pentium), the process is called 'cross assembly'. After the program in tested, it is converted to a hex file and burned into our processor (i.e. ARM).

The output of an assembly or compilation process has atleast two areas.

i) A code area. This is usually a read-only area.
ii) A data area. This is usually a read-write area.

The default area for code is Read-Only and for data it is Read-Write.

Let's understand some fundamental directives first.

10.13.1 | The AREA Directive

The first thing we do when we start assembly language programming is to define an area. There is a directive named 'AREA' for this. This directive names the area and sets its attributes. The attributes are placed after the name, separated by commas.

Example

```
AREA     SORT, CODE, READ ONLY
AREA     TABLE, DATA
```

The first area defined above is given the name SORT; it contains a code, and is read only. The word 'read only' is optional. The second AREA directive has the name TABLE and it contains data and though not mentioned will correspond to the Read Write area (as it is a data area).

10.13.2 | The ENTRY Directive

The ENTRY directive marks the first instruction to be executed within an application. Because an application cannot have more than one entry point, the ENTRY directive can appear in only one of the source modules.

10.13.3 | The END Directive

This directive tells the assembler to stop reading. Anything written after the END directive will be ignored by the assembler. So every assembly language source module must finish with an END directive, on a line by itself.

10.14 | General Structure of an Assembly Language Line

The general form of source lines in assembly language is:

`{label} {instruction|directive|pseudo-instruction} {;comment}`

Some points to keep in mind are listed as follows:

i) Instructions, pseudo-instructions and directives must be preceded by a white space, such as a space or a tab, even if there is no label. This means that they should not be written in the label space (extreme left of the line).
ii) Instruction mnemonics and register names can be written in uppercase or lowercase, but not mixed.
iii) Labels are symbols that represent addresses. The address given by a label is calculated during assembly. The assembler calculates the address of a label relative to the origin of the area where the label is defined. Assigning labels eases the programmer's burden as he does not have to concern himself with numerical values. The location counter in the assembler keeps on incrementing as labels are encountered.

Typical assembly language lines are

```
NOO     MOV R1, R2, LSL #2      ;copy the content of R2 left shifted, to R1
NUMS    DCW 2354, 5678          ;define two data half words
```

In the above two lines, NOO and NUMS are the labels, MOV (with operands) is an instruction and DCW is a directive, which is explained in the following section.

10.14.1 | Directives for Defining Data

Before we go deep into programming, we need to understand a few directives of the assembler which define and describe different kinds of data. Data which is used in a program can be bytes or words or half words. We define data and assign labels to their corresponding addresses. Defining data implies allocating space for data. The space we allocate corresponds to memory addresses, which are identified by labels. Data, when stored in memory is defined accordingly, using directives.

DCB defines data byte, DCW defines 16 bits or a half word and DCD defines a word (32 bits).

Examples

```
NUMS    DCB   9, 82, 71
NUMB    DCW   0x6787, 0x4564
NUMBR   DCD   0x00000123, 0x67890900
```

In the above, the first line shows data which are bytes. The first byte 9, has the address NUMS, 82 has the address NUMS + 1, and 71 has the address NUMS + 1.

The second line has address NUMB for the first half word, and NUMB + 2 for the second half word. In the last case, the addresses of the words are NUMBR and NUMBR + 4.

Keep in mind that a byte needs only one address, half word needs two, and a word requires four memory addresses.

10.14.2 | The EQU Directive

This is a frequently used directive, and is used to equate a numeric constant to a label. The constant may be data or address. Examples are as follows:

```
FACTR        EQU   35
BASE_ADDR    EQU   0x40000000
```

10.14.3 | Constants Allowed

The constants that can be used are numbers (decimals, hex or having any other base), characters, strings and Boolean

- Decimal., say, 346, 6748, etc.
- Hexadecimal. For example, 0x12345678, 0xFCE45, etc.
- *n_xxx* where: *n* is a base between 2 and 9 and *xxx* is a number in that base
- Characters: They are to be enclosed within single quotes, 'e', 'R', etc.
- Strings: They are characters enclosed within double quotes "mine", "non", etc.
- Boolean: TRUE or FALSE

10.14.4 | The RN Directive

The names of the general purpose registers have been introduced as R0, R1, R2, etc.

When we use them for loading operands, it is possible that we have a confusion as to which data has been loaded into which register. To ease out this problem, there is a way for giving variable names to registers. Suppose we need to use R0 for loading the value of X, and R1 for loading Y, we use the directive RN as follows:

```
X RN 0
Y RN 1
```

This method can be used for any of the registers.

```
DAT1   RN   8
DET    RN   10
```

10.15 | Writing Assembly Programs

Now, that we have got used to writing some instructions, let's get down to writing a complete program. This will let us get a feel of the programming process, after which we can learn more important instructions and write bigger and better programs.

Example 10.6

Write a program to find the sum of 3X + 4Y + 9Z, where X = 2, Y = 3 and Z = 4.

Solution

```
        AREA SUMM, CODE, READONLY
X RN 1                            ;register R1 is named X
Y RN 2                            ;register R2 is named Y
Z RN 3                            ;register R3 is named Z
        ENTRY
        MOV X,#2                  ;load X = 2 into register R1
        MOV Y,#3                  ;load Y = 3 into register R2
        MOV Z,#4                  ;load Z = 4 into register R3
        ADD R1,R1,R1,LSL#1        ;R1 = 3X
        MOV R2,R2,LSL#2           ;R2 = 4Y
        ADD R3,R3,R3,LSL#3        ;R3 = 9Z
        ADD R1,R1,R2              ;R1 = R1+R2 i.e. 3X+4Y
        ADD R1,R1,R3              ;R1 = R1+R3 i.e. 3X+4Y+9Z
STOP    B    STOP                 ;continue branching at STOP
        END                       ;end of the assembly file
```

Since this is the first complete program we are writing, it is important to make some observations regarding it.

i) SUMM is the name of the code AREA defined. The term 'Read only' is optional, as by default, a code area corresponds to the Read only memory only.
ii) As assembly language line has the label field at the left, and the opcode field to its right. For the Keil assembler, you may find that writing the word 'AREA' in the label field will generate an error message. But the directive RN is to be positioned in the label field itself. No instructions should be in the label field.
iii) The ENTRY directive should be followed by an instruction or pseudo instruction.
iv) The program involves multiplication and addition. Since the multiply instruction is a 'complex' one involving the use of special hardware (more power dissipation and more clock cycles), it is not used. Instead multiplication is achieved by the use of shift and add instructions.
v) The last instruction is an unconditional branch instruction (mnemonic 'B') and it continually branches to the same label STOP. This is done so that control does not go any instruction beyond this location. Any code has to finally be burned into ROM. Many embedded programs have their last line as this kind of self branching, since we don't want the next memory locations in code memory to be accessed.

10.16 | Branch Instructions

For any processor, branching is a very important operation. The power to change the sequence of execution is obtained by branching, which may be conditional or

Table 10.13 | List of Branch Instructions

Mnemonic	Instruction
B	Branch
BL	Branch and link
BX	Branch and Exchange
BLX	Branch Exchange with link

31 28	27 26 25	24	23
COND	1 0 1	L	Signed-immed_24

Figure 10.16 Format of a branch instruction

unconditional. Most processors have 'jump' and 'call' instructions for changing the sequence of execution. ARM does all this by different forms of a 'branch' instruction. It has the mnemonic 'B' for branch. The four different forms of branch instruction are given in Table 10.13

Let's see the usage of each of them.

Branching implies transferring control to a new memory location which is expressed as a 'label'. Hence the format of any branch instruction is B label. Branching is made conditional by appending the mnemonic B with the necessary condition.

Examples

```
        B      NEW    ;transfers control unconditionally to location NEW
STOP    B      STOP   ;continually branches to its own label STOP
        BNE    NOO    ;branch to NOO if Z flag is not set
        BHI    LUX    ;branch if high, i.e., if C = 1
```

The format of a branch instruction is as shown in Figure 10.16. Target addresses are 'relative'. What this means is that when a branch instruction is taken up, the PC (program counter) value and the value specified by the instruction are algebraically added.

The target is specified as a 24-bit signed number; this number is shifted left (logically) twice (so that the two LSB bits are zero. This makes all target addresses to be 'aligned' (Ref Secion 10.5.2). The left shifting also multiplies the number by 4. This makes the target to have 26 bits, that is, the maximum range is between +/– 2^{25} (one bit is for sign, remember). This number is added to the PC value. In short, what is done with the 24-bit immediate number, by the instruction is that *it shifts it left by two bits, sign extends it to 32 bits, and adds it to PC.* Thus, the maximum range for branching is only +/- 32 MB. ($2^{25} = 2^{20} \times 2^5$; $2^{20} = 1$ MB, $2^5 = 32$). For branch addresses beyond this range, the PC can be directly loaded with the target address. Now see this simple program which calculates the factorial of 10.

Example 10.7

```
AREA FACTO, CODE        ;define the code area
ENTRY                   ;entry point
MOV R1, #10             ;R1 = 10
```

```
        MOV R2, #1              ;R2 = 1
REPT    MUL R2, R1, R2          ;R2 = R2 xR2
        SUBS R1, R1, #1         ;R1 = R1- 1
        BNE   REPT              ;branch to REPT if Z! = 0
STOP    B   STOP                ;last line
        END
```

This is a very simple program which finds the factorial of 10. It can be used to find the factorial of any other number (except 0), provided the factorial does not exceed 32 bits in size. The technique is to multiply the number with the 'number-1' recursively. Meanwhile, a counter also decrements by 1(which is done by subtraction), and when the counter is 0, the Z flag is set. The multiplication is then stopped. The factorial is available in the register R2. The branch instruction used is a conditional one, that is, BNE which tests the Zero flag. The instruction before it, that is, SUB has been appended with the 'S' suffix to ensure the setting of flags.

Now let's see another example which uses conditional branching. This program performs division by repeated subtraction.

Example 10.8

```
        AREA DIV, CODE
        ENTRY
        MOV R1, #500        ;Move the dividend to R1
        MOV R2, #16         ;Move the divisor to R2
        MOV R3, #0          ;R3 = 0
        MOV R4, R1          ;copy the dividend to R4
REPT    SUBS R4, R4, R2     ;subtract and set flags
        ADDPL R3, R3, #1    ;add if N = 1 i.e. MSB of R$ is +ve
        BPL REPT            ;repeat the loop if the MSB is +ve
        ADDMI R4, R4, R2    ;if MSB of R4 is -ve, add R2 to R4
STOP    B    STOP
        END
```

This program performs division by repeated subtraction. Here 500 is to be divided by 16.

The method is to subtract 16 from 500 repeatedly until the result becomes negative. The branch instruction BPL REPT means Branch to label REPT if plus (PL), i.e., if N = 0.

Besides conditional branching, there are the ADD and SUB instructions also, which are conditional—the condition used is the status of the sign flag N.

The steps of the program are as follows:

i) Subtract 16 from 500, and check if the result is +ve or –ve. This can be verified by checking the N flag which corresponds to the MSB of the resultant number. The condition flags are updated by the subtraction operation (using the suffix S).
ii) If the number (in R4) is +ve, it means that subtraction can be repeated unhindered. Each time this is verified, the quotient register (R3) is incremented by 1.

iii) When the result of subtraction becomes – ve, (the condition 'MI' for minus), add the divisor to this negative number (in R3).
iv) In this problem, when 16 is subtracted 31 (0x1F) times from 500, the value in R4 is +ve. One more subtraction makes the N flag to be set, and the number R4 to be negative.
v) To this –ve number add the divisor. This makes it equal to the remainder which is 4, in this case.
vi) Thus, we get 31 (0x1F) as the quotient (in R3) and 4 as the remainder (in R4)

10.16.1 | Subroutines/Procedures

In Table 10.13, there is another form of the branch instruction which is BL standing for 'Branch and Link'. Recollect that a procedure (also called subroutines, functions, etc.) means that a new program sequence is taken up, but control returns to the original point after that. Most processors (including ARM) use stacks to store the return addresses and return instructions to handle procedure calls. ARM has an additional feature to handle procedures in a simpler manner. Recollect a register named the 'Link Register'. When a BL instruction is encountered, the PC value is changed to that of the target, but the old PC value is copied to the LR register. At the end of the procedure, the LR value can be copied back to the PC.

Now let's write a program which calls a procedure.

Example10.9

Write a program to calculate $3x^2 + 5Y^2$, where X = 8 and Y = 5

Solution

```
          AREA PROCED,CODE
          ENTRY
          MOV R2,#8              ;to calculate 3X² +5Y²
          BL SQUARE              ;call the SQUARE procedure
          ADD R1,R3,R3,LSL #1    ;3X²
          MOV R2,#5              ;R2 = 5
          BL SQUARE              ;call the SQUARE procedure
          ADD R0,R3,R3,LSL #2    ;5Y²
          ADD R4,R1,R0           ;R4 = R1+R0 i.e 3X² +5Y²
STOP      B STOP                 ;last line in the execution
SQUARE    MUL R3,R2,R2           ;the SQUARE procedure
          MOV PC,LR              ;return LR back to PC
          END
```

The salient points of this program are as follows:

i) A procedure named SQUARE has been used. This procedure uses the multiply instruction to find the square of any number. The number to be squared is passed to the procedure using the register R2. The square of the number is returned to the main program in R3.

ii) There are two numbers, X and Y, whose squares are to be found. Calling the procedure amounts to just writing the instruction BL SQUARE. This instruction will cause a branching to the procedure named SQUARE. It also copies the current PC value to the link register (LR).
iii) The procedure has only two instructions: one to perform squaring, and the other to copy the LR content back to PC. The second instruction causes a return to the main program.
iv) We need two multiplications, in addition to the squaring operation. These two, that is, $3X^2$ and $5Y^2$ are achieved by shifting and adding. The MUL instruction is used as little as possible because it takes more time, and causes higher power dissipation.
v) The last step is adding $3X^2$ and $5Y^2$ which are now in R1 and R0. The sum is available in R4.
vi) Note that the last program line to be executed is STOP B STOP, even though it is not the last line in the assembly file.

In Table 10.13 there are two more forms for the branch instruction. BX stands for Branch and Exchange. BLX is for Branch Link and Exchange. The Exchange feature is applicable when ARM and THUMB instructions are being used, and it is needed to switch from one set to another.

10.17 | Loading Constants

How is it different for ARM?

An important addressing mode for any processor is the 'immediate' mode. In this, a constant which is specified in the instruction itself is to be copied into a register, or is used as one operand in any arithmetic or logic operations.

Examples

```
MOV R1, #0x7867
ADD R1, R2, # 567
```

This seems very obvious and direct. For CISC machines, this is fine, because the immediate data can be another byte or word. But ARM has the limitation that its instruction size should nor exceed 32 bits, which means that the constant should fit in the word length of 32 bits along with the opcode, condition code, register code and other information that the instruction should carry. It is thus apparent that we can't have a 32-bit constant embedded in the instruction.

So then what is the maximum size of the constant that can be used in the immediate mode?

We would like to be able to use immediate constants as large as 32 bits. How is this done? ARM uses an ingenious technique, the idea being the use of rotation of a small number to generate a large number. We have already seen that there is a barrel shifter in the ALU. Any data processing instruction has a format as shown in Figure 10.17a. The data processing instruction format has 12 bits available for operand 2.

Figure 10.17b shows the instruction format which has been modified for using the immediate mode.

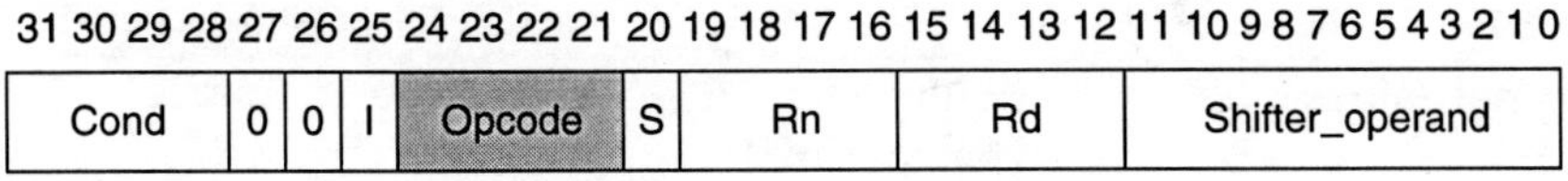

Figure 10.17a | Format of a typical data processing instruction

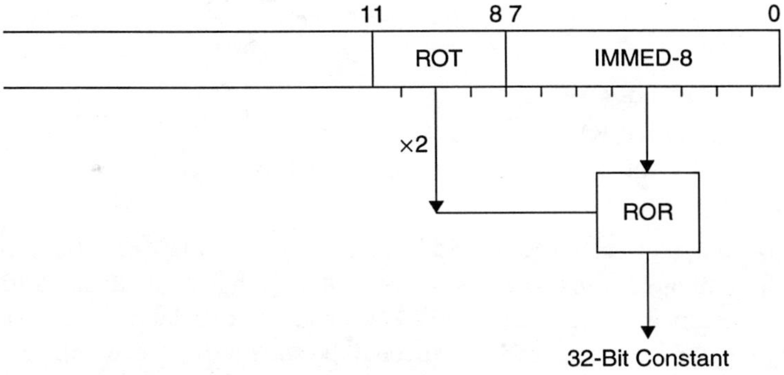

Figure 10.17b | Modification of the 'shifter operand'

When the immediate mode is needed, the 12-bit field is modified such that there is an 8-bit immediate constant which is subject to a ROR (rotate right operation). The rotate operator can use only 4 bits. But since the maximum rotation possible is 32 bits, the four bit 'rotate' operand is multiplied by 2 and then rotated. Hence, it becomes a case of '8 bits shifted by an even number of bit positions'. The rotated 8-bit number will become a 32-bit number during the data processing.

Let's try to understand how this is done.

10.17.1 | Generating a 32-bit Constant Using Rotation

Consider the steps in rotating to the right by 2, the number 0xF0 after expanding it to fill 32 bits space

Case 1

The original 8-bit number is 1111 0000

Expanding it to fill 32 bits makes it

00000000 00000000 00000000 11110000

Rotating it right by 2 makes it

00000000 00000000 00000000 00111100

i.e. 0x3C

Case 2

We can also use the MVN instruction for generating new numbers. If 0 is loaded into a register and moved into another or the same register after using the MVN instruction, we get 0xFFFFFFFF

You can try this code to verify.

Table 10.14 | The Range of Constants That Can Be Generated By the Rotation Scheme

Decimal Values	Equivalent Hexadecimal	Step Between Values	Rotate
0 – 255	0 – 0xff	1	No rotate
256, 260, 264, ..., 1020	0x100 – 0x3fc	4	Right by 30 bits
1024, 1040, 1056, ..., 4080	0x400 – 0xff0	16	Right by 28 bits
4096, 4160, 4224, ..., 16320	0x1000 – 0x3fc0	64	Right by 26 bits

```
MOV R1, #0x0
MVN R1, R1
```

Let's summarize the points regarding the generation of constants using the ARM rotation scheme.

i) A class of constants can be generated by this scheme, (Table 10.14) but all constants cannot be generated. Those that cannot be, will have to loaded directly into memory, by using the concept of 'literal pools'. We will come to that soon. (Table 10.14 shows the range of constants that can be generated by the rotation scheme)
ii) To generate the constant needed, the programmer need not specify the 8-bit immediate number, and the number of rotations to be done. He just has to write an instruction in the immediate mode. The assembler converts this instruction to the required scheme. When a constant 0x200000002 is needed, the assembler converts it to the instructions.
MOV R1, #0x22
MOV R1, R1, ROR#4, which creates the require 32-bit constants for us.
iii) The processor does not have an instruction for rotation to the left. But, rotating n times to the left is achieved by rotating (32-n) times to the right.

Example 10.9

Find the 32-bit constant generated by each of the following rotations

i) Rotate 0x40, to the right 30 times
ii) Rotate 0x56, to the left 12 times
iii) Rotate 0x6D, to the right 16 times
iv) Rotate 0x05, to the right 6 times
v) Rotate 0xFC, to the right 2 times

Solution

i) The 8-bit number is 01000000.
00000000 00000000 00000000 *01000000*; the 8-bit number in 32-bit format
00000000 00000000 00000001 00000000; the number after rotation
Thus, the constant obtained is 0x100
ii) The 8-bit number is 01010110
00000000 00000000 000000000 *01010110*; the 8-bit number in 32-bit format.
Rotating 12 times to the left is equivalent to rotating 20 times to the right
00000000 00000101 01100000 00000000; the number after rotation
The constant generated is 0x56000

Table 10.15

	8-Bit Number	ROR	Constant
iii	0x6D	16	0x6D0000
iv	0x05	6	0x14000000
v	0x3E	2	0x8000000F

The answers for iii, iv and v are in Table 10.15

From Example 10.9, we note that many 32-bit numbers can be generated by the ARM rotation scheme, but there are constants which cannot be obtained by this method. For example, the number 0x11111111 cannot be generated by rotation.

How then are such constants obtained for use in the immediate mode of addressing?

10.17.2 | Literal Pools

In computer science, specifically in compiler and assembler design, a **literal pool** is a lookup table used to hold literals during assembly and execution. But first, what exactly is a literal? In programming, a literal is a value written exactly as it is meant to be interpreted. A literal can be a number, a character or a string. For example, in the expression, x = 145, x is a variable, and 145 is a literal. Thus, literals are constants for ARM. When it is required to load a constant in a register, the assembler can help by creating a space in memory and then placing this constant in the space. From this memory space, the processor can take it and use it using load instructions. But assemblers are not guided by instructions; they use what are called pseudo instructions. In this case of making a literal pool, and taking a constant from the pool, there is a specific pseudo instruction

LDR Rd, = *const*

This pseudo instruction can construct any 32-bit numeric constant. Suppose we need to the constant 0x33333333, it is likely that we write an instructions MOV R1, # 0x33333333. With this, the assembler will give an error message that such a constant cannot be generated. To avoid such a situation, we write

LDR R1, = 0x33333333.

This is a pseudo instruction (don't confuse it with the LDR instruction, we will soon come to, there is a difference in format between the two). This will cause the assembler to check one of the following possibilities.

i) Can the constant be constructed with MOV or MVN instruction combined with rotation? If this is possible, the assembler generates the appropriate instruction, that is, an 8-bit number is rotated appropriately to get the constant in question.
ii) If the constant cannot be constructed this way, the assembler places the value in a *literal pool* and generates an LDR (load register) instruction with a program-relative address that reads the constant from this literal pool.

Example 10.10a

```
        AREA PROG1,CODE,READONLY
        ENTRY
        LDR R1, = #0x12400000
        LDR R2, = 0X00555555
        ADD R3,R1,R2
STOP    B STOP
        END
```

In Example10.10a, two constants are needed. If you run this program and check the disassembly file, you will find two interesting facts, which relate to the different ways in which these two constants are generated. The assembler realizes that the first constant can be obtained by the rotation scheme, but the second one cannot. So a literal pool is created just after the last instruction, and the constant 0x00555555 is placed therein. Then a 'load register' instruction is generated to load the constant into register.

How Is the literal pool accessed?

The literal we need is accessed from the literal pool using a PC relative mode. In this mode, only 12 bits are allowed for the 'relative number' which can be positive or negative. Thus, the literal in the pool has to be within +/– 4KB of the current PC value.

Where should the literal pool be placed?

Normally the literal pool is placed just after the END directive, which means just after the end of the program area. This is okay for normal size programs. But sometimes, programs are very large and if the literal pool is placed after the end of the program, it may be out of range (of +/– 4KB) of the LDR instruction. Such a situation implies that there should be the flexibility of placing literal pools anywhere in memory. This is done by the LTORG directive which allows us to define the origin of a literal pool.

When a pseudo instruction LDR Rd = const is encountered, the assembler checks if the constant is available and addressable in the nearest literal pool. If it is so, it takes it from the pool. Otherwise, it attempts to place the constant in the next literal pool. If the next literal pool is out of range, the assembler generates an error message. In this case, the LTORG directive is to be used to place an additional literal pool in the code. Place the LTORG directive after the failed LDR pseudo instruction, and within 4KB memory space.

Literal pools are to be placed in locations where the processor does not attempt to execute them as instructions. It is best to place them after unconditional branch instructions, or after the return instruction at the end of a subroutine. Let us see an example of a case where the LTORG directive becomes necessary.

Example10.10b

```
        AREA PROG1,CODE,READONLY
        ENTRY
        LDR R1, = 0x12400000
        LDR R2, = 0x00555555
        ADD R3,R1,R2
        SPACE  4400
STOP    B STOP
        END
```

This is a modified version of Example 10.10a. Recollect that we need to have a literal pool for the constant 0x00555555. Here, a directive called SPACE 4400 has been inserted. This directive creates an empty area of 4400 byes. Because of this, the total space occupied by the program becomes large (greater than 4400 bytes, anyway). The literal pool is usually after the program area. In this case, this will make the literal pool to be beyond the range (greater than 4KB) of the LDR R2, = 0x00555555. Hence, on assembling, the following message is seen.

error: A1284E: Literal pool too distant, use LTORG to assemble it within 4KB

In the program an error message indicating this will be obtained as above.

To avoid such a situation, we can place the literal closer to the instruction which needs the constant. See the modified version of the program.

Example 10.10c

```
        AREA PROG1,CODE,READONLY
        ENTRY
        LDR R1, = 0x12400000
        LDR R2, = 0X00555555
        ADD R3,R1,R2
        LTORG
        SPACE  4400
STOP    B STOP
        END
```

Now the program runs without error, because a literal pool has been created before the 'free space' of 4400 bytes. By the use of the LTORG directive, the required constant is found to have been placed in this pool, by the assembler. Thus, we see that the directive LTORG can be used to place literal pools wherever we want. This will become useful as programs become larger.

10.18 | Load and Store Instructions

ARM is a RISC architecture, and one of the features of RISC is that of being a 'load store' architecture. Loading is the process of getting data from memory into a register, and storing is just the reverse process. In ARM, data is brought into registers using a load instruction, and only then can it be used for data processing. After computation, the result can be 'stored' in memory. The memory in question is 'RAM' which is the read/write memory. RAM is volatile and is used for temporary storage of data in the course of computations. The only instructions which access RAM are 'load' and 'store'. All registers can be accessed using these instructions, but programmers are advised to exercise caution when accessing critical registers like the PC, SP, etc.

The syntax for load or store is

LDR/STR {<cond>}<Rd>, <addressing mode>

Rd is the source register for store and destination register for load.

The addressing mode gives us the necessary information to get the 'effective address', which is the actual memory address to be accessed. The addressing mode is indirect because the memory address is not to be specified directly in the instruction, rather a base register is mandatorily used. For the simplest case, an example of LOAD and STORE instructions are as follows:

```
LDR    R1, [R2]    ;copy into R1 the content of memory specified in R2
STR    R1, [R2]    ;store the content of R1 into the memory address specified in R2
```

This implies that the load/store instruction must be preceded by an instruction which copies the address into R2. We will soon get to know how this is done. There are various ways of specifying the effective address. The barrel shifter can be part of the address specifying mechanism.

Example 10.11

How is the effective memory address calculated in the following load and store instructions?

i) LDR R3, [R2, LSL #2]
ii) STR R9, [R1, R2, ROR #2]
iii) LDR R4, [R3, R2]
iv) STR R5, [R4, R3, ASL #4]

Solution

i) LDR R3, [R2, LSL #2]
In this the effective address is the content of R2 left shifted by 2, i.e. multiplied by 4

ii) STR R9, [R1, R2, ROR #2]
Here, the effective address is specified by R1, R2 and a right rotation. To calculate it, the content of R2 is rotated twice by 2, and then added to the content of R1.

vi) LDR R4, [R3, R2]
The effective address here is the sum of R3 and R2.

vii) STR R5, [R4, R3, ASL #4]
The effective address is the sum of the content of R4 and the arithmetically left shifted (by 4) content of R3.

10.18.1 | Bytes, Half Words and Words

Now, let's see another aspect of load and store instructions. ARM has instructions to transfer specifically a word (32 bits), half word (16 bits) or a byte (8 bits) between

Table 10.16 | List of Load and Store Instructions

LDR	Load Word	STR	Store Word
LDRH	Load Half Word	STRH	Store Half Word
LDRSH	Load Signed Half Word		
LDRB	Load Byte	STRB	Store Byte
LDRSB	Load Signed Byte		

memory and registers. There are also instructions which differentiate between signed and unsigned data.

There are instructions which clearly indicate the kind of data to be moved. See Table 10.16. From the table, we understand that we can load and store parts of a 32-bit word by using B for byte and H for half word, along with the load and store instructions.

If a memory location contains a 32-bit word, we can move the LSB (assuming little endian format) into a register by using LDRB, or the lower half of the word by using LDRH. Let's clarify this by an example.

Example 10.12

Two memory areas are being referenced and two registers are used as pointers:

R1 = 0x00000100

R2 = 0x40001200

Figures 10.18a and b show the data addresses and corresponding data.

Show the content of memory, after the execution of the following instructions:

Address	Byte Stored
0 x00000100	56
0 x00000101	23
0 x00000102	0D
0 x00000103	AE

Figure 10.18a | Address and data

Address	Byte Stored
0 x40001200	00
0 x40001201	00
0 x40001202	00
0 x40001203	00

Figure 10.18b | Address and data

i) LDR R3, [R1]
ii) LDRB R3, [R1]
iii) LDRH R3, [R1]
iv) STRB R3, [R2] given that R3 = 0xAE0D2356

For this case, show half word and word storage as well.

Solution

i) LDR R3,[R1]
In this, the complete 32-bit data in the address pointed to by R1 is copied to R3. So R3 = 0xAE0D2356

ii) LDRB R3,[R1]
In this, the byte (LSB) of the word alone is copied to R3. Since it is an unsigned byte, the remaining bytes of R3 contain 0. So R3 = 0x00000056

iii) LDRH R3,[R1]
In this, the half word (lower two bytes) of the address is copied to R3.
R3 = 0x00002356

iv) STRB R3,[R2] given that R3 = 0xAE0D2356
In this, the byte corresponding to the LSB of the data in R3 is copied to the address pointed by R2. See Tables 10.17a, b and c for byte, half word storage and word storage as well.

Table 10.17a, b and c

STRB R3, [R2]	
0 x40001200	56
	00
	00
	00

STRH R3, [R2]	
0 x40001200	56
	23
	00
	00

STR R3, [R2]	
0 x40001200	56
	23
	0D
	AE

10.18.2 | Loading Signed Numbers

Signed numbers are those whose MSB is the sign bit. For positive numbers, the sign bit is '0', whereas negative numbers are in the two's complement form and have their MSBs to be '1', When a 32-bit number is available in memory, it can be loaded into registers as signed bytes and signed half words. In these cases, the MSB of the byte part or the half word part is checked, and sign extension is done while loading it into registers

Consider the case of a word 0xCDEF8204 in memory. Let R7 be used as a pointer to that memory location. Then, observe the result of execution of the following instructions, as given in the comments column.

```
LDR      R1, [R7]    ;R1 = 0xCDEF8204.......Case 1
LDRSH    R2, R7]     ;R2 = 0xFFFF8204.........Case 2
LDRSB    R3, [R7]    ;R3 = 0x00000004...........Case 3
```

For case 1, the 32 bits are copied to R1. For case 2, only the lower 16 bits are to be copied. The MSB of the 16-bit half word is '1', and this is extended to 32 bits while copying to R2. That's how the upper 16 bits of R2 become FFFF.

For case 3, the lowest byte alone is copied. Its MSB is 0. As such, the rest of R3 is filled with zeros, i.e., the sign bit '0' is extended to fill the upper 24 bits. You can also observe in Table 10.16 that there are no store instructions for **signed bytes or signed half words.** This is because storing simply means placing numbers in memory. These numbers may be signed, unsigned data or code—it is only when the user brings it to a register, is the processing on that number done. Only then it is necessary for that number to be interpreted as signed or unsigned.

10.18.3 | Indexed Addressing Modes

In this mode, the effective address calculation can be done before a load/store is executed or afterwards. Let's see what it is all about.

10.18.3.1 | *Pre-indexed Addressing Mode*

Observe the instruction LDR R0, [R7, #4]. Here R7 is the base register and the effective address is R7 + 4. The data at this effective address is copied to R0.

Next, see the instruction STR R1, [R5, R6, LSL #2]. The effective address = R5 + R6 left shifted twice.

In the above two instructions, there is a notable feature, however. After the load/store is done, the base address content remains unchanged, that is, the effective address is not copied to the base register. But if we want the base address to contain the effective address, just suffix the instruction by the character '!' and then 'write back' occurs.

Consider the instruction LDR R2, [R6, #-8] !. In this, after the loading operation is done, R6 has the effective address written back into it.

Example 10.13

Calculate the effective addresses and explain what each instruction does.

i) STRB R2, [R6, R7, #0x24]!
ii) LDRSH R4, [R10, R11, ASR #4]

Solution

i) STRB R2, [R6, R7, #0x24]!
The effective address is the sum of the contents of R6, R7 and the number 0x24. The content of R2 is stored in the effective address. After that, the effective address is copied to R6.
ii) LDRSH R4, [R10, R11, ASR #4]
Here, the effective address is the sum of the contents of R10 and R11 after arithmetically shifting it right by 4 positions. The half word in this address is loaded to R4. The contents of the base register remains unchanged.

10.18.3.2 | *Post-indexed Addressing Mode*

In this mode, the effective address calculation is done after the execution of the specific instruction has been done.

Take the case of the instruction LDR R0, [R4], #4

Here the data pointed by the content of R4 is first copied to R0. After that, the content of R4 is changed to R4 + 4. There is no need of the '!' operation because that is exactly what post-indexing does.

Example 10.14

Let's add 10 numbers which are in memory. The numbers are 16-bit long, that is, half words, and use two byte spaces. The pre-indexed mode of addressing with write back is used to index the half words which have addresses with a spacing of 2 between them. The instruction LDRH R2, [R7, #2]! does the indexing of the 16-bit numbers.

Solution

```
        AREA DADD, CODE, READONLY
        ENTRY
        LDR R7, = TABLE      ;copy the address of Table to R7
STRT    MOV R0,#9            ;R0 = 9
        LDRH R1,[R7]         ;load 1st number from memory to R1
REPT    LDRH R2, [R7,#2]!    ;pre-indexed with writeback
        ADD R1,R1,R2         ;R1 = R1+R2
        SUBS R0,R0,#1        ;R0 = R0-1
        BNE REPT             ;repeat the addition until R0 = 0
STOP    B STOP               ;last line
TABLE   DCW 3456,7859,1234,9876,3452,3214,7864,0987,2032
        END
```

Let's examine the salient features of this program.

i) The numbers to be added are stored in code memory, just after the last line of the program.
ii) There are 10 numbers to be added. The first number is loaded into register R1 and the rest are loaded one by one into R2.
iii) R0 is used as a counter to the numbers. In a general case, if there are N numbers to be added, R0 = N-1. Here N = 10.
iv) The loading of the numbers to R2 is done using a loop. Since the numbers are half words, their addresses are to be incremented by2. This is done very efficiently by the pre-indexed addressing with write back scheme. After one half word is accessed, the effective address is written back to the base register R7 in readiness for accessing the next half word.
v) The address corresponding to TABLE is a 32-bit constant. It is calculated by the assembler, and loaded into R7 using the techniques mentioned in Section 10.17.

10.19 | Readonly and Read/Write Memory

The two memory areas defined by the compiler are 'Readonly' for code, and 'Read/write' for data. Usually this corresponds to ROM and RAM in a physical system. RAM is used for intermediate results, for temporary storage, etc., as this is volatile memory. We can store data permanently in the readonly memory, process it and copy it in RAM. In the readonly memory, data is written using directives like DCD, DCW, etc. From there, it is copied to readwrite memory using load and store instructions.

Example 10.15

```
        AREA FIRST, CODE, READONLY
        ENTRY
        LDR R7, = NUMS     ;load the address of NUMS in R7
        LDR R8, = NUMS1    ;load the address of NUMS1 in R8
        LDR R9, = NUMS2    ;load the address of NUMS2 in R9
        LDR R1,[R7]        ;load the word to R1
        STR R1,[R9]        ;store the word in R1 in NUMS2
        STR R1,[R8]        ;store the word in R1 in NUMS1
STOP    B STOP
NUMS    DCD 653451134
        AREA SECOND, DATA, READWRITE
NUMS2   SPACE 60
NUMS1   DCD 0
        END
```

In Example 10.15, three memory areas have been defined: one in readonly, and two in readwrite memory. What is accomplished is just the transfer of a word from readonly memory to readwrite memory. In readwrite memory, one part is a space of 60 bytes. The next is a word space which is initialized to 0. After the execution of the program, the number **653451134** is copied to both these spaces.

Example 10.16

```
        AREA STRIN1, CODE, READONLY
        ENTRY

STRT    LDR R1, = SOURCE   ;pointer to source string
        LDR R0, = DESTIN   ;pointer to destination string
        BL COPY            ;call procedure for copying
STOP    B STOP             ;last line of execution

COPY    LDRB R2, [R1],#1   ;Load byte and update address.
        STRB R2, [R0],#1   ;Store byte and update address.
        CMP R2, #0         ;Check for 0
        BNE COPY           ;repeat until the string is over
        MOV PC,LR          ;return to calling program
```

```
SOURCE DCB "I am sam",0

        AREA STRIN2,DATA,READWRITE
DESTIN  DCB 0
        END
```

Example 10.16 uses many of the programming aspects that we have been discussing so far. Let's have a look at the important features of this program.

i) There is an ASCII string written in readonly memory using the DCB directive. Such a string is enclosed in double quotes and each character is a byte.
ii) One readonly and one read/write memory areas have been defined.
iii) After the ASCII string, a 0 is used as a terminating character. The arrival of this 0 in R2 is used to check whether the required transfer of the string is done.
iv) The instructions for loading and storing are suffixed by 'B' which indicates that only a byte is to be transferred.
v) Post-indexed mode of addressing is used for load and store. The addresses need to be incremented only by 1, as only a byte is transferred.
vi) The instructions for loading and storing are in a procedure named COPY. The procedure is 'called' by the BL instruction which does branching and also copies the current PC to the link register. The last line of the procedure is copying the LR back to PC. This constitutes the 'return' to the main program.

10.20 | Multiple Register Load and Store

We have seen in Section 10.18 the LDR and STR instructions, which transfer data (in the form of bytes, halfwords or words) between a register and memory. Now, let's see an advanced (or let's say an extended) form of loading and storing, wherein multiple registers are involved. But only data in the form of words (32 bits) can be handled by these instruction. The mnemonic of multiple load and store is LDM/STM.

10.20.1 | The LDM Instruction

Let's talk about LDM first—it has the syntax

LDM{*cond*}*address-mode* R*n*{!},*reg-list*{^}

Rn is the base register for the load operation. The address stored in this register is the starting address for the load operation. There can be a number of modes for specifying the address. *register-list* is a comma-delimited list of symbolic register names and register ranges enclosed in braces. There must be at least one register in the list. Register ranges are specified with a dash. For example, {R0—R5, R9} is a list. The ! option is for 'write back' and the ^ option is relevant for interrupts. We will not discuss the second option here. Write back is not to be specified if the base register R*n* is in *register-list*.

Multiple register load means that multiple memory locations are to be accessed, and loaded into multiple registers. There is a 'base register' acting as a pointer for the first memory location to be accessed. This register is then incremented or decremented to point to the next memory addresses. There are four options for handling this. The base register can be **incremented or decremented by 4** (one word needs four addresses) for

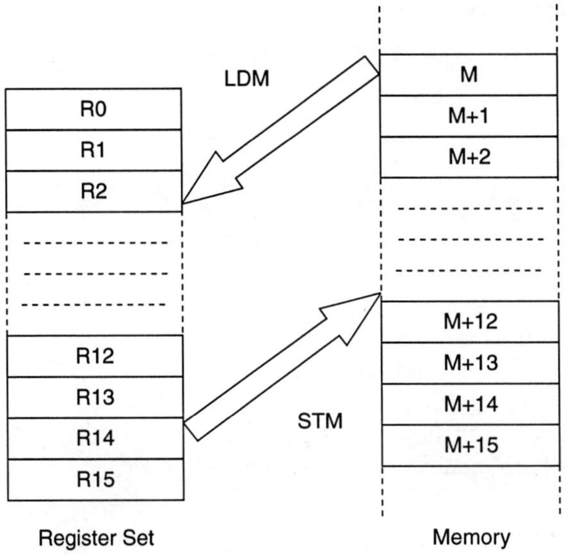

Figure 10.19 | The LDM and STM instructions

each register in the operation, and the increment or decrement can occur **before or after** the operation. The suffixes for these options are as follows:

IA – increment after
IB – increment before
DA – decrement after
DB – decrement before

Consider the instruction LDMDA R0, {R4-R9}
The base register here is R0. Let us assume it holds the number 0x45000000. The operation of this instruction is that the 32-bit word at that address is pointed by R0, and that word copied to R4. Then the address is decremented to point to the next word. So the new address is [R0-4], and this word is copied to R5. The sequence of decrementing the address and loading data from memory is done for the registers R4, R5, R6, R7, R8 and R9.

It is obvious that a single instruction replaces six LDR instructions. Is there any advantage in this? As far as execution is concerned, it is 'No'. All the six load operations have to be done. But note that only one 'instruction fetch' cycle is needed for the six load operations together. So there is definitely some savings in terms of time.

What Is the difference in operation of the following instruction?

LDMIA R10,{ R9, R1 – R5}

Here the base address is in R10, and after each data transfer, it is incremented by 4. In the destination register list, R9 is specified first, but the processor has a particular way of handling the list. The lowest register will always be loaded from the lowest address in memory, and the highest register from the highest address. Here R1 gets the data in the address pointed by R10.

10.20.2 | The STM instruction

This has the same format as the LDM instruction. Consider the instruction

STMIA R1, {R2-R4}

This will be equivalent to the instructions

STR R2, [R1]
STR R3, [R1. #4]
STR R4, [R1. #8]]

After the sequences of four stores are over, the base content does not vary, however. If you need it to be changed to that of the final address, the writeback operator '!' is to be used. So write the instruction as STMIA R1!,{R2-R4}

Now let's use the LDM and STM instructions to simply Example 10.16 which transfers bytes from one portion of memory (Readonly) to another portion (Read/write). But the multiple load/store instructions can be used only for words (32 bits). So Example 10.17 has been modified and used to move 6 words.

Example 10.17

```
        AREA STRIN1, CODE, READONLY
        ENTRY
        LDR R1, = SOURCE          ;pointer to source
        LDR R0, = DESTIN          ;pointer to destination
        LDMIA R1,{R2-R8}          ;Load six words to R2-R8
        STMIA R0,{R2-R8}          ;Store six words in destination
STOP    B STOP

SOURCE DCD 0x675889,0x1234568,0x9876543,0x2345678,0x8907653

        AREA STRIN2,DATA,READWRITE ;define the R/W memory area
DESTIN  DCD 0                      ;
        END
```

Here 6 words from the source memory have been copied to six registers using just one instruction. In the next instruction, these six words are stored in the destination memory

Note how simple, the program is.

Example 10.17 illustrates the idea that block data transfers can be simplified using the multiple register instructions. But their real importance is for stack implementation. Stacks are a necessity for any processor; stacks are needed for storing data temporarily and also for storing return addresses and register values during procedure calls. We will see this now. For those who are not very familiar with the concept of stacks, here is a brief review.

10.20.3 | Stack

A stack is an area in memory, the accessing of which is done in a special way. Most stacks are Last-In First-Out (LIFO) type stacks. This means that the last data that was stored is the first one that can be taken out. It is sequential access that is done, and not random access. Two operations are defined for a stack, that is, the PUSH, in which data is written into the stack, and POP in which data is read out and loaded into registers. The stack has a pointer to its top which is called the Stack pointer (SP). For ARM, this is register R13. This means that the address of the top of the stack is to be available in SP.

10.20.3.1 | *Types of Stacks*

Ascending/Descending and Empty/Full

An ascending stack grows upwards. It starts from a low memory address and, as items are pushed onto it, progresses to higher memory addresses. A descending stack grows downwards. It starts from a high memory address, and as items are pushed onto it, it progresses to lower memory addresses.

In an **empty stack**, the stack pointer points to the next free (empty) location on the stack, i.e., to the place where the next item to be pushed, will be stored. In a **full stack**, the stack pointer points to the topmost item in the stack, that is the location of the last item pushed onto the stack. In practice, stacks are almost always **full and descending**. Most stacks are 'Full descending' types.

Let's consider a descending stack in which SP is first decremented and then data is pushed in. The reverse occurs for the POP operation. Stacks allow data to be pushed or popped only as words (32 bits for ARM). Consider that SP = 0x50002000, and the contents of R1 and R2 are pushed in At the end of the operation we find that SP = SP-8 = 0x50001FF8. ARM does not have a mnemonic for PUSH, instead it uses the STM instruction. To simplify the use of the STM/LDM instructions corresponding to PUSH and POP for different types of stacks, Table 10.18 can be referred to.

For the kind of stack that we are talking about now, what is the instruction we can use for pushing the contents of registers R1 to R3?

The answer is STMDB SP! {R1-R3}. We need SP to be used as the base register. For pushing in, SP is first decremented, and then storing is done. So we use the suffix 'DB' along with SP. The operator '!' is used such the decremented value is available in SP.

See this simple program (Example 10.18) in which SP is initialized to 0x40000200. Some values are loaded into registers R1 to R3. Using the STMDB instruction, the content of the three registers, that is, 3 words are pushed to the stack, and will be available in memory. At the end of the program, SP will be found to have the value of 0x400001F4.

Table 10.18 | Types of Stacks and Corresponding Instructions to be Used

Stack Type	Push	Pop
Full Descending	STMFD (DB)	LDMFD (IA)
Full Ascending	STMFA (IB)	LDMFA (DA)
Empty Descending	STMED (DA)	LDMED (IB)
Empty Ascending	STMEA (IA)	LDMEA (DB)

Example 10.18

```
        AREA STCK, CODE, READONLY
        ENTRY
        LDR SP, = 0x40000200
        MOV R1,#1
        MOV R2,#2
        MOV R3,#3
        STMDB SP!,{R1-R3}
STOP    B STOP
        END
```

Now, in this program, if the STM instruction is changed to STMIA, the stack becomes an ascending stack, and the value of SP will be 0x4000200C, after program execution. Thus, it is obvious that a stack is a data structure which can be defined by software.

10.20.4 | Stacks and Subroutines/Procedures

For most processors, procedures use a stack to store the return address. A procedure is taken up by a 'CALL' instruction. This causes the action of pushing the current value of PC onto the stack. The procedure ends with a 'RETURN' instruction. This causes the PC value to be popped back.

For ARM, so far (Section 10.16.1) we have used procedures without the necessity of a stack. That is because the Link Register (LR) keeps the return address, when a procedure is called. But think of the case of nested procedures. There is only one link register for a mode, and a new procedure will overwrite the existing link register which stores the details of the previous procedure, and very soon things may go out of hand.

In such cases, a stack is a necessity. Each time a procedure is called, the PC value is saved in the LR, as is the usual case. When a nested procedure comes in, the content of the link register is pushed on to the stack, and popped out from the stack when exiting the procedure. Figure 10.20 shows the sequence of actions needed to take care of a nested procedure.

Now, let's try to understand the sequence of actions indicated by Figure 10.20.

In the main program, we define a stack by giving a value to the stack pointer (SP).

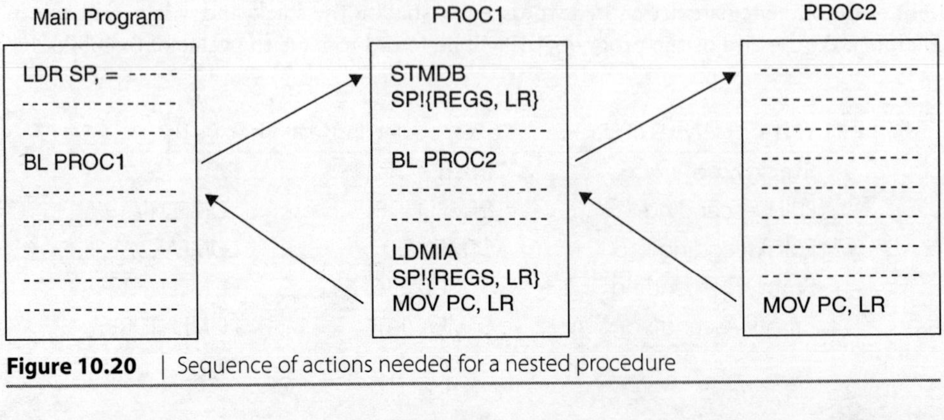

Figure 10.20 | Sequence of actions needed for a nested procedure

The main program has a procedure named PROC1 which is called by the instruction BL PROC1. This instruction **causes the current PC value to be copied to LR.** In PROC1, since we anticipate a nested procedure, we push LR and the working registers to stack using the instruction STMDB SP!,{REGS,LR}. **Thus the content of LR is safely stored in the stack.**

In the procedure PROC1, another procedure is called by the instruction BL PROC2. This instruction causes the copying of the present PC to LR. In PROC2, there is the instruction MOV PC, LR at the end. This will get the PC value back from LR, and thus execution goes back to PROC1.

At the end of PROC1, there is the stack based instruction LDMIA SP!, {REGS, LR}. This retrieves the contents of LR. This is given back to PC by the instruction MOV PC, LR. Thus, execution goes back to the main program.

Any part of memory can be defined as a stack, by simply defining the content of the stack pointer register. Let's write a procedure using a stack.

Example 10.19

```
        AREA NESTED, CODE, READONLY
        ENTRY
        LDR R7, = 0X40000000
        LDR SP, = 0x40000210   ;define SP
        MOV R1,#1
        MOV R2,#2
        MOV R3,#3
        BL PROC1               ;Call PROC1
        LDR R6,[R7]            ;load R6
STOP    B STOP

PROC1   STMDB SP!,{LR,R1-R3}   ;save registers and LR on stack
        MOV R1,#0x34
        MOV R2,#0x45
        MOV R3,#0xDC
        BL PROC2               ;call PROC2
        STR R5,[R7]            ;store R5
        LDMIA SP!,{R1-R3,LR}   ;retrieve registers from stack
        MOV PC,LR              ;copy LR to PC

PROC2   ADD R4,R2,R1           ;the nested procedure PROC2
        ADD R5,R4,R3
        MOV PC,LR              ;go back to PROC1
        END
```

Example 10.19 shows the instance of a nested procedure and the use of the stack. The example is in tune with the sequence outlined by Figure 10.20. Nothing very important is achieved by the program, But it shows how any nested procedure can be written. PROC1 changes the contents of registers R1, R2 and R3, but since they have already been saved on the stack by the STMDB instruction, their contents can be retrieved while returning to the main program.

PROC2 adds the new contents of R1, R2 and R3, and returns. In PROC1, the sum in R5 is stored in the memory location pointed by R7. Later, in the main program, this content is loaded to R6.

Example 10.20

Write a program which arranges numbers (stored in readonly memory) in ascending order, and place them in the R/W memory.

```
          AREA NUM,DATA,READONLY
          ARRAY DCD 2,7,4,5,11,17,3,15,8,6,9,19,10,23,20
          AREA COD,CODE
ENTRY
          LDR R0, = ARRAY        ;load ARRAY to R0
          LDMIA R0,{R1-R10}      ;load 10 numbers to R1 to R10
          MOV SP,#0x40000000     ;location of R/W memory
          STMIA SP,{R1-R10}      ;store the 10 numbers
          ADD SP,#40
          ADD R0,#40
          LDMIA R0,{R1-R5}       ;load next set of 5 numbers
          STMIA SP,{R1-R5}       ;store them
          MOV SP,#0x40000000     ;address of Read-write memory
          MOV R1,#0              ;Initialize counter R1 to zero
          MOV R3,SP
          LOOP1 MOV R2,#0        ;outer loop, counter from one end
          MOV R4,SP
          LOOP2 CMP R2,#14
          BEQ OUTER              ;branch to OUTER
          ADD R2,#1              ;increment the counter
          LDR R0,[R4]            ;stored as 4 bytes
                                 ;hence a jump of 4
          LDR R5,[R4,#4]
          ADD R4,#4
          CMP R0,R5              ;comparing nearby values
          BLT LOOP2
          MOV R6,R0
          MOV R0,R5              ;swapping and storing them
          MOV R5,R6
          STR R5,[R4]
          SUB R4,#4
          STR R0,[R4]
          ADD R4,#4
          B LOOP2
OUTER
          ADD R1,#1
          CMP R1,#15
          BNE LOOP1
```

```
STOP    B STOP
        END
```

This program uses the concept of 'bubble sorting'. First the 15 numbers stored in the variable ARRAY are loaded, in two different steps. After that, two loops are taken in which the first loop uses a counter from 0 to 14. The first loop traverses from one end of the array to other, and the second loop is used to compare nearby values and swap them according to which value is lesser than the other. Hence, by each iteration of the outer loop, the lowest value in the array slowly comes to the first element, and this process continues.

Conclusion

With this, we come to the end of our discussion on the architecture and assembly language programming for ARM. There are a few more instructions, pseudo instructions and directives that haven't been dealt with, but that can be learned by referring to a book fully dedicated to this processor.

KEY POINTS OF THIS CHAPTER

- ARM is the most popular of the 32-bit processors in the market.
- ARM, the company does not fabricate chips—instead it sells the design as 'Intellectual Property'.
- The ARM family consists of members ARM7, 9, 10, 11 and Cortex versions.
- Lower power dissipation and good computational capability are the chief attributes of the ARM processor.
- The processor has a large set of registers, and operates in seven modes.
- It can be programmed in assembly and one of the IDEs available is Keil RVDK.
- The barrel shifter in the ALU has a lot of relevance, as it simplifies computations.
- ARM can use data processing instructions conditionally, by suffixing S to it.
- There is a link register (LR) for simplifying procedure calls.
- It has a special mechanism for handling immediate data which is bigger than 8 bits.
- It has multiple register load and store instructions .
- Stacks are needed when nested procedures come .

QUESTIONS

1. List out the important features that make ARM ideal for embedded applications.
2. Name two aspects in the design of ARM which has made it a processor with 'low-power dissipation'.
3. What is the use of a cache for any processor?

4. What does the acronym ISA mean to you?
5. What are the advantages and disadvantages of 'pipelining'?
6. What is the penalty incurred in the case of 'unaligned' data?
7. How is 'rotation to the left' achieved in ARM?
8. How is the instruction LDR different from the pseudo instruction LDR?
9. Why is it that compare instructions don't need the suffix 'S'?
10. How is the write back operator used in the 'pre-indexed' mode of addressing?

EXERCISES

1 Write instructions for the following, without using any CISC type instruction.
   a) move into R7, a byte multiplied by 8
   b) move into R6, a word multiplied by 17
   c) move into R5, a number divided by 8
2. What do the following instructions mean and what is accomplished?
   a) ANDEQ R1, R2, R4
   b) ADDHI R2, R4, R2
   c) MOVAL R7, R5
   d) SUBME R1, R2, R7
   e) CMP R1, R2
   f) TEST R1, R3
   g) MOVGT R2, R5
   h) ADDLT R5, R6, R7
3. Write assembly language programs for the following.
   a) Find the factorial of any number (the factorial should fit in a 32-bit register)
   b) Do division using repeated subtraction
   c) Find the sum of the first 100 natural numbers. Save the result in memory
   d) Find the sum of 10 numbers stored in Readonly memory the result should be in Read/write memory
   e) Store 15 numbers in memory and arrange them in
      - descending order
      - ascending order
   f) Write a program with a procedure call using
      - without using stack
      - using stack

11 ARM—THE WORLD'S MOST POPULAR 32-BIT EMBEDDED PROCESSOR

PART II – PERIPHERAL PROGRAMMING OF ARM MCU USING C

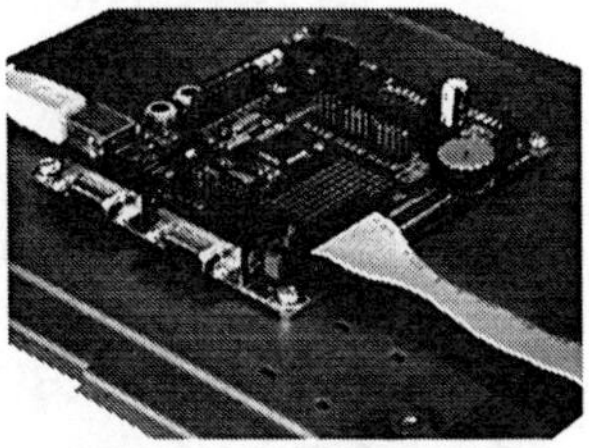

In this chapter, you will learn

- The internal architecture of LPC 2148, a typical and popular ARM7 MCU
- The buses in this MCU
- The list of peripherals inside the chip
- The memory map of the peripherals
- The programming of the GPIO
- The programming of the timer unit
- The programming of the PWM unit
- How to use the serial communication unit
- The internal structure of ARM9 and Cortex–M3

Introduction

In the previous chapter, we made a thorough study of the core of ARM. The study was not exhaustive; there are many more aspects, features and advancements introduced with each new version of the architecture. The trick is to learn more as and when you need to use the chip for a specific application. What we did in the last chapter was assembly language programming, so that the computational capabilities of ARM, the processor, are clear.

In this chapter, we take a different approach—we examine ARM as a microcontroller aka SoC (System on Chip). The application domain of this processor is in the embedded field. A number of peripherals are added inside the chip so as to make it a 'microcontroller' and as the peripherals increase in number and complexity, it is sufficient to make a complete system. The number and kind of peripherals needed depends on the application, but there are some peripherals which are more or less a standard feature in

Chapter-opening image: An ARM7 LPC2146 board.

most microcontrollers, examples are timers/counters, serial ports, general purpose I/O, etc. More advanced MCUs have I2C, SPI, RTC, PWM units and so on as internal peripherals. MCUs with more advanced cores have peripherals such as LCD controllers, CAN controllers, USB controllers, etc.

In this chapter, we will take a look at the internal block diagram and internal buses of some ARM MCUs, study a few selected peripherals and write a few programs for these peripherals.

All the programs presented in the chapter have been tested and verified on the LPC 2148 MCU using the Keil RVDK.

ARM MCUs are manufactured by different firms and so there are a variety of MCUs and peripheral boards in the market. We choose a few popular ones for our study.

We start with an MCU based on the ARM 7 core—NXP founded by Philips (the company) has manufactured and popularized the LPC 21xx series which is a set of MCUs with sufficient peripherals for a moderately complex application. Let's begin with the LPC 2148 MCU which is one member of the LPC 214x series, the other members being LPC 2141/42/44/46. Data sheets and user manuals for the series are available which give all the fine details of each and every peripheral. Some important details of the chip are given in Appendix D. The data sheet is available in the site www.pearson/lyladas/.

11.1 | Block Diagram

Figure 11.1a is the photograph of an MCB 2140 board, with the LPC 2148 and other interfaces marked on it. Figure 11.1b shows the internal block diagram of LPC 2148. Let's take a look at this block diagram, and discuss some aspects of this very complex chip.

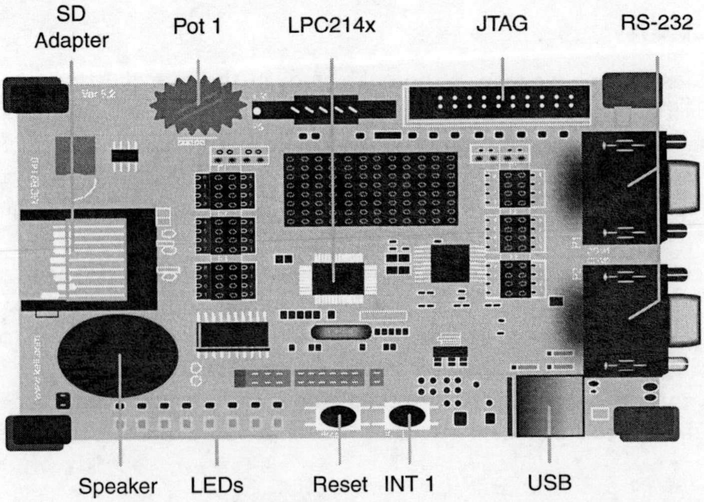

Figure 11.1a | Photograph of the LPC 2148 MCU on a MCB 2140 development board

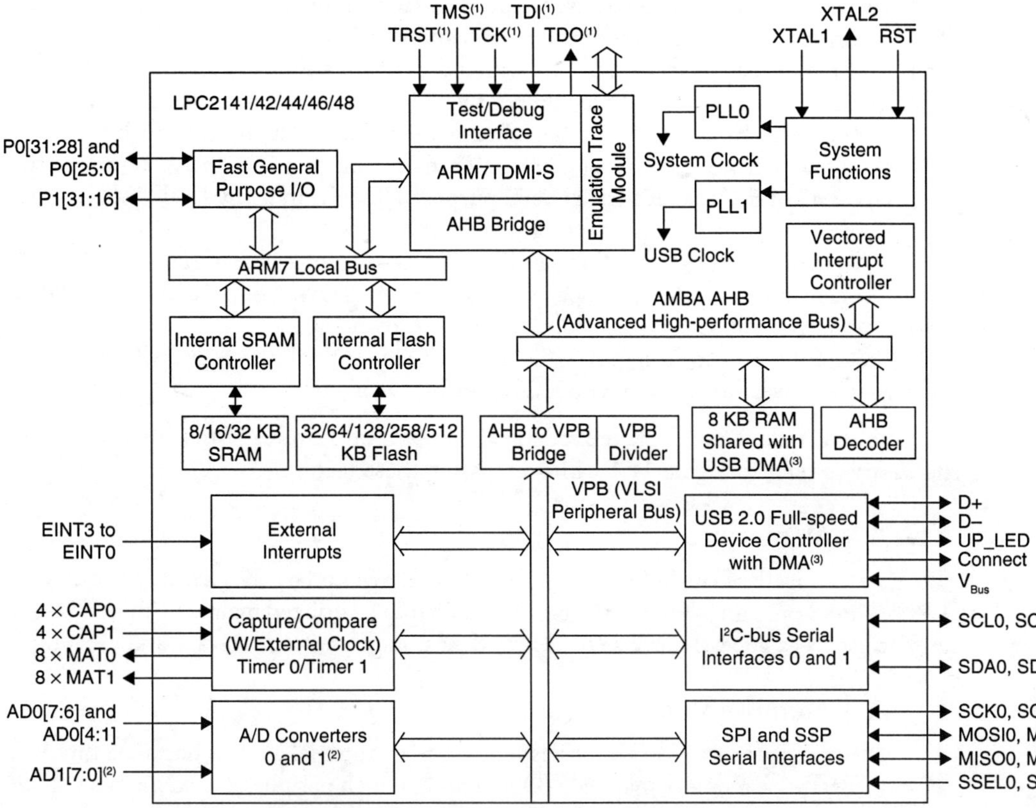

Figure 11.1b | Internal block diagram of LPC 2148

11.2 | Features of the LPC 214x Family

The different functional blocks in this SoC family (which includes the 2141/42/44/48) are shown in Figure 11.1, and let us attempt to understand some of them. The details of the ARM7 core was thoroughly covered in the previous chapter and so it is not repeated here.

The main features provided by this family are listed below. It is not necessary to go through the list comprehensively right now. Once the most important features are studied in detail, this list may be used as a back reference.

i) The core ARM 7TDMI-S in a tiny LQFP64 package
ii) 8 KB to 40 KB of on-chip static RAM
iii) 32 KB to 512 KB of on-chip flash memory
iv) 128-bit wide interface/accelerator enables high-speed 60 MHz operation
v) USB 2.0 Full-speed compliant device controller with 2 KB of endpoint RAM. In addition, provides 8 KB of on-chip RAM accessible to USB by DMA
i) 10-bit ADCs provide a total of 6/14 analog inputs
ii) Single 10-bit DAC provides variable analog output (LPC2142/44/46/48 only)

iii) Two 32-bit timers/external event counters (with four capture and four compare channels each), PWM unit (six outputs) and watchdog
iv) Low power real-time clock (RTC) with independent power and 32 kHz clock input
v) Multiple serial interfaces including two UARTs (16C550), two fast I2C-bus (400 Kbit/s), SPI and SSP with buffering and variable data length capabilities
vi) Vectored interrupt controller (VIC) with configurable priorities and vector addresses
vii) Up to 45 of 5 V tolerant fast general purpose I/O pins in a tiny LQFP64 package
viii) Up to 21 external interrupt pins available
ix) 60 MHz maximum CPU clock available from programmable on-chip PLL
x) On-chip integrated oscillator operates with an external crystal from 1 MHz to 25 MHz
xi) Power saving modes include idle and power-down
xii) Processor wake-up from power-down mode via external interrupt or BOD
xiii) Single power supply chip with POR and BOD circuits

We now take a more detailed look at the important features of the chip. It may be necessary to refer to Figure 11.1 while discussing these features.

11.2.1 | Memory

The memory available includes up to 40KB static RAM and 512KB flash. In the case of LPC2146/48 only, an 8 KB SRAM block intended to be utilized mainly by the USB, can also be used as a general purpose RAM for data storage and code storage and execution.

11.2.2 | Memory Map

The total memory space is 4 GB (corresponding to an internal address bus of 32 bits, i.e., 2^{32} = 4GB). It is a 'memory mapped I/O' system in which peripherals and memory share the same memory space.

11.2.3 | System Functions

The system functions include a crystal oscillator and a PLL (Phase Locked Loop). The oscillator frequency can be in the range of 10 to 25 MHz which can be multiplied up, to get a system frequency up to 60 MHz using the PLL. There is also the possibility of changing the system frequency dynamically (using the PLL). When the system is idling, the frequency can be scaled down to reduce power dissipation.

11.2.3.1 | *Reset*

There are two ways of resetting—a hard reset using the active low reset pin and a soft reset on account of the watchdog timer. In either case, the reset vector is the address 0x0. Reset also starts a timer designated as the 'wake up timer'. This timer ensures that a minimum delay is allowed for the system to stabilize and then only code execution is allowed to start.

11.2.3.2 | *Power Control*

One of the main features of ARM processors are their low-power dissipation Besides a basic low power design in the technological aspects, low power modes are also available: they are the idle mode and power-down mode.

Idle Mode

In the idle mode, instruction execution is suspended until either a reset or interrupt occurs.

But peripheral functions can continue operation and may generate interrupts to cause the processor to resume execution. The idle mode eliminates power used by the processor, memory systems, related controllers and internal buses.

Power-down Mode

In the power-down mode, the oscillator is shut down and the chip receives no internal clocks.

This mode can be terminated and normal operation resumed by either a reset or certain specific interrupts that are able to function without clocks. Since all dynamic operation of the chip is suspended, this mode reduces chip power consumption to almost zero.

11.2.4 | Internal Buses

11.2.4.1 | *AMBA*

'Advanced Microcontroller Bus Architecture' or AMBA is a standard defined by ARM in 1996, for on-chip buses in its SoC designs. In Figure 11.2, a number of buses can be seen which form part of AMBA. The figure shows the bus structure re-drawn to emphasize the functionality of the constituent buses of the AMBA standard. Three buses with different protocols and speeds have been defined, for catering to the different kinds of components present inside the chip.

The fastest bus is the system or the local bus, which connects the processor core with memory, as memory accesses have to be very fast. In the LPC 21xx series, serious thought has been given to the idea of speeding up special peripherals, and as such, a GPIO (General Purpose I/O) block is also connected to the local bus. This permits peripherals connected to this fast GPIO block, to use the high speed of the local bus.

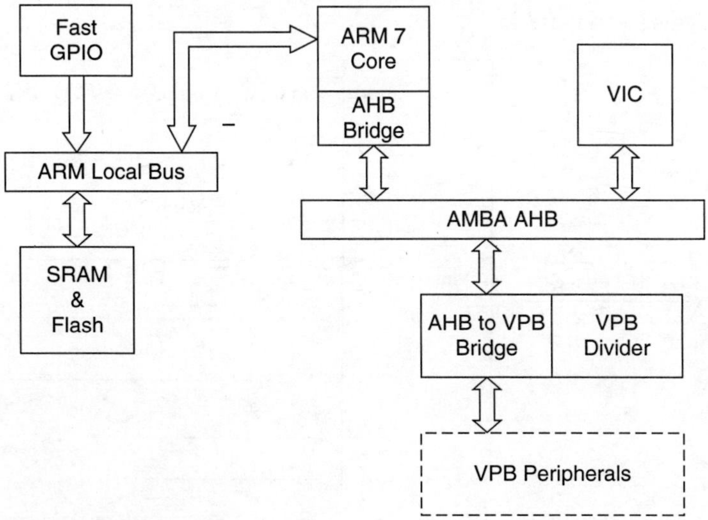

Figure 11.2 | The internal bus structure

Along with the core, an AHB bridge is seen which defines the high speed AMBA's **'Advanced High Performance Bus'** facilitating the 'Vectored Interrupt Controller'. The third bus is the VPB bus which stands for **VLSI Peripheral Bus**; there is a bridge which communicates between the low speed VPB bus and the higher speed AHB bus. The VPB is the one that connects to all the peripherals of the LPC 214x SoC.

11.2.4.2 | *The VPB Bus and Divider*

Figure 11.2 shows that there is a bridge that interfaces between the VPB and the AHB. There is also a VPB divider. This is a register whose settings can be used to divide the output frequency of the PLL so as to get a reduced clock frequency (1/2 to ¼) for the VPB peripherals which need to operate at a frequency lower than the processor. The processor clock is designated as CCLK, while the peripheral clock is called PCLK. On reset, PCLK is ¼ of CCLK.

11.2.5 | Memory Accelerator Module

Instructions are executed by fetching them from memory. In a typical MCU, program code, that is, the instructions are stored in flash memory. Flash memory is rather slow, which means that program execution gets slowed down, and so the very purpose of having a high speed processor gets defeated. The easiest solution is to have a shadow RAM as in PCs, where the content of flash is copied to RAM (on startup) so that this (fast) RAM is accessed rather than the slow flash. Such a solution can be thought out for our MCU as well, but here we are thinking of 'on-chip' flash and RAM which are limited in size—so copying program code to on-chip RAM is not a feasible solution. Another possibility is to have a fast cache on the chip, but that will need additional hardware and increase the complexity of the chip.

The final solution to this has come in the form of a module named the 'memory accelerator module'. In simple terms, the memory accelerator module (MAM) attempts to have the next ARM instruction that will be needed, in its latches in time to prevent CPU fetch stalls (see Figure 11.3).

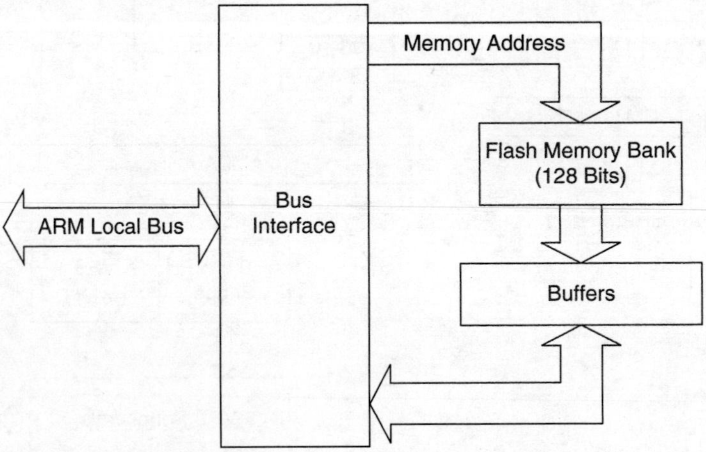

Figure 11.3 | Simplified view of the memory accelerator module

In this setup, the flash memory is arranged as a bank of 128 bits such that each access to flash allows 128 bits to be accessed. This will require the flash to be organized as 4 memory modules, where each module will have a bandwidth of 32 bits and thus effectively 128 bits at a time. In practice, the speed of memory will not get multiplied by 4, but it improves the speed over the case of having a flash memory and 32 bits access, at a time. All the extra hardware to get this done is in the memory controller, i.e., the MAM.

11.3 | Peripherals

Section 11.2 contains a list of the peripherals available in this chip. Each of the peripherals has addresses and the peripherals use the memory mapped I/O scheme of addressing– this means that both memory and I/O share the same address space. The total address space is from 0x0 to 0xFFFFFFF, i.e., a 4GB space.

The memory map of the system is as shown in Figure 11.4.

What are the notable features in this memory map?

i) The 512KB of flash (non-volatile) memory has an address starting from 0x0.
ii) The 40 KB of static RAM has the addresses starting at 0x4000 0000.
iii) There is a RAM allotted for 'USB with DMA' applications.
iv) The peripherals attached to the AHB have addresses from 0xF000 0000.
v) The peripherals attached to the lower speed VPB bus have the addresses from 0xE000 0000.

VPB Peripherals Next, we will learn how to use the peripherals of the chip. Each peripheral has a number of special function registers (SFRs) associated with it, and each SFR has a specific address. To use a specific peripheral in the way we want, the associated registers should be written with the appropriate bits.

11.3.1 | GPIO (General Purpose I/O)

If you look at the pin configuration, which is available in the manual of the chip, it will be seen that most pins have more than one function. There are three to four designations for each pin, and which of these is valid at a time depends on how the pin has been 'programmed' using the pinselect block.

There are two general purpose 32-bit ports, P0 and P1, with restrictions and features as explained below. These are the pins to which external peripherals can be connected.

11.3.1.1 | *Port 0*

Port 0 is a 32-bit I/O port with individual direction controls for each bit. 28 pins of the Port 0 can be used as general purpose bi-directional digital I/Os, while P0.31 provides digital output functions only. The operation of Port 0 pins depends upon the pin function selected via the pin connect block. Pins P0.24, P0.26 and P0.27 are 'reserved' and not available for use.

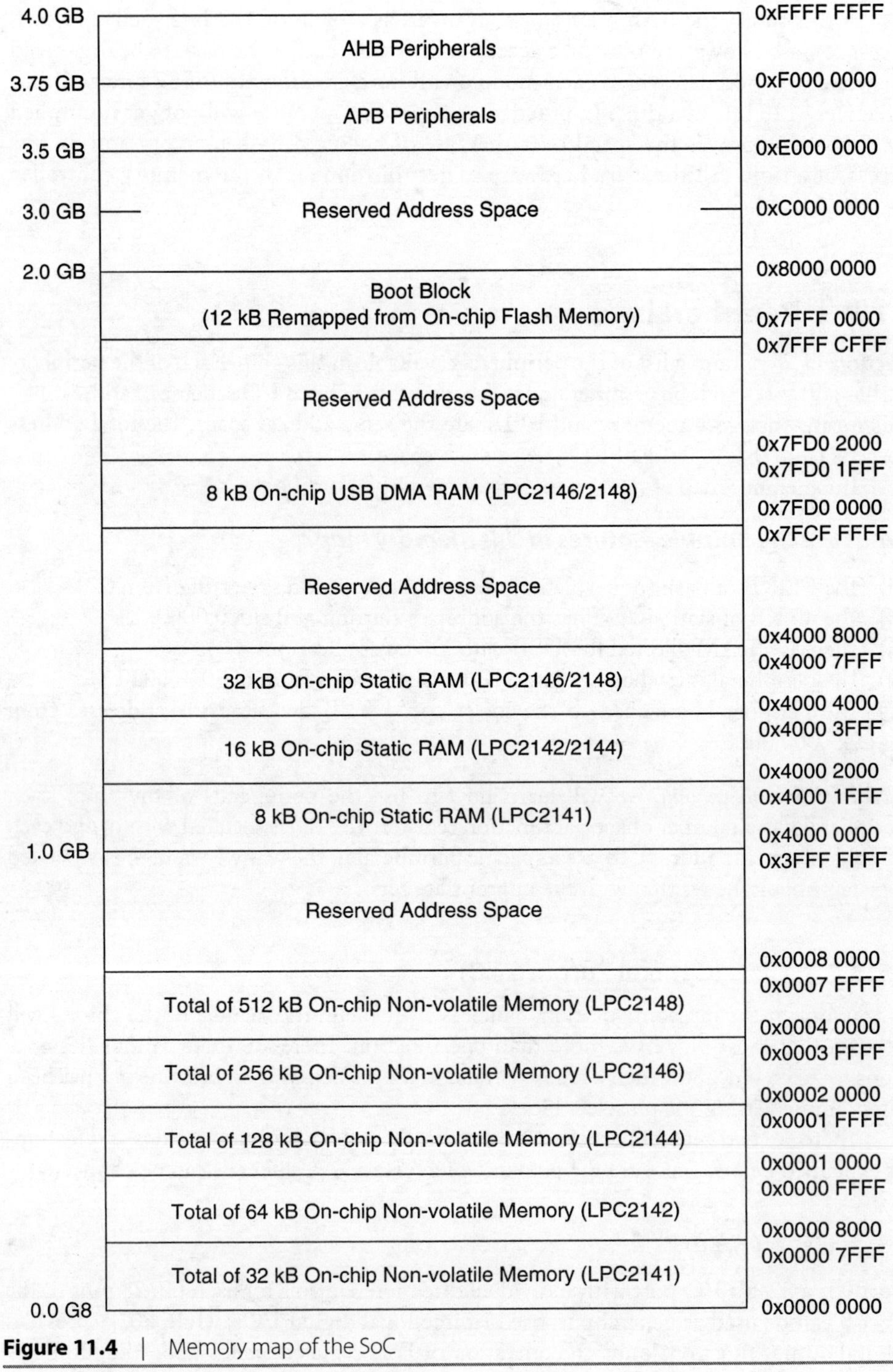

Figure 11.4 | Memory map of the SoC

11.3.1.2 | *Port 1*

Port 1 is a 32-bit bi-directional I/O port with individual direction controls for each bit. The operation of Port 1 pins depends upon the pin function selected via the corresponding pin connect block. Pins 0 through 15 are not available. Out of the remaining pins from 16 to 31, the pins 16 to 25 are 'reserved'. In effect, only very few pins of Port 1 are available and they can be used for GPIO only, because other pin functions are used for JTAG.

11.3.1.3 | *Pin Connect Block*

The purpose of this is to configure the pins to the desired functions. This acts like a multiplexer.

Let's look at it this way. Each pin of the chip has a maximum of four functions. To select one specific function for a pin, a multiplexer with two select pins, is necessary. The select pins function is provided by the bits of the PINSEL registers.

Only three 'pinselect' registers are available and needed too, because only Port 0 and half of Port 1 are available as peripheral pins. See Appendix D for details of the PINSELECT registers. As a sample, pin selection for Pin No 29, P0.5 has been shown in Table 11.1, and the selection of the pin using the Pinselect logic is shown in Figure 11.5

Table 11.1 | Pinselect Logic for P0.5

Bits of PINSEL Register	Port Pin No	Value of PINSEL Bits	Function Selected	Reset Value
11: 10	P0.5	00	GPIO	0
		01	MISO0 (SPI0)	
		10	Match 0.1 (Timer 0)	
		11	AD0.7	

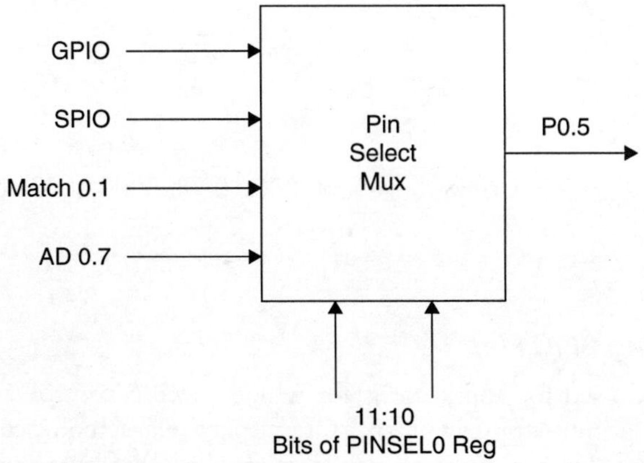

Figure 11.5 | Pinselect mux of pin P0.5

Table 11.2 | Generalization of the Function of the Pinselect Register Bits

PINSEL0 and PINSEL1	Function
00	Primary function, typically GPIO
01	First alternate function
10	Second alternate function
11	Reserved

What Table 11.1 displays is that the bits 11 and 10 of PINSEL0 register should be 00 if pin No:29 (P0.5) is to be a GPIO, 01 if it is to be used as SPIO, 10 if it is to be a match pin for Timer 0 and 11, if it is used as AD0.7.

In general, pin selection is as shown in Table 11.2

The description of a pin shows that it can have 4 possible functions. The logic on the select pins decides the functionality of the port pin. For any pin, the bit configuration '00' of the corresponding pinselect register bits program the pin to act as a general purpose I/O pin. **By default, on reset, all port pins act as GPIO pins.**

Example 11.1

Use the PINSEL0 register for activating PWM1, PWM2 and PWM3 outputs, which are at pins P0.0, P0.1 and P0.7, respectively.

Solution

Refer Appendix D, which gives the complete listing of the pin functions of the chip. PWM output pins are listed as the second alternate function of any port pin. The corresponding bits of PINSEL0 register for activating these port pins to act as PWM should be given a logic of 10. See Table 11.3.

Table 11.3

Output Function	Output Pin	Bits of PINSEL0 Register
PWM1	P0.0	1:0
PWM2	P0.7	15:14
PWM3	P0.1	3:2

Thus, PINSEL0 register has the value -0000 0000 0000 0000 1000 0000 0000 1010 = 0x0000800A

11.3.1.4 | *Using GPIO Pins*

These pins can be used for applications for which specific 'controllers/drivers' are not available inside the chip—for driving an LCD display, relays, motor controls, ON/OFF functions and so on. Four registers are available for this. They are shown in Figure 11.6 and listed as follows:

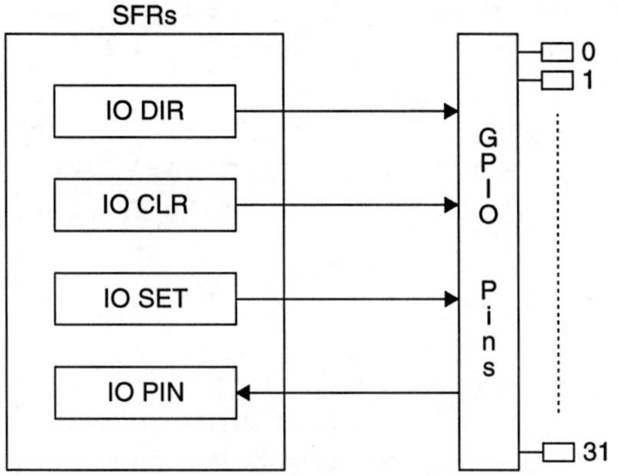

Figure 11.6 | Registers pertaining to one GPIO pin

i) **IODIR (IO Direction register):** The bit setting of this register decides whether a pin is to be an input(0) or output(1).
ii) **IOSET (IO Set register):** This register is used to set the output pins of the chip. To make a pin to be '1', the corresponding bit in the register is to be '1'. Writing zeros have no effect.
iii) **IOCLR (IO Clear register):** To make an output pin to have a '0' value, i.e., to clear it. The corresponding bit in this register has to be a '1'. Writing zeros have no effect.
iv) **IOPIN (IO Pin register):** From this register, the value of the corresponding pin can be read, irrespective of whether the pin is an input or output pin.

Example 11.2

Let us attempt to make the lower 16 GPIO pins to be output pins.

Then IODIR = 0x0000 FFFF

To send zeros to all these pins, IOCLR = 0x0000 FFFF.

Now, check the pin values in the register IOPIN, which will have the lower 16 bits to be 0.

Now, if these pins are to be set, IOSET = 0x0000 FFFF

Check the pin values in the register IOPIN, which will have the lower 16 bits to be 1.

Example 11.3

Generate an asymmetric al square wave at the lowest four pins of Port0.

```
#include <LPC214X.H>
int main(void)
{
      unsigned int x;
      for(;;)
      {
        IODIR0 = 0xFFFFFFFF;       //Make all pins as outputs
        for(x = 0;x<4;x++)         //Delay for the high part
```

```
        IOSET0 = 0x0000000F;   //Set the lowest four bits
                                 P0.0 to P0.3

      for(x = 0;x<12;x++)      //Delay for the low part
        IOCLR0 = 0x0000000F;   //Clear the lowest four
                                 bits P0.0 to P0.3
    }
}
```

Example 11.3 is a simple example to show the function of the four GPIO registers corresponding to Port 0. The use of Embedded C has been discussed in Chapter 9 and is not repeated here. This program sets and clears the lowest four bits of Port 0 at a certain asymmetric rate (note that the delays are different).

Figure 11.7 shows the output at Port pins 0.0 to 0.3, viewed in the logic analyser which is available in the 'simulator' of Keil RVDK. LEDs may be connected to the port pins and, then they will go ON and OFF at the rate determined by the delay. In the program, the OFF time is three times the ON time.

The contents of the registers in Figure 11.6 can be observed in the 'peripherals' part of the simulator.

Example 11.4

```
#include <LPC214x.h>
void wait(void)
{
      int d;
      for (d = 0; d < 1000000; d++);
}
int main(void)
{
      IODIR1 = 0x00010000;          //Make P1.16 an output
      while(1)
      {
            IOSET1 = 1<<16;         //P1.16 = 1
            wait();
            wait();
            IOCLR1 = 1<<16;         //P1.16 = 0
            wait();
      }
}
```

Example 11.4 is another program which generates a square wave at the GPIO. Here only one pin is chosen and it is P1.16. That pin is made 1 by loading '1' on the LSB of IOPIN1 register and shifting it left 16 times. Next the IOPIN1 register is cleared. This program generates a square wave at P1.16. The delay is created in a function named wait

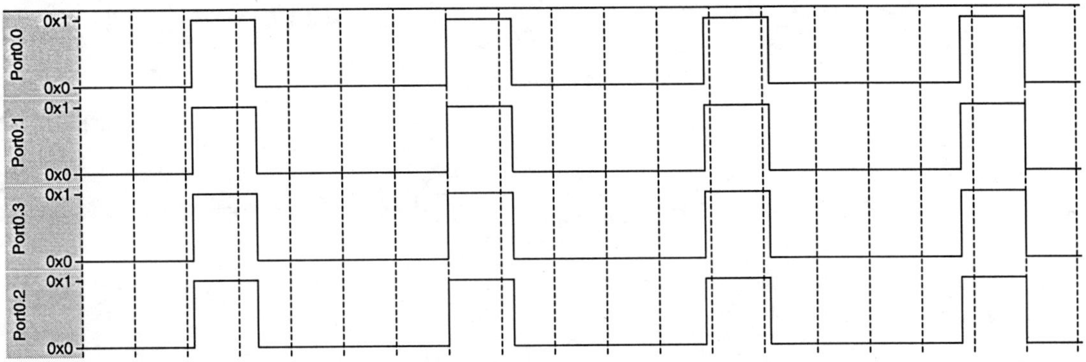

Figure 11.7 | Waveforms at the lowest four pins of Port0 for Example 11.3

and this function is then called. To make the ON time to be twice the OFF time, the wait function is called twice when the pin is '1'.

Note For both the above programs we haven't used the 'PINSELECT BLOCK' for choosing the pin function. This is not necessary, because on reset, all port pins behave as GPIO itself.

11.3.2 | The Timer Unit

Next let's study the timers/counters of LPC 2148. A timer and a counter are functionally equivalent, except that a timer uses the PCLK for its timing, while a counter uses an external source. This means that a counter is used to count external events via the capture inputs. A counter is also called a 'capture timer'.

Here, we discuss the timer function alone. There are two such units—Timer 0 and Timer 1. There are a number of registers associated with timer operations. Let's discuss the functionality of each of them for Timer 0 which we notate as T0. When we use Timer 1, we use similar registers, but with the notation T1.

The first step in timer operation is to load a number into what is called a 'match register'. Then a timer count register is started. This register keeps incrementing for each PCLK cycle or a lower rate pre-scaled cycle. When the content of this timer count register becomes equal to the value in the match register, i.e., a match occurs, the delay that occurs from the starting time can be used for our 'timing'. Figure 11.8 illustrates the idea of timing done using the timer unit.

Now, let us understand the special function registers associated with Timer 0. Keep in mind that a similar set of registers exist for Timer 1 as well.

11.3.2.1 | *Important SFRs of Timer 0*

Timer Count Register–T0TC

This is a 32-bit register, which gives it a range of counting from 0 to 0xFFFF FFFF and then wraps back to the value 0x0000 0000. This register is incremented on every tick of the clock (i.e. PCLK), if the prescale counter is made 0 (the use of the prescaler will be explained subsequently).

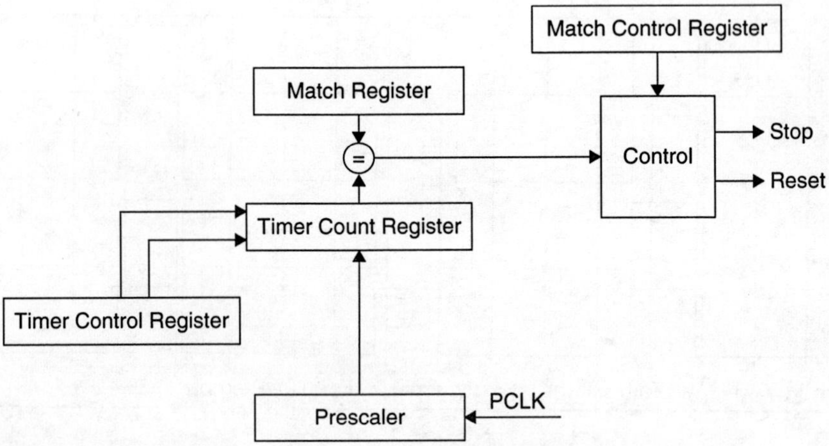

Figure 11.8 | Simplified block diagram illustrating the operation of the timer unit

Timer Control Register–T0TCR

This is an 8-bit register (Figure 11.9) in which only the lowest two bits need be used.

Bit 0–E: This bit is the Enable bit. When this bit is '1', the counter is enabled and starts. Then, the count in T0TC is incremented for every cycle of PCLK (if prescaling is not used).

Bit 1–R: This bit is the Reset bit. When '1', the counter is reset on the next positive edge of PCLK.

Match Registers (MR0 to MR3)

There are four 32-bit match registers available: MR0 to MR3. For the operation of one timer, one of the match registers may be sufficient and is used by loading a number into it.

During timer operation, the timer count register starts incrementing, and at some time, its count 'matches' with the number in the match register. When this match occurs, some action can be programmed to be done by 'configuring' the bits of the 'match control register'.

Match Control Register–T0MCR

This is a 16-bit register (Figure 11.10) used to specify the event to occur when the match occurs.

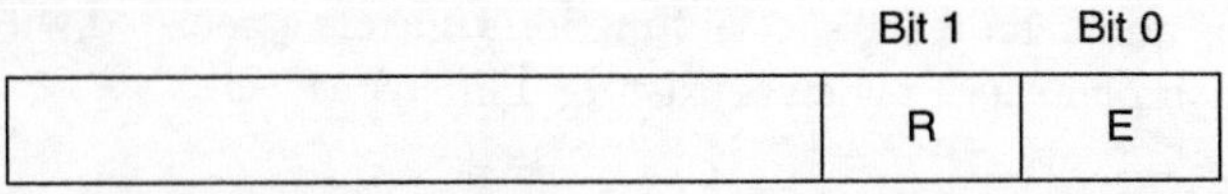

Figure 11.9 | The important bits of T0TCR

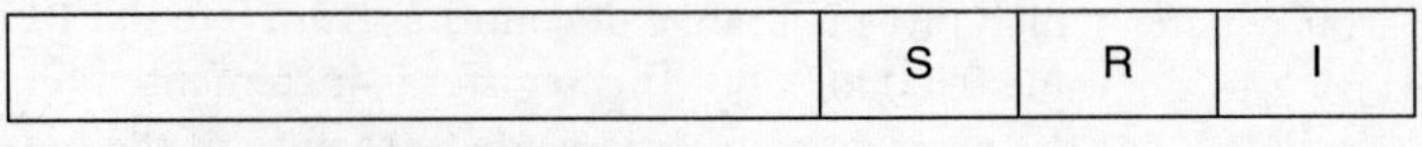

Figure 11.10 | Important bits of T0MCR

The lowest three bits are for controlling the operations related to the Match register 0. The next three are for MR1, MR2 and MR3, in that order. Remember that there are four match registers.

See the bits of the register related to Timer operation.

Bit 0–I: When '1', an interrupt is activated when match occurs
When '0', the interrupt is disabled.

Bit 1–R: When '1', the Timer count register is reset when match occurs
When '0', this feature is disabled.

Bit 2–S: When '1', the timer count (T0TC) and the pre-scale counter will be stopped when match occurs, also the Enable bit of the T0TCR is made '0'.

Let's make a simple timer for which the steps are as listed in the following section.

11.3.2.2 | *Timer Operation*

i) Load a number in a match register.
ii) Start the timer by enabling the 'E' bit in T0TCR.
iii) The timer count register (T0TC) starts incrementing for every tick of the peripheral clock PCLK (no prescaling is done).
iv) When the content of the T0TC equals the value in the match register, timing is said to have occurred.
v) One of many possibilities can be made to occur when this happens.
vi) The possibilities are to reset the timer count register, stop the timer, or generate an interrupt. This 'setting' is done in the T0MCR register.

Now let's design a very simple timer for generating a symmetric square wave at P1.16, using Timer 0.

Example 11.5

```
#include <LPC214x.h>
void wait(void);
int main(void)
{
      T0MR0 = 0x000000FF;           //Load a number in the
                                      match register
      T0MCR = 4;;                   //Stop when match occurs
      while(1)
      {
            IODIR1 = 0x00010000;    //Make P1.16 an output
                                      pin
            IOSET1 = 1<<16;         //P1.16 = 1
            wait();                 //Call the wait function
            IOCLR1 = 1<<16;         //P1.16 = 0
            wait();
      }
}
```

```
void wait(void)                          //The wait function

        T0TCR = 1;                       //Start the timer
        while(!(T0TC == T0MR0));         //Until T0TC = MR0
        T0TCR = 2;                       //Reset the counter
        T0TC = 0;                        //Make the timer count
                                           reg = 0

}
```

Explanation of Example 11.5

i) In the program, Timer 0 is used. The timer match control register (T0MCR) is written with value 04, which indicates that the timer count register is to stop when match is obtained. The match register (of Timer 0) is loaded with the number 0xFF. These two steps are the initial conditions.
ii) The pin P1.16 is chosen as the output pin. It is set to '1' initially and then the wait function (which creates a delay) is called. After one call of the wait function, P1.16 is made '0' and the wait function is called again. This causes a symmetric square wave to be obtained at this pin. Since this is a GPIO pin, it is understandable that the other pin may also be used here to get the same functionality.
iii) The wait function creates the needed delay. The timer control register (T0TCR) is loaded with the value '1', so as to enable (start) the timer counter so that the timer register T0TC increments for every clock tick of PCLK. When TOTC increments to the value 0xFF (stored in T0MR0), 'match' occurs. At this point of time, the counting is stopped, and the timer counter register is cleared.
iv) This whole sequence of events is repeated to get a continuous square wave.

11.3.2.3 | *Calculation of Timer Output Frequency*

Now let's calculate the frequency of the square wave generated. The above program has been tested on a board in which the peripheral clock (PCLK) is obtained by dividing the crystal frequency of 60MHz by 4 (using VPB register settings) Thus PCLK is 15 MHz now, and it has a period of T = 0.067 μsecs.

The function 'wait' creates a delay which is equal to 256 periods of PCLK (as T0MR0 = 0xFF), i.e., 256 x0.067 μsecs. = 17.075 μsecs. This delay is half the period of the square wave generated at P1.16. The period of the signal is thus 34μsecs and the frequency = 29.4 KHZ.

Next, change the match counter value to 0xFFFF. A similar calculation gives a frequency of 114 Hz. Figure 11.11(a) and (b) show the square waves generated for match values of 0xFF with T = 34 μS and 0xFFFF with T = 8.7msecs.

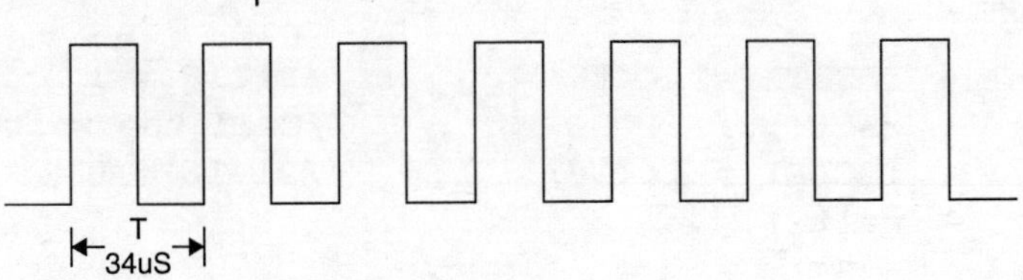

Fig 11.11a

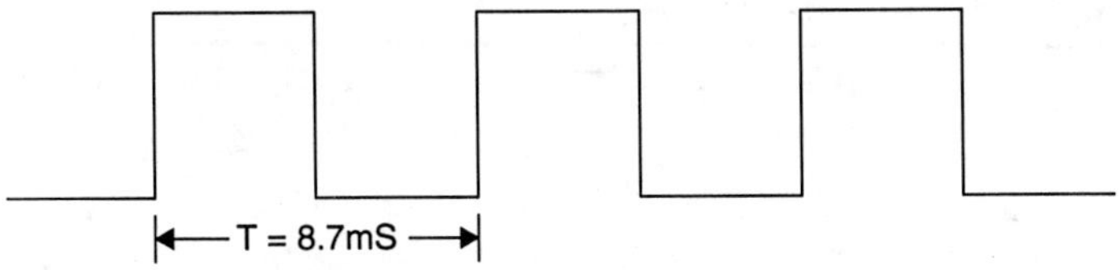

Fig 11.11b | Square wave from the timer with a) T0MR0 = 0xFF b) T0MR0 = 0xFFFF

11.3.2.4 | *Using the Pre-scaler*

To get a lower frequency output, there is the facility of using the prescale counter. There are two registers associated with 'prescaling'—the prescale counter and the prescale register.

The prescale counter increments for every PCLK, and when it counts up to the value in the prescale counter (T0PR), it allows the timer counter (T0TC) to increment its value by 1. This causes the T0TC to increment on every PCLK when PR = 0, every 2 PCLKs when PR = 1, every three PCLKs when T0PR = 2, every four PCLKs when T0PR = 3 and so on. In effect, load a number into T0PR, which will cause the output frequency to get divided.

The mechanism is like this.

i) Say the prescale counter contains a number 2. When the timer is started, the presclae counter decrements to 1 and only when it reaches 0, the timer count in T0TC is incremented by 1. Thus, the timer count is incremented once only when the prescale counter counts down from 2 to 0, i.e., in 3 clock periods of PCLK.
ii) This continues as long as the timer is enabled.
iii) For the case in Example 11.6, not using a prescale value amount to loading a number 0 into the prescale counter.

See Example 11.6, which shows the part of Example 11.5 which has been modified by the additional instruction T0PR = 1. We now get a timer frequency of 57 Hz, for T0MR0 = 0xFFFF. Without prescaling, the frequency would have been 114Hz.

Example 11.6

```
#include <LPC214x.h>
void wait(void);
int main(void)
{
      T0MR0 = 0x000FFFF;          //Load a number in the
                                    match register

      T0MCR = 4;
      T0PR = 1;                   //Stop when TC is reached
      while(1)
            ............................
            ............................
}
```

Table 11.4a | T0MR0 = 0xFFFF

T0PR	Division Factor	Frequency at P1.16
0	None	114 Hz
1	2	57 Hz
2	3	38Hz
4	5	22.8 Hz

Table 11.4b | MR0 = 0xFF

T0PR	Division Factor	Frequency at P1.16
0	None	29.4 K Hz
1	2	14.7 KHz
2	3	9.8 KHz
3	4	7.35 KHz

Tables 11.4(a) and Table 11.4(b) show the frequencies generated by Example 11.6 for match values of 0xFF and 0xFFFF, for different pre-scaling factors.

11.3.3 | Timer 0 in the Interupt Mode

Next, we write a program for Timer 0 to operate it in the interrupt mode. Example 11.7 is such a program. To understand how the interrupt mechanism is incorporated here, a brief introduction to the interrupt structure of the chip is necessary.

The discussion starts on a general note, and converges to the use of Timer 0, in the interrupt mode. This will help us to use any other peripherals in the interrupt mode by using the associated registers of the peripherals and its related interrupt registers. You can, for instance, try to write programs for PWM and UARTs in the interrupt mode. Example 11.7 is a program for generating a square wave at pin P1.16. The calculation for the frequency at this pin is the same as presented in Section 11.3.2.3.

As part of the mechanism of understanding interrupts clearly, instructions of this program are referred to, at every step of the forthcoming discussion.

Example 11.7

```
#include <LPC214x.h>
unsigned int x = 0;
__irq void Timer 0_ISR (void)
{
        x ^= 1;
        if(x)
                IOSET1 = 1<<16;         //P1.16 = 1
        else
                IOCLR1 = 1<<16;         //P1.16 = 0
```

```
        T0IR          = 0x01;          //Clear match 0 interrupt
        VICVectAddr   = 0x00000000;    //End of interrupt
}
int main(void)
{
        IODIR1 = 0x00FF0000;           //P1.16.23 defined as
                                         Outputs
        IOCLR1 = 0x00FF0000;           //P1.16 = 0
        T0TCR  = 0x00000000;           //Disable timer counter0
        T0PR   = 0x00000002;           //Prescaler value
        T0MCR  = 0x00000003;           //Enable interrupt and
                                         reset on match
        T0MR0  = 0xFF;                 // MR0 value
        VICVectAddr4 = (unsigned)Timer 0_ISR;
                                       //Set the timer ISR
                                         vector address
        VICVectCntl4 = 0x00000024;     //Set channel
        VICIntEnable = 0x00000         //Enable the TIMER-0
                                         interrupt
        T0TCR = 0x00000001;            //Enable timer counter0
        for(;;);
}
```

11.3.3.1 | *Vectored Interrupt Controller (VIC)*

See Figure 11.1 in which the block diagram of LPC 2148 has a VIC as a peripheral. It is the VIC that manages all the interrupts of the ARM core (IRQs and FIQs) as well as interrupt requests from the peripherals.

Features of VIC

- 32 interrupt request inputs
- 16 vectored IRQ interrupts
- 16 priority levels dynamically assigned to interrupt requests
- Software interrupt generation

The vectored interrupt controller (VIC) takes 32 interrupt request inputs and programmably assigns them into 3 categories: FIQ, vectored IRQ and non-vectored IRQ. The programmable assignment scheme means that priorities of interrupts from various peripherals can be dynamically assigned and adjusted.

Fast interrupt requests (FIQ) have the highest priority. If more than one request is assigned to FIQ, the VIC ORs the requests to produce the FIQ signal to the ARM processor.

Vectored IRQs have the middle priority, but only 16 of the 32 requests can be assigned to this category. Any of the 32 requests can be assigned to any of the 16 vectored IRQ slots, among which slot 0 has the highest priority and slot 15 has the lowest. Non-vectored IRQs have the lowest priority.

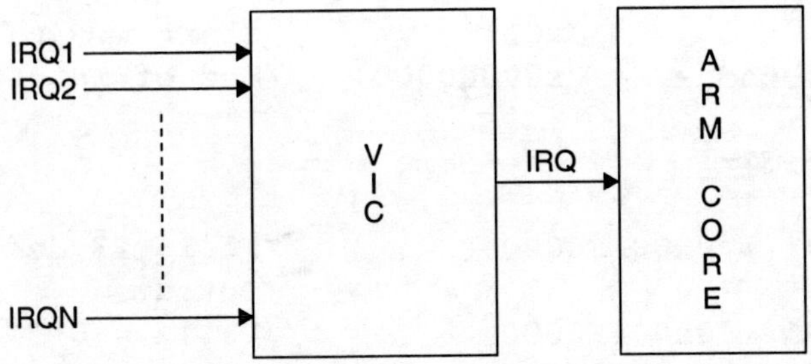

Figure 11.12 | The VIC's connection to ARM

The VIC ORs the requests from all the vectored and non-vectored IRQs to produce the IRQ signal to the ARM processor. Figure 11.12 illustrates this.

11.3.3.2 | *Interrupt Sources for the VIC*

Each peripheral device has one interrupt line connected to the VIC, but may have several internal interrupt flags. Individual interrupt flags may also represent more than one interrupt source. (See Table 11.5 which shows a part of the list of interrupt sources for the VIC) For example, Timer 0 is assigned a number '4' and has eight interrupt flags, i.e., interrupts are generated for matching due to four match registers and four capture registers, but the VIC associates Timer 0 with just one interrupt line.

Next, we will discuss briefly some of the important registers associated with the VIC.

11.3.3.3 | *Interrupt Enable Register (VIC Interrupt Enable)*

This is a read/write accessible register. This register controls the decision of which of the 32 interrupt requests and software interrupts are allowed to contribute to the generation of an interrupt.

Table 11.5 | Connection of Interrupt Sources to the VIC

Block	Flag(s)	No
WDT	Watchdog Interrupt (WDINT)	0
–	Reserved for Software Interrupts only	1
ARM Core	Embedded ICE, DbgCommRx	2
ARM Core	Embedded ICE, DbgCommTx	3
TIMER 0	Match 0 – 3 (MR0, MR1, MR2, MR3) Capture 0 – 3 (CR0, CR1, CR1, CR3)	4
TIMER 1	Match 0 – 3 (MR0, MR1, MR2, MR3) Capture 0 – 3 (CR0, CR1, CR1, CR3)	5
UART0	Rx Line Status (RLS) Transmit Holding Register Empty (THRE) Rx Data Available (RDA) Character Time-out Indicator (CTI)	6

Table 11.6 | Bit Definitions in the VIC Interrupt Enable Register for a Few Interrupt Sources

Bit	7	6	5	4	3	2	1	0
Symbol	UART 1	UART 0	TIMER 1	TIMER 0	ARM Core 1	ARM Core 0	–	WDT
Access	R/W	R/W	R/W	R/W	R/W	R/W	R/W	R/W

For example, see Table. 11.6 which is part of this registers' bit definitions for the interrupting peripherals. It seen that the bit position for Timer 0 is '4' and hence bit 4 of this register is to be set if Timer 0 is to be operated in the interrupt mode.

Example 11.7 uses the instruction

VIC Int Enable = 0x00000010; //Enable the TIMER-0 interrupt by making bit = 4

11.3.3.4 | *Vector Control Register (VIC Vect Cntl0-15)*

Only 6 bits of this register are to be used. They are lower 6 ones.

Thus, in Example 11.7 where Timer 0 is allotted the number 4, as in Table 11.7.

VICVectCntl4 = 0x00000024; //Set channel

11.3.3.5 | *Vector Address Registers (VIC Vect Add)*

These are read/write accessible registers. These registers hold the addresses of the interrupt service routines (ISRs) for the vectored IRQ slots.

In Example 11.7,

VICVectAddr4 = (unsigned)T0isr; //Set the timer ISR vector address

This instruction indicates that the ISR is at address 'T0isr' which is the starting location (address) of the ISR.

11.3.3.6 | *Using Timer 0 in the Interrupt Mode*

Besides adding the instructions corresponding to the VIC, the timer program for operating in the interrupt mode has some minor differences from its operation in the status check mode.

First of all, T0MCR is to be programmed to generate an interrupt on match. Hence the 0th bit of this register is to be set (Section11.2.2.1). So in Example 11.7,

TOMCR = 3; // generate interrupt and reset T0TC.

Table 11.7 | The lower 6 Bits of the Vector Control Register

Bits	Function	As Used in Example 11.7
4:0	The number of the selected interrupt	00100
5	Enable the chosen IRQ slot	1

11.3.3.7 | *Timer 0 Interrupt Register (TOIR)*

This register has bits for each of the matching states of MR0 to MR3. When a timer operates in the interrupt mode and a match occurs, an interrupt is generated, and the corresponding flag bit in T0IR is set. To 'clear' it, a '1' must be written into this same register. Then only will the interrupt flag be 'reset'.

Table 11.8 shows that the corresponding bit for Timer 0 in T0IR is bit 0. In Example 11.7, the instruction used is

T0IR = 0x01; // Clear match 0 interrupt

Steps of the Program (Example 11.7)

i) The operation of the timer is quite straight forward. When a match occurs, Timer 0 interrupt is activated.
ii) Program control goes the ISR T0isr, in which pin P1.16 is complemented, and the timer flag is reset.
iii) To signal the end of the interrupt, a dummy write to the VICVectAddr register is also done.
iv) Then, control goes back to the main program.

11.3.4 | The Pulse Width Modulation Unit

Pulse width modulation is basically a scene in which it is possible to control the period and duty cycle of a square wave. The duty cycle is defined as the ratio of the ON time of the pulse and the period, expressed as a %.

See Figure 11.13 which shows pulse trains at 25, 50 and 75% duty cycles.

Table 11.8 | Bits of TOIR for the Interrupts Generated When 'Match' Occurs

Bit	Symbol	Description
0	MR0 Interrupt	Interrupt flag for match channel 0.
1	MR1 Interrupt	Interrupt flag for match channel 1.
2	MR2 Interrupt	Interrupt flag for match channel 2.
3	MR3 Interrupt	Interrupt flag for match channel 3.

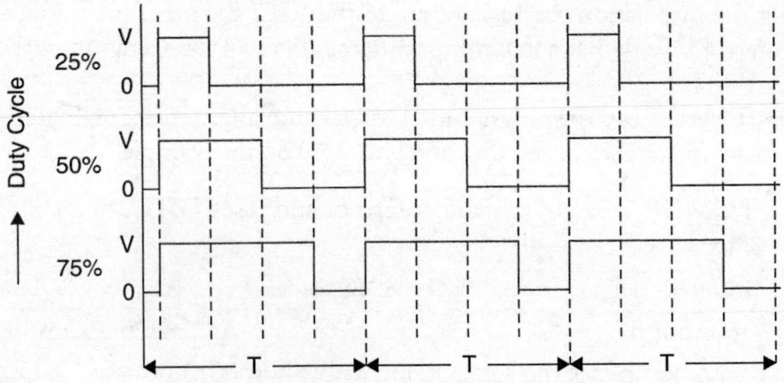

Figure 11.13 | Pulse trains at different duty cycles

When MCUs have dedicated PWM units, they have registers which can be programmed for the required frequency of the pulse train as well as the duty cycle. For this ARM7 MCU, the PWM unit works similar to a timer unit. **Also if its PWM mode is not enabled, it works only as a timer.**

There is a free running timer register (PWMTC), which matches to any of the seven 32-bit match registers (MR0 to MR6). The match register values are continuously compared to the count in the timer register which increments (with pre-scaler) when started. One match register (MR0) is dedicated to the action of deciding the frequency of the pulse train, by resetting the count upon match. The other match registers can be used for fixing the duty cycle. Thus there are six PWM output pins from which PWM signals can be simultaneously generated.

11.3.4.1 | *Single Edge Controlled PWM*

Here only the falling edge of a pulse train is controlled. Two match registers can be used to provide a single edge controlled PWM output. One match register (PWMMR0) controls the PWM cycle rate, by resetting the count upon match. The other match register controls the PWM edge position, and thus it controls the duty cycle.

Multiple PWMs can be obtained by using more than one match register. For example, refer to Figure 11.14. For this, PWMMR0 is used for specifying T. MR1 to MR6, MR3 or MR4 can be used for specifying P. Note that for all pulse trains generated at different PWM output pins, the pulse repetition rate is the same, as it is decided by the number in the match register MR0, which is common to all the pulse trains.

Rules for single edge controlled PWM outputs:

i) All single edge controlled PWM outputs go high at the beginning of a PWM cycle.
ii) Each PWM output will go low when its match value (in MR1 to MR6) is reached. If no match occurs (i.e. the match value is greater than the PWM rate), the PWM output remains continuously high.
iii) When a match occurs, actions can be triggered automatically. The possible actions are to generate an interrupt, reset the PWM timer counter, or stop the timer. Actions are controlled by the settings in the PWMMCR register.

Note In double edge controlled PWM, both the rising and falling edges of the PWM waveform are controlled by the match registers. We limit the discussion here, to just the single edge controlled PWM.

11.3.4.2 | *Calculating the Frequency*

MR0 is used to decide the frequency of the pulse train. As calculated for the timer (Section 11.3.2.3) PCLK (15 MHz) has a period of 0.067μsecs. If PWMMR0 is loaded

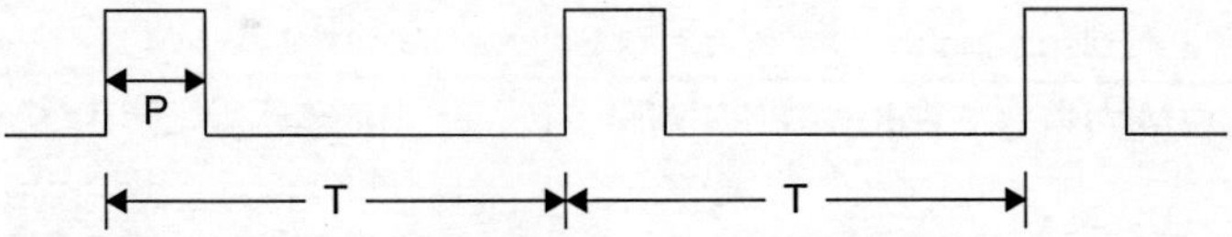

Figure 11.14 | A pulse train showing the period T and ON time P

Table 11.9 | Calculation of the Period of the Pulse for Different Values of PWMMR0

N in PWMMR0	T(μsecs)	Frequency (f) = 1/T
0xFF	256 x 0.067 = 17.152	58.3 KHz
0x 5E	95 x0.067 = 6.365	157 KHz
0x FFFF	65,536 x0.067 = 4390.8	227 Hz

with a number N, it counts from 0 to N. A match occurs after 0.067μsecx (N+1), and this is the period T of the pulse train generated. Refer Table 11.9 for a sample set of calculations.

11.3.4.3 | *Calculating the Duty Cycle*

The duty cycle is the ratio of ON period (P) to the total period T. As per Figure 11.14, it is P/T, expressed as a percentage.

There are six match registers for deciding the pulse ON time. We will consider the simplest case of single edge controlled PWM. Let's use the match register PWMMR3. In this case, when the timer count value matches the value in PWMMR3, the PWM output pin goes low. This will end the high period of the pulse. See Table11.10 for a sample calculations based on the value of MR3, for T = 6.365μsecs.

Example 11.8

Calculate the value of the value to be given in PWMMR0 andPWMMR3 to get a pulse train of period 5 ms and duty cycle of 25%.

Solution

5000 μsecs = (N+1) x.067
(N+1) = 74,626 = 0x12382
The number to be loaded in PWMMR0 is 1 less than this, i.e., it is 12381.
25% duty cycle corresponds to 1.25 msecs
(N1+1) x 0.067 μsecs = 1.25 msecs
Calculating N1 = 18,655
The number to be loaded in PWMMR3 = 18,655 = 0x48DF.

11.2.4.4 | *The PWM Output Pins*

Corresponding to the six match registers, there are six PWM output pins, and they are called the PWM channels. The pins and PWMPCR registers bits for enabling each of them are given in Table 11.11.

Table 11.10 | Calculating the Duty Cycle for Different Values of PWMMR3

N in PWMMR0	Value in PWMMR3	T_{on} (μsecs)	Duty cycle = P/T
0x5E	0xF	1.004 μsec	15.5 %
	0x2E	3.15 μsec	49.4 %

Table 11.11 | List of the PWM Output Channel and Corresponding Port Pin

PWM No	Channel No	Output Pin No
PWM1	1	P0.0
PWM2	2	P0.7
PWM3	3	P0.1
PWM4	4	P0.8
PWM5	5	P0.21
PWM6	6	P0.9

11.3.4.5 | *Control Registers of the PWM Unit*

There are a number of registers for this application, and the usage of each of them can be referred from the manual of the chip. Here, we only discuss a few.

PWMTCR This is the PWM Timer Control Register. This is an 8-bit register. Only the lower 4 bits of this register need to be used (Figure 11.15).

Bit 0–CE: COUNTER ENABLE When '1', the PWM timer counter and Prescale counter are enabled.

Bit 1–CR: COUNTER RESET 'When '1', the above mentioned PWM timer count register and Prescale counter are reset on the next positive going edge of PCLK. They remain reset until this bit is made '1'.

Bit 2: R-Reserved

Bit 3: PE-PWM ENABLE. When '1', the PWM mode is enabled. Otherwise the PWM unit acts as just a timer.

In Example 11.8, PWMTCR = 0x9

PWMPCR This is the PWM Control Register. This is a 16-bit register and is used to enable and select the type of each PWM channel.

This register enables or disables the six PWM outputs, and also chooses between double and single edge control. Bits 0, 1, 7 and 8 and 15 are unused. Table 11.12 shows the state of the bits of PWMPCR for choosing between single and double edge control.

R	PE	R	CR	CE

Figure 11.15 | Important bits of PWMTCR

Table 11.12 | Choosing Between Single and Double Edge Control Using Bits of PWMPCR

Bit No of PWMPCR	When Bit = 0	When Bit = 1
PWMPCR.2	Single edge control for PWM2	Double edge control for PWM2
PWMPCR.3	Single edge control for PWM3	Double edge control for PWM3
PWMPCR.4	Single edge control for PWM4	Double edge control for PWM4
PWMPCR.5	Single edge control for PWM5	Double edge control for PWM5
PWMPCR.6	Single edge control for PWM6	Double edge control for PWM6

Table 11.13 | The Bits of PWMPCR to be Set for Enabling the Output Pins

Enabled by Setting the Register Bit	PWM Output
PWMPCR.9	PWM1
PWMPCR.10	PWM2
PWMPCR.11	PWM3
PWMPCR.12	PWM4
PWMPCR.13	PWM5
PWMPCR.14	PWM6

Refer Table 11.13 which shows the bits of PWMPCR to be 'set' to enable the output pins on which the PWM waveform is to be obtained.

Example 11.9

What should be the value to be entered in the PWMPCR register for the following situations?

i) Single edge control for PWM3
ii) Double edge control for PWM3
iii) Single edge control for PWM1, 2 and 3

Solution

Refer to Tables 11.12 and 11.13.

i) PWM3 output to be enabled. So only bit 11 is to be enabled, and only single edge control is to be used. So PWMPCR = 0x00000800
ii) For double edge control, PWMPCR.3 should be set, and to enable PWM3 output at P0.7, PWMPCR.11 should also be set. This PWMPCR = 0x0000808
iii) Single edge control needs the corresponding bits to be '0'. For enabling the outputs of PWM 1, 2 and 3, bits 9, 10 and 11 should be set. PWMPCR = 0x00000E00;

PWMLER This is the PWM Latch Enable Register. The PWM latch enable register is an 8-bit register used to control the update of the PWM match registers when they are used for PWM generation.

When software writes to the location of a PWM match register while the timer is in PWM mode, the value is held in a shadow register. When a PWM Match 0 event occurs (normally also resetting the timer in PWM mode), the contents of shadow registers will be transferred to the actual match registers if the corresponding bit in the latch enable register has been set. At that point, the new values will take effect and determine the course of the next PWM cycle. Once the transfer of new values has taken place, all bits of the LER are automatically cleared. Until the corresponding bit in the PWMLER is set and a PWM Match 0 event occurs, any new value written to the PWM match registers has no effect on PWM operation.

Reserved	M6	M5	M4	M3	M2	M1	M0

Figure 11.16 | Bits of the PWMLER

Figure 11.16 shows the six bits of the PWMLER register, each bit enabling the latching of, match register 0 (MR0) to Match register 6, when set.

Example 11.10 uses PWMLER = 0x8, corresponding to the enabling of only PWM3 latch.

Example 11.10

```
#include<LPC214x.h>
void PWM_InIt(void)
{
      PINSEL0 | = 0x00000008;   //Enable P0.1 as PWM output
      PWMPR     = 0x00000000;   //No prescaling
      PWMPCR    = 0x00000800;   //PWM 3 single edge control,
                                  output
                                //enabled
      PWMMR0    = 0xFFF;        //Fix up the pulse repletion
                                  rate
      PWMTCR    = 0x00000009;   //Enable PWM mode and PWM
                                  timer
                                //counting
}
int main()
{
      PWM_InIt();
      while(1)
      {
            PWMMR3 = 0x2FE;     //Match value for pulse ON
                                  time
            PWMLER = 0x8;
      }
}
```

Calculating the Duty Cycle

0x2FF	=	767 in decimal
0xFFF	=	4096 in decimal
P	=	767 x.067 μsecs
T	=	4096 x.067 μsec
Duty cycle	=	P/T = 767/4096 = 18.73 %

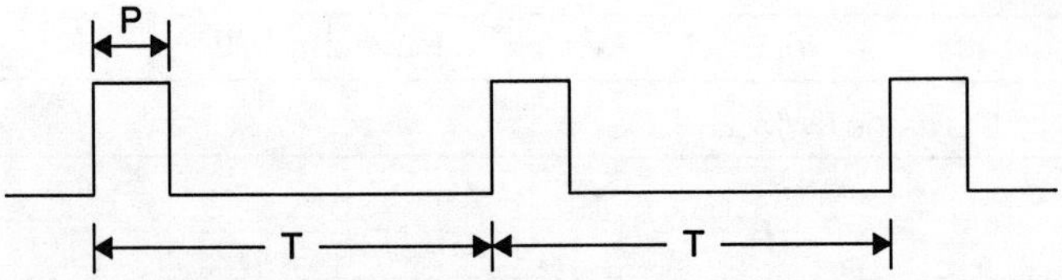

Figure 11.17 | The output waveform obtained from Example 11.10

Next, let's consider the generation of more than one PWM pulse. Example 11.11 is a program which gets PWM outputs from channels 1, 2 and 3. Note that all PWM outputs will occur at the same repetition rate.

Example 11.11

```
#include<LPC214x.h>
void PWM_InIt(void)
{
      PINSEL0 |= 0x0000800A;         //Enable PWM 1,2 and
                                       3 outputs
      PWMPR   = 0x00000001;          //Prescale value = 1
      PWMPCR  = 0x00000E00;          //Pins of PWM 1,2 and
                                       3 enabled
      PWMMR0  = 0xFF;                //Set PWM frequency
      PWMTCR  = 0x00000009;
      PWMMCR  = 0x00000002;          //Reset on PWMMR0
}
int main()
{
      PWM_InIt ();
      while(1)
      {
            PWMMR1 = 0x30;           //Pulse on time at PWM1
                                       channel
            PWMMR2 = 0x50;           //Pulse on time at PWM2
                                       channel
            PWMMR3 = 0x23;           //Pulse on time at PWM1
                                       channel
            PWMLER = 0xE;            //Latch register value
      }
}
```

T = 34.3 μsecs

Figure 11.18 shows the output pins on which the PWM signals are obtained and Figure 11.19 shows the PWM output waveforms. Since there is a prescaling factor of 1, the basic time T (calculated with a count of 0xFF) is multiplied by 2 to get T = 34. 3 μsecs. The pulse ON times are also multiplied by 2 to get values as shown in Table 11.14.

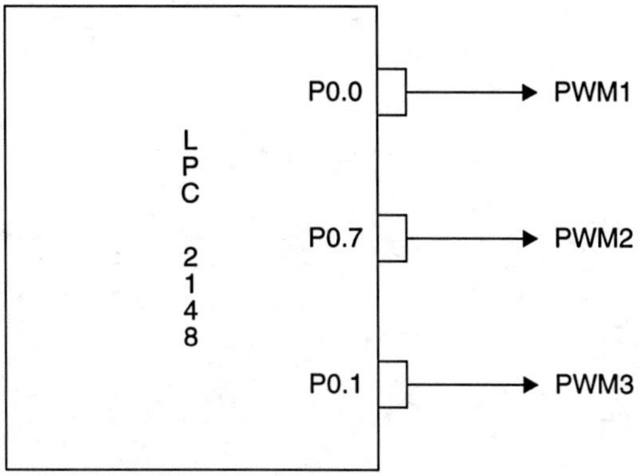

Figure 11.18 | Output pins for the PWM channels

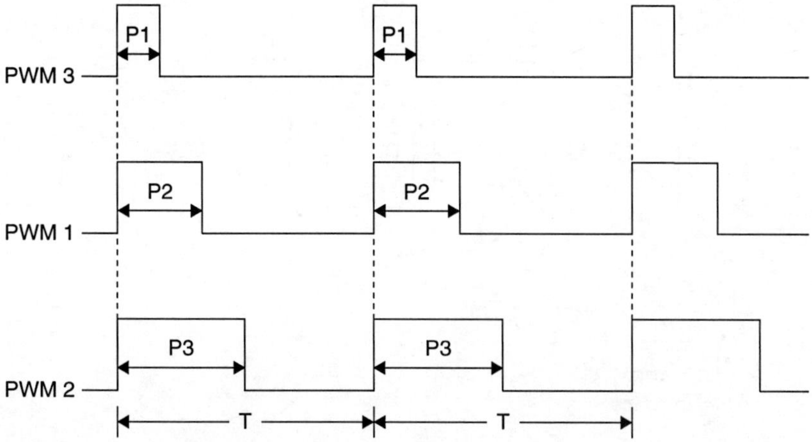

Figure 11.19 | Output waveforms from three PWM channels

Table 11.14 | Values of the Duty Cycles obtained from Example 11.11

Channel	Output Pin	P (ON Time) μ secs	Duty Cycle
PWM1	P0.0	3.38 x2 = 6.76	19.7%
PWM2	P0.7	5.42 x2 = 10.64	31.02%
PWM3	P0.1	2.41 x2 = 4.42	12.8%

11.3.5 | The UART

This chip has two UARTs, namely, UART0 and UART1. To understand the operation of these, first observe the simplified block diagram of the UARTs of the chip. For any of the registers referred herein, you must add the prefix U0 or U1 depending on which unit (UART0 or UART1) is being used. The three important units are the transmitter, receiver and the baud rate generator blocks.

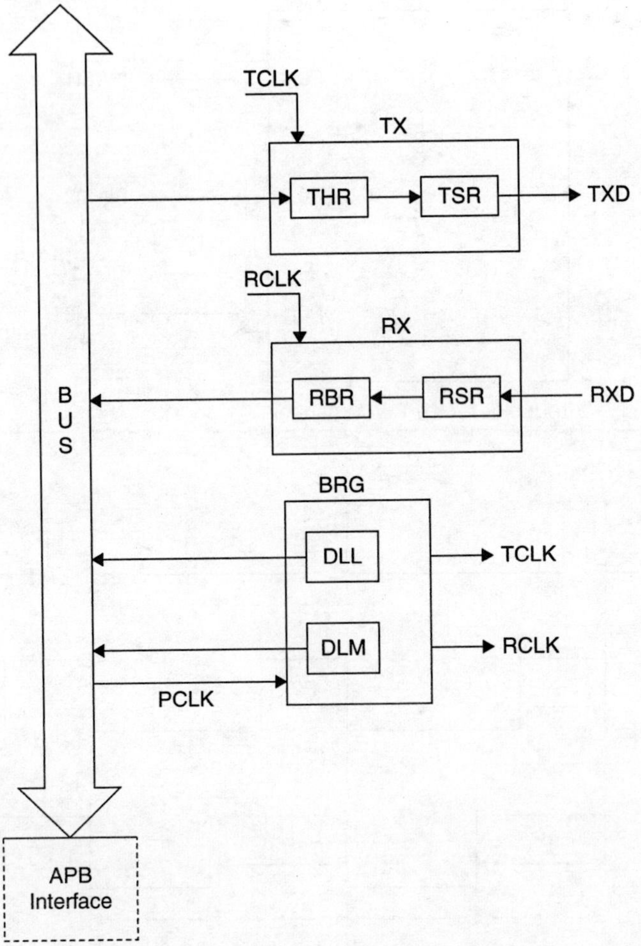

Figure 11.20 | Simplified block diagram of a UART on the chip

11.3.5.1 | *The Transmitter*

Figure 11.20 shows two registers in this block. They are the Transmitter Holding Register (THR) and the Transmitter Shift Register (TSR). When a data byte arrives in the THR, (from the CPU through the bus) it is 'framed' (by adding start and stop bits) and transferred to the TSR and sent out through the TxD pin one bit at a time, by clocking the TSR at the baud decided by the transmitter clock TCLK.

11.3.5.2 | *The Receiver*

There are two registers in the receiver block. They are the Receiver Shift Register (RSR) and the Receiver Buffer Register (RBR). The data received serially through the RxD line (at the baud decided by RCLK), is moved bit by bit into the RSR, and then transferred to the RBR after de-framing. From the RBR, it is copied to the CPU registers through the bus.

11.3.5.3 | *The BAUD Rate Generator (BRG)*

This takes PCLK as input, and generates the baud rates for the transmitter and receiver, by using the numbers in the registers DLL and DLM which function as dividers.

11.3.5.4 | *Registers of UART0*

Let us use UART0 for transferring a character string from the LPC 2148 board to a PC, using the 'hyperterminal', at a baud of 9600. Example 11.12 transmits the string 'sushmita LPC2148'. The string is moved one character at a time to the THR. Between the loading of one character and the next one, a delay is given.

It may be necessary to understand the registers used in the program to gain a full understanding of it. As such, refer to the working of each of the registers (Section 11.3.5.4) while going through the program.

Example 11.12

```
#include "LPC214x.h"
void init(void);
void delay_ms(int);
int main()
{
      int i;
      unsigned char c[] = "sushmita LPC2148 \n ";
                                    //Send data by writing to U0THR
      init();
      for(;;)
      {
            for(i = 0;i<=17;i++)
            {
                  U0THR = c[i];
                  while((U0LSR && 0x20));
                              //Check status of one bit
                                of U0LSR
                  delay_ms(250);
            }
      }
}
void init()
{
      PINSEL0 = 0x05;
      U0FCR   = 0x07;          //Enable and clear FIFOs
      U0LCR   = 0x83;          //8-N-1, enable divisors
      U0DLL   = 0x62;          //9600 baud
      U0DLM   = 0x00;
      U0LCR   = 0x03;          //8-N-1, disable divisors
}
```

```
void delay_ms(int x)
{
	int a,b;
	for(a = 0;a<x;a++)
	{
		for(b = 0;b<3000;b++);
	}
}
```

Pinselect Register (PINSEL0)

This register has been discussed earlier. In this context, only the pin selection for the TxD and RxD pins of UART0 are referred.

Table 11.15 shows that P0.0 and P0.1 are the relevant pins, PINSEL0 register selects pins P0.0 as TxD and P0.1 as RxD, by writing PINSEL0 = 0x5.

UART0 Transmit Holding Register (U0THR)

This is an 8-bit register and part of the transmit buffer, in fact, it is the topmost byte of this buffer, and new characters are to be loaded into this register for being transmitted. The data to be transmitted is written into this 'write only' register. In Example 11.12, the characters to be transmitted are loaded into this register one byte at a time, with a delay.

UART0 Divisor Latch Registers (U0DLL and U0DLM)

The UART0 divisor Latch is part of the UART0 Fractional Baud Rate Generator and holds the value used to divide the clock supplied by the fractional prescaler in order to produce the baud rate clock, which must be 16x the desired baud rate. The U0DLL and U0DLM registers together form a 16-bit divisor where U0DLL contains the lower 8 bits of the divisor and U0DLM contains the higher 8 bits of the divisor.

Example 11.12 uses U0DLL = 0x62 and U0DLM = 0x00 to get a baud rate of 9600.

Table 11.15 | Relevant Bits of the PINSEL0 Register

Bits	Port Pin	Value	Function
1:0	P0.0	00	GPIO
		01	TxD (UART0)
		10	PWM1
		11	Reserved
3:2	P0.1	00	GPIO
		01	RxD (UART0)
		10	PWM3
		11	EINT0

The calculation for these values is as follows

$$UART0_{boudrate} = \frac{PCLK}{16\times(256\times U0DLM + U0DLL)} \times \frac{MulVal}{(MulVal + DivAddVall}$$

In our case, PCLK = 15 MHz

With U0DLM = 0 and U0DLL = 0x62 (98 in decimal notation), the calculation with the above formula gives the baud rate to be 9566.32, i.e., 9600 (approx)

UART0 FIFO Control Registers (U0FCR)

This is an 8-bit register Figure 11.21 in which the important bits are as explained.

Bit 0: E: This bit must be set for enabling the Tx and Rx FIFOs

Bit 1: Rx FIFO Reset: This must be set, to clear all bytes in UART0 Rx FIFO and reset the pointer logic. This bit is self-clearing.

Bit 2: Tx FIFO Reset: This must be set to clear all bytes in UART0 Tx FIFO and reset the pointer logic. This bit is self-clearing.

Bits 7 and 6: Rx trigger level: These two bits determine how many receiver FIFO characters must be written before an interrupt is activated.

We have chosen 00.

UART0 Line Control Register (U0LCR)

The U0LCR is an 8-bit register which determines the format of the data character that is to be transmitted or received.

The bits actively used here are

i) Bits 1: 0 These two bits have been chosen to be '11' to indicate 8-bit character length
ii) Bit 2: This is made '0' to select one stop bit
iii) Bit 7: This is the Divisor Latch Access Bit (DLAB) and is set, to enable the use of the divisor latch
iv) Other bits of this register pertain to parity and break control. These have been disabled by making these bits to be '0',

Thus we have U0LCR = 1000 0011 = 0x83

UART0 Line Status Register (U0LSR)

The U0LSR is a read-only register that provides status information regarding the UART0 TX and RX blocks.

In Example 11.10, only the 5th bit of this register is used. The 5th bit shows a '1' when the transmitter holding register (U0THR) is empty. Only if the register is empty can the next byte be sent for transmission. To confirm this, U0LSR is ANDed with 0x20, and the next character is sent only after this status bit is confirmed to be high.

T (Bit 7 and 6)	Reserved (Bits 3 to 5)	Tx R (Bit 2)	Rx R (Bit 1)	E (Bit 0)

Figure 11.21 | Bits of U0FCR

With this, we conclude our discussion of serial communication. For more details of the registers used and the interrupt mode of transmission, do refer to the user manual of LPC2148.

11.3.6 | The SSP Unit

This unit performs serial communication using the SPI protocol (Refer Section 5.2.2). Appendix I contains a program which interfaces an SD card to LPC 2148 using the SSP unit. It may be necessary to refer to the manual of the chip, and gain an understanding of the registers of the SSP unit, to get a clear understanding of the interfacing program. Section 19.2 discusses a complete product developed using LPC 2148 MCU.

With this, our discussion of a typical ARM7 MCU ends. Note that the one that we have used is only one among the numerous versions of ARM7 available in the market. But a basic understanding of this chip, peripherals and programming will help in understanding any other ARM7 MCU chip.

Next we will take a look at typical ARM9 and Cortex MCUs. Going beyond the periphery of these is beyond the scope of this book. We will look at them, from a block diagram point of view, just to observe their complexity and power.

11.4 | ARM 9

The ARM9 core is a more advanced member of the ARM family (compared to ARM7). It has a 5 stage pipeline and operates at a frequency range of approximately double that of ARM7. Many ARM9 cores have DSP instructions and thus are 'Enhanced' ARM9E processors. Because the core is so powerful, it is used for more complex operations and an MCU which is based on ARM9, typically has more peripherals than an ARM7 based MCU.

Here we will take a look at a particular ARM9 board developed by NXP; it is contains an MCU of the LPC 29xx series. The user manual describes the features of this board in this way:

'The LPC 29xx combine an 125 MHz ARM968E-S CPU core, Full Speed USB 2.0 host and device (LPC 2927/29 only), CAN and LIN, 56 KB SRAM, up to 768 KB flash memory, external memory interface, three 10-bit ADCs, and multiple serial and parallel interfaces in a single chip'.

It is obvious that this is a very powerful chip with many more peripherals than the ARM7 MCU that we have just studied. Figure 11.22 shows the internal block diagram of the chip, in which you can observe its advanced features and peripheral structure.

11.5 | ARM Cortex-M3

To complete our discussion, let us look at a cortex-based MCU as well. The LPC 17xx series is an MCU series with ARM cortex M3 as its core. The following paragraphs quoted from the user manual, illustrate its main features, which are also evident from the block diagram of Figure 11.23.

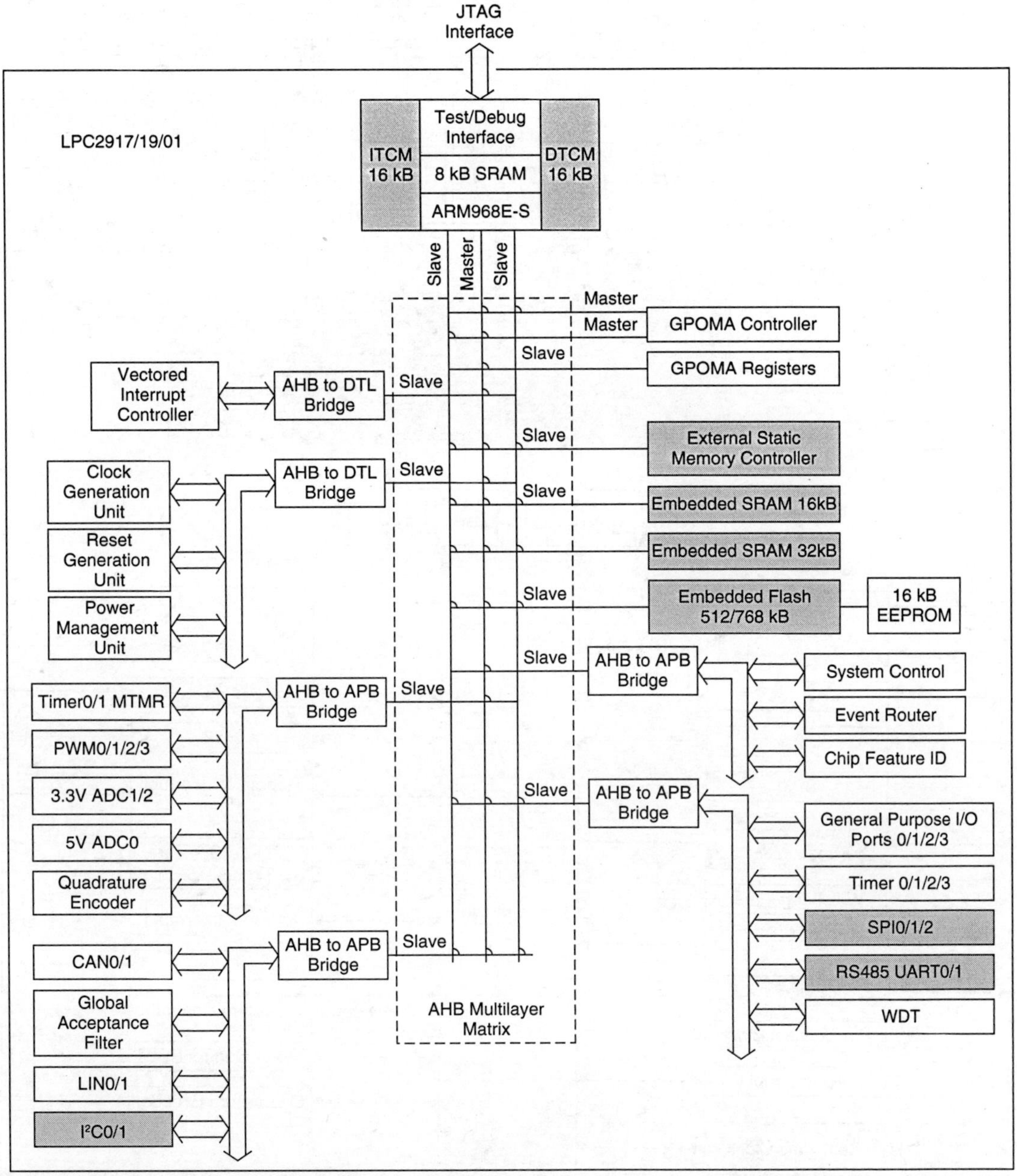

Figure 11.22 | Internal block diagram of the LPC 29xx ARM9 MCU

The LPC 17xx is an ARM Cortex-M3 based microcontroller for embedded applications requiring a high level of integration and low-power dissipation. The ARM Cortex-M3 is a next generation core that offers system enhancements such as modernized debug features and a higher level of support block integration.

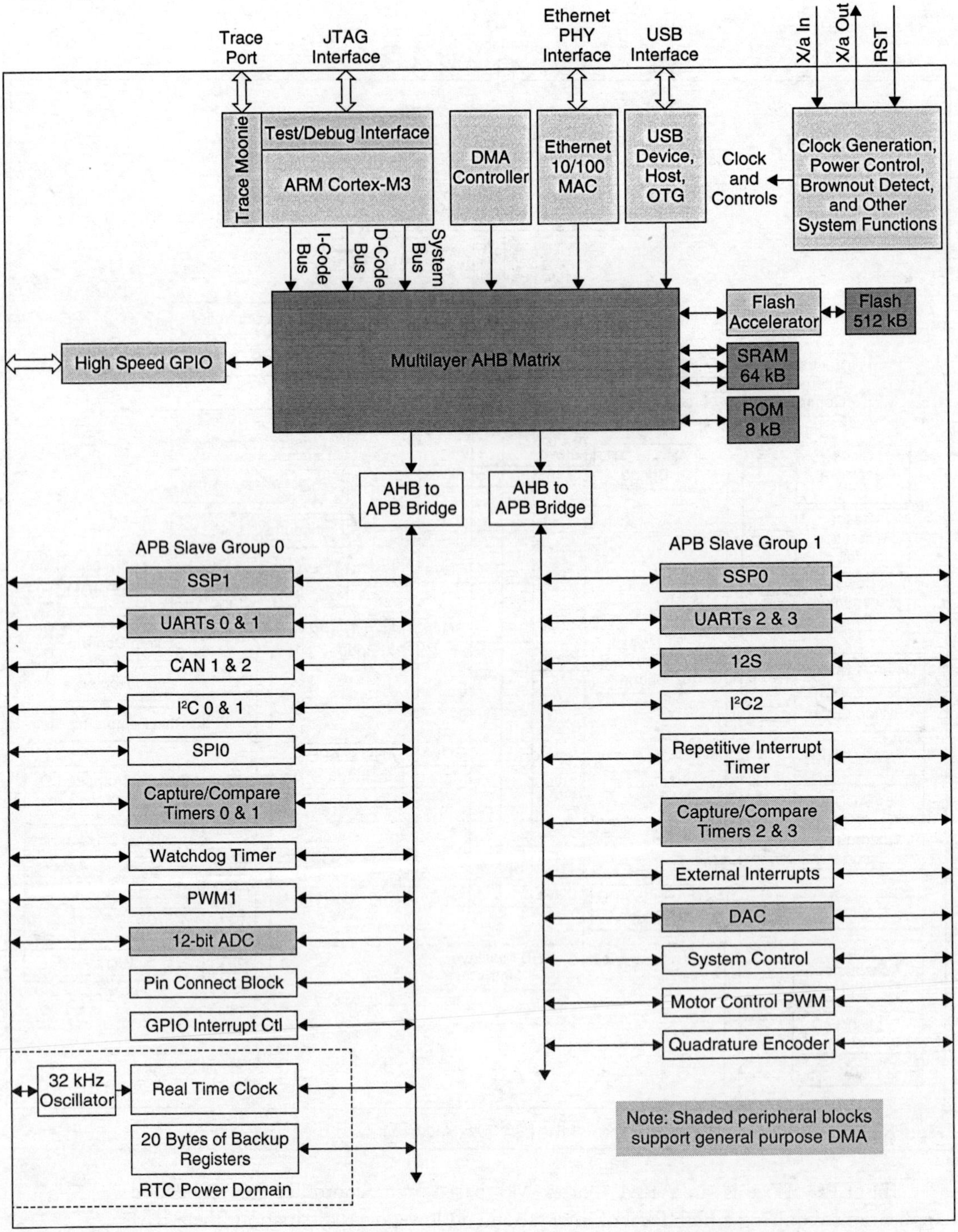

Figure 11.23 | Internal block diagram of the 17xx series of ARM–Cortex M3 MCU

High speed versions (LPC 1769 and LPC 1759) operate at up to a 120 MHz CPU frequency. Other versions operate at up to an 100 MHz CPU frequency. The ARM Cortex-M3 CPU incorporates a 3-stage pipeline and uses a Harvard architecture with separate local instruction and data buses as well as a third bus for peripherals. It also includes an internal prefetch unit that supports speculative branches.

The peripheral complement of the LPC 17xx includes up to 512 kB of flash memory, up to 64 kB of data memory, Ethernet MAC, a USB interface that can be configured as either Host, Device, or OTG, 8 channel general purpose DMA controller, 4 UARTs, 2 CAN channels, 2 SSP controllers, SPI interface, 3 I2C interfaces, 2-input plus 2-output I2S interface, 8 channel 12-bit ADC, 10-bit DAC, motor control PWM, Quadrature Encoder interface, 4 general purpose timers, 6-output general purpose PWM, ultra-low power RTC with separate battery supply, and up to 70 general purpose I/O pins.'

Conclusion

With this, we conclude our discussion of ARM peripheral interfacing. The programs in the chapter have been tested and confirmed to be working as per the specifications for which it has been designed (i.e. frequency, pulse width, etc.) Only a few peripherals of ARM7 have been discussed, but the methodology used for those blocks is expected to help in understanding the rest of them. The important point is that registers of the unit to be used are to be understood with a high degree of clarity. For ARM 9 and Cortex MCUs, only the degree of complexity has been shown–programming them can be done on similar lines, as has been done for ARM 7.

KEY POINTS OF THIS CHAPTER

- The LPC 2148 MCU belongs to the series of ARM7 MCUs of NXP, and is very popular.
- It operates with a system clock of 60 MHz, and has a large set of peripherals.
- It has three internal buses operating at different frequencies, conforming to AMBA specifications.
- There is a 'memory accelerator module' to allow fast access to program lines.
- It has two ports, the pins of which act as GPIO pins.
- Each pin is multi functional, and can be configured for a specific function by using the bits of a 'Pinselect Register'.
- There are two timers which can be used as free running interval timers or as capture timers.
- The system clock is named CCLK, and is divided to get a lower frequency peripheral clock called PCLK.
- The timers and PWMs used in the programs in the chapter have values of output frequencies, based on a PCLK of 15 MHZ.
- The PWM unit has 6 output pins from which 6 PWM pulse trains can be obtained simultaneously.

- There are two serial communication units named UART0 and UART1.
- Using the SSP unit, an SD card can be interfaced to the chip.
- ARM9 and Cortex MCUs are much more complex and powerful, and have more number of peripherals.

QUESTIONS

1. Name five peripherals in the LPC 2148 MCU.
2. What is the difference between PCLK and CCLK?
3. What is the necessity for having the MAM module? How does it function?
4. Distinguish between the power-down and idle modes of this MCU.
5. What is meant by the term 'AMBA'?
6. Differentiate between the different internal buses in terms of speed and function.
7. Look at the memory map and find out the extent of memory locations for static RAM and flash ROM.
8. For a GPIO pin to be made to act as an ON/OFF switch, which are the registers to be used. Give an example to illustrate the use of these registers.
9. How does the prescaler in a time unit function?
10. Distinguish between single and double edge PWM.

EXERCISES

Write programs to obtain the following waveforms:

1. Generate a symmetrical square wave at four pins of Port 1, using software delay.
2. Generate an asymmetric square wave at four pins of Port 0 using software delay.
3. Using Timer 1, obtain a symmetric square wave of frequency 10 KHz at one pin of Port 1, and another square wave of frequency 90 KHz at one pin of Port 0 using Timer 0. Both waveforms should be simultaneously present.
4. Using Timer 0, generate an asymmetric square waveform at four pins of Port 1. The square wave should have an ON time of 0.1 msec and an OFF time of 0.35 msec.
5. Generate PWMs at the six output pins of the PWM unit, with duty cycles of 10, 20, 30, 40, 50 and 70%.

12 PSoC-SoC FOR EMBEDDED APPLICATIONS

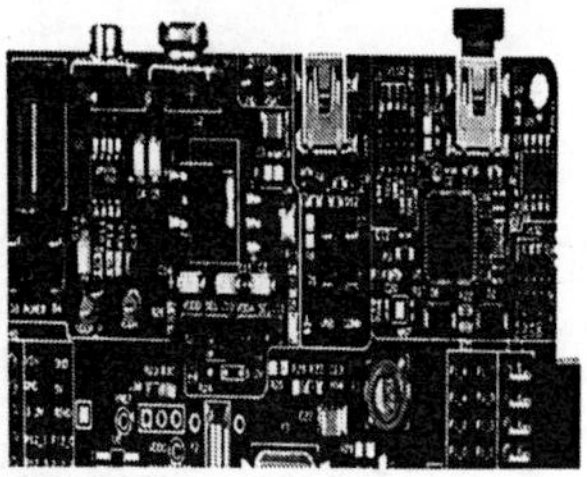

In this chapter, you will learn

- The history and application range of PSoC devices
- The distinct and special features of PSoC
- The differences between PSoC1, PSoC3 and PSoC5
- The internal architecture of PSoC1
- The GUI of PSoC Designer
- The digital blocks of PSoC1
- The working principle of Switched Capacitor circuits
- The finer details of the analog blocks
- How to do the interconnections on the GUI for digital and analog blocks
- The programming of PSoC1
- The enhancements available for PSoC3 and PSoC5

Introduction

The term SoC was mentioned in Chapter 1. So we know that an MCU with a large number of peripherals is called an SoC, for 'System on chip'. Each of the peripherals on an SoC is usually programmable, and so the term PSoC can have a general meaning. But in this chapter, we discuss a very specific product line of Cypress Semiconductors designated as PSoC. We discuss the special features of Cypress's PSoC, which has become very popular in the embedded systems world and has found many applications for itself. PSoC is a family of embedded processors with a simple 8-bit M8C core in PSoC1, a more sophisticated 8-bit 8051 core in PSoC3, and an advanced 32-bit ARM core in PSoC5.

In this chapter, we will concentrate more on the PSoC 1 architecture and usage. The aim is to introduce the reader to this series of MCUs which are versatile, easy to understand and use, and have many features that other MCUs do not possess. The best way to learn is to get a PSoC development kit and do a project based on one of the chips belonging to this family. This chapter introduces you to PSoC and analyses why PSoC is a good point to 'take off' into the embedded design world.

Chapter-opening image: A PSoC 5 development board.

12.1 | How to get a PSoC Development Kit

Look up the website http://www.cypress.com/psoc. for information on how to get a PSoC kit for academic applications. Data sheets and links to other references and forums can also be obtained here.

Development kits are available from the following distributors: Digi-Key, Avnet, Arrow and Future. The website http://www.onfulfillment.com/cypressstore/ Online Store contains development kits, C compilers and all accessories for the PSoC family.

12.1.1 | Development Kit

Figure 12.1 shows the details of the CY3210-PSoCEVAL1 evaluation kit used for the PSoC1 family of mixed signal controllers.

This PSoC1 evaluation kit features an evaluation board and MiniProg1 programming unit. The evaluation board includes an LCD module, potentiometer, LEDs, and plenty of breadboarding space. The MiniProg1 programming unit is also included with the kit and will program PSoC devices directly on the evaluation board, or on other

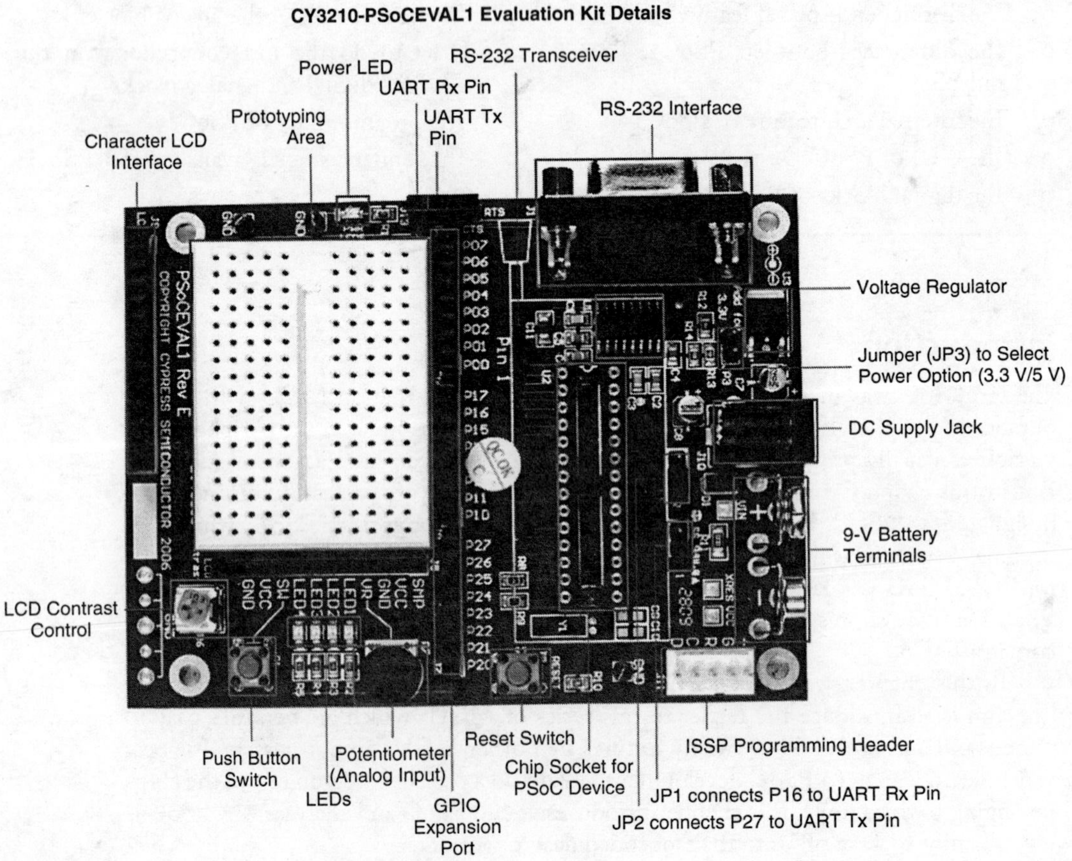

Figure 12.1 | CY3210-PSoCEVAL1 evaluation kit

boards via a 5-pin ISSP header. This programming unit is small and compact, and connects to a PC via a USB 2.0 Cable.

The kit contains the following:

i) Evaluation Board with LCD Module
ii) MiniProg1 Programming Unit
iii) PSoC Designer Software CD
iv) 28 Pin CY8C29466-24PXI PDIP PSoC Device Sample
v) 28-pin CY8C27443-24PXI PDIP PSoC Device Sample
vi) USB 2.0 Cable
vii) Getting Started Guide

12.1.2 | History and Applications of PSoC

The first PSoC chips became commercially available in 2002. Now, in 2012, PSoC has changed the profile of Cypress, the semiconductor company. Among the thousands of PSoC customers worldwide are market leaders such as HP, Cisco, Motorola, IBM, Honeywell, Samsung, LG, Lenovo, Haier, Acer, HTC, Fujitsu, Hitachi, Nintendo, Sharp, Suzuki, Philips, BMW, and Gaggia.

PSoC is used in devices as simple as Sonicare toothbrushes and Adidas sneakers, and as complex as the TV set-top box. One single PSoC, using CapSense, controls the touch-sensitive scroll wheel on the Apple iPod click wheel. An expanded list of its applications include high-definition televisions, digital cameras, remote-control hobbyist helicopters, computer mice, printers, and other PC peripherals, health and fitness equipment, automobile sound systems, satellite radios, and engine control units, medical equipment, lighting, motorized baby strollers, oscilloscope and MP3 players.

Commercial scale shipments began in 2002, and Cypress shipped its 100-millionth unit in 2006. The shipments reached 250 million units in 2007, 500 million units in 2009 and 750 million in the fourth quarter of 2010. On 12 July 2011, Cypress announced that it had shipped its one billionth PSoC unit. Obviously, PSoC is continuing its ride comfortably.

12.1.3 | What is Different About PSoC

The PSoC is an MCU with a computing engine (we call it the core) and a number of peripherals. One very distinct and special feature it possesses is that of having analog peripherals co-existing with digital ones on the same chip.

The other major distinct features are:

i) Programmable analog and digital blocks
ii) Configurable peripherals
iii) Flexible GPIOs, most of the pins can connect to any of the peripherals
iv) Configurable GPIOs—any pin can be input or output
v) GUI-based IDE for easy visualization
vi) API's for each peripheral and system resources; so less time is spent on register manual

Starting at this point, let us now list out the advantages of using PSoC, in comparison with other popular MCUs of comparable computing power.

i) For any real-world application, input signals are usually analog, and so being able to process (amplify, compare, filter, etc) them, before passing them on for digital actuation is a great boon, especially as it is all done in the same chip. This feature is pointed out as the first major highlight of PSoC. Being able to integrate analog and digital blocks on the same chip reduces the size, weight and power requirement of the final product.
ii) The second advantage is that of having an easy to use graphical IDE (Integrated Development Environment) in which the analog and digital building blocks can be selected and interconnected by the simple act of 'drag and drop'. This makes project design very easy. **PSoC Designer** is the IDE for PSoC1 and **PSoC Creator** is the IDE for PSoC3 and PSoC5.
iii) PSoC can be programmed in assembly and C and a number of functions are available in its set of APIs (for Application Programming Interfaces, refer to Section 7.6.4), which makes programming easy and 'modular'. Thus for any user module, the user has the ease of 'just looking' for the right function for his requirement. In this chapter, we use this mode of programming wherein the user manual of a particular module is referred to get the apt function for any application using a specific programmable block.
iv) The chip can use its internal oscillator and chain of multipliers and dividers, for getting any frequency as required by any of the programmable blocks. Besides that, there is the option of using an external source of frequency.

With this brief introduction, let us get started on knowing more about PSoC. As we get to understand it more, we will get accustomed to some more of its special features which will make it seem to be extremely flexible in comparison to other standard MCUs. These features are:

i) Peripherals on the chip are not fixed. A PSoC chip is blank (as far as peripherals are concerned) initially. The system designer can define what peripherals are needed for his application, and 'configure' the chip accordingly. To use any of the programmable blocks to work as the peripheral he needs, the 'drag and drop' technique of the IDE is used and the ease of using it makes the design process a very comfortable and interesting activity.
ii) For most other MCUs, the pins corresponding to the input and output of a specific peripheral are fixed as per the chip pinout. In PSoC, this does not hold true. Any GPIO pin can be used as the input or output pin of any of the peripherals of the 'user module' group (there are some restrictions in the case of analog I/O and certain pins). This simplifies the routing of signals outside the IC.
iii) PSoC has a large collection of peripherals. The user can choose from this large set, the ones that his applications need (though, limited by the number of programmable blocks and GPIO pins). The point is that for different applications, a different set of peripherals may be chosen. This is not so for any other standard MCU where a limited set of 'certain' peripherals is available for the chip, and a 'range of choice' is not available. This point will be clearer as we get to use the programmable blocks.
iv) There is an on-board power supply and the SMP unit may be used to provide power (Section 7.6.4).

v) For PSoC1, there is the 'dynamic reconfiguration' option. This means that peripherals may be changed at runtime. The point is that, if the current design is using all the programmable blocks in the first configuration, some of them may be unloaded at run time and replaced by others in the second configuration.

12.2 | The PSoC Family

The family comprises the following IC series

i) CY8C2xxxx named PSoC1 with the M8C core
ii) CY8C3xxxx named PSoC3 with the 8051 core
iii) CY8C5xxxx named PSoC5 with the ARM Cortex M3 core

There are a number of member chips in the family, and they differ in aspects like number of pins, number of digital /analog blocks, flash, RAM, IC packaging, etc.

PSoC 1

This is the first version of PSoC, that is, the original design which has been available since 2001. Its core is an 8-bit M8C (CISC) core. It uses a basic clock frequency of 24MHz (maximum), and 4 MIPS is the performance claimed by the manufacturers. There are a number of chips available which uses the PSoC1 architecture. The IDE provided for PSoC1 is the 'PSoC Designer'.

PSoC3

PSoC3 devices are based on a new, high-performance and enhanced 8-bit 8051 processor. It has a performance of 33 MIPS at 66 MHz.

PSoC5

PSoC 5 devices include a powerful 32-bit ARM Cortex M3 processor. 100 Dhrystone MIPS is the performance claimed for this. (Dhrystone is a bench mark for integer computations.)

12.2.1 | Comparing PSoC3 and 5

They have different cores and the peripheral structure is almost the same. Both of them use the PSoC Creator as their IDE. They are completely different from PSoC1 and no compatibility exists, which means that there is no way one can migrate from PSoC1 to PSoc3 or PSoC5.

12.2.2 | Focus of the Chapter

In this chapter we start with PSoC1, discuss its core, the peripherals alias user modules and write programs for some of its peripherals. The step-by-step instructions for using the PSoC Designer are given in Appendix C. Besides, that, a set of design examples for PSoC1, and also a step-by-step approach for using PSoC Creator is put up in the book website www.pearsoned.co.in/lylabdas/embeddedsystems.

This chapter is meant to facilitate a good understanding of the PSoC architecture (including programming). We will not do assembly language programming, nor discuss the cores in detail, rather our concentration will be on using the inbuilt analog and digital building blocks and programming them using C. With a good knowledge of PSoC1 and its IDE, it will be easy to use any other version of PSoC, because even if the architectures and IDE are different, the approach is the same.

PSoC3 and PSoC5 will also be discussed—but in less detail.

12.3 | PSoC1

This version is available in the CY8C 21xxx, 22xxx, 24xxx, 27xxx, 28xxx and 29xxx series. The forthcoming discussion here is more or less general and applies to all these part numbers. In this book, we use the 29xxx series to cite examples of user modules, configuration and programming.

12.3.1 | The CY8C29xxx Series

These controllers are available in different packages and pin counts, that is, there are controllers with 8, 16, 20, 24, 28, 32, 44, 48 and 100 pins. As the pinout increases, the count of the (GPIO ports) available in the chip increases. The maximum number of ports possible is 8 (for the 100 pin package). For example, the CY8C29xxx series is available in 5 packages and 5 pin counts. Figure 12.2 gives an approximate idea of this. See Table 12.1 to understand the packaging abbreviation, and Figures 12.2a to 12.2e shows the CY8C29xxx series of PSoC ICs with different pin counts and packaging.

12.3.2 | Pin Designations

Some pin designations need elaboration:

i) **AI:** Analog Input
ii) **AIO:** Analog I/O
iii) All GPIO pins (i.e. port pins) can be used for digital I/O
iv) Some pins like clock, XTAL, VDD, VSS, etc. have fixed designations. In Figure 12.2a, it can be noticed that the hardware I2C block (Section 5.2.1) can use only specific pins. (10 and 11) But the user modules realized using programmable digital blocks can use any GPIO pin. We will soon get to know how this is done.

Table 12.1 | IC Packaging Abbreviations

Abbreviation	Packaging
PDIP	Plastic Dual Inline Package
SSOP	Shrink Small Outline Package
SOIC	Small Outline Integrated Circuit
TQFP	Thin Quad Flat Pack
QFN	Quad Flat No Leads

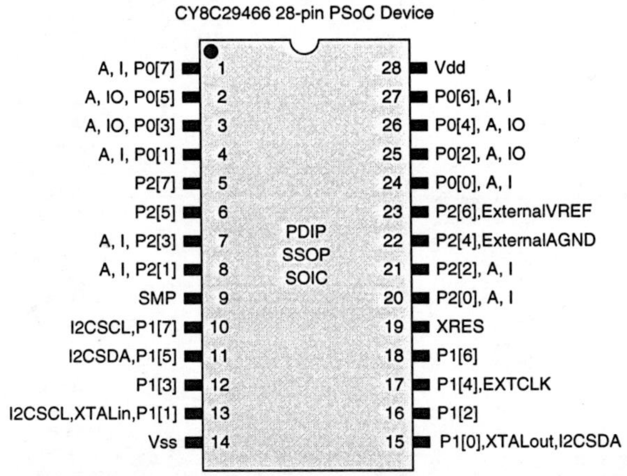

Figure 12.2a | 28 pins with 3 GPIO ports and packages PDIP, SSOP and SOIC

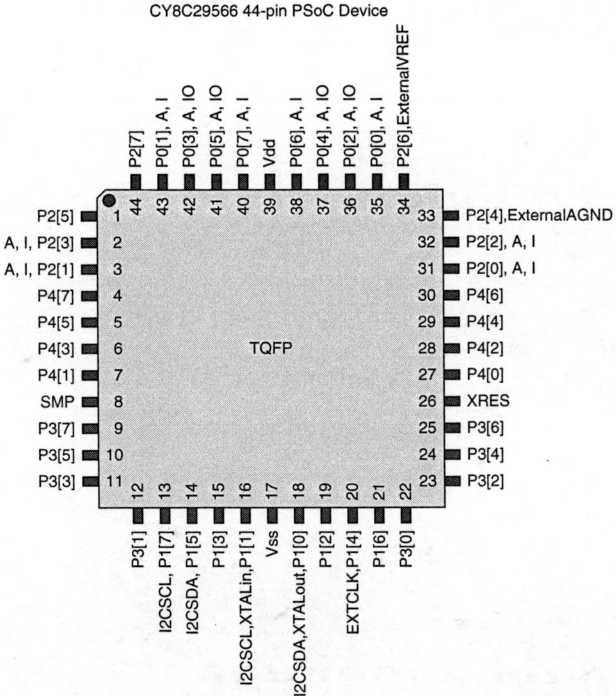

Figure 12.2b | 44 pins, 5 GPIO ports and TQFP packaging

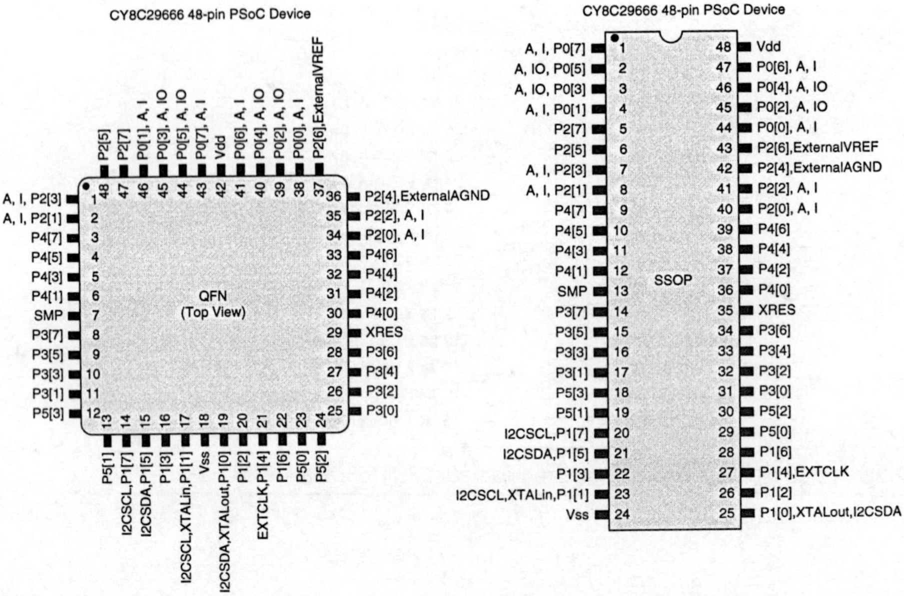

Figure 12.2c and Figure 12.2d | 48 pins–6 GPIO ports and packages QFN and SSOP

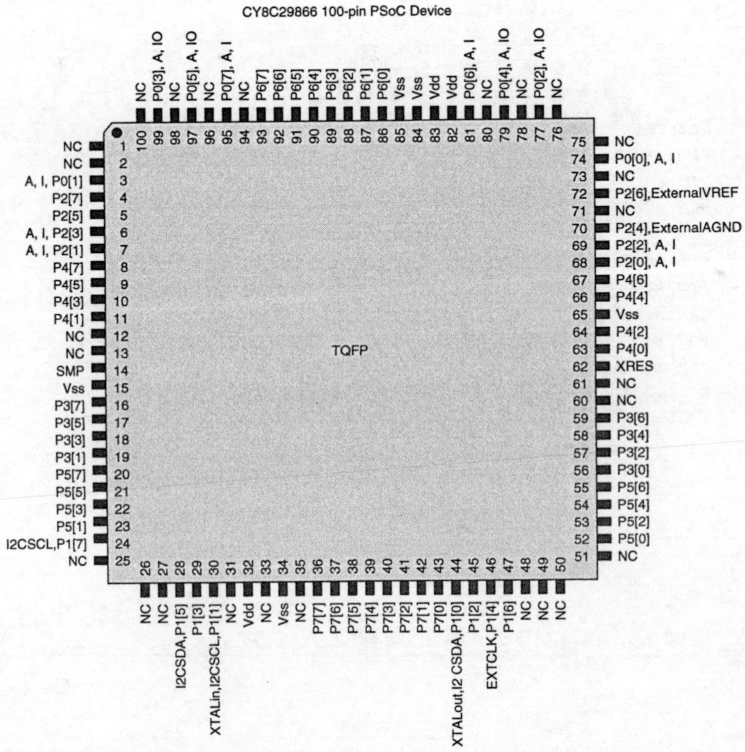

Figure 12.2e | 100 pins with 8 GPIO ports and TQFP package

12.4 | The Internal Architecture of PSoC

Figure 12.3 shows the internal block diagram of a typical PSoC1 device, with all its components which are as follows:

i) The PSoC core
ii) The digital system
iii) The analog system
iv) The system resources

Let's discuss these in detail.

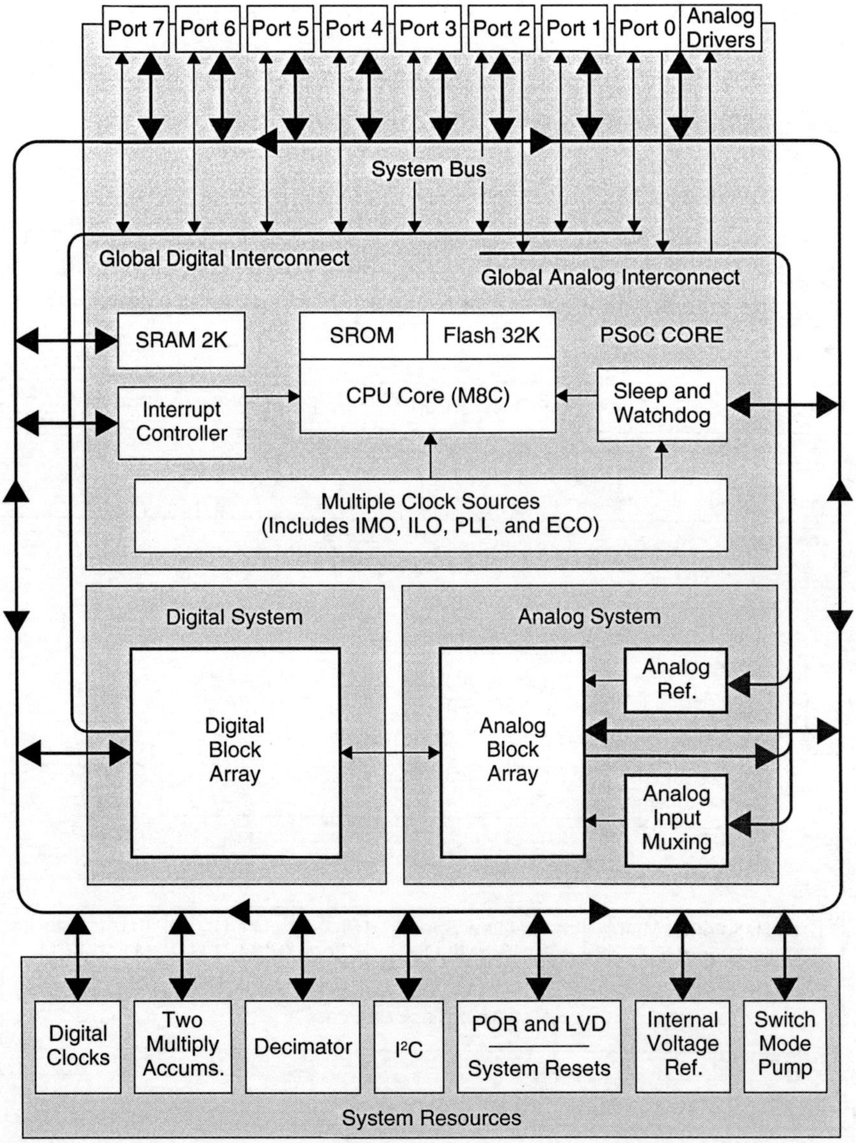

Figure 12.3 | Internal block diagram of PSoC

12.4.1 | The PSoC Core

Figure 12.4 shows the PSoC core which again is constituted by different blocks.

12.4.2 | The CPU Core (M8C)

The CPU core is an 8-bit 'Harvard' architecture (Section 2.1.2) meaning that the program space and data memory space and associated buses are separate. The M8C has five internal registers which are as follows:

i) The Accumulator (A)
ii) Index (X)
iii) Program Counter (PC)
iv) Stack Pointer (SP)
v) Flags (F)

All these are 8-bit registers except the PC which is 16-bit long.

12.4.3 | Memory

The address space of PSoC has three distinct divisions: the ROM space, the RAM space and the I/O registers. Just as in the case of any other MCU, the ROM or Flash is the one that stores program code, and is pointed by the 16-bit program counter. Figure 12.5

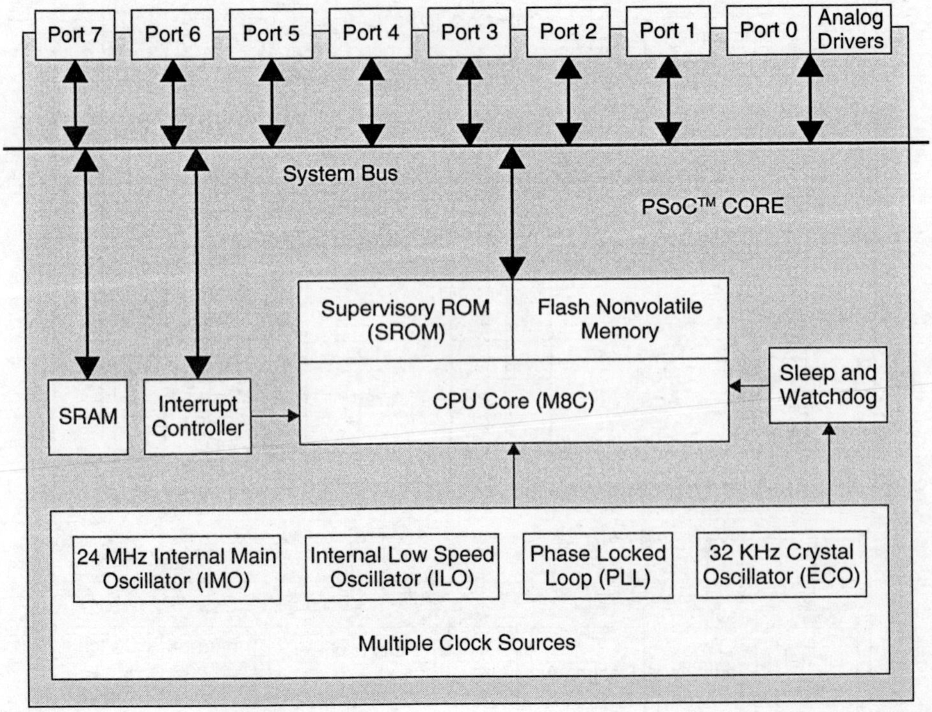

Figure 12.4 | The Core of PSoC

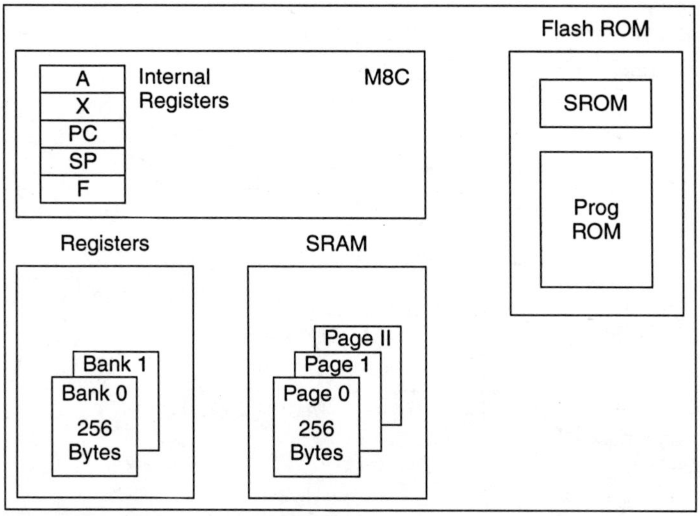

Figure 12.5 | The CPU core and memory block diagram

shows the CPU, registers and memory. The points to be assimilated while observing Figure 12.5 are as follows:

i) The maximum amount of flash possible is 32KB, but different chips (or 'parts' as they referred to) can have different flash sizes like 2, 4, 8,16 or 32 KB. The CY8C29466, for instance, has 32 KB of flash. The flash is subdivided as program ROM and supervisory ROM. This means that a part of flash memory is used for storing boot up code (supplied by the manufacturer), calibration parameters and the like. This part is called the Supervisory ROM or SROM. Normally, the application programmer does not need to access this part of ROM.
ii) The RAM is of SRAM technology and is considered as data memory. It is volatile and is used for storing intermediate results during computation. The minimum amount of RAM in any PSoC is 256 bytes. When a particular version has more than 256 bytes, it is organized as 256 byte sized pages. The CY8C29466 has 2 KB of RAM, i.e., it is organized as 8 pages.
iii) The figure shows a set of registers outside the CPU. These registers are like the SFRs (Special Function Registers) of 8051 and other MCUs; they are used for managing and configuring the programmable blocks of PSoC. This set consists of two banks of 256 bytes each, and bank switching is taken care by an XIO bit (bit 4) available in the flag register.

12.4.4 | Clock Sources

Figure 12.6 shows multiple clock sources for the chip. There is a basic clock frequency of 24 MHz, a frequency multiplier and a number of frequency dividers.

This figure shows that an internal oscillator of 24MHz, or an external oscillator with maximum frequency value of 24MHz, can be used as the system clock and also as reference, to generate a 48MHz frequency (by multiplication) or various other frequencies

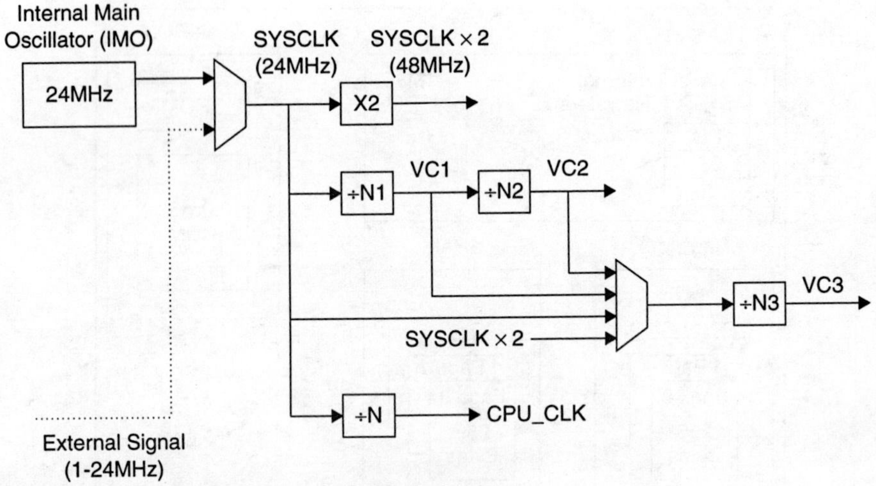

Figure 12.6 | Clock source with multipliers and dividers

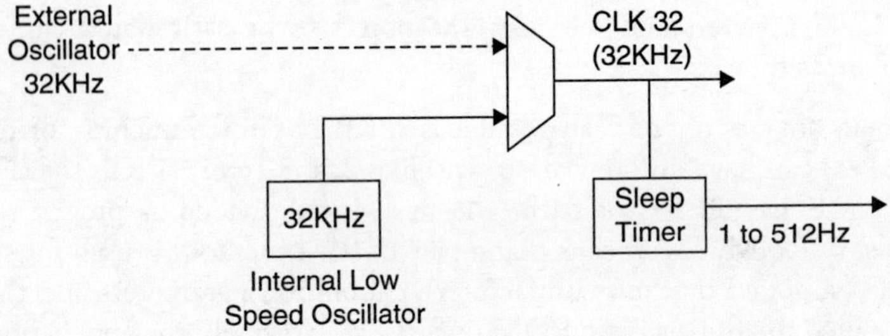

Figure 12.7 | Low frequency source for sleep timer

with a chain of dividers. The required frequencies can be got by using the values of dividers N1 and N2 which are allowed to vary from 1 to 16, and N3 from 1 to 256. The frequencies VC1, VC2 and VC3 can be used as clocks to various peripherals.

Figure 12.7 shows a lower frequency clock, which can be derived from the available internal low speed oscillator or from an external source. All these operations are selectable using the bits of an I/O register named OSSCR. The settings are available in the graphic editor as well.

Why do we need external oscillators?

The internal oscillator frequency can drift by a range of around ±2.5% (device dependent, can vary upto ±4%). When very high precision frequency generation is required, the reference frequency can be from an external source which uses a precision crystal.

Where is the frequency of 1 to 512 Hz to be used?

This is for the sleep timer which is a timer which generates periodic interrupts at any chosen rate between 1 and 512 Hz (specifically 1, 8, 64 and 512 Hz).

What is the sleep state?

Most embedded systems don't work continuously. Think of a mobile phone. It becomes active if a call or message or some other request occurs. The idea of putting an MCU to sleep is to save power when it is not doing any active computation. The only activity being done then, is the running of the sleep timer from a low frequency clock source. Once in the sleep state, the MCU is woken up periodically by interrupts from the sleep timer, (which is just like any ordinary timer) at any rate in the range of 1 to 512 Hz (as mentioned above). Besides this, the MCU can also be woken up by interrupts generated at the analog or digital inputs.

Watchdog This refers to the watchdog timer, which gets the MCU to reset, if caught in an endless loop (due to some unexpected error). Refer Section 2.2.6 for more details on this.

The other blocks in Figure 12.4 are the interrupt controller, which manages the interrupt system of the MCU (Section 2.2.9) and the PLL. The interrupt controller takes charge of 17 interrupt vectors, associated ISRs, their priorities, etc. The PLL is the 'Phase Locked Loop' which is related to the functions of generating different frequencies.

12.4.5 | The PSoC Designer

PSoC Designer is the Integrated Design Environment (IDE) used to customize PSoC to meet the specific requirements of an application. Because of the graphic environment, it accelerates the process of system design. Applications can be designed using the library of pre-characterized analog and digital peripherals in a drag-and-drop design environment. Then the design code can be written using the API libraries of each user module. Finally, the design can be debugged and tested with the integrated debug environment including in-circuit emulation and standard software debug features. To sum up, the components of the IDE include the following:

i) Application editor GUI for device and user module configuration and dynamic reconfiguration
ii) Extensive user module catalog
iii) Integrated source code editor (C and Assembly)
iv) C compiler with no size restrictions or time limits
v) Built-in debugger
vi) Integrated circuit emulation (ICE)
vii) PSoC designer supports the entire family of PSoC 1 devices

Figure 12.8 shows the PSoC Designer's graphic editor page for configuring the digital and analog blocks. This particular picture (figure) is applicable only to the 29xxx series. For any other series, the numbers of GPIO pins are not the same and so the 'picture' will be different.

Note The step-by-step guide to using this IDE is available in Appendix C.

The graphical editor allows the designer to customize the connections 'inside' the chip.

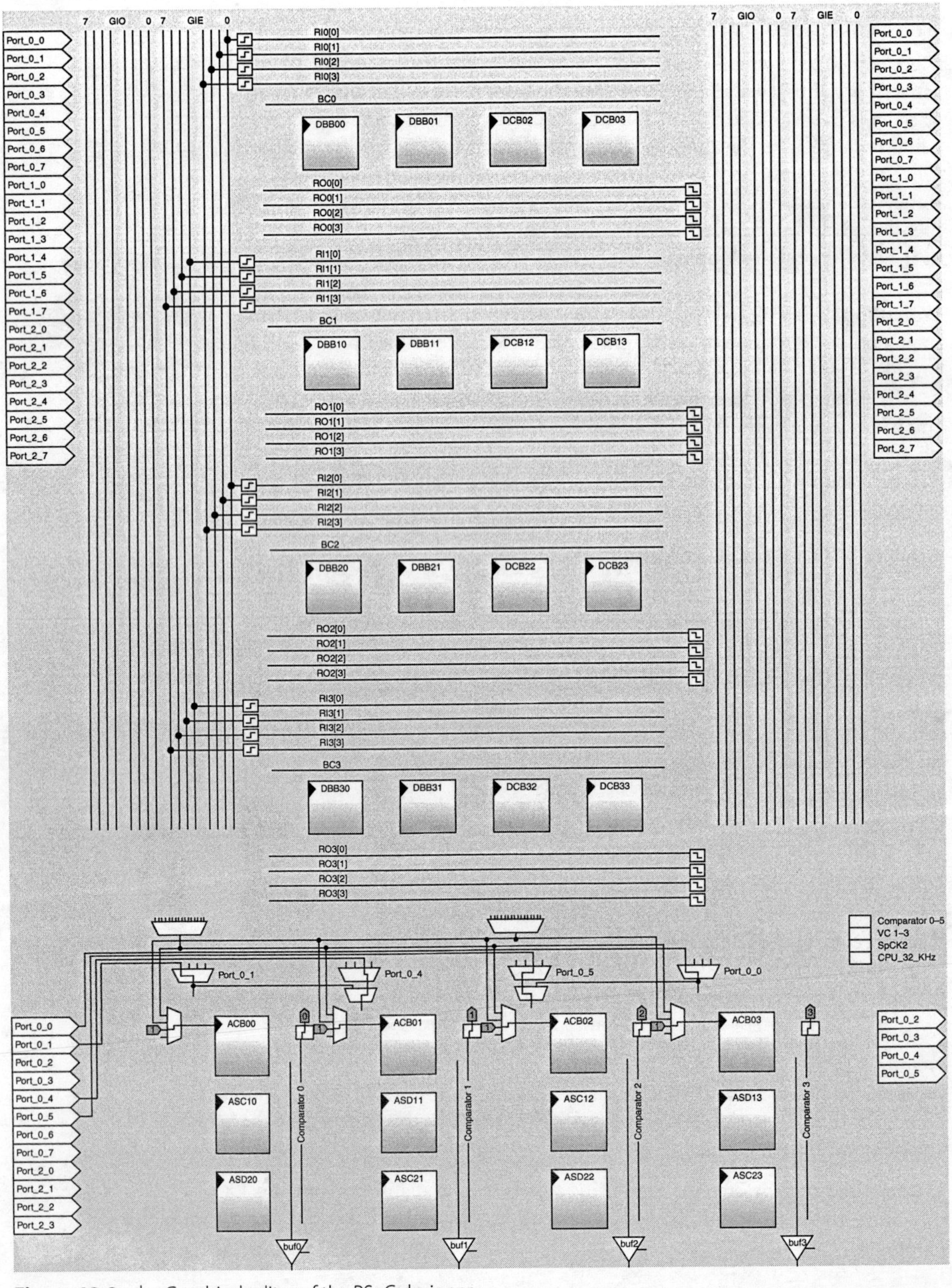

Figure 12.8 | Graphical editor of the PSoC designer

Table 12.2 | Details of Resources of the Chip Series CY9C29x66

PSoC Part Number	Digital I/O	Digital Rows	Digital Blocks	Analog Inputs	Analog Outputs	Analog Columns	Analog Blocks	SRAM Size	Flash Size
CY8c29x66	up to 64	4	16	up to 12	4	4	12	2K	32K

12.4.6 | General Purpose I/O (GPIO)

There are 8 ports defined for PSoC1. All of them are not realizable for all the parts (i.e. chips) in the family. Since each port requires 8 pins, only the 100 pin version can offer all the 8 ports. Others have port counts varying from 3 to 8. Figures 12.2a to 12.2e show the number of ports for members of the CY8C29xxx series. Each port pin has an elaborate circuitry behind it, which takes care of its logic level, as well as the load it can use. The load can be selected according to the type of driving device or incoming signal. This will be explained in greater detail soon (Section 12.6.1).

Note in Figure 12.4 that the analog driver is part of the core, though the analog blocks are not. The analog drivers are associated with Port 0, because it is the pins of this port that are used in the analog mode. Table 12.2 gives the resources available in the PSoC1 chip CY8C29x66. Note that the resources vary from part to part.

12.5 | The Digital Sub System

Now see Figure 12.9 which shows the block diagram of the digital system. It is composed of 16 digital blocks. Each block shown is an 8-bit resource, which can be used by itself to obtain an 8-bit user module, or combined with other blocks to form 16, 24 or 32-bit modules. Each digital block is blank. It is up to the designer to decide the user module to fit into any block. Let's try to understand this in greater detail.

The digital user modules available for CY829x66 are

i) PWMs (8 to 32-bit)
ii) PWMs with dead band (8 to 32-bit)
iii) Counters (8 to 32-bit)
iv) Timers (8 to 32-bit)
v) UART 8-bit with selectable parity (up to 2)
vi) SPI slave and master (up to 2)
vii) I2C slave and multi-master (one more available as a system resource)
viii) CRC (Cyclic Redundancy Check) generator (8 to 32-bit)
ix) IrDA (Infra Red communication) (up to 2)
x) PRS (Pseudo Random Sequence) generators (8 to 32-bit)

As Figure 12.9 shows, there are the **'Digital Building Blocks' (DBB)** and **'Digital Communication Blocks' (DCB)** arranged in four rows of four blocks.

In each row, the first two are DBBs and the next two are DCBs. There is one point to keep in mind, in this context. All digital components, like counters, PWM unit, PRS and CRC generators can be configured out of any free block. **On the other hand, communication components like Rx, Tx, UART and SPI can be set on the DCB blocks only. Besides these, I2C has a dedicated hardware block.**

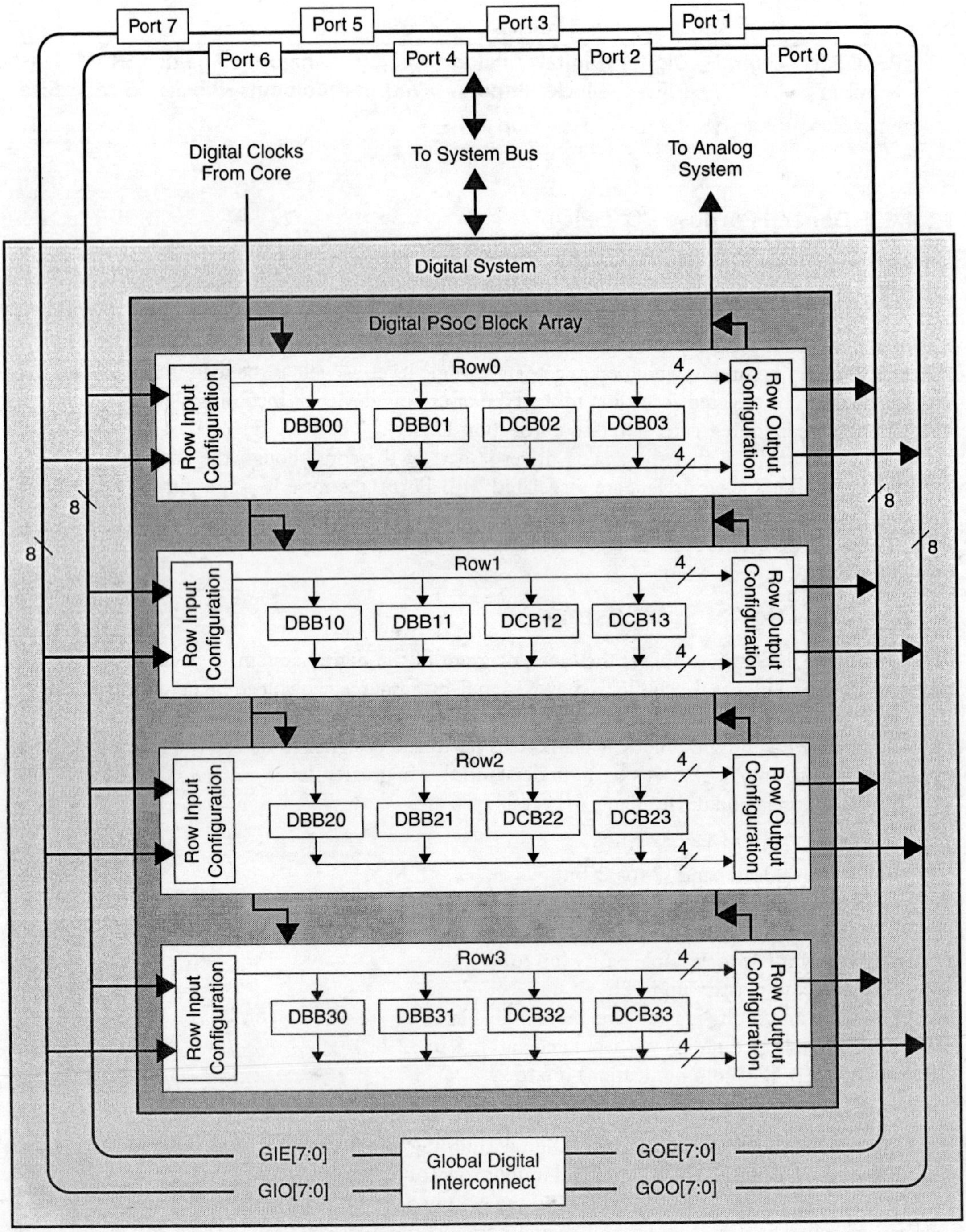

Figure 12.9 | Block diagram of the digital subsection

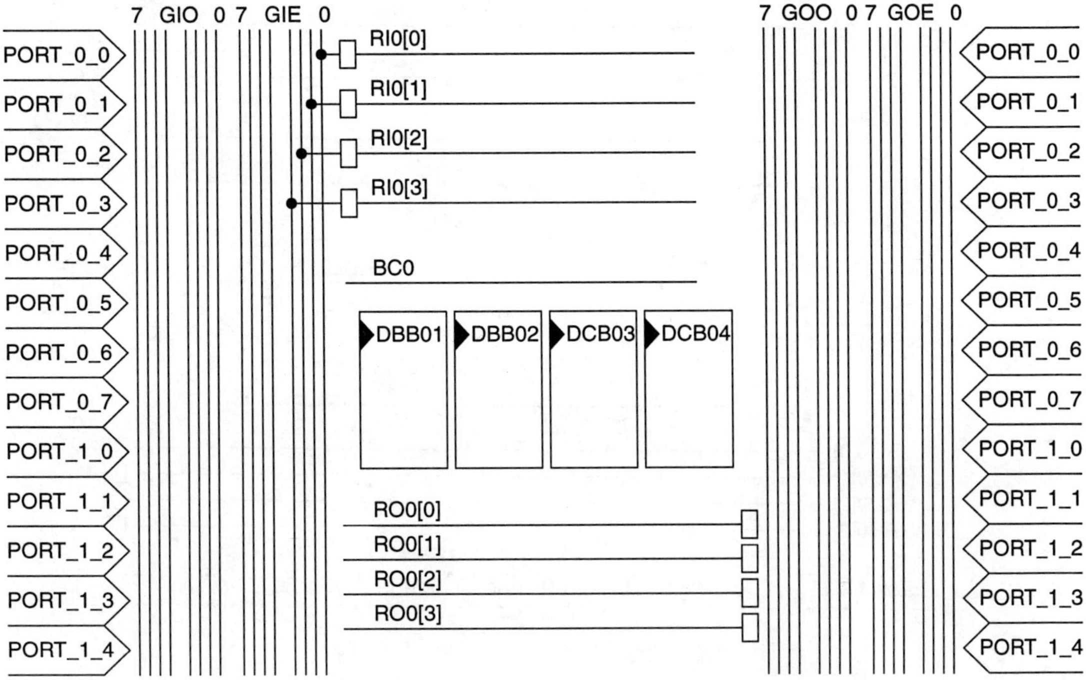

Figure 12.10 | The graphic editor page of PSoC designer for one row of digital blocks

Figure 12.10 shows the graphic editor page of PSoC designer, catering to one row of four digital blocks, the associated interconnections and a few port pins (all of them cannot be shown in this page). This figure is to be referred when we discuss various aspects of the interconnection logic. We do all interconnections using this editor.

What are the important points to note in this figure?
This figure shows just one row of four digital blocks, a set of four input rows above it, and a set of four output rows below it. There is a BC (Broad Cast) line, the GI (Global Input) lines on the left, the GO (Global Output) lines on the right and some of the port pins.

12.5.1 | Clock Input

All digital blocks need a clock as input. Figure 12.10 shows a black coloured triangular notation inside each of the blocks, which shows the clock input. One of the clock sources as discussed in Section 12.4.4, i. e., VC1, VC2, VC3, SYSCLKx2, CPU_32, etc. can be selected as the clock. There are other possibilities also. The output of one stage of a block can be used as the clock of the next stage. Figure 12.11 shows a line called BC (Broadcast), which allows any signal to be sent to various other points through the common broadcast line. The broadcast line may also be used to connect between the row lines of one group (of four digital blocks) to that of another group, say from RI0[2] to RI1[3].

The step-by-step instructions for using the PSoC designer are given in Appendix C In this chapter, the attempt is to explain the hardware and software aspects so as to

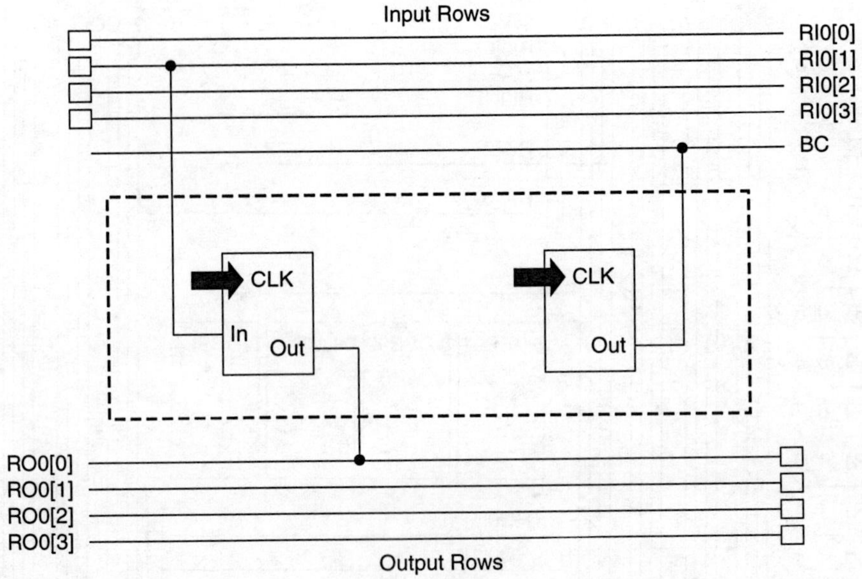

Figure 12.11 | Two digital blocks with input and output and a BC connection

facilitate a general understanding of the PSoC and it features. For that, let's use the graphic editor to define different kinds of applications.

Each of the digital blocks can be programmed using assembly language. This may be cumbersome and so the easier approach uses the graphic editor for making the connections, and writing programs in C. The PSoC API library provides, for each of the user modules, a set of functions that perform a specific task. We will use a few of them to make the concepts clear. Each user module has a number of API functions and the programmer is expected to read the manual of the module to get the right function for his requirement. Figure 12.12 contains the same information as Figure 12.10, but with a few more details added. It will be easier to use Figure 12.12 when discussing the input and output interconnections.

12.5.2 | Interconnection Structure—Input

Now refer to Figure 12.12 for the input side interconnects—there is the global bus GI with 16 bus lines, with designations of GIE and GIO. On the left of it, the port pins are seen. The interesting feature of PSoC is that the IDE provides a graphical method of choosing any GPIO pin to act as any digital input or output pin. We can make the choice of the pin and also the interconnection 'between blocks'. In essence the routing path of signals 'inside the PSoC chip' can be configured graphically.

At the input side, the global bus lines are named GIE and GIO meaning 'Global Input Even' and 'Global Input Odd'. The odd numbered bus lines connect only to odd numbered ports, i.e., to P1, P3, P5 and P7. Similar is the case for even numbered bus lines which connect to port pins of P0, P2, P4 and P6. You can see that there are only 16 GI bus lines, while there are up to 64 port lines for the chips in the series.

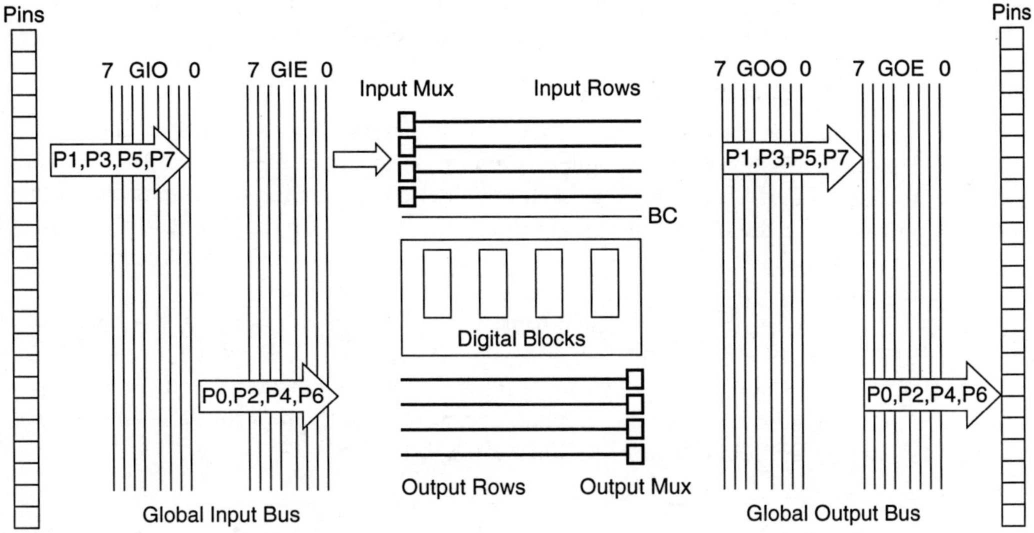

Figure 12.12 | An expanded view of Figure 12.10

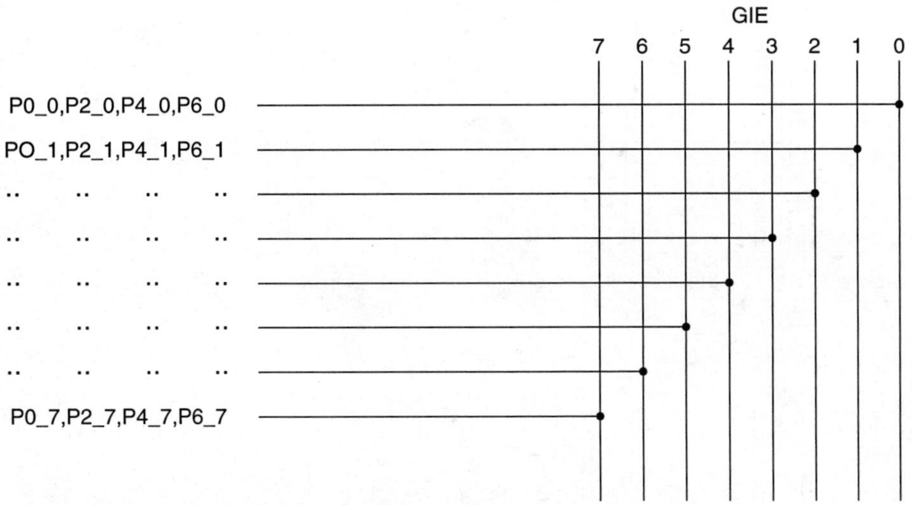

Figure 12.13 | GIE lines and the port pins that connect to each bus line

How is this managed?

The GI bus lines are for routing the signals from the input pins to the digital blocks.

The connections between the port lines and the GIE bus are as shown in Figure 12.13. What this indicates is that GIE0 is the bus line to be used for the 0th pin of any even port, GIE1 for the 1st pin of any even port pin and so on. Similar connectivity applies to other GIE bus lines. (A similar configuration of connections is applicable to the GIO lines as well, for the odd numbered ports, though).

Thus a signal from an input pin can be connected to the global bus line, and from there it has to be routed to the input point of a digital block.

How is that done?

There are multiplexers for that. A set of multiplexers carry the signal to its destination. Figure 12.14 shows the multiplexers whose output lines are notated as RI (standing for 'Row Input'). There are four such row lines corresponding to the four digital blocks in a row. For the 0th row of digital blocks, these are RI0(0), RI0(1), RI0(2) and RI0(3). This figure shows the GI bus lines at the input of the first mux (multiplexer) in the top row line.

If we need to interpret this diagram on the basis of port pins, the inputs of the multiplexer of row RI0(0) carry the signals from P0_0, P0_4, P1_0 and P1_4, see Figure 12.15 Similar thinking can be applied to the case of the other three multiplexers.

See Figure 12.16 for the complete connection for the four row lines above the digital blocks DBB00, DBB01, DCB02 and DCB03.

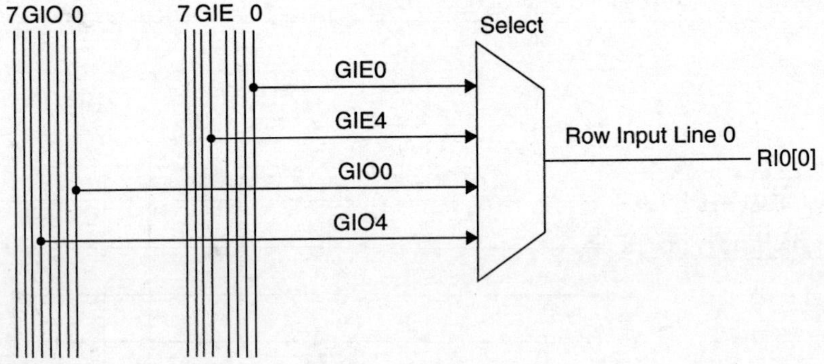

Figure 12.14 | Input bus lines to the multiplexer of row 0

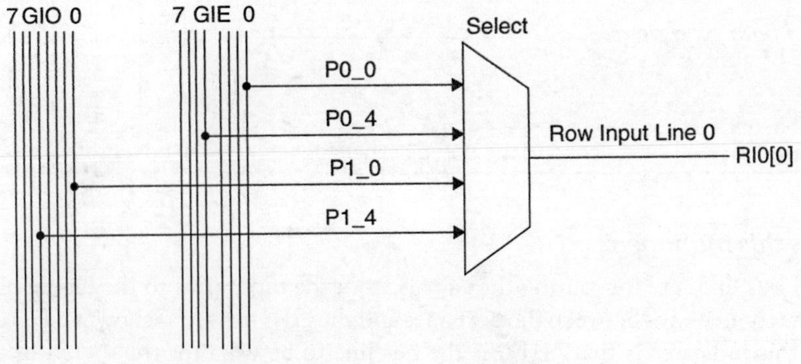

Figure 12.15 | Row 0 multiplexer and the port pins at its input

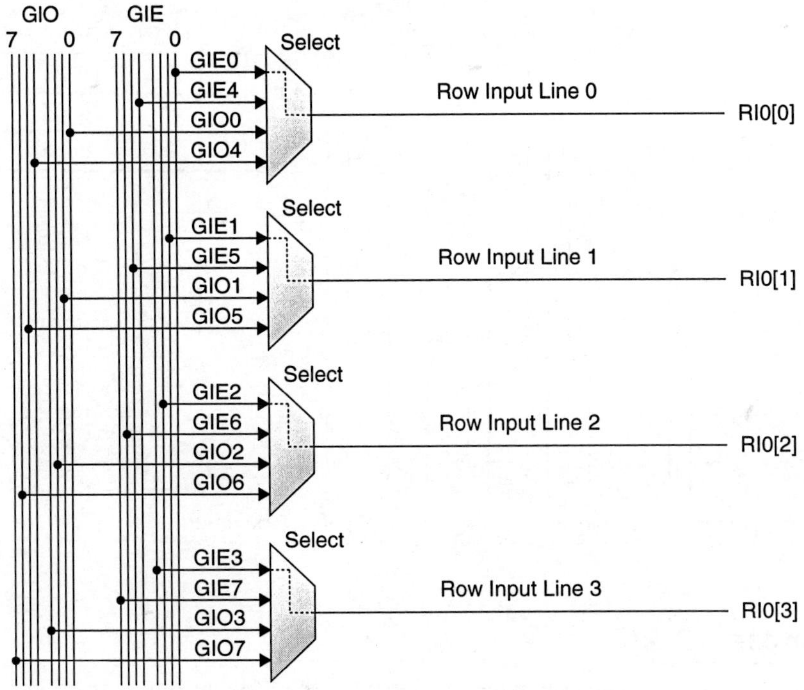

Figure 12.16 | Connections of the GIE and GIO bus lines to the input muxes

Example 12.1

Draw the routing (on the PSoC designer) for connecting input pin P0_0 to the capture input of the timer which is to be realized using DBB00

Solution

The steps are as follows

i) First 'place' the 8-bit Timer1(from the list of user modules) on DB01.
ii) Next, the connection between the global input lines and the port pin P0_0 should be made. For that, note that since P0 is an even port, the global lines to be used, belong to the GIE group. It is the 0th pin and so the GIE0 line that should be used. Establish this connection.
iii) The capture input of the timer is connected to RI0(0), since we know (Figure 12.15) that P0_0 is one of the inputs of the multiplexer whose output is RI0(0).
iv) Figure 12.17 shows this interconnection from P0_0 to GIE0 to RI0(0) to the capture input of the 8-bit Timer 1.
v) Note that the timer has been given a clock from VC1.

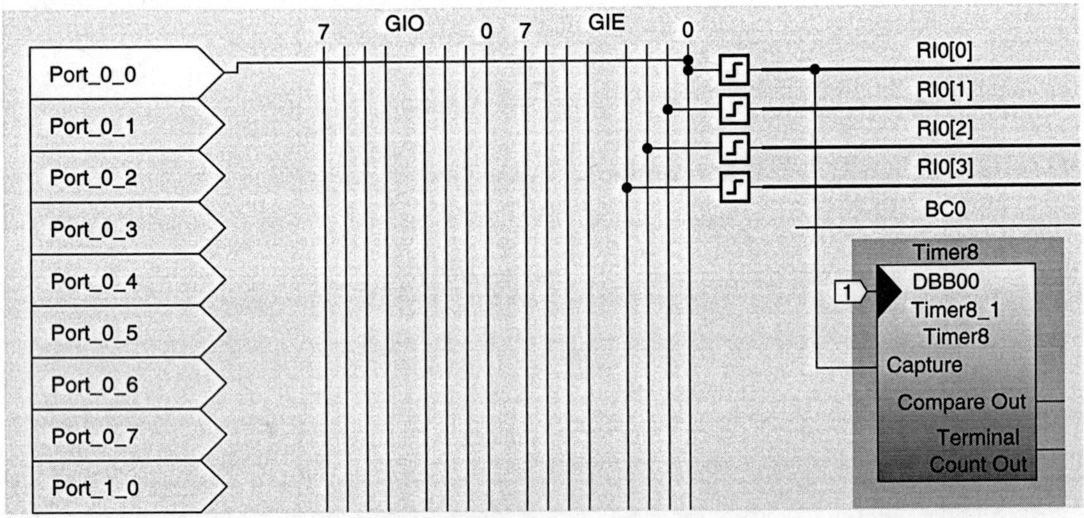

Figure 12.17 | Routing diagram from pin P0_0 to the capture pin of an 8 bit timer

Example 12.2

Explain the steps in giving an external source for the 'Enable' pin of the 8-bit PWM which has been placed at DCB02. The port pin P1_3 is used for the enable logic.

Note In this use case, the PWM output will be enabled when the external signal goes high.

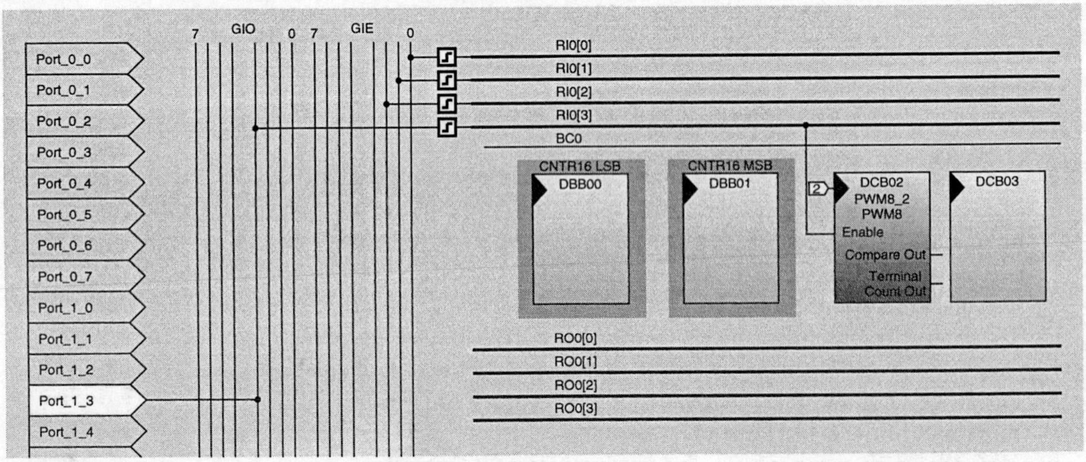

Figure 12.18 | Routing the signal from P1_3 to an input of DCB02

Solution

The steps are

i) Note that P1_3 is a pin of an odd port, and hence the bus line from GIO must be used, i.e., GI03 is connected to Port 1_3.
ii) Next, the connection from the Enable pin to RI0(3) is done, since (Figure 12.16) GIO3 is an input to the mux with output line RI0(3).
iii) Figure 12.19 shows the connections of the mux that must be selected, such that GI03 is routed to the output of the mux.
iv) VC2 is used as the clock to the PWM unit.

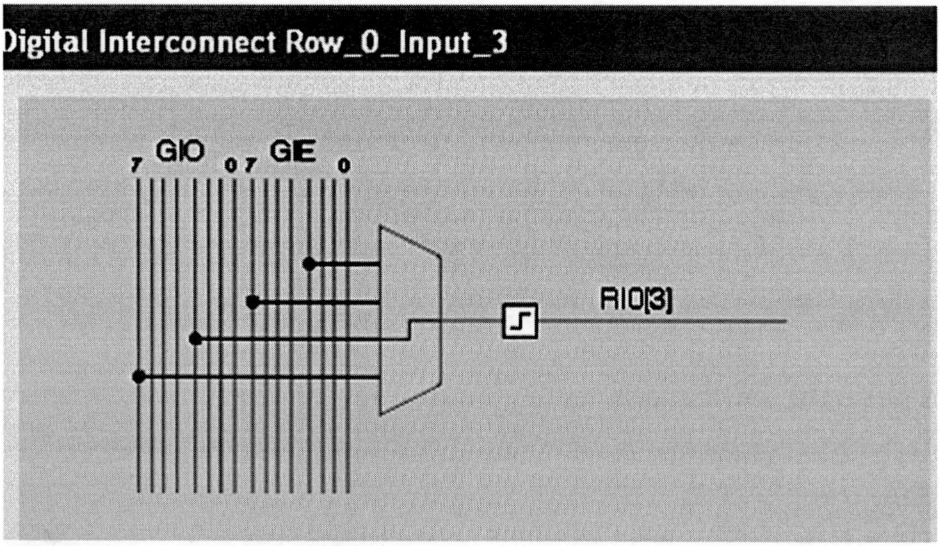

Figure 12.19 | Routing GI03 to RI0(3)

12.5.3 | Interconnection Structure—Output

Just as at the input side, there are global bus lines at the output as well. They are notated as GOE (Global Output Even) and GOO (Global Output Odd) and the connection pattern (to the port pins) is similar to that at the input side.

There are multiplexers on the output side as well, but they are slightly different from those at the input, in that additional logic functions are possible here. The output (without or without extra logic) is routed to the output pins through buffers. Note the RO0(0) to RO0(3) row line in Figure 12.10. They are the lines to be taken to the port pins through the multiplexers shown on the right hand side of each row line. These multiplexers have the options of including a logic function also, before being routed to the port pins. See Figure 12.20. This shows that logic functions of AND, NAND, etc. can be realized between one row line and its neighbouring line. The white triangles after the multiplexers are the output buffers through which the signal is routed to the GO buses and thence to the output pins.

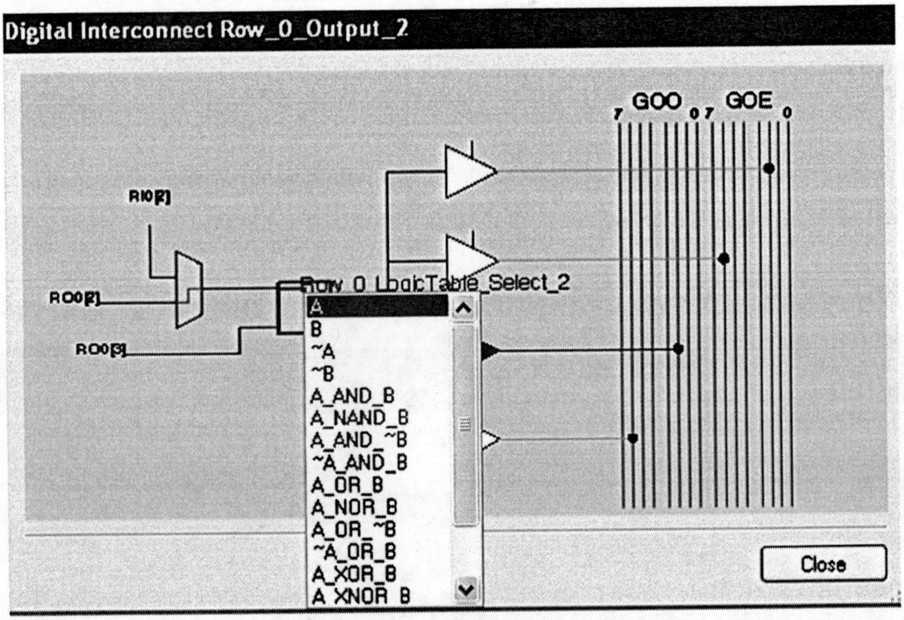

Figure 12.20 | Output side multiplexers and buffers

Example 12.3

Show the routing to use the 16-bit PWM unit to get a PWM output at port pin Port 1_2.

Solution

Figure 12.21 shows the routing. A 16-bit PWM unit uses up two of the digital blocks, DCB02 and DCB03, but the connection 'between' the two blocks is taken care of, by the PSoC internally. The following are the connections made.

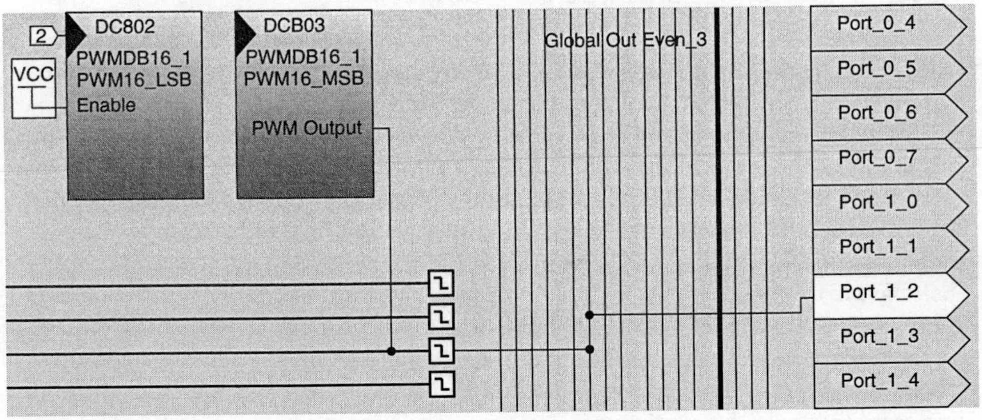

Figure 12.21 | Routing of the PWM output signal to Port 1_2

i) The clock source chosen is VC2.
ii) Active high enable is used.
iii) The PWM output is connected to RO0(3).
iv) At the output mux, no additional logic is chosen. The output of the PWM unit is sent through buffers to GO02 and from there to P1_2.

12.6 | GPIO Pins

The GPIO port pins have two basic functions

i) One is to allow the core to send information out of the PSoC device. The pin acts as an output, in this case.
ii) The second is to obtain information from outside the PSoC device. This puts the pin in the input state.

These operations are accomplished by using the bits of the port data register named PRTxDR.

The pin as an output Writes from the core to the PRTxDR register store the data state, one bit per GPIO. Then the pin drivers drive the pin in response to this data bit, with a drive strength determined by the drive mode setting.

The pin as an input For the case of an input, again the content of the PRTxDR register is referred, and the logic value at the pin is obtained in the core.

12.6.1 | Drive Modes

When using the PSoC designer, it is not necessary to know about the drive mode bits. It is only necessary to select the drive mode. For doing this 'selection', it is important to have an idea of what these drive modes mean and how the circuitry changes for each mode.

Before reading ahead, it is suggested that you refer Section 2.5 to get a clear idea of what is meant by terms like pullup, pulldown, open drain, high Z, etc. Also, on coming back here, if you find that this part is too cumbersome, skip it for the time being, and come back to it when you actually need to select drive modes for an application. For more information on PSoC drive modes, refer to http://www.cypress.com/?rID=39497&cache=0

Figure 12.22a shows the complete circuit associated with a GPIO pin. It is not necessary to try to understand this elaborate circuit—only the CMOS inverter stage at the output of the circuit need be referred, for our purpose. The drive mode is controllable by three bits PRtxDM0, DM1 and DM2 of the register associated with the pin. Refer to Table 12.3 which shows the various drive options.

Figure 12.22b shows how the output transistor stage gets modified by the DM bit settings. The diagram numbers refer to the entries in Table 12.3.

To understand the drive modes, let us name the output transistors as D1 (the upper one- the PMOS) and D2 (the lower one-the NMOS). D1 and D2 can be turned ON by setting the respective bits in the PRTxDR register. Note that only one MOS will be ON at any moment of time.

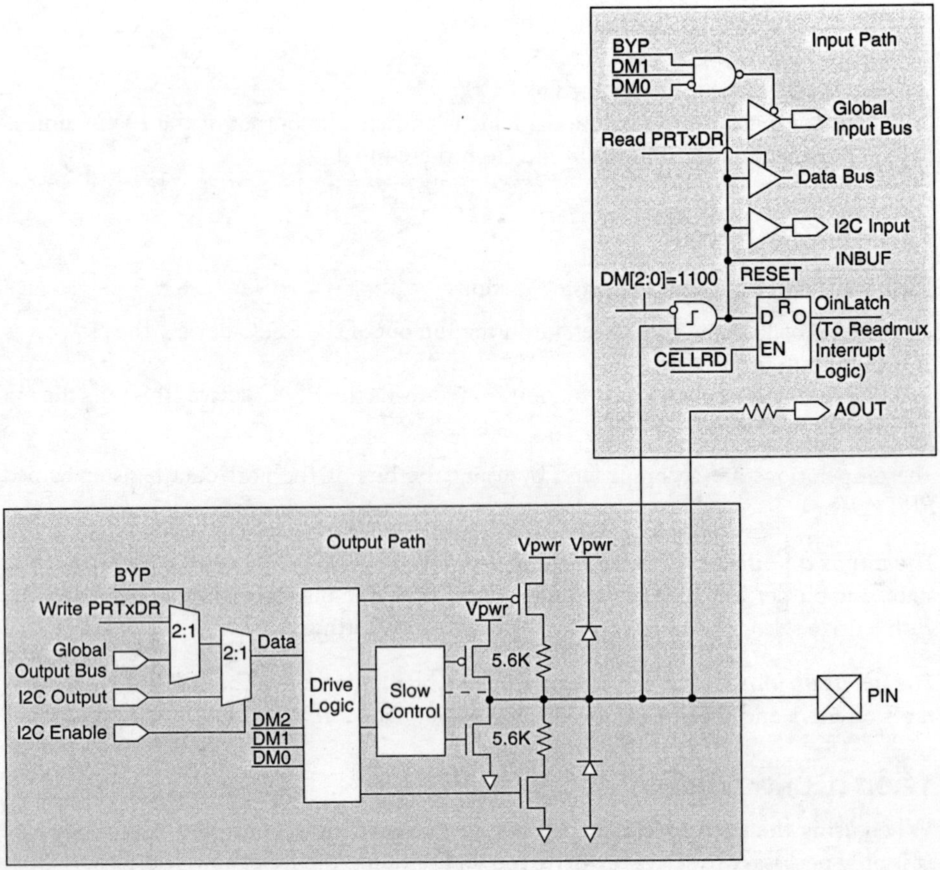

Figure 12.22a | The driver circuitry for a port pin

Table 12.3 | Drive Mode Bits and Drive Modes with Reference to Figure 12.21b

Drive Modes						
DM2	**DM1**	**DM0**	**Drive Mode**	**Diagram Number**	**Data = 0**	**Data = 1**
0	0	0	Resistive Pulldown	0	Resistive	Strong
0	0	1	Strong Drive	1	Strong	Strong
0	1	0	High Impedance	2	Hi-Z	Hi-Z
0	1	1	Resistive Pullup	3	Strong	Resistive
1	0	0	Open Drain, Drives High	4	Hi-Z	Strong (Slow)
1	0	1	Slow Strong Drive	5	Strong (Slow)	Strong (Slow)
1	1	0	High Impedance Analog	6	Hi-Z	Hi-Z
1	1	1	Open Drain, Drives Low	7	Strong (Slow)	Hi-Z

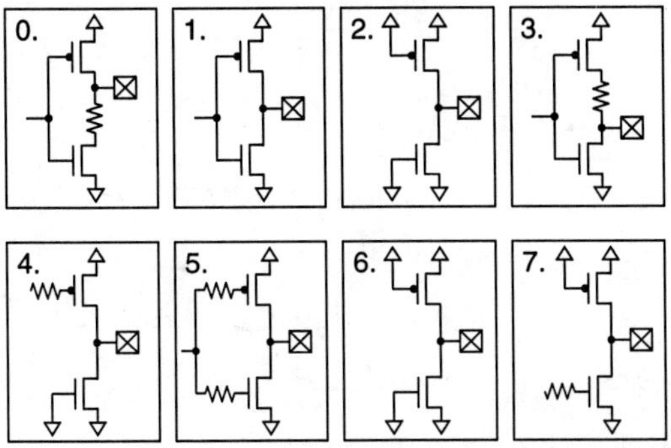

Figure 12.22b | Equivalent circuit for the output stage for the drive options of Table 12.3

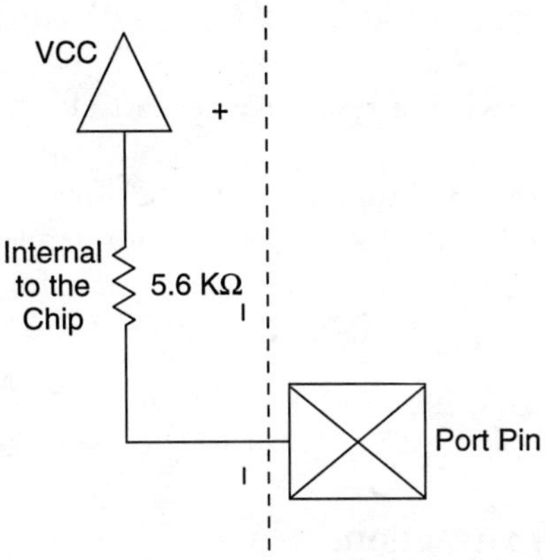

Figure 12.23 | Equivalent circuit at the pin for a resistive pullup

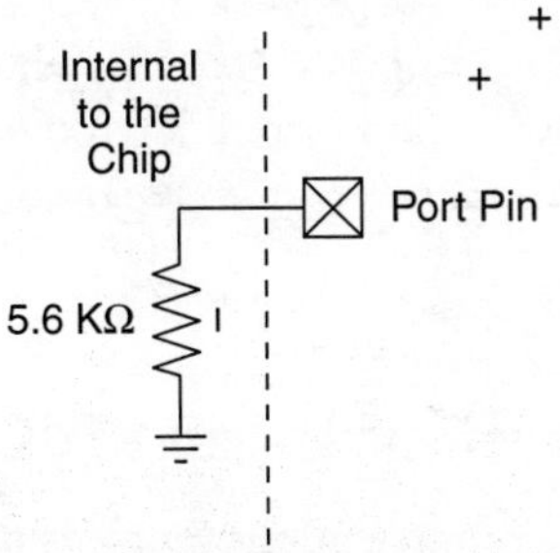

Figure 12.24 | Equivalent circuit at the pin for a resistive pulldown

i) A 'strong' drive implies that D1 or D2 is ON so that the effective load is the ON resistance of one of these, which being low, implies a 'strong' current.
ii) A resistive pullup implies that there is a resistance (5.6K) appearing in series with D1 (which is ON), and so a resistive pullup is obtained. Figure 12.23 shows this. Note that D2 will drive a strong low when it is ON.
iii) A resistive pulldown means that D2 is ON, and there is also a resistance (5.6K) that appears in series with this and connected to ground. Figure 12.24 illustrates this condition. Note that in this case, if D1 is turned ON, it will drive a strong high.

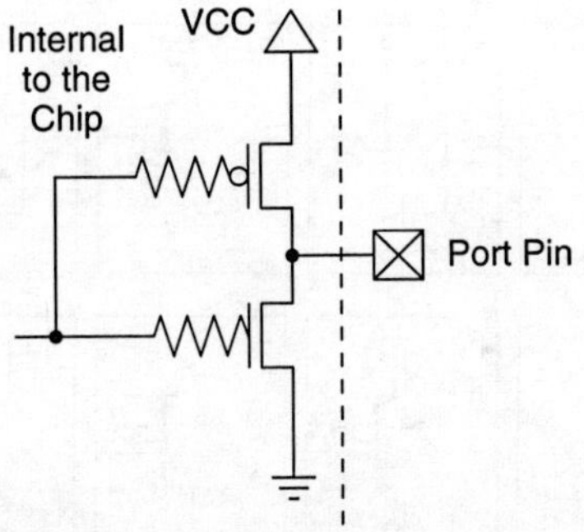

Figure 12.25 | Equivalent circuit at the pin for a slow strong drive

iv) A Hi-Z means that both D1 and D2 are OFF, and so that a very high impedance is seen at the port pin.

vi) A strong **slow** drive is when a resistance appears along with an ON transistor at the input side of the inverter and this increases the rise and fall times of switching, because of the increase in the time constant RC. This is mainly used to reduce the effect of electromagnetic radiation caused by high frequency/high slew rate signals and also to reduce the power consumption. Refer Figure 12.25. The slew control in Figure 12.22a is affected by the DM bit settings when 'slow strong' is selected.

Note For fast switching, i.e., for a strong drive, the rise and fall times are in the range of 3 to 18ns, while for the **'slow'** strong drive, it increases to the range of 10 to 25ns.

12.6.2 | Using the Drive Options

i) Hi-Z is the basic (default) input mode
ii) Strong drive is the basic (default) output mode

This mode may be changed if needed. For example, when push buttons or switches are connected at the input, resistive pullup or pulldown modes may be required to prevent a floating state. *But user modules that directly drive GPIO will have the 'right' drive options automatically configured.*

12.7 | Digital Applications Using PSoC

Now, we will have a look at two simple applications using PSoC. Understand that there are a number of user modules like counters, timers, PWM units, etc. which can be mapped on to the digital blocks, that is, the chip contains dedicated hardware for these peripherals and a number of these peripherals can run simultaneously. For example, a PWM unit, a counter and a pseudo random sequence generator can run simultaneously and produce outputs at different pins with different frequencies.

Besides such dedicated hardware, there are digital systems which are realizable using the core and the software, but need not be mapped on the digital blocks. Single LED, seven segment LED, LCD, etc. are some of them. You can refer to the user modules in the PSoC Designer for the complete list. As mentioned earlier, user module datasheets are available for each of them, which need to be read to understand the hardware connections and the usable API functions. We will start with the simplest module, that is, an LED.

12.7.1 | API Function Naming Conventions

The Application Programming Interface (API) function is to be named as

```
<Instance Name of user module>_<function> //Note the
'underscore'
```

Examples are

LED_1_Start()	; LED_1 is the name of the module and Start() is the function, with ; no parameters
LCD_Position(1, 2)	; LCD is the name of the module and Position () is the function ; with 1, 2 being the parameters used here
PWM8_1_Start	; PWM8_1 is the instance name of the module and Start() is the ; function

Note: The name LED_1, LCD, PWM8_1, etc. are names used by the IDE. But the user can change the name (there is an option available for it). For LED_1 you can change it to LED1, for instance. The API functions calling it will then start with the name LED1

LED1_Switch(1)	; LED1 is the name of the module and Switch() is the function ; with the parameter '1' being used here.

12.7.2 | The LED User Module

There is an LED module inbuilt, and a few simple functions to control it. We can choose between an active high or active low connection.

The LED User Module is just a set of simple functions to control an LED or any simple device that needs an ON–OFF control. For example, the module can be used to control a relay. Of course, you need to use a relay driver externally, since the PSoC Source/Sink current is limited).

Example 12.4

Implement a flashing LED using the inbuilt LED module.

Solution

For this, let's select P0_2 as the port pin, and 'active low', (i.e., the LED will be ON when the data bit is set to zero) in the LED_1 user module parameter settings. Also choose 'strong' for the drive option for P0_2. The interconnection is shown in Figure 12.26. Note that the only connection is to define the use of Port 0_2 for connecting the LED and none of the global buses are used.

The program to be run for switching the LED ON and OFF at a specific rate is shown below. This is the main.c file used.

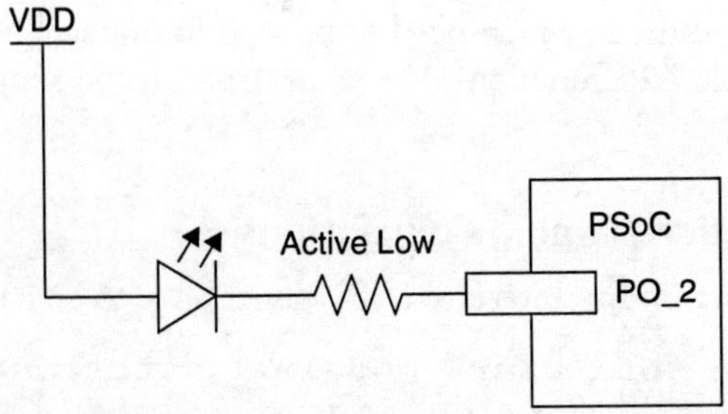

Figure 12.26 | An LED connected to P0_2

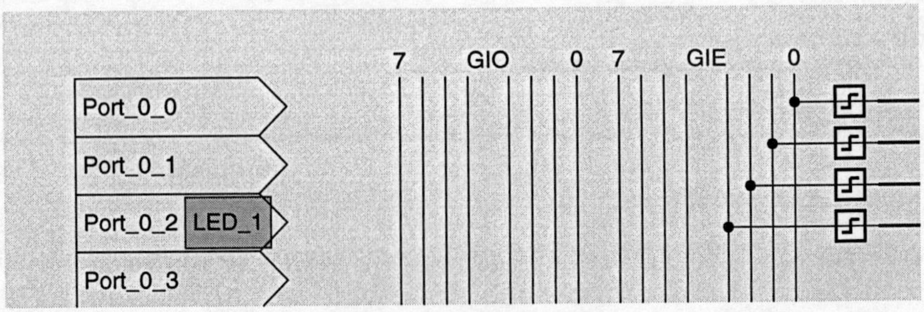

Figure 12.27 | LED_1 user module at port pin P0_2

Program

```
include <m8c.h>                 //part specific constants and
                                  macros
#include "PSoCAPI.h"            //PSoC API definitions for all
                                  User Modules
void delay(int);
void main()
{
      LED_1_Start();
      LED_1_Switch(1);          //Turn on LED
      while(1)
      {
            delay(3);
            LED_1_Invert();     //Flash LED
      }
}
void delay(sec)
int sec;
{
      int i,j,secd;
      for (secd=0;secd<=sec;secd++)
      {
            for(i=0;i<=2;i++)
```

```
                {
                        for (j= 0;j<=20480;j++)
                                {
                                }
                }
        }
}
```

Note that the functions used are LED_1_Start(), LED_1_Switch(1) and LED_1_Invert(). The delay is specified in the function named 'delay' which is written by the user. The program is burned on the flash of the chip, and the LED switches ON and OFF continuously once the Vdd is turned ON.

12.7.2.1 | *A Delay Function*

The following is another routine for creating a delay. The CPU clock (CPU_Clk) is chosen as 3MHz (SysClk/8), t=250 creates a delay of 1 ms.

Program

```
void delay_ms(unsigned char ms)
{
        volatile unsigned char t;
        while (ms--)
        {
                t = 250;
                while (t--);
        }
}
```

12.7.3 | The PWM (Pulse Width Modulation) Modules

The idea of PWM, its use and timing diagrams have been discussed in Section 3.3.2.2 Here we attempt to realize PWM using PSoC.
It is possible to have 8 or 16-bit PWM and they use one digital block (for 8-bit) or two digital blocks (for 16-bit). The other options are as follows:

i) Source clock rates up to 48 MHz
ii) Automatic reloads of period for each pulse cycle
iii) Programmable pulse width
iv) Input enables/disables continuous counter operation
v) Interrupt option on rising edge of the output or terminal count

The 8- and 16-bit PWM user modules are pulse width modulators with programmable period and pulse width. The clock and enable signals can be selected from several sources. The output signal can be routed to a pin or to one of the global output buses, for internal use by other user modules. An interrupt can be programmed to trigger on the rising edge of the output or when the counter reaches the terminal count condition.

Example 12.5

Generate a square wave using the PWM module.

Solution

Here, we choose an 8-bit PWM unit, i.e., PWM_8, use port pin P0_0 as the output pin, the drive mode 'strong' is configured automatically and, use VC3 as the clock, and '1' as Enable. Figure 12.28 shows the input and output connections of the PWM unit.

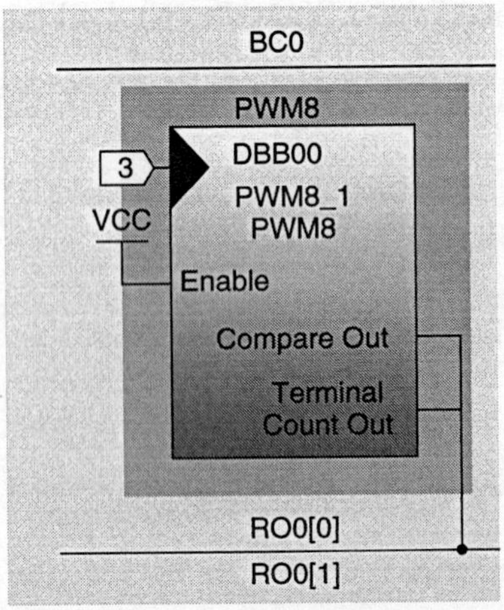

Figure 12.28 | Input and output connections of the PWM unit

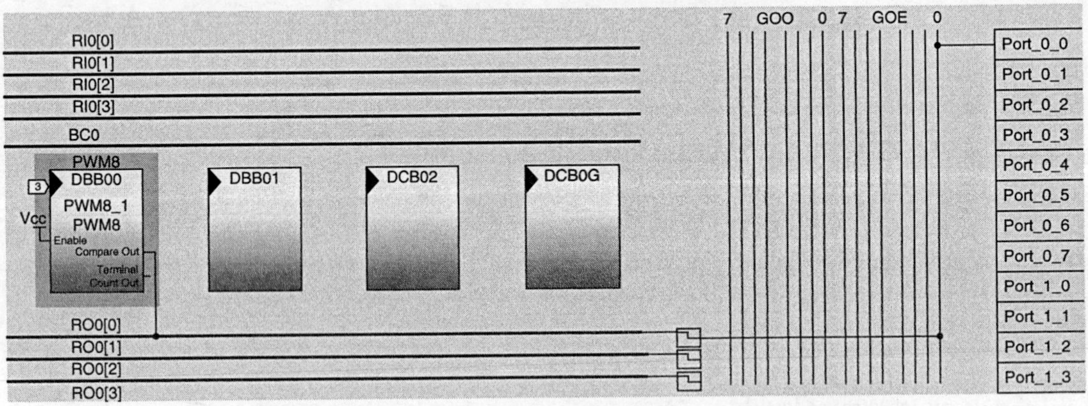

Figure 12.29 | The PWM unit with the output routed to P0_0, shown on the graphic editor

Program

```
include <m8c.h>          //part specific constants and macros
#include "PSoCAPI.h"     //PSoC API definitions for all User
                           Modules

void main()
```

```
{
        PWM8_1_Start();   //API for square wave generation
}
```

The details of the function used here, i.e., PWM8_1_Start() can be obtained from the manual of the module.

Note Once a specific peripheral, like the PWM unit, for instance, is set to start running as in Example 12.5, the CPU has no work at all. The hardware constituting the PWM unit runs continuously to generate the square wave.

PWM Settings
Period=99
Pulse width =50
Clock_Synch =Sync to Sysclk
Compare = Less Than
With this, we get a duty cycle of 50% with a frequency of VC3/100 (Since the module counts down from 99 to zero).

12.7.4 | Implement an LCD Display Design

The features of the LCD user module are

i) Uses the industry standard Hitachi HD44780 LCD display driver chip protocol
ii) Requires only seven I/O pins—four for data and three for control

There are functions provided with this module to display strings and numbers as well as to display horizontal and vertical bar graphs. The LED module is connected to one port (already pre-fixed to be Port. 2 for the development kit), see Figure 12.30.
Refer to Section 3.3.1.6 for a detailed discussion on LCD interfacing.
In the set up here, data is sent as two nibbles to save port lines. The connections between the port and PSoC pins are as shown in Table 12.5.

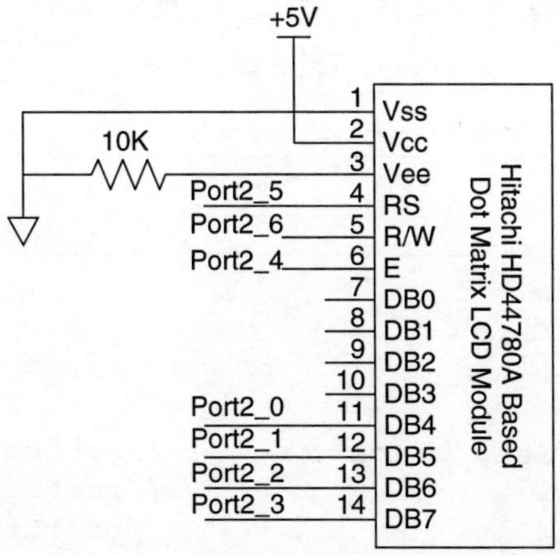

Figure 12.30 | Connection between the LCD and a PSoC Port 2 pins

Table 12.5 | Connections Between Port 2 and the LCD Pins

PSoC Pin	LCD Pin	Description
Port 2_0	DB4	Data Bit 0
Port 2_1	DB5	Data Bit 1
Port 2_2	DB6	Data Bit 2
Port 2_3	DB7	Data Bit 3
Port 2_4	E	LCD Enable
Port 2_5	RS	Register Select
Port 2_6	RW	Read/Write

Example 12.6

Implement an LCD display using the PSoC development kit.

Solution

The steps in using the LCD module are to select it from the list of user modules, and choose Port 2. The placement is as shown in Figure 12.31. Note that the LCD user module does not occupy any digital or analog blocks and also does not use any of the global buses.

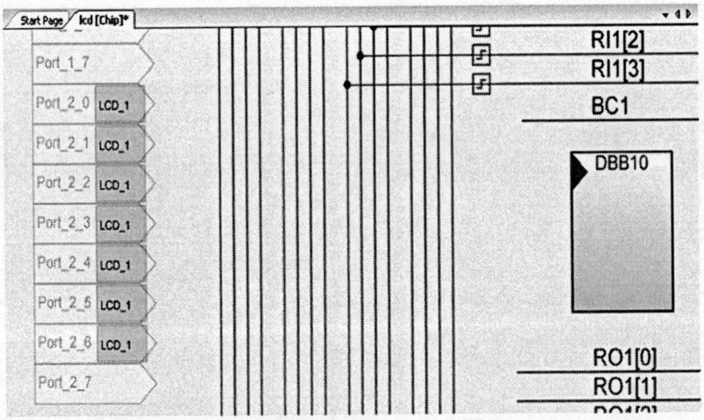

Figure 12.31 | LCD_1 module placed at Port 2 pins

Program

```
#include <m8c.h>
#include "PSoCAPI.h"
void main()
{
char str[ ] = "Lab, MTech";          //String stored in RAM
LCD_Start();                         //initialize
LCD_Position(0,4);                   //position -0th row 4th
                                       column
```

```
LCD_PrCString("Welcome to PSoC"); //Print the string
                                    stored in ROM
                                    (saves RAM
                                  //space)

LCD_Position(1,2);
LCD_PrString(str);                //Print string stored in
                                    RAM

}
The output of the display shows
'Welcome to PSoC
Lab, MTech'
```

12.8 | The Analog Section

Now, we will have a look at the analog section of PSoC. Figure 12.32 shows the block diagram of the analog system.

The analog blocks are arranged as three rows. The CY8C29x66 has four analog columns. The analog blocks are arranged as four columns and three rows. There are two types of analog building blocks.

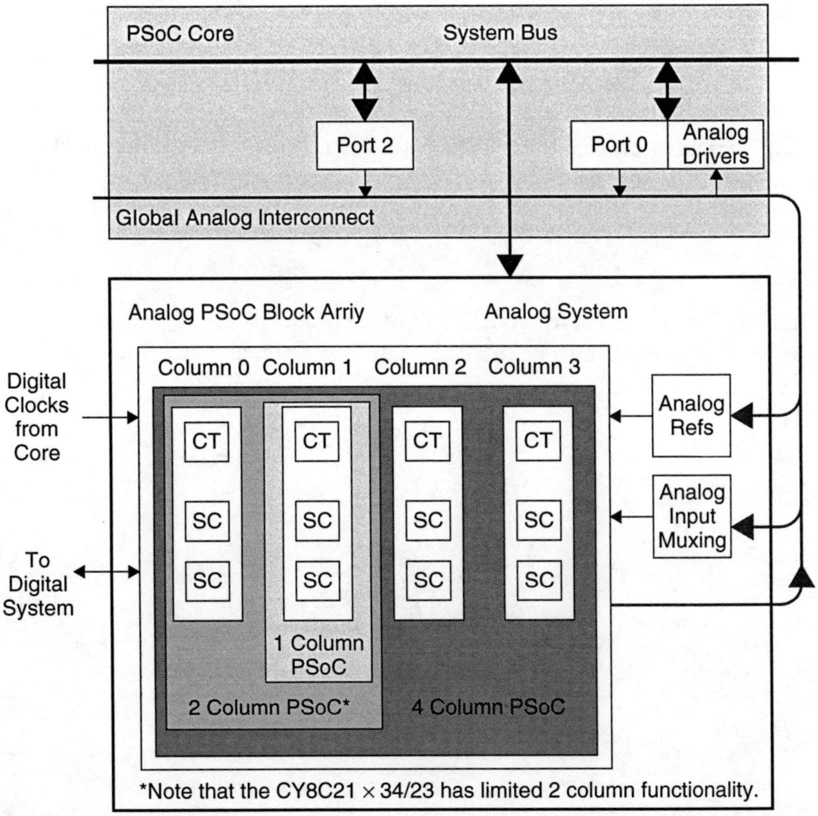

Figure 12.32 | Block diagram of the analog section

i) **The CT (Continuous Time) Blocks:** The blocks in the top row are the (CT) blocks and are used for realizing user modules like inverting amplifiers, programmable gain amplifiers (PGA), instrumentation amplifiers, comparators, etc.
ii) **The SC (Switched Capacitor) Blocks:** The lower two rows are the switched capacitor blocks. The user modules like ADCs, DACs and filters can be placed only in the SC blocks.

We should know what an SC block means before we proceed further. The next section gives a brief insight into the idea of switched capacitor circuits.

12.8.1 | Switched Capacitor Circuits

In integrated circuits, resistors are also to be fabricated along with transistors. It is quite difficult to fabricate them on an IC with a high degree of accuracy and they also take up a lot of space. In recent times, a new principle has been adopted to replace them. In this, the values can be made to depend on ratios of capacitor values (which can be set accurately), rather than absolute values (which vary between manufacturing runs). This is the driving force behind the idea of having resistors realized by switched capacitors. Let's try to understand the working principle of switched capacitor circuits.

Consider the circuit in Figure 12.33, with a capacitor connected to two switches S1 and S2 and two different voltage sources v1 and v2.

If S_2 closes with S_1 open, then S_1 closes with switch S_2 open, a charge (q is transferred from v_2 to v_1 with

$$\Delta q = C_1\left(v_2 - v_1\right) \tag{12.1}$$

If this switching process is repeated N times in a time t, the amount of charge transferred per unit time is given by

$$\frac{\Delta q}{\Delta t} = C_1\left(v_2 - v_1\right)\frac{N}{\Delta t} \tag{12.2}$$

Recognizing that the left hand side represents charge per unit time, or current, and the number of cycles per unit time is the switching frequency (or clock frequency, f_{CLK}) we can rewrite the equation as

$$i = C_1\left(v_2 - v_1\right)f_{CLK} \tag{12.3}$$

Rearranging we get

$$\frac{\left(v_2 - v_1\right)}{i} = \frac{1}{C_1F_{CLK}} = R \tag{12.4}$$

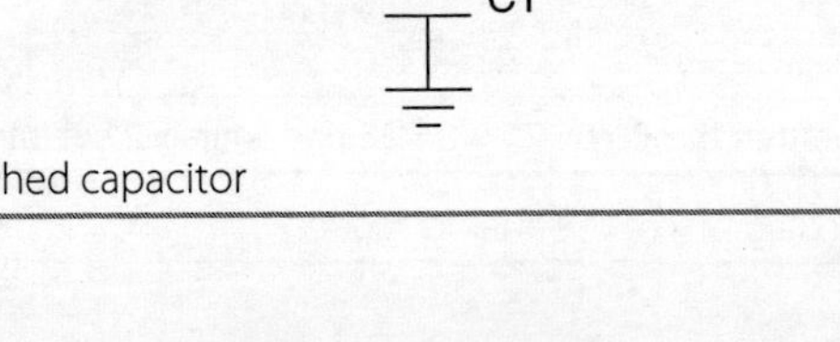

Figure 12.33 | Switched capacitor

which can be interpreted to mean that the switched capacitor is equivalent to a resistor. The value of this resistor decreases with increasing switching frequency or increasing capacitance, as either will increase the amount of charge transferred from v_2 to v_1 in a given time.

With this idea, there are switched capacitor integrators, filters, amplifiers, etc.

In integrated circuits, it is better to use this, instead of real resistors whose values are not accurate. SC blocks are accurate, require no external components and maintain a predictable response over all specified operating conditions. For switched capacitor amplifiers, for instance, the operation takes place in two phases: sampling and amplification. So the circuit needs a clock, along with the analog input. See Figure 12.34.

The advantages of switched capacitor circuits are:

i) Compatibility with CMOS technology
ii) Good accuracy of time constants
iii) Good voltage linearity
iv) Good temperature characteristics
v) 0.1% to 1% accuracy depending on the size of components

12.8.2 | SC and CT Blocks in PSoC

Thus we see that in the SC blocks, resistors are realized using the switching of capacitors. In the CT blocks, the amplifiers and comparators are realized using normal OPAMP and resistor networks. Note Figures 12.35 and 12.36 which show this. The inverting amplifier, for instance, has the circuit realization as shown in Figure 12.35 with resistors and op-Amps. The block diagram of the ADC (an SC block) shows switched capacitors instead of resistors (Figure 12.36).

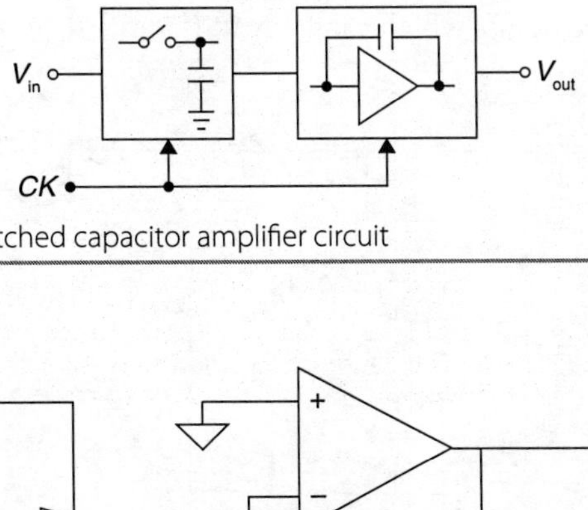

Figure 12.34 | A switched capacitor amplifier circuit

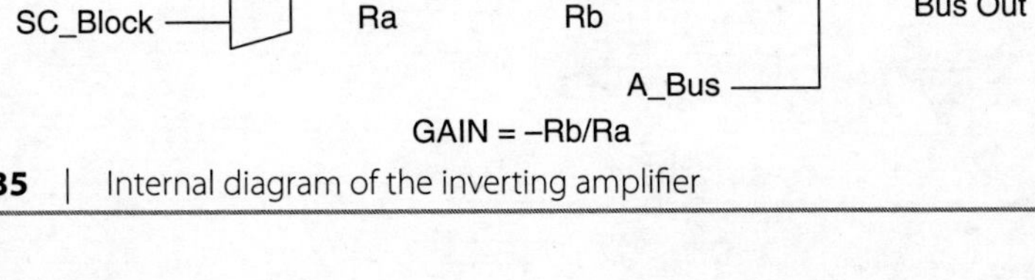

Figure 12.35 | Internal diagram of the inverting amplifier

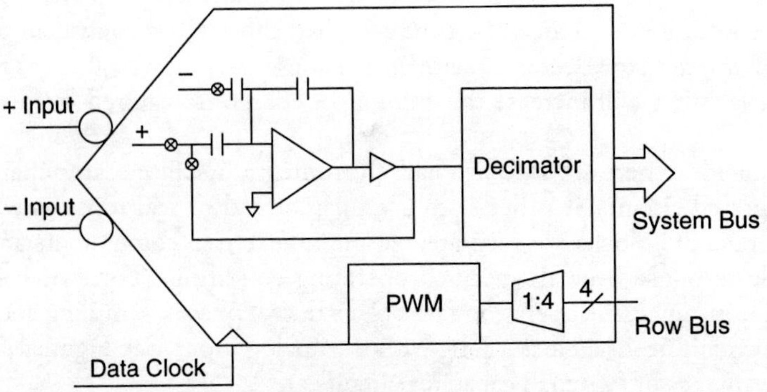

Figure 12.36 | The internal diagram of the ADC

12.8.3 | Interconnects of the Analog Section

Now let's discuss the interconnects of an analog section. Refer Figure 12.37b which is the re-drawn (for clarity) version of the analog section as viewed on the graphic editor (Figure 12.37a) of PSoC Designer. The multiplexers have been named and numbered for simplifying the explanation of the whole set up (which looks quite complicated, but is not really so).

The points to note and understand using these figures are

i) The top row contains the CT blocks—they are usually referred to as ACBs (Analog Continuous time Blocks). **Only amplifiers and comparators can use these blocks.**

ii) The next two rows contain the switched capacitor blocks of type C or type D. They are designated as ASC (type C) or ASD (type D). Having two types (C and D) imply that there are slight differences in the SC circuitry. Incidentally, type D caters to more complex circuits.

iii) There are some restrictions regarding the pins that can be used as analog input and output. Note these points which can be readily verified from the IDE.

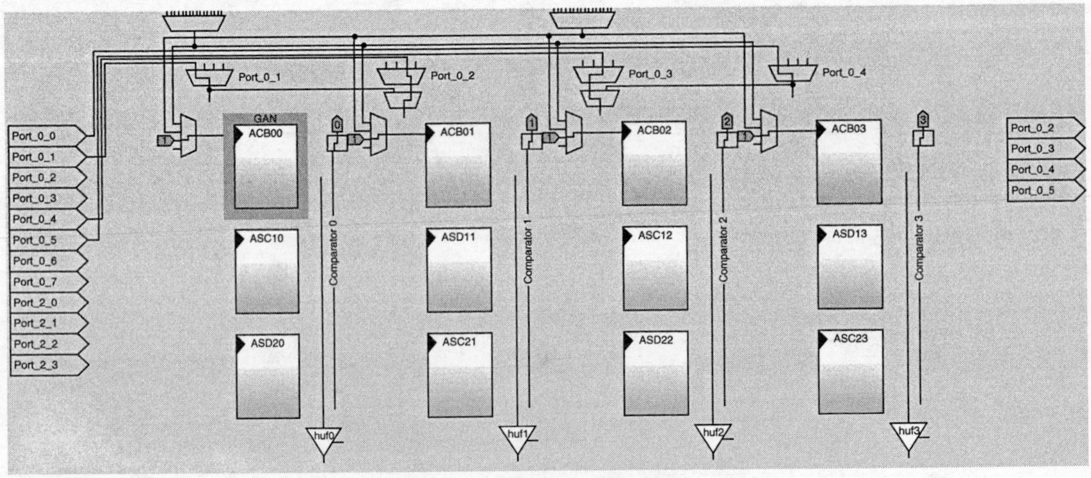

Figure 12.37a | The analog section as seen in the editor of the PSoC Designer

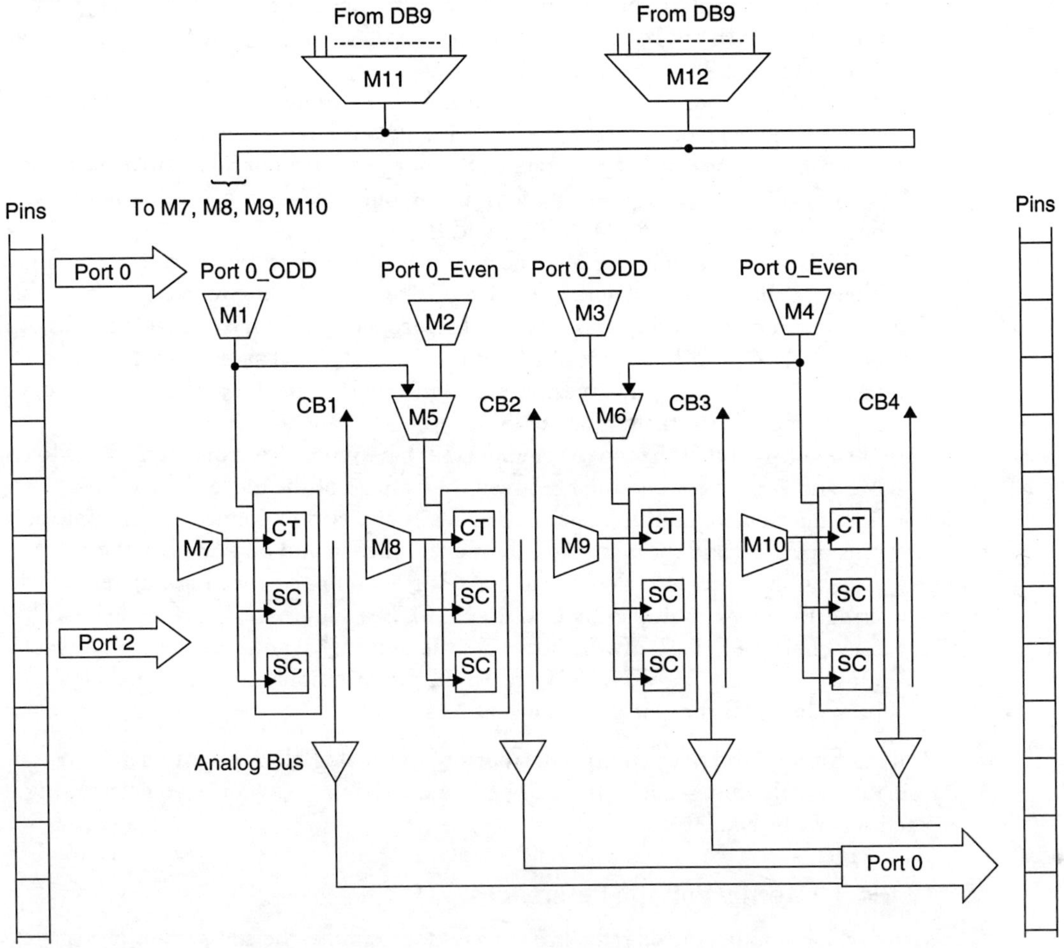

Figure 12.37b | The re-drawn version of Figure 12.35a (for ease of explanation)

– All pins of Port 0 can be used as analog inputs (if they are not used as outputs)
– The lower four pins of Port 2 can also be used as analog inputs, but only for the **left most SC blocks (rows 2 and 3 of column 1)**
– Only P0_2, P0_3, P0_4 and P0_5 can be used as analog output pins

Such restrictions are inconvenient, no doubt, but we get used to it very soon.

iv) The inputs for the CT modules (top row) can be taken from the analog input port lines of Port 0. For SC blocks which are not in column 1, or if Port 2 is not available (for instance, if it has been used already for some digital application.), inputs cannot be taken from Port_0.

How is analog input taken from an external source, then?

The solution is to take it from the outputs of the CT modules which can act as inputs to SC blocks. For example, to use an ADC (an SC block) which is to be placed in the second or third rows, the method is to choose a PGA (with a gain of 1) to be placed in one of the CT blocks. The input of the ADC is taken from the output of the PGA, which feeds into one of the SC blocks. This is made clear in Example 12.8.

v) The analog output can be taken out of the chip, through the analog bus which is then routed to an output port pin. There is only one bus line (with a buffer) for each column. This means that only one of the blocks in a column can drive an analog output, at a time. Thus there are four analog outputs which can be routed to four output port pins (P0_2, P0_3, P0_4 and P0_5)

vi) There is also a comparator bus line acting as a digital output from each column. They are shown in the figure as CB1 to CB4 corresponding to each column. This can be given 'to' any digital block. For instance, signals from two analog blocks can be compared, and the result of the comparison, a digital signal, can be passed on to some digital block,say we can use it as an enable signal for a counter or timer or similar module (in the digital section).

vii) The multiplexers at the top (M11 and M12) have inputs from digital blocks. Muxes M5 and M6 are for choosing between the outputs of the muxes M1 to M4.

viii) The input analog multiplexers (M1 to M4)) are used to connect from input port pins of Port 0 and there are separate muxes for even and odd numbered pins.

ix) Analog blocks require clocks, and there is the option of selecting different clocks using the clock multiplexers (M7 to M10). See Figure 12.38. Here ACB00 has four choices of clock, of which two are the outputs taken from the digital blocks. Others can be VC1, VC2, VC3, etc. In the figure, a signal from a digital block has been chosen as the clock.

Reading through the rules and specifications of the analog block might seem a bit confusing during the first reading, but will be found to be very easy once you start using it practically with the IDE.

12.8.4 | Internal Voltage References

Many analog resources need reference voltages,for example, the comparator needs a reference voltage with which the input voltage is to be compared, to make a decision on what the output should be. Figure 12.39 shows the choices available (in the IDE) for this.

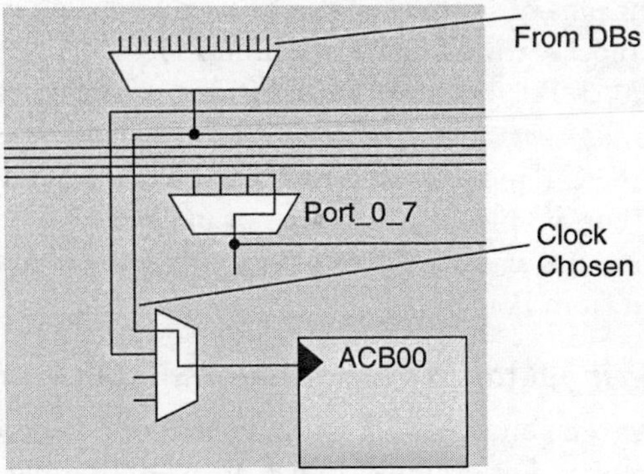

Figure 12.38 | The clock multiplexer for ACB00

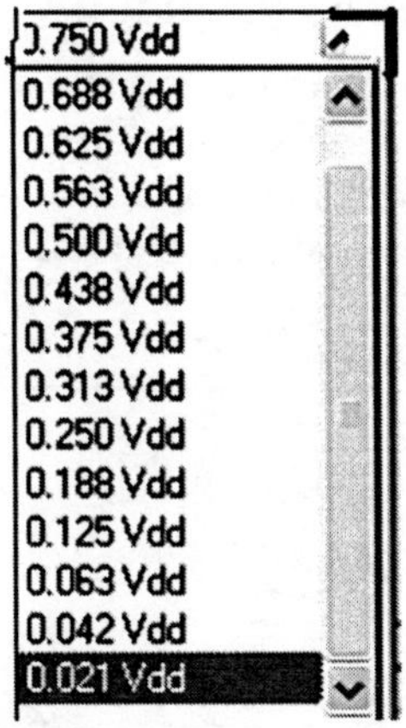

Figure 12.39 | Reference voltages available

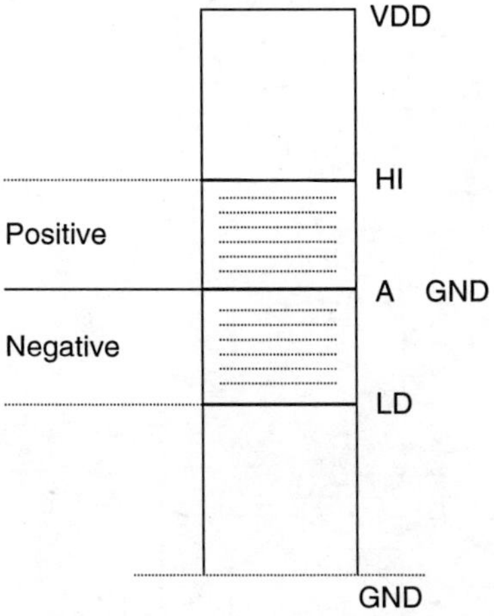

Figure 12.40 | Defining positive and negative analog voltages

As we go though the steps of design using analog blocks, we will see many requirements of 'reference voltage'. Such references are needed for comparators, ADCs, etc. and the user is allowed to choose from a list of options available. See Figure 12.39. The hardware for the reference voltage is available as part of the system resources (Section 12.9).

There is another important point to ponder on, regarding analog voltages, i.e. analog voltages can be positive or negative. For inverting amplifiers, for example, a positive input is inverted to be negative and vice versa. But PSoC supplies only voltages from 0 to +5V. So, then, how is 'negative' defined here? Figure 12.40 answers this question.

In the 0 to 5V range, VDD is the maximum and VSS (0 V) is the minimum value. Here the central voltage is considered as the 'analog ground' and notated as AGND. All voltages below that are considered as negative, and all voltages above as positive voltages.

Now let's use analog blocks for some simple applications.

12.8.5 | Programmable Gain Amplifier (PGA)

A PGA is one of the modules in the user module set of 'Amplifiers'. It implements an opamp based non-inverting amplifier with programmable gain, with 33 user-programmable gain settings (maximum is 48). For a PGA, the gain can be changed in the program. That's how its gain becomes programmable.

Example 12.7

Implement a PGA for a gain of 2.

Solution

The steps are

i) Select PGA_1 from the user module list.
ii) Select the parameters of the user module—here the input mux (M1) and the output bus is chosen as shown in Figure 12.41. The gain is chosen to be 2.
iii) In the parameter list (Figure 12.42), the reference voltage is taken as VSS (the true ground). With this, we mean that we need only positive outputs.

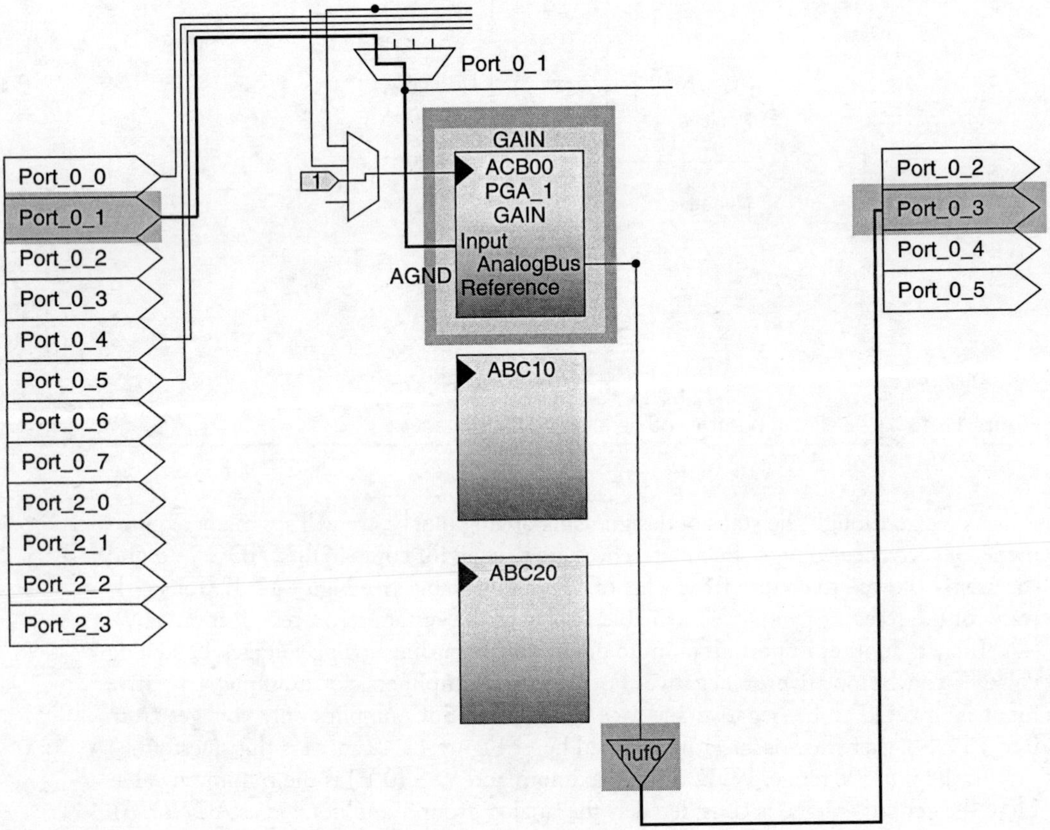

Figure 12.41 | Interconnecting the PGA to P0_1 (input pin)

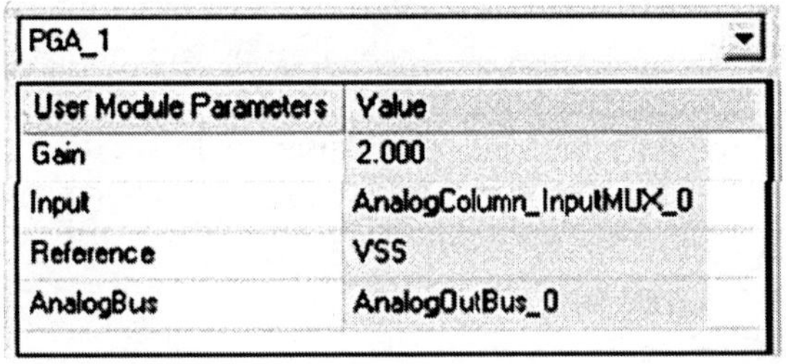

Figure 12.42 | Parameter selection for the PGA

The interconnection chosen is in Figure 12.41. Port 0_1 is chosen as the input analog pin and Port 0_3 is the output pin. The other input required for the PGA is a clock which has been chosen as VC1. The program uses two functions from the API set of the PGA.

Program

```
include <m8c.h>        //part specific constants and macros
#include "PSoCAPI.h" //PSoC API definitions for all User
Modules
void main()
{
PGA_1_Start(PGA_1_MEDPOWER);
PGA_1_SetGain(PGA_1_G2_00);
}
```

The working of the PGA can be tested by burning the code, and running the program on the development board. A variable input voltage can be applied at P0_1 and the output amplitude checked at P0_3. A gain of 2 will be obtained. The maximum output will be limited to 5V (the supply voltage). For AC, the reference must be AGND before feeding to the PSoC pin. See the '**note**' in Section 12.8.6.

12.8.6 | Implementation of an ADC

There are many types of ADCs with different resolutions, in the list of user modules. One of them may be selected.

The salient points regarding the implementation of an ADC using the PSoC are as given.

i) As mentioned in Section 12.8.3, the analog input of the ADC is not directly given to the ADC. It is applied through a PGA (with gain=1), from an input analog pin (Port 0), (Actually, the ADC which is an SC block can take analog input from Port 2. But for the kit, Port 2 is used for connecting the LCD. In this program, both the LCD and ADC are to be used, so the connection to the ADC is through the PGA). The output of the PGA is connected to the ADC input.

ii) The ADC has a digital output, the number of bits of which is dependant on the resolution of the ADC. There is no mechanism by which the digital values can be obtained at a set of output port pins directly. But the converted digital value is available in software, and API funcions may be used to obtain it. One simple method is to use the LCD API functions and display the ASCII value on an LCD which is connected to Port 2 (on the development kit).

Example 12.8

Convert an analog voltage to digital form and display it on the LCD of the kit.

Solution

The interconnection diagram is shown in Figure 12.43. Observe that, P0_1 has been chosen as the analog input pin.

Note:

i) Only positive analog voltages can be handled by the PSoC.
ii) For AC inputs which have positive and negative swings, the negative portion must be clamped and made positive (before giving it as an input to the ADC).
iii) Similarly, analog AC outputs will have a positive bias. To remove it, pass it through a capacitor to remove the positive offset.

In the figure, we find that P0_1 is the input pin. The analog input is applied to a PGA with a gain of 1. The output of this is fed to the selected ADC in the next row. There is no output for it in hardware. The ADC's API functions are used to get conversion done. The digital output in ASCII form is displayed on the LCD.

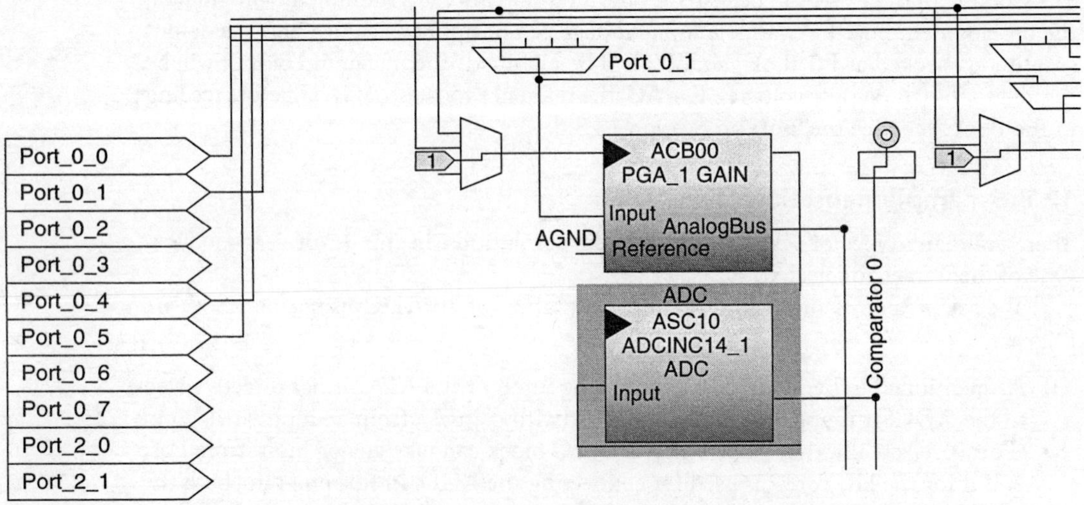

Figure 12.43 | Realization of an ADC

Program

```
#include <m8c.h>                        //part specific
                                          constants and
                                          //macros
#include "PSoCAPI.h"                    //PSoC API definitions
                                          for all User
                                          //Modules
void main()
{
      int iData;
      M8C_EnableGInt;                   //Enable global
                                          interrupts
      PGA_1_SetGain(PGA_1_G1_00);
      PGA_1_Start(PGA_1_MEDPOWER);
      ADCINC14_1_Start                  //Turn on Analog
      (ADCINC14_1_HIGHPOWER);             section
      ADCINC14_1_GetSamples(0);         //Start ADC to read
      LCD_1_Start();                    //Initialize LCD
      for(;;)
      {
      while(ADCINC14_1_fIsDataAvailable() == 0);
                                        //Wait for data to be
                                          ready
      iData = ADCINC14_1_iGetData();    //Get Data
      ADCINC14_1_ClearFlag();           //Clear data ready
                                          flag
      LCD_1_Position(0,5);              //Place cursor at
                                          row 0, col 5
      LCD_1_PrHexInt(iData);            //Print ADC data on
                                          the LCD
      }
}
```

12.9 | System Resources

Now, let's make a brief study of what are called system resources. Refer to Figure 12.44. Some of these have already been discussed earlier.

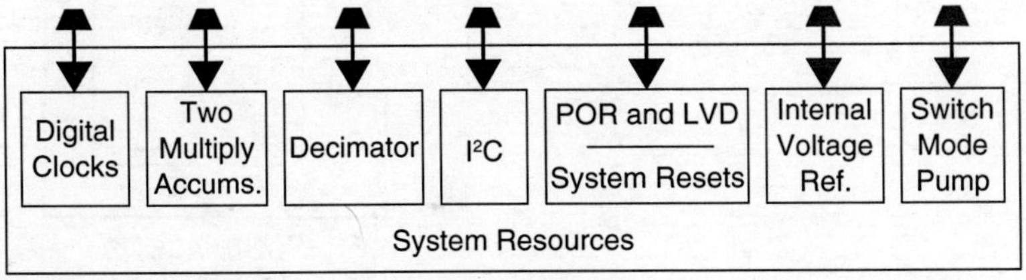

Figure 12.44 | The block diagram of system resources

i) **Digital Clocks:** This refers to the system of oscillators needed to be used as clocks for the digital as well as the analog blocks. In Section 12.4.4, these sources were explained as part of the requirement of the core. Keep in mind that the system core requires a specific clock. Besides this, the user modules need clock signals, and a chain of multipliers and dividers gives us the option to choose the value we need.

ii) **Multiply Accumulate (MAC):** For DSP applications, 'multiply and accumulate' is commonly needed. PSoC is not a DSP processor, but it provides DSP support through this hardware MAC unit. 'Multiply and accumulate' is a functionality commonly used for convolution and correlation operations.

Accumulation of products is a feature that is implemented on top of simple multiplication. When using the MAC to accumulate the products of successive multiplications, two 8-bit signed values are used for input. The product of the multiplication is accumulated as a 32-bit signed value. The user has the choice to either cause a multiply & accumulate function to take place or a multiply only function. Refer to Figure 12.45.

iii) **POR, LVD and System Resets:** POR is 'power on reset' and LVD is Low voltage detect, the same as Brown out reset which is explained is Section 2.2.3 For LVD, the threshold for reset can be selected by the user.

iv) **Power on Reset (POR):** PSoC has an active low POR. The circuitry for POR is inside the chip. When the supply voltage rises to a specified level, the chip is in the operational state.

Reset can occur from other triggers as well—one is due to the watchdog timer (refer to Section 2.2.6) It can also be caused by an internally occurring error, for instance, if during the boot sequence, it is found that the contents of flash are not valid, the chip is reset.

v) **Internal Voltage References:** The reference voltages are generated by this circuit diagram. The buffer circuit provides gain to the bandgap voltage, to produce a 1.30V reference. See Figure 12.46, which has an opamp in the noninverting configuration with a gain of $(1 + R_F/R)$. At the selected point of the potentionmeter, any voltage above the band gap can be obtained and used as the reference voltage V_{REF}.

vi) **Decimator:** This is also a hardware, mostly used for filters, i.e., in DSP applications.

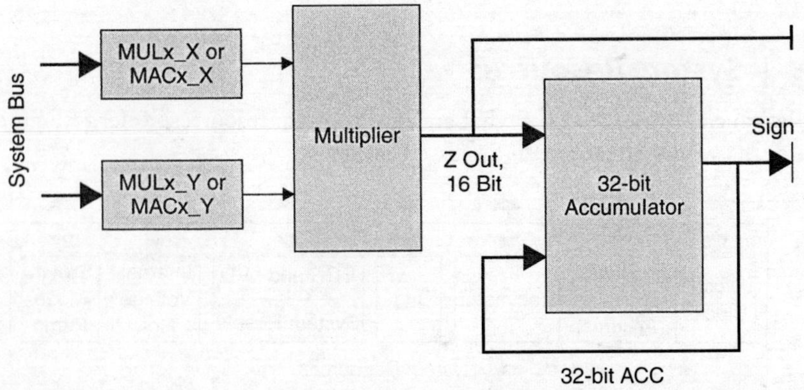

Figure 12.45 | The MAC unit

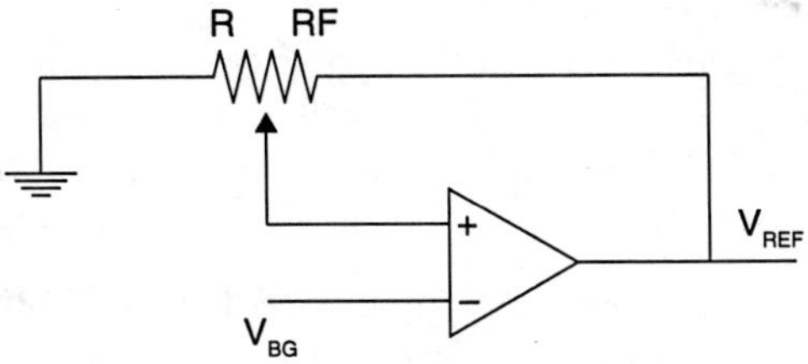

Figure 12.46 | The circuit for generating reference voltages for analog blocks

vii) I2C: The I2C is a simple two wire protocol (refer Section 5.2.1) used for serial communication between ICs. It is available as one of the user modules in the digital communication sections. We can place this user module on a digital communication block, select port pins and using the APIs supplied by the user module, I2C communication can be realized. But besides that, there is a dedicated hardware for I2C called I2HWC available as one of the system resources. Using this hardware makes I2C realization very simple and effective. Appendix J contains a detailed description of how this resource is used to facilitate communication between PSoC and an EEPROM.

viii) **Switched Mode Pump:** This is used when the PSoC operates on battery supply. A single battery voltage of 1.5V can be made to be boosted up to the level as to supply the PSoC with sufficient voltage to make it work. (In practice, it is found that the current may not be sufficient to have other chips in the circuitry, but a PSoC chip and some passive sensors can run with this boosted power supply.)

Figure 12.47 shows the circuitry associated with the switch mode pump. A battery and an inductor are connected in series at the SMP pin of the chip. A bypass capacitor of at least 0.1 μF must be connected between VDD and VSS. The inductor is charged when

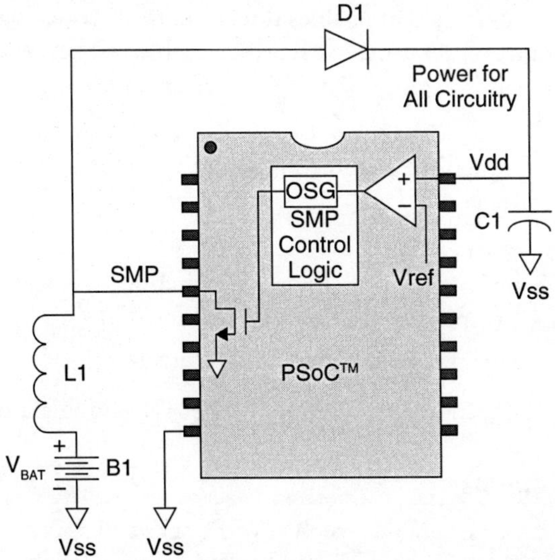

Figure 12.47 | The switched mode pump for a 20 pin PSoC chip

the internal SMP switch is on. When this switch is turned off, a flyback mode occurs and the inductor energy is released into the bypass capacitor. This is done in a periodic fashion (1.3 MHz), charging the capacitor and thus the required value of power supply voltage is obtained at the VDD point. Note that the direction of the diode is such as to get the capacitor to be charged to a positive voltage.

Note: The value of the battery voltage may go as low as 1V, but once the circuit is switched off, there is no guarantee of this set up being reliable, unless the battery voltage is at least 1.1V.

12.10 | PSoC3 and PSoC5

These two versions are the advanced versions of PSoC, to be used for more advanced applications. As mentioned in Section 12.2, they are different from PSoC1 in the core architecture as well in the IDE to be used. Appendix F gives the step-by-step instructions on how to get started on using PSoC Creator which is the IDE for PSoC3 and 5 (This Appendix is available in the website of the book).

12.10.1 | PSoC3

PSoC3 has an enhanced 8051 core. This means that its instruction set is the same as the standard 8051, but it is has a few enhancements which are as follows:

i) Pipelined RISC architecture that executes ten times faster than the industry standard 8051
ii) Most instructions executed in one or two cycles
iii) 256 bytes of internal data RAM
iv) Dual DPTR extension to the standard 8051 architecture
v) 24-bit external data space that enables access to on-chip memory and registers, and to off-chip memory
vi) New interrupt interface that enables direct interrupt vectoring
vii) New special function registers (SFRs) that enable fast access to PSoC3 I/O ports

12.10.2 | PSoC5

This has the ARM–Cortex M3 architecture with the features

i) Enhanced v7 ARM architecture, with
   - Thumb2 Instruction Set
   - 16- and 32-bit Instructions (no mode switching)
   - 32-bit ALU; Hardware multiply and divide
ii) Single cycle 3-stage pipeline; Harvard architecture

(Refer to Chapter 10 for more information on the ARM architecture)

12.10.3 | Peripherals

Figure 12.48 shows the peripheral structure of PSoC3 and 5. It shows the digital building blocks (designated as 'universal digital blocks'), the analog blocks, the core with the clocks, power management module, debug and trace and other modules which are not

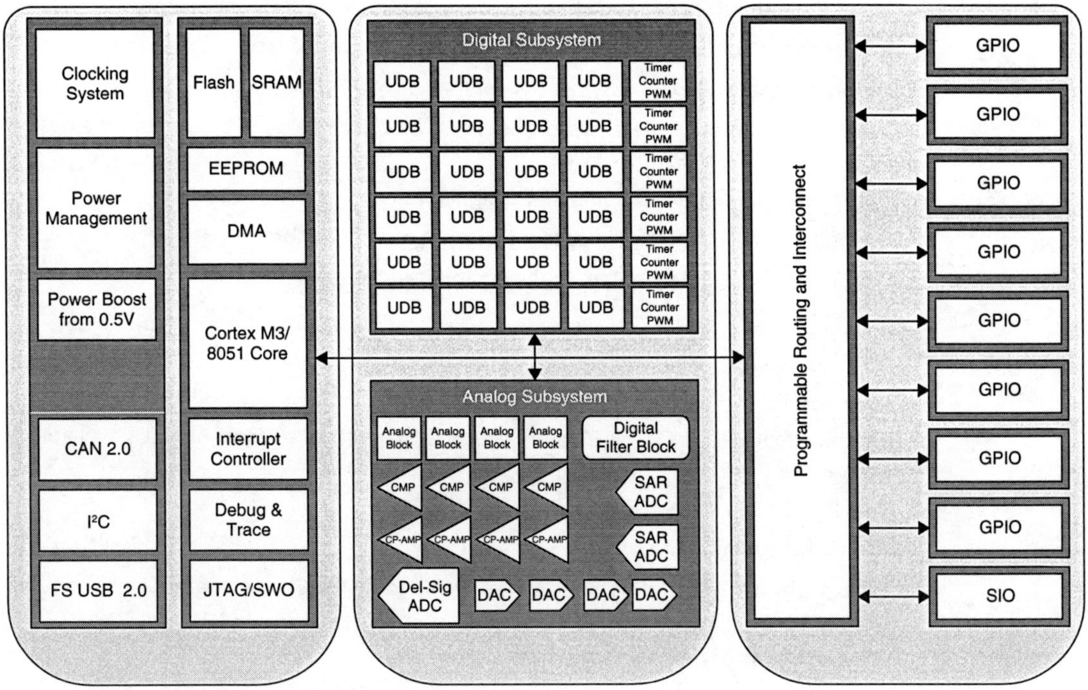

Figure 12.48 | UDBs of PSoC3 and PSoC5

present in PSoC1. There are a number of peripherals too, which are not available in PSoC1 like DMA, DAC, 20-bit ADC, USB etc. It is obvious that these two versions of PSoCs can provide a great amount of functionality for high end applications.

Conclusion

With this, we come to the end of our discussion on PSoC, in which PSoC1 has been explained in detail, while the higher versions have only been introduced. The discussion on PSoC1 is neither exhaustive nor complete. It is only meant to give an introduction to PSoC and an encouragement to those who want to try something new and innovative. There are a large number of peripherals which have just been mentioned. It is up to the user to find the right peripherals for his application and study the user manual for it, before he gets into the programming. But the point is to note that the whole process of design of an embedded system becomes very simple if PSoC is used. For high end designs, PSoC3 and PSoC5 can be used in a similar way.

KEY POINTS OF THIS CHAPTER

- PSoC is a very popular product of Cypress Semiconductors, which has a very impressive line of applications
- PSoC1 and PSoC3 are 8-bit cores, while PSoC5 is a 32-bit core
- This chapter deals with PSoC1 devices of the CY 29xxx series

- The internal structure of PSoC1 has the core, peripheral registers and memory
- Besides these, configurable digital and analog blocks are available
- Designing systems is very easy because of the use of a GUI based IDE
- Interconnections are done between the digital blocks and analog blocks, and the design is then burned on the PSoC device
- Programming is done in C, using pre-designed APIs
- Analog blocks use switched capacitor filters instead of resistors
- PSoC3 and PSoC5 are meant for high end applications

QUESTIONS

1. List three features about PSoC that makes it stand out in the crowd of MCUs available in the market.
2. How are PSoC3 and PSoC5 different from PSoC1?
3. What is the function of SROM?
4. Explain why a number of frequencies are provided by PSoC? How are these different frequencies generated.
5. What is the use of the sleep timer?
6. In the GUI of the IDE, digital blocks are named as DBB and DCB. What is the difference between the two?
7. List six peripheral functions realizable by the digital blocks.
8. In the GUI, what is the function of the GI lines? How are they connected to the Port pins?
9. How do the input and output multiplexers allow connections between port pins and digital blocks?
10. Which are the sources that can be used as clocks for the digital blocks?
11. With respect to the output circuit of a port pin, explain how resistive pullup and pulldown are achieved?
12. What is meant by a 'strong' drive?
13. Explain the naming convention used for PSoC APIs.
14. Which of the analog blocks use switched capacitors in place of resistors?
15. Suggest two cases where analog devices need 'reference voltages'.
16. In Example 12.8, what is the technique by which the analog voltage, after being converted to digital form is displayed on the LCD.
17. Where are the following two resources likely to find applications?
    (i) Decimator
    (ii) MAC unit
18. What is special about the I2C block found in the list of system resources?
19. How does the switched mode pump work?
20. List a few peripherals available in PSoC 3 and 5 which are not present in PSoC1.

EXERCISES

1. Using the PSoC designer, show the interconnect structure for realizing the following.
   i) One 8-bit timer
   ii) One 16-bit PWM
   iii) One SPI unit

   The input and output pins should also be selected.
2. Show the interconnect structure for one LED, and for a set of four LEDs.
3. Show the interconnect structure and write a program for realizing an amplifier for a gain of 12.
4. Implement a D to A converter. Show the interconnects and write a required program.
5. Generate square waves using
   i) An 8-bit timer
   ii) A 16-bit timer
6. Generate PWMs of three different frequencies and duty cycles.
7. Realize a comparator using analog blocks.

13 THE 8051 MICROCONTROLLER: THE PROGRAMMER'S PERSPECTIVE

In this chapter, you will learn

- The architecture of 8051 from a programmer's perspective
- The addressing modes of 8051
- The complete instruction set of 8051
- How to write assembly language programs using the Keil assembler

Introduction

In this chapter, we will start our study of the very popular microcontroller 8051. The programming model is discussed here while internal peripherals and their programming will be discussed in Chapter 14. Some aspects of this MCU have been used in Chapter 2 while discussing the general aspects of embedded systems. Thus a bit of overlap may be felt, but the perspective is different. Assembly language programming with worked out examples is extensively discussed in this chapter and Chapter 14. Programming using Embedded C for 8051 is included in Chapter 9.

13.1 | History and Family Details of 8051

Intel produced the 8051 microcontroller in the year 1981 calling it Intel MCS-51, the technology used for it being NMOS. Now CMOS technology has taken over and with this, relatively low-power versions of 8051 are also available. Over the years, Intel stopped manufacturing this chip (in 2007) but allowed other manufacturers to do it. Thus, we have this chip with different versions, packing and manufacturers. Chips manufactured by Atmel, Philips, Maxim (originally Dallas Semiconductors) are available with varying numbers of peripherals inside. Let's make a review of this extremely popular family of 8-bit microcontrollers. The important features of 8051 when it was first designed by Intel are as follows:

i) 8-bit data bus
ii) 16-bit address bus

Chapter-opening image: An 8051 chip.

iii) 4 register banks
iv) 32 general purpose registers each of 8 bits
v) A 16-bit program counter (PC) and data pointer (DPTR)
vi) 4 KB on chip program memory (ROM)
vii) 128 bytes on chip data memory (RAM)
viii) Two 16-bit timers
ix) Four 8-bit ports
x) 3 internal and 2 external interrupts
xi) One serial communication port (UART)
xii) Bit as well as byte addressable RAM area of 16 bytes
xiii) 12 clock cycles to constitute one machine cycle

Because of different manufacturers, many versions of the 8051 with different speeds and differing amounts of on-chip ROM are now found in the market. What is important is that although there are different flavours of the 8051, they are all compatible with the original 8051 as far as the instruction set is considered. Figure 13.1 shows the internal components of an 8051 chip.

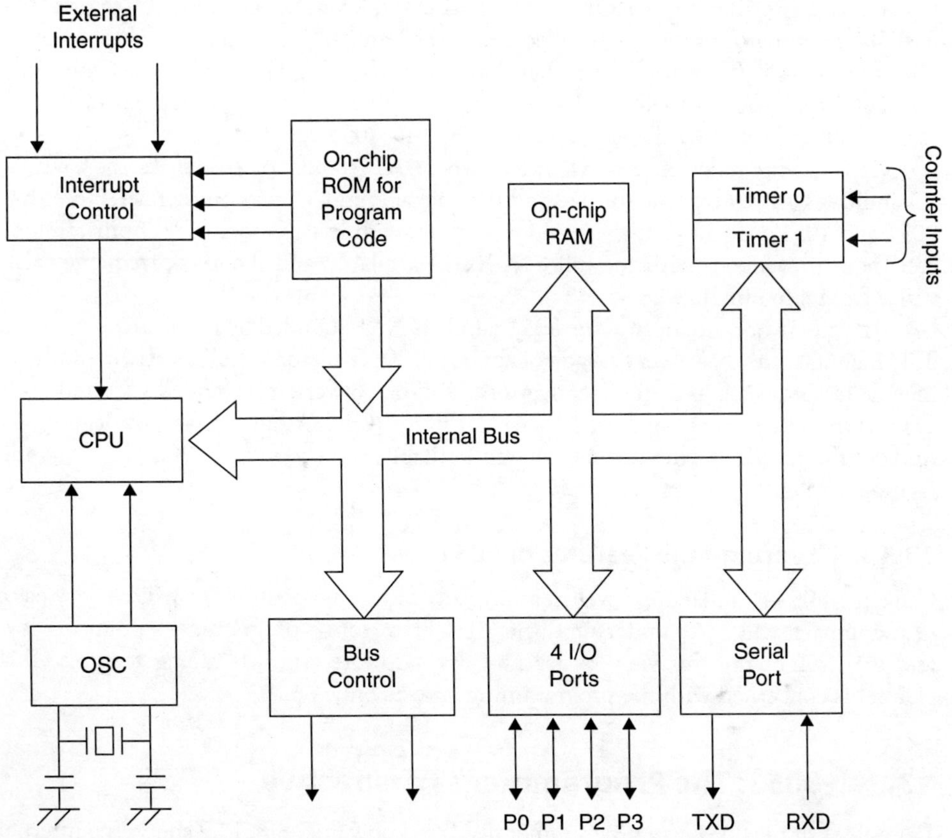

Figure 13.1 | Building blocks of a generic 8051

Table 13.1 | A List of Some 8051 Versions from Atmel

Part Number	ROM	RAM	I/O Pins	Timer	Interrupt	V_{CC}	Packaging
AT89C51	4K	128	32	2	6	5V	40
AT89LV51	4K	128	32	2	6	3V	40
AT89C1051	1K	64	15	1	3	3V	20
AT89C2051	2K	128	15	2	6	3V	20
AT89C52	8K	128	32	3	8	5V	40
AT89LV52	8K	128	32	3	8	3V	40

13.1.1 | Other Members of the Family

Two members of the family which stand out (because of being different) are the 8052 and 8031. The latter, i.e., 8031 does not have internal ROM and so is frequently denoted as a 'ROM less' 8051; it needs external ROM to burn the program designed for it. 8052 is different by having more RAM in it—128 bytes more, and also an extra timer.

When you try to buy a chip of 8051, it is likely that you will not find such a part number available. This is because 8051 has been given different numbers based on the type of ROM inside; if the ROM is UV PROM, the version is denoted 8751. If it is flash memory that is present, it is called 8951. The letter 'C' is added to the chip name, as it is based on CMOS technology rather than the NMOS used by Intel in the beginning. Thus, we find 89C51 is the chip that we might get to buy. Atmel is a popular manufacturer of 8051. Table 13.1 displays a partial list of its 8051 versions.

Consider the name AT89C51-12PC, where 'AT' stands for Atmel, 'C' for CMOS, '12' indicates 12 MHz, 'P' is for plastic DIP package, and 'C' for commercial. Note that 2051 and 1051 are scaled down versions of 8051, with less number of I/O pins, timers, etc. There are versions with the full 64K ROM available, and the clock frequency also varies from 4 to 40MHz.

Another major producer of the 8051 family is NXP founded by Philips Corporation. This manufacturer has a very large collection of 8051 microcontrollers. Their products include features such as A-to-D converters, D-to-A converters, extended I/O, and both OTP (One Time Programmable ROM) and flash ROM. As an exercise, you can try to find out the extra and extended peripherals available in the version P89C51RD2 manufactured by NXP.

13.1.2 | Learning the Features of 8051

Once the 8051 is understood well, learning any other microcontroller will be very easy. Our approach will be to understand the 8051 first, from a programmer's point of view and then to enlarge this view by learning its hardware and interfacing features. This chapter is concerned with the programming aspects only.

13.2 | 8051: The Programmer's Perspective

Let us look at the 8051, as a programmer needs to know it. Figure 13.2 shows the internal blocks which a programmer needs, to do coding. We will examine it block by block.

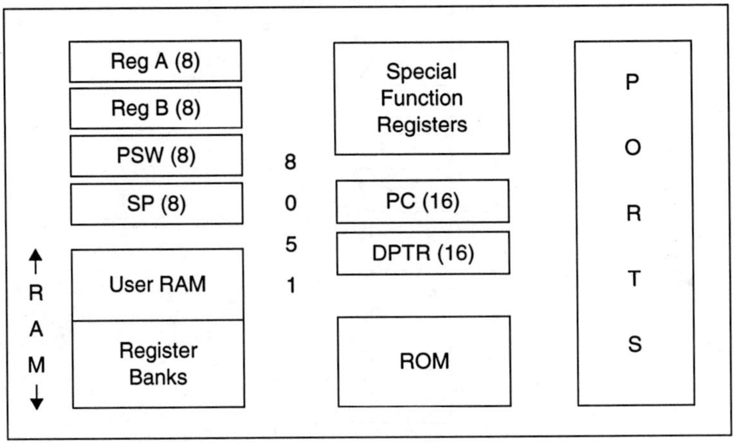

Figure 13.2 | The 8051 architecture from a programmer's point of view

In this figure, the bus connecting the blocks is not shown, but keep in mind that the data bus is 8 bits wide, while the address bus is 16 bits wide. These buses are inside the chip.

13.2.1 | Eight-bit Registers of 8051

The 8051 is an 8-bit microcontroller. This means that it can handle a maximum data width of 8 bits only. This also implies that all its data registers are 8 bits long.

The Accumulator Register 'A' The most important data register is the A register which acts as the 'accumulator'. It is mandatory that the A register carry one of the operands for all arithmetic instructions. The other operand may be in memory (RAM) or in any other register.

Register B The register B is not a frequently used register, because it can be used as an operand only for some specific operations like multiplication and division. For example, for the multiplication of two numbers, one operand should be in A, and the other should be in B. Same is the case for division. But it can store data.

Register Banks There is a set of eight registers named R0 to R7, which act as general purpose data registers. Actually, there are four sets of such registers, each set being called a register bank. But, at a particular time, only one block is operational. In conclusion, we can say that the general purpose registers available for data manipulation at any time are A, B and the current bank of eight registers. See Figure 13.3 which shows this set.

Processor Status Word (PSW) This is an 8-bit register which contains the flag bits, and also has the bits that permit 'bank switching'. We will see it in detail in the forthcoming sections.

Stack Pointer (SP) This is an 8-bit register which stores the address of the top of the stack.

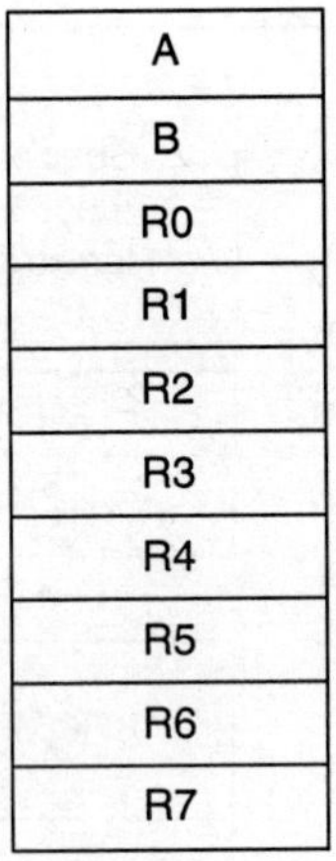

Figure 13.3 | General purpose registers

13.2.2 | Internal Memory

Internal RAM Totally, the 8051 has 256 bytes of RAM, but half of it is reserved to act as the 'special function registers', that is, the registers which are used to handle the activities of the peripherals of the device. We will discuss the SFRs in Chapter 14. The remaining 128 bytes is what is referred to as internal RAM, and it is divided into parts. The first 32 bytes act as register banks 0 to 3; each bank contains 8-data registers named R0 to R7. These registers are used for data manipulations and data movement. At a time, only one of these banks is operational. It is possible to switch from the current bank to another bank by using two bits of the PSW. By default, it is bank 0 that is the current bank. The remaining area of RAM is used simply as user RAM and can be accessed using their addresses. We will see the details as we go into programming.

Internal ROM All versions of 8051 contain some amount of ROM (except the 8031). ROM is used to store the final code that an application needs. Once a design is tested and finalized, the code is burned into ROM. Flash ROM is the type that is used nowadays. A part of ROM can store data also. There are instructions that allow us to access ROM during the course of programming. The amount of ROM available varies between chips, but the maximum possible is 64K (because the address bus is 16 bits).

13.2.3 | Sixteen-bit Registers

Program Counter (PC) This is an address register which 'sequences' instructions. This means that at any time, it points to the address of the next instruction to be fetched. Instructions are stored in ROM—hence the PC is a pointer to ROM—the maximum size of ROM is 64K, and the size of the PC is 16 bits. See Figure 13.4. On reset, the content of PC is 0, meaning that the first instruction is always taken from the address 0000.

Figure 13.4 | The program counter

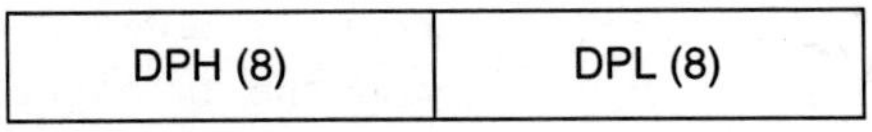

Figure 13.5 | The data pointer register

Data Pointer (DPTR) This is also an address register, and so it is 16 bits in size. However, it can be used as two 8-bit registers—DPH and DPL, with H and L standing for high and low respectively, that is, the MSB and LSB of the DPTR. See Figure 13.5.

The DPTR is used as a pointer for accessing internal ROM, and also for external memory (if added to the chip).

13.2.4 | Ports

There are four 8-bit ports for 8051, and they are named 0 to 3. There are corresponding port pins, and these are used to connect to the peripherals. The ports are designated as P0, P1, P2 and P3 and can be used with such designations in programs. They can also be designated by their RAM addresses in the SFR space.

13.3 | Assembly Language Programming

We have had just a glance at the internal structure of 8051, but with this, we can start programming. This will help to get a better view of the chip and its use. Also, as we do assembly language programming, we will get a fuller view of the internal architecture.

The general format of an assembly language instruction line is

LABEL: INSTRUCTION ;COMMENTS

In this, the label and comments are optional. The instruction consists of the opcode and the operands. The comment field needs a semicolon to indicate its presence.

For programming the 8051, different assemblers are available. In this book, all programs are tested using the Keil assembler, the details of which can be looked up in Appendix B. The evaluation version of this is freely downloadable by looking up 'Keil microvision 4' or trying the link https://www.keil.com/demo/eval/c51.htm.

13.3.1 | Modes of Addressing

As in the case of any processor, the 8051 also has various modes of addressing. Here we use the 'move' instruction to illustrate the different modes. The general format of this instruction is

MOV destination, source

The source and destination can be registers or memory. There is also the possibility of the source being a data item,that is, an immediate number.

13.3.1.1 | *Register Addressing*

In this mode, both the source and destination are registers. The registers that can be used are A, B and the registers from R0 to R7. Examples of this mode are as follows:

```
MOV A, R1          ;copy the content of register R1 to register A
MOV R3, R1         ;copy the content of R1 to R3
MOV R7, B          ;copy the content of B to R7
```

13.3.1.2 | *Immediate Addressing*

In this mode, the source is a data item and is indicated by preceding the data by a '#' symbol, indicating 'immediate'. Data can be copied to a register or a memory location, using this mode.

```
MOV A, #23H           ;copy 23H to A
MOV 34H, #2FH         ;copy 2FH to the RAM address 34H
MOV DPTR, #0F34CH     ;copy 0F34H to DPTR
```

The 16-bit DPTR can be loaded with immediate data, considering it as two 8-bit numbers being moved to DPH and DPL

```
MOV DPH, #0F3H        ;copy F3H to the upper part of DPTR,
                       i.e., DPH
MOV DPL, #4CH         ;copy 4CH to the lower part of DPTR,
                       i.e., DPL
```

Note

i) Any number is treated as a decimal number. Hexadecimal numbers are to be written suffixed with an 'H' or prefixed with 0x. For example, 91 is treated as a decimal number. If it to be considered as a hexadecimal number, it is to be written as 91H or 0x91, in programs.
ii) Hexadecimal numbers starting with the symbols 'A to F' must be preceded by a 0. Otherwise, the assembler will indicate a syntax error. For example, FEH is to written as 0FEH, in any program.

13.3.1.3 | *Direct Addressing*

In this mode, one of the operands is to be in a memory location. For the case of the MOV instruction, the content of a memory location is moved to a register or vice versa. The memory that we have is either RAM or ROM. Now, we will look into the case of addressing RAM locations. The case of ROM will be examined in Section 13.3.1.5.

Before we write any instructions, let's examine the RAM structure of 8051. The internal RAM area is 128 bytes with addresses 00 to 7FH. See Figure 13.6 which shows the RAM structure.

The first 32 bytes of RAM constitute the four register banks. For example, examine bank 0, which is the default register bank. There are eight registers named R0 to R7. Since they are part of the internal RAM, they have addresses 00 to 07 also. See Figure 13.7. Thus, the instruction MOV A, R2 can be written as MOV A,02 as well. In both the cases, the same content is being addressed.

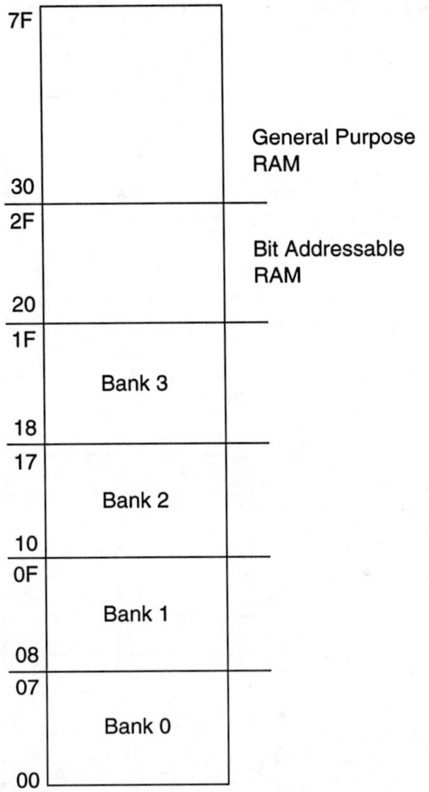

Figure 13.6 | The subdivisions of internal RAM

Similarly MOV A, R0 is the same as MOV A, 00

MOV 06, A is the same as MOV R6, A
MOV B, 04 is the same as MOV B, R4
MOV 00, 03 is the same MOV R0, R3

If bank 0 is the current bank, the other banks are just RAM locations. See the following instructions:

```
MOV 0FH, A        ;copy the content of A to RAM location 0FH
                  (this is R7 in bank 1)
MOV R1, 09        ;copy the content of RAM location 09 (R1 in
                  bank 1) to R1
MOV 70H, R4       ;copy the content of R4 to RAM location 70H
                  (beyond the banks)
MOV 17H, 14H      ;copy the content of RAM location 14H (R4 in
                  bank 2) to; 17H (R7 in bank 2)
```

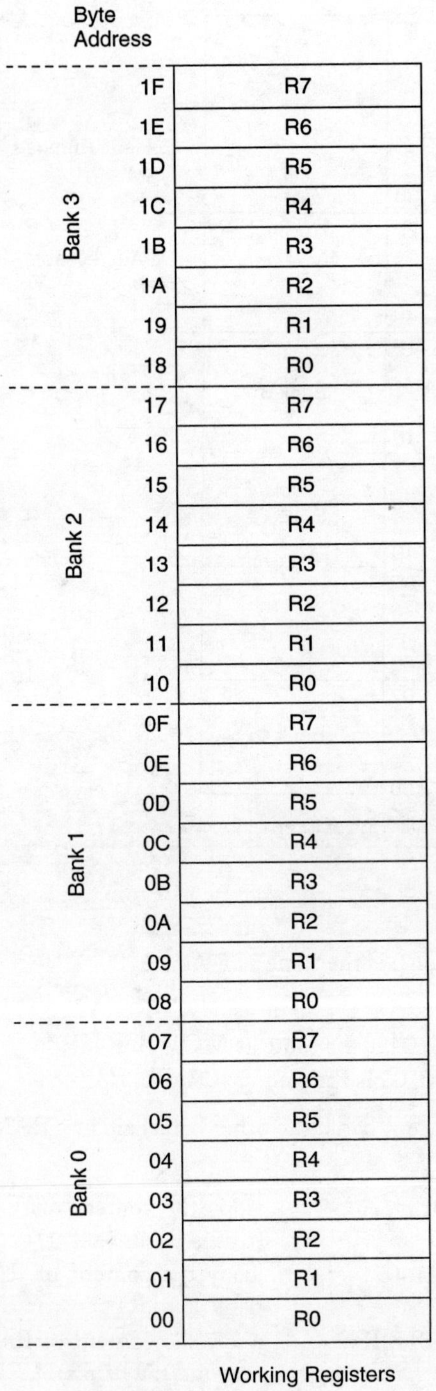

Figure 13.7 | Register banks and their RAM addresses

Example 13.1

Run the following program and explain what happens after the execution of each line of the program.

```
ORG 0
        MOV 0FH,#45H
        MOV A,0FH
        MOV R1,A
        MOV 13H,#0FEH
        MOV 12H,13H
END
```

Solution

i) The first line **ORG 0** shows the 'origin' of the program. It indicates that this program is to start from 0, that is, the address from which the first instruction will be taken up for execution.
ii) The last line END is also mandatory for any assembler. It tells the assembler to stop reading beyond this line.
iii) For each of the program lines, the result of execution is shown in the comments field.

```
MOV 0FH,#45H      ;copy data 45H to the RAM address 0FH
MOV A,0FH         ;copy the content of 0FH to A
                  ;now register A contains 45H in it
MOV R1,A          ;copy the content of A to R1
                  ;now the register R1 contains 45H
MOV 13H,#0FEH     ;move data FEH to RAM address 13H
MOV 12H,13H       ;copy the content of 13H to 12H
                  ;after program execution, both the RAM
                  ;addresses 12H and 13H contain FEH
```

13.3.1.4 | *Register Indirect Addressing*

There is an indirect method of addressing data which is in RAM, by using certain registers as pointers to the address. **However, only registers R0 and R1 are allowed to be used as pointers.**

Consider two data items residing in RAM locations 25H and 30H. R0 and R1 can be made to act as pointers to these data, by loading the address values in them. See the code snippet given as follows. The content of these RAM allocations can be copied to registers A and B using the notation '@' along with R0 and R1.

```
MOV R0, #25H    ;load 25H into R0
MOV R1, #30H    ;load 30H into R1
MOV A, @R0      ;copy to A, the contents of RAM pointed by R0
MOV B, @R1      ;copy to B, the contents of RAM pointed by R1
```

Data can also be copied to RAM locations 'indirectly', by using the pointer registers R0 and R1. But registers R0 to R7 cannot be used as destination registers in indirect addresses.

```
MOV R7, @R0      ;this gives a syntax error
```

However, using the RAM address 07 for R7 does not give any error

```
MOV 07, @R0      ;this copies to 07 (the address of R7)the contents of
                 ;RAM pointed by R0
```

Example 13.2

Examine the following program, and find out which registers and which RAM locations contain the data 7EH and EFH, after program execution. What else will be noticed?

```
ORG 0
        MOV 25H,#7EH
        MOV 30H,#0EFH
        MOV B,#88H
        MOV R0,#25H
        MOV R1,#30H
        MOV A,@R0
        MOV 07,@R0
        MOV 05H,@R0
        MOV 26H,@R1
        MOV @R0,B
END
```

Solution

In this program, R0 acts as a pointer to the data 7EH, which is in RAM address 25H. After program execution, registers A, R5 and R7 contain the data 7EH. The program does not show R5 and R7 as destinations to this data, instead their RAM addresses 05 and 07 have been used. In the Keil debugger, this data will be seen in the register list as well as in the RAM address (however, they mean the same).

The data EFH (in address 30H) is pointed by R1. The program makes this data to be copied to register B, as well as to RAM address 26H (which is beyond the address of the register banks. See Figure 13.7.

The last line of the program treats R0 as a pointer to a destination. The content of B is moved to this destination. Hence 88H will be found in the RAM address 30H.

13.3.1.5 | *Indexed Addressing*

This is a type of addressing applicable to ROM alone. It was mentioned earlier that ROM stores program code, but it can also be used to hold some data also. Usually tables and some constants are stored there, to be used by programs. Suppose we want to retrieve some of these data items, we cannot access ROM using any of the methods so far discussed.

The maximum size of ROM is 64K, and so addresses of ROM locations can be 16 bits long. In indexed addressing mode, the DPTR is used as a base address, and the accumulator is used as an offset. The effective address formed by adding the value of the base address to the offset, is the ROM address to be accessed. There is the MOVC instruction especially tailor-made for ROM access.

MOVC A, @A+DPTR is the instruction which loads the content of ROM with effective address A+DPTR, into the A register.

Consider that the ROM location 0500H is to be accessed. The instructions needed for getting data from the address are as follows.

```
MOV A, #0
MOV DPTR, #0500H
MOVC A, @A + DPTR
```

13.4 | Internal RAM

Before we go into details of active programming, it will be worthwhile to take a second look at the different subdivisions of internal RAM.

Figure 13.8 shows the memory map of the 256 bytes of internal RAM that the 8051 possesses. The upper 128 bytes from addresses 80H to FFH are addresses of the special function registers, which cater to the operation of the peripherals. Incidentally, the addresses of the A, B and SP (Stack Pointer) registers are also in this space. See Table 13.2. In programs, these addresses may be used, instead of the names, (but that may not be necessary, normally). The details of the SFRs are discussed in Chapter 14.

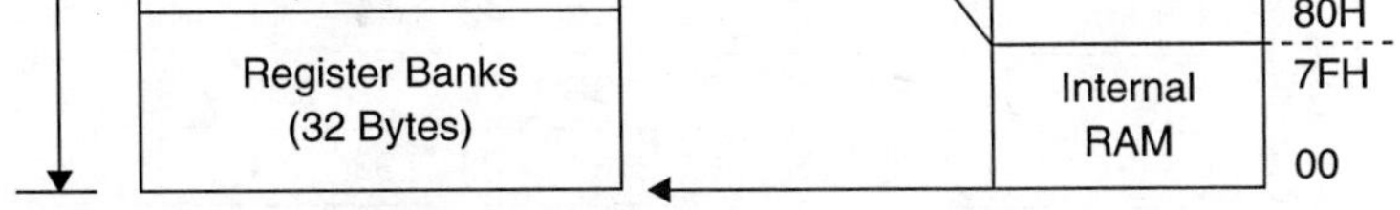

Figure 13.8 | Address map of internal RAM

Table 13.2 | Addresses of Important Registers

Register Name	Address
Accumulator (A)	E0H
B	F0H
Stack Pointer (SP)	81H

Now look at Figuere 13.8 once again. The 16 RAM addresses from 20H to 2FH are stated to be bit addressable. Figure 13.9 shows the addresses of the 'bit' locations. Note that each '**byte**' of RAM of this RAM area has an address. Within that byte, there are eight '**bit**' addresses too. For example, the byte location with address 20H can be addressed with 8 different addresses from 00 to 07, for each of the bits.

How do we differentiate between bit addresses and byte addresses?

For example, 03 is a bit address, but there is also a byte address 03.

The trick is that both use different instructions. The instructions that are applicable to bit addresses are SETB, CLR, JNB and JNB. The following instructions refer to the 'bit address' 03.

```
SETB 03
CLR 03
JB 03, NOPE
```

For byte addresses, instructions like the following apply.

```
MOV 03, #45H
MOV A, 03
MOV 03, R4
```

It is obvious that a byte is referred here.

Bit Addressable Locations

Byte Address	Bit Addresses							
2F	7F	7E	7D	7C	7B	7A	79	78
2E	77	76	75	74	73	72	71	70
2D	6F	6E	6D	6C	6B	6A	69	68
2C	67	66	65	64	63	62	61	60
2B	5F	5E	5D	5C	5B	5A	59	58
2A	57	56	55	54	53	52	51	50
29	4F	4E	4D	4C	4B	4A	49	48
28	47	46	45	44	43	42	41	40
27	3F	3E	3D	3C	3B	3A	39	38
26	37	36	35	34	33	32	31	30
25	2F	2E	2D	2C	2B	2A	29	28
24	27	26	25	24	23	22	21	20
23	1F	1E	1D	1C	1B	1A	19	18
22	17	16	15	14	13	12	11	10
21	0F	0E	0D	0C	0B	0A	09	08
20	07	06	05	04	03	02	01	00

Figure 13.9 | Addresses of the bit addressable locations of RAM

What can be done with one bit?

It can be 'set' or cleared; there are instructions available which will set or clear each individual bit of these 16-byte locations, that is, there are $16 \times 8 = 128$ bit addressable locations in the internal RAM.

Byte Addressable RAM The rest of the RAM from 30H to 7FH is addressable only as bytes. These locations can be read from or written into, using the MOV instruction in the direct or indirect addressing mode as was seen in Section 12.4.1.3.

13.5 | The 8051 Stack

All processors need a stack. A stack is a portion of memory which can act as a temporary storage location for data which will be taken back later. The stack is a special type of data structure, in that it can be accessed (read from or written to) only at the 'top of the stack'. The instructions used for this kind of access are PUSH (for writing to) and POP (for reading from). The stack is user defined, but on start up, the stack pointer register contains the number 07.

The 8051 stack is an ascending stack. This means that as data is pushed in, it grows upwards to increasing addresses. If the stack pointer contains the number 07, the stack area is defined from 08 onwards. The first data item pushed in will be stored in 08, the next in 09 and so on.

In practice, it is best to change the value of the stack pointer from 07 to a higher location. This is because register bank 1 starts at 08, and using the stack there, prevents us from being able to use bank 1. For example, the instruction MOV SP, #42H makes the stack to be defined from 43H onwards (upwards), by loading the number 42H into the stack pointer.

13.5.1 | The Push Operation

Consider the case shown in Figure 13.10, where the SP value is 42H. Assume that R3 contains the value xx and R5 contains the value yy.

Let's do the exercise of pushing in the values of R3 and R5 onto the stack. The natural way of pushing in would be to write the instructions PUSH R3 followed by PUSH R5. But 8051 does not allow us to use register names in the PUSH instruction. The address of these registers needs to be used. If register bank 0 is the one referred to, the instructions to be used are

```
PUSH 03    ;push R3
PUSH 05    ;push R5
```

The stack pointer is now incremented (after each push instruction) and the end, it has the content of 44H. Figure 13.10 shows the stack

13.5.2 | The pop operation

Now, to do popping to, say, register R7, the instruction to be used is

```
POP 07    ;pop R7
```

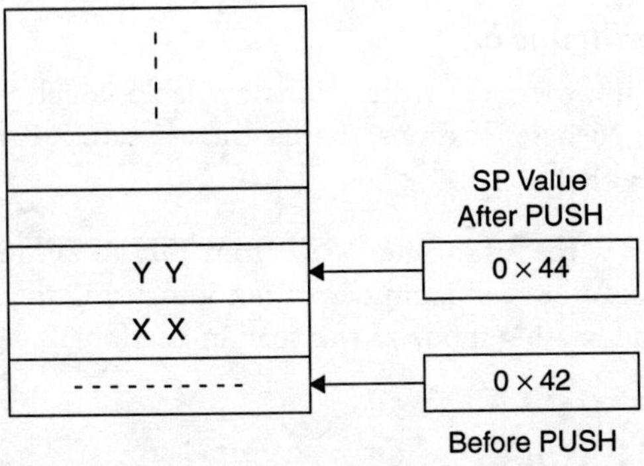

Figure 13.10 | PUSH operation for the 8051 stack

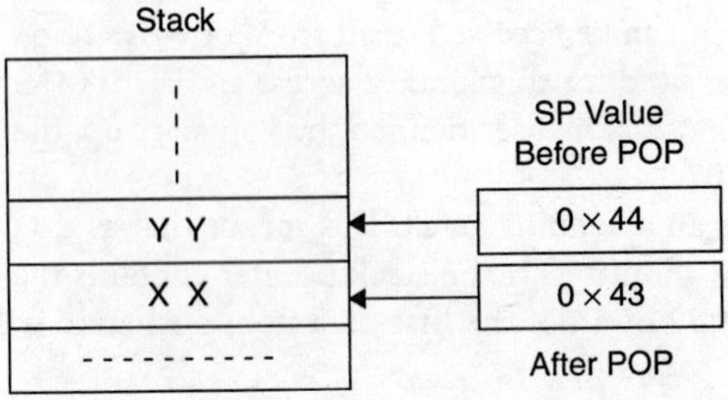

Figure 13.11 | POP operation in an 8051 stack

The SP value is decremented by one, to become 43H, and data which is on top of the stack, that is, yy, will now be in R7. See Figure 13.11.

Example 13.3

Assume that register bank 2 is now the working bank. It is needed to push the content of registers R5 and R6 to stack. It is also needed to pop out these values to A and B, respectively. Write instructions for this.

Solution

```
PUSH    15H     ;push the content of R5 of bank 2
PUSH    16H     ;push the content of R6 of bank 2
POP     0F0H    ;pop the content to B
POP     0E0H    ;pop the content to A
```

Now let's examine the salient points of this simple program

i) The addresses of the registers have been used.
ii) The content of R5 is first pushed in, and then that of R6. After this, the stack top contains the data that was in R6.
iii) The requirement is to copy the contents (through the stack) of R5 to A and R6 to B. Since the stack top contains the content of R6, the first POP operation is to pop to B.

iv) Keep in mind that for a stack, what is pushed in last is what can be popped out first.
v) The second pop operation copies the stack top contents to A.

Note There is no need to use the stack to copy the contents of one register to another. The program here uses this method only to illustrate the working of a stack.

13.6 | Processor Status Word (PSW)

This is a register with address D0H, which has the conditional flags, and also contains the bits that allows the switching of register banks, see Figure 13.12.

This register (like many other SFRs), is bit addressable, meaning that each bit can be set or cleared individually. To do that, the notation for each bit is as given in column 2 of Table 13.3.

Now let's discuss the bits of the PSW register.

The Carry Flag (CY) Bit D7, notated as PSW.7 is the carry flag. The carry flag (CY) is set if there is a carry out from the most significant bit during a calculation. For example, when 8-bit addition causes the result to be greater than 8 bits, there is a carry out from the MSB (D7), which causes this flag to be set. This flag is set also when there is 'borrow' during subtraction.

The Auxiliary Carry Flag (AC) Bit D6, notated as PSW.6 is the AC flag. This flag functions similar to the carry flag, except that the overflow is from bit D3 into D4. It thus indicates a carry out from the lower 4 bits. The need for this flag is for the Decimal Adjust (DA) instruction, which is important in BCD number calculations. There are no other instructions that directly test the state of this flag and no conditional branching is associated with this flag.

CY	AC	F0	RS1	RS0	OV	--	P

Figure 13.12 | The PSW register

Table 13.3 | Bits of the PSW and their Functions

Bit	Symbol	Bit Notation	Bit Position
Carry flag	CY or C	PSW.7	D7
Auxiliary carry	AC	PSW.6	D6
Flag 0	F0-user defined	PSW.5	D5
RS1	Register bank select 1	PSW.4	D4
RS0	Register bank select 0	PSW.3	D3
OV	Overflow flag	PSW.2	D2
R	Reserved	PSW.1	D1
P	Parity flag	PSW.0	D0

The Overflow Flag (OV) Bit D2, notated as PSW.2 is the overflow flag. This flag is set under one of the following conditions:

i) There is an overflow into the MSB (D7) from the bit of lower significance, but no carry out from the MSB,
ii) There is a carry out from the MSB, but no carry into the MSB.

This flag indicates that the result of a **signed** number operation is too large, causing the higher order bit to overflow into the sign bit, thus changing the sign bit.

The Parity Flag (P) Bit D0, notated as PSW.0 is the parity flag. The setting of this flag indicates the presence of an even number of '1' bits in the destination. For example, after a particular arithmetic or logic operation, if the destination contains the number 11100111, the parity flag is set to indicate even parity.

Have you noticed that there is no zero flag (Z) for 8051?

Well, there isn't a zero flag that a user has to take note of, but instead there are instructions which verify if the result of an arithmetic operation causes the A register to be zero, and then takes appropriate action. We will see it in the context of our discussions on the instruction set and programming.

Bank Switching The bits RS1 and RS0 (PSW. 4 and PSW.3) are used for bank switching. There are four banks of registers designated as Bank 0, Bank 1, Bank 2 and Bank 3. On start up, it is the default bank 0, which is the 'current bank'. To switch to another bank, refer to Table13.4. When bank 0 is being used, RS0 and RS1 are 00. To get to use bank 1, say, the instruction to be used just needs to set PSW.3, that is, RS0. Similarly, other banks can be used by setting /clearing these two bits.

Unused Bits of the PSW One bit, PSW.5 is available to the user to define as he deems fit or leave unused. The bit PSW.1 is reserved for future uses.

13.7 | Assembler Directives

Very soon, we will learn the instructions set of 8051, and start the programming process in dead earnest. So it is important to be aware of some of the important directives used by a typical 8051 assembler. You should already know that directives are different from instructions, in that they are non-executable statements. They just help the assembler by providing certain important information.

Table 13.4 | Bit Values for Bank Switching

RS1	RS0	Register Bank
0	0	0
0	1	1
1	0	2
1	1	3

ORG ORG is a directive which means 'origin'. In the context of assembly language programming, it defines the starting address for any item (data or code) in the program memory (ROM). We have already used the statement ORG 0 in Examples 13.1 and 13.2.

EQU This directive allows us to equate names to constants. The assembler just replaces the names by the values mentioned.

Examples

```
COST EQU 34        ;equate the label COST to 34
PRICE EQU 56H      ;equate the label PRICE by 56H
```

DB This directive stands for 'data byte' and places an 8-bit number constant at this memory (ROM) location. If labels are used for these memory locations, a 'colon' should suffix the labels.

Examples

```
NUMBER:  DB 67H     ;store the hex no.67H at a location NUMBER
FACT:    DB 90      ;store the decimal no 90 at location FACT
STRNG:   DB "MIST"  ;store the ASCII string as bytes in locations, the
                    ;starting location's name being STRNG. Note that
                    ;four bytes corresponding to four characters get
                    ;stored

LIST:    DB 34, 09, 0EH, 0FEH
                    ;store four bytes at addresses starting from
                    ;the location named LIST
```

BIT This directive equates a bit to either '1' or '0', or labels a bit which can be set or reset. When the bit is named, the name, when encountered in a program is replaced by the logic value specified.

Examples

```
FLIP BIT 0         ;the name FLIP is replaced by 0
TOG BIT 1          ;the name FLIP is replaced by 1
LIFT BIT P0.1      ;the name LIFT is replaced by the logic value of
                   ;the port pin P0.1
REE BIT PSW.5      ;the name REE is replaced by the logic value
                   ;of the register bit PSW.5
```

END This indicates that the assembler need not read beyond this.

13.8 | Storing Data in Code Memory (ROM)

We know that what we store in ROM is program code but data can also be stored and read from it, when needed. In fact, the ROM does not need to know what is stored;whatever is stored is binary numbers, either way. But when we store data, it is needed for use by the program, and therefore there should be a mechanism to read it and bring it to registers.

Example 13.4

See the following program which illustrates the use of some of the above referred directives. Data is to be stored in ROM addresses 0500H and 0800H onwards. Note that there are no instructions in this program, but only directives. Give a brief explanation on what is achieved by each of these lines .

```
ORG 0500H
      MY:         DB 89
      YOU:        DB 78, 56, 90
ORG 0800H
      ALL:        DB "5678"
      SENTNC:     DB "MY NAME"
END
```

Solution

This is only a set of directives. No instructions are involved, so 'execution' is not necessary. This data is just burned in ROM at the address 0500H and also at 0800H. In the simulator, the data is found to be in code memory, just after the program is assembled. We find data as in Tables 13.5 and 13.6.

We find another set of data from address 0800H onwards.

Table 13.5 | Data in ROM from 0500H

Label	Address in HEX	Content in HEX	Explanation
MY	0500	59	Hex value of decimal 89
YOU	0501	4E	Hex value of decimal 78
	0502	38	Hex value of decimal 56
	0503	5A	Hex value of decimal 90

Table 13.6 | Data in ROM from 0800H

Label	Address in HEX	Content in HEX	Explanation
ALL	0800	35	ASCII value of 5
	0801	36	ASCII value of 6
	0802	37	ASCII value of 7
	0803	38	ASCII value of 8
SENTNC	0804	4D	ASCII value of M
	0805	59	ASCII value of Y
	0806	20	ASCII value of space
	0807	4E	ASCII value of N
	0808	41	ASCII value of A
	0809	4D	ASCII value of M
	080A	45	ASCII value of E

13.9 | The Instruction Set of 8051

Now, let's start the assembly language programming of 8051, by first understanding the instruction set. The instructions can be divided into functional groups as follows:

i) Data transfer instructions
ii) Bit manipulation instructions
iii) Branch instructions
iv) Port manipulation instructions
v) Arithmetic instructions
vi) Logical instructions
vii) Call and return instructions

13.9.1 | Data Transfer Instructions

In any processor, moving data is of primary concern. There is a destination and a source for the movement. Data is moved between registers, memory and ports. Table 13.7 lists the data transfer instructions of 8051.

Now let's have a more detailed discussion on how and when each of these instructions is to be used.

13.9.1.1 | *MOV—Move*

Usage: MOV dest, src

For 8051, the data is 8 bits in size and so it is 8-bit data that is always moved. Let's see a few examples and the actions performed by them:

```
MOV A, B        ;copy the content of B to A
MOV A, 56H      ;copy the content of RAM location 56H to A
```

Table 13.7 | List of the Data Transfer Instructions

Sl. No.	Instruction Format	Function Performed	Flags Affected
1	MOV dest, src	Copy the content of source to destination	None
2	MOVX dest, src	Used to move from/to external data memory only	None
3	MOVC dest, src	Used to move from program memory (ROM) only	None
4	PUSH src	Copies one byte from source to stack top	None
5	POP dest	Copies one byte from stack top to destination	None
6	XCH	Exchanges data between two sources	None
7	SWAP A	Exchanges the upper and lower nibbles of A	None

```
MOV @R0, B          ;copy the content of B to the RAM address pointed by R0
MOV P0, A           ;copy the content of A to Port 0
MOV R1, #45         ;copy 45 (decimal) to R1
MOV P1, R1          ;copy the content of R1 to Port1
MOV DPTR, #4567H    ;this register is 16-bit, and it has to contain a 16-bit
                    ;address
```

13.9.1.2 | *MOVX—Move To/From External RAM*

Sometimes the 8051 needs extra RAM, as the internal data RAM in sufficient. If extra data RAM is connected externally, its content is accessed using the MOVX instruction. The DPTR is used for this instruction by loading the RAM address (to be accessed) into it. Then MOVX is used as shown as follows:

```
MOVX @DPTR, A       ;copy data from A to the address specified in DPTR
MOVX A, @DPTR       ;copy data from address specified in DPTR to A
```

13.9.1.3 | *MOVC*

The use of this instruction for accessing ROM has already been considered in Section12.4.1.5. The ROM can be external or internal. In this book, we will concern ourselves only with on-chip ROM.

13.9.1.4 | *PUSH and POP*

The use of these instructions has already been discussed in Section 12.6.

13.9.1.5 | *XCH—Exchange*

There are two instructions which perform the act of exchanging (swapping). One is 8-bit swapping, and the other is 4-bit swapping.

The format for 8-bit exchange is XCH A, byte. The byte can be another register or a memory location.

Examples

```
XCH A, R1           ;exchange the contents of A and R1
XCH A, 34H          ;exchange the contents of A and RAM address 34H
```

13.9.1.6 | *Nibble Swapping*

The format of this is XCHD A,@Ri.

This instruction exchanges the lower nibble of A and the lower nibble of the byte pointed by Ri, leaving the upper nibbles of both unchanged.

```
MOV A, #45H         ;move 45H to A
MOV 56H, #30H       ;move 30H to RAM address 56H
MOV R0, #56H        ;move 56H to R0
XCHD A, @R0         ;exchange the lower nibble of A with that @R0
```

After execution, A will contain 40H and the RAM address will contain 35H.

13.9.2 | Bit Manipulation Instructions

All microcontrollers need to address data at the bit level because they may have to deal with one bit interfaces like single switches, LEDs, relays, etc. All these devices require the setting or clearing of single bits.

Which are the bits that can be addressed individually?

i) The carry flag
ii) The bits in the bit addressable area of RAM
iii) The bits in registers that are bit addressable, e.g., PSW.1. P0.3, P2.4, ACC.0, etc.

Let's see, one by one, the instructions which allow single bits to be addressed. Refer Table 13.8 and the following examples.

Example

```
SETB ACC.0      ;set the 0th bit of the Accumulator, i.e., the A register
SETB PSW.4      ;PSW.4 = 1, i.e., RS1 = 1
SETB P2.4       ;P2.4 = 1
CLR C           ;C = 0
CLR 22H         ;clear the bit in RAM location 22H
CPL ACC.2       ;complement D2 of the A register
CPL P0.0        ;complement P0.0
ORL C, 26H      ;move to C the logical OR of content of 26H and C
MOV C, P3.2     ;move to C, the bit value of P3.2
ANL 29H, C      ;move to 29H the logical AND of content of 29H
                ;and C
```

Table 13.8 | List of Data Manipulation Instructions

Sl. No.	Instruction	Function to be Performed
1	SETB bit	Set the indicated bit
2	CLR bit	Clear the indicated bit
3	CPL bit	Complement the indicated bit
4	MOV C, bit	Move indicated bit to C (carry flag)
5	MOV bit, C	Move C (carry flag) to the indicated bit
6	ANL C, bit	Move to C, (carry flag) the logical AND of C and the indicated bit
7	ANL bit, C	Move to the bit ,the logical AND of C (carry flag) and the indicated bit
8	ORL C, bit	Move to C, (carry flag) the logical OR of C and the indicated bit
9	ORL bit, C	Move to the bit, the logical OR of C (carry flag) and the indicated bit

Example 13.5

When the MCU is powered on, the default register bank is bank 0. Write a program to switch to bank 3, and then to switch to bank 1.

Solution

On startup, it is register bank 0 which is operational, i.e., RS0 = RS1 = 0 will be the status of the bank select bits.

The bits of the PSW needed for selecting a register bank are shown as follows:

	RS1 (PSW.4)	RS0 (DSW.3)
Bank 0	0	0
Bank 1	0	1
Bank 2	1	0
Bank 3	1	1

The code lines are as follows, for switching to bank 3.

```
SETB PSW.4      ;make RS1 = 1
SETB PSW.3      ;make RS0 = 1
```

Now to switch to bank 1, it is only necessary to make RS1 = 0. The instruction for this is

```
CLR PSW.4       ;make RS1 = 0
```

13.9.3 | Branch Instructions

Branching is a very important aspect in programming, and making its actions to be 'conditional' is what gives decision-making capability to any computer. In 8051, there are unconditional, as well as conditional branch instructions. Let's have a look at these instructions. We will start with the unconditional type of the 'jump' instruction.

13.9.3.1 | *Unconditional Jump Instructions*

SJMP Target

SJMP stands for 'short jump'; it is also a 'relative' jump. What these terms mean is that the destination is expressed as a 'relative' number, and that the 'relative' number is short, that is, only 8 bits. The number is a signed number, and denotes the distance (in bytes) between the current PC value and the target (destination) address. If this number is negative, it is a backward jump, the maximum range of which is –128. If forwarding jumping is what is needed, the number is positive with a maximum range of +127.

In practice, the programmer does not need to know this relative number. He can write the label corresponding to the destination, and the assembler will calculate the 'displacement' and insert it into the machine code. To get to the target, the value of PC (when the SJMP instruction is executed) will be added to the displacement in the code, and this will be the new value of PC. Thus, control will be taken to the target address and the change of flow of the program occurs.

See the following code snippet. The target has the label THERE. When the SJMP instruction is being executed, the PC will be pointing to the next instruction in the sequence. The assembler calculates the offset to the 'THERE' label, adds it to PC and then continues execution, which is from the address THERE.

```
ORG 0
        -----------
        -----------
        SJMP THERE
        -----------
        -----------
        -----------
THERE:  ADD A, R1
        -----------
        -----------
```

LJMP Target

This is a long jump instruction, and it is not 'relative'. It is a three byte instruction; the first byte is the opcode, and the next two bytes constitute the absolute address of the target. When this instruction is executed, the current PC value is simply replaced by the 16-bit number in the instruction, which can have any value from 0 to FFFFH. Since code is written in program memory (ROM), the 16-bit number can only be as big as the actual ROM present in the chip (all 8051 chips will not have 64K ROM).

AJMP Dest

This is also a relative jump, but the range of jumping is 2K and 11 bits specify the destination range.

Unconditional jump instructions will be used later in programs which generate square waves (Section 13.12.1) Besides that, it is likely that many programs end with the following line

```
LABEL:  SJMP LABEL or
        SJMP $        which means the same
```

This instruction loops to itself continuously. This is done, because when programs are burned in ROM, execution should not proceed beyond the last instruction in the program. In the ROM, in addresses beyond the last line, random numbers (some of which are codes burned earlier) are likely to have been stored and if those get executed, it will cause havoc. To prevent this from happening, the last code line can be written using an SJMP instruction like

```
HERE:   SJMP HERE     ;loops to HERE and stays in HERE
```

13.9.3.2 | *Conditional Branch Instructions*

These are the instructions which make programming really useful. Computers are used for repetitive and conditional tasks and conditional branching is the method for it. Table 13.9 gives the list of conditional branch instructions.

Note All conditional jumps are short jumps.

Table 13.9 | List of Conditional Jump Instructions

Sl. No.	Mnemonic	Function to be Performed	Flags Affected
1	JC target	Jump if CY = 1	None
2	JNC target	Jump if CY = 0	None
3	JZ target	Jump if the register A = 0	None
4	JNZ target	Jump if the register A is not zero	None
5	JB bit, target	Jump if the bit = 1	None
6	JNB bit, target	Jump if the bit = 0	None
7	JBC bit, target	Jump if the bit = 1. Then clear the bit	None
8	DJNZ byte, target	Decrement the byte, and jump if the byte is zero	None

JC Target Jump on carry to target.

JNC Target Jump on No carry, to target.

These instructions test the carry flag, and jump to the target depending on the condition of the carry flag, as specified.

JZ Target Jump on Zero (A = 0) to target.

JNZ Target Jump on no Zero (A! = 0) to target.

Recollect that there is no Zero flag for 8051. Theses two instructions test the A register to see if it contains a non-zero number or not, and jumps to the target accordingly.

JB Bit, Target Jump to target if the specified bit is set.

JNB Bit, Target Jump to target if the specified bit is not set.

JBC Bit Target Jump to target if the specified bit is set, then clear the bit.

The bits that can be used here are bits of registers, ports or RAM.

Examples

```
JB P1.0, THERE      ;a port bit is tested and if found set, jumps
JNB ACC.4, WOW      ;a register bit is tested and if found cleared, jumps
JB 05, NOPE         ;a RAM bit is tested and if found set, jumps
```

DJNZ Byte, Target This instruction decrements the specified byte and jumps to the target if the byte becomes zero (on decrementing). The byte can be one of the registers of the register bank, or a RAM address.

Examples

```
DJNZ R2, HEER     ;decrement R2, and jump to HEER if R2! = 0
DJNZ 54H, MEER    ;decrement content of RAM 54H, and jump to MEER if ! = 0
```

Now, let's use these conditional jump instructions in programs.

Example 13.6

Write a program to fill 20 spaces in RAM with the ASCII value of '*'.

Solution

```
        ORG 0
        MOV A,#'*'          ;move the ASCII of * to A
        MOV R0,#40H         ;R0 is the pointer to address 40H
        MOV R3,#20          ;R3 = 20, is the counter
THERE:  MOV @R0,A           ;A = '*'is copied to pointed address
        INC R0              ;increment the pointer
        DJNZ R3,THERE       ;repeat 20 times, until R3 = 0
HERE:   SJMP HERE           ;stay in HERE
        END
```

This is a very direct program. The ASCII value of * is loaded in A, and moved to 20 RAM locations, by using R0 as the pointer to the starting address 30H. The pointer is incremented 20 times and at the end of the program, we find that 20 locations in RAM have this content – i.e.'*'. The counter R3 is decremented by the DJNZ instruction, and it causes jumping out of the loop once the counter is zero.

Example 13.7

Store the ASCII values of the first 10 capital letters of the alphabet in ROM locations. Bring these 10 values to RAM locations starting from 40H.

Solution

```
        ORG 0
        MOV R3,#10          ;R3 = 10
        MOV R1,#40H         ;R1 points to RAM address 40H
        MOV DPTR,#0500H     ;DPTR points to ROM address 0500H
THERE:  MOV A,#0            ;A = 0
        MOVC A,@A+DPTR      ;copy content of ROM to A
        MOV @R1,A           ;move the value in A to RAM
        INC R1              ;increment the RAM pointer
        INC DPTR            ;increment the ROM pointer
        DJNZ R3,THERE       ;repeat actions until R3 = 0
HERE:   SJMP HERE           ;stay in HERE

        ORG 0500H
        DB "ABCDEFGHIJ"
        END
```

In this example, both ROM and RAM are accessed. The ROM address (starting from 0500H) is pointed by DPTR, while the RAM address (from 40H) is pointed by R1. The directive DB at 0500H stores the required characters in ROM.

The content of ROM is brought to A and copied to RAM continuously until the counter R3 is 0.

Note that the 10 letters of the alphabets are stored as an ASCII string (in double quotes). In some (not Keil) assemblers, it is not possible to store strings like this, instead they should be stored as single characters separated by commas, i.e, 'A', 'B', 'C'... and so on.

13.9.4 | Arithmetic Instructions

The complete list of arithmetic operations of the 8051 is given in Table13.10.

Note For 8051, it is mandatory that the A register is one of the operands for addition, subtraction, multiplication and division.

13.9.4.1 | *Addition Instructions*

ADD A, src

This instruction adds the source and A, and puts the sum in A. The CY, OV and AC flags are affected.

Table 13.10 | List of Arithmetic Instructions

Sl. No.	Instruction Format	Function to be Performed	Flags Affected
1	ADD A, src	Add the source to A – result in A	OV, AC, CY
2	ADDC A, src	Add the source and C (carry flag) to A – result in A	OV, AC, CY
3	INC dest	Add 1 to the destination	None
4	SUBB A, src	Subtract the source and C from A – result in A	OV, AC, CY
5	DEC dest	Subtract 1 from the destination	None
6	MUL AB	Multiply (unsigned) the content of A and B registers – result in A (lower byte) and B (upper byte)	OV, CY
7	DIV AB	Divide (unsigned) the content of A by the content of B – result in A (quotient) and B (remainder)	OV, CY
8	DA A	Decimal adjust after addition of BCD numbers	CY
9	CLR A	A = 0	None
10	CJNE dest, source, target	Compare the source and destination, and jump to target if they are not equal	CY

```
ADD A, 32H      ;add the content of RAM address 32H to A – sum in A
ADD A, @R1      ;add the content of RAM address pointed by R1 – sum in A
ADD A, R2       ;add the content of R2 to A – sum in A
ADD A, #67      ;add 67 (decimal) to A -sum in A
```

ADC A, src

This is the 'add with carry' instruction. The source, the carry flag and A are added and the sum is put in A.

```
ADDC A, #76H ;add 76H and CY to A — sum in A
ADDC A, 56H  ;add the content of 56H and CY and A – sum in A
ADDC A, R4   ;add content of R4 and CY and A – sum in A
```

INC dest

This instruction adds 1 to the destination, which can be any register or RAM location.

No flags are affected.

```
INC R5      ;add 1 to the number in R5
INC @R0     ;add 1 to the number in the address pointed by R0
INC A       ;add 1 to the number in A
INC 43H     ;add 1 to the content in address 43H
```

Example 13.8

Add the first 20 natural numbers and store the sum in a RAM location.

Solution

```
        ORG 0
        MOV R3,#20       ;move 20 to R3
        CLR A            ;A = 0
        MOV R2,#1        ;R2 = 1
THERE:  ADD A,R2         ;A = A+R2
        INC R2           ;increment R2
        DJNZ R3,THERE    ;decrement R3, jump to THERE if R3! = 0
        MOV 40H,A        ;since R3 = 0, copy A to 40H
HERE:   SJMP HERE        ;stay in HERE
        END
```

This is quite a simple program. In this program, the numbers 1, 2, 3...... 20 are consecutively added and the sum is stored in RAM—the sum is less than 255, so one byte space is sufficient for it. R2 is used as one of the registers, and R2 is continuously incremented to get the numbers to be added.

Example 13.9

Add four 16-bit numbers which are in consecutive memory locations, assuming that the sum does not go above 16 bits.

Solution

The first part of the program simply loads the numbers in RAM locations 40H to 47H. The four numbers are 0575H,0265H,1276H,3457H. The sum is to be 4EA7H.

```
        ORG 0
        MOV R3,#4       ;counter R4 = 4
        MOV 40H,#75H    ;loading the LSB in 40H
        MOV 41H,#05H    ;loading the MSB in 41H
        MOV 42H,#65H    ;loading the LSB in 42H
        MOV 43H,#02H    ;loading the MSB in 43H
        MOV 44H,#76H    ;loading the LSB in 44H
        MOV 45H,#12H    ;loading the MSB in 45H
        MOV 46H,#57H    ;loading the LSB in 46H
        MOV 47H,#34H    ;loading the MSB in 47H
                        ;data entered in RAM
        MOV R0,#40H     ;R0 is the pointer to LSBs
        MOV R1,#41H     ;R1 is the pointer to MSBs
        MOV A,#0        ;clear A
LSB:    CLR C           ;clear C
        ADDC A,@R0      ;A = A + @R0
        JC INCRE        ;if CY = 1, jump to INCRE
BACK:   INC R0          ;increment LSB pointer
        INC R0          ;increment LSB pointer again
        DJNZ R3,LSB     ;decrement counter
        MOV R4,A        ;sum of LSBs inR4
        SJMP MSB        ;jump to MSB loop
INCRE:  INC 49H         ;the sum of CYs of LSB
        SJMP BACK       ;go back to addition loop
                        ;summing of LSBs is done
MSB:    MOV A,#0        ;clear A for MSB addition
        MOV R3,#5       ;R3 = 5 is the counter
MSB1:   ADD A,@R1       ;A = A + @R1
BACK1:  INC R1          ;increment MSB pointer
        INC R1          ;increment MSB pointer again
        DJNZ R3,MSB1    ;decrement counter
        MOV R5,A        ;sum of MSBs in R6
HERE:   SJMP HERE       ;stay in HERE
        END
```

The program first adds the LSBs. They are added taking into account the fact that their addition may lead to a carry, after adding any two numbers. Whenever a carry is generated, the RAM address 49H is incremented. The sum of the LSBs is finally copied to R4.

Then the MSBs are added. There are five numbers to be added, the fifth being the sum of the 'carry' of LSB addition. This is in address 49H and the pointer R1 points to this as the last operand.

We have used numbers which do not generate carries in the MSB addition. The sum is limited to four hex digits. The sum is finally in R4 and R5, with R4 = 0A7H and R5 = 4EH.

13.9.4.2 | *Subtraction Instructions*

SUBB A, src

This subtracts the source byte and the carry flag from A, and puts the result in A. The OV, CY and AC flags are affected. This is actually a 'subtract with borrow' instruction. There is no subtraction instruction, as such. For subtraction, the carry flag is cleared and then the operation is done.

An example of a typical set of instructions for carrying out subtraction is

```
MOV A, #78H      ;A = 78H
CLR C            ;C = 0
SUBB A, #23H     ;A = A – 23H
```

The result of this subtraction will be 55H in A

DEC dest

This instruction subtracts 1 from the destination, which can be any register or RAM location.

No flags are affected.

```
DEC R3           ;subtract 1 from the number in R3
DEC @R1          ;subtract 1 from the number pointed by R1
```

13.9.4.3 | *Multiplication Instruction*

MUL AB

This instruction multiplies two unsigned numbers—one is to be in A and the other in B. The product can be two bytes long (maximum), and it will have its lower byte in A and its upper byte in B.

The multiply instruction clears the carry flag and sets the OV flag if the product is greater than FFH.

Example

```
MOV A, #89H  ;A = 89H
MOV B, #97H  ;B = 97H
MUL AB       ;the product is 50CFH with A = CFH, B = 50H; and OV = 1
```

13.9.4.4 | *Division Instruction*

DIV AB

This instruction divides the content of A by the content of B. The quotient will be in A and the remainder in B. The CY and OV flags are affected. CY is always 0, and OV is set to 1 only when the division is invalid, that is, when B, the divisor is 0, and the result is undefined.

Example

```
MOV A, #245    ;A = 245
MOV B, #17     ;B = 17
DIV AB         ;A = 14, the quotient, B = 7, the remainder; CY = 0, OV = 0
```

13.9.4.5 | *Decimal Adjust for BCD Addition*

DA A

This is the instruction for 'decimal adjust accumulator' after BCD addition. The details of how this is done are given in Section 0.7.2.

13.9.4.6 | *Clear the Accumulator*

CLR A

This instruction clears the accumulator, and is equivalent to MOV A,#0. No flags are affected.

Example 13.10

The selling prices of 5 items are stored in ROM locations 0100H onwards. The corresponding cost prices are entered in RAM locations from 40H onwards. Calculate the average profit of the five items.

Solution

```
        ORG 0
        MOV 40H,#213        ;enters the CP in RAM 40H
        MOV 41H,#154        ;enters the CP in RAM 41H
        MOV 42H,#110        ;enters the CP in RAM 42H
        MOV 43H,#150        ;enters the CP in RAM 43H
        MOV 44H,#80         ;enters the CPs in RAM 44H
        MOV R0,#40H         ;R0 to act as pointer to 40H
        MOV R1,#50H         ;R1 to act s pointer to 50H
        MOV R3,#5           ;R3 = 5, the counter
        MOV DPTR,#0100H     ;DPTR to act as pointer to ROM
BACK:   CLR A               ;clear A
        MOVC A,@A + DPTR    ;get the data from ROM
        CLR C               ;clear carry for subtraction
        SUBB A,@R0          ;subtract CP from SP
        MOV @R1,A           ;save profit from 50H onwards
        INC R0              ;increment the RAM pointer
        INC R1              ;increment the RAM pointer
        INC DPTR            ;increment the ROM pointer
        DJNZ R3,BACK        ;repeat subtraction till R3 = 0
CALCU:  MOV R3,#5           ;R3 = 5, the counter
        CLR A               ;clear A
        DEC R1              ;decrement R1 to point to 54H
```

```
BACK1:  ADD A,@R1           ;add the profits
        DEC R1              ;decrement the RAM pointer
        DJNZ R3,BACK1       ;repeat the addition till R3 = 0
        MOV B,#5            ;B = 5, the dividend
        DIV AB              ;divide A by B
        MOV R5,A            ;move the quotient to R5
HERE:   SJMP HERE

        ORG 0100H           ;ROM address for storing the SPs
        DB 250, 167, 112, 167, 90
        END
```

The method is to get the selling prices (SP) from ROM into the A register, subtract the cost prices(CP), which are in RAM from 40H and save the corresponding profits in RAM addresses from 50H onwards. The last item will be in 54H.

The second part of the program from the label CALCU adds the five profits. During addition, R1 is used as the pointer to addresses from 54H and R1 is decremented to get the 5 items. The sum is divided by 5, to get the profit in the R5 register. See the program.

The program is logically very simple, but it includes a number of actions for 5 data items and is done by looping with a counter R3.

i) It copies the ROM contents to A
ii) It subtracts the contents of A and the contents of RAM (from 40H). This subtraction is Profit = SP – CP
iii) It stores results of the subtraction in RAM from 50H onwards
iv) It then adds contents of 5 RAM locations
v) It divides the sum by 5
vi) The quotient is moved to R5

13.9.4.7 | *Compare Instruction*

CJNE Dest, Src, Target

This instruction compares the source and destination, and if they are not equal, branches to the target address, otherwise the next instruction in the sequence is executed.

The second action that this compare action does is to grade the 'inequality' by indicating whether the destination or source is the bigger number. The carry flag is used for this; the operands, that is, the source and destination do not change in the process of comparison. The CY flag is updated according to the conditions as indicated in Table 13.11.

Table 13.11 | Condition of the Carry Flag After a Compare Instruction

Dest > source	CY = 0
Dest < source	CY = 1
Dest = source	CY = 0

But, there are some restrictions on the ways by which the source and destination can be represented. The following are the sources allowed when A is the destination register

i) the source can be an immediate data

   e.g., CJNE A, #0E4H, THERE

ii) the source can be a direct address

   e.g., CJNE A, 67H, BACK

When A is not the destination register, there are two possible cases

i) The destination can be any of the R0-R7 registers, and the source is to be an immediate data

   e.g., CJNE R3, #34H, FORE

ii) The destination is a RAM address pointed by R0 or R1 and the source is an immediate data

   e.g., CJNE @R0, #0C4H, NOPE

Example 13.11

Find the biggest of 3 numbers which are stored in RAM locations 45H, 46H and 47H. Load the biggest number in R2.

Solution

The flowchart (Figure 13.13) shows how comparison proceeds in the case of three numbers X, Y, Z.

In this program, the first number X is copied to A and the second (Y) to B. They are compared.

i) If they are equal or if A > B, then A is to be compared to the third number. For this, the third number Z is copied to B, and A and B are then compared. If A is found bigger now, then the first number X is the biggest. If A is smaller, the third number Z is the biggest.

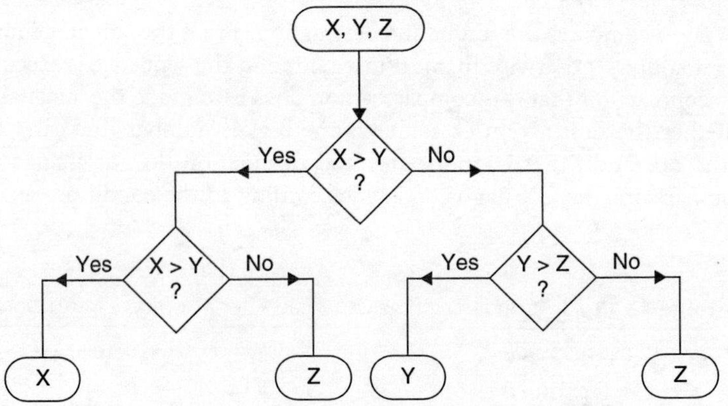

Figure 13.13 | Flowchart for the comparison of three unsigned numbers

ii) If A < B in the first comparison, then the second number is bigger, so swap the number such that the bigger number is in A. Then get the third number in B and compare them.

iii) If A < B, then the third number Z is the biggest, otherwise the second number Y is the biggest.
The biggest number is copied to the register R2.

```
        ORG 0
        MOV 45H,#0F4H       ;the first number in 45H
        MOV 46H,#0A9H       ;the second number in 46H
        MOV 47H,#98H        ;the third number in 98H
        MOV A,45H           ;copy the first number to A
        MOV B,46H           ;copy the second number to B
        CJNE A,B,AGAIN      ;compare A and B
AGAIN:  JC SWOP             ;if A < B jump to SWOP
COMP:   MOV B,47H           ;since A > B, move the third no to B
        CJNE A,B,BIG        ;compare A and B
BIG:    JC BIGR             ;if A < B, go to BIGR
        SJMP BIGG           ;since A > B, go to BIGG
SWOP:   XCH A,B             ;exchange the contents of A and B
        SJMP COMP           ;jump to COMP
BIGG:   MOV R2,A            ;copy A to R2
        SJMP HERE           ;jump to end of program
BIGR:   MOV R2,B            ;copy B to R2
HERE:   SJMP HERE           ;stay in HERE
        END
```

Example 13.12

50 bytes are stored from locations 34H onwards. Find out how many of these bytes are zero.

Solution

This is a simple program. R0 is the pointer to RAM location 34H. It is incremented to load data into A from each of the locations. After that, the JZ instruction is used to verify whether the A register has 0. Every time a 0 is loaded into A, the register R4 is incremented. At the end of the program execution, R4 has the result.

```
        ORG 0
        MOV R3,#50       ;R3 = 50, the counter
        MOV R4,#0        ;R4 = 0
        MOV R0,#34H      ;R0 is the pointer
ENTR:   MOV A,@R0        ;copy the RAM content to A
        JZ COUNT         ;if A = 0, jump to COUNT
BACK:   INC R0           ;increment R0
        DJNZ R3,ENTR     ;decrement R3, jump to ENTR if R3! = 0
        SJMP HERE        ;jump to HEE if R3 = 0
```

```
COUNT:  INC R4          ;increment R4 is a '0' is obtained
        SJMP BACK       ;jump to BACK
HERE:   SJMP HERE       ;stay in HERE
        END
```

13.10 | Port Programming

We have seen many of the important instructions, but a few more are left. They are the logical and rotation instructions, and the types involving call and return.

But before we go to that, let us learn programming involving the GPIO (General Purpose I/O) ports of the chip. There are four ports for the 8051 as can be seen in the functional pin diagram in Figure 13.14.

This diagram is meant only for understanding the port structure of 8051. You can ignore all the other pins, for the time being. Note that there are four ports—P0, P1, P2 and P3, each of which consists of 8 pins. (Note that Port 3 has dual functions associated with each of its pins.) Each of these ports can be used as inputs or outputs. On reset, all

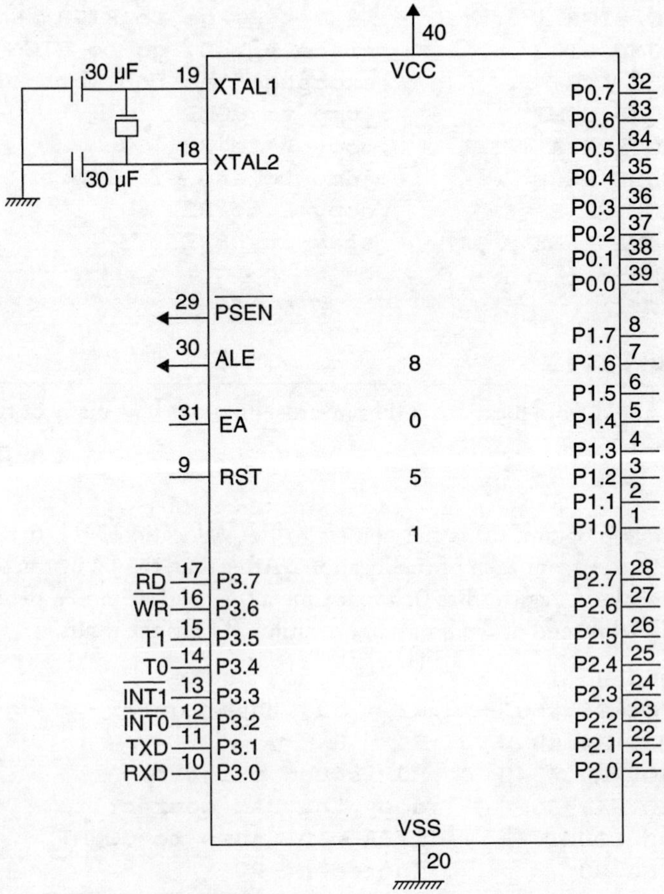

Figure 13.14 | Functional pin diagram of 8051

port pins will have logic'1'. Any data can be directly outputted to the pins, but to make them act as inputs, a '1' must be sent out on the pins–only after that, will that pin be able to accept an input signal and transfer it to the internal registers.

13.10.1 | Port Instructions

Ports can only take data in (from outside) or put data out. There are no special instructions for ports. The 8051 uses the MOV instruction for this.

```
MOV A, P1       ;copy P1 to A – here P1 is an input port
MOV P2, R1      ;copy R1 to P2 – here P2 is an output port
```

In these two cases, each of the ports has 8 bits, and all the 8 bits are taken together as a byte. But each port pin is bit addressable too, it can be set or cleared (if it is an output pin) or read in as a single pin, (for a 0 or 1), if declared to be an input pin.

For this, the nomenclature is 'portname. bit no '. For instance, we use P1.0, P2.3, P3.7, etc. meaning the 0th bit of Port 1, 3rd bit of port 2, 7th bit of port 3 and so on. Now let's do a few programs in which port pins are involved.

Example 13.13

The ports 0 and 1 are connected to two input devices. Write a program to take in data from these ports and compare them. If they are found to be equal, pin P2.0 should be set, otherwise it should be cleared.

Solution

For a port to be able to act as an input port, it should first be given a '1' on all its pins. Only after this step, will it be able to accept input data.

```
       ORG 0
       MOV P1,#0FFH        ;make P1 input
       MOV P0,#0FFH        ;make P0 input
       MOV A,P1            ;read in data at port P1
       MOV B,A             ;copy it to B
       MOV A,P0            ;read in data at port P0
       CJNE A,B,NOPE       ;compare A and B
       SETB P2.0           ;they are equal, P2.1 is set
       SJMP HERE           ;go to end of program
NOPE:  CLR P2.0            ;they are not equal, clear P2.1
HERE:  SJMP HERE           ;stay in HERE
       END
```

Example 13.14

Switches are connected to Port pins P1.6 and P1.7 as shown in Figure 13.15. They are to be monitored continuously, and if found closed, LEDs are to be lighted up or switched off (if the corresponding switch is found open), at port pins P1.0 and P1.1, respectively. Write a program to do this.

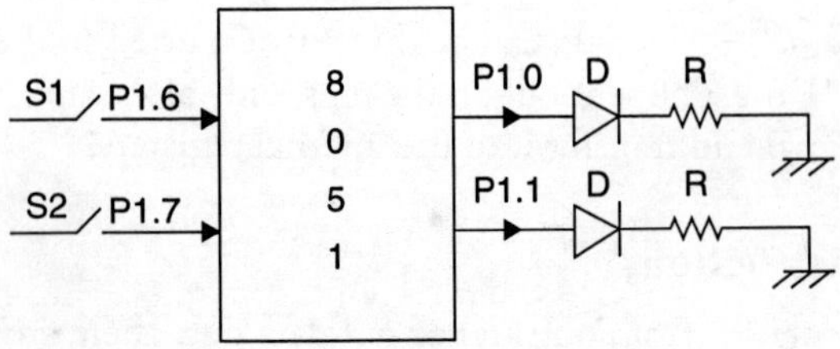

Figure 13.15 | LEDs and switches connected to an 8051

Solution

```
        ORG 0
        SETB P1.6       ;set P1.6, to make it an input
        SETB P1.7       ;set P1.7 to make it an input
        MOV C,P1.6      ;read in P1.6 and move it to C
        JNC ON          ;if C = 0 (switch closed),jump to ON
        CLR P1.0        ;if C = 1(switch open) clear P1.0
        SJMP THERE      ;jump to THERE
ON:     SETB P1.0       ;since C = 0, set the o/p pin P1.0
THERE:  MOV C,P1.7      ;read in P1.7 and move it to C
        JNC ONN         ;if C = 0, jump to ONN
        CLR P1.1        ;if C = 1 clear pin P1.1
        SJMP HERE       ;jump to HERE
ONN:    SETB P1.1       ;since C = 0, set pin P1.1
HERE:   SJMP HERE       ;stay in HERE
        END
```

Here the value of the input pin P1.6 is tested and the LED on P1.0 is lighted if the switch S1 is found closed, i.e. if P1.6 = 0 (switch closed). Then P1.0 must be made '1'. The same is the relationship between i/p pin P1.7 and o/p pin P1.1

Example 13.15

Port pin P2.2 is connected to a water level sensor, which continually senses the water level. When the level reaches a specified limit, this pin will go high. Then the following actions are to occur (See Figure 13.16).

i) Bit 05 of the RAM (in the bit addressable part) is to be set.
ii) Port pin P2.0, which is connected to a switch is to be set (this will switch off the water supply).
iii) Port pin P2.1 which is connected to a buzzer (active low) should be cleared.
iv) In the program, the port pins are given labels, and are referred by them, using the BIT directive.

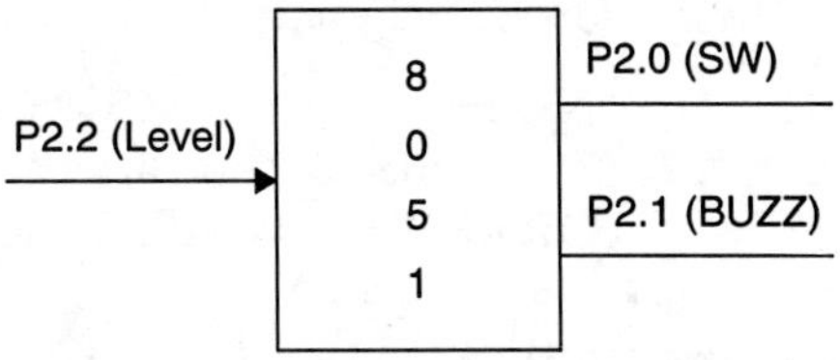

Figure 13.16 | Water level controller using 8051

```
        ORG 0
        LEVEL BIT P2.2      ;P2.2 is labelled LEVEL
        SW BIT P2.0         ;P2.0 is labelled SW
        BUZZ BIT P2.1       ;P2.1 is labelled BUZZ
        MEM BIT 05          ;RAM address 05 is labelled MEM
        SETB LEVEL          :LEVEL is made an input
NOPE:   JNB LEVEL,NOPE      ;keep monitoring LEVEL
        SETB MEM            ;set MEM if LEVEL = 1
        SETB SW             ;set SW (P2.0)
        CLR BUZZ            ;clear BUZZ (P2.1)
HERE:   SJMP HERE           ;stay in HERE
        END
```

13.10.2 | Logical Instructions

Now, let's take a quick look at the logical instructions of 8051. The list of logical instructions is shown in Table 13.12.

The points to be noted are

i) For the ANL,ORL and XRL instructions, the format is dest,src.
ii) Except for one special case, it is mandatory that the A register be the destination.

Examples

```
ANL A, #45      ;AND A with 45
ORL A, R1       ;OR A with R1
XRL A, 56H      ;XOR A with the contents of 56H
```

Table 13.12 | List of Logical Instructions

Sl. No.	Instruction Format	Function to be Performed	Flags Affected
1	ANL dest,src	Logically AND the source and destination	None
2	ORL dest,src	Logically OR the source and destination	None
3	CPL dest	Complement –i.e. logically NOT the destination	None
4	XRL dest,src	Logically XOR the source and destination	None

The special case is when a RAM address is allowed to be the destination as follows:

```
ANL 67H, #23H      ;AND the contents of RAM address 67H with 23H
ORL P1, #98H       ;OR contents of P1 (a direct address)with 98h
XRL 0E4H, A        ;XOR the contents of RAM address E4H with 23H
```

13.10.3 | Complement Instruction

Only the A register and a direct RAM address can be used as the destination

```
CPL A       ;complement the contents of A
CPL 43H     ;complement the contents of RAM address 43H
```

13.10.4 | Rotate Instructions

There are four rotate and one swap instruction for the chip. Only the A register can be used for these instructions.

Let's examine each one of them

i) **RL A:** Rotate left the contents of A
Figure 13.17 shows that the A register is rotated left and D7 appears in the D0 position after rotation.

ii) **RR A:** Rotate right the contents of A
Figure 13.18 shows that the A register is rotated right and the bit D0 is moved to D7.

iii) **RLC A:** Rotate left through carry
The A register is shifted left and bit D7 is moved to carry, while the carry bit is moved to D0 of A. See Figure 13.19.

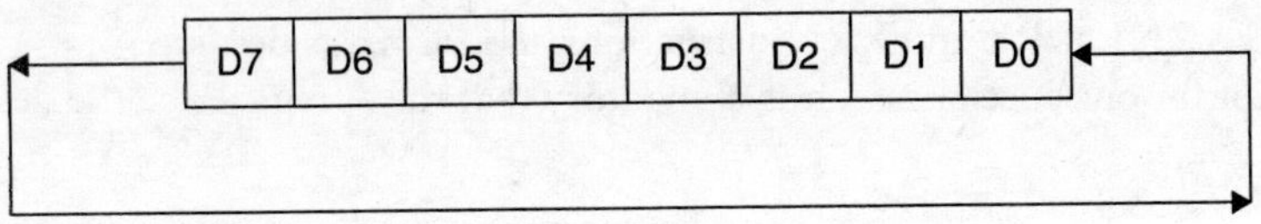

Figure 13.17 | Rotate left instruction

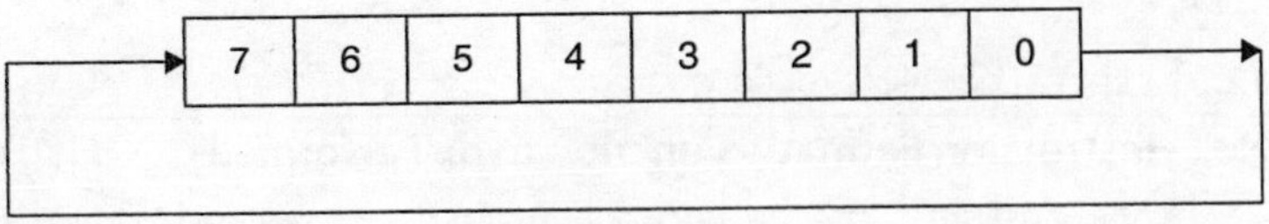

Figure 13.18 | Rotate right instruction

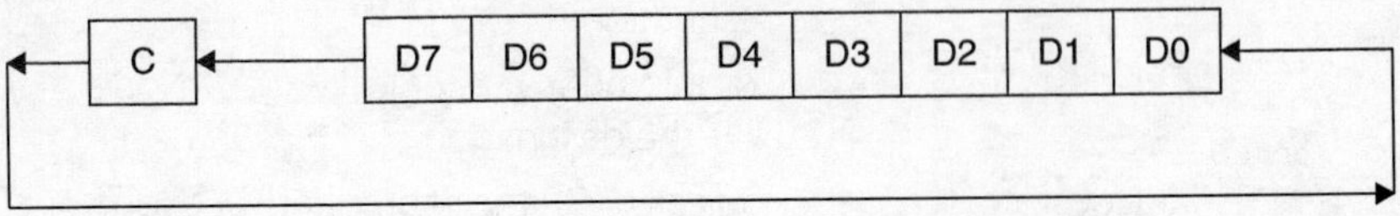

Figure 13.19 | Rotate left through carry

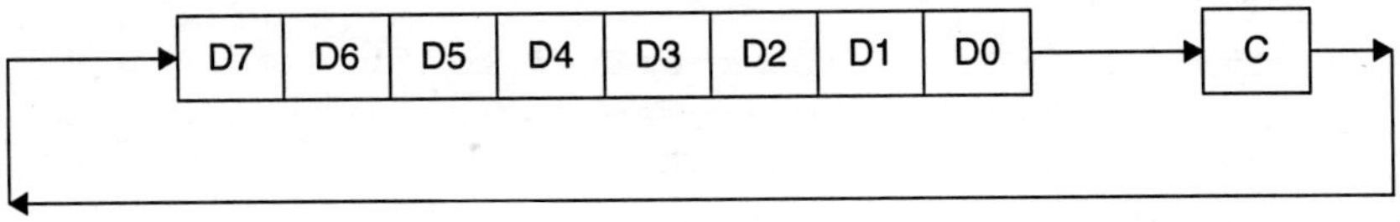

Figure 13.20 | Rotate right through carry

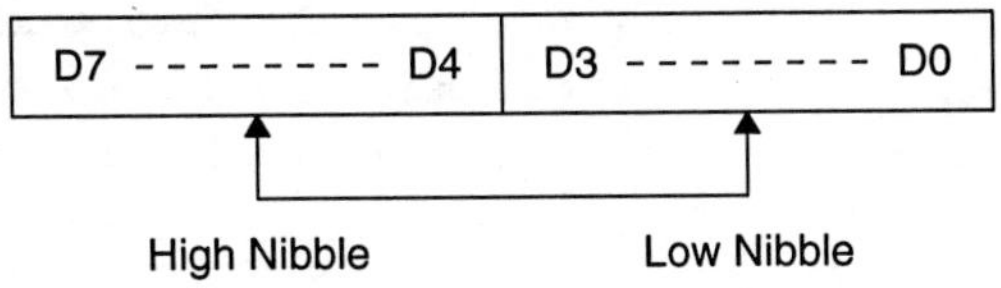

Figure 13.21 | Swapping the nibbles of the accumulator

iv) **RRC A:** Rotate right through carry
The A register is shifted right and the carry bit is moved to D7, while D0 moves into the carry. See Figure 13.20.

v) **SWAP A:** This is a special instruction where the lower and upper nibbles of A are swapped. See Figure 13.21.

Example 13.16

Read in data from port 0. Only the upper four bits of this data is needed. Take the upper four bits and send it as an output nibble to the lower four bits of port 1.

Solution

```
       ORG 0
       MOV P0,#0FFH   ;make P0 an input port
       MOV A,P0       ;move the content of Port0 to A
       ANL A,#0F0H    ;mask the lower nibble of A
       SWAP A         ;switch the upper and lower nibble of A
       MOV P1,A       ;output the content of A to P1
HERE:  SJMP HERE
       END
```

At the end of the program, the wanted data is in the lower four bits of Port 1

Example 13.17

Count the number of 1's in register R1. Take the data from a RAM location.

Solution

Here, the method is rotate A into the carry bit and check if the carry if 1 or not. If it is 1, increment a count in register R2. Finally, R2 has the count of the number of 1's in register R1.

```
        ORG 0
        MOV R1,45H      ;take data from RAM address 45H
        MOV R3,#8       ;R3 to act as a counter for 8 bits
        MOV R2,#0       ;R2 = 0
        MOV A,R1        ;copy R1 to A
ROT:    RLC A           ;rotate left
        JNC COUNT       ;if C = 0, jump to COUNT
        INC R2          ;since C = 1, increment R2
COUNT:  DJNZ R3,ROT     ;decrement until R3 = 0
HERE:   SJMP HERE
        END
```

13.11 | Subroutines (Procedures)

All the programs that we have written are straightforward, in the sense that control flows sequentially from one instruction to the next, and a change in the sequence in which a program in executed, is changed only on encountering a JUMP instruction.

But there is another way by which the execution order is changed and that is by 'one program calling another program'. The calling program is called a main program, while the called program is designated as a 'subroutine, function or procedure'. When a program has to do a task repeatedly it is better that a procedure is called whenever required. Once the procedure is executed and done with, once again the main program takes charge. See Figure 13.22. The fundamental aspects involved here are as follows:

i) The main program calls a procedure.
ii) The procedure returns control to the main program after its completion.

The first step needs a CALL instruction, and the second needs a return instruction. Let's discuss them. The 8051 has two CALL instructions, that is, the LCALL and the ACALL. The format for these instructions is

i) LCALL proc-name
ii) ACALL proc-name

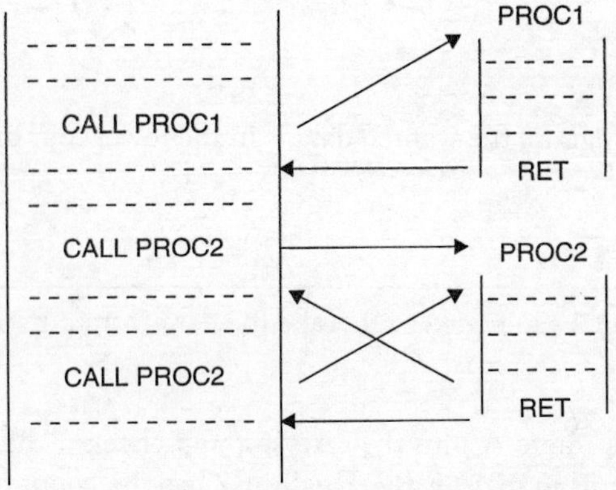

Figure 13.22 | A main program calling procedures

13.11.1 | LCALL

This is a 'long call' instruction. This means that the target program (i.e. the procedure) can be anywhere within the 64K space of program memory. This is a three byte instruction—the first byte is the opcode and the next two bytes are the two byte address of the procedure.

13.11.2 | ACALL

This is a call instruction in which the target procedure must lie within 2K range of the calling program. This is a two byte instruction, with 11 bits allotted for the address of the procedure. Thus, this instruction is used frequently, because it saves one byte of code memory.

What happens when a call occurs?

When a CALL (LCALL or ACALL) instruction is encountered, the content of PC (which is the address of the next instruction) is pushed on to the stack. The address of the procedure is copied to PC, and the next instruction that is executed will be the first instruction of the procedure. The last instruction in the procedure is RET (return). This will pop the return address from stack to PC so that control returns to the main program.

RET This instruction causes the stack top contents to be popped to PC. When a procedure was called, the return address had been pushed onto stack. The return instruction simply retrieves this. It gives back this address to the program counter.

Example 13.18

Port 0 receives BCD input data from a source. It has to be converted to ASCII form and outputted through two output ports, the lower digit at Port 1 and the upper digit at Port 2.

Write a program for this.

Solution

Consider a BCD number like, say, 89. The ASCII of this needs two bytes. The lower byte is 39H (ASCII of 9) and the upper byte is 38H (ASCII of 8).

In this program, the ASCII conversion is written as a procedure.

```
          ORG 0
          MOV P0,#0FFH      ;make P0 an input port
          MOV A,P0          ;copy P0 to A
          MOV R1,A          ;copy A to R1
          CALL ASCII        ;call the procedure ASCII
          MOV P2,A          ;the ASCII digit is at P2
          MOV A,R1          ;take the BCD no from R1
          SWAP A            ;swap the nibbles of A
          CALL ASCII        ;call procedure ASCII
          MOV P1,A          ;move the ASCII digit to P1
HERE:     SJMP HERE         ;stay in HERE
```

```
        ORG 0040H        ;origin of the procedure
ASCII:  ANL A,#0FH       ;mask the upper byte of A
        ORL A,#30H       ;OR it with 30H for ASCII
        RET              ;return
        END
```

The salient points of this program are as follows:

i) The BCD digit is got from port 0 and stored in R1. Then the lower nibble is processed. For this, the procedure ASCII is called.
ii) The procedure first masks the upper byte—if the BCD no is 89H, 09 is got
iii) Then it is ORed with 30H to get 39H, the ASCII of 9.
iv) On returning to the main program, the no is again brought to A and its nibbles are swapped, to get the upper nibble in the lower nibble position, that is, 89H becomes 98H.
v) Then the ASCII procedure masks the upper byte to get 08, and then this is ORed with 30H to get the ASCII 38H of 8.
vi) The values of ASCII numbers are outputted on P1 and P2.

Note The procedure is stored in a different location (0040H) away from the main program. That is why ORG 0040H is seen. This is not absolutely necessary. The procedure can be stored just after the main program itself.

Now, we have almost come to the end of the instruction set. In fact, just one instruction is left. It is the NOP instruction, which means 'no operation'. It does nothing, in fact, but it causes a delay of one machine cycle, and can be used to bring in an additional element of delay in 'delay loops' which we will now discuss.

13.12 | Delay Loops

Why do we need delays?

It may be required to create delays to time events, for example, we may want to output data at a port (which may be changing) every 't' seconds, say. To define 't' seconds, the microcontroller will create a delay and that can be realized by software or hardware. In the latter case, the 'timer' hardware will do this task.

But here, we will create delay using software. This simply means that we get the 8051 to execute a number of repetitive instructions. Since each instruction needs a certain amount of time for execution, the net effect of executing these instructions is to cause a delay. Nothing else is achieved with these instructions (in this context).

To create a delay, the following information must be available

i) The clock frequency of the 8051 used
ii) The number of clock cycles that constitute a machine cycle
iii) The number of machine cycles needed for each of the instructions which constitute the delay loop

Crystal Frequency Refer to Figure 13.14. You can see the pins 18 and 19 between which a crystal is to be connected. The frequency of this crystal decides the clock

Table 13.13 | Machines Cycles Expended in Executing Some Instructions

Instruction	No. of Machine Cycles
MOV Rn,#data	1
DEC Rn	1
DJNZ Rn, target	2
SJMP target	2
NOP	1

frequency for the chip. It is possible to use frequencies between 4 to 40 MHz as crystal frequencies. The frequency 11.0592 MHz is a commonly available and used crystal frequency. We will use this frequency for our calculations in this section.

Machine Cycle A machine cycle is defined as the time required for completing some part of an instruction. All instructions may require one or more machine cycles. A machine cycle will be more than one clock cycle. For 8051, a machine cycle constitutes 12 clock cycles. This standard will be used here, even though there are other versions of this chip which use less number of clock cycles.

Table 13.13 gives a list of the number of machine cycles needed for some commonly used instructions. Appendix A gives the complete list.

13.12.1 | Calculating Delay

Assume the clock frequency of f = 11.0592 MHz for the 8051. One clock period = 1/f.

$$\text{One machine cycle is } 12 \times 1/f = 1.085\ \mu \text{ secs}$$

How do we create a delay?

The method is to load a number in a register and decrement if down to zero. The amount of delay obtained depends on the number loaded.

Example 13.19

Find the delay obtained in the following loop

```
DELAY:   MOV R1,#250
HERE:    DJNZ R1,HERE
```

Solution

The MOV instruction takes 1 machine cycle, and the DJNZ instruction takes 2 machine cycles. The DJNZ instruction gets repeated 250 times.

$$\text{Total delay} = 1.085[250 \times 2 + 1] = 1.085 \times 501 = 543.585\ \mu \text{ secs}$$

The amount of delay obtained in Example 13.18 is only around half a millisecond. This is quite small. To increase the delay, two registers can be used in a nested loop configuration.

Example 13.20

Find the delay obtained in the following nested loop.

```
        MOV     R3, #50
OUTER:  MOV     R4, #255
INSIDE: DJNZ    R4, INSIDE
        DJNZ    R3, OUTER
```

Solution

Take the INSIDE loop. It creates a delay of $1.085 \times (255 \times 2 + 1) = 555$

The OUTER loop repeats the INSIDE loop 50 times to get an effective delay of $555 \times 50 = 27750$ μ secs = 27.750 m secs.

In this calculation, we have neglected the delay due to the initial instructions of

MOV R3, #255 (1 m/c cycle)
and DJNZ R3, OUTER (2 m/c cycles)

This delay = $50 \times 3 \times 1.085 = 162$ μ secs. Compared to the delay created by the double loop, this delay is negligible—and anyway, we consider the delay created by software as only approximate. So in our next examples, we will simply neglect the delay due to these 'peripheral' instructions.

Example 13.21

Write a program to generate a delay of 20 msecs using 8051.

Solution

The maximum number that can be loaded into a register is 255. From Example 13.20, it is seen that with this, the maximum delay that can be obtained is 555 μsecs. So to get a delay of 20 msecs, we should find the number of times this loop should be repeated.

To get this, the method is to divide 20 msecs by 555 μsecs
20 m secs/555 μsecs = 36
So the program is

```
        ORG 0
        MOV  R3,#36
OUTER:  MOV  R4,#255
INSIDE: DJNZ R4,INSIDE
        DJNZ R3,OUTER
```

Delay = $36 \times 255 \times 2 \times 1.085$ us = 19920 us = 19.92 m secs = 20 m secs (approx).
Figure 13.23 shows the square wave generated at pin P1.3

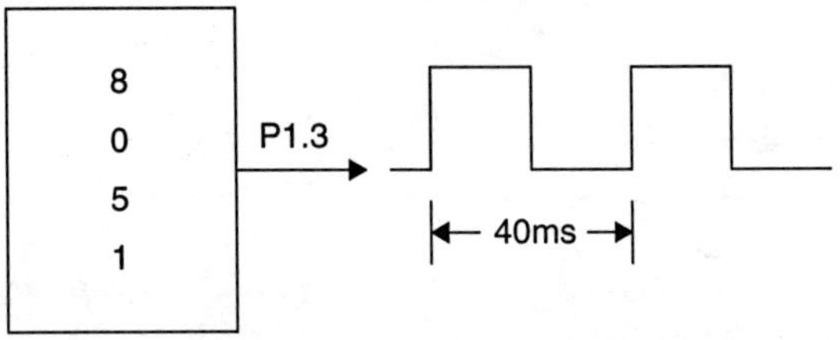

Figure 13.23 | Square wave generated at P1.3

Example 13.22

Generate a symmetrical square waveform of time period 40 m secs at P1.3.

Solution

To generate such a waveform, the pin P1. 3 should be held high for 20 msecs and low for 20 msecs. We can use the delay program of example (previous) to create the delay, we can write the delay creation part as a procedure.

```
          ORG 0
START:    SETB P1.3           ;P1.3 = 1
          ACALL DELAY         ;call the delay procedure
          CLR P1.3            ;P1.3 = 0
          ACALL DELAY         ;call the delay procedure
          SJMP START          ;jump to start
                              ;the delay procedure

DELAY:    MOV R3,#36
OUTER:    MOV R4,#255
INSIDE:   DJNZ R4,INSIDE
          DJNZ R3,OUTER
          RET
          END
```

Note that in this program, the delay procedure is written just after the main program. The last instruction of the program is actually SJMP START. It causes an infinite repetition of the program.

Example 13.23

Generate a square waveform at all the pins of port 1, with an ON time of 0.5 secs and OFF time of 1.5 secs (Figure 13.24).

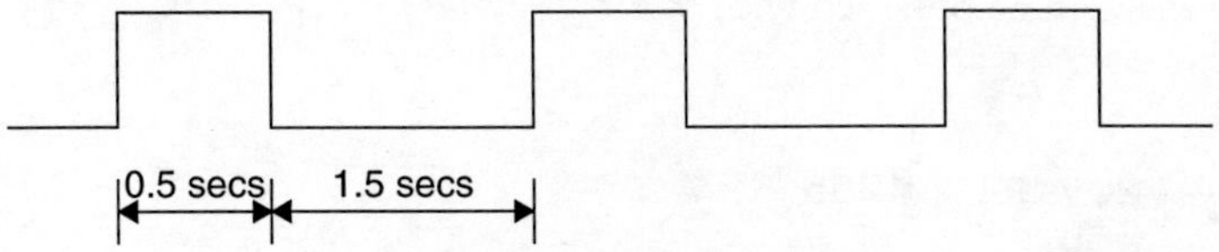

Figure 13.24 | Square wave generated at all pins of Port 1

Solution

```
               ORG 0
START:         MOV P1,#0              ;all pins of P1 made low
               ACALL DELAY_HALF       ;call a delay of 0.5 secs
               MOV P1,#0FFH           ;all pins of p1 made high
               ACALL DELAY_HALF       ;call a delay of 0.5 secs
               ACALL DELAY_HALF       ;call a delay of 0.5 secs
               ACALL DELAY_HALF       ;call a delay of 0.5 secs
               SJMP START             ;jump to START

DELAY_HALF:    MOV R2,#4
OUT_MOS:       MOV R3,#255
OUTER:         MOV R4,#255
INSIDE:        DJNZ R4,INSIDE
               DJNZ R3,OUTER
               SDJNZ R2,OUT_MOS
               RET
               END
```

We might need three registers to get a large delay of 0.5 secs. For the inner loops, let's use registers with the maximum count of 255. For the outer most loop, let the register be loaded with the number N, which we calculate as follows.

$$0.5 \times 1000 \times 1000 \ \mu \text{ secs} = \text{N} \times 255 \times 255 \times 2 \times 1.085 \ \mu \text{ secs}$$
$$500 \times 1000 = 141104 \text{ N}$$
$$\text{N} = 3.5 = 4 \text{ (approx)}$$

This will give a delay of 0.5 secs.

We call the procedure which gives a delay of 0.5 secs, as DELAY_HALF. This is just a label for the procedure, and indicates the address (in ROM) where the procedure is stored.

We write a delay procedure to get 0.5 secs delay, and call it three times to get the delay of 1.5 sec. See the complete program. The asymmetric square wave generated, can be observed at all the pins of Port 1.

13.12.2 | Using NOP

It was mentioned in Section 13.11.2, that the NOP instruction could be used in delay loops.

Example 13.24

Let's make a delay loop with just one register and 5 NOP instructions. Find the maximum delay that can be obtained with this.

Solution

```
        MOV R1, #255
HERE:   NOP
        NOP
```

```
NOP
NOP
NOP
DJNZ R1,HERE
END
```

The total delay inside the delay loop is $[255\ (1 + 1 + 1 + 1 + 1 + 1 + 2)] \times 1.085\ \mu$ secs = 1936 μ secs = 1.9 m secs

Thus, we have obtained a high delay using a NOP instruction.

Whenever an extra element of delay is needed, the NOP instruction comes in handy.

KEY POINTS OF THIS CHAPTER

- A microcontroller is a device which has a number of peripherals and memory inside the chip.
- The 8051 family has a number of members with different numbers of peripherals and different amounts of ROM, but the instruction set is the same for all of them.
- From a programmer's point of view, the registers, RAM, ROM and ports are the important entities in the chip.
- The total internal R/W memory consists of user RAM and special function register RAM
- The user RAM is referred to as internal RAM and consists of 128 bytes.
- There are four register banks, and bank switching is possible.
- The stack of 8051 is an ascending type of stack.
- The processor has data transfer, bit manipulation, arithmetic, logical, rotate and call instructions.
- The Keil assembler is a popular assembler to write and test programs, using its inbuilt simulator.
- There are different modes of addressing like register, direct, indirect and indexed modes.
- Delays can be generated using software.

QUESTIONS

1. Name at least four peripherals that a microcontroller can have.
2. What is the use of flash ROM inside the chip?
3. What is the use of register banks? How can bank switching be done?
4. Which are the registers that can be used for indirect addressing?
5. Is the 8051 stack a LIFO or FIFO stack?
6. What is the value of SP on reset?
7. What is meant by saying that a register is bit addressable?
8. What is the difference between the LJMP and SJMP instructions?
9. What is done by the instruction JB bit target?

10. Which are the two forms of the exchange instructions?
11. Which is the instruction used to create delays?
12. What is the use of the NOP instruction?

EXERCISES

1. Write a program to store the ASCII string "MY NAME IS SUSAN" IN ROM. Now bring it to RAM one byte at a time, and output it to port A, with a delay of 1 msec between each outputting action.
2. Write a program to use register bank 2 for adding ten numbers which are in RAM.
3. Take two numbers which are in ROM, multiply them, and save the product in RAM. Fix up the locations as you want.
4. Add two BCD numbers and use the DA instruction to correct the result.
5. Perform division of two numbers using repeated division.
6. Write a program to convert a hex number to decimal form.
7. Take in data from Port 1, add 10H to it, and sent it out through Port 2.
8. Read data at pins P1.2 and P1.3 and if they are both of the same logic, output '1' to P1.7. Otherwise clear P1.7.
9. Write a program to toggle all the bits of Port 1, at a rate of once per second.
10. Add two 32-bit numbers which are stored in ROM.
12. Add two 64-bit numbers which are stored in RAM.
13. Check the 50-byte locations of RAM from 30H onwards. Search for the character 'Q' in these locations and find how many times this character is present.

14 PROGRAMMING THE PERIPHERALS OF 8051

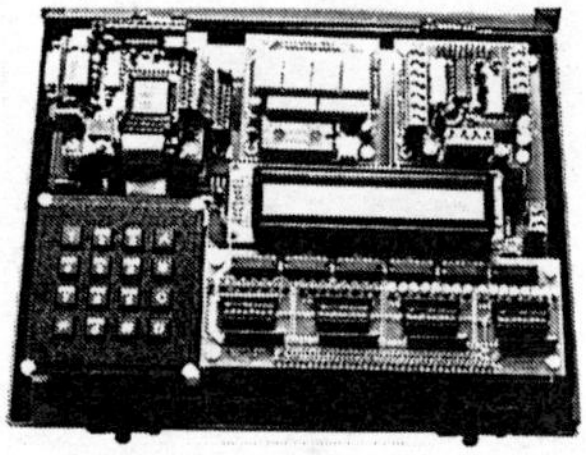

In this chapter, you will learn

- The pin diagram of 8051
- The hardware features of 8051
- The power on reset circuitry
- The concept of 'special function registers' and their uses
- The programming of timers in the polled mode
- The interrupt structure of 8051
- The programming of timers using interrupts
- How to use the serial communication interface of 8051

Introduction

In Chapter 13, our focus was on the programming aspects of 8051. Once that chapter is understood thoroughly, it becomes very easy to move on to the hardware features of 8051.

Any microcontroller needs to place most of its focus on interfacing with peripherals. External peripherals are to be controlled by programs tested and finally 'burned' in the ROM of the microcontroller. All microcontrollers have a number of inbuilt peripheral controllers (they are called peripherals, however), and the more advanced ones have more of these peripherals. The 8051 has timers/counters, interrupts and serial communication interfaces as the main internal peripherals. It has also 32 port lines to which external devices can be connected. For example, dc/stepper motors, relays, LCDS, LEDs, switches etc. can be connected to these port lines.

In this chapter, we will learn how to use timers and serial communication and also discuss the role of interrupts in these and other applications. We begin the discussion with the pin diagram of the chip.

14.1 | Pin Configuration of 8051

Figure 14.1 shows the pin configuration of 8051. Let us discuss the functions of the 40 pins of the chip (except Vcc and ground).

Chapter-opening image: An 8051 development board.

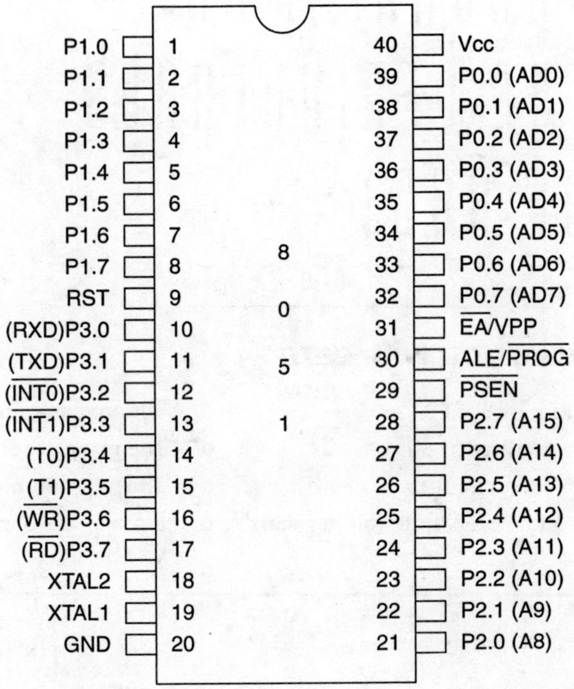

Figure 14.1 | Pin configuration of 8051

14.1.1 | The Crystal

To fix up the rate of operation of the chip, an oscillator is necessary. There is a crystal oscillator inside the chip, but it needs an external crystal to be connected between pins 18 and 19, along with two 30 pF (can vary between 20 to 40 pF) capacitors. See Figure 14.2. The chip can operate with crystal frequencies between 4 to 40MHz. The frequency of 11.0592MHz is a popular crystal frequency, because it allows serial communication using 8051 to be compatible to the baud rate of the PC.

When better performance (measured in terms of speed of execution) is needed, higher crystal frequencies may be used, but it should be kept in mind that higher clock

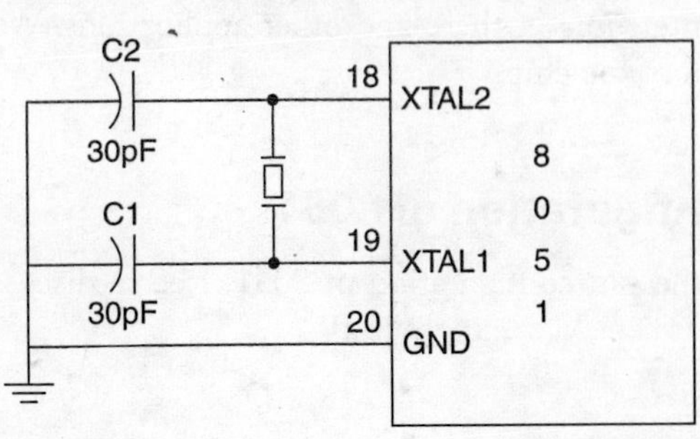

Figure 14.2 | The crystal and capacitors connected externally

speeds lead to higher power dissipation. The point to keep in mind is that very high crystal frequencies should not be used unless absolutely necessary.

14.1.2 | Power on Reset (POR)

Every processor has a (power on reset) circuit. Power on reset means when that power is switched on, the processor should be reset. Otherwise, the system may operate initially in an unpredictable fashion because flip-flops (inside the MCU) are not designed to power-on in any particular state. The meaning of reset generally implies that internal registers (constituted by flip flops) are cleared, and that the processor gets ready to execute. Because the program counter is cleared by reset, for almost all MCUs, the particular location from which the processor takes its first instruction from is 0, the first address itself. All registers (except the SP) are cleared on reset. SP has the value 07 (Section 13.5). All ports have a reset value of FFH.

Every microcontroller needs a specific pulse for reset to occur—it is specific, in the sense that the reset pulse is either high or low and also must have a minimum period. This reset pulse should appear just once, when the power is switched on, and then it should disappear. But there should be a provision for manual reset also, if necessary. There is a reset pin for the chip, but the power on reset circuit is to be provided externally. Figure 14.3 shows a typical POR circuit for the 8051, connected to the reset (RST) pin.

As the capacitor gets charged from the power supply, the voltage at the reset pin, that is, across the resistor falls exponentially as shown in Figure 14.4. This functions as the high reset pulse. It is quite likely that there is a Schmitt trigger inside the IC to convert this exponential pulse to be a pulse with steep sides (this is also shown in the figure).

The typical values used for an 8051 with a crystal frequency of 12 MHz are shown in Figure 14.3. The 8051 needs an active high pulse for reset, which is to be long enough for its oscillator to start, plus two machine cycles (this is as per the specifications given by the manufacturer). One machine cycle is 12 clock cycles. You can verify that the RC value as used in the circuit of Figure 14.3 satisfies this condition.

14.1.3 | Port Pins

8051 has 40 pins, out of which 32 pins are the general purpose I/O (GPIO) pins of the ports 0 to 3. But it can be seen that except for port1, all port lines have dual functions, that is, at any time, the pin can be used as a port pin or be used for its alternate function.

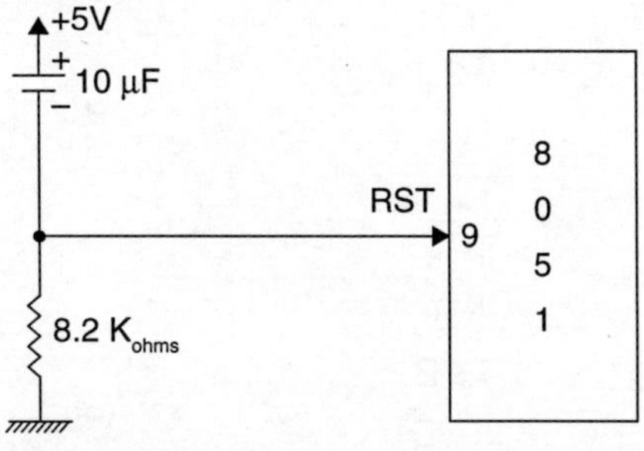

Figure 14.3 | Power-on-reset circuitry for 8051

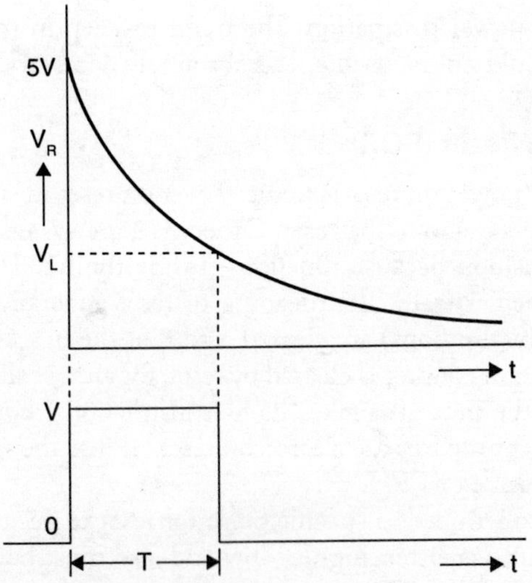

Figure 14. 4 | Discharging voltage across the resistor (at pin RST) and the reset pulse inside the chip

The alternate function of Port 2 and Port 0 are to act as 'address and data' pins for connecting external memory. This will be necessary only if the system external memory, which is relatively rare. As such, port lines of P2 and P0 can be used for connecting to peripherals. Port P1 has no 'alternate' function.

Port 3 pins have alternate functions which may or may not be used. For example, P3.2 and P3.3 have the alternate function of being external interrupt pins. P3.0 and P3.1 function as serial communication pins, and P3.4 and P3.5 have to be used as input pins for using the timer units to count external events. If interrupts or serial communication or counter functions are being used, these pins become unavailable as Port 3. Pins P3.6 and P3.7 are the write and read pins for external memory, and become unavailable as port pins, if external memory is being used. Table 14.1 lists the alternate functions of the pins of Port 3.

Table 14.1 | Alternate Functions of Port 3

Bit of P3	Alternate Function	Pin No.
P3.7	$\overline{RD}$	17
P3.6	$\overline{WR}$	16
P3.5	T1	15
P3.4	T0	14
P3.3	$\overline{INT1}$	13
P3.2	$\overline{INT0}$	12
P3.1	TxD	11
P3.0	RxD	10

14.1.3.1 | *Output Stage of Port 0*

Now let's have a look at the output stages of the ports. This is important because the output stage of Port 0 is a bit different from the other three ports.

We know that the technology used for 8051 is MOS. The output stage of Port 0 is an open drain connection which means that there is no connection between the power supply and the drain of the output transistor. So, even if the output transistor is in the cutoff state, we will not get a high level at the output unless we connect the drain of the transistor to the power source through a resistance. This resistance is called the 'pullup' resistance.

When Port 0 is to be used, separate pullup resistors be connected to each of the transistor drains because the port pins are bit addressable. Figure 14.5 shows resistors of 10 K connected to each output pin. This value has been fixed up based on the maximum current capability of the port pins, and the supply voltage (5V is assumed here).

This is the case of Port 0 alone. The other ports have internal pullups and so the port pins can be used directly.

14.1.4 | Pins for External Memory Interfacing

There are three pins which we have not touched upon. They are the pins $\overline{PSEN}$, ALE/$\overline{PROG}$ and $\overline{\text{EA}}$/VPP, and they have pin numbers 29, 30 and 31. They are associated with the connection of external memory to 8051, in case the memory (RAM and ROM) available internally are not sufficient for the intended application. The discussion of external memory interfacing is beyond the scope of this chapter, and hence we will not talk any more about these pins.

14.2 | Programming the Internal Peripherals

To use any of the internal peripherals of the chip, we should know the special function registers associated with that peripheral and the functionality of those registers. Let us take a tour of the concept of these special function registers or 'SFR's as they are referred to.

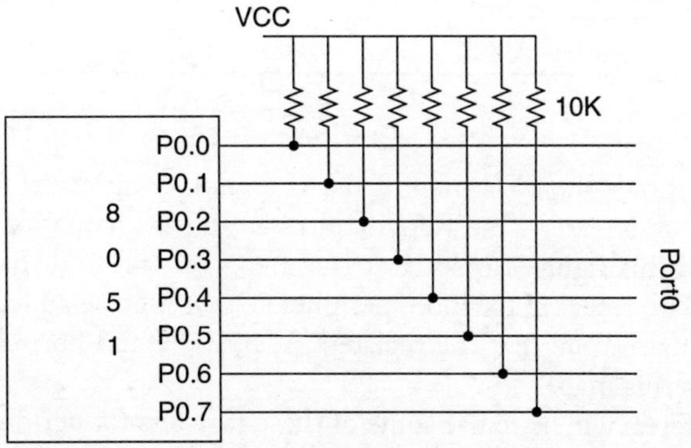

Figure 14.5 | Port 0 output stage with pullup resistors

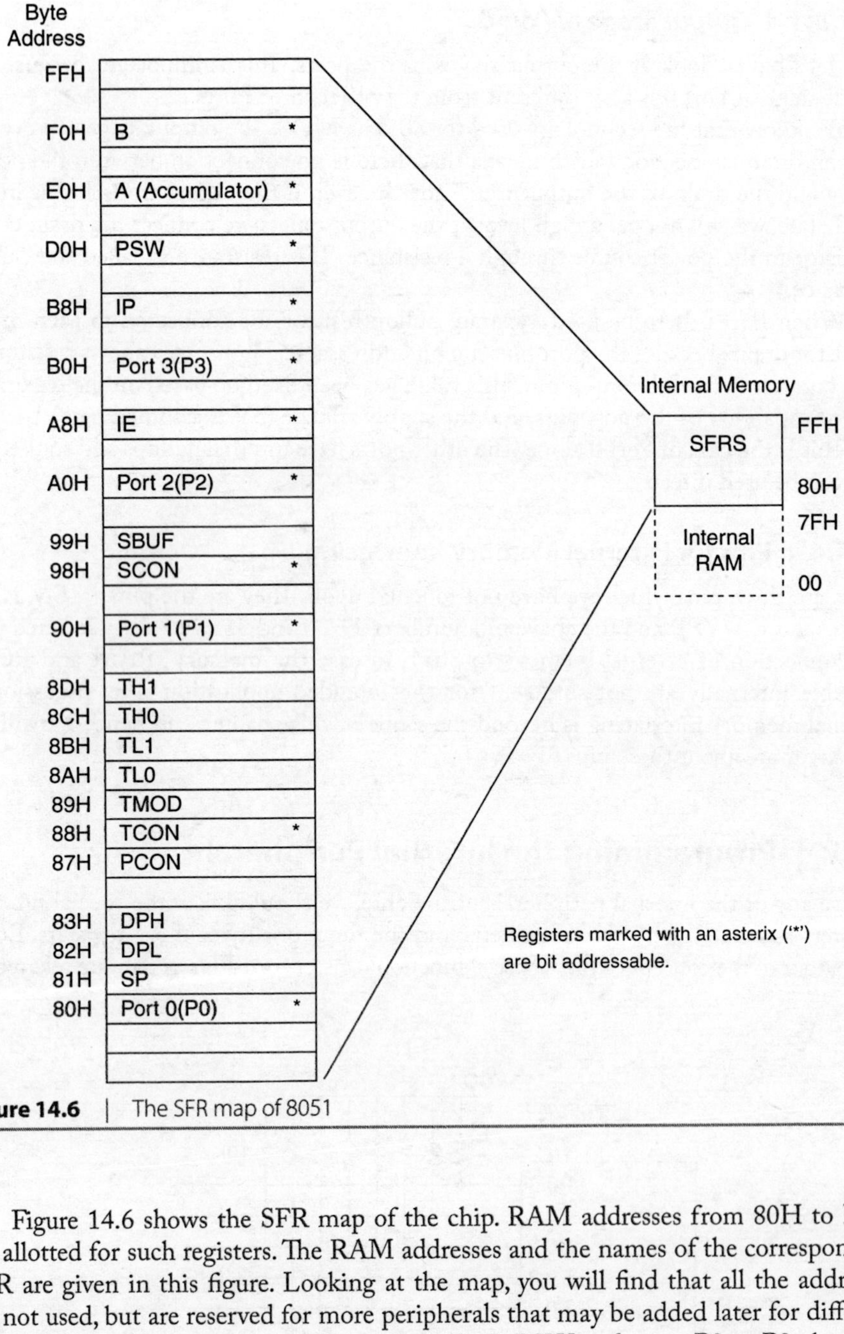

Figure 14.6 | The SFR map of 8051

Figure 14.6 shows the SFR map of the chip. RAM addresses from 80H to FFH are allotted for such registers. The RAM addresses and the names of the corresponding SFR are given in this figure. Looking at the map, you will find that all the addresses are not used, but are reserved for more peripherals that may be added later for different versions. You can also note that the registers A, B, PSW and ports P0 to P3 also have their addresses in this map.

Now, our interest will be to use some of these registers for peripheral programming. The first peripheral we learn is the timer/counter.

14.3 | Timers of 8051

The 8051 has two timer units, namely, T0 and T1. They are independent of each other and can operate simultaneously.

The functions that a timer can perform are as follows:

i) It can create a delay or an interval of time—then we call it an '**interval timer**'
ii) It can also do counting of the frequency of external signals—then, it is called an '**event counter**'

The basic difference in operation between a timer and a counter is that, for the basic timing, the former uses the clock frequency of the chip while the latter uses an external frequency.

14.3.1 | Interval Timer

What does an interval timer do?

The timer is just a hardware for creating a delay. When started, it 'runs' and by the time it stops, a delay or an interval has been created. Thus, we call this an 'interval timer'. This delay can be used just like we have done with software delays in Section 13.6.1, that is, we can generate square waves or time events.

How does the timer function?

The idea associated with a timer is very simple. A number is loaded into a timer register and the timer is given the 'start' signal. The number in the timer register keeps incrementing until it reaches the maximum possible count. This is FFH for an 8-bit register and FFFFH for a 16-bit one. In one more step, the content of the register rolls down to zero—this is the stop signal. The stop instant is indicated by a 'timer flag setting' or an interrupt. The delay in reaching this instant (from the start time) is the required delay or interval.

The important thing is that the rates at which the timer register increments, is dependant on the clock signal of the 8051. The higher the clock frequency, the faster is the rate of incrementing of the timer registers.

14.3.2 | Timer Programming

As mentioned earlier, there are two timers for the chip—Timer 0 and Timer 1. Each timer has a timer count register which is 16 bits long. It is into this timer register that we load the initial count. But since numbers can be moved only as one byte at a time, Timer 0 register has two parts—TH0 and TL0, and Timer 1 register has TH1 and TL1, where H and L correspond to the high and low bytes, respectively. See Figure 14.7a and b.

14.3.3 | The Timer Mode Register (TMOD)

The TMOD register (Timer Mode Control) is an SFR register at location 89h in the SFR space and is used to define the mode of operation.

Figure 14.8 illustrates the mode register which caters to both the timer units, the lower nibble for timer 0 operation, and the upper nibble for timer 1 operation. Writing appropriate bits in this register will let us fix up the mode of operation for the timer. This

TH0								TL0							
D15	D14	D13	D12	D11	D10	D9	D8	D7	D6	D5	D4	D3	D2	D1	D0

Figure 14.7a | Timer registers of timer 0

TH1								TL1							
D15	D14	D13	D12	D11	D10	D9	D8	D7	D6	D5	D4	D3	D2	D1	D0

Figure 14.7b | Timer registers of timer 1

MSB							LSB
Gate	C/T	M1	M0	Gate	C/T	M1	M0
Timer 1				Timer 0			

Figure 14.8 | Bit configuration of the TMOD register

Gate	C/T	M1	M0

```
Gate:  This is to be set only if the 'starting' of the
timer is to be done using hardware. When cleared,
the timer is enabled by software.
C/T:   When set, counter operation is selected
       when cleared, timer operation is selected
M1:  Mode bit 1
M0:  Mode bit 0
M1     M0
 0      0     Mode 0       :13-bit mode (seldom used).
 0      1     Mode 1       :16-bit mode
 1      0     Mode 2       :  8-bit mode (with auto reload)
 1      1     Mode 3       :  split timer mode
```

Figure 14.9 | Mode bits for a timer

register caters to both the timers. See Figure 14.9 for the meaning of each of the bits.

Figure 14.9 shows the TMOD register part for one timer. The gate pin may be made 0 in software-based timer control. For our applications here, we will make GATE = 0. Now, we select 'timer' operation, so C/T = 0. There are two mode bits to select one out of the four modes. Our interest is only in modes 1 and 2.

14.3.4 | Clock Source for the Timer

When operating as an interval timer, the clock source is the system clock itself. This frequency is divided by 12, for the timer register count to increment by 1. Let's use a clock frequency of 12 MHz. When divided by 12, effectively we get a 1 MHz source for the timer—in effect one clock tick every micro second, for the timer register to increase its count by 1.

Note If the clock frequency is 20 MHz, the clock tick for the timer occurs every 0.5/12 μsec where 0.5 μsec is the time period corresponding to the clock of 20MHz). This is a typical calculation for any clock frequency.

14.3.5 | Steps in Programming An Interval Timer

i) Write the mode control word in the TMOD register
ii) Write the count in the timer register
iii) Start the timer
iv) Wait for overflow and check the status of the timer flag
v) Stop the timer
vi) If this sequence is to repeated, reload the timer register, clear the timer flag and go to step iii

See Figure 14.10. Now let's discuss each of them steps in detail.

14.3.6 | Writing the Mode Control Word

Consider using Timer 0 in mode 1. For Timer 0, only the lower nibble of the TMOD register need be used. The upper nibble can be 0000. The lower nibble is 0001 for mode 1 usage. Thus, the mode control word is: 00000001, i.e., 01.

Example 14.1

Write the mode control words for the following cases:

i) Timer 1 in mode 1
ii) Timer 0 in mode 2
iii) Timer 1 in mode 2 and timer 0 in mode 1

Solution

Refer to Figures 14.8 and 14.9.

For all these cases, the GATE and C/T bits are to be made 0.

i) **Timer 1 in mode 1:** Timer 1 uses the upper nibble of the TMOD register, the lower nibble bits may be made 0.
   The TMOD value is to be: 0001 0000, i.e, 10H
ii) **Timer 0 in mode 2:** Timer 0 uses only the lower nibble. The TMOD value is: 0000 0010, i.e., 02
iii) **Timer 1 in mode 2 and timer 0 in mode 1:** Both the upper and lower nibbles of TMOD must be configured. TMOD is 0010 0001, i.e., 21H

14.3.7 | Mode 1 Programming

In mode 1, the timer registers TH and TL are cascaded to get a 16-bit register into which a 16-bit number can be loaded. Figure 14.10 illustrates the scenario associated with mode 1 programming.

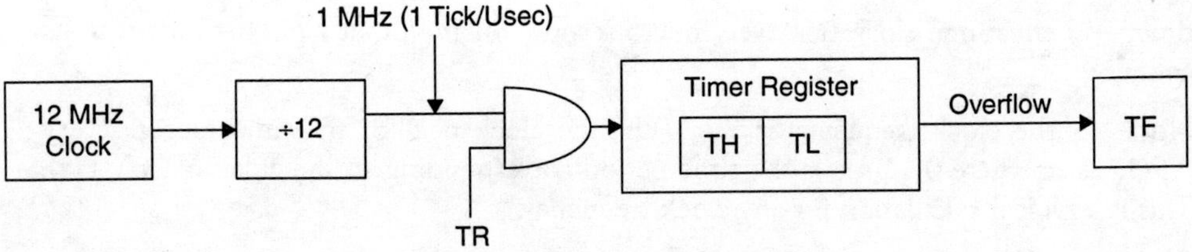

Figure 14.10 | Sequence of actions when a timer is used in mode 1

To understand mode 1 usage, refer to the 'steps in programming' in Section 14.3.5, along with Figure 14.10. The first and second steps should be clear, by now. The third step is to start the timer.

Starting the Timer

This is done in software by setting the start bit which is present in a register called the TCON (for Timer Control) register. See the relevant register bits shown in Figure 14.11

This register has 4 bits for timer operation, and they are the upper four bits. (The lower four bits are for interrupt operations, which we will discuss later). The start bit of Timer 0 is TR0 and that of Timer 1 is TR1. This register is bit addressable and TR0 may also be denoted with the symbol TCON.4 as shown in Figure 14.11.

Detecting Timer Overflow

Once the timer is started, the timer register increments, reaches the maximum and then rolls over to 0. This corresponds to the end of the timing sequence. How is this indicated? There are two timer flags in the TCON register, TF0 and TF1, as can be seen in Figure 14.11.

The flag gets set when overflow occurs. In what is called the 'polled mode', the program waits in a loop checking for the setting of this flag. There is another more efficient mechanism—the interrupt mechanism. This is discussed later in Section 14.5. For now, our focus is on the polling method. Here, when timer overflow is detected, we stop the timer (TR = 0) and re-start the timing again (TR = 1) if we want to repeat the delay cycle. An example will make all this clear.

MSB LSB

TF1	TR1	TF0	TR0	IE1	IT1	IE0	IT0

Bit	**Symbol**	**Function**
TCON.7	TF1	Timer 1 overflow flag
TCON.6	TR1	Timer 1 start bit
TCON.5	TF0	Timer 0 overflow flag
TCON.4	TR0	Timer 0 start bit

Figure 14.11 | TCON bits used for timer programming

Example 14.2

Use timer 1 in mode 1 to create a delay. Load the number 8946H in the corresponding timer register. Write a program for this, and also calculate the amount of delay obtained.

Solution

```
ORG 0
         MOV TMOD,#10H      ;load TMOD word
         MOV TL1,#42H       ;load lower byte of count
         MOV TH1,#80H       ;load upper byte of count
         SETB TR1           ;start the timer
CHECK:   JNB  TF1,CHECK     ;check if TF1 is set
         CLR TR1
END
```

This program loads the mode word, and the count value in the respective registers, i.e., TH1 and TL1. Then the timer is started. Next, the processor is in put in a loop waiting for the timer flag to be set. When the flag is set, the timer is stopped by clearing TR1.

Delay Calculation

Let's calculate the amount of this delay. The clock we use has the frequency of 12 MHz, and thus the period of one machine cycle is 1 μsec.

The timer register has the initial value of 8042H. When the timer starts, this number increases every machine cycle to 8043, 8044 .... FFFFH. The number of machine cycles expended in reaching the maximum count is FFFFH – 8042H = 7FBDH = 32,701 (in decimal). To roll to 0 from the maximum count, takes one more machine cycle, and hence the total number of machine cycles = 32,702 which corresponds to a delay of 32,702 μsecs = 32.702 msecs.

Example 14.3

Using the delay in Example 14.2, generate a square wave at pin P2.4

Solution

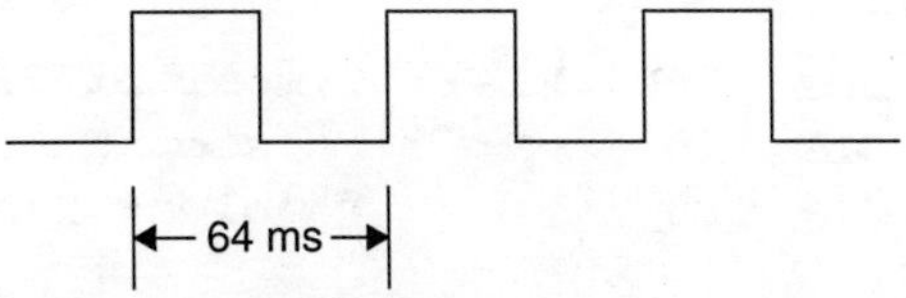

Figure 14.12 | Square wave obtained at P2.4

```
ORG 0
          MOV TMOD,#10H     ;mode 1 timer 1
BACK:     MOV TL1,#42H      ;load low byte of count
          MOV TH1,#80H      ;load high byte of count
          SETB TR1          ;start the timer
```

```
            CPL P2.4             ;complement P2.4
            ACALL DELAY          ;call delay procedure
            SJMP BACK            ;jump to BACK
DELAY:      JNB TF1,DELAY        ;jump to delay if TF1!=1
            CLR TR1              ;stop the timer
            CLR TF1              ;clear the timer flag
            RET                  ;return to main program
END
```

This program generates a square wave as shown in Figure 14.12, on pin P2.4. The delay is written as a procedure. The pin is complemented for every delay of 32 msecs.

Example 14.4

Write a program to generate a square wave of 20 msecs at pin P1.4, for an 8051 with a clock frequency of 12 MHz. Use timer 0 in mode 1.

Solution

In this problem, the delay to be generated is 10 msecs (half the time period of the symmetric square wave).

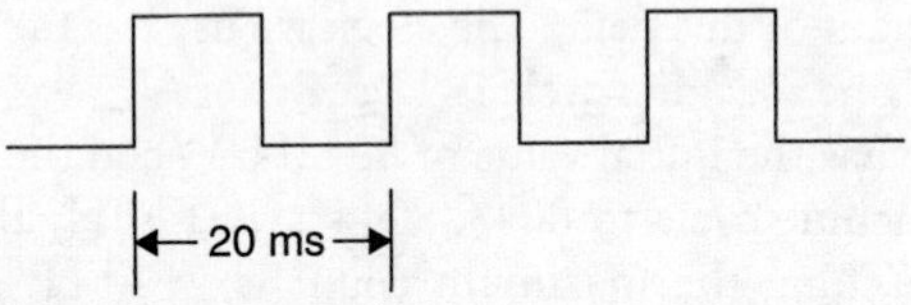

Figure 14.13 | Square wave obtained at P1.4

```
ORG 0
            MOV TMOD,#01H        ;timer 0 in mode 1
BACK:       MOV TL0,#0F0H        ;load low byte of count
            MOV TH0,#0D8H        ;load high byte of count
            SETB TR0             ;start the timer
            CPL P1.4             ;complement P1.4
            ACALL DELAY          ;call  procedure DELAY
            SJMP BACK            ;jump to BACK
DELAY:      JNB  TF0,DELAY       ;monitor TF0 until set
            CLR TR0              ;stop Timer 0
            CLR TF0              ;clear Timer flag
            RET
END
```

How do we calculate the count required for this delay?

The period of 10 msecs needs 10 msecs/1 μsec = 10000 machine cycles of the timer. Thus, the count to be loaded into the timer registers is 65536 – 10000 = 55536 = D8F0H.

This calculation is for Example 14.4. Figure 14.14 lists the steps in the calculation of the count, for a general case.

```
Now Let's generalize the steps for calculating the count, given a
delay period of 'T'. Let 't' be the machine cycle period (clock
period/12)

i)    Divide T by the machine cycle period to get.  N = T/t
ii)   Subtract N from 65,536. i.e. 65,536 -N
iii)  Convert the result of the above calculation to hex and
      this number to the 16-bit timer register.
```

Figure 14.14 | Steps in the calculation for the number to be loaded in the timer registers

Example 14.5

Find the count to be loaded in the timer register for using it in mode 1, for the following cases:

i) A delay of 1.5 msecs when the 8051 clock frequency is 12 MHz
ii) A delay of 52 msecs when the 8051 clock frequency is 12 MHz
iii) A delay of 35 msecs when the 8051 clock frequency is 20 MHz

Solution

A delay of 1.5 msecs when the 8051 clock frequency is 12 MHz

i) Here T = 1.5 msecs = 1500 μsecs
ii) t = 1 μsec
iii) N = T/t = 1500
iv) 65536 – 1500 = 64,036 = FA24H is the required count value

A delay of 52 msec when the 8051 clock frequency is 12 MHz

i) Here T = 52 msecs. = 52000 μsecs
ii) t = 1 μsec
iii) N = T/t = 52000
iv) 65536 – 52000 = 13536 = 34E0H is the required count value.

A delay of 35 msecs when the 8051 clock frequency is 20 MHz

In this case, the crystal frequency is 20MHz. To get the timer frequency, this is to be divided by 12.

20/12 = 1.667 MHz

i) t = 1/1.667 μsecs = 0.599 μsecs = 0.6 secs (approx)
ii) T = 35 msecs = 35000 μsecs
iii) N = T/t = 35000/0.6 = 58333

The required count = 65536 – 58333 = 7203 = 1C23H.

Example 14.6

Generate the following waveform: 4 msecs ON time, 13 msecs OFF time. Clock frequency = 12MHz

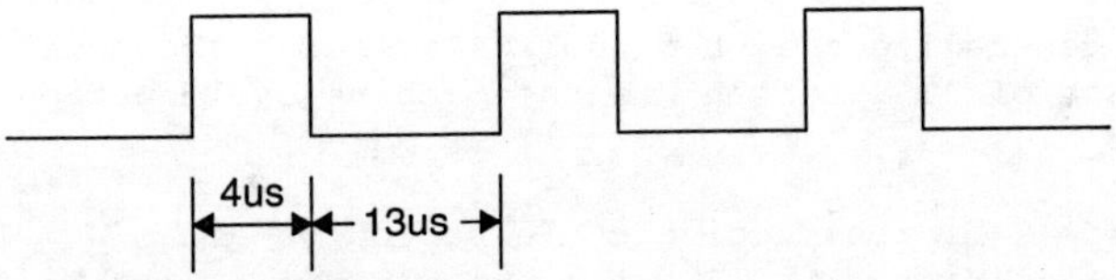

Figure 14.15 | Waveform obtained at P1.4

Solution

```
ORG 0
            MOV TMOD,#10H       ;timer 1 in mode 1
BACK:       MOV TL1,#60H        ;low byte of ON time count
            MOV TH1,#0F0H       ;high byte of ON time count
            SETB P1.4           ;P1.4 = 1
            ACALL DELAY         ;call the DELAY procedure
            MOV TL1,#38H        ;low byte of OFF time count
            MOV TH1,#0CDH       ;high byte of OFF time count
            CLR P1.4            ;P1.4 = 0
            SJMP BACK           ;jump to BACK

DELAY:      SETB TR1
NOPE:       JNB TF1,NOPE        ;loop to DELAY if TF1! = 1
            CLR TR1             ;stop timer
            CLR TF1             ;clear TF1
            RET                 ;return to main program
END
```

This is an asymmetrical waveform, and two different delays need to be calculated.

On time calculation
T = 4 msecs = 4000 μsecs
t = 1 μsec
N = T/t = 4000
Count = 65,536 – 4000 = 61536 = F060H

Off time calculation
T = 13 msecs = 13000 μsecs
t = 1 μsec
N = T/t = 13000
Count = 65,536 – 13000 = 52536 = CD38H

Example 14.7

What is the maximum delay that can be obtained using timers in mode 1 for the following cases?

i) Clock frequency of 12 MHz
ii) Clock frequency of 20 MHz

Solution

The maximum delay is possible when the timer registers are loaded with the number 0. Then the count will increment from 0 to FFFFH and then roll down to zero.

i) Clock frequency of 12 MHz
   For t = 1 μsec, this will create a delay of 65,536 × 1 μsec = 65,536 μsecs = 65.536 msecs
ii) Clock frequency of 20 MHz
   For t = 0.6 μsecs, this will create a delay of 65,536 × 0.6 μsecs = 39321 μsecs = 39.32 msecs

The issue now is how to create a delay greater than the values in Example 14.7. A simple method is to use a register with a number loaded and to have the timer action to be repeated as many times as the number in this register.

Example 14.8a

```
ORG 0
              MOV TMOD,#01H      ;timer 0 in mode 1
AGAN:         MOV R3,#08         ;R3 = 8
              CPL P2.3           ;complement P2.3
BACK:         MOV TL0,#0         ;TL0 = 0
              MOV TH0,#0         ;TH0 = 0
              SETB TR0           ;start the timer

CHECK:        JNB TF0,CHECK      ;loop to CHECK if TF! = 0
              CLR TR0            ;stop the timer
              CLR TF0            ;clear TF0
              DJNZ R3,BACK       ;reload TH and TL if R3! = 0
              SJMP  AGAN         ;jump to AGAN when R3 = 0
END
```

This example uses the R3 register loaded with the number 8. The timer registers are loaded with 0, so that the delay obtained by the timer 0 operation in mode 1 is 65.536 msecs. If this delay is repeated 8 times, 524 msecs delay, or 0.5 secs (approx) will be obtained. This program gives a symmetric square wave with a time period of 1 second.

Example 14.8b is the same as Example 14.8a. There is a slight difference in notations, however. TR0 is now written as TCON.4 and TF0 as TCON.5 (Refer to Figure 14.11). These are written as the bits of the registers TCON. This notation is also permitted by Keil. There are some assemblers (Digitck, for example) which allow only this notation. There, the words TF0, TR0, etc. are not allowed.

Example 14.8b

```
ORG 0
              MOV TMOD,#01H      ;timer 0 in mode 1
AGAN:         MOV R3,#08         ;R3 = 8
              CPL P2.3           ;complement P2.3
BACK:         MOV TL0,#0         ;TL0 = 0
```

```
            MOV TH0,#0             ;TH0 = 0
            SETB TCON.4            ;start the  timer
CHECK:      JNB TCON.5,CHECK       ;to CHECK if TF0 = 1
            CLR TCON.5             ;clear TF0 ie, TCON.5
            DJNZ R3,BACK           ;reload if R3! = 0
            SJMP  AGAN             ;jump to AGAN if R3 = 0
END
```

14.3.8 | Mode 2 Programming

In this mode, the operation is the same as mode 1 except for two aspects.

i) It is an 8-bit timer, i.e., the count values are from 0 to FFH
ii) Automatic re-loading is done

Let's examine this mode in detail.

i) In this mode, the count is to be loaded only into the TH register. The 8051 copies it to TL also.
ii) When the timer is started, it is the TL register which starts incrementing up to FFH and then rolls down to 0. The timer flag then gets set.
iii) For the timer operation to continue, the count should be re-loaded into TL. This is done automatically as the processor transfers the content of TH to TL, for a new delay cycle to start.
iv) Figure 14.16 illustrates the operation of a timer in mode 2.

Example 14.9

```
ORG 0
            MOV TMOD,#02H          ;timer 0 in mode 2
            MOV TH0,#0H            ;TH0 = 0
            SETB TR0               ;start the timer
CHECK:      JNB TF0,CHECK          ;loop to CHECK if TF0 = 0
            CLR TF0                ;clear TF0
            CPL P1.3               ;complement P1.3
            SJMP CHECK             ;jump to CHECK
END
```

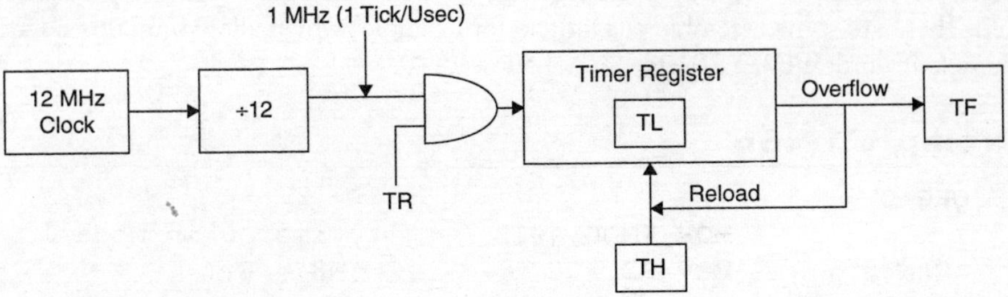

Figure 14.16 | The sequence of operation of a timer in mode 2

The program in Example 14.9 generates a square wave on pin P1.3. It uses Timer 0 in mode 2. The count loaded in TH0 is 0. **Note that, after TF0 is cleared, there is no 're-load' operation for TH0. The count is automatically re-loaded by the 8051, after the timer flag is cleared.**

Now let's calculate the frequency of the square wave, generated (assuming an 8051 with a clock frequency of 1MHz).

The count increments from 0 to 255, and then to 0.

Delay = 256 × 1 μsec = 256 μsecs
The square wave has a period of 256 × 2 = 512 μsecs, i.e., f = 0.001953 MHz
That is, 1.9 KHz. A square wave of 1.9 KHz is generated.

Example 14.10

Generate a square wave of frequency f = 50 Hz using timer 0 in mode 2. Clock frequency = 12MHz.

Solution

```
ORG 0
            MOV TMOD,#02H     ;timer 0 in mode 2
            MOV TH0,#0        ;TH = 0
REP:        MOV R0,#39        ;R0 = 39
            CPL P2.3          ;complement P2.3
            SETB TR0          ;start timer
CHECK:      JNB TF0,CHECK    ;loop to CHECK until TF = 0
            CLR TF0           ;clear TF0
            DJNZ R0,CHECK     ;repeat Timer action if R0! = 0
            SJMP  REP         ;jump to REP
END
```

50 Hz frequency corresponds to a period T = 0.02 secs.
T/2 = 0.01 secs = 10000 μsecs
With a timer in mode 2, the maximum delay possible is 256 μsecs
So an extra register is needed which repeats the timer operation 39 times (10000/256 = 39)

We have done an elaborate study of timers working in mode 1 and mode 2. Mode 0 has no special use, while mode 2 is used only for specific purposes. Now, we will go to the next application of the timer unit, that is, its use as a counter.

14.4 | Counter Programming

As a counter, the timer unit performs counting of external events. An event is a pulse, **but the source of the pulse is not the clock of the 8051, but an external source.**

Table 14.2 | Port Pins to be Used as Counter Inputs

Counter	Port Pin	Pin No.	Function
0	P3.4	14	Input for external signal
1	P3.5	15	Input for external signal

The practical application of counting is that any action can be converted into a pulse, for example, for counting people who pass through a door, a detection mechanism can generate a pulse for every person who passes through. Objects on a conveyor belt can be counted. Another application is to measure an unknown frequency

The incoming pulse train is fed in to the 8051 at the pins P3.4 or P3.5 depending on which timer unit is to be used, see Table 14.2.

14.4.1 | Measuring an Unknown Frequency

Example 14.11 is a program to measure an unknown frequency. The pulse train (whose frequency is to be measured) is fed in through P3.4 if Timer 0 is used for counting or through P3.5 for Timer 1 as a counter.

You know that a frequency is defined as the number of repetitive transitions (events) per second. The method used here is to make a 'time base' of 1 second, and then count the pulses that appear during that period.

Example 14.11 does the following

i) Makes Timer 1 to act as a timer which creates a delay of 1 second
ii) Timer 0 receives the unknown frequency at its pin P3.4
iii) Both Timer 1 and Counter 0 are started at the same time.
iv) The count in TH0 and TL0 increments as the incoming pulses come in.
v) After one second has elapsed, counter 0 is stopped, and the number in its registers (TH0 and TL0) is checked. This is the frequency of the incoming pulse train.
vi) The values of TL0 and TH0 are copied to ports.
vii) A display system will be needed to read the values.
viii) There is a limit to the maximum value of the incoming frequency which the system can measure.
ix) The 'time base' need not be for one second. Any other value of delay can be used, and interpolated for one second.
x) In the program, Timer 1 in mode 1 and a clock frequency of 12 MHz (for the 8051) have been used. R3 loaded with 16, and TH1 and TL1 loaded with 0 will give a delay of 1 second.

Example 14.11

```
STRT:     MOV TMOD,#15H      ;Timer 1 as timer
                             ;Timer 0 as counter
          SETB P3.4          ;make port P3.4 an input port
          MOV TL0,#00        ;clear TL0
```

```
            MOV TH0,#00        ;clear TH0
TIM1:       MOV R3,#16         ;R3 = 16
BACK:       MOV TL1,#0         ;load low byte
            MOV TH1,#0         ;load high byte
            SETB TR1           ;start timer 1
            SETB TR0           ;start counter 0
CHECK:      JNB TF1,CHECK      ;loop to CHECK until TF1 = 0
            CLR TF1            ;clear TF1
            DJNZ R3,BACK       ;loop to BACK until R3 = 0

            MOV A,TL0          ;1 sec has elapsed, A = TL0
            MOV P2,A           ;move A to Port2
            MOV A,TH0          ;A = TH0
            MOV P1,A           ;move A to Port1
            SJMP STRT          ;repeat
END
```

14.4.2 | Event Counting

This is to illustrate another application for a counter. There is a unit which allows only 1000 items to be sent on a conveyor belt. Once the 1000 items are got, the transit path is closed. Then a waiting (indefinite) occurs until the transit passage is open again. Port P1.0 is the pin controlling the transit. Port P1.1 senses whether the passage is open or closed.

The program tests the P1.1 pin until it is set. Then counting starts by inputting the incoming pulse train on pin P3.5 (counter input of Timer 1). Once 1000 events are counted, the timer flag is set and the transit passage is closed by the relay controlled by P1.0. See the program in Example 14.12.

Example 14.12

```
ORG 0

            SETB P3.5          ;make P3.5 an i/p pin
            SETB P1.1          ;make P1.1 an i/p pin
OPEN:       JNB P1.1,OPEN      ;test if the transit is open
            MOV TMOD,#50H      ;timer 1 as counter
            MOV TH1,#0FCH      ;high byte of count
            MOV TL1,#18H       ;low byte of count
            SETB TR1           ;start counting
CHECK:      JNB TF1,CHECK      ;test if TF1 is set
            SETB P1.0          ;closes relay if count = 1000
            CLR TR1            ;stop the counter
            SJMP OPEN
END
```

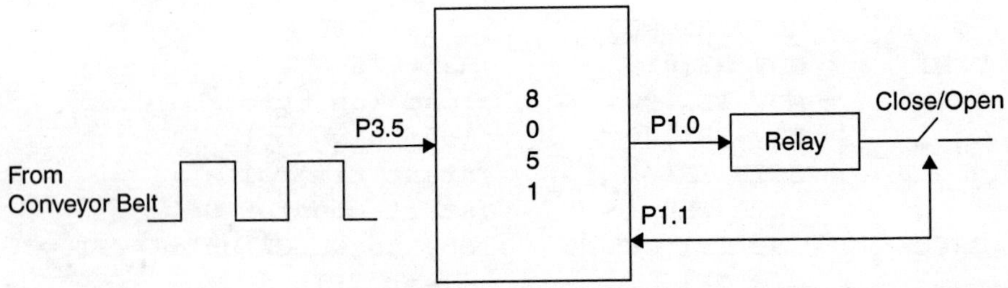

Figure 14.17 | The pins and controls for the system

In Example 14.12, how does the counter count '1000' events?

An initial count of (65,536 – 1000 = 64536 = FC18H) is loaded in the registers. For each incoming event, this count gets incremented and when it reaches the maximum, TF1 is set, which is detected.

With this, we come to the end of one part of our discussion of timers. Next, we start our study of interrupts and then timers will once again be talked about. We then will see how timers can be used more efficiently, when operated in the interrupt driven mode.

14.5 | Interrupts of 8051

Interrupts are of prime importance for any processor. In Chapter 2, the philosophy of interrupts was discussed at length, and the interrupt structure of 8086, covered in detail. In this section, we look into the operation of the 8051 interrupts. The actions that take place when an interrupt occurs is the same for all processors. So here we won't talk about the definitions of ISR, interrupt vector, etc as they have been covered in Chapter 2.

Let us see the interrupt structure of 8051. There are six interrupts for this chip, including reset. They are as follows:

i) Two external (hardware) interrupts EX0 and EX1.
ii) Two timer interrupts for Timer 0 and Timer 1
iii) One interrupt for serial interrupt, which caters to serial transmission as well as reception.
iv) Reset

All these are 'vectored' interrupts, and Table 14.3 gives the vectors of each of the interrupts. Note that only EX0 and EX1 have pins. These pins are referred to as $\overline{INT0}$ and $\overline{INT1}$.

Table 14.3 | Interrupt Vectors of 8051

Sl. No.	Interrupt	Interrupt Vector (Hex)	Pin
1	Reset	0000	9
2	External (EX0)	0003	12(P3.2)
3	Timer 0 (TF0)	000B	.....
4	External (EX1)	0013	13 (P3.3)
5	Timer 1 (TF1)	001B	.....
6	Serial	0023	.....

Refer to Table 14.3 and note the interrupt vectors. You will find there is only an 8-byte space for the ISR of INT0. Will that space be sufficient to store a program which needs to take care of an external peripheral? Quite unlikely. So usually, in the vectored location, a jump instruction is written and then control gets re-directed to some other address in memory. This is so for all the interrupt vectors.

In all our 8051 programs so far, we simply ignored the possibility that interrupts might occur. That is why we have written programs with an origin of 0 and continued sequentially in that section of memory. But if we take into account the possibility of being interrupted, our programs should NOT be written in the section of ROM where interrupt vectors are located. So what is to be done? Start up occurs at address 0, but having a jump instruction at that location bypasses the interrupt vector area. See Example 14.13.

Example 14.13

```
ORG 0                        ;this is the start up location
    LJMP STRT                ;bypass interrupt vectors

ORG 000BH                    ;interrupt vector for timer 0
    SJMP ISR_T0
ORG 40H                      ;main program  starts here
    STRT:    -----           ;main program
             -----
             -----
             -----
    ISR_T0:  -----
             -----
             -----
    RETI
END
```

In this example, what is to be observed is that the start up location is 0. At this address, a jump instruction (SJMP or LJMP or AJMP depending on the range of jumping) is written which transfers control to another location, where the main program is available. Here we have chosen 0040H for it, but any address beyond the area of the interrupt vectors can be chosen.

In the main program, the interrupts are enabled and the code therein causes a jump to an interrupt vector. Here, Timer 0 has been used for illustration. Timer 0 has the vector 000BH. When control branches there, the ISR is taken up. Since there may not be sufficient space, a jump instruction is written there which takes control to its ISR, that is, ISR_T0. The last instruction in the ISR is RETI. On executing this line, control returns to the main program, at the point where it had been interrupted.

14.5.1 | Enabling Interrupts

On startup, none of the interrupts are enabled (except reset, of course). To enable interrupts selectively, an interrupt enable (IE) register is to be loaded with the appropriate bit configuration.

EA			ES	ET1	EX1	ET0	EX0

Name	Notation	Function Performed
EA	IE.7	EA=1, enables all interrupts, but individual activation also necessary
-	IE.6	Unused
-	IE.5	Unused for 8051
ES	IE.4	ES=1, enables the serial communication interrupt
ET1	IE.3	ET1=1, enables Timer 1 interrupt
EX1	IE.2	EX1=1 enables external interrupt 1
ET0	IE.1	ET0=1 enables Timer 0 interrupt
EX0	IE.0	EX0=1 enables external interrupt 0

Figure 14.18 | Bits of the IE register

Figure 14.18 shows the bits of the IE register. This register is bit addressable and hence the notation 'IE.bit number' is used, like, say, IE.3, IE.1, etc. Setting a bit enables the specific interrupt, while clearing it, disables it. Two levels of enabling are necessary—first EA (enable all) should be set, and then the bit corresponding to the particular interrupt of our choice should be set. For example, to use Timer 0 in the interrupt mode, the bits to be set are IE.7 (EA) and IE.1 (ET0). We can use the following instructions for it.

SETB IE.7; IE.7 = 1 to enable all interrupts
SETB IE.1; IE.1 = 1 to enable Timer 0 interrupt

Example 14.14

Write the control word for enabling the two timer interrupts and the two external interrupts.

Solution

Here 5 bits of the IE register have to be set.

The IE register bit configuration is
10001111 i.e. 8FH
Instead of using individual instructions to set the five bits, one instruction will suffice
MOV IE,#8FH

14.5.2 | Using Timers in the Interrupt Mode

We have discussed timer operations in very great detail in Sections 14.3 and 14.4. There the 'polling' method was used for checking the status of the Timer flag. In the interrupt driven method, when the Timer flag is set, an interrupt is also activated, that is, control goes to the interrupt vector of the timer, and the ISR written therein is run.

Let us discuss this for Timer 0. Similar steps are applicable for Timer 1, as well.

14.5.3 | Steps in Using Timer 0 in the Interrupt-driven Mode

i) Write the IE register with the appropriate control word
ii) Start the timer, after loading appropriate words in the timer registers
iii) When TF0 is set, interrupt occurs and program control jumps to the vector 000BH
iv) The ISR therein is executed. The last instruction in the ISR is RETI, and then control returns to the main program
v) Once control branches to the interrupt vector, TF0 is automatically cleared.

Note These steps are for Timer 0, and similar steps are to be used for Timer 1.

Example 14.15

```
ORG 0
            LJMP   STRT         ;bypass the interrupt vectors

ORG 000BH                       ;interrupt vector of Timer 0
            CPL P2.4            ;complement P2.4
            RETI                ;return to main program

ORG 40H                         ;the main program is here
STRT:       MOV TMOD,#02H       ;Timer 0 in mode 2
            MOV TH0,#00H        ;load count
            MOV IE,#82H         ;IE word for timer 0
            SETB TR0            ;start timer
HERE:       SJMP HERE           ;wait in loop
END
```

Example 14.15 generates a square wave of frequency 1.9 KHz at P2.4, using Timer 0 in mode 2. The calculation of the delay is done in Example 14.9.

The ISR is very small—it is just one instruction to complement P2.4. So it is written in the area of the interrupt vector itself. If it had been bigger, a jump instruction to another location would have been necessary.

In the main program which is at ROM location 0040H, the timer and interrupt initialization instructions are written. Once the timer starts, no other activity is done by the processor. It simply waits in a loop using the instruction.

```
HERE: SJMP HERE
```

In the course of this waiting, the timer flag gets set and then the waiting is exited and the instructions in the ISR are executed. The last instruction in the ISR is RETI which takes control back to the main program instruction SJMP HERE.

Instead of simply waiting, the processor can be made to do something else. That something will then be interrupted when the timer flag is set, and the ISR is taken up. See Example 14.16, in which a port-based program (starting at label OTHER) is running along with the running of the Timer—this is the charm of using interrupts. The processor is not stuck with doing just one program. A number of tasks can be done simultaneously if separate hardware is available for each of them. Here the CPU does the port program, while the timer keeps running by virtue of it having specific hardware for that job.

Example 14.16

```
ORG 0
            LJMP STRT          ;bypass the interrupt vectors

ORG 000BH                      ;interrupt vector of Timer 0
            CPL P2.4           ;complement P2.4
            RETI

ORG 40H                        ;main program here
STRT:       MOV TMOD,#02H      ;Timer 0 in mode 2
            MOV TH0,#0FDH      ;load count
            MOV IE,#82H        ;IE word for timer 0
            SETB TR0           ;start timer

OTHER:      MOV P1,#0FFH       ;make P1 an input port
            MOV P0,#0FFH       ;make P0 an input  port
HERE:       MOV A,P1           ;read in data at port P1
            MOV B,A            ;copy it to B
            MOV A,P0           ;read in data at port P0
            CJNE A,B,NOPE      ;compare A and B
            SETB P2.0          ;P2.0 = 1 since A = B
            SJMP HERE          ;jump to HERE to repeat
NOPE:       CLR P2.0           ;P2.0 = 0
            SJMP HERE          ;jump to HERE to repeat
END
```

In this program of Example 14.16, the microcontroller performs two activities simultaneously. It generates a square wave on pin P2.4. The other activity is taking data from two ports P0 and P1 continuously, comparing them and setting pin P2.0 if they are not equal, or clearing them if they are equal.

In real time, you can find a square wave on P2.4 and a toggling of P2.0, depending on the values of data coming through Port 0 and Port 1.

Example 14.17

```
ORG 0                          ;start up here
            LJMP STRT          ;bypass the interrupt vectors
ORG         001BH              ;ISR of Timer 1
            SJMP T1_ISR        ;jump to another location

ORG 40H                        ;main program
STRT:       MOV TMOD,#10H      ;Timer 1 in mode 1
            MOV IE,#88H        ;enable Timer 1 interrupt
            SETB P1.3          ;P1.3 = 1
            SETB TR1           ;start Timer 1
HERE:       SJMP HERE          ;wait for TF1 to be set
```

```
                              ;the ISR of Timer 1
T1_ISR:   CLR TR1             ;stop Timer 1
          CPL P1.3            ;complement P1.3
          MOV TL1,#024H       ;low byte of OFF time count
          MOV TH1,#0FAH       ;high byte of OFF time count
          SETB TR1            ;start timer
          RETI
END
```

The problem in Example 14.17 uses the value of delay in Example 14.5. A symmetric square wave is to be generated using mode 1, which needs the count to be re-loaded after each cycle.

In the main program, the timer is started, but no count value is loaded into its registers. It starts with the default value of 0. The timer flag gets set and then an interrupt occurs which takes control to the label T1_ISR. Here the timer flag is cleared, and the timer is started with the actual count values in the TH and TL registers. From then on, these values are reloaded, every time the timer flag is set. The timer flag is cleared automatically, once the ISR is taken up.

Example 14.18

Generate a square wave at P1.3 using Timer 1 in the interrupt mode

Solution

```
ORG 0                         ;start up vector
          LJMP STRT           ;bypass interrupt vectors
ORG 001BH                     ;interrupt vector of Timer 1
          SJMP T1_ISR         ;jump to the ISR
ORG 40H                       ;main program is here
STRT:     MOV TMOD,#10H       ;timer 1 in mode 1
          MOV IE,#88H         ;enable Timer 1 interrupt
          SETB P1.3           ;P1.3 = 1
          SETB TR1            ;start Timer 1
HERE:     SJMP HERE           ;wait for interrupt
T1_ISR:   CLR TR1             ;stop timer
          JB P1.3,FLOW        ;test P1.3
          MOV TL1,#60H        ;if P1.3 = 0, load count low
          MOV TH1,#0F0H       ;load upper byte of count
          SJMP BACK           ;jump to BACK
FLOW:     MOV TL1,#38H        ;if P1.3 = 0,OFF time count low
          MOV TH1,#0CDH       ;high byte of OFF time count
BACK:     CPL P1.3            ;complement P1.3
          SETB TR1            ;start Timer 1
          RETI                ;return
END
```

The program of Example 14.18 generates an asymmetric waveform. The count values are taken from the calculation of Example 14.6. Since mode 1 is used here, reloading of the count values is required for the ON time as well as for the OFF time.

The steps of the program are as follows:

i) In the main program beginning at label STRT, the IE and TMOD registers are configured. The timer is started with the default count value of 0000. When the timer flag is set, control jumps to the address 001BH.
ii) In the ISR, the timer is stopped, and the value of the pin P1.3 is tested. If it is 0, the count value of F060H is loaded in the timer registers, the pin P1.3 is set, and the timer is started.
iii) Otherwise, if the value of P1.3 is '1', the count value of CD38H is loaded into the timer registers and the timer is started, after clearing the pin P1.3. This count is for the low part of the square wave. The timer starts and because of the RETI instruction just after that, control goes to the instruction SJMP HERE where waiting occurs for the timer flag to be set.
iv) When the timer flag is set, once again the ISR is taken up, and this time, the pin P1.3 is found to be low. Then the count of F060H is loaded, and since the pin P1.3 is set after this, the high portion of the square wave starts.

Example 14.19

Generate two wave forms simultaneously from pins P2.0 and P2.1.

Solution

```
ORG 0
          LJMP STRT        ;bypass the interrupt vector area

ORG 000BH                  ;interrupt vector of Timer 0
          CPL P2.0         ;complement pin P2.0
          RETI             ;return

ORG 001BH                  ;interrupt vector of Timer 1
          CPL P2.1         ;complement P2.1
          RETI             ;return

ORG 40H                    ;main program
STRT:     MOV TMOD,#22H ;TMOD for T1 and T0 in mode 2
          MOV IE,#8AH      ;T0and T1 interrupts enabled
          MOV TH0,#0AH     ;count for T0
          MOV TH1,#0CDH ;count for T1
          SETB TR0         ;start Timer 0
          SETB TR1         ;start Timer 1
HERE:     SJMP HERE        ;stay in HERE
END
```

In Example 14.19, both timers have been used. In interrupt mode, both timers can work independently. In polled mode, this is difficult as the CPU is in a loop, polling the flag of

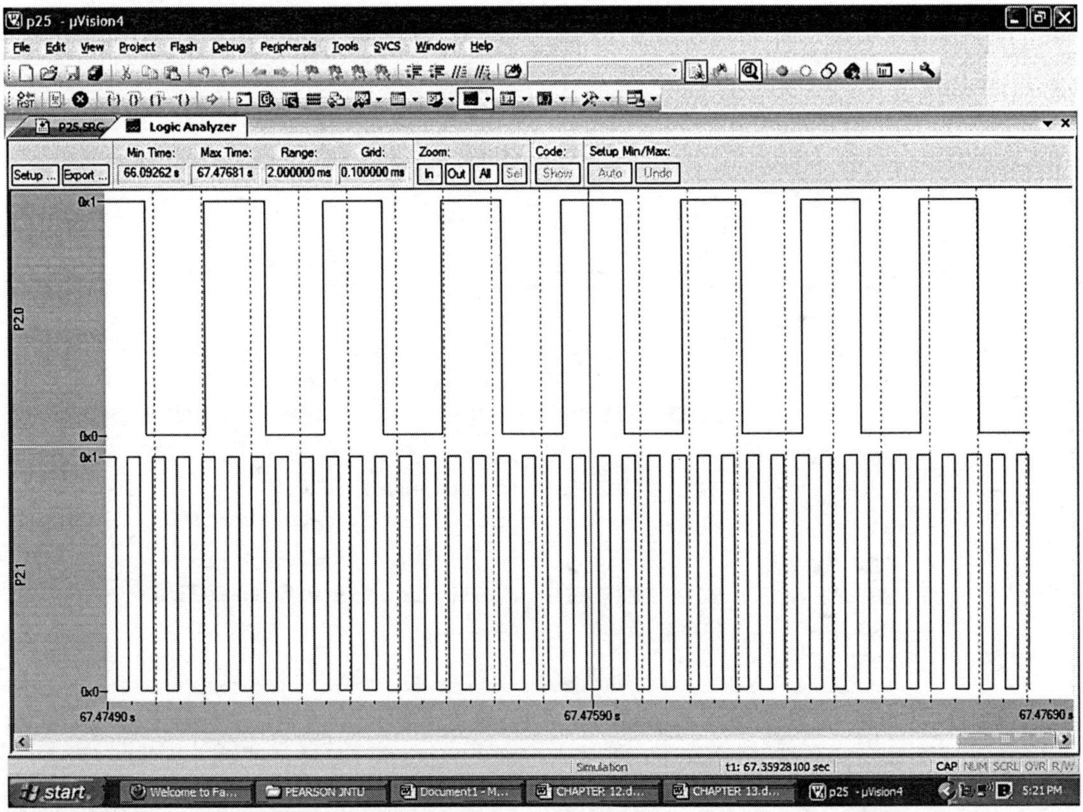

Figure 14.19 | The output signals at P2.0 and P2.1

one timer. In the interrupt mode, once a timer is started its timer register increments, the flag gets set, the interrupt is generated and the output pin is complemented. In mode 2, the re-loading of the count value is not needed and the cycle repeats. The same is the case for the other timer, as well.

Timer 0 and Timer 1, both in mode 2 have been used. Signals of two different frequencies are obtained from P2.0 and P2.1. It is up to you to calculate the frequencies of the two waveforms. Figure 14.19 shows the waveforms at P2.0 and P2.1, as seen in the logic analyser of the Keil Simulator.

14.5.4 | External Hardware Interrupts

The 8051 has two hardware interrupts, EX0 and EX1, the pins for which are P3.2 and P3.3, respectively. On reset, these pins are high, and the pins respond to a low level signal for interrupts. This means that these interrupts are low level triggered—to place an interrupt on these lines, they must be pulled low. The interrupt vectors of these interrupts are given in Table 14.3.

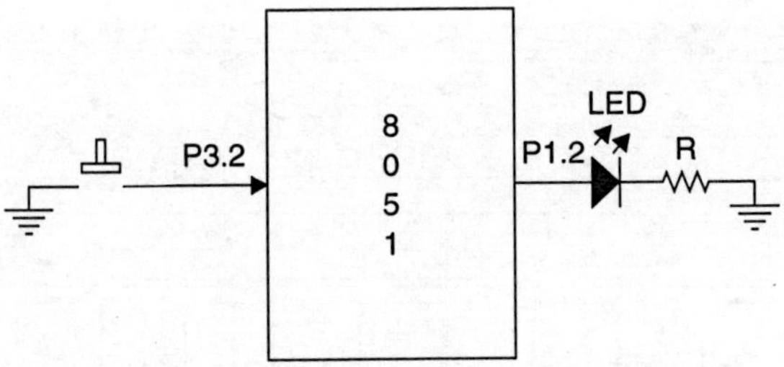

Figure 14.20 | The input and output pins as used in Example 14.19

Example 14.20

```
ORG 0                       ;start up occurs here
         LJMP STRT          ;bypass the interrupt vector area
ORG 0003                    ;interrupt vector of EX0
         CPL P1.2           ;complement P1.2
         RETI               ;return to main program
ORG 0040H                   ;main program is here
STRT:    MOV IE,#81H        ;INT0 interrupt enabled
HERE:    SJMP HERE          ;wait
END
```

Example 14.20 is a very simple program which uses EX0. Pin 3.2 is the corresponding pin to which a push button switch has been connected (Figure 14.20). When the push button switch is pressed, the pin goes low and the interrupt is activated. The corresponding ISR just complements pin P1.2 every time the switch at P3.2 is pressed. If an LED is connected to P1.2, it goes ON and OFF corresponding to the activation of the switch.

14.5.5 | Edge Triggering of the External Interrupts

From the above discussion, it is apparent that the external hardware interrupts are level triggered. However, it is possible to make them edge triggered also. For doing that, the bits of the TCON register are to be used. This register was discussed with respect to timers in Section 14.3, but only the upper nibble was in our domain of interest there. Here we look at the interpretation of the lower nibble only.

Figure 14.21 shows the bit configuration of the lower nibble of the register TCON. We can make the external hardware interrupts 1 and 0 to be edge triggered by setting the

MSB LSB

TF1	TR1	TF0	TR0	IE1	IT1	IE0	IT0

Bit	Symbol	Function
TCON.3	IE1	External interrupt 1 Flag
TCON.2	IT1	Set for edge triggering of EX1
TCON.1	IE0	External interrupt 0 Flag
TCON.0	IT0	Set for edge triggering of EX0

Figure 14.21 | Bit configuration of the lower nibble of the TCON register

bits IT1 and IT0, The edge should be a high to low transition. The flags IE1 and IE0 are set when 'edge triggered interrupts' are detected by the CPU (Note that level triggered interrupts don't affect this flag in any way). Once the ISR has completed execution (at the RETI instruction), these flags are cleared.

Example 14.21

```
ORG 0                         ;start up occurs here
          LJMP STRT           ;bypass the interrupt vector area

ORG 0003                      ;interrupt vector of EX0
          CPL P1.2            ;complement P1.2
          RETI                ;return to main program

ORG 0040H                     ;main program is here
STRT:     SETB TCON.0         ;
          MOV IE,#81H         ;INT0 interrupt enabled
HERE:     SJMP HERE           ;wait
END
```

Example 14.21 is just Example 14.20 re-written after making EX0 to be H to L edge triggered. The only additional instruction is SETB TCON.0.

Example 14.22

In this example, a square wave of 1 Hz frequency is applied to pin P3.3. This is the interrupt pin of INT1 which has been configured to be edge triggered. Figure 14.22a shows

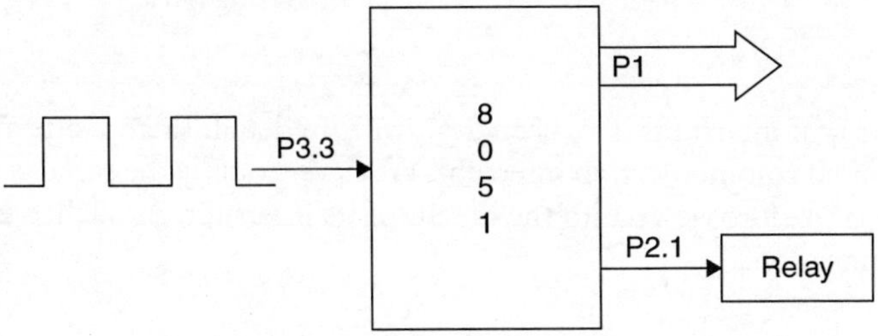

Figure 14.22a | The connections of the 8051

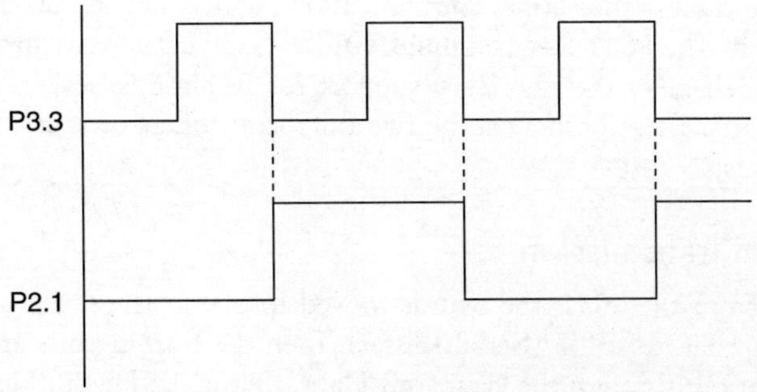

Figure 14.22b | The input waveform at P3.3 and the output waveform at P2.1

the setup. At the H to L edge of the square wave, an interrupt is generated. The ISR performs the following two actions:

i) Complements the pins of port 1 to which LEDs are connected (not shown in the figure).
ii) Complements the pin P2.1,to which a relay is connected. This relay switches ON and OFF a high power light source (not shown in the figure).

Note From Figure 14.22b it is seen that the rate of all these actions is half that of the incoming signal.

```
ORG 0                                  ;starts up at this address
            LJMP STRT                  ;bypass interrupt vectors

ORG 0013H                              ;vector of EX1
            LJMP  ISR_X1               ;jump to ISR

ORG 0040H                              ;main program starts here
STRT:       SETB TCON.2                ;make EX0 ,edge triggered
            MOV IE,#84H                ;enable EX0
            SETB P3.3                  ;P3.3 = 1
HERE:       SJMP HERE                  ;wait here

ISR_X1:     MOV A,#0FH                 ;A = 0FH
            CPL A                      ;complement A
            MOV P1,A                   ;copy A to P1
            CPL P2.1                   ;complement P2.1
            RETI                       ;return
END
```

In this section, four interrupts have been dealt with, in detail. There is one more interrupt, which is the serial communication interrupt. We have to study the serial communication facilities of 8051 before we go into the details of its interrupt. As such, our next topic is serial communication.

14.6 | Serial Communication

Here, we need to discuss the serial communication facility that the 8051 provides, and how we can use it. The 8051 has an inbuilt UART (Universal Asynchronous Receiver Transmitter), which gives the necessary support for facilitating serial communication between two points. These points can be two microcontrollers or it can be a PC and a microcontroller also.

14.6.1 | Serial Transmission

To send a byte from the 8051, the byte is moved to one of the serial communication specific registers, that is, SBUF (Serial Buffer). Then the framing bits are added to the byte and it is sent out through the 'Transmit Data', that is, Tx D (Pin No: 11. P3.1) pin of the chip. The UART hardware inside the 8051 converts the parallel data into serial form and puts it out on the T × D pin at a certain rate. This rate is called baud rate. The rate is fixed up (for the 8051) by running timer 1 in mode 2. When transmission of a byte is over, the TI (Transmit Interrupt) is also activated. Figure 14.23 shows the transmission scenario.

14.6.2 | Serial Reception

This is just the reverse of the transmission process. The data received serially through the RxD pin (Pin No:10, P3.0) is converted to parallel form by the UART and is brought into the SBUF register after stripping off the framing bits. Just the data byte is left in SBUF, and this can be moved to the A register. When reception (of a byte) is completed, the RI (Receive Interrupt) flag is set. Figure 14.24 illustrates this scenario.

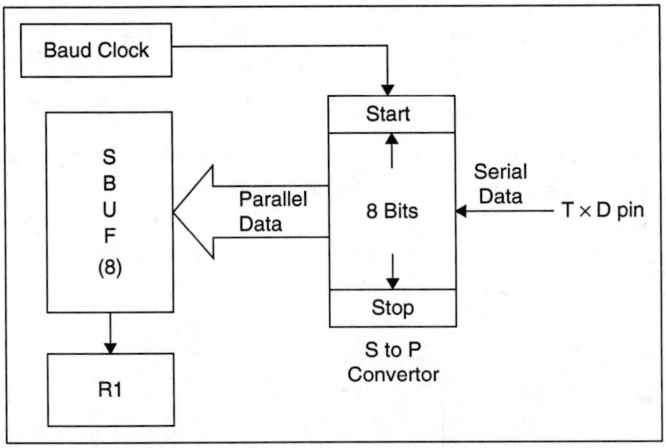

Figure 14.23 | The sequence of actions in serial transmission

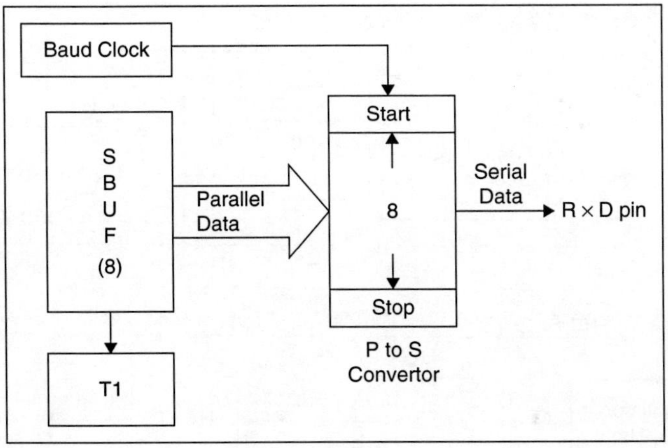

Figure 14.24 Serial reception and the sequence involved

14.6.3 | RS 232C

Serial data in raw form cannot be transmitted over long distances in TTL form. It has to be converted to the RS 232 format using the MAX 232 (or similar) chip. Many times, it may be necessary to connect a PC and an embedded board (with a microcontroller) through an RS 232C cable. Figure 14.25 shows this connection where the DB 9 connector is the PC's serial connector.

Figure 14.25 shows the part of an embedded board which contains a MAX232 IC, an MCU, the connections of the MAX232 IC to the serial data pins of the MCU, and to the DB-9 male connector of the serial port.

14.6.4 | Baud Rates

In most cases of embedded product development, there is the need for serial communication between a PC and an embedded board in which there is a microcontroller (like 8051). For PCs there are certain standard baud rates at which communication is done. To make it compatible with the PC, the baud rate setting in the 8051 should also be the same. For this, a convenient frequency of the 8051 crystal is 11.0592MHz.

How does this frequency become a convenient frequency?

Timer 1 in mode 2 is to be used for the baud rate setting for the 8051. The crystal frequency is divided by 12 to get the basic frequency for the timer. For the UART, this is to be divided by 32.
11.0592 MHz/12 = 921.6 KHz. Next, this is divided by 32 to get 28,800 Hz. This frequency is sent to Timer 1 to set the baud rate. See Figure 14.26.

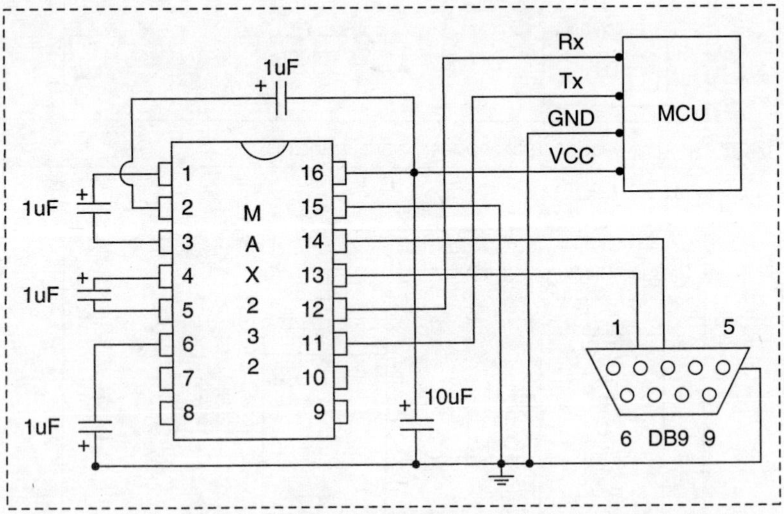

Figure 14.25 | Connections between a microcontroller and a PC using RS-232

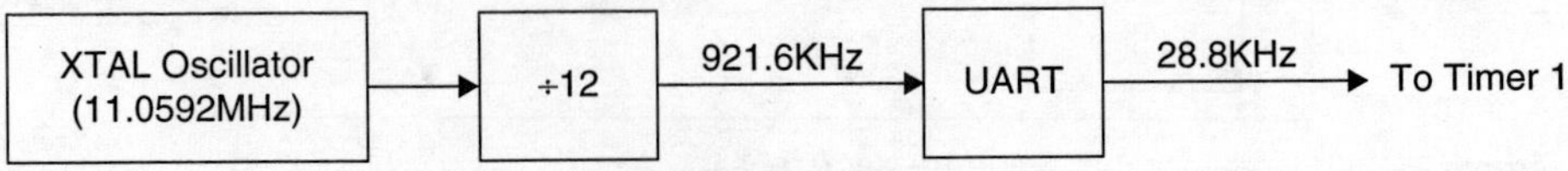

Figure 14.26 | Generation of PC compatible baud rate

Table 14.4 lists the count values to be loaded in TH1 to get some standard baud rates. To understand this table, consider the value of FDH loaded in TH1. When the counter starts, the count increases to FE, FF and then 00. Thus, three cycles of the basic clock of 28,800 will divide it by 3 to get 9600 Hz as the frequency of the signal generated by Timer 1. This is the reference frequency for serial transmission at a baud rate of 9600. The baud rate setting of the PC can be changed (in the settings window of hyperterminal). For getting the same baud rate for the 8051, we use the appropriate count in the TH1 register, as in Table 14.4.

14.6.5 | Registers in the UART of 8051

i) **SBUF (Serial Buffer):** This is an 8-bit SFR which can be written to, so as to hold the data byte to be transmitted. The instruction used is

MOV SBUF,A or
MOV SBUF,#data

In the case of reception, it holds the data byte received. Using the instruction,

MOV A,SBUF

the received byte is moved to A.

ii) **SCON (Serial Control Register):** This is an 8-bit register, whose bits can be used to configure serial communication as we need. Figure 14.27 gives the details of the bits of SCON.

Table 14.4 | Hex Values to be Loaded Into TH1 for Standard Baud Rates

Standard Baud Rates	Calculation	Hex Value in TH1
1200	28800/24	E8
2400	28,800/12	F4
4800	28,800/6	FA
9600	28,800/3	FD

SM0	SM1	SM2	REN	TB8	RB8	T1	RI

Bit	Symbol	Function
SCON.7	SM0	Specifies the mode
SCON.6	SM1	Specifies the mode
SCON.5	SM2	Clear it for normal mode set for multiprocessor mode
SCON.4	REN	Set to enable reception clear to disable reception
SCON.3	TB8	Parity bit (if used) for transmission not widely used
SCON.2	RB8	Parity bit received (Not widely used)
SCON.1	TI	Transmit Interrupt Flag Is set when (SBUF) is empty To be cleared by software
SCON.0	RI	Receive Interrupt Flag Is set when SBUF contains received data To be cleared by software

Figure 14.27 | Bit configuration of the SCON register

14.6.6 | Modes

The bits SM0 and SM1 are the mode bits of the UART. There are four possible modes, but here we will concern ourselves with the most commonly used mode, that is, mode 1 with one start and one stop bit, making the framed data to be 10 bits long. This mode is the one which is compatible with the COM port of the PC.

14.6.6.1 | *The Transmit Interrupt (TI) Flag*

For sending a data byte serially, we just load the byte into SBUF. The byte is 'framed' thereafter, by adding the start and stop bits to it. The 10-bit parallel data is converted to serial form (this is done by the UART hardware), placed on the T × D pins, one bit at a time and transmitted at the specified baud rate. First the start bit, then the data byte and finally the stop bit is sent. It is when the stop bit is being sent, that the TI flag is raised. Thus, this flag setting indicates that the transmission of the current byte is over, and that a new byte can be moved into SBUF. If the serial interrupt has been enabled (using the IE register), the TI bit being set causes an interrupt which is vectored to 0023H.

14.6.6.2 | *Steps in Transmitting Data Serially*

Let us list out the steps needed to transmit a byte through the T × D pin of 8051.

i) Configure Timer 1 in mode 2 for generating the baud rate clock
ii) Configure the SCON register for mode 1
iii) Start timer T1
iv) Move the data byte to SBUF
v) Monitor the TI flag to verify if transmission is over
vi) The data will be sent out through T × D pin at the rate decided by the baud.
vii) Clear TI
viii) If another byte is to be transmitted, go to step iv

Now let's write a program for serial transmission.

Example 14.23a uses the polling mechanism in which the TI flag status is monitored to verify if transmission is complete. In Example 14.23b the transmit interrupt has been used. Both the programs (14.22a and b) achieve the same, that is, they cause a byte to be repeatedly sent on the T × D line.

Example 14.23a

```
ORG 0
         MOV TMOD,#20H      ;timer 1 ,mode 2
         MOV TH1,#0FDH      ;baud = 9600
         MOV SCON,#50H      ;serial commn setup
         SETB TR1           ;start timer

HERE:    MOV SBUF,#'M'      ;copy 'M' to SBUF
BACK:    JNB TI,BACK        ;monitor TI
         CLR TI             ;clear TI
         SJMP HERE
END
```

Example 14.23b

```
ORG 0                         ;reset vector 0
          LJMP STRT           ;bypass interrupt vectors

ORG 0023H                     ;ISR, when TI is set
          CLR TI              ;clear TI
          MOV SBUF,#'M'       ;move 'M' to SBUF
          RETI                ;return

ORG 0040H                     ;origin of main program
STRT:     MOV TMOD,#20H       ;timer 1, mode 2
          MOV TH1,#0FDH       ;baud = 9600
          MOV IE,#90H         ;enable the serial interrupt
          MOV SCON,#50H       ;serial communication setup
          SETB TR1            ;start  Timer 1
          MOV SBUF,#'M'       ;copy 'M' to SBUF for sending
HERE:     SJMP HERE           ;wait for TI and interrupt
END
```

14.6.7 | Serial Reception

Next let's discuss serial reception. The pin for it is RxD. Data is received, with the start bit first, then the data byte and finally the stop bit. It is when the stop bit is received that the RI flag is set. This indicates that the byte received is available in SBUF and can be moved to A and then stored safely elsewhere. The setting of the RI bit activates the serial interrupt, if the interrupt had been enabled in the program (using the IE register).

14.6.7.1 | *Steps in Receiving Data Serially*

i) Configure Timer 1 in mode 2 for generating the baud rate clock
ii) Configure the SCON register for mode 1
iii) Start timer T1
iv) Clear RI
v) Monitor the RI flag to verify if reception is over
vi) When RI is raised, copy SBUF to A and then store it
vii) If another byte is to be transmitted, go to step iv

Examples 14.24a and b illustrate serial reception using the polled and the interrupt modes, respectively.

Example 14.24a

```
ORG 0
        MOV TMOD,#20H       ;Timer 1 in mode 2
        MOV TH1,#0FDH       ;count for baud = 9600
        MOV SCON,#50H       ;serial communication setup
        CLR RI              ;clear RI
        SETB TR1            ;start Timer 1
```

```
BACK:    JNB RI,BACK        ;check for RI flag
         MOV A,SBUF         ;RI = 1, copy SBUF to A
         MOV P1,A           ;copy A to P1
         CLR RI             ;clear RI for next reception
         SJMP BACK          ;jump to BACK
END
```

Example 14.24b

```
ORG 0                       ;reset location
         LJMP STRT          ;jump to STRT

ORG 0023H                   ;serial interrupt vector
         SJMP REX           ;jump to REX for ISR

ORG 0040H                   ;origin of main program
STRT:    MOV TMOD,#20H      ;Timer 1, mode 2
         MOV IE,#90H        ;enable serial interrupt
         MOV TH1,#0FDH      ;count for baud = 9600
         MOV SCON,#50H      ;serial commn. setup
         SETB TR1           ;start Timer 1
HERE:    SJMP HERE          ;wait for receive interrupt

REX:     JNB RI,EXIT        ;go to EXIT if RI is not set
         MOV A,SBUF         ;copy SBUF to A
         MOV P1,A           ;copy P1 to A
         CLR RI             ;clear RI
EXIT:    RETI               ;return to main program
END
```

Note

i) There is only one serial communication interrupt and its vector is 0023H. This caters to both transmission and reception. Thus when an interrupt comes, we need to confirm that it is reception that has occurred. **That is why the RI flag is tested in the ISR. If RI is not found to be set, then it might be that it was TI that caused the interrupt.**

ii) TI and RI are set automatically by the transmission and reception activity. But they should be cleared by software. This means that instructions to clear RI and TI should be included in the program.

iii) If reception is to be disabled throughout the course of any program execution, the bit REN in SCON can be cleared. This will disable RI and no reception will be allowed. However, transmission can be done as TI is not disabled.

Conclusion

With this, we come to the end of this chapter on timers, serial communication and interrupts. We have used most of the SFRs of the generic 8051. However, for the remaining SFRs, interested readers are advised to read other sources and the data sheet of 8051.

This chapter is meant to make you adept in the programming aspects of the inbuilt peripherals of 8051.

The 8051 has only a few internal peripherals. But it has four GPIO ports—most of these pins are free to be used, if external memory is not connected. Many peripherals like LCDs, stepper/DC motors, relays, LED displays, etc. can be connected to these pins.

KEY POINTS OF THIS CHAPTER

- The 8051 has 40 pins, in which 32 are the pins of the four ports P0 to P3.
- Three of these ports have pins with dual functions.
- The clock frequency of the chip is decided by the frequency of the crystal connected outside.
- The 'power on reset' circuitry is connected externally and provides a pulse on the reset pin.
- There are three pins devoted to the function of connecting external memory.
- The SFR map gives the list and addresses of the special function registers of the chip.
- There are two timer modules, which can be used for timing and counting.
- There are two important modes of operation for the timers.
- Timers can be operated in the polled mode or interrupt mode, of which the latter is the more efficient mechanism.
- There are 6 interrupts for 8051, including reset.
- The hardware interrupts can be made level or edge triggered.
- There is a UART inside the 8051.
- Serial communication is done through the pins T × D and R × D.
- Many more peripherals can be connected to 8051 through the GPIO pins.

QUESTIONS

1. Why is reset necessary for a processor?
2. In what way is Port 0 different from the other ports of 8051?
3. Which port has the pins for counter inputs and interrupts?
4. For a crystal frequency of 22 MHz, what is the period of the pulse train applied to the timer circuitry?
5. What are the functions decided in the mode control word of the timers?
6. Distinguish between a timer and a counter?
7. What is the role of the timer flag in the polled mode and in the interrupt mode?
8. How is mode 2 different form mode 1, in operation of timers?
9. Why is reset also considered to be an interrupt?
10. How can hardware interrupts be made to be edge triggered?
12. What is the role of SBUF in serial communication?

EXERCISES

1. Write the TMOD words for
   a) Timer 1 in mode 2 and Timer 0 in mode 1.
   b) Timer 1 in mode 0 and Timer 0 in mode 2.
2. Write programs for generating the following. Use the polled mode for timers.
   a) A pulse train of period 100 m sec on P2.6.
   b) An asymmetric pulse train of 100 μsecs ON time and 220 μsecs OFF time on P2.4.
   c) An asymmetric pulse train of 1 secs ON time and 2.3 secs OFF time at P2.6.
3. Generate the pulse trains of Problem 2 using timers in the interrupt modes.
4. Toggle all the pins of port 1 at a rate of 3 seconds.
5. When switches connected to the interrupt pins of the chip are toggled at a rate of once per 2 seconds, the LEDs connected to Port 2 are to be switched ON and OFF. Write a program for this, and comment on the rate at which the LEDs will be switched ON and OFF.
6. Write a program using interrupts for the following actions to happen simultaneously.
   a) Data at 10 ROM locations are continuously and repeatedly transmitted.
   b) Two square waves are generated simultaneously at P2.3 and P2.5.
   c) A square wave applied to the $\overline{INT0}$ pin causing an LED at pin P1.3 to toggle.

15 DSP PROCESSORS

In this chapter, you will learn

- The need for DSP processors
- The application fields of DSP processors
- The special features of DSP processors that are not present in general purpose processors
- What is meant by 'Super Harvard' architecture
- Why address calculation units are needed
- How to choose between floating and fixed point processors
- How parallelism has been incorporated in DSP processors
- The meaning of VLIW, Superscalar and SIMD architectures
- The features of the fixed point 'BlackFin' processor
- The architecture of the floating point processor 'SHARC'
- The enhancements of the massively parallel Tiger SHARC
- The high level structure of TI's TMS 320C6xxx chip
- An introduction to TI's OMAP platform

Introduction

In this book, many processors have been discussed; all of them are designated as embedded processors/microcontrollers. The key features of these processors are that of having a CPU and a number of peripherals. The 'computing power' of the chip depends on the CPU core that is present. For instance, MCUs with an ARM core are more powerful than those with an 8051 core. These kinds of processor cores are referred to as 'general purpose' cores, because they are good at ordinary, that is, general purpose arithmetic and data processing.

But for specialized arithmetic operations like fast multiply and add, floating point arithmetic, exponentiation, etc., these types of processors may fail—not in terms of accuracy of the result, but in terms of the time expended in performing these kinds of computations. The point is that, when applications demand fast results for complex math, dedicated hardware is an absolute must. This dedicated hardware with programmable features is called a DSP processor, because the applications that need such complex math are typically DSP (Digital Signal Processing) computations.

This chapter assumes that you have a basic idea of DSP and important DSP algorithms like design of FIR and IIR filters, convolution, FFT, correlation, etc.

Chapter-opening image: A BlackFin DSP kit.

15.1 | The Application Scenario

Many applications require a mixture of control-oriented DSP software. Many applications that are used in the embedded field need to use DSP computations. For example, think of a mobile phone, it deals with compressed form of audio (MP3) video and still images and thus DSP computations in 'real time' are mandatory. Many advanced mobile phones use an ARM processor, which has an instruction set with a small set of DSP instructions. But that processor may not be able to perform DSP computations in **real time,** and therefore a DSP core is also needed. Such a system is likely to use a powerful MCU for general purpose computations and an additional DSP processor. These two cores may be present as two separate chips or (as is presently getting to be the trend), a single dual core processor may be used. Such dual cores are becoming very popular, an ARM core and a DSP core is a popular combination (refer to Figure 1.7). In other cases, a DSP core with a specialized set of peripherals may be a possibility.

This being the case, let us now analyse the important aspects of DSP processors, in terms of the innovative architectural features that make such processors 'specialized' to do the tasks associated with the specific application. For this, we choose a few popular DSP processors—the BlackFin and SHARC processors manufactured by 'Analog Devices' and the TMS 320C67xx and the dual core OMAP processor of Texas Instruments. Keep in mind that all of them are high-end devices and what material that can be presented here will be very elementary and at best, may seem to just an introduction as no programming is discussed. But it is hoped that this chapter will serve to introduce important concepts regarding DSP processors in general. Implementing an application using any DSP processor requires a thorough reading and understanding of its manual, and this chapter may be read before choosing the processor for the intended application.

15.1.1 | List of Applications

Let us make a list of applications which need fast DSP. Some of them are as follows:

- Instrumentation and measurement
- Communications
- Audio and video processing
- Graphics, image enhancement, 3D rendering
- Navigation, radar, GPS
- Control—robotics, machine vision, guidance

15.1.2 | Embedded Devices and DSP

There are many embedded systems which do not need a lot of complex computations, and where signal processing does not need to be done. Think of printers, motor control systems like washing machines and dish washing machines. They need only an MCU (which may be as simple as 8051 or as complex as ARM). Whatever computation is needed is done by these MCUs which also have the 'interfacing' capability to connect to external devices.

But think of an ABS (Automatic Braking System) for an automobile. This application needs complex computations of braking dynamics and signal processing. Thus, a DSP processor is mandatory if the ABS is to react 'in time'.

The above two paragraphs indicate the importance of DSP and DSP processors for embedded systems, to justify the inclusion of this chapter in a book on embedded systems. In fact, it is in the embedded field that most of the DSP processors are used.

15.1.3 | DSP Processors

As a single unit, a DSP processor has a computational core which is similar in many ways to a general purpose processor (GPP), but has differences or enhancements to make it cater to the special requirements of DSP computations. In addition, we find that most DSP processors have peripherals just like an MCU; they have I/O capability with serial ports, SPI, I2C and parallel ports, timers, PWMs, DMA ADC, DAC and special peripherals for special applications like dedicated peripherals for video, other dedicated peripherals for audio applications and so on.

In this chapter, we will get to know the architectural aspects of some popular DSP chips. But before that, we should make a thorough study of the features of 'digital signal processors', in general, that is, the features that make such processors stand apart from GPPs and MCUs. Once these features are understood, what is left is only to study each specific chip, by noting what extra and specific capabilities each one has, besides the general features.

15.1.4 | Manufacturers of Digital Signal Processors

The two leading designers of DSP processors are Texas Instruments (TI) and Analog Devices (AD). Besides these two, Lucent and Motorola (Freescale) also have a market share in this item.

15.2 | General Features of Digital Signal Processors

15.2.1 | Fast MAC Units

DSP processors have their design aspects based on common DSP algorithms. All features that they have are 'need driven', i.e. all such features have come directly from popular signal processing algorithms. The philosophy is that these processors should be able to perform the computations involved in such algorithms much faster and more efficiently that a GPP can do it.

Think of a very common and basic DSP algorithm which is obviously, an FIR filter design. The computation involved in this is based on the formula given in Equation 15.1

$$y(n) = \sum_{i=0}^{N-1} ai \cdot x(n-i) \tag{15.1}$$

where y(n) is the current output, x (n-i) are the delayed values of inputs and the ai's are the filter coefficients. To make this point clear, let us look at an FIR filter signal flow diagram in Figure 15.1, where each Z^{-1} block causes one unit of delay.

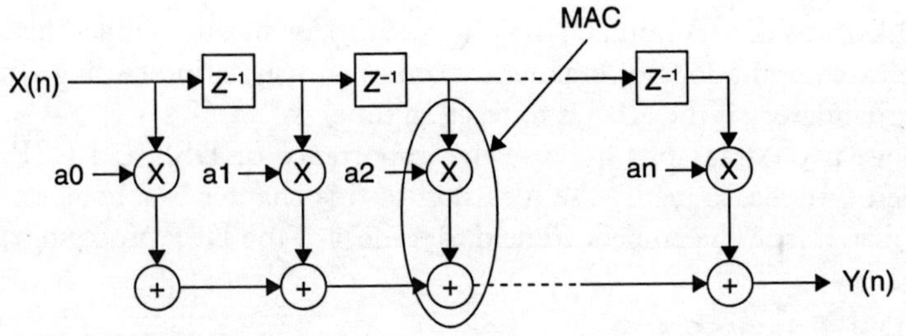

Figure 15.1 | Signal flowchart of FIR filter design

What are the operations involved here?

$$y[n] = a_0x[n] + a_1x[n-1] + a_2x[n-2] + a_3x[n-3] + a_4x[n-4] + \cdots$$

Have a look at the above equation. The mechanism of computation involved is as follows:

Signal samples arrive continuously and as they do, they and delayed versions of the earlier signal samples are multiplied with the filter coefficients and the products are added. As such, we say that a '**multiply and accumulate**' operation is necessary for an FIR filter. Similar operations are involved in IIR filter design, convolution operation, FFT, etc., and such computations are used for applications like images, sound, video, communications, etc.

An important point is that data is usually 'real time' and comes in continuously. After processing, the results should be available fast enough to guarantee 'real time' output for the system. Note that the computation is repetitive and there are no control or branching structures here. Also, since filtering, convolution and FFT are very frequently used operations, there is sufficient justification for having specialized hardware for such operations.

On the basis of these, let us list out one feature of a DSP processor which does not apply to GPPs

i) The data for processing is usually an infinite stream which is to processed in 'real time'.
ii) The probability is that intense arithmetic processing and very little of branching and control is required.

Such a necessity suggests that having hardware based 'multiply and accumulate (MAC) units' is a foremost necessity. Since $\sum xa$ is the basic filtering operation, it is imperative that 'multiplication and accumulation' be fast. This entails the need for specialized, high speed multiplication algorithms and dedicated hardware for it. There is usually a 'single cycle MAC' in which the complete operation of 'multiply and accumulate' completes within one cycle. Thus, we find that all DSP processors have MACs as a basic unit of computation. Figure 15.2 shows the internals of a MAC unit.

15.2.2 | Specialized Instructions

Operations like convolution, FFT, correlation, etc. are very frequently used, so instead of having to write a program for FFT to be done, (or a convolution), it would be very

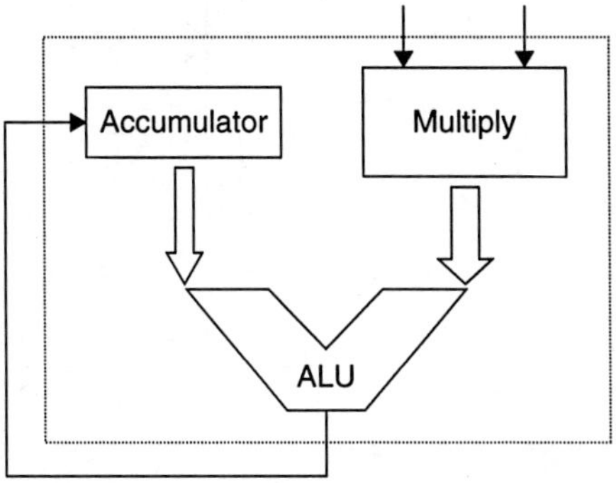

Figure 15.2 | A hardware MAC unit

convenient to have single instructions (with dedicated hardware) for such commonly used operations. For specialized DSP processors, like those which cater to specific applications like video or audio or networking, there should be 'specialized' instructions pertaining to the application scenario. We will see that some of the popular DSPs do attend to this necessity in a big way.

15.2.3 | Efficient Memory Accessing

In Section 2.1.2, the Harvard and Von Neumann architectures were discussed. All MCUs use the Harvard architecture in which the program and data memory spaces are disjoint, and separate buses access these spaces. But DSP algorithms have some special features which can be exploited to get still better performance.

A particularly innovative way of 'efficient memory access' was first implemented by Analog Devices (AD) and they called it the 'Super Harvard Architecture.' They used this feature in their SHARC series, which is actually a contraction of the terms, 'Super Harvard ARChitecture'.

What are the aspects of this 'super' architecture?

Recollect that a typical algorithm like FIR filter design repeatedly performs the same set of instructions. Thus, there is no point in fetching these instructions from program memory again and again. Instead an 'instruction cache' is included in the CPU which stores the most recent 32 instructions, and from where fast access is possible. Thus, instructions need to be taken from 'program memory' only once. For the next round of the loop repetition, the instructions can be accessed from the cache.

See Figure 15.3 in which Harvard architecture is illustrated with separate address and data buses connecting to separate data and program memory. 'Super Harvard' architecture is shown by having an 'instruction cache' within the CPU.

From the above, it is clear that the program memory bus is free, once the instructions are copied to the instruction cache. This can be used to advantage. A filtering type of operation needs a filter coefficient and a signal value for each multiplication. For each computation, the signal value comes from an external source and may be different. The filter coefficients, however, don't change. Hence the filter coefficients are stored in **program memory**, and accessed in every cycle. At the same time, the signal sample is

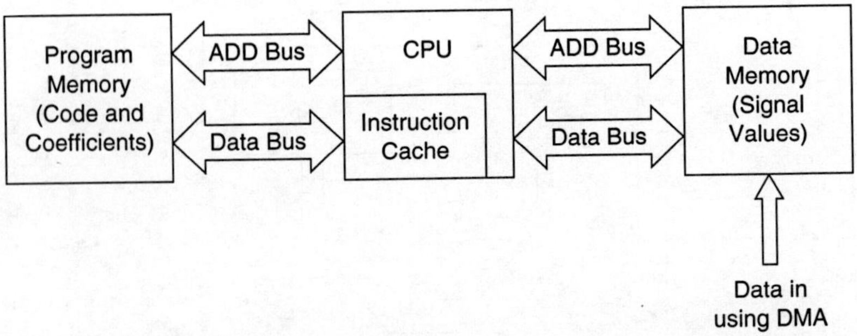

Figure 15.3 | Efficient memory architecture based on the super Harvard concept

stored in the data memory, as it comes in. Thus for one multiplication, the data memory is accessed to get the signal sample and the program memory for the coefficient, and these two accesses are done concurrently. In effect, we have the scenario in which we get the following:

i) Signal samples from data memory
ii) Coefficients from program memory
iii) Instruction from instruction cache

These three accesses occur concurrently and so we obtain 'high memory bandwidth'.

15.2.4 | DMA for Input Data

The data memory stores signal values which come in as input data. To get the signal samples fast, the I/O mechanism needs to be fast. For this, the input data is usually transferred to the data memory through a DMA (Section 2.2.10) mechanism, which means that a DMA controller is to be there, and data does not have to pass through CPU registers. Figure 15.3 shows that signal samples are brought in to the data memory using DMA.

15.2.5 | Circular Buffers

Many times, the same data (coefficients or delayed signal samples) is involved in computations. This warrants the use of circular buffers or the concept of 'circular addressing', which allows the processor to access a block of data sequentially and then automatically wrap around to the beginning address. Circular buffers allow cycling through delay elements and coefficients.

In the case of a filter, for instance, each time a new data sample appears, the Nth previous sample is discarded and the other N-1 samples are used. The method then is simply to change the pointer for the latest sample in the circular list.

What are the parameters needed for such circular buffering?

i) The pointer to the start of the circular buffer in memory.
ii) The pointer to the end of the array.
iii) The pointer to the most recent sample, which gets modified as each new sample is acquired.

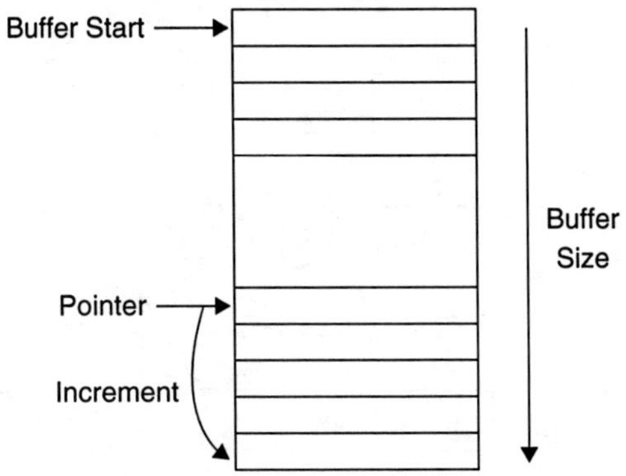

Figure 15.4 | A circular buffer

See Figure 15.4 which shows a memory area defined as a circular buffer, by these pointers.

15.2.6 | Zero-overhead Looping

Many DSP processors boast of 'zero overhead loops'. What do they mean by this? This is just a case of looping implemented in hardware so that extra memory cycles are not expended for testing and updating the loop counter. This is not a feature found in general purpose processors where Test and branch 'instructions' decide whether the loop is to be repeated or not. Getting this to be done by hardware, enhances speed for DSP processors.

15.2.7 | Multiple Execution Units

Many DSP processors have enhanced their architecture simply by increasing the number of execution units; the approach is to have more numbers of MAC units, multipliers, etc. Such an approach directly translates to higher throughput.

15.2.8 | Address Generation Units

Memory addresses are likely to be predictable in many DSP algorithms, for example, for an FIR filter design, the same coefficients are repeated in a circular buffer fashion. Addressing modes like register indirect with post-increment facility support this. Similarly, modes like auto increment, modulo (circular) and bit reverse are very helpful for DSP algorithms, where the latter is useful for FFT (please recollect the FFT algorithm to understand this). Such special requirements of signal processing algorithms warrant the inclusion of dedicated address generation/calculations units, and most DSP processors have this.

See Figure 15.5 which shows a dedicated address calculation unit which supports modulo and bit reversal arithmetic. In many processors, such units are duplicated because multiple addresses are needed in each cycle.

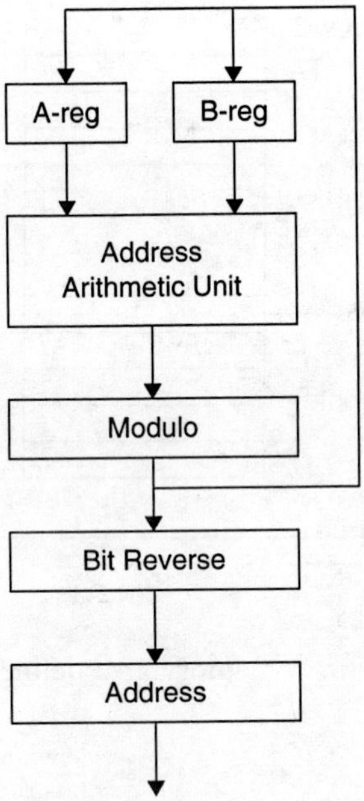

Figure 15.5 | A typical address generation unit

15.2.9 | Data Format

The data format used by DSP processors are either fixed point or floating point, meaning that there are families which are 'designated' as either fixed or floating point processors. For example, AD's BlackFin is called a fixed point processor while its SHARC family is designated as 'floating point' processors. In this context, let's try to understand the merits, demerits and the application arenas for both of them. (However, keep in mind that fixed point processors can process floating point numbers and vice versa, but a processor is specialized in processing data in the format mentioned alongside it.)

15.2.9.1 | *Fixed Point Representation*

A fixed point representation chosen is usually the two's complement form which can represent both positive and negative numbers, which may be integers or fractions. The term 'fixed point' refers to the corresponding manner in which numbers are represented, with a fixed number of digits after, or before the decimal point.DSP processors use either 16 or 32 bits for fixed point format. For a 16-bit fixed point format, one bit is allotted for the sign. So numbers from –32,768 to +32,767 may be represented. Fractional numbers within this range must also be representable, however.

How is the number 4.567 represented in the fixed point format?

There is a scaling factor involved. The number 4.567 can be taken as an integer of 4567 with a scaling factor of 1/1000. During computations, the scaling factor is to be the same for all the numbers involved—then only can integer computations be possible. Essentially, the scaling factor is the same for all values, and does not change during the entire computation. Thus in a fixed point format, the position of the decimal point gets fixed by virtue of the scaling factor.

To make the best use of the full available word length in the fixed point format, the programmer has to make some decisions:

i) If a fixed point number becomes too large for the available word length, the programmer has to scale the number down, by shifting it to the right. In the process, lower bits may drop off the end and be lost.

   To understand this point, consider a number 45678.1234. If the data width can accommodate only 6 digits, the programmer represents it as 45678.1, and thus the bits at the right are lost.

ii) If a fixed point number is small, the number of bits actually used to represent it is small. The programmer may decide to scale the number up, in order to use more of the available word length.

In both cases, the programmer has to keep a track of by how much the binary point has been shifted, in order to restore all numbers to the same scale at a later stage.

15.2.9.2 | *Floating Point Representation*

Understanding this requires a recollection of the standardized IEEE 754 format for floating point representation. The standard representation in this format, is with sign, exponent and mantissa. A 32-bit representation is called the single precision format and it has 8 bits for the exponent and 24 bits for the signed mantissa. There is also the 64-bit double precision format which has 11 bits for the sign, 52 bits for the magnitude of the mantissa and one bit for its sign. Figures 15.6 a and b show these formats.

Floating point numbers have two parts: the mantissa, which is similar to the fixed point part of the number, and an exponent which is used to keep track of how the binary point is shifted. In the standard format, the binary point comes after the second most significant bit in the mantissa. Every number is scaled by the floating point hardware, and it is the exponent that is affected by the scaling. With floating-point representation,

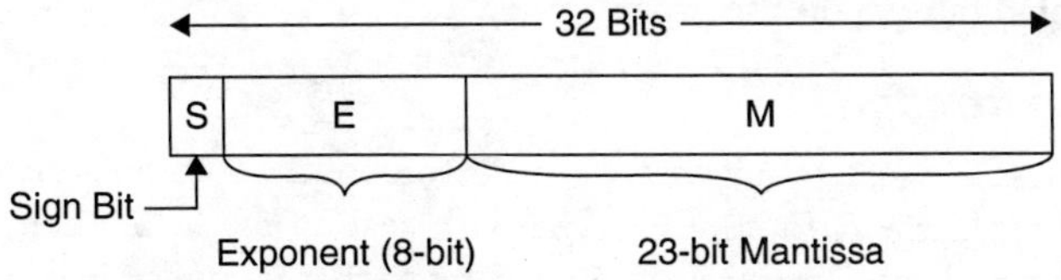

Figure 15.6a | The single precision format

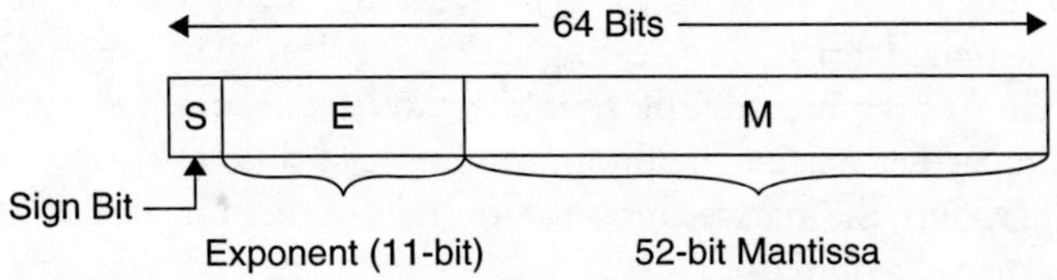

Figure 15.6b | The double precision format

the placement of the decimal point can 'float' relative to the significant digits of the number, and the exponent part takes care of it.

15.2.9.3 | *Comparing the Two Formats*

DSP processors use at least 16 bits for data in the fixed point, and 32 bits in floating point representation. Now let's make a comparison between a 16-bit fixed point format, and a 32-bit single precision floating point format.

i) **Dynamic range:** This is the difference between the largest and the smallest number that can be represented. Because of the exponent notation, the floating point representation has a very large dynamic range.

ii) **Precision:** For fixed point representation, the key point to note is that the between any number and the next one (numerically higher or lower), the 'difference' is the same for 'all numbers' irrespective of the numerical value of the number, that is, '1' between two integers.

For floating point numbers, the 'difference' between two small valued numbers and two high valued numbers is different (Refer to some literature dealing with floating point representation), being higher for the latter. But still, the gap between two adjacent values is much smaller than in fixed point notation.

How does this matter?

Every time a new number is generated as a result of a computation, (like multiplication, for instance) the number must be rounded to the next nearest value or be truncated. The actions of rounding and/or truncation naturally result in error and the end result is that it yields errors designated as 'quantization noise' - Because the gaps (between adjacent numbers) are larger for fixed-point numbers, such errors are more pronounced in that format.

As such, we can say that, floating-point processing yields much greater precision than fixed-point processing. **In short, we can conclude that the floating-point format is the ideal one when computational accuracy is a critical requirement.**

Fixed point operation can also achieve a lower quantization noise, but it requires extra effort, and this usually has to be done using software, thus reducing speed and putting an additional burden on the programmer.

What is this extra effort?

To consider such a case, lets say that we need to convert a number from a fixed point type with scaling factor R to another type with scaling factor S. Then, the underlying integer must be multiplied by R and divided by S, that is, multiplied by the ratio R/S. Thus, for example, to convert the value $4.56 = 456/100$ from a type with scaling factor $R = 1/100$ to one with scaling factor $S = 1/1000$, the number 456 must be multiplied by $(1/100)/(1/1000) = 10$, yielding the representation 1230/1000. If S does not divide R exactly (in particular, if the new scaling factor S is less than the original R), the new integer will have to be rounded. The rounding and truncation (when used) rules must be specified and used as part of the programming, and this constitutes an extra effort.

For floating point, the 'native computation' takes care of it, and no effort on the part of the programmer is required.

15.2.9.4 | *Size of Intermediate Registers*

As mentioned earlier, DSP computations are generally repetitive and many are 'MAC' operations. It is not good practice to round/truncate the product to the word length of the processor after each multiplication and/or addition. Instead, intermediate results are stored in larger registers, and only the final result is made to fit into the processor registers.

For example, for a 16-bit fixed point format, multiplication of two 16-bit numbers gives a product of 32 bits and when addition is done, overflow is also possible. In this format, the size of intermediate registers is 40 bits allowing 8 bits for cumulative overflow ($40 = 16 + 16 + 8$).

For 32-bit floating point format, multiplication of two 24-bit mantissa gives a 48-bit product. Many floating point processors have 80 bits as the size of the intermediate registers for handling the mantissa alone. (Exponents are added through separate a data path, and the accuracy is maintained because of the exponential representation.)

15.2.9.5 | *Choosing Between the Two Formats*

We see that floating point processors need larger registers and more number of I/O pins. But they have the advantage of better and more accurate results.

So what are the criteria for deciding which type of processor to use?

The answer is that is should be based on the application. Floating point processors need to be used only when computational accuracy is the most important criteria.

Consider video and audio applications, for instance. For video, the pixels are represented as integers and the processing operations used are DCT and similar transforms. The human eye is not very sensitive to small variations in image data and therefore computational accuracy is not such a critical aspect. So fixed point processors are fine for still image and video processing.

Audio data is different. The human ear is highly sensitive, and high fidelity audio needs very good computational accuracy for the innumerable filter type of calculations used for audio processing. As such, floating point processors can do a very good job here.

Table 15.1 lists out some suggestions for the choice of data format for the DSP processor to be used.

Table 15.1 | List of Applications Suggested for the Two Data Formats

Floating Point Applications	Fixed Point Applications
Radar and military applications, automotive infotainment, robotics, medical, industrial control, communications, etc.	Consumer electronics, handheld devices, image and video, automotive control

15.2.10 | Two Level Cache

Most older versions of DSP processors did not use any cache, but used multiple banks of on-chip memory and multiple bus sets to enable several memory accesses per instruction cycle.

But many modern designers have changed their mind set, and now we see many DSP processors which use a two level cache, in which Level 1 (for code as well as data) is close to the core and very fast, and Level 2 is slower, but with better performance than an off chip cache would provide. Figure 15.7 shows the two level cache for TI's TMS 320C6xxx series. AD's processors also use a similar feature.

15.2.11 | Programming Languages

Like any other processor, a DSP processor can be programmed in assembly or in high level language. The advantages and disadvantages in either case is the same as for any GPP—assembly programming is very efficient, but cumbersome, HLL programming is simpler but less efficient. Because of this principle, in the early days of DSP processors, the core programs of some applications were mandatorily done in assembly. But over the years, a lot of very efficient compilers for high level languages have come into the market, and now we find that the C programming language is the most popular programming language used, though there are some core aspects that may still merit the use of assembly language programming. The estimate is that now, around 90% programming is done in HLLs and the rest in assembly.

15.2.12 | Real-time Operating Systems

Most DSP applications need a real-time output; thus, time constraint is an issue. Also, it is quite probable that multiple tasks are being attended to, in the intended application. As such, a real-time OS is usually needed. All the new and high profile DSP processors provide good support for porting some real-time kernel. There are RTOSes supplied by the manufacturers itself (like Visual DSP++ RTOS kernel of AD).These kinds of OSes have several layers of tasking to ensure targeted performance. Beside that, context switching is made possible through hardware-based stack support.

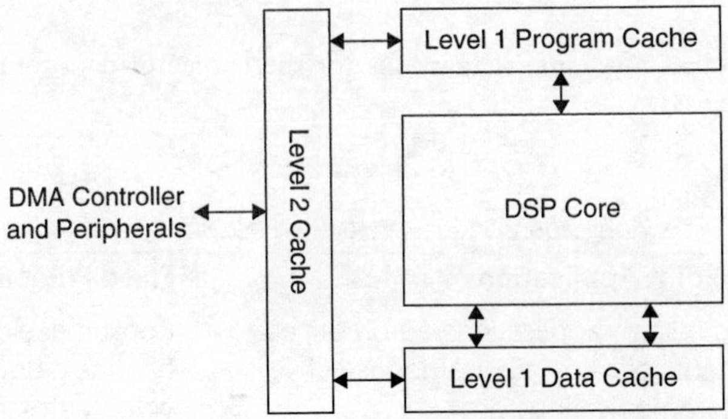

Figure 15.7 | Two level cache structure of modern DSPs

15.2.13 | Power Dissipation

The biggest application of DSP processors are in the embedded market, where low-power dissipation is the biggest and most emphasized figure of merit. All established manufacturers are taking special care to utilize every trick in the trade to bring down the number that specifies the power rating. The methods include the ability to vary both the voltage and frequency of operation so as to lower significantly, the overall power consumption. Since the power consumed is proportional to the square of the voltage (which is proportional to the power supply voltage), varying the supply voltage results in a substantial reduction in power consumption. This translates directly into longer battery life for portable appliances. Besides this, there are power down and idle modes (like any MCU) and provision for gated clocks, etc. All these come under the title of 'dynamic power management' techniques.

15.2.14 | Streamlined I/O and Specialized DSP Peripherals

Most processors have high speed parallel and serial I/O facility with DMA and low latency interrupt and interrupt controllers, etc. Besides that, serial communication ports like I2C and SPI are available in most DSP processors which allow fast access from SD cards and similar storage mediums.

Besides such common peripherals, some DSP processors have special peripherals which cater to specific applications. For example, a DSP processor which is recommended for video should have specialized peripherals and connectors for this. A processor specialized for network and telecommunications has bidirectional link ports.

15.2.15 | Parallelism in the Processor Architecture

This is a very important point and most manufacturers are finding more and more innovative means for improving 'parallelism' in the architecture itself, so that the throughput is increased in proportional to the parallelism introduced. What is aimed at, is to get more operations done (and results obtained) per unit time.

What are the methods sought for this?

i) Increase the number of operations that can be performed in each instruction.

   This idea leads to what can be classified as 'complex' instructions; each instruction leads to many operations being done. Such a typical complex instruction needs just one 'fetch' operation, following which it is decoded and all the operations corresponding to it gets done and results are obtained.

ii) Increase the number of instructions that can be issued and executed in every cycle.

   In this case, many simple instructions are issued in one cycle and many functional units execute them in parallel. Let us examine this aspect in greater detail. There are two sub divisions for this architectural feature. They are the superscalar and VLIW architectures.

15.2.15.1 | *The Superscalar Architecture*

This is a common feature in many high-end general purpose GPPs. For example, Pentium, which is commonly termed a superscalar processor, is a two-way superscalar, while there are processors which are 4-way superscalar. The difference is that the former can issue and execute up to 2 instructions per cycle, while the latter can do the same with 4 instructions.

Superscalar architectures have multiple execution units which execute different instructions simultaneously—these functional units may not be uniform—for Pentium, for example, one unit is more powerful (computationally) than the other.

15.2.15.2 | *The VLIW Architecture*

In the DSP world, however, the idea of 'multiple instructions' has mostly been implemented using VLIW (Very Long Instruction Word) rather than superscalar architectures. In this method, many instructions are bundled together as one word, and all these instructions are executed simultaneously. Obviously, there are multiple execution units which can function in parallel.

Some characteristics of such an architecture are

i) Each set consists of simple instructions.
ii) Instruction scheduling is done at compile-time and not at run-time so as to guarantee deterministic behaviour.
iii) DSP performance for a wide range of algorithms is easily adaptable to such a set.
iv) The architecture is scalable, that is, more execution units could be added to allow a higher number of instructions to be executed in parallel.

A good example of this approach is TI's TMS320C62xx. This VLIW processor has up to 256 bits of instruction words at a time, breaks them into as many as eight 32-bit sub instructions, and passes them to its eight independent computational units. See Figure 15.8.

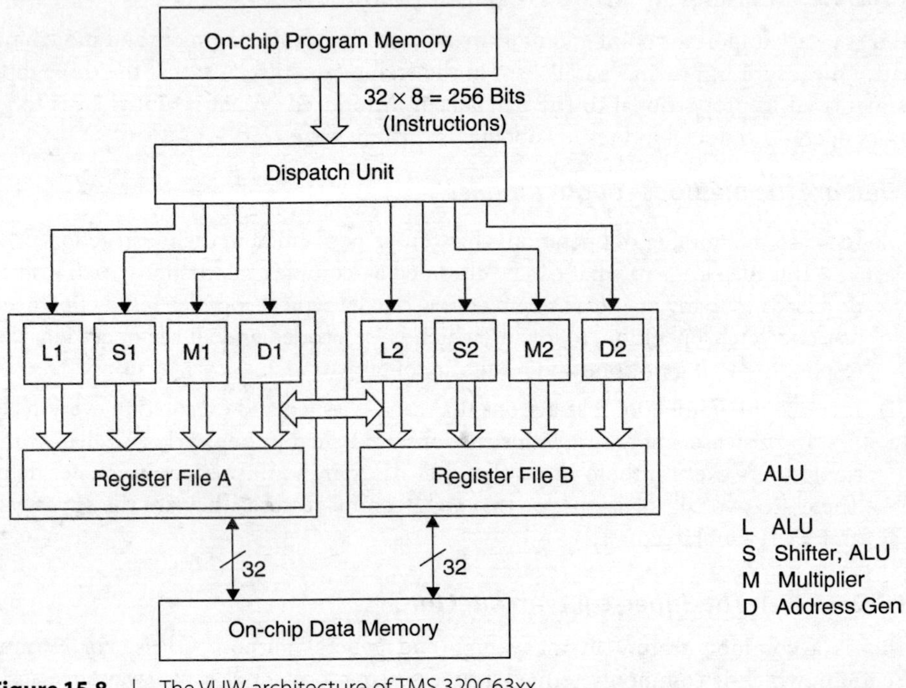

Figure 15.8 | The VLIW architecture of TMS 320C63xx

It is possible (but not mandatory) that all the eight units are active simultaneously, and the processor executes eight sub instructions in parallel. But in most cases, it may not be possible to have all the execution units to be functional at the same time. The number of active units may be less than 8, then. For VLIW to be effective, it is necessary that there is sufficient parallelism in the code to occupy the many execution units.

Examples of modern VLIW processors are from major DSP vendors—TI's TMS320C6xxx series, Analog Devices' Tiger SHARC and the joint venture of Motorola and Lucent known as StarCore. VLIW and superscalar processors often suffer from higher energy consumption compared to conventional DSP processors, but speed is the main emphasis in such designs and high speed processing is made possible with such designs.

15.3 | SIMD Techniques

VLIW is an architectural feature that utilizes ILP, that is, 'Instruction Level Parallelism'. There is another method for an increased throughput, and that uses 'data parallelism' where multiple data is operated upon by the same instruction. This technique is labelled SIMD which means 'Single Instruction Multiple Data'. It is a technique which can be added as an additional capability for a DSP processor, and for some processors (like SHARC), there is the possibility of switching ON or OFF the SIMD section.

It is likely that you have heard about the MMX (MultiMedia eXtension) instructions of Pentium, which utilizes SWAR (SIMD Within A Register). Such concepts are used in DSP processors also.

To understand this concept, think of monochrome image data which is one byte long. A 64-bit register operates on 8 data items as in Figure 15.9 where 8 bytes (each byte being an independent data item) are packed in a register. Such a grouped data can be operated upon by a single instruction, where, for example, addition is done to another packed data byte register. Figure 15.9 shows a 64-bit register with 8 bytes. Note that this register can also be used for four 16-bit operands, or two 32-bit operands or one 64-bit operand.

In many DSP processors, because data involved is of the kind that can be packed together, this makes sense. Many of the DSP and multimedia applications use vectors of packed 8, 16 and 32-bit integers, and also floating-point numbers that allows potential benefits of SIMD architectures,

AD's Tiger SHARC is a DSP processor which uses the VLIW architecture with SIMD capabilities. Figure 15.10 shows the six execution units of this processor, grouped in two sets of three. In the figure, the MAC instruction is shown to be operating in the SIMD mode.

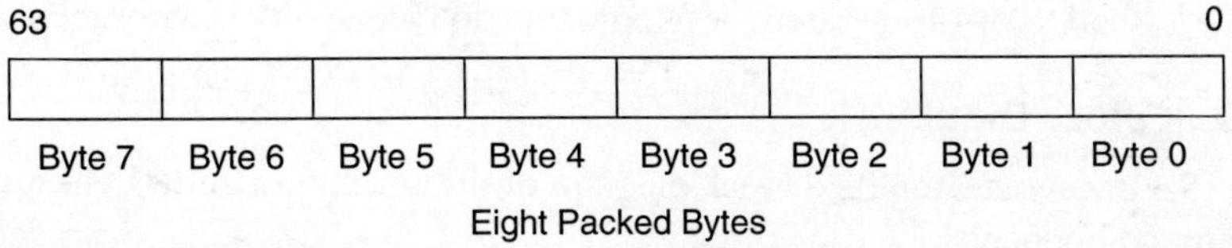

Figure 15.9 | SIMD within a register

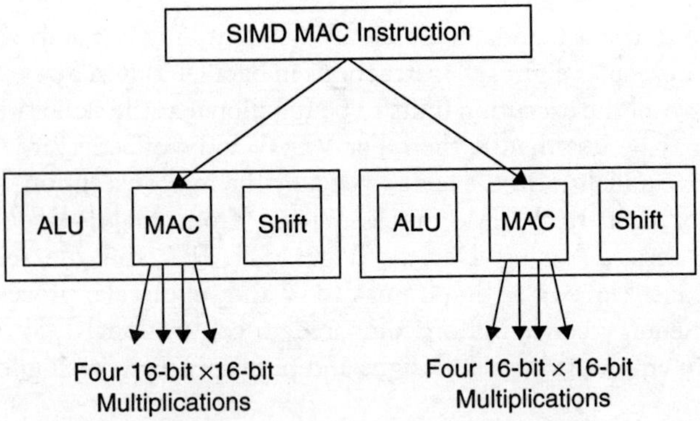

Figure 15.10 | Illustrating the SIMD architecture used in SHARC

With this, we come to the end of our discussion of the features of DSP processors. We will soon find that most DSP chips of the current times possess these features. With this background, it will be easier to understand the next sections which deal with a few popular DSP processors. We cannot do a detailed study of any of these chosen processors here.

15.3.1 | The BlackFin Fixed Point Processor

The BlackFin series of DSP processors is manufactured by Analog Devices, Inc. The first processor of this series is ADSP–BF 535 which was released in 2000 followed in March 2003 by three pin-compatible devices, the ADSP-BF531, ADSP-BF532 and ADSP-BF533. In January 2005, Analog Devices introduced three BlackFin processors with embedded connectivity: ADSP-BF536, ADSP-BF537 and ADSP-BF534. Over the years, a number of processors of this series have been released, with the same basic architecture but slight differences and enhancements, in terms of peripherals and increased clock speed (in the range of 300 MHz).Now there are dual core processors also in this series, one of which is BF561.

Let's examine the salient features of the BlackFin architecture.

i) Its ISA is based on a 32-bit RISC-like instruction set
ii) It has dual 16-bit MAC units for signal processing
iii) It has an 8-bit instruction set for video processing
iv) It possesses SIMD features
v) It application scenario ranges from image and video to control systems
vi) It has specialized instructions for accelerated video and image processing
vii) It has advanced memory management support for embedded operating systems
viii) It can act as a 32-bit MCU with 32-bit registers and has a large range of peripherals.
ix) It is supported by ADI's CROSSCORE development tool chain, which includes the VisualDSP++ Integrated Development and Debugging Environment (IDDE).

15.3.2 | Block Diagram

Figure 15.11 shows a simplified block diagram of the BlackFin family. Let's examine its important components.

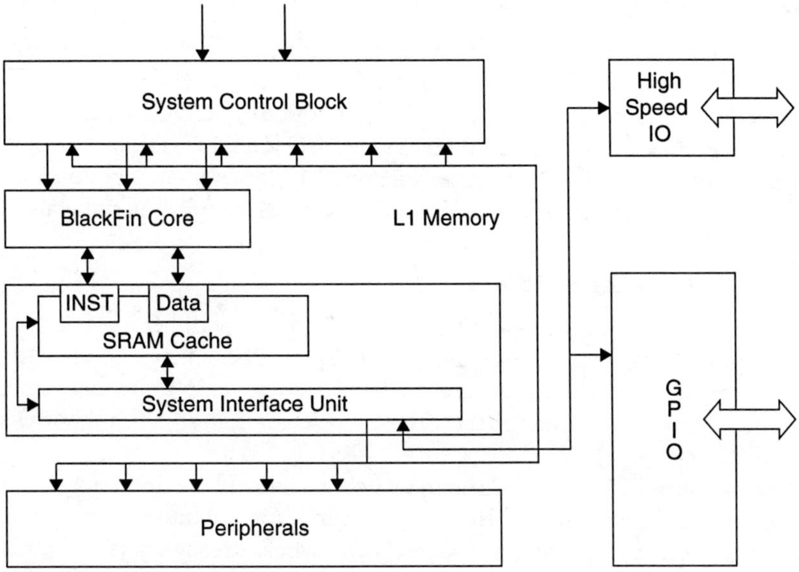

Figure 15.11 | Simplified block diagram of BlackFin

15.3.2.1 | *The Core*

This is the central processing unit. At the core, BlackFin processors have a 16-bit, dual MAC architecture with 32-bit registers and 64-bit internal data paths.

This core is surrounded by high-speed memory and high-speed peripherals.

15.3.2.2 | *Memory*

It has a two level cache structure as explained in Section 15.2.9. Both the L1 and L2 memories are dual-ported so that information can be simultaneously incoming and outgoing. This allows maximum throughput without having the core to be affected by memory transfers. Both Level 1 (L1) and Level 2 (L2) memory blocks are SRAMs. Each memory can be configured as SRAM, cache or a combination of both. Besides the caches, there is a scratch pad SRAM (see Figure 15.12).

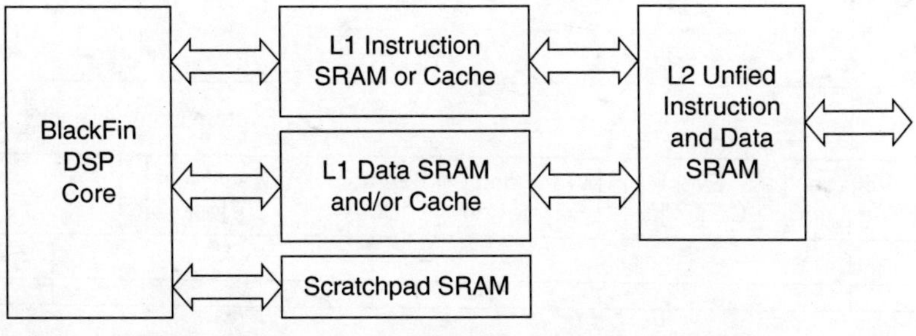

Figure 15.12 | The memory structure of BlackFin

15.3.2.3 | *Peripherals*

There are a number of peripherals for the processor. At the minimum, there are 100 Mbps serial ports (SPORTs), a high-speed parallel peripheral interface (PPI) capable of moving digital video on and off chip, UART with IrDA support, SPI port, GPIO pins and DMA controllers. In Figure 15.11 GPIO and High speed I/O are shown as separate blocks, but they form part of the peripheral structure. Figure 15.13 shows a set of peripherals which any BlackFin will have. Advanced members of the series have more peripherals.

15.3.2.4 | *System Control Block*

The system control block is shown to be separate from the peripheral block. It includes a software-programmable, on-chip phase-lock loop (PLL) that allows software to control the core and system clock speeds. There is an on-chip switching regulator to provide software control of core voltages. These blocks result in significant power savings (Section15.2.12).

An event controller, watchdog timer, real-time clock, JTAG interface, etc. are also part of the system control block. The event controller is for interfacing with external inputs, like for instance, it accepts a square wave whose frequency is to be measured by the timer unit. The JTAG unit is to assist in testing and debugging. There is a block called 'memory DMA' which is the DMA controller which allows DMA between different memory blocks. Figure 15.14 shows the system control block.

15.3.3 | Instruction Set

This list below explains the kind of instructions available for the processor:

i) It uses both 16- and 32-bit instructions
ii) Arithmetic instructions can take operands from the data registers, the pointer registers, the accumulators or immediate operands

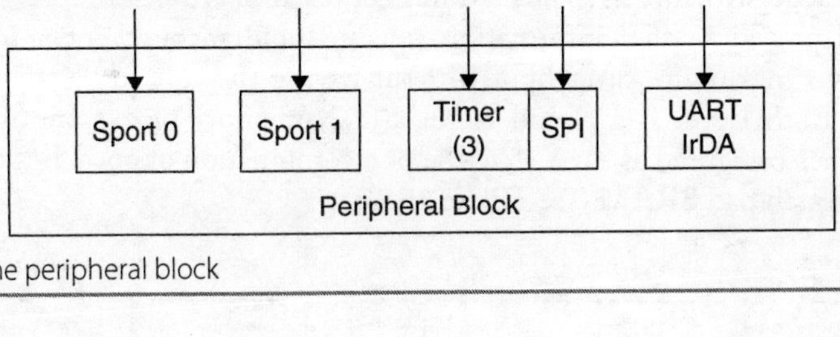

Figure 15.13 | The peripheral block

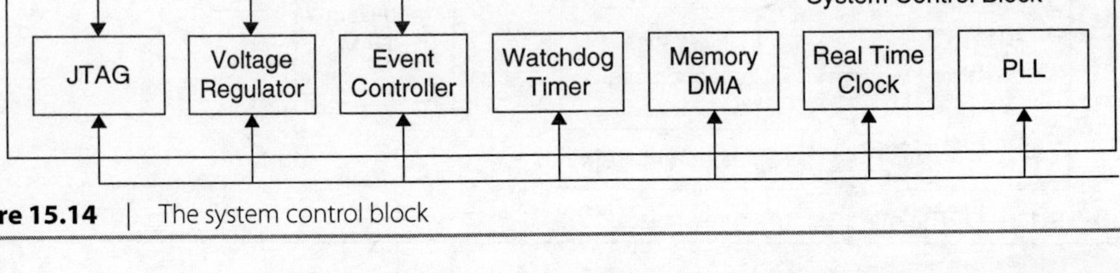

Figure 15.14 | The system control block

iii) It also support SIMD operations
iv) It supports multi-length instruction encoding
v) Control-type instructions are encoded as compact 16-bit words
vi) Mathematically intensive signal processing instructions are encoded as 32-bit values
vii) Intermix and link 16-bit control instructions with 32-bit signal processing instructions are bundled into 64-bit groups to maximize memory packing

15.3.4 | System Development Using BlackFin

The core's performance and architectural partitioning allow development of a complete, high performance DSP system that could incorporate either AD's Visual DSP Kernel (VDK) RTOS or any other industry recognized real-time operating systems—all within a single processor environment.

15.3.5 | Dual Core BlackFin

There are dual core BlackFin Processors, and they add flexibility and concurrency to tasks. There are applications in which different tasks can run on each of the cores. While one core runs the operating system or kernel, the other core is dedicated to the application's high-intensity processing functions. The ability to segment these types of functions allows parallel design processes, and thus dual cores help in achieving better performance.

15.3.6 | Evaluation Boards

The manufacturer has released a number of evaluation boards for easy product development using BlackFin processors. Figure 15.15 is a photograph of an ADSP BF-533 evaluation board.

So far we have done two things:

i) Discussed DSP processors and their features in general
ii) Discussed the architecture of the BlackFin DSP processor

Figure 15.15 | A BlackFin evaluation board

Next, a set of features of a specific BlackFin is listed below. This list is not meant to be studied, but only to be browsed through. It is put in here, just to give you a feel as to what to expect to find in a typical DSP processor. While browsing, it might be interesting to relate the list to the features listed in Section 15.2 and verify your understanding of the characteristics of this processor.

This list applies to the BlackFin DSP BF-21535, which is recommended (by the manufacturer) to be used for networking and digital imaging.

15.3.7 | Features of BF-21535

15.3.7.1 | *Processor Core*

i) 300 MHz high performance DSP core
ii) Dual 16-bit MACs, supporting 600 MMACs of sustained performance
iii) Two 32-bit ALUs
iv) Two 40-bit accumulators
v) Four 8-bit video ALUs
vi) Parallel address computational DAGs for circular buffer and bit reversed addressing support
vii) 40-bit shifter for bit manipulation and data interleaving
viii) Flexible software controlled dynamic power management
ix) RISC-like register and instruction model for ease of programming and compiler-friendly support
x) Enhanced multimedia instructions for media-rich processing
xi) Advanced debug, trace and performance monitoring support

15.3.7.2 | *Memory*

i) 768 Mbytes unified address memory map
ii) 308 Kbytes of on-chip memory
 - 16 Kbytes of dual-ported L1 instruction SRAM/cache
 - 32 Kbytes of dual-ported L1 data SRAM/cache
 - 4 Kbytes of high speed scratchpad SRAM
 - 256 Kbytes of full speed, low latency, dual-ported L2 SRAM
iii) Memory management unit providing memory protection
iv) Memory controller providing glueless connection to multiple banks of SDRAM, SRAM, FLASH or ROM
v) Flexible memory initialization capability (boot from SPI, serial port, external memory source or second stage PCI load)

15.3.7.3 | *Peripherals and System Control Block*

i) 32-bit 33 MHz PCI V2.2 compliant bus interface with both master and slave support
ii) USB device V1.1 compliant controller supporting up to eight endpoints
iii) Event handler
iv) Two UARTs with auto baud capability (one UART includes support for IrDA®)
v) Four 32-bit timer/counters—three of which

vi) Two SPI compatible ports support PWM, pulsewidth and event count modes
vii) Two dual-channel, full-duplex synchronous serial ports (SPORTS)
viii) 12-channel DMA controller and memory DMA controller capable of internal, external and PCI transfers
ix) Real-time clock
x) Watchdog timer
xi) 16 general purpose I/O
xii) Debug/JTAG interface
xiii) On-chip PLL capable of 1_ to 31_ frequency multiplication

15.3.7.4 | Targetted Applications

i) Automotive
ii) Broadband access
iii) Central office/network switch
iv) Digital imaging and printing
v) Global positioning systems
vi) Industrial signal processing
vii) Instrumentation/telemetry
viii) Internet appliances
ix) Modem solutions
x) Personal branch exchanges (PBX)
xi) Telecommunications
xii) Video conferencing
xiii) VoIP phone solutions

Figure 15.15 shows a photograph of the development platform BlackFin BF-533.

15.4 | The SHARC Floating Point Processor

This is a floating point processor developed by Analog Devices. It is based on the 'Super Harvard' architecture mentioned in Section 15.2.3. The series boasts of possessing all the advantages that a floating data format gives (Section 15.2.8). There are a number of processors in the SHARC series which have the architectural features as listed below.

15.4.1 | Common Architectural Features of SHARC

i) CISC philosophy
ii) SIMD architecture
iii) 32/40-bit IEEE Floating-Point Math
iv) 32-bit Fixed-Point Multipliers with 64-bit Product & 80-bit Accumulation
v) All Computations Are Single-Cycle
vi) 32 Address Pointers Support 32 Circular Buffers
vii) Six Nested Levels of Zero-Overhead Looping in Hardware
viii) DMA Allows Zero-Overhead Background Transfers at Full Clock Rate Without Processor Intervention

All the above characteristics have been made clear in Section 15.2, and so we will not dwell on them again.

The series has been identified to have four generations, of which the fourth generation includes the ADSP-21486, ADSP-21487, ADSP-21488 and ADSP-21489, and the manufacturers claim increased performance, hardware-based filter accelerators, audio and application-focused peripherals and new memory configurations capable of supporting the latest audio processing algorithms. All devices in this generation are pin-compatible with each other and completely code-compatible with all prior SHARC Processors.

In 2010, a few newer SHARC processors were launched, which the manufacturers call the 'fifth generation'. They are SHARC 2147x and SHARC 2148x with operating frequencies of 266 MHz and 400 MHz, respectively. As the current design trend is focused towards low power, these designs also have 'low power' as their claims along with more efficient memory usage.

15.4.2 | The Tiger SHARC

The Tiger SHARC processor was released in the year 1998, and is considered to be the most powerful member of AD's SHARC floating point family. It has incorporated many features that constitute the current trends in DSP processor. Its design is optimized for telecommunications infrastructure, such as cellular telephone base stations and xDSL central-office equipment.

A typical Tiger SHARC ADSP-TS101S has the following characteristics:

i) It is a RISC architecture and can boast of being 'superscalar plus VLIW' with SIMD capability.
ii) It provides native support for 8, 16 and 32-bit fixed, as well as floating point data types on a single chip.
iii) It has large on-chip memory, providing extremely high internal and external bandwidths.
iv) Its dual compute blocks provide the necessary capabilities to handle a vast array of computationally demanding large signal processing tasks.

Figure 15.16 shows the architectural block diagram of the Tiger SHARC

15.4.3 | The Architecture of Tiger SHARC

15.4.3.1 | *Two Computational Units*

The two computation units each contain the functional units of multiplier, an ALU, and a shifter which use 32- or 64-bit inputs and support both floating-point and fixed-point data. Each computation unit has a register file with thirty-two 32-bit data registers. For 64-bit inputs, two 32-bit registers are concatenated to form one 64-bit value. Data transfers and some outputs from the multiplier can be up to 128 bits wide. Note that 128-bit destinations are formed by concatenating four consecutive 32-bit registers.

i) The Tiger SHARC becomes an SIMD machine when its two computational units are controlled by a single instruction which usually specifies an arithmetic operation carried out on several data items.

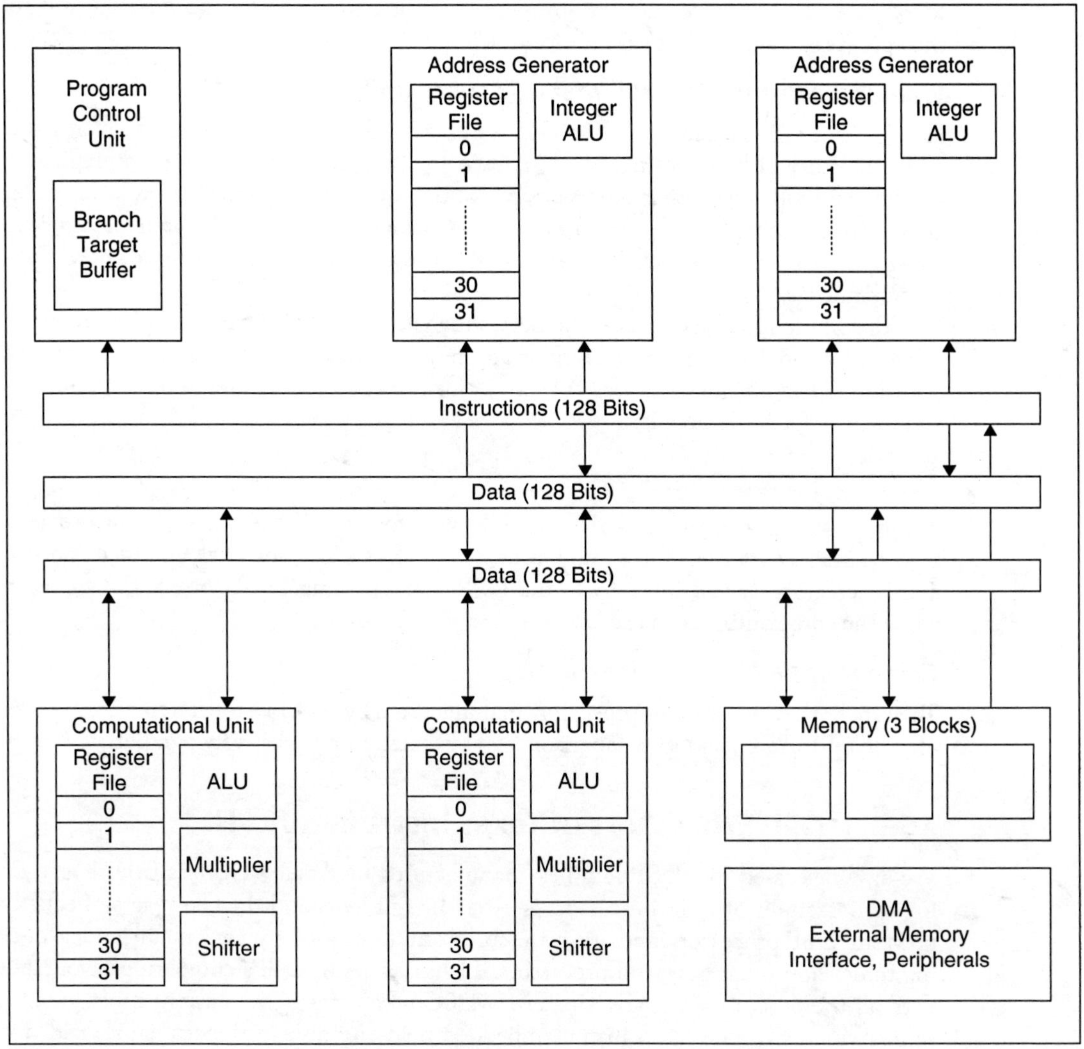

Figure 15.16 | Internal architecture of Tiger SHARC

ii) To handle diverse data types of video, audio, image, etc., the processor has allowed the 32-bit registers to be used as two 16 bit, four 8-bit or a single 32-bit register.
iii) On chip memory is divided into three banks: one for code and two for data.
iv) To get data into its two computational units, the processor uses two address generators, which are integer ALUs. They do address calculations (Section 15.2.7)

15.4.3.2 | *The Program Control Unit*

The program control unit manages program structure and program flow by supplying addresses to memory for instruction fetches. Contained within the program sequencer, is the 'Instruction Buffer (IB)' which caches up to five fetched instruction lines waiting to execute. The sequencer extracts an instruction line from the IB and distributes it to the appropriate computational unit for execution.

What is the Branch Target Buffer (BTB) used for?

A BTB is a unit usually found in GPPs–Pentium, for instance. The buffer stores the address history of branches taken, and is used for 'branch prediction'. Branch prediction is usually used in superscalar processors which do not have the patience to wait until the condition for taking (or not taking) a branch, is evaluated. So, one of the branches is taken using the statistics of previous history. The BTB stores the target addresses of previously taken branches.

The whole idea is to reduce the delays involved in conditional branching by making guesses about the branch directions and target addresses. Such ideas are commonly used in GPPs, but not in most DSP processors. Refer to some literature on computer architecture for more details.

15.4.3.3 | *DMA Controller*

The processor has an on-chip DMA controller with fourteen DMA channels, and provides zero-overhead data transfers without processor intervention. The DMA controller operates independently and invisibly to the DSP core, enabling DMA operations to occur while the core continues to execute program instructions.

Comparing SHARC and Tiger SHARC

They are both floating point processors manufactured by AD, but the latter is more complex than SHARC, and in comparison, can be stated to be 'massively parallel'.

15.5 | DSP Processors of Texas Instruments (TI)

We have discussed two DSP families, manufactured by Analog Devices. Another leading manufacturer of DSP processors is Texas Instruments and they have sets of equally powerful DSP processors, and are in the forefront of technology, continually endeavouring to develop more powerful processors. TI has its set of DSPs comparing favourably with all the processors of AD. The TMS 320C6xxx series is the current most popular series, which is widely used in the embedded field and also in the academic field (for study purposes). Figure 15.17 is the photograph of the evaluation board of the DSP processor TMS 320C6713.

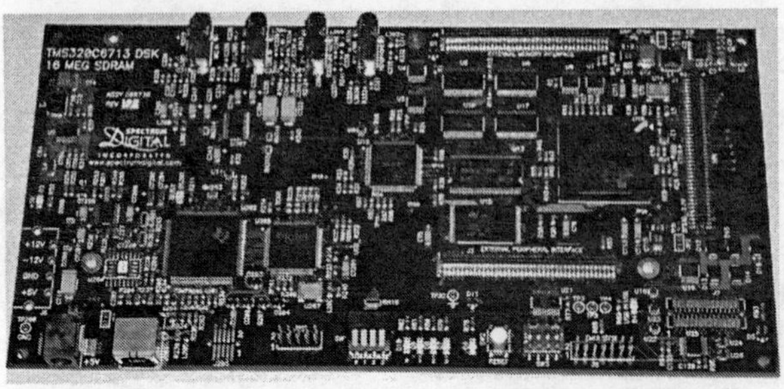

Figure 15.17 | Photograph of the TMS 320C6713 evaluation board

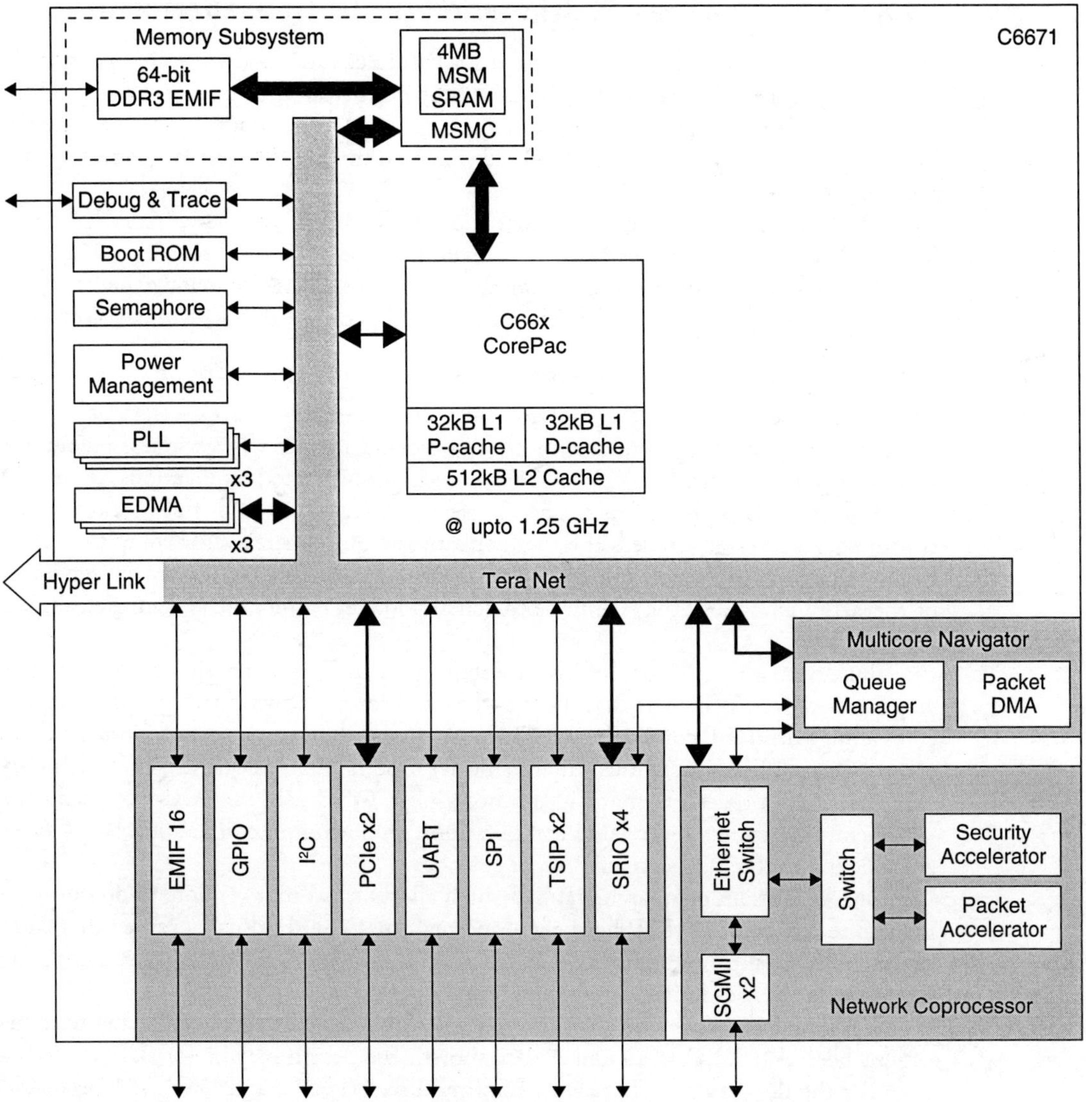

Figure 15.18 | High level block diagram of TI's TMS 320C 6671 showing its peripherals

Figure 15.18 is the high level block diagram of TMS320C6671 which is rated to be as good, or even better, than the Tiger SHARC.

Like Tiger SHARC, this processor is also targeted for the telecommunications and network field, and its peripheral structure indicates this.

Right now, our interest is not in going into the details of this DSP processor. It is up to you to find out more details about this, or any other DSP processor you might use. That should be a trivial task considering that you have had a good exposure to peripherals and also the key characteristics of a DSP processor. We will now move on to an introduction to TI's current most sophisticated DSP platform.

15.6 | OMAP (Open Multimedia Applications Platform)

This is an SoC in which a GP core and a DSP core co-exist and work in unison such that the user gets the best of both worlds. It is obvious from the name that this product is aimed at the multimedia market. In fact, it has also been endorsed for the wireless market, and is widely used for handheld devices and mobile receivers which need multimedia processing.

OMAP1 started with an ARM core and a DSP core. Over the years, ARM cores from ARM 9 to different versions of Cortex have been used. Also from OMAP 4 onwards, the ARM processors are themselves dual core. There are many generations of OMAP too—from OMAP 1 to OMAP 5. The DSP core used is a TMS 320 core.

What is the motivation for producing such highly complex SoCs?

The factors are the market competitiveness and the increased expectations of the consumer. The following is quoted from TI's technical paper: 'The wireless revolution is moving rapidly beyond voice to include such sophisticated applications as mobile e-commerce, real-time Internet, speech recognition, audio and full-motion video streaming. As a result, wireless Internet appliances require increasingly complex mobile communications and signal processing capabilities. And while consumers expect state-of-the-art functionality, they continue to demand longer battery life and smaller, sleeker products.'

Thus, what the OMAP SoC is expected to perform is faster signal processing at very lower power. Why is it that there is the need for a platform with general purpose cores along with DSP cores? The two kinds of processors, though part of the same SoC, can perform different activities. Interfacing with peripherals is one aspect, and highly complex signal processing math is another aspect. Obviously the ARM cores do the peripheral interfacing and related computations, while complex signal processing tasks are assigned to the DSP core.

OMAP uses an open architecture, which allows third part vendors to do development. The design of OMAP has been done such that any third party can easily take it and adapt it to suit his applications. A set of APIs which developers can use, allow different kinds of OSes to be ported on to it and develop many products.

See Figure 15.19 which shows the way a design proceeds. There can be many applications here: A1, A2, A3, A4 and A5 are shown. The design may be for audio, video or web. For the design team, there are MM (multimedia) APIs and DSP APIs available. Within the OMAP, an embedded OS (in the Figure 15.19, the term GPP OS is used), and a DSP OS are both required to ensure that both types of tasks are well supported for multitasking and timing constraints. The OS adapters make use of the APIs provided by the OEM (Original Equipment Manufacturer, here TI). The power of OMAP and the tool support available ensures easy design of complex systems.

How can a student use an OMAP platform?

There are various boards available for the OMAP platform. These boards have a number of peripherals and connectors. Open source OSes like versions of Linux can be ported on to this board, and projects can be done very easily. To get the DSP part to be working in step with the ARM core, a DSP OS many also have to be ported. For support for all these, support web sites of the manufacturer of the boards as well as TI are accessible.

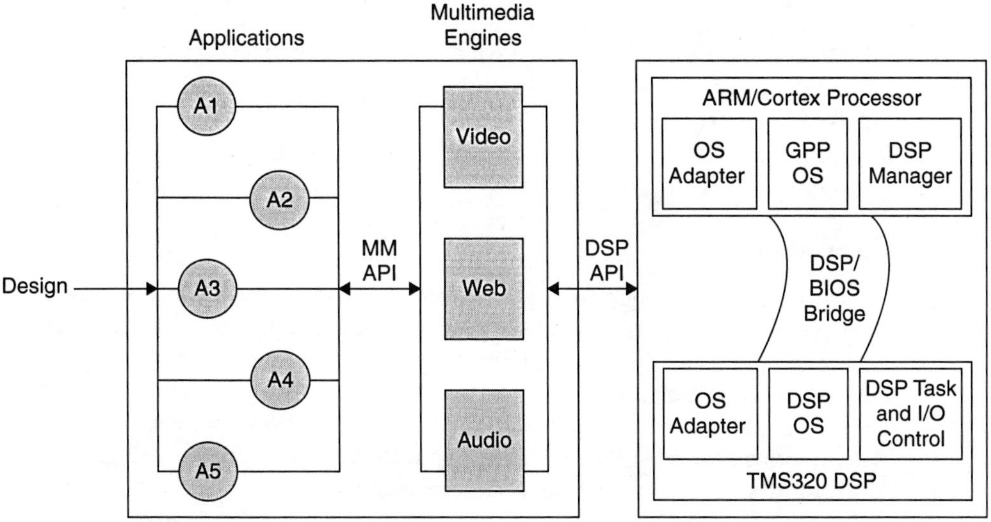

Figure 15.19 | Design sequence using OMAP

Since powerful processors are available on the platform, multimedia projects can be easily done using this. There are various open source programming languages too, for easy application development at the student level. Platforms like the Beagle board, Hawk board, Panda board etc are available, and OpenCV is a language easily usable for image applications. One such application is included in the list of projects (Section.19.1).

Figure 15.20 is a photograph of a beagle board which has the OMAP SoC and interfacing chips, connectors, slots for external memory and SD cards, etc.

Figure 15.20 | Photograph of a beagle board

The specification of the OMAP SoC used here are listed below:

i) **Processors:** DM 3730 (Digital Media Processor) with ARM Cortex-A8 core and TMS 320C64xx DSP processor
ii) **ARM Frequency:** 1 GHz
iii) **DSP Frequency:** 800 MHz

Conclusion

What we should conclude from this chapter is that DSP processors are very different from GPPs. In most cases, such DSP processors are used in embedded applications and so cost and power dissipation are important figures of merit. Many application-specific DSP processors are also available, which can be used efficiently and easily for the application in hand. So there are some DSPs which are best for video, some others for audio and still others for telecommunication applications and so on. Choosing the right one suited for the application leads to a successful design.

KEY POINTS OF THIS CHAPTER

- DSP processors are a very important component in embedded systems, where signal processing is involved.
- They have applications in video, audio, wireless, networking, automotive and communication fields.
- The design of DSP processors is quite different from that of general purpose processors.
- They have dedicated MAC units, specialized instruction sets and multiple execution units.
- For efficient memory accesses, they use the Super Harvard architecture.
- Their speed of operation depends to a certain extent, on the presence of DMA, circular buffers and zero overhead loops.
- They have address generation units for generating multiple addresses in the same memory cycle.
- DSP processors have either the fixed point or floating point data formats.
- Caches, RTOSes, streamlined I/O, etc. are the characteristics of modern DSP processors.
- Parallelism is achieved in the architecture by VLIW, SuperScalar and SIMD techniques.
- AD's BlackFin is a popular series of fixed point processors.
- AD's SHARC is a family of floating point processors, in which Tiger SHARC is a massively parallel processor.
- TI's TMS 320C 6xxx series is widely used in many modern applications.
- The new OMAP dual core SoC is gaining ground in most multimedia applications.

QUESTIONS

1. What is the role of DSP processors in the field of embedded systems?
2. What is the justification for dedicated MAC units in DSP processors?
3. How does the 'Super Harvard' architecture contribute to increased memory bandwidth?
4. For what types of computations are circular buffers needed?
5. Compare the two data formats generally used in DSP processors?
6. How is a choice made on the data format to be used for an application?
7. Why are fast DMA and interrupts mandatory for DSP processors?
8. Distinguish between VLIW and superscalar architectures.
9. Does SIMD prove to be useful for all types of computation?
10. Suggest an application field in which BlackFin processors are likely to perform very well.
11. What aspects of Tiger SHARC gives it a description of being 'massively parallel'?
12. What are the reasons for the high popularity of OMAP SoCs?

EXERCISES

1. List 10 BlackFin processors which are single core and five which are dual core.
2. Find out at least five products in which OMAP SoCs are used.
3. Find out where SHARC processors have their widest use.

PART-IV

DESIGN AND PERFORMANCE ASPECTS

16 AUTOMATED DESIGN OF DIGITAL ICs

In this chapter, you will learn

- A brief history of IC development
- The classification of digital ICs
- The different types of programmable logic devices
- The difference between custom and semi-custom ASICs
- The concepts in modelling and designing an ASIC
- The complete ASIC design flow

16.1 | History of Integrated Circuit (IC) Design

The semi-conductor industry started its evolution with the advent of diodes and transistors (in the 1970s) gradually leading to the development of the first integrated circuits (ICs). First, a few logic gates (1 to 10) in one single package constituted small scale integration (SSI). Over the years, the gradual development of IC technology led to MSI (medium scale integration), LSI (large scale integration) and now VLSI (very large scale integration).We now see 64 bit microprocessors, SRAM and other functional units all integrated in the same silicon chip, with many millions of transistors in it. The number of transistors in one package keeps on increasing as new design technology trends emerge.

Looking back at history, it can be recalled that it was bipolar technology that was used in the beginning of the semiconductor revolution. Gradually, NMOS and PMOS and finally CMOS (complementary MOS) picked up the trail and currently, all these different technologies co-exist, even though CMOS has established its dominance, because of its features of low-power consumption and high packing density (more transistors in unit area). There is even BiCMOS technology—this is a combination of bipolar and CMOS technology. The advantage of bipolar technology is that it can sustain higher voltages compared to MOS, so for such applications (like power electronics) bipolar or BiCMOS devices can be used.

16.2 | Types of Digital ICs

Figure 16.1 shows a rough classification for the digital ICs that we generally use. Let's have a detailed discussion on what the terms used in the diagram mean to us.

Chapter-opening image: A Virtex-4 FPGA development board.

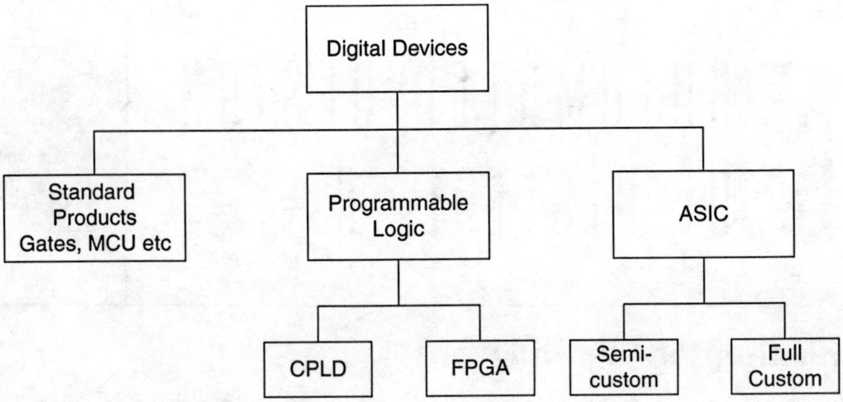

Figure 16.1 | Classification of digital ICs

16.2.1 | Standard Products

We are used to making use of standard ICs for the various applications that we design; we use ICs of gates, counters, multiplexers, MCUs, etc. and look up data sheets for the specifications of these ICs. The term used for such ICs is 'standard product' or 'standard part'. Such ICs are manufactured in bulk and sold in large quantities. They are more or less 'general purpose' as far as their application domain is concerned, and their design is standard.

16.2.2 | ASIC (Application Specific Integrated Circuit)

Next, we come to the definition of ASICs and try to establish that they are different from standard ICs. ASICs are manufactured for specific applications. A video codec, audio codec, controllers for specific devices, etc. are examples of ASICs. These may not be manufactured in bulk. Product manufacturers fix the specifications, and ASIC designers design them according to the spec given. Note that two different product manufacturers (who may be producing different brands of TVs or MP3 players, for example) may give two different 'specs' for the video codec that they need. This also implies that an ASIC is built for one and only one customer, that is, the embedded product manufacturer who has given the specifications for the design. For instance, an ASIC for a specific line of cell phones of a specific company can be used only for that product line.

Thus, an ASIC is likely to be proprietary by nature and not available to the general public. ASIC design is a 'specific' design, and entails more work and is more time-consuming and expensive. It may happen that once a product (e.g. cellphone, music player, etc) becomes very popular, the ASICs used in them have to be manufactured in bulk, that is, they become a 'standard product', then such ASICs are called ASSP (Application Specific Standard Product).

16.2.2.1 | *Classification of ASICs*

Thus, we see that ASICs are just ICs made for specific applications. The design and manufacture of all ICs have to go through a cycle starting from 'specification' to 'fabrication and testing'. We will soon go in detail into that sequence. Keep in mind that complex design of MPUs and MCUs which are meant to be 'standard parts' as well as ASICs for specific designs, go through the same sequence, when it is a 'new design' that is being implemented.

Custom Design

This is a design which starts from scratch. This means that the designer has only 'transistors' as his basic unit of design. He designs bigger circuits with this basic unit. Note that, this gives very high flexibility and freedom to the designer, but also a lot of hard work and time is involved. The ASIC designer (along with his team) customizes all the features of the IC, all the time trying to get the maximum performance from every element in the design which may have analog circuits, digital circuits, memory, etc. Each new generation of microprocessors and memory is designed in this way. Analog parts of ICs are also made this way.

Semi-custom Design

A semi-custom design, on the other hand, is easier. Units available in a 'library' are used to make a final design. Most ASICs are semi-custom designs.

In this, the designer uses the 'logic cells' from a library. Thus, the basic unit of design is not the transistor, but logic circuits (AND gates, OR gates, multiplexers, and flip-flops, for example) known as standard cells. These standard cells are designs which have already been tested and verified, and thus the design team has an easier time and consequently, a faster design ensues. Small cells can be combined to make 'megacells' and these could be stacked and arranged as the designer wishes, and then the designer does the interconnections only.

16.2.3 | Programmable Devices

They are ICs available that are programmable and are classified as PLDs (programmable logic devices) or FPGAs (field programmable gate arrays).

16.2.3.1 | *PLDs*

They implement AND-OR logic. They can be customized for any specific application. When a PLD has a flip flop at the output, it becomes a sequential PLD as in Figure 16.2.

The basic building block of a PLD is the macrocell. Figure 16.3 shows a typical macrocell with a AND-OR programmable array, a FF, a clock, a controlled (using the output enable, OE pin) buffer and inputs. Thus, a PLD contains a number of macrocells which are programmable.

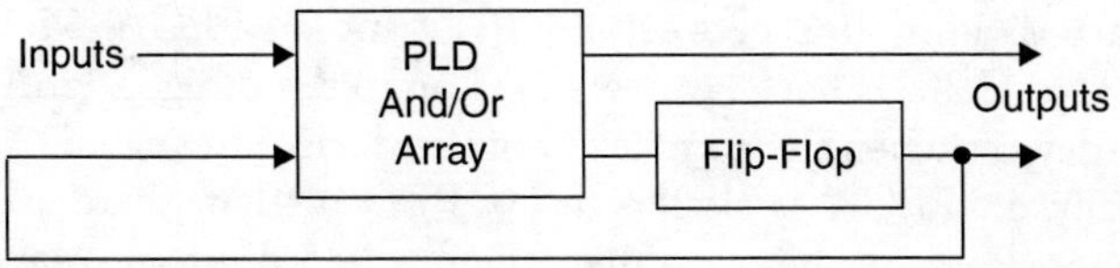

Figure 16.2 | A sequential PLD

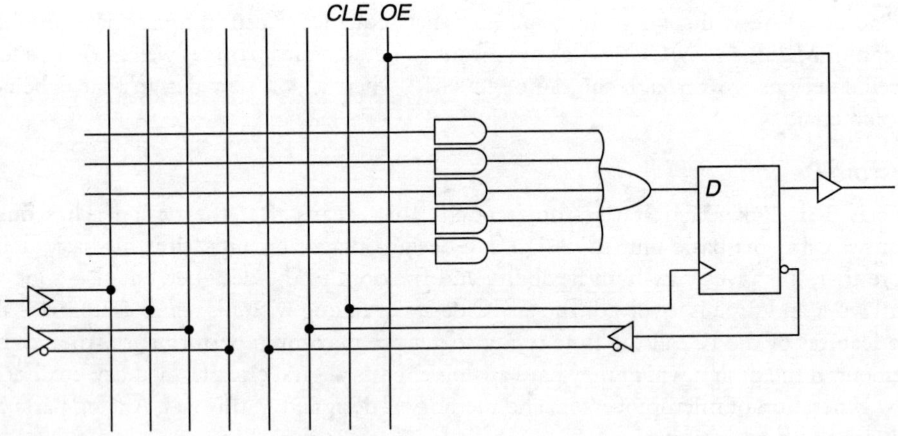

Figure 16.3 | Schematic of a typical macrocell

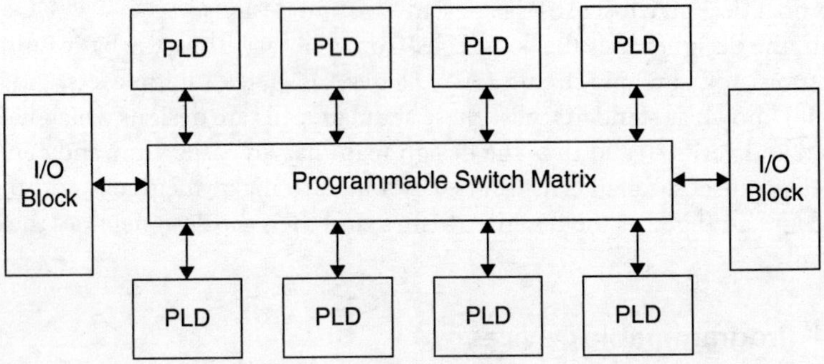

Figure 16.4 | A CPLD made up of a number of PLDs

When small PLD blocks are combined, they become a 'complex PLD (CPLD)', and cater to bigger applications. Figure 16.4 shows a CPLD made up a number of PLDs. The I/O blocks indicate the presence of programmable logic behind each I/O pin. The switch matrix is a 'programmable interconnect'. It receives inputs from the I/O block and directs it to the individual macrocells. Similarly, selected outputs from macrocells are sent to the output pins as needed.

16.2.3.2 | *FPGA*

This is also a programmable device and is considered to be a 'step above' CPLDs. But there is no sharp dividing line between a CPLD and an FPGA. Most manufacturers who used the word CPLDs have now switched on to the designation FPGAs, for their programmable devices when the complexity of the devices increased.

Conceptually, an FPGA is similar to a CPLD in that, there are macrocells and programmable interconnects between them. Figure 16.5 illustrates the essential characteristics of an FPGA, showing the logic blocks, I/O pads and the routing channel.

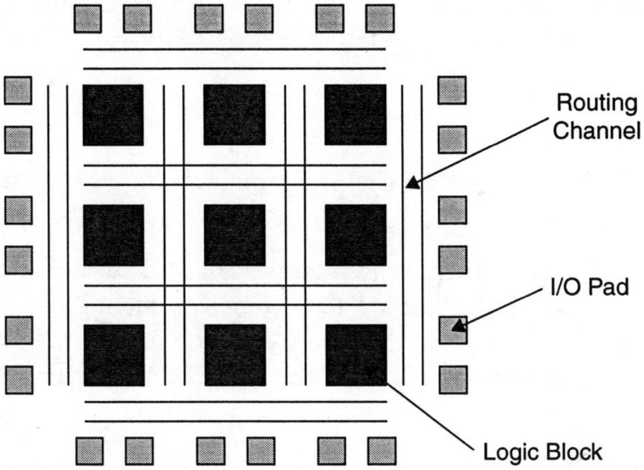

Figure 16.5 | The basic structure of an FPGA

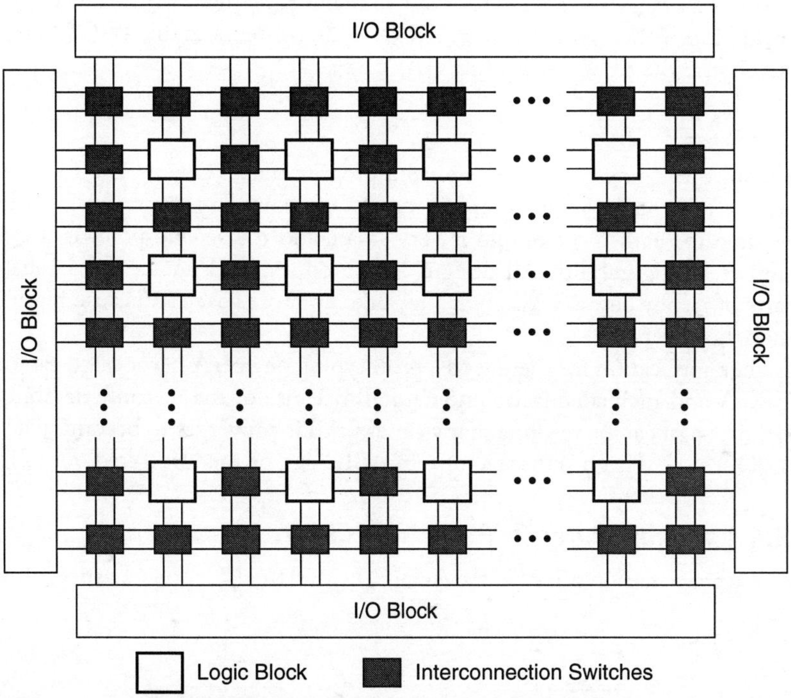

Figure 16.6 | The internal structure of an FPGA unit

Figure 16.6 is an expanded view of an FPGA, the features of which can be listed as below:

i) The basic logic cells and the interconnects are programmable
ii) The structure is a regular array of programmable basic logic cells that can implement combinational as well as sequential logic

iii) A matrix of programmable interconnects surrounds the basic logic cells
iv) Programmable I/O cells are associated with the I/O pins

16.2.3.3 | *Types of FPGAs*

In terms of the technology used for the programmable 'interconnects,' there are two types of FPGAs.

i) **Anti-fuse:** See Fig 16.7. The link is what we call 'anti-fuse'. The anti-fuse doesn't conduct initially, but can be 'burned' to become conducting. The anti-fuse behaviour is thus opposite to that of the fuse, hence the name. It is obvious that such FPGAs can be programmed only once; they are OTP (One Time Programmable) devices.

ii) **SRAM FPGAs:** This type has an interconnect made of SRAM transistors, which conduct or does not conduct according to the logic 'burned' on it. Such FPGAs lose their 'configuration' once power is switched OFF. To avoid that, there is always a PROM along with the FPGA chip (outside it), which stores the configuration information. When power is switched ON, the contents of this PROM are used to re-configure the SRAM-based FPGA.

Why FPGAs?

The question that comes is why do we need programmable devices like FPGAs? Why not fabricate ICs for the required application? One point in favour of using FPGAs is that the 'time to market' the design is very small, and the second point is that of flexibility and re-configurability. All designs in a product need not be FPGA-based, but some parts of it may be FPGA-based. They take up more space and cause higher power dissipation, however.

Another application for them is as a prototyping device. A new design can be tested on an FPGA and its inadequacies understood. Because of the re-configuarabilty of the FPGA, the design can be re-done many times until it converges to becoming a satisfactory one. Once the design is satisfactory, an ASIC can be manufactured out of it.

16.2.3.4 | *Manufacturers of FPGAs and CPLDs*

Some of the big names in this field are Actel, Altera, Atmel, Cypress, Lattice, Quicklogic, Xilinx, etc.

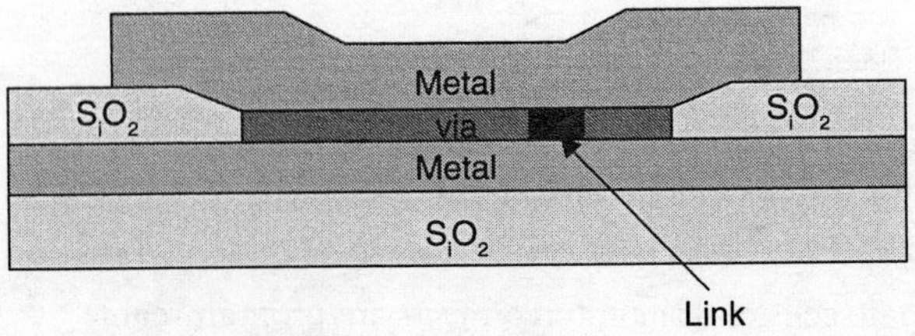

Figure 16.7 | The anti-fuse type FPGA

16.3 | ASIC Design

Let's now go into the details of ASIC design. Note that design is fully automated—there are EDA (Electronic Design Automation) tools available for each and every stage—the designer can manually intervene, but the automation tools take care of most issues. So let's go to the various steps, in this automated design. We first discuss the design with a set of simple steps, like a design done for a small application in an academic environment. After that, we will make a review of design as done in the ASIC design industry.

When a design is to be done, the first point is to have a 'requirement' specified. This amounts to having a functional description of the circuit we need. Aspects like area, power, speed, etc. may also be added to make the specification complete. The functional description is called a behavioral model. This model contains the information on how the circuit behaves, i.e., with this, we have a list of inputs and a list of outputs and a function which maps between the two. Figure 16.8 illustrates the concept of a behavioral model. We will delve more deeply into it.

Our first concern is—how do we represent circuit behaviour?

There are different methods:truth tables, schematic entry and hardware description languages. Only the latter (HDLs) will be good enough for a reasonably robust design of complex digital hardware. Note that there are no HDLs for analog design, though 'mixed signal design' is being considered using HDLs.

16.3.1 | Hardware Description Languages

Hardware description languages started becoming popular towards the beginning of the 1980s; around that time, many manufacturers started developing their own versions of HDLs, but soon it became clear that without some sort of standardization, compatibility issues would soon create confusion in the market. At that point of time, IEEE stepped in and set about the task of standardizing two popular HDLs: they are VHDL (Very High speed integrated circuit Hardware Description Language) and Verilog. Both these HDLs are popular in the hardware design world.

HDLs are syntactically similar to a high level language (HLL) like C. But there is an important difference. An HLL like C is a sequential programming language, meaning that always the second statement is 'executed' after the first statement is executed. Execution flow is sequential. But this is not so for HDLs. Note that hardware is concurrent, that is, all parts of a circuit function simultaneously. Thus, 'concurrency' is a key aspect in the HDL scenario and the idea of 'execution' does not have any relevance here, as ultimately the hardware is to be 'configured' by the HDL program statements.

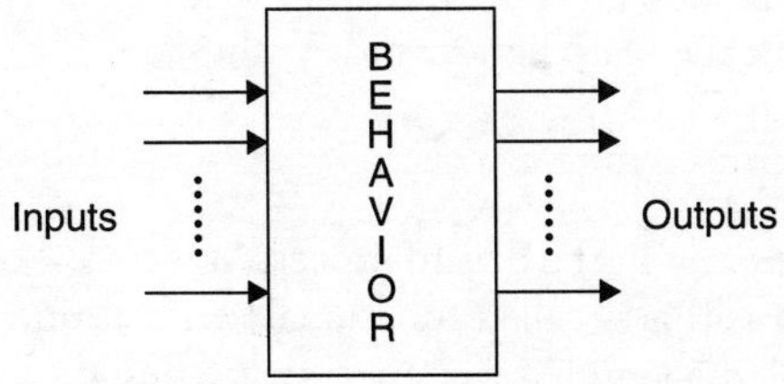

Figure 16.8 | The behavioural model

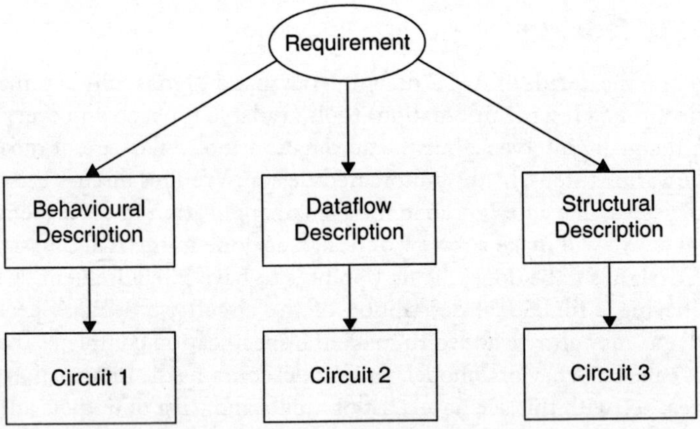

Figure 16.9 | The three different models for expressing circuit functionality

16.3.2 | Architectural Models

There are three architectural models for specifying the functionality of a circuit, as shown in Figure 16.9.

i) **Behavioural model:** In this, the behaviour is expressed in sequential form using constructs similar to that of 'C'—like, if then, for, case statements, etc. This is actually a simple way for expressing the behaviour—it doesn't directly convert to hardware—we say that the sequential model is not fully 'synthesizable'.
ii) **Data flow model**: In this model, the behaviour is expressed in terms of a set of 'concurrent' statement which shows the logical relationship between the output and input ports.
iii) **Structural model**: In this, the actual hardware components for the design are identified, and the interconnection between these components is defined by the statements in the structural model.

Figurre 16.9 shows that for a particular requirement, any of the three models can be used, and may lead to three different circuits, all of them satisfying the required functionality. It is also possible to use a combination of these models for a design. If a comparison is needed, one can say that the easiest (to visualize and express) is the behavioural model, but the most efficient and exact one is the structural model.

Once the program is written and checked for syntactic correctness, the first part of design is considered to be done.

The next stages are called simulation and synthesis.

16.3.3 | Simulation

Before proceeding further on in the design process, it is necessary to verify the functional correctness of the design. This is called functional verification.

For this, a tool called a simulator is used, or the designer writes a test bench using the HDL itself. A simulator is mostly (but not always) a waveform simulator, and shows the visual display of input and output waveforms. If the input stimuli are supplied, the corresponding output waveforms are seen in the simulator, for the circuit under test. The test bench written by the designer also performs the same actions of generating input stimuli and obtaining the output signals. The designer can verify 'design correction' from this step.

16.3.4 | Synthesis

A synthesis tool is available as part of the automation software. Figure 16.10 shows that synthesis converts a design to an actual hardware diagram. We say that the synthesis tool converts the HDL design to an **RTL level design**, and then to a **gate level netlist**. The design is also mapped to the standard cells, in this stage.

See Figure 16.10 which clarifies the ideas of modelling, simulation and synthesis. Before processing further, let's make ourselves clear about the two highlighted terms:

i) **RTL:** This stands for 'Register Transfer Logic'. This implies that any design can be broken up into a synchronous (register) part and a combinational part. Bringing a functional design to such a setup is called RTL design. See Figure 16.11 which shows that a circuit generally can be split up as a sequential part and a combinational counterpart. This level of expression of circuit functionality is what we mean by the term 'RTL level'.

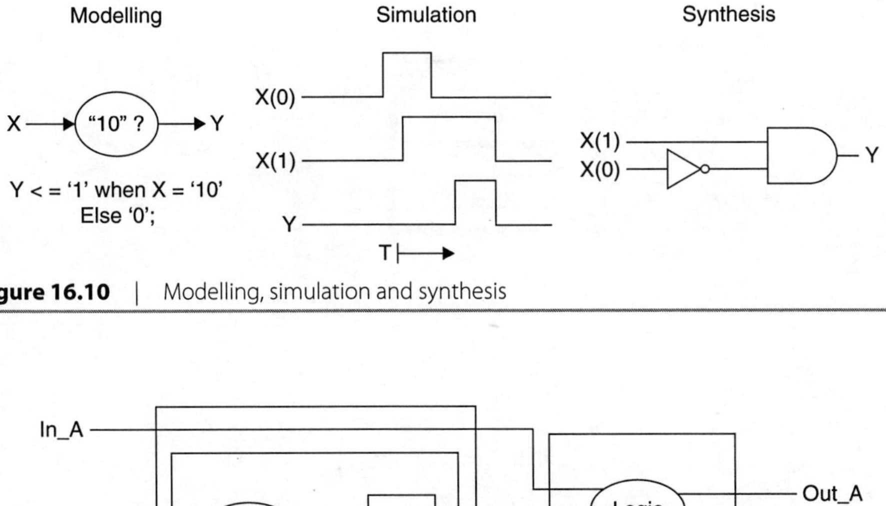

Figure 16.10 | Modelling, simulation and synthesis

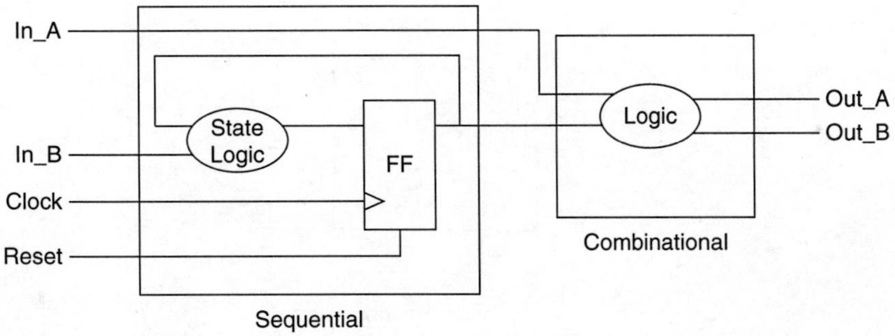

Figure 16.11 | An RTL level design

ii) **Gate level netlist:** Dividing the RTL level further down takes us to gates and wires. This is called a gate level 'netlist'. The term 'net' simply means 'electronic wires' and the list of wires (inputs, outputs and interconnections) is called a netlist. At the logic level, the design is expressed as a list of logic gates and the interconnections between them. Figure 16.12 expresses design at the various levels of abstraction.

The aim of design is to convert a behavioural model to a logic level netlist and this has been achieved now. For a particular device, a set of standard cells are available in the library which are to be used for making the ASIC. Mapping the design to the available cells is called 'technology mapping'. This part is also done by the EDA tool after synthesis.

The sequence of steps in design that we have done so far is called 'front end design'. The steps as seen in Figure 16.13 are explained below.

16.3.5 | Front End Design Steps

Design Entry Entering the design using an HDL.

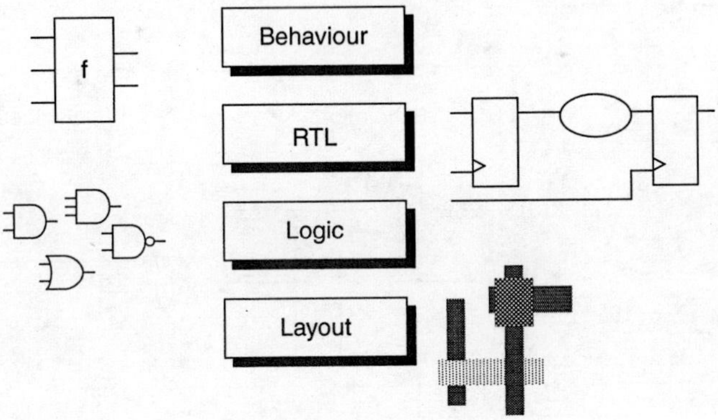

Figure 16.12 | Design expressed at different levels of abstraction

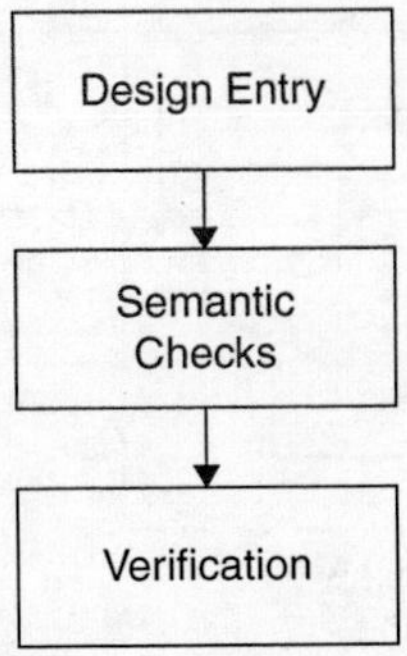

Figure 16.13 | Steps in front-end design

Semantic Checks

i) Design entry needs to be checked for language correctness.
ii) This phase can also be used to check the synthesizability of code, i.e., whether the code can lead to practical hardware.
iii) It is important to check synthesizability, as the RTL should be mapped to standard cells using synthesis tools later in the flow.

Design Verification

i) Verification is the process where the design is tested against the specification.

What do we do with the 'netlist' obtained after the front-end design?

There are two options.

i) One is to burn it onto an FPGA; thus, the FPGA gets configured to act functionally as per the designed model.

Note Keep in mind that SRAM FPGAs are re-configurable. At some later stage, this design can be 'overwritten' by another one, and the FPGA gets re-configured as per the new design. For example, if our first design had been a decade counter, the FPGA acts as a counter to count from 0 to 9. Later, if we want to change it to a 64 bit shift register, we only need to write the design for a shift register using HDL, synthesize it and burn it into the FPGA. It now functions as a shift register.

ii) The other option is to make an ASIC out of this; this means that it is to be fabricated as a chip. For this, a few additional steps are required. The layout, that is, the floor plan and routing have to be done before giving the design to the fab (fabrication unit) for final fabrication and delivery as an IC. This part is called 'back-end design'.

16.3.6 | Back-end Design Steps

Layout The layout is a set of patterns in which the transistors and their connections are laid out, i.e., finalized.

Floor Plan It defines the following:

i) The aspect ratio of the chip
ii) The placement of the cells
iii) The positions of the I/O pad

Routing In this, the interconnections between and within the cells are finalized.

There are CAD tools for all these steps, but manual intervention is sometimes necessary to make the design optimal. Once all these steps are over, the design can be sent to the fabrication unit which delivers the design in the form of an IC.

16.4 | ASIC Design: The Complete Sequence

Now that the general idea of design is more or less clear, let's refer to Figure 16.14 to understand the design in greater detail. This flowchart corresponds to the steps of design as done in the ASIC design industry. In such a setup, the 'front end' and 'back end' design

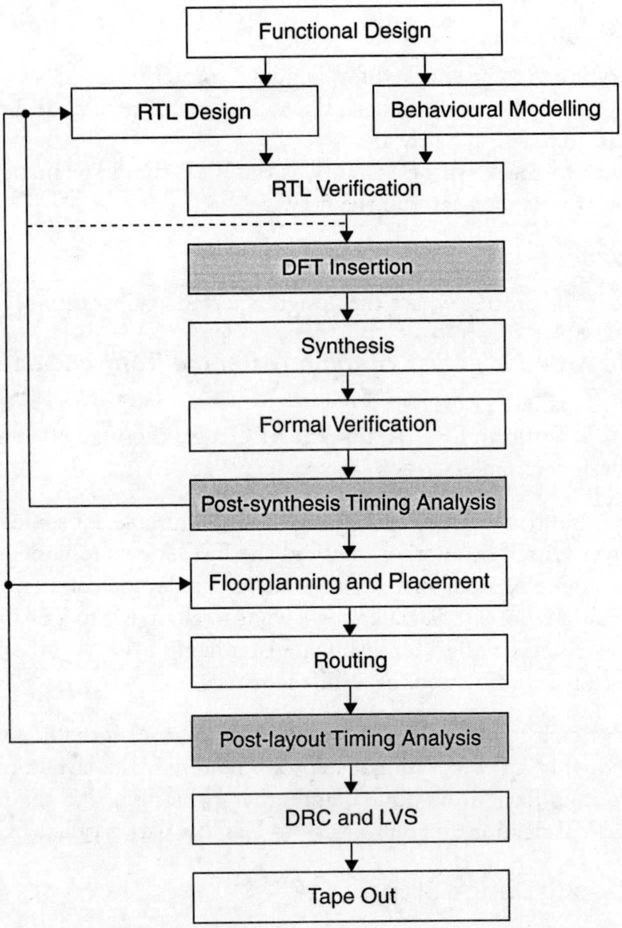

Figure 16.14 | The complete ASIC design flow

teams are separate. For the front-end design, the RTL design and verification are also done by different teams.

It starts like this. A customer is usually a product designer who needs 'the' ASIC as one of the ICs to be incorporated in his product. The customer lays out his requirement to the designer. There is no need for any specific format for this, except that the designer is made very clear about the requirements and specifications of the product his team is to deliver.

The next steps are as in the flowchart of Figure 16.14.

i) **Functional design:** This is made using any HDL.
ii) **RTL design**: This is obtained at the end of the synthesis stage, after a simple simulation check done by the RTL design team.
iii) **Behavioural model**: The verification team keeps ready a model for the functionality of his design, i.e., it could be just a set of statements indicating the expected output for a set of input conditions.

iv) **RTL verification**: Then, the RTL is verified against the behavioural model prepared by the verification team. This step is also called 'validation'. If the RTL design does not match the behavioural model, re-design is done by the RTL team. This sort of feedback mechanism is practised until the complete design is 'validated'.

v) **DFT insertion**: The term 'DFT' and its relevance need explanation. DFT stands for 'Design For Testability'. This is a very important aspect of modern ICs which are very complex. Take the case of a microprocessor, for instance. Once it is manufactured, it is assumed to be a functionally perfect chip. But in a big lot of many such chips, it is quite likely that some of them are faulty—the faults must have crept in at the manufacturing stage. The process of confirming that an IC is fault-free is called 'testing' or post-silicon validation. To be able do this later, extra 'testing circuits' are inserted into the design, and these extra test circuits are called DFT circuits. They are added to the RTL, after functional verification is over.

vi) **Logic synthesis**: This corresponds to technology mapping, where the RTL is mapped to the standard cells in the library. After this, the gate level netlist is available.

vii) **Formal verification**: This stage attempts to prove mathematically that all requirements are met, and that certain undesired behaviours like deadlock do not occur. There are formal verification tools to check whether the RTL and the logic netlist are equivalent.

viii) **Post-synthesis timing analysis:** So far, 'timing' had not been considered at all. Now at this stage, preliminary timing results after synthesis are analysed and checked against the project performance requirements.

If needed, the RTL design and synthesis options are modified, and the synthesis is repeated. This is shown in Figure 16.15 by the feedback loop.

ix) **Layout design**: The next two stages are for layout preparation, and includes floor planning, placement and routing. The EDA tools do this, but manual routing is allowed if the designer feels it necessary.

x) **Post-layout timing analysis**: Now, once again timing results are again compared with performance requirements. If it doesn't fit, the floorplan can be changed or the placement run with other parameters. See the feedback loop which shows that RTL design/layout can be modified again.

xi) **DRC:** This stands for 'Design Rule Check'. This confirms that the layout made conforms to the rules of the foundry (fab unit) in which the ASIC is to be fabricated.

xii) **LVS:** This mean 'Layout Versus Schematic'. This is another formal verification check between the post-synthesis netlist and the final layout.

xiii) **Tape out**: The process of handing over the resulting layout to the semi-conductor fabrication plant (foundry) is called *tape out*.

Suppliers of EDA tools

Synopsys, Cadence, Chrysalis, Avanti, Xilinx, Mentor Graphics, Magma, Co-Ware, Altera, etc. are some important vendors of EDA tools for digital design.

KEY POINTS OF THIS CHAPTER

- ICs were initially fabricated using bipolar technology, but now CMOS technology rules over the silicon industry.
- Digital ICs are classified as standard products, ASIC and programmable logic
- Complex programmable devices are of two types: CPLDs and FPGAs.
- FPGAs use either the anti-fuse or SRAM technology.
- ASIC design has two parts: front-end and back-end design.
- Front-end design consists of design and verification.
- Back-end design comprises layout, placement and routing.
- The complete ASIC design flow is complex with many steps.

QUESTIONS

1. Why is CMOS technology preferred for IC manufacture? List two points in favour of CMOS.
2. What, in your view, is special about an ASIC?
3. Distinguish between custom and semi-custom design of ASICs.
4. What, in your understanding, is a CPLD?
5. Compare anti-fuse and SRAM FPGAs in terms of performance.
6. Which parts of an FPGA are programmable?
7. What is the basic difference between an HDL and an HLL used for software development?
8. Distinguish between simulation and synthesis.
9. Differentiate between front-end and back-end design.
10. In which stages of the ASIC, is design flow 'timing' verified?

EXERCISES

1. List 10 ICs which are considered as 'standard products'.
2. Find the names/details of five ASICs and the application they perform.
3. Name two CPLDs and two FPGAs each, of five manufacturers.
4. Find the names of the design tools provided by the following EDA vendors. Also specify which aspect of ASIC design these tools perform.

   i) Synopsis
   ii) Cadence
   iii) Mentor Graphics
   iv) Xilinx
   v) Altera

17 HARDWARE SOFTWARE CO-DESIGN AND EMBEDDED PRODUCT DEVELOPMENT LIFECYCLE MANAGEMENT

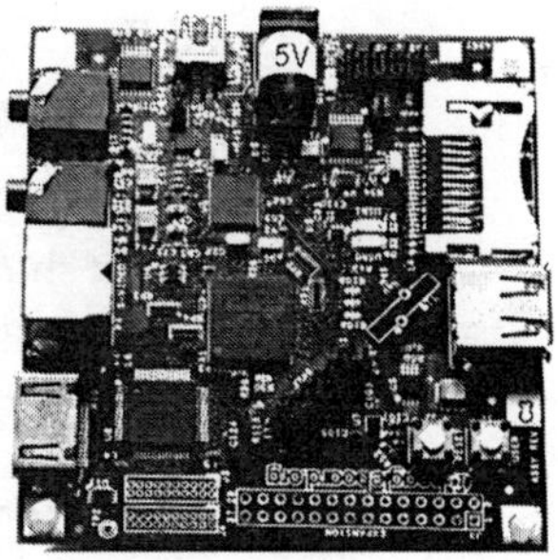

In this chapter, you will learn

- The relevance of hardware–software co-design
- The steps in the co-design process
- The commonly used models for expressing system functionality
- The meaning of EDLC management and why it is necessary
- The eight different phases of EDLC
- A few important EDLC models

Introduction

This chapter is meant to provide an overview of two important topics: the first is that of the current viewpoint with respect to embedded system design. Over the years, it has been realized that a system that employs both hardware and software should not consider each of them as separate and isolated aspects. There can be profitable trade-offs between the two, and they need to be looked at as mutually dependant, and therefore the current thinking is that design should be a co-design, in which the two partners, i.e., the hardware and software design teams, continually communicate and interact, with the willingness to make modifications and corrections at every stage of the design process. We will also take a look at some of the models available for system design.

The second topic that we touch upon is entitled 'Embedded Product Lifecycle' (EDLC) management. Here we trace the flow of the development process from the point of time when the idea of developing a product germinates. The next phases are the designing, producing and launching of the product into the market. After a period

---

Chapter-opening image: A Beagle board.

of time, this product, like everything else in this world, reaches the end of its useful life, and then it retires and dies, and then the manufacturer has the option to launch a better product of the same line. Thus, a lifecycle starts from an 'idea' and ends with retirement/ death and possible rebirth. We will study a few popular models also, of EDLC.

17.1 | Hardware Software Co-design

Considering all the previous chapters as different but related aspects of embedded systems, it should now be very clear that the design of an embedded system involves both 'hardware and software'. They are two essential parts of the design and in the current scenario, both of them are equally important because in embedded system design of complex systems, hardware and software design influence each other and therefore should be done in a structured and systematic way. The term 'co-design' implies that hardware and software design be considered concurrent and be done together.

This is different from the earlier thinking that hardware be designed first and software be taken care of later and then ported into the hardware. Because of the growing complexity of embedded systems, techniques for supporting hardware software co-design have been developed in order to permit the joint specification, design and synthesis of mixed hardware software systems. The terms 'co-simulation', 'co-synthesis', etc. will also be discussed. Having a properly functioning system is not the only point-goals with respect to cost, performance and reliability, but must also be attained.

What are the factors in the current design scene which support co-design?

i) The availability of hardware components like processors which are programmable—MCUs, DSP processors, etc.—fall into this category.
ii) The availability of re-configurable hardware like FPGAs and CPLDs.

For the above devices, design is made easy because of efficient C compilers and hardware description languages that automate design using simulation and synthesis tools.

In the context of co-design, the terms 'co-simulation' and 'co-synthesis' come into picture.

17.1.1 | Steps in Co-design

The sequence of steps involved is shown in Figure 17.1. The first step in any design is the step of making a 'requirements specifications'. The list of requirements includes functional aspects and non-functional aspects like speed, power, cost, etc. Making a very clear specification is a very important step and a successful implementation depends to a very great degree on this.

17.1.1.1 | *Functional Design*

Any system should be 'functionally' correct. For this to be ensured, the 'behaviour' of the system should be specified correctly. This means that the behavioural model should be made first. A set of inputs, a set of outputs, and the mapping between the two constitutes the behaviour, and is equivalent to 'defining the system'. The block 'system model' in Figure 17.1 implies the functional design of the system.

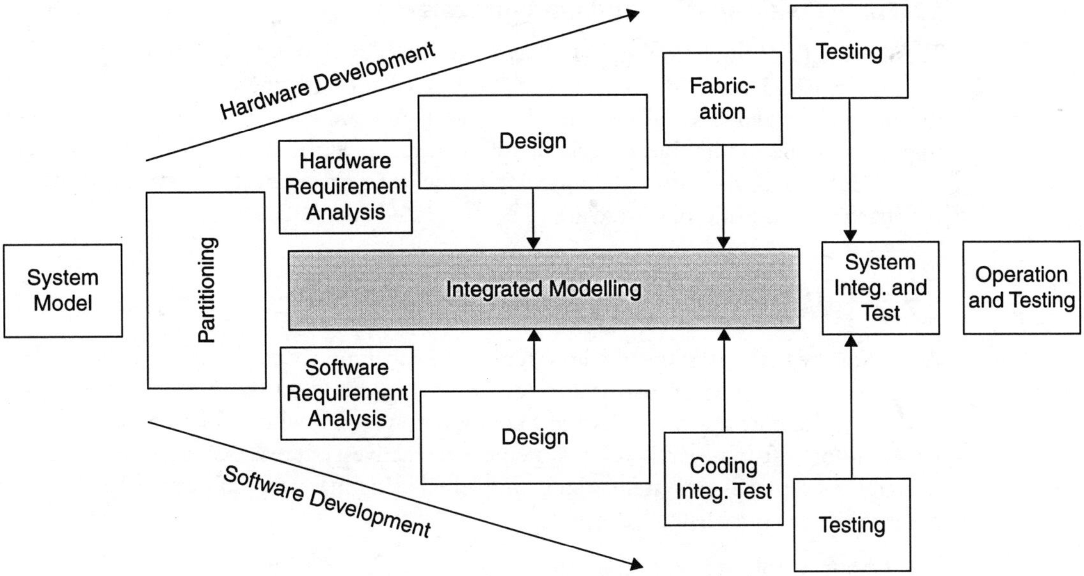

Figure 17.1 | Co-design illustrated with the steps in the development process

This will be an architecture independent description of the system functionality. This description is independent of HW and SW, and several system representations may be utilized.

17.1.1.2 | *Mapping/Partitioning*

The next step is to divide the functionality into two parts for the purpose of implementation, that is, into hardware and software. This is called partitioning. This is a very critical step because the decision on which parts are best implemented in hardware and which in software, makes an impact on factors like speed, power, performance, etc. of the product. Since we are talking about 'co-design', it is important to realize that this partitioning does not cause the design to diverge into two entirely separate and independent parts. In fact, there is continual interaction between the two partitions as illustrated by the block 'integrated modelling' of Figure 17.1.

Partitioning also means that the design is broken down into smaller units, each of which has a defined 'functionality'. The whole functional block is 'partitioned' into smaller blocks which are then realized. This idea applies to hardware as well as software.

The term 'mapping' also implies a similar idea. It is just that a particular function is mapped to, that is, assigned to be performed by a specific block.

17.1.1.3 | *Design of Hardware and Software*

As seen in Figure 17.1, hardware and software design proceeds in two separate directions. But there is continuous interaction between these two design teams, such that feedback, correction and re-design is done. Once the software and hardware designs are completed, the system is integrated and tested, and then put into operation.

17.1.2 | Co-simulation and Co-synthesis

These two terms 'simulation' and 'synthesis' have been used in Sections 16.3.3 and 16.3.4 with reference to ASIC design. Here, the prefix 'co' for both these activities mean that simulation and synthesis of both hardware and software should be done more or less together. Simulation implies the testing of functionality without the actual 'implementation'. Synthesis means the final 'realization' of the designed product. Co-synthesis means that both software and hardware are to be integrated and realized.

17.2 | Modelling of Systems

Any system, whether it is the whole system or the sub-units thereof, needs to be modelled.

A model is a conceptual notion for expressing the function of a system. Keep in mind that the unit that we talk of is a computational unit, which is finally realizable as hardware or software. Embedded systems are reactive systems, that is, systems which respond to events. Such systems can be modelled using many techniques, some of which fall into the category listed below:

i) Data/control diagrams
ii) Concurrent models
iii) Finite state machines

Now we will go into more details of these models.

17.2.1 | Data Flow Diagram

In such a model, it is the flow of data alone that is taken into consideration. Such a model is data driven. Take a look at Figure 17.2, which shows the flow of data in a communications system.

The points to note are:

i) Each box is a subsystem which is 'data driven'.
ii) A particular box obtains data as input from the previous block.
iii) Each functional block may need to wait till it gets processed data from the previous block.

Figure 17.2 is meant only to illustrate the concept of 'data flow' through these blocks.

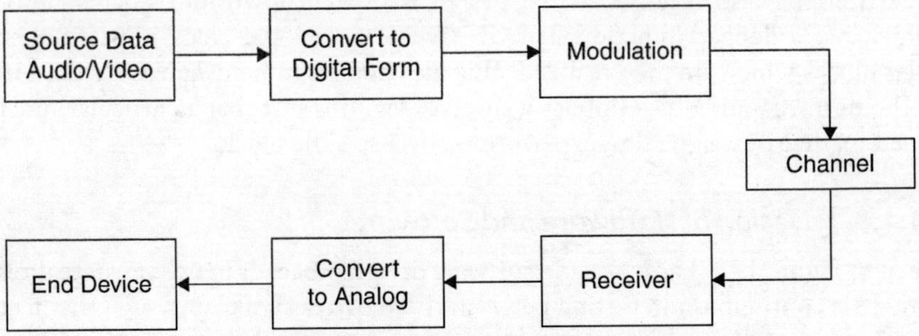

Figure 17.2 | Flow of data through a digital communications system

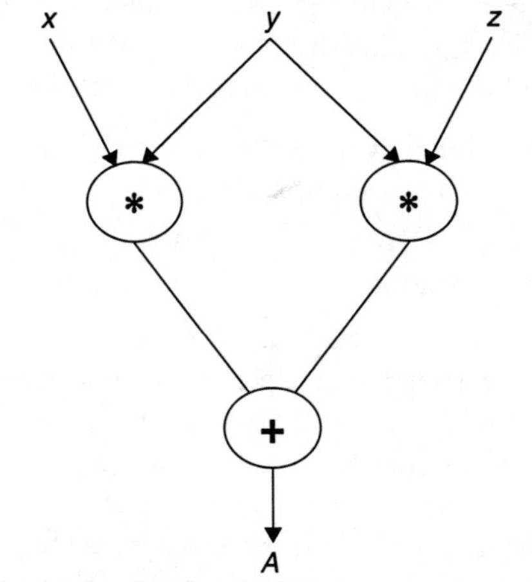

Figure 17. 3 | Data flow diagram for $A = xy + yz$

Now we see an actual 'data flow diagram' for a simple calculation A = xy + yz. Figure 17.3 is the corresponding data flow diagram.

17.2.1.1 | *Control/Data Flow Graph*

This is a data flow graph with 'control' added to it. Conditional processing activities fit into this type of graph. For example, consider this computation

$x <= a \times b;$
if ($x > 100$)
$y <= a - c;$
else
$y <= a + c;$

Figure 17.4 shows the data flow diagram for this.

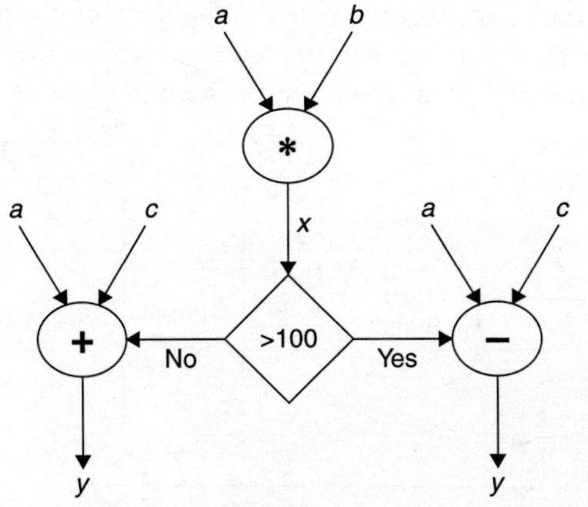

Figure 17.4 | A data flow graph with control

Now, what do we do with this kind of a system model? Do we realize these DFDs in hardware or software? The answer is that they can be realized in either ways and that would have been decided at the time of 'partitioning' in the first level.

Note How is such a graph different from a 'flow chart'? The answer is that a flowchart represents 'control flow' only, while a DFG shows 'data flow'.

17.2.2 | Concurrent Processes

Concurrent processes are units in which activities are scheduled to happen concurrently. Each activity may be referred to as a process with communication being possible between these processes. Whether the activities are performed 'actually' in parallel or it is 'pseudo parallelism' that occurs, depends on the system.

The idea of concurrency has been discussed in detail with respect to 'operating systems' in Chapter 7. If concurrency is to be thought of, for software, it is important to understand that software does not mean just 'code'. In reality, software for a system implements a system of concurrent processes. The tools for software design should ensure the correct implementation for inter-process communications with synchronization.

In hardware design also, the idea of concurrency appears. Since all parts of a circuit are to work in parallel, the design of hardware finally boils down to writing code with 'concurrent statements' or 'concurrent processes'. There is communication between these processes/statements and the hardware is finally realized from such concurrent code which leads to a hardware structure.

17.2.3 | Finite State Machines

This is a very commonly used system model suggested for the design of hardware and software. A state machine is a very simple concept, but as the system complexity grows, the model tends to become slightly unmanageable. The idea of a 'state machine' is that, on the occurrence of events, the 'state' of the machine changes. (A state can be thought of as a stored information possessed by the system, like for instance, the contents of a number of registers). Thus, most real-world problems can be represented by such machines with 'finite states' and hence the terminology 'Finite State Machines' (FSMs).

In Figure 17.5, the current state is taken as the 'state' of this sytem. When an event, i.e., an input x appears, it interacts with the current state in the 'next state logic' block, and a new state is generated. For very simple machines, the output is the state itself. Thus,

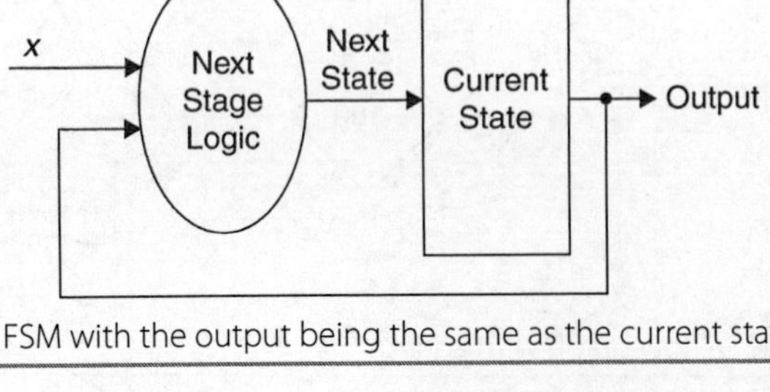

Figure 17.5 | An FSM with the output being the same as the current state

an FSM is defined by three quantities, i.e., 'input, output and state'. It is the change in input which functions as the required 'event'.

For biggers systems, theres is an 'output logic' block. For each change of state, the output changes,depending on the function represented by the 'output logic block'. This is shown in Figure 17.6.

A very commonly quoted example in embedded system design using FSMs is the seat belt control used in cars. See Figure 17.7. When the driver turns on the ignition, he is expected to fasten the seat belt within a certain time (Timer 1). If the seat belt is not fastened by then, an alarm is generated. This continues until the key is turned off or the seat belt is put on or the alarm time (Timer 2) expires.

Another popular example of the FSM is the design of a traffic light control. Figure 17.8 shows the FSM of such a sytem in which the three lights of red,green and yellow remain ON for times decided by Timers 1, 2 and 3. When the time for that state elapses, the next state is taken on, the ouput changes and this sequence continues. The output for each of the states is R,G and Y and they are '1', only for that state. This translates into saying that, once the green light is ON, it remains ON for a time decided by Timer 2. When Timer 2 expires, the green light goes OFF and the yellow light becomes ON, and the current state is YELLOW and so on.

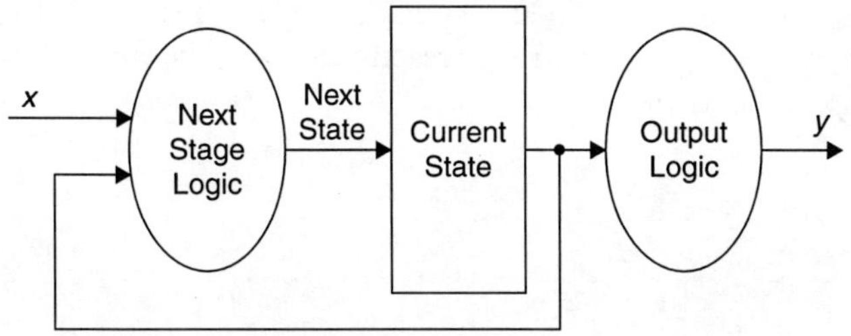

Figure 17.6 | An FSM with an output logic clock

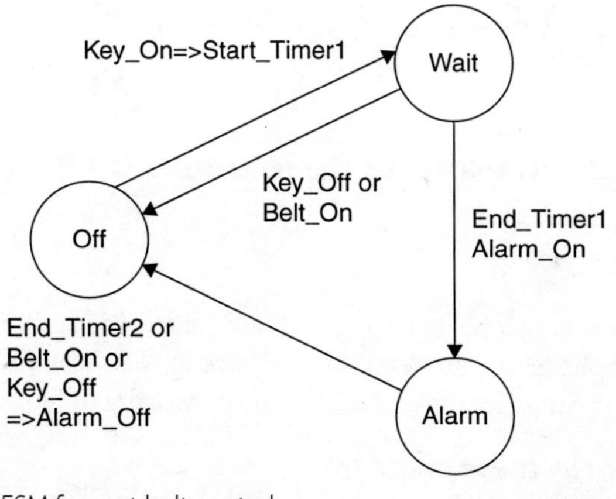

Figure 17.7 | An FSM for seat belt control

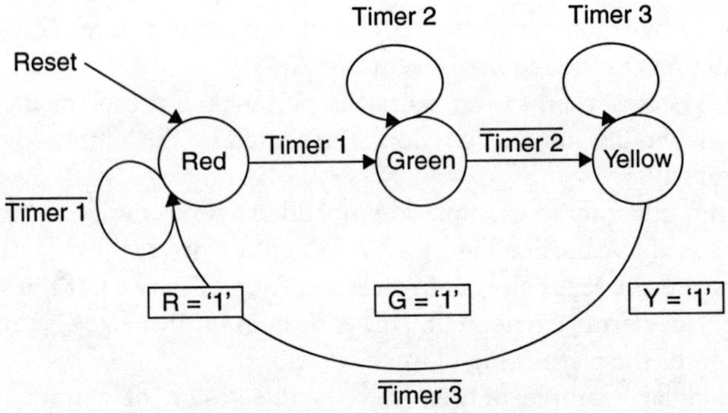

Figure 17.8 | An FSM for a traffic signalling system

The above two are very simple examples of modelling using FSMs. These systems can be designed very easily in software or in hardware by using the constructs of a hardware description language.

The advantages of FSMs for modelling are that they are simple to visualize, but the disadvantage is that as systems become complex, the large number of states become unmanageable.

In this section, what has been attempted is to give an exposure to three different types of models that can be used to design reactive systems like embedded systems. Three other modelling methods are

i) Petri nets
ii) Object-oriented systems
iii) Behaviour trees

Conclusion

We have just had a brief introduction to the concept of hardware software co-design as is applicable to embedded systems. We now move on to the next aspect of embedded system design, which is EDLC management, where EDLC stands for 'Embedded Product development Life-Cycle'.

17.3 | Embedded Product Development Lifecycle Management

What is EDLC?

This can be better explained by an example. Consider the idea of building a house. How does a person go about it? A number of phases have to be successfully surpassed in order to have a house built and then furnished, and made worthy of being lived in.

What do we mean by these phases?

Refer to Figure 17.9 to have an idea of the flow of these phases.

Figure 17.9 | The different phases involved in building a house

Figure 17.10 | The visualization of our dream house

Dreaming We start with a dream, and that dream builds up gradually. Consider that our dream house looks like the house in Figure 17.10. As we go on with our daily grind, we do our visualization of our dream house—we visualize its size, appearance, key features, innovative aspects and also the timeframe within which we want to complete it.

Planning This has two parts (i) Budget and (ii) Architectural design

i) **Budget:** Once we are sure that we want to build the house of our dreams, we move on to the next step . The first part is of course the affordability. We make an estimate of how much our dream house will cost us, and we also look for sources for the amount we need—bank loans, matured term deposits and any other possible sources.

ii) **Architectural design:** Next, we find the right people for it. First, an architect is sought to design the house. While the design is being done, we have frequent discussions with the architect, and the plan gets modified as the discussions proceed. The stage of planning is time-consuming, because we, in the role of the user will surely insist on the many features we need. The designer should be able to tell us whether they are feasible within the budget of money and time. In effect, the feasibility study is done in this stage.

Structural Work The first stage of implementing the design is to build the structure of the house which needs resources. The resources include the building materials and the workers to do the construction. Procuring materials and managing the construction works is a big hassle and we would like to be free of it. We then opt to have a supervisor who does the management of the construction project. Of course, we keep a tab on the way the manager handles the show. We also have frequent discussions with him, ask his opinion while insisting on getting our viewpoint. We also try to ensure that the time schedule is maintained (very difficult, in practice).

Inspections Inspections are a very important part of the house construction process, for it ensures that every element of the building is done correctly. This is done by someone who is an expert, who gives his comments and feedback which we try to incorporate.

Finishing Work Once the structural work is over, the finishing work is to taken up—this includes plastering, plumbing, electrification, carpentry, flooring and painting work. This is a phase in which a lot of decision-making is involved. The options for flooring tiles, plumbing items, wood work, etc. are so many, that we have to make decisions based on affordability and quality. This is a very critical phase of the house construction, and the appearance of the final product depends on the right decisions taken during this stage. This phase is also difficult with respect to time management. Things don't get going as per schedule, usually.

Interior Design Now, let's assume the house construction is over and the house is ready to be lived in. Well, not yet. To make a house truly liveable, interior design, furnishing and garden design are to be done. It is likely that in this phase, the supervisor does not have much of a role. It is the family members who makes decisions in consultation with an interior design and gardener.

Living Our family moves in, and it is after this that the real 'feedback' is obtained, about the decisions that had been made earlier. But sadly, nothing can be changed now and everyone has to adjust and 'live with' whatever flaws had crept in, at some stage of these seven phases of house building.

17.3.1 | Embedded Product Development

Assuming that you have read through the whole process of building a house, compare it to the phases of building an embedded product. The phases of development may not be similar, but the same mechanism of planning and development is at work here too. The example was presented to explain why the 'big bang model' of product development may not be the best model.

What is the big bang model?

It is the case when

i) The developer receives the list of requirements
ii) The developer works in isolation for some time
iii) The developer delivers the result to the customer
iv) The developer hopes the client is satisfied

But developing a sophisticated embedded product is not done by just one person. There are hardware and software developers, managers, aesthetic designers (to design the appearance and user interface), etc. And of course, the most important person is the customer who spells out the features and capabilities expected for the end product.

Why is EDLC management considered to be important?

The embedded systems industry is now very large and can compete well (not in volume, though) with the software industry. In the early phases of the 'embedded revolution', an embedded product was not really a 'big deal'. The product was usually small and did not involve high-end technology or a large set of people working together to build it. But all that has changed. Now, such products are developed by the major players in the market—they employ the best people and use the best technology available—both for hardware and software. You know the names of the big players in the market for a product such as the mobile phone. There are many high-end products as well as small, dedicated and very useful products also in the market.

While developing a product, well-established companies usually have a definite plan of action and a cycle of well-defined activities from the beginning to the end. How well this action plan and activities are done, does reflect on the final product. This is one reason why we get better products from better manufacturers. The reason is not only because they are likely to utilize better technology and have better designers—they also follow 'best practices' for product development.

There are benchmarks using which companies can be rated. Such benchmarks are used by software companies as well as embedded product development companies. Why some companies have better ratings and deliver better products is because they follow the best models for 'product development'. See Figure 17.11 which suggests some of the factors that must be taken into consideration and planned before a product is manufactured and launched into the market.

For the software industry, development models are clustered under the title SDLC. SDLC has been widely studied, documented and researched upon. Since the embedded industry is a related field, it is quite logical that similar models be used for product development here also. It may be worthwhile to realize that even small manufacturers can use these models to improve the quality of their products as well to ensure that delivery schedules are met. This helps to ensure that the product can hold on strongly against fierce competition.

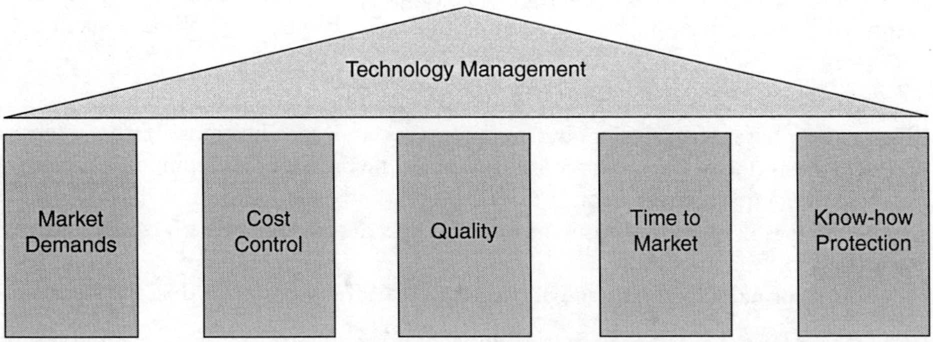

Figure 17.11 | Important factors in technology management

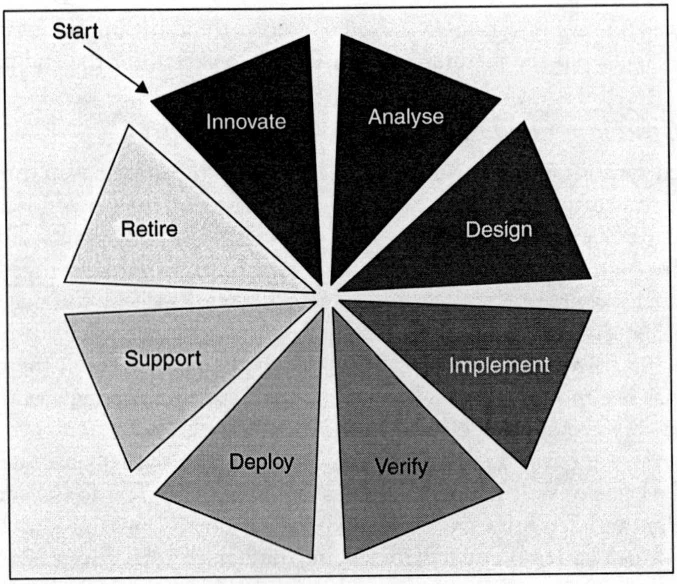

Figure 17.12 | Phases of EDLC

17.3.2 | Phases of the Design and Development of an Embedded Product

Now that the necessity and flow of EDLC has been elaborated, let's get into the act of formalizing a set of stages/phases in the lifetime of an embedded product. Figure 17.12 shows all the eight phases involved.

17.3.2.1 | *Innovate/Conceptualize*

This is the stage when the idea of a product takes shape. New and innovative ideas and concepts are sought, the market is studied, and various technological aspects are considered. This is the phase of 'dreaming', when a company wonders whether it can introduce an entirely new product or a 'me too' product. The latter terminology is used in the case when a product is already available in the market, but a company contemplates on the plan of introducing its own version of the product with minor changes and advancements. If the market and technology trends are favourable, the next phase is taken up.

17.3.2.2 | *Analyse the Requirements*

This is the phase of analyzing the requirements and specifications of the intended product, and is one of the most critical aspects of the product development lifecycle.

Requirements management is a well-established practice in industries. A set of requirements is finalized in consultation with a specific customer (if any) or by performing a 'user' study.

This is formally the first stage of the lifecycle of the product. In this, the steps are:

i) Make a formal and thorough feasibility study including the investment and returns expected.

ii) Make a list of requirements of the product including its specifications. The specifications should include the electrical and mechanical specifications. Other aspects like packaging, appearance and user interface should also be listed.
iii) Analyse the requirements and make sure they can be implemented practically.

17.3.2.3 | *Design the Intended Product*

In this phase, the steps are

i) Propose a prototype
ii) Partition the prototype design into hardware and software
iii) Do functional modelling for the hardware and software

17.3.2.4 | *Implement the Design*

The steps here are

i) Choose the hardware components
ii) Design the hardware
iii) Generate the code and test it
iv) Integrate the hardware and software and test it

17.3.2.5 | *Perform Verification*

The verification intended here is a 'system level verification'. The integrated system is verified against the 'requirements' made in phase (ii) to confirm that they match.

17.3.2.6 | *Formalize and Deploy*

In this phase, aspects like field trials, reliability and quality tests are conducted. After these are successfully completed, the product is 'deployed' in the market. If the product was built for a specific customer, it is supplied to the customer after training suitable number of personnel for using the product.

This stage is critical because making inroads into the market is the most important expectation regarding a product. Companies with proven track records have an easier time in this phase. Remember how the iPhone was awaited by eager customers, and so Apple did not have to do much of marketing for its product. Smaller and newer product manufacturers have a tougher time during this phase.

17.3.2.7 | *Sustain and Support*

Once the product is launched into the market, it is very important to collect feedback from users, provide support to understand the product better, and give solutions for bugs detected in this phase. A maintenance group should be in action all the time, along with a marketing team to improve the image of the product.

17.3.2.8 | *Retire*

This is an obvious stage for any product. No concept or product lasts forever. In today's dynamic world, rapid obsolescence of electronic products is the rule rather than the exception. This phase should be expected and the company should be ready to allow 'retirement' for the product, before it dies a natural death. But in either case, there is always the necessity and possibility of 'rebirth'. If the manufacturer is smart enough, he can foresee the end of the useful life of the product. He is then ready to give a rebirth to the product in a new, fresh and advanced form, with new ideas, concepts and features in place and ready to take on the challenges in the changed market.

We have now made a framework for EDLC, i.e., the mandatory phases/stages have been identified, understood and listed. Next, these phases will be correlated to the different 'lifecycle models' popularly used. These models are well-known and widely used in the software industry. Some of these models have been adopted by the embedded industry also. We will discuss only a few important and pertinent models, and the discussion will be brief and 'to the point'. Our attempt will be to fit the models to the framework developed in Section.17.3.2.

Note In these models, we use only the six phases from 2 to 7 of Section 17.3.2.

17.4 | Lifecycle Models

17.4.1 | The Waterfall Model

This is the classical lifecycle model. The waterfall lifecycle approach is based on the serialization of development phases. One phase 'flows' into the next, and thus the name.

Figure 17.13 shows the Phases 2 to 6 of Section 17.3.2 depicted in order. The waterfall lifecycle model has the advantage of easy scheduling and is direct and easy to understand.

De-merits

i) All requirements must be known before hand, as there is no phase which goes back and makes a correction.

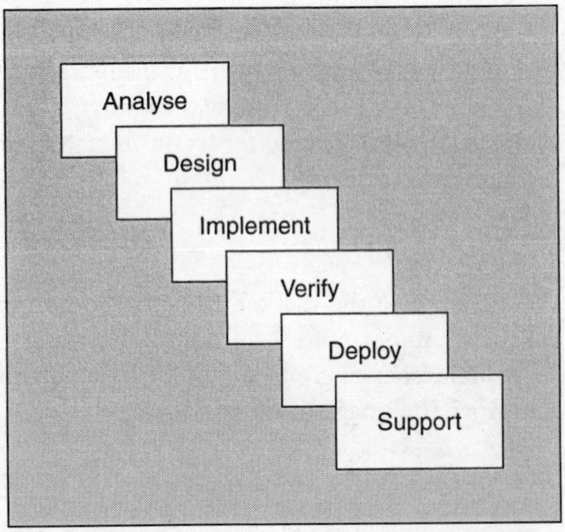

Figure 17.13 | The waterfall model

ii) There is no opportunity for a customer to preview and correct the system. He gets the product at the end of all the phases, and this may be too late to incorporate any changes.

17.4.1.1 | *Waterfall Model with Backflow*

There is a waterfall model with backflow, in which each phase has a backflow. In this, as is seen Figure 17.14, corrections to the immediate previous stage is possible based on the feedback at the end of each phase. In the figure, only the most important stages of design, implementation and testing have been shown.

17.4.2 | The V Model

In this model, each phase has corresponding test or *V*alidation counterpart.This simply means that tests are conducted at each phase before proceeding to the next.

Advantages

i) It emphasizes planning for verification and validation of the product in the early stages of development.
ii) The deliverable at each stage is a tested one.
iii) Once each phase is tested and verified, it is marked as a milestone in the development process.

Disadvantages

i) It does not easily handle dynamic changes in requirements
ii) It does not contain risk analysis activities

17.4.3 | The Iterative Model

Such a model can be thought of as a waterfall model which executes many times, and that each iterative 'turn of the wheel' results in a prototype. Such incomplete models are subject to testing and analysis and then a re-design. Thus the design 'evolves' iteratively. This is a useful notion because it takes note of 'reality' in which each phase is not perfect the first time through.

Such a model is flexible and 'risk' management is automatically taken care of.

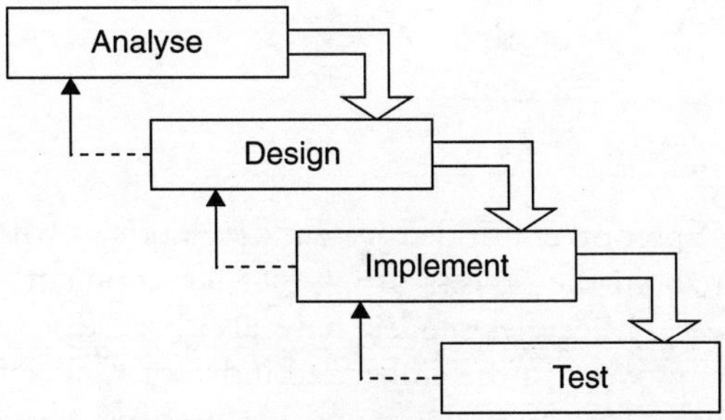

Figure 17.14 | The waterfall model with backflow

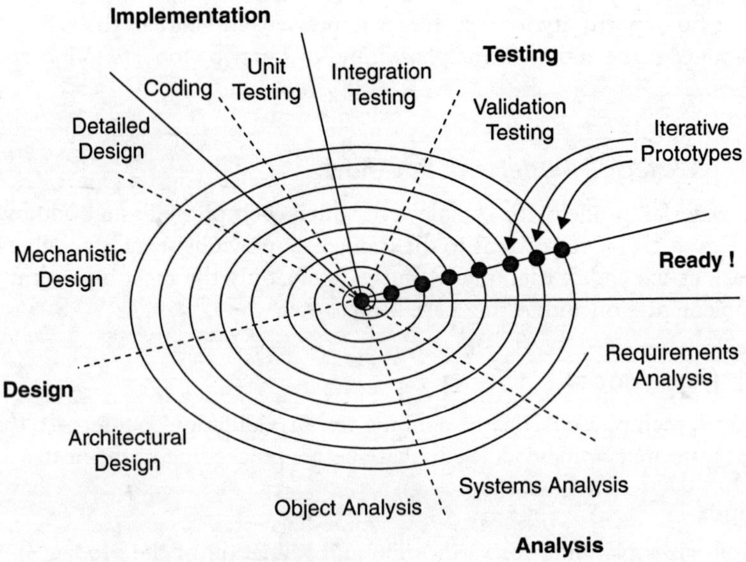

Figure 17.15 | The spiral lifecycle model

What is 'risk' in this context?

The point is that the scope and difficulty of the task at hand is not well-understood at the point at which the venture is taken up. The reasons are that

i) The customer is not clear about what he want and keeps changing his requirements as the project progresses.
ii) New trends and technology appears, and there is the need to incorporate these also, in the product.
iii) Designers and developers may be inexperienced in this domain.

It is obvious that the iterative model covers and manages these factors very well, and thus risk management is ensured.

Barry Boheim published his work on iterative lifecycles which he referred to as the 'spiral lifecycle' as in Figure 17.15. The dots in each 'round' show the prototype developed, after that round of activity. Then, the wheel is turned, and it goes through the cycle again, and a next and better prototype is developed. This continues until the final product is declared to be 'READY'.

Conclusion

We conclude this chapter on embedded system development with this. This was meant just to give an idea about the process of product development, which is a mixture of hardware and software. Lifecycles models have also been discussed to aid the understanding of how things work in the embedded industry. Only a few models have been touched upon because, doing an in depth and comprehensive study on all the available models does not seem worthwhile in the academic field, though having a general idea of such an aspect is advantageous.

KEY POINTS OF THIS CHAPTER

- In the current scenario, it is important that hardware and software be designed in unison, and this is called co-design.
- Once functionality is partitioned as hardware and software, they are designed separately, but there is continuous interaction between the two teams.
- Some of the models for expressing system functionality are data flow diagrams, finite state machines, concurrent processes, petri nets, etc.
- EDLC is similar to SDLC which is used in the software industry.
- There are eight phases for EDLC, and all these phases are to be managed well.
- Some of the popular models for lifecycle management are the waterfall model, V model, spiral model, etc.

QUESTIONS

1. What is the meaning of the terms 'co-design', 'co-simulation' and 'co-synthesis'?
2. Explain what is meant by design partitioning/mapping.
3. How are data flow diagrams different from flowcharts? Use an example to explain.
4. Why are FSMs popular in embedded system design?
5. What is the relevance of 'lifecycle management' for any product?
6. With reference to Figure 17.11, explain what the following terms mean for product development.
   i) Know–how protection
   ii) Time to market
7. Why does a product have a retirement phase? What does rebirth mean in this context?
8. What are the flaws of the simple waterfall model?
9. How does 'risk' come in here?
10. Why is the iterative model an improvement over older models?

EXERCISES

1. Make a thorough study of other models used in the software industry for lifecycle management.
2. Find out the meaning of the words 'Agile model' and 'extreme programming'.
3. Is the Agile model suitable for use in the embedded industry?

18 EMBEDDED DESIGN: A SYSTEMS PERSPECTIVE

In this chapter, you will learn

- The concept of 'need' for a product
- The importance of awareness about the user of a product
- The feasibility of user requirements
- The importance of mechanical and interface design of a product
- The concept of 'ergonomics' and its importance in product design
- The steps of hardware design including PCB design
- The concept of 'Design For Manufacturability'
- The concept of 'Design For Testability'
- The important steps involved in product testing

Introduction

'**Systems perspective**' refers to the thinking that the 'relationship' between the parts of a system is more important than the parts by themselves. Thus comes the relevance of the statement that '*the whole is more than just the sum of the individual parts*'. The systems perspective focuses on the difference between a disconnected set of parts versus a collection of parts that work together to create a functional whole. A number of components interact with each other to form a complete system and when the state of one component changes, it has an effect on the others. In this chapter, we look at embedded design with this point of view.

Some typical examples of embedded system, as mentioned in Chapter 1, are the washing machine, air conditioner, microwave oven, digital camera, etc. Components used for embedded design like micro-controllers, memory, etc., which we have been continually talking about all through this book, are not at all visible to the user in any of these applications. Then the question arises as to how we can we say that the above-mentioned appliances are examples of embedded systems. The other side of the question is, how do we say that these components are the parts of those systems. Obviously, the user is unaware (and probably unconcerned, too) of anything but the 'working' of the appliance he has purchased, its functionality, its capabilities and also its aesthetic appearance. Figure 18.1 shows a set of appliances in the list of embedded products.

Chapter-opening image: 'Insect' robotic platform (Courtesy: Nex Robotics, Mumbai).

Author of the chapter: Raghu C. V., Assistant Professor, Department of Electronics and Communications, NIT, Calicut.

Figure 18.1 | Embedded products—mobile phone, camera, toy robot, laser printer (Courtesy: www.clipart.com)

Thus comes the philosophy of looking at the 'system as a whole' from the top. A very essential quality for any system designer is to be able to visualize the system from this perspective. It is to be clearly understood that all the parts work together to make the complete system. It is similar to saying that the heart, brain, liver and a lot of other parts make the complete human body. Even though they are parts of human body, individually they cannot perform much. Each of these parts has its own specified functionality and when working in unison, they contribute to make a 'whole' human being.

Similarly, all the parts of an embedded system, which have been explained in previous chapters, have their own specific functionalities; but they should work together to make the complete system. This process of arranging the individual parts (each with well-defined individual functionalities), such that a particular application is 'realized', is the process of 'system design'.

18.1 | A Typical Example

Now let's see how the functionality of a household appliance like a washing machine (Figure 18.2) is realized. The function of a washing machine is to wash clothes and then squeeze the water out of it. Looking from the top, from a systems perspective, we do not observe any 'electronics' coming into the picture. But we know for sure that some electrical/electronics and mechanical components are mandatorily used. This obviously means that the 'non-electronic' functions are implemented electronically.

How is this done?

The mechanism of washing clothes is this: Clothes, along with water and detergent, are put in the tumbler (washing tub) and vigorously shaken to wash out the dirt from them, The same action, with just clothes and water, is equivalent to 'rinsing'. Now for 'drying', the water particles in the clothes can be squeezed out by centrifugal force. So we need to have the clothes to be rotated or 'spinned', (as it is referred to). Figure 18.3 shows a washing machine in which the wash cycle is started by putting clothes in it.

Figure 18.2 | A typical fully automated washing machine

Figure 18.3 | Starting the 'wash cycle' by putting clothes into the wash tub (Courtesy:www.clipart.com)

Clearly, washing and drying are simply translated to the action of rotating a motor which is a function that can be performed by an electronic (aka electrical) component, i.e., the motor. Adding more features, like controlling water flow, controlling the time of the wash or rinse cycle, controlling the speed of rotation, etc., can be simply done by proper electronic control of the motor control unit. Thus, all the activities involved in 'washing clothes' are simply and easily controlled by such an electronic control unit.

There is of course, a mechanical system also involved. The motor action causes the 'wash tub' and spin tub to be in motion. Thus, we see that the design of the washing machine involves electronic control, electrical actuation (by motors), mechanical motion, and containers (tubs) into which clothes, water and soap can be deposited.

We have used the example of a washing machine to describe the idea of how a product like a washing machine becomes an 'embedded system'. A similar thinking can be applied to other products as well.

18.2 | Product Design

Here we lay out a step-by-step procedure for designing an embedded product.

18.2.1 | The Concept of 'Need'

Now the question before us, is how we go about the arrangement of component parts to realize a product. It cannot be done in a haywire fashion—obviously, it has to be a well-defined process. We will start with the philosophical question of 'necessity'. As is said, 'necessity is the mother of invention', and so all design should start from a 'need'/'necessity'.

From where does 'need' originate?

It can be from different sources.

- A new company is likely to want to develop a product which will give them a good launching point. This company will first make a proper study to identify the kind of product which is likely to give them a good start. A good market survey should be done before deciding on the product.
- Another situation of need is that an existing company wants to expand its area of business. They also should do a good market survey to identify the new area for expansion. It may also be another way. A company gets to know about a business opportunity in some product area and decides to develop the product which fills that gap.
- Another case is of a personal need. An individual may want a product for his personal need. For example, a person who has a habit of listening to music just before sleeping may need an automatic control mechanism for his music system. He wants the audio player to switch off just as soon as he drops off to sleep. He can ask a designer to develop a product exactly satisfying his requirements.
- This idea may be expanded to the case of companies, as well. A company may approach another company to design a product for them—for reasons like cost benefit, lack of man power, lack of technology, etc. Of course, the first company must have identified the need before. But as far as the designer company is concerned, the 'need' comes from the requirement of the 'customer' company.
- Yet another reason for starting a new design is to modify an already existing product. It may be to correct some inadequacies, to add new features, to reduce cost, to improve the performance (reduce power, improve speed of operation, etc.), etc.

- A company might decide to come up with a new product even with a reason that its competitor company has come up with a similar product. The first company is already in the market, selling its product. The second company comes up with some extra features— now the first company is forced to add these features in their product also in order to sustain its market. These are situations that continually occur in the highly competitive product market
- Other cases are when people design products as a hobby. Students may do a product design (project) as their academic need, others design products in order to participate in some competitions and so on.

To sum up, we say that a product design will start only with a 'reason' behind it.

18.2.2 | Requirements

Once we have the reason to start a product design, what else we need to start the design? The 'requirements' of the intended design is the next item. For example, for designing a washing machine, we need at least the following information:

- The quantity of clothes that the machine can wash at a time
- The voltage from which it is supposed to work
- Is it to be fully automatic or semi-automatic?

Listing together such information is called the 'requirements' of the intended product.

18.2.3 | User's Perspective

From where do these requirements come from?

Many a time, when we do academic projects, it is the usual practice that 'we, the product designer', decide the features of the product that we plan to design. But for a commercial product design point of view, this approach is not right. A product is for the use of a customer (the user) and it is 'his' satisfaction that makes the product successful. Only he knows what he wants. So the basic features of any product are the 'requirements' of the user of that product. So, identification of the probable user of the product and a good interaction with him are essential steps that need to be followed at the starting of any design. Figure 18.4 implies that the set of users (for a particular product) may be a large group of people with different tastes and preferences.

As discussed at the beginning of this chapter, there is a lot of variety in the types of users. So the 'requirement list' that the designer initially gets as a result of a 'user study' will also have a lot of diversity. For example, the common man, is unlikely to be aware of technical aspects of a product, however, simple they may be. For instance, asking such a user about the 'working voltage' of a product does not help, because he is totally unconcerned about that factor. He will be happy as long as the product works at all times of the day, when there is 'line supply'. So it is the designer's duty and responsibility to clearly understand the 'actual requirements' that the user might be looking for.

For example, the user simply wants to get all his clothes washed every day. He may not be concerned about 'how many kilograms of clothes' that he might put to wash. It is the designer's duty to understand whether it is 2Kg, 5Kg, or 10Kg. Getting the right

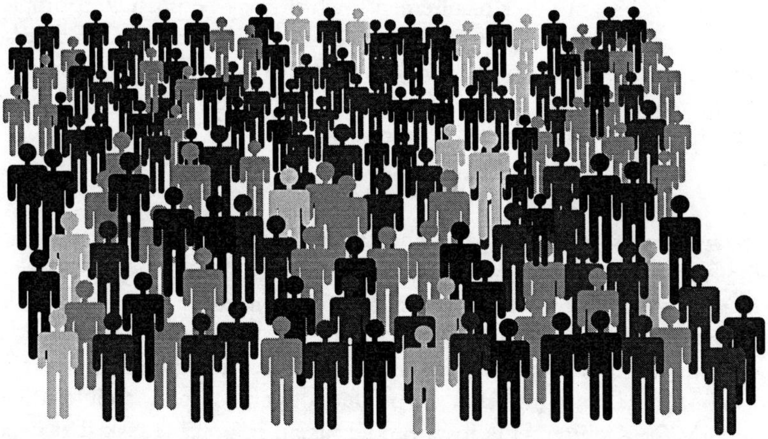

FIGURE 18.4 | A large set of users with diverse requirements

information is possible only with proper interaction with the user. But if the customer is another company, then it is possible that more clear requirements are obtained.

18.2.4 | User Research

Asking questions, collecting filled up questionnaires etc., from prospective users constitute what is called 'user study', and companies perform such studies before venturing to design a new product.

Many a time, a user might want a lot of things without having a holistic view of what he/she really needs. This is not an underestimation of the user in any way. It only means that the research team's interaction with the user should lead to the user becoming clearer about his needs. To understand this, a very strong foundation of user research is required while designing anything. The focus is on seeking out the real users, knowing them and finally understanding their needs.

Many forms of research methodologies like contextual enquiry, ethnographic research, focus groups, quantitative research, etc. are used as part of this exercise. The list is long, but the basic fact is that everything depends on the kind of product and what it demands is to clearly understand the users' needs, analyse them and interpret them into functional requirements as a starting point to begin work on the product design.

18.2.5 | Feasibility Study

It is not that all the requirements of the user can be satisfied in a product. Examine the following situations.

- Users can ask for a week-long battery backup for a mobile phone. (They may be happier if there is no need to re-charge it at all!)
- A user says he wants a touch screen on a mobile phone whose targeted cost is just one thousand rupees!

These are two different cases. The first one may not be technically possible; the second one may be possible, but with a higher budget.

Then, there are certain other requirements, which may be possible to implement if more time is available for delivery. It is again the designer's (or the associated persons, i.e., marketing/management team in a company) duty to convince the user about these aspects.

Finally, the requirements emerge as a compromise between the user and the designer keeping feasibility and cost to be well balanced.

18.2.5.1 | *Special Requirements*

So far, we have been talking only about general requirements of a specific product, which would come from the user. But there are some other requirements which are decided by the type of the product. For example, a product in the bio-medical area should satisfy certain safety standards, a mobile phone may have to satisfy some other standards like restriction on the radiation levels, a car should have restricted emission/certain safety levels and so on. These are things that the product design company should be aware of.

Thus, fixing the requirements for a product is an important task that needs to be done very carefully. Awareness about the market and end users, proper interaction with them, experience, technical knowledge, and above all, common sense are all required to finalize a list of requirements/features of the product to be designed.

18.2.6 | Specifications

Once we have the clear requirements, we are ready to start the technical work associated with the product design. The first step in this is to convert the requirements to what is known as 'technical specifications'. Look at it this way. The user research has given us the requirements in the 'language' of the user, which is not technical. For example, the user might have said that his requirement is a washing machine to wash 7Kg of clothes; a cell phone user requires a battery backup of two days.

The above requirements have to be converted to the technical language pertaining to the product. The requirement of washing '5 Kg clothes' for the washing machine may be converted to a washing tumbler size of diameter X and height Y of a material of type M. The 'battery backup time' may be converted to the 'ampere hour' of the battery and power dissipation of the total circuit. Converting the user's requirements to this form amounts to making the 'technical specification' of the product.

But still we are not in a position to start the design. As we know, a product consists of different parts. A hardware circuit as the heart of the product and software to control/monitor its activities are not all that 'design' entails. The mechanical parts associated with the products have also to be designed. Even if there are no parts like motors, actuators, etc. associated with it, the external casing is an unavoidable part in any product. A good amount of time and effort are to be expended for deciding these specifications also.

Now, once the technical specifications have been finalized, we have to decide the optimum way to achieve them. The next decision to be taken is—which parts can be implemented in hardware, which parts in software (Refer Section 17.1). For example, we may be able to control the speed of rotation of the tumbler in a washing machine using a gear mechanism. It may also be possible by controlling the speed of the motor directly using hardware/software. So at this point of time, we have to split (map) the complete technical specification to hardware specifications, software specifications and mechanical specifications. The process of mapping the 'requirements' to 'specifications' may be represented as in Figure 18. 5.

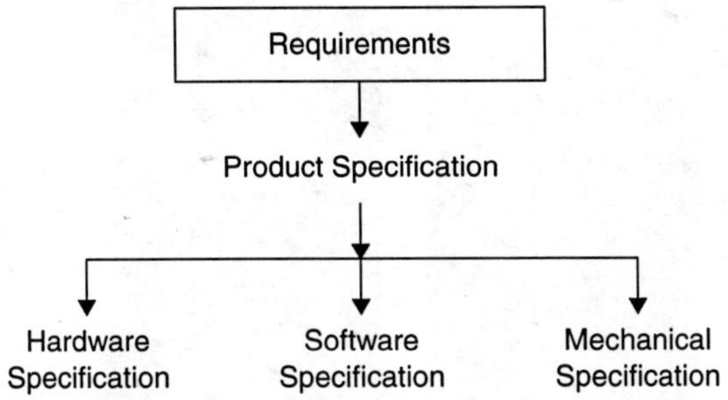

Figure 18.5 | Converting the 'requirements' to 'technical specifications'

18.3 | The Design Process

Once the specifications are clear, the design process can be started. As shown in Figure 18.5, the technical specification is split into three parallel paths—hardware specification, software specification and mechanical specification. So without further clarification, it is can be understood that the design process also proceeds through three different paths. But, are they three independent paths as shown in the figure? Can we proceed with them independently? The answer is an obvious NO. As discussed in the 'Introduction', the design itself is 'arranging different parts in such a way that they work together as a whole to perform a specified task'. So the design process also cannot be independent. There needs to be mutual understanding between these three paths in order to have a good system (Section. 17.1).

18.3.1 | The Starting Point

At this point, it would be interesting to ask the following questions to a group of prospective buyers:

- How many of you bought your washing machine after finding out which processor is being used in it?
- How many of you bought your microwave oven after checking the amount of memory used in it?

We can be sure with a reasonable amount of confidence, that the answers to these questions would be near to zero (there may be exceptions though).

So then, what are the aspects of a product that attract the user (at least in the initial stages)? It is basically the 'look', that is, the appearance of the product and special features associated with it that attracts customers. These features do not include parameters like processor speed, RAM capacity, software algorithms used, etc. Though the special features are actually the result of using better processors, a large RAM, superior algorithms, etc., the customer is not really aware of such things. What this points to is that, the difference between the features that a user will look for and the detailed technical parameters should be properly understood.

There are different types of products. Let us first take an example of a product which needs good aesthetic appeal and convenience in handling, that is, the user is

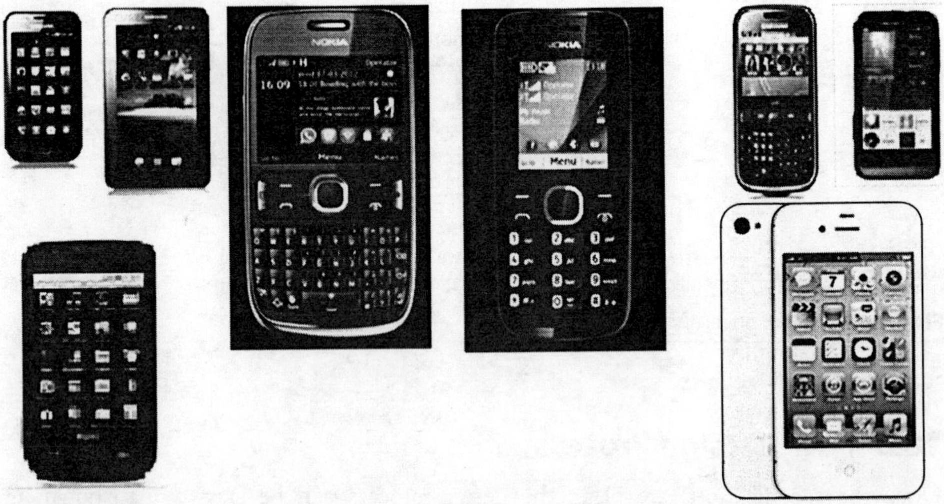

Figure 18.6 | A galaxy of mobile phones to choose from (Courtesy: www.google.com)

very much concerned about the appearance and 'interface'. A mobile phone is a good example in this group where a sleek appearance creates the first impression, the list of new and advanced features is the second point and finally the interface, that is, the convenience with each feature is accessible follows it. See Figure 18.6 which illustrates a sample of the galaxy of phones available for a prospective buyer.

The other extreme is the class of products for critical applications, like those used for space application, where the physical appearance is not important. Rather, the functionality, reliability, ruggedness, etc. are the important parameters. These products would be designed for proper physical size, structure, fault-free performance, etc. Similarly bio-medical products like pacemakers and ECG machines should be designed for the smallest size possible. They should also be designed for proper user safety, ruggedness, low power, accuracy, etc.

From the above discussions, it is clear that mechanical and aesthetic features (physical look, size, structure, strength, etc.) are very important in any class of products. So it would turn out to be a better choice to start the design with the mechanical/aesthetic design. (Ultimately, this is how the final product will look like!) Now let us look into another important aspect of the 'usability' of a product.

18.3.2 | Ergonomic Design

The term 'ergonomics' is one that engineers are unlikely to be familiar with. But when a product is to be designed, especially if it is a new design, the product designer should ensure that 'ergonomic principles' have been 'looked into and adhered to', in the overall design.

What is ergonomics?

The word 'ergonomics' comes from two Greek words:

i) ERGO: meaning work
ii) NOMOS: meaning laws

It is defined and elaborated in this way:

'Ergonomics is a branch of science drawn from physiology, engineering and psychology studies. Ergonomics is a science focused on the study of human fit, and seeks to reduce the fatigue and discomfort that might result from the use of a product. It seeks to harmonize the functionality of tasks with the human requirements of those performing them'.

Ergonomic design focuses on the compatibility of 'objects and environments' with the 'people' using them. The principles of ergonomic design can be applied to objects used in daily life and in the workspace. **At work, school or at home, when products fit the user, the result can be more comfort, higher productivity and less stress.**

Ergonomics should be an integral part of design, manufacturing and use. Mass production of products does not take into account that humans come in various shapes and sizes. When a chair is designed, its shape and size should be such that it is comfortable for the expected class of users. Desks and chairs for school kids should obviously be designed differently from furniture for use in plush offices.

Good ergonomic design may be difficult (but not impossible) when mass production of the product is done. In that case, anthropometric measurements should be a guide for design.

18.3.2.1 | *Anthropometric Measurements*

Anthropometry is the science that measures the range of body sizes in a population. When designing products, it is important to remember that people come in many sizes and shapes. Anthropometric data varies considerably between regional populations. For example, North European populations tend to be taller, while Indian and Chinese populations tend to be shorter.

How does all this affect product design?

For instance, a washing machine designed for the Indian user might have a different 'height' from one designed for a North European user.

With anthropometric data available, any item meant for 'mass production' may be designed better. While designing a mobile phone, its size, position of its keys/buttons, etc., are decided after considering the size of a human palm. Note that this 'size' varies with gender and the race of the population. The design of a computer mouse also has ergonomics playing an important role in it. It needs to take into account the size of the human hand, the movements that a mouse does and how those movements cause 'fatigue' in the user, etc. See Figure 18.7 which shows three headphones. The design of headphones needs very detailed anthropometric data, obviously.

Ergonomic design is easier if a product is designed for a restricted class of users. Headphones for kids and headphones for adults need to have different measurements. A mobile phone for senior citizens might need a different set of features as compared with those that a younger group of people want. So why not have different designs for the two classes?

18.3.2.2 | *Examples of Ergonomic Designs*

As a general case, all designs should be good ergonomic ones. Ergonomics entails matching the design of physical devices to the needs and characteristics of the human body.

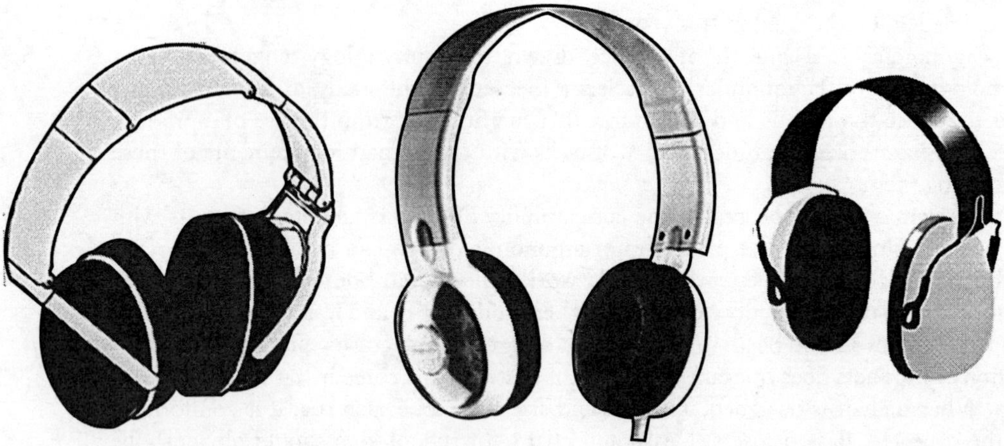

Figure 18.7 |Picture of headphones illustrating the need for anthropometric data for their design

One of the most frequently and widely used devices in modern life is the telephone (landline and mobile). Business professionals are forced to spend gruelling hours talking on the phone. A good ergonomic design of a telephone receiver definitely helps to reduce fatigue.

Take a look at Figure 18.8 which shows a good ergonomic design for a telephone handset which can be held across the saddle, with the handset matching the curves of the hand. Using such a receiver while talking for long hours is likely to reduce fatigue, compared to the case of having to use a badly designed handset.

Observe Figure 18.9, this is a mobile 'concept phone' fashioned by designer Heiki Juvonen for Nokia. It supports a bulky lower half, with all the bulk at the lower half and

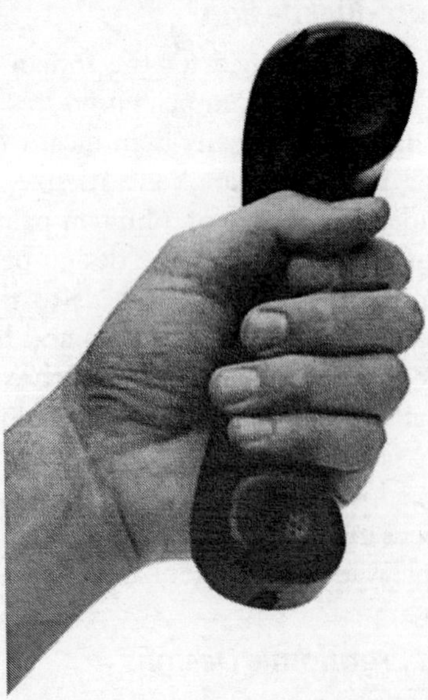

Figure 18.8 | An ergonomically designed telephone handset

Figure 18.9 | A 'concept phone' designed for just one aspect alone (Courtesy: http://www.symbian-freak.com/news).

a sleek thin display at the top. This design claims to be ergonomically pleasing to hold, though obviously not comfortable while carrying in a pocket.

Ergonomics is becoming increasingly important in the design and use of computer peripherals. Consider the use of a keyboard, at which many people spend most of their working time. Most conventional keyboards cause painful and even permanent injuries to the spine, fingers, and neck and wrist joints. Now there are keyboards available which aim to get the hands and wrists in the right position. There are many manufacturers (including Microsoft) who offer 'ergonomic keyboards' (at a higher price, though). See Figure 18.10.

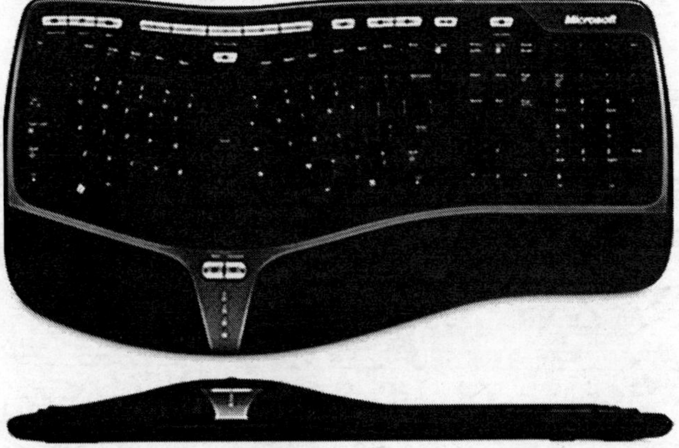

Figure 18.10 | Photograph of a natural ergonomic keyboard developed by Microsoft (Courtesy: http://www.microsoft.com/hardware).

18.3.3 | Mechanical and Interface Design

Now, coming back to the steps in product design, we can say that it is the mechanical and interface design which decides the overall arrangement of all the parts in a product. It decides how the product should look like and how it would interact with the user.

The mechanical design provides answers to questions of what should be its size, how much it should weigh, what materials are to be used, etc. The actual mechanical design steps and theory of mechanical design are out of scope of this book. We only try to look at the mechanical design from an electronics engineer's point of view.

18.3.3.1 | *Interface Design*

Interface design is very important and it is meant to enhance 'usability' of the product. To understand this point, think about the 'usability' of the cell phone. We would all like to have phones in which we can navigate **easily** to get the service we want. We want the keypad/touch screen to look sleek, the fonts used in the menu to be pleasing and clear, having matching background and foreground colours and so on. All these are taken care of by the 'interface designer'. Figure 18.11 shows a user navigating the menu using the keys of a mobile phone.

The interface design of a system decides the overall arrangement of the components, especially the components which interact with the user in the system. For example, the position of connectors, switches, display, cables, etc. are decided by the interface designer. This is the input for the electronics engineer for the placement of these and related components on the PCB.

18.3.3.2 | *Mechanical Design*

The total size of the product is the result of the mechanical design. This creates restrictions to the electronic engineer such as the size of the PCB (Printed Circuit Board), and the size of the components that can be used in this product design. This may make his life tough. For example, since the size and shape of the PCB is decided by the mechanical design, all electronic components used in the design have to be put together on this PCB, and this might lead to the necessity of minimizing the number of components,

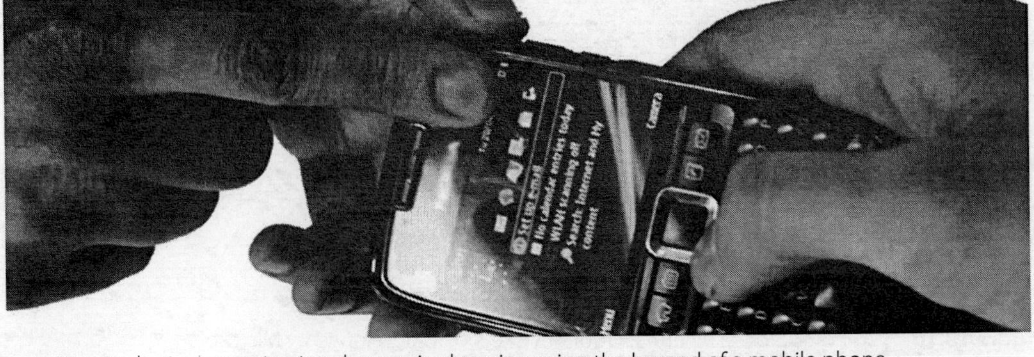

Figure 18.11 | A user navigating the required service, using the keypad of a mobile phone

causing restrictions on component package selection, connector size selection, routing restrictions and so on.

Mechanical design imposes restrictions on the length, width and height of the system. Component height, stacking of PCBs, screw height, distance between different parts (case and PCB, two PCBs, etc.), size of connectors used, etc. all have to be finalized within these dimensional restrictions.

The mechanical design should also take care of the thermal behaviour of the system. For that, the positioning of holes for the flow of heat to the outside world, placement and size of the fans (if required), size and alignment of heat sinks (again, if required), etc. have to be given due importance. These matters decide the placement of at least the major components of the system. Also components like heat sinks and fans demand more size, height and weight for the system.

The product may have to satisfy EMI/EMC (ElectroMagnetic Interference/ ElectroMagnetic Compatibility) standards and other safety standards. The number of holes, size of the holes, materials, etc. affect this.

Mechanical design also decides the strength of the product, the final product assembly time (e.g., imagine the time to assemble a system with more than 10–12 screws), etc. It also decides the accessibility of repairable parts. For example, a battery-operated system should have a provision for easy access to the cells for easy replacement, etc.

A class of products where more stringent mechanical requirements would appear are bio-medical products like pacemakers, underwater products, etc. In these, the mechanical design should provide proper sealing of the entire product.

In short, the mechanical and interface design provides the base of the product design and the entire system is built on this framework.

18.3.4 | Software Design

Design principles, the entire design cycle, design techniques, etc. of software design have been covered to a certain extent in Chapter 17. From an electronic designer's point of view, the software is used to control the entire system. The software performance of a system is decided by the computational capability of the processor, memory capacity, etc. So, to a certain extent, software design influences the selection of the processor, memory, clock speed, etc. It also influences the decision on the kind of buses to be used.

18.3.5 | Hardware Design

Hardware design is the main job of the electronics engineer. The starting point of hardware design is the hardware specifications. This specification would simply be a translation of the requirements to be satisfied by the system. For example, consider a 'specification' saying that the device should operate from a 9V re-chargeable battery and that once charged, the device should operate at least for 8–10 hrs without another charging operation. Another example is that the motor should be able to rotate a tumbler of a specific weight with a specific speed. The speed should be variable, etc. These are all typical examples of specifications.

The very first job is to understand the specifications clearly and to make a high level design from it. High level design implies dividing the design into sub-parts, that is,

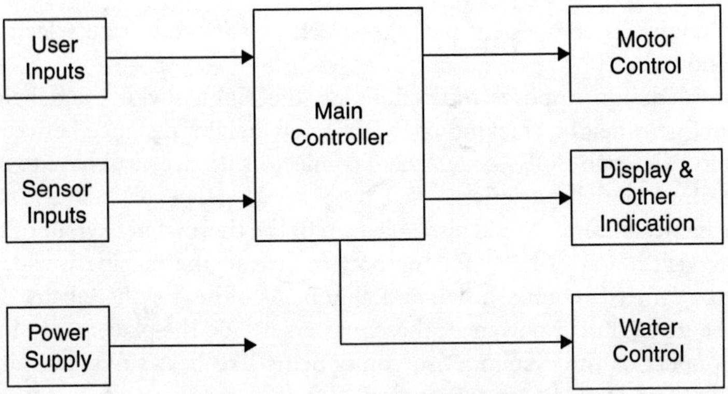

Figure 18.12 | High level block diagram of a washing machine

functional mapping (Section 17.1) For example, a washing machine design may be divided into sub-parts as listed below.

- The major controller section
- The motor control section
- The user inputs and outputs
- The sensor inputs
- The valve control section
- The power section

A probable high level block diagram of a washing machine would be as shown in Figure 18.12.

The next step is to go to the detailed hardware design. In this process, all the high level blocks are further sub-divided. The electronic components to be used are identified in this step. Here the term 'hardware design' is used to represent the task of dealing with the 'real electronic parts'. It is here that the electronic design in paper form is converted to a physical form. The designer needs to identify the electronic components which would carry out each and every functionality.

18.3.5.1 | *Component Selection*

Now the electronic components to be used in the product are selected. The first and foremost criteria are the functionality of each individual component. Each component should be able to perform the required functionalities under the conditions specified. After browsing through various references and data sheets, the complete list of components is converged to.

The designer has to make a selection matrix for each and every component to be used. The design matrix may include comparison criteria like:

- Basic functionalities
- Additional features
- Cost
- Voltage and current
- Special clocks and other signals

- Size and weight
- Power
- Technologies used
- Availability
- Company reputation
- Previous experience

But the items in the list and the importance of the entries in each column depends on the specific product. For example, for a component which is to be used in space applications, functionalities, previous experience, reliability, size and weight, etc. would be important factors, while cost may not be a deciding factor. But for a component that is to be used in a commercial product like the mobile phone, audio player, etc. cost is an important factor.

Re-usability, bulk use, etc. are also important factors which need to be considered during component selection. For example, an organization will be designing different category of products. So during a component selection, the very first question would be whether a similar component is already used in any of the previous designs. If a very new component is to be selected, this question would change to 'Will it be possible for the same component to be used for any of the future designs?'

There are some advantages in thinking on this line. An already used component is a well-proven one. So there is no risk of reliability for that particular component. Also as the quantity of a component increases, its purchase cost comes down considerably. This factor may even lead to a non-optimized component selection. For example, a CPLD or FPGA with additional capacity could be used in a product because of the factor that the same component is already used in a previous product. A resistor with additional wattage capacity may be selected for a design because it is already used before and hence the quantity for purchase will increase. These are all industrial and commercial concerns—not strictly technical.

The next step is to interconnect these components to make the required circuit.

18.3.6 | Schematic Design

Schematics is the pictorial/symbolic representation of a circuit diagram. It indicates the interconnection between the components. The components used and interconnection between them are represented using symbols and interconnecting wires, respectively. So all the components used in the design need to have its corresponding symbol in the schematics. Thus, the first step in schematic design is 'symbol creation'. Specific computer-aided tools are used for schematics design. They are commonly known as CAD (Computer-Aided Design) tools. Orcad is very common tool used for this purpose. Mentor graphics, Altium, etc. are some of the popular schematic design tool vendors.

18.3.6.1 | *Schematic Symbol Creation*

A schematic symbol is the pictorial/symbolic representation of a component used in the design. Each component has its symbolic representation. These are similar to the common symbols that we use to represent resistors, capacitors, inductors, transistors, etc. Complex ICs are also represented by their corresponding symbols.

A schematic symbol of a component contains only its external interface details, that is, the pin details. This means that an IC with 676 pins has 676 external interface points in the symbol also. For ease of use, pins of similar functionalities are grouped together in a symbol. Also there is the practice to have different sub-parts for a symbol. Essentially, this means that the complete pin details of a single IC will be represented using multiple entities. Here also some kind of logical grouping may be used. That is, one entity has all the power supply pins, the second entity has the timing pins, another entity has the communication pins, etc.

It is the designer's responsibility to make sure that all pins of a component are included in its symbol. So the 'pin details' given in the device data sheet is to be carefully analysed for this symbol creation. The symbol of a component needs to be created considering the fact that it will be used in future designs also. That means that even if all the pins of an IC are not used in one particular design, still it is a good practice to include all the pins in a symbol so that it may be used in other designs.

18.3.6.2 | *Schematic Design Process*

It is the process in which the components are interconnected using wires. It is similar to the way in which a circuit is drawn on paper. This interconnection should consider all the design aspects of a circuit. The most important factor is the functionality itself. Different components are connected to perform specific tasks. Input/output directions of the pins, electrical compatibility between the pins, specific design requirements like pulling the pin to supply voltage/ground, etc. are some of the design aspects to be taken care of.

All the components used in a circuit need not be present in a single sheet in the design tool. There may be multiple page schematics. In such cases, the interconnections are represented by careful naming of the wires in different pages. That is, in a schematic tool, nets (i.e. electronic wires) with the same name will be interconnected together. Figure 18.13 a–e, shows the different pages of a schematic design.

This process contains the real technical aspects of the design. The designer should consider basic electrical/electronic/mechanical theory while doing such designs. For example, terminations for impedance matching, de-coupling capacitors to avoid power supply noise, etc. are some of the design factors which need to be considered while doing the schematic design. Current limiting resistors, filter capacitors, and voltage dividers are some other components that may be included in the schematics. The voltage and current limitations and requirements of the components also need to be considered while designing.

18.3.7 | PCB Layout

The selected components are now to be placed on a board and connected together according to the designed schematics. These two requirements are satisfied by a printed circuit board (PCB). It not only provides electrical connectivity between the components, but also provides proper mechanical support for them. The functionalities of a PCB are listed below:

- Signal distribution
- Power distribution
- Mechanical support
- Environmental protection

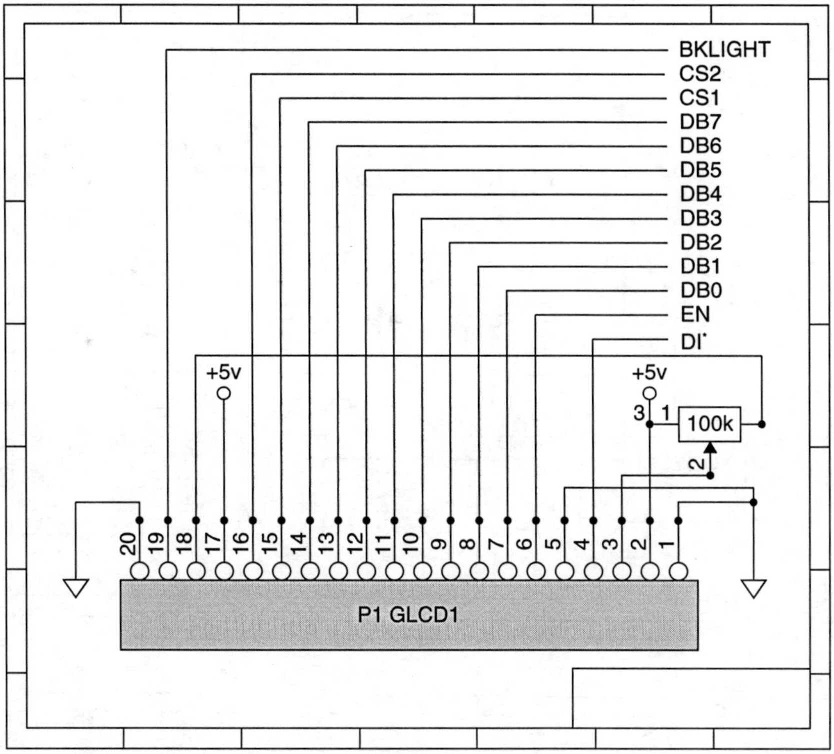

(a)

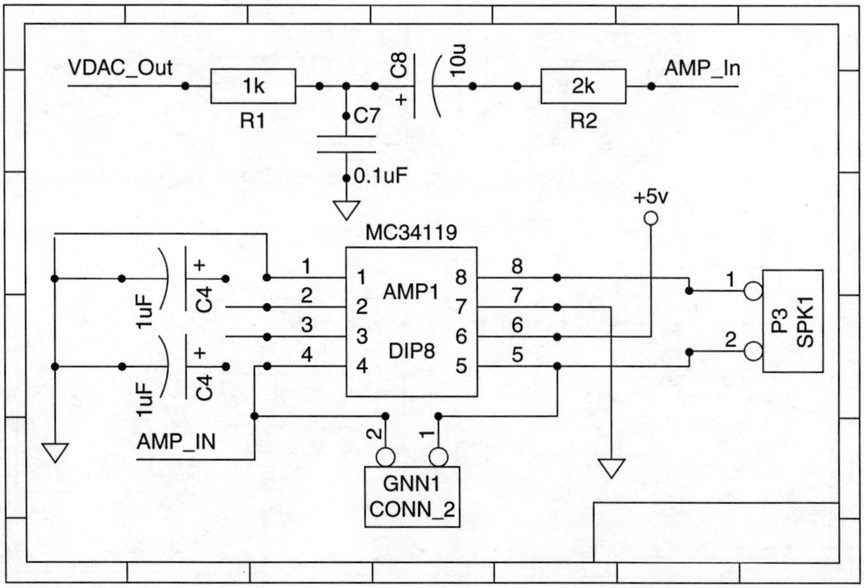

(b)

Figure 18.13a–e | Continued

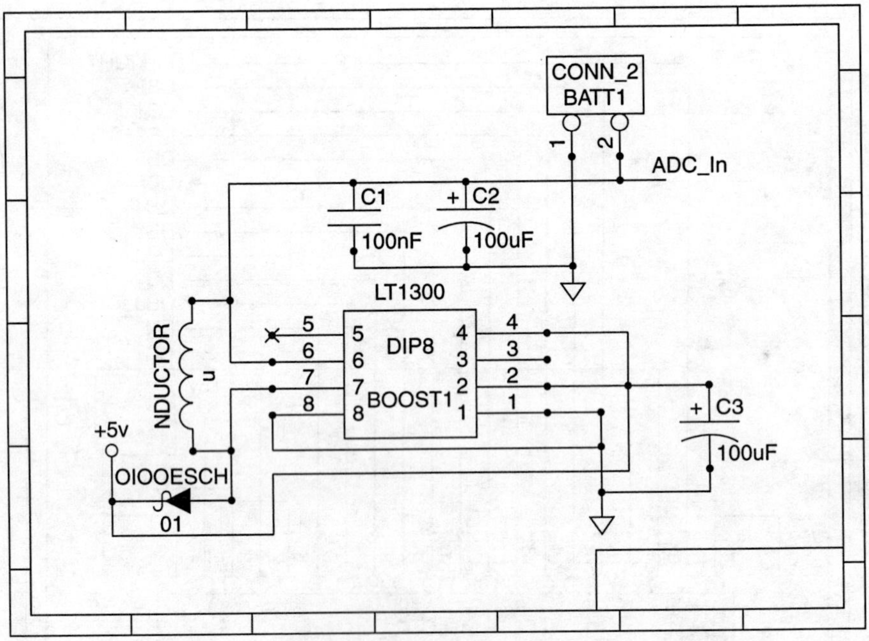

(c)

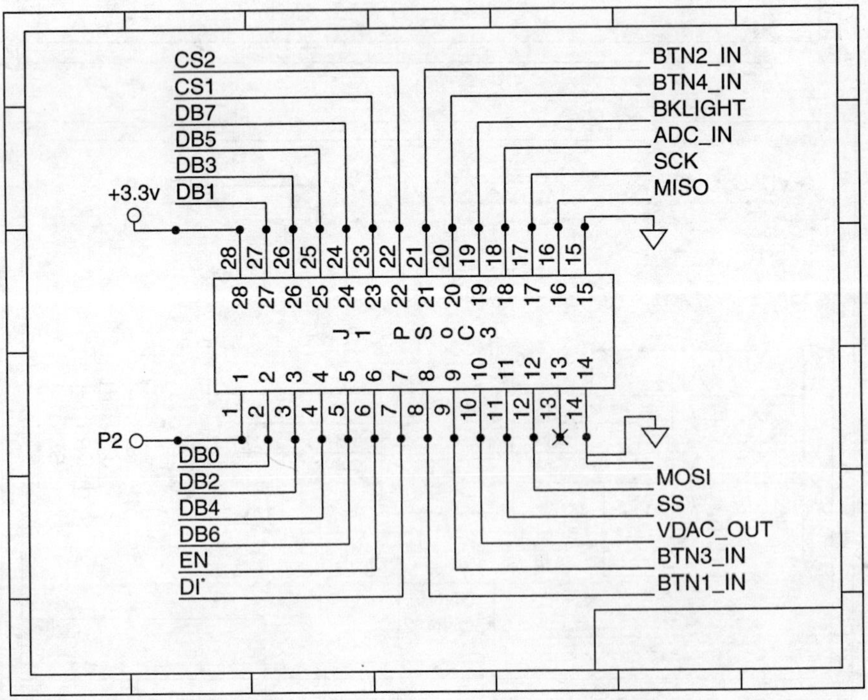

(d)

Figure 18.13a–e | Continued

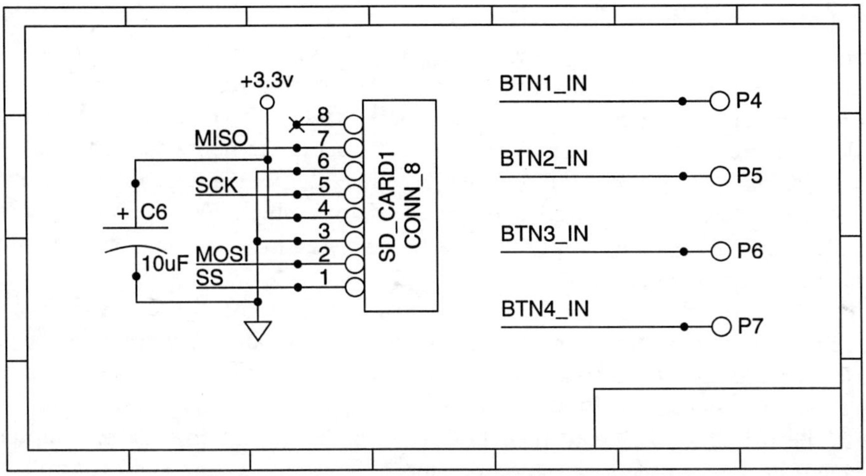

(e)

Figure 18.13a–e | Different pages of the schematic design of a hardware

18.3.7.1 | *PCB Design*

PCB design is the first step in converting the virtual world of components in the schematics, to the real world. That means that, in PCB design we consider the components in their real nature. In contrast, in the schematic design the components are represented by their symbols.

The first step in the PCB design process is to fix the board shape and dimensions (recollect that this had already been done at the time of mechanical design). This is the basis on which the layout is made.

PCB design is a three-step process. It consists of component foot print creation, component placement and routing.

18.3.7.2 | *Foot Print Creation*

It is similar to the process of symbol creation in a schematic design. The schematic symbol is the electrical representation of a component while the PCB footprint is its real-world representation. It is created with the actual dimensions of the component. The dimensions like size of the chip, pitch and size of the leads, etc. need to be accurately used while creating the foot print of a component. The foot print represents the 'location' on the PCB, where the component is to be mounted. That clearly indicates that the foot print dimensions should match the real physical component. The 'mechanical dimensions' provided in the device data sheet is the reference document for the foot print designer.

Each foot print has separate names. The same foot print may be used by different components in a design. For example, most of the resistors and capacitors use the same foot print. All ICs with DIP14 package will have the same foot print and so on. That means the foot print is not for a specific component but for a specific package. It is the designer's responsibility to make sure that the correct foot print is assigned to each component.

18.3.7.3 | *Component Placement*

Component placement means 'arranging the foot prints in correct order inside the PCB outline'. There are a lot of factors to be considered during this placement. The most important of them is to ensure the logical correctness of the placement. A common practice is to group the components logically. For instance, components associated with a particular functionality may be grouped together. The user interface parts like displays and switches may be placed at board edges, for example. Another criterion is to ensure 'ease' in routing. The components should be placed in such a way that the routing between them becomes easy.

In most cases, there will be components which need to be placed at specific locations. This is likely to be fixed by some restrictions in the product. For example, the connectors, switches, LEDs, etc. may have to be placed at a fixed location. This would have been fixed by the mechanical/interface design of the product. That is, these components have to be placed according to their positions on the casing. So usually, component placement begins by placing such components first. After this, the main controller IC (MCU) is placed approximately at the centre of the board so that there is sufficient space for placing other peripherals surrounding it.

There are cases where some components need to be mandatorily placed close to another set of components. For example, termination resistors have to be placed close to the source or the destination, and de-coupling capacitors and reference clock sources are to be placed very close to the relevant IC. (The reader may refer other books to understand the reason for such requirements.)

Yet another requirement may be to 'avoid' placing certain components close to certain others. For example, analog circuit components are usually to be placed far away from digital components; noise generating components should be placed away from noise sensitive components and so on.

It is very difficult to list all the possible requirements in this discussion. The point to keep in mind is that component placement cannot be done randomly. There should be a logical reason/justification for each placement. Even simple reasons like aesthetics of a board with well-arranged components play a major role in this matter.

18.3.7.4 | *PCB Routing*

PCB routing is the process in which the properly placed components are interconnected according to the circuit. In a very simple sense, it is a process by which the actual circuit is made. But the real challenge lies in the process of routing. Let's list out some of the points which make routing cumbersome:

- The very first issue is the space available for routing. All the nets (the technical term for the interconnections) in the circuit need to be routed in the limited space available on the PCB. As the circuit becomes more and more complex, the number of nets increases and the situation becomes complicated. The total size of the PCB is already fixed and hence the total space for routing is also fixed. So it is the designer's responsibility to accommodate all the nets in this available space.
- Another constraint comes from the requirements like minimum separation between two adjacent nets. If the nets are made closer than a 'defined' limit, electrical coupling

between them ensue. Additionally, there are constraints for the spacing between component pads. As in the case of component placement, this also leads to routing constraints like separation between noise generating and noise-sensitive nets.

- The minimum width of a net is another point to be thought about. More number of nets may be included in one area if the width of these nets is reduced. But reducing the width of a net can possibly lead to issues like manufacturing difficulty, reduced current carrying capacity of the nets, etc.
- Another point of concern is the impedance of the nets, especially the nets of the power supply and ground. As the impedance of a net increases, the voltage drop across it increases and hence the downstream circuits may not get sufficient voltage. This is applicable for both DC and AC (signal) currents present on the board. This implies that both the resistance and inductance of a net are equally important. The increased impedance of ground lines could lead to issues like ground bounce. These things lead to concepts like power plane, ground plane, etc.
- Yet another area of concern is the loop area of a signal. Any signal travelling from one point to another has a return path associated with it. The area of the loop through which this travel occurs should be minimum. A larger loop area naturally leads to higher antenna effect causing the circuit to transmit or receive more noise.

18.3.7.5 | *PCB Layers*

According to the routing space, PCBs can be classified into three—single layer, double layer PCB and multilayer PCB.

- A single layer PCB is the one in which routing is done only on one side of the PCB. (Components may be placed on the other side).
- A double layer PCB is the type in which routing is done both the sides of the PCB.
- A multilayer PCB is the one in which routing is done in more than two layers—there are layers sandwiched between the two outer layers. The interconnection between these layers is made through interconnecting via.

Again, a detailed discussion of all the technical issues associated with routing is beyond the scope of this chapter. But the point to be noted is that, routing does not simply mean taking copper lines (tracks) from one point to another—a lot of thought and effort is needed to get it right. Figures 18.14a and b show the front and back side of the PCB layout corresponding to the schematic design of Figure 18.13.

18.3.8 | PCB Manufacturing and Assembly

18.3.8.1 | *PCB Manufacturing*

All that we have talked so far, are related to the 'virtual world', that is, all those processes were done using EDA (Electronic Design Automation) tools. PCB manufacturing is the process where the 'real' PCB is made. The design done using the layout tool is now converted to a real, 'physical' PCB. There are a lot of processes involved and process technologies available for PCB manufacturing. Chemical processes, laser processes, etc. are used for PCB manufacturing. The reader is advised to refer to other sources for details of

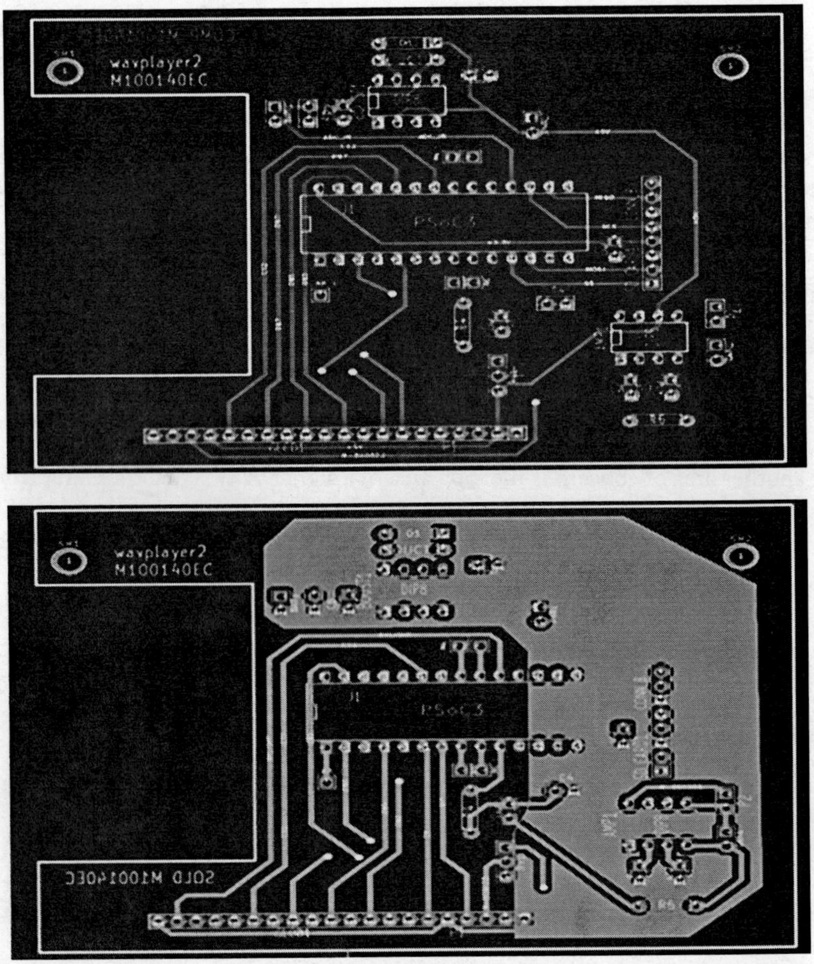

Figure 18.14a and b | PCB layout—front side and back side

PCB manufacturing. Figure 18.15a and b are photographs of the PCB mode using the layout of Figure 18.14.

18.3.8.2 | *Design for Manufacturability (DFM)*

Design for manufacturability (DFM) is an important concept that needs to be taken care in any PCB design. All designs that a designer does should be 'manufacturable'. In this context, what we mean is that, the PCB manufacturer should be able to manufacture the PCB that has been designed. It is the designer's responsibility to make sure that he does not include any aspect that the manufacturer finds impossible to implement.

For example, according to the technology available with the manufacturer, there is a minimum track width that he can make; there may a maximum number of layers, minimum/maximum via size, minimum/maximum separation between tracks or tracks and vias, pads and tracks, etc. Materials with which the PCB is to be made is another

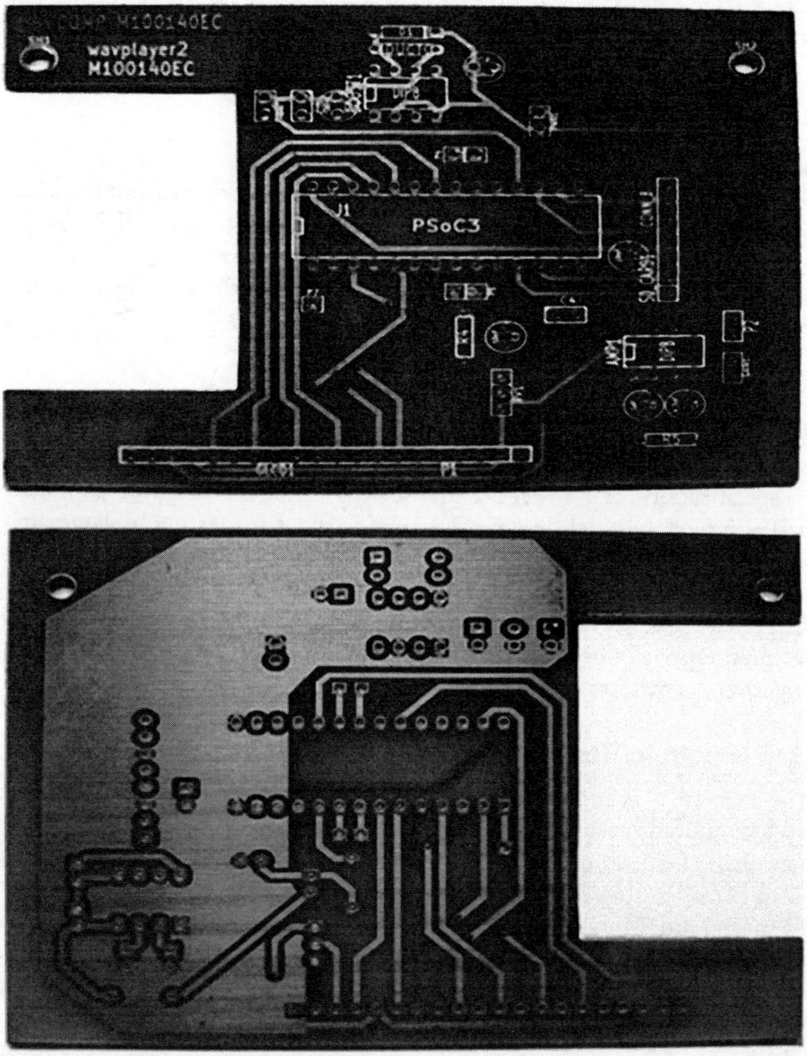

Figure 18.15a and b | Front side and back side of the PCB manufactured from the layout of Figure 18.14

point to be taken care of. There are different materials used for PCB manufacturing with varying reliability, cost, strength, flammability, etc. The designer should consider these points while designing the PCB and ensure that the PCB can be manufactured according to the design.

18.3.8.3 | *PCB Assembly*

The electronic components are then to be assembled on the PCB that has been manufactured. Soldering is the common process used for this. Manual soldering is the normal process; but it is not suitable for a product design, if the number of components on the

PCB is very large. The small size of electronic components also make manual soldering very difficult. Automated machine soldering is used in such cases.

There are two different types of components used:

i) Through hole components
ii) Surface mount components

As the name implies, a 'through hole' component is inserted from one side of the PCB and is soldered on the other side. But a surface mount device (SMD) is soldered on the surface itself. That means that it does not have any part to be inserted to the other side of the PCB. Obviously, surface mount devices are small and they help to accommodate more components in a small area.

18.4 | Testing

Testing is the process by which it is confirmed that the designed product meets all the required specifications. It is a very important step in product design. It is estimated that around 70–75% of the total design cycle time is spent for testing. A large amount of money is also spent for this. It is the product manufacturers' responsibility to make sure that their product is launched to the market without any faults/errors. Discovering bugs and faults after a product lands in the market is likely to be a very costly mistake for any manufacturer, especially because it causes irreparable damage to the reputation of the company. This is why testing is considered to be a very crucial stage.

18.4.1 | Design for Testabiliy (DFT)

DFT (Section 16.4) is another important concept in product design. All the features of a product should be testable. There should be some well-defined method to test all the available features of the item under design. This aspect of 'testability' is to be taken into consideration during the design phase itself. If a feature cannot be tested directly, special provision should be given in the design to test it in some indirect way. Special components/circuits/software are usually added initially itself in the total design. Even if this does affect the cost, real estate and time, the effort spent on this is worth the trouble as this will lead to a systematic testing, and thus a truly reliable product.

18.4.2 | Levels of Testing

Testing is done at different levels. It spans from the basic circuit testing to the complete product testing. In the industry, once hardware and software design is complete, test teams separately test hardware and software. There are limitations for these testing processes. All features may not be tested at this first stage. Once the basic functionalities are confirmed, there is hardware–software integrated testing. The software is ported to the hardware and it is then this testing is done.

Once the second level testing is over, the product is tested in the 'simulated real scenarios'. Individual features are tested in detail. All possible error-prone situations are simulated and tested.

There is another level of testing, which is called regression testing, where the product is tested in a regressive manner. The same feature is tested multiple times to make sure that the product passes the test always, or at least the failure percentage is within the allowed limit.

Next, the product is tested for all **'corner cases'**, which means conditions which occur rarely. The product is also tested in extreme conditions like minimum voltage, maximum load, maximum temperature, etc.

18.4.3 | Reliability and 'Standards' Testing

Reliability testing means that the product is tested to make sure that it performs its functionality for the specified **'life time** of the product'. Obviously it cannot be tested for the entire time duration equal to the expected life time. Therefore, it is tested for shorter time durations in elevated conditions. The successful completion of such a test provides the manufacturer a confidence about the reliability of the product. For instance, the product is continuously tested for 48 or 72 hours with full load, minimum voltage and a high temperature. These conditions will be above the maximum specified value. The test condition depends on the standard requirements, experience, company practice, etc.

Most products will have to meet certain standards according to the application. So the requirements in the 'defined standard' need to be tested and certified by an external agency. Special types of testing like vibration testing, shock testing, etc. are included in this.

18.4.4 | Field Trials

The testing cycle is not complete without performing field trials. The product is now tested in the real-working conditions for a specified amount of time. There may be some pre-fixed customers for performing this task. This is not just about testing the 'functionality' alone. Different modes of operations, the indications, user inputs, etc. also need to be tested.

18.4.5 | Signature Testing

Testing for an un-successful condition is equally important as that of a successful condition. This means a product should be tested for invalid inputs, invalid conditions, etc. to make sure that it will refuse to function in such situations.

18.5 | Bulk Manufacturing

The product samples manufactured initially are mainly used for different kinds of testing and are called 'prototypes' of the product. There can be different levels of prototypes—first prototype, second prototype, etc. The product is ready for bulk manufacturing after rigorous testing, correcting errors, proper certifications, etc. are done on the prototype. For this purpose, different parts like PCB, casing, etc. are manufactured in bulk and different tasks like PCB assembly, software porting, mechanical assembly, etc. are performed in bulk. The total time taken for all these processes affects the manufacturing time and hence the cost of the total product. So while designing different parts, especially those that need to be assembled, the time for such assembly should be considered. The aim of the designer should be to minimize the time for each process during bulk manufacturing.

18.5.1 | Manufacturing Tests

It is not possible to perform the entire test cycle on all the pieces of the product after manufacture. The normal practice is to conduct a selected set of tests (A representative set for the entire test cycle) on all the individual pieces of the product, and to perform the entire test cycle on selected pieces (again representatives of the lot—1 in 100 or 1 in 1000, etc.). This manufacturing test process is automated, usually.

18.5.2 | Yield

There is no guarantee that all the individual pieces manufactured will come out as usable products. Some of them will definitely be found to be useless because of bad components, manufacturing issues, quality of parts used, etc. The measure of the final usable pieces to the total number of pieces manufactured is the 'yield'. So obviously the main aim of any designer-cum-manufacturer should be to maximize the yield during bulk manufacturing. Using of reliable components, simple manufacturing steps, use of commonly available, easily processable and quality materials, etc. are some of the steps towards achieving high yield.

18.5.3 | Product packing/Delivery

Finally, once the product is ready for delivery it has to be packed properly and then delivered to the customer. The safety of the product during transportation is the main concern during packing. Other issues like ESD (Electro Static Discharge), etc. are also matters of concern at this stage. It is the manufacturer's responsibility to make sure that the final customer gets a 'quality' product.

Conclusion

Through this chapter, the various steps involved in product design have been introduced. These are the steps involved in realizing a product, and they are **general** steps. Different manufacturers have variants of these steps. In addition, it is to be well understood that, these processes are neither open loop nor sequential in the real scenario, even though the explanation has been given sequentially. This means that feedback from one process goes to any of the previous steps (Section 17.4.3). If any issues are found, they are corrected immediately. That is, all these are iterative processes. It is not that each step will start only once the previous steps are completed. There is continual overlap between different steps. This contributes to making an iterative model for design.

This chapter is meant only to sensitize the reader about these steps. The 'details' in each phase involved are not explained comprehensively. The reader is advised to refer various other documents/text books to get the details involved in these processes.

KEY POINTS OF THIS CHAPTER

- Embedded product design is a well-structured and systematic process.
- It starts with a list of requirements which is converted to 'specifications'.
- Ergonomic principles should be adopted in product design to make it comfortable for users.
- Besides electronic design, mechanical and interface design are also involved, and they are equally important.
- Hardware design includes component selection and schematic design, which is converted to a PCB layout, with which the PCB is manufactured.
- After the PCB is made, packaging is done.
- Around 75% of the design cycle time is allocated to testing.
- The aim of product design and manufacture is to get a high yield.

QUESTIONS

1. Give typical examples of embedded systems.
2. What is the importance of 'need for a product'? From where does the need originate?
3. Why is feasibility study required in product design?
4. What is the difference between user requirements and product specifications?
5. How is 'ergonomic design' important in product design? Give examples for good and bad ergonomic designs.
6. What is meant by anthropometric measurements? How does it affect a product design?
7. Why is mechanical and interface design of an electronic product important? Explain in detail.
8. What are the various considerations to be taken during component selection for a product design?
9. What is the difference between the schematic symbol and layout symbol of a component?
10. What are the functions of the PCB in an electronic product?
11. What are the various considerations to be taken during component placement?
12. What are the various considerations to be taken during PCB routing?
13. What is the difference between single layer, double layer and multi-layer PCBs?
14. What is meant by 'design for manufacturability?' How is this concept important in product design?
15. What is 'design for testability?' How is this concept important in product design?
16. Why do you say that testing is critical for a product? What are the probable consequences of insufficient testing?
17. What are the different types of testing done after a product is ready?
18. How is the expected life time of a product tested?
19. What is the difference between prototype manufacturing and bulk manufacturing?
20. What is meant by the term 'yield'? How is it important?

EXERCISES

1. Identify some typical embedded systems. Try to come up with its probable design—block diagrams, components used, mechanical and interface design, software algorithm, etc.
2. Perform a user research in a field of your interest. Come up with user requirements for a probable product, do a study about feasibility of all these requirements and finally come up with a probable product specification.
3. Observe some of the products available in the market. Study the 'ergonomics' in their design. Study how each interface of this product (all different types—key pads, display, connectors etc.) matter, in enhancing its usability.
4. Identify a CAD tool which can be used for schematics and PCB design. Design a small circuit using this and then design its corresponding PCB.
5. Visit an electronic product design firm and perform a detailed study about different steps they follow during the complete design. Compare it with the steps discussed here.

PART-V
PROJECTS

19 ACADEMIC PROJECTS

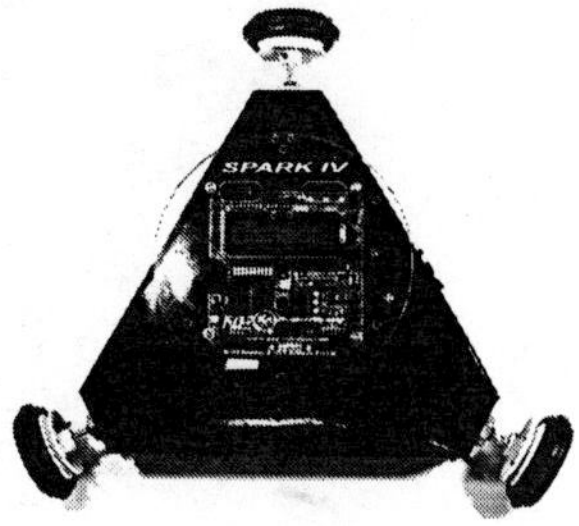

In this chapter, you will learn

- The concept of vision controlled robots
- How to use MATLAB in a PC to generate the control signals for a robot
- How to develop an autonomous vision controlled robot using a Beagle board
- How to design and implement an audio player using an ARM 7 MCU
- How to interface a PIC MCU to GPS and GSM modules for an accident alert system

Introduction

In this chapter, three projects done at the academic level, by students of NITC are discussed. All of them are hardware implementations with software embedded into powerful MCUs. The discussion here is brief, but more details of the projects are put up in the website of the book which is www.pearson.com/lybdas/embedded systems.

19.1 | Project No: 1

Vision Controlled Robots

(Team: Nithin Gopinath, Jayalal Vijayan, Ashwin Harikumar, Kurian Abraham, Ebin George)

19.1.1 | Introduction

There are two implementations in this project:

i) The movement of a ball is tracked using control signals obtained by visual processing in MATLAB using a PC. The drive signals for the robot are provided by a PIC MCU and motor driving hardware.
ii) A vision controlled robot moves in response to signs provided by different sign boards. This is an 'autonomous' robot. The signal processing is done using the OMAP processor in a 'Beagle board'. (Refer to Section 15.6). The driving signals for the robot are provided by the GPIO pins of the Beagle board.

Chapter-opening image: 'Spark 4' robotic platform (Courtesy : Nex Robotics, Mumbai).

19.1.2 | Robots and Vision

Visual servo-control refers to the use of computer vision data to control the motion of a robot. Visual (image-based) features such as points, lines and regions can be used to enable the alignment of a manipulator/gripping mechanism with an object. Hence, vision is a part of a control system where it provides feedback about the state of the environment. It relies on techniques from image processing, computer vision and control theory.

Vision is a useful robotic sensor data, since it mimics the human sense of vision and allows for non-contact measurement of the environment. Typically visual sensing and manipulation are combined in an open-loop fashion, 'looking and then moving'. The accuracy of the resulting operation depends directly on the accuracy of the visual sensor and the robot end-actuators. An alternative to increasing the accuracy of these subsystems is to use a visual feedback loop that will increase the overall accuracy of the system—a principal concern in most applications.

19.1.3 | Aim of the Project

Objectives

Two different and separate problems have been tackled.

i) To design and develop a robot which can be controlled using serial communication with a PC and using an on-board processor.
ii) To implement visual control in robot using MATLAB and OpenCV.

19.1.4 | Problem Specification

Two different and separate problems have been tackled.

i) Implement a 'ball following robot' which should be able to follow a particular coloured ball using an on-board camera. The main aim of implementing this in the first stage is to make sure that the robot is able to follow at least one colour properly in real time as in the later stages it has to choose between different colour patterns and then decide its motion.
ii) Implement a vision-guided robot which is capable of identifying specific patterns (which are provided to guide the robot) in different colour backgrounds and intelligently processes this information to reach its destination point. In this project, we have used arrows in particular colour backgrounds. For example, if the robot sees an arrow in a yellow background, it moves to the direction as shown by the arrow.

19.1.5 | System Description

The system for vision controlled machine (VCM)/robot consists of.

i) **Image acquisition setup:** It consists of a video camera, web camera or an analogue camera with suitable interface for connecting it to processor.
ii) **Processor:** It consists of either a personal computer or a dedicated image processing unit like a DSP kit or an embedded processor like OMAP3530.
iii) **Image analysis:** Certain tools are used to analyse the content in the image captured and derive conclusions, e.g., locating position of an object.

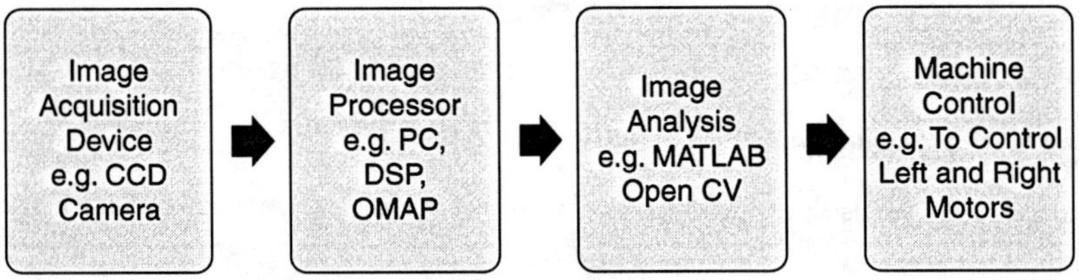

Figure 19.1 | Block diagram of a vision controlled robot

iv) **Machine control:** After making the conclusion, mechanical action is to be communicated using serial or parallel port of a PC to control left and right motors of a robot to direct it towards the ball. Figure 19.1 elaborates the set-up.

19.1.6 | Image (Video) Capture

Image capturing can be done using video camera available in various resolutions, e.g., 640 × 480 pixels. Generally, there are two types of cameras available: Digital cameras (CCD–charge coupled device and CMOS sensor-based) and analogue cameras. Digital cameras generally have a direct interface with computer (USB port), but analogue cameras require suitable grabbing card or TV tuner card for interfacing with PC.

19.1.7 | Image Analysis

Image analysis consists of extracting useful information from the captured images. We first decide the characteristics of the object to look for, in the image. This characteristic of the object must be as robust as possible. Generally, for the purpose of tracking or identifying the object we utilize:

i) Colour
ii) Intensity
iii) Texture or pattern
iv) Edges—circular, straight, vertical stripes
v) Structure—arrangement of objects in a specific manner

19.1.7.1 | *Quantitative/Statistical Analysis of Image*

i) Centre of gravity—point where the desired pixels can be balanced
ii) Pixel count–a high pixel count indicates the presence of object
iii) Blob–an area of connected pixels

19.1.8 | The Matrix

Images are stored in a computer in the form of 2D matrices, which represent the locations of all pixels. All images have an X component and a Y component. If the image is black and white (binary), either a 1 or a 0 will be stored at each location. If the colour is gray scale, it will store a range of values. If it is a colour image (RGB), it will store sets of values. The less the amount of colour involved is, the faster can the image be processed. For many applications, binary images can give information for image processing.

19.1.9 | Image Processing Techniques

In this section, an overview of the various techniques used has been presented.

19.1.9.1 | *Thresholding*

In this method, we isolate and create a new image based on the captured image with (say) only two values of intensity 0 and 255. These values are given to the different pixels based upon certain conditions. For example, if you want your robot to follow a yellow-coloured ball, all those pixels which have RGB values with a comparatively dominant percentage of yellow will be given the intensity value 255 and the rest pixels as zero. This would give a gray scale image which shows only the location of the ball (provided there are no yellow-coloured objects in the environment).

19.1.9.2 | *Middle Mass and Blob Detection*

Blob detection is an algorithm used to determine if a group of connecting pixels are related to each other. This is useful for identifying separate objects in a scene. Blob detection, would, for example, be useful for counting people in an airport lobby, or fish passing by a camera. Middle mass, on the other hand, would be useful for a baseball catching robot, or a line following robot. If there is only one blob in a scene, the middle mass is always located in the centre of an object.
But if there were two or more blobs, each blob is labelled as a separate entity. Then the middle mass can be found for each separately labelled blob.

19.1.10 | Ball Following Robot

The ball following robot is to be connected to the PC and the image processing is done in the PC using MATLAB.

19.1.10.1 | *Machine Control Code using MATLAB*

Machine control consists of controlling a robot based on the conclusion derived from image analysis. To achieve this using PC, its parallel port or serial port can be used for driving the robot. For example, H-bridge PWM control can be extensively used for right and left motor. Serial port can be used for transferring data, which necessitates a micro-controller on the robot to interpret the data.

19.1.10.2 | *Video Capture*

MATLAB has in-built functions for providing video capture. Any camera connected to the PC can be accessed through the *videoinput* function in MATLAB. Then we can use the *getdata* function for accessing frames (images) from the video. For example, vid = videoinput ('winvideo',1,'YUY2_160x120'); AB = getdata (vid,1); The execution of this code results in one frame (image) stored in variable AB in YUV format with resolution 160x120.

19.1.10.3 | *Serial Port*

If you have to transmit one byte of data, the serial port will transmit 8 bits as one bit at a time. The advantage is that a serial port needs only one wire to transmit the 8 bits (while a parallel port needs 8). Figure 19.2 shows a serial part connector.

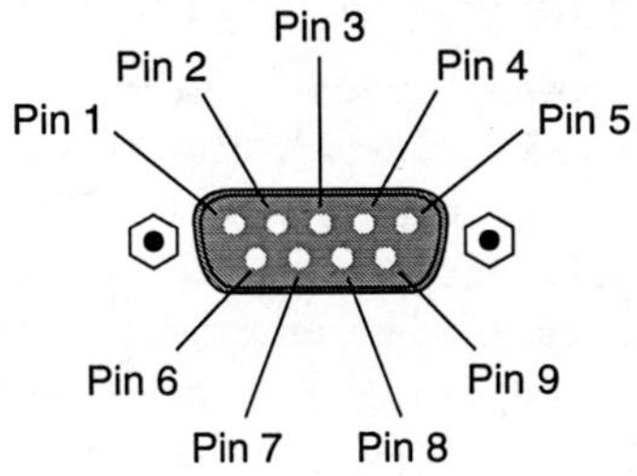

Figure 19. 2 | Serial Port

Pin 3 is the Transmit (TX) pin, pin 2 is the Receive (RX) pin and pin 5 is Ground pin. Other pins are used for controlling data communication in case of a modem. For the purpose of data transmission, only the pins 3 and 5 are required. (© Nex Robotics Pvt. Ltd. http://www.nex-robotics.com/workshop.html.) At the receiver side, you need a voltage level converter called as RS232 IC which is a standard for serial communication. And to interpret the serial data, a microcontroller with UART (Universal asynchronous receiver transmitter) is required aboard the robot. Most of the microcontrollers like AVR ATMEGA 8, Atmel/Philips 8051 or PIC microcontrollers have a UART. The UART needs to be initialized to receive the serial data from PC. (Refer Section 5.3.3.)

In this case, the microcontroller is connected to the motor driver ICs which controls the right and left motors. After processing the image, and deciding the motion of the robot, transmit codeword for left, right, forward and backward to the microcontroller through the serial port (say 1-Left, 2-Right, 3-Forward, 4-Backward).

MATLAB code for accessing the serial port is as follows:

```
>> ser= serial('COM1','BaudRate',9600,'DataBits',8);
>> fopen(ser);
```

To send data through the serial port, the available commands

```
>> fwrite (ser,1); % for left motion
>> fwrite (ser,2); % for right motion
```

You can close the port in case there are other applications using this port using the *fclose* command.

```
>> fclose(ser);
```

The microcontroller has an output port whose pins can be used to control the driver IC. Thus, the microcontroller interprets the serial data from the PC and suitably controls the motors through the output pins and the motor driver or H-bridge.

19.1.11 | Signboard Guided Autonomous Robot

The Beagle Board, which has the OMAP3530 as its processor is used for the signboard-guided robot. The image processing is done in the processor and the necessary control signals are generated at the general purpose I/O (GPIO) pins of the Beagle Board. These outputs are first level-shifted and given to the driver ICs for the motors.

19.1.11.1 | *Beagle Board (Refer to Section 15.6)*

The Beagle Board is a low-power, low-cost, fan-less single board computer with laptop-like performance produced by Texas Instruments in association with DigiKey. The heart of the Beagle Board used here is an OMAP 3530 SoC. The main processor the OMAP3530 includes an ARM Cortex-A8 CPU which can run Windows CE, Linux or Symbian. Here in our case we have used a Linux distribution called *Angstrom.*

The Beagle Board is also equipped with a single SD/MMC card slot supporting SDIO, a USB On-The-Go port, an RS-232 serial connection. The operating system, Angstrom was loaded in to the SD/MMC. The USB port is connected to the WebCam which gives input images to the processor. The communication between the computer and the Beagle Board was done using the RS-232 serial communication port available on-board.

The board uses up to 2 W of power and can be powered from the USB connector or a separate 5 V power supply. Because of the low-power consumption, no additional cooling or heat sinks are required.

19.1.11.2 | *On-board Memory for the Beagle Board*

The Micron POP memory is used on the Beagle Board and is mounted on top of the processor. The key function of the POP memory is to provide:

i) 2GB NAND x 16 (256MB)
ii) 2GB MDDR SDRAM x32 (256MB @ 166MHz)

No other memory devices are on the Beagle Board. It is possible, however, that additional memory can be added to Beagle Board by installing a NAND-based device in the SD/MMC slot or use the USB OTG port and a powered USB hub to drive a USB thumb drive or hard drive. Support for this is dependent upon driver support in the OS.

19.1.12 | RS 232 Serial Communication

Support for RS232 via UART3 is provided by a 10 pin header on the Beagle Board for access to an on-board RS232 transceiver. Connection to the header is through a 10 pin IDC to 9 pin D-sub cable. Communication with the Beagle Board is done through the serial port. For this, a 9 pin RS 232 flat cable was used. Also a serial to USB converter was used so as to connect it to the USB port of the PC.

19.1.13 | MMC/SD

A 6 in 1 SD/MMC connector is provided as a means for expansion.

One of the nice features is that the OMAP3530 can be booted from the SD/MMC. In order to boot from MMC/SD, the card must be a 3V 4-bit card. By holding the user button and forcing a reset, the Beagle Board will boot from the SD/MMC. Even though the NAND may have a program in it, if a card is placed in the MMC slot, it will try to boot from it first. If it is not there, it will boot from NAND.

19.1.14 | Angström OS

As mentioned earlier, the Beagle Board is a low cost, low power fan-less single board computer with laptop-like performance. So like any other system, the Beagle Board also requires an operating system. The main processor, the OMAP3530 includes an ARM Cortex-A8 CPU which can run Windows CE, Linux or Symbian. Here we have used Angstrom which is a Linux distribution. The advantage of Linux distributions over Windows CE and other proprietary software is that they are open source and hence there is a vast resource and support base in the Internet.

19.1.15 | Setting Up the Operating System

The Ångström distribution contains four major components. They are shown below in the order in which you must copy them to the SD card, as the boot-loaders must appear first on the card:

i) First-stage boot-loader
ii) Second-stage boot-loader
iii) Linux boot image (uImage)
iv) Linux file system

By default, the Beagle Board's firmware contains the first stage boot-loader or X-loader. Any further editing of X-loader can be done using a signed MLO file which is loaded into the MMC card from where the X-loader is loaded. X-loader bootstraps the system only enough to load the second-stage boot-loader, which otherwise would not fit into memory.

The second stage boot loader is called as u-boot or the universal boot-loader. It is provided in Beagle Board's flash memory. U-boot initializes the system, and boots the Linux kernel. It can also be run from the console.

The Linux boot image, named *uImage*, finally boots the Linux kernel, which resides in the Linux file system in the /boot directory.

Once the kernel is booted using uImage, it initializes the drivers and devices and also mounts the file system.

19.1.15.1 | *Partitioning the MMC Card*

You must create two disk partitions on the SD card.

i) **FAT file system:** The first partition is dedicated to a FAT partition that hosts the boot-loaders and the kernel image. FAT is used for the boot partition, because it is a very basic file system that is straightforward and well understood by the Beagle Board by default, requiring no intelligence from the boot-loader or operating system. The boot-flag of this partition is set so that the files are loaded once the MMC is inserted into the Beagle Board.
ii) **Ext3 file system:** The remaining part of the card is dedicated to an ext3 File system. It contains the file system associated with the operating system. The Linux root file system, however, can be in any file system format understood by the Linux kernel. Here ext3 File system has been used which is understood by Angstrom.

19.1.15.2 | *Copying Files onto MMC*

Once we are done with the partitioning the MMC, the next step is to copy the files into these partitions. The copying of the files should be done in the same order as mentioned below.

i) Copy MLO onto the bootable FAT partition
ii) Copy u-boot.bin onto the bootable FAT partition
iii) Copy uImage onto the bootable FAT partition
iv) Extract the root file system into the ext3 partition

Once this is done, unmount the MMC and its ready to be inserted into the Beagle Board.

19.1.15.3 | *Booting LINUX*

The term *booting* is short for *bootstrapping*, which refers to the process by which a newly reset computer prepares itself to load an operating system. In modern and powerful systems, this process is often relegated to the BIOS but in small, resource-constrained systems such as the Beagle Board a slightly different, multi-step process is followed because of constrained memory.

This process often involves three stages. A small, *first-stage* boot-loader, which fits neatly into the small ROM provided on the system, locates and loads a larger, *second-stage* boot-loader into RAM. The second-stage boot-loader initializes the system and boots the operating system.

Type the following lines at the U-boot prompt to set the environment variables for booting from the card:

```
setenv bootargs 'console=ttyS0,115200n8 root=/dev/mmcblk0p2 rw rootwait'
setenv bootcmd 'mmcinit; fatload mmc 0 80300000 uImage; bootm 80300000'
boot
```

Note that you can write these environment variables to memory to instruct the Beagle Board to boot always from flash memory by typing *saveenv* before booting with the boot command.

19.1.15.4 | *Auto-boot*

In order to make the robot intake images, process them and move accordingly automatically on boot-up (power on), we have to run a bash script on boot-up. Usually, the OS looks into the init.d folder in the root file system to find out which all programs have to be run on boot-up. So, the bash script containing the shell command to run the object file of this code is saved in this location.

```
#! /bin/sh
cd <path to file>
./<filename>
```

19.1.16 | Hardware

There is a DC motor control circuit which is a standard circuit. (Refer Section 3.3.2.3.) Besides this, there is a level shifter which is realized as below.

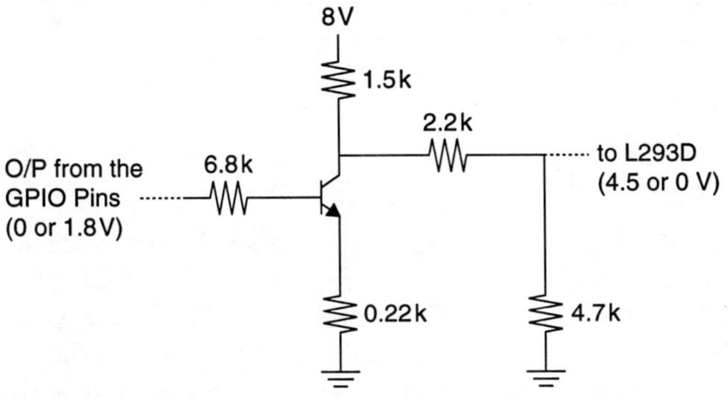

Figure 19. 3 | Level-shifter Circuit

19.1.16.1 | *Level Shifter Circuit*

The level shifter is implemented using a very simple transistor circuit. (Refer Figure 19.3.)

The circuit shown above is a transistor circuit in common-emitter configuration. It works as an inverter circuit, that is, the circuit gives us an output of 4.5V when the input to the transistor circuit is 0V and it gives us an output of 0V when the input is 1.8V.

Thus, a low GPIO out would result in a 4.5 V output from the transistor which enables the driver circuit and the motor is turned on. So summing up, the motor is turned on when the GPIO out is low.

19.1.16.2 | *Design*

i) $V_C = 8V$ at Vin = 0V
ii) $V_{CE} = 0.2V$ at Vin = 1.8V
iii) Take $R_C = 1.5k$
iv) We get
   - $R_E = 220$ ohms
   - $R_B = 6.8k$
v) As we have utilized the same 8V supply used for the motors, the output will be 8V when the input is 0 (cut-off). Hence, we have used an additional potential divider of ratio 1:2 in order to get the output voltage around 4.5V.

19.1.17 | Vision Guided Robot Algorithm

19.1.17.1 | *Algorithm*

Image capture

The video captured by the camera mounted on the robot is transferred to the PC or processor for analysis.

i) In the case of the ball following robot which is connected to the PC, this is done with the help of MATLAB *videoinput* function. Also using the MATLAB *getdata* function, frames (images) of the video are obtained in the software working environment.

ii) In the case of signboard guided robot which has on-board processor, this is done using *CapturefromCAM* function of OpenCV library.

Processing the Image

Once the image is obtained, the next step is processing it.

i) In case of a robot following a coloured ball, we use thresholding. This function will be based on the colour of the ball to be followed, i.e., the RGB points close to the specific colour of the ball in the RGB colour space will be isolated and they will be given intensity value 255 in the output image, whereas the other RGB values are given intensity value 0 in the output image. The centroid of all such high intensity values in the output image is found out and that gives the image-based position of the ball relative to the robot.
ii) In case of a signboard guided robot, the robot has to identify signboards of a particular case (e.g. yellow) and move in the direction of the sign. Hence, we threshold the image for the yellow pixels in the frames captured. Then, the centroid of the pixels corresponding to the arrow is calculated.

Intelligence

i) In case of a ball following robot, the ideal condition is that the ball should be in the middle portion of the span of the view of the camera (and hence the captured images). Any deviation would mean error, and the robot must do whatever is necessary to nullify this error. So the robot should be given the necessary control signals by the program to move in the corresponding direction. An interesting problem comes up when the ball moves out of the span of view of the camera. In this case, the robot will have to estimate the position of the ball. This can be done by analysing previous frames and finding out the last noted position of the ball.
ii) In case of a signboard guided robot, the robot simply moves in the direction of the arrow. This is done by checking the position of the centroid of the arrow with respect to the centre of the signboard. For example, if the arrow's centroid is more to the left of the sign, then the direction is decoded as left.

Generation of Control Signals

The intelligence of the system (i.e. the software) analyses the situation and finds out the best course of action. This has to be actuated through the robot and hence the necessary control signals are to be generated by the program.

i) In case of the ball following robot, if the ball is found to be positioned towards the right of the robot, the program should generate the code such that the robot turns towards its right till the ball comes in the middle of its view.
ii) In case of the signboard guided robot, the program simple generates control signals to the motors so that the robot moves in the direction of the signboard.

19.1.18 | Implementation of the Robots

19.1.18.1 | *Ball Following Robot Connected to a PC*

Software Implementation

We wrote a program in MATLAB which did the following things:

i) Take data from the on-board camera which was connected to the PC using USB port.
ii) Process the image to detect the pixels corresponding to any particular colour (RED) using the Euclidean distance method.
iii) Find the centroid of all such pixels.
iv) Compute the deviation of the centroid of the target from the centre of the camera frame.

Using this code, we also performed a simulation of the actual intended motion of the robot. Refer Figure 19.4.

Based on the value of the error, the robot had to move left, right or centre. If the error value is below the threshold set for straight movement, the robot is to move straight. If not, the robot would turn to the left if the error was positive and to the right if the error was negative. We represented the motor movement using a MATLAB graphical representation.

The line shown in Figure 19.4, would be in the second quadrant (indicating that the robot would turn left) if the ball was on the left of the robot. If it was on the right, the line would be in the second quadrant. If the ball was in the 'centre' region, the line would lie on the y-axis (indicating that the robot would move forward).

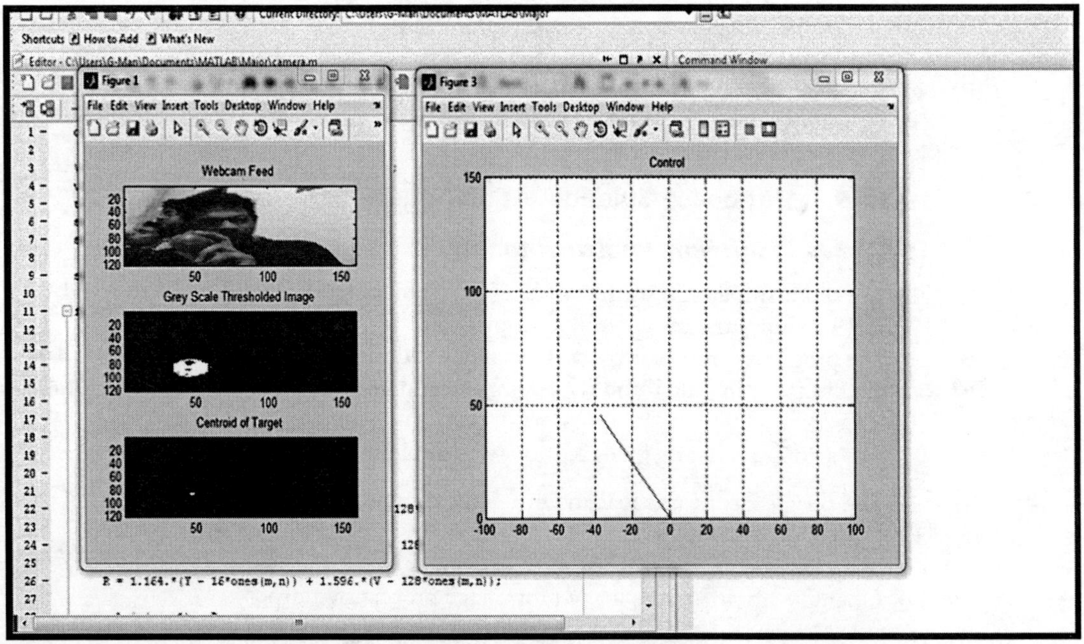

Figure 19.4 | Software implementation of ball-following robot

Hardware Implementation

In this section, the robot design has been described.

i) The robot was implemented using the PIC18F4550 microcontroller.
ii) Webcam used was *mercury viewpoint click* camera.

The on-board camera was connected to the PC using USB cable and the robot (PIC) was connected to the PC using serial cable.

Drive Platform Motors

i) Choose to use 2 DC motors for front wheel drive and castor wheel at the rear
ii) Motors require 12V, commonly available from batteries
iii) DC motors chosen are with sufficient torque

Wheels

i) Small rubber wheels designed for stability
ii) Commonly available

Communication Subsystem

Communication of robot can be made possible using serial port communication.

Batteries and Power Subsystem Batteries

i) Choose NiMH batteries
ii) Reliable, have high mAh capacity, built for continuous operation
iii) 7805 voltage regulator giving constant output 5V
iv) Ideal voltage for digital circuits
v) Regulator provided with heat sink for improved heat dissipation
vi) L293D IC motor driver used

19.1.19 | Signboard Guided Autonomous Robot

19.1.19.1 | *Software Implementation*

First we did a simulation of the working of the signboard-guided robot in MATLAB. Figure 19.5 shows the results of the simulation.

The program thresholds the yellow colour and identifies the signboard. Then it finds out the direction in which the sign points to and generates the necessary motor signal (Turn Left).

The actual signboard-guided Robot was implemented:

i) The Beagle Board was loaded with Angström operating software
ii) USB and webcam drivers were loaded
iii) The OS was then loaded with GCC compiler
iv) OpenCV libraries were loaded for image processing purposes

We wrote a program in Open CV which did the following things:

i) Take data from the on-board camera which was connected to the Beagle Board using USB port.

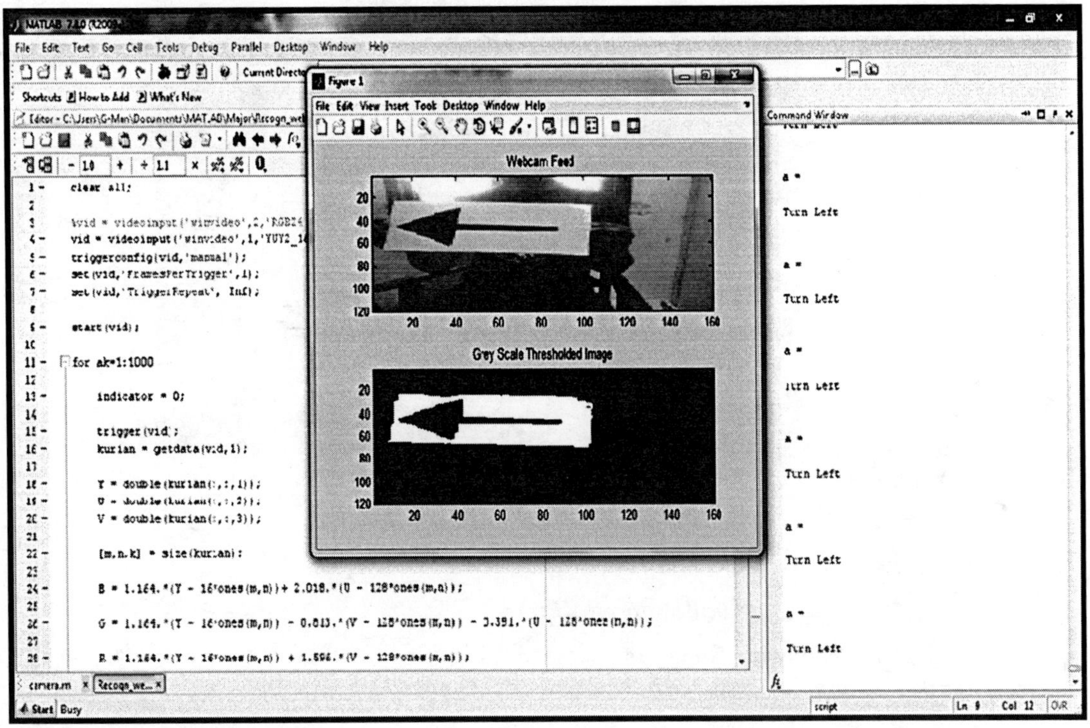

Figure 19.5 | MATLAB simulation

ii) Process the image to detect the pixels corresponding to the colour of the sign board (YELLOW) using the Euclidean distance method.
iii) Find the centroid of all other pixels inside the signboard (which correspond to the arrow).
iv) Compute the deviation of the centroid of the target from the centre of the signboard.
v) Depending on whether the centroid is displaced more to the left/right/above/below the centre of the signboard, the program generates the necessary control signals on the GPIO pins of the Beagle Board.

19.1.19.2 | *Hardware Implementation*

The robot was implemented using the following:

i) Webcam—*Mercury Viewpoint Click* camera.
ii) Beagle Board consisting of
    - OMAP3530 processor
    - USB ports
    - Serial ports
    - Expansion header with general purpose I/O (GPIO) pins
iii) Level-Shifter Circuit (Common Emitter Configuration) using Transistor BC547.
iv) L293D driver IC for driving the motors
v) 2 DC motors (100 rpm) for front wheel drive and castor wheel at the rear

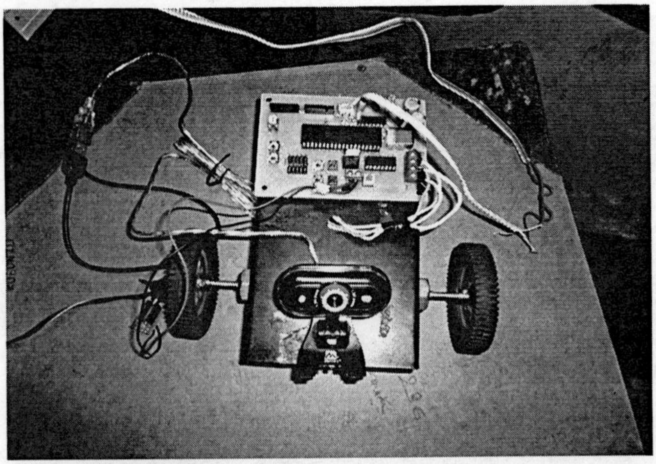

Figure 19.6 | Ball following robot

19.1.20 | Results

19.1.20.1 | *Ball Following Robot*

The 'Ball Following Robot' was successfully implemented as shown in Figure 19.6. The robot was found to successfully follow the coloured (RED) ball.

19.1.20.2 | *Signboard-guided Robot*

The 'Signboard-guided Robot' was successfully implemented as shown in Figure 19.7. The robot was found to successfully identify the signboard, understand the direction and move accordingly.

Figure 19.7 | Vision-guided robot

19.2 | Project No: 2

Arm-based Audio Player

(Sushmita Dandeliya, M.Tech.)

19.2.1 | Introduction

This project aims to build a digital audio player which can be used where high quality audio is desired. It uses an SD/MMC card for storing audio files. The player is based on the ARM processor, which has the advantage of high-speed operation and low-power requirement. The ARM7TDMI-based LPC2148 MCU running at 60MHz frequency has been chosen.

This player contains an audio codec chip (VS10XX) to decode audio formats like MP3, WAV, Ogg-vorbis and Wma format. The ARM processor reads the audio files from the SD/MMC card and sends it to the code chip. The codec decodes the audio format and converts it into analog form using an inbuilt DAC, and then sends it to a headphone or speaker. An LCD display is used to show the play/pause and volume icons, and push buttons are used as the user interface. Figure 19.8 is the block diagram of the unit.

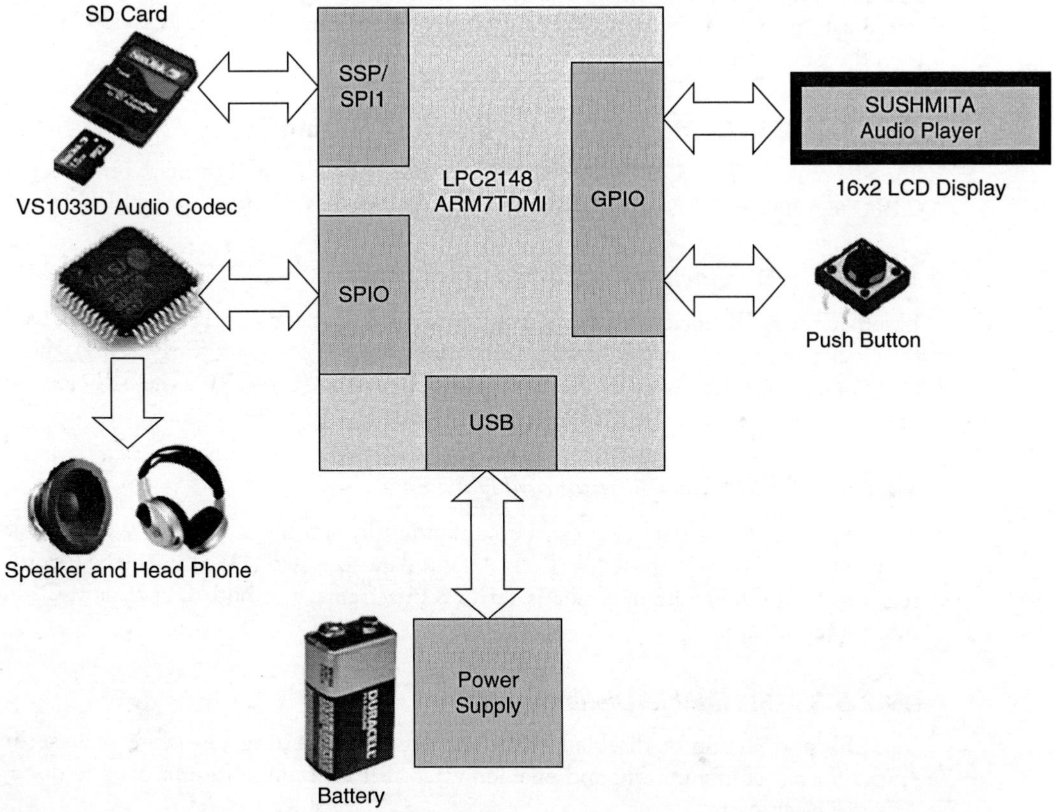

Figure 19.8 | The block diagram of the ARM-based audio player

19.2.2 | The Microcontroller

In this project, the LPC2148 microcontroller is selected because it has all the required interfaces for this application. It contains ARM7TDMI core that is the best choice due to its 32-bit architecture and large memory for program and data. The MCU runs at a frequency of up to 60 MHz maximum. The operating voltage of LPC2148 is 3.3V only.

19.2.3 | The Interfaces Required

This design requires SSP, SPI and GPIO interfaces. LPC2148 microcontroller contains 2 SPI (Serial Peripheral Interface) interfaces, SPI0 and SPI1/SSP. SPI0 has been used for interfacing the audio codec and SSP (Synchronous Serial Port) used to interface the microSD card. Four bit GPIO interface is used to interface the 16x2 LCD.

19.2.4 | Memory Unit

A microSD card stores the audio files. This microSD card is connected to the MCU through the SSP (Synchronous Serial Port) interface that contains four lines, which are MISO (Master in Slave Out), MOSI (Master Out Slave In), SCLK (Serial Clock) and SSEL (Slave Select). The MCU selects the slave using the SSEL line and sends the initialization commands to the SD card on the MOSI line when SCLK is 400KHz and then the card starts sending data to the MCU on the MISO line.

19.2.5 | GPIO Settings (SSP/SPI1 Interface Settings)

The SPI pins, CLK, CS, MOSI and MISO, need to be configured through pin select and GPIO registers, PINSEL1, IODIR0 and IOSET0, before configuring the SPI interface.

19.2.5.1 | *SPI Clock Pre-scale and Clock Rate*

Based on the APB clock (PCLK) setting in the APB divider control register (APBDIV), the clock pre-scale can be set through SSP Clock pre-scale register (SSPCPSR), and the clock rate can be controlled in the SSP control 0 register (SSPCR0). The SPI clock rate in the project is set to 2.14 MHz for the SD card.

19.2.5.2 | *SPI Frame Format and Data Size*

The SPI format and data size can be configured by setting the proper clock polarity bit (CPOL) and clock phase bit (CPHA) and data size field (DSS) in the SSP control registers (SSPCR0). The data size is set to 8 bits/frame, and both CPOL and CPHA bits are set to zero.

19.2.5.3 | *SPI Enable/Disable*

The SSP port should be disabled before the GPIO pin setting, clock pre-scale setting, frame format configuration, and enabled after all the configuration setting is done to ensure a clear start.

Figure 19.9 shows the connections between the SD card and the LPC 2148.

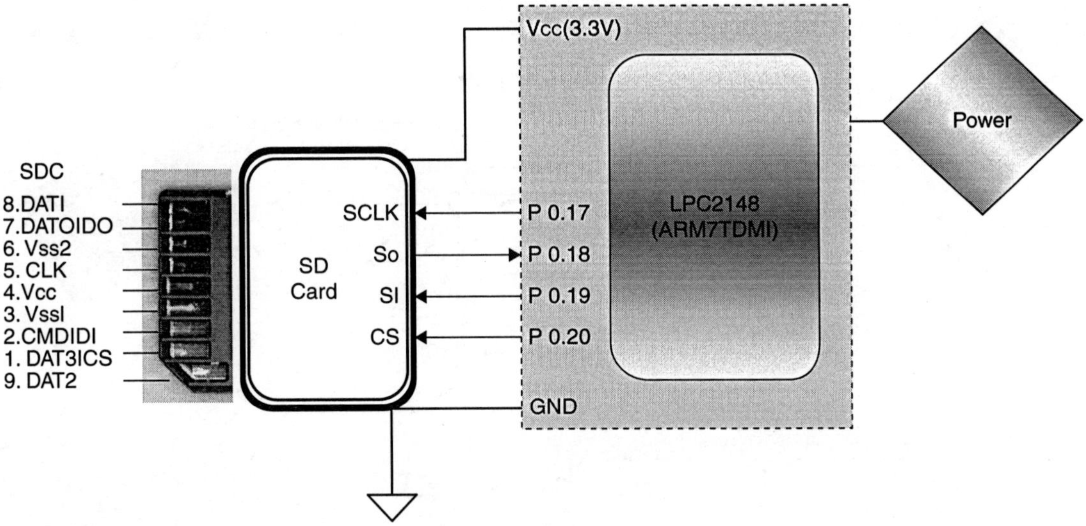

Figure 19.9 | SD card interface with LPC2148

19.2.6 | Basic SD Commands

i) CMD0 IDLE_STATE, reset the card to idle state
ii) CMD1 SEND_OP_COND, ask the card in idle state to send their operation conditions contents in the response on the MISO line. Any negative response indicates the media card cannot be initialized correctly.
iii) CMD16 SET_BLOCKLEN, set the block length (in bytes) for all the following block commands, both read and write. In the sample program, the data length is set to 512 bytes.
iv) CMD17 READ_BLOCK, read a block of data that its size is determined by the SET_BLOCKLEN command.
v) CMD24 WRITE_BLOCK, write a block of data that its size is determined by the SET_BLOCKLEN command.

For initializing the SD card and accessing data from that, various API's are used.

sd_init( ) is used for initializing SD card. It uses SPI_Send function for sending 80 clk pulses to the card. After that, CMD0 (Go idle state) is send to card to put it in idle state. Then CMD1 (SET_OP_COND) and CMD16 (SET_BLOCK_LENGTH) are sent, and the response is checked after each command.

sd_read_block( ) is used to read data from the SD card based on the block number. It uses SPI_Send() to send CMD17(READ_SINGLE_BLOCK) to the SD card first, check the response of the CMD17. If the response is successful, use SPI_ReceiveByte() repeatedly to read the data back from the SD card. The iteration of the SPI_ReceiveByte() is 512 (block length) + 2 (two-byte checksum). The return value of sd_read_block() indicates the status of the command and data response, zero is succeed and non-zero is failure.

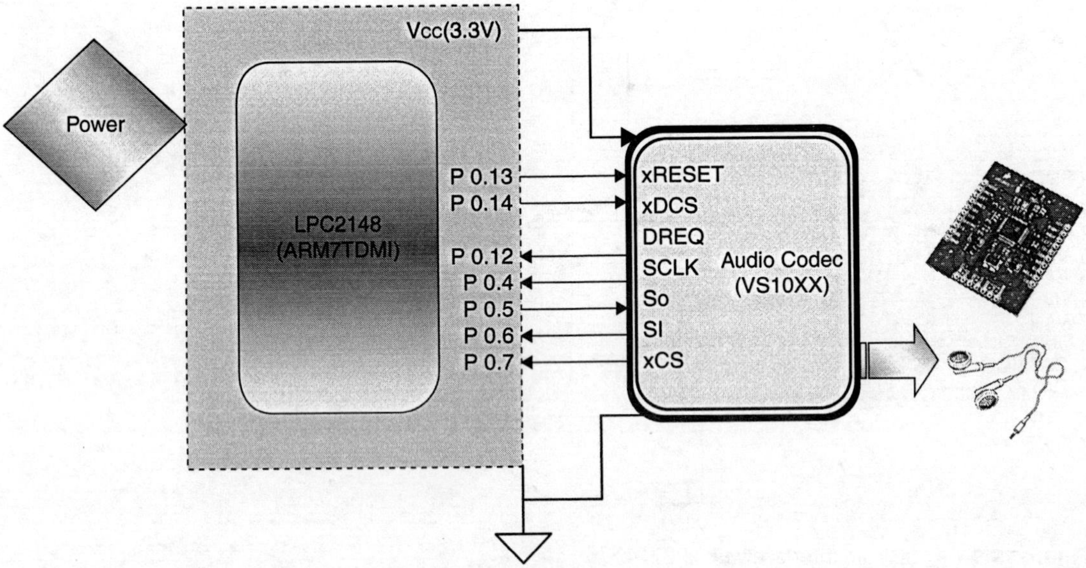

Figure 19.10 | Audio codec interfacing with LPC2148

19.2.7 | The Audio Codec

VS1033d is a single-chip MP3/AAC/WMA/MIDI audio decoder and ADPCM encoder. This chip is selected because of good sound quality and has inbuilt DAC and amplifier as well. It has inbuilt features of volume, bass and treble control. In addition to playing music, it also has the feature of recording.

The VS1033 receives its input bit stream through a serial input bus, to which it listens, as a system slave. The input stream is decoded and passed through a digital volume control to an 18-bit oversampling, multi-bit, sigma-delta DAC. The decoding is controlled via a serial control bus. In addition to the basic decoding, it is possible to add application specific features, like DSP effects, to the user RAM memory.

The audio codec is connected through the SPI0 (Serial Peripheral Interface) and three general purpose pins to the LPC2148 MCU. It contains xReset, Bsync and DREQ pins and SPI pins. When xReset and Bsync pins are inputs for the codec and DREQ is the output for the codec, it sends the status of the Codec (Data and Command FIFO is Empty or Not). The MCU checks the DREQ status after sending each command. The codec, after decoding the data, converts it into analog form and then sends it to the audio jacks which is connected through the right, left and Gbuf pins. Figure 19.10 shows the interfacing between the MCU and the codec.

19.2.8 | The SPI0 Interface Settings

i) **GPIO settings:** The SPI0 pins, CLK, CS, MOSI and MISO need to be configured through pin select and GPIO registers, PINSEL1, IODIR0 and IOSET0, before configuring the SPI interface.

ii) **SPI clock pre-scale and clock control:** Based on the VPB clock (PCLK) setting in the VPB divider control register (VPBDIV), the clock pre-scale can be set through SPI clock pre-scale register (S0SPCCR). This register controls the frequency of a master's SCK. The register indicates the number of PCLK cycles that make up an SPI clock. The value of this register must always be an even number. The SPI clock rate in this project is set to 3.74 MHz for audio codec.
iii) **SPI mode and operation control:** The SPI mode and data bits per transfer can be configured through setting the MSTR and bitEnable bits of S0SPCR register. Proper clock phase control is done by setting (CPOL) and (CPHA) bits in the SPI control registers (S0SPCR). The number of bits/transfer is set by BITS bit in S0SPCR register. Both CPOL and CPHA bits are set to zero.
iv) xReset, xDCS, DREQ pins are initialized as normal GPIO pins where DREQ is initialized as input and others as output by configuring the IODIR register.

19.2.9 | Test Mode

To make the audio codec to work in the test mode from a 16-bit SCI_Command, SM_TESTs bit should be high and xTEST pin should be always connected to IOVDD or it should be high. Otherwise the data request pin will behave strangely.

Steps for playing audio files:

i) Release vs1033d from reset
ii) Write a suitable value at SCI_CLOCKF (0x9800) using xCS
iii) Write SCI_MODE register as (0x8000)
iv) Write volume register SCI_VOLUME with a suitable value between 0x0000 to 0xfefe, where 0x0000 is the value for highest volume and 0xfefe for lowest or mute
v) Set SCI_BASS with a suitable value for bass and treble variation
vi) Send the file data to SDI using xDCS whenever DREQ is high. Data should send in a 32 byte buffer at a time after checking DREQ status

19.2.10 | The 16 × 2 LCD Display

As a display panel, a 16 × 2 LCD module is used. This has an HD44780 LCD controller inbuilt. It contains a RAM to generate and save sixty four 8 bits characters while using 5x8 dots for one character. It supports a low-power operation from 2.7 to 5.5V but to display something on LCD display ($V_{cc} - V_{contrast}$) 5v voltage is required. That can be obtained by a negative voltage of 2V at contrast pin by using a charge pump circuit.

Here the LCD is interfaced to the LPC2148 by 7 GPIO pins. 4 GPIO pins are for 4 data and 3 pins for RS, RW, EN pins of LCD. The LCD is interfaced in 4 bits mode in which only 4 data pins are required. (Section 3.3.1.6). Figure 19.11 shows the LCD interface.

The charge pump input is taken from Timer 0 external match output. To make the timer0 to toggle at external match, T0EMR register's 14th and 15th bits are set as 11. Also the T0MR0 register is initialized with value 0x4F to keep the frequency at 100 KHz. So the Timer0 works as an oscillator with 100 kHz frequency and this is given to the charge pump circuit which produces a negative voltage that is applied to the contrast pin of the LCD.

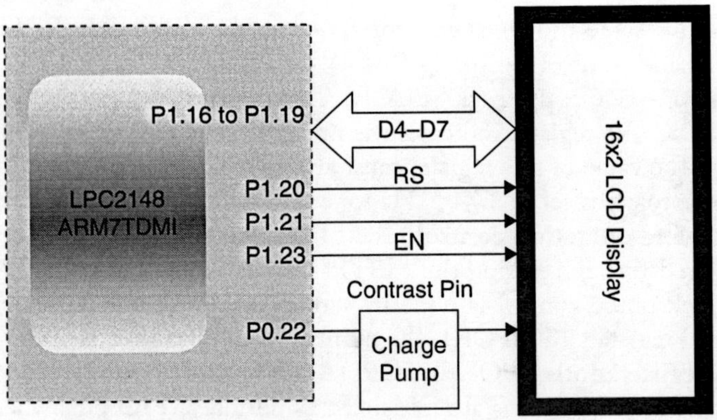

Figure 19.11 | 16 × 2 LCD interfacing with LPC2148

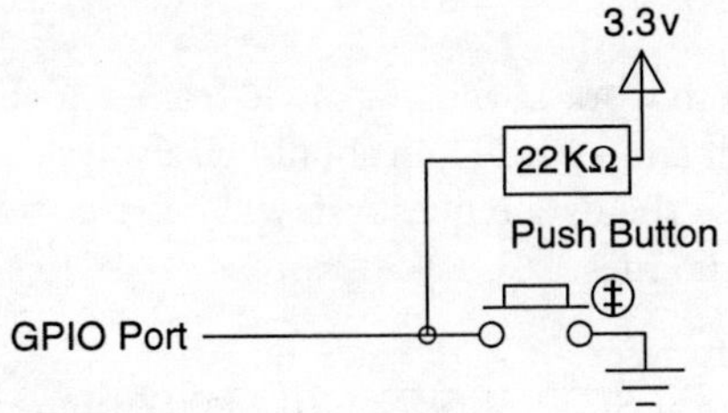

Figure 19.12 | Push button interface with port pin

19.2.11 | Push Buttons

Push buttons are used for user interface and to control the features of the audio player. Push buttons are used for the following functions: play/pause, volume increase, volume decrease, bass increase and treble increase.

These push buttons are connected through the GPIO ports of LPC2148 microcontroller. All are pulled up and become low when pressed. Otherwise they are at high level. Figure 19.12 shows the push button circuit.

For interfacing push buttons to the LPC2148 the IODIR register bits should be zero for the ports used for push buttons. Then the status of the push button is checked by the IOPIN register.

19.2.12 | Algorithm

i) Initialize the clock prescaler (VPBDIV) at some value.
ii) Select Timer0 as capture output at port 0.22 be setting PINSEL1 register.
iii) Set the direction of all input and output ports, i.e., xRESET, xCS, xDCS as output and DREQ as input by setting the bits of IODIR0 register.
iv) Initialize SSP interface by initializing all registers of this interface and sets the frequency 2.25 MHz.

v) Initialize the SPI interface for audio codec at 3.74 MHz clock frequency as master.
vi) Initialize the 4-bit data pins for 16x2 LCD.
vii) Clear LCD.
viii) Release vs1033d from reset.
ix) Write a suitable value at SCI_CLOCKF (0x9800) using xCS.
x) Write SCI_MODE register as (0x8000).
xi) Write some initial value to VOL register.
xii) Initialize SD Card by sending 80 clock pulses and other initializing commands and fix block length.
xiii) Read a block of 512 Kb and save it into a temporary buffer.
xiv) Check for button pressed (Play/Pause).
xv) If pressed print 'Playing' on LCD and send data from 512 Kb buffer to audio codec. by SPI interface in a form of 32byte at a time.
xvi) Check for DREQ status after sending each 32 byte.
xvii) Check for the switch press again. If pressed data sending is paused and song pauses playing.
xviii) Print 'Pause'.
xix) Check for volume and bass/treble buttons simultaneously.
xx) If any button is pressed LCD will print the particular instruction and player will work accordingly.

19.2.13 | Results

The player is completed, and packaged as a product. Figures 19.13 to 19.16 show the product in various stages of completion.

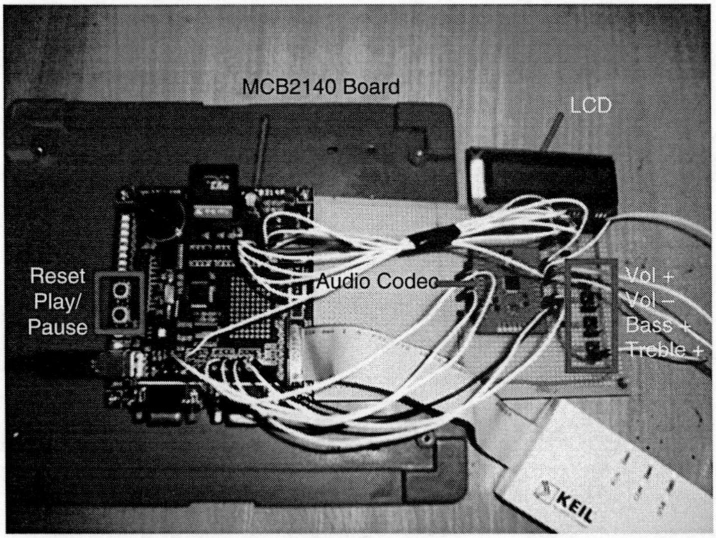

Figure 19.13 | ARM-based audio player with MCB2140 board and general purpose PCB

Figure 19.14 | ARM-based audio player with MCB2140 board and PCB for audio codec, and LCD fixed above the board

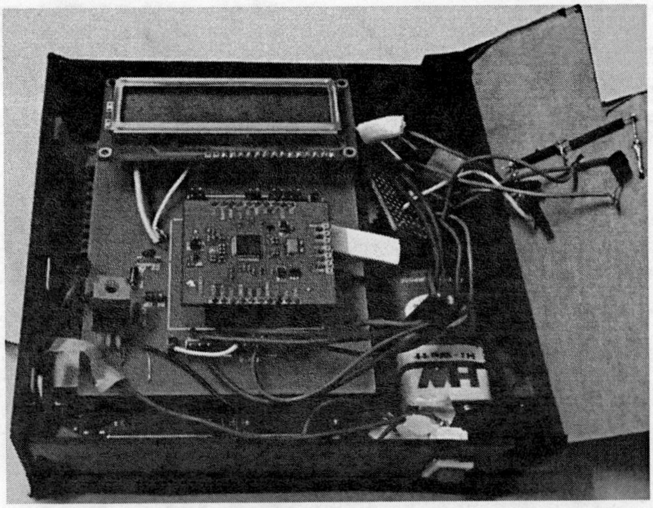

Figure 19.15 | The hardward placed inside the package

Figure 19.16 | The packaged product

19.3 | Project No: 3

Automatic Vehicle Accident Alert System (Avaas)

(Team: Fahim Bin Basheer, Jinu J. Alias, Mohammed Favas C., Navas V., Naveed Farhan K.)

19.3.1 | Introduction

We hear a lot about accidents happening these days. Many of the accident victims die on the spot or on their way to hospitals. Timely intervention by paramedics and relatives may help save their lives. The objective of this project is to provide a solution for helping these accident victims. A system is designed to work automatically without any human interference. This will especially be useful in cases when an accident occurs in a remote place or at night. This can also be helpful at times of emergencies like heart attack, getting lost, etc., where, the driver or co-passengers can inform others about their location for help.

This project aims to automatically locate the site of accident and alert concerned people. The system consists of sensors to identify the situation, locate the position, process this information and send the request for help. The expected design constraint would be to recognize the situation based on the inputs from various sensors, failure of which will give false alarms. There is also provision for giving an emergency signal by the user.

19.3.2 | Problem Statement

For providing timely help to accident victims, the proposed system should automatically identify a case of accident and pass on the emergency information to the authorities and relatives. It should be done automatically as the person involved in the accident may not be in a state to send the information. The problem can be divided into three steps.

i) **Detect:** The proposed system should be able to automatically detect an accident at the instant it happens.
ii) **Locate:** The location of accident must be identified.
iii) **Transmit:** The proposed system must be able to inform the responsible authorities about the accident and its location, so that help arrives very fast.

19.3.3 | The Solution

The proposed system is a completely automated one, which requires minimum human intervention. As mentioned in the problem definition section, there are three main steps in this system: identifying the accident, locating the position and transmitting the information. There are certain parameters that change during accidents which can be detected using sensors that measure these changing parameters. The position of the accident is located using GPS data as it is freely available, and this information about the location of the bike (the vehicle) is sent through the GSM network.

19.3.4 | Overview of the Project

Various scenarios of motor cycle accidents have been studied thoroughly. Accidents in motor cycles include head-on collisions, collision on the sides or from back, and losing control after skidding. Usually, the rider is thrown from the seat and the vehicle falls down. Keeping in mind all these possibilities, we decide the parameters that should be measured to confirm the occurrence of an accident. Some of the observations are:

i) The deceleration of the vehicle can be measured using an accelerometer. This acceleration value compared with the braking of the vehicle at normal braking is used to analyse whether sudden braking is applied and also if collision has occurred.
ii) Impact at various points can be measured using impact sensors. They will provide data regarding the state of collision and also measure its magnitude. They have to be placed at various points where impact is large and can be measured easily.
iii) A tilt meter can be used to get information regarding the inclination of the bike. This can be used to detect whether the vehicle has fallen or not.

So from the above observations, the various sensors used in this project are:

i) Accelerometer
ii) Piezo impact sensor
iii) Tilt meter

If an accident has occurred, the sensors would give output signals which if above a certain threshold value, would identify the occurrence of an accident as per the algorithm defined. Then the data regarding the location of the motorcycle is acquired using a GPS (Global Positioning System) module. This data will be available as coordinates of the location. This is got from satellites revolving around the earth and is a renowned technology. And then this information along with the details of vehicle is send to some previously set phone numbers. These numbers can include police control room,

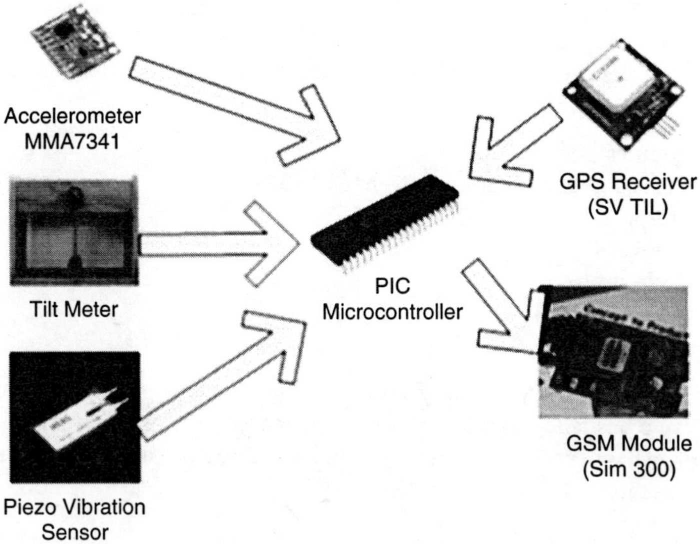

Figure 19.17 | The block diagram of the system

ambulance services and some of the victims' relatives. Hardware requirements for this system would be the various sensors (mentioned above) to measure the accident, the embedded system used to process the output signal for analysing the situation, GPS system to get the regarding location and GSM system which has prioritized list of numbers to send the information. Figure 19.17 is the block diagrem of the system. Figure 19.18 illustrates the mechanism by which 'communication' is achieved.

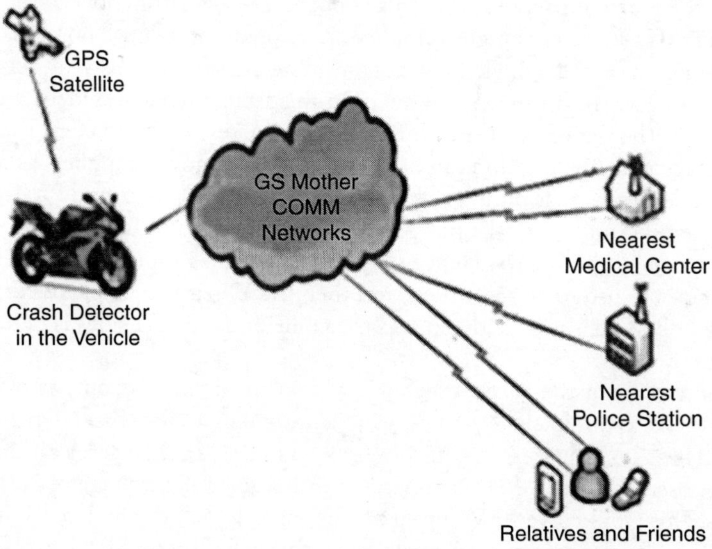

Figure 19. 18 | The network diagram

The software requirements are the data processing algorithms to arrive at a conclusion, application to get data from the GPS system, software to send the text message and also process the coordinates into text and add it to the information being sent.

Modules used in the project are:

i) Sensor modules
   - Triple axis accelerometer module-MMA7341
   - Piezo impact sensor
   - Tilt meter
ii) GPS module
iii) GSM module
iv) Microcontroller module (PIC18F542)

An additional accessory to the system would be a beaming light and sound so that if the motorcycle has fallen to a bushy place, the people nearby would know that something wrong has happened. The light and sound should sound an alarm. It will also help the emergency team to locate the position.

19.3.5 | Implementation

19.3.5.1 | *Decision-making*

The decision making algorithm is explained in Figure 19.19. The next task is to include the sensors which are the accident detection tools to the problem. The sensors can be taken to give high output when the symptoms for an accident occur and low output when they are absent. The algorithm hence should be checking for the high input at the pins. This can be implemented by making the pins as input pins in the program. The algorithm checks continuously if the accelerometer or the piezo sensor gives an output. This occurs when the vehicle suddenly decelerates above threshold or an impact occurs at the position of the piezo impact sensor. If this happens, the algorithm now checks for the tilt of the vehicle. If tilt meter is high it implies an inclination of above 60°. This is checked for some time since the vehicle may not fall down instantaneously (a delay of about 7 seconds is included). If it is also high within this time, then an accident is assumed to have occurred. The data from GPS (location coordinates) is then taken. The previously stored message with the location can be sent to as many mobile numbers as required.

The accelerometer has outputs corresponding to 3-axes (X, Y and Z). The direction in which the bike moves is taken as X. Usually if the bike collides, the acceleration is likely to happen in the X-axis. Hence only this is taken as input. Later on, if the collision from sides is also to be accounted, and then the Y-axis can be included. But for the time being only X-axis is considered and the collision from the sides is detected by the impact sensor.

The output from the accelerometer is analog in nature. An output of above 2.5g (1g = 9.8m = s2) is not likely to occur during a normal bike ride. This reference value can be adjusted based on the various collision tests on bikes. For 2.5g acceleration, an output of 2.8V is observed. An LM311 comparator with a reference voltage of 2.8V is used to detect this. This would give a 5V output at this value, which is a high level input.

The piezo impact sensor gives a voltage output when there is force acting on it. This can also be calibrated to suit real-life situations. The sensor is assumed to give 1V output

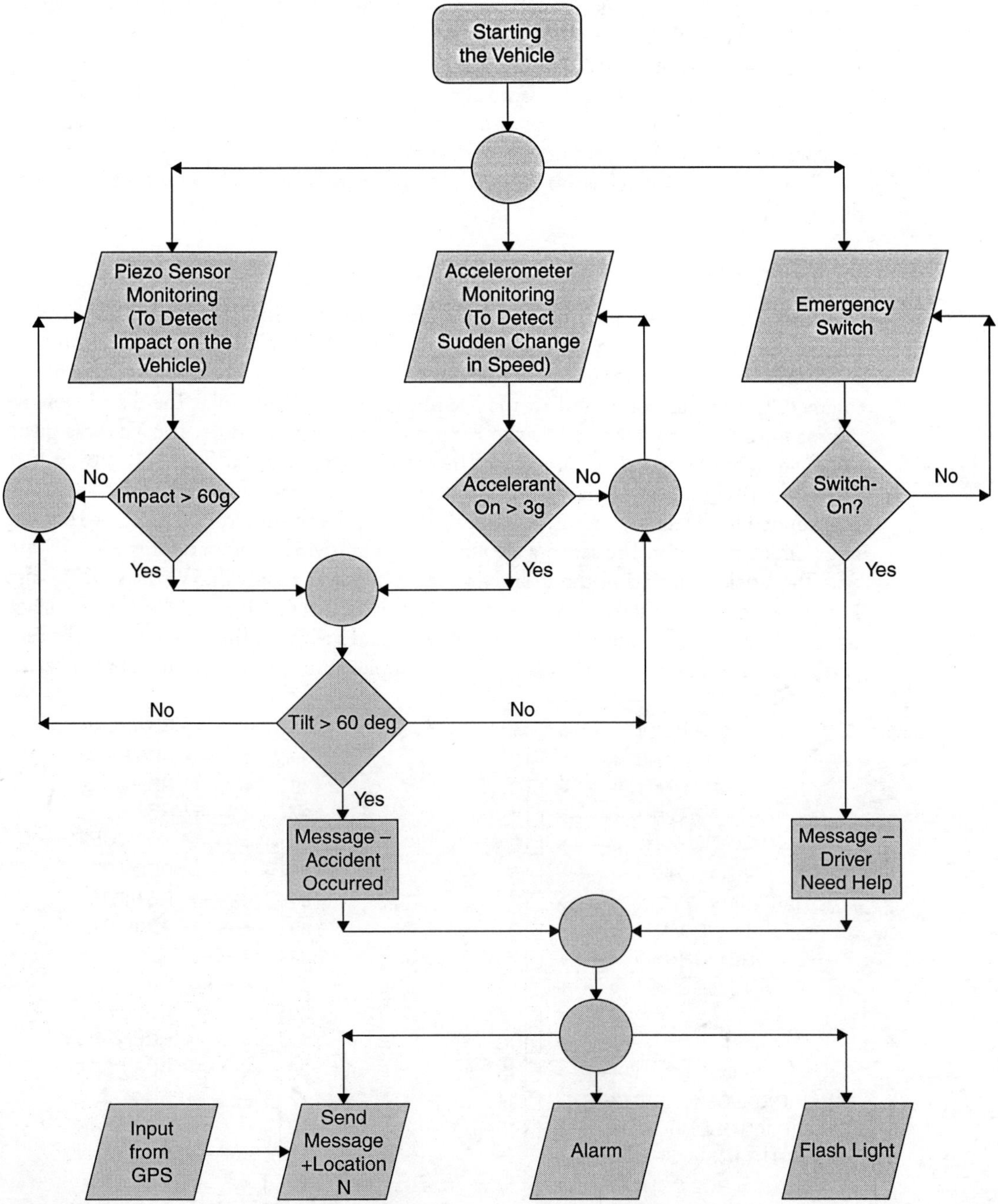

Figure 19.19 | Decision-making algorithm

for an impact. This is also measured by using the same LM311 comparator, but with a reference voltage of 1V.

The main feature is that commercial manufacturers can calibrate various sensors or even use better sensors using the same algorithm. The most efficiently calibrated design will be the most effective. This project only uses the most probable values got from various sources and they have not been tested in real life.

The tilt sensor switches on when there in an inclination above 60°. This can be directly fed into a pin.

19.3.6 | Using the PIC MCU

The final design was decided based on the algorithm. The MCU used is PIC 18F452, the pin configuration of which is given in Figure 19.20. The PIC was first set up with a 20MHz clock and normal operation (PIN 1 connected to Vcc). The Rx pin of the microcontroller was connected to the Tx pin of the GPS module. The Tx pin of the microcontroller was connected to the Rx pin of the GSM module. The Vcc was given as 5V and ground was also connected. The sensors were given to PORT B setting it as input. The PIC has the property that it detects a floating PIN as a high input. Hence, it is grounded to detect low input. A 10 K resistor was connected to the ground. This acts as a pulldown resistor. The sensors are connected via LM311 comparator.

The accelerometer and the tilt meter require a power supply of 5V. The LM311 also has the power requirement of 5V. The reference voltage is set in the LM311 using a voltage divider circuit. This is done using a potentiometer and a resistor. The outputs from the sensors are fed through a resistor. This circuit was implemented and tested on a bread-board.

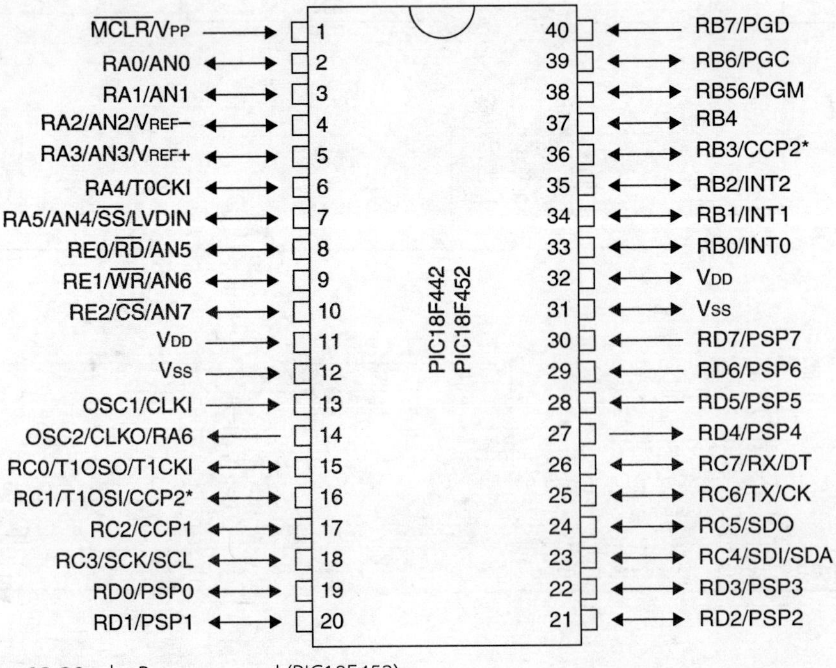

Figure 19.20 | Processor used (PIC18F452)

The circuit diagram is shown in Figure 19.21. The circuit has features like alarm (buzzer) and flashing lights (LEDs). This is required to locate the position when the accident occurs in a remote position at night. This can be changed to powerful flashing lights and high sound speakers. But in this project only a demo is implemented. The LEDs and the buzzer are driven by a BC547 circuit which provides the required current.

A voltage regulator (LM7805) was also provided to convert a 12V supply to 5V. A reset circuitry was also designed to manually reset the PIC without using power off.

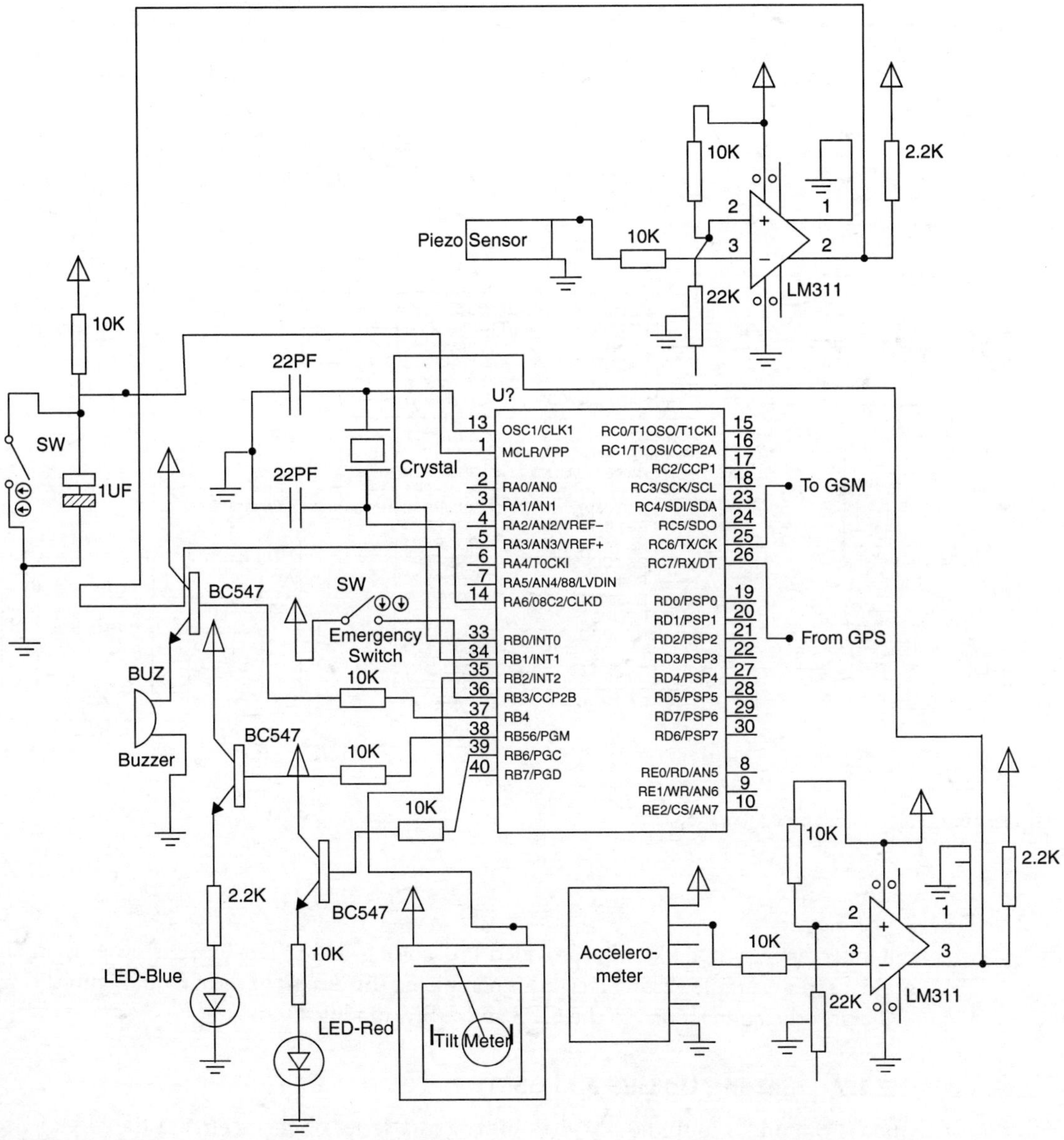

Figure 19.21 | Circuit diagram of the system

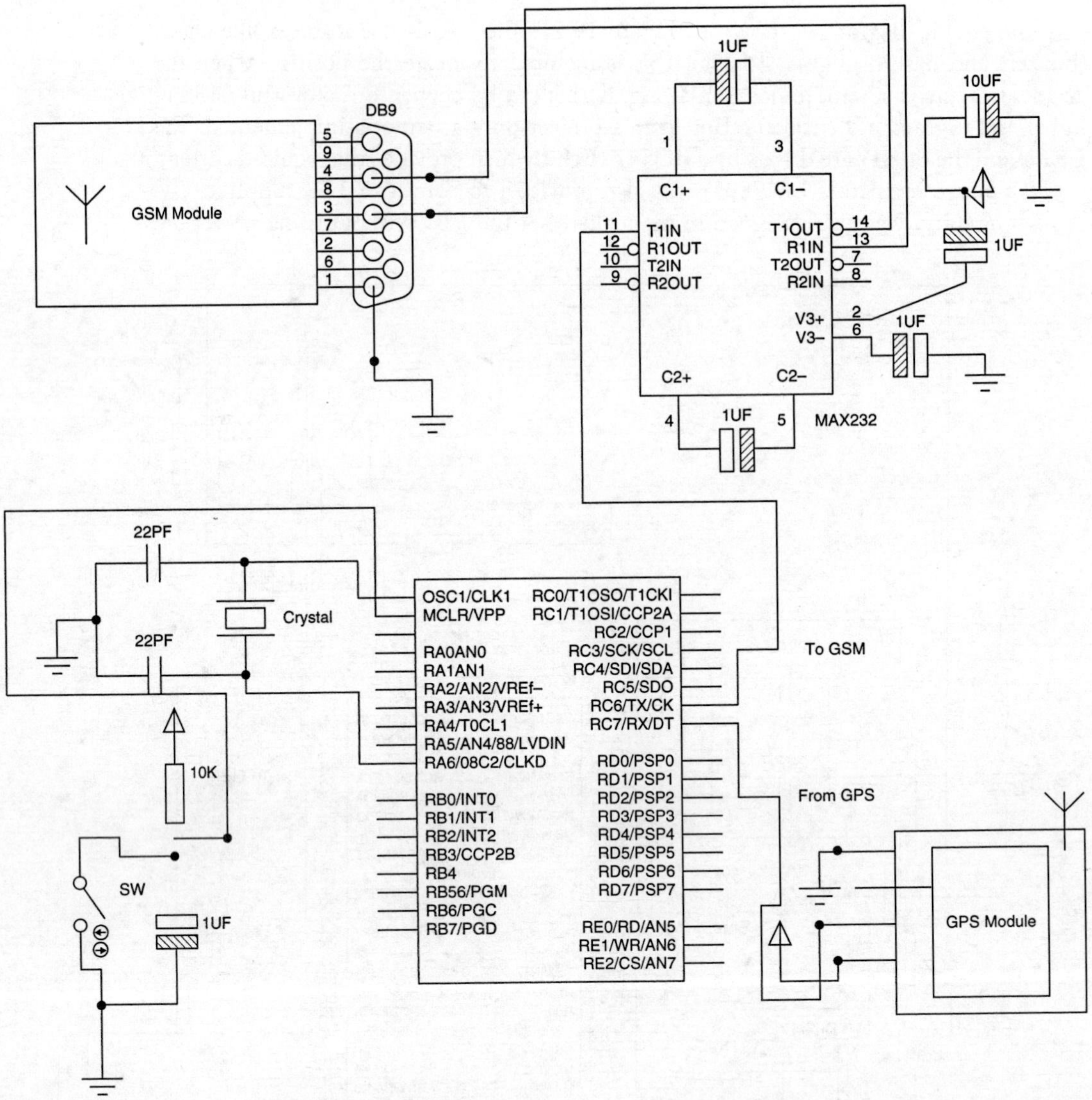

Figure 19.22 | Circuit for GPS and GSM

An emergency switch was also provided for sending SMS alert in cases other than an accident (for example getting lost). This completed the design of the circuit. Figure 19.22 elaborates the connections to the GPS and GSM modules.

19.3.7 | Setting Up GPS and GSM

The GPS module continuously gives in data as a series of characters via the UART Tx pin. This consists of unnecessary data as well. The data coming out from the module is:

```
$GPRMC,112958.000,A,0958.9621,N,07617.0536,E,0.66,160.96,190110,,,A*67
$GPVTG,160.96,T,,M,0.66,N,1.23,K,A*35
$GPGGA,112959.000,0958.9622,N,07617.0535,E,1,6,1.37,10.0,M,-93.4,M,,*45
$GPGSA,A,3,31,30,24,10,26,21,,,,,,,1.66,1.37,0.92*07
$GPRMC,112959.000,A,0958.9622,N,07617.0535,E,1.33,157.11,190110,,,A*6C
$GPVTG,157.11,T,,M,1.33,N,2.46,K,A*3F
```

From this, the strings starting with $GPRMC or $GPGGA contains the required location coordinates. A comparison algorithm that checks for $GPGGA and then takes only the value of the location coordinates from the string was formulated. This data can be stored in the internal memory of the microcontroller.

The UART communication of the GPS module is by default at 9600 baud. This is setup in the microcontroller as well. The module is set to work in default settings. The data comes out through the Tx pin. This is directly connected to the Rx pin of the microcontroller. No data is needed to be sent for the functioning of this module.

The GSM module also works via the UART. This also had a baud rate of 9600. The communication is initiated via AT commands. This was also tested to work using the hyper terminal. The algorithm is to initiate the GSM modem, bring it to the SMS mode and then send the required data. The location coordinates stored previously is also appended to this and sent.

The communication with both the GPS and GSM modules uses a baud rate of 9600. The GPS requires only the Rx pin and the GSM modem communication can be setup using the Tx pin of the microcontroller. Hence, the one and only UART port (Tx and Rx) is sufficient to communicate with both. Thus, the use of multiplexer and associated complexities can be avoided.

The GPS module requires a power supply of 5V. The GSM module has got its own power supply. The UART output of GSM module is taken via a DB-9 connector (3.25V for high and -3.25V for low). This has to be converted to TTL levels (5V for high and 0V for low). This was done by using a level converter circuit (using MAX232). This MAX232 IC required a power supply of 5V.

After successfully testing on a bread board, a PCB was assembled for the whole system. The PCB was designed using the software ORCAD. Figure 19.23 is the picture of the PCB designed to mount the circuit hardware.

19.3.8 | Observations and Conclusions

The project was completed in various stages as has been previously explained. Each stage had a unique result that led to the next stage. The successive stages led to the completion of the project and the various intermediary results were observed. Figure 19.24(a) to (d) illustrates the simulation results and the implementation.

In order to develop AVAAS (Automatic Vehicle Accident Alert System), three main sub-problems were identified: identifying the accident (using sensors), finding the location of the vehicle and sending the information to the concerned. All these sub-problems are joined to make an optimal solution for the whole problem. In this project work, a platform for emergency rescue in case of an auto crash was designed and a prototype was developed and tested. Various challenges have been encountered. The system was tested to operate optimally in order to reduce the golden time for arrival of aid when every second counts.

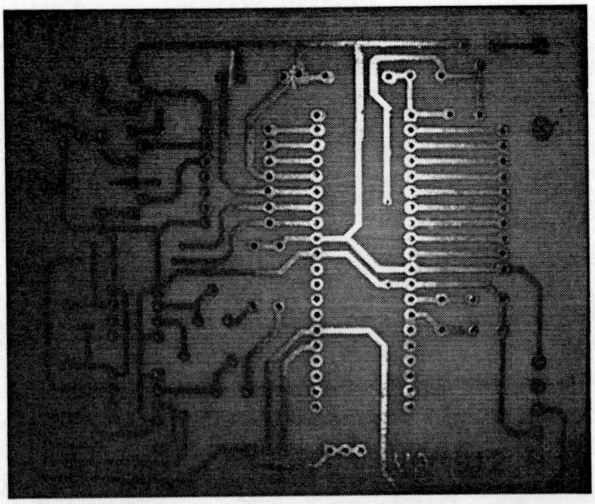

Figure 19.23 | PCB design

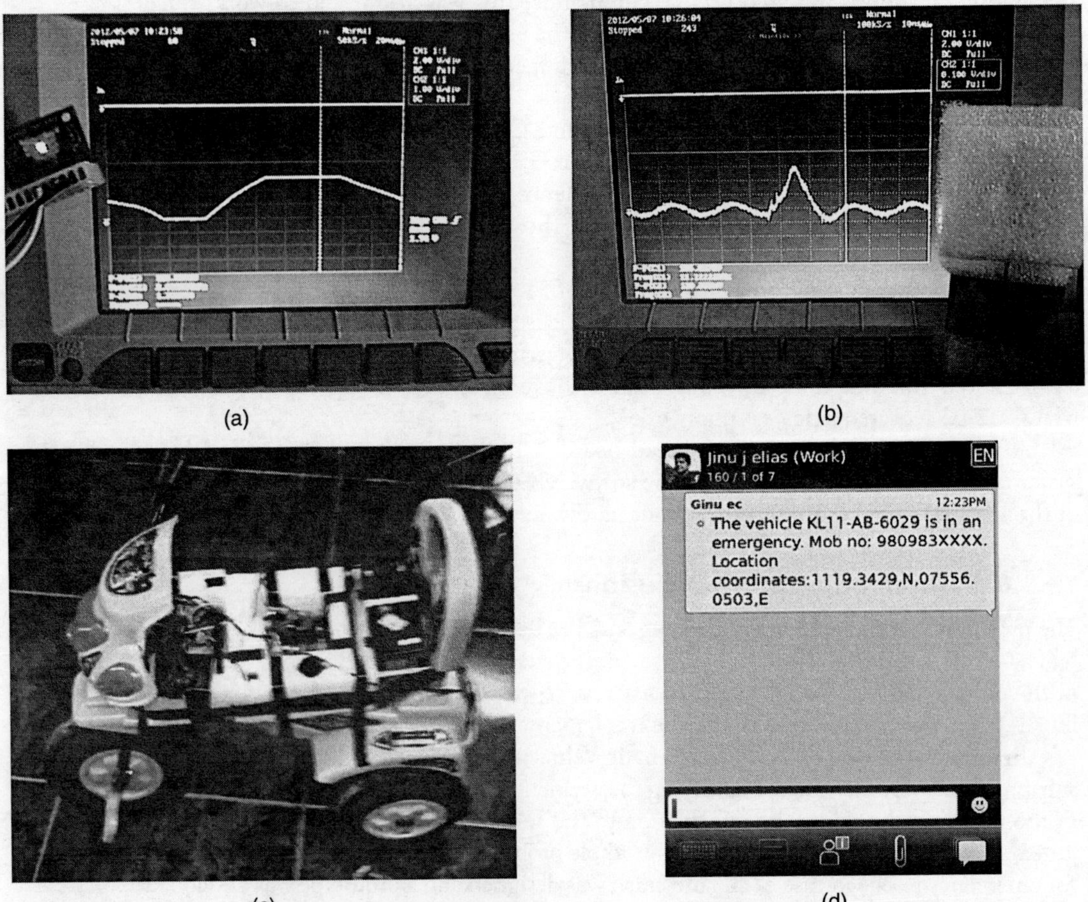

(a) (b) (c) (d)

Figure 19.24 | (a) Output of accelerometer, (b) output of Piezo sensor, (c) prototype of the system implemented on a tricycle, (d) the message sent

19.3.9 | Future Scope

This project is implemented by taking into consideration only the data that was available from various sources. But the practical implementation considering a real accident scenario has not been done. Simulation of various types of accidents and changing the design to make it efficient can be done in future.

The system can be commercialized by including the various options. For example, integrating the system to the Internet can make the design more efficient and also more precise. This can be done using the GPRS system available in the GSM module. This will help to monitor the accidents and develop a better traffic system.

The implementation of features like voice call, video call, measuring the various parameters digitally and monitoring the vehicle right from the beginning of the journey will add new dimensions in this system and help to ensure road safety.

Conclusion

Three projects in which there are four embedded implementations have been briefly discussed here. The salient points of most of the previous chapters are used in these projects. Two of the implementations use the PIC MCU, one uses ARM7 and one is based on the OMAP dual core processor. These projects have been included in the book, to show that anyone with a reasonable knowledge of embedded theory coupled with strong motivation, can develop embedded products which perform very well.

KEY POINTS OF THIS CHAPTER

- Four practically implemented embedded systems are discussed in this chapter.
- In the ball following robot, the software is run in MATLAB in a PC, and a serial cable connects the PC to the robot which is implemented using a PIC MCU and DC motors.
- In the vision controlled 'autonomous' robot, the complete implementation is done using a Beagle board, into which a Linux OS is booted, and programs are written in OpenCV.
- An ARM based audio player with an audio codec is implemented, which gives very good audio re-play.
- Using a PIC MCU, and GSM and GPS modules, an automatic alert system is implemented.
- These four projects encapsulate many of the concepts discussed in previous chapters.

QUESTIONS

1. Is it possible to use MATLAB to control the movement of a robot?
2. What have you understood about 'blob detection'?
3. Why is it necessary for an OS to be ported in the Beagle board used in the vision guided robot?
4. Why is a level shifter used in project no:1 of this chapter?

5. What is the difference between a NAND flash and NOR flash?
6. What protocol is used for communicating between the SD card and ARM in Project No. 2?
7. List the sensors used in Project No. 3.
8. How do each of the sensors indicate the occurrence of an accident?
9. What information is obtained from the GPS module?
10. What is the role of the GSM module in Project No. 3?

EXERCISES

1 Design a system for home security using a GSM module for sending information for alerts.
2. Design a system for home security with Zigbee and GSM included in it.
3. Design a system which can activate all the apparatus at home (AC, fan ,TV etc) from a remote point. Will a GSM module be useful here?

APPENDIX A

THE INSTRUCTION SET OF 8051

Arithmetic Operations

Mnemonic		Description	Bytes	Cycles
ADD	A,Rn	Add register to A	1	1
ADD	A,direct	Add direct byte to A	2	1
ADD	A,@Ri	Add indirect RAM to A	1	1
ADD	A,#data	Add immediate data to A	2	1
ADDC	A,Rn	Add register to A with Carry	1	1
ADDC	A,direct	Add direct byte to A with Carry	2	1
ADDC	A,@Ri	Add indirect RAM to A with Carry	1	1
ADDC	A,#data	Add immediate data to A with Carry	2	1
SUBB	A,Rn	Subtract register from A with Borrow	1	1
SUBB	A,direct	Subtract direct byte from A with Borrow	2	1
SUBB	A,@Ri	Subtract indirect RAM from A with Borrow	1	1
SUBB	A,#data	Subtract immediate data from A with Borrow	2	1
INC	A	Increment A	1	1
INC	Rn	Increment register	1	1
INC	direct	Increment direct byte	2	1
INC	@Ri	Increment indirect RAM	1	1
DEC	A	Decrement A	1	1
DEC	Rn	Decrement register	1	1
DEC	direct	Decrement direct byte	2	1
DEC	@Ri	Decrement indirect RAM	1	1
INC	DPTR	Increment Data Pointer	1	2
MUL	AB	Multiply A and B (A x B => BA)	1	4
DIV	AB	Divide A by B (A/B => A + B)	1	4
DA	A	Decimal Adjust A	1	1

Logical Operations

Mnemonic		Description	Bytes	Cycles
ANL	A,Rn	AND register to A	1	1
ANL	A,direct	AND direct byte to A	2	1
ANL	A,@Ri	AND indirect RAM to A	1	1
ANL	A,#data	AND immediate data to A	2	1
ANL	direct,A	AND A to direct byte	2	1
ANL	direct,#data	AND immediate data to direct byte	3	2
ORL	A,Rn	OR register to A	1	1
ORL	A,direct	OR direct byte to A	2	1
ORL	A,@Ri	OR indirect RAM to A	1	1
ORL	A,#data	OR immediate data to A	2	1
ORL	direct,A	OR A to direct byte	2	1
ORL	direct,#data	OR immediate data to direct byte	3	2
XRL	A,Rn	Exclusive-OR register to A	1	1
XRL	A,direct	Exclusive-OR direct byte to A	2	1
XRL	A,@Ri	Exclusive-OR indirect RAM to A	1	1
XRL	A,#data	Exclusive-OR immediate data to A	2	1
XRL	direct,A	Exclusive-OR A to direct byte	2	1
XRL	direct,#data	Exclusive-OR immediate data to direct byte	3	2
CLR	A	Clear A	1	1
CPL	A	Complement A	1	1
RL	A	Rotate A Left	1	1
RLC	A	Rotate A Left through Carry	1	1
RR	A	Rotate A Right	1	1
RRC	A	Rotate A Right through Carry	1	1
SWAP	A	Swap nibbles within A	1	1

Data Transfer

Mnemonic		Description	Bytes	Cycles
MOV	A,Rn	Move register to A	1	1
MOV	A,direct	Move direct byte to A	2	1
MOV	A,@Ri	Move indirect RAM to A	1	1
MOV	A,#data	Move immediate data to A	2	1
MOV	Rn,A	Move A to register	1	1
MOV	Rn,direct	Move direct byte to register	2	2

Mnemonic		Description	Bytes	Cycles
MOV	Rn,#data	Move immediate data to register	2	1
MOV	direct,A	Move A to direct byte	2	1
MOV	direct,Rn	Move register to direct byte	2	2
MOV	direct,direct	Move direct byte to direct byte	3	2
MOV	direct,@Ri	Move indirect RAM to direct byte	2	2
MOV	direct,#data	Move immediate data to direct byte	3	2
MOV	@Ri,A Move	Move A to indirect RAM	1	1
MOV	@Ri,direct	Move direct byte to indirect RAM	2	2
MOV	@Ri,#data	Move immediate data to indirect RAM	2	1
MOV	DPTR,#data16	Load Data Pointer with 16-bit constant	2	1
MOVC	A,@A+DPTR	Move Code byte relative to DPTR to A	1	2
MOVC	A,@A+PC	Move Code byte relative to PC to A	1	2
MOVX	A,@Ri	Move External RAM (8-bit addr) to A	1	2
MOVX	A,@DPTR	Move External RAM (16-bit addr) to A	1	2
MOVX	@Ri,A	Move A to External RAM (8-bit addr)	1	2
MOVX	@DPTR,A	Move A to External RAM (16-bit addr)	1	2
PUSH	direct	Push direct byte onto stack	2	2
POP	direct	Pop direct byte from stack	2	2
XCH	A,Rn	Exchange register with A	1	1
XCH	A,direct	Exchange direct byte with A	2	1
XCH	A,@Ri	Exchange indirect RAM with A	1	1
XCHD	A,@Ri	Exchange low-order Digit indirect RAM with A	1	1

Boolean Variable Manipulation

Mnemonic		Description	Bytes	Cycles
CLR	C	Clear Carry flag	1	1
CLR	bit	Clear direct bit	2	1
SETB	C	Set Carry flag	1	1
SETB	bit	Set direct bit	2	1
CPL	C	Complement Carry flag	1	1
CPL	bit	Complement direct bit	2	1
ANL	C,bit	AND direct bit to Carry flag	2	2
ANL	C,/bit	AND complement of direct bit to Carry flag	2	2
ORL	C,bit	OR direct bit to Carry flag	2	2
ORL	C,/bit	OR complement of direct bit to Carry flag	2	2
MOV	C,bit	Move direct bit to Carry flag	2	1
MOV	bit,C	Move Carry flag to direct bit	2	2

Program and Machine Control

Mnemonic		Description	Bytes	Cycles
ACALL	addr11	Absolute subroutine call	2	2
LCALL	addr16	Long subroutine call	3	2
RET		Return from subroutine	1	2
RETI		Return from interrupt	1	2
AJMP	addr11	Absolute Jump	2	2
LJMP	addr16	Long Jump	3	2
SJMP	rel	Short Jump (relative addr)	2	2
JMP	@A+DPTR	Jump indirect relative to DPTR	1	2
JZ	rel	Jump if A is Zero	2	2
JNZ	rel	Jump if A is Not Zero	2	2
JC	rel	Jump if Carry flag is set	2	2
JNC	rel	Jump if No Carry flag	2	2
JB	bit,rel	Jump if direct Bit is set	3	2
JNB	bit,rel	Jump if direct Bit is Not set	3	2
JBC	bit,rel	Jump if direct Bit is set and Clear bit	3	2
CJNE	A,direct,rel	Compare direct to A and Jump if Not Equal	3	2
CJNE	A,#data,rel	Compare immediate to A and Jump if Not Equal	3	2
CJNE	Rn,#data,rel	Compare immediate to register and Jump if Not Equal	3	2
CJNE	@Ri,#data,rel	Compare immediate to indirect and Jump if Not Equal	3	2
DJNZ	Rn,rel	Decrement register and Jump if Not Zero	2	2
DJNZ	direct,rel	Decrement direct byte and Jump if Not Zero	3	2
NOP		No operation	1	1

Notes on Data Addressing Modes

Rn	Working register R0-R7
direct	128 internal RAM locations, any I/O port, control or status register
@Ri	Indirect internal RAM location addressed by register R0 or R1
#data	8-bit constant included in instruction
#data16	16-bit constant included in instruction
bit	128 software flags, any I/O pin, control or status bit

Notes on Program Addressing Modes

addr16	Destination address may be anywhere in 64-kByte program address space
addr11	Destination address will be within same 2-kByte page of program address space as first byte of the following instruction
rel	8-bit offset relative to first byte of following instruction (+127, −128)

Information from Intel Application Note AP-69

APPENDIX B

USING THE KEIL μVISION4 TOOLS FOR 8051 AND ARM

The latest version of RVDK (Real View Development Kit) supplied by Keil is μvision4, The evaluation version of this is freely downloadable by looking up 'Keil μ Vision 4' or from the links

https://www.keil.com/demo/eval/c51.htm for 8051 and
https://www.keil.com/demo/eval/arm.htm for ARM

The evaluation version can be used for simulation, and the only limitation it has is that a memory limitation of 2K for program code for 8051, and 32K for ARM.

The 'Real View Development Kit (RVDK) of Keil' is a tool chain consisting of assemblers, compilers, debuggers, simulators etc for many chips of many families—it caters to the 8051 family, ARM and many more families of chips. It can be used for C programming of embedded devices as well as assembly language programs.

For 8051

In Chapters 13 and 14, a number of assembly programs have been discussed and the Keil tool has been mentioned. In Chapter 9, C programs are covered.

In this appendix, the steps in using this tool are discussed.

The discussion covers the step-by-step approach for using this tool for

i) assembly language and
ii) C language programming,
iii) building and debugging.

A particular device of a specific family has to be chosen, and for this explanation we choose the 8951 chip of Atmel.

Assembly Language Programming of 8051

Creating a Project

First make a folder in which your programs will be saved.

Then, open μvision4 and click the 'Project' menu and then 'New μ Vision Project' in it, as illustrated in Fig A-B.1

Browse, and get to the folder in which you will save it. Name the project FIRST. and it will be saved as FIRST.uvproj. (You can use any other name, this is just an example.)

With this, the device selection page will be opened and it will look like it is seen in Fig A-B.2.

Scroll, and choose Atmel, and a list of the names of chips of the 8051 family will be seen.

Select the device you want—here we click on 89C51 as pointed in Fig A-B.3.

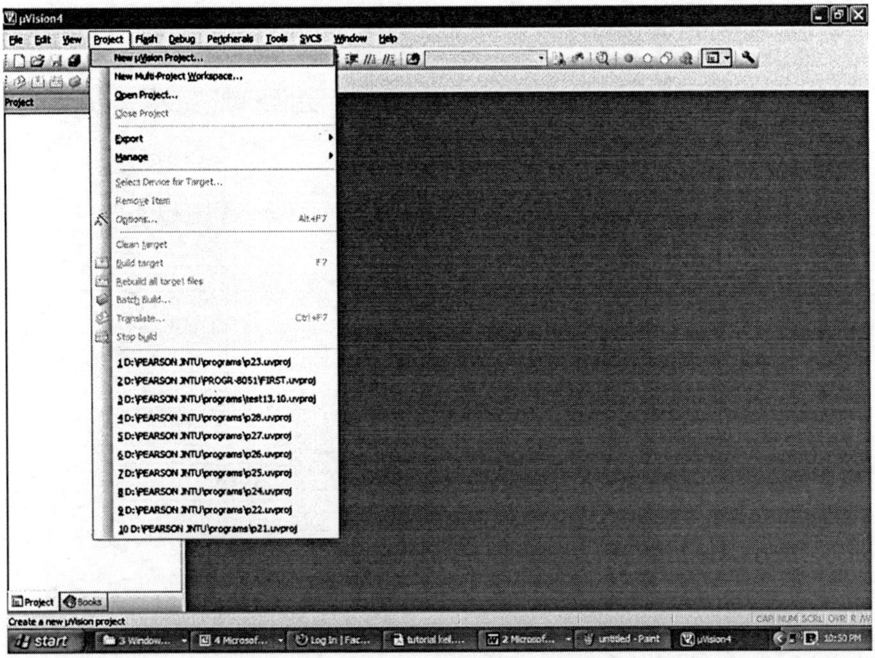

Figure A-B.1

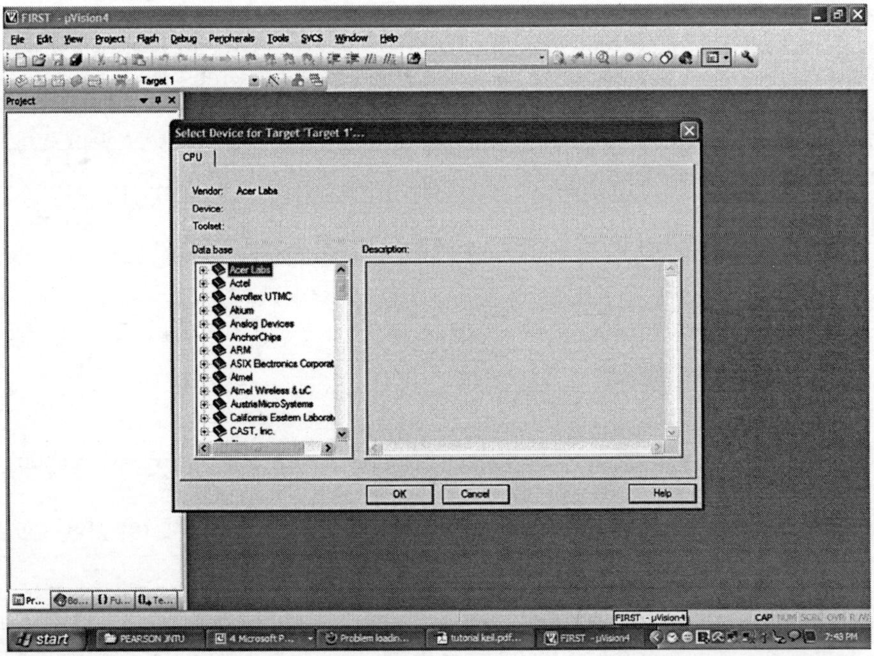

Figure A-B.2

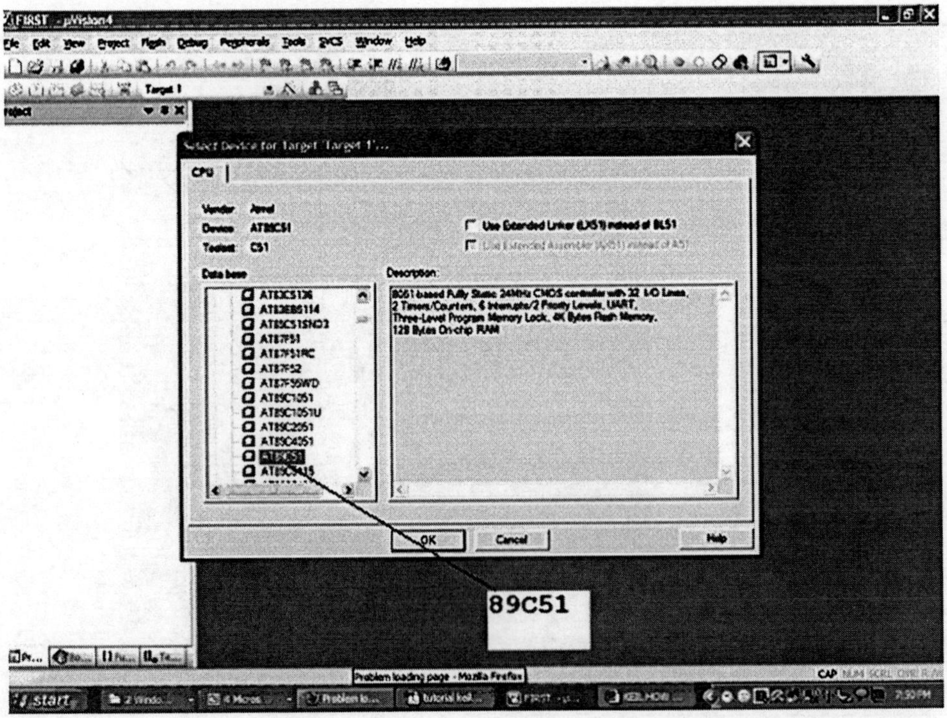

Figure A-B.3

The next screen will ask the question 'Copy Standard 8051 startup code to Project Folder and Add File to Project?' This can be answered as 'No', as we don't need it for assembly language programming (For C programs, we answer 'Yes)'.

Next, click on the File Tab and choose New. The editor opens and you can type your program here. This is an example program chosen.

```
ORG 0
STRT:   MOV A,#45H
        MOV R1,#23H
        ADD A,R1
        MOV 45H,A
HERE:   SJMP HERE
END
```

Type this program and save it as FIRST.src. Any filename can be chosen, but the extension should be .src.

The next step is to add the filename to the source. For that, look to the left, in the project workspace. Click the + sign on the left of 'Target1' and get 'Source Group 1'.

Right click on it to get the screen as shown in Fig A-B.4

Click on 'Add files to group source Group 1', browse for 'src files and choose the file FIRST.src.-. This is shown in Fig A-B.5. Click Add and then Close. After this, if you click the '+' on the left of Source Group 1, this filename will be seen there.

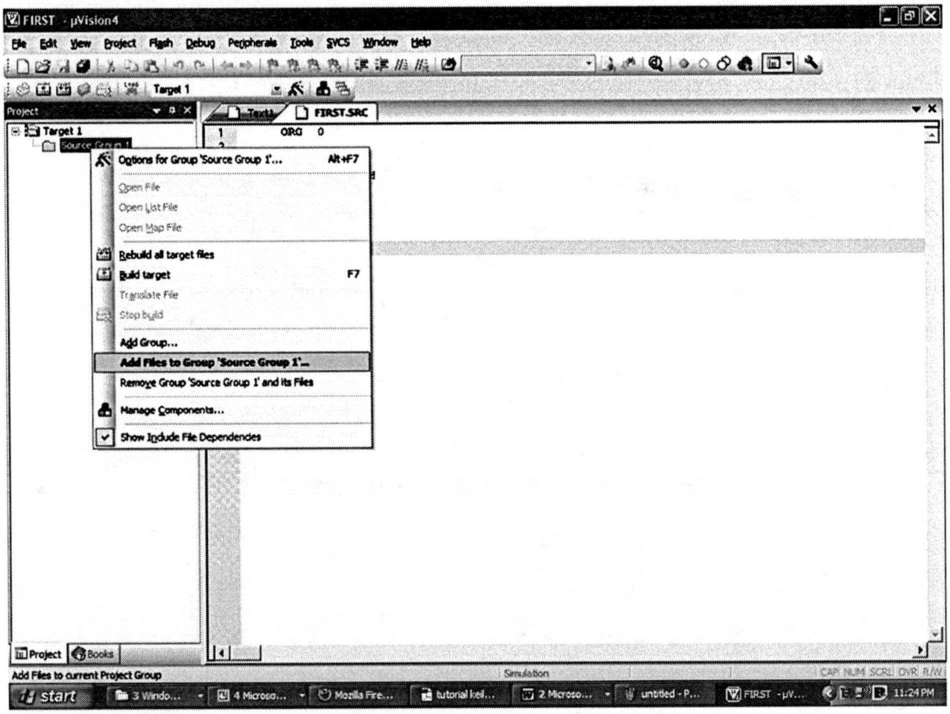

Figure A-B.4

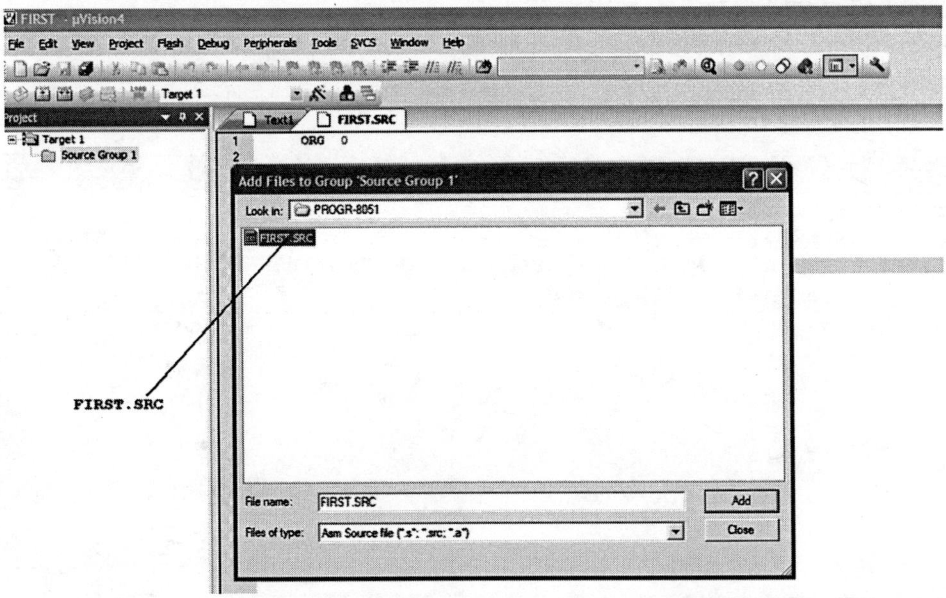

Figure A-B.5

Next, we need to assemble this file. Click on the Project tab, and get the 'Build file' Option or 'Build all files'. Click on it, and the output window will open as shown in Fig A-B.6.

Since there are no errors, the message is that of 0 errors and 0 warnings. In case of any error, it will be listed as in Fig A-B.7

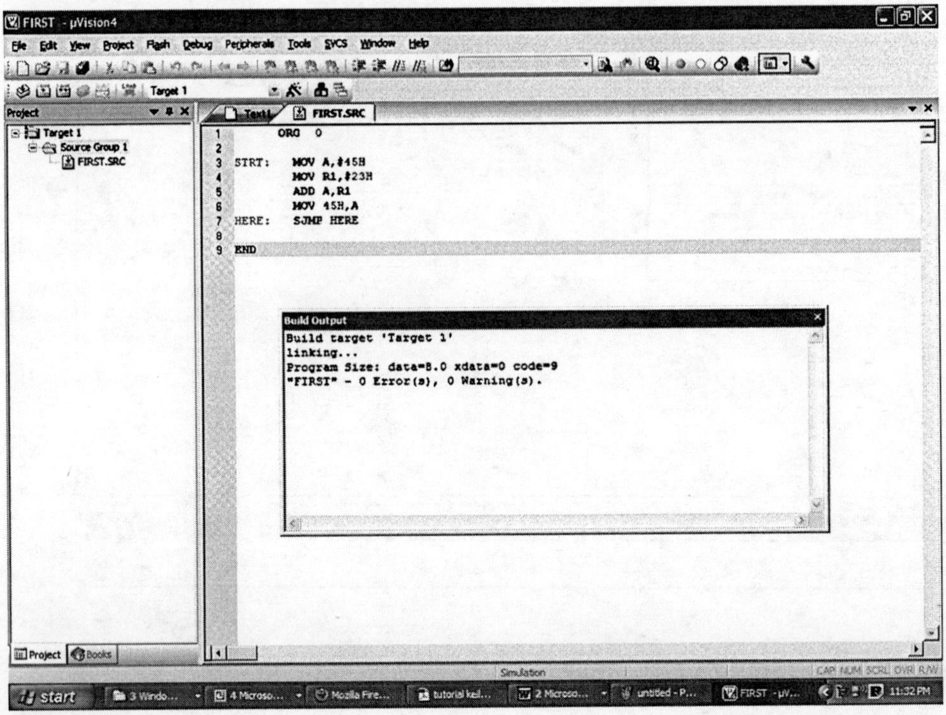

Figure A-B.6

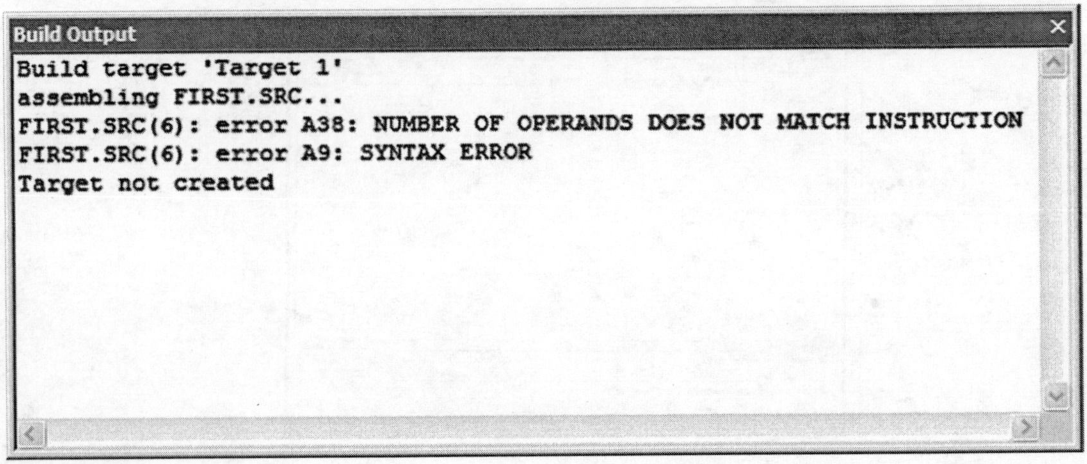

Figure A-B.7

Debugging

Once building is done, we can do debugging. This is the option by virtue of which it is possible to view the contents of memory, registers, observe output waveform etc.

There are actually a lot of things we can do, but only a few will be considered here. The rest of the options can be tried out easily, referring to the 'Help' menu.

Go to the Debug tab, and click on 'Start/Stop Debug session'.

The following actions are the result:

i) A small window opens with the message EVALUATION MODE:
   Running with code size limit : 2K
ii) Click Ok and the debug session starts with a number of windows getting open. See Fig A-B.8.

You can open/close these windows using the View menu. The registers, memory, output, disassembly window, etc can be opened or closed using 'View'.

Fig A-B.8 shows the debug screen with the disassembly window, register window and Memory 2 window. In the memory window, typing c: 0x0000 (and pressing ENTER) gives us the content of ROM. and typing d: 0x00 displays the content of RAM.

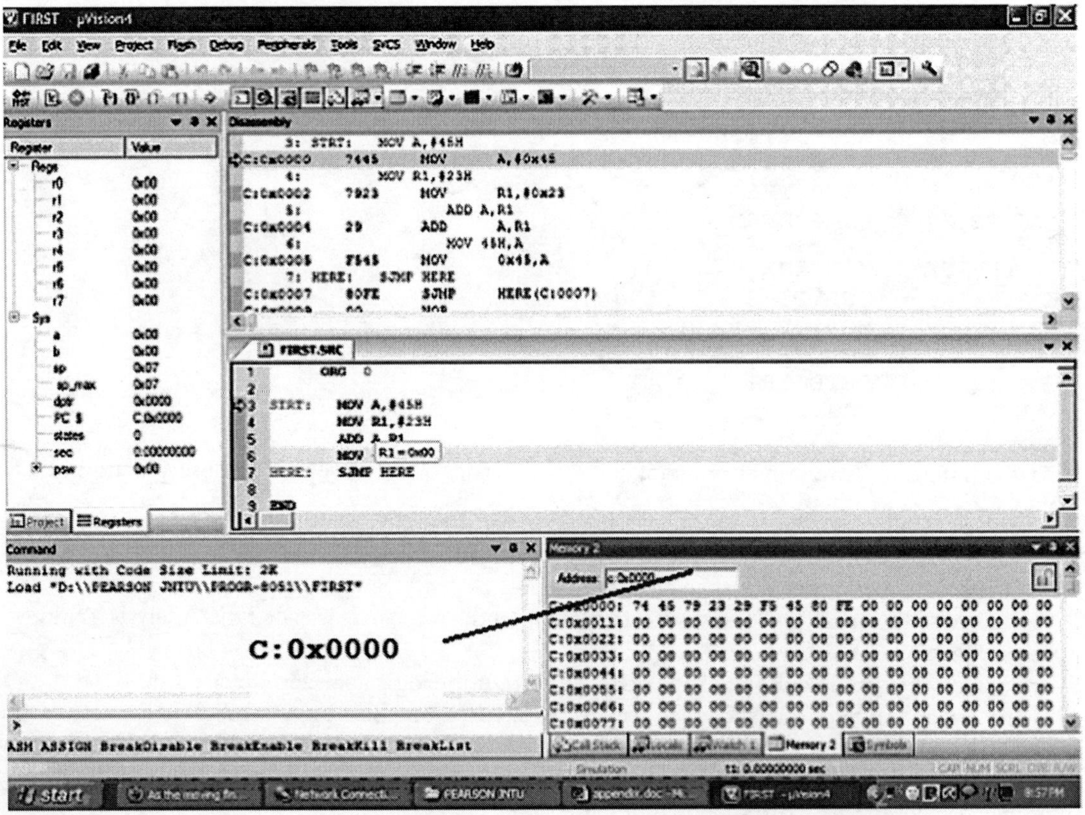

Figure A-B.8

For checking the content of RAM, type d:0x00 in the memory window.

Single Stepping

The easiest thing to do is to 'single step' and get one instruction executed, and then check the contents of registers and memory. For that, go to the Debug tab and click 'Step' or press F11. This activity is very interesting, as you will be able to observe the result of the execution of each instruction. Just after pressing FI, examine the content of the register or memory which is involved in the instruction executed. You will see how the content has changed.

If peripherals are involved in the program, go to the Peripherals tab and click on timers or I/O or serial ports, and single step through the program. All these actions become quicker, easier and fun with practice. The easiest is the GPIO peripheral window which shows the ON-OFF condition of all the pins.

Using the Logic Analyser

We conclude this appendix by giving some tips on using the logic analyzer which allows us to view waveforms. The following program is used to discuss this.

```
ORG 0
                      LJMP STRT

ORG       001BH
                SJMP   T1_ISR

ORG     40H
STRT:           MOV TMOD,#10H

                MOV IE,#88H
                SETB P1.3
                SETB TR1
HERE:           SJMP HERE

 T1_ISR :       CLR TR1
                CPL P1.3
                MOV TL1,#24H
                MOV TH1,#OFAH
                SETB TR1
END              RET1
```

This is an interrupt driven timer program and a symmetric square wave is to be observed at pin P1.3

Steps

Build the program and then start the debug session.

You can see a 'red and yellow' waveform symbol on the toolbar. It is called the 'Analysis Window'. Click and open it.

Click on the 'setup window 'on the open window of the logic analyzer. Refer Fig A-B.9.

The set up box alone is shown in Fig A-B.10. Click on the square symbol at the left of the X symbol. A bar gets highlighted. On this bar, write P1.3 (for the output pin), then click Hexadecimal display and write '0' in the Shift Right box. You can select the color in the color box and the display type may be chosen to be 'Bit' as shown in Fig A-B.11.

Click close, then go to the Debug menu and click on Run.

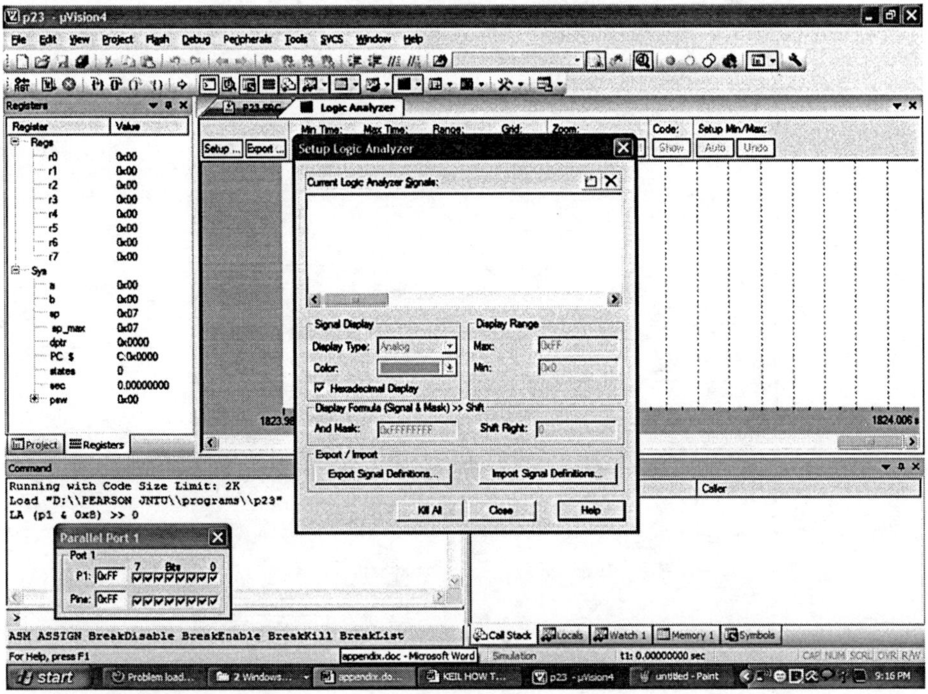

Figure A-B.9

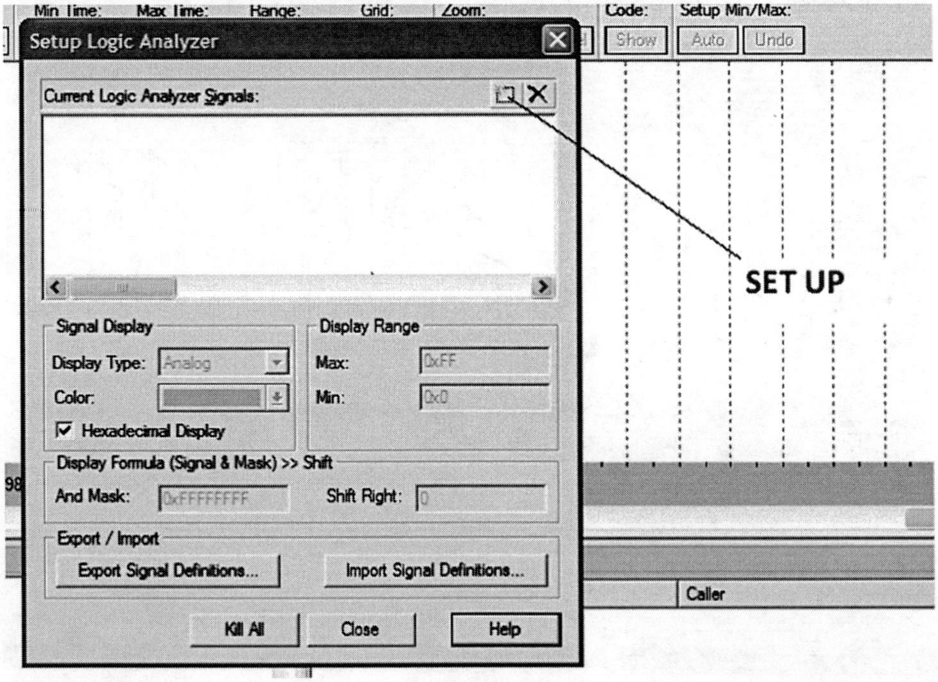

Figure A-B.10

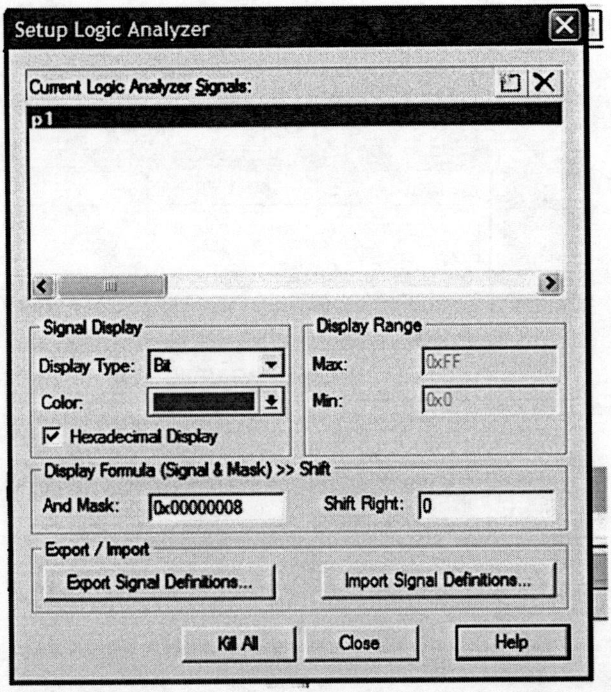

Figure A-B.11

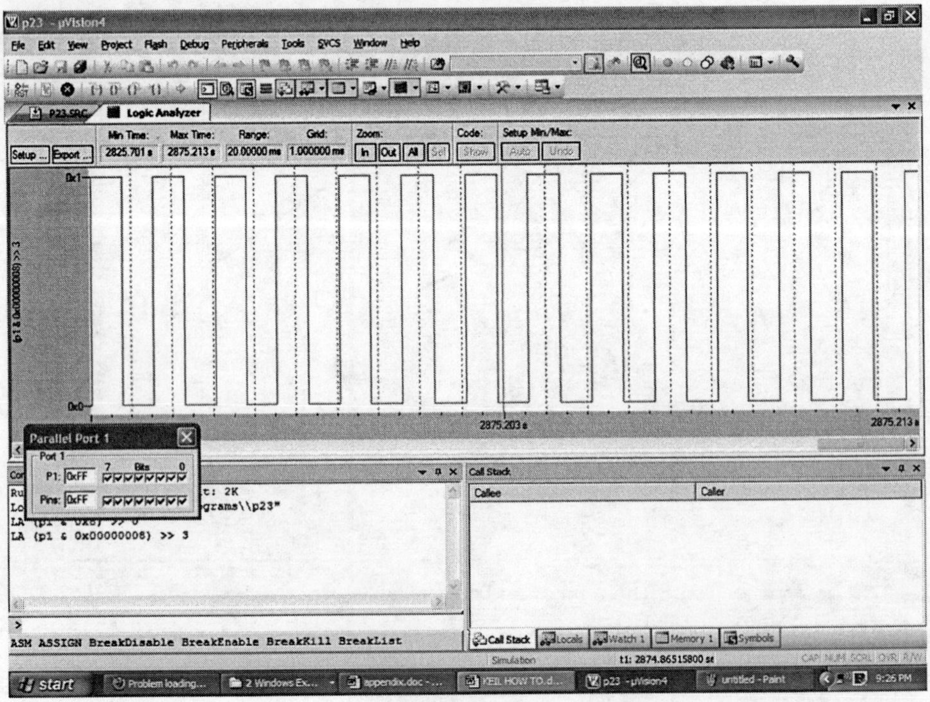

Figure A-B.12

The waveform at P1.3 will be displayed on the window. This waveform can be zoomed out and in, as you wish. If you want a stationary waveform, after Run, you can click on Stop and then click the logic analyzer window again. Fig A-B.12 shows the displayed waveform for the program used.

Fig A-B.12 shows the debug window with the logic analyzer. Incidentally, the peripherals window is also open showing the state of Port 1. (The disassembly and registers window have been closed).

All the square waveform generation examples of Chapter 12 and 13 have been tested using this logic analyzer. By reading more about this in the RVDK manual, a greater understanding of the debugging support facilitated by the Keil tools can be gained.

Using the Keil RVDK for C Programming of 8051

The steps in using the IDE for C programming is similar to what has been discussed for assembly language programming. There is a difference in one step, however.

Refer back to Fig A-B.3 and the discussion following it, which is quoted below.

"The next screen will ask the question 'Copy Standard 8051 startup code to Project Folder and Add File to Project?' This can be answered as 'No', as we don' t need it for assembly language programming (For C programs, we answer 'Yes)'."

The point is that, for C programs, we need to include the startup file as well. After this step, the C program is written into the editor and saved as filename.c. Then this filename is added to the project. You will find that there are two files in the source group. One is the startup file, and the other is the C file.

After this, the building and debugging is exactly the same as discussed for assembly language programming.

For ARM

For using Keil RVDK for ARM, you must download the relevant software for ARM using the following link

https://www.keil.com/demo/eval/arm.htm

Programs discussed in Chapter 10 (assembly) and Chapter 11 (C programming) can be tested in this simulator.

After installing the tool chain, it can be used in the same way as discussed for 8051. The difference comes only in the choice of the device. One of the ARM chips must be chosen. In Chapter 11, the ARM MCU used is LPC 2148, belonging to NXP. This can be chosen. The steps in saving, building and debugging are similar to that used for 8051.

The points to keep in mind are:

i) For C programming, a 'start up file' is to be included.
ii) For assembly programming, a start up file' is NOT to be included.
iii) To know the contents of memory during debugging, find the address of RAM and flash ROM from the memory map of the device. For LPC 2148, ROM starts at 0x00000000 and RAM at 0x40000000. Type one of these numbers in the memory window to read the content of the corresponding memory.

A step-by-step procedure for using RVDK for ARM is made available in the website of the book, which is www.pearsoned.co.in/lylabdas/embeddedsystems.

APPENDIX C

A STEP-BY-STEP GUIDE FOR USING THE PSoC DESIGNER

PSoC Designer™ is two tools in one. It combines a full featured integrated development environment (IDE) (the Chip-Level Editor) with a powerful visual programming interface (the System-Level Editor). The two tools require and support two different design processes.

In the Chip-Level Editor you specify exactly how you want the device configured. This allows you direct access to all of the features of your PSoC device and complete control over the routing, system resource use, and firmware development:

i) Choose a base device to work with.
ii) Choose user modules that configure the PSoC device for the functionality you need in your system.
iii) Configure the user modules for your chosen application and connect them to each other and to the proper pins.
iv) Generate your project. This prepopulates your project with APIs and libraries that you can use to program your application.
v) Program in C for rapid development, assembly language to get every last drop of performance, or a combination of both.

The **Chip-Level Editor** allows you to work directly with the resources available on a PSoC device, select and configure user modules, such as analog to digital converters (ADCs), timers, amplifiers, and others, and route inputs, outputs, and other resources to and from them.

In the **System-Level Editor** you solve design problems the same way you might think about the system:

i) Select input and output devices based upon system requirements.
ii) Add a communication interface and define the interface to the system (registers).
iii) Define when and how an output device changes state based upon any/all other system devices.
iv) Based upon the design, automatically select one or more PSoC Mixed-Signal Controllers that match system requirements.
v) PSoC Designer completely and correctly generates all embedded code, then compiles and links it into a programming file for a specific PSoC device.
vi) You can then open the project in Interconnect view to review and further configure your design.

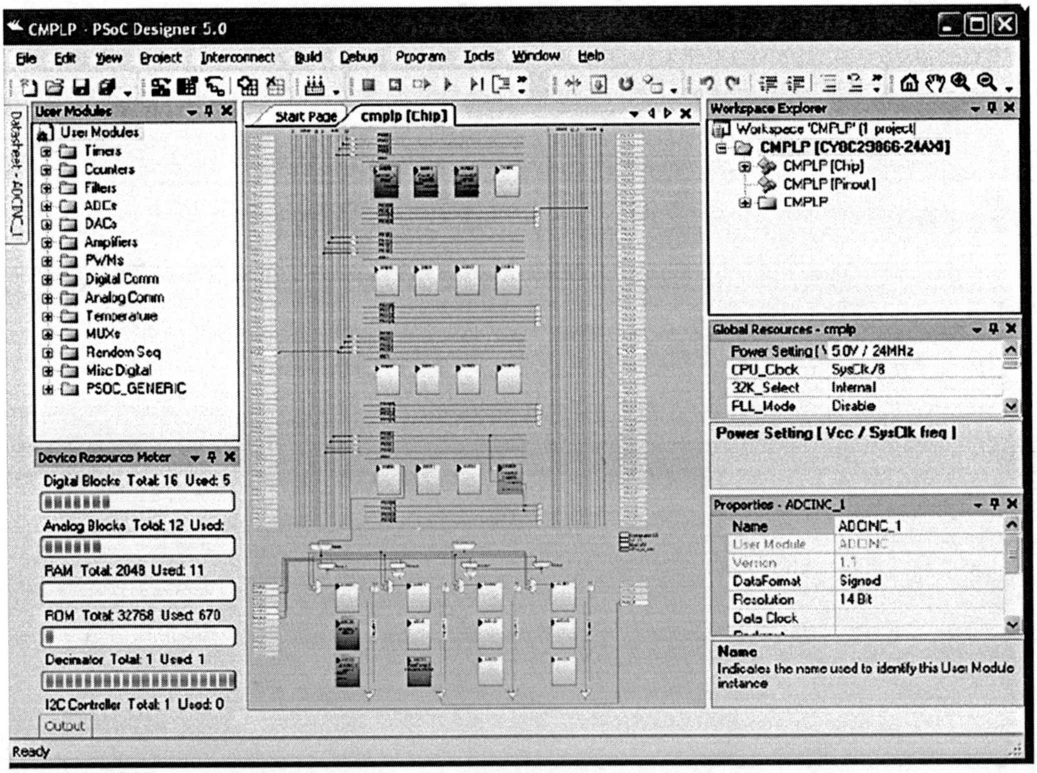
CMPLP - PSoC Designer 5.0
File Edit View Project Interconnect Build Debug Program Tools Window Help
User Modules
User Modules
Timers
Counters
Filters
ADCs
DACs
Amplifiers
PWMs
Digital Comm
Analog Comm
Temperature
MUXs
Random Seq
Misc Digital
PSOC_GENERIC
Start Page
cmplp [Chip]
Workspace Explorer
Workspace 'CMPLP' (1 project)
CMPLP [CY8C29866-24AXI]
CMPLP [Chip]
CMPLP [Pinout]
CMPLP
Global Resources - cmplp
Power Setting [5.0V / 24MHz
CPU_Clock SysClk/8
32K_Select Internal
PLL_Mode Disable
Power Setting [Vcc / SysClk freq]
Device Resource Meter
Digital Blocks Total: 16 Used: 5
Analog Blocks Total: 12 Used:
RAM Total: 2048 Used: 11
ROM Total: 32768 Used: 670
Decimator Total: 1 Used: 1
I2C Controller Total: 1 Used: 0
Output
Properties - ADCINC_1
Name ADCINC_1
User Module ADCINC
Version 1.1
DataFormat Signed
Resolution 14 Bit
Data Clock
Name
Indicates the name used to identify this User Module instance
Ready

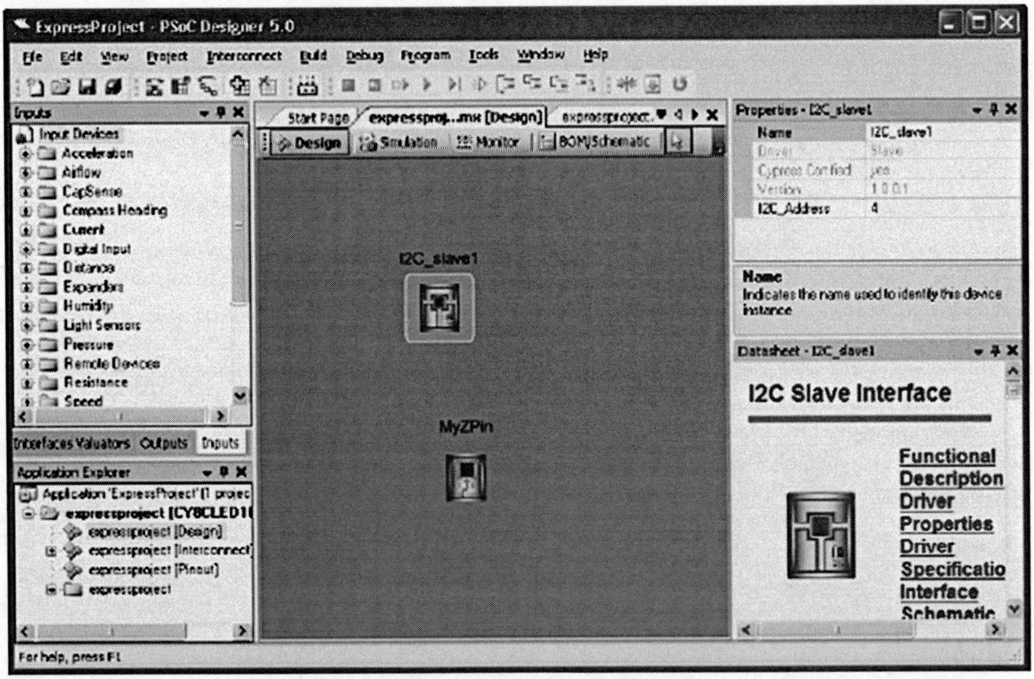
ExpressProject - PSoC Designer 5.0
File Edit View Project Interconnect Build Debug Program Tools Window Help
Inputs
Input Devices
Acceleration
Airflow
CapSense
Compass Heading
Current
Digital Input
Distance
Expanders
Humidity
Light Sensors
Pressure
Remote Devices
Resistance
Speed
Interfaces Valuators Outputs Inputs
Application Explorer
Application 'ExpressProject' (1 projec
expressproject [CY8CLED1
expressproject [Design]
expressproject [Interconnect]
expressproject [Pinout]
expressproject
Start Page
expressproj...mx [Design]
Design
Simulation
Monitor
BOM/Schematic
I2C_slave1
MyZPin
Properties - I2C_slave1
Name I2C_slave1
Driver Slave
Cypress Certified yes
Version 1.0.0.1
I2C_Address 4
Name
Indicates the name used to identify this device instance
Datasheet - I2C_slave1
I2C Slave Interface
Functional
Description
Driver
Properties
Driver
Specificatio
Interface
Schematic
For help, press F1

Chip-Level Design

In the **Chip-Level** view you specify exactly how you want the device configured. This allows you direct access to all of the features of your PSoC device and complete control over the routing, system resource use, and firmware development:

Create a Project

In order to program the desired functionality into a PSoC device, you need to first create a project directory in which the files and device configurations reside.

Step 1: To start a new project, select **New Project** from the **File** menu.

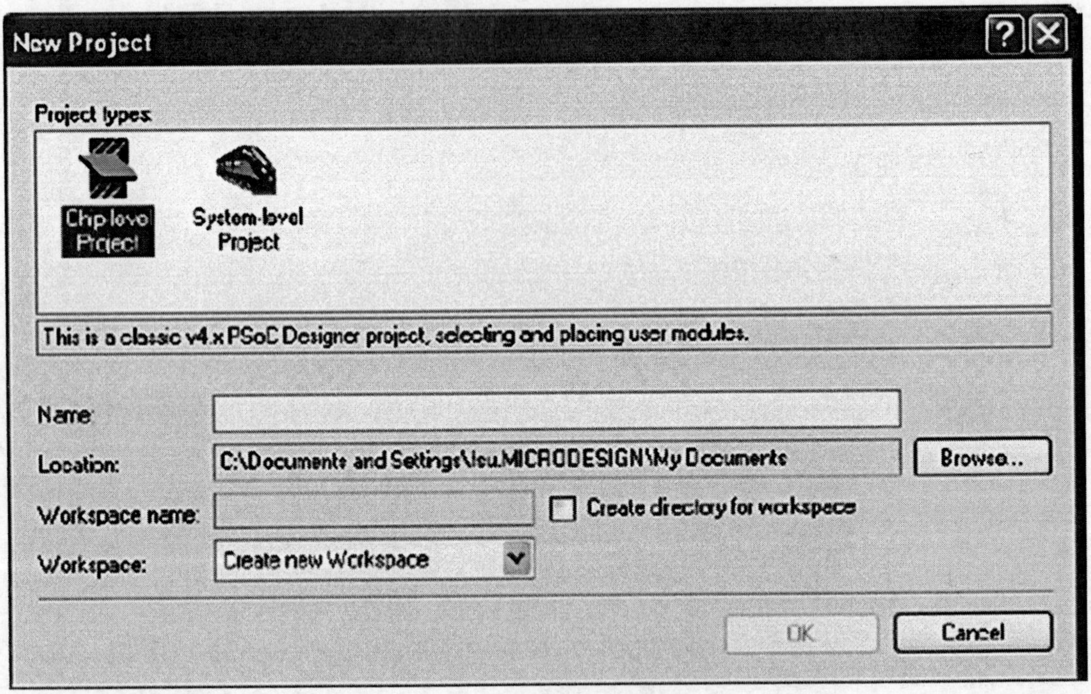

Step 2: Choose a name and location for the project. By default, a project is created inside a workspace with the same name as the project; the project is stored in the project directory. If you plan to create multiple projects in a single workspace (for example, if your project will use multiple PSoC devices), click **Create a directory for workspace** and supply a name for the first project. When you are finished, click **Next**.

Step 3: In the Select Project Type dialog box, click View Catalog to access a detailed list of available parts.

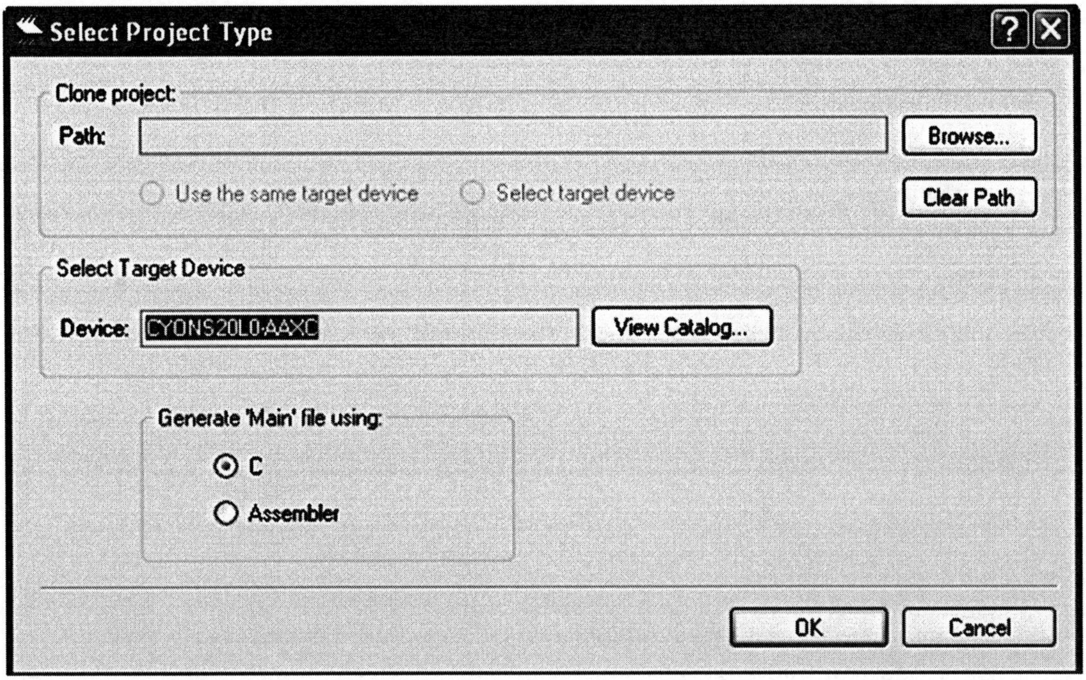

Step 4: In the Parts Catalog Dialog Box, highlight your part of choice. Tabs at the left and characteristic selections along the top narrow the list of devices. You have several options in this dialog box including layout display, viewing part image, and sorting part selection.

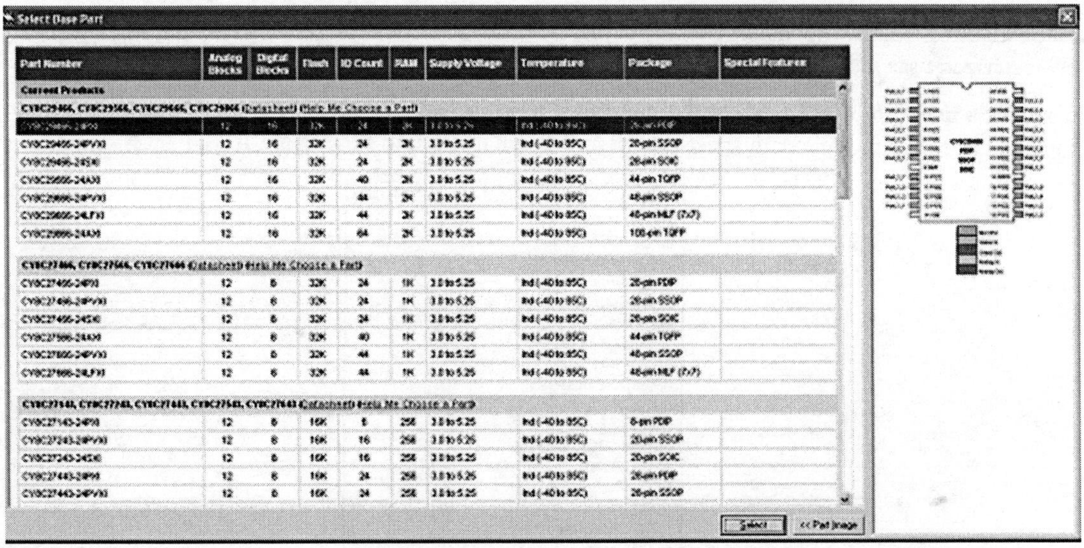

Clone a Project

Cloning a project is used when you want to convert an existing project to a different PSoC part. The part is referred to as the "base" part. You can clone an existing project at any point of its existence: before, during, or after device configuration, assembly-source programming, or project debugging. Cloning copies the existing project but allows you to change the base device. Use the cloning method to move an existing project from one directory to another, rather than physically moving the files.

You must use the cloning method to change parts within a part family in the middle of a project design. Refer to the Application Notes on the Cypress web site for assistance.

To clone an existing project:

i) From the **File** menu, select **New Project**. You can only clone a Chip-Level project. Select **Chip-Level**.
ii) Select a name and location for your new application and click **OK**.
iii) In the Clone project box click browse and find the .SOC or .CMX file of the project you want to clone.
iv) Choose whether you want to choose a new base device or not. If you do, select View Catalog to select a new device.
v) Choose C or assembler for the language of the main file. Click **OK**.

Step 5: Once you select a part, click **C** or **Assembler**, in the Select Project Type dialog box, to designate the language in which you want the system to generate the "main" file.

Step 6: Click **OK**. Your workspace directory with folders is created and is listed in the Workspace Explorer. If the Workspace Explorer is not visible, choose **Workspace Explorer** from the **View** menu.

Design Entry in PSoC Designer IDE Software

Placing User Modules

Device Editor window opens on clicking Finish. On the Left side, there are pre-configured and pre-characterized user module library for creating the mixed signal system. As per our block diagram

To place a user module: Locate the desired user module in the the user module catalog. Each user module has a user module data sheet that describes what it is and how to use it.

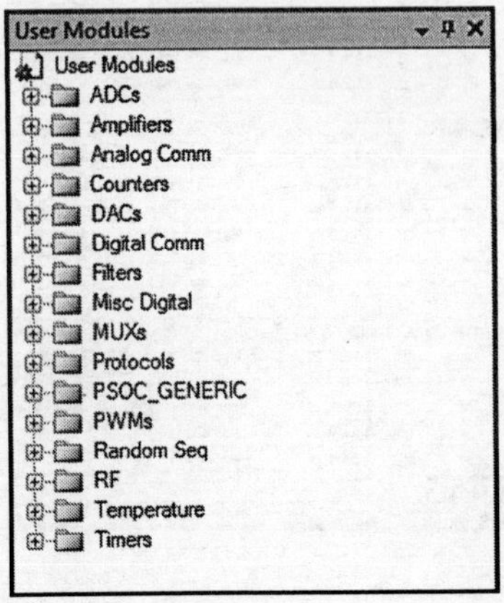

If we want add **LCD, PGA, ADC** module from the **Misc Digital, amplifiers, and ADC's respective** module Library as shown in below diagram.

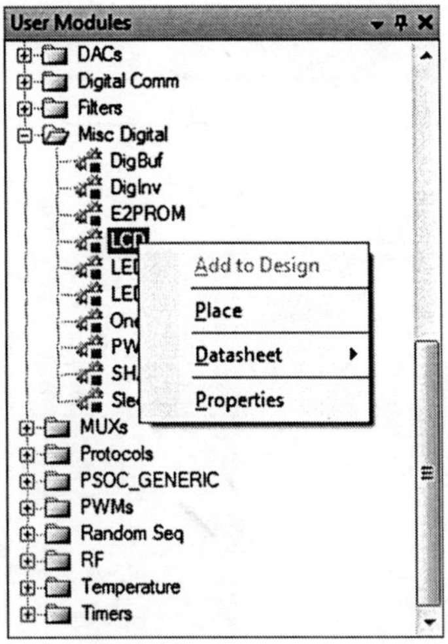

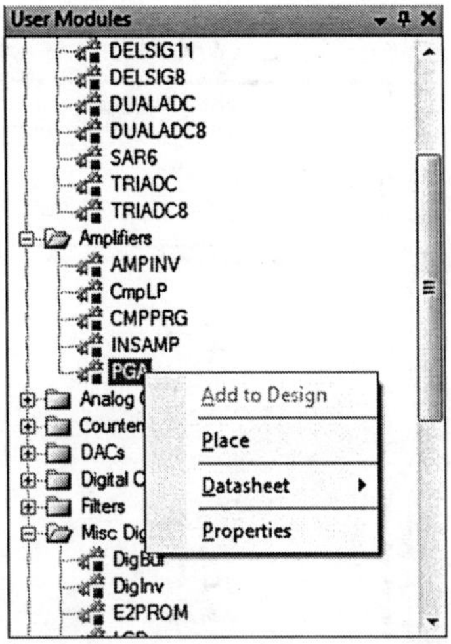

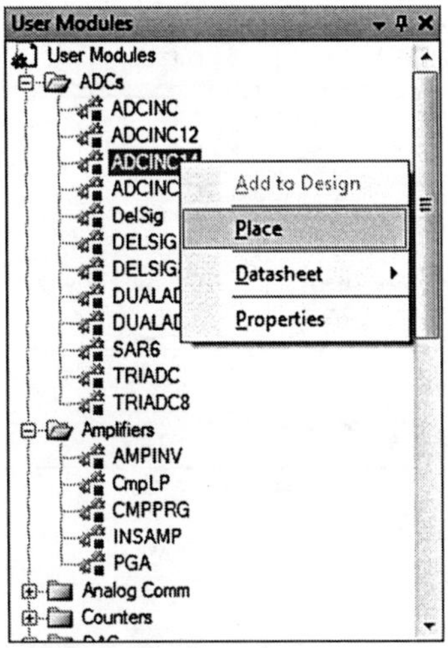

All the modules are added in the user module tray.

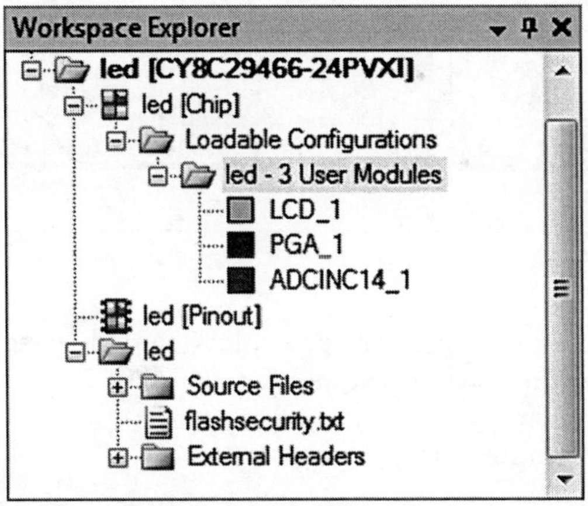

The selected user module block diagram and datasheet is displayed below the user module tray. Click on the Interconnect symbol in the toolbar. It shows the interconnect window for inter connecting and routing the signals to the output pins.

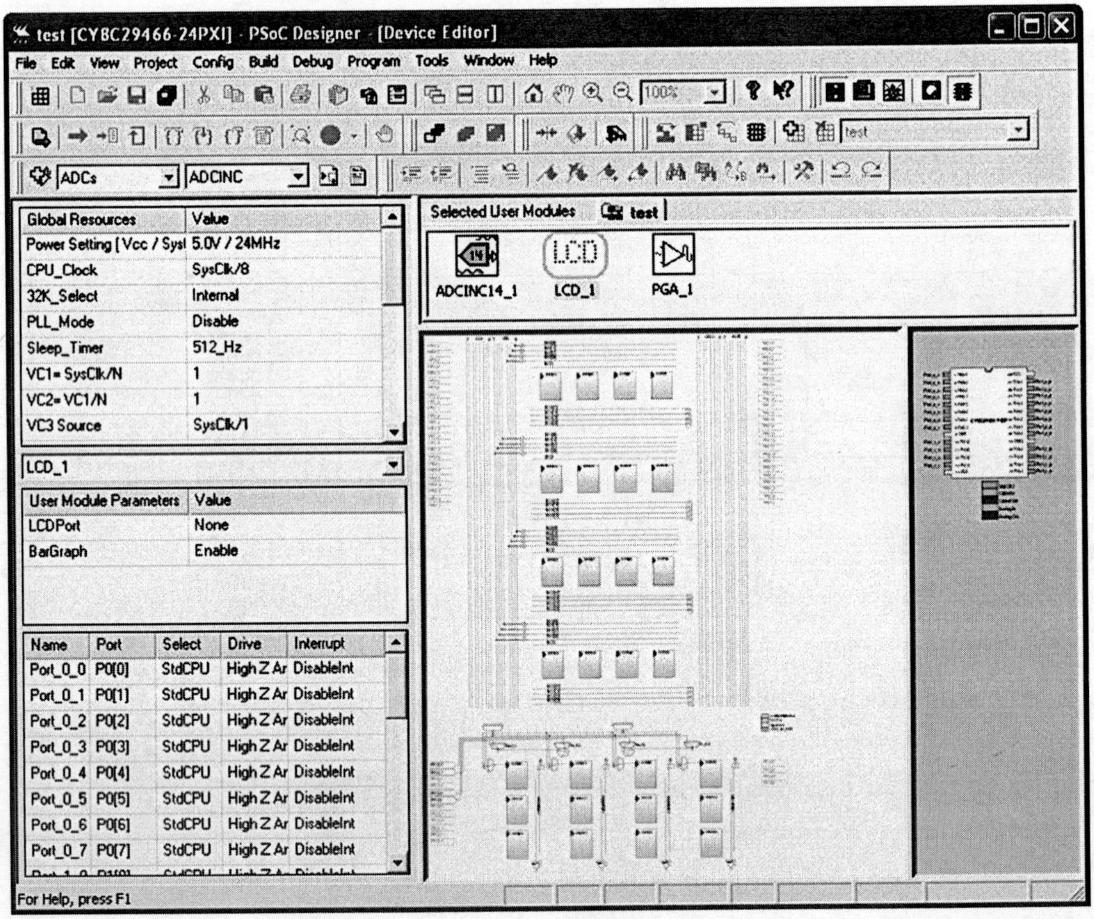

Interconnect View

Global Resources

Global Resources are hardware settings that determine the underlying operation of the part. For example, the CPU clock designates the clock speed of the M8C. Note that Global Resource options differ slightly for each device family.

To update and save Global Resources:

i) Click each drop-arrow (in parameter value fields) and make your selections. Some parameters in Global Resources are specified as integer values (such as 24V1 and 24V2). Set these values by clicking the up/down arrows or double-clicking the value and typing over them. If you enter an out of range value, you see a dialog box specifying the acceptable range. Click **OK** to close the dialog box.

ii) The current settings for the Global Resources can be saved as default settings. Right-click on any Global Resource name and select **Update Default Values.** This action saves all Global Resource settings to the \Preferences directory under the PSoC Designer installation path. Use these settings for any other project by right-clicking any Global Resource name and selecting **Restore**

Default Values: If no custom default values are saved, then the menu item and the right-click to Restore Default Settings restore the factory default Global Resource Settings. The Global Resources available in PSoC Designer are shown and described briefly. Different PSoC Devices have different global resources. The figure shown is typical.

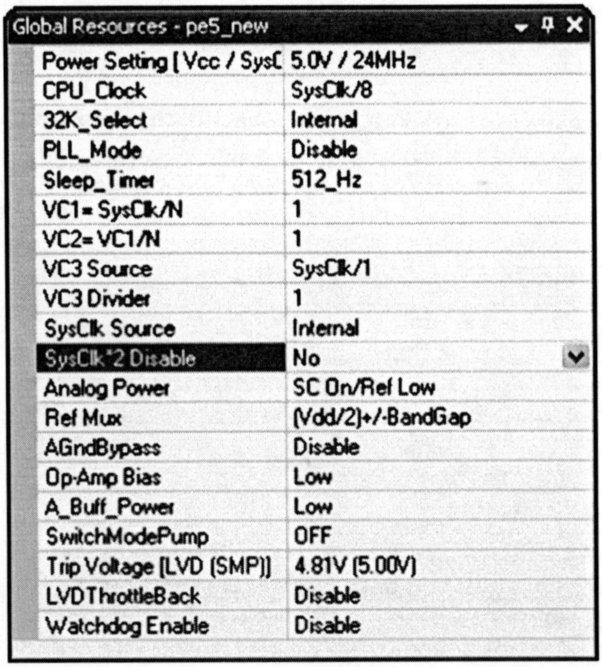

CPU Clock

The CPU clock sets the frequency of the instruction clock to the M8C core. This clock is based off SysClk. (Note: SysClk is the internal 24 MHz clock on 25xxx/26xxx parts.) You can choose one of several divisions of this clock if you want a slower operation frequency. Before you start thinking that faster is always better, take into account that a slower processor uses less power and is more noise immune. Make sure that you take your power supply into account, as the slower speeds allow you to operate the processor over a larger voltage range without risking bad fetches from Flash memory. The 24 MHz speed may also require some adjustments to your project if you are using 25xxx/26xxx parts.

The CPU clock specifies the timing of the instruction clock. This global setting asserts bits 0–2 of the OSC_CR0 register in bank 1. The available settings are as follows:

24 MHz SysClk / 1
12 MHz SysClk / 2
6 MHz SysClk / 4
3 MHz SysClk / 8
1.5 MHz SysClk / 16
750 KHz SysClk / 32
185.5 KHz SysClk / 128
93.75 KHz SysClk / 256

32K_Select, PLL_Mode

The 32K_Select and PLL_Mode refer to the use of an external 32.768 kHz crystal on pins P1[0] and P1[1]. If you select **Internal** then the micro assumes no external crystal is present to use and these two I/O pins are available for normal use. If you choose **External**, then the micro tries to drive a crystal at those pins. The PLL_Mode option allows you to phase lock the internal oscillator with the external crystal. This gives you a higher accuracy on your internal 24 MHz

Sleep Timer

The sleep timer resource allows you to adjust the frequency of the sleep timer. The sleep timer allows the processor to periodically awake from a low-power state to do a quick poll on any desired inputs or conditions to see if it's time to exit sleep or just time to go back to sleep. A slower sleep period saves power, but also means that you will have a slower response waking up from the lower power state.

VC1, VC2, VC3 (24V1 and 24V2 on Older Parts)

The VC clocks are available to use as timing sources for digital blocks, and switched cap clocking signals. The VC1 (24V1) is derived from SysClk and has the potential to divide by integer values up to 16. VC2 (24V2) is derived from VC1 and has the potential to divide by interger values up to 16. VC3 (only present on newer parts) has four sources: VC1, VC2, SysClk, or SysClk*2. VC3 has the potential to divide by 256. VC3 also can be an interrupt to the processor on terminal count.

SysClk Source, SysClk*2 Disable

These resources don't exist on the 25xxx/26xxx parts. It allows you to select a source for your SysClk. It can be the internal 24 MHz oscillator or an external source. If SysClk*2 isn't used in your project, you have the ability to disable it.

Analog Power

This allows you to turn your switched cap blocks on and off. It also allows you to set a power level for the reference voltage. The default setting for this resource is SC On/Ref Low, meaning the switched cap blocks are on and the reference voltage is at a low setting.

Ref Mux

The ref mux can seem a little confusing. For beginning users of the PSoC I would recommend having this setting at Vcc/2 ± Vcc/2. This allows your analog-to-digital converters to work from GND to Vcc and your gain stages to work as you would probably expect. The ref mux sets the reference levels that are used in the analog blocks of the PSoC. There are also some options to use external pins to set these levels.

AGND Bypass

Enabling the AGND bypass in conjunction with placing a capacitor from Port2[4] to GND helps to reduce noise levels on the internal AGND signal of the PSoC.

Op-Amp Bias

The op-amp bias is left low for most projects. A high setting gives you a faster slew rate, but less voltage swing.

A_Buff_Power

This is a power setting for the analog output buffers. Choices are low or high. High power can mean a more stable voltage.

Switch Mode Pump

This option allows you to control whether the switch mode pump is enabled or disabled on the PSoC. The switch mode pump is used with a simple circuit to pump up a low voltage source to a voltage level where the PSoC can operate.

Voltage [LVD(SMP)]

The trip voltage allows you to set two levels. LVD is the level at which a low voltage detection circuit will trip. This is similar to a brown out voltage level that you've seen on other microcontrollers. The SMP is the level at which the switch mode pump starts to transition to pump the voltage back up to a safe level.

LVD ThrottleBack

LVD ThrottleBack doesn't exist on the 25xxx/26xxx parts. It is designed to slow down processor operation at lower voltages to help with accurate operation.

Supply Voltage

The supply voltage option allows you to select between the two expected operating voltages. This option is used to determine oscillator trim values for the internal oscillator.

Watchdog Enable

The watchdog enable option is used in boot.asm generation to decide whether the watchdog timer should be enabled by default.

Specifying Interconnects

Interconnectivity allows communication between user modules, PSoC blocks, pins, and other onchip resources. Connections are shown as lines between elements, special symbols, or flag connectors. Flag connectors are used when the connection is made to a point where drawing a line results in a cluttered display, with the legend indicating the origin of the connection. Connections to pins are shown as lines from interconnection buses. The interconnection bus structure depends on the PSoC device selected and can consist of one or more levels of buses between the digital PSoC blocks and the pins. Connections between analog PSoC blocks and pins are made through the analog input muxes and output buses. Pin names are duplicated in several places, since they are multifunctional, and are highlighted when used with lines showing their current connection state. The location of the pin to which a line is drawn indicates the usage of the pin. Lines drawn to the pins on the left edge indicate that the pins are used as inputs, while the right edge indicates the pins are used as output. Pins in the upper groups indicate connection to the digital network, while lower groups indicate analog connections. Lines drawn from multiple locations on the same pin indicate that the shown combination is electrically valid. To specify interconnections, click the **Interconnect** folder in the Workspace Explorer. User module interconnections consist of connections to surrounding PSoC blocks, output bus, input bus, internal system clocks and references, external pins, and analog output buffers. Multiplexers may also be configured to route signals throughout the PSoC block architecture.

Digital PSoC blocks are connected through the Global_IN and Global_OUT buses to external pins and to other digital PSoC blocks. There are eight Global_IN and eight Global_OUT bus lines, numbered 0 through 7. For external pin connections, the number of the Global bus line corresponds to the bit number of the associated port. For example, Global_IN_0 can connect to pins associated with P0[0], P1[0], P2[0], etc. The Global_OUT buses can drive the inputs to other digital PSoC blocks. However, all Global_OUT lines do not reach all digital PSoC blocks. When setting output parameters to the Global_OUT lines, only one PSoC block drives a single

Global_OUT line at a time. Global_OUT lines used by a user module are not available to other user modules for output. For example, if two timer user modules are placed and the first timer is set to use Global_OUT_1 for output, attempting to set the output for the second timer to Global_OUT_1 fails.

Connecting User Modules

These procedures show you how to make certain types of connections.

Global In

Global In connections apply to a PSoC device in this manner:

- Global In: Input Port Connections.
- All other PSoC devices as Global In Odd and Global In Even: Input Port Connections and Global Connections.

To set Global In connections:

i) Click on the target Globalxxx vertical line.

ii) Select the pin to connect to.

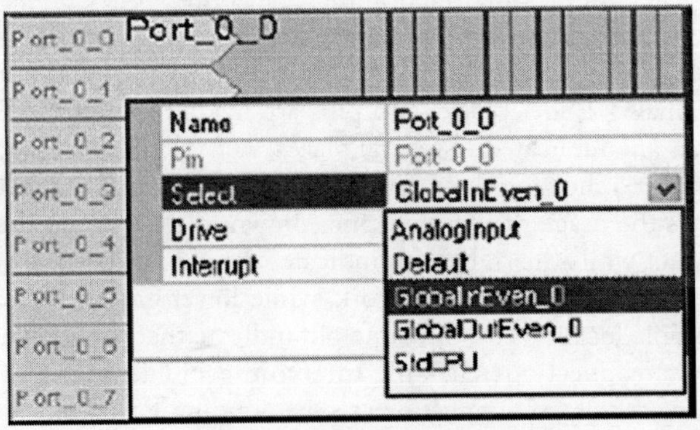

iii) Select the global input to output connection (if active).

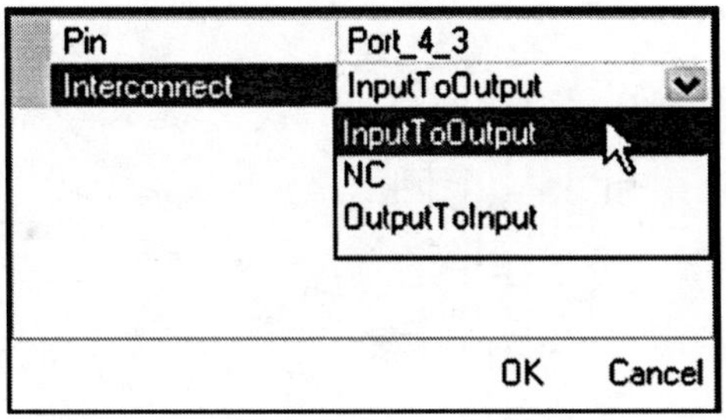

iv) Click **OK.**

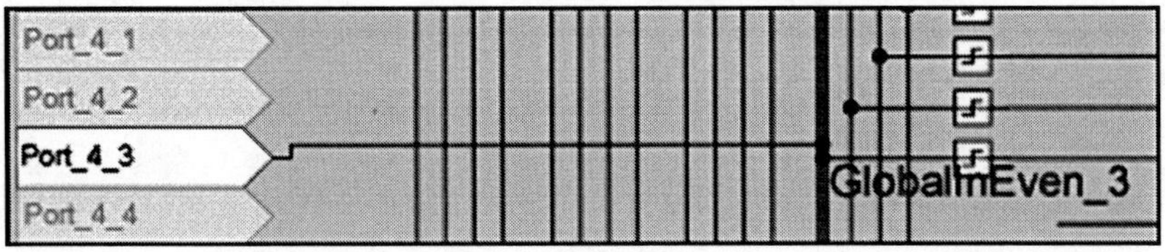

You see a line connecting the digital input port to the global vertical line.

Global Out

Global Out connections apply to a PSoC device in this manner:

- Global Out: Output Port Connections.
- All other PSoC devices as Global out Odd and Global Out Even: Output Port Connections and Global Connections.

To set Global Out connections:

i) Click on the target Globalxxx vertical line.
ii) Select the global input to output connection (if active) and the port.
iii) Click **OK.**
You see a line connecting the digital output port to the global vertical line.

Digital Interconnect Row Input Window

The Digital Interconnect Row Input window connections do not apply to CY8C25xxx/26xxx parts.

Connection to Global Input

To set a Connection to Global Input:

i) Click on the white box or the line of the target Row_x_Input_x.

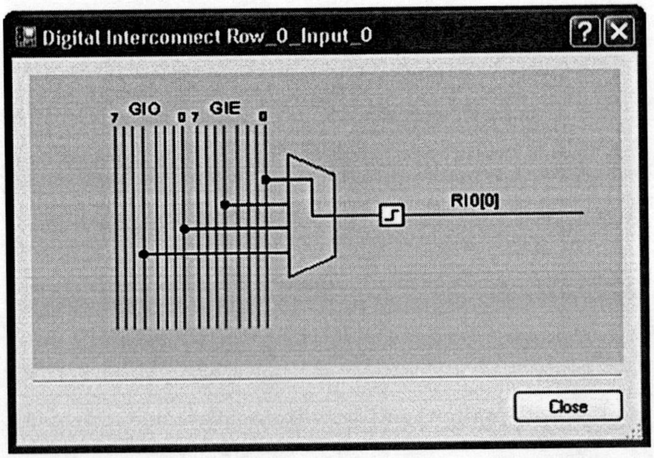

ii) Click on the Row_x_Input_x Mux in the Digital Interconnect Row Input floating window and select a Global Input from the menu. (You immediately see a connection from the mux to the Global Input vertical line.) In this floating window you can also click the white box to toggle the Synchronization value for Row_x_Input_x. Options include SysClk_Sync and Async.

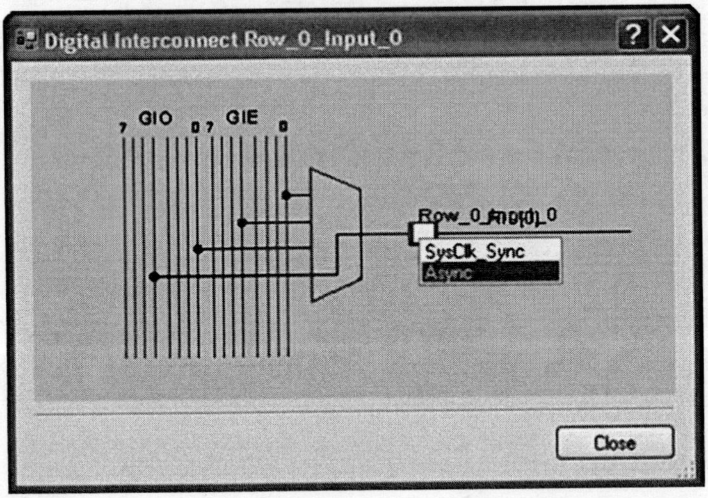

Digital Interconnect Row Output Window

Digital Interconnect Row Output Window connections do not apply to CY8C25xxx/26xxx parts.

Row Logic Table Input

To set Row Logic Table Input connections:

i) Click on the target Row_x_Output_x Logic Table Box.

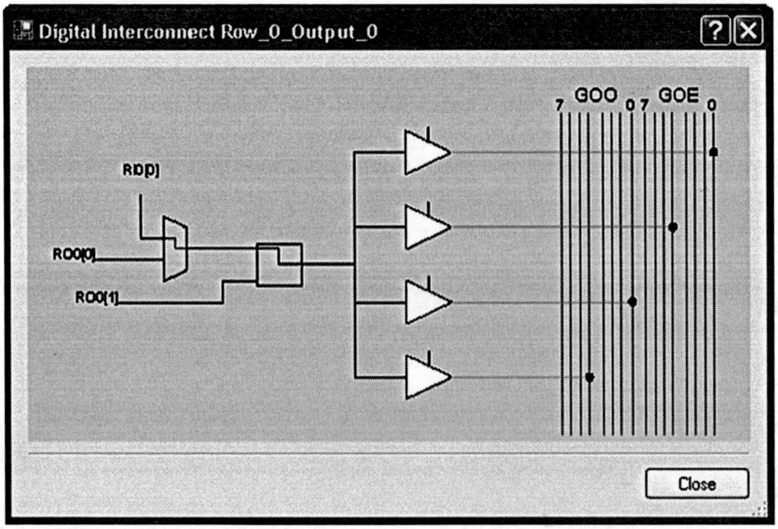

ii) Click on the Row_x_LogicTable_Input_0 Mux in the Digital Interconnect Row Output floating window and select an input or output option from the menu.
iii) Click **Close** when finished.

Row Logic Table Select

To set Row Logic Table Select connections:

i) Click on the target Row_x_Output_x Logic Table Box.
ii) Click on the Row_x_LogicTable_Select_x logical operation box in the Digital Interconnect Row

Output floating window and select an option from the menu

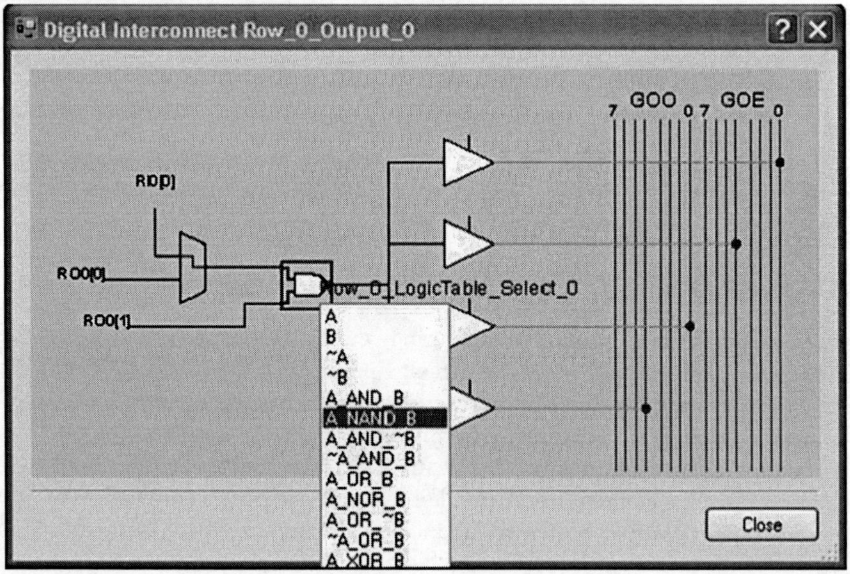

Connection to Global Output

To set connections to Global Output:

i) Click on the target Row_x_Output_x Logic Table Box.
ii) Click on the target Row_x_Output_x_Drive_x triangle in the Digital Interconnect Row Output floating window and select an option from the menu. Once you open the Digital Interconnect Row Global Output window, you can select Row Logic Table Input, Row Logic Table Select, and Connections to Global Output without closing the window.

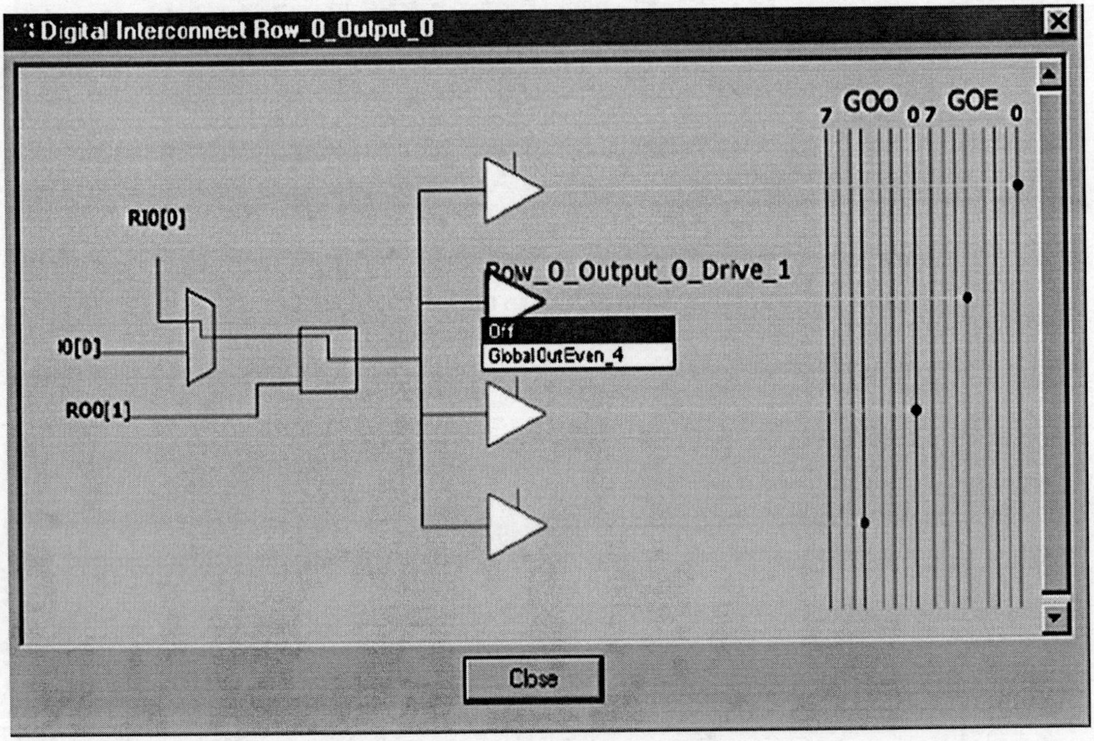

iii) Click the **Close** button when finished.

You see a connection from the Row_x_Output_x Logic Table Box to the chosen GlobalOutEven_x vertical line.

Specifying the Pinout

Specifying the pinouts is the next step to configuring your target device. This converts the pins to the Configurable PSoC resources. To restore the default Pinout, click the Restore Default Pinout button. Be careful when connecting to pins. The pin settings can be modified either by setting elements to connect to pins or by setting the pin directly. Setting the pin directly connects the pin to the appropriate element and disconnects it from any other element. To have multiple connections to the same pin, make connections from the element to the pin. For example, suppose a connection to a pin, an analog input mux and an analog output buffer, simultaneously, is desired. P0[2] can connect to the analog input mux for column 1 and to the analog output buffer for column 3. The connections must be made from the analog input mux and the analog output buffer. Setting the pin to Default disconnects the pin from both digital buses, but does not affect analog connections.

Port Connections

You make port connections in three ways:

- Click the port icons and make settings in the device interface
- Click the pin and make settings in the device Pinout
- Change port-related fields in the Global or User Module properties windows These procedures show you how to make certain types of port connections.

Analog Input

To set Analog Input connections.

i) Click on the target Port_0_x.
ii) From the **Select** menu select **AnalogInput**.

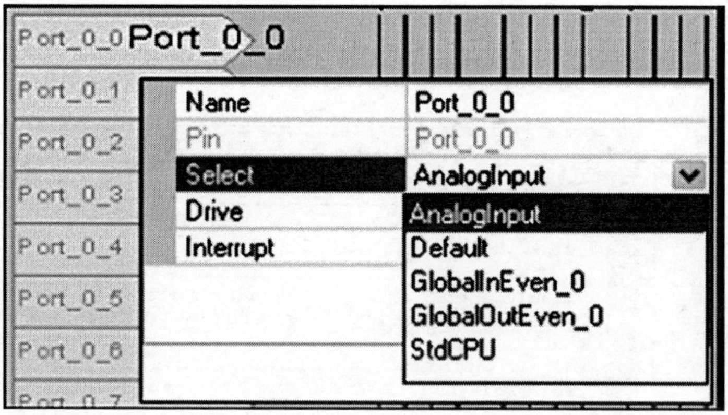

Default Input

To set Default Input connections:

i) Click on the target Port_x_x.
ii) From the **Select** menu select **Default**.

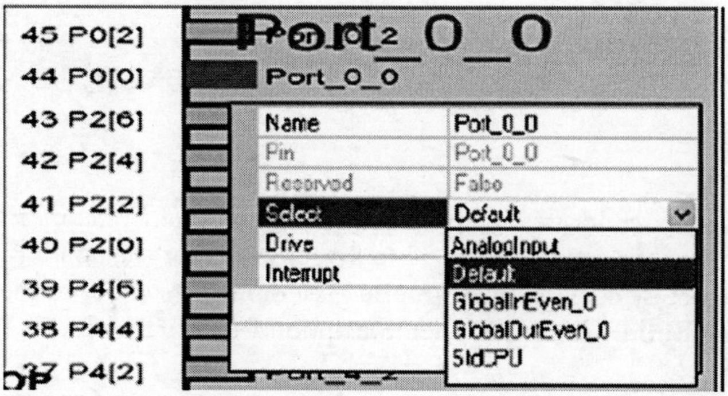

Click on the Generate Application symbol on toolbar buttons. By clicking on this button, it starts creating the user configuration PDF file for project and generate the **"main.c"** file.

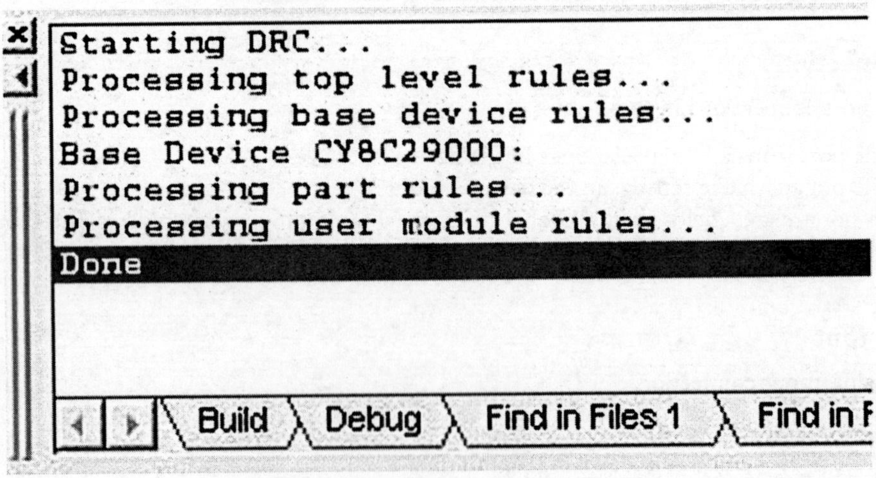

On the left side of the Application Editor window, there is a project files hierarchy. Under **Source Files** select the **main.c** file. Open it by double clicking on it.

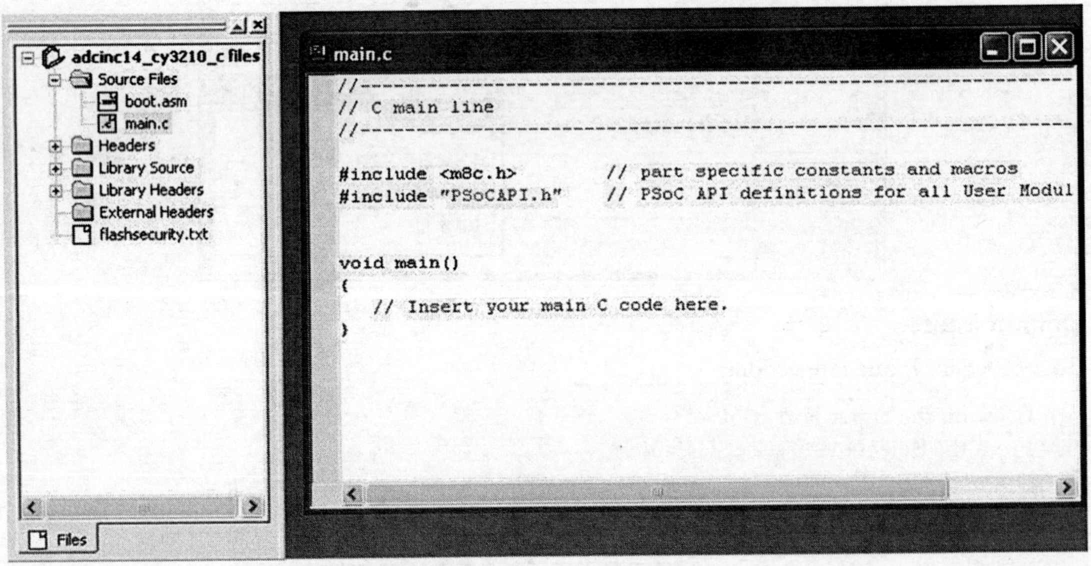

Building

During building, the compiler locates and process all design files, generates message and reports related to the current building of the project. Steps 53 to 57 guide you for the building of the design file.

Compile the project by clicking on **Compile/Assemble** symbol in the toolbar. You can also compile the project by **Build>Compile/Assemble** option from menu bar.

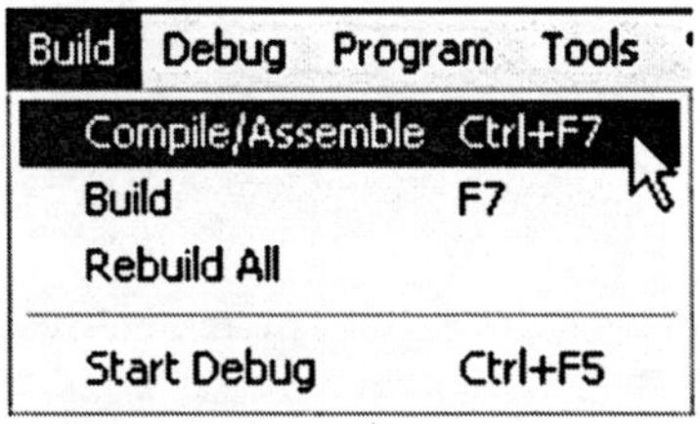

Compilation is successful, when 0 errors and 0 warnings message appears on the screen.

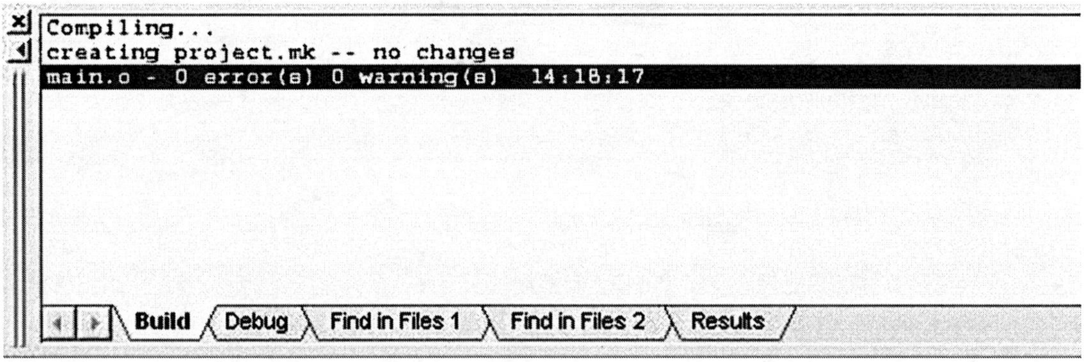

Click on the **Build** symbol on the toolbar buttons. You can also build the project by clicking on **Build> Build** option.

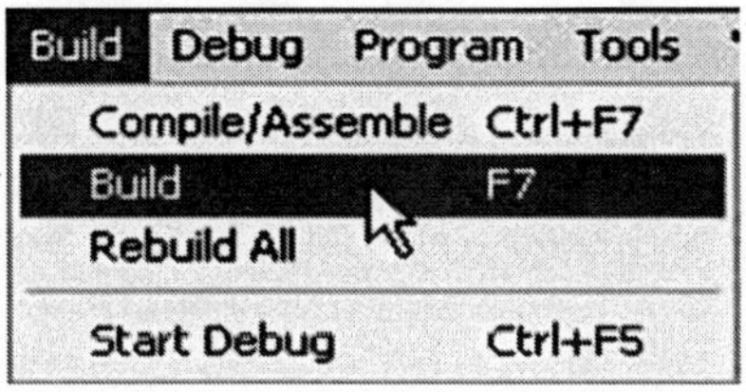

When building is successful, you will see 0 errors and 0 warning message on the screen.

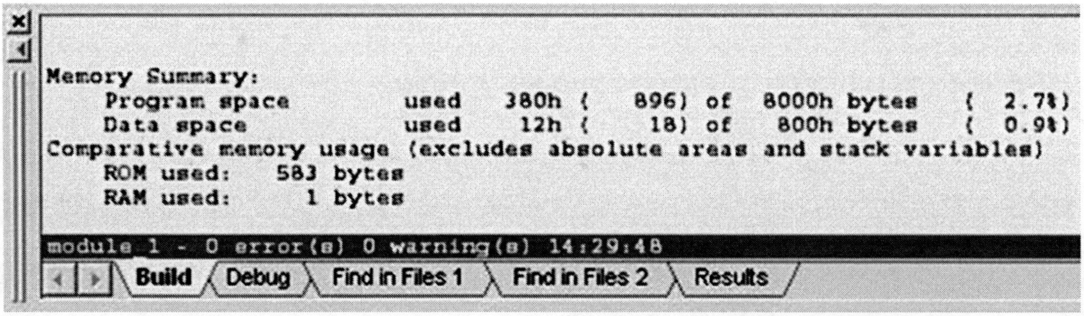

Programming

Now we shall program the PSoC on the board using PSoC Programmer IDE.

i) Before starting the programmer, connect the board using PSoC MiniProg1 to the USB port of the PC.
ii) Select Program Part from the Program menu or click on the **Program Part** symbol on the toolbar buttons.

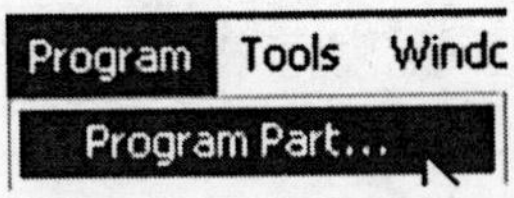

APPENDIX D

PIN CONFIGURATION AND PINSELECT REGISTERS OF LPC 2148

Pin Description for LPC2141/2/4/6/8

Pin description for LPC2141/2/4/6/8 and a brief explanation of corresponding functions are shown in Table A-D.1.

Table A-D.1 | Pin Description

Symbol	Pin	Type	Description
P0.0 to P0.31		I/O	**Port 0:** Port 0 is a 32-bit I/O port with individual direction controls for each bit. Total of 28 pins of the Port 0 can be used as a general purpose bi-directional digital I/Os while P0.31 provides digital output functions only. The operation of port 0 pins depends upon the pin function selected via the pin connect block.
			Pins P0.24, P0.26 and P0.27 are not available.
P0.0/TXD0/	19	I/O	**P0.0** — General purpose digital input/output pin
PWM1		O	**TXD0** — Transmitter output for UART0
		O	**PWM1** — Pulse Width Modulator output 1
P0.1/RxD0/	21	I/O	**P0.1** — General purpose digital input/output pin
PWM3/EINT0		I	**RxD0** — Receiver input for UART0
		O	**PWM3** — Pulse Width Modulator output 3
		I	**EINT0** — External interrupt 0 input
P0.2/SCL0/	22	I/O	**P0.2** — General purpose digital input/output pin
CAP0.0		I/O	**SCL0** — I^2C0 clock input/output. Open drain output (for I^2C compliance)
		I	**CAP0.0** — Capture input for Timer 0, channel 0
P0.3/SDA0/	26	I/O	**P0.3** — General purpose digital input/output pin
MAT0.0/EINT1		I/O	**SDA0** — I^2C0 data input/output. Open drain output (for I^2C compliance)
		O	**MAT0.0** — Match output for Timer 0, channel 0
		I	**EINT1** — External interrupt 1 input
P0.4/SCK0/	27	I/O	**P0.4** — General purpose digital input/output pin
CAP0.1/AD0.6		I/O	**SCK0** — Serial clock for SPI0. SPI clock output from master or input to slave

Symbol	Pin	Type	Description
		I	**CAP0.1** — Capture input for Timer 0, channel 0
		I	**AD0.6** — A/D converter 0, input 6. This analog input is always connected to its pin
P0.5/MISO0/	29	I/O	**P0.5** — General purpose digital input/output pin
MAT0.1/AD0.7		I/O	**MISO0** — Master In Slave OUT for SPI0. Data input to SPI master or data output from SPI slave
		O	**MAT0.1** — Match output for Timer 0, channel 1
		I	**AD0.7** — A/D converter 0, input 7. This analog input is always connected to its pin
P0.6/MOSI0/	30	I/O	**P0.6** — General purpose digital input/output pin
CAP0.2/AD1.0		I/O	**MOSI0** — Master Out Slave In for SPI0. Data output from SPI master or data input to SPI slave
		I	**CAP0.2** — Capture input for Timer 0, channel 2
		I	**AD1.0** — A/D converter 1, input 0. This analog input is always connected to its pin. Available in LPC2144/6/8 only.
P0.7/SSEL0/	31	I/O	**P0.7** — General purpose digital input/output pin
PWM2/EINT2		I	**SSEL0** — Slave Select for SPI0. Selects the SPI interface as a slave
		O	**PWM2** — Pulse Width Modulator output 2
		I	**EINT2** — External interrupt 2 input
P0.8/TXD1/	33	I/O	**P0.8** — General purpose digital input/output pin
PWM4/AD1.1		O	**TXD1** — Transmitter output for UART1
		O	**PWM4** — Pulse Width Modulator output 4
		I	**AD1.1** — A/D converter 1, input 1. This analog input is always connected to its pin. Available in LPC2144/6/8 only
P0.9/RxD1/	34	I/O	**P0.9** — General purpose digital input/output pin
PWM6/EINT3		I	**RxD1** — Receiver input for UART1
		O	**PWM6** — Pulse Width Modulator output 6
		I	**EINT3** — External interrupt 3 input
P0.10/RTS1/	35	I/O	**P0.10** — General purpose digital input/output pin
CAP1.0/AD1.2		O	**RTS1** — Request to Send output for UART1. Available in LPC2144/6/8 only.
		I	**CAP1.0** — Capture input for Timer 1, channel 0
		I	**AD1.2** — A/D converter 1, input 2. This analog input is always connected to its pin. Available in LPC2144/6/8 only.
P0.11/CTS1/	37	I/O	**P0.11** — General purpose digital input/output pin

Symbol	Pin	Type	Description
CAP1.1/SCL1		I	**CTS1** — Clear to Send input for UART1. Available in LPC2144/6/8 only.
		I	**CAP1.1** — Capture input for Timer 1, channel 1.
		I/O	**SCL1** — I2C1 clock input/output. Open drain output (for I^2C compliance)
P0.12/DSR1/	38	I/O	**P0.12** — General purpose digital input/output pin
		I	**DSR1** — Data Set Ready input for UART1. Available in LPC2144/6/8 only.
		O	**MAT1.0** — Match output for Timer 1, channel 0.
		I	**AD1.3** — A/D converter input 3. This analog input is always connected to its pin. Available in LPC2144/6/8 only.
P0.13/DTR1/	39	I/O	**P0.13** — General purpose digital input/output pin
MAT1.1/AD1.4		O	**DTR1** — Data Terminal Ready output for UART1. Available in LPC2144/6/8 only.
		O	**MAT1.1** — Match output for Timer 1, channel 1.
		I	**AD1.4** — A/D converter input 4. This analog input is always connected to its pin. Available in LPC2144/6/8 only.
P0.14/DCD1/	41	I/O	**P0.14** — General purpose digital input/output pin
EINT1/SDA1		I	**DCD1** — Data Carrier Detect input for UART1. Available in LPC2144/6/8 only.
		I	**EINT1** — External interrupt 1 input
		I/O	**SDA1** — I2C1 data input/output. Open drain output (for I2C compliance) **Note:** LOW on this pin while RESET is LOW forces on-chip boot-loader to take over control of the part after reset.
P0.15/RI1/	45	I/O	**P0.15** — General purpose digital input/output pin
EINT2/AD1.5		I	**RI1** — Ring Indicator input for UART1. Available in LPC2144/6/8 only.
		I	**EINT2** — External interrupt 2 input.
		I	**AD1.5** — A/D converter 1, input 5. This analog input is always connected to its pin. Available in LPC2144/6/8 only.
P0.16/EINT0/	46	I/O	**P0.16** — General purpose digital input/output pin
MAT0.2/CAP0.2		I	**EINT0** — External interrupt 0 input.
		O	**MAT0.2** — Match output for Timer 0, channel 2.
		I	**CAP0.2** — Capture input for Timer 0, channel 2.

Symbol	Pin	Type	Description
P0.17/CAP1.2/	47	I/O	**P0.17** — General purpose digital input/output pin
SCK1/MAT1.2		I	**CAP1.2** — Capture input for Timer 1, channel 2.
		I/O	**SCK1** — Serial Clock for SSP. Clock output from master or input to slave.
		O	**MAT1.2** — Match output for Timer 1, channel 2.
P0.18/CAP1.3/	53	I/O	**P0.18** — General purpose digital input/output pin
MISO1/MAT1.3		I	**CAP1.3** — Capture input for Timer 1 channel 3.
		I/O	**MISO1** — Master In Slave Out for SSP. Data input to SPI master or data output from SSP slave.
		O	**MAT1.3** — Match output for Timer 1, channel 3.
P0.19/MAT1.2/	54	I/O	**P0.19** — General purpose digital input/output pin
MOSI1/CAP1.2		O	**MAT1.2** — Match output for Timer 1, channel 2.
		I/O	**MOSI1** — Master Out Slave In for SSP. Data output from SSP master or data input to SSP slave.
		I	**CAP1.2** — Capture input for Timer 1, channel 2.
P0.20/MAT1.3/	55	I/O	**P0.20** — General purpose digital input/output pin
SSEL1/EINT3		O	**MAT1.3** — Match output for Timer 1, channel 3.
		I	**SSEL1** — Slave Select for SSP. Selects the SSP interface as a slave.
		I	**EINT3** — External interrupt 3 input.
P0.21/PWM5/	1	I/O	**P0.21** — General purpose digital input/output pin
AD1.6/CAP1.3		O	**PWM5** — Pulse Width Modulator output 5.
		I	**AD1.6** — A/D converter 1, input 6. This analog input is always connected to its pin. Available in LPC2144/6/8 only.
		I	**CAP1.3** — Capture input for Timer 1, channel 3.
P0.22/AD1.7/	2	I/O	**P0.22** — General purpose digital input/output pin.
CAP0.0/ MAT0.0		I	**AD1.7** — A/D converter 1, input 7. This analog input is always connected to its pin. Available in LPC2144/6/8 only.
		I	**CAP0.0** — Capture input for Timer 0, channel 0.
		O	**MAT0.0** — Match output for Timer 0, channel 0.
P0.23/VBUS	58	I/O	**P0.23** — General purpose digital input/output pin.
		I	**V_{BUS}** — Indicates the presence of USB bus power.
P0.25/AD0.4/	9	I/O	**P0.25** — General purpose digital input/output pin
Aout		I	**AD0.4** — A/D converter 0, input 4. This analog input is always connected to its pin.
		O	**Aout** — D/A converter output. Available in LPC2142/4/6/8 only.

Symbol	Pin	Type	Description
P0.28/AD0.1/	13	I/O	**P0.28** — General purpose digital input/output pin
CAP0.2/ MAT0.2		I	**AD0.1** — A/D converter 0, input 1. This analog input is always connected to its pin.
		I	**CAP0.2** — Capture input for Timer 0, channel 2.
		O	**MAT0.2** — Match output for Timer 0, channel 2.
P0.29/AD0.2/	14	I/O	**P0.29** — General purpose digital input/output pin
CAP0.3/ MAT0.3		I	**AD0.2** — A/D converter 0, input 2. This analog input is always connected to its pin.
		I	**CAP0.3** — Capture input for Timer 0, Channel 3.
		O	**MAT0.3** — Match output for Timer 0, channel 3.
P0.30/AD0.3/	15	I/O	**P0.30** — General purpose digital input/output pin.
EINT3/CAP0.0		I	**AD0.3** — A/D converter 0, input 3. This analog input is always connected to its pin.
		I	**EINT3** — External interrupt 3 input.
		I	**CAP0.0** — Capture input for Timer 0, channel 0.
P0.31	17	O	**P0.31** — General purpose output only digital pin (GPO).
		O	**UP_LED** — USB Good Link LED indicator. It is LOW when device is configured (non-control endpoints enabled). It is HIGH when the device is not configured or during global suspend.
		O	**CONNECT** — Signal used to switch an external 1.5 kΩ resistor under the software control (active state for this signal is LOW). Used with the Soft Connect USB feature. **Note:** This pin MUST NOT be externally pulled LOW when RESET pin is LOW or the JTAG port will be disabled.
P1.0 to P1.31		I/O	**Port 1:** Port 1 is a 32-bit bi-directional I/O port with individual direction controls for each bit. The operation of port 1 pins depends upon the pin function selected via the pin connect block. Pins 0 through 15 of port 1 are not available.
P1.16/	16	I/O	**P1.16** — General purpose digital input/output pin
TRACEPKT0		O	**TRACEPKT0** — Trace Packet, bit 0. Standard I/O port with internal pullup.
P1.17/	12	I/O	**P1.17** — General purpose digital input/output pin
TRACEPKT1		O	**TRACEPKT1** — Trace Packet, bit 1. Standard I/O port with internal pullup.
P1.18/	8	I/O	**P1.18** — General purpose digital input/output pin
TRACEPKT2		O	**TRACEPKT2** — Trace Packet, bit 2. Standard I/O port with internal pullup.

Symbol	Pin	Type	Description
P1.19/	4	I/O	**P1.19** — General purpose digital input/output pin
TRACEPKT3		O	**TRACEPKT3** — Trace Packet, bit 3. Standard I/O port with internal pullup.
P1.20/	48	I/O	**P1.20** — General purpose digital input/output pin
TRACESYNC		O	**TRACESYNC** — Trace Synchronization. Standard I/O port with internal pullup.
			Note: LOW on this pin while $\overline{\text{RESET}}$ is LOW enables pins P1.25:16 to operate as Trace port after reset
P1.21/	44	I/O	**P1.21** — General purpose digital input/output pin
PIPESTAT0		O	**PIPESTAT0** — Pipeline Status, bit 0. Standard I/O port with internal pullup.
P1.22/	40	I/O	**P1.22** — General purpose digital input/output pin
PIPESTAT1		O	**PIPESTAT1** — Pipeline Status, bit 1. Standard I/O port with internal pullup.
P1.23/	36	I/O	**P1.23** — General purpose digital input/output pin
PIPESTAT2		O	**PIPESTAT2** — Pipeline Status, bit 2. Standard I/O port with internal pullup.
P1.24/	32	I/O	**P1.24** — General purpose digital input/output pin
TRACECLK		O	**TRACECLK** — Trace Clock. Standard I/O port with internal pullup.
P1.25/EXTIN0	28	I/O	**P1.25** — General purpose digital input/output pin
		I	**EXTIN0** — External Trigger Input. Standard I/O with internal pullup.
P1.26/RTCK	24	I/O	**P1.26** — General purpose digital input/output pin
		I/O	**RTCK** — Returned Test Clock output. Extra signal added to the JTAG port. Assists debugger synchronization when processor frequency varies. Bi-directional pin with internal pullup.
			Note: LOW on this pin while $\overline{\text{RESET}}$ is LOW enables pins P1.31:26 to operate as Debug port after reset
P1.27/TDO	64	I/O	**P1.27** — General purpose digital input/output pin
		O	**TDO** — Test Data out for JTAG interface.
P1.28/TDI	60	I/O	**P1.28** — General purpose digital input/output pin
		I	**TDI** — Test Data in for JTAG interface.
P1.29/TCK	56	I/O	**P1.29** — General purpose digital input/output pin
		I	**TCK** — Test Clock for JTAG interface. This clock must be slower than 1/6 of the CPU clock (CCLK) for the JTAG interface to operate.

Symbol	Pin	Type	Description
P1.30/TMS	52	I/O	**P1.30 —** General purpose digital input/output pin
		I	**TMS —** Test Mode Select for JTAG interface.
P1.31/$\overline{\text{TRST}}$	20	I/O	**P1.31 —** General purpose digital input/output pin
		I	**$\overline{\text{TRST}}$ —** Test Reset for JTAG interface.
D+	10	I/O	USB bidirectional D+ line.
D-	10	I/O	USB bidirectional D- line.
$\overline{\text{RESET}}$	57	I	**External reset input:** A LOW on this pin resets the device, causing I/O ports and peripherals to take on their default states, and processor execution to begin at address 0. TTL with hysteresis, 5 V tolerant.
XTAL1	62	I	Input to the oscillator circuit and internal clock generator circuits.
XTAL2	61	O	Output from the oscillator amplifier.
RTCX1	3	I	Input to the RTC oscillator circuit. Can be left floating if the RTC is not used.
RTCX2	5	O	Output from the RTC oscillator circuit. Can be left floating if the RTC is not used.
VSS	6, 18, 25, 42, 50	I	**Ground:** 0 V reference
VSSA	59	I	**Analog Ground:** 0 V reference. This should nominally be the same voltage as VSS, but should be isolated to minimize noise and error. This pin must be grounded if the ADC/DAC are not used.
VDD	23, 43, 51	I	**3.3 V Power Supply:** This is the power supply voltage for the core and I/O ports.
VDDA	7	I	**Analog 3.3 V Power Supply:** This should be nominally the same voltage as VDD but should be isolated to minimize noise and error. This voltage is used to power the ADC(s) and DAC (where available). This pin must be tied to VDD when the ADC/DAC are not used.
VREF	63	I	**A/D Converter Reference:** This should be nominally the same voltage as VDD but should be isolated to minimize noise and error. Level on this pin is used as a reference for A/D convertor and DAC (where available). This pin must be tied to VDD when the ADC/DAC are not used.
VBAT	49	I	**RTC Power Supply:** 3.3 V on this pin supplies the power to the RTC.

Pin Function Select Register 0 (PINSEL0 - 0xE002 C000)

The PINSEL0 register controls the functions of the pins as per the settings listed in Table A-D.2. The direction control bit in the IO0DIR register is effective only when the GPIO function is selected for a pin. For other functions, direction is controlled automatically.

Table A-D.2 | Pin Function Select Register 0 (PINSEL0 - Address 0xE002 C000) Bit Description

Bit	Symbol	Value	Function	Reset Value
1:0	P0.0	00	GPIO Port 0.0	0
		01	TXD (UART0)	
		10	PWM1	
		11	Reserved	
3:2	P0.1	00	GPIO Port 0.1	0
		01	RxD (UART0)	
		10	PWM3	
		11	EINT0	
5:4	P0.2	00	GPIO Port 0.2	0
		01	SCL0 (I^2C0)	
		10	Capture 0.0 (Timer 0)	
		11	Reserved	
7:6	P0.3	00	GPIO Port 0.3	0
		01	SDA0 (I^2C0)	
		10	Match 0.0 (Timer 0)	
		11	EINT1	
9:8	P0.4	00	GPIO Port 0.4	0
		01	SCK0 (SPI0)	
		10	Capture 0.1 (Timer 0)	
		11	AD0.6	
11:10	P0.5	00	GPIO Port 0.5	0
		01	MISO0 (SPI0)	
		10	Match 0.1 (Timer 0)	
		11	AD0.7	
13:12	P0.6	00	GPIO Port 0.6	0
		01	MOSI0 (SPI0)	
		10	Capture 0.2 (Timer 0)	
		11	Reserved or AD1.0	
15:14	P0.7	00	GPIO Port 0.7	0
		01	SSEL0 (SPI0)	
		10	PWM2	
		11	EINT2	

Bit	Symbol	Value	Function	Reset Value
17:16	P0.8	00	GPIO Port 0.8	0
		01	TXD UART1	
		10	PWM4	
		11	Reserved or AD1.1	
19:18	P0.9	00	GPIO Port 0.9	0
		01	RxD (UART1)	
		10	PWM6	
		11	EINT3	
21:20	P0.10	00	GPIO Port 0.10	0
		01	Reserved or RTS (UART1)	
		10	Capture 1.0 (Timer 1)	
		11	Reserved or AD1.2	
23:22	P0.11	00	GPIO Port 0.11	0
		01	Reserved or CTS (UART1)	
		10	Capture 1.1 (Timer 1)	
		11	SCL1 (I2C1)	
25:24	P0.12	00	GPIO Port 0.12	0
		01	Reserved or DSR (UART1)	
		10	Match 1.0 (Timer 1)	
		11	Reserved or AD1.3	
27:26	P0.13	00	GPIO Port 0.13	0
		01	Reserved or DTR (UART1)	
		10	Match 1.1 (Timer 1)	
		11	Reserved or AD1.4	
29:28	P0.14	00	GPIO Port 0.14	0
		01	Reserved or DCD (UART1)	
		10	EINT1	
		11	SDA1 (I^2C1)	
31:30	P0.15	00	GPIO Port 0.15	0
		01	Reserved or RI (UART1)	
		10	EINT2	
		11	Reserved or AD1.5	

Pin Function Select Register 1 (PINSEL1 - 0xE002 C004)

The PINSEL1 register controls the functions of the pins as per the settings listed in Table A-D.3. The direction control bit in the IO0DIR register is effective only when the GPIO function is selected for a pin. For other functions direction is controlled automatically.

Table A-D.3 | Pin Function Select Register 1 (Pinsel1 - Address 0Xe002 C004) Bit Description

Bit	Symbol	Value	Function	Reset Value
1:0	P0.16	00	GPIO Port 0.16	0
		01	EINT0	
		10	Match 0.2 (Timer 0)	
		11	Capture 0.2 (Timer 0)	
3:2	P0.17	00	GPIO Port 0.17 0	
		01	Capture 1.2 (Timer 1)	
		10	SCK1 (SSP)	
		11	Match 1.2 (Timer 1)	
5:4	P0.18	00	GPIO Port 0.18	0
		01	Capture 1.3 (Timer 1)	
		10	MISO1 (SSP)	
		11	Match 1.3 (Timer 1)	
7:6	P0.19	00	GPIO Port 0.19	0
		01	Match 1.2 (Timer 1)	
		10	MOSI1 (SSP)	
		11	Capture 1.2 (Timer 1)	
9:8	P0.20	00	GPIO Port 0.20	0
		01	Match 1.3 (Timer 1)	
		10	SSEL1 (SSP)	
		11	EINT3	
11:10	P0.21	00	GPIO Port 0.21	0
		01	PWM5	
		10	Reserved or AD1.6	
		11	Capture 1.3 (Timer 1)	
13:12	P0.22	00	GPIO Port 0.22	0
		01	Reserved or AD1.7	
		10	Capture 0.0 (Timer 0)	
		11	Match 0.0 (Timer 0)	
15:14	P0.23	00	GPIO Port 0.23	0
		01	VBUS	
		10	Reserved	
		11	Reserved	
17:16	P0.24	00	Reserved	0
		01	Reserved	

Bit	Symbol	Value	Function	Reset Value
		10	Reserved	
		11	Reserved	
19:18	P0.25	00	GPIO Port 0.25	0
		01	AD0.4	
		10	Reserved or Aout(DAC)	
		11	Reserved	
21:20	P0.26	00	Reserved	0
		01	Reserved	
		10	Reserved	
		11	Reserved	
23:22	P0.27	00	Reserved	0
		01	Reserved	
		10	Reserved	
		11	Reserved	
25:24	P0.28	00	GPIO Port 0.28	0
		01	AD0.1	
		10	Capture 0.2 (Timer 0)	
		11	Match 0.2 (Timer 0)	
27:26	P0.29	00	GPIO Port 0.29	0
		01	AD0.2	
		10	Capture 0.3 (Timer 0)	
		11	Match 0.3 (Timer 0)	
29:28	P0.30	00	GPIO Port 0.30	0
		01	AD0.3	
		10	EINT3	
		11	Capture 0.0 (Timer 0)	
31:30	P0.31	00	GPO Port only	0
		01	UP_LED	
		10	CONNECT	
		11	Reserved	

Pin Function Select Register 2 (PINSEL2 - 0xE002 C014)

The PINSEL2 register controls the functions of the pins as per the settings listed in Table A-D.4. The direction control bit in the IO1DIR register is effective only when the GPIO function is selected for a pin. For other functions direction is controlled automatically.

Table A-D.4 | Pin Function Select Register 2 (PINSEL2 - 0xE002 C014) Bit Description

Bit	Symbol	Value	Function	Reset Value
1:0	-	-	Reserved, user software should not write ones to reserved bits. The value read from a reserved bit is not defined.	NA
2	GPIO/DEBUG	0	Pins P1.36-26 are used as GPIO pins.	$\overline{\text{P1.26}}/\overline{\text{RTCK}}$
		1	Pins P1.36-26 are used as a Debug port.	
3	GPIO/TRACE	0	Pins P1.25-16 are used as GPIO pins.	$\overline{\text{P1.20}}/\overline{\text{TRACESYNC}}$
		1	Pins P1.25-16 are used as a Trace port.	
31:4	-	-	Reserved, user software should not write ones to reserved bits. The value read from a reserved bit is not defined.	NA

Pin Function Select Register Values

The PINSEL registers control the functions of device pins as shown below. Pairs of bits in these registers correspond to specific device pins.

Table A-D.5 | Pin Function Select Register Bits

PINSEL0 and PINSEL1 Values	Function	Value After Reset
00	Primary (default) function, typically GPIO port	00
01	First alternate function	
10	Second alternate function	
11	Reserved	

The direction control bit in the IO0DIR/IO1DIR register is effective only when the GPIO function is selected for a pin. For other functions, direction is controlled automatically. Each derivative typically has a different pinout and therefore a different set of functions possible for each pin. Details for a specific derivative may be found in the appropriate data sheet.

BIBLIOGRAPHY

A BDTI white paper on 'The Evolution of DSP Processors', Berkeley Design Technology Inc., 2000.

Abhiman Hande, University of Texas, Dallas, Zigbee Tutorial, 2005.

Abraham Silberchatz, Peter Baer Galvin, Greg Gagne, *Operating System Principles*, Seventh Edition, John Wiley & Sons, 2006.

Andrew N. Sloss, Dominic Symes, Chris Wright, *ARM System Developer's Guide, Developing and Optimizing System Software*, Elseiver, 2008.

Arezou Mohammadi and Selim G. Akl, *Technical Report No. 2005–499 Scheduling Algorithms for Real-time Systems*, 2005.

Atmel CAN the ultimate CAN Controller, Tutorial, 2004.

Bhatt P. C. P. 'Lecture notes on Operating Systems/Inter-Process Communication', IISc, Bangalore, 2004.

Bill Moyer, Member, IEEE. *Low-power Design for Embedded Processors, Proceedings of the IEEE*, Vol. 89, No. 11, November 2001.

Bruce Jacob, *Cache Design for Embedded Real-time Systems*, Embedded Systems Conference, Summer 1999. Danvers MA, June 30, 1999.

C. L. Liu and J. W. Layland, 'Scheduling Algoritms for Multiprogramming in a Hard-real-time Environment', *Journal of ACM*, Vol. 20, No. 1, January 1973.

Clifford W. Mercer, Lecture notes on 'An Introduction to Real-time Operating Systems: Scheduling Theory', 1992.

Dania A. El-Kebbe Salaheddine, 'Aperiodic Scheduling in a Dynamic Real-time Manufacturing System', IEEE Real-Time Embedded System Workshop, December 3, 2001.

Data Sheet for GP2D120 Optoelectronic Device, Sharp Corporation, 2006.

Data sheet for H21A1/H21A2/H21A3 Phototransistor Optical Interrupter Switch, Fairchild Semiconductors, 2001.

Data sheet for K817P/ K827PH/ K847PH Vishay Semiconductors Optocoupler with Phototransistor Output, Vishay Semiconductors.

Data sheet for LPC1769/68/67/66/65/64/63, 2011.

Data sheet for LPC 2148, 2010.

Data sheet for LPC29xx ARM9 Microcontroller with CAN and LIN, 2008.

Data sheet for MAX 1169, Maxim Integrated Products, 2010.

Data sheet for Optical Encoders, Bourns® Sensors & Controls, 2004.

Data Sheet of ADSP-TS201 TigerSHARC® Processor Hardware Reference, Analog Devices Inc., 2009.

Data Sheet of Blackfin Embedded Processor ADSP-BF531/ADSP-BF532/ADSP-BF533, Analog Devices Inc., 2011.

Data Sheet of TMS320C674x/OMAP-L1x Processor Peripherals Overview, Texas Instruments, 2011.

Dogan Ibrahim, *Advanced PIC Microcontroller Projects in C*, Elseiver, 2008.

Flash Memory Guide, Kingston Technologies, 2004.

Gary Nutt, *Operating Systems*, Third Edition, Pearson Education, 2004.

Gene Frantz, TI Principal Fellow, Business Development Manager; Ray Simar, Fellow and Manager of Advanced DSP Architectures, Texas Instruments. *Comparing Fixed- and Floating-Point DSPs*, 2004.

Greg Osborne, *Embedded Microcontrollers and Processor Design*, Pearson Education, 2012.

Jagbeer Singh, Bichitrananda Patra, Satyendra Prasad Singh, 'An Algorithm to Reduce the Time Complexity of Earliest Deadline First Scheduling Algorithm in Real-time System', *International Journal of Advanced Computer Science and Applications*, Vol. 2, No. 2, February 2011.

Jan Axelson, *USB Mass Storage: Designing and Programming Devices and Embedded Hosts*, ebook.

Jinzhong Niu, 'Lecture notes on Operating Systems/Process Concept and State', 2003.

John A. Stankovich, R. Rajkumar, *Real Time Operating Systems*, Kluwer Academic Press, 2004.

Joseph Liu, *The Definitive Guide to the ARM CORTEX-M3*, Second Edition, Newnes, 2010.

LPC2104/2105/2106 User manual, 2008.

Luddy Harrison, 'Processor Presentation Series of AD's BlackFin Processor', University of Illinois, 2005.

Lyla B. Das, *Microprocessors and Microcontrollers*, Pearson Education, 2011.

Lyla B. Das, *The x86 Microprocessors, Architecture, Programming and Interfacing (8086 to Pentium)*, Pearson Education, 2010.

M. H. Klein, et al., *A Practitioners' Handbook for Real-time Analysis: Guide to Rate Monotonic Analysis for Real-time Systems*, Boston, MA: Kluwer Academic Publishers, 1993.

Manual for KS0108B 64CH Segment Driver for Dot Matrix LCD, Samsung Electronics, 2012.

Michael J. Pont, *Embedded C*, Pearson Education, 2007.

Michael J Pont, *Embedded C*, Pearson Education, 2007.

'Micro Processor Report: Tigersharc Sinks Teeth Into VLIW' *Journal of Micro Designer Sources*, December 7, 1998.

Qing Li with Caroline Yao, 'Real Time Concepts for Embedded Systems', CMP Books, 1971.

Radhakrishnan P., Senior ASIC-Core Development Engineer, Lecture notes on 'ASIC Design Flow', Toshiba, 2000.

Robert Ashby, *Designer's Guide to the Cypress PSoC*, Elseiver, 2005.

Sanjoy Baruah, 'Fairness in Periodic Real-time Scheduling', *Proceedings of the Real-time Systems Symposium*, IEEE Computer Society Press, Pisa, Italy, December 1995, pp. 200–209.

Shibu K. V., *Introduction to Embedded Systems*, Tata McGraw Hill, 2010.

ShoreTel Ergonomic Phones White paper, www.shoretel.com, 2003.

Tammy Noergaard, *Embedded Systems Architecture: A Comprehensive Guide for Engineers and Programmers*, Elseiver, Newnes, 2006.

'The Tigersharc DSP Architecture', *Journal of IEEE Micro*, February 2000.

Tiemen Spits and Paul Werp, White paper on 'OMAP Technology Overview', Texas Instruments, 2000.

Trevor Martin, *The Insiders Guide to ARM based Micrcontrollers,* Hitex Development tools, 2005.

User manual for LPC17xx, 2011.

Vishay Manual for Graphical LCD, 2002.

Wayne Wof, *Computers as Components, Principles of Embedded Computing System Design*, Elseiver, 2008.

White paper on 'ASIC Design Flow', Nokia, 2009.

White paper on 'Choosing a DSP Processor', Berkeley Design Technology Inc., 2000.

White paper on 'Comparing TI's TMS320C6671 DSP with ADI's ADSP-TS201S TigerSHARC® Processor', Texas Instruments, 2012.

White paper on 'Standard Cell ASIC to FPGA Design Methodology and Guidelines, Altera Inc., 2009.

William Hohl, *ARM Assembly Language Fundamentals and Techniques*, CRC Press, 2009.

William Stallings, *Operating Systems, Internals and Design Principles*, Fifth Edition, Pearson Education, 2006.

http://82.157.70.109/mirrorbooks/kerneldevelopment/0672327201/ch01lev1sec2.html.

http://www.acroname.com/robotics/info/articles/sharp/sharp.html September 2011.

http://www.analog.com/en/content/fixed-point_vs_floating-point_dsp/fca.html.

http://www.autotantra.com/misc/2008/17/bosch-plans-on-introducing-anti-lock-brake-system-in-india-by-2009/.

http://www.autotantra.com/misc/2008/17/bosch-plans-on-introducing-anti-lock-brake-system-in-india-by-2009/.

http://www.bdti.com/InsideDSP/2011/10/20/NvidiaQualcomm, Feb, 2012.

http://www.bluetooth.com.

http://www.bores.com/courses/intro/chips/6_dsp32c.htm, Feb, 2012.

http://www.comptechdoc.org/basic/basictut/osintro.html.

http://www.computer.howstuffworks.com/brain-computer-interface.htm.

http://www.cyberiapc.com/os/.

http://www.dspguide.com/ch1.htm, Feb, 2012.

http://www.ece.cmu.edu/~ece749/docs/whatMakesAGoodRtos.pdf.

http://www.eetimes.com/design/embedded/4023891/Low-Power-Design.

http://www.eetimes.com/discussion/beginner-s-corner/4023908/Introduction-to-Serial-Peripheral-Interface.

http://www.electronics-tutorials.ws/io/io_5.html, September 2011.

http://www.ergonomics4schools.com/lzone/anthropometry.htm.

http://www.esacademy.com/en/library/technical-articles-and-documents/miscellaneous/i2c-bus/general-introduction/i2c-bus-protocol.html.

http://www.freewebs.com/maheshwankhede/basic.html, September 2011.

http://www.geocities.com/dinceraydin/lcd/gfxintro.htm, April 2012.

http://www.gigaom.com/mobile/video-nvidias-tegra-2-powering-the-lg-optimus-2x/.

http://www.iue.tuwien.ac.at/phd/entner/node34.html.

http://www.kpsec.freeuk.com/555t.

http://www.mashable.com/2010/10/06/ide-guide/.

http://www.mcmanis.com/chuck/robotics/tutorial/index.html, September 2011.

http://www.microcontrollershop.com/An%20Embedded%20Tools%20Introduction.php.

http://www.mitros.org/p/projects/encoder/ September 2011.

http://www.mydigitallife.info/sony-launches-newest-portable-navigation-systems/.

http://www.nbb.cornell.edu/neurobio/land/STUDENTPROJ/1999to2000/gurnee/index.htm#lcddisp.

http://www.nex-robotics.com.

http://www.oled-display.net/how-works-the-oled-technology, September 2011.

http://www.omimo.be/encyc/buyersguide/rtos/what_good_rtos_abstract.htm.

http://www.pcmag.com/article2/0, 2817, 2386274, 00.asp.

http://www.radio-electronics.com/info/data/semicond/memory/eeprom-basics-tutorial.php.

http://www.scribd.com/doc/38634832/9/TYPES-OF-DSP-PROCESSORS, Feb, 2012.

http://www.shree-electronics.com/interfacing_relays.htm September 2011.

http://www.slashgear.com/tags/omap4/, February, 2012.

http://www.slideshare.net/moto_modx/theevo1, Feb, 2012.

http://www.socialbarrel.com/samsung-unveils-arm-cortex-a15-based-exynos-5250-chip/28219/, February 2012.

http://www.societyofrobots.com/sensors_encoder.shtml September 2011.

http://www.societyofrobots.com/sensors_sharpirrange.shtml, September 2011.

http://www.symbian-freak.com/news/008/11/nokia_s_shape_bringing_ergonomics_to_phones.htm.

http://www.usbmadesimple.co.uk/ums_1.htm.

http://www10.edacafe.com/book/ASIC/CH01/CH01.php.

http://www2.imse-cnm.csic.es/vmote/english_version/deteccion_texturas.php.

INDEX

A

B

C

D

G

H

N

O

P

Q

R

S

T

U

V

W

X

Y

Z